Encyclopedia
of the
American Constitution

Original 1986 Editorial Board

Encyclopedia
of the
American Constitution

SECOND EDITION

Edited by
LEONARD W. LEVY
and
KENNETH L. KARST

ADAM WINKLER, Associate Editor for the Second Edition

DENNIS J. MAHONEY, Assistant Editor for the First Edition

JOHN G. WEST, JR., Assistant Editor for Supplement I

MACMILLAN REFERENCE USA
An imprint of the Gale Group
New York

Macmillan Library Reference USA
1633 Broadway
New York, NY 10019

Printed in the United States of America

Printing Number
10 9 8 7 6 5 4 3 2 1

Library of Congress Cataloging-in-Publication Data
Encyclopedia of the American Constitution / edited by Leonard W. Levy and Kenneth L.
Karst.—2nd ed. / Adam Winkler, associate editor for the second edition.
    p. cm.
    Includes bibliographical references and indexes.
    ISBN 0-02-864880-3 (hard cover : alk. paper)
        1. Constitutional law—United States—Encyclopedias.   I. Levy, Leonard Williams,
1923–   II. Karst, Kenneth L.   III. Winkler, Adam.
    KF4548 .E53   2000
    342.73—dc21   00-029203

This paper meets the requirements of ANSI-NISO Z39.48-1992 (Permanence of Paper).

FAIR COMMENT

See: Libel and the First Amendment

FAIR HEARING

In numerous contexts the Constitution requires the state to afford its citizens DUE PROCESS, which frequently includes an adversarial voicing of opposed contentions. "Fair hearing" in this broadest sense could thus include both the specific constitutional guarantees that attach to criminal trials and the more general requirement that civil litigation meet minimal standards of fairness. Among lawyers, however, the term more narrowly refers to the procedure that must be afforded to persons involved not in judicial trials but in some less formal dispute with the state. Speaking to that issue, the Supreme Court has asked when the Constitution requires any process and what that process should be. For some time the Court focused on the first question, assuming that if any process was due, it would resemble a formal trial; later decisions emphasized the flexibility of appropriate process.

For due process requirements to attach to any proceedings, they must, by involving governmental action that threatens life, liberty, or property, fall within the requirements of the Fifth and FOURTEENTH AMENDMENTS. Following in the wake of the welfare state, the Court has expanded its definition of property to include entitlements to various government benefits (for example, welfare and disability payments, tenured positions in state employment). Many threatened deprivations of such benefits consequently require due process, and the question becomes what that process must be. The Court has never answered that question in categorical terms, insisting that each situation calls for a rather individualized judgment. It has, however, suggested some minimal criteria and a set of factors to be considered in striking the balance from case to case. In deciding what process is due, one must consider "first, the private interest . . . affected by the official action; second, the risk of an erroneous deprivation of such interest through the procedures used, and the probable value, if any, of additional or substitute procedural safeguards; and finally, the government's interest, including the function involved and the fiscal and administrative burdens that the additional or substitute procedural requirements would entail" (MATHEWS V. ELDRIDGE, 1976). These factors represent an attempt to arrive at conclusions about two aspects of process: timing and elaborateness.

At a minimum, due process requires notice that tells the person threatened with deprivation the reason for the action and how he can challenge its factual and legal bases. Usually notice and such an opportunity must precede the deprivation, but even this proposition is not invariable; thus in a case of a threat to public health or other emergency situation, a seizure could occur first and notice and hearing afterward.

More difficult than the question of the timing of the required process is its nature. Because the Court has been unable to articulate guidelines applicable to all situations, it defines appropriate processes on a case-by-case basis. Consequently one can fully understand the requirements of due process only by sampling a large number of cases. It is, however, possible to suggest some rough guidelines and some distinctions. The first might be the line between situations requiring formal adjudicatory hearings, as for the termination of WELFARE BENEFITS in GOLDBERG V. KELLY (1970), and those that do not: the more serious the deprivation, the more likely the Court is to require a trial-type hearing. Even when such a hearing is not required, one can further differentiate situations according to the formality of the process required: the state must provide a written statement of reasons for ending disability benefits and give the recipient a chance to respond (*Mathews v. Eldridge*), but a school official need engage only in a brief oral conversation before suspending a student, as in GOSS V. LOPEZ (1975). Indeed, the Court has approved procedures that are not even adversarial in the normal sense, for example, an expulsion proceeding in which a medical student has an opportunity to demonstrate her medical skills to several local doctors over several days. (See BOARD OF CURATORS V. HOROWITZ.)

The consequence of such flexibility is that a constitutionally "fair hearing" need not entail a hearing at all, and even if it does that hearing may occupy various points along a continuum of adjudicatory formality. Such flexibility results from the Court's attempts, once it has concluded that due process attaches, to tailor the process to the situation at hand, taking some account of the stakes for the adversaries and of the goals of process. Some commentators have criticized the Court for the narrowness of its focus, arguing that the goals of process include the dignity of the participants as well as the accuracy of the result; the Court has seemed unpersuaded of this point.

The constitutional focus on fair hearings in administrative law has drawn attention to a number of areas presenting similar profiles—to which, however, due process does not apply, either because the institutions involved are private or because life, liberty, or property is not threatened. Nevertheless, under the influence of the constitutional cases many institutions (such as private schools or trade associations) have adopted processes that resemble those that might be required if due process did apply. Some of these procedures have resulted from legislation or regulation and an occasional judicial decision using COMMON LAW; others have come voluntarily. In either case the consequence has been a softening of the lines between the practices of public and private institutions; there is thus a sense in which one can speak of a fair hearing as a practice (though not a constitutional requirement) of many areas of institutional life.

If fairness does not always require a hearing, it is nevertheless true that the constitutional ideal described by the term has permeated many areas of life where neither fairness nor a hearing is constitutionally required. The result, in a society of large institutions and sometimes uncertain responsibility for decisions, has been a requirement taking many forms but having at its basis the idea that persons about to be adversely affected have the right to know why and to respond.

STEPHEN C. YEAZELL
(1986)

Bibliography
FRIENDLY, HENRY   1975   Some Kind of Hearing. *University of Pennsylvania Law Review* 123:1267–1317.
MASHAW, JERRY L.   1976   The Supreme Court's Due Process Calculus for Administrative Adjudication in *Mathews v. Eldridge:* Three Factors in Search of a Theory of Value. *University of Chicago Law Review* 44:28–59.
VERKUIL, PAUL   1975   The Ombudsman and the Limits of the Adversary System. *Columbia Law Review* 75:845–861.

FAIR HOUSING LAWS

See: Open Housing Laws

FAIR LABOR STANDARDS ACT
52 Stat. 1060 (1938)

The Fair Labor Standards Act (FLSA), usually called the federal wage and hour law, was adopted in 1938. For all covered employees the act required the payment of a minimum wage (initially 25 cents an hour) and time and one-half for all hours worked over forty a week. Child labor was forbidden under certain circumstances. The act prohibited the shipment in INTERSTATE COMMERCE of goods produced under substandard conditions. There were numerous and complicated exemptions.

The constitutionality of the act under the COMMERCE CLAUSE was sustained by the Supreme Court in UNITED STATES V. DARBY LUMBER CO. (1940). Since then the act has been amended many times, principally to increase periodically the minimum wage, which reached $3.35 an hour in 1981, to expand coverage, and to provide more effective enforcement.

The act originally covered employees engaged in commerce or in the PRODUCTION of goods for commerce. Production was defined to include activities necessary to the actual production.

Coverage based on engagement in commerce includes employees engaged in the actual movement of commerce, such as transportation, shipping, and communications. It also includes employees whose work involves the distribution or receipt of goods across state lines. The Supreme Court upheld application of the act to employees who did construction or repair work on interstate instrumentalities and even to employees who prepared plans and specifications for the construction or repair of interstate instrumentalities.

Under the extended production definition, many fringe activities were found necessary to production. Thus, the Court upheld application to employees of an office building occupied by a corporation which at other locations produced goods for commerce and to employees of an independent contractor washing windows in industrial plants that produced goods for commerce.

These decisions, although they involved statutory construction, demonstrated the enormous scope of the commerce power even under coverage formulas less extensive than that used to describe the constitutional maximum, "affecting" commerce. The breadth of the Court's holdings led Congress in 1949 to amend the statute to confine the extended production definition to activities "closely related" and "directly essential" to production.

The reduced coverage effectuated by this change was largely nullified, however, by a 1961 amendment providing for "enterprise" coverage. Before 1961 coverage was determined for each employee; thus, some employees of an employer could be covered while others were not. "Enterprise" coverage extended to all an employer's employees, if at least two employees were covered individually and the enterprise did a requisite annual dollar volume of business. The constitutionality of "enterprise" coverage was upheld by the Court in *Maryland v. Wirtz* (1967).

Other aspects of the act have also received expansive interpretation. Thus, the term "employee" has been defined in accordance with "economic reality" rather than COMMON LAW rules, and applied to persons who in other contexts would be independent contractors. These cases illustrate the peculiar American phenomenon of defining "employee" differently under various statutes, so that an employee may be covered under one statute and not under another.

What constitutes compensable work time has presented a special problem under the FLSA. In *Armour & Co. v. Wantoch* (1944), involving firefighters, the Court held that inactive waiting time was compensable work time. Time spent in travel between the mine entrance and the underground cutting face was held compensable in *Tennessee Coal, Inc. & Railroad v. Muscoda Local* (1944). Finally, in *Anderson v. Mt. Clemens Pottery Co.* (1946), the Court required payment for time spent by employees walking between the factory gate and their work place. Many lawsuits were promptly filed claiming billions of dollars in back wages. Congress responded by enacting the Portal-to-Portal Act of 1947, which distinguished between an employee's compensable principal activity and noncompensable preliminary and after-working activities. Employers were thus absolved in most cases from liability under the *Mt. Clemens Pottery* decision. The Court held,

however, that time spent changing clothes, when necessitated by the nature of the work, is a principal activity and thus compensable.

The FLSA applies on a work week basis. Overtime is required for hours in excess of forty a week. The required time and one-half premium is applied to the employee's "regular rate of pay" which is determined by dividing the total weekly compensation (including straight wages plus all fringe benefits) by the number of hours worked. Because employee pay plans are of great variety, determination of the regular rate of pay frequently is a difficult problem.

Among the principal exemptions from the FLSA are executive, administrative, and professional employees (which terms have special definitions), employees of small retail or service establishments, and some employees engaged in agriculture. Special provision is made for learners, apprentices, students, and the handicapped.

The act is enforced by individual employee suits for back wages, or suits by the secretary of labor seeking an INJUNCTION as well as back wages. Individual suits are preempted by suits by the secretary. Liquidated DAMAGES are authorized. TRIAL BY JURY is available in employee suits, but generally is denied in combined injunction-back-wage suits by the secretary. The FLSA is unique in labor legislation in providing criminal prosecution for willful violators. Such actions are handled by the Justice Department, but have not been a major aspect of the statute's enforcement.

Originally the FLSA applied only to private employment. In 1966 it was extended to employees of state hospitals and schools; this extension was sustained in *Maryland v. Wirtz* (1967). In 1974 Congress extended the FLSA to almost all state and local government employees. In NATIONAL LEAGUE OF CITIES V. USERY (1976) the Court held that the TENTH AMENDMENT protected state sovereign functions against commerce power regulation and overruled *Maryland v. Wirtz. Usery* in turn was overruled by GARCIA V. SAN ANTONIO METROPOLITAN TRANSIT AUTHORITY (1985). Congress responded the same year with legislation authorizing states and cities to reimburse employees for overtime with compensatory time off in lieu of cash payment.

In 1938 the principal purpose of the FLSA was to combat the Depression by increasing the purchasing power in the hands of the lowest-paid workers. Thus, it has been called the original antipoverty law. Fifty years later, the wisdom of the act and its effect on the economy are still debated, but the FLSA survives as a permanent and major piece of American labor legislation.

WILLIAM P. MURPHY
(1986)

Bibliography

PLAYER, MACK   1975   Enterprise Coverage under the Fair Labor Standards Act: An Assessment of the First Generation. *Vanderbilt Law Review* 28:283–347.

WILLIS, ROBERT N.   1972   The Evolution of the Fair Labor Standards Act. *University of Miami Law Review* 26:607–634.

FAIRNESS DOCTRINE

Born out of a progression of decisions by the Federal Communications Commission (FCC) and then codified by Congress in 1959, the fairness DOCTRINE requires a BROADCASTING license holder "to operate in the public interest and to afford reasonable opportunity for the discussion of conflicting views on issues of public importance." Although the doctrine was upheld against a FIRST AMENDMENT challenge in RED LION BROADCASTING COMPANY V. FCC (1969), it has been perceived increasingly as an intrusive exception to the First Amendment, with diminishing justification.

The doctrine, applicable to radio and television licensees and to some cable operators, requires a licensee that presents a controversial issue to provide a reasonable amount of time for contrasting viewpoints. A less frequently litigated aspect of the doctrine requires affirmative coverage of issues important to the public. Finally, the doctrine assures persons who are disparaged on the airwaves a limited right to respond.

The doctrine reflects a distinction in the way Congress and the courts have conceived of newspapers, on the one hand, and broadcasters on the other. Thus, in MIAMI HERALD V. TORNILLO (1974) the Supreme Court held unconstitutional on First Amendment grounds a Florida statute that required a newspaper to grant a right of reply to persons attacked in its columns. The Court did not distinguish *Red Lion* but ignored it.

Recently a campaign to narrow, if not eliminate, the fairness doctrine has gained momentum. When the fairness doctrine was in full sway, its justification was a supposed scarcity of the channels available for transmission of broadcast signals. Those who wished to communicate by the printed word were not curtailed by government action or the rationing of resources. On the other hand, the number of channels for radio and television transmission was demonstrably limited. Cable television and other new technologies have undermined the "scarcity" justification for regulation by providing abundant new channels.

Some have argued that the spectrum of broadcasting channels is a public resource, and thus that the federal government can insist that a private user of that resource give voice to many speakers. In another perspective, emphasis on the right of the licensee to be an unencumbered

editor is misplaced. Expressing this view, in *Red Lion*, the Court said that "it is the right of the viewers and listeners, not the right of broadcasters, which is paramount." (See LISTENERS' RIGHTS.)

Recent commentary has proposed quite a different solution to the "fairness" issue: setting aside segments of broadcast time, or even whole channels, for public access. Owners of broadcasting stations would have no editorial control over these "soapboxes of the air." Broadcasters generally consider the fairness doctrine a badge of second-class citizenship in the ranks of the press. The FCC, in the early 1980s, confined the fairness doctrine's scope and considered its repeal. As an interim measure the FCC announced that asserted violations would not be adjudicated individually, but would be considered when a broadcaster sought renewal of a license. Still, despite these limits, the doctrine continues to influence the culture of television. Producers of national and local television news programs take great care to present at least two sides of important controversial issues.

MONROE E. PRICE
(1986)

Bibliography

BOLLINGER, LEE   1976   Freedom of the Press and Public Access: Toward a Theory of Partial Regulation of the Mass Media. *University of Michigan Law Review* 75:1–42.

FAIRNESS DOCTRINE
(Historical Development and Update)

From its establishment in 1934 the Federal Communications Commission (FCC) discouraged broadcast station owners from airing biased presentations of controversial issues. In 1939 the National Association of Broadcasters (NAB) echoed the FCC's fair treatment approach. Responding at least in part to Father Charles Coughlin's controversial anti-Semitic broadcasts, NAB adopted a voluntary code that discouraged stations from editorializing and encouraged balanced treatment of controversial issues. In 1940 the FCC applied these principles in its *Mayflower* decision, which banned on-air editorializing by station owners involved in BROADCASTING. Although the FCC's no-editorializing policy was never challenged in the courts, scholars have long criticized it as a clear violation of broadcasters' FIRST AMENDMENT rights.

In 1946 the FCC promulgated "The Blue Book," in which it suggested that broadcasters had an affirmative duty to cover subjects of a controversial nature. At this point NAB lobbied the FCC to overturn its *Mayflower* decision and to recognize a broadcasters' right to editorialize. In 1949 the FCC agreed to permit editorializing, but continued its commitment to fair treatment of controversial issues in its "Report on Editorializing," which included what came to be known as the "fairness doctrine." The doctrine required broadcasters to cover controversial issues of public importance and provide a reasonable opportunity for the presentation of opposing viewpoints on these issues. Broadcasters preferred blanket permission to editorialize and complained about the fairness doctrine on FREEDOM OF SPEECH grounds. However, the FCC enforced fairness doctrine violations only at license renewal time and even then was extremely reluctant to deny renewal on that basis. The lack of official enforcement of the doctrine left it constitutionally unchallenged until the 1960s.

In the 1960s the FCC increased its enforcement of the fairness doctrine, and it developed further the principle that fairness required broadcasters to offer response time to persons personally attacked by commentators. When the FCC ordered a station to provide response time for such an attack, the station brought a First Amendment challenge in RED LION BROADCASTING CO., INC. V. FCC (1969). The Supreme Court upheld the fairness doctrine as justified by the governmental interest in allocating and regulating the broadcast spectrum as a scarce resource. The constitutional significance of *Red Lion* is the lower degree of scrutiny given to laws burdening the First Amendment rights of broadcasters.

Since *Red Lion*, however, judges, scholars, and policymakers have expressed increasingly shrill opposition to the scarcity rationale for government regulation of broadcasting, with commentators arguing either that the rationale was never sound or that technological change has rendered it no longer sound. Heeding these calls, a deregulatory FCC abolished the fairness doctrine in 1987. It found that the doctrine was inconsistent with the FCC's mission to regulate broadcasting in the public interest, and that the doctrine had a CHILLING EFFECT on speech in violation of the First Amendment. The U.S. Court of Appeals for the District of Columbia Circuit reviewed this decision in *Syracuse Peace Council v. FCC* (1989), but it did not reach the First Amendment question, holding that the FCC had acted within its discretion when abolishing the doctrine, which was not required by statute.

The Supreme Court declined to review *Syracuse Peace Council*, and the Court has avoided revisiting *Red Lion*. Nonetheless, the Court has expressed skepticism about the continuing vitality of the scarcity rationale as applied to broadcasting. In addition, the Court has chosen not to extend *Red Lion* to new media. In TURNER BROADCASTING SYSTEM, INC. V. FCC (1994), the Court applied heightened scrutiny to regulations of the cable industry, and in *Reno v. ACLU* (1997), the Court declined to apply *Red Lion* to regulation of the INTERNET. Scholars seeking to justify new

media regulation have frequently turned from the scarcity rationale to other regulatory rationales, such as intrusiveness in the home and the need to protect children from violence.

In the late 1980s Congress tried twice to enact the fairness doctrine into law, but opposition from Presidents RONALD REAGAN and GEORGE H. W. BUSH on First Amendment grounds thwarted these efforts. A Republican Congress is unlikely to seek reenactment of the fairness doctrine, but a Democratic Congress with a Democratic President could conceivably revive it. The doctrine's demise appears to have encouraged the development of talk radio, which some scholars interpret as evidence that the doctrine did in fact chill speech.

Today the fairness doctrine is but a legacy that lives on in the Supreme Court's *Red Lion* PRECEDENT, which itself reflects an earlier era of First Amendment jurisprudence rather than current scholarly thinking on the subject.

AMY L. TORO
(2000)

Bibliography

BARRON, JEROME A.   1989   What Does the Fairness Doctrine Controversy Really Mean? *Hastings Communications/Entertainment Law Journal* 12:205–44.

HAZLETT, THOMAS W. and SOSA, DAVID W.   1997   Was the Fairness Doctrine a "Chilling Effect"?: Evidence from the Postderegulation Radio Market. *Journal of Legal Studies* 26:279–301.

KRATTENMAKER, THOMAS G. and POWE, L. A., JR.   1985   The Fairness Doctrine Today: A Constitutional Curiosity and an Impossible Dream. *Duke Law Journal* 1985:151–176.

ROWAN, FRED   1984   *Broadcast Fairness, Doctrine, Practice and Prospects.* New York: Longman.

SIMMONS, STEVEN J.   1978   *The Fairness Doctrine and the Media.* Berkeley: University of California Press.

FAIR RETURN ON FAIR VALUE

The DOCTRINE of a fair return on a fair value, which the Supreme Court propounded in SMYTH V. AMES (1898), provided that any government regulation of rate schedules charged by railroads or utilities must allow a reasonable profit or fair rate of return based on a fair valuation of the property. The principal considerations were the original cost of the property, and the cost of reproducing it at the time of the rate regulation. Having entered the business of supervising the details of ratemaking, the Court remained in that business until 1944.

The Court first provided the basis for the doctrine by equating rate regulation with EMINENT DOMAIN: just compensation must accompany a TAKING OF PROPERTY, and to the Court a rate regulation was comparable to a taking. In

CHICAGO, MILWAUKEE, AND ST. PAUL RAILWAY COMPANY V. MIN-NESOTA (1890) the Court declared that the failure to allow a company to charge reasonable rates for the use of its property constituted an unconstitutional taking of property or a violation of SUBSTANTIVE DUE PROCESS OF LAW comparable to a taking. In REAGAN V. FARMERS' LOAN AND TRUST COMPANY (1894) the Court voided rates because they were fixed so low that they virtually took property without compensation. (See GRANGER CASES.) In *Smyth v. Ames* the Court, in a unanimous opinion by Justice JOHN M. HARLAN, proclaimed that a company was entitled to receive a reasonable profit based on the rates it could charge and that a reasonable rate must be determined by the fair value of the property. To ascertain that value, Harlan declared that among the matters to be considered "and given such weight as may be just and right in each case" are the following: "the original cost of construction, the amount expended in permanent improvements, the amount and market value of its bonds and stock, the present as compared with the original cost of construction, the probable earning capacity of the property under particular rates prescribed by statute, and the sum required to meet operating expenses. . . ."

Prior to WORLD WAR I, the Court usually relied on original costs in determining whether a particular rate schedule yielded a fair return. The Court switched to reproduction costs after the war, when prices and costs rose, thereby challenging more rates. *Smyth*'s vague and flexible standards allowed the Court to act as it wished, without restraints. In UNITED RAILWAYS & ELECTRIC COMPANY V. WEST (1930), for example, the Court voided rates allowing a profit of 6.26 percent on the ground that anything less than 7.5 percent was "confiscatory."

Fair value governed fair return standards against the opposition of Justices LOUIS D. BRANDEIS and OLIVER WENDELL HOLMES, who attacked the doctrine as legally and economically unsound. In 1939, Justices FELIX FRANKFURTER and HUGO L. BLACK called for the rejection of the doctrine, and in 1942 the Court indicated that the determination of property value, although useful, was not indispensable. Finally, in FEDERAL POWER COMMISSION V. HOPE NATURAL GAS (1944), the Court rejected the fair value doctrine. Thereafter the Court permitted government ratemaking bodies to fix rates without judicial interference, on condition that the ratemaking process respected PROCEDURAL DUE PROCESS.

LEONARD W. LEVY
(1986)

Bibliography

HALE, ROBERT L. 1952 *Freedom through Law.* New York: Columbia University Press.

FAIR TRIAL

The requirement of a fair trial in criminal proceedings has its constitutional source in the due process clause of the Fifth and FOURTEENTH AMENDMENTS, which declares that no person shall be deprived of "life, liberty, or property, without DUE PROCESS OF LAW." Other provisions of the BILL OF RIGHTS deal explicitly with particular aspects of a criminal trial. Historically, the coverage of those provisions has tended to expand, narrowing the application of the more general provision. The "incorporation" of provisions of the Fifth and SIXTH AMENDMENTS into the due process clause of the Fourteenth Amendment is especially noteworthy in this respect, having had the effect of eliminating the need for fair-trial analysis of issues in state cases covered by those provisions. While important elements of a fair trial are thus treated individually, the requirements can be summarized generally as a hearing before a competent, impartial tribunal, at which the prosecutor does not present the government's case inaccurately or unfairly and the defendant has an opportunity to present his case fully and effectively.

Ordinarily, any judge of a court having JURISDICTION is presumed to be competent to hear a criminal case. However, a judge is presumed not to be impartial if he has a substantial personal interest in a verdict against the defendant. The requirement of a fair trial prohibits a judge from sitting in that circumstance. In *Tumey v. Ohio* (1927) the Supreme Court held invalid a local practice assigning the mayor of a village as judge in criminal cases, because the compensation for his judicial services and other income for the village accrued only if the defendant were convicted and a fine imposed. In *In re Murchison* (1955) the Court overturned convictions for criminal contempt following a trial before the same judge who was the defendants' accuser and the principal witness against them.

The Sixth Amendment gives a criminal defendant the right to be tried by an "impartial jury." That provision, which applies to federal and state trials, entitles the defendant to a jury selected from a representative cross-section of the community, without inclusions or exclusions because of sex, nationality, race, or other impermissible classifications. (See JURY DISCRIMINATION.) The jury finally chosen need not have any particular composition or be representative of the community as a whole.

The defendant must have a reasonable opportunity to uncover bias or prejudice of an individual juror. This is afforded by VOIR DIRE, the examination of prospective jurors. The trial judge or the prosecutor and defense counsel question the members of the jury panel to reveal any basis for disqualification in the particular case. The trial judge has broad discretion to direct the conduct and scope of the examination, provided it is adequate to ensure the jurors' impartiality. Counsel for either side may challenge a juror "for cause" if there is a basis for disqualification and then exercise a limited number of "peremptory" challenges without explanation. In an effort to secure an impartial jury, the prosecutor may, under the DOCTRINE of SWAIN V. ALABAMA (1965), exercise peremptory challenges on the basis of group factors such as race or nationality.

However fair the formal means for ensuring an impartial tribunal, a trial conducted in an atmosphere of mob violence or insistent public pressure for conviction does not meet the constitutional standard. (See MOORE V. DEMPSEY.)

The Sixth Amendment gives a criminal defendant the RIGHT TO BE INFORMED OF THE ACCUSATION. This right, which is essential to a fair trial, requires that the statement of the offense charged identify the criminal conduct and the circumstances of the alleged crime precisely enough for the defendant to prepare his defense.

Although the constitutional guarantee of a fair trial does not ordinarily entitle the defendant to PRETRIAL DISCLOSURE of the EVIDENCE against him, all jurisdictions allow limited pretrial DISCOVERY of evidence and some allow rather full discovery subject only to special exceptions. Whenever evidence against the accused is disclosed, the defendant is entitled to enough time to prepare to meet it; if evidence is not disclosed before trial, the defendant may be entitled to a continuance. Furthermore, as the Court held in *Wardius v. Oregon* (1973), the defendant cannot be obliged to disclose evidence before trial unless the prosecution has a reciprocal obligation; fundamental fairness requires that discovery be "a two-way street."

Most of the evidentiary requirements of a fair trial are now subsumed under the CONFRONTATION and COMPULSORY PROCESS clauses of the Sixth Amendment, which, as incorporated into the Fourteenth, are applied to state criminal trials. A defendant has the rights "to be confronted with the witnesses against him" and "to have compulsory process for obtaining witnesses in his favor." As part of his right to hear and challenge the evidence against him, the defendant has a right to be present at the trial. (He may lose this right by absenting himself voluntarily or interfering with the orderly conduct of the trial.) Like other constitutional rights, the right to be present cannot be unnecessarily burdened; accordingly, since *Estelle v. Williams* (1976) a defendant cannot be required to appear at trial in prison clothing. Where jurors have obtained information from a person who did not appear as a witness, some courts have treated the event as a violation of the right to confront witnesses.

The confrontation clause also limits the use of out-of-court statements of persons who are not present in court. With few exceptions, an available witness must testify in person, so that he can be cross-examined by the defense.

If a witness is not available, his out-of-court statement can be used as evidence only if there are indications of reliability sufficient to satisfy the purpose of confrontation at trial. (See HEARSAY RULES.)

The right to compulsory process assures the defendant that he will be able to present evidence favorable to his case. On occasion, the Supreme Court has held that the application of a state procedural requirement or the trial judge's conduct of the trial denied the defendant an opportunity to present critical evidence and has reversed the conviction, relying on the compulsory process clause or directly on the due process clause.

The Sixth Amendment gives a defendant the right "to have the assistance of counsel for his defense," which requires that counsel be appointed for an INDIGENT defendant in any case in which a sentence of imprisonment is imposed. Before this provision was made applicable to the states by incorporation into the Fourteenth Amendment, an indigent state defendant had a right to appointed counsel only if counsel were necessary to a fair trial. The appointment of counsel was required for defendants who were unable to defend themselves effectively because of their ignorance, or illiteracy, or youth, or because the circumstances of the case made professional skills essential; capital cases were invariably deemed to require the appointment of counsel. Since the decisions in GIDEON V. WAINWRIGHT (1963) and ARGERSINGER V. HAMLIN (1972), the RIGHT TO COUNSEL applies alike in federal and state cases. It is possible although unlikely that in a minor case in which the Sixth Amendment's provision was inapplicable, the defense would be so difficult and complex that counsel would be required for a fair trial.

The requirements of a fair trial embodied in the due process clause continue to govern the conduct of the prosecution, which is not the subject of another, particular provision of the Bill of Rights. Although the prosecution is responsible for the presentation of the case against the defendant, its concern must be, as the Court said in BERGER V. NEW YORK (1967), "not that it shall win a case, but that justice shall be done. . . . It is as much [the prosecutor's] duty to refrain from improper methods calculated to produce a wrongful conviction as it is to use every legitimate means to bring about a just one."

The prosecutor's obligation of fairness requires him to avoid conduct calculated or likely to mislead the jury. The knowing use of false evidence, including testimony of a witness, is ground for reversal of a conviction. If the prosecutor knows that a witness has testified falsely about a material fact, he must take steps to correct the falsehood. The obligation not to use false evidence extends to the government as a whole; even if the prosecutor at trial is unaware that evidence is false, a blameworthy failure of the police or others in the prosecutor's office or elsewhere in the government to avoid or remedy the falsehood is a denial of a fair trial.

The prosecutor has a parallel obligation to disclose evidence favorable to the defendant if, as the Court said in *United States v. Agurs* (1976), the "evidence is obviously of such substantial value that elementary fairness requires it." The constitutional obligation of fairness does not require the prosecution to disclose all evidence that might possibly be helpful to the defense. The test following a conviction is whether the undisclosed evidence "creates a REASONABLE DOUBT that did not otherwise exist." The duty to disclose evidence in response to a specific request by the defense is greater; if the evidence is material at all the prosecutor must either honor the request or inform the court of his refusal.

Aside from his obligation to present the evidence fully, the prosecutor must avoid arguments or conduct before the jury that might mislead it or prejudice it against the defendant. In his opening and closing arguments as well as his questioning of witnesses, the prosecutor is expected not to depart from the evidence or to lead the jury away from a dispassionate judgment based on the evidence. Isolated improper remarks of a prosecutor usually are not deemed to have denied a fair trial, especially if they do not appear to have been a deliberate violation and the trial judge has taken corrective action such as instructing the jury to disregard the remarks. In order to determine whether the standard of fair trial has been met, the prosecutor's conduct is examined in the context of the whole trial.

In a number of situations, the demands of a fair trial are opposed by conflicting demands based on the FIRST AMENDMENT's protection of FREEDOM OF THE PRESS. Pretrial publicity of a case may make it more difficult or impossible to impanel an impartial jury. A fair trial does not require that jurors have been entirely ignorant of the facts of a case but only that, having in mind the news coverage and atmosphere of the community, they be able to decide according to the evidence. The Supreme Court has occasionally reversed a conviction because members of the jury were presumed to have, or acknowledged that they had, strong preconceptions of the defendant's guilt because of extensive coverage of the case in local news media.

A similar problem has sometimes arisen during trial. In *Sheppard v. Maxwell* (1966) the Supreme Court concluded that prejudicial pretrial publicity in the news media as well as the "carnival atmosphere" created by the media in and around the courtroom during trial had denied the defendant a fair trial. In ESTES V. TEXAS (1965) the Court concluded that television coverage of portions of a sensational trial that had also been the subject of massive pretrial publicity was impermissible. There is, however, no absolute constitutional prohibition against radio, television, or photographic coverage of a trial, which may, as the Court held in CHANDLER V. FLORIDA (1981), be allowed if it is conducted in a manner consistent with a fair trial.

The Supreme Court held, in RICHMOND NEWSPAPERS, INC. V. VIRGINIA (1980), that the First Amendment protects the right of the public to attend criminal trials. (In contrast, the right to a PUBLIC TRIAL in the Sixth Amendment is a right of the defendant alone.) Therefore, all other measures for ensuring a fair trial, such as sequestration of witnesses or jurors, must be considered before the public can be excluded, whether or not the defendant asks for exclusion. The Court has indicated strongly that a trial court should exercise its authority in whatever manner will afford a fair trial without closing it to the public.

Unlike some of the more particular provisions of the Bill of Rights that have to do with criminal process, the requirement of a fair trial retains the flexibility of a general standard and is not susceptible to precise definition by a set of rules. While important aspects of a fair trial are covered by other constitutional provisions, some remain within the ambit of the general standard. Jurisprudentially, the principal difference is that, unlike some particular constitutional rules, the general standard does not invalidate a conviction for a single instance of prejudicial error or unfairness. Rather it is set in the context of the whole trial, and a conviction will be reversed only if the trial as a whole was unfair. The standard of a fair trial also serves as a reminder of the government's relationship with an individual even when it seeks to convict him of a crime and as the repository of changing or enlarged conceptions of what fairness in the criminal process requires.

LLOYD L. WEINREB
(1986)

Bibliography

AMERICAN BAR ASSOCIATION   1968   *Standards Relating to Fair Trial and Free Press.* New York: Institute of Judicial Administration.

FELLMAN, DAVID   1976   *The Defendant's Rights Today.* Madison: University of Wisconsin Press.

KAMISAR, YALE; LaFAVE, WAYNE R.; and ISRAEL, JEROLD H.   (1965) 1986   *Modern Criminal Procedure.* St. Paul, Minn.: West Publishing Co.

LEVY, LEONARD W.   1974   *Against the Law.* New York: Harper & Row.

WEINREB, LLOYD L.   (1969) 1987   *Criminal Process.* Mineola, N.Y.: Foundation Press.

FAMILY AND THE CONSTITUTION

Family relations have an uncertain, even ambivalent constitutional status in Supreme Court decisions. If the Constitution protects the family against external interference, it also permits the establishment of public moral standards to regulate social relations among adults and to protect children from apparently harmful parental conduct.

This ambivalence appeared early. In MEYER V. NEBRASKA (1923) the Supreme Court opined that FOURTEENTH AMENDMENT "liberty" included the right "to marry, establish a home and bring up children." The Court did not explain, however, why this right stopped short at monogamy. In REYNOLDS V. UNITED STATES (1878) it had upheld Congress's power to forbid POLYGAMY in the TERRITORIES notwithstanding the religiously grounded objections of Mormon settlers. Nor did the Court subsequently explain how the right "to bring up children" was consistent with the compulsory STERILIZATION of a woman considered retarded by state authorities upheld in BUCK V. BELL (1927). One discernible principle did unify these early cases: the Constitution protects only family relations that judges consider "normal" and "wholesome." This principle might occasionally lead judges to substitute their views of normality for legislative impositions (as in *Meyer* where the state had forbidden schoolroom teaching of children in any language but English); it hardly serves, however, as a MAGNA CARTA for the protection from state interference of family sanctity and autonomy.

The prospect that constitutional doctrine might be elevated to serve this broader protective purpose emerged in the 1960s, as cases involving family relations began to appear in unprecedented numbers on the Supreme Court's docket. But in fact the decided cases exemplify the same conflicting strains as before. The first of the modern cases was GRISWOLD V. CONNECTICUT (1965), striking down a state law that prohibited anyone including married couples from using contraceptives. The Court spoke of marriage as "intimate to the degree of being sacred" and found a constitutionally protected " RIGHT OF PRIVACY surrounding the marriage relationship." In subsequent cases, however, the Court has been reluctant to extend this familial privacy right beyond the conventionally conceived marriage bond. Although EISENSTADT V. BAIRD (1972) recognized the right of unmarried persons to practice contraception, in *Doe v. Commonwealth's Attorney* (1976) the Court summarily affirmed a lower court's rejection of a constitutional attack on a state law criminally proscribing homosexual relations even among consenting adults in private. Similarly in *Belle Terre v. Boraas* (1974) the Court upheld a municipal ZONING restriction excluding communal families unless they were "related by blood, adoption or marriage"; and yet in MOORE V. CITY OF EAST CLEVELAND (1977) the Court struck down zoning restrictions that limited residence to nuclear families and excluded multigenerational families with blood ties. The theme that runs through these two zoning cases and through *Griswold* and

Doe is that the Constitution protects "families" when they reflect conventional social definitions of decency and morality.

The Court does not unquestioningly defer to legislative conceptions of appropriately conventional family relations. The Court has struck down familial regulations reflecting RACIAL DISCRIMINATION as in LOVING V. VIRGINIA (1967), or SEX DISCRIMINATION regarding alimony entitlements as in *Orr v. Orr* (1979), or required consent for adoptive placement as in *Caban v. Mahammed* (1979). But even in these cases the Justices appear guided more by their own conceptions of appropriate social conventions for family relations than by any principle of protection of individuals against state interference with their autonomous choices in family matters.

The constitutional status of parent-child relations is the result of similar conflicting impulses. In the adult relations cases, the underlying conflict is essentially between principles of individual autonomy and of community, between the individual's FREEDOM OF INTIMATE ASSOCIATION and the right of a group to define and enforce common standards of conduct on every group member. For state regulation of parent-child relations, these same conflicting principles are at stake, but the conflict extends even into these principles' very definition.

Thus the state can plausibly claim that it must restrict parental conduct to protect and enhance the child's developing capacity for individual autonomy. The claim is implicit in compulsory education laws, in laws permitting state intervention to override parental directives in disputes between parent and child (particularly adolescent children), and in laws proscribing child abuse or neglect. Parents, however, can plausibly claim that a child's capacity to develop as an autonomous individual is impaired by state impositions on parental conduct beyond the most minimal standards to protect the child's physical integrity. Thus even if constitutional DOCTRINE should give priority to individual autonomy over communitarian claims in adult relations, this priority does not resolve disputes regarding state regulation of parental conduct when both the state and the parents can plausibly claim to speak for the child's developing capacity for individual autonomy.

These disputes have occurred in three different contexts: claims by state authorities that parents' conduct was harmful to children; claims by parents that their children were harmed by state conduct, particularly in public schools; and claims by children, particularly older children, that state authorities should take their sides in disputes with their parents. In none of these contexts do the decided cases yield consistent constitutional principles.

The unresolved tension between competing principles was particularly evident in two Supreme Court decisions in successive terms that considered the application of constitutional norms to state abuse and neglect statutes. In *Santosky v. Kramer* (1982) the Court held that states must meet a higher burden of proof than the ordinary civil standard before the parent-child relationship could be terminated on grounds of harmful parental conduct; but in *Lassiter v. Department of Social Services* (1981) the Court had held that the parental relationship was not of sufficient constitutional weight to require the appointment of counsel to give indigent parents effective assistance against state actions for termination.

A similar if less blatant inconsistency is evident in the Court's rulings regarding the rights of parents to constrain state impositions on their children in public schools. Thus in INGRAHAM V. WRIGHT (1977) the Court ruled that school officials were free to inflict corporal punishment on students notwithstanding parental objections that the punishment was physically and psychologically harmful to their children; but in WISCONSIN V. YODER (1972) the Court had ruled that school officials could not require Amish children to attend secondary schools in the face of their parents' objections that this imposition was harmful to the children and inconsistent with the parents' views on proper child-rearing practices.

In the Amish case, the Court emphasized the religious basis for the parents' claims, a factor that might serve to distinguish the parents' claim in the corporal punishment case. But parental claims to preclude state interference in their decisions regarding children were not similarly honored, notwithstanding the religious grounding of such claims, in PLANNED PARENTHOOD V. DANFORTH (1976) where the parents objected to their unmarried pregnant daughters' wish to obtain an abortion. The minors' abortion and the Amish case might be distinguished on the ground that the pregnant minors openly disagreed with their parents while the Amish students apparently concurred with theirs. But this view of the abortion case—that the Constitution not only permits but requires state intervention to protect the autonomous wishes of older children from being overridden by their parents—cannot readily be squared with the Court's subsequent ruling in PARHAM V. J. R. (1979) essentially upholding parents' authority to confine their adolescent children in psychiatric institutions, notwithstanding the children's objections and claims for independent judicial protection.

These decisions raise at least the suspicion that the same guiding principle is at work in these parent-child-state cases as appeared in the cases regarding state regulation of adult familial relations—the principle that the Justices are not prepared to find constitutional protection for family status as such but only for those families whose conduct meets the Justices' particular approval. This principle could explain the Court's deference to Amish parents who generally succeed in imposing rigid behavioral con-

trols on their children, as the Court repeatedly stressed in *Yoder*, or its deference to parents' wishes to confine their socially disruptive children in psychiatric institutions. A judicial preference for such behavior controls might also explain the Court's refusal to defer to parents' objections to school corporal punishment or to parents' resistance to abortions when they had failed effectively to constrain their unmarried daughters' indulgence in sexual relations.

The Court has not been unanimous in these cases, and no Justice has explicitly defended this particular child-rearing principle as a constitutional norm. Yet the logical plausibility of this harmonizing principle does suggest that current constitutional doctrine gives no special status to family relations as such, either between parents and child or among adults. The occasional rhetorical flourishes in Supreme Court opinions about the "constitutional sanctity" of the family does not yet reflect any consistent constitutional principle.

ROBERT A. BURT
(1986)

Bibliography

BURT, ROBERT A. 1979 The Constitution of the Family. *The Supreme Court Review* 1979:329–395.
GOLDSTEIN, J. et al. 1973 *Beyond the Best Interests of the Child.* New York: Free Press.
——— 1979 *Before the Best Interests of the Child.* New York: Free Press.
KARST, KENNETH L. 1980 The Freedom of Intimate Association. *Yale Law Journal* 89:624–692.

FARETTA v. CALIFORNIA
422 U.S. 806 (1975)

In *Faretta* the Supreme Court reversed the conviction of a defendant forced to accept the services of a public defender in a FELONY case, holding that the Sixth Amendment guarantees the right to self-representation when a defendant "knowingly and intelligently" requests it.

This is a major decision about the WAIVER OF CONSTITUTIONAL RIGHTS because the argument of the state and the dissent was that society has an interest in a FAIR TRIAL, independent of the defendant's desires. Recognition of such an interest would necessarily mean that the trial judge must have discretion to reject even a knowing and intelligent waiver of the RIGHT TO COUNSEL.

Standby counsel may be appointed over the defendant's objection to aid him should he request help at the trial, or to intervene if the termination of self-representation becomes necessary.

BARBARA ALLEN BABCOCK
(1986)

FARRAND, MAX
(1869–1945)

Anyone who cares seriously to study the work of the CONSTITUTIONAL CONVENTION OF 1787 owes a debt to Max Farrand. Farrand, professor of history at Stanford (1901–1908) and Yale (1908–1925) Universities and later director of research at the Huntington Library, compiled and edited all the known *Records of the Federal Convention* (1911, revised 1937). That work was more influential than his narrative history books, which were intended for undergraduate or popular audiences.

DENNIS J. MAHONEY
(1986)

FAY v. NOIA
372 U.S. 391 (1963)

The Great Writ of HABEAS CORPUS allows state prisoners to seek federal court review of constitutional errors made at their trials, but the JUDICIAL CODE requires EXHAUSTION OF REMEDIES in state court, in order to preserve comity between state and federal courts. Charles Noia's 1942 murder conviction was based solely on a coerced confession procured in violation of his FOURTEENTH AMENDMENT rights to DUE PROCESS. He chose not to file a state APPEAL, however, because he feared that a new trial might end in a death sentence. Years later, he sought review of his due process claim in state courts, but they held that his original failure to appeal was a procedural default that barred further review. In *Fay*, a 6–3 Supreme Court held that his failure was not a "deliberate bypass" of state procedures and thus no bar to habeas corpus relief.

Justice WILLIAM J. BRENNAN, speaking for the majority, posited a "manifest federal policy" that liberty rights should not be denied without the fullest opportunity for federal JUDICIAL REVIEW. The concept of comity could not justify denying habeas corpus relief for failure to exhaust a remedy no longer available. As for the state's interests in insuring finality of criminal judgments, or exacting compliance with its procedures through default rules, these could not outweigh the "ideal of fair procedure" and the historic habeas corpus policy favoring the free exercise of federal judicial power to enforce this ideal. Finally, the state's rejection of Noia's claim could not be treated as an ADEQUATE STATE GROUND, for this jurisdictional deference would unduly burden the vindication of federal rights. Only when a defendant deliberately evaded state adjudication would FEDERALISM concerns justify the denial of habeas corpus review.

As dissenting Justice JOHN MARSHALL HARLAN noted, *Fay* marked a dramatic expansion of federal power to supervise state criminal justice. The concepts of exhaustion and adequate state grounds were modified to make room for a generous view that excused defendants from uncalculated WAIVER OF CONSTITUTIONAL RIGHTS in state proceedings. The "deliberately bypassing" defendant was a rare one, and *Fay*'s scope freed most defendants from forfeiting their rights through procedural defaults of every kind. Simultaneously, the WARREN COURT's application of the Fourth, Fifth, and Sixth Amendments to the states codified a Bill of Rights for criminal defendants. *Fay* insured a broad federal path of enforcement for these new guarantees, in an era when the state path of review was not always open or receptive to constitutional claims.

The BURGER COURT era brought a less hospitable federal climate for criminal defendants and, not surprisingly, also brought a corresponding change in the habeas corpus barometer, emerging clearly in WAINRIGHT V. SYKES (1977). *Fay*'s deliberate bypass rule did not endure as an exclusive measure of federalism interests, because a new "manifest" federal policy came to elevate the state's interest in finality above the ideal of fair procedure. With this new federalism, the whole point of habeas corpus review was transformed from the protection of constitutional rights to the protection of those with a claim to innocence.

CATHERINE HANCOCK
(1986)

Bibliography

COVER, ROBERT M. and ALEINIKOFF, T. ALEXANDER 1977 Dialectical Federalism: Habeas Corpus and the Court. *Yale Law Journal* 86:1035–1102.

FBI

See: Federal Bureau of Investigation

FEDERAL . . . ACT

See also under word following "Federal"

FEDERAL BUREAU OF INVESTIGATION

The Federal Bureau of Investigation (FBI) is a division of the Department of Justice supervised by the attorney general. Although a CABINET officer since the 1790s, the ATTORNEY GENERAL did not oversee federal law enforcement and did not even head a federal department until congressional legislation of 1870 created the Department of Justice. The attorney general's responsibilities originally involved arguing major cases before the Supreme Court and advising the President on constitutional questions. The combination of the RECONSTRUCTION experience with the enactment of legislation regulating INTERSTATE COMMERCE in 1887 and preventing corporate mergers in 1890, however, led attorneys general to recognize the need for experienced investigators to secure evidence to prosecute violators of the ANTITRUST and interstate commerce laws. Accordingly, in July 1908 Attorney General Charles Bonaparte, by EXECUTIVE ORDER, created a special investigation division within the Department of Justice, the Bureau of Investigation, formally renamed the Federal Bureau of Investigation in 1935.

Thereafter, the FBI's investigative reponsibilities increased as new laws expanded the definition of interstate commerce crime (the MANN ACT of 1910 and the Dyer Act of 1919) and law enforcement responsibilities (laws criminalizing kidnapping and bank robbing) and barred specified political activities that threatened the nation's internal security (the ESPIONAGE ACT of 1917 and the Smith Act of 1940). Yet this expansion raised no unique constitutional question both because it was legislatively mandated and because the Supreme Court upheld the constitutionality of the Espionage and Smith Acts, which impinged on speech and association.

The FBI's activities have raised constitutional issues because of the Bureau's monitoring of "subversive" activities, particularly since 1936. In striking contrast even to the abusive PALMER RAIDS of 1920, which had been based on the 1918 Immigration Act's alien deportation provisions, after 1936 the FBI did not seek evidence to effect prosecution; and its "intelligence" investigations were authorized solely under secret executive directives (President FRANKLIN D. ROOSEVELT's oral directive of August 1936) or public executive orders (President HARRY S. TRUMAN's March 1947 order establishing the Federal Employee Loyalty Program). In acquiring intelligence about dissident activities, the FBI's purposes became either to service White House interests and those of the increasingly powerful FBI director or, in the case of federal loyalty-security programs, to anticipate espionage by identifying "potentially disloyal" federal employees. In time, the FBI's dissemination activities extended beyond the executive branch—at first, during the 1940s, informally and then after the 1950s formally, to governors and to carefully selected reporters, columnists, prominent national leaders, and members of Congress. Rather than prosecuting individuals for violating federal laws, the FBI instead brought about the dismissal of "subversive" employees by disseminating information on state employees to state governors under a code-named Responsibilities Program and by exposing publicly other "subversives," often through covert assistance to the HOUSE COMMITTEE ON UN-AMERICAN ACTIVITIES, Senator Joseph McCarthy, and the Senate In-

ternal Security Subcommittee. Adopting a more aggressive tack after 1956, FBI officials instituted two other formal programs, COINTELPRO and Mass Media, both having as their purpose the discrediting of targeted organizations and their adherents.

These programs were not subject to JUDICIAL REVIEW both because they had no law enforcement purpose and because they were conducted secretly. Furthermore, these covert efforts to "harass, disrupt and discredit" targeted organizations or to disseminate derogatory information about political activists to favored journalists, members of Congress, Presidents, governors, and prominent citizens were based on a commitment to contain political change.

The FBI's activities raised other constitutional questions in view of some of the Bureau's investigative techniques. Despite the legislative ban against WIRETAPPING of the COMMUNICATIONS ACT of 1934 and the FOURTH AMENDMENT prohibition of UNREASONABLE SEARCHES and seizures, from 1940 forward the FBI installed wiretaps and bugs and conducted break-ins when investigating "subversive" activities and at times during sensitive criminal investigations. These techniques were authorized under secret directives issued either by Presidents (Franklin Roosevelt's May 1940 authorization of wiretapping), the attorney general (Herbert Brownell's May 1954 authorization of bugging), or solely by the FBI director (J. EDGAR HOOVER's 1942 authorization of break-ins). Theoretically, information so obtained could not be used for prosecution. However, two individuals inadvertently uncovered the FBI's ELECTRONIC EAVESDROPPING at a time when they were the subjects of criminal inquiries. Intercepted messages included attorney-client conversations, and in both cases, the disclosures led the courts to overturn the defendants' convictions.

Contrary to the rationale that gained currency during the 1960s of inherent presidential powers, when FBI officials first employed these electronic surveillance techniques in the 1940s they privately conceded their illegality and accordingly sought to preclude public discovery of potentially controversial practices. For example, when outlining how requests for his approval to conduct break-ins were to be submitted, FBI Director Hoover characterized this technique as "clearly illegal." Because break-ins offered the opportunity to acquire otherwise unobtainable information about "subversive" activities (membership and subscription lists, financial records, correspondence and memoranda), Hoover was willing to risk use of this technique. To avert discovery, however, the FBI director devised a special records procedure, "Do Not File," to ensure the undiscoverable destruction of such records and further to allow FBI officials to affirm, in response to congressional SUBPOENAS or court-ordered DIS-

COVERY motions, that a search of the FBI's "central records system" uncovered no evidence of illegal conduct. This FBI practice raised additional constitutional question insofar as, beginning in the late 1950s, break-ins were employed during some criminal investigations.

ATHAN THEOHARIS
(1992)

(SEE ALSO: *McCarthyism.*)

Bibliography

THEOHARIS, ATHAN and COX, JOHN STUART 1988 *The Boss.* Philadelphia: Temple University Press.
UNGAR, SANFORD 1975 *FBI.* Boston: Atlantic/Little, Brown.

FEDERAL COMMON LAW, CIVIL

In the English legal tradition to which this country is heir, judge-made COMMON LAW—law developed by courts in the absence of applicable LEGISLATION—has played a critical role in the determination of rights, duties, and remedies. But because our federal government is one of limited, delegated powers, the questions whether and under what circumstances the federal courts are empowered to formulate federal common law have been the subject of much debate. Although it is now settled that the federal courts do have such authority in civil matters, the debate continues over the sources of that authority and the proper scope of its exercise.

The Supreme Court's decision in ERIE RAILROAD CO. V. TOMPKINS (1938) marks a watershed in the evolution of this problem. Prior to that decision, the federal courts did not strive to develop a federal, or national, common law binding on the states and indeed on occasion denied that it existed (*Wheaton v. Peters*, 1834; *Smith v. Alabama*, 1888). Yet the Supreme Court, in SWIFT V. TYSON (1842), upheld the authority of the federal courts, in cases within the DIVERSITY JURISDICTION, to determine certain controversies on the basis of "general principles and doctrines" of jurisprudence and without regard to the common law decisions of the state courts. Thus, during the reign of *Swift v. Tyson*, the federal courts exercised considerable common law authority over a variety of disputes, ultimately extending well beyond the interstate commercial controversy involved in *Swift* itself and involving matters apparently not subject to federal legislative power. The decisions rendered in these cases, however, did not purport to bind the state courts, and the result was often the parallel existence of two different rules of law applicable to the same controversy, with the governing rule dependent on the forum in which the controversy was adjudicated.

Historians disagree on the justification—statutory and constitutional—of the *Swift* decision. In one view, the decision was not rooted in contemporary understanding of the nature of the common law but instead represented the use of judicial power to aid in the redistribution of wealth to promote commercial and industrial growth. A contrasting position is that the decision was fully consistent with the perception of the time that the common law of commercial transactions was not the command of the sovereign but rather was both the embodiment of prevailing customs and a process of applying them to the case at hand.

There is general agreement, however, that the Court expanded *Swift* well beyond its originally intended scope and that its OVERRULING, in *Erie*, reflected a very different perception of the proper role of the federal courts. The Court in *Erie*, speaking through Justice LOUIS D. BRANDEIS, concluded that there was no "general" federal common law—that the Rules of Decision Act, originally section 34 of the JUDICIARY ACT OF 1789, required adherence to state decisional or common law in controversies such as *Erie* itself, a case that fell within federal JURISDICTION solely on the basis of the parties' diversity of citizenship.

But the *Erie* decision helped bring to the surface the existence of what has been called a "specialized" federal common law, operating in those areas where the application of federal law seems warranted even though no federal constitutional or legislative provision points the way to a governing rule. Indeed, on the very day that *Erie* was decided, the Court in *Hinderlider v. La Plata River & Cherry Creek Ditch Co.* (1938), again speaking through Justice Brandeis, said that "whether the water of an interstate stream must be apportioned between the two States is a question of 'federal common law' upon which neither the statutes nor the decisions of either State can be conclusive."

What is the source of the authority to formulate federal common law—law that, unlike decisions rendered pursuant to *Swift*, binds state and federal courts alike? To some extent, the source may be traced to specific constitutional provisions, such as the grant of ADMIRALTY AND MARITIME JURISDICTION in Article III, or the prohibition of unreasonable SEARCHES AND SEIZURES in the FOURTH AMENDMENT. (See BIVENS V. SIX UNKNOWN NAMED AGENTS, declaring the existence of a damage remedy for a Fourth Amendment violation.) But the line between CONSTITUTIONAL INTERPRETATION, on the one hand, and the exercise of common law authority, on the other, is indistinct, and there is often disagreement among both judges and commentators about the function the courts are performing. The significance of this disagreement is more than semantic, for the ability of the legislative branch to modify or reject a Supreme Court ruling is plainly more circumscribed if the ruling is seen to be required by the Constitution than if the ruling is a common law one authorized but not compelled by the FUNDAMENTAL LAW.

In other instances, the source of judicial authority may be found in a particular federal statute. Infrequently, the congressional command is explicit, as in the mandate in Rule 501 of the Federal Rules of Evidence that in certain cases questions of evidentiary privilege "shall be governed by the principles of the common law as they may be interpreted by the courts of the United States in the light of reason and experience." More often, the legislative direction is, at best, implicit and the judicial role may be viewed as that of implementing federal legislative policy by filling the gaps left by the legislation itself. Once again, the line between statutory construction and the exercise of common law authority is not easily drawn.

In a significant number of cases, the exercise of authority to formulate federal common law is difficult to trace to a specific provision in the Constitution or in a statute. In such cases, the authority may be attributed more broadly to the nature of the judicial process, to the structure of our federal constitutional system, and to the relationships created by it. The authority, in other words, may be rooted in necessity. As Justice ROBERT H. JACKSON put it, concurring in *D'Oench Duhme Co. v. F.D.I.C.* (1942): "Were we bereft of the common law, our federal system would be impotent. This follows from the recognized futility of attempting all-complete statutory codes and is apparent from the terms of the Constitution itself."

Some examples of the exercise of this authority may help to clarify its scope. Perhaps most important is the category of those interstate or international disputes that, in the words of the Supreme Court, "implicate conflicting rights of States or our foreign relations" (*Texas Industries, Inc. v. Radcliff Materials, Inc.*, 1981). Such disputes do not always fall within the specific jurisdictional grants of Article III applicable to certain interstate or international controversies. In any event, the existence of a conflict between the interests of two states may make it inappropriate for the law of either to govern of its own force. And controversies affecting our relations as sovereign with foreign nations may require a single federal response rather than a cacophony of responses rooted in varying state laws. (See ACT OF STATE DOCTRINE.)

Another leading instance of the exercise of common law authority embraces controversies involving the rights, obligations, or proprietary interests of the United States. In such controversies, especially those arising in the administration of nationwide programs, formulation of federal common law may be warranted by the need for uniform treatment of the activities of the federal government or, more modestly, for some degree of federal supervision of the application of state law to those activities.

The amorphous origins and uncertain scope of the federal common law power underscore the need to recognize certain limitations that are anchored in the concerns of FEDERALISM and of SEPARATION OF POWERS. The first of these concerns focuses on the interests of the states in preserving a measure of autonomy on matters properly within their sphere—interests reflected in the TENTH AMENDMENT. Because federal law is often interstitial in character—written against a background of state laws governing basic human affairs—the concern for federalism supports a presumption that state law ought not to be displaced in the absence of a clear legislative direction, a sharp conflict between the state law and federal program, or the existence of a uniquely federal interest requiring protection. To some extent, this presumption is supported by and reflected in the provision of the Rules of Decision Act that state laws shall constitute the rules of decision except where otherwise required by the Constitution or by federal treaty or statute. But the last phrase of that act—limiting its command to "cases where they (the rules of decision) apply"—gives the provision a circularity that affords little guidance to the resolution of particular problems of potential conflict between federal and state authority.

Even when the exercise of federal authority is warranted, a careful balancing of state and federal interests may lead to the adoption of state laws rather than to the imposition of a uniform federal rule, so long as the state laws in question are compatible with federal interests. Such results were reached, for example, in *De Sylva v. Ballentine* (1955), involving a definition of "children" under the Federal Copyright Act, and *United States v. Kimbell Foods, Inc.* (1979), dealing with the priority of federal government liens arising from federal lending programs.

The second concern—that of separation of powers—springs from the belief that the primary responsibility for lawmaking should rest with the democratically elected representatives in the legislative branch. At a time when the common law function was seen in terms primarily of the application of established customs and usages, the concern for the proper separation and allocation of federal powers had less force than it does today, when there is more emphasis on the creative potential of the common law. Moreover, the separation of powers question is not unrelated to the regard for state interests, since the bicameral federal legislature is structured in such a way as to protect the states against action that might be taken by a legislature apportioned solely on the basis of population.

Concern that the courts not usurp a function that is properly legislative has led to an emphasis on LEGISLATIVE INTENT in many instances in which the federal courts have been asked to articulate new rights or develop new remedies not specifically provided for by statute. Moreover, the Supreme Court has stressed the ability of Congress to displace federal common law with statutory regulations, even in some instances in which the source of authority is the Constitution itself.

The problems inherent in the exercise of common law power have been highlighted in the Supreme Court's struggle with the question of implied remedies for federal constitutional or statutory violations. Since *Bivens v. Six Unknown Named Agents* (1971), the Court has generally been willing to allow a person harmed by unconstitutional action to sue for damages, despite the lack of any constitutional or statutory provision for suit. But persons harmed by violations of federal statutes have frequently been held unable to obtain relief in the absence of an express statutory remedy or strong evidence of legislative intent to permit such a remedy.

In both types of cases the Supreme Court has perhaps too readily yielded its authority to exercise a principled discretion in determining whether traditional common law remedies should be available to implement federal policy. The tendency toward formalistic insistence on a remedy for every wrong in cases involving constitutional violations, and toward ritualistic invocation of legislative intent in order to deny a remedy in cases of statutory infractions, suggests a relinquishment of the judicial responsibility that lies at the heart of our common law heritage.

DAVID L. SHAPIRO
(1986)

Bibliography

BATOR, PAUL; MISHKIN, PAUL J.; SHAPIRO, DAVID L.; and WECHSLER, HERBERT (1953) 1973 and 1981 Supp. *Hart and Wechsler's The Federal Courts and the Federal System.* Pages 691–832. Mineola, N.Y.: Foundation Press.

BRIDWELL, RANDALL and WHITTEN, RALPH U. 1977 *The Constitution and the Common Law.* Lexington, Mass.: Lexington Books.

FIELD, MARTHA A. 1986 Sources of Law: The Scope of Federal Common Law. *Harvard Law Review* 99:883–984.

FRIENDLY, HENRY J. 1964 In Praise of Erie—And of the New Federal Common Law. *New York University Law Review* 39: 383–422.

FREYER, TONY ALLAN 1979 *Forums of Order: The Federal Courts and Business in American History.* Greenwich, Conn.: Jai Press, Inc.

HILL, ALFRED 1967 The Law-Making Power of the Federal Courts: Constitutional Preemption. *Columbia Law Review* 67:1024–1081.

HORWITZ, MORTON J. 1977 *The Transformation of American Law, 1780–1860.* Pages 211–252. Cambridge, Mass.: Harvard University Press.

REDISH, MARTIN H. 1980 *Federal Jurisdiction: Tensions in the Allocation of Judicial Power.* Pages 79–107. Indianapolis: Bobbs-Merrill.

FEDERAL COMMON LAW OF CRIMES

One of the leading Jeffersonian jurists, ST. GEORGE TUCKER, noted with alarm that Chief Justice OLIVER ELLSWORTH and Justice BUSHROD WASHINGTON had laid down the general rule that the COMMON LAW was the unwritten law of the United States government. The question whether the Constitution adopted the common law, Tucker wrote,

is of very great importance, not only as it regards the limits of the JURISDICTION of the *federal courts;* but also, as it relates to the extent of the powers vested in the *federal government.* For, if it be true that the common law of England has been adopted by the United States in their national, or federal capacity, the jurisdiction of the *federal courts* must be co-extensive with it; or, in other words, *unlimited:* so also, must be the jurisdiction, and authority of the *other branches* of the federal government [Tucker, *Blackstone's Commentaries*, 1803, I, 380].

Tucker's answer to the question was that the JUDICIAL POWER OF THE UNITED STATES under Article III was limited to the subjects of congressional legislative power and that common law did not give jurisdiction in any case where jurisdiction was not expressly given by the Constitution. Tucker's view eventually prevailed, but it was probably not the view of the Constitution's Framers.

Article III extends the judicial power of the United States to all cases in law and EQUITY arising under the Constitution, treaties, and "Laws of the United States." The latter phrase could include common law crimes. At the CONSTITUTIONAL CONVENTION OF 1787, the Committee of Detail reported a draft declaring that the Supreme Court's jurisdiction extended to "all Cases arising under the Laws passed by the Legislature of the United States." The Convention without dissenting vote adopted a motion striking out the words "passed by the Legislature." That deletion suggests that "the Laws of the United States" comprehended the common law of crimes, as well as other nonstatutory law.

The legislative history of the JUDICIARY ACT OF 1789 suggests a similar conclusion. A draft of that statute relating to the jurisdiction of both the federal district and federal circuit courts (sections nine and eleven as enacted) gave these courts "cognizance of all crimes and offenses that shall be cognizable under the authority of the United States and *defined by the laws of the same.*" The italicized phrase, deleted from the act's final text, might have restricted criminal jurisdiction to statutory crimes. Whether a federal court was to apply a federal common law of crimes or apply the common law of the state in which a crime was committed is not clear.

What is clear is that the first generation of federal

judges assumed jurisdiction in cases of nonstatutory crimes. Justice JAMES WILSON, an influential Framer of the Constitution, at his state's ratifying convention had endorsed federal prosecutions at common law for criminal libels against the United States. In 1793 he instructed a federal GRAND JURY on the virtues of the common law, which included, he said, the law of nations. The grand jury indicted Gideon Henfield for breaching American neutrality by assisting a French privateer in the capture of a British ship; the INDICTMENT referred to "violation of the laws of nations, against the laws and constitution of the United States and against the peace and dignity of the United States." ALEXANDER HAMILTON prepared the indictment, which Attorney General EDMUND RANDOLPH (another Framer) helped prosecute. Justice Wilson, joined by Justice JAMES IREDELL and Judge RICHARD PETERS, constituted the federal CIRCUIT COURT that tried Henfield's nonstatutory offense. Henfield, having been at sea when President GEORGE WASHINGTON proclaimed American neutrality, pleaded ignorance. Secretary of State THOMAS JEFFERSON, who had urged Henfield's prosecution and endorsed Wilson's opinion as to the indictability of the offense, explained that the jury acquitted because the crime was not knowingly committed. JOHN MARSHALL, in his *Life of Washington,* described the prosecution as having been based on an offense "indictable at common law, for disturbing the peace of the United States."

Subsequent common law prosecutions were not so fuzzy. In 1793 a federal grand jury indicted Joseph Ravara, a consul from Genoa, for attempting to extort money from a British diplomat. Justice Wilson, joined by Peters, ruled that the circuit court had jurisdiction, although Congress had passed no law against extortion. Justice Iredell argued that the defendant's diplomatic status brought him within the exclusive ORIGINAL JURISDICTION of the Supreme Court. Ravara was tried in 1794 by a circuit court consisting of Jay and Peters, who instructed the jury that the offense was indictable at common law, part of the LAW OF THE LAND. The jury convicted. In 1795 a federal court in New York, at the instigation of Attorney General Randolph, indicted Greenleaf, the editor of the *New-York Journal,* for criminal libel, a common law crime. The case was dropped, but in 1797 the editor was again indicted for the same crime and convicted by a court presided over by Chief Justice Oliver Ellsworth, an influential Framer and chief author of the Judiciary Act of 1789. In Massachusetts in 1797 Ellsworth ruled that the federal circuit court possessed jurisdiction over crimes against the common law, which the laws of the United States included, and therefore might try persons indicted for counterfeiting notes of the Bank of the United States (not then a statutory offense).

In the same year a federal grand jury followed Justice Iredell's charge and indicted a congressman, Samuel J. Cabell, for the common law crime of SEDITIOUS LIBEL, but the prosecution was aborted for political reasons. In 1798, before Congress passed the Sedition Act, prosecutions for seditious libel were begun against Benjamin Bache, who soon died, and John Burke, who fled the country before Justice WILLIAM PATERSON could try him. In 1799 Ellsworth and Iredell, in separate cases, told federal grand juries that the federal courts had common law jurisdiction over seditious libel and, in Ellsworth's words, over "acts manifestly subversive of the national government." He added that an indictable offense need be defined only by common law, not statute.

The sole dissenting voice in this line of decision was that of Justice SAMUEL CHASE in *Worrall's Case* (1798), where the common law indictment was for attempted bribery of a federal official. Judge Peters disagreed with Chase's argument that no federal common law of crimes existed, and the jury convicted. Chase, however, changed his opinion in *United States v. Sylvester* (1799), when he presided over a common law prosecution for counterfeiting. Thus, Chief Justices Jay and Ellsworth and Justices Wilson, Paterson, Iredell, and Chase endorsed federal court jurisdiction over common law crimes. The Jeffersonians, by then, vehemently opposed such views, arguing that only the state courts could try common law crimes. When Jefferson was President, however, Judge Pierpont Edwards, whom he had appointed to the federal district court in Connecticut, sought and received common law indictments against several persons for seditious libel against the President and the government. Jefferson knew of the common law prosecutions by the federal court and did not criticize them or take any actions to halt them, until he learned that one of the defendants could prove the truth of his accusation that the President had once engaged in a sexual indiscretion. The prosecutions were dropped except for those against Hudson and Goodwin, editors of Hartford's *Connecticut Courant,* who challenged the jurisdiction of the federal court.

By this time the administration had a stake in a ruling against federal jurisdiction over common law crimes. After much government stalling until a majority of Jeffersonian appointees controlled the Supreme Court, UNITED STATES V. HUDSON AND GOODWIN was finally decided in 1812. Without hearing ORAL ARGUMENTS and against all the precedents, a bare majority of the Court, in a brief opinion by Justice WILLIAM JOHNSON, ruled that the question whether the federal courts "can exercise a common law jurisdiction in criminal cases" has been "settled in public opinion," which opposed such jurisdiction. Moreover, the Constitution had not expressly delegated to the federal courts authority over common law crimes. "The legislative authority of the Union must first make an act a crime, affix a punishment to it, and declare the Court that shall have jurisdiction of the offense."

Justice JOSEPH STORY, who had not made known his dissent at the time, did so in a circuit opinion in 1813 and forced a reconsideration of the rule of *Hudson and Goodwin*. In *United States v. Coolidge* (1816), decided without argument, Johnson, noting that the Court was still divided (Marshall and Washington probably supported Story), refused to review the 1812 decision in the absence of "solemn argument." Thus the great question was resolved without reasoned consideration, to the enormous detriment of the power of the United States courts to define criminal acts.

Although "judge-made" or nonstatutory federal crimes disappeared after the *Coolidge* decision, federal courts continued to exercise common law powers to enforce law and order within their own precincts (see CONTEMPT POWER) and continued to employ a variety of common law techniques, forms, and writs in the enforcement of congressionally defined crimes. The FEDERAL RULES OF CRIMINAL PROCEDURE reflect that fact, as does *Marshall v. United States* (1959). By its "supervisory powers" over lower federal courts and, through them, over federal law enforcement officers, the Supreme Court can still be said, loosely, to exercise an interstitial common law authority with respect to federal crimes.

LEONARD W. LEVY
(1986)

Bibliography

CROSSKEY, WILLIAM W.   1953   *Politics and the Constitution in the History of the United States*, 2 vols. Chaps. 20–24. Chicago: University of Chicago Press.

GOEBEL, JULIUS, JR.   1971   *Antecedents and Beginnings to 1801*. Volume 1 of Freund, Paul, ed., *The Oliver Wendell Holmes Devise History of the Supreme Court*. New York: Macmillan.

PRESSER, STEPHEN B.   1978   "A Tale of Two Judges: Richard Peters, Samuel Chase, and the Broken Promise of Federalist Jurisprudence." *Northwestern Law Review* 73:26–111.

TUCKER, ST. GEORGE   1803   Blackstone's Commentaries, with Notes of Reference to the Constitution and Laws of the Federal Government of the United States and of the Commonwealth of Virginia, 5 vols. Philadelphia: Young & Small.

WARREN, CHARLES   1923   "New Light on the History of the Federal Judiciary Act of 1789." *Harvard Law Review* 37:49–132.

WHARTON, FRANCIS, ed.   1849 (1970)   *State Trials of the United States During the Administrations of Washington and Adams.* New York: Burt Franklin.

FEDERAL COMMUNICATIONS COMMISSION

See: Broadcasting; Communications Act;
Regulatory Agencies

FEDERAL COMMUNICATIONS COMMISSION v. LEAGUE OF WOMEN VOTERS

See: Government Speech

FEDERAL COMMUNICATIONS COMMISSION v. PACIFICA FOUNDATION
438 U.S. 726 (1978)

In *FCC v. Pacifica Foundation* the Court held that limited civil sanctions could constitutionally be invoked against a radio broadcast containing many vulgar words. The Court stressed that its holding was limited to the particular context, that is, to civil sanctions applied to indecent speech in an afternoon radio broadcast when, the Court assumed, children were in the audience. The opinion did not address criminal sanctions for televised or closed circuit broadcasts or late evening presentations, nor did it illuminate the concept of indecent speech except to suggest that occasional expletives and Elizabethan comedies may be decent enough even in the early afternoon.

STEVEN SHIFFRIN
(1986)

FEDERAL COURTS IMPROVEMENT ACT
96 Stat. 25 (1982)

This act reorganized several specialized federal courts. It merged the former COURT OF CLAIMS and COURT OF CUSTOMS AND PATENT APPEALS into a new UNITED STATES COURT OF APPEALS FOR THE FEDERAL CIRCUIT, transferring to the new court the former courts' JURISDICTION, and staffing it with the judges of the superseded courts. The Federal Circuit is a CONSTITUTIONAL COURT, staffed by twelve judges with life terms.

The act also created a new CLAIMS COURT to handle the trial functions formerly performed by commissioners (later called trial judges) of the old Court of Claims. The Claims Court is a LEGISLATIVE COURT; its sixteen judges serve for fifteen-year terms. Appeals go to the Federal Circuit.

KENNETH L. KARST
(1986)

Bibliography

SYMPOSIUM 1983–1984 The Federal Courts Improvement Act. *Cleveland State Law Review* 32:1–116.

FEDERAL CRIMINAL LAW

In the past two decades, Congress has enacted many new types of criminal statutes, such as the RACKETEER INFLUENCED AND CORRUPT ORGANIZATIONS ACT (RICO) and the continuing criminal enterprise and money-laundering offenses. New approaches to criminal penalties and sentencing have also been adopted, including criminal forfeiture, high mandatory sentences, and the sentencing guidelines. Although the government has been prosecuting these new crimes and penalties, often in combination, for many years, with few exceptions their constitutionality has not been tested in the Supreme Court.

The Constitution as applied to the substantive federal criminal law is largely dormant. The Supreme Court infrequently agrees to review cases raising issues of interpretation of federal criminal statutes. Even rarer is the case in which the Court agrees to consider the constitutionality of a substantive criminal statute. And cases in which the Court holds either substantive criminal legislation or prosecutorial action to be unconstitutional are rarer still. This is not for want of a large number of federal criminal cases in which such issues are raised, nor for a lack of applicable constitutional provisions or doctrines against which federal criminal statues and prosecutions can be tested—for example, DOUBLE JEOPARDY, VAGUENESS, and CRUEL AND UNUSUAL PUNISHMENT.

There have been a few recent exceptions to the prevailing pattern. In *Grady v. Corbin*, a 1990 decision arising out of a state drunk driving-criminal homicide prosecution, the Supreme Court adopted a revised double-jeopardy test that, among its most important effects, may have an impact on federal RICO and continuing criminal enterprise prosecutions.

Before *Grady*, the principal test for determining whether the Constitution was violated by successive prosecutions under two different criminal statutes for the same criminal act or transaction was the doctrine described in *Blockburger v. United States* (1932): that the double-jeopardy prohibition is not violated if each of the statutes involved in the two prosecutions requires proof of a fact that the other statute does not.

The effect of *Blockburger* has been generally to permit separate prosecutions growing out of the same conduct (even if the essence of the charges are similar) as long as they were based on different federal criminal statutes. In the federal criminal context, the *Blockburger* standard is easily met; there is little coherence or consistency in the way federal crimes are drafted, and the nature of most of these statutory offenses is such that they have elements quite different from all others.

In *Grady*, the Court ruled that the *Blockburger* test should still be applied in the first instance. If this standard is satisfied by a comparison of the elements of the two offenses, it is to be followed by a further inquiry under which the subsequent prosecution is barred if "the government, to establish an essential element of an offense charged in that prosecution, . . . prove[s] conduct that constitutes an offense for which the defendant has already been prosecuted."

Rather than focusing, as does *Blockburger*, on the statutory elements alone, this latter test requires a comparison of what the prosecutor attempts to prove at both of the trials. Justice WILLIAM J. BRENNAN, writing for the majority in *Grady*, took pains, however, to note that "[t]his is not . . . [a] same evidence test. The critical inquiry is what conduct the . . . [government] will prove, not the evidence . . . [it] will use to prove that conduct."

Depending on its subsequent interpretation, application of the *Grady* test could impose an important restriction on the government's ability to prosecute RICO and continuing criminal-enterprise cases. The RICO offense is committed when a person conducts the affairs of an enterprise (a continuing conspiratorial group or legal entity, such as a corporation or a governmental agency) through a pattern of racketeering activity that involves the commission of two or more related predicate offenses.

Before *Grady*, the government could, and often did, prosecute RICO cases relying on predicate offenses for which the accused had previously been tried and convicted (and even offenses of which the accused had been acquitted). *Grady*'s abandonment of *Blockburger* as the exclusive test of double jeopardy in successive-prosecution cases can be argued to bar the use as predicate offenses in RICO (and, for similar reasons, in continuing criminal enterprise cases) of crimes for which the accused has previously been tried. If the *Grady* test is applied as Justice ANTONIN SCALIA, in dissent, suggested it would be—that is, "where the charges arise from a single criminal act, occurrence, episode, or transaction, they must be tried in a single proceeding"—the decision will have the effect of barring separate trials of a RICO charge and the predicate offenses on which the RICO count is based.

An early post-*Grady* decision, *United States v. Esposito* (1990), handed down by a federal court of appeals, has taken a contrary view, however, holding that *Grady* does not bar a prosecution of the predicate crimes where there has been a prior acquittal on the related RICO charge. *Esposito* relied mainly on the earlier Supreme Court decision in *Garrett v. United States* (1985), a case only briefly cited in *Grady*.

Garrett involved the double-jeopardy implications of a continuing criminal-enterprise prosecution where the facts underlying a prior conviction of marijuana importation were used to prove one of the three predicate offenses on which the continuing criminal-enterprise charge was based. The Supreme Court ruled that the double-jeopardy prohibition was not violated where the prior conviction was only one incident of conduct that occurred on two single days during the five-year course of conduct that was the basis for the continuing criminal-enterprise charge.

Although *Garrett* seems to be a relevant precedent in deciding on the effect of *Grady* on RICO and continuing criminal-enterprise prosecutions, the question remains whether, after *Grady*, *Garrett* is still good law and, if so, whether in a RICO or continuing criminal-enterprise prosecution, the government in proving conduct underlying a prior conviction as a predicate offense is trying to "establish *an essential element* of . . . [the] offense charged in that prosecution" (emphasis added).

Grady does not affect another application of the same *Blockburger* test—its use as the constitutional standard for determining whether separate punishments can be imposed for offenses tried together. Accordingly, even after *Grady*, there is no constitutional bar to the practice of prosecuting, along with a RICO count, separate predicate offenses (even those based in essentially the same harmful conduct) whose statutory elements differ from each other and those in the RICO statute and, following conviction on all of the charges, imposing separate punishments for each of the several crimes.

Grady is a modern rarity, a constitutional decision that may impose a substantive restriction on the enforcement of the federal criminal law, but there is a chance that it will not remain very long on the books. It was a 5–4 decision, with Justice Scalia, joined by Justices SANDRA DAY O'CONNOR, ANTHONY M. KENNEDY, and Chief Justice WILLIAM H. REHNQUIST dissenting. Given the close division in the case, the subsequent retirement of the author of the majority opinion, Justice Brennan, and the fact that the Court's articulation of double-jeopardy doctrine seems to be continually evolving, the case is a possible candidate for early overruling.

Apart from *Grady*, no other recent significant constitutional decision has served to restrict the use of the many innovative federal crime statutes and punishments enacted during the past two decades. The closest that the Court has come recently to such a decision is Justice Scalia's concurring opinion in *H.J., Inc. v. Northwestern Bell Telephone Co.* (1989) (joined by the same three Justices who joined him in dissent in *Grady*), in which he raised doubts about whether a key element of the RICO statute—the "pattern" requirement in the "pattern of racketeering activity" phrase—meets the constitutional proscription against vagueness in criminal statutes.

The *H.J.* decision itself involved a civil action under the provision of the RICO statute that authorizes a private treble-damage suit to be brought by a person injured by a criminal RICO violation. Justice Scalia noted that because RICO has criminal applications "as well," it "must, even in its civil applications, possess the degree of certainty required for criminal laws." A corollary follows from this proposition. A decision in a civil RICO suit that the "pattern of racketeering" phrase used in defining the criminal violation is constitutionally infirm would apply equally in the criminal context. Thus, a constitutional decision that might in its immediate impact serve to insulate business people from treble-damage actions could also serve to protect organized-crime figures from federal criminal prosecution. Of course, it remains to be seen whether the concurring opinion in *H.J.* will gain another adherent and ripen into a constitutional restriction on the breadth of the RICO statute.

An innovative aspect of the RICO and drug statutes, the punishment of criminal forfeiture, was recently considered in *Caplin and Drysdale, Chartered v. United States* (1989), where the Court held that neither the Fifth nor the Sixth Amendment exempts from forfeiture assets that a criminal defendant proposes to use to pay defense counsel. In a related case, *United States v. Monsanto* (1989), the Court upheld the constitutionality of a pretrial order freezing such assets in a defendant's possession.

A more central constitutional challenge to criminal forefeiture, litigated in some of the courts of appeals, but yet to be considered by the Supreme Court, is the question as to whether, given the nature and circumstances of the offense, a forfeiture might be grossly disproportionate under the Eighth Amendment's cruel and unusual punishment clause.

Under the RICO statute, the prosecutor may seek forfeiture of the convicted person's entire interest in an enterprise the affairs of which were carried on in violation of the statute; the statutory forfeiture provision contains no limitation. Moreover, once the accused is convicted, forfeiture is mandatory; the judge has no discretion to reduce the amount. Thus, a person who owns all or most of a corporation and violates the federal criminal law, for example, by accepting or paying some kickbacks may, as a result of a RICO conviction, forfeit his or her entire interest in the corporation to the government.

In *United States v. Busher* (1987), taking to heart the Supreme Court's ruling in SOLEM V. HELM (1983) (the Eighth Amendment "prohibits not only barbaric punishments, but also sentences that are disproportionate to the crime committed"), the Ninth Circuit Court of Appeals ruled that the Eighth Amendment limits extreme criminal forfeitures under RICO (and under the drug laws) to insure that the punishment imposed is not "disproportionate to the crime committed." Some of the other circuits have ruled similarly.

None of these decisions has been reviewed by the Supreme Court. However, the Court has agreed to consider an appeal on an Eighth Amendment ground in a drug case that might shed some light on the forfeiture punishment issue. In *Harmelin v. Michigan,* the Court will decide whether a mandatory term of life imprisonment without parole imposed on a person with no prior criminal record, who has been convicted of possession of slightly more than a pound of cocaine, violates the eighth amendment proscription against cruel and unusual punishment. The case will be considered in the 1990–1991 term.

There has been one recent important constitutional decision affecting a key element in the federal criminal enforcement system, MISTRETTA V. UNITED STATES (1989), where the Court sustained the United States Sentencing Commission against a constitutional challenge claiming that the legislation setting up the Commission delegated excessive legislative power to the Commission and violated separation of powers doctrine.

In 1984, with a view to eliminating excessive disparity in federal sentences, the Congress enacted the Sentencing Reform Act setting up the Sentencing Commission as an independent body in the Judicial Branch, with authority to establish binding Sentencing Guidelines that, based upon detailed factors relating to the offense and the offender, provide for a range of determinate sentences for all federal offenses.

In *Mistretta,* the Court ruled that the Sentencing Reform Act sets forth "more than . . . [the] 'intelligible principle' or minimal standards" that are required under traditional nondelegation doctrine prohibiting excessive delegations of legislative authority: "Developing proportionate penalties for hundreds of different crimes by a virtually limitless array of offenders is precisely the sort of intricate, labor-intensive task for which delegation to an expert body is especially appropriate."

While recognizing that the Sentencing Commission "unquestionably is a peculiar institution within the framework of our Government," the Court rejected the argument that the structure of the Commission violated separation of powers doctrine insofar as it required Article III judges, who sit on the Commission with other nonjudicial appointees selected by the President, to exercise legislative authority; and also required those judges to share their judicial rulemaking authority with nonjudges; and threatened judicial independence insofar as the President is given authority to remove the judges from the Commission.

Mistretta is a significant decision since it sustains against constitutional attack the basic structural change relating to federal sentencing that Congress had effected by enacting the Sentencing Reform Act. Although there are further constitutional issues that may be raised in cases

applying the guidelines—for example, whether the guidelines violate due process insofar as they restrict judicial discretion to weigh individual factors in sentencing—the message of *Mistretta* is that the Sentencing Commission and its guidelines are here to stay.

Although *Mistretta* is significant, it is also *sui generis.* It is a unique decision relating to a new institutional structure and does not detract at all from the observation made earlier that the Constitution is largely dormant as applied to the substantive federal criminal law.

Of course, given the current makeup of the Court, public attitudes toward crime, and the historical reluctance of the Court to adjudge substantive federal criminal legislation unconstitutional, even were the Court to agree to review the constitutionality of these new measures, it would be unlikely that any of them would be found invalid. Still, even if declarations of unconstitutionality are unlikely, it would be helpful to the bench and bar if the Court were to review these issues with greater frequency.

The import of the Court's general reluctance to review many issues of statutory interpretation and the constitutionality of substantive federal criminal laws and related issues (while inexplicably continuing frequently to delve deeply into the minutiae of Fourth Amendment search and seizure issues) goes far beyond the direct effect of the Court's failure to consider the relevant issues; it influences the lower federal courts, which see many more federal criminal cases than the high court, and it may also be having an impact on the Congress.

Not surprisingly, federal district courts and courts of appeals generally do not give extended consideration to claims challenging the constitutionality of the new federal criminal statutes such as RICO. Correspondingly and perhaps more importantly, they also appear generally not even to be influenced very much by constitutional values in their interpretation of federal criminal statutes. This may not be unexpected in a climate created by a high court that itself is paying little attention to such issues. Yet in a system of judicial review, one expects constitutional values to be applied not only as a basis for determining the validity of criminal statutes, but as an element influencing, in appropriate cases and to a limited extent, issues of statutory interpretation.

In recent years, Congress has legislated an explosion in federal criminal statutes. At the same time, the legislature seems to be paying less and less attention to statutory details and has even become careless in the drafting process. In 1984, 1986, and 1988, Congress enacted comprehensive legislative packages encompassing a large number of federal criminal subjects; in the 1988 legislation, for example, a significant number of the provisions were directed to correcting drafting errors in the earlier legislation. Although it is not possible to demonstrate any direct linkage between the Supreme Court's inattention to the federal criminal law and the increase in legislative action in this area and the corresponding increase in drafting sloppiness, one might expect the Congress to be affected in its actions if the Court were to enter this arena more frequently.

Were the Court more actively to review and perhaps occasionally invalidate federal legislative or executive action in the criminal sphere affecting substantive interests, the effect might go far beyond the specific issues being decided. It might influence federal judges' approach to issues of interpretation of federal criminal statutes and also affect the kinds of cases prosecutors bring and the kind of positions they take in cases being brought. Most important, it could influence the Congress and have a significant impact on the form and content of future federal criminal legislation.

NORMAN ABRAMS
(1992)

Bibliography

ABRAMS, NORMAN   1986   *Federal Criminal Law and Its Enforcement*. St. Paul, Minn.: West Publishing Co.

——— 1989   The New Ancillary Offenses. *Criminal Law Forum* 1:1–39.

KURLAND, ADAM H.   1989   The Guarantee Clause as a Basis for Federal Prosecution of State and Local Officers. *Southern California Law Review* 62:367–491.

LYNCH, GERARD E.   1987   Rico: The Crime of Being a Criminal, Parts I & II, Parts II & III. *Columbia Law Review* 87:661–764, 920–984.

FEDERAL CRIMINAL LAW
(Update)

If a constitutional snapshot is taken of the current status of the federal criminal law, the picture that emerges is somewhat changed from a decade ago. It continues to be the case that the Supreme Court does not with great frequency label as unconstitutional federal prosecutorial action, judicial penalties, or federal criminal statutes under the DOCTRINES of DOUBLE JEOPARDY, CRUEL AND UNUSUAL PUNISHMENT, excessive fines, or void for VAGUENESS, but there have been some new developments.

Although the Court is reviewing fewer criminal cases overall, the Justices are addressing more federal criminal cases, particularly those involving key issues of STATUTORY INTERPRETATION or questions arising under the SENTENCING guidelines and criminal forfeiture. This activity has marginally increased the number of cases in which the Court has addressed constitutional issues in a federal criminal context.

In 1993, in *United States v. Dixon*, the Court OVERRULED its earlier decision in *Grady v. Corbin* (1990) that had established a new test for double jeopardy in a successive prosecution context. Grady had applied a "same conduct" test as a supplement to the *Blockburger* test which provides that in successive prosecution cases, if each of the statutes involved in the two prosecutions contains an element that the other does not, double jeopardy does not bar the second prosecution. In *Dixon*, a majority of the Court ruled that *Grady* had been wrongly decided and reinstated the *Blockburger* test as the exclusive means of adjudging whether the double jeopardy standard has been violated in a successive prosecution context.

The Court also applied the double jeopardy clause in cases involving both civil sanctions and criminal prosecution. As in the *Grady* and *Dixon* cases, the Court overruled a decision that had won the Court's approval only a handful of years earlier.

In *Hudson v. United States* (1997), which involved administrative sanctions imposed against bankers followed by their indictment for the same conduct, a majority of the Court "largely disavowed" the approach developed in 1989 in *United States v. Halper*. The Court adopted a two-pronged test for determining whether double jeopardy barred the second prosecution. Were the administrative sanctions imposed intended by Congress to be civil? If so, were they nevertheless punitive in nature or effect despite the congressional intent? Only the "clearest proof" would suffice to overturn the legislative intent. In both *Dixon* and *Hudson*, the Court returned to an approach that is easier to apply; one that focuses mainly on the statutory setting rather than the particular circumstances of the case; one that makes it more difficult for a defendant to sustain a claim of double jeopardy.

Because forfeiture is now part of a number of federal criminal statutes, it should not surprise that during this period, the Court also addressed constitutional issues regarding the use of this sanction. First, in *Alexander v. United States* (1993), the Court held that criminal forfeiture is "no different, for Eighth Amendment purposes, from a criminal fine," and in the same year in *Austin v. United States*, relying in part on *Halper*, the Court ruled that CIVIL FORFEITURE is limited by the excessive fines clause of the Eighth Amendment if at least part of its purpose was punishment.

Subsequently in *United States v. Usery* (1996), the Court ruled that, for purposes of the double jeopardy clause, civil IN REM forfeitures under the drug laws and money laundering statutes were not punitive and not to be treated as criminal. The approach used in *Austin* was thus restricted to the excessive fines clause.

Then in 1998, in *United States v. Bajakajian*, the Court applied the excessive fines clause to strike down the criminal IN PERSONAM forfeiture of $357,144 that the defendant had been transporting out of the country without reporting it as required by federal law. The majority concluded that the forfeiture of the "property involved in the [failure to report] offense" constitutes punishment and is thus a fine within the meaning of the excessive fines clause. The majority proceeded to use the same standard applied under the cruel and unusual punishments clause—gross disproportionality—as the test of constitutionality under the fines clause.

While the double jeopardy and excessive fines clauses have been applied by the Court in recent federal criminal cases, the void for vagueness doctrinal area continues to be quiescent. One case is worth mentioning because it involved what the Sixth Circuit Court of Appeals described as the "most ambiguous of federal criminal statutes." In *United States v. Lanier* (1997), the Court unanimously rejected a vagueness challenge to Title 18, section 242, which makes it a federal crime for a person acting willfully and under COLOR OF LAW to deprive another of rights protected by the Constitution. A local judge who allegedly sexually assaulted several women in his chambers had been charged with a violation of section 242.

The Supreme Court stated that the "touchstone" of vagueness doctrine is "whether the statute, either standing alone or as construed, made it reasonably clear at the relevant time that the defendant's conduct was criminal." The Court remanded the case to the Court of Appeals to determine whether, in light of preexisting law, the unlawfulness of the judge's behavior under the Constitution was apparent. The decision appears to leave open the possibility of a wide-ranging use of section 242 to address conduct not covered by other federal criminal statutes, and it suggests that the Court is not likely to restrict on vagueness grounds other broad criminal statutes found in the Federal Criminal Code.

In its recent constitutional decisions affecting the federal criminal law, the Supreme Court has shown a willingness to strike down prosecutorial action and judicial penalties, but it has not invalidated criminal statutes on substantive grounds. That the Court has been closely divided in many of its recent constitutional rulings, and that dissenting Justices (not always the same group) have not been reluctant to overrule recent PRECEDENTS when they later obtain a majority, does not bode well in the near term for the stability, certainty, and predictability of federal criminal law.

NORMAN ABRAMS
(2000)

Bibliography
AMAR, AKHIL R. 1997 Double Jeopardy Law Made Simple. *Yale Law Journal* 106:1807–1848.

JEFFRIES, JOHN C., JR. 1985 Legality, Vagueness and the Construction of Penal Statutes. *Virginia Law Review* 71:189–244.
KING, NANCY J. 1996 Portioning Punishment: Constitutional Limits on Successive and Excessive Penalties. *University of Pennsylvania Law Review* 144:101–196.
THOMAS, GEORGE C., III 1995 A Blameworthy Act Approach to the Double Jeopardy Same Offense Problem. *California Law Review* 83:1027–1070.

FEDERAL ELECTION CAMPAIGN ACTS

Presidential Election Campaign Fund Act
85 Stat. 497 (1971)

Federal Election Campaign Act
86 Stat. 3 (1971)

Federal Election Campaign Act
88 Stat. 1263 (1974)

The success of constitutional democracy depends upon the integrity and autonomy of the electoral process. But whether that integrity is threatened more seriously by wealthy individuals and organizations than by regulations that prevent individuals and organizations from using their resources to promote candidates and policies is a matter for debate. During the 1970s several attempts at campaign finance "reform" were enacted, resulting in an almost complete switch from private to public financing at least of the presidential general election campaigns.

Two reform statutes were enacted in 1971: the Federal Election Campaign Act (FECA) and the Presidential Election Campaign Fund Act. The former required any committee receiving or spending more than $1,000 in a campaign for federal office to register with the federal government and publish reports of contributions and expenditures. It also prohibited contributions under names other than that of the actual donor and limited total expenditures on campaign advertising. The second statute created a fund of public money to replace private contributions in financing presidential election campaigns. By means of a "check-off" device, taxpayers would nominally designate one dollar of their annual federal income tax payment for the election campaign fund. Acceptance of these public funds precluded a party or campaign committee from accepting any private contributions.

The FECA of 1974 was an extremely comprehensive effort to regulate the "time, place, and manner" of electing federal officials. Among the provisions of the 1974 act were: maximum spending limits for presidential nominating and general election campaigns; federal matching funds for qualifying candidates in major party nominating campaigns; complete federal funding of major party candidates in the general election campaign; limits on contributions of individuals, organizations, and political action committees to campaigns for Congress and for the presidential nominations; limits on campaign spending per state in presidential nomination campaigns; and rigorous accounting and reporting requirements for campaign finance committees. In addition, the 1974 act created a six-member Federal Elections Commission to enforce the other provisions of the act; the commission was to comprise members appointed by the President, the speaker of the House of Representatives, and the president pro tempore of the Senate.

The Supreme Court heard major constitutional challenges to the 1974 act even as the first campaign was being conducted under it. In BUCKLEY V. VALEO (1976) the Court held unconstitutional the method of appointment of the commission (because the Constitution grants to the President alone the power to appoint federal officers) and all the spending limitations imposed other than as a condition for receiving federal matching funds. The rationale for the latter holding was that the commitment of funds in support of a candidate or cause was a form of expression protected under the FIRST AMENDMENT.

The tendency toward public financing of electoral campaigns, with accompanying regulation, works to the advantage of incumbents and to the disadvantage of challengers, who usually need to spend more than their opponents to overcome the advantages of incumbency. The scheme for financing and regulating the presidential election campaigns serves to insulate the two major parties from challenges by third parties or independent candidates. While claiming to protect the people from the "fat cats," federal politicians have taken steps to protect themselves from the people.

DENNIS J. MAHONEY
(1986)

Bibliography

ALEXANDER, HERBERT E. 1980 *Financing Politics: Money, Elections and Political Reform.* Washington, D.C.: Congressional Quarterly.

FEDERAL ENERGY AGENCY v. ALGONQUIN SNG, INC.
426 U.S. 548 (1976)

A unanimous Supreme Court, through Justice WILLIAM J. BRENNAN, upheld the constitutionality of oil import licensing fees imposed under the Trade Expansion Act (1962) and the Trade Act (1974). Under those statutes the President was authorized to "adjust" imports of commodities if the importation was in such quantities or under such conditions as to threaten national security. This was not an improper DELEGATION OF POWER, as the laws established preconditions for and limits upon its exercise. Furthermore, the court ruled, license fees were as acceptable a means of adjusting levels of importation as quotas.

DENNIS J. MAHONEY
(1986)

FEDERAL FARM BANKRUPTCY ACT

See: Frazier-Lemke Acts

FEDERAL GRANTS-IN-AID

Federal grants-in-aid are subventions to state or local governments, private institutions, or individuals in support of a wide variety of undertakings. Early in the nineteenth century, governmental transfers of land were used to support road construction and agricultural education. Cash grants to states for diverse functions, such as vocational EDUCATION, forest fire prevention, and maternal health, came of age in the decades preceding the NEW DEAL. The public welfare programs established in 1935 greatly expanded the federal role in state finances. But it is the proliferation of categorical grants since 1960 that has rendered them the principal instrument of federal influence over social services and urban affairs. This recent extraordinary growth reflects an unplanned series of fragmented national responses to state fiscal inadequacy in the face of increased demand for collective goods.

Most of the current 500 or so national grant programs are intergovernmental, and federal monies under them constitute about one-quarter of the annual expenditures of both state and local governments. Notwithstanding federalism-inspired movements toward less directive federal grants, known as REVENUE SHARING and block grants, most aid programs remain categorical, with narrowly defined undertakings and detailed conditions imposed on the receiving agencies.

Grants are made pursuant to Congress's broad discretion to spend for the GENERAL WELFARE and common defense. Like other national powers, grant-making authority rests on permissive and expansive constitutional principles established during the post-New Deal era of judicial reaction and retreat, typified by such cases as STEWARD MACHINE CO. V. DAVIS (1937) and *Oklahoma v. Civil Service Commission* (1947). The recurrent use of grant conditions to impose national solutions on traditionally local issues suggests that the political safeguard of FEDERALISM constraining Congress in the use of national regulatory power is less operative in the exercise of grant-making authority. (See TAXING AND SPENDING POWER.)

For many years intergovernmental relationships in grant programs were understood to be administrative, co-operative, professional, and donative. Consequently, federal judges declined to intervene in grievances founded on grant programs. This aloofness markedly changed with the advent of antipoverty litigation in the late 1960s, when courts acknowledged that private beneficiaries of public WELFARE BENEFITS were entitled to relief against state and local laws and practices inconsistent with federal grant conditions. Litigation over grants soon became a staple of federal court dockets, with suits by federal grantor agencies and local government grantees as well as by private parties. The judicial decisions, while providing a novel and potent injunctive remedy, broadly construed and uniformly validated federal goals and conditions. Federal courts thus placed their stamp of approval on Congress's expansive use of federal grants.

Grants differ from regulation in that they entail expenditures, not direct commands and sanctions, as the inducement for conforming activity. Because of this difference, courts maintain that state and local governmental participation in grant-in-aid programs is voluntary, not coerced. They consequently reject attacks on grant conditions, on the ground that onerous or intrusive requirements can be avoided by the "simple expedient" of not yielding and of refusing the grant. This choice of the state or city is largely fictional in light of citizen-industry mobility and the competition among states for resources. But courts cannot intelligibly resolve the question of whether federal grants have overborne the "free will" of government units.

On several recent occasions Congress has further reduced the difference between grants and regulation through the creation of new grant-in-aid directives without additional federal funding. Instead of monetary inducements, Congress has chosen to condition continuation of eligibility under well-established, and usually large, aid programs on conformity with its new requirements. This tying arrangement has the look of regulation, but its validity seems beyond question so long as there is a plausible relationship between the new program or condition and the national purposes of the older one.

For example, states may be required to supplement or to provide welfare payments in order to remain eligible for large Medicaid health care grants; the justification is that income maintenance and health-care support once were within a single grant program, and, more fundamentally, that subsistence payments significantly affect the health of the impoverished. Similarly Congress has tied the availability of federally insured mortgages to state participation in a flood control program; has tied the entire portmanteau of federal health dollars to state adoption of an elaborate apparatus for health systems planning and cost control; and has tied highway grants to state regulation of billboards, state enforcement of a federal speed limit, and state adoption of a national minimum age for drinking. There may be constitutional limits on tying new conditions to older grant programs, but the limits remain unenforced and unexplored.

The basic constitutional constraint on grant conditions is that they must be relevant to the purpose of a grant program. Here, as elsewhere, Congress has an exceedingly large discretion to determine relationships between means and goals. Fair treatment of private beneficiaries and efficiency are the two primary categories of relatedness, and they obviously can carry a good deal of baggage. In addition, Congress of late has established a web of elaborate "cross-cutting" conditions applicable to all or most grant-in-aid programs concerning, for example, the handicapped, environmental impacts, labor and procurement standards, citizen participation, merit hiring, and CIVIL RIGHTS. Administrative enforcement of grant conditions played a major role in the DESEGREGATION of southern schools. To be sure, many of these restrictions would fall within congressional powers under the COMMERCE CLAUSE and the FOURTEENTH AMENDMENT, but there is significance in Congress's casting them as grant-in-aid conditions. The judicial assumption that states have the option not to accept the grants apparently makes it easier for Congress to impose new and controversial obligations on the states.

The TENTH AMENDMENT limit established in NATIONAL LEAGUE OF CITIES V. USERY (1976) has not been applied to grants founded on the spending power, no doubt because such a ruling would eviscerate the current system of federal grants. Numerous federal grant conditions directly affect the structure and operation of state and local governments. Grant programs not only pervasively alter the spending priorities of governmental units, but, through the imposition of conditions, also allocate power between state and local governments (and occasionally between governors and legislatures), dictate hiring practices and employment benefits, and, by barring partisan political activity, limit the occasions on which officials administering departments having grants may be elected.

There is, finally, the Supreme Court's assimilation of grant programs to regulatory ones in its holding that state laws inconsistent with the terms of federal grants are invalid under the SUPREMACY CLAUSE. Although not fully explicated, this theory has been used repeatedly to warrant injunctive relief against grantee noncomplicance with national conditions. Traditionally, federal administrative enforcement of grant conditions had been exceptionally lax, perhaps designedly so. Third-party suits for injunctive relief have altered this convention, while enlarging the role of federal courts in monitoring and enforcing grant programs. As a consequence, there is now more law and less discretion defining and governing the relationships under national grants.

LEE A. ALBERT
(1986)

Bibliography

LAPIERRE, D. BRUCE   1983   The Political Safeguards of Federalism Redux. *Washington University Law Quarterly* 60:779–1056.

MAXWELL, J. and ARONSON, J. R.   (1965) 1977   *Financing State and Local Government.* Washington, D.C.: Brookings Institution.

FEDERAL IMMUNITY ACT
68 Stat. 745 (1954)

The growing tendency in the early 1950s of witnesses before congressional committees to refuse to testify by relying on the Fifth Amendment's RIGHT AGAINST SELF-INCRIMINATION led Congress in 1954 to amend previous statutes and provide revised immunity arrangements. The purpose of the measure was to bypass the Fifth Amendment by giving Congress the power to grant a reluctant witness immunity from prosecution and compel the individual to testify. Either house of Congress by majority vote or a congressional committee by a two-thirds vote could grant immunity from prosecution to a witness in a national security investigation, provided an order was first obtained from a United States District Court judge. The statute required the attorney general to be given advance notification and an opportunity to offer objections. The law also permitted UNITED STATES DISTRICT COURTS to grant immunity to witnesses before courts or GRAND JURIES. Witnesses thus immunized faced the choice of testifying or going to jail. The Fifth Amendment could not be raised as a barrier to compulsory testimony.

In ULLMAN V. UNITED STATES (1956) the Supreme Court sustained its constitutionality.

PAUL L. MURPHY
(1986)

(SEE ALSO: *Immunity Grant.*)

FEDERALISM

Federalism is a political system in which different levels of government agree to share power in governing the same territory. Constitutional federalism in the United States refers both to the constitutional provisions for the national and the state governments to exist and to perform particular functions in the federal system of governance, and to the sets of relationships—among states, and between states and the federal government—for which the Constitution provides a framework. JUDICIAL REVIEW of federalism refers to the limits on federal and state action that courts will enforce on behalf of the federal structure of the Constitution.

Constitutional Federalism.   Constitutional federalism in the United States emerged out of practical experiences under the ARTICLES OF CONFEDERATION and political exigencies. Experience showed that greater centralization was essential, but the political leadership of the states would not have been prepared to give up their states' self-governing powers to a separate and entirely national government. This pragmatic reality is reflected in the assumption, in many parts of the Constitution, that the states will continue as separate governments, each having a legislature, an executive authority, and courts. The provisions for selecting members of Congress presuppose that state legislatures exist; the provisions for calling forth the militia presuppose an executive authority in each state; and the SUPREMACY CLAUSE presupposes a state judiciary. Even the FOURTEENTH AMENDMENT, which substantially changed the balance of powers between the national and the state governments, contemplates the continued existence of the states as self-governing entities. Section 2 of the Fourteenth Amendment, which penalizes states for VOTING RIGHTS discrimination in elections of members of the state legislature or for state executive or judicial officers, contemplates not only the states' existence but also the continued operation of the three branches of state government.

U.S. federalism has been the subject of theoretical debate from its beginnings. FEDERALIST No. 39 described the provisions of the Constitution as partly national and partly confederated. *Federalist* No. 59 offered a political theory of the value of federalism: it would serve as a "double security" for the preservation of liberty, with each level of government presumably having motives to check abuses by the other. In *United States Term Limits v. Thornton* (1995), the influential concurrence of Justice ANTHONY M. KENNEDY linked U.S. federalism to coexisting CITIZENSHIPS (state and federal) and political accountability, emphasizing that both state and national government representatives are selected by the people and that each level of government is accountable to the people.

Among the values claimed for federalism as a constraint on national power are (1) its liberty-preserving, tyranny-preventing possibilities, (2) the potential for decentralized government to maximize the satisfaction of individual preferences by allowing citizens to choose among diverse regimes by moving from one to another, (3) the opportunities for more active political participation at lower levels of government whose units are smaller, (4) the possibilities for developing cross-cutting allegiances among different groups in society, given that state boundaries for the most part do not correspond to such deeply divisive characteristics as race, religion, or language, and (5) the greater prospects offered by decentralization for useful innovation in government design and policy. But whether constitutional constraints on national power actually serve these goals remains contested. National power in the last half-century has been an important force for liberty and equality as against tyrannical policies of state-sponsored racial SEGREGATION, though in recent years some state or local jurisdictions have moved ahead of federal policies in advancing CIVIL RIGHTS for gays and lesbians. Vigorous federal action, especially in economic or environmental spheres, can sometimes avoid "races to the bottom" that would constrain rather than enhance state choices, though whether states would race to the bottom, or to the top, in some important areas of regulation remains in contest. If the only significant politics is at the national level, participation in state or local politics may be less meaningful. Cross-cutting allegiances may be temporary products of contingent demographic distributions rather than a value of federalism itself. And, some would say, experimentation can be achieved through nationally directed but decentralized programs.

Debate over the "value" of federalism in the United States continues. Edward Rubin and Malcolm Feeley, for example, argue that federalism, as a constraint on national power, is a "national neurosis," grounded in history but serving no current constitutional value, and thus should never be the basis for invalidating or interpreting a federal statute. At another pole, scholars such as Steven Calabresi argue that judicial enforcement of federalism-based limits on national power is as important as judicial enforcement of individual rights–based limits. Still others, such as Larry Kramer, explore the federal structure's empirical effects on national politics and governance.

A related controversy has developed over the basis, and scope, of judicial enforcement of federalism-based limits on state regulation under the DORMANT COMMERCE CLAUSE doctrine. Values of diversity and efficiency have been invoked in favor of more relaxed review of state programs; public choice analysis, on the other hand, has been invoked to support judicial enforcement of "bargains" among the states that will be economically advantageous in the long run to all if cheating can be avoided. There is disagreement both about the source of the limits (e.g., whether from the grant of power to Congress over INTERSTATE COMMERCE or from the PRIVILEGES AND IMMUNITIES of citizenship clause in Article IV) and over the value of some of the more recent manifestations of federalism-based invalidations of state regulatory action (especially those in the area of ENVIRONMENTAL REGULATION). Justices ANTONIN

SCALIA and CLARENCE THOMAS have sought, from ORIGINALIST or TEXTUALIST perspectives, to unravel the COMMERCE CLAUSE as a source of judicially imposed restraints on the states, while upholding judicially enforced bans on state discrimination against out-of-staters or interstate commerce under the privileges and immunities clause, or the import–export clause.

Judicial Review of National Action. The debate over the values of federalism is only loosely linked to debate over the role of judicial review. While those who see no value in the maintenance of federal structures may be opposed to judicial enforcement of purported federalism-based limits on national or state power, those who see value in federalism are nonetheless of very different minds on the proper role of judicial review. Building on Herbert Wechsler's work, some argue that federalism values are adequately protected by the structural role of the states in the national political process, or even that federalism challenges to national action should be regarded as lacking JUSTICIABILITY. Others, including Barry Friedman and Vicki Jackson, argue that the historical embeddedness of federalism, RULE OF LAW concerns, or the constitutionally prescribed functions of the states, contemplate some judicially enforceable federalism-based limits on national power. And still others, including Roderick Hills, Jr., argue for judicial enforcement of federalism-based limits to promote accountability and efficiency in national decision-making.

Despite proclamations of the death of federalism in the 1970s, the 1990s have seen a renewed willingness by the Supreme Court to invalidate federal laws based on federalism concerns. Two somewhat distinct lines of cases can be identified, one dealing with federal regulations that apply to the states as such, and the other dealing with federal regulation of the activity of private entities.

(i) Federal Regulation of State Governments. In *Maryland v. Wirtz* (1966), the Court held that the commerce clause authorized federal regulation of the employment practices of state governments, and upheld an extension of the federal minimum wage law to a limited group of state and local government public employees. But in NATIONAL LEAGUE OF CITIES V. USERY (1974), the Court found merit in TENTH AMENDMENT objections to Congress's further extension of the federal minimum wage law to municipal transit workers. Under *National League of Cities*, the Tenth Amendment barred federal action if it regulated states as such, affecting attributes of state sovereignty in areas of traditional government function, without compelling federal need. Seeking to apply this standard, the lower courts reached conflicting decisions on a range of questions and for several years the Court declined to invalidate other extensions of federal law to the states. Then, in GARCÍA V. SAN ANTONIO METROPOLITAN

TRANSIT AUTHORITY (1985), the Court, by a 5–4 vote, OVER-RULED *National League of Cities*. It concluded that the effort to identify traditional government functions protected by the Tenth Amendment was inconsistent with federalism's dynamic potential, and that the national political process would generally be sufficient to protect the interests of the states. *García* was widely read as an abandonment by the Court of federalism-based judicial review of national action.

Instead, in the 1990s, the Court began to abandon the premise of *García*. In GREGORY V. ASHCROFT (1991), a STATUTORY INTERPRETATION decision holding the federal AGE DISCRIMINATION law inapplicable to state judges, the Court wrote at length about the values of federalism and the need for a constrained national government. In NEW YORK V. UNITED STATES (1992), the Court held unconstitutional a federal statute that required a state by a certain date either to designate a site for disposal of radioactive WASTE or to assume liabilities of private generators and holders of radioactive waste in the state, a choice that the Court found to be an effort to coerce or "commandeer" the state legislature. According to the OPINION OF THE COURT by Justice SANDRA DAY O'CONNOR, the 1787 Constitution abandoned federal power to regulate the states as such, substituting for it federal power to regulate private persons. Moreover, the Court suggested, to permit Congress to require states to legislate would confuse the lines of political accountability. *García*'s basic rationale was ignored, and its holding distinguished and narrowed. The statute upheld in *García*, the Court said, was one generally applicable to private as well as state entities. In *Printz v. United States* (1997), the Court extended the anticommandeering rule of *New York* to invalidate a federal law requiring local law enforcement authorities to perform background checks on gun purchasers. Distinguishing this case from the well-settled obligation of state courts to entertain federal claims, the Court held that the federal government cannot require state executive or legislative bodies to enforce or administer federal law. As of this writing, the Court has granted CERTIORARI in a case challenging Congress's power to require states to limit their own disclosures of drivers' records and raising the question whether Congress, under Article I, can enact laws that regulate but do not "commandeer" the states.

City of Boerne v. Flores (1997) suggests that the Court's reinvigoration of federalism as a limit on national action will also apply to Congress's power under the Fourteenth Amendment. *Flores* held that Congress exceeded its powers under the FOURTEENTH AMENDMENT, SECTION 5 in enacting the RELIGIOUS FREEDOM RESTORATION ACT (RFRA), which prohibited state and local governments from applying generally applicable laws in ways that substantially burdened religious practice, unless the laws met the "com-

pelling interest" test of STRICT SCRUTINY. First, the Court held that Congress lacked power to treat conduct that, under the Court's caselaw, did not violate the free exercise clause as if it did violate that clause. Moreover, the Court held, although Congress does have some power to impose prophylactic measures prohibiting conduct that does not itself violate section 1 of the Fourteenth Amendment in order to prevent other conduct that does, such a remedial or preventive use of the section 1 power must be proportional and congruent to actual violations. It concluded that the sweep of RFRA was broader than any record of such violations would warrant and thus found RFRA unconstitutional, while also suggesting that Congress had violated SEPARATION OF POWERS principles in acting on a theory different from the theory previously approved by the Court in enforcing rights under the Fourteenth Amendment. (*Flores* carried to its logical extreme might suggest that, had Congress sought to outlaw racial segregation by the states after PLESSY V. FERGUSON (1896) was decided but before *Plessy* was in substance overruled by BROWN V. BOARD OF EDUCATION (1954), Congress's action could have been challenged as violating the separation of powers.) Two 1999 decisions by the Court expanded on *Flores*, holding unconstitutional, as not supported by the due process clause of the Fourteenth Amendment, Congress's abrogation of ELEVENTH AMENDMENT immunity on claims for PATENT infringement and Lanham Act violations.

(ii) Federal Regulation of Private Activity. In the years following the NEW DEAL, the Court upheld federal power under the commerce clause to regulate a wide range of private activities, in areas ranging from civil rights to crimes such as loansharking. The Court's reasoning appeared to allow little room either for consideration of the interests of states or the effect of federal LEGISLATION on the balance of powers between national and state governments. Nor did the Court engage in rigorous judicial scrutiny of congressional motives or reasons for acting. But in UNITED STATES V. LÓPEZ (1995), for the first time since the New Deal, the Court struck down a federal law regulating private behavior as beyond Congress's ENUMERATED POWERS. The statute prohibited possession of a firearm within 1,000 feet of a school, but included no explicit findings supporting a connection to interstate commerce or otherwise linking the prohibited action to an enumerated source of federal power. Invoking the notion of dual sovereignty, in which the states needed to have a sphere of regulation that the federal government was not involved in, the Court held that the connection to interstate commerce was too obscure, the rationales for upholding the law too sweeping, and the subject matter too closely connected to areas traditionally regulated by the states to pass constitutional muster.

(iii) Related Cases. In addition to these lines of cases

lection of the National Government. *Columbia Law Review* 54:543–560.

FEDERALISM, CONTEMPORARY PRACTICE OF

The Supreme Court does not enforce constitutional FEDERALISM. Rather, it enforces sufferance federalism, that is, federalism as determined by Congress, a weak form of federalism in which state laws govern particular subjects only so far as Congress decides and in which Congresss controls such subjects as it sees fit. The Court also does not now recognize any significant distinction between taxing a state and taxing a private business; the former may be subjected to national taxes imposed by Congress in any circumstance applicable to the latter. And the Court interprets the SPENDING POWER not as a limited power enabling the government to defray the expenses of its own operations and programs but as a power available to Congress to use to eliminate diversity among state laws according to its own choice. At the same time, the Supreme Court also deems Congress to possess power to restrict the means by which state or LOCAL GOVERNMENTS might attempt to raise their own revenue for their own programs, without depending on appropriations from Congress. This renders each state dependent on such funds as Congress may see fit to budget, with such strings attached as Congress decides as a way to force changes in laws otherwise not subject to its control. In brief, in the aggregate of its federalism decisions the Court acts overall as an agency of the national government on federalism questions. "Judicially constrained dual federalism" does not accurately describe federalism in the United States. Rather, "sufferance federalism"—federalism to such extent as the national government decides to be appropriate—is the system virtually de jure in the United States.

Several examples of mere sufferance federalism have been provided in four recent decisions of the Supreme Court. Instructive on the point is *South Dakota v. Dole* (1987), which sustained an act of Congress that disapproved state statutes permitting any person over eighteen years of age to purchase beer. Congress desired that the minimum state drinking age should be raised to twenty-one. The means selected by Congress were efficient to this end. It reduced federally appropriated matching highway funds to any state in which the lawful minimum drinking age was lower than Congress desired the state legislature to enact and reduced these funds by such a fraction as Congress could be confident would be sufficiently harsh that no state could hold out against the penalty thus imposed.

The Court, over two dissents, rejected the view that the spending power is a power merely to meet the government's own operating BUDGET as a national government (the view JAMES MADISON had held). It also rejected the view that Congress's power was at most a power to set the conditions of a general or a specific program it would be willing to help fund (e.g., the construction of such highways as would be built to congressional specifications of design, quality, and materials). Rather in *Dole* the Court accepted the additional view that the spending power is available to Congress to use as an oblique power for the "indirect achievement of objects which Congress is not empowered to achieve directly." It is a power, in short, to require states to adopt the same substantive law on a given subject as their neighbors have, insofar as Congress sees fit, or be penalized under federal programs of assistance at such level of disadvantage Congress is confident will be sufficient to bring about the change it desires in their laws. As illustrated by the *Dole* case, the Court thus acts as an *active* department in federalism matters, that is, an enforcing department of the national government, validating Congress's preferences not merely in respect to its own laws but in respect to the content of state law as well. The three other major federalism decisions by the Court in the most recent five years (1985–1990) are of the same general hue.

In *South Carolina v. Baker* (1988), for example, the Court sustained an act of Congress eliminating the federal tax deductibility of interest income received on bearer bonds issued by state or local governments, bonds commonly used as a means of financing state or local operations. In sustaining this act, the Court overruled its own unanimous holding in POLLOCK V. FARMERS' LOAN TRUST (1895). Then, going beyond the facts of the case and the immediate legal question, Justice WILLIAM J. BRENNAN volunteered that Congress might also forbid states from attempting to raise revenue by issuing such bonds *at all.* In Justice Brennan's view, if Congress felt that such bonds would be a hindrance to its own collection of national taxes, it might outlaw their use by the states. To the objection that this would leave the states effectively subject to Congress ("sufferance federalism"), Justice Brennan was unfazed: "[S]tates must find their protection from congressional regulation through the national political process, not through judicially defined spheres of [respective national and state powers]."

In a related federalism development involving the ELEVENTH AMENDMENT and state immunity from suits brought by private parties in federal court, a majority of the Court overruled still another unanimous and equally long-standing contrary decision. It held that Congress could subject states to money DAMAGE CLAIMS in federal courts without their consent or waiver of SOVEREIGN IMMUNITY despite the Eleventh Amendment, which as applied by the Court a full century earlier in *Hans v. Louisiana* (1890), was deemed by the Court to preclude such FEDERAL JURISDICTION. In this third new case, *Pennsylvania v. Union Gas Co.* (1989) the Court thus reinterpreted the Constitution to favor congressional power once again.

The fourth case in the Court's recent quartet is of the same character. In GARCIA V. SAN ANTONIO METROPOLITAN TRANSIT AUTHORITY (1985), the Court overruled its own decision that was then less than a decade old, holding that Congress may directly command the terms of state employment to the same extent it had presumed to regulate wages and hours in private employment. The case overruled was NATIONAL LEAGUE OF CITIES V. USERY (1976).

In large measure, however, these developments are not thematically new, despite the fact that three of the four constituitonal federalism cases involved such complete inconsistencies with the Supreme Court's own prior decisions as to require its previous interpretations of the Constitution to be set aside. Rather, the passing terms of the Supreme Court have but hardened what has been, overall, a one-way twentieth-century trend. Writing in 1950 in the *Virginia Law Review*, the distinguished constitutional historian EDWARD S. CORWIN summarized the developments in "The Passing of Dual Federalism." His conclusions were accurate even for the time:

> [T]he Federal System has shifted base in the direction of a consolidated national power. . . . [The] entire system of constitutional interpretation touching the Federal System is today in ruins. Today neither the State Police Power nor the concept of Federal Equilibrium is any "ingredient of national legislative power," whether as respects subject-matter to be governed, or the choice of objectives or of means for its exercise. [Today] "Cooperative Federalism" spells further aggrandizement of national power. . . . Resting as it does primarily on the superior fiscal resources of the National Government, Cooperative Federalism has been, to date, a short expression for a constantly increasing concentration of power at Washington in the instigation and supervision of local policies.

To be sure, even as implied in Corwin's article a half-century ago, the system of dual federalism was not originally expected to be administered by the Supreme Court in this one-sided fashion. Rather, in theory, it spoke to the Constitution's original differential apportionment of legislative powers (between the national and state governments) and a certain equilibrium in different spheres of respective national and constrained state powers that was meant to be held in place under the superintendence of the Supreme Court. The powers constitutionally apportioned were separated between limited—albeit important—powers under congressional control and the larger number left to the separate determination by legislature

within each state. Subjects not believed to require a common regime of uniform national regulation—and thus not identified in Article I or elsewhere as subject to congressional disposition—were reserved from the national government to such differential treatment as the domestic law of each state might reflect. Madison characterized this basic arrangement in THE FEDERALIST #45: "The powers delegated by the proposed Constitution to the federal government are few and defined. Those which are to remain in the State governments are numerous and indefinite."

The Supreme Court, while fully expected to grant full enforcement to acts of Congress within its ENUMERATED POWERS ("few and defined"), was equally expected to withhold enforcement from any not within them. Indeed, it was the latter obligation of the courts that was particularly emphasized in the course of the RATIFICATION debates. In Pennsylvania, JAMES WILSON put the point reassuringly in the following terms: "If a law should be made inconsistent with those powers vested by this instrument in Congress, the judges, as a consequence of their independence, and the particular powers of government being defined, will declare such law to be null and void." In *The Federalist* #78, ALEXANDER HAMILTON specifically adverted to the federalism-checking function of the courts: "If it be said that the legislative body [Congress] are themselves the constitutional judges of their own powers, . . . it may be answered that this cannot be the natural presumption, where it is not to be collected from any particular provision in the constitution. . . . It is far more rational to suppose that the courts were designed to be an intermediate body between the people and the legislature, in order, among other things, to keep the latter within the limits assigned to their authority." In the Virginia convention, JOHN MARSHALL took the same view: "If they [Congress] were to make a law not warranted by any of the powers enumerated, it would be considered by the judges as an infringement of the Constitution which they are to guard. They would not consider such a law as coming under their jurisdiction. *They would declare it void.*"

Moreover, according to Marshall, a law that might nominally come within the limits of some enumerated power vested in Congress should—and would—be held void by the courts if it were discoverable that it was but a means to effectuate a control over a matter not entrusted to Congress, a matter reserved to the internal disposition of each state. On the very point of policing the equilibrium of federalism against abuse by congressional indirection in the exertion of its powers (as in *South Dakota v. Dole*), Marshall insisted in MCCULLOCH V. MARYLAND on the obligation of the judges to disallow the attempt: "[S]hould congress, under pretext of executing its powers, pass laws for the accomplishment of objects not trusted to the [national] government it would become the painful duty of this tribunal, should a case requiring such a decision come before it, to say, that such an act was not the law of the land." This is the same position Justice FELIX FRANKFURTER repeated concretely, dissenting in *United States v. Kahriger* (1953): "[W]hen oblique use is made of the taxing power as to matters which substantively are not within the powers delegated to Congress [in this instance, whether gambling within a state ought or ought not be suppressed—a commonplace criminal law subject of state and local law and nowhere entrusted to Congress to decide], the Court cannot shut its eyes to what is obviously, because designedly, an attempt to control conduct which the Constitution left to the responsibility of the States, merely because Congress wrapped the legislation in the verbal cellophane of a revenue measure."

The constitutional checks felt to be desirable in respect to state laws not subject to congressional pleasure were in turn expressly (albeit quite narrowly) provided for principally in the special provisions of Article I, section 10 (forbidding state EX POST FACTO LAWS or impairing the OBLIGATION OF CONTRACT). Later, to be sure, between 1865 and 1870, these limitations were significantly enlarged in the Civil War amendments—in respect to which Congress is given strong powers of enforcement. However, subject to these limitations and such others as might be variously reflected internally in each state in keeping with its own constitution as interpreted by the states' own courts (rather than as the federal courts might want), it was the varietals of state law—not national law—that were meant to occupy the fields not given to Congress to command.

The main check against persistent immoderation of state law (for example, criminal law, family law, TORTS, local business regulation, trusts and estates) lay not in any possible PREEMPTION by Congress—it being understood that there was no such general power of preemption provided or vested in Congress by the Constitution. Instead, the main check that might keep the character of state laws from reaching extremes not forbidden by the constitution itself inhered in the porousness of state boundaries and the freedom of state citizens to move away from a state to a different state, taking their skills and personal property with them. Any persistent tendency toward immoderation in state legislation was thus constrained to the extent it was deemed constitutionally desirable to have it constrained—not by a supererogatory general authority in Congress, but by the consciousness of each state that it could not prevent its citizens from considering the comparative advantage of a different state or veto the free movement of persons and of personal property within the United States.

In contrast, modern federalism, or sufferance federalism, eliminates this alternative check on state laws, as it tends also to eliminate differences among the states themselves. Insofar as processes of democratic centralism (Congress) can impose uniform preemptive national legislation regardless of subject matter (as the Constitution is now construed by the Supreme Court to permit—largely via the COMMERCE CLAUSE), such difference as any particular state law might provide as a contrast with that of some other state can be made of no consequence even within that state. Whatever the state law may permit to those within that state, it remains true that even all those moving to or residing in that state must reckon with the separate and enforceable prohibition Congress has already enacted and made applicable to them as a matter of federal law, a law fully enforceable via the federal courts. They must therefore conform to that law, rather than merely to the law of the state, regardless of where they reside. And insofar as Congress has been persuaded to regulate them in keeping with how others (though not including the state of their residence) may want them to be regulated by federal law, it will make no difference where they attempt to go. However, even more obtains under sufferance federalism than this. Because powers vested in Congress are interpreted to permit it to effectively determine the very content of state laws (as they are now so interpreted in general), then to the extent that INTEREST GROUPS and states with influence in Congress find themselves embarrassed or vexed by some distinction the internal laws of some few other states provide by way of contrast with themselves, they may act through Congress to compel the legislatures in every state to revise those states' own laws to conform to the preference already adopted in their states. Either way, then, such differences as may tend to exhibit themselves in certain laws of different states even today remain subject to congressional sufferance and elimination, if, as, and when Congress so decides.

It is the interpretive stance of the Supreme Court (e.g., on the scope of the power to "regulate commerce among the several states," equating it with a power to regulate or prohibit whatever may affect commerce, whether or not it is commerce that Congress cares about in the particular case) and not the literal abrogation of JUDICIAL REVIEW on the federalism question that is solely responsible for the change to sufferance federalism in the United States. The Court continues to be nominally willing to review substantive federalism, but it invariably sustains such preemptions of directions or commands that Congress presumes to enact as long as Congress goes through certain formal motions in the course of enacting its bills; however, it is not a refusal to hear or to entertain the case as such. This distinction might appear to be merely scholastic insofar as the practical results would appear to be the same as though the Court had abrogated judicial review of federalism cases. But it is more than scholastic precisely because the Court's current position does not leave the merits of the federalism objection unaddressed; rather, it denies the merits of those objections—that is, it decides the cases in which they arise. Accordingly, an amendment currently being pressed in thirty-three state legislatures (approved by fifteen legislatures, by one house in six others, and pending in twelve more) that, if proposed and ratified, would require the Court to address and decide the merits of federalism objections in cases otherwise appropriately raising such questions, would change nothing at all. Proposals of this sort proceed on a misunderstanding of judicial behavior on the Supreme Court. Sufferance federalism in the United States is not the result of the nonreviewability of federalism cases arising under the Constitution; rather, it is the result of the Supreme Court's own disposition to find that it is merely this form of federalism the Constitution of the United States provides.

WILLIAM W. VAN ALSTYNE
(1992)

Bibliography

CORWIN, EDWARD 1950 The Passing of Dual Federalism. *University of Virginia Law Review* 36:1–23.

EPSTEIN, RICHARD 1989 The Proper Scope of the Commerce Clause. In Ellen Frankel Paul, ed., *Liberty, Property, and Government*. Albany: State University of New York Press.

PATTERSON, JAMES 1969 *The New Deal and the States: Federalism in Transition*. Princeton, N.J.: Princeton University Press.

STERN, ROBERT 1973 The Commerce Clause Revisited—The Federalization of Intrastate Crime. *Arizona Law Review* 15: 271–285.

VAN ALSTYNE, WILLIAM 1985 The Second Death of Federalism. *Michigan Law Review* 83:1709–1733.

——— 1987 Federalism, Congress, the States and the Tenth Amendment: Adrift in the Cellophane Sea. *Duke Law Journal* 87:769–799.

——— 1989 Dual Sovereignty, Federalism and National Criminal Law: Modernist Constitutional Doctrine and the Nonrole of the Supreme Court. *American Criminal Law Review* 26:1740–1759.

FEDERALISM, HISTORY OF

Reflecting on the achievements of the CONSTITUTIONAL CONVENTION, JAMES MADISON, wrote in 1831 that the Framers had lacked even "technical terms or phrases" to describe accurately the governmental system they designed. Prior to 1787, the term "federal" had been used to signify confederation, a system in which SOVEREIGNTY remained with the constituent states that ceded certain elements of authority to a central government—and in which the central authority's legislature merely could propose measures to the states for approval. By contrast, in what was known as "consolidated" government, typical of the modern European nation-state, the central authority was the repository of sovereignty and the power of the locally based units of government depended entirely upon it. The Founders departed from all the historical precedents in both these modes, Madison declared, to produce a system that was "a novelty and a compound." It is this system that we know as American federalism, with its combination of features associated with both the consolidated (or unitary) nation-state and the old-style confederational form of government.

Nearly two centuries of colonial history in North America had afforded only rare examples of cooperation and coordination that presaged even in a remote way the system devised in 1787. In 1643, Plymouth, Massachusetts, Connecticut, and New Haven formed a league called the United Colonies of New England. Commissioners appointed by the four governments dealt with boundary questions, missions to the Indians, and even coordination of military operations in the Indian war of 1675–1676; but the organization soon faded into obscurity. The only serious effort at united action after that time and involving surrender of any colonial powers was the abortive Albany Plan of Union of 1754. Designed by BENJAMIN FRANKLIN and THOMAS HUTCHINSON, the plan would have created a council of the colonies and an executive appointed by the Crown. In addition to being empowered to declare war, conclude treaties with the Indian nations, and regulate territories outside the existing colonial boundaries, the council would have been given authority to impose taxes. But the plan foundered, with not a single colonial assembly giving assent to the proposal.

Certain qualities of the British colonial system itself had foreshadowed American federalism. Although formal authority remained squarely in the hands of the British government, still the colonies were given significant latitude in governing their own affairs. The sudden centralization of power after 1763, when the British decided to tighten the reins and impose new taxes and administrative reforms, precipitated the Revolutionary crisis. Even the exigencies of newly declared independence and armed conflict with Britain had not induced the American states, however, to surrender claims to sovereignty in the interest of national unity. Indeed, the ARTICLES OF CONFEDERATION specifically provided that each state would retain "its sovereignty, freedom, and independence, and every power, JURISDICTION and right, which is not by this confederation expressly delegated to the United States, in Congress assembled." Article III, moreover, described the government only as "a firm league of friendship." The notorious weaknesses of government under the Articles, leading to demands for basic reform by 1786–1787, derived from precisely this perpetuation of the states' prerogatives.

What the Convention sought to create in 1787 was a system in which some measure of sovereignty would be retained for the states; but the national government would be given powers ample enough to govern effectively, operate directly upon the citizens, and establish the nation as a credible presence in international affairs. The continued existence of the states as separate legal entities was an essential component of the original understanding embodied in the Constitution. Structural features that assured the states of great influence included the system of REPRESENTATION in Congress (including equal representation for each state in the Senate), the AMENDING PROCESS, and the voting by state in the House of Representatives in presidential elections not resolved in the ELECTORAL COLLEGE.

Equally important was the concept of enumerated powers. The jurisdiction of the proposed national government, wrote Madison in THE FEDERALIST #39, extended "to certain enumerated objects only, and [left] to the several states a residuary and inviolable sovereignty over all other objects." The "general principle" underlying enumeration of the central government's powers, as JAMES WILSON later wrote, was "that whatever object was confined in its nature and operation to a particular State ought to be subject to the separate government of the States; but whatever in its nature and operation extended beyond a particular State, ought to be comprehended within the federal jurisdiction." On this principle was designed Article I, section 8, with its enumeration of the specific powers of Congress, including control over foreign and INTERSTATE COMMERCE, coinage, and the military and naval forces; the power to establish roads and post offices, inferior federal courts, and an organized militia; and authority as well to declare war and conclude treaties, to create a federal district as the seat of government, and to govern TERRITORIES and regulate property of the United States. Specific limitations were also embraced in the original document of 1787: the prohibition against import and export taxes, grants of TITLES OF NOBILITY, BILLS OF ATTAINDER, suspension of HABEAS CORPUS except during rebellions or invasions, or congressional interference with the slave trade for a period of twenty years. Demarcating the boundaries of the states' authority were provisions in Article I, section 10, that prohibited the states from enactment of EX POST FACTO LAWS, bills of attainder, or laws impairing the OBLIGATION OF CONTRACT. The Constitution also forbade the states from entering into treaties or imposing duties or tonnage fees without permission of Congress.

The seeds of controversy over the proper reach of the bounds of national power were to be found, however, in the GENERAL WELFARE CLAUSE and in the NECESSARY AND PROPER CLAUSE. Article VI, moreover, included the SUPREMACY CLAUSE, holding that all laws and treaties made under the Constitution "shall be the supreme Law of the Land." Opponents of the Constitution cited all these provisions as evidence that the Constitution could easily justify a dangerous centralization of power, overwhelming the states and rendering their alleged residual sovereignty a nugatory matter. A new tyranny, according to this view, could easily be the result of consolidated, unitary government.

Anticipating exactly such objections, the Framers built into the federal design a guarantee of a REPUBLICAN FORM OF GOVERNMENT to each state. The PRIVILEGES AND IMMUNITIES, and extradition provisions further buttressed state authority. The most important consequence of concern about the centralization of power and potential tyranny, however, was the movement for a BILL OF RIGHTS. The first nine amendments, together with the original provisions of the Constitution prohibiting the states from enacting bills of attainder or abrogating contracts, represented an effort to establish national ideals of justice—defining boundaries beyond which government must respect the rights of individual citizens. The Bill of Rights served to reinforce federalism itself as a bulwark of defense for liberty against concentrated governmental power.

What values were intended to be served by this new system of federalism, a system described by a New York judge in 1819 as a "complex and peculiar structure" that permitted the states and the national government to move "in different spheres but occupying the same territorial space, operating upon and for the benefit of the same people"? The first value, designed to protect liberty and to give republican principles full play, was maintenance of government "close to the people." The champions of the Constitution contended that by giving a continuing—and vital—role to the states, popular oversight of governmental operations would be effective and there would be a high degree of participation in public affairs. These same contentions have been heard ever since in the arguments for a federal division of powers in American government.

A second value given a high place in the rationale for federalism was diversity itself. Regional differences in cultural values and local preferences on matters of law and policy would be permitted and find expression when important powers of government remained with the states. Providing in this manner for diversity meant, as Justice LOUIS D. BRANDEIS argued in NEW STATE ICE COMPANY V. LIEBMANN (1932), that "a single courageous state may, if its citizens choose, serve as a laboratory, and try novel social and economic experiments without risk to the rest of the country."

Efficiency was another value intended to be promoted by federalism. Loading all the functions of government upon authority at the center is not only potentially dangerous to liberty; it is also potentially the cause of congestion, complexity, and ineffectiveness. Even unitary, consolidated governments find it necessary to devolve certain functions on subnational or local authority. As Madison wrote in *The Federalist* #14, even if the states were to be abolished, "the general government would be compelled, by the principle of self-preservation, to reinstate them in their proper jurisdiction." What distinguishes a system founded on the principles of federalism from a consolidated system, however, is that federalism recognizes the legitimacy of exclusive state claims to some meaningful autonomy in important areas of law and policy. Power to control at least some of the things that really matter, in the regulation of society's affairs, must be left to the states.

A notable distinguishing feature of American federalism, consistent with the effective pursuit of these values, is the provision for constitutional amendment. What seemed a rational division of authority in the largely agrarian-commercial nation of 1787 will not be rational (or even minimally workable) two hundred years later in an integrated industrial nation with over fifty times the population of 1787. Most of the major changes in the American federal system, both in formal doctrine and in actual governmental practice, have occurred in response to that problem. By a remarkable insight of the Framers, expressed through the amendment process explicitly and the judicial processes by implication, they provided mechanisms for successful adaptation to changing circumstances and national values.

The principles of a federal system require that major changes in the boundaries of authority between the states and the national government should be accomplished by the prescribed amendment process. Such fundamental change should not occur through a process of ordinary legislation or mere administrative innovations in policy. The actual operation of the American system has sometimes conformed to this ideal: fundamental change in the structure of powers within the system were initiated, for example, by the CIVIL WAR and RECONSTRUCTION amendments. Yet at other times basic changes in federal-state relationships were effected without resort to the amendment process. Even the THIRTEENTH, FOURTEENTH, and FIFTEENTH AMENDMENTS, for example, ratified decisions already made on the bloody battlefields of the Civil War. The doctrine of IMPLIED POWERS was a judicial invention in MCCULLOCH V. MARYLAND (1819). The dramatic swing in antebellum interpretation of the COMMERCE CLAUSE—first the MARSHALL COURT's nationalistic interpretation; then, the TANEY COURT's assertion of DUAL FEDERALISM and con-

current powers—came about by judicial innovations in doctrine. Vast changes in law and policy, not least the abandonment of economic due process and the emergence of new presidential EMERGENCY and WAR POWERS, have occurred since 1933 without benefit of constitutional amendments.

Provisions for accommodating new states in the course of national expansion is another important feature of the federal scheme. The thirteen original states took the chance, in effect, that they would be confronted by new sectional alignments and powerful interests hostile in some measure to their own. It was a certainty that each new state taken into the Union would significantly dilute the power of the original states in the Senate, and, as population grew in newer areas, would dilute even more their power in the House of Representatives and in the Electoral College. This provision for the admission of new states underlined the values fundamental to the original understanding: government close to the people, diversity, and efficiency.

A legacy of the Founders not easily separated from their creation of a federal system is the "federal creed" that has been as influential in shaping political behavior as constitutional provisions have been in shaping the dynamics of government. By "federal creed" is meant habitual skepticism with regard to centralized power. It was expressed vividly in Walt Whitman's *Leaves of Grass*:

> To the States or any of them or any city of the States,
> *Resist much, obey little.*
> Once unquestioning obedient, once fully enslaved, no nation state, city of this earth, ever afterward resumes its liberty.

These lines express a political reality of the nineteenth century, namely, that whenever a policy was considered, debate typically centered not only on the wisdom of the policy itself but also on the cognate question: what level of government—the states or Washington—ought legitimately to have responsibility? It was the enduring popular commitment to the values of federalism, some historians contend, that kept the nation from accepting full-scale reorganization as a consolidated, unitary government in the Civil War years. Instead, despite such centralizing measures as the wartime banking laws and the postwar adoption of the Fourteenth Amendment, there remained a strong faith in the desirability of a meaningful "state sovereignty." The culture of federalism was expressed in the enigmatic pronouncement of the Supreme Court in TEXAS V. WHITE (1869) that "the Constitution in all its provisions looks to an indestructible Union composed of indestructible states." Similar convictions about the states' continuing importance found voice in COLLECTOR V. DAY, two years later, when the Court asserted that surviving aspects of state sovereignty made the states "as independent of the general government as [it] is independent of the states."

Opponents of centralized power appealed to such convictions in the late nineteenth century and early twentieth century, when they argued for narrow construction of the commerce clause and found in the due process clause of the Fifth Amendment authority for declaring unconstitutional congressional regulatory measures. The same federal creed led many reformers in the Progressive era to prefer uniform state codes to outright imposition of uniformity in law by congressional action. In the New Deal years and down to the present day, moreover, opponents of the welfare and regulatory features of modern policy have expressed their views in terms that extolled state sovereignty and deplored the centralizing of power in Washington as contrary to the Framers' intent.

The variety and ingenuity of such arguments have led many commentators to conclude that the federal creed is a convenient, all-purpose shield behind which to advocate special-interest positions. The most egregious example in the nation's history has been the invocation of STATES' RIGHTS as a justification for policies of RACIAL DISCRIMINATION. Conservative jurists also created a constitutional void within which neither the national government nor the states could legislate to regulate economic interests; federalism became the handmaiden of laissez-faire. Inconsistency in the application of federal principles in the 1920s led THOMAS REED POWELL to remark that "the sacred slogan of states' rights is easily forgotten when employers wish their laborers sober but unctuously invoked when they wish them young" (a reference to southern opposition to child-labor laws and support of national prohibition). In the post-WORLD WAR II era, moreover, some of the most outspoken champions of "small government" and states' rights, and opponents of the nationalization of economic and social policy, have also been most consistently in favor of massive increases in the size of the national armed forces and even of federal surveillance of political activists and other infringements on CIVIL LIBERTIES.

Even if one concedes that federalism can be a smokescreen behind which special interests can pursue selfish aims or hide inconsistencies, the prominence of the traditional values of federalism in political rhetoric indicates that such arguments are regarded as effective. They are, in effect, appeals to the values of a "federal" political culture: American political consciousness retains inherited and much reiterated notions that certain important values are best served by decentralization of power.

Some prominent contemporary students of American federalism claim that the abstract concept of separate governments (state and national), with separate responsibilities and constituencies, is—and indeed always has been—a fiction. According to this view, despite the "fiction" of ENUMERATED POWERS there has always been an overlap of responsibilities and a significant measure of federal-state sharing of power. "Dual federalism"—the concept of state and national governments occupying distinct, separate spheres of authority—is in this version of our history only a myth. Contrary to this view is another that contends that until 1861 the federal system in actuality functioned much as the model of "dual federalism" prescribed, and after the Civil War, there began a progressive centralization of power which continued until the 1980s.

The evaluation of such contending views depends upon analysis not only of doctrinal development but also of the system's practical operation. How has government actually behaved, and to what extent has power been centralized or decentralized in important areas of policy, at different stages of the nation's history? In fact, the story of American federalism is one of progressive centralization. Except for the overarching continuity infusing the whole record—the progressive centralization of power, step by step—distinct stages in the history of federalism indicate fundamental discontinuities.

The first stage was the period from the founding, in 1787–1789, to the Civil War. In this period, a remarkable array of governmental functions were exclusively, or nearly so, in the hands of the states. Power was diffused, and what "sharing" was found tended to be confined to the most superficial types of cooperation between state and national governments. Criminal law, definition of the requirements of due process, prison management, and criminal punishment were all state functions. So was the definition of property rights, confined only by the contract clause decisions of the Supreme Court. The power of EMINENT DOMAIN was exercised by the states virtually without a check by federal authority. Public education and labor relations, even slavery, were state matters. The states controlled the content of commercial law, family law, and such COMMON LAW matters as the rules of torts, nuisance, and liability. Also decentralized were CORPORATION law, most of taxation policy, and the design and control of the nation's transport system. At no other time after 1861 were the theoretical maxims of dual federalism so closely approximated by government in action.

The decentralization of real power before 1861 persisted even though the Marshall Court was handing down a series of landmark "nationalizing" decisions that lay the doctrinal groundwork for centralization. Even the Marshall Court left the door open for robust state regulatory activity. By the late 1830s, moreover, the Taney Court had begun to develop the doctrine of "concurrent powers," and it had shored up the STATE POLICE POWER with its decision in CHARLES RIVER BRIDGE V. WARREN BRIDGE (1837). Congress simply abstained from acting in many areas of policy that had been left open to it by the Marshall Court's doctrines. The state governments, therefore, held the reins in many vital areas of policy; the structure and dynamics of power were decentralized. One consequence of this decentralization was significant state-to-state variation in the substantive content of law in property, labor, family, and criminal law. The differences between law in slave states and free states were only the most dramatic illustration of such diversity.

The period from 1861 to 1890 was the second stage in the development of American federalism. Formal constitutional change came with the Civil War and had transforming doctrinal and practical consequences, deriving from the Thirteenth, Fourteenth, and Fifteenth Amendments. Meanwhile, Congress in the 1860s was enacting CIVIL RIGHTS laws, instituting an income tax (terminated after the war), inaugurating a national banking system, subsidizing transcontinental railroad projects, and expanding the size and reach of the federal bureaucracy generally. Thus power was centralized at an entirely unprecedented level, both in control of the economy and in protection of individual rights. Laws expanding the jurisdiction of the federal courts further concentrated power in the national government. In 1887, the INTERSTATE COMMERCE ACT inaugurated federal ADMINISTRATIVE LAW and centralized the regulation of the railroads. In 1890, the SHERMAN ACT marked the beginning of federal business law. Although such measures continued the centralizing trend in the distribution of real power, nonetheless elements of dual federalism persisted: property law, criminal justice, family relations, labor law, and most of an infant system of business regulation all remained nearly exclusively with the states.

The third stage of American federalism occupied the years 1890–1933. It was an era of accelerating centralization of policy responsibilities—although diversity persisted and the states did continue to exercise a wide-ranging discretionary authority, without substantial federal interference or direction, in many areas of law. Large-scale aid for irrigation in the West commenced with the Carey Act of 1894; and the Newlands Act of 1902 established an even larger national policy presence in that area. The PURE FOOD AND DRUG ACT (1906) signaled a trend toward exercise of the NATIONAL POLICE POWER, augmenting controls imposed through use of the TAXING AND SPENDING POWER, POSTAL POWER, and commerce power. Both the Federal Reserve Act of 1913 and the CLAYTON ANTITRUST ACT of 1914 greatly extended federal administrative law, displacing state regulatory powers. Over the next seventy years, one of the most influential changes was the SIXTEENTH AMENDMENT, which set the stage for the national government's use of income taxes as a major source of revenues. Midway in this period, moreover, came the dramatic temporary expansion of centralized power occasioned by WORLD WAR I. Although the conservative dominance of Congress in the Republican 1920s slowed the centralizing trend, even in that decade new responsibilities were assumed or expanded by the national government. They included the institution of FEDERAL GRANTS-IN-AID to the states for infant and maternity care, and expansion of the federal roads program, established earlier. The 1920 Transportation Act and the Federal Power Act of the same year also enlarged the regulatory powers of the federal government.

Ironically, these expansions of centralized power occurred in counterpoint with recurrent expressions of dual federalism and LIMITED GOVERNMENT doctrines by the Supreme Court. The most important initiatives of Congress struck down by the Court were the income tax instituted in 1893 and the 1916 KEATING-OWENS CHILD LABOR ACT. Matters such as labor relations were "entrusted to local authority" by the Constitution, the Court asserted in HAMMER V. DAGENHART (1918); child labor was "a purely local matter in which federal authority does not extend," and to permit Congress to regulate child labor risked permitting "our system of government [to] be practically destroyed"! Yet the same judges who subscribed to such doctrines of federalism also adhered to the doctrine of economic due process. Hence, when the Court reviewed regulatory and welfare legislation enacted by the states, it frequently struck down such laws under the Fourteenth Amendment. The Court thus immunized many business interests against regulation by either the state or the national government. The federal judiciary's activism in the cause of laissez-faire and dual federalism, ironically, was evidence of a negative type of centralization: the Supreme Court stood as censor of the states in vital social and economic matters.

Against this background of mixed constitutional doctrine and new centralizing initiatives, intergovernmental relations in the modern "sharing" mode emerged. Its most important feature was grants of cash aid to the states. Congress often tied strings to such aid, requiring planning of state programs and some degree of auditing by federal officers. By 1920, eleven programs were paying $30 million annually to the states—about 2.5 per cent of state revenues, or about a tenth the proportion paid by such grants-in-aid in the early 1980s—with most of the payments representing highway construction funds.

In the field of civil rights, the Court made only a small dent in the solid shield of states' rights behind which Jim Crow legislation, disfranchisement of blacks, and control of racial violence remained the exclusive responsibility of state governments. In the South, white supremacy reigned. In the area of FREEDOM OF SPEECH and FREEDOM OF THE PRESS, however, there was some movement by the

Court toward applying Fourteenth Amendment constraints on state action.

The fourth stage of American federalism's development embraced the NEW DEAL and World War II years, from 1933 to 1945. This period witnessed the wholesale centralization of policy responsibilities, a movement spurred by the worst economic depression in the nation's history and by four years of total mobilization for war. In the wake of centralizing initiatives by Congress came a dramatic shift in constitutional doctrine by the Supreme Court. To be sure, the Court initially erected doctrinal barriers to the innovations of FRANKLIN D. ROOSEVELT's New Deal administration; but by 1937–1938 a modern "constitutional revolution" had occurred without benefit of formal constitutional amendment. The Court discarded the doctrine of economic due process, and it adopted an interpretation of the commerce clause that validated unprecedented expansion of federal interventions in the economy and of social welfare and relief programs.

One policy area after another that previously had been in the states' hands came into the domain of federal action. Congress made agriculture a managed sector beginning in 1933; and the NATIONAL INDUSTRIAL RECOVERY ACT had much the same effect in the manufacturing sector from 1933 to 1935. The TENNESSEE VALLEY AUTHORITY ACT inaugurated regional development under federal auspices, and national programs proliferated in the conservation and reclamation fields. The WAGNER ACT of 1935 established a comprehensive federal policy of collective bargaining in labor relations, instituting national administrative law in the labor field; and by 1938 wages and hours legislation had augmented the basic labor law by setting uniform national standards. Congress authorized massive federal relief and subsidized work programs; and the SOCIAL SECURITY ACT and unemployment-compensation legislation of 1935 marked a new era of nationally sponsored and directed welfare policy. The net of federal regulatory power was thrown over many areas of industry formerly controlled, if at all, by the states: BROADCASTING, trucking, waterways, the securities exchanges, and previously unregulated segments of the banking industry. Meanwhile grants-in-aid—and the model of COOPERATIVE FEDERALISM of which they were an essential component—began to dominate federal-state relationships. True "sharing," in which the bulk of funding came from Congress, thus became a prominent feature of the working federal system; yet decisions tended to be made at the center, both as to policy and as to funding, with the states exercising administrative functions and serving as conduits for federal money.

Still, except for the three and a half years of war, when emergency powers extended to the national control of virtually every feature of the nation's life, the states remained a source of diversity in the American system of government. Yet the number and the significance of policy areas under their control had been so reduced that a new-modeled federal system had clearly become dominant.

The final stage in the history of federalism dates from 1945 to the present day. Its main feature, at least until the administration of RONALD REAGAN beginning in 1981, was a continued trend toward centralization. Four characteristics of this centralization movement are particularly important. First is the permanent status of large-scale standing military forces, their support taking as much as half of the federal government's operating expenses—something without precedent in peacetime prior to 1940. Second is the tendency toward stronger federal guarantees of civil rights. All three branches of government contributed to the civil rights expansion. The executive branch enforced racial integration of the armed forces and required AFFIRMATIVE ACTION programs of firms taking government contracts. Congress defined new guarantees of rights in areas such as PUBLIC ACCOMMODATIONS, and employment; it also enacted legislation under which executive departments instituted affirmative action and equal opportunity policies in labor relations, education, and other areas. The judiciary played a leading role, with the line of DESEGREGATION cases elaborating the principles of BROWN V. BOARD OF EDUCATION (1954). The Court also carved out new areas of federal constitutional rights, such as the RIGHT OF PRIVACY and rights against SEX DISCRIMINATION.

The third major characteristic of centralization since 1945 is the rapid growth in the 1960s and 1970s, and the continued importance since then, of federal grants-in-aid to the states. The design and initiation of new grant programs, especially those associated with the "Great Society" measures of the LYNDON B. JOHNSON administration, led some analysts to speak of a "near monopolization of innovation by the central government" as a novel form of primary centralization. A fourth characteristic of post-1945 centralization is the continued enlargement of the scope of congressional regulatory concerns. Congress instituted far-reaching controls over air and water pollution, occupational health and safety, food and drug quality, and energy resources. Despite a strong movement in the Jimmy Carter and especially the Reagan years toward "deregulation," the federal regulatory presence in the mid-1980s remained far greater than that of the 1950s.

The Supreme Court seldom has stood in the way of such trends. Indeed, its role has been that of leader in the REAPPORTIONMENT and civil rights areas. In reviewing regulatory measures, only once since 1937 has the Court invoked states' rights or the commerce clause in such a way as to limit congressional power; that one exception was NATIONAL LEAGUE OF CITIES V. USERY (1976), a decision of limited application although notable for its assertion of the rights of the states "as states." Some state activities, the Court held, were beyond the reach of national wage and hour standards. Yet the Court has validated all other federal regulatory measures.

The scores of modern grant-in-aid programs have included many that bypassed the state governments: federal funds were awarded directly to cities and local special-purpose districts. Another hallmark of recent intergovernmental relations is what may be termed "managerialism," taking the form of program realignments, reliance on new budgeting concepts, oversight of programs by regional-level federal offices, and increased attention by Congress to the quality of governmental services at all levels. In 1958, Congress created the Advisory Commission on Intergovernmental Relations, which became a major proponent of reforms in aid programs and also an exemplar of the new-style managerialism in action.

Successive Presidents have championed the realignment of powers and policy responsibilities, as between the nation and the states. Thus Lyndon Johnson called for a "creative federalism" that would involve private-sector institutions as well as all levels of government in jointly administered programs. Some of Johnson's Great Society program complicated intergovernmental relations by permitting community organizations to challenge the existing governmental and political establishments. A reaction to the Johnson-era programs and politics was embodied in RICHARD M. NIXON's call for a "new federalism." His proposals took the form of combining increased executive power with increasing reliance on REVENUE SHARING and "block grants" instead of categorical or conditional grants-in-aid. Although during Jimmy Carter's administration general revenue sharing was continued, the President sought to reemphasize the problems of major urban centers and depressed minority populations; he also sought to impose tighter control on grants-in-aid, to assure the realization of congressional objectives.

Ronald Reagan announced his own brand of "new federalism" on taking office in 1981. Both in his rhetoric and by administrative actions, he sought to turn the clock back dramatically on many features of modern federalism. National political dialogue was infused, for the first time in many years, with an orthodox small-government, anticentralist ideology little heeded since New Deal days. Previous Republican Presidents—DWIGHT EISENHOWER, Nixon, and GERALD R. FORD—had all accepted in varying degrees, and even expanded in some respects, the permanent legacy of the New Deal. But in the 1980s, Reagan led a much more deeply rooted challenge to some of the welfare state and regulatory state foundations of the modern federal system. At the same time, he endorsed legislation designed to curb the authority of the federal courts, especially in the civil rights and CRIMINAL PROCEDURE areas; and he gave his support to constitutional amendments designed to permit school prayer in public schools, to require balanced BUDGETS, and to permit the states to prohibit abortions. Reagan's programs underlined his admiration for the constitutional doctrines and policies of federalism dominant in Republican circles in the 1920s.

Once again, therefore, in the Reagan years, federalism was at the center of political debate in America; and once again, the values of federalism were being invoked for purposes that transcended the mere reordering of federal-state relationships. The classic concerns of federalism in theory—diffusion of power, diversity, liberty, efficiency—remained in the forefront of public attention. How to square the ideals expressed in the original understanding with the social and economic realities of the late twentieth century remained a profoundly important issue.

HARRY N. SCHEIBER
(1986)

Bibliography

BEER, SAMUEL   1973   The Modernization of American Federalism. *Publius* 3:49–95.

DAVIS, RUFUS   1978   *The Federal Principle: A Journey through Time in Quest of Meaning.* Berkeley: University of California Press.

GRODZINS, MORTON   1966   *The American System: A New View of Government in the United States,* ed. Daniel Elazar. Chicago: Rand, McNally.

MACMAHON, ARTHUR W., ed.   1955   *Federalism: Mature and Emergent.* New York: Columbia University Press.

PATTERSON, JAMES   1969   *The New Deal and the States: Federalism in Transition.* Princeton, N.J.: Princeton University Press.

SCHEIBER, HARRY N.   1975   Federalism and the American Economic Order, 1789–1910. *Law & Society Review* 10:57–118.

———— 1978 American Federalism and the Diffusion of Power. *University of Toledo Law Review* 9:619–680.

WALKER, DAVID   1981   *Toward a Functioning Federalism.* Cambridge, Mass.: Winthrop.

WRIGHT, DEIL   1978   *Understanding Intergovernmental Relations.* North Scituate, Mass.: Duxbury Press.

FEDERALISM, THEORY OF

The American federal system came into existence when the United States declared its independence in 1776. Indeed, the very process of declaring independence involved a series of reciprocal initiatives and actions on the part of the colonies; the CONTINENTAL CONGRESS declared independence for all thirteen colonies in one act, federal to the extent that the declaration itself was a culmination of this interplay and was undertaken by delegates from the states, each state speaking with one voice.

The foundation of the United States was a federal act par excellence, involving a consistent and protracted interplay between the colonies (later states) and the Congress, which they created as a single, national body to speak in their collective name. In the year that the representatives of the people of the colonies collectively declared the independence of the United States, other representatives of the same people were reconstituting the colonies themselves as states. Four colonies—New Hampshire, South Carolina, Virginia, and New Jersey—adopted state CONSTITUTIONS in 1776 before the adoption of the DECLARATION OF INDEPENDENCE, and four more—Pennsylvania, Maryland, Delaware, and North Carolina—did likewise before the year was out. Within sixteen months, all the former colonies except Massachusetts had adopted constitutions.

At one time this fact was used to argue that considerable disagreement existed over whether the states preceded the Union. Today it is generally agreed that both came into existence simultaneously—in the original federal act of the United States as such. In sum, all of the ambiguities of diversity in unity endemic to federalism were present at the creation. Even local governments (in this case the towns and counties) participated in the constitutional drafting and ratifying processes.

As Americans moved westward, they created new states "from scratch," in virtually every case establishing local and territorial institutions under the aegis of the federal government, but generally as a result of local initiatives. Ultimately, these new polities, with their new populations, would be admitted to the federation as states, fully equal to their sisters under the Constitution. Thus the American federation expanded from the Atlantic to the Pacific by settling what were, to white Americans, empty lands and organizing them politically.

The last of the forty-eight contiguous states was admitted in 1912; and Alaska and Hawaii, the two noncontiguous states, were added in 1959 and 1960, respectively, after relatively long periods of territorial status. In the same decade, the United States embarked upon a new experiment in federalism by creating a category of commonwealth or "free associated state," whose people, as American citizens, voted to associate their polity with the United States under a special charter. This new arrangement was devised for Puerto Rico, which became the first "free associated state" in 1952. In 1976 a similar arrangement was made with the Northern Mariana Islands. In both cases small, populated TERRITORIES sought that status to increase their autonomy, not to diminish it. (See COMMONWEALTH STATUS.)

Historically, then, the United States model is that of a political entity that was federal from its founding. The American states did not have to find a common cultural denominator because they had one from the first. All of their regimes were of the same character and their level of economic development was roughly equal. No plan for intercolonial union was ever put forth that was not federal in character. The American colonial period, indeed, had been a period of incubation for a uniquely American approach to governance, which properly can be termed "federal democracy."

Federal democracy is the authentic American contribution to democratic thought and republican government. Its conception represents a synthesis of the Puritan idea of the covenant relationship as the foundation of all proper human society and the constitutional ideas of the English natural rights school of the seventeenth and early eighteenth centuries. Contractual noncentralization—the structured dispersion of power among many centers whose legitimate authority is constitutionally guaranteed—is the key to the widespread and entrenched diffusion of power that remains the principal characteristic of and argument for federal democracy.

Federal democracy is a composite notion that includes a strong religious component. The religious expression of federalism was brought to the United States through the theology of the Puritans, who viewed the world as organized through the covenants that God had made with mankind, binding God and man into a lasting union and partnership to work for the redemption of the world, but in such a way that both parties were free, as partners must be, to preserve their respective integrities. Implicit in the Puritan view is the understanding that God relinquished some of His own omnipotence to enable men to be free to compact with Him.

According to federal theology, all social and political relationships are derived from that original covenant. This theological perspective found its counterpart in congregationalism as the basis of church polity and the town meeting as the basis of the civil polity. Thus, communities of believers were required to organize themselves by covenant into congregations just as communities of citizens were required to organize themselves by covenant into towns. The entire structure of religious and political organization in New England reflected this application of a theological principle to social and political life.

Even after the eighteenth-century secularization of the covenant idea, the behavioral pattern resurfaced on every frontier, whether in the miners' camps of southwestern Missouri, central Colorado, and the mother lode country of California, in the agricultural settlements of the upper Midwest, or in the wagon trains that crossed the plains, whose members compacted together to provide for their internal governance during the long trek westward.

It should not be surprising that Americans early became socialized into a kind of federalistic individualism that recognized the subtle bonds of partnership linking individuals even as they preserved their individual integrities. William James was later to write about the federal character of these subtle bonds in his prescription for a pluralistic universe as a "republic of republics."

In strictly governmental terms, federalism is a form of political organization that unites separate polities within an overarching political system, enabling all to maintain their fundamental political integrity and distributing power among general and constituent governments so that they all share in the system's decision-making and executing processes. In a larger sense, federalism represents the linking of free people and their communities through lasting but limited political arrangements to protect certain rights or liberties and to achieve specific common ends while preserving their respective integrities. To reverse the order, federalism has to do, first and foremost, with a relationship among entities, and then with the structure that embodies that relationship and provides the means for sustaining it. Originally federalism was most widely recognized as a relationship to which structural questions were incidental; but since the creation of the American federal system, in which a new structure was invented to accommodate that relationship, federalism has become increasingly identified in structural terms. This usage in turn has contributed to a certain emphasis on legal and administrative relations between the units and to a neglect of the larger question of the relationships federalism is designed to foster throughout the polity.

Although, in a strictly constitutional sense, American federalism is a means by which the national government shares authority and power with the states, the influence of federal principles actually extends far beyond the institutional relationships that link the federal, state, and local governments. The idea of the federal commonwealth as a partnership is a key principle of federalism and the basis of its integrative powers. Like all partnerships, the commonwealth is bound by a compact—the Constitution—that sets the basic terms of the partnership to insure, among other things, the preservation and continued political viability of its basic political units.

The principle of partnership has been extended far beyond its simple sense of a relationship between the federal and state governments. It has come to serve as the guiding principle in most of the political relationships that tie institutions, groups, interests, and individuals together in the American system. The term "partnership" describes a relationship that allows the participants freedom of action while acknowledging the ties that require them to function in partnership.

Partnership implies the distribution of power among several centers that must negotiate cooperative arrangements with one another in order to achieve common goals.

Although the basic forms of the partnership are set forth in the United States Constitution, the actual character of the federal system is delineated, maintained, and made functional only partly by constitutional devices. The role of the Constitution (and of its primary interpreters, the courts) should not be minimized; yet equally important is the way in which the institutions and purposes of federalism are maintained through the political process. The political process, as it affects the federal-state-local relationship most directly, is made manifest through four basic political devices: territorial democracy, the dual system of laws and courts, the POLITICAL PARTY system, and the system of public-private "complexes."

The basic pattern of political organization in the United States is territorial. That is to say, American politics is formally organized around units of territory rather than economic or ethnic groups, social classes, or the like. The nation is divided into states, and the states are divided into counties, and the counties are divided into townships or cities or special districts, and the whole country is divided into election districts of varying sizes. This organization means that people and their interests gain political identity and formal representation through their location in particular places and their ability to capture political control of territorial political units.

A second basic device is the multiple system of laws and courts tied to the federal division of powers. In the nation as a whole, state law is the basic law. Federal law is essentially designed to fill in the gaps left by the existence of fifty different legal systems. Thus both state and federal courts are bound by state-made law unless it is superseded by the Constitution or by federal statutory law. The complexity of this system is compounded by the nature of the dual court structure, with each state and the federal government having its own complete court system. The federal courts have asserted extensive superiority in interpreting the manner in which the United States Constitution protects the rights of American citizens (who, of course, are also citizens of their states). Led by the United States Supreme Court, which is constitutionally placed at the apex of both court systems, the federal courts interpret federal law, review the work of the state courts, and enforce the laws of the states in which they are located in cases that come under federal JURISDICTION.

The third basic political channel is the party system. The Democratic and Republican parties represent two broad confederations of otherwise largely independent state party organizations that unite on the national plane primarily to gain public office. Despite the greater public attention given to the national parties, the real centers of party organization, finance, and power are on the state and local planes. This noncentralization of the parties helps to maintain generally noncentralized governments and to perpetuate a high degree of local control even in the face of "big government." Thus the party system is of great importance in maintaining the basic structure of American politics and basic American political values, including those of federalism.

The fourth political device, the system of public-private "complexes," is partly reflected in the character of interest group activity. The partnership system extends outward to include private elements as well as governments—both public nongovernmental bodies, such as civic, philanthropic, educational, health, and welfare associations, and private profit-making bodies. These private associations and bodies often work so closely with their governmental allies that it is difficult to distinguish where the public interest ends and the private interest begins.

As a federation, the United States differs from a confederation of essentially separate political systems where the overarching authority is deliberately weak. At the same time, in the noncentralized American system, there is no central government with absolute authority over the states, but there is a strong national or general government coupled with strong state and local governments that share authority and power, constitutionally and practically.

The first important feature of a federation, following the American pattern, is the fundamental role and importance of the federal constitution as an organic law. The American Constitution reflects a federal approach to political SOVEREIGNTY, rejecting the idea that states or governments are sovereign as such, and holding that the people are the ultimate repositories of sovereignty and that governments have only "powers," delegated to them by the people. That approach precludes any notion of IN-HERENT POWERS. Under the Constitution, all powers possessed by the federal government are delegated to it by the people. The federal government has no inherent powers, although, as a result of those delegated, it gains some inherent extensions of its power. So, for example, because the people have delegated to the federal government the power to conduct some aspects of FOREIGN AFFAIRS, the President is understood to have acquired certain IMPLIED POWERS to negotiate with foreign governments. Once the people delegated the principal power, the implied power flowed automatically, but the second is theoretically dependent upon the first. From time to time, Presidents have claimed that they have inherent powers in the fields of foreign affairs and defense that are not subject to constitutional limitations but, rather, flow from the status of the United States as a sovereign state. Although the United States Supreme Court has recognized the existence of inherent powers, it has clearly limited them. This approach has been possible in the United States because of the dual character of the American founding, which enabled Americans to avoid confronting the issue of sovereignty head on.

Accordingly, as ANDREW C. MCLAUGHLIN suggested, the American federal system was designed to provide for the government of a large civil society without reliance upon hierarchical principles. In its original form, the American political system was designed as a matrix of polities, an indefinite number of structured political arenas linked to one another within the framework provided by the national and state constitutions. These arenas were to be distinguished from one another not on the basis of being "higher" or "lower" in importance but on the basis of the relative size of the constituencies they served. It was further assumed that the arenas were essentially equal, because size, of itself, was no measure of importance. Tasks were designed to be assumed or shared within the matrix on the assumption that sometimes a smaller arena is more appropriate than a larger one and that sometimes the reverse is true. The federal government was constitutionally mandated to serve the largest arena and to maintain the entire structure by assuring the continuity of the matrix itself. The role of the state governments in serving the basic divisions in the matrix was affirmed in the constitutional arrangement, and the states established local governments to serve the smallest arenas. Today the matrix consists of thousands of local arenas within the national framework, divided into fifty basic units—the states of the federal Union.

The American system has increasingly emphasized CO-OPERATIVE FEDERALISM rather than DUAL FEDERALISM as the basis of its operations. The American pattern of federalism has been cooperative since its beginnings, because since its inception most powers and competences have been treated as concurrent, shared by the various planes of government. In Morton Grodzins's terms, it is not a layer cake but a marble cake. Therefore, in the American polity, it is especially difficult to define what is exclusively in the federal sphere of competence, or in the state sphere, or in the local sphere.

The American federal system is at once extraordinarily simple and unusually complex. The simplicity of the federal system lies in a formal structure of federal, state, and local governments and in the outline of formal relationships between them. The complexity of the system lies in the myriad relationships that have developed between the governments and those who make them work. People often tend to take it for granted that national problems are handled in Washington; state problems in the state capital; and local problems at city hall or in the county courthouse. But, although it is easy to say that this is how things should be, it is well-nigh impossible to take a specific issue or function and to determine that it is exclusively national, state, or local.

The constitutional place of the states in the federal system is determined by four elements: the provisions in the federal and state constitutions that either limit or guarantee the powers of the states vis-à-vis the federal government; the provisions in the federal Constitution that give the states a role in the composition of the national government; the subsequent interpretations of both sets of provisions by the courts (particularly the United States Supreme Court); and the unwritten constitutional traditions that have evolved informally and have only later been formally recognized through the first three, directly or indirectly. The federal constitutional provisions outlining the general position of the states must always be taken into consideration even if some of them can be transcended through politics in specific situations. The specific limitations and guarantees of state powers fall into four basic categories: general concern for the integrity of the states as well as their subordination to the Union; some brief provisions ensuring the states a role in the common defense; a delineation of the role of the states in the two central areas of positive governmental activity at home, management of commerce and raising of revenues; and a description of state responsibilities in the administration of justice.

The procedure by which the basic status of the Union may be revised is found in Article V of the United States Constitution.

Similar procedures are found in most federal constitutions in the world. They underline one of the paramount characteristics of a federation: the revision of the basic status of the union is not totally dependent on the member states. Individual states have no right to veto changes adopted through the accepted procedure. When they oppose an amendment to the constitution—or demand an amendment—they are not sure to win.

One of the most important features of American federalism lies in the impossibility of the member states to abandon the federation. As the Civil War dramatically affirmed, there is no right of SECESSION. The United States Supreme Court, responding to that war, set down the accepted definition of the American federation in TEXAS V. WHITE (1869): "The Constitution in all its provisions, looks to an indestructible Union, composed of indestructible States."

Another characteristic of federalism in the United States is the existence of federal norms, whether legal, administrative, or judicial, that bear directly upon the federation citizens, without any need of intervention of the member states. The architects of the American system recognized that a successful federal system, something more than a loose confederation of states, required that both the national and the state governments be given substantial autonomy. They also recognized that each had to have some way to influence the other from within as well as through direct negotiation. The federal government has the power to deal directly with the public, that is to say, with the citizenry of the states. The states, in turn, have a

major role in determining the composition of the federal government and the selection of those who make it work.

DANIEL J. ELAZAR
(1986)

Bibliography

ELAZAR, DANIEL J. 1962 *The American Partnership: Intergovernmental Cooperation in the Nineteenth Century United States.* Chicago: University of Chicago Press.
——— 1984 *American Federalism: A View from the States.* New York: Harper & Row.
GRODZINS, MORTON 1966 *The American System: A New View of Government in the United States.* Chicago: Rand McNally.
HART, HENRY and WECHSLER, HERBERT 1953 *The Federal Courts and the Federal System.* Mineola, N.Y.: Foundation Press.
MCLAUGHLIN, ANDREW C. (1932) 1972 *The Foundations of American Constitutionalism.* Gloucester, Mass.: Peter Smith.
OSTROM, VINCENT 1971 *The Political Theory of the Compound Republic.* Blacksburg: Virginia Polytechnic Institute, Center for the Study of Public Choice.
VILE, M. J. C. 1961 *The Structure of American Federalism.* Oxford: Oxford University Press.
WRIGHT, DEIL S. 1978 *Understanding Intergovernmental Relations.* North Scituate, Mass.: Duxbury Press.

FEDERALISM AND CIVIL RIGHTS

In the scheme of the United States Constitution, the concept of FEDERALISM requires respect for the distinct legal authorities and diverse cultures of the separate states, but the concept of CIVIL RIGHTS requires adherence to uniform rules emanating either directly from the national Constitution or indirectly from various congressional enactments. The two concepts are thus bound in a structural tension.

This tension has persisted since the RECONSTRUCTION amendments, when the national government first seriously began to create federal civil rights that could be asserted against the states. These rights, together with the expansion of federal JUDICIAL POWER necessary to enforce them, were self-conscious efforts to eradicate aspects of the indigenous culture of the southern states traceable to the institution of SLAVERY. Federal civil rights were thus born in a burst of national centralization.

Ironically, these rights were interpreted by courts in such a way as to permit racial subordination to endure even in the absence of slavery. The FOURTEENTH AMENDMENT in particular was understood to establish civil rights that were primarily economic in nature, most notably the right of FREEDOM OF CONTRACT. In the era after LOCHNER V. NEW YORK (1905), federal courts were so persistent in using this right to strike down social reform legislation in the states that Thomas Reed Powell was moved to "question whether judicial centralization is not pushed to an extreme under our federal system."

In this context, the values of federalism acquired a distinctively progressive cast. In 1932, for example, Justice LOUIS D. BRANDEIS, in his dissent in NEW STATE ICE COMPANY V. LIEBMANN, gave his influential and ringing defense of federalism as a "laboratory" for "novel social and economic experiments." When, after the constitutional crisis of the NEW DEAL, the Supreme Court backed off from its enforcement of laissez-faire economic rights, these same federalist values led some to challenge the Court's creation of a vigorous regime of noneconomic civil rights. In ADAMSON V. CALIFORNIA (1947), for example, Justice FELIX FRANKFURTER opposed Justice HUGO L. BLACK's proposal to "incorporate" the guarantees of the BILL OF RIGHTS into the Fourteenth Amendment for application against the states. Frankfurter argued that the INCORPORATION DOCTRINE would "tear up by the roots much of the fabric of law in the several States, and would deprive the States of opportunity for reforms in legal process designed for extending the area of freedom."

In this way the values of federalism became associated with conservative opposition to the establishment of federal noneconomic civil rights. This association reached its apex when the concept of STATES' RIGHTS was used to challenge the legitimacy of BROWN V. BOARD OF EDUCATION (1954, 1955) and the CIVIL RIGHTS MOVEMENT, a conjunction that came close to discrediting the values of federalism as effective limitations on the establishment of civil rights.

Certainly by the mid-1960s, as the nation committed itself to the recognition and implementation of civil rights, the values of federalism were in eclipse. The Supreme Court incorporated virtually all of the Bill of Rights into the Fourteenth Amendment for application against the states, and it aggressively enlarged its interpretation of the scope and application of those rights. The incorporation of most of the FOURTH AMENDMENT, Fifth Amendment, and Sixth Amendment forced the states to comply with uniform national standards in the area of CRIMINAL PROCEDURE. The Court's expansion of FIRST AMENDMENT guarantees of FREEDOM OF SPEECH and RELIGIOUS LIBERTY resulted in the invalidation of numerous state regulations that had heretofore been deemed perfectly acceptable reflections of local culture. And the Court's firm commitment to rights of racial and ethnic equality effectively outlawed the Jim Crow culture of the southern states. Congress significantly participated in this process of establishing national civil rights through its enactment of the CIVIL RIGHTS ACT OF 1964, the CIVIL RIGHTS ACT OF 1968, and the VOTING RIGHTS ACT OF 1965.

By the end of the WARREN COURT era, the rhetoric of federalism had virtually disappeared from the ongoing debate about the substance of civil rights. For example, when the BURGER COURT deliberated whether the EQUAL PROTECTION clause should require STRICT SCRUTINY of gender classifications, it argued the question almost entirely in terms of the independent merits of the position, rather than in terms of the effect that such scrutiny would have on the ability of diverse states to enact laws that reflected distinct cultural attitudes toward controversial issues of gender equality. Similarly, when the Burger Court in ROE V. WADE endowed women with the constitutional right to have an ABORTION, it barely discussed the implications of the decision for the values of federalism.

The end of the 1960s witnessed a political renaissance of the values of federalism, a renaissance that later intensified during the presidency of RONALD REAGAN. This renaissance found judicial expression in debates over the reach of federal judicial power, rather than in debates over the nature of the substantive civil rights protected by that power. Thus, both the Burger Court and the REHNQUIST COURT invoked values of federalism in order to curb the authority and accessibility of federal courts, which the Warren Court had greatly expanded in an attempt to enforce fully the civil rights that it had recognized.

For example, in an important line of cases that originated with YOUNGER V. HARRIS, the Burger Court invoked the principles of "our Federalism" in order to limit the availability of federal EQUITY relief. The Court explained these principles as a "notion of "comity,' that is, a proper respect for state functions," and the belief that the nation "will fare best if the States and their institutions are left free to perform their separate functions in their separate ways." The Court invoked similar notions of COMITY to justify restrictions on ACCESS TO THE COURTS for federal writs of HABEAS CORPUS, expansive interpretations of state immunity from federal judicial power under the ELEVENTH AMENDMENT, strict presumptions against waivers of that immunity, and limitations on the authority of federal courts to issue injunctions broadly restructuring state and local government institutions. The tension between civil rights and federalism thus continued, although in a somewhat modulated key.

That tension may profitably be analyzed by inquiring into the values served by the concepts of civil rights and federalism. Civil rights, at least those that emanate from the Constitution, serve mainly to protect persons from the exercise of governmental authority. The persistent image is that of individuals safeguarded by courts from the domination of an overpowering government. From this perspective, it makes no difference whether government power is exercised at the state or federal level.

Yet federalism is committed to the proposition that it is usually preferable to exercise power at the local rather than national level. There are many different rationales for this preference, ranging from efficiency to experimentation. But there are two justifications that are most directly responsive to the values underlying the claim for civil rights.

The first accepts the premise that it is vitally important to protect individual liberty from the excesses of state power, but it views courts as, in the long run, unreliable institutions for securing that protection. Individual freedom is better served, so the argument runs, by establishing the states as centers of power that are competitive with the federal government, in the expectation that the resulting diffusion of power will effectively check the potential for abusive government. To establish the states as independent centers of power, however, requires ceding to them autonomy from a uniform regime of civil rights emanating from the federal government. On this account, then, the resolution of the tension between civil rights and federalism ought to depend upon how the long-term benefits to civil rights anticipated from the structural arrangements of federalism compare against the short-term benefits that would result from judicial enforcement of federal civil rights.

The second justification for federalism strikes deeper, for it denies that the image underlying the rationale for civil rights is adequate as a description of local state governments. State governments, according to this argument, are closer to the people and hence more fully realize the values of political participation. Thus, they should not be pictured as overreaching and impersonal governments estranged from their citizens, but rather as more nearly authentic communities, in which political processes both form and express genuine social commitments. The national imposition of uniform civil rights would therefore be both unnecessary and deeply disruptive of these positive local processes. On this account, then, the resolution of the tension between civil rights and federalism ought to depend upon whether states can more accurately be described as representing authentic and inclusive communities or as impersonal and potentially oppressive governments.

Given the difficult and perplexing nature of these inquiries, it is clear why the tension between federalism and civil rights has endured, and in all likelihood will continue to do so.

ROBERT C. POST
(1992)

Bibliography

POST, ROBERT C. 1988 Justice Brennan and Federalism. In Harry N. Scheiber, ed., *Federalism: Studies in History, Law and Policy*, pp. 37–45. Berkeley, Calif.: Berkeley Press.
POWELL, THOMAS REED 1931 The Supreme Court and State Police Powers, 1922–1930. *Virginia Law Review* 17:529–556.
RAPACZYNSKI, ANDRZEJ 1985 From Sovereignty to Process: The Jurisprudence of Federalism After *Garcia. Supreme Court Review* 43:29–38.
SANDALOW, TERRANCE 1980 Federalism and Social Change. *Law and Contemporary Problems* 43:29–38.

FEDERALISM AND ENVIRONMENTAL LAW

Environmental protection was viewed as a state or local responsibility until the post–WORLD WAR II era when pollution problems assumed national scope. Congress responded initially by providing financial assistance to encourage state and local governments to control pollution. Federal grants for construction of municipal sewage treatment plants were the most prominent of these programs. The perceived failure of state and local regulation led Congress during the 1970s and 1980s to establish comprehensive national regulatory programs to protect the environment.

Most of the federal laws employ a "cooperative" FEDERALISM approach in which a federal agency establishes minimum national standards that states may opt to implement or to leave implementation to federal authorities. The Clean Air Act, the Clean Water Act, the Safe Drinking Water Act, and federal hazardous waste LEGISLATION require the Environmental Protection Agency (EPA) to set minimum national standards, while authorizing delegation of authority to administer these programs to states. In states that fail to receive program delegation, the laws are administered by federal authorities.

Most federal environmental laws allow states to adopt more stringent standards than the federally mandated minimum. However, in a few instances Congress has chosen to preempt inconsistent state standards, usually when regulating products that are distributed nationally, such as chemicals regulated under the Toxic Substances Control Act and pesticide labels mandated under the Federal Insecticide, Fungicide, and Rodenticide Act.

The rise of the federal regulatory infrastructure has generated environmental policy conflicts between federal and state authorities. Four types of constitutional issues have arisen in conflicts over environmental federalism. First, states have argued that some federal environmental regulations impermissibly infringe on state SOVEREIGNTY in violation of the TENTH AMENDMENT. In NEW YORK V. UNITED STATES (1992), the Supreme Court struck down a federal requirement that states "take title" to any low-level radioactive waste generated within their borders if they had not made arrangements by a certain date for access to a disposal site for such waste. The Court found that the requirement violated the Tenth Amendment by "comandeering" the states' legislative processes to compel states to enact and enforce a federal regulatory program. Few federal environmental laws are vulnerable to Tenth Amendment challenges because most offer states a choice between regulating an activity according to federal standards or having state law preempted by federal regulation.

This "cooperative federalism" approach is less intrusive on state sovereignty than direct PREEMPTION. Congress also may condition the receipt of federal funds on state participation in federal environmental programs, which is a proper use of Congress's SPENDING POWER and consistent with the Tenth Amendment so long as the conditions bear some relationship to the purpose of the federal spending. Thus, the Clean Air Act's denial of federal highway funds to states that fail to meet national air quality standards is constitutional.

The Court's decision in UNITED STATES V. LÓPEZ (1995) that Congress's regulatory authority under the COMMERCE CLAUSE of Article I, section 8, extends to intrastate activities only when they substantially affect INTERSTATE COMMERCE has spawned a second set of challenges to federal environmental regulations. Arguments that some federal environmental laws exceed Congress's authority by regulating noncommercial activity that is wholly intrastate have been rejected by most courts because of the potential cumulative impact of even localized environmental damage.

A third source of constitutional limitations on federal authority is the ELEVENTH AMENDMENT, which makes states immune from suits for damages in federal court. In *Seminole Tribe of Florida v. Florida* (1996), the Court held that Congress cannot abrogate state SOVEREIGN IMMUNITY by exercising its authority under the commerce clause. This overruled the Court's prior decision in *Pennsylvania v. Union Gas Co.* (1989), which had held that a state could be liable for the costs of environmental remediation under the federal "Superfund" law.

In a fourth set of cases, beginning with PHILADELPHIA V. NEW JERSEY (1978), the Court has used the DORMANT COMMERCE CLAUSE to strike down state laws that restrict the disposal of waste originating out-of-state or that seek to channel solid waste flows to local facilities, as in *C & A Carbone, Inc. v. Town of Clarkstown* (1994).

While federal regulations now dominate the field, states continue to play an important role in implementing and enforcing national environmental policy under a system of cooperative federalism.

ROBERT V. PERCIVAL
(2000)

(SEE ALSO: *Environmental Regulation; Waste, Pollution, and Federalism.*)

Bibliography

DWYER, JOHN P. 1995 The Practice of Federalism Under the Clean Air Act. *Maryland Law Review* 54:1183–1225.

ESTY, DANIEL C. 1996 Revitalizing Environmental Federalism. *Michigan Law Review* 95:570–653.

PERCIVAL, ROBERT V. 1995 Environmental Federalism: Historical Roots and Contemporary Models. *Maryland Law Review* 54:1141–1182.

PERCIVAL, ROBERT V.; MILLER, ALAN S.; SCHROEDER, CHRISTOPHER H.; and LEAPE, JAMES P. 1996 *Environmental Regulation: Law, Science, and Policy*, 2nd ed. Boston, Mass.: Little, Brown.

STEINZOR, RENA I. 1996 Unfunded Environmental Mandates and the "New (New) Federalism": Devolution, Revolution, or Reform? *Minnesota Law Review* 81:101–227.

FEDERALISM AND SHARED POWERS

FEDERALISM and SEPARATION OF POWERS are the two principal techniques in America for dividing political power. Federalism allocates power between the national government and the states; separation of powers distributes power among three branches of the national government and within each of the state governments. Although these divisions of power characterize national and state government, many essential functions of government are shared. Justice ROBERT H. JACKSON deftly noted in YOUNGSTOWN SHEET & TUBE CO. V. SAWYER (1952), "While the Constitution diffuses power the better to secure liberty, it also contemplates that practice will integrate the dispersed powers into a workable government. It enjoins upon its branches separateness but interdependence, autonomy but reciprocity." Jackson directed his observation to the doctrine of separation of powers, but it applies equally well to federalism.

Independence from England in 1776 left the thirteen American states without a central government. Under the ARTICLES OF CONFEDERATION, drafted in 1777 but not ratified until 1781, each state retained "its sovereignty, freedom and independence," with the exception of a few powers expressly delegated to the national government. Various attempts were made over the years to bring a measure of effectiveness to the Confederation, but it was finally agreed after the ANNAPOLIS CONVENTION in 1786 to meet in Philadelphia the following year "to devise such further provisions as shall appear to them necessary to render the constitution of the Federal Government adequate to the exigencies of the Union."

The delegates at Philadelphia rejected MONTESQUIEU's theory that republican government could function only in small countries. He had argued that as a country increased in size, popular control must be surrendered, requiring aristocracies for moderate-sized countries and monarchies for large countries. JAMES MADISON, in THE FEDERALIST #10, made precisely the opposite argument: that republican government was more likely the larger the territory. In a small territory, a dominant faction could gain control. "Extend the sphere," Madison reasoned, "and you take in a greater variety of parties and interests; you make it less probable that a majority of the whole will have a common motive to invade the rights of other citizens."

Critics of the 1787 Constitution claimed that it promoted a national or consolidated form of government instead of preserving the independence of the states. An exceptionally blunt challenge came from the Virginia ratification convention, where PATRICK HENRY attacked the opening words of the Constitution: "What right had they to say, *We, the people?* . . . Who authorized them to speak the language of, *We, the people,* instead of, *We, the states?*" Madison answered these critiques in *Federalist* #39, pointing out that the Constitution contained features of a national character but also vested some power directly in the states. The proposed Constitution, he said, "is, in strictness, neither a national nor a federal Constitution, but a composition of both." By "federal" Madison meant *con*federal: a confederation of sovereign states, such as existed under the Articles of Confederation.

The Philadelphia Convention wrestled with two rival proposals. The VIRGINIA PLAN called for a strong central government, while the NEW JERSEY PLAN advocated a confederation with few national powers. The latter attracted little support. The GREAT COMPROMISE, promoted by OLIVER ELLSWORTH of Connecticut, combined two antagonistic ideas: representation by population in the HOUSE OF REPRESENTATIVES and equal voting power for each state in the SENATE. He explained to the Convention on June 29, "We were partly national; partly federal. The proportional representation in the first branch [the House] was conformable to the national principle & would secure the large States agst. the small. An equality of voices [in the Senate] was conformable to the federal principle and was necessary to secure the Small States agst. the large. He trusted that on this middle ground a compromise would take place."

The compromise gave the central government the power to collect taxes, regulate commerce, and declare war, along with other express functions, including the NECESSARY AND PROPER CLAUSE to carry into effect the ENUMERATED POWERS. National powers are reinforced by the SUPREMACY CLAUSE in Article VI, section 2: "This Constitution, and the laws of the United States which shall be made in pursuance thereof; and all treaties made, or which shall be made, under the authority of the United States, shall be the supreme law of the land; and the judges in every State shall be bound thereby, anything in the constitution or laws of any State to the contrary notwithstanding." Article I, section 9, prohibits the national government from taxing articles exported from any state

or preferring the ports of one state over another, while Article I, section 10, prohibits a number of state actions, including entering into any treaty, alliance, or confederation; coining money; passing any BILL OF ATTAINDER or EX POST FACTO LAW; impairing the OBLIGATION OF CONTRACTS; or laying any IMPOSTS or duties on imports or exports without the consent of Congress, except what is "absolutely necessary" to execute its inspection laws.

The TENTH AMENDMENT provides that the powers "not delegated to the United States by the Constitution, nor prohibited by it to the States, are reserved to the States respectively, or to the people." The Articles of Confederation gave greater protection to the states, which retained all powers, except those "expressly delegated" to the national government. When it was proposed in 1789 that the same phrase be inserted in the Tenth Amendment, Madison objected to the word "expressly" because it was impossible to delineate every function and responsibility of the federal government. There had to be, he said, room for IMPLIED POWERS "unless the Constitution descended to recount every minutiae." On the force of his argument, the word "expressly" was eliminated from the Tenth Amendment. In MCCULLOCH V. MARYLAND (1819), Chief Justice JOHN MARSHALL relied on Madison's argument in upholding the power of Congress to establish a national bank, even though that power is not expressly included in the Constitution.

The suggestion that the Tenth Amendment contains substantive powers for states, even to the point of reinserting the word "expressly," has been made in such cases as *Lane County v. Oregon* (1868) and HAMMER V. DAGENHART (1918). In MISSOURI V. HOLLAND (1920), however, the Supreme Court denied that the TREATY POWER was restricted in any way "by some invisible radiation from the general terms of the Tenth Amendment," and Justice HARLAN F. STONE, in UNITED STATES V. DARBY LUMBER COMPANY (1941), dismissed the Tenth Amendment as a "truism," meaning only "that all is retained which has not been surrendered." Nevertheless, the decisions in *Fry v. United States* (1975) and NATIONAL LEAGUE OF CITIES V. USERY (1976) demonstrate that the Tenth Amendment retains vitality.

Many of the turf battles between the national government and the states have been fought over the scope of the COMMERCE CLAUSE. Commercial friction among the states after 1776 was a principal reason for discarding the Articles of Confederation and adopting a government with greater national powers. The enumerated powers given to Congress in Article I include the power to "regulate commerce with foreign nations, and among the several States, and with the Indian tribes." In GIBBONS V. OGDEN (1824), Chief Justice Marshall advanced a broad interpretation of the power of Congress to regulate commerce, but over the years, the Court employed other doctrines to distinguish between national and state powers. At times the two levels of government could exercise CONCURRENT POWERS. States were able to regulate commerce within their borders unless preempted by Congress. The Court also created the doctrine of exclusive JURISDICTIONS, promoting the theory of DUAL FEDERALISM, under which the states and the national government exercised mutually exclusive powers.

These doctrines appeared to be increasingly artificial with the rapid nationalization of the American economy. Traditional boundaries between INTRASTATE COMMERCE and INTERSTATE COMMERCE were swept aside when the operations of railroads, agriculture, and livestock acquired national structures. The Court even held that Congress could regulate actions inside a state that were simply related to interstate commerce. During World War I and World War II commercial and economic activities that normally fell within the jurisdiction of the states were controlled by the federal government.

During the period of SUBSTANTIVE DUE PROCESS, which lasted from the 1890s to 1937, the Supreme Court struck down a number of regulatory efforts by Congress and state legislatures on the theory that the statutes interfered with the "liberty of contract," a fiction created by the judiciary to limit governmental power. Statutes enacted to establish minimum wages and maximum hours, to protect children from harsh labor practices, or to create better working conditions were regularly invalidated by state and federal courts.

Those judicial doctrines were eventually cast aside during the NEW DEAL revolution, especially after the COURT-PACKING PLAN in 1937. Although at one period the Court struck down congressional statutes because they invaded "local" activities within the control of state governments or because "manufacturing" was considered by the judiciary as local and thus beyond congressional control, these barriers to national action were eventually removed. A series of rulings, such as *NLRB v. Jones & Laughlin Steel Corp.* (1937) and *United States v. Darby Lumber Company* (1941), gave solid support to Congress's interpretations of its powers under the commerce clause. In PRUDENTIAL INSURANCE COMPANY V. BENJAMIN (1946), a chastened Court offered this revealing assessment: "The history of judicial limitation of congressional power over commerce, when exercised affirmatively, has been more largely one of retreat than of ultimate victory."

In *National League of Cities v. Usery* (1976), the Supreme Court appeared to resuscitate state SOVEREIGNTY and the Tenth Amendment. The case involved the decision of Congress to extend federal hours-and-wages standards to state employees. In *Maryland v. Wirtz* (1968), the Court had upheld the extension of federal minimum wages and overtime pay to state-operated hospitals and schools. It even upheld, in *Fry v. United States* (1975), the short-term power of the President to stabilize wages and salaries for state employees. Nevertheless, *National League* refused to permit federal minimum-wage and maximum-hour provisions to displace state powers in such "traditional governmental functions" as fire prevention, police protection, sanitation, public health, and parks and recreation. This 5–4 decision overruled *Wirtz* on the ground that the congressional statute threatened the independent existence of states. In his dissent, Justice WILLIAM J. BRENNAN objected that the Court had delivered "a catastrophic judicial body blow at Congress' power under the Commerce Clause."

The Court's bifurcation between "traditional" and "nontraditional" governmental functions spawned confusion in the lower courts. Many of the efforts of federal district courts to apply the standard in *National League* were rejected by the Supreme Court. Finally, in *Garcia v. San Antonio Metropolitan Transit Authority* (1985), Justice HARRY A. BLACKMUN, whose concurrence had provided the fifth vote in *National League*, swung in the other direction to join with the four dissenters in overruling *National League*. He called attention to the frustrating struggle in federal and state courts to distinguish between traditional and nontraditional functions. He called the criteria in *National League* "unworkable," "inconsistent with established principles of federalism," and "both impracticable and doctrinally barren." Because of this decision, the protection of federalism has been left largely to the political process of Congress. The tone of the four dissents, however, suggests that *Garcia* might be living on borrowed time, reflecting the position of older members of the Court: Blackmun, Brennan, THURGOOD MARSHALL, BYRON R. WHITE, and JOHN PAUL STEVENS. WILLIAM H. REHNQUIST, the author of *National League*, offered this advice in his *Garcia* dissent: "I do not think it incumbent on those of us in dissent to spell out further the fine points of a principle that will, I am confident, in time again command the support of a majority of this Court."

Although the position of the Court on *National League* and *Garcia* might be in a state of flux and easily reversible, the judgment of ANTONIN SCALIA during his nomination hearings in 1986 to be Associate Justice seems well grounded in history: "The primary defender of the constitutional balance, the Federal Government versus the states, . . . the primary institution to strike the right balance is the Congress. . . . The court's struggles to prescribe what is the proper role of the Federal Government vis-à-vis the State have essentially been abandoned for quite a while."

LOUIS FISHER
(1992)

Bibliography

ADVISORY COMMISSION ON INTERGOVERNMENTAL RELATIONS 1988 *State Constitutional Law: Cases and Materials.* Washington, D.C.: U.S. Government Printing Office.

ANTON, THOMAS J. 1989 *American Federalism and Public Policy.* Philadelphia: Temple University Press.

CONLAN, TIMOTHY 1988 *New Federalism: Intergovernmental Reform from Nixon to Reagan.* Washington, D.C.: Brookings Institution.

O'BRIEN, DAVID M. 1989 Federalism as a Metaphor in the Constitutional Politics of Public Administration. *Public Administration Review* 49, no. 5:411–419.

FEDERALISM IN HISTORICAL PERSPECTIVE

See: Devolution and Federalism in Historical Perspective

FEDERALIST, THE

In the eight months following the adjournment of the CONSTITUTIONAL CONVENTION OF 1787, ALEXANDER HAMILTON, JAMES MADISON, and JOHN JAY wrote a series of eighty-five essays in support of the proposed Constitution. These essays were published in newspapers and as a two-volume book under the title *The Federalist*. This work was intended to influence voters electing delegates to the ratifying conventions and the delegates themselves; and the length, detail, and subtlety of its argument suggest an additional intention of enlightening later generations. While some contemporaries thought other, simpler and briefer, writings better calculated to influence the decision of 1787–1788, *The Federalist* was regarded as a work of enduring value by THOMAS JEFFERSON ("the best commentary on the principles of government which ever was written"), GEORGE WASHINGTON, and others. It has remained the most comprehensive and profound defense ever written of the American form of government; and it has been, as Chief Justice JOHN MARSHALL wrote in MCCULLOCH V. MARYLAND (1819), "justly supposed to be entitled to great respect" by courts engaged in "expounding the constitution."

The first section of *The Federalist* (#2 through #14) explains the advantages of a union as compared to independent American states. A large country is better suited than small countries to avoid or win wars, to pursue profitable commercial arrangements, and to raise revenue. Moreover, a large country's relative freedom from fear of war makes it more likely to preserve a free government. (Small countries facing frequent wars eventually accept the risk of being less free in order to be more safe.) Most novel was *The Federalist's* claim that a popular form of government would be more likely in a large country than in a

small country to secure private rights and the public good. MONTESQUIEU and the Anti-Federalist writers who quoted him acknowledged that large countries ruled by monarchs enjoyed certain advantages in FOREIGN AFFAIRS, but insisted that only small republics could enjoy the internal advantages of a patriotic citizenry ruling itself for its own good. In the famous *Federalist* #10 Madison argued that even in the smallest republic the citizenry is not an "it" but a collection of diverse individuals. Those individuals' rights deserve protection, but their passions and interests can unite them in groups that oppose the rights of others or the public good. Madison offered a twofold defense of a large republic. First, the diversity of a large country makes it less likely that any single group will constitute a majority of the voters and therefore be able to oppress other groups by virtue of the republican principle of majority rule. Second, in a large republic elections will be more likely to choose "fit characters" who will pursue the public good. The conclusion that republican government was possible, indeed better, in a large country served to reconcile the unpleasant necessities that seem to require largeness with the deep-rooted desire to have a popular government.

Essays #15 through #36 explain the necessity of "energetic" government. Although the national government has limited purposes, it must be able to tax and raise armies. Under the ARTICLES OF CONFEDERATION, Congress could demand the necessary money and men but had to address its demands to the state governments, whose disobedience could not be punished and whose compliance therefore could not be counted on. The decisive innovation of the new Constitution was the government's ability to address its commands to individual citizens, each of whose inability to contemplate forcible resistance made him respectful of "the arm of the ordinary magistrate." By defending this innovation in the name of FEDERALISM, *The Federalist* transformed the meaning of that term. Whereas others regarded true federalism as requiring what Montesquieu called a "society of societies"—that is, a union composed of and ruling over political communities rather than individuals—*The Federalist* regarded that as a prescription for disunion, thus deserving the name "antifederal" for its inevitable tendency.

The prospect that the new government would be able to exercise its nominal powers and coerce citizens raised the question of how such an energetic government could be confined to its proper purposes and restrained from oppression. *The Federalist* did not look to a careful enumeration of granted or excluded powers to control the government, because mere "parchment" would do little by itself and because certain formidable powers (for example, taxation) could not be excluded or even limited in their extent. The government could only be controlled by being "well modeled," by having a "general genius" and "internal structure" that made it trustworthy. This meant first of all that the government was "wholly popular"; its whole power was entrusted to the representatives of the people, and could therefore be controlled by the people in elections. *The Federalist* #37 through #84 explains the "conformity of the proposed Constitution to the true principles of republican government."

The fact that popular elections permit the people to "oblige the government to control itself" exhausts neither *The Federalist*'s prescription for a well-modeled government nor its argument for popular government. For one thing, the people are vulnerable to rulers who deceive them, misuse their powers between elections, or cancel elections. "A dependence on the people is no doubt the primary control on the government; but experience has taught mankind the necessity of auxiliary precautions." The auxiliary precautions are of various sorts, but all are designed to make ambition counteract ambition, so that no ruler's love of power is given free rein. A SEPARATION OF POWERS, legislative, executive, and judicial, insures that the people will be ruled in accordance with known laws that are enforced even against those who adopt them. The executive's VETO POWER both preserves this functional separation and, together with the legislature's BICAMERALISM, inhibits hasty lawmaking. The judiciary enjoys a tenure of GOOD BEHAVIOR to fortify judges in their task of preventing illegal executive acts and unconstitutional legislative acts. This last activity, now known as JUDICIAL REVIEW, was given its first sustained intellectual defense by Hamilton in *The Federalist* #78. Hamilton insisted on the court's duty to enforce the Constitution as law and indeed, because it was solemnly and authoritatively adopted by the people, as superior to the laws passed by the legislature, even if the legislature's laws were supported or instigated by the people themselves. The legislature's power of IMPEACHMENT provided a remedy against abuse of this judicial authority, or of the President's formidable powers. And the existence of state and national governments with independent powers to serve their own distinct objects gives each a platform and a motive to expose the other's encroachments.

The Federalist defended such auxiliary precautions (that is, precautions in addition to the people's electoral power) as reducing the chance that the government would betray and oppress the people as a whole. A more difficult problem, already explained in *The Federalist* #10, was that the people are not a whole, and that rulers elected by the majority might oppress the rights of minorities. The longer terms of senators, Presidents, and judges enabled them to oppose sudden and transient unjust impulses of the majority. A grateful people might reward such service once the heat of passion had cooled, or an excellent ruler might do his duty without reward; but the Constitution's insti-

tutions could not defend against an enduring majority's unjust passion or interest—hence the importance of a large country's diversity in making such majorities less likely.

The Federalist defends the "particular structure" of the Constitution not only as discouraging oppression but as encouraging good government. The task of a good national government is to secure the nation against foreign and domestic violence and to regulate its commerce so as to promote the general welfare. These activities in turn serve the most fundamental object of government, which is justice, meaning the protection of each individual's right to exercise his own faculties in the acquisition of property and in other activities. Thus an important accomplishment for any government is that it not itself be a source of injustice, that it achieve "the negative merit of not doing harm."

Further, positive merit of doing some good is encouraged by the Constitution's creation of offices in relatively small numbers and with relatively long terms, so as to encourage more capable candidates to seek office and to be elected and (more important) to put those elected in a situation in which they feel a personal motive to do some good. The experience officials could gain in office would help them devise means to promote the public good; and the distance of the people from direct rule would enable them to judge dispassionately and retrospectively the merit of their officials' policies according to their experience of the apparent effects of those policies. In the best case, officials moved by "the love of fame, the ruling passion of the noblest minds" would have an opportunity to "undertake extensive and arduous enterprises for the public benefit." Even in more ordinary cases, a durable senate would tend to foster stability in the laws and a single executive would be able to enforce them energetically.

The Federalist's defense of these institutions does not, however, deduce them entirely from the requirements of safe and good government. By those standards, *The Federalist* would not have found indefensible the "mixed" government of England, whose popularly elected House of Commons permits the people to restrain the government from oppression, whose king is an energetic executive, and whose House of Lords provides a source of stability and of protection for the rights of a minority. *The Federalist* emphatically defends the "strictly republican," "wholly popular" character of the American Constitution, which is made necessary by "that honorable determination, which animates every votary of freedom, to rest all our political experiments on the capacity of mankind for self-government." Not a knowledge of human fitness for self-government but an assertion of that fitness, or a knowledge of the human impulse to assert that fitness, justifies popular government. To protect the faculties of men requires protecting their faculty of passionately defending their own opinions, respecting their "pretension" to rule. *The Federalist* defended the American Constitution not only for its likely service of the interests of Americans but also for its tendency to "vindicate the honor of the human race."

The Federalist remains America's most important political book because it offers an explanation and defense of our form of government written by men who could not take the goodness or permanence of that regime for granted. Americans who study *The Federalist* today may find not only new reasons to appreciate the Constitution they inherit but also an account of government somewhat different from that assumed in contemporary opinion. For example, to *The Federalist* justice means impartial protection of the right to exercise one's faculties, not equal provision for the satisfaction of one's needs or desires. CONSTITUTIONALISM means that the people's solemn choice of their own form of government can be overridden only by a new, deliberate popular choice, not silently and gradually improved by judges trying to make the Constitution a living document. And REPRESENTATION is an arrangement that allows an opinionated people to select capable rulers and periodically pass formal judgment on their service of the public good, not an imperfect simulation of ancient direct democracy or a primitive version of modern opinion polling. *The Federalist* is thus both a source of understanding and appreciation of the American Constitution and a guide to reflection on its subsequent development.

DAVID F. EPSTEIN
(1986)

Bibliography

ADAIR, DOUGLASS 1974 *Fame and the Founding Fathers.* New York: Norton.

DIAMOND, MARTIN (1963) 1972 The Federalist. Pages 631–651 in Leo Strauss and Joseph Cropsey, eds., *History of Political Philosophy.* Chicago: Rand McNally.

EPSTEIN, DAVID F. 1984 *The Political Theory of The Federalist.* Chicago: University of Chicago Press.

FEDERALISTS

Arguments about the meaning of the Constitution can be dated to the controversy over its adoption or to the congressional debates of 1789 about the power to remove subordinate executive officials. But not until the conflict over ALEXANDER HAMILTON's proposal to create a BANK OF THE UNITED STATES did these disputes assume a partisan configuration and begin to take the form of two conflicting modes of CONSTITUTIONAL INTERPRETATION. When Hamilton's proposal came before the HOUSE OF REPRESENTATIVES in February 1791, Congressman JAMES MADISON remem-

bered that the CONSTITUTIONAL CONVENTION OF 1787 had specifically declined to add the right to charter CORPORATIONS to the list of Congress's powers. Madison contended that incorporation of a bank was not an exercise of any of the delegated powers and could not be justified on other grounds without confiding an "unlimited discretion" to a limited regime and threatening its gradual transmutation into a unitary national system. Disturbed by Madison's objections, President GEORGE WASHINGTON requested the opinions of his principal advisers before he signed the bill. EDMUND RANDOLPH and Secretary of State THOMAS JEFFERSON agreed with their Virginia friend. Elaborating Madison's insistence that to step beyond the constitutional enumeration was "to take possession of a boundless field of power, no longer susceptible of any definition," Jefferson maintained that the incorporation of a bank was not a regulation of the nation's commerce, not a tax, and not a borrowing of money. To derive the power from the "general phrases," he continued, would render the enumeration useless, reduce the Constitution "to a single phrase," and, in practice, authorize the federal government to do anything it pleased.

Hamilton's rebuttal of his colleagues, which persuaded Washington to sign the bill, erected the essential framework for the BROAD CONSTRUCTION of the document that would prevail throughout the 1790s. In fact, the reasoning and phrasing of this great opinion would be closely followed by JOHN MARSHALL in MCCULLOCH V. MARYLAND in 1819. "If the *end* be clearly comprehended within any of the specified powers, and if the measure have an obvious relation to that *end,* and is not forbidden by any particular provision of the Constitution," Hamilton maintained, "it may safely be deemed to come within the compass of the national authority." Insisting that the Constitution's grant of sovereign powers necessarily implied a power to decide which means were most appropriate to federal ends, the secretary of the treasury rejected Jefferson's contention that the boundaries of federal power would be washed away if "NECESSARY AND PROPER" was construed to mean "convenient," "useful," "requisite," and "needful." A liberal interpretation of this phrase was vital, he observed, to an effective federal system: "The means by which national exigencies are to be provided for . . . are of such infinite variety, extent, and complexity that there must, of necessity, be great latitude of discretion in the selection and application of those means."

Hamilton's opinion on the national bank began with the assumption "that every power vested in a government is in its nature *sovereign,* and includes . . . a right to employ all the means requisite and fairly applicable to the attainment of the ends." It was not to be denied, the secretary argued, "that there are *implied* as well as *express powers.*" Similar assumptions underpinned his "Letters of Pacificus" in 1793, with their defense of the inherent power of the chief executive to issue the Neutrality Proclamation. And yet, a "liberal" or "broad" construction of the reach of federal powers only partially describes the general tendency of Federalist interpretations of the Constitution. While the party was in power, Hamilton and other leaders generally assumed that the enduring dangers to the new regime would issue for the most part from the states' continual encroachments on the federal government's preserve and from a democratic people's tendency to favor an increasing concentration of the powers of the central government itself in the popularly elected lower house. Thus, the Federalists did seek as broad and flexible a definition of the general government's authority as reason would admit. They also usually attempted to defend the independence and prerogatives of the executive and the courts against encroachments by the Congress, which the Framers had intended to be more immediately responsive to the people. The most important constitutional collisions of the decade can all be helpfully illuminated in these terms. So could Federalist resistance to the Jeffersonians' repeal of the JUDICIARY ACT OF 1801, when many argued that the tenure of judges during GOOD BEHAVIOR should not be subverted by an abolition of their posts.

After 1793, foreign policy and its domestic repercussions dominated the intensifying party conflict, and Hamilton's defense of presidential leadership initiated an extended public argument about the meaning of the clause that vested "the executive power . . . in a President of the United States." "Pacificus" interpreted this phrase as granting an inherent body of executive prerogatives to the head of the executive department, "subject only to the *exceptions* and *qualifications*" defined by the Constitution. Writing as "Helvidius" at Jefferson's request, Madison condemned this doctrine as derived from the theory and practice of monarchical Britain and as striking "at the vitals" of a republican Constitution. Hamilton's interpretation, he insisted, would enable an ambitious President to take the country into war without congressional consent.

In practice, the conduct of the first two administrations did establish lasting precedents for firm executive direction of the country's international relations. In 1796 the House of Representatives asked Washington for documents relating to JOHN JAY's negotiation of a commercial treaty with Great Britain. Some members hoped to defeat the unpopular treaty by declining to appropriate the money necessary to carry it into effect. Washington's refusal to submit the papers to the House, which had no constitutional role in making treaties, was consistent with his general practice of an active leadership in foreign-policy concerns. JOHN ADAMS's decision to initiate a diplomatic resolution to hostilities with France, undertaken in

the face of active opposition from his CABINET and from Federalists in Congress, was yet another potent contribution to the chief executive's command of his department and to presidential guidance in this field.

The diplomatic impasse that resulted in the naval war with France—undeclared but authorized by acts of Congress—also ended in the most ferocious constitutional collision of the decade. Fearing French collusion with their Jeffersonian opponents, as well as with a host of recent immigrants to the United States, Federalists in Congress took advantage of the patriotic fury sparked by revelation of the XYZ Affair to pass a range of crisis legislation. Their opponents sharply criticized the Alien Acts of 1798, which authorized the President—without judicial process and merely on suspicion—to deport any ALIEN whose presence he considered dangerous to the United States. But the Republicans reserved their most ferocious condemnations for a controversial companion law, aimed at the repression of domestic opposition.

The Sedition Act of 1798 made it a criminal offense to "write, print, utter, or publish . . . any false, scandalous, and malicious writing or writings against the government of the United States, or either House of Congress of the United States, or the President of the United States, with the intent to defame [them] or to bring them . . . into contempt or disrepute." To the Republicans, whose opposition culminated in the VIRGINIA AND KENTUCKY RESOLUTIONS, this legislation was a flagrant violation of the limits of Congress's delegated powers and of the FIRST AMENDMENT. Little less objectionable, they thought, were prosecutions grounded on the supposition that there was, in any case, a federal COMMON LAW of SEDITIOUS LIBEL.

The crisis laws of 1798 were major threats to private rights and public liberties as these would later be defined. Together with the argument for the existence of a FEDERAL COMMON LAW OF CRIMES, they were supreme examples of the readiness of many Federalists to broaden federal authority by means of constitutional constructions that advanced a sweeping doctrine of inherent sovereign powers along with a constricted reading of the BILL OF RIGHTS. In defense of the Sedition Law, the Federalists contended that the First Amendment's guarantee of FREEDOM OF THE PRESS extended only to a prohibition of true censorship (or PRIOR RESTRAINT), not to prosecutions in the aftermath of publication. Because the act provided that the truth of a seditious utterance would be an adequate defense—and because it allowed juries, rather than judges, to decide whether such an utterance was libelous or not—the Sedition Act, its advocates maintained, was actually a liberalization of existing common law. These arguments did not disguise the Federalists' desire to break an opposition that was intensifying as danger of a French invasion disappeared. Neither did they hide the party's underlying fear of the results of open political competition; that fear was amply justified by the defeat of 1800.

From the LOUISIANA PURCHASE TREATY through the War of 1812, growing numbers of beleaguered Federalists retreated from the party's early, broad construction of the Constitution. In 1803 a few objected to the treaty, not because they shared the President's concern that there was no explicit constitutional foundation for the acquisition, but because the treaty promised that a territory not within the boundaries of the original United States (and likely to support their Jeffersonian opponents) would in time be granted statehood. If such a promise were constitutional at all, they argued, it lay within the prerogative of Congress. After 1808, with slighter strain, a larger number of Federalists bitterly denounced Jefferson's embargo, the Enforcement Acts, and other efforts to compel the warring European powers to respect the country's rights as a neutral. Congress's constitutional authority to regulate the nation's commerce, they maintained, did not include the power to prohibit it entirely. Moreover, the EMBARGO ACTS produced a vast extension of executive authority and nearly dictatorial intrusions by the military and the revenue collectors into the nation's economic life, violating both the spirit of the Constitution and the FOURTH AMENDMENT guarantees against UNREASONABLE SEARCHES and seizures. To New Englanders especially, the long experiment with economic warfare, which was pressed in a variety of ways through the next three years, seemed evidence of Jeffersonian hostility to commerce in general and to New England as a region. For them, accordingly, a narrow definition of the commerce power proved a milepost on a general withdrawal into constitutional interpretations that the Federalists had once condemned.

The quick retreat into a narrow, sometimes tortured understanding of the Constitution was primarily, though not exclusively, a sectional response to the Republican ascendancy in national affairs. Although this doctrinal switch ended by discrediting the party as a whole, it won approval neither from the Federalist judiciary nor from many of the greatest architects of Federalist ideas. After the commencement of the War of 1812, the Massachusetts legislature, governor, and courts, building on the compact theory of the Constitution, insisted that the state executive, not Congress, should determine whether an "invasion" authorized the federal government to call forth the militia. All the New England states impeded federal employment of these forces, practicing state interposition in a way that even the Virginia and Kentucky legislatures had never actually attempted. Regional resistance to the war extended to flirtations with SECESSION or a separate peace and culminated in the HARTFORD CONVENTION of December 1814. This effort to extort concessions in the midst of war discredited the Federalists beyond redemption and na-

tionalized a constitutional interpretation that all New England states had once condemned. The constitutional amendments the convention urged would have gravely weakened the effective federal regime, which was the most impressive legacy of Federalist administrations. Yet, even as the party died, the nationalistic constitutional construction of its greatest years were winning the endorsement of the MARSHALL COURT.

LANCE BANNING
(1992)

(SEE ALSO: *Alien and Sedition Acts; Commerce Clause; Foreign Affairs; Implied Powers; Jeffersonianism; Militia Clause; Republicanism; Treaty Power.*)

Bibliography
MILLER, JOHN C.   1960   *The Federalist Era, 1789–1801.* New York: Harper & Row.
SMELSER, MARSHALL   1968   *The Democratic Republic, 1801–1815.* New York: Harper & Row.
SMITH, JAMES MORTON   1956   *Freedom's Fetters.* Ithaca, N.Y.: Cornell University Press.

FEDERAL JUDICIAL APPOINTMENTS, TENURE, AND INDEPENDENCE

In the federal judicial system the appointment and tenure of judges are governed by the Constitution and by statutes enacted by Congress. Neither the Constitution nor Congress controls the structure of state judicial systems or the appointment and tenure of judges of those courts; under state laws, judges are variously popularly elected or appointed by the governor or another state officer, with or without the consent of the legislature, a commission, or a confirming election. State judges do not have life tenure.

Federal courts are classified as "Article III courts," also known as CONSTITUTIONAL COURTS, and "Article I courts," also known as LEGISLATIVE COURTS. The constitutional courts are those courts specified in Article III, section 1, vesting the JUDICIAL POWER of the United States "in one supreme Court, and such inferior Courts as the Congress may from time to time ordain and establish." These judges have lifetime tenure and compensation that cannot be reduced during their judicial service. Legislative courts encompass the remaining adjudicative tribunals that are congressionally established but do not have all of the characteristics required by Article III. Judges of legislative courts are appointed for terms of years; the jurisdiction of those courts is not coextensive with Article III courts' jurisdiction.

Except for recess appointments by the President to fill

vacancies when the Senate is not in session (Article II, section 1), constitutional Justices and judges hold their offices "during good behavior," as Article III provides. In UNITED STATES EX REL. TOTH V. QUARLES (1955), the Court held that the GOOD BEHAVIOR clause guarantees such judges lifetime tenure, subject to removal only by IMPEACHMENT.

Article II, section 2, requires nomination of Article III Justices and judges by the President "with the advice and consent of the Senate." The role of the Senate under the ADVICE AND CONSENT clause has been debated since the CONSTITUTIONAL CONVENTION OF 1787. The clause was adopted as a compromise in the closing days of the Convention as an alternative to proposals to grant appointing power to the President alone or to the Senate alone; the delegates did not discuss the meaning of the clause.

Senators have variously interpreted their constitutional obligations in proceedings to confirm presidential nominations to the judiciary. Some senators have treated their task as little more than a procedural formality unless the nominee is egregiously unfit for the judicial post to which he or she has been named or a serious flaw in the candidate's background is revealed during the deliberations. Other senators have expansively interpreted their responsibility to "advise" the President, including the advice that the President's choice is wrong. The history of confirmation battles strongly suggests that the fate of a particular nominee more often depends on the political views of the senators than on intellectual differences over CONSTITUTIONAL INTERPRETATION. Apart from the individual characteristics of the nominee and the personal and political philosophies of the senators who act on a nomination, the outcome of the process is heavily influenced by the sensitivity of the judicial post to which the candidate has been named, the existing composition of that particular court, the relative power of the President and the Senate at the time of the nomination, and the prevailing national political climate. The closest senatorial scrutiny is usually given to nominees for the Supreme Court. The obvious reason is the tremendous importance of the Court. Less obvious is that senatorial courtesies do not have the same significance in confirmation of Supreme Court nominees as they do in nominations to district courts and courts of appeals. In the latter instances, the opposition of one senator from the nominee's home state is usually enough to doom confirmation, especially if the senator is a member of the President's political party.

Scant attention was given to the public interest in judicial confirmations before 1929 because, until then, the Senate acted upon all nominations in closed executive session unless the hearing was ordered open by a two-thirds vote of the Senate. Except in rare instances, such as the nomination of Justice LOUIS D. BRANDEIS in 1916 and of

Justice HARLAN FISKE STONE in 1925, the necessary votes could not be mustered. The Senate rules were amended in 1929 to open all confirmation hearings.

Even after hearings were open, they were usually quiet events. Nominees were not called to appear before the SENATE JUDICIARY COMMITTEE until 1939, when the nomination of FELIX FRANKFURTER was under consideration. Although he initially declined to appear, he later testified and was unanimously approved by the Senate. Since then, with few exceptions, nominees to Article III courts are routinely called to, and do testify before, the Judiciary Committee. The addition of televised hearings probably has not changed confirmation results, but at a minimum it has heightened the drama of controversial appointments and encouraged oratory.

Although the confirmation process is now generally available in living color, the roles of the actors in the prenomination process are neither public nor well known. The large cast includes the President, the inner circle of the White House, senators who are not members of the Judiciary Committee, congressional delegations, the ATTORNEY GENERAL, the Department of Justice, the Federal Bureau of Investigation, the American Bar Association, and sometimes others.

Presidential means and motives for selecting nominees to the Supreme Court defy facile description. Supreme Court vacancies occur unpredictably and sporadically. For example, no vacancies on the Court appeared during President JIMMY CARTER's term, but Justice POTTER J. STEWART's retirement gave President RONALD REAGAN his first appointment to the Court within a few months of his assuming office.

History gives substance to Justice Felix Frankfurter's description of Supreme Court nominations as "that odd lottery." Sometimes the presidential motivation for a particular appointment is evident, even if the means by which the person came to presidential attention are not. Thus, President HERBERT HOOVER's reason for nominating CHARLES EVANS HUGHES as CHIEF JUSTICE in 1930 was the economic plight of the country and his belief that Hughes would forward views that would help the President's economic policies. On the other hand, the source of President ULYSSES S. GRANT's choice of Caleb Cushing is known, but his motives in selecting him are not. The nominee was seventy-four years old, and his political philosophy was unknown. President Grant withdrew the nomination after he discovered Cushing's ties to the Confederacy. Both the source and motive are occasionally clear, as is true of President LYNDON B. JOHNSON's nomination of Solicitor General THURGOOD MARSHALL.

History permits only a few generalizations about presidential choices for the Supreme Court. For example, the nominee will almost always be a member of the political party of the President, and in making selections the President will rely on the advice of trusted friends within and outside his administration and of those persons whose support, or nonopposition, will be needed to confirm the nominee or to assist the President in achieving other objectives on his political agenda.

Presidents have sometimes selected candidates for lower courts without initial outside consultation. Usually, however, the President makes his choice from a list of potential nominees submitted to him. For district courts, typically a nomination is initiated by a senator of the candidate's home state if the senator is of the President's political party. When no senator of the candidate's home state is of the President's party, the names may be suggested by the state governor, leaders of the President's party, members of the congressional delegation, or members of his administration. President Carter encouraged all senators to use regional or local panels to gather and submit potential nominees for district courts before making recommendations to him. Some senators still use such panels, although the White House has not recently urged them to do so.

Proposals for appointments to courts of appeals are initiated by an analogous process. Because courts of appeals' geographical jurisdiction is not confined within state lines, as the jurisdiction of a district court is, more senators have a say in these appointments than in appointments of district judges. Senators of the President's party continue to play an important initiating role, but some degree of senatorial courtesy is also extended to other senators in the affected states. President Carter departed from prior practice by issuing an EXECUTIVE ORDER establishing a nationwide commission, with panelists chosen from all states within each circuit to propose nominations. Senators could propose nominees in addition to those proposed by panels. The Reagan administration abolished the commission, relying instead on members of his administration and selected senators to perform the task, a process that more nearly resembled the practices before President Carter.

When potential nominees have been reduced to a short list, the candidates are screened by the Department of Justice and discussed with key senators and with leaders of the congressional delegation of the President's party. The Federal Bureau of Investigation is directed to search the background of potential nominees to discover evidence that might disqualify the candidate or embarrass the administration. Further screening is usually done by White House personnel to whom the President has delegated that task.

If all these preliminary tests look positive, the names on the short list will be submitted to the American Bar Association's Standing Committee on Federal Judiciary to test their professional qualifications. Committee rankings of district and circuit judge nominees are self-explanatory: "exceptionally well qualified," "well qualified," "qualified," and "not qualified." The rating system for Supreme Court nominees describes the candidates as "well qualified," "not opposed," and "not qualified." In committee parlance, "not opposed" means that the nominee is considered barely qualified. Presidents do not have to accept these ratings, but it is rare that a nomination has been forwarded to the Senate when the candidate has received poor grades from the Bar Association.

Appointments and tenure of judges to Article I courts do not follow the same scenario. Article I courts display almost as many variations as Charles Darwin's "singular group of finches," and Congress has adapted the system to each of the jurisdictional environments in which these courts sit. Even a partial taxonomy of Article I courts reveals their jurisdictional diversity: the district courts of the Canal Zone, Virgin Islands, Guam, and Northern Mariana Islands; the High Court of American Samoa; certain AD-MINISTRATIVE AGENCIES with adjudicative powers; the United States COURT OF MILITARY APPEALS; the TAX COURT; the bankruptcy courts; and the local judiciary of the DISTRICT OF COLUMBIA. Appointment to these courts is made variously by the President, with or without senatorial confirmation, and, in the instance of the bankruptcy courts, by federal district judges. Judges of these courts serve designated terms in office, rather than having life tenure.

The constitutional legitimacy of Congress's establishing courts other than Article III courts has been repeatedly questioned from the early days of our Republic. The issue first came before the Supreme Court in AMERICAN INSURANCE COMPANY V. CANTER (1828), testing the constitutionality of Congress's creating TERRITORIAL COURTS staffed by judges without life tenure. Chief Justice JOHN MARSHALL, writing for the Court, held that Congress had the power to create "legislative courts," having judges of limited tenure with jurisdiction that was not coextensive with that of Article III courts. Since then, the Court has had second thoughts about the vexing constitutional restrictions on congressional delegation of jurisdiction to adjudicative tribunals that do not have all of the characteristics of Article III courts. Although the former Court of Claims survived constitutional attack when the Supreme Court held that it was a peculiar Article III court in *Glidden Co. v. Zdanok* (1962), the reorganized bankruptcy courts did not fare so well in NORTHERN PIPELINE CO. V. MARATHON PIPE LINE CO. (1982), in which a sharply divided Court struck down part of the legislative grant of jurisdiction to bankruptcy courts as an unconstitutional delegation of Article III jurisdiction.

Although appointments to the federal judiciary are heavily politicized, federal judges are thereafter completely independent of the politics that brought them to the bench, as some Presidents have unhappily learned when their appointees have not followed the philosophies they anticipated. Despite the divorce of the judges from politics, judges and Justices have not always been removed from the political realm. For example, in 1790, Chief Justice JOHN JAY and Associate Justice OLIVER ELLSWORTH temporarily shed their robes to represent the government in treaty negotiations with France and England. Chief Justice WILLIAM HOWARD TAFT actively participated in helping President WARREN G. HARDING select federal judges, and Chief Justice EARL WARREN in 1962 chaired the commission investigating the assassination of President JOHN F. KENNEDY. A number of Justices have been continuing confidants of Presidents and assisted them in formulating national policies.

Inevitable tensions are generated between independence and politics because the judiciary depends on Congress to authorize needed judgeships, to pay judicial salaries and authorize and pay for nonjudicial personnel assisting courts, and to provide for courtrooms and courthouses. Justices and judges commonly testify before Congress and write and speak on such issues affecting the judiciary and the administration of justice. Statutes and canons of judicial ethics announce rules designed to avoid collisions between independence and political influences.

Particularly sensitive conflicts are also generated when the need for judicial independence must be balanced against the need to sideline judges who are physically or mentally unable to perform their duties and to discipline errant federal judges short of impeachment. Little controversy has arisen from involuntarily retiring judges for disability. A storm of criticism followed the enactment of the 1980 Judicial Councils Reform and Judicial Conduct and Disability Act, which empowered a panel of judges to investigate complaints against a federal judge accused of "conduct prejudicial to the effective expeditious administration of the business of the courts" and authorized the panel to impose discipline, short of removal from office, if the panel should find wrongdoing. The act was attacked on two grounds: for infringing the constitutional freedom of judges from removal by procedures other than impeachment, and for posing a threat that such disciplinary proceedings could be used to subject judges to reprisals for unpopular decisions. Nonetheless, the statute has been sustained, and the opponents' fears of retaliation have not been realized.

The independence of the judiciary implies more than political neutrality. Numerous statutes, rules, and ethical principles seek to preserve judicial independence by foreclosing parties to litigation and other persons from improperly influencing judicial decisions. With a few carefully guarded exceptions, litigants, their lawyers, and others are forbidden to contact a judge about a pending case without prior permission and without contemporaneously informing all parties and their lawyers about the existence and substance of any such communications. Both civil and criminal penalties are used to punish persons who violate those rules.

SHIRLEY HUFSTEDLER
(1992)

(SEE ALSO: *Appointing and Removal Power, Presidential; Appointments Clause.*)

Bibliography

EDWARDS, DREW E. 1987 Judicial Misconduct and Politics in the Federal System: A Proposal for Revising the Judicial Councils Act. *California Law Review* 75:1071–1092.

FOWLER, W. GARY 1984 Judicial Selection Under Reagan and Carter: A Comparison of Their Initial Recommendation Procedures. *Judicature* 67:265–283.

FREUND, PAUL A. 1988 Appointment of Justices: Some Historical Perspectives. *Harvard Law Review* 101:1146–1163.

SLOTNICK, ELLIOT E. 1988 Federal Judicial Recruitment and Selection Research: A Review Essay. *Judicature* 71:317–324.

FEDERAL JUDICIAL ROLE

Article III of the Constitution creates the federal judicial system, defines its boundaries, and describes the characteristics of its judges. The Constitution specifically vests JUDICIAL POWER in "one supreme court" and authorizes Congress to create lower federal courts. Article III defines "federal judicial power" in reference either to subject matter (extending to "all Cases in Law and Equity, arising under this Constitution, the Laws of the United States, and Treaties made" and to admiralty) or to the parties in the case (e.g., cases involving ambassadors, states, or citizens of different states).

Article III also describes attributes of federal judges "of both the supreme and inferior Courts." Such judges hold their offices during "good Behavior" and their salaries are protected against diminution. The GOOD BEHAVIOR clause is now understood as providing these judges with life tenure, subject to IMPEACHMENT and removal by the U.S. SENATE. The compensation clause has been a source of debate about whether congressional withholding of benefits, such as cost-of-living increases and forms of insurance, constitute infringements of constitutional protections.

Although the Constitution is open-ended about the existence of lower federal courts, Congress has many times since 1789 exercised its powers to create a lower federal judiciary and to reorganize the structure of and mandates to that judiciary. The federal judiciary was initially comprised only of district judges and Supreme Court Justices (who upon occasion joined together to create CIRCUIT COURTS). By early in the twentieth century, the federal judiciary had become a three-tiered structure, consisting of trial judges (district judges), intermediate appellate judges (circuit judges), and nine Supreme Court Justices. As of the 1920s, some 120 men held those positions; in several instances, a single federal district judge served the entire state.

Since the CIVIL WAR, Congress has steadily increased the role of the federal courts by exercising its constitutional powers to enact federal statutory rights and to vest enforcement powers in the government and/or private actors, authorized to file claims in federal courts. FEDERAL JURISDICTION is typically concurrent with state courts rather than exclusive. The federal court docket includes cases involving a wide array of subject matters, both civil and criminal, "arising under" federal law and including securities regulation, environmental laws, consumer protection, CIVIL RIGHTS, and pension and WELFARE benefits.

Given congressional decisions to expand the role of federal law, the federal judiciary has also needed to grow. Although one reading of the Constitution would have permitted such growth to occur only by the creation of more life-tenured, salary-guaranteed judges (what I term "constitutional judges" because, pursuant to Article III, they are nominated by the President, confirmed by the Senate and enjoy the structural protections detailed in the Constitution), neither the Congress nor the federal courts have insisted on that understanding of Article III.

Rather, beginning in the 1930s and blossoming since the 1960s, two other sets of "federal judges" have gained federal adjudicatory power. One group—magistrate and bankruptcy judges—are specified by statutes and work within Article III; these judges are selected by the constitutional judges and serve for renewable terms. A second set of judges—administrative law judges bearing a variety of titles—are also creatures of statute but are typically annexed to the agencies for which they decide cases, and their employment is governed by civil service provisions. Note that both sets of these statutory judges serve without constitutional protection for either their terms of office or their salaries.

In short, the three-tiered pyramid of the federal courts from the early part of the twentieth century has been replaced by a four-tiered system, with some 1,600–2,000 constitutional judges holding positions on the Supreme, intermediate appellate, and district courts, joined within Article III courts by another 750 statutory judges (magistrate and bankruptcy judges) who also work at the trial level, below or akin to the district court. The four tiers are supported by a staff of some 30,000, working in more than 500 court buildings. That structure is, in turn, augmented by two major groups of add-ons. First, some 2,000 administrative judges staff "courts" that are located in agencies. Second, arbitrators, mediators, and "neutrals" have been provided more recently under federal law, as both statutory and constitutional judges promote the use of alternative dispute resolution (ADR) in federal courts and in administrative agencies.

Reflective of the advent of ADR, the modes of judging have also shifted over the twentieth century. In 1938, the first uniform FEDERAL RULES OF CIVIL PROCEDURE were promulgated for all federal trial courts. Those rules specified a pretrial process that has since become the focus of contemporary litigation. Judges from the 1930s to the 1950s did not much use their powers under this discretionary pretrial rule. However, in the 1950s, when faced with what were then called "protracted cases" and what are now called "large-scale" or "complex" litigations, a group of judges within the federal judiciary began to advocate greater judicial control over attorneys. In the 1950s, the federal judiciary began systematic training—judicial education—to encourage judges to become "managerial judges." Judges were initially reticent to promote settlement of cases, but over the decades, leaders of the federal judiciary became increasingly insistent that the judicial role should encompass settlement efforts. The shift of role (from adjudicator to manager to settler) is reflected in a series of revisions during the 1980s and 1990s of civil procedure rules and in the enactment by Congress of statutes calling for additional efforts at management and for alternative dispute resolution in federal courts.

Just as the federal courts and Congress have worked in concert to enlarge the number of federal judges and to alter their daily practices, so have the federal courts and Congress reshaped the doctrinal requirements of Article III. The creation and institutionalization of a diverse set of federal judges result from congressional enactment of LEGISLATION for such judges, and also from federal judicial interpretation of Article III to permit the delegation of a range of judicial tasks to statutory judges who have neither life tenure nor salary protections. Early in the twentieth century, life-tenured judges were hesitant to permit much delegation, insisting, for example, on their own authority to review, de novo, certain kinds of facts as part of the "essential attributes of judicial power." More recently, however, life-tenured judges have upheld congressional statutes providing for trials (with parties' consent) by magistrate judges; conveying substantial powers to bankruptcy judges; authorizing administrative judges to hear related state claims in certain instances; and even, in narrow circumstances, permitting final decisionmaking power by arbitrators. In other words, creative readings of Article III have enabled the manufacture of federal judges outside its parameters. The charter for such judges is not unlimited; the Supreme Court insists on vaguely described constraints and some commentators argue that "Article III values" require access to life-tenured judges at least upon appeal of certain cases. But the decisions in the second half of the twentieth century recognize an ever- growing role for statutory federal judges.

In addition to the elaboration of tiers of judging, alteration of the modes of judging, and reinterpretation of Article III during the twentieth century, the federal judiciary also developed a corporate identity. In the early 1920s, Congress authorized a Judicial Conference, composed of senior appellate judges, to meet to consider systemic issues. In 1939, at the behest of the judiciary, Congress created the Administrative Office of the United States Courts to enable the judiciary to take on the staff work— budgeting, supplies, reports to Congress on the docket— that previously had been performed by the executive branch. In the early years of these institutional structures, federal judges saw their judicial role as limiting their dealings with Congress. Invoking constitutional obligations of adjudication, the federal judiciary as an institution generally declined to comment on legislation other than bills seeking additional judgeships or governing court procedure. In later years, the Judicial Conference began to take an active role in attempting to shape national policy about federal jurisdiction and to promote its vision of the federal courts' mandate and the work appropriate for life-tenured judges. In the 1970s, the federal judiciary started issuing "impact statements" arguing the likely effects of proposed legislation. In the 1990s, the Judicial Conference put forth its own Long Range Plan, making more than ninety recommendations to Congress. That plan's central premise is that federal courts should have limited jurisdiction; thus, Congress should adopt a presumption against creating new civil or criminal federal causes of action.

Because Article III's limitations of federal judicial power are tied to congressional powers to create federal law, the federal judicial role is closely linked to conceptions of congressional powers. During the last decade of the twentieth century, the Supreme Court revisited rulings made in the context of reviewing NEW DEAL and civil rights legislation. In a series of cases, the Court held that, when conferring jurisdiction on federal courts, Congress had exceeded its powers under either the COMMERCE CLAUSE, the FOURTEENTH AMENDMENT, or general FEDERALISM principles, or that Congress had failed to heed the limitations imposed by the ELEVENTH AMENDMENT's SOVEREIGN IMMUNITY provisions. During the same decade, Congress also imposed new limitations on federal jurisdiction. These laws curtailed access for prisoners seeking review of their sentences through HABEAS CORPUS proceedings, and for immigrants contesting decisions by the U.S. Immigration and Naturalization Service. Congress has also limited the remedial authority of courts to enforce CON-SENT DECREES mandating improved conditions in prisons. Litigants challenging the constitutionality of such restrictions have generally lost; the federal courts have thus far upheld most of these provisions. Federal judicial institutional advocacy for restrictions on federal jurisdiction are thus echoed in federal adjudication imposing or upholding such limits.

In sum, when one considers the federal judicial role, recurrent themes emerge, some that span this country's constitutional history and others that have arisen during the twentieth century. Debated, at the constitutional level, are the allocation of labor among adjudicatory bodies (state, federal, and tribal courts and administrative agencies) and among tiers of federal judges; the degree of deference owed to other court systems or state and local government officials (often referred to as "COMITY" and sometimes as "federalism"), to Congress and the executive (sometimes termed "SEPARATION OF POWERS"), to state executive officials, and to lower echelon judges within the system; and the respective roles of Congress and the courts in determining the permissible boundaries of federal judicial and LEGISLATIVE POWER. The issues that have come to prominence during the twentieth century include the boundaries, if any, of the federal judicial role as an administrative organization (using its corporate voice to advance a programmatic agenda developed by the Judicial Conference) and the question of how to deploy constitutional judges (as contrasted with statutory federal judges).

In light of such developments, Article III's description of federal judicial power requires reconsideration. Conventional constitutional discourse assumes that Article III is the paradigm of judicial independence and represents the pinnacle of political safeguards. Judicial independence on the federal side is often invoked in contrast to the perceived thinner protections afforded many state judges, serving for terms and by election.

But these distinctions recede when one considers the fit between the constitutional terms of federal judicial power and the current structures and deployment of that power. Article III—as read by judges chartered under its aegis—provides nothing for hundreds of federal judges existing outside its purview and little by way of institutional protection to the judiciary as an organization. Although judicial–congressional interactions have often resulted in agreements about how to expand resources, the growing reliance on statutory judges increases judicial dependence on Congress and leaves a large group of federal judges with authority to render an array of judgments but lacking attributes of independence associated with federal adjudication. On the other hand, given the willingness of life-tenured judges on the lower courts to delegate portions of their adjudicatory tasks elsewhere, and to assume roles as multipurpose dispute resolvers pressing for settlements that reduce their roles as adjudicators, Article III's structural protections insulate actors decreasingly committed to formal adjudicatory roles that enable public scrutiny of their exercise of the power of judgment.

The growing distance between Article III's description and the practices of federal adjudicators raises normative questions. Article III stands for the concept of a distinct judicial branch of government and for the ability of individual judges to render judgment independent from fear of economic retribution. Should that constitutional commitment be elaborated in the context of statutory federal judges, so that the transfer of judicial power to them is conditioned on the creation of structural protections akin to those afforded constitutional judges? If not, by what terms can one assess the role allocation between constitutional and statutory judges? The Constitution, as currently interpreted, offers little guidance on either issue. Understandings of the DUE PROCESS clause provide a conception that all judges must be impartial, but standards for impartiality of agency judges are not exacting. And, while invoking "Article III values," the Supreme Court has approved most delegations to nonconstitutional judges, and the federal judiciary as an agenda setter has pressed for expansion of those judges' roles. If adjudicatory processes are to retain political and legal significance in the coming decades, the jurisprudence of Article III, intertwined with understandings of constitutional mandates for due process, will require significant development.

JUDITH RESNIK
(2000)

Bibliography

FALLON, RICHARD H.; MELTZER, DANIEL J.; and SHAPIRO, DAVID L. 1996 *Hart and Wechsler's The Federal Courts and the Federal System*, 4th ed. Westbury, N.Y.: Foundation Press.

JACKSON, VICKI C. 1998 Federalism and the Uses and Limits of Law. *Harvard Law Review* 111:2180–2259.

JUDICIAL CONFERENCE OF THE UNITED STATES 1995 *Long Range Plan for the Federal Courts.* Washington, D.C.: Committee on Long Range Planning.

MONAGHAN, HENRY P. Constitutional Fact Review. *Columbia Law Review* 85:229–276.

RESNIK, JUDITH 1982 Managerial Judges. *Harvard Law Review* 96:374–448.

SYMPOSIUM 1998 Congress and the Courts: Jurisdiction and Remedies. *Georgetown Law Journal* 86:2445–2636.

FEDERAL MORTGAGE MORATORIUM ACT

See: Frazier-Lemke Acts

FEDERAL POWER COMMISSION

See: Regulatory Agencies

FEDERAL POWER COMMISSION v. HOPE NATURAL GAS COMPANY
320 U.S. 591 (1944)

In SMYTH V. AMES (1898) the Supreme Court saddled state REGULATORY COMMISSIONS with a specious DUE PROCESS rule for setting public utility rates. Forty-six years later the Justices repudiated the rule of a FAIR RETURN ON FAIR VALUE. Prior to *Hope*, the Court relied primarily on original construction costs and reproduction costs as a means of determining property value.

Justice WILLIAM O. DOUGLAS, speaking for a 5–3 Court, based rate regulation on the POLICE POWER. Douglas declared: "In so far as the power to regulate involves the power to reduce net earnings, it must involve the power to destroy." He adhered to the recent trend of decisions which removed the Court from such determinations. Without mentioning *Smyth*, Douglas accorded regulatory commissions broad power to choose methods of evaluating property: "The Constitution does not bind rate-making bodies to the service of any single formula or combination of formulas." Henceforth, the determination of the reasonableness of a rate would be made by looking to the "end result" or "total effect." This pragmatic approach returned the burden of decision to the commissions because a rate order was "the product of expert judgment," carrying a presumption of validity. Even the dissenters did not feel bound to adhere to *Smyth;* they disagreed over the applicable statutory standard. In *Hope*, the Court eliminated judicial obstruction to effective administrative rate regulation.

DAVID GORDON
(1986)

FEDERAL PROTECTION OF CIVIL RIGHTS

Although the story of federal protection of CIVIL RIGHTS is most conveniently told chronologically, two themes warrant separate mention. First, federal protection of civil rights has a paradoxical relationship with STATES' RIGHTS. All civil rights legislation has been opposed or limited in response to the argument that the federal government ought not involve itself in areas of state responsibility. The Supreme Court repeatedly has voiced this concern and, in the past, invalidated civil rights legislation partly on this ground. Deference to state law enforcement prerogatives

Comminssion, at the administration's request, promulgated stringent rules against discrimination in terminals. Armed with the CIVIL RIGHTS ACTS OF 1957 and 1960, the Civil Rights Division established by the 1957 Act conducted massive voter registration suits but secured only token improvements in black registration. Sometimes the judges blocking progress were Kennedy appointees. In November 1962 President Kennedy issued an executive order prohibiting discrimination in public housing projects and in projects covered by direct, guaranteed federal loans. And in executive orders in 1961 and 1963 Kennedy both required AFFIRMATIVE ACTION by government contractors and extended the executive branch's antidiscrimination program in federal procurement contracts to all federally assisted construction projects.

Soon after LYNDON B. JOHNSON succeeded to the presidency, he publicly endorsed Kennedy's civil rights legislation. Due in part to his direct support, Congress enacted the CIVIL RIGHTS ACT OF 1964, the most comprehensive civil rights measure in American history. The act outlaws discrimination in public accommodations, in federally assisted programs, or by large private employers, and it extends federal power to deal with voting discrimination. Title VII of the act created a substantial new federal bureaucracy to enforce antidiscrimination provisions pertaining to employment. The 1964 act also marked the first time that the Senate voted cloture against an anti-civil rights filibuster.

Despite the efforts of the Kennedy and Johnson Justice Departments, the Civil Rights Acts of 1957, 1960, and 1964 proved inadequate to protect black VOTING RIGHTS. Marches and protests to secure voting rights led to violence, including an infamous, widely reported confrontation in Selma, Alabama, in which marchers were beaten. In March 1965, President Johnson requested new voting rights legislation. He included in his speech to the nation and a joint session of Congress the words of the song of the civil rights movement, "We shall overcome," thus emphasizing the depth of the new federal involvement in civil rights. By August, the VOTING RIGHTS ACT OF 1965 was in place. Within ten years of its passage many more than a million new black voters were registered without great fanfare, with corresponding gains in the number of black elected officials. In 1968, after the assassination of Martin Luther King, Jr., Congress enacted a fair housing law as part of the CIVIL RIGHTS ACT OF 1968.

Unlike the Reconstruction civil rights program, Congress's 1960s civil rights legislation survived judicial scrutiny. In a series of cases from 1964 to 1976, the Supreme Court both sustained the new civil rights program and revived the Reconstruction-era laws. In *Katzenbach v. McClung* (1964) and HEART OF ATLANTA MOTEL V. UNITED STATES (1964) the Court rejected constitutional attacks on the public accommodations provisions of the 1964 act. In SOUTH CAROLINA V. KATZENBACH (1966) and KATZENBACH V. MORGAN (1966) the Court rebuffed state challenges to the VOTING RIGHTS ACT OF 1965. And in JONES V. ALFRED H. MAYER CO. (1968) and RUNYON V. MCCRARY (1976) the Court interpreted the CIVIL RIGHTS ACT OF 1866 to fill important gaps in the coverage of the 1964 and 1968 acts.

With the passage and sustaining of the 1964, 1965, and 1968 acts and the revival of the 1866 act, the legal battle against RACIAL DISCRIMINATION at least formally was won. The federal civil rights program encompassed nearly all public and private purposeful racial discrimination in public accommodations, housing, employment, education, and voting. Future civil rights progress would have to come through vigorous enforcement, through programs aimed at relieving poverty, through affirmative action, and through laws benefiting groups other than blacks.

Just as the civil rights movement was running out of traditional civil rights laws to support, two other issues brought federal civil rights protection near its outer limits. The comprehensive coverage of federal civil rights laws did not eliminate the inferior status of blacks in American society. Pressure mounted for assistance in the form of affirmative action programs. But these programs divided even the liberal community traditionally supportive of civil rights enforcement. Affirmative action, unlike antidiscrimination standards, meant black progress at the expense of what many believed to be legitimate opportunities of innocent individuals. In its most important aspects affirmative action survived the initial series of statutory and constitutional attacks.

In the 1970s, civil rights enforcement became engulfed in another controversy: whether to bus school children for purposes of desegregation. (See SCHOOL BUSING.) President RICHARD M. NIXON's 1968 "Southern strategy" included campaigning against busing. Within six months of Nixon's inaugural, the Justice Department for the first time opposed the NAACP LEGAL DEFENSE AND EDUCATION FUND in a desegregation case. But under the pressure of Supreme Court decisions, and given the momentum of the prior administration's civil rights efforts, the Nixon administration did help promote new levels of southern integration. The administration, however, continued to lash out at "forced busing."

School desegregation also triggered a legislative backlash. In the 1970s the Internal Revenue Service, under the pressure of court decisions, sought to foster integration by denying tax benefits to private segregated academies and their benefactors. Congress, however, intervened to limit the Service's use of funds for such purposes. Similarly, Congress restrained executive authority to seek busing as a remedy for school segregation.

In the 1960s and 1970s, federal protection of civil rights

reached beyond race. In the Age Discrimination in Employment Act, the AGE DECRIMINATION ACT OF 1975, the REHABILITATION ACT OF 1973, and other measures, Congress acted to protect the aged and the handicapped. And the Equal Pay Act of 1963, the Civil Rights Act of 1964, and the EDUCATION AMENDMENTS OF 1972 increased federal protection against sex descrimination. In each of these areas, attachment of antidiscrimination conditions to federal disbursements became a significant vehicle for civil rights enforcement.

THEODORE EISENBERG
(1986)

Bibliography

BERMAN, WILLIAM C. 1970 *The Politics of Civil Rights in the Truman Administration.* Columbus: Ohio State University Press.

BRAUER, CARL M. 1977 *John F. Kennedy and the Second Reconstruction.* New York: Columbia University Press.

CARR, ROBERT K. 1947 *Federal Protection of Civil Rights: Quest for a Sword.* Ithaca, N.Y.: Cornell University Press.

GRESSMAN, EUGENE 1952 The Unhappy History of Civil Rights Legislation. *Michigan Law Review* 50:1323–1358.

HARVEY, JAMES C. 1973 *Black Civil Rights During the Johnson Administration.* Jackson: University and College Press of Missouri.

KONVITZ, MILTON R. 1961 *A Century of Civil Rights.* New York: Columbia University Press.

LITWACK, LEON F. 1979 *Been in the Storm So Long: The Aftermath of Slavery.* New York: Knopf.

FEDERAL QUESTION JURISDICTION

Article III of the Constitution provides that the JUDICIAL POWER OF THE UNITED STATES shall extend to all "Cases . . . arising under this Constitution, the laws of the United States, and Treaties. . . ." This power is called federal question jurisdiction, because typically it entails the construction, application, or enforcement of federal law, including federal COMMON LAW. Performance of this function includes interpretation of the Constitution itself; thus federal question jurisdiction provides the jurisdictional basis for the federal courts' important power of JUDICIAL REVIEW. It is also the means by which Congress can secure a sympathetic and uniform interpretation of federal laws.

Although Congress has the power to make exceptions to the Supreme Court's APPELLATE JURISDICTION over federal questions, it currently makes few of them. A few federal trial court decisions, such as those remanding cases to state court following removal, are unreviewable. The Supreme Court reviews state court decisions only when they are FINAL JUDGMENTS that have been rendered by the highest state court in which judgment is available. Such a judgment will not be reviewed if it rests on an independent and ADEQUATE STATE GROUND or if it lacks a substantial federal question (for example, raises only a federal issue already resolved in an earlier case).

Apart from these restrictions, the appellate federal question jurisdiction extends to every federal issue, factual or legal, part of the plaintiff's case or part of a defense, in either a civil or a criminal case. Even if federal law appears in a case solely because a state statute refers to and incorporates it, the Supreme Court may exercise its federal question jurisdiction if it finds an independent federal interest in assuring proper interpretation of the incorporated federal matter.

In contrast, when Congress first created the lower federal courts in 1789, it authorized them to hear only a few federal question cases of special importance, such as PATENT suits and suits involving treaty rights. After the CIVIL WAR, Congress realized that state courts would be reluctant to enforce newly created federal CIVIL RIGHTS, and authorized the federal courts to hear the enforcement actions. Then, in 1875, Congress used almost the exact language of Article III to empower federal courts to hear "all suits of a civil nature . . . arising under the Constitution or laws of the United States, or treaties made. . . ." The 1875 act, known as the general federal question statute, required that at least $500 be in controversy in the suit, a requirement that was increased gradually over time.

Notwithstanding the breadth of the general federal question statute, Congress has continued to enact more limited laws authorizing federal jurisdiction over particular kinds of federal questions. These laws, designed to aid in enforcing the vast array of federal rights created in recent decades, have not required any amount in controversy. The range of these specialized federal question statutes is so great that by 1970 few federal question cases drew only upon the general statute. In 1976 Congress eliminated the amount in controversy requirement for the only remaining significant group of such cases, suits alleging unconstitutional conduct by federal officers; and in 1980, it repealed the requirement altogether.

Because Congress's legislative powers are enumerated and limited, a complaint filed in federal court frequently invokes a combination of state and federal law. The issue then arises whether the federal element warrants labeling the case one that "arises under" federal law. For a federal court to have federal question jurisdiction, this inquiry must be determined affirmatively, both under Article III and under the general federal question statute.

Although some Supreme Court decisions, notably Justice BENJAMIM N. CARDOZO's opinion in *Gully v. First National Bank* (1936), have announced an equally demanding construction for both the Constitution and the statute, the currently accepted view is that the statute should be construed more narrowly than Article III despite the near identity of their language. In other words, Congress has a broad power but is assumed not to have exercised all of it. Interpretations of Article III have required that the plaintiff invoke some federal law to support a part of the claim for relief, whether or not the federal right is actually disputed by the defendant. (See OSBORN V. BANK OF UNITED STATES.) In a theory known as "protective jurisdiction," some judges and scholars have advanced the view that Congress should have the power to confer federal question jurisdiction even over a case arising under state law, when the claim implicates a strong, legitimate federal interest. The Supreme Court has not yet been required to decide whether Article III extends this far, although in some fields, such as BANKRUPTCY, the Court has approved federal question jurisdiction over suits involving only minor elements of federal law.

The Supreme Court has struggled to develop a narrower interpretive principle for the general federal question statute, seeking to allow adequate implementation of federal policy while avoiding an unnecessary deluge of cases into federal courts. For example, the statute is read to require the plaintiff's reliance on federal law to be revealed in the complaint according to traditional rules of pleading. It also appears that if plaintiff's reliance on federal law is not at the forefront of the claim, as when there is a dispute over present property rights that at some remote time had their source in federal law, jurisdiction will be denied under the general statute even though Congress could constitutionally confer it more specifically. Also, if the plaintiff relies on, refers to, and incorporates state law, the Court may refuse to allow the claim into federal court under the general statute because federal law will not be sufficiently at issue.

No single principle explains all the cases interpreting the general federal question statute. Despite this confusion, most types of cases have been classified either within or outside the federal question jurisdiction. To determine whether a new type of case combining federal and state elements falls within the statute's scope, the courts pragmatically assess the degree of federal interest in the subject matter of the litigation, the relative prominence of state and federal issues, and the likely burden on the federal judicial system of accepting jurisdiction in cases of that type.

The federal question jurisdiction authorized in Article III encompasses cases removed from state to federal court upon the defendant's assertion of a federal defense. Congress has not, however, conferred such broad federal question removal jurisdiction upon the federal courts. With a few exceptions, it has limited removal to cases that fall within original federal question jurisdiction under the general statute.

CAROLE E. GOLDBERG-AMBROSE
(1986)

Bibliography

COHEN, WILLIAM   1967   The Broken Compass: The Requirement That a Case Arise "Directly" under Federal Law. *University of Pennsylvania Law Review* 115:890–916.
MISHKIN, PAUL J.   1953   The Federal "Question" in the District Courts. *Columbia Law Review* 53:157–196.

FEDERAL RULES OF CIVIL PROCEDURE

Article I of the Constitution empowers Congress to "constitute" lower federal courts and thus, by conventional assumption, to regulate practice and procedure in the cases heard in those courts. When the lower federal courts were first created in 1789, Congress enacted a law, known as the Conformity Act, that required each federal trial court to follow, in civil actions at law, the procedural rules of the state in which it was situated. By contrast, Congress directed the Supreme Court to promulgate federal procedures for federal admiralty and EQUITY cases respectively.

Under the Conformity Act, hypertechnical and arbitrary state procedures hampered the federal courts. Also, uniform procedures were not available for administration of federal law nationwide under the general FEDERAL QUESTION JURISDICTION first conferred on the federal courts in 1875. Finally, in 1934, Congress adopted the Rules Enabling Act, which authorized the Supreme Court to promulgate federal procedural rules, subject to a congressional veto. Both Congress's power to delegate this authority and the Supreme Court's power to exercise it, consistent with the CASE OR CONTROVERSY requirement of Article III, have been upheld.

In accordance with the Act, the Supreme Court issued the Federal Rules of Civil Procedure in 1938. Congress declined to veto them. The new rules combined law and equity into a single form of action while preserving the SEVENTH AMENDMENT right to TRIAL BY JURY on any issue that would have been so tried before the merger. While they incorporated state law with respect to some matters, such as provisional remedies, the rules also made important innovations, such as simplified pleading, liberal joinder of claims and parties, and greater emphasis on pretrial discovery of facts. Many state procedures have come to resemble the Federal Rules. And the new joinder rules have resulted in enlargement of the definition of a "case" for purposes of determining ANCILLARY and PENDENT JURISDIC-

TION in the federal courts. In 1966, admiralty actions were made subject to the Federal Rules of Civil Procedure, as amended to retain a few specialized rules for suits designated as admiralty actions in the pleadings.

Special constitutional problems have arisen when the Federal Rules have been employed in diversity actions. Congress and the federal courts do not have general substantive lawmaking power over cases simply because they are within the DIVERSITY JURISDICTION. Thus, when a Federal Rule of Civil Procedure differs from the procedural rule that would be applied in state court, and the difference in rules could affect the outcome of the case, the question arises whether the Federal Rule exceeds federal lawmaking authority and impermissibly intrudes on reserved state power. In *Hanna v. Plumer* (1963) the Supreme Court held that so long as a rule is "rationally capable of classification" as procedural, it is an appropriate subject of legislation under Congress's Article I power to create and regulate the lower federal courts, even though the rule may also affect substantive rights. It is unlikely that the Supreme Court, which promulgates the rules of civil procedure, would decide that those rules are not rationally classifiable as "procedural."

CAROLE E. GOLDBERG-AMBROSE
(1986)

Bibliography

WRIGHT, C.   1976   *Federal Courts*, 3rd ed. St. Paul, Minn.: West Publishing Co.

FEDERAL RULES OF CRIMINAL PROCEDURE

After the FEDERAL RULES OF CIVIL PROCEDURE (1938) established a uniform set of procedures for the trial of civil cases in federal courts, Congress authorized the SUPREME COURT to make rules for the trial of federal criminal cases as well. With two Justices dissenting, the Supreme Court adopted the rules in 1944 and submitted them to Congress, which, by silence, approved them.

Before adoption of the rules, the trial of federal criminal cases was regulated by a varying and uncertain mixture of state and federal rules. The first achievement of the Federal Rules was simplification and clarification. The second was uniformity: the same rules would govern the major aspects of federal criminal trials all over the country. The federal appellate courts would now need to know only one body of procedural law, and all federal defendants would now enjoy similar rights and bear similar burdens.

Certain of the changes worked by the rules—for example, the substitution of a simplified complaint for the old, highly technical forms of INDICTMENT, and the consolidation of defense motions under a single heading—were clear gains by any measure. But probably the most significant achievement of the rules was to focus national attention on the regulation of the criminal process, which has consumed an enormous amount of professional and public attention ever since. Surely it was no accident that *McNabb v. United States* (1943), holding inadmissible a statement obtained from a suspect whom federal officers illegally detained, was decided while the rules were being considered; nor that *McNabb* was later reaffirmed in *Mallory v. United States* (1957) on the basis of Rule 5. (See MCNABB-MALLORY RULE.)

The rules have played a significant part in the expansion and clarification of defendants' rights: as an independent source of law, as a model for constitutional judgments, and as a means by which constitutional judgments could be elaborated. Two examples are illustrative. Rule 11, governing guilty pleas, was used as a guide in constitutional decision making and was itself amended to reflect and to elaborate case law. Rule 41, governing SEARCH WARRANTS, has likewise been modified to elaborate Supreme Court holdings, with respect, for example, to the permissible objects of search, and has also been used as a guide by the Court.

The administration, amendment, and interpretation of the Federal Rules have been heavily charged with constitutional significance, especially in a time of fundamental rethinking of the relation between government and the accused. For the most part this process has been carried on in a public and openminded way, largely immune from politically motivated oversimplifications.

JAMES BOYD WHITE
(1986)

Bibliography

MOORE, JAMES WILLIAM and WAXNER, MARVIN   1985   *Rules of Criminal Procedure*. Volume 8 of *Moore's Federal Practice*, 2nd ed. New York: Matthew Bender.

FEDERAL TEST ACTS
12 Stat. 430 (1862)
12 Stat. 502 (1862)
13 Stat. 424 (1865)
23 Stat. 21 (1868)

Early in the CIVIL WAR northern state and federal officials on an ad hoc basis administered oaths of allegiance to civilians suspected of disloyalty. In June 1862 Congress enacted the "jurors' test oath" which required persons sitting on federal GRAND and PETIT JURIES to swear to future loyalty and that they had not, in the past, voluntarily supported or given "aid or comfort" to the rebellion. The "Ironclad Test Oath" statute, enacted by Congress in July 1862, required all federal officeholders, except the President and vice-president, to swear they had "never voluntarily borne arms against the United States," aided the rebellion, nor "sought nor accepted nor attempted to exercise" any office under the Confederacy. In 1864 the United States SENATE required that its members take this oath. In 1865 the "ironclad oath" was extended to attorneys practicing in federal courts, but in *Ex parte Garland* (1867) (one of the TEST OATH CASES) this extension was declared unconstitutional. From 1864 until 1868 the "ironclad oath" kept former Confederates from holding federal offices or being seated in Congress. After 1868 the Republican-dominated Congress allowed exceptions for members of their party (and later Democrats) who had served the Confederacy. The "jurors' oath" was used to prevent former Confederates from serving on juries until the repeal of all test oaths in 1884.

PAUL FINKELMAN
(1986)

Bibliography

HYMAN, HAROLD M. 1954 *Era of The Oath: Northern Loyalty Tests During the Civil War and Reconstruction.* Philadelphia: University of Pennsylvania Press.

FEDERAL TORT CLAIMS ACT
60 Stat. 842 (1946)

The Federal Tort Claims Act, enacted in 1946, relinquished an important part of the SOVEREIGN IMMUNITY of the United States and was part of a larger twentieth-century trend toward relaxing absolute barriers to suits against governments and officials. By this act, the United States consented to be sued for its agents' torts when private persons would be liable for such torts under the law of the place where the tort occurred. But the act fell short of imposing liability for all torts of United States agents. Generally, the tort must be compensable under state law. In addition, the act excluded liability for a vague category of behavior known as "discretionary functions." As originally enacted, the act also excluded liability for many torts that might arise in the context of law enforcement, including assault, battery, false imprisonment, and false arrest. In 1974, however, the Intentional Tort Amendment Act expanded government liability to include these and other torts. The act continues to exclude liability for def-

amation, misrepresentation, deceit, and interference with contract rights.

THEODORE EISENBERG
(1986)

Bibliography

SCHUCK, PETER H. 1983 *Suing Government: Citizen Remedies for Official Wrongs.* New Haven, Conn.: Yale University Press.

FEDERAL TRADE COMMISSION

See: Regulatory Agencies

FEDERAL TRADE COMMISSION v. GRATZ
253 U.S. 421 (1920)

Section 5 of the FEDERAL TRADE COMMISSION ACT outlawed, but did not define, "unfair methods of competition." Justice JAMES MCREYNOLDS, for a 7–2 Supreme Court, upheld a contract exclusively binding customers to one supplier. Confining Federal Trade Commission (FTC) orders against unfair methods to those previously found illegal (a HOLDING reversed in 1934), the courts, not the commission, were henceforth to determine what section 5 meant. Justice LOUIS D. BRANDEIS, joined by Justice JOHN H. CLARKE, dissented. They would have voided this practice, contending that "the Act left the determination to the Commission." They agreed that courts might determine whether—based on FTC findings—a practice was unfair, but they cautioned against overturning commission decisions without substantial reason.

DAVID GORDON
(1986)

(SEE ALSO: *Economic Regulation; Regulatory Agencies.*)

FEDERAL TRADE COMMISSION ACT
38 Stat. 717 (1914)

When the decisions in STANDARD OIL COMPANY V. UNITED STATES (1911) and *United States v. American Tobacco* (1911) demonstrated that trusts could be dissolved, public calls for a policy regulating combinations and monopolies increased. Responding to President WOODROW WILSON's appeal, Congress created the Federal Trade Commission (FTC) on September 26, 1914. The act created no criminal offenses; the commission would advise business on how to conform to a policy of competition. Congress vested the commission with broad powers of investigation and recommendation regarding enforcement of the ANTITRUST laws, but the act did not cover banks or common carriers. (See INTERSTATE COMMERCE ACT.) Consisting of five commissioners, the FTC is a quasi-judicial tribunal whose findings of fact, if supported by testimony, are binding on the courts and whose decisions are reviewable there.

In furtherance of its goal of fostering competition, section 5 stated that "unfair methods of competition in commerce and unfair or deceptive acts or practices in commerce are hereby declared illegal." Intentionally vague, this provision relied on judicial decisions and experience to give it meaning. By outlawing methods, it improved upon earlier statutes which prohibited only specific acts. Other sections (6 and 9) granted the commission power to require compliance: it could require written responses to inquiries, secure access to corporate books and records, and subpoena witnesses.

DAVID GORDON
(1986)

(SEE ALSO: *Federal Trade Commission v. Gratz.*)

FEINER v. NEW YORK
340 U.S. 315 (1951)

Feiner was convicted of BREACH OF THE PEACE for derogatory remarks concerning President HARRY S. TRUMAN which provoked hostility and some threats from a "restless" crowd. Two police officers, fearing violence, ordered Feiner to stop. When he refused, they arrested him. Feiner marked the post-1920s Court's first use of the CLEAR AND PRESENT DANGER rule to uphold the conviction of a speaker. Chief Justice FRED M. VINSON spoke for the majority. JUSTICE FELIX FRANKFURTER's concurrence urged a balancing approach to replace the danger rule. This case, like TERMINIELLO V. CHICAGO (1949), raised the HOSTILE AUDIENCE problem.

MARTIN SHAPIRO
(1986)

FELONY

The most common classification of crimes is between MISDEMEANORS and felonies. The Constitution does not control the definitions of felony and misdemeanor; the distinction usually is made by a state statute, or, in a few instances, by state constitution. Federal statutes define the scope of federal felonies and misdemeanors.

A state statute commonly will define a felony as a crime for which a person may be imprisoned in a state penitentiary (rather than a local jail) or as an offense for which a person may be imprisoned for a minimum length of time (such as six months or one year). The distinction between a felony and a misdemeanor may determine whether a police officer had statutory authority to arrest a person without a warrant, which state court has jurisdiction over a criminal charge, or whether the defendant will be subject to punishment under a habitual criminal statute which provides for increased punishment after conviction for several felonies.

Although the distinction between felonies and misdemeanors is an important one under state law, it is not significant for constitutional law purposes. There are three constitutional provisions, applicable to the prosecution of criminal cases, whose meaning or impact is dependent in part upon the seriousness of the crime charged, not upon the felony-misdemeanor distinction. These provisions are the Fifth Amendment GRAND JURY clause, the Sixth Amendment RIGHT TO COUNSEL, and the Sixth Amendment right to TRIAL BY JURY.

The Supreme Court has held that the FOURTEENTH AMENDMENT does not incorporate the Fifth Amendment's grand jury clause; that clause, therefore, is not applicable to state or local criminal prosecutions. In *Ex parte Wilson* (1885) the Supreme Court defined the federal crimes to which the grand jury clause applied as those "punishable by imprisonment at hard labor" in a federal penitentiary. Federal statutes and the FEDERAL RULES OF CRIMINAL PROCEDURE define a federal felony as any federal offense punishable by imprisonment for a term exceeding one year. A federal felony prosecution must be initiated by a grand jury indictment. Someone charged with a federal misdemeanor may be prosecuted based on either an INFORMATION filed by the federal prosecutor or a grand jury indictment.

The Sixth Amendment guarantee of a right to counsel in all criminal prosecutions applies to the states through the Fourteenth Amendment. The Supreme Court has held that the Sixth Amendment also gives an INDIGENT defendant the right to have the government provide him with an attorney in some, but not all, criminal cases. A defendant convicted of a crime cannot be sentenced to imprisonment for even one day unless he has had the opportunity to be represented by counsel at his trial. The government, however, need not appoint attorneys for indigent persons who are convicted of crimes that in fact are not punished by imprisonment. The determination whether the state is required to appoint counsel to represent an indigent defendant is not based on a felony-misdemeanor distinction. A state is not required to provide counsel to an indigent defendant charged with a serious crime so long as the conviction in fact does not result in imprisonment. Any right to an attorney in a case in which incarceration is not imposed would be based upon a case-by-case DUE PROCESS analysis.

The Sixth Amendment also provides that an accused person has a right to "an impartial jury." The jury trial provision of the Sixth Amendment has been incorporated into the Fourteenth Amendment; it governs both state and federal prosecutions. Although the Sixth Amendment refers to the right to a jury trial in "all criminal prosecutions," the Supreme Court has ruled that the accused has a right to a jury trial, rather than a trial before a judge, only when he is charged with an offense that is not "petty." The Court has held that any offense punishable by incarceration for more than six months cannot be deemed "petty." Thus, regardless of the sentence a defendant actually receives, if the defendant is accused of an offense for which there is a possible sentence of more than six months of incarceration, he has a Sixth Amendment right to a trial by jury. The Supreme Court has not explained how courts are to distinguish between "petty" and "nonpetty" offenses where the crime is punishable by no more than six months' imprisonment.

JOHN E. NOWAK
(1986)

Bibliography

LaFave, Wayne, and Israel, Jerold 1984 *Criminal Procedure.* St. Paul, Minn.: West Publishing Co.

FEMINIST THEORY

Feminist theory encompasses such a large and diverse body of work that it can no longer be described succinctly. A partial definition might stress the relationships among and between, on the one hand, women, women's experience, perceptions and treatment of women, gender as a social category, masculinity and femininity, and sexuality, and, on the other, social and personal identity, language, religion, economic and social structures, law, philosophy, and knowledge. The multifaceted nature of current feminist theory has even led many feminists to use the term "feminist theories." This diversity also marks the use of feminist theory with respect to law.

Feminists trained in law tend to describe their theoretical work as "feminist legal theory" or "feminist jurisprudence." The early development of the field, in the late 1970s and early 1980s, was closely tied to traditional legal categories and analysis, even while it posed a significant challenge to the traditional use of such categories and methods. Its existence was made possible by the movement of significant numbers of women into the legal profession, and especially onto law school faculties, and by

changes in interpretation of constitutional doctrine wrought by the CIVIL RIGHTS MOVEMENT. The extent of these changes began to manifest itself in *Reed v. Reed* (1971), in which the Supreme Court first interpreted the EQUAL PROTECTION clause as demanding significant justification for laws that formally discriminated against women. At first, then, feminist jurisprudence concerned itself primarily with elaboration of what equality might mean for women; a large proportion of the scholarship in the field remains focused on this question. However, in the 1990s the directions of feminist legal theory are likely to respond more to developments in feminist theory than to developments in legal theory or doctrine.

In some way all feminist theory concerns itself with describing, explaining, criticizing, and changing the social condition of women as a class from the perspective of, and on behalf of, all women. This project is pursued, however, in radically different ways, posing several kinds of challenges to traditional constitutional JURISPRUDENCE and practice: doctrinal, culture, textural, and structural.

Feminist theory criticizes constitutional doctrine primarily for its failure to center, or often even to consider, women's experience in fashioning, elaborating, and applying rules presented as "neutral." Decisions such as *Geduldig v. Aiello* (1974)—in which a majority of the Supreme Court rejected an equal protection challenge to the exclusion of pregnant women from a state disability insurance plan, finding the exclusion based on medical condition rather than on sex—are used to demonstrate the extent to which nonfeminist interpretations of equal protection treat as irrelevant or unimportant experiences that many women consider quite important to them as women. While agreeing on this criticism, however, feminist theorists tend to disagree among themselves on whether constitutional law should attempt to develop more "truly neutral" doctrines, what such doctrines might be like, and whether neutrality itself is possible or desirable.

Cultural challenges to constitutional law are of two primary types. Some theorists suggest that the replacement of a predominantly white male judiciary, legislature, and practicing bar with a profession that more closely represents the sex and race composition of the general population would tend to change law and legal practice in a variety of ways. Attempts to test these propositions range from examination of the opinions of women jurists, such as Supreme Court Justice SANDRA DAY O'CONNOR, to documentation of shifts in political language, to interviews with, and observations of, female lawyers. Other theorists abstract certain characteristics thought to be associated with women and attempt to elaborate the potential effects of a closer integration of such characteristics into constitutional law. Both of these types of cultural critique often draw on Carol Gilligan's suggestion that an "ethic of care," with its attendant focus on responsibility, connection, and relationship, could validly be added to the "ethic of justice" that biases both moral and legal theory toward an exclusive focus on rights, autonomy, and individualism.

Textual criticism focuses on the language of law, especially law's written texts. Judicial opinions, legislation, and even the Constitution itself may be read as examples of literary production not fundamentally dissimilar from novels, plays, or newspaper articles. Some feminist textual criticism examines language as it communicates certain assumptions about the appropriateness or relevance of women's presence or experience, and shares with doctrinal criticism the project of identifying the sex bias concealed under seemingly neutral practices. This type of criticism has led to some minor changes in legal language (e.g., the replacement of "reasonable man" with "reasonable person"), as well as to textual revisions with more substantive force, such as recrafting jury instructions on self-defense so that their language does not presume the situation of one man resisting another. More literary-oriented theory focuses on the use and deployment of words, images, and metaphors that may be understood as gendered, either in their conscious association with traditional notions of masculinity and femininity or in their historical or psychosocial association with sexuality, sexual courtship, or heterosexual intercourse. Such theorists find within legal texts a process of dichotomization between male and female and a hierarchical ordering of male over female that mirror the insights of structural theories.

Finally, feminist theory also examines both conceptual and rhetorical structures within law and the structure of law itself. Probably the most widely disseminated insight to arise from feminist theory with respect to law is the critique of the process by which law divides human life into a "public" realm, in which law, justice, equality, and politics are thought to be appropriate, and a "private" realm, in which ideals of harmony, sacrifice, and intimacy are to be protected from public scrutiny. The feminist critique of this public-private distinction makes several key points: (1) Legal actors, such as courts, which are themselves "public," decide where the line will be drawn between public and private, and thus shape "the private" through public actions. (2) The association of men with the public sphere and women with the private sphere is used to legitimize women's exclusion from the political life of the nation. (3) When women's experience with intimacy is one of violence—marital rape, wife battering, incest, or sexual coercion—the public-private distinction operates not to protect women's privacy from public scrutiny but to block women's ability to hold male intimates publicly accountable for their violence. (4) The very process of dichotomization that makes it possible to think of public and private life as two separate spheres reflects and strengthens the notion that women and men are fundamentally, necessarily, and naturally different, separate, and unequal. This critique has obvious implications for STATE ACTION doctrine, the choice to place women's reproductive rights under the rubric of the RIGHT OF PRIVACY, and interpretations of what PROCEDURAL DUE PROCESS requires in a variety of situations.

Other structural critiques question traditionally presumed relationships between the state and the individual, law and society, normality and deviance, identity and politics, freedom and coercion, and the subjective and objective. The results of these inquiries have led some feminists to characterize the state, the law, or both as "male" in the social, rather than biological, sense of that term.

The Constitution plays a major role in creating or maintaining the structures critiqued by feminist theory. Feminist theory suggests that the Framers' constitution of a polity that excluded women of all races and classes, as well as men of certain races and classes, did not simply result in a partial realization of a vision that could, over time, be extended to those who had been left out. Instead, that decision created gaps and contradictions within the very definitions of what it means to be a polity, to create and limit a government, to "promote the general welfare," and even what it means to subscribe to a rule of "laws, not men [sic]."

CHRISTINE A. LITTLETON
(1992)

(SEE ALSO: *Constitution as Literature; Gender Rights; Women in Constitutional History; Woman Suffrage.*)

Bibliography

DuBois, Ellen et al. 1985 Feminist Discourse, Moral Values and the Laws—A Conversation. *Buffalo Law Review* 34:11–87.

Kay, Herma Hill and Littleton, Christine A. 1988 Feminist Jurisprudence: What Is It? When Did It Start? Who Does It? Pages 844–887 in Herma Hill Kay, ed., *Sex-Based Discrimination*, 3rd ed. St. Paul, Minn.: West Publishing Co.

Littleton, Christine A. 1987 Reconstructing Sexual Equality. *California Law Review* 75:1279–1337.

MacKinnon, Catharine A. 1989 *Toward a Feminist Theory of the State.* Cambridge, Mass.: Harvard University Press.

Sherry, Suzanna 1986 Civic Virtue and the Feminine Voice in Constitutional Adjudication. *Virginia Law Review* 72:543–616.

West, Robin L. 1988 Jurisprudence and Gender. *Chicago Law Review* 55:1–72.

Williams, Patricia 1988 On Being the Object of Property. *Signs* 14:5–24.

Williams, Wendy 1985 Equality's Riddle: Pregnancy and the Equal Treatment/Special Treatment Debate. *New York University Review of Law and Social Change* 13:325–380.

FERGUSON v. SKRUPA
372 U.S. 726 (1963)

This decision is often cited as a leading modern example of the Supreme Court's permissive attitude toward ECO-NOMIC REGULATION challenged as a violation of SUBSTANTIVE DUE PROCESS.

Kansas prohibited "the business of debt adjusting" except as an incident of the practice of law. The Court unanimously upheld this statute against a challenge to its constitutionality. Justice HUGO L. BLACK wrote for the Court. Any argument that the business of debt adjusting had social utility should be addressed to the legislature, not the courts. "We refuse to sit as a "super legislature to weigh the wisdom of legislation." The Court had given up the practice, common during the years before WEST COAST HOTEL CO. V. PARRISH (1937), of using "the "vague contours' of the Due Process Clause to nullify laws which a majority of the Court believed to be economically unwise." Justice Black, unlike many of his brethren, carried this same view of the judicial function into other areas of CONSTITUTIONAL INTERPRETATION; see his dissents in GRISWOLD V. CONNECTICUT (1965) and HARPER V. VIRGINIA BOARD OF ELECTIONS (1966).

In *Ferguson* Justice JOHN MARSHALL HARLAN concurred separately on the ground that the law bore "a rational relation to a constitutionally permissible objective." Apparently Justice Harlan wanted to maintain some level of judicial scrutiny of economic regulations, even if it were only the relaxed RATIONAL BASIS standard, and thought the Black opinion suggested a complete abdication of the judicial role in such cases.

KENNETH L. KARST
(1986)

FESSENDEN, WILLIAM PITT
(1806–1869)

A Maine lawyer, congressman (1841–1843; 1853–1854), senator (1854–1864; 1865–1869), and secretary of the treasury (1864–1865), William Pitt Fessenden chaired the Senate Finance Committee during the CIVIL WAR and later the Joint Committee on Reconstruction. Although sympathetic to many radical goals, Fessenden always demanded strict adherence to constitutional principles. Thus, he opposed aspects of the EMANCIPATION PROCLAMATION, the legal tender acts, the CONFISCATION ACTS, and the TENURE OF OFFICE ACT. Although Senate majority leader, he voted to acquit ANDREW JOHNSON in his 1867 IMPEACHMENT trial, because he did not believe the President had committed an impeachable offense within the meaning of the Constitution.

PAUL FINKELMAN
(1986)

Bibliography
JELLISON, CHARLES ALBERT 1962 *Fessenden of Maine, Civil War Senator.* Syracuse, N.Y.: Syracuse University Press.

FEUDALISM
AND THE CONSTITUTION

When the Framers referred to feudalism in the FEDERALIST, that abstraction served as a model of decentralized rule. Otherwise, they would have agreed with JOHN ADAMS, who in 1765 had authored a short dissertation on the topic: feudalism, merged perniciously with Romish religion, was what the Puritans left behind them in England; released from ignorance, dependence, and extreme poverty, their descendants were free to follow "the true map of man." This view was later endorsed by leading interpreters of "American exceptionalism." More recent research has shown it to be incomplete. Among the COMMON LAW hierarchies that ordered the relations of persons throughout medieval society, those in religious and commercial affairs were removed by the time Adams wrote and were now governed by Parliament. Other hierarchies remained; WILLIAM BLACKSTONE enshrined them as "private relations"—husband and wife, parent and child, master and servant, guardian and ward—still under the aegis of the courts. These survived the AMERICAN REVOLUTION.

The English development was transplanted into the United States as every state and territory except Louisiana received English common law and statutes into its own legal system. Ancient privileges still intact became VESTED RIGHTS, protected by the SEPARATION OF POWERS against legislative tampering. Following old rules of STATUTORY INTERPRETATION, and newer constitutional limitations, nineteenth-century judges read women's inheritance acts to preserve their husbands' interests against express language to the contrary, nullified maximum-hours statutes as invasions of FREEDOM OF CONTRACT between masters and servants, and struck down state liberty laws for violating slaveholders' common-law right of recaption.

The stubbornness of inherited hierarchy in the face of ideological and social democratization characterizes important constitutional struggles of the twentieth century. Among the most tumultuous was the conflict between employers and employees over the establishment of trade unions. Before the NEW DEAL, most judges held union activity to violate the master's ancient and constitutionally endorsed rights in the workplace. These rights were at issue in the COURT-PACKING "crisis" of 1936, finally resolved in *NLRB v. Jones & Laughlin Steel Co.,* in which the Supreme Court upheld an act of Congress giving an employee a right to a reinstatement proceeding under the WAGNER ACT, a right "unknown to the common law."

Feudal privileges remained prominently on display in the setting of the family. Not until 1943 was a husband's common law right over the possession of his wife's earnings finally terminated. Justices on the REHNQUIST COURT have relied on Blackstone's codification of "private relations" between parents and children to support opinions on subjects ranging from ABORTION to school drug SEARCHES AND SEIZURES. In general, however, sufficiently pointed LEGISLATION in this realm will prevail.

These hierarchies by no means exhaust the feudal content of the Constitution. The writs of CERTIORARI, MANDAMUS, and HABEAS CORPUS, by which constitutional rights might be vindicated, are of medieval vintage. Habeas corpus, "the Great Writ," for instance, was put to its oldest purpose, of securing a party's custody rather than his or her release, in the case of slaves, and after the CIVIL WAR, of apprentices, children, and wives. The three branches of state, as well as the arrangements of FEDERALISM, redact, in their basic design, the intricate network of jurisdictions that was English government under Henry VII and his forebears.

KAREN ORREN
(2000)

Bibliography

ADAMS, JOHN   1765   An Essay on Canon and Feudal Law. In John Holroyd, Earl of Sheffield, ed., *Observations on the Commerce of the American States with Europe and the West Indies.* New York: Research Reprints (1783/1970).

BROWN, ELIZABETH GASPAR   1964   *British Statutes in American Law, 1776–1836.* Ann Arbor: University of Michigan Press.

HARTZ, LOUIS   1955   *The Liberal Tradition in America.* New York: Harcourt, Brace.

HURD, ROLLIN C.   1876   *Treatise on the Right of Personal Liberty.* Albany, N.Y.: W. C. Little.

SEDGWICK, THEODORE   1857   *A Treatise on the Rules Which Govern the Interpretation and Application of Statutory and Constitutional Law.* New York: J. S. Voorhies.

FEW, WILLIAM
(1748–1828)

William Few represented Georgia at the CONSTITUTIONAL CONVENTION OF 1787 and signed the Constitution. He attended the Convention irregularly (leaving to attend Congress), spoke infrequently, and served on only one committee. He afterward served as a senator and federal judge.

DENNIS J. MAHONEY
(1986)

FIELD, DAVID D.
(1805–1894)

David Dudley Field, older brother of Justice STEPHEN J. FIELD, won a number of important cases before the Supreme Court in his career as a highly successful lawyer, EX PARTE MILLIGAN (1866), *Cummings v. Missouri* (1867), and UNITED STATES V. CRUIKSHANK (1876) among them. His appearance on behalf of Jay Gould and Jim Fisk in the celebrated Erie Railroad scandal brought him popular criticism and charges of misconduct from his peers. He would later represent the Tweed Ring when his free services were rejected by the prosecution. As one biographer remarked, Field "was essentially a protestant, an originator, a breaker of precedents."

Field devoted his last decades to codification of municipal and international law. He also played a fundamental role in reforming the substantive and procedural codes of New York State; those codes would serve as models for many other states. He served as president of the American Bar Association, 1888–1889.

DAVID GORDON
(1986)

FIELD, STEPHEN J.
(1816–1899)

Stephen Johnson Field is a massive figure in the history of the United States SUPREME COURT. Appointed by ABRAHAM LINCOLN in 1863 following six years of distinguished service on the California Supreme Court, Field remained on the bench until 1897 and established a record for length of tenure since surpassed only by WILLIAM O. DOUGLAS. For two generations he preached a radically new gospel of constitutional interpretation that fused natural law concepts, a theory of adjudication based on formally bounded categories of public power and private right, and a designing foresight about the Court's unique capacity to shape American public life. Field's contributions to American constitutional development are conventionally summed up in the phrase laissez-faire CONSTITUTIONALISM. But his profound impact on the institutional character of the Court outlasted his doctrinal formulations. Field was arguably the Court's first self-conscious "activist," and he was certainly the first Justice to describe judicial protection of substantive rights as a democratic endeavor. "As I look back over the more than a third of a century that I have sat on this bench," Field wrote in his valedictory letter, "I am more and more impressed with the immeasurable importance of this court. Now and then we hear it spoken of as an aristocratic feature of a Republican government. But it is the most Democratic of all. Senators represent their states, and Representatives their constituents, but this court stands for the whole country, and as such it is truly "of the people, by the people, and for the people" It was this fundamentally new conception of the Court's position in the American system of government and the manifold ways Field acted upon it during his long career that prompted EDWARD S. CORWIN to describe him as "the pioneer and prophet of our modern constitutional law."

Field's jurisprudence was essentially a constitutional version of the equal rights creed expounded by ANDREW JACKSON in his veto of the bill rechartering the Second Bank of the United States. Field understood democracy in terms of "the natural equal rights of the citizen," particularly equality in the marketplace; he was quick to distinguish the common good of the whole people from the focused demands of interest seekers that sometimes generated legislation favoring some and discriminating against others. Since the Court, like the President, represented "the whole country" rather than a narrow constituency, Field claimed that JUDICIAL REVIEW of legislation was at once the moral equivalent of the executive veto and a consummately democratic power. His two most famous opinions resonated with the substantive concerns of antebellum Jacksonians. The first was designed to protect the rights of the many against legal privileges granted to a few. Dissenting in the SLAUGHTERHOUSE CASES (1873) Field denounced the "odious monopoly" produced by legislative skulduggery in Louisiana and claimed that the newly adopted FOURTEENTH AMENDMENT would become "a vain and idle enactment, which accomplished nothing" if the Court continued to permit state legislatures "to farm out the ordinary avocations of life" to favored corporations. In the second, POLLOCK V. FARMERS LOAN & TRUST CO. (1895), Field resisted a statute that, in his view, was designed to enable the many to steal from the few under color of law. There he attacked the mildly progressive federal tax on incomes as an "assault on capital . . . the stepping stone to others, larger and more sweeping, till our political contests . . . become a war of the poor against the rich; a war constantly growing in intensity and bitterness." If Field had been successful in persuading his colleagues to conceptualize the case as he did, the income tax would have been invalidated not because it was a DIRECT TAX but on the ground that its graduated rates violated the Constitution's requirement that "all duties, imposts and excises shall be uniform throughout the United States." For

Field, uniformity mandated equal treatment; the chief defect of the statute was that it created a different rule for rich and poor, thereby violating the first principle of republicanism articulated by his Jacksonian mentors.

Field's penchant for pouring his ideological predispositions into open-ended textual phrases such as "uniform" and "due process" was apparent to colleagues throughout his career. Many were alarmed by his expansive conception of the judicial function; some regarded him as a dangerous man. DAVID DAVIS called him a "damned rascal" in 1866 and HORACE GRAY likened him to a "wild bull" three decades later. HENRY B. BROWN said he was "a man of great determination and indomitable courage, though lacking in judicial temperament." Yet it was impossible to ignore him. What made Field so formidable was his skill in translating the featureless generalities of the Constitution into a coherent system of principled standards. He had an uncanny ability to diagnose recurrent problems almost immediately and to frame rules derived from the COMMON LAW or the structure of the federal system that accommodated his value-laden premises. He anticipated future controversies and supplied mutually consistent solutions to all of them. For Field, these solutions were neither contingent nor variable; they were "true."

Few of the twenty-eight men with whom Field sat on the bench perceived the whole truth in precisely the way he did. But every Justice shared at least some of his premises, and most were willing to articulate one or more of his pet doctrinal formulations in an opinion for the Court. With each new handhold Field secured, however, his colleagues found it increasingly difficult to resist the entire array of rules he had proposed at the outset. The analogies linking each component of his system to the others were very compelling. As late as 1890, Field remained confident that the whole truth, as he understood it, would eventually be embraced by the Court. "[A]ny grave departure from the purposes of the Constitution . . . will not fit harmoniously with other rulings," he explained at the Centennial Celebration of the Organization of the Federal Judiciary. "[I]t will collide with them, and thus compel explanations and qualifications until the error is eliminated. . . . [T]ruth alone is immortal, and in the end will assert its rightful supremacy."

The system of rules Field proposed for integrating the Fourteenth Amendment into the existing corpus of constitutional law was breathtaking in scope. It also had a deceptively simple and, in its day, alluring structure. First, he called for a clear and immutable boundary between the public and private spheres in order to forestall legislation that emptied one pocket only to fill another. Here the operable phrase in the amendment was not due process so much as "take property." Beginning in the *Slaughterhouse Cases*, Field claimed that some businesses were purely private while others were public in "use." Firms that necessarily "held franchises of a public character appertaining to government," such as those that exercised the EMINENT DOMAIN power or occupied the public rivers or public streets, were public in "use." Consequently government might confer monopoly privileges on such firms, subsidize their operations with tax funds, and regulate their rates of charge. But manufacturers, food processors, warehouse operators, and other businesses that did not need to exercise public franchises were purely private. Those businesses had to be open to all entrants as a matter of common right and their operations could be subject neither to price regulations nor to public subsidy. In the GRANGER CASES (1877) Field added one corollary to this scheme. When government regulated the rates of firms public in "use," he asserted, the prices fixed must be subject to judicial review in order to ensure that service to the public was not "required without reward, or upon conditions amounting to the TAKING OF PROPERTY for PUBLIC USE without compensation." The Court's duty, he said, was "to draw the line between regulation and confiscation."

Field repeatedly claimed that judicial application of these doctrines required no great departure in constitutional interpretation. All the Court had to do was constitutionalize under the Fourteenth Amendment and apply in a systematic fashion the principles of "general constitutional law" articulated by SAMUEL F. MILLER in *Pumpelly v. Green Bay Co.* (1872) and LOAN ASSOCIATION V. TOPEKA (1874). There the Court proscribed exercises of the eminent domain and tax powers that amounted to "robbery," in the one case by designating irreparable injury to property as a taking and in the other by barring public spending "for purposes of private interest instead of public use." When the Court refused to apply the same principles to the POLICE POWER under the Fourteenth Amendment in the *Granger Cases,* Field dissented. "Of what avail is the constitutional provision that no State shall deprive any person of property except by DUE PROCESS OF LAW," he asked, "if the State can, by fixing the compensation which he may receive for its use, take from him all that is valuable in the property?" Beginning in STONE V. FARMER'S LOAN AND TRUST CO. (1886), however, the majority made one concession after another to Field's position. By 1898 only the doctrine of business AFFECTED WITH A PUBLIC INTEREST, which Field considered dangerously protean, remained to be pulled down before "the truth . . . asserted its rightful supremacy."

The second component of Field's Fourteenth Amendment system dealt with intergovernmental relations. His general theory was based on the Jacksonian principle of DUAL FEDERALISM: "a national government for national purposes, local governments for local purposes," and each "sovereign" within its assigned sphere such that neither was dependent upon or subordinate to the other nor, indeed, capable of clashing with it as long as the powers of each were properly defined. Thus Field eagerly joined majorities that imposed implied limitations on Congress's MONETARY POWER in *Lane County v. Oregon* (1869), its taxing power in COLLECTOR V. DAY (1871), and its commerce power in UNITED STATES V. E. C. KNIGHT CO. (1895). Beginning in *Tarble's Case* (1871) he also developed implied limitations on the states' authority to impair the national government's independent energy in the exercise of its "acknowledged powers." Yet Miller, speaking for the majority in the *Slaughterhouse Cases,* claimed that the Fourteenth Amendment threatened to unravel these "main features of the federal system." What frightened Miller most was the assumption that if the Court had JURISDICTION to protect FUNDAMENTAL RIGHTS under the amendment's first section, Congress must have jurisdiction to enact statutes affecting the same rights under the fifth section vesting it with power "to enforce, by appropriate legislation" the amendment's substantive provisions. One reason the majority gutted the PRIVILEGES OR IMMUNITIES clause, then, was to avoid articulating doctrine that might ultimately "fetter and degrade the State governments by subjecting them to the control of Congress."

In Field's view, the *Slaughterhouse* majority was afraid of a phantom, for a STATE ACTION doctrine could stay the hand of Congress without disturbing the Court's jurisdiction. Here the operable phrase in the text was: "No State shall make or enforce any law." The Fourteenth Amendment, he asserted in dissent, only "ordains that [fundamental rights] shall not be abridged by State legislation." "The exercise of these rights . . . and the degree of enjoyment received from such exercise," he added in anticipation of UNITED STATES V. CRUIKSHANK (1876), "are always more or less affected by the condition and the local institutions of the State, or city, or town where he resides." These rights had never been a concern of the United States and the amendment did not make them one. The enabling clause in the fifth section, whatever its meaning, could not constitutionally enlarge the modest accretion to national authority envisioned by the first section. Because the amendment was not a grant of power but a series of limitations on state legislation, moreover, the Court could readily distinguish between national remedies for prohibited state action (laws that were not "true" exercises of the eminent domain, taxing, and police powers reserved to the states) and inappropriate acts of Congress invading the sphere of state authority. In practical application, the amendment would affect the federal system in a way comparable to the clauses of the Constitution forbidding the states from passing EX POST FACTO, laws, and laws impairing the obligation of contracts.

The WAITE COURT tentatively endorsed the state action

doctrine in *Cruikshank,* and invoked it with a vengeance in UNITED STATES V. HARRIS (1883) and the CIVIL RIGHTS CASES (1883). These decisions not only assuaged previous doubts about Congress's authority to use the Fourteenth Amendment as a grant of power but also prompted the Court to reconsider Field's blueprint for judicial intervention in government-business relations. Meanwhile, Field elaborated the third component of his Fourteenth Amendment theory. It addressed what he called INVIDIOUS DISCRIMINATION. Here Field was a singularly important pioneer, for he decided the federal case of first impression on circuit. At issue in *Ho Ah Kow v. Nunan* (1879) was the San Francisco "queue ordinance" requiring county prisoners to have their hair cropped. As it was "universally understood" that the regulation had been designed "to be enforced only against [the Chinese] race," Field explained, the ordinance violated the equal protection clause. This decision, along with Field's 1882 opinion striking down an anti-Chinese laundry ordinance, supplied the conceptual foundations for the Court's ringing proclamation of the antidiscrimination principle in YICK WO V. HOPKINS (1886).

Yet Field's understanding of "invidious discrimination" did not compel state governments to be colorblind. Dissenting in STRAUDER V. WEST VIRGINIA (1880), where the Court invalidated a statute that limited jury service to whites, Field claimed that the equal protection clause dealt only with the CIVIL RIGHTS described in *Ho Ah Kow.* It "leaves political rights . . . and social rights . . . as they stood previous to its adoption." "Civil rights," he explained, "are absolute and personal and [a]ll persons within the jurisdiction of the State, whether permanent residents or temporary sojourners, whether young or old, male or female, are to be equally protected." But nobody in the *Strauder* majority was prepared to hold that the Fourteenth Amendment forbade the states from excluding Chinese aliens, women, or children from the jury box. The conclusion was inescapable that jury service could not be regarded as a "civil right," for which the amendment mandated "universality of the [equal] protection secured," but only as a "political right . . . conditioned and dependent upon the discretion of the elective or appointing power, whether that be the People acting through the ballot, or one of the departments of their government." The "social rights" to which Field only alluded in the *Strauder* stood on a similar footing. The capacity of individuals to marry or to have access to public goods such as libraries and schools had always been regulated by law on the basis of age, sex, race, and citizenship. "Such legislation is not obnoxious to the [equal protection] clause of the 14th Amendment," he said, "if all persons subject to it are treated alike under similar circumstances and conditions."

The *Strauder* majority flatly rejected the classification of rights that Field proposed. "The Fourteenth Amendment makes no attempt to enumerate the rights it is designed to protect," WILLIAM STRONG declared for the Court. "It speaks in general terms, and those are as comprehensive as possible." But once again a Field dissent proved to be prophetic. Three years later, speaking for a unanimous Court in PACE V. ALABAMA (1883), Field held that antimiscegenation laws were not forbidden by the Fourteenth Amendment as long as both parties received the same punishment for their crimes. Equal protection mandated equal treatment, not freedom of choice; antimiscegenation laws restricted the liberty of blacks and whites alike. Underlying this ruling was an unarticulated premise of enormous importance: the legal classification "Negro" was not suspect per se. The doctrine of SEPARATE BUT EQUAL enunciated in PLESSY V. FERGUSON (1896) followed almost as a matter of course, especially after the Court had distinguished "civil rights" from "social rights" under the THIRTEENTH AMENDMENT in the *Civil Rights Cases.* Even Field's distinction between "civil rights" and "political rights" eventually got incorporated into the Court's Fourteenth Amendment jurisprudence, albeit in a form substantially different from what he proposed in *Strauder.* The Waite Court conceded from the outset that jury selection officials might constitutionally employ facially neutral yet impossibly vague tests of good character, sound judgment, and the like. In the absence of state laws expressly restricting participation to whites, JOHN MARSHALL HARLAN explained in *Bush v. Kentucky* (1883), the Court had no choice but to presume that jury commissioners had acted properly. When the "civil right" of equal opportunity to pursue an "ordinary trade" was at issue in *Yick Wo,* however, the Court unanimously invalidated the law not only because it had been administered with "an evil eye and an unequal hand" but also because it lacked adequate standards for controlling the discretion of public officials authorized to license the regulated trade.

Simply to sketch the basic contours of Field's jurisprudence is to suggest the degree to which his views, forged into a coherent system at an astonishingly early date and reiterated with great force throughout his record-shattering tenure on the Court, shaped the course of American constitutional law. His associates resisted the whole "truth," as Field understood it, to the very end, and Harlan predicted that he would spend even the final days with "his face towards the setting sun, wondering . . . whether the Munn case or the eternal principles of right and justice will ultimately prevail." Yet appellate judging in America is inherently a collective enterprise. The remarkable thing about Field's career is not that he failed to win every battle but that he eventually celebrated so many victories when the stakes were so very high. What endured was his claim that the Court was "the most [d]emocratic of all" governmental institutions. By acting on that belief Field not only transformed the character of judicial power in America but also influenced debate on the Court's legitimate role long after the structure of doctrine he helped to forge had been annihilated.

CHARLES W. MCCURDY
(1986)

Bibliography

CORWIN, EDWARD S. 1909 The Supreme Court and the Fourteenth Amendment. *Michigan Law Review* 7:643–672.

GRAHAM, HOWARD J. 1968 Everyman's Constitution: Historical Essays in the Fourteenth Amendment, the "Conspiracy Theory," and American Constitutionalism. Madison: State Historical Society of Wisconsin.

MCCURDY, CHARLES W. 1975 Justice Field and the Jurisprudence of Government-Business Relations. *Journal of American History* 61:970–1005.

SWISHER, CARL B. 1930 *Stephen J. Field: Craftsman of the Law.* Washington, D.C.: Brookings Institution.

FIELD v. CLARK
143 U.S. 649 (1892)

This is a leading case on the subject of DELEGATION OF POWER. The Tariff Act of 1890 authorized the President to suspend its free-trade provisions indefinitely as to countries discriminating against American products. The Supreme Court held, 7–2, that though the act invested the President with discretion, it did not invest him with "LEGISLATIVE POWER"; Congress had fixed adequate standards for his guidance.

Field is also often cited as a POLITICAL QUESTION precedent. Appellants argued that the enrolled act contained one section that the HOUSE OF REPRESENTATIVES had not passed. The Court refused to examine this question; the act's transmission by the congressional leadership and its enrollment by the secretary of state conclusively established its content.

LEONARD W. LEVY
(1986)

FIFTEENTH AMENDMENT
(Framing and Ratification)

In January 1869 adult black males could vote in only twenty states. Blacks had received the franchise in ten states of the South under the Reconstruction Act of March 1867 as part of the price of readmission to the Union set by the Republicans in Congress. Because Republicans also controlled the state government of Tennessee, blacks were enfranchised there. But many lived in the ex-slave border states that had been loyal to the Union, and they were not enfranchised. In the North, most blacks did not have the right to vote; however, there were minor exceptions in those states where the black population was small. The New England states except Connecticut allowed black suffrage, as did four midwestern states, Wisconsin, Nebraska, Minnesota, and Iowa. But especially in the lower North, where most northern blacks lived, white voters in REFERENDUM after referendum had rejected their unrestricted enfranchisement. Indeed in 1868 the issue of black suffrage was thought to be so dangerous and debilitating to the Republican party that at the party's national convention the framers of the platform devised a double standard by endorsing black voting in the South while trying not to antagonize white voters in the North: thus each northern state could decide black suffrage without federal interference, but southern states must accept black voting as a matter of national policy.

In the presidential election of 1868 Republican candidate ULYSSES S. GRANT captured most of the electoral vote and the Republicans retained control of Congress. But beneath the surface the situation was not reassuring. Grant's electoral victory was much greater than his popular vote (only 52 percent). Without the southern black voter Grant would have lost the popular, though not the electoral, vote. In state after state Grant squeaked by with narrow margins. Indeed, a switch of a mere 29,862 votes out of the 5,717,246 cast for the two major party candidates (.52 percent) would have made the Democratic candidate president. Moreover, the Democrats gained seats in the HOUSE OF REPRESENTATIVES in Washington. And Republican majorities in state after state were slim indeed. Finally, Republican politicians throughout the South reported that little reliance could be placed on the southern black voter in the long run because of strong white influence and intimidation and because of black poverty, illiteracy, and inexperience. Danger signals in the South, defeats in state referenda in the North, and a narrow escape from defeat in the presidential election of 1868 taught the Republicans that their platform pledge to the North had to be ignored. Something must be done by the final session of the Fortieth Congress before the Democrats arrived in force.

The Republicans decided it was necessary to augment their strength by enfranchising more blacks, who could be expected to vote Republican en masse. Although egalitarians had begun the advocacy of black enfranchisement, politicians had made its achievement possible. Two years before, Congress had enfranchised blacks in the South because the Republicans then needed southern black votes to counter southern white votes. Now the Republicans also needed the support of northern and border blacks, especially in closely balanced states, and were willing to run limited risks and promote political reform in order to maintain power.

Therefore, during early 1869 the Republicans in the lame-duck Congress pressed for a constitutional amendment to secure impartial manhood suffrage in every state, thereby avoiding further popular rejection in state referenda. They opted for the usual but more indirect method of having Republican state legislatures that were still in session ratify the amendment. Thus they avoided the risk of possible rejection by special conventions.

The amendment finally passed Congress in late February 1869 after a number of compromises. To secure enough moderate votes, the sponsors had to omit a clause that would have outlawed property qualifications and LITERACY TESTS. Such a clause was dispensable because the tests would affect more Negroes in the South than in the North, and because the proponents of the amendment were intent primarily upon securing the northern Negro voter for the Republican party. For the same reasons, they omitted any provision banning RACIAL DISCRIMINATION in qualifications for officeholding. A provision for federal authority over voter qualifications was defeated, and so the potential for evasion in the southern and border states was left wide open.

The legislative history of the Fifteenth Amendment indicated no triumph of radical idealism but rather served to demonstrate its failure—a fact underscored by the fury and frustration of that band of radicals who had favored idealistic and uncompromising reforms. A moderate measure, the amendment had the support of those who understood the limits of party power and who had practical goals in mind; they took into account the possible difficulties of ratification. Time was short, the pressures were great, and the options were limited.

The primary objective—the enfranchisement of blacks in the northern and border states—was clearly understood, stated, and believed by the politicians, the press, and the people during the time when the amendment was framed and then considered by the state legislatures. As the abolitionist organ, the *National Anti-Slavery Standard*, declared, "evenly as parties are now divided in the North, it needs but the final ratification of the pending Fifteenth Amendment, to assure . . . the balance of power in national affairs." A black newspaper, the Washington *New National Era*, predicted the same for the border states. Indeed, most newspapers both in the North and in the South during 1869 and 1870 unequivocally, incontrovertibly, and repeatedly spoke of the Republican objective of ensuring party hegemony by means of the Fifteenth Amendment. Moreover, congressmen and state legisla-

tors, in arguing for passage and ratification, referred again and again to the partisan need for those votes. The southern black, already a voter, was not irrelevant; an important secondary purpose of the amendment was to assure the continuance of black suffrage in the South by forbidding racial discrimination as to the franchise in a virtually unrepealable amendment to the federal Constitution. Still, the anticipated importance of the black electorate in the North and in the borderland was clearly the overriding concern.

To be sure, the political motives of many Republican politicians were not incompatible with a sincere moral concern. The idealistic motive reinforced the pragmatic one: there was no conflict at the outset between the ideal and the practical or between the interests of the black electorate and those of the Republican party. A radical Republican congressman declared, "party expediency and exact justice coincide for once." A black clergyman from Pittsburgh observed that "the Republican Party had done the negro good but they were doing themselves good at the same time." Indeed, the amendment as framed was both bold and prudent: bold in enfranchising blacks despite concerted opposition and in ordering change by establishing constitutional guidelines; prudent in adapting methods to circumstances so that the amendment would not only pass Congress but also be ratified by the states.

Although the struggle over ratification lasted only thirteen months, it was hard going and the outcome was uncertain until the very end. To be sure, ratification was easy in safe Republican territory (New England and most of the Middle West) and in the South where Republican legislators did their duty. But the fight was especially close in the Middle Atlantic states and in Indiana and Ohio, where the parties were competitive and a black electorate had the potential for deciding victory or defeat. In the Democratic border states and on the Pacific Coast, where racial feeling ran high, Republicans feared that pushing the amendment would lose them votes; so they refrained from pressing for ratification in these regions. Nevertheless, in clear-cut conflicts of interest between state and national Republican party organizations, the national party was everywhere victorious. Mutinies in Rhode Island and Georgia were suppressed. The amendment had the backing of the Grant administration, with its rich patronage. By endorsing the amendment in his inaugural address, Grant placed the indispensable prestige of the presidency behind it; he then went beyond pronouncements by swinging Nebraska to ratify it. Those Republican politicians who held or aspired to hold national office added the weight of their influence. As one Ohioan advised, "By hook or by crook you must get the 15th amendment through or we are gone up."

The Fifteenth Amendment became law on March 30,

1870. Republican euphoria followed the hard battle for ratification. Grant, in his message to Congress, wrote that the amendment "completes the greatest civil change and constitutes the most important event that has occurred since the nation came to life." Blacks everywhere celebrated; they regarded the Fifteenth Amendment as political salvation, as a solemn written guarantee that would never be abridged. They now felt secure, protected by both the vote and the "long strong arm of the Government." Whites believed that since the Negro was now a citizen and a voter, he could take care of himself. Antislavery societies throughout the country disbanded, now confident that equality before the law was sufficient and that in any event, "no power ever permanently wronged a voting class without its own consent." But subsequent events made a mockery of such predictions in the South where Democrats denied blacks the franchise for almost a century.

WILLIAM GILLETTE
(1986)

Bibliography

GILLETTE, WILLIAM (1979) 1981 *Retreat from Reconstruction, 1869–1879.* Baton Rouge: Louisiana State University Press.
——— (1965) 1969 *The Right to Vote: Politics and the Passage of the Fifteenth Amendment.* Baltimore: Johns Hopkins University Press.
MITTRICK, ROBERT 1985 *A History of Negro Voting in Pennsylvania during the Nineteenth Century.* Unpublished Ph.D. dissertation, Rutgers University, chap. 5.

FIFTEENTH AMENDMENT
(Judicial Interpretation)

The judicial interpretation of the Fifteenth Amendment has been closely intertwined with that of the FOURTEENTH AMENDMENT, largely in a Southern context. Within a year of ratification (1870) Congress passed three FORCE ACTS forbidding both public and private interference with voting on the basis of race or color. Federal officials tried hard at first to enforce these laws, but they were daunted by hostility in the South and growing indifference in Congress and the Supreme Court. Prosecutions dropped sharply in 1874; RECONSTRUCTION ended in 1877; the Jim Crow era of systematic SEGREGATION began around 1890; and the conspiracy provisions of the Force Acts were dropped in 1894.

From Reconstruction to WORLD WAR I the Supreme Court showed more ingenuity in voiding VOTING RIGHTS actions than in upholding them. Although it was willing, under Article I, section 4, to uphold convictions and damage awards for ballot box fraud in federal elections, as in EX PARTE YARBROUGH (1884), it would not allow INDICTMENTS for conspiracy to bribe, even in federal elections as in JAMES V. BOWMAN (1903). It steadfastly refused to uphold convictions for private interference with voting rights in state or local elections in UNITED STATES V. REESE (1875) and UNITED STATES V. CRUIKSHANK (1876), or to uphold civil actions for a state official's refusal to register blacks, in *Giles v. Teasley* (1904).

The Court did shrug off arguments in *Myers v. Anderson* (1915) that the Fifteenth Amendment was itself void for diluting the votes of enfranchised whites and thereby depriving their states of equal suffrage in the Senate without their consent. But it did almost nothing to thwart the new franchise restrictions of the Jim Crow era—literacy, property, POLL TAX, residence, character, and understanding tests—designed to cull black and upcountry white voters. (See WILLIAMS V. MISSISSIPPI.) Only in GUINN V. UNITED STATES (1915) did it strike down a GRANDFATHER CLAUSE exempting descendants of 1867 voters from Oklahoma's LITERACY TEST—without, however, striking down the test itself. *Guinn* had no practical impact on voting registration, but it was important for serving notice that the Fifteenth Amendment bars subtle as well as blatant discrimination.

The Court moved against white PRIMARY ELECTIONS with more deliberation than speed. Party primary elections emerged in response to the regional party monopolies, Republican in the North, Democratic in the South, which followed the "realigning" election of 1896. By World War I, primaries were universal. The dominant party's nomination became the choice that counted, and general elections merely rubber-stamped the dominant party's nominee. This trend was earliest and most pronounced in the South. It weakened party discipline, lowered turnout drastically in general elections, strengthened the dominance of plantation whites, and froze out blacks almost completely.

Blacks challenged this exclusion in a famous series of Texas cases. In NIXON V. HERNDON (1927) and NIXON V. CONDON (1932) NAACP attorneys successfully attacked statutes barring blacks, and letting the parties bar blacks, from voting in primary elections. Counsel for both sides in *Herndon* argued the Fifteenth Amendment, but Justice OLIVER WENDELL HOLMES, speaking for a unanimous Court, found the statute instead a "direct and obvious infringement of the Fourteenth." The Court followed this precedent in *Condon.*

In attacking the discriminatory law under the Fourteenth, rather than the denial of a voting right under the Fifteenth, the Court ignored its earlier view that the pertinent section of the Fourteenth was not intended to protect voting rights. (See MINOR V. HAPPERSETT.) It also left

Texas free to repeal the *Condon* statute, while permitting the Democrats to exclude blacks legally through their own "private" action. (See GROVEY V. TOWNSEND.)

The Court returned to the Fifteenth Amendment to overrule *Grovey* in SMITH V. ALLWRIGHT (1944), finding STATE ACTION in laws governing the timing and conduct of primary elections and by the "fusing [in UNITED STATES V. CLASSIC (1941)] of primary and general elections into a single instrumentality for the choice of officers." Later, in TERRY V. ADAMS (1953), the Court extended this concept of "fusion into a single instrumentality" to invalidate a whites-only "preprimary" election used by the Jaybird party since 1889 to capture Democratic nominations in a Texas county.

Without the white primary, segregationist whites had only franchise restrictions to block black votes. These restrictions had reduced black registrations by a third in the nineteenth century, but they had only limited and temporary effect by the 1950s. Black literacy was up, and only three of the eleven Southern states—Alabama, Mississippi, and Louisiana—retained blatantly discriminatory literacy tests. These the Court struck down, along with nondiscriminatory tests where blacks had been segregated in inferior schools.

Congress greatly aided in expanding the black vote with jucidial protection in the CIVIL RIGHTS ACTS of 1957, 1960, and 1964, and especially with the VOTING RIGHTS ACT OF 1965, which authorized suspension of state literacy and character tests and provision of federal examiners to register blacks where discrimination was found. In 1970, congress wholly forbade literacy tests as a condition on voting in state elections.

Though the Court took almost seventy-five years to give the Fifteenth Amendment much practical effect, its interventions since World War II have greatly changed both the constitutional and political landscapes. *Smith v. Allwright*, with its broad reading of the Fifteenth Amendment looking through form to substance foreshadowed such great Fourteenth Amendment cases as SHELLEY V. KRAEMER (1948) and BROWN V. BOARD OF EDUCATION (1954). GOMILLION V. LIGHTFOOT (1960), which struck down a racial GERRYMANDER under the Fifteenth Amendment, was a bridge to BAKER V. CARR (1962).

Opening the primaries and the franchise to blacks brought them out of political exile. Black registration in the South, only five percent in 1940, grew to twenty-eight percent in 1960 and sixty-three percent in 1976, narrowing the gap between black and white registrations from forty-four percent to five percent. Black elected officials in the South increased from fewer than 100 to more than 1,000. White politicians stopped waving ax handles, standing in the doorways of segregated schools, and using terms like "burrhead" in public debate. The Court's enforcement of the Fifteenth Amendment may properly be described as late, but not little.

WARD E. Y. ELLIOTT
(1986)

Bibliography
ELLIOTT, WARD E. Y. 1975 *The Rise of Guardian Democracy: The Supreme Court's Role in Voting Rights Disputes, 1845–1969.* Cambridge, Mass.: Harvard University Press.
KEY, V. O., JR. 1949 *Southern Politics.* New York: Knopf.
KOUSSER, J. MORGAN 1974 *The Shaping of Southern Politics: Suffrage Restriction and the Establishment of the One-Party South, 1880–1910.* New Haven, Conn.: Yale University Press.
LAWSON, STEVEN F. 1976 *Black Ballots: Voting Rights in the South, 1944–1969.* New York: Columbia University Press.

FIFTH AMENDMENT

See: Double Jeopardy; Due Process of Law; Grand Jury; Right Against Self-Incrimination; Taking of Property

FIGHTING WORDS

In CHAPLINSKY V. NEW HAMPSHIRE (1942) the Supreme Court upheld the conviction of a Jehovah's Witness who called a policeman "a God damned racketeer" and "a damned Fascist," holding that "fighting words"—face-to-face words plainly likely to provoke the average addressee to fight—were not protected by constitutional free speech guarantees. Viewed narrowly, the fighting words doctrine can be seen as a per se rule effectuating the CLEAR AND PRESENT DANGER principle, relieving the government of proving an actual INCITEMENT by taking the words themselves as decisive. Taken broadly, *Chaplinsky* strips "four-letter words" of free speech protection. "It has been well observed," Justice FRANK MURPHY said, "that such utterances are no essential part of any exposition of ideas, and are of such slight social value as a step to the truth that any benefit that may be derived from them is clearly outweighed by the social interest in order and morality."

The modern tendency of the Court has been to extend partial FIRST AMENDMENT protection to even the "excluded" areas of speech. To the extent that *Chaplinsky* refuses protection to four-letter words because they offend against taste or morality, it has been limited by recent decisions such as COHEN V. CALIFORNIA (1971), *Gooding v. Wilson* (1972), and *Rosenfeld v. New Jersey* (1972). The Justices appear to have been engaging in ad hoc analysis of what persons in what situations are entitled to a measure of protection from the shock to their sensibilities generated by words that, in the language of *Chaplinsky*, "by their very utterances inflict injury."

The shock aspect of four-letter words is obviously related to the shock element in OBSCENITY. In FCC V. PACIFICA FOUNDATION (1978) the Court upheld FCC regulation of "indecent" broadcasting that involved "patently offensive" four-letter words but was not obscene. While admitting that the words in question would warrant constitutional protection under certain circumstances, the Court held that in view of their capacity to offend, their slight social value in the conveying of ideas, and the intrusive character of speech broadcast into the home, their repeated use might constitutionally be banned at least in time slots and programming contexts when children might be listening.

The recent decisions suggest that outside the direct incitement to violence context the Court is prepared to balance PRIVACY against speech interests where four-letter words are at issue. Where statutes go beyond prohibiting incitement to violence, and also bar cursing or reviling, or using opprobrious, indecent, lascivious, or offensive language, they are likely to be held unconstitutionally vague or overbroad. (See *Lewis v. New Orleans*, 1974.)

MARTIN SHAPIRO
(1986)

(SEE ALSO: *Balancing Test; Freedom of Speech.*)

Bibliography

KONVITZ, MILTON 1978 *Fundamental Liberties of a Free People.* Chap. 17. Westport, Conn.: Greenwood Press.
SHEA, THOMAS 1975 Fighting Words and the First Amendment. *Kentucky Law Journal* 63:1–22.

FILIBUSTER

A filibuster is the strategic use of delay to block LEGISLATION, to force an amendment, or to prompt other action by the U.S. SENATE. Filibusters occur in the Senate, but not in the U.S. HOUSE OF REPRESENTATIVES, because only the Senate allows unlimited debate on any measure, and no motion exists by which a simple majority of senators can bring any debatable measure to a vote. The only way the Senate can vote on any matter subject to filibuster over the objection of even a single senator is to obtain CLOTURE (an end of debate) under Senate Rule XXII, which requires the votes of 60 senators.

Contrary to popular belief, a filibuster today is seldom conducted through actual extended speech on the Senate floor, but is accomplished rather by a senator threatening to speak indefinitely if a matter is brought before the Senate for a vote. Consequently, a filibuster occurs when senators credibly threaten the Senate leadership that they possess the requisite 41 votes to block cloture under Rule XXII. The widespread use of filibuster threats has effectively increased the number of votes it takes to enact controversial legislation from 51 (or 50 plus the Vice-President's vote) to 60. A majority of senators cannot change this because any revision of Rule XXII requires a vote of two-thirds of the Senate.

The conventional objection to the filibuster is that it is antimajoritarian and thus antidemocratic. The supermajority requirement of Rule XXII, however, is not alone among Senate procedures that are antimajoritarian. Notably, Senate rules empower committees to determine the content of proposed legislation and to decide whether legislation reaches the floor for a vote. Over the years, committees have exercised their power to block or divert action favored by majorities of the House and Senate. The filibuster may counteract the antimajoritarian aspects of the committee system by enabling individual senators to block legislation favored by a committee or to force changes rejected by a committee. Thus, the filibuster may work not so much against majority rule as against other forms of minority power.

The attacks on the constitutionality of the filibuster nonetheless focus on its antimajoritarian character. The Constitution is silent on the topic of filibusters; it neither authorizes nor prohibits them. There are two aspects of the filibuster rule that may be unconstitutional: one is that it requires a supermajority to enact legislation; the second is that a supermajority is required to change the voting rules. As to the first, the strongest arguments against the constitutionality of filibuster are textual. The Constitution specifically requires a supermajority vote in only seven situations. This enumeration of the instances where a supermajority was required suggests that the Framers assumed that a simple majority vote in each house would suffice for all other congressional action. Other constitutional provisions support the argument that the constitution makes a majority vote sufficient for action in the Senate. For instance, the provision specifying that a two-thirds vote can override a presidential VETO of legislation suggests that the Framers assumed that a majority vote would be sufficient for action by the Senate.

The problem with this textual argument is that the Constitution explicitly grants the Senate the power to determine its own rules and procedures. The list of instances in which the Constitution specifies that a supermajority is required does not compel the Senate to act by majority vote at all other times. Rather, the Senate is free to adopt its own rules for voting on all other matters.

The stronger argument against the constitutionality of the Senate rules regarding the filibuster lies in the supermajority requirement for changing Rule XXII. Senators can filibuster efforts to amend the Senate rules and Rule XXII requires agreement of two-thirds of those present and voting to obtain cloture on any motion to amend the rules. The Senate that adopted Rule XXII attempted to restrict the ability of all future Senates to change it. The entrenchment of the filibuster violates a fundamental constitutional principle that one legislature cannot bind a subsequent one. The popular sovereignty and legislative accountability upon which American democracy is premised are frustrated when one session of the legislature can prevent or limit action by future sessions, thus preventing the people's elected representatives from enacting laws favored by their constituents.

CATHERINE L. FISK
ERWIN CHEMERINSKY
(2000)

(SEE ALSO: *Supermajority Rules.*)

Bibliography

EULE, JULIAN N. 1987 Temporal Limits on the Legislative Mandate: Entrenchment and Retroactivity. *American Bar Foundation Research Journal* 1987:379–459.

FISK, CATHERINE and CHEMERINSKY, ERWIN 1997 The Filibuster. *Stanford Law Review* 49:181–254.

MCGINNIS, JOHN O. and RAPPAPORT, MICHAEL B. 1995 The Constitutionality of Legislative Supermajority Requirements: A Defense. *Yale Law Journal* 105:483–511.

FILLMORE, MILLARD
(1800–1874)

A Buffalo, New York, lawyer and WHIG politician, Millard Fillmore was elected vice-president in 1848 and became President when ZACHARY TAYLOR died in 1850. Unlike Taylor, Fillmore enthusiastically supported passage of the COMPROMISE OF 1850 which he believed necessary to preserve the Union. His administration was particularly vigorous in enforcing the Fugitive Slave Law through the Christiana Treason Trials, and prosecutions of those involved in the Shadrach Rescue, the Jerry Rescue, and the abortive Sims Rescue. Fillmore was not renominated by the Whigs in 1852 and ran unsuccessfully as a Know-Nothing in 1856.

PAUL FINKELMAN
(1986)

Bibliography

RAYBACK, ROBERT J. 1959 *Millard Fillmore: Biography of a President.* Buffalo, N.Y.: Buffalo Historical Society.

FINAL JUDGMENT RULE

By congressional statute the federal courts of appeals are permitted, in the usual case, to exercise their APPELLATE JURISDICTION only over final judgments of the district courts. An additional provision authorizes review of district court orders granting, denying, or otherwise dealing with INJUNCTIONS, and of certain other INTERLOCUTORY orders less frequently given. Furthermore, a district judge may certify an interlocutory order for review by the court of appeals, and that court can, in its discretion, review such a nonfinal order. The Supreme Court's appellate jurisdiction over cases coming from the state courts also is limited to final judgments of those courts. (The Supreme Court is not limited by this final judgment rule in hearing cases coming to it from a federal court of appeals; it can grant CERTIORARI in any case "in" the court of appeals.)

The final judgment rule, which aims at avoiding piecemeal appellate review, has so many judge-made exceptions that it has aptly been called "a permeable screen." Thus, a "collateral" order, unrelated to the merits of the case, may be reviewed if it presents an issue that might never be decided if the final judgment rule were strictly applied. Similarly, if rigorous application of the rule would do irreparable injury to some important federal policy, the Supreme Court has held that a nonfinal order can be reviewed. And in UNITED STATES V. NIXON (1974) the Court permitted review of a nonfinal order of a district court ordering the President of the United States to turn over the "Watergate tapes," in order to avoid putting the President to the "unseemly" choice between obeying the order and refusing and being cited for contempt. It is hard to avoid the conclusion that the final judgment "rule" has been made into a technique for allowing review of those interlocutory orders the Supreme Court thinks should be reviewed even though they are not final.

KENNETH L. KARST
(1986)

Bibliography

WRIGHT, CHARLES ALAN 1983 *The Law of Federal Courts*, 4th ed. Pages 697–717, 739–743. St. Paul, Minn.: West Publishing Co.

FIREFIGHTERS LOCAL UNION NO. 1784 v. STOTTS
467 U.S. 561 (1984)

The City of Memphis, Tennessee, laid off white firefighters with more seniority to protect the positions of less senior blacks who had been employed under a "race conscious" AFFIRMATIVE ACTION plan. The white firefighters sued, alleging that their seniority rights were explicitly protected by the CIVIL RIGHTS ACT OF 1964.

Justice BYRON R. WHITE, writing for the Supreme Court's majority, agreed, noting that "mere membership in the disadvantaged class is insufficient to warrant a seniority award; each individual must prove that the discriminatory practice had an impact on him." White thus affirmed the proposition, which is explicit from the plain language of Title VII, that rights vest in the individual and not in the racial class, and that this fact demands a close fit between injuries and remedies. White's opinion raises some doubt about the power of courts to fashion classwide remedies where, as in race-conscious affirmative action plans, benefited individuals are not required to demonstrate individual injury. This case signals an important move toward the restoration of the principle that rests at the core of liberal jurisprudence—that rights adhere to the individual, and not to the racial class that one happens to inhabit.

EDWARD J. ERLER
(1986)

FIRST AMENDMENT

The First Amendment today protects the overlapping realms of the spirit—of belief, emotion, and reason—and of political activity against intrusion by government. The amendment directly forbids federal violation of the individual's RELIGIOUS LIBERTY, freedom of expression, FREEDOM OF ASSEMBLY, and associated political liberties. The amendment indirectly forbids state violation because it is held to be incorporated into the FOURTEENTH AMENDMENT's restrictions upon the powers of the states. The body of law presently defining First Amendment liberties has been shaped not so much by the words or intent of the original sponsors as by the actors and events of much later history. The story is one of the continual expansion of individual freedom of expression, of the FREEDOM OF THE PRESS, and, until 1980, of widening SEPARATION OF CHURCH AND STATE.

The CONSTITUTIONAL CONVENTION OF 1787 saw no need to include guarantees of religious liberty, FREEDOM OF SPEECH, or other human rights. Most of the Framers believed in some such rights but supposed that the powers proposed for the new federal government were so severely limited by specific enumeration as to leave scant opportunity for either Congress or President to threaten individual liberty. The threats would come from state law and state governments. For protection against these, the Framers looked to the constitutions of the individual states. In the struggle for RATIFICATION OF THE CONSTITUTION, however, those who feared abuse of federal power exacted an undertaking that if the proposed Constitution were ratified by the states, the first Congress would be asked to propose amendments constituting a BILL OF RIGHTS. The First Amendment is thus the first and most far-reaching of the ten articles of amendment submitted by JAMES MADISON, proposed by Congress, and ratified by three-quarters of the states in 1791 solely as restrictions upon the new federal government, the powers of which were already severely limited.

The assumption that the amendment would have only a narrow function made it possible to ignore fundamental differences that would produce deep divisions more than a century later, after the amendment had been extended to the several states. The colonists held a variety of religious beliefs, though nearly all were Christian and a majority were Protestant. Whatever the limits of their tolerance back home in their respective states where one church was often dominant, they had reason to understand that the coherence of the federal union could be fixed only if the new federal government were required to respect the free exercise of religion. The men of South Carolina with their state-established religion and of Massachusetts with religion appurtenant to their state government could therefore support a prohibition against any *federal* ESTABLISHMENT OF RELIGION shoulder to shoulder with the deist THOMAS JEFFERSON and other eighteenth-century rationalists who opposed any link between church and state. Similarly, in applying ROGER WILLIAMS's vision of "the hedge or wall of separation between the garden of the church and the wilderness of the world," there was originally no need to choose between his concept of protection for the church against the encroachments of worldly society and Jefferson's concept of protection for the state against the encroachments of religion.

The conditions and political assumptions of 1791 also made it easy to guarantee "the freedom of speech or of the press" without accepting or rejecting the Blackstonian view that these guarantees bar only licensing and other previous restraints upon publication, leaving the government free to punish SEDITIOUS LIBELS and like unlawful utterances. Because the original amendment left the states unhampered in making and applying the general body of civil and criminal law, except as the people of each state might put restrictions into its own constitution, there was no need to consider how the First Amendment would affect the law of LIBEL and slander, the power of the judges to punish CONTEMPT of court, or the operation of laws punishing words and demonstrations carrying a threat to the public peace, order, or morality. Such questions could and would arise only after the First Amendment was extended to the states.

The fulcrum for extending the First Amendment to the states was set in place in 1868 by the adoption of the Fourteenth Amendment, which provides in part: ". . . nor shall any State deprive any person of life, liberty or property without DUE PROCESS OF LAW."

The effects of the new amendment upon religious and political liberty and upon freedom of expression were slow to develop. As late as 1922 the Court declared in *Pruden-*

tial Insurance Co. v. Cheek that "neither the Fourteenth Amendment nor any other provision of the Constitution of the United States imposes upon the States any restrictions about "freedom of speech." Within another decade, however, the First Amendment's guarantee of freedom of expression had been incorporated into the Fourteenth by judicial interpretation. INCORPORATION of the other clauses, including the prohibition against laws "respecting an establishment of religion," followed somewhat later. Today the First Amendment restricts both state and federal governments to the same extent and in the same fashion.

Yet the historic sequence is important. Many questions of First Amendment law cannot be resolved truly in terms of the original intention because the questions could not arise while the original assumption held. Resolution of the issues was thus postponed until the middle decades of the twentieth century, an era in which liberalism, secularism, and individualism dominated American jurisprudence.

Disparate strains of thought were merged even in the writing of the First Amendment. Subsequent events, including current controversies, have poured new meaning into the words, yet the juxtaposition of the key phrases still tells a good deal about the chief strains in the philosophy underpinning and binding together guarantees of several particular rights.

The Framers put first the prohibition against any law "respecting an establishment of religion or prohibiting the free exercise thereof." The sequence attests the primacy ascribed to religion. The colonists belonged to diverse churches. Many had fled to the New World to escape religious oppression. Rigid though some might be in their own orthodoxy, probably a majority rejected the imposition of belief or the use of government to stamp out heresy. Certainly, they rejected use of federal power.

It was natural for the authors of the amendment to link "the freedom of speech, or of the press" with freedom of religious belief and worship. The one church was breaking up in late sixteenth- and seventeenth-century Britain. New faiths were emerging based upon individual study of the Holy Word. The man or woman who has discovered the road to salvation has a need, even feels a duty, to bring the gospel to others. Liberty of expression benefits more than the speaker. Suppression would deny the opportunity to hear and read the word of God, and thus to discover the road to salvation. Modern legal analysis recognizes the importance of the hearers' and readers' access to information and ideas in cases in which the author's interest lacks constitutional standing or would, if alone involved, be subject to regulation. (See LISTENERS' RIGHTS.)

Concern for a broader spiritual liberty expanded from the religious core. The thinking man or woman, the man or woman of feeling, the novelist, the poet or dramatist, and the artist, like the evangelist, can experience no greater affront to his or her humanity than denial of freedom of expression. The hearer and reader suffer violation of their spiritual liberty if they are denied access to the ideas of others. The denial thwarts the development of the human potential, the power and responsibility of choice. Although concerned chiefly with religion, JOHN MILTON stated the broader concern in *Areopagitica* (1644), the single most influential plea, known to the Framers, for unlicensed access to the printing press.

The Enlightenment gave the argument a broader, more rationalistic flavor. Thomas Jefferson and other children of the Enlightenment believed above all else in the power of reason, in the search for truth, in progress, and in the ultimate perfectibility of man. Freedom of inquiry and liberty of expression were deemed essential to the discovery and spread of truth, for only by the endless testing of debate could error be exposed, truth emerge, and men enjoy the opportunities for human progress.

After JOHN STUART MILL one should perhaps speak only of the ability to progress *toward truth*, and of the value of the process of searching. The compleat liberal posits that he has not reached, and probably can never reach, the ultimate truth. He hopes by constant search—by constant open debate, by trial and error—to do a little better. Meanwhile he supposes that the process of searching has inestimable value because the lessons of the search—the readiness to learn, the striving to understand the minds and hearts and needs of other men, the effort to weigh their interests with his own—exemplify the only foundation upon which men can live and grow together.

It was not chance that America's most eloquent spokesman for freedom of speech, OLIVER WENDELL HOLMES, was also a profound skeptic. Dissenting in ABRAMS V. UNITED STATES (1919), he wrote:

> When men have realized that time has upset many fighting faiths, they may come to believe even more than they believe the very foundations of their own conduct that the ultimate good desired is better reached by free trade in ideas—that the best test of truth is the power of the thought to get itself accepted in the competition of the market, and that truth is the only ground upon which their wishes safely can be carried out. That at any rate is the theory of our Constitution.

On the far side of the First Amendment's guarantee of freedom of speech and of the press one finds the political rights "peaceably to assemble, and to petition the Government for a redress of grievances." (See FREEDOM OF PETITION; FREEDOM OF ASSEMBLY AND ASSOCIATION.) The juxtaposition recalls that freedom of speech and of the press have a political as well as a spiritual foundation; and that the First Amendment protects political activity as part of and in addition to the world of the spirit. American thought, especially in Supreme Court opinions, puts the greater emphasis on the political function of free expression. In *Garrison v. Louisiana* (1964), for example, the Court explained that "speech is more than self-expression; it is the essence of self-government." ALEXANDER MEIKLE-JOHN, perhaps the foremost American philosopher of freedom of expression, argued that whereas other constitutional guarantees are restrictions protecting the citizens against abuse of the powers delegated to government, the guarantees of freedom of speech and of the press hold an absolute, preferred position because they are measures adopted by the people as the ultimate rulers in order to retain control over the government, the people's legislative and executive agents. James Madison, the author of the First Amendment, expressed a similar thought in a speech in 1794. "If we advert to the nature of Republican Government, we shall find that the censorial power is in the people over the Government, and not in the Government over the people."

Despite the eloquence of Justice Holmes, most of us reject the notion that the ability of an idea to get itself accepted in free competition is the best test of its truth. Some propositions seem true or false beyond rational debate. Some false and harmful, political and religious doctrines gain wide public acceptance. Adolf Hitler's brutal theory of a "master race" is sufficient example. We tolerate such foolish and sometimes dangerous appeals not because they may prove true but because freedom of speech is indivisible. The liberty cannot be denied to some persons and extended to others. It cannot be denied to some ideas and saved for others. The reason is plain enough: no man, no committee, and surely no government, has the infinite wisdom and disinterestedness accurately and unselfishly to separate what is true from what is debatable, and both from what is false. To license one to impose his truth upon dissenters is to give the same license to all others who have, but fear to lose, power. The judgment that the risks of suppression are greater than the harm done by bad ideas rests upon faith in the ultimate good sense and decency of free people.

Constitutional law has been remarkably faithful to this philosophy in dealing with both religious and political ideas. In the prosecution of the leader of a strange religious cult for obtaining money by false pretenses, as in UNITED STATES V. BALLARD (1963), the truth or falsity of the leader's claims of miraculous religious experiences is legally irrelevant; conviction depends upon proof that the defendant did not believe his own pretenses. Similarly, although distaste for political ideology may have influenced some of the decisions in the 1920s affirming the convictions of anarchists and communists for advocacy of the overthrow of the government by force and violence, the social, political, or religious activists seeking changes

that frighten or annoy all "right-minded" people receive wide protection in their resort to the SIT-INS, PICKETING, marches, mass demonstrations, coarse expletives, affronts to personal and public sensibilities, and other unorthodox vehicles that are so often their most effective means of expression. Such methods of expression may prejudice opposing public and private interests because of the time, place, or manner of communication, regardless of the content of the message; therefore, the amendment allows regulation of particular forms of expression, or of expression at a particular time or place, regardless of content, provided that the restriction protects important interests that cannot be secured by less restrictive means. The courts have typically scrutinized such restrictions, however, with an eye zealous to condemn as unconstitutional any statute or ordinance ostensibly designed to protect the public peace and order but phrased in such loose words as either to deter constitutionally protected expression or to invite discrimination by police, public prosecutors, or judges against radical "troublemakers" and other unpopular minorities. Thus, the American Nazis were secured the right to parade in uniform with swastikas in an overwhelmingly Jewish community many of whose residents had fled the Holocaust.

Distrust of official evaluation of the worth of ideas may also lie behind the decisions barring regulation of political debate in the interest of "fairness" or equality of opportunity. In BUCKLEY V. VALEO (1976), holding that the freedom of speech clause bars laws restricting the dollars that may be spent in a political campaign, the Court observed: "The concept that government may restrict the speech of some elements of our society in order to enhance the relative voice of others is wholly foreign to the First Amendment." Similarly, in MIAMI HERALD V. TORNILLO (1974) the Court held a state law granting a political candidate a right of space in which to reply to a newspaper's attacks upon his or her record to be unconstitutional interference with the editorial freedom of the newspaper. Only in the area of BROADCASTING has the Court thus far recognized that realization of the ideal of free competition of ideas may be irreconcilable with total freedom from regulation in an era in which the public's chief sources of ideas and information are expensive media of mass communication, which are often under monopolistic control. Federal statutes and regulations subject radio and television broadcasters to loosely defined duties to present public issues fairly and to give a degree of access to political candidates and parties.

Although only deliberately false religious or political representations fall wholly outside the First Amendment, the law is more willing to try to separate the worthless from the valuable in the field of literature and the arts. The amendment gives no protection to "obscene" publications. For many years the definition of OBSCENITY was broad enough to cover works containing individual words or short passages that would tend to excite lustful thoughts in a particularly susceptible person. This standard condemned *Lady Chatterley's Lover, An American Tragedy,* and *Black Boy.* From 1930 to 1973 the legal definition of obscenity was gradually narrowed so tightly that many jurists concluded that the First Amendment would protect the most prurient of matter unless it was "utterly without redeeming social value." After 1973 changes in the composition of the Court led to a somewhat less permissive formulation. A work is obscene if a person applying contemporary community standards would find that it appeals to the prurient interest; if it represents or describes ultimate sexual acts, excretory functions, or the genitals in a patently lewd or offensive manner; and if it lacks serious literary, artistic, political, or scientific value. YOUNG V. AMERICAN MINI THEATRES (1976) suggests that explicitly sexual books and motion pictures, even when not obscene, may be regulated as to the places and perhaps the time and manner of their distribution in ways that are forbidden for other materials.

These exceptions from the principle that bars any branch of government, including the judiciary, from judging the value of ideas and sensations seem attributable partly to the emphasis that American law puts upon the political values of the First Amendment, partly to the diminishing but still traditional concern of government for public morals, and partly to the actual or supposed links between producers and distributors of commercial pornography and the criminal underworld.

So long as one is dealing with beliefs and expressions separable from conduct harmful to other individuals or the community, the essential unity of the philosophical core of the First Amendment makes it unnecessary to distinguish for legal purposes among religious beliefs, political ideologies, and other equally sincere convictions. In upholding the First Amendment privilege of Jehovah's Witnesses to refuse to join other school children in a daily salute to the United States flag, the Court pointedly refrained from specifying whether the privilege arose under the free exercise clause or the guarantee of freedom of speech: ". . . compelling the flag salute and pledge . . . invades the sphere of intellect and spirit which it is the purpose of the First Amendment to reserve from all official control." (See FLAG SALUTE CASES.) Test oaths, like particular beliefs, cannot be required for holding public office or receiving public grants. In upholding the conviction of a Mormon for POLYGAMY in REYNOLDS V. UNITED STATES (1879), despite his plea that the free exercise clause protected him in obeying his religious duty, the Supreme Court sought to erect this distinction between the realm of ideas and the world of material action into a constitu-

tional principle: "Congress was deprived of all legislative power over mere opinion, but was left free to reach actions which were in violation of social duties or subversive of good order."

As the guarantees of the freedoms of speech and press and of free exercise of religion seek to bar hostile governmental intrusion from the realm of the spirit, so do modern interpretations of the establishment clause bar state sponsorship of, or material assistance to, religion. In the beginning religion and established churches were dominant forces in American life. Nearly all men and women were Christians; Protestants were predominant. In South Carolina the Constitution of 1778 declared the "Protestant religion to be the established religion of this State." Church and state were intertwined in Massachusetts. Where there was no official connection, both the laws and practices of government bore evidence of benevolent cooperation with the prevailing creeds. SUNDAY CLOSING LAWS were universal. Oaths were often required of state officials. Legislative sessions began with prayer. The crier in the United States Supreme Court still begins each session by invoking divine blessing. The coinage states, "In God We Trust." Church property was and remains exempt from taxation. As public education spread, prayers and Bible-reading became the first order of each school day.

These traditional links between church and state were challenged after incorporation of the First Amendment into the Fourteenth Amendment, not only by anticlerical secularists but also by religious minorities whose members were set apart by official involvement in religious practices and who were fearful that their isolation would hamper full assimilation into all aspects of American life and might stimulate INVIDIOUS DISCRIMINATION. The Supreme Court was then forced to choose among the competing strains of religious and political philosophy whose adherents had agreed only that the federal government, but not the States, should be barred from "an establishment of religion." The majority's inclination during the years 1945–1980 toward Jefferson's strongly secular, anticlerical view of the wall of separation between church and state led to two important lines of decision.

One line bars both state and federal governments from giving direct financial aid to sectarian primary and secondary schools even though the same or greater aid is given to the public schools maintained by government. The decisions leave somewhat greater latitude not only for aid to parents but also to include religious institutions in making grants for higher education. (See GOVERNMENT AID TO SECTARIAN INSTITUTIONS.)

The second important line of decisions required discontinuance of the widespread and traditional practice of starting each day in the public schools with some form of religious exercise, such as saying an ecumenical prayer or reading from the Bible. The latter decisions provoked such emotional controversy that in the 1980s, more than two decades after the decisions were rendered, fundamentalist groups were actively pressing for legislation abolishing the Supreme Court's JURISDICTION to enforce the establishment clause in cases involving school prayer, thus leaving interpretation of the clause to the vagaries of judges in individual states. (See RELIGION IN PUBLIC SCHOOLS.)

Even though the line between the realm of the spirit and the world of material conduct subject to government regulation is fundamental to the jurisprudence of the First Amendment, the simple line between belief and conduct drawn in the polygamy cases was too inflexible to survive as a complete constitutional formula. Religious duties too often conflict with the commands of civil authority. Conversely, the public has compelling interests in the world of conduct that sometimes cannot be secured without interference with the expression of ideas.

Two cases suggest the line limiting constitutional protection for religious disobedience to the commands of the state. In WISCONSIN V. YODER (1972) the Supreme Court held that the free exercise clause secured Amish parents the privilege of holding fourteen- and fifteen-year-old children out of high school contrary to a state compulsory attendance law but pursuant to their religious conviction that salvation requires simple life in a church community apart from the world and worldly influence. The Court's constitutional, judicial duty—the Court said—required balancing the importance of the interests served by the state law against the importance to believers of adherence to the religious practice in question. Striking such a balance, the Court held in *Negre v. Larsen* (1971) that a faithful Roman Catholic's belief that the "unjust" nature of the war in Vietnam required him to refuse to participate did not excuse his refusal to be inducted into the armed forces.

When belief is invoked to justify otherwise unlawful conduct, it may become significant that the First Amendment speaks of the free exercise of "religion," but not of other kinds of belief held with equal sincerity. In UNITED STATES V. SEEGER (1965) the Court skirted establishment clause questions by refusing to make any distinction between the teachings of religion and other moral convictions for the purposes of the Selective Service Act. That act exempted from military service CONSCIENTIOUS OBJECTORS opposed to war in any form by reason of their "religious training and belief" and defined such belief as one "in relation to a Supreme Being involving duties superior to those arising from any human relation." A majority held that, despite the references to religion and a belief in a Supreme Being, the exemption extended "to any belief that occupies a place in the life of its possessor parallel to

that filled by the orthodox belief in God of one who clearly qualifies for the exemption." In the *Yoder* case, on the other hand, the opinion of the Court by Chief Justice WARREN E. BURGER, calling upon the example of Henry D. Thoreau, stated that a "philosophical and personal" belief "does not rise to the demands of the Religion Clauses." Perhaps this declaration of orthodoxy puts an end to the question, but in an age of subjectivism it is likely to press for fuller debate and deliberation.

Where religious objectors seek exemption from laws of general application, both federal and state governments must walk a narrow line. On the one hand, the free execise clause may require exception. On the other hand, excepting religious groups from laws of general application may be an unconstitutional "establishment of religion." Here again the decisions call for ad hoc balancing of the individual and public interests affected by the particular legislative act.

The requirement of self-preservation exerts the strongest pressures upon government to violate the realm of the spirit by suppressing the publication of ideas and information. Here, as in other areas, judicial elaboration of the First Amendment has been increasingly favorable to freedom of expression.

The expansion of the freedom by interpretation began within a decade from ratification. WILLIAM BLACKSTONE had taught that the freedoms of speech and press were freedoms from PRIOR RESTRAINTS, such as licensing, and did not bar subsequent liability or punishment for unlawful words, including seditious libels. Dispute arose when Congress enacted a Sedition Act and the Federalist party then in office prosecuted the editors of journals supporting their political opponents, the Jeffersonian Republicans, for publishing false, scandalous, and malicious writings exciting the hatred of the people. (See ALIEN AND SEDITION ACTS.) Thomas Jefferson and James Madison led the attack upon the constitutionality of the Sedition Act by drafting the VIRGINIA AND KENTUCKY RESOLUTIONS declaring that the act violated the First Amendment. The lower federal courts followed the orthodox teaching of Blackstone, upheld the act, and convicted the Republican editors. Jefferson pardoned them after his election to the presidency. Still later, Congress appropriated funds to repay their fines. Events thus gave the speech and press clauses an interpretation extending the guarantees beyond mere prohibition of previous restraints. The Supreme Court subsequently ratified the teaching of history.

The modern law defining freedom of expression began to develop shortly after WORLD WAR I when pacifists and socialists who made speeches and published pamphlets urging refusal to submit to conscription for the armed forces were prosecuted for such offenses as willfully obstructing the recruiting or enlistment service of the United

States. In affirming the conviction in SCHENCK V. UNITED STATES (1919), Justice Holmes coined the famous CLEAR AND PRESENT DANGER test: "The question in every case is whether the words used are of such a nature as to create a clear and present danger that they will bring about the substantive evils that Congress has a right to prevent." When Justice Holmes wrote these words, they gave little protection to propaganda held subversive by dominant opinion. Speaking or circulating a paper, the Justice held, is not protected by the First Amendment if the "tendency" of the words and the intent with which they are uttered are to produce an unlawful act. Later, after Justice Holmes's sensitivity to the dangers of prosecution for words alone had been increased by the prosecution of tiny groups of anarchists and communists for holding meetings and distributing political pamphlets in time of peace, criticizing the government, and preaching its overthrow by force and violence, he and Justice LOUIS D. BRANDEIS in a series of dissenting opinions tightened their definition of "clear and present danger" and laid the emotional and philosophical foundation for the next generation's expansion of the First Amendment guarantees. Justice Brandeis's eloquent opinion in WHITNEY V. CALIFORNIA (1927) is illustrative:

> Those who won our independence by revolution were not cowards. They did not fear political liberty. To courageous, self-reliant men, with confidence in the power of free and fearless reasoning applied through the processes of popular government, no danger flowing from speech can be deemed clear and present, unless the incidence of the evil apprehended is so imminent that it may befall before there is opportunity for full discussion. If there be time to expose through discussion the falsehood and fallacies, to avert the evil by the processes of education, the remedy to be applied is more speech, not enforced silence. Only an emergency can justify repression. Such must be the rule if authority is to be reconciled with freedom. Such, in my opinion, is the command of the Constitution. It is, therefore, always open to Americans to challenge a law abridging free speech and assembly by showing that there was no emergency justifying it.
>
> Moreover, even imminent danger cannot justify resort to prohibition of these functions essential to effective democracy, unless the evil apprehended is relatively serious. . . . There must be the probability of serious injury to the state. Among freemen, the deterrents ordinarily to be applied to prevent crime are education and punishment for violations of the law, not abridgement of the rights of free speech and assembly.

In the 1920s a majority of the Justices consistently rejected the views expressed by Justices Holmes and Brandeis. GITLOW V. NEW YORK (1925) held that (1) a state, despite the First Amendment, may punish utterances inimical to the public welfare; (2) a legislative finding that a class of utterances is inimical to the public welfare will be accepted by the Court unless the finding is arbitrary or capricious; (3) the Court could not set aside as arbitrary or capricious a legislative finding that teaching the overthrow of the government by force or violence involves danger to the peace and security of the State because the spark of the utterance "may kindle a fire that, smoldering for a time, may burst into a sweeping and destructive conflagration"; and (4) the Court would not consider the kind or degree of evil threatened by a particular utterance if it fell within a class of utterances found by the legislature to be dangerous to the state.

Ironically, in the very years in which the Court was deferential to legislative restrictions upon radical political expression, the Court was going behind legislative judgment to invalidate minimum wage laws, the regulation of prices and other restrictions upon FREEDOM OF CONTRACT. Beginning in 1937, however, a philosophy of judicial self-restraint became dominant among the Justices. "We have returned to the original proposition that courts do not substitute their social and economic beliefs for the judgment of legislative bodies, who are elected to pass laws," the Court declared in FERGUSON V. SKRUPA (1963). (See JUDICIAL ACTIVISM AND JUDICIAL RESTRAINT.)

Such sweeping denigration of JUDICIAL REVIEW put civil libertarians in a dilemma. On the one hand, the need for consistency of institutional theory cautioned against activist judicial ventures even under the First Amendment. On the other hand, self-restraint would leave much CIVIL LIBERTY at the mercy of executive or legislative oppression. The only logical escape was to elevate civil liberties to a "preferred position" justifying standards of judicial review stricter than those used in judging economic regulations. The dissenting opinions by Justices Holmes and Brandeis seemed to point the way. Three rationales were offered:

(i) In a famous footnote in UNITED STATES V. CAROLENE PRODUCTS COMPANY (1938), Justice HARLAN FISKE STONE suggested that legislation restricting the dissemination of information or interfering with political activity "may be subject to more exacting judicial scrutiny . . . than most other types of legislation" where the legislation "restricts those political processes which can ordinarily be expected to bring about the repeal of undesirable legislation." The rationale fails to justify STRICT SCRUTINY in cases involving religious liberty, freedom of expression in literature, entertainment, and the arts, and other nonpolitical, personal liberties.

(ii) "Personal liberties" deserve more stringent protection than "property rights." The rationale does not explain why holding property is not a preferred "personal" liberty.

(iii) Stricter review is appropriate in applying the First Amendment, and the First when incorporated into the Fourteenth, because the guarantees of the First Amendment are more specific than the general constitutional prohibitions against deprivation of life, liberty, or property without due process of law. The difference in specificity is considerable, but its relevance is less obvious. Justice HUGO L. BLACK stood almost alone in the supposition that the language of the First Amendment could be read literally. (See ABSOLUTISM.) Perhaps the most that can be said is that the Bill of Rights marks particular spheres of human activity for which the Framers deemed it essential to provide judicially enforced protection against legislative and executive oppression. During the debate in Congress, James Madison observed: "If they [the Amendments] are incorporated into the Constitution, independent tribunals of justice will consider themselves in a peculiar manner the guardian of those rights; they will be an impenetrable bulwark against every assumption of power in the Legislative or Executive. . . ."

At bottom all the rationales assert that the ultimate protection for minorities, for spiritual liberty, and for freedom of expression, political activity, and other personal liberties comes rightfully from the judiciary. In this realm the political process, filled with arbitrary compromises and responsive, as in some degree it must be, to short-run pressures, is deemed inadequate to enforce the long-range enduring values that often bespeak a people's aspirations instead of merely reflecting their practices.

Propelled by this judicial philosophy, the Court greatly expanded the First Amendment guarantees of freedom of expression. The Court avowedly adopted the strict Holmes-Brandeis "clear and present danger" test for judging whether prosecution for a subversive utterance is justified by its proximity to activities the government has a right to prevent. The amendment bars restrictions upon the publication of information or ideas relating to public affairs because of harm which the government asserts will result from the impact of the message unless the government shows pressing necessity to avoid an immediate public disaster. The case of the Pentagon Papers (1971) illustrates the principle. (See NEW YORK TIMES V. UNITED STATES.) A consultant to the Department of Defense, cleared for access to classified information, gave copies of highly secret papers describing military operations and decision making to newspapers for publication. The Department of Justice upon instructions from the President asked the courts to enjoin publication, making strong representations that the risks of injury to national interests included "the death of the soldiers, the destruction of alliances, the greatly increased difficulty of negotiation with our enemies, the inability of our diplomats to negotiate . . . and the prolongation of the war." All the weight of these executive representations was insufficient to induce the Court to bar disclosure.

After 1940 the PREFERRED FREEDOMS theory coupled with the incorporation of the First Amendment into the Fourteenth led to Supreme Court review and invalidation or modification of many familiar state statutes and well-established COMMON LAW doctrines restricting or penalizing sundry forms of expression: libel and slander, contempt of court, obscenity, BREACH OF THE PEACE, and laws limiting access to the streets, parks, or other public places for the purposes of expression. A short reference to the law of contempt will illustrate the trend.

The interest in the impartial disposition of judicial business solely upon the evidence and arguments presented in court often conflicts with the interest in free discussion of public affairs. Newspaper editorials and like public pressures upon a judge may improperly influence or seem to influence the disposition of a pending judicial proceeding. In English and early American law such publications were enjoinable and punishable as contempt of court. Today the First Amendment is held to protect such expression. Similarly, the English law and some American decisions treated the pretrial publication of EVIDENCE as contempt of court where, as in a notorious criminal case, the publicity might reach actual or prospective jurors and serve to make it difficult to assure the accused a FAIR TRIAL and a jury verdict based solely upon the evidence presented in the court room. The Supreme Court has now set its face firmly against GAG ORDERS forbidding newspapers to print or broadcast or publicize confessions or other damaging evidence before their admissibility has been determined and they have been received in court.

The heavy emphasis that constitutional law puts upon the role of the First Amendment in the operation of representative government has led some commentators to ascribe special significance to the amendment's particular mention of "the freedom of the press" in addition to the more general guarantee of "the freedom of speech." In a crowded society, newspapers, radio, and television not only are the most effective vehicles for disseminating ideas and information but also have by far the best, if not the only, adequate resources for gathering information concerning the conduct of public affairs by the vast and omnipresent agencies of government. Starting from this premise, proponents of a "structural view" of the First Amendment argue that the special functions of the "fourth estate" entitle its members to special protection. Some of the claims to exemption from laws of general applicability have been patently excessive, such as the claims to exemption from antitrust laws, labor relations laws, and wage and hour regulation. With much greater force but scarcely greater success, the media have claimed that the First Amendment protects reporters in refusal to disclose their sources or give unpublished information to a court or GRAND JURY in compliance with the general testimonial obligation of all citizens. (See REPORTER'S PRIVILEGE.) On the other hand, the near-immunity from liability for libels upon public figures which the Court has granted to the press under the First Amendment has not yet been extended by that Court to other writers and publishers.

The words of the First Amendment move from religion to speech and press and then to the purely political rights of free assembly and petition for redress of grievances. Denials of the rights of assembly and petition have been infrequent. The express mention of a "right of the people peaceably to assemble" is also taken, however, to symbolize the much broader freedom of association that the amendment is held to secure.

The freedom of association thus far held to be protected by the First Amendment, while broad, is narrower than the freedom of individuals to associate themselves for all purposes in which they may be interested, the right debated by Thomas Hobbes and Jean-Jacques Rousseau, on one side, and, on the other side, by JOHN LOCKE. The enactment of labor relations acts securing employees the right to form, join, and assist labor unions made it unnecessary for workers to appeal to a constitutional right of freedom of association. Only the antitrust laws barring unreasonable restraints on competition impose substantial restrictions upon business combinations. In consequence, the decisional law treats association as a necessary and therefore protected incident of other First Amendment liberties: speech, political action, and religious purposes. Associations formed to provide legal services in litigation have been treated as "political" not only in the plausible instances of suits to establish civil liberties and CIVIL RIGHTS but also in the incongruous instances of actions for damages for personal injuries.

Legislative efforts to outlaw associations formed for religious or political purposes have been infrequent, except in the case of the Communist party. A decision in 1961 sustained the power of Congress to require the party to register and disclose its membership as a foreign-dominated organization dedicated to subversion of the government, but the sanctions directed at members, for example, denial of passports and employment in defense facilities, were held unconstitutional. Associations and their members have had more occasion to complain of coerced disclosure under disclosure laws and in LEGISLATIVE INVESTIGATIONS. Prima facie the First Amendment protects privacy of association. Governmentally compelled disclosure must be justified by a showing of important public purpose. Where the unpopularity of the association makes it likely that disclosure will result in reprisals, an even stronger justification may be required. Similarly, a state must justify by a strong public purpose any interference with the conduct of a religious organization's or political party's internal affairs.

Any pressure for substantial new growth in First Amendment interpretation will probably come in three areas. First, the amendment was intended and has nearly always been construed as a prohibition against active government interference. Today government has a near-monopoly upon much information essential to informed self-government. Although FREEDOM OF INFORMATION ACTS may at least partially satisfy the need, there is likely to be pressure to read into the First Amendment's explicit verbal barrier to abridgment affirmative governmental duties to provide access to official proceedings and even to supply otherwise inaccessible information in the government's possession.

Second, in the crowded modern world broadcasters, newspapers, and other media of mass communication dominate the dissemination of information and formation of public opinion. New technologies make prediction hazardous, but the concentration of control over the most influential media appears to be increasing. In this context the old assumption, that the widest dissemination of information and freest competition of ideas can be secured by forcing government to keep hands off, is open to doubt. Such questions as whether the First Amendment permits government regulation to secure fair access to the mass media and whether the amendment itself secures a right of access to media licensed by government may well multiply and intensify.

Third, the electoral influence of political advertising through the mass media, coupled with its high cost, gives great political power to the individuals and organizations that can raise and spend the largest sums of money in political campaigns. Even though decisions already rendered tend to accord political expenditures the same protection as speech, important future litigation over legislative power to limit the use and power of money in elections seems assured. (See CAMPAIGN FINANCING.)

The First Amendment secures the people of the United States greater freedom against governmental interference in the realms of the spirit, intellect, and political activity than exists in any other country. The future may bring shifts of boundary lines and emphasis. A threat to national survival could revive earlier restrictions. Generally speaking, however, the modern First Amendment appears to meet the nation's needs.

ARCHIBALD COX
(1986)

(SEE ALSO: *Children and the First Amendment.*)

Bibliography

ABERNATHY, GLENN 1961 *The Right of Assembly and Association.* Columbia: University of South Carolina Press.
CHAFEE, ZECHARIAH, JR. 1948 *Free Speech in the United States.* Cambridge, Mass.: Harvard University Press.

Cox, Archibald 1981 *Freedom of Speech in the Burger Court.* Cambridge, Mass.: Harvard University Press.

Emerson, Thomas I. 1970 *The System of Freedom of Expression.* New York: Random House.

Howe, Mark Dewolfe 1965 *The Garden and the Wilderness.* Chicago: University of Chicago Press.

Konvitz, Milton 1957 *Fundamental Liberties of a Free People: Religion, Speech, Press, Assembly.* Ithaca, N.Y.: Cornell University Press.

Levy, Leonard W. 1963 *Freedom of Speech and Press in Early American History: Legacy of Suppression.* New York: Harper & Row.

——— 1972 "No Establishment of Religion: The Original Understanding." Pages 169–224 in *Judgments: Essays in American Constitutional History.* Chicago: Quadrangle.

Meiklejohn, Alexander 1960 *Political Freedom: The Constitutional Powers of the People.* New York: Harper & Bros.

Pfeffer, Leo 1967 *Church, State, and Freedom.* Rev. ed. Boston: Beacon Press.

Stokes, Anson Phelps 1950 *Church and State in the United States.* 3 Vols. New York: Harper & Bros.

——— 1964 *Church and State in the United States.* Rev. ed., with Leo Pfeffer. New York: Harper & Row.

FIRST AMENDMENT
(Update 1)

Within the legal culture, the First Amendment is typically understood to protect from government abridgment a broad realm of what might be called "symbolic activity," including speech, religion, press, association, and assembly. Because these symbolic activities are intertwined with many other activities that the government is clearly empowered to regulate—for instance, education and economic relations—the courts have experienced considerable difficulty in distinguishing impermissible infringement on First Amendment freedoms from legitimate exercises of government authority. Much of Supreme Court doctrine in the First Amendment area is an attempt to develop and refine precisely this sort of distinction.

One dominant principle that has informed the Supreme Court's doctrinal development of this distinction is the principle of content neutrality. The principle of content neutrality suggests that government must be neutral as to the conceptual content of speech, religion, press, and symbolic activity in general. Hence, according to First Amendment doctrine, it is only in extreme circumstances and for the most important reasons that the Court will allow government to regulate symbolic activity because of its conceptual content. The converse of this judicial principle is that the Court will recognize a relatively broad governmental power to regulate symbolic activity because of its effects or its form. Putting these two principles side by side, the result is that content-based regulation is often found unconstitutional, whereas content-neutral regulation is often found to be constitutional. These two broad imperatives with their sharply divergent implications for case outcomes place great conceptual pressure on distinguishing the content-based from the content-neutral, or more specifically on distinguishing the conceptual or substantive content of symbolic activity from its form and effects.

Although there has been no shortage of attempts, both scholarly and judicial, to specify and refine the gist of this distinction, First Amendment doctrine remains relatively undeveloped and unstable in dealing with this recurrent tension. Indeed, the Supreme Court seems continually to shift the terrain for making the predicate determination of whether the government action is content-based or content-neutral. Often the Justices are divided on the question whether the critical content-neutrality determination should be made with respect to the express or apparent state interest, the underlying governmental intent or motivation, the statutory or regulatory description of the symbolic activity, the judicial description of the symbolic activities actually affected, or the judicial description of symbolic activities conceivably affected. Although the Supreme Court has fashioned numerous diverse and detailed doctrines to specify the appropriate grounds on which to make the content-neutrality determination, there is so much of this doctrine and it is so obviously overlapping that ample room remains for disagreement among the Justices, the advocates, and the commentators about how to characterize and hence decide particular First Amendment cases. The result is that in the 1980s the First Amendment—especially in the area of religion—has followed the FOURTH AMENDMENT in an entropic proliferation of fragmentary, ephemeral, and highly bureaucratized doctrine.

In consequence, it has become easy for Justices to find ample legal resources to disagree about whether some particular government action is content-neutral. The result is that a government action that is described as content-based by one group of Justices will often be characterized as effect-based or form-based by another group of Justices. Often the Justices will disagree about whether—and if so, to what extent—the conceptual content of a symbolic activity is divisible from its form or effects. In making determinations about whether some government action is content-neutral and in deciding to what extent the conceptual content of symbolic activity is distinguishable from its form, there is virtually no guiding Supreme Court doctrine. The result is that the importance of political ideology in the production of the legal conclusions of the Justices has become relatively transparent in the First Amendment area.

In *Texas v. Johnson* (1989), for instance, the Court overturned the conviction of a flag burner on the ground that the FLAG DESECRATION statute was aimed at suppressing speech on the basis of its content. Counsel for Texas had argued that the statute was aimed at preserving the flag as a symbol of nationhood and national unity. The majority concluded that this state interest was an instance of content-based suppression because it singled out for punishment those messages at odds with what Texas claimed to be the flag's meaning. For the majority, the state interest was intricately related to the content-based suppression of certain ideas. The dissent by Chief Justice WILLIAM H. REHNQUIST (joined by Justice BYRON R. WHITE and Justice SANDRA DAY O'CONNOR), by contrast, viewed flag burning in less conceptual, less content-oriented terms. The dissent characterized flag burning as "a grunt and a roar"—not an essential part of the expression of ideas. Unlike the majority, these dissenters characterized the form and the content of the flag burner's protest as easily divisible. Indeed, the dissenters argued that the defendant could easily have chosen any number of vehicles other than flag burning to express his views. Accordingly, for the dissenters the Texas flag desecration statute merely removed one of these vehicles from the defendant's arsenal of available forms of expression.

This pattern of conflicting characterizations of state interests aimed at content, on the one hand, or form or effect, on the other, recurs frequently throughout the law of FREEDOM OF SPEECH and FREEDOM OF THE PRESS. For instance, in *American Booksellers Assn., Inc. v. Hudnut* (1986), Judge Frank Easterbrook of the Seventh Circuit Court of Appeals, struck down the Indianapolis version of an antipornography civil rights ordinance originally drafted by Catharine MacKinnon and Andrea Dworkin. The ordinance defined PORNOGRAPHY as the graphic sexually explicit subordination of women and provided various civil rights remedies for injured parties. The proponents of the ordinance emphasized the subliminal socializing effects of pornography. They described pornography as harmful in its institutionalization of a subordinate role and identity for women. The proponents of the ordinance thus emphasized the material, constitutive, and hence instantaneous manner in which pornography visits its injurious effects on women. Judge Easterbrook, however, characterized the ordinance as based on content viewpoint, for the ordinance had the explicit aim and effect of condemning the view that women enjoy pain, humiliation, rape, or other forms of degradation. Judge Easterbrook noted that the harmful effects of poronoraphy, like the effects of political views, depend upon—and are indeed indivisible from—the conceptual content of pornography.

In the related context of zoning restrictions on adult theaters, the Court, in CITY OF RENTON V. PLAYTIME THEATERS, INC. (1986), upheld a zoning ordinance that prohibited adult motion picture theaters from locating within 1,000 feet of a residential zone, church, park, or school—the effect being to exclude such theaters from approximately ninety-four percent of the land in the city. Writing for the Court, Chief Justice Rehnquist rejected the view that this ordinance was content-based and instead found that the "predominate intent" was to prevent undesirable secondary effects such as crime or decrease in property value. On the basis of this conception of predominant intent, the Chief Justice classified the zoning ordinance as one that did not offend the fundamental principle against content-based regulation. By contrast, Justice WILLIAM J. BRENNAN, dissenting with Justice THURGOOD MARSHALL, argued that the ordinance's exclusive targeting of adult motion picture theaters—theaters that exhibit certain kinds of motion pictures—demonstrated the absence of content neutrality. For the dissent, the content-based character of the regulation was further evidenced by indications of the city council's hostility to adult motion pictures and by the failure of the ordinance to target other activities that could conceivably give rise to the undesirable secondary effects.

These divergences among the judges and commentators are readily understandable, given that as yet no coherent basis has been provided to distinguish content-neutral from content-based regulation or to specify the extent to which content is divisible from form or effect in the various kinds of symbolic activities. The absence of a coherent basis for such a distinction permits political preferences concerning the speech at issue and the importance of governmental interests at stake to play a role, though not necessarily a determinative role, in the decisions of the courts.

The same kind of politicization, the same problem of distinguishing content-neutral from content-based regulation, and the same tendency to produce more complex context-specific doctrine has been evident in the Supreme Court's treatment of religion cases. In COUNTY OF ALLEGHENY V. ACLU (1989), for instance, the Court fragmented over the constitutionality of two religious displays on public property during the Christmas-Hanukkah season. One display was of a crèche; the other display exhibited a Christmas tree and a menorah. On the basis of some exceedingly fine distinctions, the various opinions established that the menorah exhibition was constitutional while the crèche was not.

The importance of the distinction between content, on the one hand, and form and effect, on the other, was especially evident in the judicial disagreement over the constitutionality of the crèche display. Writing at times for the Court, for a plurality, and for himself, Justice HARRY A. BLACKMUN concluded that the display of a crèche on public property during the Christmas season violated the ESTABLISHMENT CLAUSE because it endorsed a patently Christian message. Focusing on the message conveyed by the display, Justice Blackmun noted that the crèche was accompanied by the words "Glory to God in the Highest" and that unlike the crèche in the case of LYNCH V. DONNELLY (1984), there was nothing in the context of the display to detract from the crèche's religious message. Accordingly, Justice Blackmun concluded that the government was endorsing a religious message in violation of the establishment clause. One group of dissenting and concurring justices, Justice ANTHONY M. KENNEDY, Justice White, and Justice ANTONIN SCALIA, rejected Justice Blackmun's establishment clause requirement of no government endorsement of religion. Turning away from an inquiry into the meaning of the government display of a crèche, this group of Justices focused attention on the effects of the crèche: they noted that there was no evidence of coerced participation in religion or religious ceremonies or of significant expenditures of tax money. On the whole then, the judicial disagreement here also organized itself around the determination of whether it is the conceptual meaning of the government action that matters or its forms and effect.

In the area of freedom of the press, the distinction between content-based and content-neutral regulation also plays an important role. In *Arkansas Writers' Project, Inc. v. Ragland* (1987) the Court found unconstitutional a state law that imposed taxes on general-interest magazines but exempted newspapers and religious, professional, trade, and sports journals. The Court found this selective taxation scheme particularly disturbing because the different treatment accorded to the various magazines depended upon their content. The dissent of Justice Scalia and Chief Justice Rehnquist, by contrast, focused on the form and the effects of the tax scheme. Noting that the tax scheme merely withheld an exemption from the disfavored magazines, the dissent refused to equate the denial of an exemption to regulation or penalty on the disfavored magazines. The dissent noted that unlike direct regulation or prohibition, the denial of a subsidy was unlikely to be coercive. Focusing next on the effects of the tax scheme, the dissent noted that the tax was so small that it would be unlikely to inhibit the disfavored magazines. The dissent closed by hinting that given the indivisibility of form from subject matter in written material, it would not be possible to insist on a principled—that is, neutral—basis to distinguish permissible from impermissible subsidization.

It would be an overstatement to say that all of First Amendment doctrine turns upon the distinction between content-based regulation, on the one hand, and form-based or effect-based regulation, on the other. But the distinction does play an important role in the jurisprudence of the First Amendment. And yet, despite the important role played by this distinction, the Court has failed

thus far to provide any coherent interpretation of the distinction. Indeed, at times, individual Justices deny the very possibility of making such a distinction—as in the selective yet oft-repeated claim that in a given symbolic context, form and effect are indeed inseparable from content.

PIERRE SCHLAG
(1992)

(SEE ALSO: *Extremist Speech; Freedom of Assembly and Association; Freedom of Petition; Religious Liberty; Separation of Church and State.*)

Bibliography
BOLLINGER, LEE 1986 *The Tolerant Society.* New York: Oxford University Press.
GREENAWALT, KENT 1988 *Religious Convictions and Political Choice.* New York: Oxford University Press.
LEVY, LEONARD W. 1985 *Emergence of a Free Press.* New York: Oxford University Press.
——— 1986 *The Establishment Clause: Religion and the First Amendment.* New York: Macmillan.
SHRIFFRIN, STEVEN 1990 *The First Amendment, Democracy, and Romance.* Cambridge: Harvard University Press.
TRIBE, LAURENCE H. 1988 *American Constitutional Law,* 2nd ed. Pages 785–1061, 1154–1301. Mineola, N.Y.: Foundation Press.

FIRST AMENDMENT
(Update 2)

As a general matter, the Supreme Court has held that laws directly restricting the freedom of individuals to express particular messages because those messages might have harmful or undesirable effects are presumptively—perhaps conclusively—unconstitutional. Indeed, the Court has not upheld a direct restriction on speech because it might persuade readers or listeners to engage in criminal activity since DENNIS V. UNITED STATES (1951); it has not upheld a direct restriction on speech because the ideas expressed might provoke a HOSTILE AUDIENCE response since FEINER V. NEW YORK (1951); and it has never upheld a direct restriction on the publication of truthful information because its disclosure would interfere with public or private interests in keeping the information confidential.

This powerful presumption against content-based restrictions on the FREEDOM OF SPEECH derives from the Court's judgment that such laws are particularly likely to distort public debate, to be enacted for constitutionally "improper" reasons (such as hostility to or disagreement with the particular views suppressed), and to be defended in terms of considerations that are thought to be inconsis-

serve in the new Congress. Eleven of the first senators and nine congressmen had been delegates to the federal convention, and fourteen senators and twice as many congressmen had served in state ratifying conventions. GEORGE WASHINGTON told Lafayette that the new Congress "will not be inferior to any Assembly in the world."

The whole country anxiously anticipated the meeting of Congress at Federal Hall in New York City on March 4, 1789. However, much to the chagrin of Federalists, neither house had a quorum on the appointed day. Almost a month elapsed before the HOUSE OF REPRESENTATIVES attained a quorum on April 1, followed five days later by the SENATE; at this time, a joint session of Congress performed its constitutionally assigned function of counting the presidential electoral votes. George Washington was declared President by a unanimous vote, while JOHN ADAMS, a distant second, was proclaimed vice president. Messengers were sent to Washington and Adams as Congress made plans for their reception and inauguration.

Early in April the House elected Frederick A. Muhlenberg of Pennsylvania speaker and John Beckley of Virginia clerk. The Senate elected JOHN LANGDON of New Hampshire president pro tempore and Samuel A. Otis of Massachusetts secretary. The House voted to hold open sessions except on sensitive matters such as Indian or military policy, whereas the Senate chose to keep its sessions closed. Two delegations came to the House under a cloud; opponents formally contested the elections of William Loughton Smith of South Carolina and the entire New Jersey delegation. Acting under Article I, section 5, of the Constitution, the House investigated the elections and declared that Smith and the New Jersey congressmen had been duly elected. The Senate, acting under Article I, section 3, drew lots to determine which senators would have initial terms of two, four, or six years that would give the Senate its distinctive staggered election every second year.

A week before Washington's inauguration, the Senate debated the titles to be given the President and vice president. Advocates of grandiose titles, such as "His Highness the President of the United States of America, and Protector of their Liberties," felt that the new republic needed such titles to command the respect of European nations. The House, however, disagreed, and the first conference committee settled the matter when the Senate agreed to the simple title of "Mr. President." The debate set the tone for the new government and symbolically marked a clear break with monarchy.

As expected, the House of Representatives initiated most legislation and the Senate became primarily a revisory body. The House proposed 143 bills to the Senate's 24. Except for the JUDICIARY ACT OF 1789, the Residency bill, and the act establishing the postmaster general, all major legislation originated in the House. Because neither house established a system of standing committees, each bill was submitted to an ad hoc committee that drafted legislation which was then considered by the committee of the whole.

The first bill enacted by Congress required all federal and state officials to take an oath to support the new Constitution. Within two years, Congress created the executive departments, provided for the federal judiciary, set the country's finances in order, proposed a federal BILL OF RIGHTS, approved a federal tariff, reenacted the NORTH-WEST ORDINANCE, took over the states' lighthouses, and passed legislation for NATURALIZATION and COPYRIGHTS and PATENTS.

Early in Congress's first of three sessions, James Madison notified the House that he intended to introduce amendments to the Constitution. With little support from other congressmen who thought that the consideration of amendments was premature, Madison persevered; and on August 24, the House sent seventeen amendments in the form of a bill of rights to the Senate. The Senate combined some of Madison's amendments, tightened the language of others, and eliminated the amendments prohibiting the states from infringing on the freedoms of conscience, speech, and press and the right to jury trial. On September 25, 1789, Congress approved twelve of Madison's amendments, which were sent to the states for their legislatures to adopt.

Unquestionably, the most controversial issues during the First Congress centered on the secretary of the treasury's *Report on Public Credit*. In his report ALEXANDER HAMILTON proposed the funding of the federal debt, the federal assumption of the states' debts, the levying of an excise on distilled spirits, and the incorporation of a federal bank. No one denied the responsibility of the federal government to pay its own debt; however, some congressmen, led by Madison, opposed paying the debt at face value to speculators who had over the years accumulated a large percentage of the outstanding federal securities at greatly depreciated prices. Madison advocated paying speculators only a fraction of the face value of their holdings while providing partial compensation to the original holders. Madison also led the fight against other aspects of Hamilton's plan, arguing that the Constitution gave Congress no authority to take over the states' debts or to create a bank. To a great extent, the debate over these issues centered over a strict or broad interpretation of the Constitution. Did Congress only have delegated powers or, as Hamilton argued, did the NECESSARY AND PROPER CLAUSE allow Congress to exercise implied powers? President Washington agreed with Hamilton's broader interpretation and refused to veto the bank bill. Madison, in fact, had earlier compromised his strict interpretation of the Constitution by supporting the federal assumption of state debts in exchange for northern support for the movement of the federal capital from New York City, first to Philadelphia for ten years, and then permanently to a site on the banks of the Potomac River.

Precedents were also set by the First Congress in establishing the relationship between the Senate and the President. With some hesitation, the Senate welcomed President Washington to its chamber as he presented the Treaty of New York with the Creek Nation for ratification. The Senate felt uncomfortable with the executive waiting in its chamber for an immediate adoption of the treaty, and the President disliked the Senate's insistence on examining the treaty in greater detail. Washington vowed never again to present a treaty in person. Except in one case, the Senate confirmed Washington's appointments. A protracted debate occurred over the President's power to dismiss department heads without the Senate's approval. The controversy ended when John Adams broke a tie vote on a motion to strike wording from a foreign-relations bill giving the President the right of removal. By not specifying this right in terms of a congressional grant, Congress strengthened the presidency while restricting the Senate's executive power.

In two short years the new Congress had assuaged the fears of Anti-Federalists and stifled their attempts to call a second constitutional convention. Congress had breathed life into the new Constitution, set legislative precedents, created a structure of government, enacted the first phases of Hamilton's financial plan, and established working relationships between its two houses, between itself and the other two branches of the federal government, and between the federal government and the states. The actions of the First Congress, particularly its handling of the financial morass left by the Revolution, divided the new nation economically and ideologically and set the groundwork for the first nationwide political parties. John Trumbull wrote to Vice President Adams that "In no nation, by no Legislature, was ever so much done in so short a period for the establishing of Government, order public Credit & general tranquility." It was an auspicious beginning.

JOHN P. KAMINSKI
(1992)

Bibliography

BAKER, RICHARD ALLAN   1989   The Senate of the United States: "Supreme Executive Council of the Nation," 1787–1800. *Prologue* 21:299–313.

BICKFORD, CHARLENE BANGS and BOWLING, KENNETH R.   1989 *Birth of the Nation: The First Federal Congress 1789–1791.* Madison, Wis.: Madison House.

SILBEY, JOEL H.   1987   "Our Successors Will Have an Easier Task": The First Congress under the Constitution, 1789–1791. *This Constitution* 17:4–10.

SMOCK, RAYMOND W.   1989   The House of Representatives: First Branch of the New Government. *Prologue* 21:287–297.

FIRST CONTINENTAL CONGRESS, DECLARATIONS AND RESOLVES OF
(October 1, 1774)

The Coercive or Intolerable Acts, passed by Parliament in 1774, threatened colonial self-government. The Boston Port Act sought to starve Boston into paying a tax on tea and making reparations for the "Boston Tea Party." The Massachusetts Government Act altered the charter of the colony: it stripped the lower house of power to choose the upper house, which became the creature of the royal governor; it took from the town meetings the power to choose jurors and vested that power in sheriffs appointed by the governor; and it banned all town meetings not approved by the governor. The Administration of Justice Act allowed the governor to transfer to England trials involving the enforcement of revenue acts. The Quartering Act and the Quebec Act also contained provisions deemed reprehensible by many colonists.

To decide on measures for the recovery of American liberties, delegates from all colonies but Georgia assembled in Philadelphia. After defeating the plan of union proposed by JOSEPH GALLOWAY, the congress adopted a statement that defined the American constitutional position on the controversies with Parliament. Congress grasped a rudimentary principle of FEDERALISM, asserted various American rights, and condemned as "unconstitutional" the Coercive Acts and all the acts by which Parliament sought to raise a revenue in America. Rejecting Parliament's claim of unlimited power to legislate for America, the congress repudiated TAXATION WITHOUT REPRESENTATION and any parliamentary governance over "internal polity" but recognized Parliament's power to regulate "external commerce." Congress also grounded American rights, for the first time, in "the immutable laws of nature" as well as the British CONSTITUTION and COLONIAL CHARTERS. Among the rights claimed were free government by one's own representatives, TRIAL BY A JURY of the VICINAGE according to the COMMON LAW, FREEDOM OF ASSEMBLY and petition (holding town meetings), freedom from standing armies in time of peace, and, generally, the rights to life, liberty, property, and all the liberties of English subjects. The document was a forerunner of the first state bills of rights.

LEONARD W. LEVY
(1986)

Bibliography

BURNETT, EDMUND CODY 1941 *The First Continental Congress.* Pages 33–59. New York: Macmillan.

FIRST NATIONAL BANK OF BOSTON v. BELLOTTI
435 U.S. 765 (1978)

Although the Supreme Court had extended FIRST AMENDMENT protections to newspapers that were organized as CORPORATIONS, this was the first case to hold explicitly that the FREEDOM OF SPEECH was not a "purely personal" right such as the RIGHT AGAINST SELF-INCRIMINATION and so might be claimed by corporations. In this case and in VIRGINIA STATE BOARD OF PHARMACY V. VIRGINIA CITY CONSUMER COUNCIL (1976), the Justices adopted the position that where there is a willing speaker, he may be protected by the First Amendment not so much because of his own speech interest but because of the societal interest in maximizing the stock of information upon which the public may draw. Thus a banking corporation was held to have speech rights because limiting its speech would limit the electorate's access to vital information.

After defeat of a REFERENDUM authorizing a personal income tax, which was attributed by some to corporation-funded advertising, Massachusetts adopted a statute forbidding a corporation to spend money for the purpose of influencing the vote on referenda not directly affecting the corporation, including referenda on individual income taxation. In the face of this obvious attempt of protax legislators to muzzle their opponents, Justice LEWIS F. POWELL for the Court had little trouble concluding under a BALANCING TEST that the asserted state interests in preserving the integrity of the electoral process were not compelling and that the statute was not narrowly drawn to protect the interests of stockholders.

The dissent by Justices BYRON R. WHITE, WILLIAM J. BRENNAN, and THURGOOD MARSHALL sounds the theme of a legitimate state interest in limiting the influence of money on elections raised in BUCKLEY V. VALEO (1976). Justice WILLIAM H. REHNQUIST dissented alone on STATES' RIGHTS grounds.

With the recognition of corporate speech rights and the recognition of some First Amendment protection for COMMERCIAL SPEECH, the Court set the stage for a whole new area of freedom-of-speech jurisprudence, particularly in the light of the high levels of corporate institutional and issue advertising engendered by environmental, energy, and deregulation policies. Among the difficult problems are the rights of stockholders who oppose advertised corporate stances and the extent to which laws against false and misleading advertising constitutionally can be applied to advertisements that do more than offer a product for sale.

MARTIN SHAPIRO
(1986)

FIRST WORLD WAR

See: World War I

FISHER, SYDNEY GEORGE

See: Commentators on the Constitution

FISKE, JOHN
(1842–1901)

A conservative Yankee educated at Harvard, where he later taught, John Fiske was a man of letters who published about a book a year, as many on science, philosophy, and religion as on history. He was essentially a great popularizer. His books were captivatingly written, bold in interpretation, and widely read. His most influential work as a historian was *The Critical Period in American History, 1783–1789* (1888), which vividly depicted the weaknesses and deficiencies of the United States under the ARTICLES OF CONFEDERATION. For Fiske the Constitution was "a Fifth Symphony of statesmanship" that saved the nation from Balkanizing into petty states.

LEONARD W. LEVY
(1986)

FITZPATRICK v. BITZER
427 U.S. 445 (1976)

This case concerned Congress's power to modify states' ELEVENTH AMENDMENT immunity from suit in federal court. In the 1972 amendments to Title VII of the CIVIL RIGHTS ACT OF 1964, Congress extended Title VII to forbid employment discrimination by state employers. In *Fitzpatrick*, in an opinion by Justice WILLIAM H. REHNQUIST, the Court held that Congress, in exercising its FOURTEENTH AMENDMENT powers, and despite the Eleventh Amendment, could subject states to suit in federal courts for discriminatory behavior. *Fitzpatrick* was an important counterpoint to *Employees v. Department of Public Health and Welfare* (1973) and EDELMAN V. JORDAN (1974), cases that had held that other federal statutes were not meant to abrogate the states' Eleventh Amendment immunity.

THEODORE EISENBERG
(1986)

FITZSIMONS, THOMAS
(1741–1811)

An Irish-born Roman Catholic and a successful merchant, Thomas FitzSimons signed the Constitution as a Pennsylvania delegate to the CONSTITUTIONAL CONVENTION OF 1787. He spoke infrequently and always in favor of a strong national government to foster and regulate commerce. He served in the first three Congresses under the Constitution, where he supported ALEXANDER HAMILTON's policies.

DENNIS J. MAHONEY
(1986)

FIVE KNIGHTS' CASE

See: Petition of Right

FLAG BURNING

See: Flag Desecration

FLAG DESECRATION

The American flag, as a unique symbol embodying national pride and patriotism, evidences the unity and diversity which the country represents, and the varying ideals and hopes of its people. By the same token, the flag has frequently been used by those who wish to communicate opposition to—or even ridicule of—government policies.

Congress has enacted statutes that prescribe how the flag may be displayed and disposed of, and how and for what purposes it may be used. Many state laws prohibit flag "desecration" (casting "contempt" on a flag by "mutilating, defacing, defiling, burning or trampling upon" it) and "improper use" of flags (placing on a flag "any word, figure, mark, picture, design, drawing or advertisement").

In *Halter v. Nebraska* (1907) the Supreme Court upheld a state statute prohibiting flag desecration and use of the flag for advertising purposes. But that decision was rendered twenty years before the Court applied the FIRST AMENDMENT to the States, and it was not dispositive when protesters later challenged the constitutionality of flag desecration statutes.

In *Smith v. Gorguen* (1973), the Court reversed a conviction for wearing an American flag on the seat of the pants, ruling that the Massachusetts flag desecration statute was void for VAGUENESS. In *Spence v. Washington* (1974) the Court invalidated a Washington statute prohibiting the affixing of a symbol to the flag, holding that the display of a flag with a peace symbol superimposed on it

was protected free expression. The *Spence* decision was consistent with other cases in which the Supreme Court recognized SYMBOLIC SPEECH as a form of activity protected by the First Amendment. On the other hand, the Court has upheld statutes forbidding flag burning, concluding as in *Sutherland v. Illinois* (1976) that they rested on a "valid governmental interest unrelated to expression—that is, the prevention of breaches of the peace and the preservation of public order."

NORMAN DORSEN
(1986)

FLAG DESECRATION
(Update)

The word "desecration" has religious overtones. It means defiling the sacred. Flag burning is the secular equivalent of the offense of BLASPHEMY, a verbal crime signifying an attack, by ridicule or rejection, against God, the Bible, Jesus Christ, Christianity, or religion itself. Flag burning is comparable to a verbal attack on the United States. Burning the nation's symbol signifies contempt and hatred by the flag burner of the things he or she believes the flag stands for, such as colonialism, imperialism, capitalism, exploitation, racism, or militarism. To the overwhelming majority of Americans, however, the flag embodies in a mystical and emotional way the loyalty and love they feel for the United States. With few exceptions we venerate the flag because it symbolizes both our unity and diversity; our commitment to freedom, equality, and justice; and perhaps above all, our constitutional system and its protection of individual rights.

Like blasphemy, therefore, flag burning tests the outermost limits of tolerance even in a free society. Burning the flag is a most offensive outrage that stretches to the breaking point the capacity of a nation to indulge dissidents. But that same form of desecration is not only an act of vandalism; it is symbolic expression that claims the protection of the free speech clause of the FIRST AMENDMENT. Therein lies the problem and the paradox: should the flag represent a nation whose people have a right to burn its revered symbol?

Imprisoning flag burners would not mean that book burning and thought control are next. We know how to distinguish vandalism from radical advocacy; we would not regard urinating on the Jefferson Memorial or spray painting graffiti on the Washington Monument as a form of constitutionally protected free speech. Special reasons exist for protecting the flag from the splenetic conduct of extremists. A society should be entitled to safeguard its most fundamental values, but dissenters have a right to express verbal opposition to everything we hold dear. Yet, nothing is solved by saying that it is better to live in a country where people are free to burn the flag if they wish, rather than in a country where they want to burn it but cannot. We know the difference between suppressing a particularly offensive mode of conduct and a particularly offensive message. The problem is, however, that the particular mode of conduct may be the vehicle for communicating that offensive message. To suppress the message by suppressing the conduct involves governmental abridgment of a First Amendment freedom. So the Supreme Court held in *Texas v. Johnson* in 1989.

In 1984 in Dallas, Gregory Johnson, a member of the Revolutionary Communist Youth Brigade, a Maoist society, publicly burned a stolen American flag to protest the renomination of RONALD REAGAN as the Republican candidate. While the flag burned, the protesters, including Maoists, chanted, "America, the red, white, and blue, we spit on you." That the flag burning communicated an unmistakable political message was contested by no one. The police arrested Johnson not for his message but for his manner of delivering it; he had violated a Texas statute that prohibited the desecration of a venerated object by acts that seriously offended onlookers.

State appellate courts reversed Johnson's conviction on ground that his conduct constituted constitutionally protected SYMBOLIC SPEECH. Given its context—the Republican convention; Reagan's foreign policy; the protestors' demonstrations, marches, speeches, and slogans—Johnson's burning the flag was clearly speech of the sort contemplated by the First Amendment. The Texas courts also rejected the state's contention that the conviction could be justified as a means of preventing breach of the public peace. In fact, the state admitted that no BREACH OF THE PEACE occurred as a result of the flag desecration. The Supreme Court, 5–4, affirmed the judgment of the Texas Court of Criminal Appeals.

Justice WILLIAM J. BRENNAN, spokesman for the majority, showed his political savvy by emphasizing that the courts of the Lone Star State, where red-blooded John Wayne patriotism flourishes, recognized "that the right to differ is the centerpiece of our First Amendment freedoms." Government cannot mandate a feeling of unity or "carve out a symbol of unity and prescribe a set of approved messages to be associated with that symbol." Brennan added that although the First Amendment literally forbids the abridgment of only "speech," the Court had labeled as speech a variety of conduct that communicated opinions, including the wearing of black arm bands to protest war, a sit-in by blacks to protest racial segregation, picketing, and the display of a red flag. Indeed the state conceded that Johnson's conduct was politically expressive. The question was whether that expression could be constitutionally proscribed, like the use of FIGHTING WORDS calculated to provoke a breach of peace. Apart from the fact that no breach occurred here, Brennan reminded, a prime function of free speech is to invite dispute. The "fighting words" doctrine had no relevance in this case because the message communicated by flag burning did not personally insult anyone in particular.

Whether the state could justify the conviction as a means of preserving the flag as a symbol of nationhood and national unity depended on the communicative impact of the mode of expression. Brennan insisted that the restriction on flag desecration was "content-based." Johnson's political expression, he declared, was restricted because of the content of the message that he conveyed. This point is important and unpersuasive. As Chief Justice WILLIAM H. REHNQUIST for the dissenters said, burning the flag was no essential part of the exposition of ideas, for Johnson was free to make any verbal denunciation of the flag that he wished. He led a march through the streets of Dallas, conducted a rally on the front steps of the city hall, shouted his slogans, and was not arrested for any of this. Only when he burned the flag was he arrested. Texas did not punish him because it or his hearers opposed his message, only because he conveyed it by burning the flag.

Brennan replied that by punishing flag burning the state prohibited expressive conduct. "If there is a bedrock principle underlying the First Amendment," he wrote, "it is that the Government may not prohibit the expression of an idea simply because society finds the idea itself offensive or disagreeable." By making an exception for the flag, Texas sought to immunize the ideas for which it stands. Whatever it stands for should not be insulated against protest. In the context of this case, the act of flag burning constituted a means of political protest. Compulsion is not a constitutionally accepted method of achieving national unity.

Brennan believed that the flag's deservedly cherished place as a symbol would be "strengthened, not weakened, by our holding today. Our decision is a reaffirmation of the principles of freedom and inclusiveness that the flag best reflects, and of the conviction that our toleration of criticism such as Johnson's is a sign and source of our strength." This was the Court's strongest point.

Texas v. Johnson provided Court watchers with the pleasure of seeing judicial objectivity at work, for the Court did not divide in a predictable way. The majority included Justices ANTONIN SCALIA and ANTHONY M. KENNEDY, Reagan-appointed conservatives, whereas the dissenters included Justice JOHN PAUL STEVENS, a liberal moderate. Stevens wrote his own dissent. He believed, oddly, that public desecration of the flag "will tarnish its value." He also thought that the Texas statute that the Court struck down did not compel any conduct or profession of respect for any idea or symbol. The case had nothing to do with disagreeable ideas, he said; it involved offensive conduct that diminishes the value of the national symbol. Texas prosecuted Johnson because of the method he used to express dissatisfaction with national policies. Prosecuting him no more violated the First Amendment than prosecuting someone for spray painting a message of protest on the Lincoln Memorial.

Rehnquist's dissent was suffused with emotional theatrics about the flag and patriotism. His point was that the flag was special, as two hundred years of history showed. Even if flag burning is expressive conduct, he reasoned, it is not an absolute. But he thought it not to be expressive conduct. Flag burning was no essential part of any exposition of ideas, he claimed, but rather was "the equivalent of an inarticulate grunt" meant to antagonize others. By the same reasoning, however, one might say that flag flying is also a grunt of patriotism. That does not alter the point that flag burning is malicious conduct—vandalism rather than speech.

Zealous politicians, eager to capitalize on their love for the flag and opposition to those who burned it, sought to gain political advantage from the Court's opinion. President GEORGE BUSH, a war hero, had helped spur a paroxysm of patriotism in 1988 by assaulting his opponent for having vetoed a bill that would have compelled teachers to lead their students in a Pledge of Allegiance every day. Bush, having made a photo opportunity of visiting a flag factory in 1988, made another after the decision in *Texas v. Johnson*, by holding a ceremony in the White House rose garden. Accepting a replica of the Iwo Jima Memorial, depicting the marines hoisting the flag on a bloody wartime site, Bush condemned flag burning as a danger to "the fabric of our country" and demanded a constitutional amendment outlawing desecration of the flag.

Cynical observers shouted "cheap politics" and criticized the President and his supporters for trying to cover up problems concerning the savings and loan scandals, the deterioration of the nation's schools, the ballooning national debt, the urban underclass, and the army of homeless beggars in American cities. Bush's opponents declared that he sought to desecrate the Constitution by indulging in escapist politics and seeking the first revision of the BILL OF RIGHTS in two centuries. Many conservatives in Congress agreed that tampering with the Bill of Rights was not the way to treat the problem of flag burning. Democrats, who felt obligated to "do something" at the risk of being branded unpatriotic, offered the Flag Protection Act of 1989, and so headed off the amendment movement. The new act of Congress provided that whoever knowingly mutilates, defaces, physically defiles, or burns the flag shall be fined or imprisoned for a year, or both.

Members of the "lunatic left" promptly defied the act of Congress by burning the flag on the Capitol steps for the benefit of the TV cameras. Shawn Eichman and company got the publicity they wanted and were arrested. They quickly filed motions to dismiss, on grounds that the act of Congress was unconstitutional; that is, the flag they burned symbolized their freedom to burn it. The government asked the Supreme Court to reconsider its holding in *Texas v. Johnson* by holding that flag burning is a mode of expression, like fighting words, that does not enjoy complete protection of the First Amendment.

The Court, by the same 5–4 split, refused to alter its opinion. Brennan, again the majority spokesman, acknowledged that the government may create national symbols and encourage their respectful treatment, but concluded that it went too far with the Flag Protection Act "by criminally proscribing expressive conduct because of its likely communicative impact." Desecrating the flag was deeply offensive to many people, like virulent racial and religious epithets, vulgar repudiations of conscription, and scurrilous caricatures, all of which came within the First Amendment's protection, notwithstanding their offensiveness.

The government sought to distinguish the Flag Protection Act from the state statute involved in *Johnson*, on the theory that the act of Congress did not target expressive conduct on the basis of the content of its message. The government merely claimed its authority to protect the physical integrity of the flag as the symbol of our nation and its ideals. Brennan replied that destruction of the flag could in no way affect those ideals or the symbol itself. The invalidity of the statute derived from the fact that its criminal penalties applied to those whose treatment of the flag communicated a message. Thus, *United States v. Eichman*, resulting in the voiding of the act of Congress, was a replay of *Johnson*.

Stevens, for the dissenters, recapitulated his previous contentions. He believed that the majority opinion concluded at the point where analysis of the issue ought to begin. No one, he declared, disagreed with the proposition that the government cannot constitutionally punish offensive ideas. But, he argued, certain methods of expression, such as flag burning, might be proscribed if the purpose of the proscription did not relate to the suppression of ideas individuals sought to express, if that proscription did not interfere with the individual's freedom to express those ideas by other means, and if on balance the government's interest in the proscription outweighed the individual's choice of the means of expressing themselves. Stevens expatiated on the flag as a symbol and insisted that the government should protect its symbolic value without regard to the specific content of the flag burner's speech. Moreover, Eichman and the other dissidents were completely free to express their ideas by means other than flag burning. Stevens apparently missed the point that Eichman had a right to choose his own means of communicating his political protest. What disturbed Stevens most was the belief that flag burners actually have damaged the symbolic value of the flag. And he added the following in a veiled allusion to the shenanigans of would-be amenders of the Constitution: "Moreover, the integrity of the symbol has been compromised by those leaders who seem to advocate compulsory worship of the flag even by individuals whom it offends, or who seem to manipulate the symbol of national purpose into a pretext for partisan disputes about meaner ends."

Every nation in the world has a flag, and many of them, including some democracies, have laws against desecrating their flag. No other nation has our Bill of Rights. The year 1991 marked the 200th anniversary of its ratification. It requires no limiting amendment. The American people understand that they are not threatened by flag burners, and the American people prefer the First Amendment undiluted. They understand that imprisoning a few extremists is not what patriotism is about. Forced patriotism is not American. Flag burning is all wrong, but a lot of wrongheaded speech is protected by the Constitution. When the nation celebrated the bicentennial of the Bill of Rights, it celebrated a wonderfully terse, eloquent, and effective summation of individual freedoms. Time has not shown a need to add "except for flag burners." That exception, as the Court majority realized, might show that the nation is so lacking in faith in itself that it permits the Johnsons and Eichmans to diminish the flag's meaning. They are best treated, as Brennan urged, by saluting the flag that they burn or by ignoring them contemptuously.

LEONARD W. LEVY
(1992)

Bibliography

GREENAWALT, KENT 1990 O'er the Land of the Free: Flag Burning as Speech. *UCLA Law Review* 37:925–947.
KMIEC, DOUGLAS W. 1990 In the Aftermath of *Johnson* and *Eichman*. *Brigham Young University Law Review* 1990:577–638.

When Brooks and her family were evicted from their apartment, a city marshal had her goods stored with Flagg Bros. Ten weeks later, Flagg Bros. wrote to Brooks, demanding payment of storage charges and threatening to sell her goods to satisfy the charges accrued. Brooks brought a CLASS ACTION against Flagg Bros. for damages and injunctive relief under federal CIVIL RIGHTS laws claiming DUE PROCESS and EQUAL PROTECTION violations. (See Injunction.) The Supreme Court held, 5–3, that the proposed sale did not amount to state action; thus there had been no constitutional violation.

Justice WILLIAM H. REHNQUIST wrote for the majority, as he had done in other recent cases strengthening the state action limitation. The proposed sale did not fit the "public function" DOCTRINE of state action (here renamed the "sovereign function" doctrine), because the function of dispute resolution historically had not been the exclusive province of the states. Nor had the state authorized or encouraged the use of this creditor's remedy in such a way as to take responsibility for its exercise. The Uniform Commercial Code "permits but does not compel" a warehouse operator's threat to sell goods stored and merely announces the circumstances in which the state will not intervene with that private sale.

Justice WILLIAM J. BRENNAN did not participate in the decision. Justice JOHN PAUL STEVENS dissented, joined by Justices BYRON R. WHITE and THURGOOD MARSHALL. The distinction between state permission and state compulsion was untenable, Stevens argued; on the Court's theory, for example, the state could "announce" its intention not to intervene when a finance company entered a private home to repossess property, with no finding of state action. He also argued persuasively that the "exclusive sovereign function" notion had no basis in the Court's prior decisions. What the state had done here was to "order binding, nonconsensual resolution of a conflict between debtor and creditor"—which is "exactly the sort of power with which the Due Process Clause is concerned."

KENNETH L. KARST
(1986)

FLAGG BROS., INC. v. BROOKS
436 U.S. 149 (1978)

Brooks is one of a series of BURGER COURT decisions reestablishing the STATE ACTION limitation as a barrier to judicial enforcement of FOURTEENTH AMENDMENT rights against private persons acting under state authority. The Uniform Commercial Code, as adopted in New York, authorizes a warehouse operator to sell goods stored in order to pay overdue warehousing charges. This notion of a "warehouseman's lien" is an ancient COMMON LAW remedy.

FLAG SALUTE CASES
Minersville School District v. Gobitis
310 U.S. 586 (1940)
West Virginia Board of Education v. Barnett
319 U.S. 624 (1943)

The Supreme Court's encounter in the early 1940s with the issue of compulsory flag salute exercises in the public schools was one of the turning points in American constitutional history. It presaged the civil libertarian activism that culminated in the WARREN COURT of the 1960s.

The flag salute ceremony developed in the latter half of the nineteenth century. In the original ceremony the participants faced the flag and pledged "allegiance to my flag and the republic for which it stands, one nation indivisible, with liberty and justice for all." While repeating the words "to my flag" the right hand was extended palm up toward the flag. Over the years the ceremony evolved slightly, with minor changes of wording and with the extended arm salute dropped in 1942 because of its similarity to the Nazi salute. At this point in its evolution, however, the salute had official standing; Congress had prescribed the form of words and substituted the right hand over the heart for the extended arm.

Beginning in 1898 with New York, some states began requiring the ceremony as part of the opening exercise of the school day. The early state flag salute laws did not make the ceremony compulsory for individual pupils, but many local school boards insisted on participation. Many patriotic and fraternal organizations backed the flag salute; opposition came from civil libertarians and some small religious groups. The principal opponents of the compulsory school flag salute were the Jehovah's Witnesses, a tightly knit evangelical sect whose religious beliefs commanded them not to salute the flag as a "graven image."

The Witnesses were blessed with legal talent. "Judge" Joseph Franklin Rutherford, who had become head of the sect, brought in Hayden Covington, who, as chief counsel for the Witnesses in the *Gobitis* litigation and in many other cases influenced the development of First Amendment doctrine.

The first flag salute case to reach the Supreme Court came out of Minersville, a small community in northwest Pennsylvania. Because of Rutherford's bitter opposition to required flag salute exercises, Lillian and William Gobitis stopped participating in the ceremony in their school and were expelled.

The argument for the Gobitis children was that requiring them to salute the flag, an act repugnant to them on religious grounds, denied that free exercise of religion protected against state action by the DUE PROCESS clause of the FOURTEENTH AMENDMENT. Arguments for the Minersville School Board relied on REYNOLDS V. UNITED STATES (1878), JACOBSON V. MASSACHUSETTS (1905), and the doctrine that a religious objection did not relieve an individual from the responsibility of complying with an otherwise valid secular regulation. The Gobitis children won in the lower federal courts, but the Supreme Court granted CERTIORARI.

The Court in the spring of 1940 had a very different cast from that which had survived FRANKLIN D. ROOSEVELT's effort to "pack" it three years before. Of the hard-core,

pre-1937 conservatives only Justice JAMES C. MCREYNOLDS remained. Chief Justice CHARLES EVANS HUGHES and Justices HARLAN F. STONE and OWEN J. ROBERTS also remained. With them, however, were five Roosevelt appointees: FELIX FRANKFURTER, HUGO L. BLACK, WILLIAM O. DOUGLAS, STANLEY F. REED, and FRANK MURPHY. On three previous occasions the Court had sustained compulsory flag salutes against religious objection in PER CURIUM opinions. Whether because of the extraordinary persistence of the Jehovah's Witnesses or because of the nonconformance of the lower federal courts in this case, the Justices now gave the matter full dress consideration.

Speaking for the majority Justice Frankfurter concluded that "conscientious scruples have not, in the course of the long struggle for religious toleration, relieved the individual from obedience to a general law not aimed at the persecution or a restriction of religious beliefs."

To Justice Stone, dissenting, the crucial issue was that the Gobitis children were forced to bear false witness to their religion. The flag salute compelled the expression of a belief, and "where that expression violate[d] religious convictions," the free exercise clause provided protection.

The reaction to the decision in the law reviews was negative. In the popular press the reaction was mixed but criticism predominated. Most important, the decision seems to have produced a wave of persecution of Jehovah's Witnesses which swept through the country. *Gobitis* emboldened some school authorities. The State Board of Education of West Virginia in January 1942 made the salute to the flag mandatory in the classrooms of that state.

Meanwhile, new decisions of the Supreme Court, notably the 5–4 division of the Justices in *Jones v. Opelika*, raised the hopes of opponents of the mandatory flag salute. Hayden Covington sought an INJUNCTION barring enforcement of West Virginia's new rule against Walter Barnett and other Jehovah's Witness plaintiffs. After a three-judge District Court issued an injunction, the State Board of Education appealed to the Supreme Court.

The case was argued on March 11, 1943, and the decision came down on June 14. Justice ROBERT H. JACKSON, who had joined the Court after *Gobitis*, wrote for a 6–3 majority, overruling the prior decision. Chief Justice Stone was with Jackson, as were Justices Douglas, Black, and Murphy, who had changed their minds. Justice Frankfurter, the author of *Gobitis*, wrote a long and impassioned dissent.

For Justice Jackson and the majority the crucial point was that West Virginia's action, while not intended either to impose or to anathematize a particular religious belief, did involve a required affirmation of belief: "If there is any fixed star in our constitutional constellation, it is that no official, high or petty, can prescribe what shall be orthodox in politics, nationalism, religion, or other matters of opinion or force citizens to confess by word or act their faith therein." West Virginia was pursuing the legitimate end of enhancing patriotism, but had not borne the heavy burden of justifying its use of coercive power.

Justice Frankfurter began his dissent by noting that were the matter one of personal choice he would oppose compulsory flag salutes. But it was not for the Court to decide what was and was not an effective means of inculcating patriotism. West Virginia had neither prohibited nor imposed any religious belief. For Frankfurter this fact was controlling, and he reminded his brethren that a liberal spirit cannot be "enforced by judicial invalidation of illiberal legislation."

Barnett was a landmark decision in the strict sense of that overworked word. By 1943 the Roosevelt Court had largely completed its task of dismantling the edifice of SUBSTANTIVE DUE PROCESS erected by its predecessors to protect economic liberty. Now the Court set out on the path to a new form of JUDICIAL ACTIVISM in the service of individual rights. *Barnett* was the first long step on that path.

Barnett had doctrinal significance both for FREEDOM OF SPEECH and for RELIGIOUS LIBERTY. Jackson's opinion suggested that there were significant limitations on the kinds of patriotic affirmations that government might require, and the decision also moved away from the "secular regulation" rule that had dominated free exercise doctrine.

Barnett also had a significant effect on the Supreme Court. Justice Frankfurter was deeply offended by the majority's treatment of his *Gobitis* opinion and even more alarmed at what he regarded as a misuse of judicial power. The split between the activist disposition of Justices Black and Douglas and the judicial self-restraint championed by Frankfurter date from *Barnett*.

RICHARD E. MORGAN
(1986)

Bibliography

MANWARING, DAVID R. 1962 *Render unto Caesar: The Flag Salute Controversy.* Chicago: University of Chicago Press.

FLAST v. COHEN
392 U.S. 83 (1968)

A WARREN COURT landmark regarding the JUDICIAL POWER OF THE United States, *Flast* upheld taxpayer STANDING to complain that disbursements of federal funds to religious schools violate the FIRST AMENDMENT prohibition of an ESTABLISHMENT OF RELIGION. The decision carved an exception from, but did not overturn, the rule of FROTHINGHAM V. MELLON (1923) that federal taxpayers lack a sufficiently

individual or direct interest in spending programs to be allowed to attack them in federal court. To Justice JOHN MARSHALL HARLAN's dissenting chagrin, the Court so ruled knowing that Congress, cognizant of *Frothingham*, had decided against granting taxpayers a right to JUDICIAL REVIEW of federal support for religious education.

The Court was unanimous on one fundamental point: the taxpayers in *Flast* presented an Article III "case." (See CASES AND CONTROVERSIES.) For the majority, Chief Justice EARL WARREN reaffirmed the traditional Article III requirement of a "personal stake in the outcome of the controversy," but deemed that requirement satisfied whenever a taxpayer claims that Congress exercised its TAXING AND SPENDING POWER in derogation of specific constitutional limits on that power. The Court found the establishment clause a specific limit, because, historically, the clause was designed to block taxation to support religion.

Dissenting, Justice Harlan could not agree that taxpayers challenging spending, rather than their tax liability, had a personal stake. They had no financial stake, because victory would only change how the government's general revenues are spent—not their tax bill. Nor was the Court's exception tailored to the requirement of a personal stake. A taxpayer's interests did not vary with the power Congress exercised in appropriating funds or with the constitutional provision ("specific" or not) invoked to oppose the expenditures. For Harlan, the taxpayer's interest in government spending was not personal but public—a citizen's concern that official behavior be constitutional. Nonetheless, he thought the "public action" would satisfy Article III, apparently because the parties were sufficiently adversary. But because "public actions" would press judicial authority vis-à-vis the representative branches to the limit, he concluded the Court should not entertain them without congressional authorization.

The bearing of SEPARATION OF POWERS on taxpayer standing was the pivotal dividing point in *Flast*. Justice WILLIAM O. DOUGLAS, too, thought *Flast* a public action, the attempt to distinguish *Frothingham* a failure, and the requirements of Article III met. But he found *Frothingham* deficient, not *Flast*, for he perceived the judicial role as enforcement of basic rights against majoritarian control without awaiting congressional authorization—even in "public actions." Chief Justice Warren's view fell between the Harlan and Douglas poles by disavowing the connection between standing and the separation of powers. Justiciability requires that a suit be appropriate in form for judicial resolution and implicates separation of powers, said Warren, but standing, with its focus on the party suing, not the issues raised, looks only to form.

Under the BURGER COURT, separation of powers considerations have resurfaced in TAXPAYER SUITS, stunting the potential growth of *Flast* into the mature "public action."

Typical of the Burger Court approach was VALLEY FORGE CHRISTIAN COLLEGE V. AMERICANS UNITED FOR SEPARATION OF CHURCH AND STATE (1982). The *Flast* landmark has become a historical marker.

JONATHAN D. VARAT
(1986)

FLETCHER v. PECK
6 Cranch 87 (1810)

Fletcher was the Court's point of departure for converting the CONTRACT CLAUSE into the chief link between the Constitution and capitalism. The case arose from the Yazoo land scandal, the greatest corrupt real estate deal in American history. Georgia claimed the territory within her latitude lines westward to the Mississippi, and in 1795 the state legislature passed a bill selling about two-thirds of that so-called Yazoo territory, some 35,000,000 acres of remote wilderness comprising a good part of the present states of Alabama and Mississippi. Four land companies, having bribed every voting member of the state legislature but one, bought the Yazoo territory at a penny and a half an acre. Speculation in land values was a leading form of capitalist enterprise at that time, provoking an English visitor to characterize the United States as "the land of speculation." Respectable citizens engaged in the practice; the piratical companies that bought the Yazoo included two United States senators, some governors and congressmen, and Justice JAMES WILSON. In a year, one of the four companies sold its Yazoo holdings at a 650 percent profit, and the buyers, in the frenzy of speculation that followed, resold at a profit. But in 1796 the voters of Georgia elected a "clean" legislature which voided the bill of sale and publicly burned all records of it but did not return the $500,000 purchase price. In 1802 Georgia sold its western territories to the United States for $1,250,000. In 1814 a Yazooist lobby finally succeeded in persuading Congress to pass a $5,000,000 compensation bill, indemnifying holders of Yazoo land titles.

Fletcher v. Peck was part of a twenty-year process of legal and political shenanigans related to the Yazoo land scandal. Georgia's nullification of the original sale imperiled the entire chain of Yazoo land speculations, but the ELEVENTH AMENDMENT made Georgia immune to a suit. A feigned case was arranged. Peck of Massachusetts sold 15,000 acres of Yazoo land to Fletcher of New Hampshire. Fletcher promptly sued Peck for recovery of his $3,000, claiming that Georgia's nullification of the sale had destroyed Peck's title: the acreage was not his to sell. Actually, both parties shared the same interest in seeking a judicial decision against Georgia's nullification of the land titles—the repeal act of 1796. Thus, by a collusive suit

based on DIVERSITY OF CITIZENSHIP, a case involving the repeal act got into the federal courts and ultimately reached the Supreme Court. The Court's opinion, by Chief Justice JOHN MARSHALL, followed the contours of Justice WILLIAM PATERSON's charge in VAN HORNE'S LESSEE V. DORRANCE (1795).

Although the fraud that infected the original land grants was the greatest scandal of the time, the Court refused to make an exception to the principle that the judiciary could not properly investigate the motives of a legislative body. (See LEGISLATION.) The Court also justifiably held that "innocent" third parties should not suffer an annihilation of their property rights as a result of the original fraud. The importance of the case derives from the Court's resolution of the constitutionality of the repeal act.

Alternating in his reasoning between extraconstitutional or HIGHER LAW principles and constitutional or textual ones, Marshall said that the repealer was invalid. Before reaching the question whether a contract existed that the Constitution protected, he announced this doctrine: "When, then, a law is in its nature a contract, when absolute rights have been vested under that contract, a repeal of the law cannot devest those rights. . . ." In the next sentence he asserted that "the nature of society and of government" limits legislative power. This higher law doctrine of judicially inferred limitations protecting vested rights was the sole basis of Justice WILLIAM JOHNSON's concurring opinion. A state has no power to revoke its grants, he declared, resting his case "on a general principle, on the reason and nature of things: a principle which will impose laws even on the Deity." Explicitly Johnson stated that his opinion was not founded on the Constitution's provision against state impairment of the OBLIGATION OF CONTRACTS. The difficulty, he thought, arose from the word "obligation," which ceased once a grant of lands had been executed.

The difficulty with Marshall's contract clause theory was greater than even Johnson made out. The clause was intended to prevent state impairment of executory contracts between private individuals; it had been modeled on the provision of the NORTHWEST ORDINANCE, which had referred to "private contracts, or engagements *bona fide*, and without fraud previously formed." What was the contract in this case? If there was one, did its obligation still exist at the time of the repeal bill? Was it a contract protected by the contract clause, given that it was a land grant to which the state was a party? If the land grant was a contract, it was a public executed one, not a private executory one. The duties that the parties had assumed toward each other had been fulfilled, the deal consummated. That is why Johnson could find no continuing obligation. Moreover, the obligation of a contract is a creature of state law, and the state in this instance, sustained by its courts, had recognized no obligation.

Marshall overcame all difficulties by employing slippery reasoning. A contract, he observed, is either executory or executed; if executed, its object has been performed. The contract between the state and the Yazoo land buyers had been executed by the grant. But, he added, an executed contract, as well as an executory one, "contains obligations binding on the parties." The grant had extinguished the right of the grantor in the title to the lands and "implies a contract not to reassert that right." Moreover, the Constitution uses only the term "contract, without distinguishing between those which are executory and those which are executed." Having inferred from the higher law that a grant carried a continuing obligation not to repossess, he declined to make a distinction that, he said, the Constitution had not made. Similarly he concluded that the language of the contract clause, referring generally to "contracts," protected public as well as private contracts. Marshall apparently realized that the disembodied or abstract higher law doctrine on which Johnson relied would provide an insecure bastion for property holders and a nebulous precedent for courts to follow. So he found a home for the VESTED RIGHTS doctrine in the text of the Constitution.

Marshall seemed, however, to be unsure of the text, because he flirted with the bans on BILLS OF ATTAINDER and EX POST FACTO laws, giving the impression that Georgia's repeal act somehow ran afoul of those bans, too, although the suit was a civil one. Marshall's uncertainty emerged in his conclusion. He had no doubt that the repeal act was invalid, but his ambiguous summation referred to both extraconstitutional principles and the text: Georgia "was restrained, either by general principles which are common to our free institutions, or by the particular provisions of the Constitution. . . ." He did not, in the end, specify the particular provisions.

In the first contract clause decision by the Court, that clause became a repository of the higher law DOCTRINE of vested rights and operated to cover even public, executed contracts. The Court had found a constitutional shield for vested rights. And, by expanding the protection offered by the contract clause, the Court invited more cases to be brought before the judiciary, expanding opportunities for judicial review against state legislation.

LEONARD W. LEVY
(1986)

Bibliography

MAGRATH, C. PETER 1966 *Yazoo: Law and Politics in the New Republic, The Case of Fletcher v. Peck.* Providence, R.I.: Brown University Press.

FLORIDA BAR v. WENT FOR IT, INC.
515 U.S. 618 (1995)

The Supreme Court upheld, 5–4, a Florida Bar rule prohibiting direct-mail solicitation of personal injury or wrongful death clients within thirty days of the event that was the basis for the claim. Justice SANDRA DAY O'CONNOR, writing for the majority, found that the regulation served the state's significant interests in protecting injured or grieving people from unwanted invasions of their privacy, and in avoiding harm to the reputation of the legal profession. She relied on a Florida Bar survey that purported to show that the public was deeply offended by the solicitations in issue. Justice ANTHONY M. KENNEDY, writing in dissent, challenged the merits of the survey, and the degree to which the rule actually served the state interests that justified it.

JAMES M. O'FALLON
(2000)

(SEE ALSO: *Attorney Speech; Commercial Speech.*)

FOLEY v. CONNELIE
435 U.S. 291 (1978)

New York excluded ALIENS from employment as state troopers. In an opinion by Chief Justice WARREN E. BURGER, the Supreme Court held, 6–3, that this discrimination did not violate the EQUAL PROTECTION clause of the FOURTEENTH AMENDMENT. The Court took its cue from OBITER DICTA in SUGARMAN V. DOUGALL (1973) concerning "political community." Although the admission of aliens for permanent residence showed congressional intent to grant them full participation in earning a livelihood and receiving such state benefits as welfare and education, the "right to govern" could be limited to citizens. Police officers, like high executive officials, exercise discretionary governmental power, whose abuse can have "serious impact on individuals." (The Chief Justice may have had a vision of an alien trooper inviting a citizen to spreadeagle over the hood of a car.)

Justices THURGOOD MARSHALL, WILLIAM J. BRENNAN, and JOHN PAUL STEVENS dissented: the "execution of broad public policy" mentioned in *Sugarman* had not included the day-to-day execution of the law but the formulation of broad policy. The disloyalty of aliens could not be conclusively presumed.

KENNETH L. KARST
(1986)

FOOD, DRUG, AND COSMETIC ACT
52 Stat. 1040 (1938)

Grounded on the COMMERCE CLAUSE, this act was a sweeping revision of the PURE FOOD AND DRUG ACT of 1906. It passed Congress after a five-year struggle and then only because of an uproar caused by nearly one hundred deaths from a new drug. Despite extensive compromise, this act substantially strengthened earlier legislation, affording greater consumer protection. Different chapters of the law dealt at length with food, drugs, and cosmetics, expanding coverage and increasing penalties. The act prohibited shipment in INTERSTATE COMMERCE of adulterated or misbranded products and broadened the definition of these terms. Indicative of the act's thrust, one section authorized the secretary of agriculture to establish standards of quality for foods to "promote honesty and fair dealing in the interest of consumers." Misbranding received special attention: imitations were to be clearly marked, flavoring or coloring additives noted, and the use of habit-forming ingredients was to be indicated on the label. Drugs had to meet federal formulations or disclose the differences. New drugs would have to pass rigorous tests. Congress partly remedied one of the act's weaknesses, a less stringent control over false advertising, in the Wheeler-Lea Act of the same year. The Supreme Court sustained the act in UNITED STATES V. SULLIVAN (1947).

DAVID GORDON
(1986)

FOOD LION, INC. v. AMERICAN BROADCASTING CO. (ABC)
194 F. 3d 505 (4th Cir. 1999)

For the purpose of filming material for the ABC television network's *Prime Time Live* program, two reporters obtained jobs at a Food Lion store by misrepresenting their mission. Using concealed cameras, they obtained damaging footage of food handling and storage conditions. Food Lion sued unsuccessfully to bar the broadcast, and later sought large damages for lost business and consumer confidence.

Food Lion advanced two claims—that ABC personnel had breached a duty of loyalty owed to an employer, and that ABC had engaged in unfair and deceptive trade practices—including the alleged fabrication of conditions shown in the film. A federal judge held that such claims were not barred by the FIRST AMENDMENT, even as applied to gathering and disseminating truthful information that held obvious public interest.

A jury awarded Food Lion more than $3 million in damages. The judge sharply reduced the award, to $315,000. ABC appealed even that smaller damage amount on FREEDOM OF SPEECH and FREEDOM OF THE PRESS grounds.

In late October 1999, a panel of the U.S. Court of Appeals for the Fourth Circuit reduced the damage award to a nominal $2, ruling that Food Lion's tort-based claims represented a constitutionally forbidden "end-run" around First Amendment protections for the news-gathering activities of journalists. The absence of any LIBEL claims, or any showing that the camera crew's conduct had been unlawful, undoubtedly made such a judgment easier for the court of appeals.

ROBERT M. O'NEIL
(2000)

(SEE ALSO: *Journalistic Practices, Tort Liability, and the Freedom of the Press.*)

FORCE ACT
4 Stat. 632 (1833)

Restive over the threat to slavery that they saw implicit in the growth of federal power, South Carolinians devised doctrines of NULLIFICATION and SECESSION in response to the Tariff Act of 1828. When the Tariff of 1832 failed to satisfy their demands for reduction, a special convention adopted an Ordinance of Nullification (1832), nullifying the tariff. President ANDREW JACKSON responded with his PROCLAMATION TO THE PEOPLE OF SOUTH CAROLINA (1832), denouncing the theory of secession, and with a request to Congress to enact legislation that would simultaneously avoid a military clash with the state over the collection of duties and permit a more prompt resort to federal force if confrontation could not be evaded.

Congress responded with the Force Act (Act of 2 March 1833), reaffirming the power of the President to use federal military and naval force to suppress resistance to the enforcement of federal laws, even if the source of resistance was the state itself. The act empowered him to call up states' militias after issuing a proclamation calling on those obstructing to disperse. It also permitted him to revise the procedure for collecting customs duties. Though South Carolina subsequently nullified the Force Act, federal authority had been vindicated.

WILLIAM M. WIECEK
(1986)

Bibliography

FREEHLING, WILLIAM W. 1966 *Prelude to Civil War: The Nullification Controversy in South Carolina, 1816–1836.* New York: Harper & Row.

FORCE ACTS
16 Stat. 140 (1870)
16 Stat. 433 (1871)
17 Stat. 13 (1871)

Congress enacted three statutes in 1870 and 1871 to protect the right of blacks to vote in the southern states and to suppress anti-RECONSTRUCTION terrorism. They are sometimes called the Enforcement Acts. The Act of May 31, 1870, prohibited all forms of infringement of the RIGHT TO VOTE, not merely the exclusion prohibited by the FIFTEENTH AMENDMENT, and made nightriding a federal FELONY. The Act of February 28, 1871, provided for federal supervision of voter registration and congressional elections to prohibit ballot-box frauds and intimidation of black voters. The Act of April 20, 1871, commonly called the Ku Klux Klan Act, provided civil remedies to persons deprived of rights and privileges secured by the federal Constitution; prohibited violent resistance to federal authority, in order to protect civilian and military officials enforcing Reconstruction measures; authorized the President to use militia and federal military force to suppress insurrections and domestic violence when a state was unable to do so; defined "rebellion" against the federal government; and provided that when the president proclaimed that a rebellion exists, he could suspend the writ of HABEAS CORPUS in the rebellious district. Under authority of the Klan Act, President ULYSSES S. GRANT proclaimed nine counties in South Carolina to be in rebellion during October 1871, suspended the writ of habeas corpus, and used federal troops to suppress violence there and elsewhere in the South. The Klan Act was instrumental in breaking the power of the Klans and other terrorist organizations for the time being.

In UNITED STATES V. REESE (1876), the Supreme Court held sections of the 1870 Act unconstitutional on the grounds that "the Fifteenth Amendment does not confer the right of suffrage upon any one." The Court anticipated its later STATE ACTION doctrine in UNITED STATES V. CRUIKSHANK (1876), voiding INDICTMENTS under the Klan Act on the grounds that the FOURTEENTH AMENDMENT "adds nothing to the rights of one citizen as against another. It simply furnishes a federal guaranty against any encroachment by the States." The Court held parts of the Klan Act unconstitutional in UNITED STATES V. HARRIS (1883) because they were directed at the actions of private persons, not at the states or their officers. (These decisions have lost most of their force today. See UNITED STATES V. GUEST, 1966.) Later Congresses in 1894 and 1909, hostile to the goals of Reconstruction, repealed most of the 1870 Act and the Klan Act, but the prohibitions of conspiracies and nightriding survive today in the United States Code, and the civil remedies provided by the Klan Act are today the foundation for an overwhelming majority of federal court lawsuits challenging the constitutionality of actions of state officers. (See SECTION 1983, TITLE 42, UNITED STATES CODE.)

WILLIAM M. WIECEK
(1986)

Bibliography

HYMAN, HAROLD M. 1973 *A More Perfect Union: The Impact of the Civil War and Reconstruction on the Constitution.* New York: Knopf.

FORD, GERALD R.
(1913–   )

Gerald Rudolph Ford, Jr., a graduate of the University of Michigan and Yale University Law School, served in the HOUSE OF REPRESENTATIVES from 1949 to 1973. A moderately conservative Republican who opposed most social welfare legislation but supported all of the CIVIL RIGHTS ACTS, Ford was his party's floor leader in the House from 1965 to 1973. Among his more controversial undertakings in that capacity was his attempt to secure the IMPEACHMENT of Supreme Court Justice WILLIAM O. DOUGLAS in 1970.

President RICHARD M. NIXON appointed Ford vice-president of the United States when the office fell vacant in 1973; this was the first application of procedures set forth in the Twenty-Fifth Amendment. When Nixon resigned the presidency in August 1974, Ford succeeded him, thereby becoming the first President to serve without winning a national election. In September 1974 Ford granted Nixon a full pardon for any offense against the United States that he might have committed while in office. (See WATERGATE AND THE CONSTITUTION.)

As President, Ford used the VETO POWER extensively, disapproving some forty-eight bills. In 1974, after Congress failed to act, Ford granted conditional AMNESTY to VIETNAM WAR deserters and draft evaders, exercising the presidential PARDONING POWER. His dispatch of Marines to free the freighter *Mayaguez* from Cambodia in May 1975 demonstrated that the "consultation" provisions of the WAR POWERS RESOLUTION OF 1973 did not prevent the COMMANDER-IN-CHIEF from taking decisive action in an emergency. Ford sought election in his own right in 1976 but was narrowly defeated by JIMMY CARTER.

DENNIS J. MAHONEY
(1986)

FORD v. WAINWRIGHT
477 U.S. 399 (1986)

The Supreme Court held, 5–4, that the infliction of CAPITAL PUNISHMENT on an insane prisoner violates the ban on

CRUEL AND UNUSUAL PUNISHMENTS imposed by the Eight Amendment and the FOURTEENTH AMENDMENT. Justice THURGOOD MARSHALL for the majority applied the principle that the Eighth Amendment recognizes the evolving standards of decency of a maturing society. No state today permits the execution of the insane. Even at the time of the adoption of the BILL OF RIGHTS, the COMMON LAW disapproved execution of the insane because it lacked retributive value and had no deterrence value. Marshall ruled that Florida's procedure for determining a condemned prisoner's sanity failed to rely on the judiciary to ensure neutrality in fact-finding.

The dissenting Justices contended that the Eighth Amendment did not mandate a right not to be executed while insane. Justice WILLIAM H. REHNQUIST observed that at common law the executive controlled the procedure by which the sanity of the condemned prisoner was judged. The dissenters refused to endorse a constitutional right to a judicial determination of sanity before the death penalty could be imposed. Justice LEWIS F. POWELL was the swing vote in this case. He agreed that the Eighth Amendment prohibited the execution of the insane, but declined to endorse Justice Marshall's virtual requirement of a judicial proceeding to determine sanity.

LEONARD W. LEVY
(1992)

FOREIGN AFFAIRS

The words "foreign affairs" are not to be found in the United States Constitution. There are scattered references to "commerce with foreign nations," to TREATIES and ambassadors, to the law of nations, but there is nothing to suggest that the relations of the United States with other nations form a significantly discrete constitutional category. Yet every major theme of constitutional jurisprudence is played differently in respect of foreign affairs. Foreign affairs provide a unique exception to the dogma that the federal government has only the powers expressly enumerated in the Constitution. For the relations of the United States with other countries, FEDERALISM is virtually irrelevant and the United States is essentially a unitary state. The separation and allocation of authority among the branches of the federal government for conducting foreign affairs are different from what they are in respect to domestic matters. Individual rights, strongly safeguarded by the Constitution in the internal life of the country, bow quite readily before the foreign interests of the United States. In this and in other respects foreign affairs discourage JUDICIAL REVIEW and intervention, the hallmark of United States constitutionalism.

The Constitution vests some foreign affairs powers in the federal government in the same manner in which it vests domestic powers, by bestowing them on one or another of the three branches of that government. Thus, Congress in Article I, section 8, is given the power to regulate commerce with foreign nations, to define offenses against the law of nations, and to declare war. The President has the power under Article II, section 2, to appoint ambassadors and make treaties (with the ADVICE AND CONSENT of the Senate). The JUDICIAL POWER of the United States extends, according to Article III, section 2, to cases arising under treaties, and to certain controversies involving foreign states, their public ministers, or their citizens. Many powers of government relating to foreign affairs, however, are not mentioned: for example, the power to control IMMIGRATION, to regulate ALIENS in the United States or United States nationals abroad, to assert the rights of the United States and to respond to claims by other governments, to participate in the international process of developing customary law, to make international agreements other than treaties, to recognize states and governments, or generally to determine national policy and attitudes on friendship and intercourse with other nations. While some missing powers can plausibly be inferred from ENUMERATED POWERS, others cannot, and, under general principles, powers not enumerated and not fairly to be inferred from expressed powers were not granted to the federal government: the legislative powers of Congress are limited to those "herein granted" (Article I, section 1), and the powers not delegated to the United States are reserved to the states or to the people by the TENTH AMENDMENT. Yet the federal government has exercised all these foreign affairs powers and others from the beginning, and no one has doubted that the federal government had that authority, and that the states did not.

In foreign affairs, then, the principle that the federal government has only the enumerated powers does not apply. All foreign affairs are delegated to the federal government as though that were expressly provided. A hundred years ago the Supreme Court, in CHAE CHAN PING V. UNITED STATES (1889), held, for example, that Congress has the power to regulate immigration because the power to exclude or admit aliens is inherent in the nationhood and SOVEREIGNTY of the United States. In UNITED STATES V. CURTISS-WRIGHT EXPORT CORP. (1936) the Supreme Court expounded a special constitutional principle:

> The broad statement that the federal government can exercise no powers except those specifically enumerated in the Constitution, and such implied powers as are NECESSARY AND PROPER to carry into effect the enumerated powers, is categorically true only in respect of our internal affairs. In that field, the primary purpose of the Constitution was to carve from the general mass of legislative powers *then possessed by the states* such portions as it was

thought desirable to vest in the federal government, leaving those not included in the enumeration still in the states. . . . And since the states severally never possessed international powers, such powers could not have been carved from the mass of state powers but obviously were transmitted to the United States from some other source. . . .

As a result of the separation from Great Britain by the Colonies acting as a unit, the powers of external sovereignty passed from the Crown not to the colonies severally, but to the colonies in their collective and corporate capacity as the United States of America. . . .

The Union existed before the Constitution, which was ordained and established among other things to form "a more perfect Union." Prior to that event, it is clear that the Union, declared by the ARTICLES OF CONFEDERATION to be "perpetual,' was the sole possessor of external sovereignty and in the Union it remained without change save in so far as the Constitution in express terms qualified its exercise. The Framers' Convention was called and exerted its powers upon the irrefutable postulate that though the states were several their people in respect of foreign affairs were one. . . .

It results that the investment of the federal government with the powers of external sovereignty did not depend upon the affirmative grants of the Constitution. The powers to declare and wage war, to conclude peace, to make treaties, to maintain diplomatic relations with other sovereignties, if they had never been mentioned in the Constitution, would have vested in the federal government as necessary concomitants of nationality. . . . As a member of the family of nations, the right and power of the United States in that field are equal to the right and power of the other members of the international family. Otherwise, the United States is not completely sovereign. The power to acquire territory by discovery and occupation . . . the power to expel undesirable aliens . . . the power to make such international agreements as do not constitute treaties in the constitutional sense . . . , none of which is expressly affirmed by the Constitution, nevertheless exist as inherently inseparable from the conception of nationality. This the court recognized, and . . . found the warrant for its conclusions not in the provisions of the Constitution, but in the law of nations.

Although the theory underlying *Curtiss-Wright* has been criticized, it has never been questioned by the Supreme Court. In any event, the DOCTRINE resulting from the theory—plenary power of the federal government in matters relating to foreign affairs, beyond those explicitly granted in the Constitution—is firmly established. The Supreme Court has not often found it necessary to resort to "sovereignty" or "nationhood" as a source of power for the federal government. In large part, the foreign activities of the federal government that have come to court are amply supported by enumerated powers of Congress or the President, by powers reasonably implied in enumer-

ated powers, or by construction of the Constitution as a whole. But sovereignty, nationhood, and their implications in international law and in the practice of other nations are ever available as a source of authority to supply any lack of enumerated power for the federal government in matters relating to foreign affairs. The network of regulation of immigration and of aliens in the United States, for a principal example, rests ultimately on United States sovereignty, and other exercises of authority not easily rooted in enumerated powers have been supported as exercises of "the foreign affairs powers" of Congress, with citations to *Curtiss-Wright*.

The powers expressly conferred upon branches of the federal government, and those additional powers implied in sovereignty, give the federal government full authority to act in the United States and for the United States in respect to its foreign affairs. Since plenary power has been delegated, state authority, STATES' RIGHTS, even state immunity (except in remote, hypothetical respects) do not limit federal authority in foreign affairs. When the federal government acts, its action is supreme, superseding any inconsistent state law. Federal action may also preempt, "occupy a field," excluding state action even if it is not inconsistent.

Some state actions in foreign affairs are excluded by Article I, section 10, even when the federal government has not acted. A state may not make a treaty. It may enter into an "Agreement or Compact" with a foreign nation only with the consent of Congress. Although here, as for other purposes, the difference between a treaty and another international agreement is uncertain, presumably if Congress should consent to an agreement by a state with a foreign government the agreement would not be successfully challenged as being a treaty to which Congress could not consent. An agreement requiring the consent of Congress may be formal or informal, even tacit. But, by analogy to doctrine that has developed in cases such as *Virginia v. Tennessee* (1893), with respect to compacts between states of the United States, probably a state may make a compact with a foreign government without congressional consent if the agreement does not tend to "the increase of political power in the states, which may encroach upon or interfere with the just supremacy of the United States."

The states are limited also by implication of the grant to Congress of power "to regulate commerce with foreign Nations and among the several States." Although that doctrine of implied limitations developed principally in respect of INTERSTATE COMMERCE it applies in essentially the same way to FOREIGN COMMERCE. The COMMERCE CLAUSE bars regulation by the states that excludes or discriminates against foreign commerce, or burdens such commerce unduly, as determined by weighing the local against the national interest. The courts continue to monitor such state regulations.

A single case, *Zschernig v. Miller* (1968), has held, more broadly, that even if the federal government has not acted, and even if there is no undue burden on foreign commerce, a state may not intrude on the federal monopoly in foreign affairs. In that case Oregon law required state courts to deny an inheritance to an alien unless the court were satisfied that the government of the alien's state of nationality would allow a United States national to inherit in reciprocal circumstances, and that the alien would be allowed to enjoy his inheritance without confiscation. That state law, the Supreme Court ruled, was impermissible under the Constitution because it involved the state courts in sitting in judgment on the policies of foreign governments. No other case has been decided on that principle.

"In respect of foreign relations generally, State lines disappear. As to such purpose the State . . . does not exist," the Supreme Court said in UNITED STATES V. BELMONT (1937). But while federal authority in foreign affairs is plenary, it is not exclusive. Federal law generally is superimposed on a network of state law; state law of property and contract, state tort and criminal law, state corporate law, tax law, and estate law govern activities and interests that implicate or impinge on foreign trade and other foreign relations of the United States. If in principle all of that state law could be superseded or excluded by federal statute or treaty, it has not been and could not effectively be done in fact, and foreign relations continue to be greatly affected by state law. State influence is reflected also in the system of selection of the national government—the President, the Senate, and the House of Representatives—and particular state interests weigh heavily in the determination of national interest by every branch of the federal government. Increasingly, states have also entered, independently if informally, on the international scene by commercial missions to promote local produce and industry abroad, and by participation in international cultural activities.

The principal field of constitutional uncertainty and the focus of constitutional controversy in foreign affairs have been the respective powers and authority of President and Congress.

The Framers of the Constitution, reflecting the painful lessons of the early years of independence, created the office of President and vested it with "executive power." They gave the President authority to appoint ambassadors and to make treaties but required that he obtain the advice and consent of the Senate. They designated the President the COMMANDER-IN-CHIEF of the army and navy. At the same time the Framers gave Congress the power to impose tariffs and otherwise regulate commerce with foreign nations; to define and punish piracy and other offenses against the law of nations; and to declare war. Other general powers given to Congress reach to foreign as well as domestic matters: the powers to tax and spend, to borrow and regulate the value of money, to establish post offices, to authorize and appropriate funds, to create and regulate a federal bureaucracy, and to make other laws necessary and proper to carry out the power of Congress and other federal powers.

Both Congress and the presidency have developed and changed, the President in particular now exercising his constitutional authority through a huge bureaucracy. The enumerated powers of each branch have grown as the United States has grown and achieved its large place in a transformed world. But the division of authority between President and Congress remains today essentially as it was expressly prescribed by the Framers. Although the President may propose, and his proposals weigh heavily, Congress exercises its expressed powers as they have developed. Congress decides whether the United States shall be at war or at peace, and passes the laws necessary to prepare for war, and to wage war successfully, and to deal with the consequences of war. Congress regulates "commerce with foreign nations"—trade, transportation, communication, and other intercourse—in its innumerable forms. Congress enacts laws to effectuate the powers of the federal government deriving from the sovereignty and nationhood of the United States. It passes laws constituting national policy toward other nations, for example, laws fixing the rights of their nationals in the United States or in our coastal waters. It also passes laws regulating our relations with other nations, for example, the 1976 statute determining the immunity of foreign governments in American courts. Congress enacts the laws—including any federal criminal law—necessary and proper for carrying out its own foreign affairs powers, the country's treaty obligations, and the foreign affairs powers of the President, including laws protecting the processes for making foreign policy or conducting foreign relations, *e.g.*, statutes protecting classified documents, or forbidding the harassment of foreign diplomats or the picketing of foreign embassies. Congress also uses its general lawmaking powers for foreign as for domestic affairs. Congress decides how much to spend for defense, and how much for foreign aid and to which countries. Its power to borrow money and to regulate the value of money (of the United States and that of other countries) has major transnational applications and implications. By its authority to establish post offices Congress has approved American participation in an international postal system; it has used its authority over PATENTS and COPYRIGHTS to authorize dealing with them by international arrangements. Congress appropriates money for the BUDGET of the State Department, or to pay our obligations to the United Nations. Congress creates and regulates the Foreign Service. It investigates so that it can legislate (or not legislate).

For his part, the President (not Congress) makes treaties and appoints ambassadors (with the consent of the Senate) and receives ambassadors. Only the President acts as commander-in-chief of the armed forces; only he can take care that the laws are faithfully executed. A few powers have been inferred from those listed: for example, only the President speaks for the United States to other nations and only the President negotiates with other nations. The President recognizes governments, enters into diplomatic relations with them or terminates these relations, and gives his ambassadors their instructions and receives their reports.

There is more to foreign affairs, however, than is accounted for in the express allocations of the Constitution, and issues have arisen as to matters not clearly implied in those allocations or where argument can support allocation to one of the political branches as plausibly as to the other. The President makes treaties, but who can terminate them on behalf of the United States? Congress declares war, but who can decide to terminate a war? Who can make international agreements other than treaties, or otherwise commit the power and resources of the United States? Who can deploy forces for purposes short of war? Who can determine those general principles, guidelines, and attitudes that go to make up "foreign policy?"

There is no ready principle of allocation of authority between Congress and President, or of CONSTITUTIONAL INTERPRETATION generally, to determine to whom these unmentioned yet clearly federal powers are assigned. In domestic affairs the principle of allocation of authority between Congress and the President is reasonably clear: Congress makes the law; the President executes the law. In foreign affairs that principle of allocation did not obtain even in the original conception, and surely it does not as the two branches have developed. Clearly, the President has substantial authority to "legislate," to determine national policy, as well as to execute it. The President makes foreign policy when he makes treaties and other international agreements; he also makes law, since international agreements create international law, and some treaties and agreements have domestic effect and are the LAW OF THE LAND under the SUPREMACY CLAUSE. The President makes foreign policy also in representing the United States in the international arena—by recognizing states or governments and deciding on the character of relations with them; by making or responding to international claims; by declaring the attitudes of the United States, many of which he can implement or reflect in actions on his own authority. Inevitably, the President makes foreign policy also by the manner in which he conducts foreign relations.

The President and Congress have asserted opposing principles of constitutional jurisprudence to determine allocation of the unallocated federal powers in foreign affairs. The President has claimed a source of plenary authority in that he is the "sole organ of the United States in its international relations." He has argued that Article II, section 2, of the Constitution vests in him not only the power to execute laws but the whole "executive power" of the United States. It is urged that the Framers understood the executive power to include the whole of foreign relations, except insofar as the Constitution expressly limits the President's authority (as by requiring that he obtain the consent of the Senate to appoint ambassadors or to make treaties), or has expressly given some foreign affairs power to Congress, such as the power to regulate foreign commerce or to declare war. Congress, on the other hand, has claimed that its constitutional authority over foreign "commerce" includes all aspects of intercourse with foreign nations; by that authority, and by its control of war and peace, it has been claimed, Congress is the principal political organ of the nation and has all the authority of the United States in international relations except that expressly given to the President.

The competing constitutional doctrines have rarely come to court and the issue remains largely unresolved in principle. Constitutional history, however, has supplied some of the answers that constitutional law has left unanswered. From the beginning, many powers not expressly delegated by the Constitution have flowed to the President and have made his the predominant part in the foreign policy process. Presidential authority grew early and steadily by a kind of "accretion." Even when United States diplomatic missions abroad were few and United States international relations simple and minimal, the conduct of foreign affairs was a continuing process, and it raised issues every day. These came to the President, through his ambassadors and his secretary of state; Congress did not hear of them unless the President saw necessary or fit to tell Congress. The early issues—whether to declare our neutrality in European wars, or send a misbehaving French minister home—were not matters which the Constitution expressly left to Congress or expressly denied to the President. They did not call for general policy best reflected in formal legislation or resolution, but for ad hoc judgment and particular measures tailored to the case. Sometimes decision was urgent, and the President was always "in session" while Congress was not, and could readily or easily be informed and convened, especially in the conditions of communications and transportation of the early days. The President could act quickly and informally, often discreetly or secretly, while action by Congress would have been public and formal, slow and sometimes unduly dramatic. Often, unless the President acted, the United States could not act at all.

And so President GEORGE WASHINGTON declared neutrality, President JAMES MONROE his famous doctrine; later Presidents opened Japan, traded in China, intervened in Latin America. Presidents appointed "agents" (without Senate consent), concluded EXECUTIVE AGREEMENTS (without consent of Congress or the Senate), sent troops abroad, expanded intelligence and "covert activities," acted in the world arena for the United States, making its policies, committing its honor and credit. What early Presidents did became precedents for their successors to do likewise or to exceed. What successive Presidents did became the basis for assertions of authority to do them, supported in constitutional terms in the President's "foreign affairs power" often implemented by his power as commander-in-chief.

Congress contributed to the steady growth of presidential power. Congress early recognized and confirmed the President's control of daily foreign intercourse, and the resulting monopoly of information and experience promoted the President's claim of expertise and Congress's sense of inadequacy. A growing practice of informal consultations between the President and congressional leaders disarmed them as well as members of Congress generally, and helped confirm presidential authority to act without formal congressional participation. Often Congress later ratified or confirmed what the President had done, as in the KOREAN WAR. And repeatedly it delegated its own huge powers to the President in broad terms, so that he could later claim to act under the authority of Congress as well as his own, as in the VIETNAM WAR.

Congress has never formally conceded all these unspecified powers to the President. At most Congress has silently acquiesced in his power to act. Frequently, Congress asserted authority for itself to act in areas where the President also claimed authority. For example, although in 1945, President HARRY S. TRUMAN, without congressional participation, claimed for the United States the resources of its continental shelf, Congress in 1976 acted to declare an exclusive 200-mile fishing zone for the United States, and did so against the wishes of the executive branch. At times, Congress has also insisted on its authority to preclude, supersede, or control presidential action. In foreign affairs, as elsewhere, it has insisted that the President must execute the laws that Congress enacts and must spend (not impound) money that Congress appropriates. In foreign as in domestic affairs Congress has repudiated EXECUTIVE PRIVILEGE when its committees have sought information or documents. In foreign affairs, too, Congress has provided for LEGISLATIVE VETO to recoup delegation of authority and to oversee executive execution of the law. Whether the general invalidation of the legislative veto (IMMIGRATION AND NATURALIZATION SERVICE V. CHADHA, 1983) will totally bar its use in foreign affairs legislation as well is yet to be determined.

A principal unresolved issue between President and Congress has been the claimed authority of the President to deploy the armed forces of the United States. The issue has not been about the WAR POWERS, expressed in the Constitution. The power to decide for war or peace is indisputably with Congress: Congress can declare war or authorize it by other resolution; it can decide for limited war, and though Presidents have claimed plenary authority as commanders-in-chief, theoretically Congress can probably regulate the conduct of war in general though perhaps not in detail. Wars apart, Presidents have claimed authority to deploy the armed forces for political ends and have done so on numerous occasions, sometimes engaging them in hostilities short of war. In Korea in 1950–1952 troops were engaged in war, President Truman claiming authority to act under a treaty—the UNITED NATIONS CHARTER—and Congress soon acquiesced in and ratified his action. In Vietnam, Congress gave two Presidents blanket authority to engage in hostilities. Members of Congress have often challenged the President's authority, although Congress has rarely done so formally. After Vietnam, however, in the WAR POWERS RESOLUTION adopted over President RICHARD M. NIXON's veto, Congress purported to regulate the power of the President to deploy armed forces in circumstances where they are or might be engaged in hostilities. Although Presidents have questioned the resolution's constitutionality, they have acquiesced in principle, but in several instances they may not have respected the resolution in fact.

The power that Presidents have claimed to enter into international agreements or otherwise commit the United States has also been an unresolved subject of controversy. Again, it is not the treaty power, expressed in the Constitution, that has raised serious issues. The President can make a treaty if the Senate consents, and the Senate can ask for changes and impose other relevant conditions upon its consent. The power to terminate treaties has been exercised by the President, often on his own authority. A challenge to the President's authority to terminate the treaty with the Republic of China (Taiwan) in 1979 did not prevail, although the Supreme Court did not decide the merits of the controversy in GOLDWATER V. CARTER (1980).

Since the beginnings of the nation, Presidents have made many international agreements other than by treaty. An agreement authorized or approved by resolution of Congress, by majority vote in both Houses (rather than by consent of two-thirds of the Senate to a treaty), is the equivalent of a treaty for virtually all purposes. But Presidents have also made agreements on their own authority. Some authority to do so is conceded. It is not disputed that the President can make agreements as commander-in-chief during war (for example, an armistice). He can make agreements also to implement his established foreign affairs power, for example, agreements incidental to recognizing a foreign government, as in the Litvinov agreements with the Union of Soviet Socialist Republics in 1933. (See UNITED STATES V. BELMONT; UNITED STATES V. PINK.) At least some other international agreements have been held to be within his authority, for example, the Iranian Hostages Agreement, since, the Supreme Court said, in DAMES & MOORE V. REGAN (1981), the President's exercise of authority to resolve international claims had been acquiesced in by Congress. On the other hand, some agreements clearly require Senate consent (to a treaty) or congressional approval. There has been no authoritative determination, nor any accepted guidelines, as to which agreements the President can make on his own authority and which he cannot. The suggestion that "important" agreements cannot be made by the President alone is not self-defining, and Presidents have in fact made "important" agreements alone, especially when they desired to keep them confidential. The Senate has expressed its sense that the President cannot commit the forces or resources of the United States except by treaty or pursuant to act of Congress. Congress has considered numerous bills to regulate international agreements by the President on his own authority. But it has legislated only a limited measure, requiring the executive branch to transmit any executive agreement to Congress, if only to a congressional committee in confidence.

In general, Presidents and Congress have worked together even when Congress is not controlled by the President's POLITICAL PARTY. That party politics "stop at the water's edge" and do not trouble American foreign relations is not wholly true, and in the view of many would not be desirable. But throughout most of our national history the dominant voices in the two major parties have not differed sharply in foreign policy, and Congress has more or less willingly followed the President's lead, while Presidents have tried to lead chiefly where Congress would not be too reluctant to follow.

The respective authority of the political branches apart, there have been other constitutional issues relating to treaties and other international agreements. Some early issues have been resolved. Treaties and other international agreements, like other acts of the United States government, are subject to the BILL OF RIGHTS and other constitutional limitations. There are no limitations on the subject matter of such agreements other than those implied in the fact that there must be a bona fide agreement between the United States and one or more other nations in a matter related to foreign policy interests of the United States. A treaty or other agreement may deal with matters that might otherwise be regulated by the states or by congressional statute.

Treaties and international agreements have their own place in constitutional law. Some treaties or agreements are "self-executing": they are intended to be enforced by the executive or applied by the courts without waiting for implementation by Congress. Whether a treaty is self-executing is a matter of interpretation of the agreement, usually determined by the intent of the United States government in the matter. If a treaty or other agreement is self-executing it will be treated like a federal law, supreme over state law and superseding any earlier, inconsistent federal law. But the treaty is not superior to later federal law, and although the courts will interpret a statute, where fairly possible, consistently with international obligations of the United States, when Congress passes a law clearly inconsistent with a pre-existing treaty, the courts will apply the later statute, in effect putting the United States in default on its international obligation.

The role of the courts in foreign affairs is not essentially different from their role in domestic affairs. The JURISDICTION OF THE FEDERAL COURTS under Article III of the Constitution extends to cases arising under treaties of the United States as well as those arising under other international agreements of the United States or under customary international law. Foreign affairs may be implicated also in cases arising under the Constitution and various laws of the United States. The federal courts have jurisdiction also over "cases affecting Ambassadors, other public ministers and consuls," and over controversies between a foreign state or foreign citizen and a state or citizen of the United States, but such controversies have not loomed large in the history of the Constitution or of our foreign relations.

Thanks to both political and institutional limitations, the judicial prerogative of invalidating acts of the political branches has not troubled United States foreign affairs. Most constitutional issues in foreign affairs, including some big issues of competition between President and Congress, rarely come to court because in general there is not the required CASE OR CONTROVERSY and there is no one with the necessary STANDING to raise the issue. Challenge to an exercise of national authority in foreign affairs on grounds of "states' rights" is generally futile in view of the established monopoly of the federal government. Foreign affairs have also been a principal source of the POLITICAL QUESTION DOCTRINE, under which the courts have declared some foreign affairs issues "political" and therefore not justiciable. Federalism does provide the court a role relevant to foreign affairs when they scrutinize state activities that, a private party claims, unduly burden foreign commerce or that may be inconsistent with or preempted by congressional policy.

The courts exercise their usual lawmaking function in foreign affairs also. In addition to interpreting the Constitution and laws, the courts have determined and developed the maritime law which remains largely judge-made. They have also developed rules, if only for their own guidance, such as the " ACT OF STATE" DOCTRINE, that courts will not sit in judgment on the acts of a foreign state in its own territory, as in *Banco Nacional de Cuba v. Sabbatino* (1964). Courts also make foreign relations law when they determine and apply customary international law. "International law is part of our law, and must be ascertained and administered by the courts of justice of appropriate jurisdiction, as often as questions of right depending on it are duly presented for their determination," the Court said in *The Paquete Habana* (1900).

Nothing in the Constitution suggests that the rights of individuals in respect of foreign affairs are different from what they are in relation to other exercises of governmental power. But although arguments that individual rights and protections are fewer and narrower in foreign affairs than elsewhere have not prevailed in principle, constitutional guarantees sometimes look different and afford less protection.

In principle, constitutional safeguards apply in foreign as in domestic affairs and apply to governmental activities abroad as at home. The Bill of Rights limits the Congress and the President, foreign affairs legislation as well as treaties and other international agreements. Even temporary or unauthorized aliens in the United States are entitled to the protections of the Bill of Rights, for example, the safeguards for those accused of crime. But where an individual right is not absolute but might be outweighed by an important public interest, national interests in war and peace, and even lesser concerns of foreign relations, would have important weight in the balance. So, for example, courts have upheld prohibitions on picketing near embassies (*Frend v. United States*, 1938), or the cancellation of a passport of someone engaged in systematically identifying U.S. intelligence agents abroad (AGEE V. HAIG, 1981).

In regard to foreign relations as to other matters, DUE PROCESS OF LAW requires fair procedures, and that requirement applies to aliens as to citizens, in the United States or abroad. Trial under the authority of the United States, at least in time of peace, must provide a jury, RIGHT TO COUNSEL, and other constitutional safeguards for those accused of crime. An alien in the United States, subject to DEPORTATION on grounds prescribed by law, is entitled to a FAIR HEARING, and the government must prove by clear, unequivocal, and convincing evidence that the alien is deportable on the grounds provided by Congress. But an alien seeking admission to the United States is due no process beyond consideration and decision by the designated administrative officer.

Due process also limits the substance of what government can do, requiring that it not be "unreasonable, arbitrary or capricious, and [that] the means selected have real and substantial relation to the object sought to be attained," as the Court said in NEBBIA V. NEW YORK (1934).

Courts have long refrained, however, from invalidating economic and social regulations, and they are even less likely to do so in matters affecting foreign relations. But SUBSTANTIVE DUE PROCESS protects also a person's liberty, and here the constitutional limitation has been greater, and judicial deference to the political branches far less. The Supreme Court declared in KENT V. DULLES (1955) that the RIGHT TO TRAVEL abroad is "a part of the liberty of which the citizen cannot be deprived without due process of law." In AFROYIM V. RUSK (1967) the Court invalidated a statutory provision making it a crime for members of certain communist organizations to obtain or use a passport, because the law "too broadly and indiscriminately restricts the right to travel and thereby abridges the liberty guaranteed by the Fifth Amendment." However, in *Agee v. Haig* the Court upheld withdrawal of a passport from one who systematically exposed the identity of United States intelligence agents. And to date the courts have held that even an alien lawfully admitted and long resident in the United States can be deported for whatever reasons commend themselves to Congress.

The EQUAL PROTECTION OF THE LAWS is required in foreign affairs matters as elsewhere. States cannot discriminate against aliens to deny them WELFARE BENEFITS, EDUCATION, access to the general civil service, or the right to practice their profession. States may not deny educational opportunities even to "undocumented" alien children, not lawfully admitted to the United States (*Plyer v. Doe*, 1982). But a state may reserve for citizens jobs as teachers, policemen, other "peace officers" (including deputy probation officers), and others involved in "the political function of governing." (See FOLEY V. CONNELIE; AMBACH V. NORWICK.) Some state discriminations against aliens are invalid because inconsistent with, or preempted by, the immigration laws or other acts of Congress (HINES V. DAVIDOWITZ, 1941; TAKAHASHI V. FISH & GAME COMMISSION, 1948). Unlike the states, however, Congress can limit the federal Civil Service to citizens, and may discriminate against aliens in other respects that do not infringe their basic rights. An act of Congress or treaty may give some rights to aliens on the basis of reciprocity, *i.e.*, that the country of which the alien is a national give such benefits to United States citizens.

Aliens may be denied the right to acquire some kinds of property or invest in some kinds of enterprises in the United States. But an alien (other than an enemy alien in time of war) may not be deprived of his property without due process of law, and it cannot be taken for public use without JUST COMPENSATION.

The constitutional provision that property not be taken for public use without just compensation may have special application in foreign affairs. The United States has frequently in its history entered into an agreement with another government to settle claims of United States citizens against that government. Although the settlements sometimes did not have authorization or approval by the individual claimants, and often gave them only partial recovery, the courts have upheld such agreements as within the authority of the President to make, and have rejected claims that the agreements deprived the claimants of property without just compensation. But where private claims are sacrificed by the United States in settlement of other national interests, as was apparently the case in the early French spoliation cases, and as was claimed in the Iranian Hostages Agreement, the courts may yet find that there has been a taking of the claims requiring compensation.

There is much uncertainty in the constitutional law of foreign relations but it should not be exaggerated. The abiding uncertainties lie principally—almost wholly—in the separation, distribution, and fragmentation of powers between the President and Congress (or between President and Senate), a division different from those prevailing in domestic affairs. Some of the uncertainties and conflicts arise out of different constitutional interpretations, which might in theory be resolved but are not likely to be resolved soon, for courts are reluctant to step into intense confrontation between President and Congress or inhibit either when the other does not object. If the courts do speak to such "separation" issues occasionally, they are likely to reach for the narrowest ground, resolving as little as possible.

Much of the controversy in the conduct of foreign affairs, moreover, does not stem from constitutional uncertainty, but rather reflects what the Framers intended, or were willing to accept, when they separated powers and subdivided functions. If Congress refuses to authorize an anti-ballistic missile program requested by the President, if the President vetoes a tariff adopted by Congress, if the Senate refuses consent to a human rights treaty negotiated by the President, the controversy does not involve competition for constitutional power but the kind of conflict "prescribed" by the Constitution. There is no constitutional issue when the complaint is not that the Constitution has been violated but that it is not working to taste. For a contemporary example, the real complaint in the national crisis over Vietnam was not that the President usurped constitutional power, but that, acting within his powers, he virtually compelled Congress to go along. That is a complaint against the Constitution.

That under a less-than-certain and less-than-happy constitutional arrangement, the conduct of foreign relations continues to function with reasonable effectiveness owes in substantial part to extraconstitutional arrangements, including varieties of congressional committees and staff that have become integral to the foreign policy process.

But the Framers thought they had good reasons for prescribing limits to cooperation, even some conflict. If effective government, in foreign relations as elsewhere, requires cooperation, democratic government, in foreign relations as elsewhere, abhors congressional abdication, and even enjoins it to provide legal opposition. The President provides initiative and efficiency, but Congress is the more representative branch and brings to bear the influence of public opinion, diversity, concern for local and individual rights. At its best, there is a counterpoint of presidential expertise and some inexpert congressional wisdom producing foreign policy and foreign relations not always efficient but supporting larger, deeper national interests.

LOUIS HENKIN
(1986)

(SEE ALSO: *Congress and Foreign Policy.*)

Bibliography

CORWIN, EDWARD S. 1957 *The President: Office and Powers.* 4th rev. ed. New York: New York University Press.

HENKIN, LOUIS 1972 *Foreign Affairs and the Constitution.* Mineola, N.Y.: Foundation Press.

LOFGREN, CHARLES A. 1972 War-Making Power Under the Constitution: The Original Understanding. *Yale Law Journal* 81:672–797.

MCDOUGAL, MYRES S. and LANS, ASHER 1954 Treaties and Congressional-Executive or Presidential Agreements: Interchangeable Instruments of National Policy. *Yale Law Journal* 54:181–351, 534–615.

Report of the Commission on the Organization of the Government for the Conduct of Foreign Policy, and Appendices. 1975.

SOFAER, ABRAHAM D. 1976 *War, Foreign Affairs and Constitutional Power.* Cambridge, Mass.: Ballinger Publishing Co.

WRIGHT, QUINCY 1922 *The Control of American Foreign Relations.* New York: Macmillan.

FOREIGN AFFAIRS
(Update)

In the last decade of the twentieth century there have been several important developments in the constitutional balance affecting U.S. foreign relations. The most conspicuous changes have involved the relative power of the Congress (especially the U.S. SENATE) and the President. The political weakness of President WILLIAM J. CLINTON has permitted a resurgence of the Senate Foreign Relations Committee and a significant expansion of the Senate's role under the TREATY POWER, with a corresponding diminution of executive authority with respect to that power. Congress has also continued to use its LEGISLATIVE POWER and appropriations power to specify details of foreign policy (maintaining a trend beginning with the Democratic Congress elected after WATERGATE). With respect to the WAR POWERS, Clinton has continued the past practice of executive-initiated uses of military force in limited engagements where the risk of American casualties was small. However, Clinton seems to have been especially cautious in this area. He has defended executive authority under the Constitution less vigorously than his immediate predecessor, GEORGE H. W. BUSH. Finally, the Supreme Court has revived judicial enforcement of principles of FEDERALISM, which in turn may call into question the virtually unlimited scope (subject to the BILL OF RIGHTS) of the federal treaty power. The basic lines of authority among the political branches, and the near total formal supremacy of the federal government over the states in foreign affairs, continued to be well established and uncontroversial. Political controversy affects issues at the margins, but the political weakness of the Clinton administration illustrates the vulnerability of EXECUTIVE POWER to the vicissitudes of domestic politics.

The Chair of the Senate Foreign Relations Committee, Senator Jesse Helms of North Carolina, has used his influence in recent years to block important ambassadorial appointments by Clinton, most predominantly when he blocked Clinton's nominee for Ambassador to Mexico. By declining to schedule hearings on important appointments and treaties, he also forced a reorganization (and diminution in stature) of that part of the executive branch dealing with arms control and foreign economic assistance. In 1999, the Senate rejected U.S. adherance to the Comprehensive Nuclear Test Ban Treaty, which had been a central part of the Clinton foreign policy program. In addition, the Senate has asserted its power in significantly expanded ways to attach conditions to its resolutions of ratification to arms control and INTERNATIONAL HUMAN RIGHTS treaties in ways unappealing to the executive branch. For example, the Senate has attempted to assure that no U.S. domestic law will be affected by human rights treaties. By attaching extensive and detailed conditions to arms control treaties the Senate has also successfully asserted its prerogative, albeit over protests by Clinton, in four distinct areas.

Historically, the executive branch has concluded treaty amendments of a technical, administrative, or minor substantive nature, on the basis of its own constitutional authority, and has likewise adjusted treaty relations to take account of the break-up of states and state succession. In addition, the executive branch has historically exercised the prerogative of determining whether to seek required legislative support for international agreements through the Article II procedure or, alternatively, through an act of Congress. In its interaction with the Senate over adjusting two major arms control treaties, however, the Clinton administration may have contributed to the erosion of executive authority on all these points.

First, the administration agreed to submit an agreement dealing with conventional weapons in Europe—the CFE Flank Agreement—to the Senate for its approval under Article II of the Constitution, abandoning its earlier decision to seek simple legislative approval from both houses of Congress. In doing so Clinton made two conceptually distinct concessions. He first acceded to the Senate's hitherto unsupportable position that "militarily significant" agreements had to be submitted to the Senate as Article II treaties rather than to Congress as Congressional–Executive agreements. Second, he failed to preserve executive prerogative to choose which constitutional procedure—Article II or an Act of Congress—to follow. The Clinton administration's concessions were qualified but the end result was that Clinton capitulated to an assertion of Senate power that is unsupported by historical practice.

Third, the Clinton administration accepted the Senate's position that the executive cannot subsequently change "shared understandings" between the executive branch and the Senate. Clinton thereby accepted, as a correct statement of constitutional law, the "Biden Condition" that grew out of the attempt by President RONALD REAGAN to amend the Anti-ballistic Missle (ABM) Treaty unilaterally under the guise of a "reinterpretation" of the treaty. The Biden Condition restricts the ability of the executive to change the interpretation of a treaty provision if it has made an "authoritative statement" of that provision's meaning to the Senate during the ratification process, such that there is a "shared understanding" of that meaning. The condition apparently applies even if the adjustment in interpretation of the provision is based on changed circumstances and is entirely uncontroversial. The consequence of this concession may be to restrict the future ability of the executive to adjust treaty relations in the normal course of diplomacy.

Finally, Clinton agreed to and then complied with a Senate condition that was both unrelated to the treaty under consideration and arguably unconstitutional as well. The condition in question—"Condition 9"—dealt with an agreement that would have extended obligations under the 1972 ABM Treaty to several new states, and also changed obligations under the treaty to account for the break-up of the Soviet Union. Condition 9 required the President to submit this agreement to the Senate for ADVICE AND CONSENT. When the Senate consents to ratification of a treaty, it may without question attach conditions to its consent that relate to the treaty obligations that it accepts and, more controversially, to associated domestic matters and the domestic effect of the treaty in question. On the other hand, the Senate presumably has no authority to condition its consent on presidential action wholly unrelated to the treaty. Condition 9 fell in the middle of this spectrum in that it related to an entirely different treaty, the ABM Treaty, although that treaty also dealt with arms control and was therefore loosely related to the subject matter of the treaty to which Condition 9 was attached. The agreement also would have adjusted the operation of the ABM Treaty to take account of the breakup of the Soviet Union. Normally such matters involving the succession of states would be settled by EXECUTIVE AGREEMENT pursuant to the President's constitutional foreign affairs authority, but under Condition 9 this agreement must be submitted to the Senate.

The role of Congress in authorizing the use of military force has also continued to fluctuate, and the constitutional debate over the scope of congressional authority, executive prerogative, and the war power has continued as well. In defending executive power the Clinton administration has at times seemed more solicitous of Congress than prior administrations. For example, the legal opinion justifying military intervention in Haiti relied principally on arguments based on statutory authority rather than relying on generalized claims of constitutional authority as had often been done in the past. On the other hand, the President conducted an air war against Yugoslavia, and stated a willingness to use ground forces, without formal congressional authorization. Congress had indicated support for the President's policy, and the air war was crafted to minimize the risk of American casualties.

With respect to the power of Congress to declare war, recent scholarship has called into question the proposition that Congress has the ultimate power to determine whether the country will wage war or maintain peace. This proposition was based on the ORIGINAL INTENT of the Framers, which does not now seem to be so clear as it was to those who were passionately opposed to the VIETNAM WAR. The text of the Constitution gives Congress the power to "declare" war, but a declaration of war is different from making, initiating, or deciding upon war. It is different both semantically and in legal meaning. The intent of the Framers on this point is inscrutable. The sole drafting change in the relevant text at the CONSTITUTIONAL CONVENTION was to change Congress's war power from "make" to "declare." That change by itself plainly suggests a narrowing of Congress's power. The change may have been made for a different reason, or for no substantive reason at all, but it is one that under the normal canons of legal interpretation would be given some significance. Whether the change was designed to curtail congressional power or to clarify the COMMANDER-IN-CHIEF clause depends on inferences from isolated statements that seem at best inconclusive. In the end the record consists mostly of silence from which contradictory inferences can be drawn—ei-

ther that "more people would have protested if they had understood that the President was given power to initiate war," or that "initiating war was an executive power that was so ingrained in the political and legal context that the Framers just naturally assumed that the President had that power as a result of being vested with the 'executive power.' "

In addition, original intent as commonly applied is a fragile basis for interpreting the Constitution in the context of contemporary foreign relations. Terms like "war" or the "executive power" do not have meanings fixed for all time in the eighteenth century. Subsequent practice by the political branches can provide a new gloss on original intent. A good example is the Senate's role to "advise" in the making of treaties. President GEORGE WASHINGTON and his successors effectively reinterpreted the original understanding to eliminate the Senate's formal role during the course of a negotiation, and the Senate has concurred for 200 years. Another example is the Framers' assumption that all treaties would be "self-executing" and applied by the courts as rules of decision, as is literally required by Article VI. Chief Justice JOHN MARSHALL created a category of non-self-executing treaties in the case of *Foster and Elam v. Neilson* (1829). Similarly the term "war," which in any event seems especially ambiguous and indeterminate, seems to have been reinterpreted over the course of two centuries. Perhaps there is a distinction between big wars and little wars, or offensive wars and defensive responses, or wars and police actions. Perhaps the use of small-scale military force for foreign policy purposes is not "war" at all. Looking at historical practice, especially since WORLD WAR II, one could conclude that the political branches have made some of those distinctions, reserving Congress's role to approving major wars in advance when such a decision was possible under the circumstances. The role of Congress in the GULF WAR supports this distinction. In other, minor war decisions Congress has acquiesced to presidential initiation of military action and has confined its role to influence through the authorization and appropriations process.

Even the way the debate is framed is misleading. The issue is normally described as one of reconciling Congress's so-called war power based on the declare war clause with the President's commander-in-chief power. This presentation of the issue in this way is at least incomplete, because both Congress and the President have many additional powers that bear on the question of how the use of military force must be authorized under the Constitution. In fact, Congress is intimately involved in the decisions to use military force, in focused and specific ways, through its authorization and appropriation functions. In recent years, Congress also has enhanced its role informally through the legislative process, for example in a procedure negotiated by Congress and the President for prior consultation in connection with continued authorization and appropriations for UNITED NATIONS Peacekeeping forces.

In the 1990s, the Supreme Court revived judicial enforcement of STATES' RIGHTS and principles of federalism. These decisions may call into question the virtually unlimited scope of the treaty power (subject to the Bill of Rights) derived from MISSOURI V. HOLLAND (1920). Treaties dealing with human rights, government procurement, ENVIRONMENTAL REGULATION, and criminal law raise many federalism concerns. A conspicuous manifestation of the states' disregard of federal treaty obligations is their regular failure to notify criminal defendants of their rights under consular treaties to contact their consuls. The executive branch has neither sought LEGISLATION nor taken other action to implement these obligations via-à-vis the states, and in the case of *Breard v. Greene* (1998), the Supreme Court declined to intervene in the execution of a Paraguayan national by the state of Virginia, even though Virginia had violated this U.S. treaty obligation, which is entitled to supremacy over state law by virtue of Article VI, and even though the International Court of Justice and the U.S. Secretary of State had requested a STAY OF EXECUTION pending further proceedings in the Hague. Several states have violated and continue to violate this treaty obligation, and it may be unclear under the federalism decisions of the REHNQUIST COURT whether the federal government has constitutional power to require otherwise.

PHILLIP R. TRIMBLE

(2000)

Bibliography

BRADLEY, CURTIS A. 1998 The Treaty Power and American Federalism. *Michigan Law Review* 97:390–461.

HENKIN, LOUIS 1996 *Foreign Affairs and the Constitution*, 2nd ed. Mineolo, N.Y.: Foundation Press.

TRIMBLE, PHILLIP R. 1997 The War Power Twenty-Five Years Later. *UC Davis Journal of International Law and Policy* 3: 183–190.

TRIMBLE, PHILLIP R. and KOFF, ALEXANDER W. 1998 All Fall Down: The Treaty Power in the Clinton Administration. *Berkeley Journal of International Law* 16:55–70.

YOO, JOHN C. 1996 The Continuation of Politics By Other Means: The Original Understanding of War Powers. *California Law Review* 84:167–305.

FOREIGN COMMERCE

The Constitution grants to Congress the power "To regulate Commerce with foreign Nations, and among the several States. . . ." A few cases in the 1800s indicated that the power to regulate foreign commerce was the same as the power to regulate INTERSTATE COMMERCE. Later, in *Brolan v. United States* (1915), the Supreme Court indicated that the power given Congress to regulate foreign commerce was so complete that it was limited only by other portions of the Constitution. So the Court upheld Congress in its regulating, prohibiting, and taxing commerce with other nations while sometimes restricting its power to regulate interstate commerce.

Today the issue is of no significance. The power of Congress to regulate interstate commerce is so great as to make any distinctions meaningless. Congress need only concern itself with the specific constitutional restrictions on the foreign commercial power: those preventing the taxation of exports and giving any preference to the ports of one state over those of another state.

In *Japan Line, Ltd. v. Los Angeles* (1979), however, the Court held that the foreign COMMERCE CLAUSE may serve to limit state taxation in cases in which the interstate commerce clause would not. The Court held invalid a nondiscriminatory, apportioned, state property tax on the value of shipping containers belonging to a Japanese shipping company. The Court said that the tax would have been valid if it had been applied to interstate shipments, but was not here because the containers were taxed on full value in Japan and the Court had no authority to require apportioned taxation in foreign lands. The Court said that state taxes on foreign commerce had to meet all the tests for interstate commerce; in addition, the Court must inquire whether even with apportionment a substantial risk of international multiple taxation persists, and whether the tax prevents the federal government from speaking with one voice when regulating commerce with foreign governments.

EDWARD L. BARRETT, JR.

(1986)

(SEE ALSO: *State Regulation of Commerce; State Taxation of Commerce.*)

Bibliography

HENKIN, LOUIS 1972 *Foreign Affairs and the Constitution.* Pages 69–71. Mineola, N.Y.: Foundation Press.

NOWAK, JOHN E.; ROTUNDA, RONALD D.; and YOUNG, NELSON J. 1980 *Handbook on Constitutional Law.* Pages 129–131. St. Paul, Minn.: West Publishing Co.

FOREIGN POLICY

See: Congress and Foreign Policy; Congressional War Powers; Foreign Affairs; Senate and Foreign Policy

FORFEITURE

See: Civil Forfeiture

FORSYTH COUNTY, GEORGIA v. NATIONALIST MOVEMENT
505 U.S. 123 (1992)

Forsyth County, Georgia had described itself as "the whitest county in America," and when some ninety CIVIL RIGHTS demonstrators staged a march, about 400 counterdemonstrators broke up the march, throwing rocks and bottles. The next weekend the civil rights marchers returned, 20,000 strong, protected from 1,000 opponents (including members of the Ku Klux Klan and the Nationalist Movement) by 3,000 police officers and National Guardsmen. The protection cost $670,000, a small part of which was paid by the county. The county commissioners then adopted an ordinance requiring a permit for parading, conditioned on a permit fee of up to $1,000, depending on the expense incident to maintaining public order. Two years later the Nationalist Movement sought a permit to hold its own march on the birthday of MARTIN LUTHER KING, JR. The county demanded a permit fee of $100, based not on anticipated costs of policing but on the cost of ten hours of administrative work. In the previous year such fees had ranged from $5 (for the Girl Scouts) to $100 (for the Nationalist Movement). The Movement sued to enjoin the county from imposing the fee, lost in the District Court, but won in the U.S. Court of Appeals. The Supreme Court affirmed, 5–4.

For the majority, Justice HARRY A. BLACKMUN concluded that the ordinance was invalid because it gave "standardless discretion" to the licensing official, whose decision was unreviewable. Such a power carried the risk that the official might vary the fee according to his like or dislike for the parade's message content, or his anticipation of the degree of hostility to that content. Chief Justice WILLIAM H. REHNQUIST, for the dissenting Justices, would have upheld the ordinance against a facial attack on the basis of COX V. NEW HAMPSHIRE (1941), and would withhold judicial intervention until the ordinance was given a message-content-based application.

KENNETH L. KARST
(2000)

(SEE ALSO: *Freedom of Speech.*)

FORTAS, ABE
(1910–1982)

Abe Fortas of Tennessee, a graduate of Yale Law School, became a NEW DEAL lawyer. As undersecretary of state, he opposed the removal and internment of Japanese Americans. In 1946 Fortas cofounded a Washington law firm whose corporate clients made him rich and influential, but he contributed his time to defending the rights of underdogs and alleged security risks. One client, LYNDON B. JOHNSON, became a close friend. Fortas continued as his adviser after Johnson became President, and Johnson later appointed Fortas to the Supreme Court.

Justice Fortas served for less than four years, from October 4, 1965, to May 14, 1969. In 1968, President Johnson nominated him to serve as Chief Justice of the United States, succeeding EARL WARREN, but a Senate delay in confirming him, initiated primarily by Republicans eager to save the appointment in case a Republican was victorious in November, caused Fortas to withdraw from consideration before the 1968 Supreme Court Term opened. Before that term was over, Justice Fortas had resigned his seat because of revelations of alleged improprieties in his financial activities.

Four years away from practice is a very brief period in which to develop an overall judicial philosophy. Nevertheless, Fortas developed a distinctive style, notable for flowery prose, the artful phrase, and emphasis on the underlying facts of the particular case. He also developed distinctive positions on particular issues.

Fortas's FIRST AMENDMENT analysis was the most well-developed aspect of his constitutional theory. He disparaged the speech-conduct distinction adhered to by Justice HUGO L. BLACK and others; Fortas thought both speech and conduct could warrant First Amendment protection. But while he gave full protection in cases like TINKER V. DES MOINES INDEPENDENT COMMUNITY SCHOOL DISTRICT (1969) to nonviolent, nondisruptive speech and conduct, he believed, as he said in *Barker v. Hardway* (1969), that speech or conduct that is "violent and destructive interference with the rights of others" falls outside the scope of First Amendment protections. In drawing this line in individual cases, Fortas focused tightly on the specific facts of the case. For instance, in *Brown v. Louisiana* (1966), the arrest of demonstrators for conducting a SIT-IN in a segregated public library was unconstitutional because the particular sit-in was "neither loud, boisterous, obstreperous, indecorous, nor impolite."

Those who disagreed with Fortas's approach asked, as in ADDERLEY V. FLORIDA (1966), whether the *type* of demonstration at issue could be disruptive and so was legitimately subject to state prohibition. Fortas reached opposite conclusions by weighing the potential for violence only of the *particular* demonstration involved. He thus gave greater protection to expression in cases the Supreme Court reviewed. But his opinions gave little guidance, simply reporting his own reactions to the facts of the case. Moreover, Fortas occasionally strayed from this approach. Dissenting in *Street v. New York* (1969), he was willing to affirm a conviction under a state FLAG DESECRATION statute, not because the particular flag-burning threatened disorder but because a government seeking to avoid fire hazards could have prohibited all public burning. There, Fortas stated "action, even if clearly for serious protest purposes, is not entitled to the pervasive protection that is given to speech alone." Seemingly, it again was reaction to the particular factual situation that stirred Fortas, but he was unable to articulate persuasively the reasons for the particular sanctity he attached to the American flag.

When appointed, Fortas already was well-known as the victorious attorney in GIDEON V. WAINWRIGHT (1963), establishing indigents' RIGHT TO COUNSEL in criminal cases. As a Justice, he continued to stress procedural regularity and the need for law enforcement officers to obey the law. He was not afraid to extend protections further than the WARREN COURT majority, as he urged in ALDERMAN V. UNITED STATES (1969) and *Desist v. United States* (1969). One example is the Fifth Amendment RIGHT AGAINST SELF INCRIMINATION which the majority limited to evidence of a testimonial or communicative nature in SCHMERBER V. CALIFORNIA (1966) and UNITED STATES V. WADE (1967). Fortas disagreed, saying it violated the privilege to subject a defendant to blood tests, or to make him repeat words uttered by the perpetrator of the crime, or to give a handwriting sample. His principle was that the privilege forbade compelling any evidence the gathering of which requires "affirmative, volitional action" on the part of the defendant. He applied that test in a somewhat conclusory fashion, however, maintaining that the accused could be made to stand in a LINEUP, "an incident of the state's power to ARREST, and a reasonable and justifiable aspect of the state's custody resulting from the arrest."

In EPPERSON V. ARKANSAS (1968) Fortas, for the Court, struck down an Arkansas statute that prohibited teaching evolution. *Epperson* suggests that the fact that a prohibition owes its existence to a particular religious dogma or religious campaign may be sufficient to invalidate it under the ESTABLISHMENT OF RELIGION clause—a position that Fortas might have preferred as an explanation for the invalidity of anti-abortion legislation, had he remained on the Court to decide that issue. That case and those in which Fortas championed the rights of children, such as *Tinker* and his landmark opinion IN RE GAULT (1967), or suggested the desirability of parents making some important decisions with their children rather than having a state-prescribed rule, such as *Ginsburg v. New York* (1968) (dissent), foreshadowed themes that have since proved important in other contexts (health services, EDUCATION, contraception, and abortion, for example). They suggest that Fortas would have had much to contribute

to the Court had his service not been so limited in duration.

MARTHA A. FIELD
(1986)

Bibliography

GRAHAM, FRED 1969 Abe Fortas. Pages 3015–3027 in Leon Friedman and Fred L. Israel, eds., *The Justices of the United States Supreme Court, 1789–1969*. New York: Chelsea House.

MASSARO, JOHN 1982–1983 LBJ and the Fortas Nomination for Chief Justice. *Political Science Quarterly* 97:603–621.

SHOGAN, ROBERT 1972 *A Question of Judgment: The Fortas Case and the Struggle for the Supreme Court*. Indianapolis: Bobbs-Merrill.

FOSTER FAMILIES

When a parent is unable to care for a child, the parent may temporarily transfer care and custody of the child to a public or charitable agency. Care and custody may also be transferred by court order when, for example, a parent has abused or neglected a child. The agency may place the child with an adult who is licensed and paid by the state to provide the child with care. The caretaker is commonly called a "foster parent." Voluntary relinquishment and foster care are regulated by statute and by contracts between the natural parent and the agency, and the agency and the foster parent. By statute and contract, children are removable from a foster home on short notice when the agency determines that the best interests of the child would be served by reunification with a natural parent, placement in another foster home, or adoption by a person other than the foster parent.

In theory, foster placement is intended to be short term and is not expected to engender strong emotional bonds between the foster parent and child. Nevertheless, foster placements often last a long time, and a foster parent and child may become deeply attached to one another. Consequently, foster parents have challenged removal procedures on the ground that they infringe FOURTEENTH AMENDMENT DUE PROCESS rights of the foster parent and child. Despite their initial contractual undertaking to relinquish the child to the agency upon demand, foster parents assert that a constitutionally protected liberty interest arises when a psychological parent–child relationship does in fact develop in foster placement. In the leading case, *Smith v. Organization of Foster Families for Equality and Reform (OFFER)* (1977), foster parents challenged New York removal procedures. The Supreme Court held that, even assuming the existence of a liberty interest in the foster family relationship, the removal procedures employed by New York were not constitutionally defective.

The Court observed that *OFFER* does not involve "arbitrary government interference in . . . family- like associations" but instead entails a potential collision of private liberty interests. The interest of natural parents in regaining their children may directly conflict with the interest of foster parents in keeping the children. The best the state can do in drafting removal provisions is give due respect to all interests, which New York had done.

Deciding the question left unanswered by *OFFER*, the U.S. Court of Appeals for the Second Circuit in *Rivera v. Marcus* (1982) held that a person who entered a foster care agreement to care for younger half-siblings had a constitutionally protected liberty interest in preserving the integrity of the family from state removal of the children, and that the Connecticut removal provisions did not adequately respect this interest. Acknowledging that several other circuits had concluded that foster parents do not possess a constitutionally protected liberty interest in the integrity of the foster family, *Rivera* relied, in part, on the biological relationship between the caregiver and her half siblings. Similarly, *Rodriguez v. McLoughlin* (1998), a federal district court decision, found a liberty interest where a child had spent all his life with the foster parent and the foster parent had signed an agreement to adopt the child before the child was removed from the foster home.

GRACE GANZ BLUMBERG
(2000)

Bibliography

CHAMBERS, DAVID L. and WALD, MICHAEL S. 1985 *Smith v. OFFER.* Pages 114–117 in Robert H. Mnookin, ed., *In the Interest of Children: Advocacy, Law Reform, and Public Policy.* New York: W.H. Freeman.

MNOOKIN, ROBERT H. and WEISBERG, D. KELLY 1995 *Child, Family and State*, 3rd ed. Boston: Little, Brown and Co.

FOURTEENTH AMENDMENT
(Framing)

The Fourteenth Amendment to the United States Constitution consists of a variety of provisions addressed to several problems that arose when the CIVIL WAR and the abolition of slavery transformed the American political order. One sentence—"No State shall make or enforce any law which shall abridge the PRIVILEGES OR IMMUNITIES of citizens of the United States; nor shall any State deprive any person of life, liberty, or property without DUE PROCESS OF LAW; nor deny to any person within its jurisdiction the EQUAL PROTECTION OF THE LAWS"—has become the text upon which most twentieth-century constitutional law is a gloss. But this sentence may not have been the most important part of the amendment as it was conceived by its framers, adopted by Congress, and ratified by the states between 1865 and 1868.

The sentence was addressed most pointedly to one of the lesser problems that Congress faced in the winter of 1865–1866. During that winter congressional legislation protecting the CIVIL RIGHTS of former slaves had been vetoed by President ANDREW JOHNSON in part, he contended, because the Constitution entrusted the protection of civil rights to the states. The Republican proponents of the CIVIL RIGHTS ACT OF 1866 mustered the necessary two-thirds vote to override the veto, but doubt remained about the power of the federal government to protect civil rights. The quoted sentence in section 1 of the Fourteenth Amendment was written, at least in part, to resolve that doubt.

Another concern of some Northerners in the winter of 1865–1866 was that some future Congress might repudiate the debt that the federal government had amassed during the Civil War or might undertake to pay the Confederate debt or compensate former slaveholders for the loss of their slaves. Section 4 of the amendment guaranteed the national debt, prohibited the payment of the Confederate debt, and barred compensation to slaveholders.

However, the most urgent task that the Thirty-ninth Congress confronted when it began its first session in December 1865 was to establish governments in the South that would be loyal to the Union and send loyal representatives to Congress. The problem was compounded by the ratification of the THIRTEENTH AMENDMENT, which not only abolished slavery but also put an end to the original Constitution's THREE-FIFTHS CLAUSE. With the abolition of slavery, the former slaves would be fully counted as part of the population of the former Confederate states; as a result those states would have more power in Congress and the ELECTORAL COLLEGE than they had had before the Civil War. Something had to be done to insure that the war did not increase the political power of the disloyal groups that had brought the war about.

Three solutions were advanced to prevent those who had lost the Civil War from enhancing their power as a result of it. One was to confer the franchise on Southern blacks, whose votes were expected to bring about the election of loyal candidates. A second solution was to deny political rights—both the right to vote and the right to hold office—to some or all who had participated in the rebellion against national authority. This scheme would increase the number of districts in which Union loyalists had a majority or at least some power to tip the electoral balance in favor of loyal candidates.

A third solution was to alter the basis of representation: to base a state's number of representatives in the House and hence its votes in the Electoral College not on total population but on the number of people eligible to vote. Thus, if a state excluded blacks from the right to vote, they would not be counted in determining its representation in Congress and its vote in the Electoral College. Thus the abolition of slavery and the end of the three-fifths compromise would reduce Southern political power in Congress unless Southern states gave blacks the right to vote and hence a share in that power.

The JOINT COMMITTEE ON RECONSTRUCTION, established by CONCURRENT RESOLUTIONS of the House and Senate in the opening days of the Congress, sought to put the possible solutions into some sort of order. Four members of this fifteen-man committee were most prominent in its activities: JOHN A. BINGHAM and THADDEUS STEVENS from the House and WILLIAM PITT FESSENDEN and JACOB M. HOWARD from the Senate.

At the third meeting of the Joint Committee on January 12, 1866, Bingham proposed a constitutional amendment that would give Congress "power to make all laws necessary and proper to secure to all persons in every State within this Union equal protection in their rights of life, liberty and property." The proposal was referred to a subcommittee which eight days later returned it to the Joint Committee in the following form: "Congress shall have power to make all laws necessary and proper to secure to all citizens of the United States, in every State, the same political rights and privileges; and to all persons in every State equal protection in the enjoyment of life, liberty, and property." In this form the proposal addressed two of the problems then pending, because it gave Congress power to protect civil rights and to legislate VOTING RIGHTS for blacks. This proposal, however, was never presented to Congress. The committee spent two weeks debating its language, finally agreeing on February 3 to the following: "The Congress shall have power to make all laws which shall be necessary and proper to secure to citizens of each State all privileges and immunities of citizens in the several States [Art. IV, Sec. 2]; and to all persons in the several States equal protection in the rights of life, liberty and property [5th Amendment]." A key issue that subsequent judges and scholars have long debated is whether this change in language was meant to deprive Congress of power to legislate black suffrage or merely to put that power into more acceptable language.

On the same day that the subcommittee submitted the early version of the amendment to the Joint Committee, it also submitted a proposal basing representation on population, but further providing "[t]hat whenever the elective franchise shall be denied or abridged in any State on account of race or color, all persons of such race or color shall be excluded from the basis of representation." Thus, the total package as of January 20 not only gave Congress power to legislate civil rights and black suf-

frage—power which Congress might or might not exercise—but also deprived a state of representation based on its black population if blacks were not given suffrage either by Congress or by the state. The package, as altered by the language change of February 3, was submitted to the full House as two separate constitutional amendments.

On February 28, the House postponed consideration of the Bingham amendment conferring legislative power on Congress, and never again considered that amendment as a separate entity. Earlier it had passed and sent to the Senate the amendment depriving states of representation if blacks were denied the right to vote. The Senate, however, never acted on the proposal. Thus, by the end of February 1866, the two forerunners of the Fourteenth Amendment had come to nought.

Both reappeared in slightly different language, however, in the omnibus measure which the Joint Committee presented to both houses of Congress on April 30, 1866. Section 1 of the measure was the sentence containing today's privilege and immunities, due process, and equal clauses, while section 2 reduced the representation of states who denied the right to vote to males over the age of twenty-one. Section 3 deprived all persons who had voluntarily supported the Confederate cause of the right to vote in federal elections prior to 1870, while section 4 dealt with the war debt. Section 5 gave Congress power to enforce the other four sections.

The omnibus amendment passed the House as proposed, but it faced difficulties in the Senate. When it emerged from the Senate on June 8, it had been changed in two significant respects. One of the changes added to section 1a . . . definition of CITIZENSHIP. The Senate also weakened section 3; instead of disfranchising those who had supported the Confederacy, it merely barred from federal office those Confederate supporters who prior to the Civil War had taken an oath to support the Constitution.

After the House had concurred on June 13 in the Senate's changes, the amendment was sent to the states. Twelve days later, on June 25, Connecticut became the first state to ratify. Five additional states ratified the amendment in 1866, and eleven added their RATIFICATIONS in January 1867. By June of 1867, one year after the amendment had been sent to the states, a total of twenty-two had ratified it.

Ratification by six more states was needed, however, and that did not occur until July 1868. By that time two of the states that had previously ratified the amendment, New Jersey and Ohio, had voted to withdraw their assent. Nonetheless Congress ruled that their ratifications survived the subsequent efforts at withdrawal and remained valid. On July 28, 1868, Secretary of State WILLIAM SEWARD accordingly proclaimed the Fourteenth Amendment part of the Constitution of the United States.

In recent decades, historians and judges have extensively debated three questions about the meaning which the Thirty-Ninth Congress and the ratifying states attached to the Fourteenth Amendment, especially to section 1. First, does section 1 give Congress power to protect voting rights? Second, does section 1 overrule BARRON V. BALTIMORE (1833) and require the states to abide by the provisions of the BILL OF RIGHTS? Third, does section 1 prohibit compulsory racial SEGREGATION?

Did section 1 of the Fourteenth Amendment give Congress power to protect voting rights? The Justices of the Supreme Court have been divided in their answer to this question, although the weight of historical scholarship leans toward the view that section 1 was not concerned with voting rights. As the above summary of the progress of the amendment in Congress suggests, resolution of the issue depends on whether the privileges and immunities language in section 1 was meant to alter the substance or only the form of an earlier version of the section, which explicitly gave Congress power to secure to all citizens in every state "equal political rights and privileges." The question can never be answered definitively, for the substitution was made in committee and the committee left no record of its reasoning. The record of congressional debates is equally ambiguous. When the present language of section 1 was on the floor, some congressmen suggested that the section gave Congress power to protect voting rights, but others disagreed. Similarly, some congressmen claimed after the amendment had been adopted that it gave them power to legislate protection of voting rights—and again others disagreed.

Was section 1 meant to overrule *Barron v. Baltimore* and compel the states to abide by the provisions of the Bill of Rights? Justice HUGO L. BLACK, relying on explicit statements during congressional debates that the section would accomplish that end, declared in a dissenting opinion in *Adamson v. California* (1947) that the Fourteenth Amendment did incorporate the Bill of Rights and apply it to the states. Some scholars have supported Black's position. However, two years after *Adamson* Charles Fairman wrote an article challenging Black. Fairman noted that many states in the 1860s did not follow procedures mandated by the Bill of Rights, but that no one during state ratification proceedings seemed concerned that adoption of the Fourteenth Amendment would require changes in state practice. He thought it probable that, if the states were concerned that the amendment, through INCORPORATION of the Bill of Rights, would require changes in their practices, they would at least have discussed the issue. He concluded from the lack of discussion that the amendment had no such purpose. The view of several recent scholars has been that, in light of the conflicting and insubstantial evidence, the question raised by Justice Black can never be conclusively answered.

Finally, there is the question whether section 1 was intended to prohibit racial segregation. After asking the litigants in BROWN V. BOARD OF EDUCATION (1954) to address this question, the Court concluded that the historical evidence was too ambiguous to permit an answer. Some scholars, however, have been more confident. Raoul Berger concluded that the framers of the amendment did not intend to prohibit racial segregation. On the other hand, ALEXANDER BICKEL had argued some years earlier that the framers had consciously framed section 1 in broad, open-ended language that would permit people in the future to interpret it as prohibiting the practice of segregation. The historical record itself is sparse. During the debates in Congress on the amendment, little was said about segregation. Earlier, however, Congress had engaged in lengthy debates about the legality of segregation on DISTRICT OF COLUMBIA streetcars. Moreover, school segregation was opposed by some members of Congress, notably CHARLES SUMNER who had been counsel in ROBERTS V. CITY OF BOSTON, an 1849 school desegregation case. In the 1860s, however, Congress was permitting racially segregated schools to exist in the District of Columbia.

Questions about whether the Thirty-Ninth Congress and the states that ratified the Fourteenth Amendment intended it to protect voting rights, make the Bill of Rights binding on the states, or outlaw segregation can never be answered confidently. All that the person who inquires into the historical record in search of an answer can do is make a guess—a guess more likely to reflect his political beliefs than to reflect the state of the historical record. The questions that judges and historians have asked about the original meaning of the Fourteenth Amendment are simply the wrong ones, because they do not address the issues that Congress and the ratifying states in fact debated and decided during the era of Reconstruction.

On one point of political philosophy, nearly all Americans of the 1860s agreed. President Andrew Johnson stated the point in his 1865 State of the Union address: "Monopolies, perpetuities, and class legislation are contrary to the genius of free government, and ought not to be allowed. Here there is no room for favored classes or monopolies; the principle of our Government is that of equal laws. . . . We shall but fulfill our duties as legislators by according "equal and exact justice to all men, special privileges to none." Innumerable Republicans argued that the purpose of section 1 of the Fourteenth Amendment was to enact this political principle into law. John A. Bingham, the draftsman of section 1, said what others repeated: that he proposed "by amending the Constitution, to provide for the efficient enforcement, by law, of these "equal rights of every man"—of "the absolute equality of all men before the law." Even Democrats from former slave states accepted the principle that the law should treat all persons equally. There was neither division nor sustained debate in the Thirty-Ninth Congress over the contrary principle that people who are in fact the same should receive equal treatment before the law and that people who are different may be treated differently. The issue on which Republicans and Democrats divided was whether black people, in essence, were equal to white people or inherently inferior.

Garrett Davis, a Democratic senator from Kentucky, used typical racist rhetoric. During an 1866 debate on the question whether blacks should be permitted to vote in the District of Columbia, Davis said:

[T]he proposition that a nation of a superior race should allow an inferior race resident in large numbers among them to take part in their Government, in shaping, and controlling their destinies, is refuted by its mere statement. And the further proposition that a nation composed of the Caucasian race, the highest type of man, having resident in it more than four million negroes, the lowest type, of which race no nation or tribe, from the first dawning of history to the present day, has ever established a polity that could be denominated a Government, or has elaborated for itself any science or literature or arts or even an alphabet, or characters to represent numbers, or been capable of preserving those achievements of intellect when it has received them from the superior race; such a proposition is, on examination, revolting to reason, and in its practical operation would be productive of incalculable mischief.

Republicans responded to this "prejudice," which "belong[ed] to an age of darkness and violence, and is a poisonous, dangerous exotic when suffered to grow in the midst of republican institutions." Jacob M. Howard, a key member of the Joint Committee, told the Senate:

For weal or for woe, the destiny of the colored race in this country is wrapped up with our own; they are to remain in our midst, and here spend their years and here bury their fathers and finally repose themselves. We may regret it. It may not be entirely compatible with our taste that they should live in our midst. We cannot help it. Our forefathers introduced them, and their destiny is to continue among us; and the practical question which now presents itself to us is as to the best mode of getting along with them.

Justin Morrill of Vermont added: "We have put aside the creed of the despot, the monarchist, the aristocrat, and have affirmed the right and capacity of the people to govern themselves, and have staked the national life on the issue to make it good in practice. . . . To deny any portion of the American people civil or political rights common to the citizen upon pretense of race or color, is to ignore the fundamental principles of republicanism." The only proper policy for the Government, according to Lyman Trumbull, chairman of the Senate Judiciary Committee, was "to legislate in the interest of freedom. Now, our laws are to be enacted with a view to educate, improve, enlighten, and Christianize the negro; to make him an independent man; to teach him to think and to reason; to improve that principle which the great Author of all has implanted in every human breast, which is susceptible of the highest cultivation, and destined to go on enlarging and expanding through the endless ages of eternity."

Trumbull and his fellow Republicans understood that God had created blacks as the equals of whites and that, if the law gave blacks an opportunity, they would demonstrate their equality. The Republicans made this equalitarian faith the basis of the Fourteenth Amendment. Although the faith was forgotten within a decade of the Fourteenth Amendment's ratification, it still offers a perspective from which to begin analysis of the issues of Fourteenth Amendment jurisprudence that confront us today.

WILLIAM E. NELSON
(1986)

(SEE ALSO: *Abolitionist Constitutional Theory.*)

Bibliography

BERGER, RAOUL 1977 *Government by Judiciary: The Transformation of the Fourteenth Amendment.* Cambridge, Mass.: Harvard University Press.

BICKEL, ALEXANDER M. 1955 The Original Understanding and the Segregation Decision. *Harvard Law Review* 69:1–65.

FAIRMAN, CHARLES 1949 Does the Fourteenth Amendment Incorporate the Bill of Rights? The Original Understanding. *Stanford Law Review* 2:5–173.

HYMAN, HAROLD M. and WIECEK, WILLIAM M. 1982 *Equal Justice under Law: Constitutional Development 1835–1875.* New York: Harper & Row.

JAMES, JOSEPH B. 1956 *The Framing of the Fourteenth Amendment.* Urbana: University of Illinois Press.

TEN BROEK, JACOBUS 1951 *The Antislavery Origins of the Fourteenth Amendment.* Berkeley: University of California Press.

FOURTEENTH AMENDMENT, SECTION 5
(Framing)

The FOURTEENTH AMENDMENT was proposed by Congress in 1866 and ratified in 1868. Section 1 made persons born in the nation citizens and prohibited states from abridging the PRIVILEGES AND IMMUNITIES of citizens of the United

States and from denying DUE PROCESS or EQUAL PROTECTION to any person. Section 5 gave Congress the power to enforce the amendment by appropriate legislation. However, in 1866, the exact scope of the enforcement power was not clear. Particularly, it was unclear whether the amendment was designed to reach purely private action and conspiracies or only those in which state officials were involved. Controversy on this question has continued from 1866 to the present.

Although the debates on the Fourteenth Amendment did not emphasize the mechanics of the enforcement authorized by section 5, broad themes in the debate were clearly relevant to enforcement. Most members of the RE-PUBLICAN PARTY insisted on protection for FUNDAMENTAL RIGHTS of American citizens, were committed to a federal system that required states to respect basic rights, and were unwilling for the federal goverment to supplant the basic jurisdiction of the states over crimes and civil matters. At the same time, Republicans were determined to protect blacks and loyalists in the South.

A prototype of the Fourteenth Amendment written by Republican JOHN A. BINGHAM provided congressional power to pass all laws necessary to secure all persons equal protection in their rights to life, liberty, and property. Several Republicans objected to the prototype because they thought it would allow federal statutes broadly to supplant state civil criminal law. Bingham denied that was his purpose and said he intended to authorize Congress to punish state officers for violations of the BILL OF RIGHTS. Bingham's prototype was recast with limitations on the states in section 1 and the enforcement power in section 5. Bingham explained that the final version of the amendment would allow Congress to protect the privileges and immunities of citizens and the inborn rights of every person when these rights were abridged or denied by unconstitutional acts of any state.

Although Republicans generally believed that state laws denying privileges or immunities, due process, or equal protection could be struck down by the courts, they expected Congress to take a direct and substantial role in enforcing the guarantees of section 1. Many believed that the equal protection clause required the states to supply the protection of the laws to blacks, Unionists, Republicans, and others who faced private violence.

Republicans thought enforcement could reach state officials who violated the rights secured by the amendment. One object of the Fourteenth Amendment was to ensure that Congress had the power to pass the CIVIL RIGHTS ACT OF 1866. That act had punished persons who, under color of state law or custom, had deprived citizens of the rights it guaranteed. Senator LYMAN TRUMBULL, chairman of the SENATE JUDICIARY COMMITTEE and manager of the civil rights bill in the Senate, thought that state judges who maliciously violated rights secured in the act were subject to prosecution.

In 1871, Congress considered an act to deal with terrorism by the Ku Klux Klan. The most difficult issue confronting the Congress was whether the power to enforce the Fourteenth Amendment under section 5 allowed Congress to make private action a crime. Republicans generally supported provisions that would punish those, like state officers, who deprived persons of rights, privileges, and immunities of citizens of the United States under COLOR OF LAW. However, Democrats and several leading Republicans objected to provisions designed to reach private acts and private conspiracies to deny constitutional rights. They insisted that the power to enforce the Fourteenth Amendment was limited to STATE ACTION or, some Republican dissenters thought, to cases where the state failed to supply equal protection. Congressional critics pointed to the change from the prototype of the Fourteenth Amendment, which granted Congress power to secure equal protection in life, liberty, or property, to the amendment's final version, which provided restriction on the states in section 1 together with congressional power to enforce the amendment in section 5.

According to the state-action argument, Congress had less power to reach private terrorism intended to deny constitutional rights than the Supreme Court in 1842 had found it had to punish private individuals who interfered with the return of FUGITIVE SLAVES.

In 1871, most Republicans thought the states had the duty to protect their citizens against politically or racially motivated violence and that private individuals who interfered with this duty could be punished. As finally passed, the 1871 act punished private individuals who conspired to deprive persons of equal protection or equal privileges or immunities or who conspired to interfere with state officials supplying equal protection. In this form, the act secured the support of Republicans who had expressed constitutional doubts. Still, in UNITED STATES V. HARRIS (1883), the United States Supreme Court held a section of the 1871 act unconstitutional because it reached conspiracies by private persons to deny constitutional rights and did so regardless of how well the state had performed its duty of equal protection. In 1966, in the midst of a second RECONSTRUCTION, six Justices suggested that Congress could reach some private conspiracies designed to interfere with constitutional rights. In JONES V. ALFRED H. MAYER CO. (1968) the Supreme Court recognized power in Congress to enforce the THIRTEENTH AMENDMENT by prohibiting private racial discrimination in housing contracts. Still, the power of Congress to reach private conduct under the Fourteenth Amendment remains controversial.

MICHAEL KENT CURTIS
(1992)

Bibliography

AVINS, ALFRED 1967 The Ku Klux Act of 1871: Some Reflected Light on State Action and the Fourteenth Amendment. *Saint Louis University Law Journal* 11:331–381.

CARR, ROBERT K. 1947 *Federal Protection of Civil Rights.* Ithaca, N.Y.: Cornell University Press.

FRANTZ, LAURENT B. 1964 Congressional Power to Enforce the Fourteenth Amendment Against Private Acts. *Yale Law Journal* 73:1352–1384.

HYMAN, HAROLD and WIECEK, WILLIAM 1982 *Equal Justice Under Law.* New York: Harper & Row.

KACZOROWSKI, ROBERT J. 1985 *The Politics of Judicial Interpretation: The Federal Courts, Department of Justice and Civil Rights 1866–76.* New York: Chelsea House.

ZUCKERT, MICHAEL 1986 Congressional Power Under the Fourteenth Amendment—The Original Understanding of Section Five. *Constitutional Commentary* 3:123–155.

FOURTEENTH AMENDMENT, SECTION 5
(Judicial Construction)

Section 5 of the FOURTEENTH AMENDMENT empowers Congress to "enforce, by appropriate legislation" the other provisions of the amendment, including the guarantees of the DUE PROCESS and EQUAL PROTECTION clauses of section 1. Congress can, of course, enact criminal penalities or provide civil remedies to redress violations of the due process and equal protection clauses. The more difficult issue is whether the Fourteenth Amendment enforcement power is large enough to allow Congress to forbid conduct that does not violate due process or equal protection.

In the CIVIL RIGHTS ACT of 1875, Congress made RACIAL DISCRIMINATION in "inns, public conveyances . . . , theatres and other places of public amusement" a crime. The CIVIL RIGHTS CASES (1883) held that the Fourteenth Amendment enforcement power did not provide sufficient support for the law. Congress only had the power under section 5 to "enforce" the amendment, which forbade only discrimination by the state. Therefore, legislation outlawing a "private wrong" was beyond the enforcement power. The same limit applies to the enforcement power in section 2 of the FIFTEENTH AMENDMENT, for section 1 of that amendment is similarly interpreted to forbid only state abridgment of the right to vote.

Despite the holding of *Civil Rights Cases*, it has been settled that the Fourteenth Amendment gives Congress power to prohibit some behavior by private individuals. In UNITED STATES V. GUEST (1966) six Justices agreed to an OBITER DICTUM that Congress can "punish private conspiracies that interfere with fourteenth amendment rights, such as the right to utilize public facilities." That concept supports provisions of 1968 legislation that make it a federal crime for private individuals to deny others, "because of . . . race, color, religion or national origin," their rights to attend public schools or participate in programs provided or administered by the state.

It is less clear whether the holding of the *Civil Rights Cases* is still valid in denying Congress the power, under section 5 of the Fourteenth Amendment, to control private conduct that is not connected to any relationship between the victim and the states. No Supreme Court decision since *Guest* has spoken to that question. Because Congress has a wide range of other legislative powers available to it, this abstract question probably will not be answered in the foreseeable future. The CIVIL RIGHTS ACT OF 1964, for example, went further than the law invalidated in the *Civil Rights Cases*, outlawing discrimination by hotels, restaurants, and private employers. The 1964 Act was upheld, in *Katzenbach v. McClung* (1964), under Congress's broad power to regulate INTERSTATE COMMERCE. The commerce power also supports 1968 federal legislation regulating private housing discrimination.

One question concerning the scope of the Fourteenth Amendment enforcement power may be more than academic. In cases like NATIONAL LEAGUE OF CITIES V. USERY (1976) and GARCIA V. SAN ANTONIO METROPOLITAN TRANSIT AUTHORITY (1985), questions have been raised about the constitutionality of federal laws that impose obligations directly on state governments—for example, that the state pay its workers a minimum wage. It may be necessary to decide whether legislation imposing some obligations on state or LOCAL GOVERNMENTS can be sustained under the Fourteenth Amendment enforcement power. The Court has concluded in *City of Rome v. United States* (1980) that the three constitutional amendments enacted following the CIVIL WAR—the THIRTEENTH AMENDMENT, the Fourteenth Amendment, and the Fifteenth Amendment—"were specifically designed as an expansion of federal power and an intrusion on state sovereignty." Thus, constitutional limits on national power imposed to protect state sovereignty are inapplicable to legislation authorized by these amendments. In *City of Rome* the Court upheld federal VOTING RIGHTS legislation requiring the city to obtain approval of the United States ATTORNEY GENERAL before it could reduce the size of its city council.

The power to provide "remedies" to prevent violations of the Fourteenth and Fifteenth Amendments allows Congress to invalidate some state laws that courts otherwise would have sustained. State LITERACY TESTS for voters are a clear example. The Supreme Court upheld literacy tests as a requirement for voters in *Lassiter v. Northampton County Board of Elections* (1959). Federal voting rights laws, however, have since suspended all state literacy tests. The Court sustained that legislation in OREGON V. MITCHELL (1970). Congress could reasonably find that the states had used literacy tests to engage in racial discrimination. Even if literacy tests for voting did not themselves violate the Constitution, Congress decided that they were being used to violate the Fifteenth Amendment. Congress could then invalidate all literacy tests as a remedy to prevent racial discrimination in voting.

Modern cases have uniformly sustained federal laws enacted to provide broad remedies for possible violations of the Fourteenth and Fifteenth Amendments. There has been more controversy concerning the question of whether Congress has power to interpret the guarantees of section 1 of the Fourteenth Amendment. In KATZEN-BACH V. MORGAN (1965) the Court sustained a provision of the VOTING RIGHTS ACT OF 1965 that suspended literacy tests for voting in New York by persons who had completed six grades of school in Puerto Rico. The Court sustained that legislation, in part on the ground that Congress could decide that New York's literacy test law, which waived the test only for citizens who had completed six grades of school in the English language, violated the equal protection clause of section 1 of the Fourteenth Amendment. Two dissenters argued that only courts could interpret the Constitution and warned that the power to interpret the Constitution's guarantees of liberty could authorize Congress to dilute those guarantees as well as amplify them.

The continuing authority of the interpretive theory of *Katzenbach v. Morgan* is now in some doubt. Amendments to the Voting Rights Act in 1970 extended the right to vote to eighteen-year-olds in both state and federal elections, interpreting the equal protection clause to declare that it was unconstitutional to deny them the right to vote because of their age. Different 5–4 majorities of the Court in *Oregon v. Mitchell* upheld the statute as applied to federal elections and invalidated it as applied to state elections. Four of the Justices would have upheld the statute in its entirety, while four would have held that Congress lacked the power to change the voting age in either state or federal elections. The specific issue of voting age has, of course, been mooted by enactment of the TWENTY-SIXTH AMENDMENT the following year. Since 1970 Congress has not relied on the interpretive theory in enactments enforcing the Fourteenth and Fifteenth Amendments.

WILLIAM COHEN
(1992)

Bibliography
BICKEL, ALEXANDER M. 1966 The Voting Rights Cases. *Supreme Court Review* 1966:79–102.
COHEN, WILLIAM 1975 Congressional Power to Interpret Due Process and Equal Protection. *Stanford Law Review* 27:603–620.
COX, ARCHIBALD 1971 The Role of Congress in Constitutional Determination. *University of Cincinnati Law Review* 40:199–261.

FOURTEENTH AMENDMENT AS A NEW CONSTITUTION

The FOURTEENTH AMENDMENT transformed—reconstructed—the meaning of the Framers' Constitution. This transformation is most visible in the interpretations now given to the BILL OF RIGHTS. At the Founding, the first ten Amendments were primarily structural, emphasizing STATES' RIGHTS and majoritarian POPULAR SOVEREIGNTY. These amendments applied only against federal officials (as the Supreme Court made clear in the 1833 case of BARRON V. CITY OF BALTIMORE), and were never described by the antebellum Court as the "Bill of Rights." The Fourteenth Amendment changed all that. The Amendment aimed to make the various rights and freedoms of the original bill applicable against state and local governments—what twentieth-century jurists call "incorporation" of the Bill of Rights. In the process, the amendment reshaped the meaning of these rights, giving Americans a new birth of freedom featuring national protection more than states' rights, and minority rights more than majority rule. Only after and because of this amendment does it make sense to call the original amendments a true "Bill of Rights" for individuals and minorities. In addition, the amendment affirmed the idea of national CITIZENSHIP; highlighted the key value of equality (a word notably absent from the Framers' Constitution); sought to penalize denial of VOTING RIGHTS of black men; and tried to give Congress a broad substantive role in protecting liberty and equality.

The Founding Fathers forged their Constitution and early amendments in the afterglow of the AMERICAN REVOLUTION. That revolution showcased POPULISM and FEDERALISM—the people collectively had acted to throw off the yoke imposed on them by government officialdom, and democratic local regimes had banded together to help their citizens fight off an arrogant imperial center. Liberty held hands with localism—the rallying cry of "no taxation without representation" sounded in federalism as well as freedom, affirming the rights of local, representative legislatures even as it denied power to the central Parliament. Classical political theory also suggested that democracy thrived in small settings, and could not easily extend over a vast continent encompassing a large and diverse population. Thus, the patriots' initial scheme of government featured a loose-knit confederation of sovereign states with little effective central power. When these ARTICLES OF CONFEDERATION proved too weak to hold America together, the Federalists proposed a new Constitution that they claimed would vindicate the principles of the revolution. Beginning with the words "We the People," the Constitution in both word and deed stressed popular sovereignty: the words became law by ratification in popular conventions via a process that was more participatory than anything before in the planet's history (though still woefully underinclusive from a modern-day perspective). The document also showcased federalism, limiting power of the central government to enumerated domains, and retaining important roles for states as constituent parts of the new system.

But Anti-Federalist critics of the Constitution remained skeptical, and demanded additional safeguards in the form of a Bill of Rights. As originally crafted, this bill focused less on individualistic liberty, and more popular sovereignty and states' rights. No phrase appeared in more of the first ten amendments than the phrase "the people," echoing the PREAMBLE and emphasizing popular rule. At its core the FIRST AMENDMENT right of "the people" to assemble affirmed the sovereign people's collective entitlement to assemble in constitutional conventions and other political conclaves, the SECOND AMENDMENT right of "the people" to keep and bear arms stressed the collective authority of the citizenry to check a standing army that might seek to tyrannize, and the NINTH AMENDMENT and TENTH AMENDMENT served as a reminder of the rights retained and reserved to "the people." (The FOURTH AMENDMENT spoke of "the people" but counterbalanced this collective noun with two individualistic references to "persons." The key collective idea of this amendment was that juries of ordinary citizens, representing the people, would help keep abusive officials in check by holding these officials liable for unreasonable SEARCHES AND SEIZURES.) The original bill was equally emphatic about states' rights. For example, the First Amendment affirmed that Congress lacked all enumerated power to regulate the press or religion in the states—and the ESTABLISHMENT CLAUSE prevented the federal government not only from establishing a national church but also from disestablishing state churches. Likewise, the Ninth and Tenth Amendments stressed the idea of the federal government's limited ENUMERATED POWERS. Perhaps the central idea of the original bill was the idea of TRIAL BY JURY, explicitly affirmed in the Fifth Amendment's guarantee of GRAND JURIES, the Sixth Amendment's protections of criminal PETIT JURIES, and the SEVENTH AMENDMENT's embrace of civil juries, and implicitly affirmed in many other provisions. The Founding-era jury was a populist and provincial institution, empowering ordinary citizens against government professionals (judges and prosecutors), and localists against centralizers. The key idea of the jury was not simply the right to be tried, but the right to try—the right of the people themselves to take part in government administration.

This Revolutionary-era vision was revised in the aftermath of the CIVIL WAR. The antebellum experience had proved that states could also threaten liberty, especially when SLAVERY dominated politics. Slave states had become increasingly oppressive in their efforts to prop up a legal regime of human bondage—stifling abolitionist FREEDOM OF SPEECH, suppressing antislavery preachers, invading the RIGHT OF PRIVACY, and violating virtually every right and freedom that Americans held dear. A new Bill of Rights was needed to affirm national rights against states, and individual rights against overweening local majoritarianism. Congressman JOHN A. BINGHAM drafted Section I of the Fourteenth Amendment to make clear that henceforth no state should be allowed to abridge fundamental PRIVILEGES AND IMMUNITIES of Americans, such as freedom of speech, RELIGIOUS LIBERTY, and the rest of the rights and freedoms mentioned in the original Bill of Rights. Although the Supreme Court disregarded this ORIGINAL INTENT for many years, twentieth-century Justices eventually came around to Bingham's view, using the amendment's DUE PROCESS clause rather than, as Bingham would have had it, its privileges or immunities clause (which the Court effectively buried in the 1873 SLAUGHTERHOUSE CASES). Today, virtually all the provisions of the first eight amendments apply against state and local governments, except for rules regarding guns, grand juries, and civil juries.

In the process of incorporating the bill against the states, modern judges have also—and quite properly, given the spirit of RECONSTRUCTION—reshaped the meaning of various rights. Whereas Founding-era liberty emphasized majority rule and popular sovereignty, the Reconstruction generation cared more about the individual and minority groups, such as the unpopular speaker (like Frederick Douglass or Harriet Beecher Stowe down South) and the religious outsider (like many of the abolitionists). States' rights were less central to Reconstructors, and so the Tenth Amendment properly plays a smaller role today than it did at the Founding. The local institution of the jury—which was central after a revolution born in localism—seems somewhat less central today in the wake of the more nationalistic Civil War amendments. Another example—which goes beyond current DOCTRINE but illustrates the general theme of this transformation— comes from the Second Amendment. The Founding generation intended to affirm the rights of local militias to resist an imperial army, in the spirit of Lexington and Concord and Bunker Hill. The Reconstruction generation had a different view, understandably less hostile to a central army and less enamored of local militias. Reconstructors believed in a different individualistic right to firearms: blacks must be entitled to keep guns in their homes to ward off Klansmen and other ruffians. In short, modern views about the Bill of Rights owe a great deal to the Reconstruction vision of nationalist, individualistic liberty—even though conventional wisdom often reads these themes (anachronistically) back into the Founding.

Beyond its transformation of the Bill of Rights, the Fourteenth Amendment aimed to reconstruct the Framers' Constitution in several other key ways—not all of which have proved successful. The amendment's first sentence established a national definition of citizenship and affirmed the centrality of national BIRTHRIGHT CITIZENSHIP. Section 1 went on to affirm the civil equality of all persons via an EQUAL PROTECTION clause that has come to play an enormous role in the twentieth century on behalf of racial minorities and women. Whereas the Framers had rewarded slavery—for every new slave born or imported, a slave state would gain clout in the U.S. HOUSE OF REPRESENTATIVES and ELECTORAL COLLEGE—section 2 of the Fourteenth Amendment sought to penalize states that disenfranchised blacks by reducing their congressional REPRESENTATION. (This section inserted the word "male" into the Constitution for the first time, outraging many suffragists such as SUSAN B. ANTHONY and ELIZABETH CADY STANTON. Other suffragists at the time supported the amendment, noting that its first section protected all citizens and persons, male and female alike). Sections 3 and 4 sought to reduce the political and economic clout of slave owners and leading Confederates; and section 5 aimed to give broad power to Congress to implement the amendment's vision. Early Congresses tried to use this power to help blacks in the South, but the late-nineteenth-century Court stepped in to limit congressional Reconstruction. More recently, in the 1997 *City of Boerne v. Flores* case, the Court declared that Congress has a more limited role under section 5— a result that is hard to defend on grounds of text and original intent, and that is in sharp tension with THIRTEENTH AMENDMENT case law.

AKHIL REED AMAR
(2000)

(SEE ALSO: *Bill of Rights in Modern Application; Incorporation Doctrine.*)

Bibliography
AMAR, AKHIL REED 1998 *The Bill of Rights: Creation and Reconstruction.* New Haven, Conn.: Yale University Press.
CURTIS, MICHAEL KENT 1986 *No State Shall Abridge: The Fourteenth Amendment and the Bill of Rights.* Durham, N.C.: Duke University Press.
MEYER, HOWARD N. 1973 *The Amendment That Refused to Die.* Radnor, Penn.: Chilton Book Co.

FOURTH AMENDMENT

The Fourth Amendment gives citizens the "right . . . to be secure" in their "persons, homes, papers, and effects" by prohibiting the government from engaging in unreasonable SEARCHES AND SEIZURES. The nature and scope of this "right" depends on how the Supreme Court resolves three central questions of Fourth Amendment jurisprudence: which government information-gathering techniques merit Fourth Amendment regulation, what type of regulation applies to these "searches" and "seizures" to ensure their "reasonableness," and what remedies follow Fourth Amendment violations.

The amendment's text yields no answers to the questions of coverage and remedy. It does not specify the criteria for determining whether a particular governmental practice qualifies as a Fourth Amendment "search" or "seizure." Nor does the amendment say whether the evidentiary products of "unreasonable" Fourth Amendment activity should be excluded from a defendant's criminal trial to deter future governmental violations of the amendment. The Supreme Court resolved this latter problem when it "read" an exclusionary remedy into the Fourth Amendment in WEEKS V. UNITED STATES (1914) and applied it to the states in MAPP V. OHIO (1961).

The amendment does provide some clues as to what constitutes "reasonable" Fourth Amendment activity because its "warrant" clause identifies the conditions that must be satisfied for the issuance of a valid SEARCH WARRANT or ARREST WARRANT. The government must show a neutral magistrate that it has PROBABLE CAUSE for believing that it will find what (or whom) it is looking for and that the seizure of such EVIDENCE serves a legitimate governmental purpose. The warrant must contain a particular description of the place to be searched or person or items to be seized. The violation of these guidelines could provide the exclusive or primary criteria for assessing what constitutes an unreasonable search or seizure prohibited by the first clause of the amendment. But the text certainly does not dictate this interpretation, and the Court has not consistently embraced this "warrant" model of Fourth Amendment regulation.

To aid its interpretation of the text, the Supreme Court has sought to ascertain the goals and concerns of those who drafted and ratified it. Translating the "Framers' intent"—when it can be discovered—to a radically different social, cultural, and institutional context is, however, an exercise of dubious value. We know that the Framers wanted to eliminate GENERAL WARRANTS because such warrants placed few limits on the scope of the search or on what could be seized. More generally, the Framers wanted to confine the nascent federal government's powers. However, their vision of what those powers entailed bears little resemblance to the vast regulatory capacities of the modern welfare state. Drawing comparisons between their concerns and ours works only at the highest level of generality. The vague principles generated by such analogies cannot resolve the difficult interpretive questions the Court faces when it applies the amendment to governmental functions and uses of modern technology the Framers could not have imagined.

These intractable uncertainties in the text and historical record help explain why the Supreme Court has rarely relied on a "Framers' intent" methodology to resolve the three central questions of Fourth Amendment jurisprudence. Instead, the Court's fundamental interpretive strategy is to identify and balance the competing values implicated by this restraint on governmental power.

To resolve the threshold question of whether a particular governmental information-gathering practice constitutes Fourth Amendment activity, the Court has identified the individual "interests" protected by the Fourth Amendment and then determined whether that practice significantly implicates these Fourth Amendment values. A Fourth Amendment "seizure" of a person's tangible "effects" takes place when the government interferes with an individual's legitimate property interests. A fourth amendment "seizure" of a person occurs when the governmental agent takes some action that restrains a REASONABLE PERSON's liberty of movement. A Fourth Amendment "search" occurs when the government intrudes on the individual's REASONABLE EXPECTATION OF PRIVACY as to the place searched (including the individual's body) or information examined.

The Court's test for evaluating what constitutes a reasonable expectation of privacy comes from Justice JOHN MARSHALL HARLAN's CONCURRING OPINION in KATZ V. UNITED STATES (1967). Harlan articulated "a twofold requirement, first that a person have exhibited an actual (subjective) expectation of privacy and, second, that the expectation be one that society is prepared to recognize as "reasonable." Harlan subsequently rejected the subjective component of his test, and the Court endorsed his rejection of it in *Hudson v. Palmer* (1984). Focusing on the individual's subjective expectations is unsatisfactory because the government can destroy our actual privacy expectations by engaging in the very type of intrusive surveillance practices that the amendment was designed to regulate. Harlan insisted that the question of reasonable privacy expectations demanded a normative inquiry into the types of privacy expectations a free society *should* protect. Or, as Anthony Amsterdam put it, the Court should determine "whether if the particular form of surveillance practiced by the police is permitted to go unregulated by constitutional restraints, the amount of privacy and freedom remaining to citizens would be diminished to a compass inconsistent with the aims of a free and open society."

Amsterdam's inquiry reminds us of the risks generated by the Court's decision *not* to subject some governmental information-gathering activity to constitutional constraints. When the courts hold that a surveillance practice does not qualify as Fourth Amendment activity, the government may employ the practice against any citizen without any basis for believing either that the citizen merits governmental scrutiny or that such attention will promote any legitimate public interest. Amsterdam's query brilliantly characterizes the ultimate issue implicated by this threshold question of Fourth Amendment coverage; it does not, however, provide any guidelines for resolving the coverage question.

First, application of Amsterdam's formulation requires an empirical prediction about how the police will use (or abuse) the information-gathering technique if it is not subject to any constitutional regulation. But whose prediction of future police behavior should govern? A majority of the Justices on the WARREN COURT feared potential abuse of unregulated police power against racial and ethnic minorities. In contrast, a majority of the Justices on both the BURGER COURT and the REHNQUIST COURT appear more sanguine about the police's good-faith use of unregulated surveillance tactics.

Second, Amsterdam's characterization of the ultimate normative judgment does not tell us *whose* norms should define what counts as a loss of privacy that is "inconsistent" with the aims of a free society. Do these norms come from some independent political theory about the minimal amount of privacy and liberty necessary for a free society; from a moral theory about the minimal privacy due to any human being; or from current majoritarian preferences as expressed by customs, laws, and moral conventions?

The Rehnquist Court does not appear to be relying on any independent normative account of the minimal privacy expectations necessary for a free society in its Fourth Amendment coverage decisions. According to the Court, individuals cannot legitimately demand privacy protection for information that they "knowingly" expose to the public. Thus, in *California v. Ciraolo* (1986) and *Florida v. Riley* (1989) the Court concluded that citizens cannot reasonably demand some privacy protection from governmental aerial surveillance of the private property adjoining their homes so long as these flights operate at altitudes where private flights frequently occur. By "exposing" their activity in this area to view from private aircraft, citizens have assumed the risk that this information will be disclosed to the public and therefore have no legitimate privacy expectation against unregulated govermental snooping. Similarly, in CALIFORNIA V. GREENWOOD (1988), the Court concluded that no Fourth Amendment search occurs when governmental agents rummage through people's discarded trash, because they have exposed that trash (and all the information about their lives that can be gleaned from its inspection) to any private citizen who wishes to examine it.

The question-begging nature of the Court's "assumption of risk" analysis hardly suggests that the Justices are relying on any coherent theoretical account of privacy. The Court fails to ask whether individuals have any meaningful choice to avoid exposure of some information to private third parties in these cases. How, for example, are homeowners supposed to protect their backyards from those curious airline passengers armed with high-powered binoculars? More importantly, the empirical risks of disclosure that citizens assume as to some private third party (for example, the scavenger going through their trash) cannot resolve the normative question of what risks of disclosure they should bear when the government is the information-gatherer. Must we incinerate our own trash to keep the government from rummaging through it to learn the most intimate details about our lives? Must we remain indoors behind shrouded windows to prevent the government from learning what we might otherwise do in our backyards? Why, in short, must information remain secret before we can demand that the government have some good reason for gaining access to it?

All of these objections have considerable force if the Fourth Amendment's privacy norms derive from some coherent theoretical account. But why does the constitution endorse any particular theoretical account about how to determine what constitutes a reasonable expectation of privacy? What if a majority of American citizens approved of these decisions because they accurately reflected their own judgments about what types of privacy expectations should be considered legitimate? Admittedly, the majority's normative judgments might reflect the public's acquiescence to a range of intrusive governmental information-gathering practices that have gradually lowered its normative expectations. But there are other possible explanations for such majoritarian views.

Majoritarian preferences about the degree of desirable protection from unregulated government surveillance may reflect an assessment of how much privacy and liberty is lost from the high incidence of crime in our communities. People who live in a drug-infested high-crime area might be happy to have the police engage in suspicionless searches of their trash in hope that these unregulated practices will generate more drug arrests, more convictions, and a lower level of criminal activity in their neighborhoods. In short, the majority might be willing to forgo some protection from unregulated governmental intrusions into their lives to increase their protection from violent criminal intrusions.

Linking a "reasonable expectation of privacy" test to majoritarian preferences is, of course, very problematic. Courts will have difficulty determining whether majoritarian preferences reflect acquiescence to intrusive governmental practices or considered judgments about the best trade-off between different types of privacy losses. Moreover, "majoritarian" calculations of this trade-off are suspect because the losses of privacy and liberty from governmental intrusion probably will not be equally distributed among all citizens. Finally, basing Fourth Amendment privacy norms on majoritarian preferences offers no constitutionally mandated minimal floor of privacy protection against the government. If crime sufficiently threatened the basic fabric of society, the majority might prefer a trade-off that gave governmental authorities the powers of a police state. If the majority expressed these preferences in a political process that gave equal weight to all citizens' choices, the Court could not invalidate any resulting crime-control legislation without appealing to some independent normative privacy theory.

The conclusory nature of the Court's analysis in cases like *Ciraolo* and *Greenwood* precludes any confident conclusion about the sources from which the Court is deriving its privacy-expectation norms. Indeed, the incoherence of these opinions might be the inevitable product of the Court's refusal to rely exclusively on either majoritarian preferences or some normative privacy theory to justify its coverage decisions.

However, an examination of the Rehnquist Court's answers to the second central question of Fourth Amendment jurisprudence—the type of regulation applicable to governmental practices that are covered by the amendment—strongly suggests that the Court's "reasonableness" analysis reflects current societal assessments of when these practices are cost-justified.

What constitutes a "reasonable" search or seizure depends in part on the nature of the Fourth Amendment "interest" or "right" at stake. Consider the RIGHT OF PRIVACY implicated by governmental intrusions into our bodies. The Supreme Court faced this issue in *Winston v. Lee* (1985) when it decided that a court-approved surgery to remove a bullet that could link the individual to a crime constituted an unreasonable search and seizure.

The Court could have justified this decision by viewing bodily privacy as a right of personhood that merits respect and protection regardless of the beneficial social consequences that might be generated by its impairment. A court-ordered surgical procedure performed for nonmedical reasons against the individual's will would constitute an "unreasonable" search because it violated this norm.

Instead, the Court said that a search's reasonableness "depends on a case by case approach, in which the individual's interests in privacy and security are weighed against society's interests in conducting the procedure." In this case, the balance tipped in the individual's favor. The state did not need the incriminating bullet because it already possessed sufficient independent evidence of Lee's guilt to secure his conviction. While acknowledging that an intrusion into bodily privacy might be so egregious and life-threatening that it would be deemed unreasonable on that basis alone, the Court endorsed a utilitarian cost-benefit-balancing analysis to determine the reasonableness of intrusive BODY SEARCHES in future cases.

Winston offers an extreme example of a general judicial trend to view Fourth Amendment values in liberty, property, and privacy as "individual interests" that will be protected from state interference only when doing so will promote our general welfare. In theory, a comprehensive utilitarian calculation of whether a particular search was "reasonable" might consider several factors, including: the strength of the Fourth Amendment interest that is being impaired, the degree of its impairment, the strength of the societal interest at stake, the extent to which the Fourth Amendment activity under review actually furthers that societal interest, and whether the government could further that societal interest by means that intruded less on the individual's Fourth Amendment interests.

But who should balance these competing interests? From what sources should the balancer derive the standard for determining how much social cost the protection of the individual's Fourth Amendment interests is worth? And what kinds of regulatory guidelines should follow from this balancing methodology?

Courts could defer to majoritarian resolutions of such questions in those cases where majoritarian preferences are expressed through political processes that treat all individual choices with equal weight. Under such a "fair process" model, the Court might limit its constitutional inquiry to determining whether the manner by which these trade-off judgments were reached provided a fair opportunity for all interests, values, and alternatives to be considered by politically accountable decision makers. Searches and seizures would be unreasonable if the political process for making the cost-benefit judgment was flawed by some form of discrimination or if the trade-off judgment was delegated to the "arbitrary" discretion of officers in the field who do not qualify as "democratically accountable" officials.

Deriving Fourth Amendment norms exclusively from majoritarian preferences (even those expressed by a well-functioning democratic process) remains problematic for those who view the Constitution as a source of rights and principles that are designed in part to check majoritarian will. But what is the alternative if an assessment of reasonableness requires a cost-benefit analysis? Some commentators have suggested that the Framers of the Fourth Amendment have already done all the necessary balancing of competing interests and that their judgments are reflected in the amendment's warrant-clause requirements.

According to this "warrant" model of Fourth Amendment regulation, the probable cause requirement embodies the Framers' balancing judgment of what constitutes a reasonable search or seizure. Prior judicial authorization ensures that a neutral magistrate, and not the officer in the field, will decide whether the probable cause standard is satisfied. The warrant also controls the discretion of governmental field agents because its particular description of what can be searched and seized limits the scope of their justifiable intrusion.

The Warren Court appeared to embrace this warrant model; it treated searches and seizures without probable cause and most warrantless Fourth Amendment activity as presumptively unreasonable. That Court identified only two narrowly defined exceptions (STOP AND FRISK and ADMINISTRATIVE SEARCHES) where it was willing to engage in its own balancing analysis to assess the reasonableness of Fourth Amendment activity that did not satisfy the warrant clause's requirements.

In TERRY V. OHIO (1968) the Court applied a watered-down version of probable cause (individualized reasonable suspicion) to justify warrantless investigative seizures (stops) and protective searches (frisks) that were less intrusive than ARRESTS and full evidentiary searches. But these stop-and-frisk cases retained a core Fourth Amendment criterion for assessing reasonableness: the government had to demonstrate an individualized factual basis for engaging in Fourth Amendment activity.

The Warren Court's second deviation from the warrant model of regulation came in CAMARA V. MUNICIPAL COURT (1967), where it recognized that governmental civil regulatory interests may render some administrative searches reasonable even in the absence of any individualized factual bases for conducting them. *Camara* upheld the reasonableness of housing-code inspection searches even though there were no individualized ground for believing that the homes searched contained code violations. Having concluded that an individualized suspicion requirement would destroy the state's ability to promote its valid civil regulatory interest, the Court sustained the constitutionality of housing-code inspections conducted in conformity with "reasonable administrative or legislative standards" that limited the discretion of inspectors in the field.

The Burger and Rehnquist Courts have shown a far greater willingness to engage in their own context-specific balancing of competing interests to decide what constitutes reasonable Fourth Amendment activity. At a rhetorical level, they have not explicitly repudiated the warrant model of regulation for criminal cases. However, they have greatly expanded the range and scope of Fourth Amendment intrusions governed by the *Terry* exception to probable cause. On the basis of individualized reasonable suspicion, the police may now "frisk" the passenger compartment of cars to look for dangerous weapons and conduct protective "sweep" searches of homes to look for dangerous accomplices of the person they have arrested. Moreover, the Court has watered down the quality of the evidence needed to establish reasonable suspicion by holding in *Alabama v. White* (1990) that police corroboration of nonincriminating details from an anonymous tip may satisfy the standard of founded suspicion.

More importantly, the Court has greatly expanded both the rationale and scope of the administrative search doctrine. In several decisions, the Court has used a balancing approach to justify intrusive searches and seizures without a warrant, probable cause, or even individualized suspicion where the governmental interest furthered by the search is viewed as particularly compelling. Two significant themes emerge from these cases.

First, the Court has dispensed with individualized suspicion as a minimal Fourth Amendment requirement even in contexts in which such a requirement would not preclude the government from promoting the societal interests at stake. Thus, in NATIONAL TREASURY EMPLOYEES UNION V. VON RAAB (1988), the Court upheld the constitutionality of suspicionless DRUG TESTING of employees who were in or were seeking certain sensitive positions within the Customs Service. The Court found mandatory urine testing reasonable despite the absence of any showing that the Service had a drug problem or that a founded suspicion standard would prevent the Service from adequately dealing with any problem it did have.

Second, the Court has not confined its interest-balancing approach to civil regulatory searches and seizures. Despite language in *Von Raab* that some special "governmental need" beyond the normal imperatives of law enforcement must be shown for interest balancing to be appropriate, the Court used interest balancing in MICHIGAN DEPARTMENT OF STATE POLICE V. SITZ (1990) to uphold the reasonableness of seizures of all drivers at sobriety checkpoints. The Court did not concern itself with whether these suspicionless seizures better promoted the detection and deterrence of drunk driving than did police patrols that stopped drivers on the basis of individualized reasonable suspicion. Nor did the availability of less intrusive police practices that served the same societal interests render these checkpoint stops unreasonable. In essence, this law enforcement seizure was "reasonable" because the state's compelling interest in fighting drunk driving outweighed the individual's interest in liberty that was only "minimally" intruded on by a momentary detention and examination for signs of intoxication.

When the Court uses this interest-balancing approach, it never identifies the source of its standard for assessing why the state interest outweighs the individual's Fourth Amendment interests. But opinions like *Sitz* strongly suggest that the Court is relying on its interpretation of majoritarian assessments of when searches and seizures are cost-justified. The Court certainly is not making its own probing cost-benefit analysis. Instead, it defers to the judgments of upper-level law enforcement officials concerning the most appropriate use of their scarce law enforcement resources because the Fourth Amendment "was not meant to transfer [such decisions] from politically accountable officials to the courts." Left unstated is the assumption that the tenure of "politically accountable" officials depends on their ability to gauge accurately majoritarian preferences about the appropriate trade-off between individual and societal interests. Left unexamined is whether the political process generating these trade-off decisions has fairly considered the competing interests at stake or adequately examined alternative ways to accommodate them. The Court appears to be using a "fair process" model in name only to legitimate majoritarian preferences concerning what constitutes cost-justified Fourth Amendment activity.

The Court's Fourth Amendment jurisprudence reflects a fundamental tension within constitutional law concerning two different functions that can be served by constitutional principles in a democratic system. The Court sometimes treats the Constitution as a source of norms whose justification is not linked either to the satisfaction of majoritarian preferences or to the promotion of general social welfare. When the Court views the Fourth Amendment from this perspective, its determination of what constitutes "reasonable" Fourth Amendment activity will sometimes frustrate majoritarian preferences. Recently, the Court has viewed the Constitution's requirements as embodied in the expression of the preferences that emerge from a democratic process. The Rehnquist Court, however, does not engage in any searching inquiry about the nature of the process that generated these preferences; it simply assumes that a well-functioning democratic process was in place. When the Court views the Fourth Amendment from this more positivistic perspective, it shows far greater deference to the judgments and actions of the governmental actors subject to the amendment's constraints.

PETER ARENELLA
(1992)

(SEE ALSO: *Fourth Amendment, Historical Origins of; Search and Seizure; Unreasonable Search.*)

Bibliography

AMSTERDAM, ANTHONY G.   1974   Perspectives on the Fourth Amendment. *Minnesota Law Review* 58:349–477.
LAFAVE, WAYNE   1987   *Search and Seizure: A Treatise on the Fourth Amendment*, 2nd ed. Vols. 1–3. St. Paul, Minn.: West Publishing Co.

SCHULHOFER, STEPHEN J. 1989 On the Fourth Amendment Rights of the Law-Abiding Public. *Supreme Court Review* 1989:87–163.

WASSERSTROM, SILAS J. and SEIDMAN, LOUIS M. 1988 The Fourth Amendment as Constitutional Theory. *Georgetown Law Journal* 77:19–112.

FOURTH AMENDMENT
(Update)

During the 1990s, the Supreme Court continued to confront the central issues of the Fourth Amendment's scope: what conduct is covered by the Amendment, what regulations apply to that conduct, and how those limitations are to be enforced.

Just as the Court had earlier taken a narrow view of what the word "searches" means in the Fourth Amendment, in recent years the Court has given the "seizures" term a limited construction, again confining within too narrow a compass those police activities subject to the Amendment's restrictions. Illustrative is *Florida v. Bostick* (1991), holding that the state court erred in finding a seizure occurred during a suspicionless bus sweep involving confrontation and interrogation of the passengers. The Court objected that the state decision inappropriately (1) used the Court's previous test of whether "a reasonable person would have believed that he was not free to leave," which the Justices deemed inapplicable to one who had no desire to leave the bus; and (2) treated the on-bus locale of the encounter as especially significant. But the Court's own analysis was flawed. When police undertake a bus sweep, they act with the obvious connivance of the common carrier to which bus travelers have entrusted their care, thereby creating a highly coercive situation unlike any contact that might occur between two private citizens, contrary to the more common forms of nonseizure police–citizen encounters.

This police dominance has a uniquely heavy impact on interstate bus travelers precisely because they do not, as a practical matter, have available the range of avoidance options that pedestrians might use. Abandoning one's journey by leaving the bus is not feasible, so that the passenger's only remaining privacy-protection option is obstinate refusal to respond to the officers' questions. But the dynamics of the situation make a nonconforming refusal to cooperate an unlikely choice, especially when it is considered that bus transportation is used largely by people with low incomes and little influence.

When the Court determines the "reasonableness" of conduct amounting to a search or seizure, typically it balances the individual's interests in privacy and security against society's interests. The latter interests are usually crime detection and sometimes crime prevention, but yet another is ensuring that police are not unduly endangered while carrying out their duties, as reflected in the rules governing SEARCH INCIDENT TO AN ARREST and frisk incident to a stop. The Court's decisions in the 1990s, involving concern about police safety in other settings, highlight two competing considerations: (1) a risk of death or serious injury to police is less tolerable than a risk that some crimes will remain undetected, so that police authority to act in their own protection must generally be more broadly stated; and (2) general grants of authority to the police to act for their own protection are nonetheless undesirable when the contemplated activity is highly intrusive on individual privacy and freedom. The Court's efforts to thread a line between those two considerations are reflected in three decisions. *Maryland v. Wilson* (1997) held that passengers as well as drivers may be required to exit a vehicle incident to a traffic stop, because such minimal added intrusion is justified in the interest of the officer's safety. *Richards v. Wisconsin* (1997) rejected a state's blanket rule that police, for their own safety, could make a NO-KNOCK ENTRY when they are executing a SEARCH WARRANT regarding a felony drug crime, because such a broad category "contains considerable overgeneralization." *Maryland v. Buie* (1990) considered protective sweeps incident to in-premises arrests. The Court deemed it necessary to create a two-pronged test whereby police were given automatic authority to look into "spaces immediately adjoining the place of arrest" but were required to show facts warranting reason to believe persons posing danger were present before undertaking a more extensive sweep.

One shining beacon in our Fourth Amendment history is the brilliant argument of JAMES OTIS, JR., against writs of assistance, when he railed against the "power that places the liberty of every man in the hands of every petty officer." These words are an apt description of one of the most pervasive law enforcement techniques of the 1990s: An officer stops a vehicle on the highway (often as a result of a selection process that takes into account nothing other than the driver's race) for an insignificant traffic violation that would not provoke any police response but for the officer's desire to determine (by a plain-view observation, a consent search, or summoning a drug-detection dog) whether the vehicle contains drugs. This practice raises the important question of whether the Fourth Amendment's "reasonableness" requirement necessitates only that there be some factual basis for the action taken (such as the traffic violation), or whether in addition it is necessary that the conduct not be arbitrary or pretextual. That question was answered in the traffic-stop case of *Whren v. United States* (1996), which may turn out to be the Court's most significant, and most unfortunate, Fourth Amendment decision of the 1990s. The Court in *Whren* reached three startling conclusions: (1) the pretextual nature of a traffic stop, even if shown by the subjective motivation of the officer, and even when absent such motivation no Fourth Amendment intrusion would have been made, does not make the stop unreasonable, (2) a showing of a departure from usual practice, again producing an intrusion a reasonable police officer would not have made, also does not constitute a Fourth Amendment violation, and (3) there is no violation even when, as in *Whren*, the departure is clearly shown by a deviation from a police regulation limiting the circumstances in which Fourth Amendment intrusions are permissible.

WAYNE R. LAFAVE
(2000)

(SEE ALSO: *Search and Seizure; Unreasonable Search.*)

Bibliography

LAFAVE, WAYNE R. 1996 *Search and Seizure: A Treatise on the Fourth Amendment*, 3rd ed. Vols. 1–5. St. Paul, Minn.: West Publishing Co.

FOURTH AMENDMENT, HISTORICAL ORIGINS OF

Appended to the United States Constitution as part of the BILL OF RIGHTS in 1789, the Fourth Amendment declares that "The right of the people to be secure in their persons, houses, papers and effects against UNREASONABLE SEARCHES and seizures shall not be violated, and no warrants shall issue but upon PROBABLE CAUSE, supported by oath or affirmation, and particularly describing the place to be searched and the persons or things to be seized." In identifying the "specific" warrant as its orthodox method of search, the amendment constitutionally repudiated its antithesis, the GENERAL WARRANT.

The general warrant did not confine its reach to a particular person, place, or object but allowed its bearer to arrest, search, and seize as his suspicions directed. In 1763, a typical warrant by the British secretaries of state commanded "diligent search" for the unidentified author, printer, and publisher of a satirical journal, *The North Briton, No. 45*, and the seizure of their papers. At least five houses were consequently searched, forty-nine (mostly innocent) persons arrested, and thousands of books and papers confiscated. Resentment against such invasions ultimately generated an antidote in the Fourth Amendment and is crucial to its understanding.

General warrants and general searches without warrant had a lengthy pedigree. In 1662, a statute codified WRITS OF ASSISTANCE that allowed searching all suspected places for goods concealed in violation of the customs laws. Such writs had been used since at least 1621 and themselves absorbed the language of royal commissions that had for centuries authorized general searches without warrant. Similarly promiscuous searches had existed for numerous applications: the pursuit of felons, suppression of political and religious deviance, regulation of printing, medieval craft guilds, naval and military impressment, counterfeiting, bankruptcy, excise and land taxes, vagrancy, game poaching, sumptuary behavior, and even the recovery of stolen personal items.

Colonial America copied Britain's machinery of search but varied its applications. Most jurisdictions instituted general searches to collect taxes, discourage poaching, capture felons, or find stolen merchandise. In the southernmost colonies, general searches without warrant blossomed into a comprehensive system of social regulation of the civilian population by quasi-military "slave patrols."

Although general warrants were the basic method of search, numerous restraints qualified their operation. Writs of assistance were invalid at night; certain areas of legislation touching the guilds and excises confined the general searches involved to the persons vocationally concerned. Yet such measures were not a comprehensive guarantee, systematically applied. Moreover, social philosophy outweighed civil libertarianism as a motive for the most conspicuous restraints, for while general "privy searches" plagued the poor, the elite enjoyed immunity from whole classes of similar searches. Covered by a thin veneer of restraints different from the specific warrant, the centrality of the general search remained starkly visible. Conversely, although specific warrants existed in legal manuals, they were rare before 1750, thereby indicating that they were not the intended constitutional successor to the general warrant.

English legal thinkers, however, expressed far greater hostility to the general warrant than did the law itself. As early as 1589 Robert Beale charged that the general search warrants used by the "High Commission" against Puritans violated MAGNA CARTA (1215). In the next two centuries, such titans of English law as Sir EDWARD COKE, Sir Matthew Hale, and Sir WILLIAM BLACKSTONE embellished similar themes with citations from the COMMON LAW.

Such evidence, however, was more embroidery than substance. Magna Carta was a profoundly feudal document that said nothing on the intersection of searches, houses, and warrants. The master case usually cited against the general warrant, *Semayne's Case* (1602, 1604), actually drew a rigid line exempting the Crown from the protections elsewhere extended against invasion of the dwelling by private citizens. Unlike later scholars, the court had there emphasized that a man's house was *not* his castle against the government.

Like legal theorists, ordinary critics of the general

search did not identify the specific warrant as its solution. Those whose houses were searched were more likely to execrate being searched than the generality of the authorizing warrant. Indignation that the victim of a general search was a member of the nobility deflected hostility from the search process and implied that it could properly be inflicted on the overwhelming majority who were not nobles. Ubiquitous laments that pregnant wives had miscarried during violent searches simply substituted appeals to the reader's sympathy for criticism of the absence of the concrete laws against such actions. Yet these very mythologies provided legitimacy and impulse for a right against unreasonable SEARCH AND SEIZURE. Although the Magna Carta of the thirteenth century said nothing against general searches, that of the eighteenth century had swollen into a formidable ideological weapon against them.

The movement against general warrants accelerated from 1761 to 1787. The *North Briton* controversy culminated in dozens of trials and in resolutions by the House of Commons against the use of those warrants. In *Wilkes v. Wood* (1763) and *Huckle v. Money* (1763–1765), CHARLES PRATT (Lord Camden) and WILLIAM MURRAY (Lord Mansfield), the chief justices of the Courts of Common Pleas and King's Bench, respectively, condemned the general warrants of search and arrest used by the secretaries of state as incompatible with statute, natural justice, the common law, and Magna Carta. A dozen derivative cases surrounding *Entick v. Carrington* ended in decisions against the seizure of personal papers. (See WILKES CASES.)

Writs of assistance came under attack in the American colonial courts. JAMES OTIS, a fiery young Massachusetts attorney, made a brilliant "higher law" assault on the writs in PAXTON'S CASE (1761). Although Otis lost, most colonial courts refused to issue such writs when requuired to do so by the Townshend Act of 1767, and a series of pamphlets beginning with JOHN DICKINSON's *Farmer's Letters* joined in the assault. Eight states inserted some guarantee against general warrants in their constitutions of 1776–1784. Finally, four state conventions urged a corresponding restraint on searches by the new national government in ratifying the federal Constitution of 1787. JAMES MADISON of Virginia duly responded by including what became the Fourth Amendment among the Bill of Rights which he proposed to Congress on June 8, 1789.

Neither Britain nor the separate American states, however, immediately abolished general searches. Rhetorical implications notwithstanding, the British abandoned only the isolated form of general warrants issued by state secretaries. Writs of assistance and other kinds of statutory general SEARCH WARRANTS survived, for no comprehensive statute to the contrary ever emerged from the House of Commons. Despite their constitutions, the American states retained general search warrants not only as devices

for [prosecuting the American Revolution] but also for a wide range of other purposes into the 1780s.

Although the right against unreasonable search and seizure has lengthy British roots, its cornerstone, the confinement of all searches, seizures, and arrests by warrant to the particular place, persons, and objects enumerated, derives from Massachusetts. A cluster of Massachusetts statutes and court decisions from 1756 to 1766, the third stage in a century-long process, uniformly restrained searches and arrests to the person or location designated in the warrant. Legislation in the 1780s extended this specificity to the objects of seizure. The Fourth Amendment is thus the marriage of an ancient British right and a new, colonial interpretation that vastly extended its meaning.

WILLIAM J. CUDDIHY
(1986)

Bibliography

CUDDIHY, WILLIAM and HARDY, B. CARMON 1980 A Man's House Was Not His Castle: Origins of the Fourth Amendment to the United States Constitution. *William and Mary Quarterly* 3: 371–400.
LASSON, NELSON 1937 *The History . . . of the Fourth Amendment.* Baltimore: Johns Hopkins University Press.

FRAENKEL, OSMOND K.
(1888–1981)

Trained at Columbia University Law School, Osmond Kessler Fraenkel made his mark on American constitutional law as a CIVIL LIBERTIES advocate. He was counsel for the New York Civil Liberties Union from 1934 to 1955 and for the AMERICAN CIVIL LIBERTIES UNION from 1955 to 1977. During most of that time he was also an official of the National Lawyers Guild. In addition to being involved in much of the important civil liberties litigation of his time, Fraenkel wrote four books, including *Our Civil Liberties* (1945) and *The Supreme Court and Civil Liberties* (1960), as well as many law review articles.

DENNIS J. MAHONEY
(1986)

FRANK, JEROME N.
(1889–1957)

Jerome Frank held important positions in FRANKLIN D. ROOSEVELT'S NEW DEAL, pioneered American legal realism, taught at Yale Law School, and served on the United States Court of Appeals for the Second Circuit from 1941 until his death in 1957. During this period the Second Circuit was one of the most illustrious courts in the nation's history. On the court Frank developed a highly refined concept of his role as intermediate appellate judge. His decisions greatly influenced the United States Supreme Court by crystallizing and focusing legal issues and by articulating major considerations of precedent and policy. His opinions, even if written as concurrences or dissents, frequently became the law of the land when the Supreme Court followed Jerome Frank's lead. When the VINSON COURT and WARREN COURT protected CIVIL LIBERTIES, they often relied on the spadework of lower federal judges, prominently including Jerome Frank.

In his opinions Frank frequently addressed the Supreme Court as an advocate—urging, persuading, coaxing, and cajoling the Court to move in desired directions. At the same time, he recognized the limits imposed by his subordinate position, and he gracefully accepted those bounds. Frank faithfully followed Supreme Court precedent, but, if a rule seemed misguided, he would criticize the DOCTRINE and urge the Supreme Court to reexamine it. *United States v. Roth* (1956) illustrates Frank's technique. Although he considered a federal OBSCENITY statute unconstitutional, several Supreme Court decisions had assumed the statute's validity without squarely facing the issue. In a new challenge to the law, Frank did not dodge these earlier rulings by describing them as OBITER DICTA. Rather, he followed them and voted to uphold the convictions. At the same time, in a concurrence, he analyzed the serious constitutional issues with a coherence and lucidity that has not yet been surpassed. Frank's seminal effort anticipated many later Supreme Court cases which, over the next two decades, relied on Frank's opinion and reasoning. (See *Roth v. United States*, 1957.)

Protection for civil liberties was a persistent theme in Frank's judicial opinions. He believed that republican government maximized free choice and affirmed the dignity of the individual. On the Second Circuit he struggled to protect this vision. He regularly challenged the Supreme Court to expand the definition of, and protection for, civil liberties. For instance, he tried valiantly to humanize IMMIGRATION and DEPORTATION laws which perennially had treated ALIENS cavalierly. Frank wrote his most passionate opinions in the area of criminal law and procedure. He considered ELECTRONIC EAVESDROPPING a dangerous invasion of privacy which should be limited by the FOURTH AMENDMENT's prohibition on UNREASONABLE SEARCHES and seizures. His skepticism about the accuracy of the law's fact-finding processes led him to believe that courts wrongly convicted many innocent persons. He thought that police investigation practices frequently degenerated into brutal "third degree" tactics which coerced confessions in violation of the Fifth and Sixth Amendments. Following in Frank's path, the Supreme Court moved to curb prolonged POLICE INTERROGATIONS and to control offensive police practices. The progressive constitutionalization of American criminal process secured by the Vinson and Warren Courts reflected not merely the judgment of a majority of the Supreme Court but rather a broader legal movement led prominently by Jerome Frank.

ROBERT JEROME GLENNON
(1986)

Bibliography

GLENNON, ROBERT JEROME 1985 *The Iconoclast as Reformer: Jerome Frank's Impact on American Law.* Ithaca, N.Y.: Cornell University Press.

FRANK v. MANGUM
237 U.S. 309 (1915)

Vicious anti-Semitism and bitter resentment against encroaching industrialization joined in Atlanta, Georgia, in the spring of 1913. Leo Frank, a young Jewish businessman from the North, was arrested and convicted of murdering a thirteen-year-old girl in a factory he superintended. Prejudice, disorder, and blatant public hostility characterized the trial and its coverage. The Georgia Supreme Court denied Frank a new trial, 4–2, dismissing claims of procedural errors, irregularities, and the trial judge's stated doubts about Frank's guilt.

Justices JOSEPH R. LAMAR and OLIVER WENDELL HOLMES each turned down requests for WRITS OF ERROR on procedural grounds (though Holmes was not convinced that Frank had received DUE PROCESS), as did the entire Supreme Court, without opinion. Frank then petitioned for a writ of HABEAS CORPUS because mob domination had effectively denied him PROCEDURAL DUE PROCESS. The Court likewise denied this relief, 7–2. Justice MAHLON PITNEY declared that habeas corpus could not be substituted for a writ of error to review procedural irregularities. Further, when Frank neglected to object during the trial, he effectively waived the right to claim a denial of due process later. Justices Holmes and CHARLES EVANS HUGHES dissented, pointing to the lack of a FAIR TRIAL: "Mob law does not become due process of law by securing the assent of a terrorized jury." Less than two months after the Georgia governor commuted his death sentence to life imprisonment, Frank was kidnapped from prison and lynched. That he was innocent of the crime for which he was convicted is no longer doubted.

The Supreme Court subsequently embarked on a series of decisions insuring the observance of the constitutional safeguards of procedural due process. In MOORE V. DEMPSEY (1923), the turning point, Holmes wrote for the Court, permitting the use of habeas corpus as a means of preserving criminal defendants' rights. *Frank*'s rule of forfeiture through failure to object, however, returned with only slight modification in WAINWRIGHT V. SYKES (1977).

In 1982 a witness came forward and stated that shortly after the murder he had seen another man carrying the victim's body. In 1986 the governor of Georgia posthumously pardoned Leo Frank.

DAVID GORDON
(1986)

Bibliography

DINNERSTEIN, LEONARD 1968 *The Leo Frank Case.* New York: Columbia University Press.

FRANKFURTER, FELIX
(1882–1965)

The immigrant son of Austrian Jews, Felix Frankfurter acquired a legendary reputation as a lawyer, law professor, intellectual gadfly, and presidential adviser even before President FRANKLIN D. ROOSEVELT named him to the Supreme Court in 1939. Unable to speak or write a word of English when he entered the public schools of New York City in the 1890s, he was graduated with honors from City College of New York and compiled a distinguished record at the Harvard Law School, where he fell under the influence of Dean James Barr Ames's historical methods, absorbed the constitutional theories of JAMES BRADLEY THAYER, and generally adopted the social and cultural trappings of the New England Brahmins, without their intellectual boorishness or political conservatism.

As a law professor at Harvard, Frankfurter introduced several generations of students to constitutional and ADMINISTRATIVE LAW, and invented a new field of study: the JURISDICTION of the federal courts. His students and protégés, including Dean Acheson, JAMES LANDIS, David Lilienthal, and Tom Corcoran, populated the federal bureaucracy from the days of WOODROW WILSON to those of JOHN F. KENNEDY. His 1917 report on the deportation of striking miners from Arizona by local vigilantes and his severe criticism of the procedural unfairness of the COMMONWEALTH V. SACCO & VANZETTI (1921) showed his deep concern for CIVIL LIBERTIES and political reform. That he should come to be known, at the end of his judicial career, as a conservative on many of these issues reflected not a weakening of personal convictions, but a strongly held view about the proper limits of the judicial function.

Frankfurter served on the Court between the two great periods of JUDICIAL ACTIVISM in this century. He arrived on the bench two years after the HUGHES COURT, retreating from its activism of 1935–1936, laid to rest the DUE PROCESS clause and the COMMERCE CLAUSE as instruments of judicial control over legislative ECONOMIC REGULATION. His retirement and replacement in 1962 by ARTHUR J. GOLDBERG permitted the Warren Court to enter its most activist phase through the expansion of due process and EQUAL PROTECTION to provide Americans with extensive new CONSTITUTIONAL REMEDIES against governmental encroachments upon personal liberties.

Frankfurter deplored both the conservative activism of the Hughes years and the liberal activism of the Warren era. From 1939 until 1962, he attempted to discover some middle ground for the Court to occupy that would be intellectually respectable, politically defensible, and morally satisfying. Although his ultimate posture of institutional self-restraint won him few plaudits from liberals and captured the fancy of only a minority among the legal intelligentsia, it had the virtue of predictability.

He rejected the PREFERRED FREEDOMS doctrine articulated by Justice HARLAN FISKE STONE in UNITED STATES V. CAROLENE PRODUCTS CO. (1938), where the latter urged the Court to adopt a two-tiered system of JUDICIAL REVIEW that would take the justices out of the business of shaping economic policy at large but expand their role as the arbiters of civil liberties, race relations, and criminal justice. When passing upon all constitutional questions, Frankfurter responded, the Justices should always act with restraint, avoid ultimate issues of power, and insist only upon a RATIONAL BASIS test for legislation, whether the challenged law concerned filled milk, labor relations, FREEDOM OF SPEECH, or CRIMINAL PROCEDURE. This judicial posture led Frankfurter to uphold a broad range of social and economic measures adopted by the states and the federal government after 1940, but it also earned him the enmity of constitutional liberals when he applied the same tolerant standards to less enlightened manifestations of the political process, including the SMITH ACT, the McCarran Act (see INTERNAL SECURITY ACT), a GROUP LIBEL statute, and the investigative techniques of the HOUSE COMMITTEE ON UN-AMERICAN ACTIVITIES.

Frankfurter also spurned Justice HUGO L. BLACK's arguments for incorporating the BILL OF RIGHTS into the FOURTEENTH AMENDMENT's due process clause. Like Frankfurter, the Alabama-born justice wished to chain the arbitrary power of judges in the wake of the Great Depression's constitutional crisis, and he urged the Court to replace "the vague contours of due process" with the specific prohibitions and guarantees of the first nine amendments. But beneath Black's façade of positivistic neutrality, Frankfurter suspected, there beat the heart of a judicial fundamentalist, moved by the plight of the poor and the oppressed but no less unbending than PIERCE BUTLER's or GEORGE SUTHERLAND's. Frankfurter eschewed mechanical formulas such as Black's, and he believed that the INCORPORATION DOCTRINE lacked any historical basis in the

Fourteenth Amendment. Incorporation, he feared, would encourage the Supreme Court to impose a single code of criminal procedure upon the states and would establish a more rigid judicial tyranny than even the conservative "Four Horsemen" had espoused during the 1930s.

From BETTS V. BRADY (1942) to MAPP V. OHIO in 1961, he insisted that the framers of the Fourteenth Amendment had not intended to subject state criminal proceedings to the precise requirements of the federal Bill of Rights. That amendment, he argued in *Adamson v. California* (1947), was "not the basis of a uniform code of criminal procedure federally imposed. . . . In a federal system it would be a function debilitating to the responsibility of state and local agencies."

But this did not mean for Frankfurter that the Supreme Court of the United States had no obligation to review state criminal convictions under the due process clause. That clause, he believed, represented no explicit commands, but a requirement of fairness and reasonableness, above all, a prohibition against official conduct that "shocked the conscience" or offended contemporary standards of civilized behavior. Within this broad, subjective framework, the states had flexibility to manage their own affairs in the realm of criminal justice. Police officers could not, in the absence of friends or counsel, interrogate a suspect for days and claim that his confession had been voluntary; they could not recover physical evidence with the aid of a stomach pump (as in ROCHIN V. CALIFORNIA, 1952); or place a listening device in a suspect's bedroom (as in IRVINE V. CALIFORNIA, 1953, dissenting opinion). But due process did not require, in Frankfurter's judgment, that the state provide legal counsel in all felony cases; exclude evidence seized illegally by the police; or refrain from executing a person after a first attempt had failed, although he had strong personal objections to all of these practices (*Louisiana ex rel. Francis v. Resweber*, 1947, concurring opinion; *Mapp v. Ohio*, 1961, dissenting).

An early high point of Frankfurter's doctrinal influence came in the summer of 1940, when, over Stone's lone dissent, the Justices rejected a FIRST AMENDMENT—due process attack on the mandatory flag salute in the public schools of West Virginia. Within a year of that decision, however, Frankfurter's majority disintegrated. (See FLAG SALUTE CASES.) Led by Black and WILLIAM O. DOUGLAS, a coalition of from five to six Justices carved out a generous area of constitutional protection for both religious and political minorities under the First Amendment and the due process clause. This same majority also began to impose sharp limitations upon the conduct of state criminal trials and local police methods and to afford state prisoners greater ACCESS to federal courts by means of HABEAS CORPUS proceedings.

Throughout his judicial career, Frankfurter remained skeptical of absolutes. He preached a gospel of relativism and "balancing" that usually encouraged judicial modesty and retrenchment, yet, he too could be a fundamentalist on many constitutional questions. Few Justices took more literally the First Amendment's prohibition against an ESTABLISHMENT OF RELIGION, and his views in EVERSON V. BOARD OF EDUCATION (1947) and MCCOLLUM V. BOARD OF EDUCATION (1948) remained as uncompromising as Black's on freedom of speech. He abhorred CAPITAL PUNISHMENT and used every weapon in his considerable legal arsenal to set aside convictions that carried the death penalty.

Moreover, he consistently championed the FOURTH AMENDMENT by refusing to bend its language to accommodate SEARCHES AND SEIZURES made without a valid warrant or PROBABLE CAUSE as demonstrated by his dissenting opinion in UNITED STATES V. RABINOWITZ (1950). Finally, although he resisted the extension of the EXCLUSIONARY RULE to the states via the due process clause, he expected federal judges, prosecutors, and law enforcement officials to follow a strict code of fairness and decency when confronting persons accused or suspected of crimes (*McNabb v. United States*, 1943, see MCNABB-MALLORY RULE; *Nye v. United States*, 1941; *Rosenberg v. United States*, 1953, dissenting opinion).

In addition to institutional self-restraint, Frankfurter found in FEDERALISM—perhaps the oldest of our constitutional values—a major, articulate premise of his jurisprudence. His concern for maintaining the vitality of local governmental units distinguished him sharply from most other post-1937 Justices. "The states," he wrote, nine years before joining the Court, "need the amplest scope for energy and individuality in dealing with the myriad problems created by our complex industrial civilization. . . . For government means experimentation. To be sure, constitutional limitations confine the area of experiment. But these limitations are not self-defining and were intended to permit government. Opportunity must be allowed for vindicating reasonable belief by experience. The very notion of our federalism calls for the free play of local diversity in dealing with local problems." From 1939 until 1962, he attempted to apply these convictions.

A great many of Frankfurter's conflicts with other Justices, often viewed as disputes over civil liberties or judicial self-restraint, actually focused for him upon questions of federalism. A good example is the famous 1941 case of BRIDGES V. CALIFORNIA, which, many scholars agree, marked a turning point in his relationship with Justice Black and remains a landmark in the Court's post-1937 concern for civil liberties. In *Bridges*, speaking through Black, the Court reversed contempt sentences imposed by California judges upon a militant union leader and the Los Angeles *Times* for out-of-court publications that the local courts believed had disrupted pending cases. Unless such statements represented a CLEAR AND PRESENT DANGER to the orderly administration of justice, Black wrote, the due process clause (incorporating the First Amendment's protection of speech and press) prohibited judicial punishment of this kind.

Frankfurter took issue with Black on several points, but the heart of his dissenting opinion reflected powerful federalist concerns for the independence and autonomy of local courts. "We are, after all," he noted, "sitting over three thousand miles away from a great state, without intimate knowledge of its habits and its needs, in matters which do not cut across the affirmative powers of the national government. . . . How are we to know whether an easy-going or stiffer view of what affects the actual administration of justice is appropriate to local circumstances?" Nine months earlier, in a similar contempt case that did not raise the problem of a direct conflict with state courts, Frankfurter had no difficulty in joining an opinion by Justice Douglas in *Nye v. United States* (1941) that sharply curtailed the power of federal judges to punish disruptive litigants. For Frankfurter, what distinguished *Nye* from *Bridges* was not the First Amendment, "the clear and present danger" test, or the degree of judicial misconduct involved, but the simple matter of the constitution's limited reach into the processes of state courts.

A passionate New Dealer, Frankfurter consistently upheld the power of Congress, acting under the commerce clause, to regulate the nation's economic affairs, even when these regulations touched activities within the traditional domain of the states. He sustained, for example, the judgment of the National Labor Relations Board that local newspaper boys, employed by the Hearst chain, were "employees" within the coverage of the WAGNER (NATIONAL LABOR RELATIONS) ACT, and he agreed that the administrator of the FAIR LABOR STANDARDS ACT could entirely prohibit homework in the embroidery industry as a reasonable means to enforce minimum wage decrees.

At the same time, he tended to read congressional regulation of commerce as permitting complementary state legislation, except where the national legislature acted with clarity to preempt local regulations. He insisted that Congress speak with precision on this matter, and he abhorred judicial expansion of congressional intentions, especially where the results limited local authority. In *Cornell Steamboat Co. v. United States* (1944), for instance, he rejected Black's interpretation of the 1940 Transportation Act that gave the Interstate Commerce Commission authority to fix the rates of tugboats operating on the Hudson River, where ninety-five percent of their business took place between New York ports, but where they passed briefly over the territorial waters of New Jersey. He rejected the idea that Congress had intended in the Wagner Act to exempt union officials from state regu-

lation that did not touch directly upon the employee-employer relationship. In close cases, he often supported a solution that expanded federal authority the least.

In commerce clause cases, despite his concern for maintaining local authority, he refused to endorse the extreme views of Justice Black and others, who mechanically endorsed state economic regulations in the absence of specific federal legislation preempting certain fields. He voted to overturn, for example, Arizona's Train Limit Law and he likewise objected to a local milk ordinance that discriminated against competing products pasteurized beyond five miles of the city. On the other hand, he often allowed the states considerable latitude when they attempted to tax or regulate other aspects of interstate commerce, and he did not support wholeheartedly the economic nationalism of Justice ROBERT H. JACKSON, with whom he disagreed in cases such as *Duckworth v. Arkansas* (1941); *Northwest Airlines v. Minnesota* (1944); and *H. P. Hood & Sons v. DuMond* (1949; dissenting).

Frankfurter believed that federalism required the national judiciary, above all the Supreme Court, to respect the autonomy, sagacity, and integrity of state courts. He was a strong supporter of Justice LOUIS D. BRANDEIS's views (which had become law in ERIE V. TOMPKINS, 1938) that required federal judges to apply state law in cases involving diversity of state citizenship, and he often voted to restrict the role of federal courts in this area. (See DIVERSITY JURISDICTION.) State courts, he believed, could efficiently and honestly protect the interests of nonresidents. The Supreme Court should not construe federal statutes in such a manner as to preempt local judicial procedures unless that construction seemed inescapable. For instance, he rejected the idea that Congress intended in the federal bankruptcy laws to strip local courts of their control over their own procedures. "The state courts belong to the States," he wrote. "They are not subject to the control of Congress though of course state law may in words or by implication make the federal rule for conducting litigation the rule that should govern suits to enforce federal rights in the state courts."

America's continuing racial ordeal probably tested the limits of his deference to state authority more severely than did any other constitutional issue. An early member of the NAACP and the first Justice to hire a black clerk, he detested racial discrimination in all of its forms. Yet he refused to interpret the Reconstruction-era CIVIL RIGHTS ACTS to impose criminal and civil penalties on local officials who abused their authority and acted in a hostile manner against minorities. In SCREWS V. UNITED STATES (1945), Frankfurter, dissenting, argued that Congress had intended in the Reconstruction statute to attack only discrimination sanctioned by positive state laws, not the abuse of authority by local officials. "We should leave to the States," he said, "the enforcement of their criminal law, and not relieve States of the responsibility for vindicating wrongdoing that is essentially local or weaken the habits of local law enforcement by tempting reliance on federal authority for an occasional unpleasant task of local enforcement."

Two decades later, Frankfurter still reaffirmed these views in MONROE V. PAPE (1961), when the Court sustained a civil action against several Chicago police officers who invaded a black family's home and illegally arrested a member of the household without a SEARCH WARRANT. The conduct of the police infuriated him, but in Frankfurter's judgment they had not acted with the approval of state law and therefore they could not be sued under the federal statute for damages. "To be sure," he wrote, "this leaves certain cases unprotected. . . . But the cost of ignoring the distinction in order to cover those cases—the cost, that is, of providing a federal judicial remedy for every constitutional violation—involves preemption by the National Government . . . of matters of intimate concern to state and local government."

History treated neither Justice Frankfurter nor his federalism kindly. By means of the commerce clause and its TAXING AND SPENDING POWERS, the federal government continued to absorb more and more authority at the expense of the states, usually with the Supreme Court's approval. Horrified by local police brutality and by the failure of local political elites to eradicate racial SEGREGATION, the federal judiciary became a powerful instrument of social reform in the decade after Frankfurter left the bench. Even during his tenure, American society was not usually prepared to pay the price of his attachment to federalism. As the *Screws* and *Monroe* cases demonstrated, the price could be very high: the inability of the national government to correct glaring denials of constitutional rights that the states themselves refused to correct, and the failure of the states to correct local ills of a kind already eliminated in the conduct of the national government.

From the perspective of many of his colleagues, Frankfurter too often sacrificed efficiency, uniformity, and morality on behalf of an archaic devotion to localism. They hoped to create a new world of prodigious economic growth and humanitarian social policy, where the enlightened judiciary helped to sweep away the provincial forces of commercial and political reaction. For Justice Frankfurter, however, federalism remained both a constitutional command as well as a viable method for ordering American life through the slower process of self-education and social experimentation.

Frankfurter enlivened American politics and immeasurably enriched the nation's legal literature for a half-century. "There is some talk here of replacing him on the Supreme Court," James Reston wrote when he retired in 1962, "but this is as silly as the doctor's bulletins. They may eventually put somebody in his place, but they won't replace him."

MICHAEL E. PARRISH
(1986)

Bibliography

FREEDMAN, MAX, ed. 1967 *Roosevelt and Frankfurter: Their Correspondence, 1928–1945.* Boston: Little, Brown.

HIRSCH, HARRY N. 1981 *The Enigma of Felix Frankfurter.* New York: Basic Books.

LASH, JOSEPH P. 1975 *From the Diaries of Felix Frankfurter.* New York: Norton.

PARRISH, MICHAEL E. 1982 *Felix Frankfurter and His Times.* Volume One. New York: Macmillan.

PHILLIPS, HARLAN B., ed. 1960 *Felix Frankfurter Reminisces.* New York: Reynal & Co.

FRANKLIN, BENJAMIN
(1706–1790)

Benjamin Franklin, president of Pennsylvania, was the oldest delegate to the CONSTITUTIONAL CONVENTION OF 1787. A beloved elder statesman of the young Republic, Franklin lent prestige to the Convention by his presence. His signature on the new Constitution was a symbol of the continuity of revolutionary principles and a warranty of the democratic character of the document.

Franklin's public career began in 1736, when he was appointed clerk of the Pennsylvania Assembly, and lasted for more than half a century. He served as a member of the assembly and as postmaster of British North America even while pursuing a private career as a printer and inventor.

In 1754, as a delegate to the Albany Congress, Franklin proposed the "Albany Plan" of colonial union. Under his plan, the British Crown would have appointed a president-general and the colonial legislatures would have chosen delegates to a Grand Council with power to raise an army and navy, to make war and peace with the Indian tribes, to control commerce with the Indians, and to levy taxes and customs duties to pay the expenses of the union. The plan, one of the earliest moves toward American FEDERALISM, was too consolidated to find support in the colonies and too democratic to be acceptable in England.

From 1757 to 1762, and again from 1766 to 1775, Franklin was the agent in England of Pennsylvania and several other colonies. In that capacity he explained to Parliament American opposition to the Stamp Act, that is, to TAXATION WITHOUT REPRESENTATION, and persuaded WILLIAM PITT to propose a plan of colonial union within the British Empire.

Returning to Pennsylvania in 1775, Franklin was named a delegate to the Second Continental Congress, where, in July, he proposed ARTICLES OF CONFEDERATION establishing a "league of friendship" among the colonies with a Congress that would exercise considerable legislative power. The following year he served on the committee that drafted the DECLARATION OF INDEPENDENCE.

From 1776 to 1785, Franklin served as minister of the United States to France (and was accredited to several other European governments as well). He negotiated the French military and financial assistance that was crucial to the success of the Revolution, and he carried out a propaganda campaign to win European support for the American cause. In 1781 he was named a commissioner to the peace negotiations that resulted in the Treaty of Paris and formal British recognition of American independence.

At the Constitutional Convention, Franklin was a conciliator and mediator. Although, at eighty-one, he was in failing health and had to have his speeches read by fellow delegate JAMES WILSON, Franklin attended almost all sessions. Such proposals as he put forward (for example, unicameral legislature, plural executive, elected judges, unpaid officials) were too radical to attract much support; but Franklin, with his humorous anecdotes and his commitment to the Union, served the Convention well by cooling tempers and encouraging compromise.

According to a legend, which serves as a warning still, Franklin, emerging from the Convention, was asked, "What have you given us?" "A republic," he replied, "if you can keep it."

DENNIS J. MAHONEY
(1986)

Bibliography

VAN DOREN, CARL 1938 *Benjamin Franklin*. New York: Viking.

FRAZEE v. ILLINOIS DEPARTMENT OF EMPLOYMENT SECURITY
489 U.S. 829 (1989)

This case expanded the protection of the free-exercise clause of the FIRST AMENDMENT by allowing a Christian to refuse work on the Sabbath without being denied unemployment benefits. Earlier, the Court had held that such benefits may not be denied to persons whose religious beliefs obligated them to refuse work on the Sabbath, but in all the PRECEDENTS, such as SHERBERT V VERNER (1963), the claimant had belonged to a religious sect or particular church. Frazee was not a member of either and did not rely on a specific religious tenet. The Illinois courts therefore upheld the denial to him of unemployment compensation.

Unanimously, the Supreme Court sustained Frazee's free-exercise right. He had asserted that he was a Christian, and no authority had challenged his sincerity. As a Christian, he felt that working on Sunday was wrong. The Court held that a professing Christian, even if not a church-goer or member of a sect, was protected by the free-exercise clause from having to choose between his or her religious belief and unemployment compensation. Denial of compensation violated the clause.

LEONARD W. LEVY
(1992)

FRAZIER-LEMKE ACTS
Federal Farm Bankruptcy Act
48 Stat. 1289 (1934)
Farm Mortgage Moratorium Act
49 Stat. 942 (1935)

Congress passed the Federal Farm Bankruptcy Act in June 1934 in an effort to stem the flow of foreclosures caused by the Depression. Enacted as an amendment to a general bankruptcy act of 1898, the first Frazier-Lemke Act allowed bankrupt farmers two choices. Under the first, court-appointed appraisers would assess the "fair and reasonable value, not necessarily the market value" of the property, which the debtor could then repurchase within six years according to a graduated scale of interest. Alternatively, a court could halt all proceedings for five years, during which time the debtor would retain possession "provided he pays a reasonable rent annually," preserving the right to buy it after five years.

Within a year a unanimous Supreme Court struck down the act as a TAKING OF PROPERTY belonging to the creditor without JUST COMPENSATION in LOUISVILLE JOINT STOCK LAND BANK V. RADFORD (1935). Congress passed a second Frazier-Lemke (Farm Mortgage Moratorium) Act in August 1935, effectively similar legislation to which they added a declaration of emergency and a discretionary provision allowing courts to shorten the stay of proceedings during which time the creditor retained a lien on the property. This act received the Court's approval in WRIGHT V. VINTON BRANCH OF MOUNTAIN TRUST BANK OF ROANOKE (1937).

DAVID GORDON
(1986)

FREEDMAN v. MARYLAND
380 U.S. 51 (1965)

Although the Supreme Court often remarks that the FIRST AMENDMENT imposes a heavy presumption against the validity of any system of PRIOR RESTRAINT on expression, the Court has tolerated state censorship of motion pictures through advance licensing. Typically, such a law authorizes a censorship board to deny a license to a film on the ground of OBSCENITY. Other substantive standards ("immoral," "tending to corrupt morals") have been held invalid for VAGUENESS. In addition, the Court insists that the licensing system's procedures follow strict guidelines designed to avoid the chief evils of censorship. *Freedman* is the leading decision establishing these guidelines.

In a test case, a Baltimore theater owner showed a concededly innocuous film without submitting it to the state censorship board, and he was convicted of a violation of state law. The Supreme Court unanimously reversed the conviction. The *Freedman* opinion, by Justice WILLIAM J. BRENNAN, set three procedural requirements for film censorship. First, the censor must have the burden of proving that the film is "unprotected expression" (for example, obscenity). Second, while the state may insist that all films be submitted for advance screening, the censor's determination cannot be given the effect of finality; a judicial determination is required. Thus the censor must, "within a specified brief period, either issue a license or go to court to restrain showing of the film." Advance restraint, before the issue gets to court, must be of the minimum duration consistent with orderly employment of the judicial machinery. Third, the court's decision itself must be prompt. Maryland's statute failed all three parts of this test and accordingly was an unconstitutional prior restraint. Justices WILLIAM O. DOUGLAS and HUGO L. BLACK, concurring, would have held any advance censorship impermissible.

KENNETH L. KARST
(1986)

FREEDMEN'S BUREAU

Congress created the Bureau of Refugees, Freedmen, and Abandoned Lands in March 1865, assigning it the disposition of rebels' lands and distribution of emergency relief to freed blacks and refugees of both races uprooted by the CIVIL WAR. Though the Freedmen's Bureau was the first federal human-services organization, its establishment reflected Congress's resistance to constitutional innovation, combined with the pervasive nineteenth-century belief that relief and welfare were beyond the constitutional authority of the federal government. Hence the Bureau was a public-private hybrid, drawing its personnel from the army, assisted by volunteers from the various private relief and welfare organizations working with blacks and soldiers in the South.

The 1865 Act provided that the agency would expire a year after cessation of hostilities. In February 1866, Congress enacted a bill to extend the Bureau's life indefinitely. The bill permitted the President "to extend military protection and jurisdiction over all cases" in which blacks were denied CIVIL RIGHTS enjoyed by whites or were punished in ways whites were not. This provision reflected Republicans' resentment at the de jure and de facto discrimination against blacks in the South, especially that authorized by the BLACK CODES. Democrats and other conservatives denounced trials before military commissions or "courts" composed of Freedmen's Bureau agents, citing the absence of guarantees of INDICTMENT or PRESENTMENT as violative of the prohibition against military trials of civilians implied in the Fifth Amendment. Republicans countered that the bill was authorized by the enforcement clause (section 2) of the recently ratified THIRTEENTH AMENDMENT. The bill thus provided the first opportunity to explore the meaning and extent of this new provision. President ANDREW JOHNSON vetoed the bill, charging its Republican sponsors with racial favoritism and a disregard of FEDERALISM. Congress narrowly sustained the veto, but a similar bill became law four months later over his veto.

In existence until 1874, the Bureau helped blacks to adjust to freedom in the turbulent conditions of the postwar South.

WILLIAM M. WIECEK
(1986)

Bibliography

NIEMAN, DONALD G. 1979 *To Set the Law in Motion: The Freedmen's Bureau and the Legal Rights of Blacks, 1865–1868.* Milwood, N.Y.: KTO Press.

FREEDOM OF . . .

See also under Right . . .

FREEDOM OF ASSEMBLY AND ASSOCIATION

The FIRST AMENDMENT's "right of the people peaceably to assemble" and the FOURTEENTH AMENDMENT have supplied a basis for federal protection of undefined FUNDAMENTAL RIGHTS from violation by the states. In the landmark case of UNITED STATES V. CRUIKSHANK (1876), the Supreme Court, in the course of allowing some lynchers to escape federal prosecution, said by way of OBITER DICTUM that the right peaceably to assemble was an attribute of CITIZENSHIP under a free government that antedated the Constitution, and that it was a privilege of national citizenship provided that the assembly in question concerned matters relating to the national government. (See PRIVILEGES AND IMMUNITIES.)

With respect to STATE ACTION, the right of peaceable assembly is now regarded as a Fourteenth Amendment DUE PROCESS right. Thus, in DEJONGE V. OREGON (1937), the Supreme Court reversed a conviction for CRIMINAL SYNDICALISM under an Oregon statute of a man who had participated in a peaceful meeting called by the Communist party for a lawful purpose, on the grounds that the due process clause of the Fourteenth Amendment had been violated. Chief Justice CHARLES EVANS HUGHES wrote for a unanimous Court: "The right of peaceable assembly is a right cognate to those of free speech and free press and is equally fundamental," and "peaceable assembly for lawful discussion cannot be made a crime," no matter under whose auspices the meeting is held.

In addition, the rights of assembly and petition are mentioned in rather standardized language in all but two of the fifty state CONSTITUTIONS. The first such statement appeared in the North Carolina constitution of 1776, and the New Hampshire constitution of 1784 began the practice of adding the word "peaceable" to the right of assembly guarantee. Furthermore, the constitutions of Missouri, New Jersey, and New York specifically guarantee a particular form of association, the right of employees to bargain collectively through representatives of their own choosing; the North Carolina constitution forbids "secret political societies" as being "dangerous to the liberties of a free people"; and there is a declaration in the Georgia constitution, of dubious validity, that "freedom from compulsory association at all levels of public education shall be preserved inviolate."

The right of assembly, like nearly all other rights, is not and cannot be regarded as without limit. As Justice LOUIS D. BRANDEIS wrote in 1927, concurring in WHITNEY V. CALIFORNIA, "although the rights of free speech and assembly are fundamental, they are not in their nature absolute. Their exercise is subject to restriction, if the particular restriction proposed is required in order to protect the State from destruction or from serious injury, political, economic or moral." The right of assembly does not protect an unlawful assembly, usually defined in American law as a gathering of three or more people for the purpose of committing acts that will give firm and courageous people in the neighborhood grounds to apprehend a BREACH OF THE PEACE. It must be shown that those who assembled intended to do an unlawful act or a lawful act in a violent, boisterous, or tumultuous manner. Thus the right to engage in peaceful PICKETING is protected by the Constitution, but picketing in a context of violence or having the purpose of achieving unlawful objectives, may be forbidden.

In American law the right of assembly extends to meetings held in such PUBLIC FORUMS as the streets and parks. This point was first spelled out in HAGUE V. C.I.O. (1939), extending constitutional protection to street meetings since, in the words of Justice OWEN J. ROBERTS, streets "have immemorially been held in trust for the use of the public and, time out of mind, have been used for purposes of assembly, communicating thoughts between citizens, and discussing public questions." Public authorities may be given the power to license parades or processions on the public streets as to time, place, and manner, provided that the licensing law does not confer an arbitrary or unbridled administrative discretion upon them. (See PRIOR RESTRAINT.) In addition, Justice Roberts wrote in CANTWELL V. CONNECTICUT (1940) that "When a CLEAR AND PRESENT DANGER of riot, disorder, interference with traffic upon the public streets, or other immediate threat to public safety, peace, or order, appears, the power of the State to prevent or punish is obvious." Thus, a leading decision has upheld the right to assemble on the grounds of a state house, but the Court has drawn the line at the picketing of a courthouse or holding a demonstration on jail grounds. The Court extended the concept of the right of assembly in RICHMOND NEWSPAPERS, INC. V. VIRGINIA (1980) by ruling invalid a state judge's order barring all members of the public and the press from the courtroom where a murder case was being tried, on the grounds that the First Amendment rights of speech, press, and assembly were violated.

Although the right of association is not mentioned specifically either in the United States Constitution or in the state constitutions, it is now recognized through judicial interpretation of various constitutional clauses, particularly those dealing with the rights of assembly and petition, the right of free press, and the privileges and immunities of citizens. The first forthright recognition by a majority of the Supreme Court that due process embraces the right to freedom of association, as distinguished from the more limited concept of assembly, came in NAACP V. ALABAMA (1958), although the idea had been advanced in several earlier minority opinions. In the *Alabama* case, the Court unanimously held unconstitutional a statute that required the NAACP to give to the state's attorney general the names and addresses of all its members, reasoning that such compelled disclosure of affiliation could constitute an effective restraint on freedom of association. Justice JOHN MARSHALL HARLAN wrote: "Effective advocacy of both public and private points of view, particularly controversial ones, is undeniably enhanced by group association, as this Court has more than once recognized by remarking upon the close nexus between the freedoms of speech and assembly. . . . Of course, it is immaterial whether the beliefs sought to be advanced by association pertain to political, economic, religious or cultural matters, and state action which may have the effect of curtailing the freedom to associate is subject to the closest scrutiny." In later years the Supreme Court, in a series of decisions, protected the NAACP's associational rights from various forms of harassment, subtle as well as heavy-handed, by local authorities.

A leading case involving education was SHELTON V. TUCKER (1960), where the Supreme Court, by a 5–4 vote, declared unconstitutional an Arkansas statute requiring every teacher in the public schools to file annually an affidavit listing all organizations to which the teacher belonged or contributed money during the preceding five years, because disclosure of every associational tie undoubtedly impaired the teacher's right of free association. Furthermore, in *Healy v. James* (1972), the Court upheld the right of a student association to receive university recognition, including access to various campus facilities, even though the president of the college regarded the group's philosophy as abhorrent; the Court added that the university might lawfully require the group to agree to obey reasonable rules relating to student conduct.

The Court took an even more generous view of the right of association in GRISWOLD V. CONNECTICUT (1965), in which a state anticontraceptive statute was held unconstitutional. Justice WILLIAM O. DOUGLAS reasoned that the statute operated directly on the intimate relationship of husband and wife, thus invading the right of association broadly construed. In his opinion there was a first suggestion that although the right of association grows out of the PENUMBRA of the First Amendment, its scope is larger and extends to the marriage relationship. (See FREEDOM OF INTIMATE ASSOCIATION.)

The right of association, however vital it may be in a society committed to maximum freedom of speech and action, is not absolute but is subject to reasonable limitations required by substantial public interests. For example, the right of workers to organize and bargain collectively through representatives of their own choosing is firmly established in statute and judge-made law. But trade unions are not free to organize or participate in SECONDARY BOYCOTTS, since Congress did not intend "to immunize labor unions who aid and abet manufacturers and traders in violating the SHERMAN ACT. . . ." (See ALLEN BRADLEY CO. V. LOCAL UNION #3.) On the other hand, the Court has ruled that a labor leader cannot be required to secure a license to give a speech soliciting new members.

The right to form or engage in the activities of POLITICAL PARTIES is protected by the constitutional right of association. "The First Amendment," the Supreme Court said in BUCKLEY V. VALEO (1976), "protects political association as well as political expression." In that case the Court upheld a federal statute imposing limitations on contributions to political parties, on the theory that the limitations were designed to prevent corruption and the appearance of corruption, and to open up the political system to candidates who lacked access to large amounts of money. In addition, the right of political association extends to members of minor parties as well as to the two major parties. Many cases hold that government may protect the right to vote in party primaries, and ensure that voters cast ballots of approximately equal weight, but the two large parties are not obliged to apportion national convention delegates among the states according to the ONE PERSON, ONE VOTE concept, because party strength varies from state to state, and the parties must have the freedom to operate effectively. Similarly, the Supreme Court has ruled that a national party convention is not bound by state law and state judicial power in deciding which of two slates of delegates from a state should be seated. A state does have the power to decide upon the strength a party must demonstrate in order to get a place on the election ballot, but such a statute may not impose a rigid and arbitrary formula that applies equally to sparsely settled and populous counties, and unreasonably large signature requirements will not be permitted. Furthermore, the Supreme Court has conceded that, in order to protect the integrity of the electoral process, states may require some sort of party registration during a reasonable period before a primary election is held. Similarly, a state may require that candidates for party nominations pay filing fees, but the fees must not be so excessive as to be patently exclusionary.

Finally, in the unusual case of *Elrod v. Burns* (1976), a bare majority of the Court read something new into party membership by holding that in discharging persons in non-civil service positions because they were Republicans, the newly elected Democratic sheriff of Cook County was placing an unconstitutional restraint on freedom of belief and association. This ruling does not apply, however, to persons holding policymaking positions involving broad functions and goals.

Membership in the Communist party or subversive organizations has for some years posed complex issues of constitutional law. (See SUBVERSIVE ACTIVITIES AND THE CONSTITUTION.) In AMERICAN COMMUNICATIONS ASSOCIATION V. DOUDS (1950), the Court upheld a section of the TAFT-HARTLEY ACT of 1947 which denied access to the facilities of the National Labor Relations Board to any union whose officers were members of the Communist party. The Court reasoned that the act validly protected INTERSTATE COMMERCE from the obstruction caused by political strikes and applied only to those who believed in the violent overthrow of the government as a concrete objective and not merely as a prophecy. Similarly, in SCALES V. UNITED STATES (1961), the Court upheld the clause in the SMITH ACT of 1940 making membership in any organization advocating the overthrow of government by force or violence (in that instance, membership in the Communist party) a criminal offense. But the Court stressed that it was reading the statute to mean that the Smith Act did not proscribe mere membership in the Communist party as such but only membership of an individual who knew of the party's unlawful purposes and specifically intended to further those purposes; the proscribed membership must be active and not nominal, passive, or merely theoretical. This construction of the Smith Act was fully consistent with the position the Court had taken in YATES V. UNITED STATES (1957). The distinction between INCITEMENT and abstract teaching was underscored by the Court in the important case of BRANDENBURG V. OHIO (1969), which held the Ohio Criminal Syndicalism Act unconstitutional. Thus, mere membership in the Communist party, without more, cannot be made a predicate for the denial of a passport, or a job in a defense facility, or of public employment. The Court has recognized that membership may be innocent, and that groups may change their positions from time to time.

Whether unions or other associations may engage the services of such regulated professionals as doctors and lawyers has been the subject of much recent litigation. Because the practice of medicine is subject to comprehensive and detailed regulation by the state under its POLICE POWER for compelling reasons, a state statute prohibiting laymen from forming CORPORATIONS for the delivery of medical care has been upheld on the theory that limiting the formation of such corporations to licensed physicians tends to preserve important doctor–patient relationships and prevents possible abuses which may result from lay control.

The constitutionality of regulation of lawyers presents more complex issues. The Supreme Court has ruled that a state may lawfully compel all lawyers in the state to belong to an integrated bar, and a state bar association may be authorized to discipline a lawyer for personally soliciting clients for pecuniary gain, although the Court ruled in BATES V. STATE BAR OF ARIZONA (1977) that a state, through its bar association, may not forbid lawyers to engage in truthful advertising of routine legal services. Furthermore, the Court held in KONIGSBERG V. STATE BAR OF CALIFORNIA (1961) that a state may refuse to admit to the practice of law a candidate who refuses to reply to questions regarding membership in the Communist party, although the Court has also ruled that there must be a showing of knowing, active membership before an applicant can be excluded on this ground.

The Supreme Court has decided that such associations as trade unions, the NAACP, and the AMERICAN CIVIL LIBERTIES UNION may employ lawyers to provide legal services for their members. In Brotherhood of Railroad Trainmen v. Virginia ex rel. Virginia State Bar (1964), the Court held that a union has an associational right to advise injured members to use the services of specific approved lawyers. Moreover, a labor union is constitutionally entitled to employ a licensed attorney on a salary basis to represent any of its members who desire his services in prosecuting workers' compensation claims. In NAACP V. BUTTON (1963), the Court upheld the right of this association to finance certain types of litigation through its own staff of lawyers. The Court noted that NAACP litigation is not a mere technique for resolving private differences but a means of achieving the lawful objective of legal equality. Similarly, the Court has affirmed the right of the American Civil Liberties Union to employ attorneys in the pursuit of its objectives.

The right of association has been explored in a wide variety of other situations. Many years ago, in Waugh v. Board of Trustees of the University of Mississippi (1915), the Supreme Court held constitutional a Mississippi statute prohibiting Greek-letter fraternities and other secret societies in all public educational institutions of the state, on the theory that this was a reasonable moral and disciplinary regulation which the legislature might believe would save the students from harmful distraction. Several state appellate courts have sustained the validity of such regulations as applied to high schools. In New York ex rel. Bryant v. Zimmerman (1928), the Supreme Court upheld a state statute, aimed at the Ku Klux Klan, which required all secret oath-bound organizations having over twenty members to supply to a designated public official a roster of its members and a list of its officers. In NAACP V. ALABAMA (1958), holding unconstitutional a similar disclosure requirement of the NAACP, the Court noted that the Zimmerman decision "was based on the particular character of the Klan's activities, involving acts of unlawful intimidation and violence, which the Court assumed was before the state legislature when it enacted the statute, and of which the Court itself took judicial notice." (See COMMUNIST PARTY V. SUBVERSIVE ACTIVITIES CONTROL BOARD.) On the other hand, in Lanzetta v. New Jersey (1939), the Court ruled unconstitutional a state statute that purported to make it illegal to associate with gangsters, on the ground that the key words in the statute were so vague, indefinite, and uncertain that it lacked the specificity required of penal enactments.

Although the right of association as such is not mentioned in the Constitution, it holds a firm, indeed expanding, place in American constitutional law. This right is partly an emanation from the First Amendment's cognate guarantees of freedom of speech and assembly, partly a privilege or immunity of citizenship, and partly a by-product of democratic voting and representative government. However the right of association is tied to the text of the Constitution, it is regarded by the judges as such a fundamental right that doubts are resolved in favor of protecting the right of association from governmental restraints.

DAVID FELLMAN
(1986)

Bibliography

ABERNATHY, GLEN 1961 *The Right of Assembly and Association.* Columbia: University of South Carolina Press.
FELLMAN, DAVID 1963 *The Constitutional Right of Association.* Chicago: University of Chicago Press.
HORN, ROBERT A. 1956 *Groups and the Constitution.* Stanford, Calif.: Stanford University Press.
KALVEN, HARRY, JR. 1965 The Concept of the Public Forum. *Supreme Court Review* 1965:1–32.
RAGGI, REENA 1977 An Independent Right to Freedom of Association. *Harvard Civil Rights-Civil Liberties Law Review* 12:1–30.

FREEDOM OF ASSOCIATION

The freedom of association derives from the free speech and free assembly provisions of the FIRST AMENDMENT, and it protects the right of persons to enter into relationships with one another unhampered by intrusive governmental regulation. More precisely, the freedom of association encompasses two distinct guarantees: the FREEDOM OF INTIMATE ASSOCIATION and the freedom of expressive association. The freedom of intimate association protects "certain kinds of highly personal relationships," such as marriage. The freedom of expressive association, on the other hand, protects "the right to associate with others in pursuit of a wide variety of political, social, economic, educational, religious, and cultural ends."

In recent cases the Court has made clear the limits of these two guarantees with respect to ANTIDISCRIMINATION LAWS. In *Roberts v. United States Jaycees* (1984) and *Board of Directors of Rotary International v. Rotary Club* (1987), the Court rejected arguments by both the Jaycees and Rotary International that laws prohibiting SEX DISCRIMINATION could not be applied to them without violating their members' freedom of association. Both organizations limited their regular membership to men. The Court held that neither the freedom of intimate association nor the freedom of expressive association protected this type of discrimination by the organizations in question. The freedom of intimate association did not apply at all because both organizations tended to have unlimited memberships and open meetings. The freedom of expressive association may have been implicated, but not sufficiently to override the government's COMPELLING STATE INTEREST to eradicate discrimination. As the Court said in *Rotary*, "The evidence fails to demonstrate that admitting women . . . will affect in any significant way the existing members' ability to carry out their various purposes."

In *New York State Club Association v. New York City* (1988), the Court turned back yet another free association challenge to an antidiscrimination law. New York City prohibits discrimination on the basis of race, gender, and other grounds by any "place of public accommodation, resort or amusement," but exempts from this restriction any group "which is in its nature distinctly private." In 1984 the city passed a new law providing that no groups shall be considered private if it "has more than four hundred members, provides regular meal service and regularly receives payment . . . from or on behalf of nonmembers. . . ." The new law exempted religious and benevolent associations from this provision. A consortium of private clubs and associations challenged the ordinance, claiming that it abridged on its face both the First Amendment and the EQUAL PROTECTION clause. The Supreme Court unanimously disagreed.

Writing for the Court, Justice BYRON R. WHITE argued that the First Amendment facial challenge failed both because the law was not invalid in all its applications and because its provisions were not overbroad. Under the previous rulings in *Roberts* and *Rotary*, the law clearly could be applied constitutionally to some of the groups that challenged it, and no evidence was presented showing that the law applied impermissibly to a substantial number of other groups. White acknowledged that the law still might be unconstitutional as applied to certain associations, but noted that these groups maintained the right to sue in order to invalidate particular applications of the ordinance. White also rejected the consortium's equal protection challenge, arguing that the city council could have reasonably believed that exempted religious and benevolent groups differ from those covered by the ordinance because of the level of business activity conducted by the groups.

No member of the Court has dissented in these cases, but Justice SANDRA DAY O'CONNOR has tried to clarify when discriminatory activities might be protected by the freedom of expressive association. In *Roberts* and again in *New York*, O'Connor filed concurring opinions that sought to distinguish expressive associations from commercial ones. An expressive association exists to promote a particular message; thus, according to O'Connor, it should be protected by the full force of the First Amendment against state control of its membership. A commercial association, however, exists primarily to engage in certain commercial activities, and the protection afforded it by the Constitution subsequently should be much more limited. In O'Connor's view, groups like the Jaycees are predominantly engaged in commercial activities; hence, the freedom of expressive association should not exempt them from rational state regulations such as antidiscrimination laws. In contrast, gender-exclusive groups such as Boy Scouts or Girl Scouts probably should be protected as expressive associations because "even the training of outdoor survival skills or participation in community service might become expressive when the activity is intended to develop good morals, reverence, patriotism, and a desire for self-improvement."

JOHN G. WEST, JR.
(1992)

FREEDOM OF CONTRACT

Freedom of contract in the United States means that the law accepts and protects broad scope for private individuals and business firms to decide the uses of economic resources in seeking profits. Through the country's history, sharp controversies have centered on exercise of freedom of contract as it has affected concerns for the worth of individuals, the vitality of private markets, the natural and social environment, and the structure of practical as well as formal legal power in the society. Few other concepts touch as many dimensions of the history of American public policy and constitutional law.

The law's attention to freedom of contract has centered on fostering and sustaining the private market as a major institution of social control (ranking in importance with the law itself). Even the assessment of the interactions of freedom of contract and other values, not defined in market, has typically resulted from community reactions to the effects of market operations. Thus, to examine the place of freedom of contract in constitutional law entails examining the roles and working character of the market.

Law and public policy have historically responded to four salient characteristics of private contract activity in market, carrying both constructive and damaging aspects. These responses have provided the institutional setting within which the substantive legalconstitutional meaning of freedom of contract has emerged.

(1) Under the protection of the law of contract, private contract activity seeking profit in market energizes private will in producing and distributing goods and services. This activity promises efficiency in allocating limited resources, partly because the actors are motivated to obtain the most output for the least input, and partly because market bargaining allows flexibility in coordinating a great volume and diversity of private decisions. In the country's constitutional tradition, social and political values also favor freedom of contract. Proponents argue that individuals gain self-respect from the initiatives of will they exercise in markets, as well as courage to participate in and criticize government because their means of livelihood are not dependent on official favor. The law reflects this appraisal of positive values by presuming the legality of private contracts until a challenger demonstrates their unlawfulness, and by casting some constitutional protections around private contract activity and the property interests it produces. (See CONTRACT CLAUSE; SUBSTANTIVE DUE PROCESS; TAKING OF PROPERTY; ECONOMIC REGULATION AND THE CONSTITUTION.) But the driving dynamic of private contract activity is the focused self-interest of the bargainers. We value this dynamic because it counters the inertia prevalent in social relationships, but it largely ignores the impact of bargains on people other than the bargainers. A factory producing to meet its contractual obligations may deposit in a handy stream industrial wastes harmful to the public's interest in pure drinking water or recreational opportunities. The law responds to this narrow focus of the market with ENVIRONMENTAL REGULATIONS, the constitutionality of which may or may not be challenged.

(2) Large-scale markets cannot operate by barter but require use of money (including money-measured credit). Law responds to this need by regulating the money supply. But the money calculus required by extended contract activity carries dangers of a bias in identifying and weighing matters of public interest. Public opinion, public policymakers (including judges), and market-oriented pressure groups seeking to influence legislators and other public officers tend to identify interests deserving law's promotion or protection only with interests readily calculable in dollar terms. Thus, nineteenth-century COMMON LAW readily gave JUDGMENT for money damages if a factory failed to deliver promised goods to a buyer but was grudging in recognizing a community right to redress for more diffuse detriments—hard to measure in dollars—caused by the factory's deposit of industrial waste in a nearby stream. Today's public policy, with the blessings of today's constitutional law, increasingly seeks to offset the bias injected by a monetized calculus of interests by legislating to protect diffuse values and establishing administrative agencies to implement them.

(3) Whether tailored to particular transactions or standardized as in such commercial instruments as promissory notes or warehouse receipts, private contracts can be multiplied to any number of dealings and varied to shifting conditions of supply and demand. Contracts and the market thus permit flexible adaptation to changes in the conditions of the economy and the parties. Public policy recognizes the value of this adaptability in the law's readiness to enforce such terms of dealing as the parties choose and in legalconstitutional doctrine protecting the play of market competition. However, when change proceeds in this manner, its increments are so small that even the parties, let alone the environing society, may not be aware that the accumulation of relatively limited incremental

shifts is producing basic alterations in the social context which no one has predicted, assessed, or chosen to bring about.

(4) Private contracting parties and the markets in which they operate typically work within the distribution of wealth and income in society as they find it. Contract and property law reinforce this distribution; only in rare hard cases will courts set aside a bargain as unconscionable, and normally they will not examine the adequacy of the consideration a party accepted in return for what he promised to perform. But underlying the social utility of freedom of contract and the resource-allocations role of markets lies an assumption: that private bargainers enjoy a considerable range of practical and legal options in dealing with each other. Great inequalities of wealth may grossly distort some bargaining relations, so that freedom of contract becomes illusory and markets sharply accentuate inequalities of bargaining power. While constitutional law only rarely addresses such inequalities (see INDIGENTS; WEALTH DISTRIBUTION), it consistently validates legislation to this end. (See SUBSTANTIVE Due Process; ECONOMIC REGULATION; COMMERCE CLAUSE.) Sometimes lawmakers seek to encourage private organization of countervailing power, as in the law regarding COLLECTIVE BARGAINING between management and LABOR. Sometimes they interpose between focused centers of private market power and diffused bodies of customers a public bargaining agency, as in the law of public utilities. Such legal interventions and their constitutional underpinnings depart from an abstract model of freedom of contract in order to promote more real freedom of bargaining.

The span from the 1880s through the 1920s witnessed increased resort to state and national law to correct imperfections of private contract activity in market. In this period opponents of government intervention made "freedom of contract" a code phrase for imposing constitutional and other limits on legal regulation. This emphasis has been so prominent in past policy debate that there is danger of equating the idea of freedom of contract with limitations on the use of law. In fact, law operates at least as much to promote market activity as to regulate it. A realistic assessment of the relation of constitutional law to freedom of contract must recognize the range of such promotional roles of legal processes.

By the late eighteenth century, in this country of abundant land, the law of land titles made land fully transferable and thus readily marketable—thus promoting private contract activity. By the mid-nineteenth century, common law had established a strong presumption in favor of the legality of private agreements for market dealing. By the second half of the nineteenth century, state legislatures were actively removing the common law disability of married women to make binding contracts. The married women's property acts may have responded more to the wish of the husband's creditors to acquire effective pledge of the wife's assets to secure her husband's debts than to any concern for sex equality. Still, these statutes enlarged the potential scope for contract activity in market.

Legal development, often supported by constitutional law, has consistently fostered entrepreneurial energy. Contract law legitimized and standardized a growing range of trade documents and instruments for capital investment. In three respects law especially promoted increased reach and pervasive effect of private contract activity. Though often inefficiently, law provided a money supply to facilitate increased volumes of trade. Particularly under the commerce clause of the national Constitution, Congress and the Supreme Court protected markets of sectional or national scope against intrusion of state parochial interest. (See STATE REGULATION OF COMMERCE; STATE TAXATION OF COMMERCE.) With increasing liberality lawmakers made the device of incorporation available for the general run of business, providing means for mustering and directing otherwise scattered assets. (See CORPORATIONS AND THE CONSTITUTION.)

Many individuals had only their labor to offer in market, and only their wages to spend. For them law gave other positive promotion to freedom of contract. In the nineteenth century, statutes created mechanics' liens, exempted workers' tools from creditors' execution, and abolished imprisonment for debt. In the twentieth century, legislation created administrative agencies to implement laws designed to help consumers get money's worth for their purchases. The most dramatic expansion of freedom of contract for labor was the abolition of SLAVERY. Fulfillment of the substance of that policy through the THIRTEENTH AMENDMENT and the supplementary provisions of the FOURTEENTH AMENDMENT and the CIVIL RIGHTS ACT OF 1866 had a long and tortured history, but the general line of policy was clear. In the 1960s, CIVIL RIGHTS legislation gave that policy additional impetus, placing the affirmative support of law behind opening markets for labor, goods, and services free of barriers raised on grounds of race, sex, or religion. (See FEDERAL PROTECTION OF CIVIL RIGHTS; EMPLOYMENT DISCRIMINATION.)

Granted that law plays positive, promotional roles in fostering markets, freedom of contract also insists that law protect a substantial area of autonomy for private contract and market activity, to allow operative room for the efficiency criteria which legitimize private contract and market functions. Threats of invasion of this zone come from both private and official power. Accordingly the autonomy that public policy provides for private contract and private markets has two dimensions, relating to private and to official action.

The law protects market autonomy against private interference not only by enforcing contractual obligations through damages or other relief against breach of contract but also by providing sanctions against interference by outsiders with the performance of those obligations. Furthermore, an elaborate body of statutory, judge-made, and ADMINISTRATIVE LAW offers criminal and civil sanctions against efforts to defeat market bargaining by achieving monopoly, or by fixing prices or other terms of trade, or by engaging in such predatory forms of competition as geographical price discriminations so as to limit or destroy competition. (See ANTITRUST AND THE CONSTITUTION.)

More controversy has surrounded the creation of legalconstitutional protections of limited autonomy for private contract activity in market as against interventions by government. Experience shows two quite different sources of concern. Some battles over legal regulation are fought on claims that one set of private interests seeks to handicap another by persuading a legislature to create barriers to free competition as when producers of dairy products obtained laws regulating the sale of oleomargarine. Other battles are fought on claims that in pursuing nonmarket objectives, such as protecting public health, lawmakers impose unreasonable costs on market-measured profitseeking—as when environmental regulations are opposed on the ground that they hamper "productivity" (meaning that they limit money-measured gains of regulated firms). Common to both types of concern is the objection that law is used in ways that interfere with economic efficiency defined according to the profit and loss calculus of the immediate bargainers in a competitive private market. "Efficiency" in this sense and freedom of contract are the same thing.

Common law imposes some limits on freedom of bargainers to set terms for which they may invoke the law's support and sets the standards for determining what constitutes an enforceable contract. Generally, however, the courts presume that private bargains are valid. The principal legal battlegrounds for defending freedom of contract against official invasion lie in constitutional law. Both national and state constitutions limit legislative restrictions on the freedom of private contract.

The national and state constitutions forbid government to take private property for PUBLIC USE without JUST COMPENSATION. These guarantees primarily protect property titles rather than contracts not yet performed. However, they help safeguard private contract activity; contracts that call for performance over time are likely to require commitments of assets which bargainers will not make if they do not consider the commitments secure against government appropriation. Some uncertainty attends the definition of what public action amounts to a "taking." However, these guarantees do not require government to pay all costs incurred by those subjected to laws regulating economic affairs. Particularly, when government intervenes in a situation where some detriment will in fact occur to either of two competing private interests whether government acts or not, there is no "taking" requiring compensation when the law determines which interest must bear the burden. (See TAKING OF PROPERTY.)

The national Constitution forbids any state to make a law that impairs the OBLIGATION OF CONTRACTS. This clause limits only retroactive state legislation; it does not affect state laws that operate only on future events. No comparable clause limits the Congress, and the Supreme Court applies a presumption of constitutionality to federal statutes of retroactive impact. (See RETROACTIVITY OF LEGISLATION.) The CONTRACT CLAUSE has not figured in so much litigation as the constitutional guarantees of DUE PROCESS and EQUAL PROTECTION OF THE LAWS. Where litigants invoke the clause, however, judges generally give it firm application in the types of situation that most directly challenge respect for outstanding private agreements in market—that is, where a retroactive state statute undertakes to readjust the terms of a contract or its legal context in order to give one party what the legislature in hindsight sees as a socially more acceptable exchange. The usual case of this kind has arisen when a legislature intervenes to relieve distressed debtors of the full measure of claims or remedies afforded their creditors. Moreover, the Supreme Court requires a state to enforce a contract between the state itself and a private party when the retroactive change has given the state an economic advantage not conferred by the original terms. On the other hand, the Supreme Court treats the contract clause more flexibly when the prime object of the challenged legislation appears to be not to alter terms of dealing between the bargaining parties but to protect public interests in a healthy social context without which private contracts have no meaning. Care for social context may include care for preserving the market itself. Thus the Supreme Court upheld a state statute that imposed a limited moratorium on foreclosing mortgages contracted before the statute was passed, where the Court was persuaded that the legislature reasonably believed the moratorium necessary not mainly to benefit mortgagors but to save the general economy from destruction by averting distress sales of land that would undermine the financial integrity of the banking and insurance systems of the state. (See HOME BUILDING AND LOAN ASSOCIATION V. BLAISDELL.) The Court has taken a like approach where the challenged legislation seeks to safeguard other than market interests; thus it has sustained against contract clause challenges retroactive legislation that, in the interest of public morals, abrogated an earlier statutory charter for a lottery and that, to protect public health, abrogated an earlier statutory charter for a slaughterhouse.

Another relatively specific constitutional limit on state legislation affecting freedom of contract developed under the COMMERCE CLAUSE of the national Constitution. The core purpose of granting Congress authority to regulate INTERSTATE COMMERCE was to use national law to protect from parochial state legislation contract activity that ranged over state lines into markets of interstate scope. Congress has used this authority notably to provide uniform national regulation of the terms on which private business provides interstate transportation and communication services. Most often, however, the commerce clause has operated to limit state interference with interstate contract activity through the United States Supreme Court. In the Court's construction, the commerce clause of its own force authorizes judges to rule invalid state legislation that discriminates against or unduly burdens interstate transactions. The Court most strictly limits state laws that in their terms or by their practical effect lay legal or economic burdens on dealings in an interstate market that they do not impose on intrastate transactions. Here the Court puts on the supporter of a challenged state statute a heavy burden of persuading the Court that some overriding local public interest warrants legislation that thus singles out interstate dealing for special regulation. But if a nondiscriminatory state statute affects interstate transactions for a nonmarket purpose, such as protecting public safety on the highways, it enjoys the benefit of a presumption of constitutionality, so that the challenger must persuade the Court that local interests are insufficient to warrant the regulation.

Constitutional guarantees of due process and equal protection are the protections most often invoked on behalf of substantial autonomy of private contract activity in market, as against government intervention. At the threshold of any examination of this body of constitutional law stands an issue of institutional legitimacy. Anglo-American political tradition includes high regard for public policy that favors initiatives of private will in the economy. JOHN LOCKE gave this tradition classic expression in seventeenth-century England, asserting that the individual normally needs no official license before he may make productive use of natural resources. Locke recognized that legislation might properly care for "commonwealth" interests, and particularly that the elected legislature might exercise the power to tax for public purposes. But the legislative authority, he said, was held in "trust," permitting the legislature to act only for the public interest (foreshadowing the Supreme Court's later standard of SUBSTANTIVE DUE PROCESS) and by equal laws. Of course, this English inheritance did not provide authority for judges to hold invalid legislation that infringed standards of public interest and equal protection. When judges in the United States asserted that authority—with some limited

warrant in the history of adoption of the national Constitution—it was another, long step for them to conclude that the guarantee of due process of law included judicial protection of some extent of private contract autonomy. In its origins, "due process of law" meant assurance of fair procedures for applying law, not authority of courts to set limits on the substantive content of the policy legislatures might adopt. And the core historic meaning of the equal protection standard referred to application of law rather than to its substantive classifications. However, by the mid-twentieth century, some seventy-five years of Supreme Court practice had outweighed historic doubts; the live issue in the twentieth century is, rather, how the Court will use the authority it has staked out for itself. The fact that judges were able to extend their power of review beyond historic foundations attests to the strength of values which conservative opinion in the past has put on freedom of contract in market. On the other hand, the doubt which history has cast on the political legitimacy of the expanded judicial role correspondingly helps account for the limits set by the Court since the 1930s on its exercise of JUDICIAL REVIEW of economic regulations challenged as violations of due process and equal protection.

Early in the development of the doctrine of substantive due process, in *Powell v. Pennsylvania* (1888), the Court set sharp limits on the scope of judicial review. There a state had banned the sale of oleomargarine, for the declared goals of protecting public health and preventing fraud on consumers. The Court ruled that it would uphold the statute unless the challenger showed beyond a reasonable doubt that the legislature could not reasonably find that the act was an appropriate means to serve some public interest. Nonetheless, in some cases judges, especially state courts interpreting state constitutions, will enforce respect for some degree of autonomy of private contract activity in market. In some cases parties have successfully rebutted the strong presumption of constitutionality by showing that one set of business interests has won the law's favor simply in order to obtain a legal advantage against other socially useful competitors. Such resort to law violates the social justification of legally protected freedom of contract: the promotion of efficient allocation of limited resources through market competition. Thus, in a later case, where the challenger demonstrated that an anti-oleomargarine statute had no reasonable basis in protecting health or preventing fraud, the Wisconsin court held, in *John F. Jelke Co. v. Emery* (1927), that the act violated constitutional standards of due process and equal protection.

In counterpoint with the pattern of judicial self-restraint indicated by *Powell v. Pennsylvania*, over the span from about 1890 into the mid-1930s the Supreme Court developed three other interrelated doctrinal lines which promoted aggressive judicial protection of private contract autonomy.

First, the Court identified freedom of private contract as a key component of the "liberty" protected by the due process and equal protection clauses. The founding decision was ALLGEYER V. LOUISIANA (1897). There the Court held unconstitutional a Louisiana statute forbidding performance of a contract to insure property in the state with a company not licensed to do business there. The Court ruled that in denying the parties the liberty to make the contract the statute violated limits that the due process clause put on the substantive policies which the legislature might enact into law.

Second, in the standard of substantive due process the Court found warrant for a judicial veto over legislative goals. Judicial scrutiny of these goals had two aspects. One concerned the relationship between private contract and the social context in which the contracting went on. Even in decisions most restrictive of legislative power, the Supreme Court did not deny that legislation might properly pay some regard to the impact of private contract activity on the lives and concerns of individuals or groups other than the contracting parties. However, the Court often spoke of legislative authority as the sum of a limited, closed number of categories of goals traditionally recognized as serving public interest, notably protection of health, safety, or morals. (See STATE POLICE POWER; NATIONAL POLICE POWER). The indication was that a statute would violate substantive due process if its objective did not fit handily under one of these familiar designations. Conspicuous in this approach were *Adair v. United States* (1908), COPPAGE V. KANSAS (1915), and WOLFF PACKING COMPANY V. COURT OF INDUSTRIAL RELATIONS (1923). These rulings refused to recognize promotion of peace in management-labor relations as a sufficient public-interest goal to sustain statutes that outlawed employment contracts binding employees not to join a union or providing for compulsory arbitration of labor disputes.

The third aspect of heightened judicial scrutiny of statutory goals was more specific. Substantive due process demanded that legislation serve what the Court regarded as the general welfare. A statute might appear to serve one of the judicially approved public-interest goals, such as protection of health. But also, it might have the purpose or likely effect of bringing about a different distribution of gains and costs among private bargainers than might result if bargainers operated simply within the frame of common law contract and property law. Between about 1890 and the mid-1930s many decisions treated the presence of a purpose or effect to alter the distribution of gains and costs among private bargainers as enough to show that a challenged statute did not meet the due process standard of serving the public interest; the redistributive character

of such a statute made it "class legislation" or an effort, forbidden by constitutional law, to "take property from A and give it to B." Judges would accept statutes that protected groups commonly recognized as subject to exceptional hazards or weaknesses in bargaining power. Thus, in HOLDEN V. HARDY (1898), the Supreme Court upheld a statutory limit on working hours of men mining coal underground, emphasizing the well-known special hazards of the occupation and the accepted fact that in practice the employers fixed the terms of the employment contracts. So, too, in MULLER V. OREGON (1908), the Court sustained a working hours limit for women, to protect a class which the judges saw as peculiarly dependent. But where a statute apparently sought to offset the weak bargaining power of workers in situations not conventionally regarded as deserving law's special care, the fact that the statute would confer particular benefit on labor was taken as enough to show a lack of justifying public interest. Such was the Court's approach in LOCHNER V. NEW YORK (1905), which held invalid a statutory limit on working hours of bakers. Of similar character was Court doctrine that confined statutory regulation of prices and services of private contractors to what judges regarded as businesses AFFECTED WITH A PUBLIC INTEREST—those conventionally deemed public utilities. On this basis, in TYSON V. BANTON (1927) and in RIBNIK V. MCBRIDE (1928), the Court held invalid statutes regulating resale prices of theater tickets and fees of employment agencies.

There was unreconciled tension between many of these decisions and the approach taken in *Powell v. Pennsylvania.* In *Powell,* the fact that the statutory ban on selling oleomargarine might serve both the private, competitive interest of sellers of butter and the public interest in health was held insufficient to invalidate the regulation. In *Powell,* the favored private interest was that of one set of businessmen, the sellers of butter. In *Lochner* and in *Ribnik,* the interest the statutes immediately protected was that of labor. So, also, in *Adair, Coppage,* and *Wolff Packing,* the interest of labor suffered when the challenged legislation was upset. The pattern suggested a definite bias of policy.

Between 1890 and the mid-1930s the Supreme Court also usually required a positive showing of a "real and substantial" relation between the legislature's goal and the means it provided to reach the goal. That the Court could conceive of other, less burdensome means of achieving the desired result was likely, as in *Lochner v. New York,* to be treated as a distinct and sufficient basis for invalidating the statute. The climax of both lines of doctrine—regarding challenges to the end or to the means adopted by the legislature—came in ADKINS V. CHILDREN'S HOSPITAL (1923), when the Supreme Court held unconstitutional legislation setting minimum wages for women workers.

There a Court majority in effect repudiated the presumption of constitutionality by declaring that "Freedom of contract is . . . the general rule and restraint the exception; and the exercise of legislative authority to abridge it can be justified only by the existence of exceptional circumstances." As late as MOREHEAD V. NEW YORK EX REL. TIPALDO (1936), a Court majority in effect reaffirmed the *Adkins* approach, but a new alignment of Justices repudiated that approach in WEST COAST HOTEL V. PARRISH (1937).

The Court's readiness through some forty years after 1890 to upset legislation limiting freedom of contract had serious implications for the role of legislatures and the interests legislatures sought to advance or protect. But we should not exaggerate the impact of judicial review. One inventory counts 197 cases between 1899 and 1937 in which the Supreme Court invalidated state or federal regulations under the standard of substantive due process, but another estimate notes that between 1889 and 1918 the Court upheld some 369 challenged statutes enacted under the state police power. Other tallies emphasize the more vigorous use of the judicial veto in the later years of the forty-year span; one count finds fifty-three state police power acts held invalid between 1889 and 1918, while another shows almost 140 laws held unconstitutional between 1920 and 1930. All such inventories must be seen in a wider perspective; a great bulk of economic regulatory legislation never came under constitutional challenge in lawsuits.

However, in a sharp turnabout beginning in the mid-1930s, the Court disavowed these enlargements of judicial protection for autonomy of private contract in market. In NEBBIA V. NEW YORK (1934) it ruled that a legislature might regulate pricing practices outside the field of traditional public utilities if legislators could reasonably find that regulation would serve a public interest. In UNITED STATES V. CAROLENE PRODUCTS COMPANY (1938), it ruled that no particular sanctity attached to the "liberty" or "property" interests involved in private contract activity; all regulatory legislation affecting ordinary commercial transactions enjoyed the presumption of constitutionality. *Nebbia* also made clear that there is no closed category of public interests to which legislatures may extend protection; even if a statute intervenes in private contract activity for a purpose not within familiar concerns with public health, safety, or morals, it is valid unless the judges determine that no reasonable legislators could find justification for it. Finally, in WEST COAST HOTEL COMPANY V. PARRISH (1937), the Court expressly overruled the formula declared in *Adkins;* that a statute limits freedom of contract does not cast on its supporter a burden of justifying it; rather, the general presumption of constitutionality applies.

The Court's permissive modern doctrine leaves the autonomy of private contract activity mostly in the hands of the legislature. Given the realities of the legislative process, in two respects this outcome implies a lessening of the preferred status of the private market. Statute law tends to speak more and more for interests of the general social context, as in regulation of burdens—such as air or water pollution—which private contract activity otherwise may place on parties outside the bargaining circle. Less appealing is the practical operation of the presumption of constitutionality to allow special interest lobbies to obtain legal favors, protected by plausible arguments of action taken for a presumed public interest. But this increased scope for lobby influence seems an inescapable cost of a proper division of functions between legislatures and courts in the area of economic regulation. In a more favorable light, the presumption of constitutionality as the Supreme Court defines it means that a statute is not invalid merely because in serving some public interest it may operate concurrently to provide special gain to some private interest. This result seems appropriate. Concurrence of public and private gain from legislation is so common in this society of diverse, interweaving interests that judges would substantially abrogate the legislative function if they held that such parallel effects alone made a statute unconstitutional.

Finally, we should recall that constitutional law is by no means the whole of what determines the realities of freedom of contract. In the second half of the twentieth century several factors other than direct legal regulation work to reduce, or at least realign, the operation of the freedom of contract. One element is the growth in relative economic importance of large-scale business corporations. In a big corporate organization many decisions that once would have been made by private bargains over supply of goods and services now occur through relations of hierarchy, as boards of directors instruct managers and managers plan and instruct subordinates. Thus, much resource allocation is done through internal discipline of firms, rather than by transactions in market. This internalizing of decisions has generated new concerns about the balance of power among affected interests. Such concerns have prompted new government regulation, as in the WAGNER (NATIONAL LABOR RELATIONS) ACT, in legislation governing corporate finance and administered by the Securities and Exchange Commission, and in the regulation of workplace safety under state and federal laws.

Statutes and administrative regulations now standardize many areas of contract dealing, sometimes providing optional standard forms, sometimes requiring adherence to forms fixed by law. Thus, large areas which are still governed by contract, in the sense that parties enter into relationships only by exchange of consents, are nonetheless areas in which individuals and firms no longer bargain out the details of their transactions. Such is the case with most contracts of insurance, contract relations between corporate stockholders and their corporations, collective bargaining contracts for the supply of labor, and lending contracts.

From the 1930s on, national monetary and fiscal policy has greatly affected the practical scope of freedom of private contract. Government's roles in providing and regulating the money supply are not neutral ones; the qualities of public monetary policy affecting rates of deflation or inflation profoundly affect the extent to which people can control their affairs by private bargains. Similarly, as government enlarges the reach of its TAXING AND SPENDING POWERS, it enlarges or restricts practical freedom of private contract. Government-induced transfer payments—payment of interest on public debt, or payments of Social Security allowances or of unemployment compensation—shift purchasing power among groups. Government spending on goods or services for its own needs removes some proportion of material or labor from the field of private contract in market. In the late twentieth century the cumulative effects of public monetary and fiscal programs spell substantial complication of the patterns of private contract activity and public resource allocation, in comparison with the patterns that existed from the late eighteenth century to the end of the nineteenth century. Freedom of contract in the United States continues to stand for important propositions concerning the structure and working procedures of society, but the content of the idea has undergone significant change from the vision of society held by John Locke or by the Justices of the Supreme Court who spoke for strict judicial review of economic regulations between the 1890s and the middle 1930s.

JAMES WILLARD HURST
(1986)

Bibliography

CHANDLER, ALFRED D., JR. 1977 *The Visible Hand.* Cambridge, Mass.: Belknap Press of Harvard University Press.

FRIEDMAN, LAWRENCE M. 1973 *A History of American Law.* New York: Simon & Schuster.

HORWITZ, MORTON J. 1977 *The Transformation of American Law, 1760–1860.* Cambridge, Mass.: Harvard University Press.

HURST, JAMES WILLARD 1982 *Law and Markets in United States History.* Madison: University of Wisconsin Press.

JACOBS, CLYDE 1954 *Law Writers and the Courts.* Berkeley: University of California Press.

MACAULAY, STEWART 1963 Non-Contractual Relations in Business: A Preliminary Study. *American Sociological Review* 28: 55–67.

PAUL, ARNOLD M. 1960 *Conservative Crisis and the Rule of Law: Attitudes of Bar and Bench, 1887–1895.* Ithaca, N.Y.: Cornell University Press.

POUND, ROSCOE 1909 Liberty of Contract. *Yale Law Journal* 18:454–487.

TRIBE, LAURENCE H. 1978 *American Constitutional Law.* Chap. 8. Mineola, N.Y.: Foundation Press.

TWISS, BENJAMIN R. 1942 *Lawyers and the Constitution: How Laissez Faire Came to the Supreme Court.* Princeton, N.J.: Princeton University Press.

FREEDOM OF INFORMATION ACT
80 Stat. 378 (1966)

The Freedom of Information Act of 1966 establishes a public disclosure policy for information in the custody of the executive branch of the federal government. It authorizes public access to government records and provides administrative and judicial APPEAL of decisions to withhold them. The law mandates that unreleased executive branch records be made available on request; however, it permits the withholding of information in nine categories upon government justification. Among them are classified national security information, information protected by other statutes, internal advisory memoranda, invasions of privacy, certain law enforcement records, and certain confidential business information.

The idea of a freedom of information law was first championed by journalists concerned with the effects of government censorship and discretionary bureaucratic secrecy on FREEDOM OF THE PRESS and the accountability of public officials. After eleven years of congressional hearings, the Freedom of Information Act was passed in 1966, amending the Administrative Procedures Act which had allowed the withholding of almost all government records. Initial compliance with the new law fell short of congressional expectations, and effectuating amendments were passed over a presidential veto in 1974.

As the keystone of "open government" legislation, the act was the first of several statutes that subject certain records and activities of the federal government to public scrutiny. These include the Federal Advisory Committee Act of 1972, the PRIVACY ACT of 1974, the Government in the Sunshine Act of 1976, and the Presidential Records Act of 1978.

The freedom of information policy established by the law does not flow from an express, constitutional RIGHT TO KNOW. Some controversy surrounds the question of whether a public right to know is merely political rhetoric or is an unenumerated constitutional right protected by the NINTH AMENDMENT. A majority of the Justices of the Supreme Court concluded, in RICHMOND NEWSPAPERS, INC. V. VIRGINIA (1980), that the FIRST AMENDMENT gave the public a right of access to criminal trials, which rests on the traditional importance of citizen scrutiny of the judicial trial process. In a separate opinion, Justice WILLIAM J. BREN-

NAN argued that the theory of citizen participation in self-government also supports the right, and that this logic is not confined to access to courtrooms. In another CONCURRING OPINION, Justice JOHN PAUL STEVENS pointed out that in this case the Court recognized for the first time a protected right of access to important government information.

EXECUTIVE PRIVILEGE is embodied in several exemptions to the 1966 Act. Although the scope of the privilege remains in dispute, the Supreme Court in OBITER DICTUM in UNITED STATES V. NIXON (1974) recognized the authority to withhold military and diplomatic national security information, as well as internal memoranda that are advisory and not factual in nature. Later that year, in his veto message returning the 1974 amendments to Congress, President Ford declared that the provision for judicial review of executive branch determinations as to national security classification violates constitutional principles. However, the government has never pressed that argument in litigation.

Individuals have found the act useful for obtaining business information and as an alternative to judicial discovery. Open government policies have affected administrative behavior. Federal law enforcement practices were somewhat restrained after dubious covert investigative activities were disclosed. A government study following the 1974 amendments found that attitudes in the bureaucracy had become more positive toward the release of information and that the quality of some government work had improved because of public scrutiny.

EVERETT E. MANN, JR.
(1986)

Bibliography

MANN, EVERETT E. 1984 The Public Right to Know Government Information: Its Affirmation and Abridgment. Ph.D. dissertation, Claremont Graduate School.

FREEDOM OF INTIMATE ASSOCIATION

Since the 1960s the Supreme Court has decided scores of cases dealing with marriage and divorce, family relationships, the choice whether to procreate, and various forms of intimate association outside the traditional family structure. Although the factual settings of these cases and their opinions' doctrinal explanations have been diverse, in the aggregate they represent the emergence of a constitutional freedom of intimate association.

The Court had asserted as early as MEYER V. NEBRASKA (1923) and PIERCE V. SOCIETY OF SISTERS (1925) that the Constitution protected the freedom to marry and raise one's children, and SKINNER V. OKLAHOMA (1942) had subjected a compulsory STERILIZATION law to STRICT SCRUTINY. But the modern beginning for the freedom of intimate association was Justice WILLIAM O. DOUGLAS's opinion for the Court in GRISWOLD V. CONNECTICUT (1965). Although that case involved a prosecution of the operators of a BIRTH CONTROL clinic for dispensing advice on contraception and the means to achieve it, the focus of the opinion was a married couple's right to use contraceptive devices. Justice Douglas located that right in a "zone of privacy," created by "penumbras" of various specific guarantees in the BILL OF RIGHTS. He did not specify the scope of the new RIGHT OF PRIVACY, and one product of Griswold has been a distinguished body of literature rich with suggested approaches to that issue. In Griswold itself, however, the chief object of constitutional protection was the marital relationship.

Griswold has become a major precedent for several lines of doctrinal development. The right to marry has been recognized as a SUBSTANTIVE DUE PROCESS right in LOVING V. VIRGINIA (1967) and ZABLOCKI V. REDHAIL (1978). The right to use contraceptives has been extended to unmarried persons in EISENSTADT V. BAIRD (1972) on an EQUAL PROTECTION theory, and even the right to advertise and sell them has been defended in CAREY V. POPULATION SERVICES INTERNATIONAL (1977) on the basis of the FIRST AMENDMENT and the privacy right of potential buyers, married or not. These protections of intimate relationships outside marriage have been complemented by heightened scrutiny of legislative classifications visiting disadvantage on the status of ILLEGITIMACY. Griswold's most famous doctrinal outgrowth was ROE V. WADE (1973), which squarely placed the new constitutional right of privacy within the liberty protected by substantive due process, and held that the right included a woman's freedom to choose to have an ABORTION.

Here as elsewhere, constitutional doctrine has followed in the wake of social change. After World War II the movement for racial equality accelerated, bringing new awareness and new acceptance of a cultural diversity extending well beyond differences based on race. By the 1970s the feminist movement had succeeded in engaging the nation's attention and changing attitudes of both men and women toward questions of "woman's role," and in particular toward marriage and the family. The white, middle-class "housewife marriage," with the father working and the mother and children at home in a one-family suburban house, may still be the image most often called to mind by general references to "the family." The image, however, represents less than half of America's population. The "wife economy" is now obsolete; increased longevity will place further strains on lifetime marriage; women now know they can choose marriage without motherhood, or motherhood without marriage; racial and ethnic minorities will not again accept the idea that the diversity of their forms of intimate association is merely pathological. Indeed, large numbers of middle-class white couples are openly living together without marrying. What has changed is not so much the fact of diversity as the range of the acceptable in intimate association.

A strong egalitarian theme runs through our society's collective recognition of these changes; it is natural that both due process and equal protection have provided doctrinal underpinnings for the freedom of intimate association. As abstractions, "liberty" and "equality" may sometimes be in tension, but here they have nourished each other. As the civil rights movement sought to advance equality under the banner of "freedom," so the abortion rights movement has sought a new status for women under the banner of "choice."

Taking account of doctrinal development in this area, the Supreme Court, in its opinion in *Roberts v. United States Jaycees* (1984), referred for the first time to a "freedom of intimate association." "[C]ertain kinds of highly personal relationships," said the Court, had been afforded substantial constitutional protection: "marriage; childbirth; the raising and education of children; and cohabitation with one's relatives." The Court noted that these relationships tended to involve relatively small numbers of persons; a high degree of selectivity in beginning and maintaining the affiliations; and "seclusion from others in critical aspects of the relationship." Their constitutional protection reflected "the realization that individuals draw much of their emotional enrichment from close ties with others. Protecting these relationships from unwarranted state interference therefore safeguards the ability independently to define one's identity that is central to any concept of liberty."

For half a century the Court has performed much of its judicial interest-balancing by adjusting the STANDARDS OF REVIEW of the constitutionality of legislation. As the *Jaycees* opinion noted, heightened judicial scrutiny results when the Court perceives the importance of the values or interests impaired when government restricts freedom or imposes inequality. The Court has spoken of procreation as a "basic" right, and has labeled "fundamental" both the right to marry and the freedom of choice "whether to bear or beget a child." To understand what these characterizations may imply for the constitutional status of other forms of intimate association, it is necessary to ask why REPRODUCTIVE AUTONOMY and the freedom to marry are so important. To answer that question requires analysis of the substantive values that may be at stake in intimate associations.

The term "intimate association" is used here to mean a close and familiar personal relationship with another that is in some significant way comparable to a marriage or family relationship. Its connecting links may take the form of living together in the same quarters, or sexual intimacy, or blood ties, or a formal relationship, or some mixtures of these, but in principle the idea of intimate association also includes close friendship, with or without any such links. The values of intimate association are undeniably elusive; they are not readily reducible to items on a list. Yet such an exercise is implicit in any attempt to illuminate the principle underlying the decisions on marriage and reproductive choice. The potential values in intimate associations can be grouped in four clusters: society, caring and commitment, intimacy, and self-identification.

Intimate association implies some expectation of access of one person to another's physical presence, some opportunity for face-to-face encounter. A couple's claim of the right to live together, with or without a sexual relationship, directly implicates this interest in another's society; so does a divorced parent's claim of a right of access to a child in a former spouse's custody, or a prison rule wholly denying visitation rights. Other impairments of the interest in an intimate's society are indirect, as when welfare aid to a mother's family is terminated because she is living with a man. The latter case offers opportunity for manipulation; it might be characterized as a denial of no more than a money payment, or as a denial of the society of an intimate. To allow a claim of constitutional right to turn on such question-begging seems intolerable; yet that is just what the Supreme Court typically does in cases of indirect interference with the values of intimate association. Concededly, not every impairment of the freedom to enjoy an intimate's society requires the same degree of justification, but there is little to be said for distracting attention from substantive interest-balancing by engaging in definitional legerdemain.

For most people, mutual caring and commitment are the chief values of intimate association. Caring implies commitment, for it requires an effort to know another, trust another, hope for another, and help another develop. The commitment in question is not a legal commitment enforceable by law, but a personal commitment, the sense that one is pledged to care for another and intends to keep the pledge. It is possible to be committed to an association one has not chosen; a young child exercises no choice in forming an association with her family and yet may feel wholly committed to them. Still, the value of commitment is usually heightened for the partners to an intimate association when they know there is real and continuing choice to maintain the association. The caring partner continually reaffirms her autonomy and responsibility by choosing the commitment, and the cared-for partner gains in self-respect by seeing himself through his partner's eyes as one who is worth being cared for. Furthermore, although commitment means an expectation of constancy over time, it is not paradoxical to say that effective legal shelter for this value must offer protection to casual intimate associations as well as lasting ones. Such a casual association may ripen into a durable one, and the value of commitment is fully realizable only in an atmosphere of freedom to choose whether a particular association will be fleeting or enduring. Finally, to limit the law's protection to lasting intimate associations would require intolerable inquiries into private behavior and private intentions.

Intimacy, in the context of intimate associations, is more than privacy in its ordinary sense of nondisclosure. When we speak of intimate friends, or of persons who share an intimate relationship, we refer to the intimacy of a close and enduring association, that is, intimacy in the context of caring and commitment. This sort of intimacy is something that a person can share with only a limited number of others, for it requires time and effort to know another and deal with her as a whole person.

Intimate associations are powerful influences over the development of most people's personalities. Not only do these associations give an individual his best chance to be seen (and thus to see himself) as a whole person rather than an aggregate of social roles; they also serve as statements to others. As the legal consequences of cohabitation come to approximate those of marriage, and as divorce becomes more readily available, marriage itself takes on a special significance for its expressive content as a statement that the couple wish to identify with each other. The decision whether to have a child is also a major occasion for self-identification. To become a parent is to assume a new status in the eyes of oneself and others. Plainly the freedom to choose one's intimate associations is at the heart of this notion of association-as-statement. And, just as the freedom of political nonassociation is properly recognized as a FIRST AMENDMENT right, the freedom not to form an intimate association is similarly linked to the freedom of expression.

These four sets of intimate associational values—society, caring and commitment, intimacy, and self-identification—coalesce in an area of the human psyche that is awkward to discuss in lawyers' language. Yet even before the *Jaycees* opinion the Supreme Court had occasionally suggested its awareness of the reasons why such values are important. In *Eisenstadt*, for example, Justice WILLIAM J. BRENNAN spoke of "unwarranted governmental intrusion into matters so fundamentally affecting a PERSON as the decision whether to bear or beget a child." Although the word "person" usually is no more than a prosaic reference to an individual, its use in this passage resonates in the registers of matters personal and the human personality. If freedoms relating to marriage and family and

reproductive choice are "fundamental," the reason is that these concerns lie close to the center of one's sense of self.

Not all governmental restrictions on associational freedom are intrusive in the same degree on the values of intimate association. The constitutional freedom of intimate association is not a rule for decision but an organizing principle, demanding justification for governmental intrusions on close personal relationships in proportion to the magnitude of invasion of intimate associational values. One complicating feature of this interest-balancing is that the law's interference with the freedom of intimate association usually is not direct. Instead, government typically conditions some material benefit (employment, inheritance, welfare payments, Social Security) on the candidate's associations in fact or formal associational status.

In DANDRIDGE V. WILLIAMS (1970), for example, a state proportioned welfare benefits to family size but set an absolute limit on aid to any one family. The Supreme Court, treating the law as a restriction on money payments and ignoring its potential effects on family size, subjected it only to RATIONAL BASIS scrutiny. In CLEVELAND BOARD OF EDUCATION V. LAFLEUR (1974), however, pregnant school teachers were required to take a long maternity leave. The Court, emphasizing the right to procreate, rigorously scrutinized the law under the IRREBUTTABLE PRESUMPTIONS doctrine. This sort of question-begging without explanation, far from being aberrational, has been the norm for the Court's treatment of indirect restrictions on intimate association. It is not unusual for the Court to conceal its interest-balancing behind definitional assumptions.

When a state conditions a benefit on a formal associational status such as marriage or legitimacy of parentage, a further analytical complication arises. The state controls entry into the status as well as its legal consequences. Judicial evaluation of such a restriction on benefits must take into account the ease of entry. Alternatively, a law restricting entry into a formal associational status must be evaluated partly on the basis of the consequences of the status, including eligibility for benefits. The opportunities for circular reasoning are evident; only close attention to the associational values at stake will permit noncircular resolutions. The formal status of marriage, for example, must be seen not merely as a bureaucratic hurdle on the road to material benefits but also as a statement of the partners' commitment and self-identification.

In protecting the freedom of intimate association the Supreme Court has followed several different doctrinal paths. The *Griswold* opinion drew on the First Amendment's freedom of political association partly by way of analogy and partly in support of the Court's "zone of privacy" theory. Later decisions have both extended *Griswold*'s results in the name of equal protection and recharacterized its right of privacy as a substantive due process right. For a brief time in the 1970s the Court even used the rhetoric of PROCEDURAL DUE PROCESS and irrebuttable presumptions to defend the freedom of intimate association—a development which some Justices called a disguised form of equal protection or substantive due process. Today the freedom's most secure doctrinal base is substantive due process; yet both the First Amendment and the equal protection clause counsel judicial sensitivity to the need to protect intimate associations that are unconventional or that may offend majoritarian morality. In a society that expresses its cultural diversity in a rich variety of family forms and other personal relationships, these constitutional claims of freedom and equality will overlap.

Whatever its doctrinal context, a claim to freedom of intimate association depends on the nature and magnitude of the intrusion into the substantive values of intimate association, weighed against the governmental interests asserted to justify the intrusion. To give life to this abstraction it is necessary to examine the freedom of intimate association in operation as an organizing principle in particular subject areas. The Supreme Court's decisions can be grouped in seven overlapping categories: marriage and husband-wife relations; divorce; nonmarital relationships; procreation; illegitimacy; family autonomy; and homosexual relationships.

The Supreme Court's clear recognition of a constitutional right to marry by no means forecloses a state from regulating entry into marriage. Some restrictions, in fact, promote the principle of associational choice: minimum age requirements, for example, or requirements demanding minimum competency to understand the nature of marriage. Other restrictions aimed at promoting public health, such as mandatory blood tests, also seem likely to pass the test of strict judicial scrutiny. It is less clear that the balance of state interests against the freedom of associational choice should uphold a prohibition against POLYGAMY, or a refusal to allow homosexuals a status comparable to marriage, or a prohibition on marriage between first cousins. Yet it is safe to predict that homosexual marriage will not gain judicial blessing in the immediate future, and that the constitutionality of incest and polygamy laws will not be questioned seriously in any future now foreseeable. The Supreme Court, after all, is an instrument of government in a human society. Still, in theory, any direct state prohibition of marriage must pass the test of strict scrutiny, and indirect restriction on the right to marry requires justification proportioned to the restriction's likely practical effects as a prohibition.

The freedom of intimate association speaks not only to state interference with the right to marry but also to state intrusion into the relations between husband and wife. A marriage is more than a list of contractual duties; the partners deal with each other on many levels, both practical and emotional, and their relations are necessarily diffuse rather than particularized, exploratory rather than fixed. Spouses who are committed to stay together in an intimacy characterized by caring need to heal their relationship for the future, not settle old scores. Long before *Griswold* recognized a married couple's constitutional right to autonomy over the intimacies of their relationship, our nonconstitutional law largely maintained a "hands-off" attitude toward interspousal disputes. This tradition once supported a system of patriarchy now discredited; today the values of intimate association counsel the state to leave the partners to an ongoing marriage alone and let them work out their own differences—or, if they cannot, to terminate the marriage with a minimum of state interference.

Although the Supreme Court has not formally recognized a constitutional "right to divorce" comparable to the right to marry, both in principle and in practical effect such a right can be derived from the Court's decisions. The freedom of intimate association demands significant justification for state restrictions on exit from a marriage. The relevance to divorce of the associational value of self-identification is evident. Even the value of commitment bears on such a case, and not merely because divorce is the legal key to remarriage. For those who choose to stay married, their commitment is heightened by the knowledge that it is freely chosen. The Constitution apart, state laws setting conditions for divorce have virtually eliminated the requirement of a showing of one partner's fault. The restrictions that remain concern ACCESS TO THE COURTS, and involve limitations such as filing fees, as in BODDIE V. CONNECTICUT (1971), or RESIDENCE REQUIREMENTS, as in SOSNA V. IOWA (1975).

When a marriage terminates, nothing in the principle of associational choice militates against judicial enforcement of interspousal contracts governing the division of property. Once the union is dissolved, application of the usual rules of contract law to postdissolution obligations threatens none of the values of intimate association and demands no special justification. (Issues of child custody, which do require careful balancing of associational values, are discussed along with other parent–child questions.)

When a couple live together in a sexual relationship without marrying, the associational values of society, caring, and intimacy are all present in important degrees. Although the couple's association may not be so definitive a statement of self-identification as marriage would be, such a statement it surely is. Even the commitment implicit in such a union, although it may be tentative, usually is not trivial. If the couple see the union as a trial marriage, it takes on the instrumental quality that the *Griswold* court saw in sexual privacy. The Supreme Court's decisions on contraception and abortion have extended that right of privacy to unmarried persons. In 1968 the Court construed federal welfare legislation to prevent a state from terminating a mother's benefits merely because she had a man, not her husband, living in the house; Justice Douglas, concurring, would have held the state's attempted regulation of the mother's morals a denial of equal protection, by analogy to the Court's then recent decisions on illegitimacy. Some classifications based on marital status plainly are unconstitutional.

It seems no more than a matter of time before the Court, recognizing the expansion of the boundaries of the acceptable in intimate association, follows the logic of the contraception cases and holds invalid state laws forbidding fornication and unmarried cohabitation. Many lower courts have reached similar results, typically without addressing constitutional issues. Most of the cases have involved the claims of unmarried women denied employment, or child custody, or admission to the bar because they were living with men. The freedom of intimate association is, in important part, a product of the movement for equality between the sexes.

So are the Supreme Court's decisions on reproductive choice. "Birth control is woman's problem," said Margaret Sanger in 1920; it still is. The right to procreate, which another generation's Court called "one of the basic civil rights to man," is now matched with the constitutional right of man and woman alike to practice contraception and with a woman's right to have an abortion, even over her husband's objection. Although the right to choose "whether to bear or beget a child" is not reducible to an aspect of the freedom of intimate association, it is in part an associational choice. Given today's facility of contraception and abortion, generally one can choose whether to be a parent. The *Skinner* opinion properly connected marriage and procreation. An unmarried couple living together recognize this linkage when they decide to marry because they "want to have a family." Children are valued not only for themselves and the associations they bring but also as living expressions of their parents' caring for—and commitment to—each other. The decision whether to have a child is, in part, a choice of social identification and self-concept; it ranks in importance with any other a person may make in a lifetime.

Not only the right to be a parent, protected in *Skinner*, but also the right to choose to defer parenthood or to avoid it altogether implicates the core values of intimate association. *Griswold* and its successor decisions, defending these values in the context of nonassociation, protect men and women—but particularly women—against the enforced intimate society of unwanted children, against an unchosen commitment and a caring stained by reluctance, against a compelled identification with the social role of parent. Coerced intimate association in the shape of forced child-bearing or parenthood is no less serious an invasion of the sense of self than is forced marriage.

Griswold and its successors also protect the autonomy of a couple's association, whether it be a marriage or an association of unmarried intimates. The point was explicitly made in the *Griswold* opinion concerning marital autonomy, and *Eisenstadt v. Baird* (1972) effectively gave unmarried couples the same power to govern the intimacies of their association. What emerges from these decisions, along with *Skinner* and *LaFleur*, is not an absolute rule but a requirement of appropriate justification when the state burdens the decision whether to procreate.

The Supreme Court has focused on equal protection in dealing with the constitutionality of laws defining the incidents of illegitimacy. There is obvious unfairness in visiting unequal treatment on an illegitimate child in order to express the state's disapproval of her parents. Yet the freedom of intimate association suggests an additional perspective: the unfairness of state-imposed inequality between persons in traditional marriage-family relationships and those in other comparable forms of intimate association. In particular, the illegitimacy laws discriminate against unmarried women and their children—as, indeed, such laws have done from their medieval beginnings. The principle of legitimacy of parentage assumes not only that a child needs a male link to the rest of the community but also that the claim of the child's mother to social position depends on her being granted the status of formal marriage. In historical origin and in modern application, the chief function of the law of illegitimacy is to assure male control over the transmission of wealth and status. Deviance from the principle of legitimacy is most likely in subgroups whose fathers lack wealth and status; it is no accident that the incidence of illegitimacy in our society is highest among the nonwhite poor.

As increased numbers of middle-class couples live together without marrying, surely there will be changes in the legal status of unmarried mothers and their children. In the perspective of the freedom of intimate association, the constitutional basis for the whole system of illegitimacy appears shaky. If the informal union of an unmarried couple is constitutionally protected, the relationship between that union's children and their parents is also protected. Significant impairment of the substantive values of such an intimate association must find justification, in proportion to the impairment, in state interests that cannot be achieved by other less intrusive means.

Ever since *Meyer v. Nebraska* (1923) and *Pierce v. Society of Sisters* (1925) judges and commentators have assumed that the Constitution protects the autonomy of the traditional family against excessive state interference. Those two decisions rested on substantive due process grounds, and they have been cited often by the Supreme Court during the modern revival of substantive due process as a guarantee of personal liberty. When a family is united concerning such matters as the children's education, only a COMPELLING STATE INTEREST will justify state interference with the family's choice.

When a family is not united, however, the constitutional principle of family autonomy is an imperfect guide. Generally, the law assumes that children prosper under their parents' control. For very young children, this assumption is little more than a corollary of the family autonomy principle. As children mature, however, it becomes sensible to speak of the continuing family relationship as a matter of choice. Within the family that stays together, parent–child relations are, from some point in a child's teenage years forward, a matter of intrafamily agreement. Even when parental discipline is the rule, it rests on the child's consent, once the child is capable of making an independent life. Not surprisingly, the Supreme Court held invalid a state law giving an unmarried minor female's parents the right to veto her decision to have an abortion. (See PLANNED PARENTHOOD OF MISSOURI V. DANFORTH.)

The freedom of intimate association thus counsels severe restrictions on the state's power to intervene either to enforce parental authority or to oppose it—just as considerations of intramarital associational choice and harmony dictate that state intervention into the husband-wife relationship be limited to cases of urgent necessity, such as wife abuse. Conceding that most children want and need parental discipline, it remains true that invoking the state's police officers and juvenile halls to enforce that discipline is destructive of the values of intimate association. For mature children, those values depend on their willingness to identify with their parents and to be committed to maintaining a caring intimacy with them. In cases of a parent's incapacity or serious neglect, state intervention into the zone of family autonomy may be constitutionally justified. Yet removals of children from parental custody and terminations of parental rights are extreme measures, intruding deeply into the values of intimate association—not only for parents but also for children. The most compelling justification is therefore required for so drastic a state intervention, justification found in the child's needs, not any interest the state may have in punishing parental misbehavior. The Supreme Court's refusal in LASSITER V. DEPARTMENT OF SOCIAL SERVICES (1981) to extend the full reach of the RIGHT TO COUNSEL to indigent parents in termination proceedings seems an unstable precedent.

While a marriage lasts, the law is no more likely to interfere in interspousal disputes over child-rearing than it is in other controversies between husband and wife. When a marriage ends, an agreement between the separating parents over child custody usually will prevail, absent some overriding factor such as the associational choice of a mature child. A custody contest upon divorce, involving competing claims of rights of association, demands discretionary, whole-person evaluations rather than application of specific rules of law. The Constitution comes to bear on such decisions only marginally, as appellate courts seek to assure that trial judges do, in fact, consider the whole persons before them and do not disqualify parents from custody by informally substituting unconstitutional "rules" for the discretion that is appropriate. Such a "rule," for example, might disqualify on the basis of a parent's race—or, as in PALMORE V. SIDOTI (1984), the race of the parent's spouse—or religion, or unmarried cohabitation, or sexual preference. *Stanley v. Illinois* (1972) is an instructive analogy; there the Supreme Court held that a law disqualifying a natural father from custody of his illegitimate child upon the mother's death was an unconstitutional irrebuttable presumption of unfitness.

It is now established beyond question that the "liberty" protected by the two due process clauses protects "freedom of personal choice in matters of marriage and family life"—Justice POTTER STEWART's words, concurring in *Zablocki v. Redhail* (1978). If the logic of that freedom extends beyond formal marriage and beyond the nuclear family, the reason is that the human family is a social artifact, not an entity defined in nature. In MOORE V. CITY OF EAST CLEVELAND (1977) a plurality of four Justices admitted the traditional "extended family" into the circle of due process protection, and that opinion is now regularly cited as if it were an OPINION OF THE COURT. The freedom Justice Stewart described is comprehensible only in the light of intimate associational values that are also found in families that depart significantly from traditional models. One result of the movement for women's liberation has been the increased adoption of alternative living arrangements: couples living together outside marriage; single mothers with children, sometimes combining with other similar families. Other groupings such as communes for the young and the old are responses to what their members see as the failings of traditional arrangements. These people do not risk prosecution under cohabitation laws or other "morals" statutes; they may, however, risk the loss of material benefits.

Any governmental intrusion on personal choice of living arrangements requires substantial justification, in proportion to its likely influence in coercing people out of one form of intimate association and into another. In DEPARTMENT OF AGRICULTURE V. MORENO (1973) the Supreme Court demanded such justification for a law denying food stamps to households composed of "unrelated" persons, and found it lacking. Yet in *Village of Belle Terre v. Boraas*

(1974) the Court made no search for justification beyond minimum rationality, and upheld a ZONING ordinance designed to screen out nontraditional families and applied to exclude occupancy of a home by six unrelated students. In design, the *Belle Terre* ordinance was a direct assault on the freedom of intimate association, an attempt to stamp out forms of personal association departing from a vision of family life that no longer fit a large proportion of the population. *Belle Terre's* standing as a precedent surely will weaken as the Court comes to take seriously its own rhetoric about "family" values in nontraditional families. One occasion for such rhetoric was the opinion in *Smith v. Organization of Foster Families* (1977), recognizing the values of intimate association in a foster family.

Laws prohibiting homosexual conduct are only rarely enforced against private consensual behavior. The middle-class homosexual couple thus have each other's society, including whatever sort of intimacy they want; they care for each other and are committed to each other in the degree they choose. What government chiefly denies them is the dignity of self-identification as equal citizens, along with certain forms of employment and other material benefits that may be reserved for partners to a formal marriage.

Whatever may have been the original purpose of laws forbidding homosexual sex, today one of their chief supports is a wish to regulate the content of messages about sexual preference. One fear is that the state, by repealing its restrictions, will be seen as approving homosexual conduct. The selective enforcement of these laws is itself evidence that one of the main policies being pursued is the suppression of expression; the laws are enforced mainly against those who openly advertise their sexual preferences. The immediate practical effect of this enforcement pattern is to penalize public self-identification and expression, some of which is political expression in support of "gay liberation." Even thoroughgoing enforcement would severely impair expression, along with the values of caring and intimacy. For a homosexual, a violation of these laws is the principal form that a sexual expression of love can take.

The denial of the status of marriage, or some comparable status, does not merely limit homosexuals' opportunities for expressive self-identification; material benefits also are frequently conditioned on marriage. Some commentators argue that a state's refusal to recognize homosexual marriage raises a problem of sex discrimination, and others contend that homosexuality should be regarded as a SUSPECT CLASSIFICATION for equal protection purposes. In any case, the heart of the constitutional problem lies in the freedom of intimate association. Although the denial of formal recognition of a homosexual couple's union may not demand the same compelling justification that would be required by a total prohibition of homosexual relations, it nonetheless seems unlikely that government could meet any requirement of justification that was not wholly permissive.

The burden of justification is of critical importance in the area of regulation of homosexual conduct, precisely because most such regulations are the product of folklore and fantasy rather than evidence of real risk of harm. If, for example, the state had to prove that a lesbian mother, by virtue of that status alone, was unfit to have custody of her child, the effort surely would demonstrate that the operative factor in the disqualification was not risk of harm, but stigma. The results of serious constitutional inquiry into harms and justifications in such cases are easy to predict. First, however, that serious inquiry must be made, and the Supreme Court showed in *Doe v. Commonwealth's District Attorney* (1976) that it was not eager to embark on that course.

The freedom of intimate association serves as an organizing principle mainly by focusing attention on substantive associational values. In a given case, the impairment of those values is matched against the asserted justifications for governmental regulation. Those justifications are hard to discuss systematically, for they can be asserted on the basis of a range of interests as broad as the public welfare. One cluster of justifications, however, deserves attention: the promotion of a political majority's view of morality. The state may claim a role in socializing its citizens, and especially the young, to traditional values. When a legislature prohibits unmarried cohabitation or homosexual relations or other disapproved forms of intimate association, it does so primarily to promote a moral view and to protect the sensibilities of those who share that view. The freedom of intimate association does not wholly disable government from seeking these ends; however, as *Griswold* and its successor decisions show, neither can the state defeat every claim to the freedom of intimate association simply by invoking conventional morality.

The judicial interest-balancing appropriate to the evolution of many claims of freedom of intimate association thus must consider not only degrees of impairment of associational values but also questions of the kind raised by GOVERNMENT SPEECH cases involving official promotion of particular points of view. There is a difference, for example, between a "baby bonus" designed to assist parents with child-rearing and a state's offer of cash to any woman entering an abortion clinic, conditioned on her agreement to forgo an abortion. To say that the difference is one of degree is to remind ourselves that the judicial function in constitutional cases is one of judgment. The freedom of intimate association is not a machine that, once set in motion, must run to all conceivable logical conclusions. It is instead a constitutional principle, requiring significant justification when the state seeks to lay hands on life-defining intimate associational choices.

KENNETH L. KARST
(1986)

Bibliography

BURT, ROBERT A. 1979 The Constitution of the Family. *Supreme Court Review* 1979:329–395.

Developments in the Law—The Constitution and the Family 1980 *Harvard Law Review* 93:1156–1383.

GERETY, TOM 1977 Redefining Privacy. *Harvard Civil Rights-Civil Liberties Law Review* 12:233–296.

GLENDON, MARY ANN 1977 *State, Law and Family*. New York: North-Holland Publishing Company.

KARST, KENNETH L. 1980 The Freedom of Intimate Association. *Yale Law Journal* 89:624–692.

SYMPOSIUM 1975 Children and the Law. *Law and Contemporary Problems* 39, no. 3:1–293.

—— 1979 Children and the Law. *University of California, Davis Law Review* 12:207–898.

—— 1985 The Legal System and Homosexuality—Approbation, Accommodation, or Reprobation? *University of Dayton Law Review* 10:445–813.

TRIBE, LAURENCE H. 1978 *American Constitutional Law*. Chap. 15. Mineola, N.Y.: Foundation Press.

WILKINSON, J. HARVIE, III and WHITE, G. EDWARD 1977 Constitutional Protection for Personal Lifestyles. *Cornell Law Review* 62:563–625.

FREEDOM OF PETITION

The freedom to petition the government for redress of grievances was recognized in MAGNA CARTA in 1215 and was well established in English law before the American Revolution. The king would summon Parliament to supply funds for the running of government and Parliament developed the habit of petitioning for a redress of grievances as the condition of supplying the money. The growing recognition of the right of subjects as well as of Parliament to petition the Crown culminated in the explicit affirmation in the English BILL OF RIGHTS of 1689 "That it is the right of the subjects to petition the King and all commitments and prosecutions for such petitioning are illegal."

In the United States Constitution, the FIRST AMENDMENT protects "the right of the people peaceably to assemble, and to petition the Government for a redress of grievances." Historically, the FREEDOM OF ASSEMBLY was regarded as ancillary to the right of petition, as if the amendment guaranteed the right to assemble *in order to* petition the government. This view was expressed by the Supreme Court in UNITED STATES V. CRUIKSHANK (1876). Today, however, the right of assembly has independent significance equal to that of the FREEDOMS OF SPEECH, PRESS, and religion. (See DEJONGE V. OREGON.) The right to petition has

received less judicial attention than the other First Amendment rights. Nevertheless, it is one of the freedoms protected by the DUE PROCESS clause of the FOURTEENTH AMENDMENT against infringement by the states. (See HAGUE V. CIO.) Comparable protections of the right of petition are found, expressly or by clear implication, in the constitutions of all the states. And the right to petition Congress for redress of grievances has been recognized as one of the privileges of national CITIZENSHIP protected against state infringement by the PRIVILEGES OR IMMUNITIES clause of the Fourteenth Amendment. (See TWINING V. NEW JERSEY.)

The right of petition includes the right not only to approach public officials directly with requests for redress of grievances but also to circulate petitions for signature so as to generate mass pressure on the Congress and other public bodies. It is in this context that the right of petition may have its greatest contemporary significance. For the exercise of the right of petition involves the exercise of other First Amendment rights, including not only the right of expression but the right of other people to be exposed to the ideas expressed in the petition. The act of preparing and circulating a petition is itself an exercise of the freedom to associate with others for the expression of political and other opinions. Justice WILLIAM J. BRENNAN, dissenting in *Boston v. Glines* (1980), remarked: "The petition is especially suited for the exercise of all these rights: It serves as a vehicle of communication; as a classic means of individual affiliation with ideas or opinions; and as a peaceful yet effective method of amplifying the views of the individual signers." As with other First Amendment rights, the freedom of petition cannot be infringed in the absence of a compelling governmental interest justifying the infringement; the right of petition is an essential component of the political liberties protected by the First Amendment.

CHARLES E. RICE
(1986)

FREEDOM OF RELIGION

See: Religious Liberty

FREEDOM OF SPEECH

Freedom of speech is guaranteed in the American Constitution by the FIRST AMENDMENT. Adopted in 1791 as the first provision of the BILL OF RIGHTS, the First Amendment reads (excluding the clauses on religion): "Congress shall make no law ... abridging the freedom of speech, or of the press, or the right of the people peaceably to assemble, and to petition the Government for a redress of grievances." Although the provision names four specific rights—freedom of speech, FREEDOM OF THE PRESS, FREE-DOM OF ASSEMBLY, and FREEDOM OF PETITION—the several guarantees have never been clearly differentiated; rather the First Amendment has been construed as guaranteeing a composite right to freedom of expression. The term "freedom of speech," therefore, in popular usuage as well as in legal doctrine, has been considered roughly coextensive with the whole of the First Amendment.

The precise intentions of the framers of the First Amendment have never been entirely clear. The debates in Congress when the amendment was proposed do not throw much light upon the subject. The right to freedom of speech derives from English law and tradition. And it is agreed that the English law of the time, following the lapse of the censorship laws at the end of the seventeenth century, did not authorize advance censorship of publication. The English law of SEDITIOUS LIBEL, however, did provide punishment, after publication, for speech that criticized the government, its policies or its officials, or tended to bring them into contempt or disrepute. These features of English law were under severe attack, both in England and in the American colonies, but whether the First Amendment was meant to abolish or change them has been a matter of dispute. Similarly, the application of the First Amendment to other aspects of free speech, such as civil libel, OBSCENITY, and the like, remained obscure.

Passage of the ALIEN AND SEDITION ACTS in 1798, which incorporated much of the English law of seditious libel, stimulated public discussion of the meaning of the First Amendment. The constitutional issues, however, never reached the Supreme Court. Nor, despite widespread suppression of speech at certain times in our history, such as took place during the abolitionist movement, the CIVIL WAR, and the beginnings of the labor movement, did the Supreme Court have or take the occasion to address in any major way the development of First Amendment doctrine. The reason for this failure of the constitutional guarantee to be translated into legal action seems to lie partly in the fact that the Bill of Rights had been construed by the Court to apply only to action of the federal government, not to state or local governments; partly in the fact that, insofar as suppression emanated from federal sources, it was the executive not the legislature that was involved; and partly in the fact that the role of the courts in protecting CIVIL LIBERTIES had not matured to the point it has reached today.

In any event this state of affairs ended at the time of WORLD WAR I. Legislation enacted by Congress in 1917 and 1918, designed to prohibit interference with the war effort, raised clear-cut issues under the First Amendment. Beginning in 1919, a series of cases challenging the wartime legislation came before the Supreme Court. These were followed by cases arising out of the Red scare of the early 1920s. In 1925, in *Gitlow v. United States*, the Court accepted the argument that the First Amendment was applicable to the state and local governments as a "liberty" that could not be denied without DUE PROCESS OF LAW under the FOURTEENTH AMENDMENT. It also became clear that, while the First Amendment literally refers only to "Congress," its provisions extend not only to the legislature but to the executive and judicial branches of government as well. As the First Amendment has come to be applied to more and newer problems growing out of the operation of a modern technological society, there has developed an extensive network of principles, legal rules, implementing decisions, and institutional practices which expand and refine the constitutional guarantee.

The fundamental values underlying the concept of freedom of speech, and the functions that principle serves in a democratic society, are widely accepted. They have been summarized in the following form:

First, freedom of speech is essential to the development of the individual personality. The right to express oneself and to communicate with others is central to the realization of one's character and potentiality as a human being. Conversely, suppression of thought or opinion is an affront to a person's dignity and integrity. In this respect freedom of speech is an end in itself, not simply an instrument to attain other ends. As such it is not necessarily subordinate to other goals of the society.

Second, freedom of speech is vital to the attainment and advancement of knowledge. As JOHN STUART MILL pointed out, an enlightened judgment is possible only if one is willing to consider all facts and ideas, from whatever source, and to test one's conclusion against opposing views. Even speech that conveys false information or maligns ideas has value, for it compels us to retest and rethink accepted positions and thereby promotes greater understanding. From this function of free speech it follows that the right to express oneself does not depend upon whether society judges the communication to be true or false, good or bad, socially useful or harmful. All points of view, even a minority of one, are entitled to be heard. The MARKETPLACE OF IDEAS should be open to all sellers and all buyers.

Third, freedom of speech is a necessary part of our system of self-government. ALEXANDER MEIKLEJOHN, the leading exponent of this view of the First Amendment, stressed that under our Constitution, sovereignty resides in the people; in other words, the people are the masters and the government is their servant. If the people are to perform their role as sovereign and instruct their government, they must have access to all information, ideas, and points of view. This right of free speech is crucial not only in determining policy but in checking the government in its implementation of policy. The implication of this position is that the government has no authority to determine what may be said or heard by the citizens of the community. The servant cannot tell the master how to make up its mind.

Fourth, freedom of speech is vital to the process of peaceful social change. It allows ideas to be tested in advance before action is taken, it legitimizes the decision reached, and it permits adaptation to new conditions without the use of force. It does not eliminate conflict in a society, but it does direct conflict into more rational, less violent, channels. From this it follows, in the words of Justice WILLIAM J. BRENNAN in NEW YORK TIMES V. SULLIVAN (1964), that speech will often be "uninhibited, robust, and wide-open."

There is also general agreement that speech is entitled to special protection against abridgment by the state. Freedom of thought and communication are central to any system of individual rights. Most other rights of the person against the collective flow from and are dependent upon that source. Moreover, speech is considered to have less harmful effects upon the community—to be less coercive—than other forms of conduct. And, as a general proposition, the state possesses sufficient power to achieve social goals without suppressing beliefs, opinions, or communication of ideas. Hence, in constitutional terms, freedom of speech occupies a "preferred position."

One further background factor should be noted. Toleration of the speech of others does not come easily to many people, especially those in positions of power. As Justice OLIVER WENDELL HOLMES remarked in ABRAMS V. UNITED STATES (1919), "If you have no doubt of your premises or your powers and want a certain result with all your heart you naturally express your wishes in law and sweep away all opposition." Hence the pressures leading to suppression of speech are widespread and powerful in our society. The mechanisms for protecting freedom of speech, therefore, must rely heavily upon an independent judiciary, standing somewhat outside the fray, and upon the creation of legal DOCTRINES that are precise and realistic.

The principal controversies that have engaged our system of freedom of speech have concerned the formulation of these implementing rules. In general the issues have centered on two basic questions. The first is what kind of conduct is to be considered "speech" entitled to special protection under the First Amendment. The second concerns what degree of protection, or encouragement, must be given that speech under the constitutional mandate.

As to the first question—the issue of coverage—it has been argued from time to time that certain categories of speech are totally outside the purview of the First Amendment. Thus it has been contended that totalitarian and racist groups should not be permitted to advance antidemocratic ideas. The argument has been that political groups that would destroy democratic institutions if they came to power should not be entitled to take advantage of these institutions in order to promote their cause; only those who adhere to the rules of the game should be allowed to participate. Similarly it has been urged that racist speech violates the dignity and integrity of fellow persons in the community, performs no social function, and should not be tolerated in a civilized society dedicated to human rights.

While this position has been strongly urged it has not prevailed in the United States. For both theoretical and practical reasons the concept of freedom of speech has been interpreted to mean that all persons should be allowed to express their beliefs and opinions regardless of how obnoxious or "fraught with death" those ideas may be. As a matter of principle, all ideas must be open to challenge; even totalitarian and racist speech serves a useful purpose in forcing a society to defend and thereby better comprehend its own basic values. Moreover, groups that promote totalitarian or racist ideas do not operate in a political vacuum. Their speech reflects fears, grievances, or other conditions which society should be aware of and in some cases take action to deal with. Suppression of such speech simply increases hostility, diverts attention from underlying problems, and ultimately weakens the society.

In practical terms, experience has shown that it is difficult or impossible to suppress any set of ideas without endangering the whole fabric of free speech. The dividing line between totalitarian and racist speech, on the one hand, and "acceptable" speech, on the other, cannot be clearly drawn and thus is open to manipulation. The apparatus necessary to suppress a political movement—involving government investigation into beliefs and opinions, the compiling of dossiers, the employment of agents and informers—inevitably creates an atmosphere damaging freedom of all speech. Frequently actions ostensibly directed against the outlawed group are merely a pretext for harassment of unwanted political opposition. Most important, once the dike has been broken all unorthodox or minority opinion is in danger. The only safe course is to afford protection to all who wish to speak.

The Supreme Court, accepting the prevailing view, has consistently taken the position that antidemocratic forms of speech are within the coverage of the First Amendment. Thus, while upholding the conviction of the Communist party leaders under the Smith Act for advocating overthrow of the government by force and violence in DENNIS V. UNITED STATES (1951), the Court never suggested that the defendants were not entitled to the protection of the First Amendment. Likewise in BRANDENBURG V. OHIO (1969) racist speech by members of the Ku Klux Klan was given full First Amendment protection. The viewpoint taken by the Court was perhaps most dramatically formulated by Justice Holmes when he said in *Gitlow v. New York:* "If in the long run the beliefs expressed in proletarian dictatorship are destined to be accepted by the dominant forces of the country, the only meaning of free speech is that they should be given their chance and have their way."

It has also been contended that the coverage of the First Amendment should be limited to speech that relates to "political issues." Meiklejohn, who emphasized the role of the First Amendment in the process of self-government, advocated this interpretation, although he ultimately reached a broad definition of "political speech." Other commentators, arguing for a similar limitation, have adopted a far more restrictive concept of "political speech." The position has not, however, been accepted. For one thing, the proposed restriction has no inner logic; virtually all speech has political overtones or ramifications. In any event, there is no convincing reason for restricting the coverage of the First Amendment in this way. Speech concerned with literature, music, art, science, entertainment, ethics, and a host of other matters serves the functions sought by the First Amendment and should be equally entitled to its protection. The Supreme Court has consistently so held.

Other, narrower, categories of speech have also been said to be excluded from First Amendment coverage. In CHAPLINSKY V. NEW HAMPSHIRE (1942) the Supreme Court observed that restrictions on speech that was obscene, profane, libelous, or involved FIGHTING WORDS had "never been thought to raise any Constitutional problem." But this OBITER DICTUM has been eroded in the course of time. Obscenity is still, in theory, excluded from First Amendment protection; but in formulating the definition of "obscenity" the Court has brought constitutional considerations back into the decision. The exception for profanity has been disregarded. The dictum concerning libel has been expressly overruled. And the "fighting words" exemption, which has been narrowly construed to apply only to face-to-face encounters, turns more on the proposition that "fighting words" are not really speech at all than upon a concept of exclusion from First Amendment protection. Thus virtually all conduct that can be considered "speech" falls within the coverage of the First Amendment.

There are certain areas of speech where, although the First Amendment is applicable, the governing rules afford somewhat less protection than in the case of speech generally. These areas include speech in military institutions, which are not structured according to democratic principles, and speech by or addressed to children, who are "not possessed of that full capacity for individual choice which is the presupposition of First Amendment guarantees." COMMERCIAL SPEECH, that is, speech concerned solely with buying or selling goods or services for a profit, was at one time excluded from First Amendment protection. It is now covered by the First Amendment but is entitled to less stringent safeguards than noncommercial speech.

The most controversial aspect of the coverage question concerns not whether conduct that is recognized as speech is exempted from First Amendment protection but what conduct is to be considered speech and what is to be held non-speech, or "action," and hence not protected by the First Amendment. The resolution of this problem poses obvious difficulties. Clearly some verbal conduct, such as words exchanged in planning a CRIMINAL CONSPIRACY, does not constitute "speech" within the intention of the First Amendment. Likewise some nonverbal conduct, such as operating a printing press, is an integral part of the speech which it is the purpose of the First Amendment to protect. Some conduct, such as PICKETING, combines elements of speech and action.

Two approaches to this dilemma are possible. One is to attempt to define "speech" or "action" in light of the values and functions served by the First Amendment. The other is to abandon any effort at a sharp definition of "speech" and to hold that any conduct containing an "expressive element" is within the coverage of the First Amendment. The advantage of the first approach is that it allows the development of more clear-cut rules for protecting conduct found to be "speech," that is, all "speech" or most "speech" could be fully protected without the need for devising elaborate qualifications difficult to apply. The advantage of the second approach is that it avoids the necessity of making refined, and in some cases unpersuasive, distinctions between "speech" and "action." The Supreme Court has, on the whole, tended to follow the second path of analysis. However, in the overwhelming majority of cases where First Amendment protection is invoked, there is no serious question but that the conduct involved is properly classified as "speech."

The second major problem in interpreting and applying the First Amendment is the determination of what degree of protection from government interference, or encouragement by government, is to be afforded "speech." Most of the controversy over the meaning of the First Amendment has involved this issue. The Supreme Court has varied its approach from time to time and no consistent or comprehensive theory has emerged. The question arises in a great variety of situations, and only a brief summary of some of the principal results is possible.

The starting point is that, as a general proposition, the government cannot prohibit or interfere with speech because it objects to the content of the communication. Legitimate government interests must be achieved by methods other than the control of speech. Thus speech that is critical of the government or its officials, that interferes with government efficiency, that makes the attainment of consensus in the society more difficult, that urges radical change, or that affects similar societal interests cannot be abridged.

Somewhat less stringent rules have been applied where the speech is of such a character as to lead to concern that it will provoke violence or other violation of a valid law. Many of the Supreme Court decisions have involved issues of this nature, and a series of legal doctrines emerged. In the earlier cases, mostly growing out of legislation designed to prevent interference with the conduct of World War I or to suppress emerging radical political parties, the Court adopted a BAD TENDENCY TEST under which any speech that had a tendency to cause a violation of law could be punished. Such a test, of course, gives very little protection to nonconforming speech. Subsequently, on the initiative of Justices Holmes and LOUIS D. BRANDEIS, the Court accepted the CLEAR AND PRESENT DANGER TEST. Under this doctrine speech could be penalized only when it created a clear and present danger of some significant evil that the government had a right to prevent. In some cases the Court has used an ad hoc BALANCING TEST, by which the interest in freedom of speech is balanced against the social interest in maintaining order. Ultimately the Court appears to have settled upon the so-called *Brandenburg* test. "[T]he constitutional guarantees of free speech and free press," the Court said in *Brandenburg v. Ohio*, "do not permit a State to forbid or proscribe advocacy of the use of force or of law violation except where such advocacy is directed to inciting or producing imminent lawless action and is likely to incite or produce such action." An approach which attempts to separate "speech" from "action" and gives full protection to speech has never appealed to a majority of the Justices. But the Court has progressively tightened the originally loose restrictions on the government's power to punish militant political rhetoric.

In recent years the question has been posed in various forms whether or not speech can be curtailed where it may cause injury to NATIONAL SECURITY. The term "national security" has never been precisely defined and could of course include virtually every aspect of national life. Generally speaking it is clear that the usual First Amendment principles apply in national security cases; the society must seek to achieve national security by methods that do not abridge freedom of speech. Nevertheless, qualifications of the general rule have been urged with increasing vigor. The chief issues have involved publication of information alleged to jeopardize national security and the conduct of intelligence agencies seeking to acquire information relating to national security matters.

The Supreme Court in NEW YORK TIMES V. UNITED STATES (1971) (the Pentagon Papers case), a landmark decision in this area, rejected attempts by the government to enjoin the *New York Times* and the *Washington Post* from publishing a secret classified history of the VIETNAM WAR obtained illicitly by a former government employee, despite government claims that publication would cause "grave and irreparable injury" to the national security. The decision rested on the ground that the government had not met the "heavy burden of showing justification for the imposition of [a PRIOR] RESTRAINT." The majority were unable to agree, however, upon a single theory of the case. Three Justices thought that an INJUNCTION against publication of information should never, or virtually never, be allowed, but others, including the dissenters, would have accepted less rigorous standards. In *United States v. United States District Court* (1972), another critical decision in the national security area, the Court ruled that government intelligence agencies were bound to adhere to constitutional limitations (in that case the FOURTH AMENDMENT) in gathering information pertaining to national security, but it expressed no opinion as to "the issues which may be involved with respect to activities of foreign powers or their agents." The degree to which the Supreme Court will accept claims to national security as ground for qualifying First Amendment rights thus remains uncertain.

Cases where the exercise of free-speech rights runs into conflict with other social or individual interests frequently come before the Supreme Court. Interests invoked as ground for limiting speech have included the right of an accused person to obtain a FAIR TRIAL free from prejudice caused by adverse newspaper publicity; the interest of society in assuring fair elections through regulation of contributions and expenditures in political campaigns; the patriotic interest of the community in protecting the American flag against desecration by political dissenters; the aesthetic interests of the public in maintaining certain areas free from unsightly billboards; and many others. Where the countervailing interest is an appealing one the Court has tended to apply a balancing test: individual and social interests in freedom of speech are balanced against the opposing interests at stake. Likewise, where a government regulation is ostensibly directed at some other objective but has the effect of restricting speech, as in the case of government LOYALTY-SECURITY PROGRAMS or LEGISLATIVE INVESTIGATIONS, the balancing test is usually employed.

The balancing test has come to assume various forms. When most protective of free speech it requires that the government (1) has the burden of justifying any restriction on speech (2) by demonstrating "compelling" reasons and (3) showing that less intrusive means for advancing the government interest are not available. On the other hand, in some cases the balancing test is applied without giving any special weight to First Amendment considerations. The consequence of using a balancing test is that the outcome in any particular case is difficult to predict. Thus in BUCKLEY V. VALEO (1976) the Supreme Court held, in substance, that limitations on the amount of funds that can be contributed to a candidate in a political campaign are permissible but limitations on expenditures are not. Moreover, the balancing test is such a loose standard that, in times of stress, it might afford very little protection to freedom of speech. Thus far, however, the balances struck by the Court have given a substantial degree of support to free-speech rights.

Special rules for measuring the protection accorded speech have evolved in several areas. With respect to laws punishing obscene publications the Supreme Court, as noted above, still adheres to the theoretical position that obscenity is not covered by the First Amendment but it does take constitutional factors into account in determining whether or not a particular publication is obscene. As set forth in MILLER V. CALIFORNIA (1972), the current definition of obscenity is "(a) whether the average person, applying contemporary community standards, would find that the work, taken as a whole, appeals to the prurient interest; (b) whether the work depicts or describes, in a patently offensive way, sexual conduct specifically defined by the applicable state law; and (c) whether the work, taken as a whole, lacks serious literary, artistic, political, or scientific value." In practical application, as nearly as it can be articulated, the *Miller* test allows regulation only of "hard-core pornography."

The Supreme Court has also imposed substantive limitations upon actions for libel. Criminal libel laws have been narrowly construed and, although a GROUP LIBEL law was upheld in BEAUHARNAIS V. ILLINOIS (1952), subsequent developments have cast doubt upon the present validity of that decision. In the field of civil libel the Supreme Court held, in *New York Times v. Sullivan*, that public officials could maintain a suit for libel only when they can establish that a damaging statement about them was not only false but was made with "actual malice," that is, "with knowledge that it was false or with reckless disregard of whether it was false or not." Later the "actual malice" rule was extended to "public figures." As to others, namely "private individuals," the Court has held that the state or federal government could adopt any rule respecting libel so long as it required at least a showing of negligence on the part of the defendant. Although the Court in recent years has tended to take a narrow view of who is a "public figure," and the costs of defending libel actions frequently operate as a restraint upon speech, the curtailment of public discussion through libel laws has been somewhat held in check.

Constitutional doctrine for reconciling the right to freedom of speech with the RIGHT OF PRIVACY remains unformed. In most respects the two constitutional rights do not clash but rather supplement each other. Conflict may arise, however, at several points, such as where a communication contains information that is true, and hence is not covered by the libel laws, but relates to the intimate details of an individual's personal life that are not relevant to any issue of public concern. The scope of the constitutional right of privacy has never been clearly delineated. Nor has the Supreme Court ever held that the right of privacy prevails over the right to freedom of speech. Nevertheless the issue is a recurring one and sooner or later an accommodation between the two constitutional rights will have to be formulated.

The degree of protection afforded speech under the First Amendment may also hinge on various other factors. Where the physical facilities for communication are limited, and the government is therefore forced to allocate available facilities among those seeking to use them, the government has the power, indeed the obligation, to lay down certain conditions in order to assure that the scarce facilities will be used in the public interest. This is the situation with respect to radio and television BROADCASTING where, at least at the present time, the number of broadcast channels is limited. On this theory, government regulations such as the FAIRNESS DOCTRINE, requiring that broadcasting stations give adequate coverage to public issues and that such coverage be fair in accurately reflecting opposing views, have been upheld by the Supreme Court. Such regulatory powers, however, extend only to what might be termed a "macro level" of intervention. The government may require that a broadcasting station devote a certain proportion of its time to public interest programs, but it may not censor or determine the content of particular programs, that is, it may not exercise control at the "micro level."

Likewise special considerations enter when a person seeking to exercise rights to freedom of speech is an employee of the government or is confined in a government institution such as a mental hospital or a prison. Here the relationship of the individual to the government is somewhat different from the relationship of the ordinary citizen to the general community; the goals and interests of the particular institution involved are entitled to more immediate recognition. The Supreme Court has dealt with these issues by applying a balancing test, but the weights have been cast largely on the government side of the scales.

One further aspect of government attempts to regulate the content of speech should be noted. The letter and spirit of the EQUAL PROTECTION clause have had an important bearing upon the right to freedom of speech. The equal protection element guarantees the universality of the rules protecting the right to speak. It means that the government cannot differentiate, at least without a compelling reason, between speakers on the basis of the content of their communications. Hence if the government allows a patriotic organization to march down the main street of town it must grant equal opportunity to unpopular or radical organizations. If it grants the use of a public building for a meeting to a group of one political persuasion it must grant the same use to all political groups. This combination of the First Amendment and the equal protection clause thus helps to assure that unorthodox speech will receive the same treatment as conventional speech.

Apart from attempts to control the content of speech, government regulation has also dealt with various issues in the administration of the free speech system. Thus the requirement of a permit to hold a meeting in a public building, or to conduct a demonstration that may interfere with traffic, clearly constitutes a justifiable regulation. Likewise, a municipal ordinance may legitimately keep soundtrucks from operating in a residential area during certain hours of the night. It is frequently said that "time, place, and manner" restrictions on speech are permissible so long as they are "reasonable." Such generalizations, however, are overbroad. In many situations, "time, place, and manner" restrictions can be used to curtail freedom of speech to the same degree as content regulations. And to accord them all validity would be inconsistent with the basic premise that the right of free speech is entitled to a preferential position among competing interests. A more precise statement of the applicable legal doctrine would be to say that administrative regulations dealing with physical incompatibilities between the exercise of free speech rights and other interests are permissible. Thus government could validly allocate use of the streets between those seeking to hold a demonstration and those using the streets for passage. And the physical intrusion of noises from soundtrucks would also be subject to control. The principle for resolving such physical conflicts is not mere "reasonableness" but a fair accommodation between the competing interests.

Other legal doctrines play an important role in maintaining the system of freedom of speech. Thus the courts have held that the rules against undue VAGUENESS or OVERBREADTH in legislation or administrative regulation will be applied with special rigor where First Amendment rights are affected. And the prohibition in the Fourth Amendment against UNREASONABLE SEARCHES and seizures is given added force when invoked to protect freedom of speech. Perhaps the most significant supportive doctrine of this nature is the rule against prior restraint. Attempts by the government to prevent publication in advance, through a system of censorship, an injunction, or similar measures, are presumptively invalid and rarely allowed. Thus the silencing of speech before it is uttered—a par-

ticularly effective form of suppression—is normally not available as a method of control.

The constitutional doctrines thus far discussed have been of a negative character in that they have been directed against government interference with freedom of speech. In recent years, however, increasing attention has been given to questions relating to the affirmative side of the constitutional guarantee: to what extent does the First Amendment allow or require the government to encourage or promote a more effective system of free speech? These issues are important because of growing distortions within the system. More and more, as the mass media have become concentrated in fewer hands and have tended to express a single economic, social, and political point of view, the concept of a marketplace of diverse ideas has failed to conform to original expectations. The problems are difficult to solve because they involve using the government to expand freedom of speech while at the same time continuing to prohibit the government from controlling or inhibiting speech.

Not only does government itself engage in speech, for example, through schools and libraries and the statements of officials (see GOVERNMENT SPEECH), but government also promotes the freedom of speech in many ways. One of the most significant involves assuring access to the means of communication. The courts have gone some distance in recognizing the obligation of government to make facilities for communication available. Thus the courts have held that the streets, parks, and other public places must be open for meetings, parades, demonstrations, canvassing, and similar activities. Other public facilities have likewise been considered PUBLIC FORUMS and available, to the extent compatible with other uses, for free speech purposes. At one time the Supreme Court ruled that SHOPPING CENTERS and malls, privately owned but open to the public, could not exclude persons seeking to engage in speech activities. However, the Court later withdrew from this position. A very limited right of access to radio and television, justified by the scarcity principle, has been upheld. On the other hand, the Court has refused to allow a right of access to the columns of privately owned newspapers, on the grounds that intervention of this nature would destroy the independence of the publisher. Expansion of a right of access, without jeopardizing the rights of those already using the facilities of communication, remains a critical problem, the solution to which appears to depend more upon legislative than judicial action.

Affirmative governmental promotion of speech also takes the form of subsidies. Government contributions to educational, cultural, research, and other speech activities are widespread. Most of these subsidies have gone unchallenged in the courts. In *Buckley v. Valeo*, however, the Supreme Court did consider the constitutionality of legislation providing for the public financing of presidential election campaigns, upholding that measure upon the grounds that the use of "public money to facilitate and enlarge public discussion . . . furthers, not abridges, pertinent First Amendment values." The decision apparently accepts the basic validity of all government funding that can be found to promote public discussion. Nevertheless certain limitations on the power of government to finance nongovernment speech would seem to be clear. Thus government subsidy of religious speech would certainly be prohibited under the religion clauses of the First Amendment. And although the government would be free to choose at the "macro" level of intervention, that is, to determine the nature of the speech activity to be subsidized, it would have no power to intervene at the "micro" level, that is, to control the content of a particular communication. Likewise some rules against INVIDIOUS DISCRIMINATION, though giving government more leeway than when it is undertaking to regulate speech, would certainly apply. Development of these and other limiting principles, however, remains for the future.

Further support for affirmative promotion of speech rests on the constitutional doctrine of the RIGHT TO KNOW. The concept of a right to know includes not only the right of listeners and viewers to receive communications but also the right of those wishing to communicate to obtain information from the government. In earlier decisions the Supreme Court rejected right-to-know arguments that news reporters had a constitutional right to be admitted to prisons in order to observe conditions and interview inmates. But in RICHMOND NEWSPAPERS V. VIRGINIA (1980) the Court, changing directions, ruled that the public and the press could not be excluded from criminal trials, thereby holding for the first time that some right to obtain information from the government existed. How much further the Court will go in compelling the government to disclose information remains to be seen. Most likely the right of would-be speakers to obtain information from the government will continue to rest primarily upon FREEDOM OF INFORMATION and sunshine laws.

Efforts to expand and improve the system of free speech by affirmative governmental action, although they incur serious risks, remain essential to the continued vitality of the system. Major progress in this area will probably depend, however, more on legislative than judicial action.

The right to freedom of speech embodied in the First Amendment has expanded into an elaborate constitutional structure. This theoretical framework has some weaknesses. At some points it does not extend sufficient protection to speech, and at other places loosely formulated doctrine may not stand up in a crisis. On the whole, however, the legal structure provides the foundation for a workable system. The extent to which freedom of speech is actually realized in practice depends, of course, upon additional factors. The underlying political, economic, and social conditions must be favorable. Above all, freedom of speech, a sophisticated concept, must rest on public interest and understanding.

THOMAS I. EMERSON
(1986)

Bibliography

CHAFEE, ZECHARIAH, JR.   (1920) 1941   *Free Speech in the United States.* Cambridge, Mass.: Harvard University Press.
DORSEN, NORMAN et al.   1976   Emerson, Haber and Dorsen's *Political and Civil Rights in the United States,* 4th ed. Vol. 1. Boston: Little, Brown.
EMERSON, THOMAS I.   1970   *The System of Freedom of Expression.* New York: Random House.
HAIMAN, FRANKLYN S.   1981   *Speech and Law in a Free Society.* Chicago: University of Chicago Press.
HUDON, EDWARD G.   1963   *Freedom of Speech and Press in America.* Washington, D.C.: Public Affairs Press.
LEVY, LEONARD W.   1960   *Legacy of Suppression.* Cambridge, Mass.: Harvard University Press.
MEIKLEJOHN, ALEXANDER   (1948) 1960   *Political Freedom.* New York: Harper.
MILL, JOHN STUART   1859   *On Liberty,* R. B. McCallum, ed., London: Oxford University Press.
NIMMER, MELVILLE B.   1984   *Nimmer on Freedom of Speech.* New York: Mathew Bender.
REDISH, MARTIN H.   1984   *Freedom of Expression: A Critical Analysis.* Charlottesville, Va.: Michie Co.

FREEDOM OF SPEECH
(Update 1)

Although the Supreme Court decided almost thirty cases addressing freedom of speech issues between 1985 and 1989, most of these decisions merely reaffirmed or only modestly refined existing doctrine. Perhaps most important, the Court in this period continued to invoke its content-basedcontent-neutral distinction as a central precept of FIRST AMENDMENT jurisprudence. For purposes of this distinction, a content-based restriction may be defined as a law that limits speech because of the message it conveys. Laws that prohibit SEDITIOUS LIBEL, ban the publication of confidential information, or outlaw the display of the swastika in certain neighborhoods are examples of content-based restrictions. To test the constitutionality of such laws, the Court first determines whether the speech restricted occupies only "a subordinate position on the scale of First Amendment values." If so, the Court engages in a form of categorical balancing, through which it defines the precise circumstances in which each category of LOW-VALUE SPEECH may be restricted. In this manner, the Court deals with such speech as false statements of fact, commercial advertising, FIGHTING WORDS, and OBSCENITY. If the Court finds that the restricted speech does not occupy "a subordinate position on the scale of First Amendment values," it accords the speech virtually absolute protection. Indeed, outside the realm of low-value speech, the Court has invalidated almost every content-based restriction it has considered in the past thirty years.

Content-neutral restrictions, the other half of the content-basedcontent-neutral distinction, limit expression without regard to the content of the message conveyed. Laws that restrict noisy speeches near a hospital, ban billboards in residential communities, or limit campaign contributions are examples of content-neutral restrictions. In dealing with such restrictions, the Court engages in a relatively open-ended form of balancing: the greater the restriction's interference with the opportunities for free expression, the greater the government's burden of justification.

It may seem odd that the Court uses a stricter standard of review for content-based restrictions (other than those involving low-value speech) than for content-neutral restrictions, since both types of restrictions reduce the sum total of information or opinion disseminated. The explanation is that the First Amendment is concerned not only with the extent to which a law reduces the total quantity of communication but also—and perhaps even more fundamentally—with at least two additional factors: the extent to which a law distorts the content of public debate, and the likelihood that a law was enacted for the constitutionally impermissible motivation of suppressing or disadvantaging unpopular or "offensive" ideas. These two factors, which are more clearly associated with content-based than with content-neutral restrictions, explain both why the Court strictly scrutinizes content-based restrictions of high-value speech and why it does not apply that same level of scrutiny to all content-neutral restrictions. As indicated, most of the Court's decisions about freedom of speech from 1985 to 1989 reaffirmed this basic analytical structure.

Perhaps the two most important Supreme Court decisions in the realm of freedom of speech in this era were HUSTLER MAGAZINE V. FALWELL (1988) and *Texas v. Johnson* (1989). In *Hustler Magazine* the Court held that the First Amendment barred an action by the nationally known minister Jerry Falwell against *Hustler* magazine for a "parody" advertisement. The ad contained a fictitious interview with Falwell in which he allegedly said that he had first engaged in sex during a drunken rendezvous with his mother in an outhouse. The Court held that a public figure may not recover DAMAGES for the intentional infliction of emotional harm caused by the publication of even gross,

outrageous, and repugnant material. In *Johnson* the Court held that an individual may not constitutionally be prosecuted for burning the American flag as a peaceful political protest. The Court explained that "if there is a bedrock principle underlying the First Amendment, it is that the Government may not prohibit the expression of any idea simply because society finds the idea itself offensive or disagreeable." Justice ANTHONY M. KENNEDY observed in a concurring opinion, "It is poignant but fundamental that the flag protects those who hold it in contempt." In each of these decisions, the Court emphatically reaffirmed the central structure of free speech analysis and declined the invitation significantly to expand the concept of low-value speech.

Although *Hustler Magazine* and *Johnson* involved expansive interpretations of freedom of speech, in at least three other areas in this era the Court appreciably narrowed the scope of First Amendment protection. First, there is the issue of COMMERCIAL SPEECH. Although the Court once had held that commercial advertising is of such low value that it is entirely outside the protection of the First Amendment, the Court overturned that doctrine in 1974 and held that commercial advertising is entitled to substantial—though not full—First Amendment protection. Specifically, the Court held that government may not constitutionally ban the truthful advertising of lawfully sold goods and services on the "highly paternalistic" ground that potential consumers would be "better off" without such information. More recently, however, the Court has retreated from this position. Indeed, in POSADAS DE PUERTO RICO ASSOCS. V. TOURISM COMPANY OF PUERTO RICO (1986), which involved restrictions on advertising for lawful gambling activities, the Court held that even truthful advertising of lawful goods and services can be extensively regulated or banned in order to discourage "undesirable" patterns of consumption.

Second, the Court in recent years has increasingly granted broad authority to local governments to regulate expression that is sexually explicit, but not legally obscene. Although failing to classify sexually explicit expression as low-value speech, the Court has repeatedly sustained restrictions that curtail such expression in a discriminatory manner. In CITY OF RENTON V. PLAYTIME THEATRES (1986), for example, the Court upheld a city ordinance prohibiting adult-film theaters from locating within 1,000 feet of any residential zone, church, park, or school, even though this effectively excluded such theaters from more than 95 percent of the entire area of the city.

Third, in dealing with speech in "restricted environments," such as the military, prisons, and schools, which are not structured according to traditional democratic principles, the Court has increasingly deferred to the judgment of administrators in the face of claimed infringements of First Amendment rights. In BETHEL SCHOOL DIS-TRICT V. FRASER (1986), for example, the Court upheld the authority of a public high school to discipline a student for making a campaign speech that contained sexual innuendo; in HAZELWOOD SCHOOL DISTRICT V. KUHLMEIER (1988) the Court upheld the authority of a public high school principal to exclude from a student-edited school newspaper stories dealing with pregnancy and with the impact of divorce on students; in *Turner v. Safley* (1987) the Court upheld a prison regulation generally prohibiting correspondence between inmates at different institutions; and in *Thornburgh v. Abbott* (1989) the Court upheld a Federal Bureau of Prisons regulation authorizing wardens to prevent prisoners from receiving any publication found to be detrimental "to the security, good order or discipline of the institution." These decisions are in sharp contrast to earlier decisions that granted considerable protection to the freedom of speech even in such restricted environments. It should be noted that the Court's recent inclination to grant broad deference to administrative authority is evident not only in its restricted environment decisions but also in decisions dealing with PUBLIC FORUMS and with the speech of PUBLIC EMPLOYEES.

Although not involving the Supreme Court, there was extensive debate and activity with respect to several other free speech issues between 1985 and 1989. First, there has been considerable controversy concerning the law of LIBEL AND THE FIRST AMENDMENT. In NEW YORK TIMES V. SUL-LIVAN (1964) the Court held that in order to prevent the chilling of "uninhibited, robust and wide-open" debate, public officials could not recover for libel without proof that the libelous statements were false and that they were published with a knowing or reckless disregard of the truth. In recent years, critics have maintained that *New York Times* not only has prevented injured plaintiffs from obtaining judicial correction of published falsehoods but also has produced excessive damage awards against publishers. These critics argue that *New York Times* has thus effectively sacrificed legitimate dignitary interests of the victims of libel without protecting the "uninhibited, robust, and wide-open" debate the rule was designed to promote. Such criticism has provoked a wide range of proposals at both the state and national levels for either judicial or legislative reform. The most common and most intriguing of these proposals calls for the recognition of a civil action for a declaration of falsity, which would require no showing of fault on the part of the publisher but would authorize no award of damages to the plaintiff.

A second area that has generated increased attention in recent years concerns the advent and expansion of cable television. REGULATORY AGENCIES and state and federal courts have confronted a broad range of issues arising out of the cable revolution, including the regulation of sexually explicit programming, the applicability of political "fairness" principles, the constitutionality of mandatory access and "must carry" rules, the regulation of subscription rates and franchise fees, and the constitutionality of government restrictions on the number of cable systems. Most fundamentally, the expansion of cable television may ultimately undermine the "scarcity" rationale for government regulation of radio and television BROADCASTING.

Perhaps the most interesting and most controversial development in recent years relating to freedom of speech concerns the issues of obscenity and PORNOGRAPHY. Sixteen years after the 1970 Report of the Commission on Obscenity and Pornography, which found "no evidence that exposure to explicit sexual materials plays a significant role in the causation of delinquent or criminal behavior," a new government commission, the Attorney General's Commission on Pornography, concluded that there is indeed a causal relationship between exposure to sexually violent material and aggressive behavior toward women. This conclusion, which stirred immediate controversy among social scientists, led the 1986 commission to recommend additional legislation at both the state and federal levels and more aggressive enforcement of existing antiobscenity laws.

In a related development, many feminists in recent years have actively supported a more extensive regulation of pornography. Distinguishing "obscenity," which offends conventional standards of morality, from "pornography," which subordinates women, such feminists as Catharine MacKinnon and Andrea Dworkin have proposed legislation that would restrict the sale, exhibition, and distribution of pornography, which they define as "'the sexually explicit subordination of women, graphically depicted, in which women are presented dehumanized as sexual objects, as sexual objects who enjoy pain, humiliation or rape, as sexual objects tied up, or cut up or mutilated or physically hurt, or as whores by nature."

This type of legislation poses a profound challenge to free speech. Opponents maintain that these laws constitute censorship in its worst form and that they are nothing less than blatant attempts to suppress specific points of view because they offend some citizens.Supporters of such legislation maintain that pornography is of only low First Amendment value, that it causes serious harm by shaping attitudes and behaviors of violence and discrimination toward women, and that it is futile to expect "counter-speech" to be an appropriate and sufficient response to such material. Although the courts that have considered the constitutionality of this kind of legislation have thus far held it incompatible with freedom of speech, the pornography issue will no doubt continue to generate constructive debate about the occasionally competing values of equality, dignity, and freedom of speech for some time to come.

GEOFFREY R. STONE
(1992)

(SEE ALSO: *Balancing Test; Child Pornography; Dial-a-Porn; Feminist Theory; Flag Desecration; Pornography and Feminism.*)

Bibliography

BOLLINGER, LEE C.   1986   *The Tolerant Society: Freedom of Speech and Extremist Speech in America.* Oxford: Clarendon Press.

KALVEN, HARRY, JR.   1988   *A Worthy Tradition: Freedom of Speech in America.* New York: Harper & Row.

STONE, GEOFFREY R. et al.   1986   *Constitutional Law,* Chap. 7. Boston: Little, Brown.

FREEDOM OF SPEECH
(Update 2)

Questions about freedom of speech can be divided into questions of coverage (or scope) and questions of protection (or strength). The question of coverage is the question, logically primary, whether some act, event, behavior, state of affairs, or case is indeed a free speech case at all. The question of protection, which follows, is the question of how much protection against legislative, executive, or judicial control an act has by virtue of the decision that it is an act covered by the concept of freedom of speech and thus covered by the free speech clause of the FIRST AMENDMENT.

In the earlier years of American free speech theory and adjudication, questions of protection were overwhelmingly more important than questions of coverage. Although it may seem that this reverses the logical relationship between coverage and protection, the initial focus on the degree of protection, primarily from the period between 1919 and 1969, was premised on the implicit understanding that the coverage of the free speech clause of the First Amendment was well-understood and non-controversial. With virtually no question, free speech during this period, starting with such 1919 cases as SCHENCK V. UNITED STATES (1919) and ABRAMS V. UNITED STATES (1919) and then going through McCarthy-era cases such as DENNIS V. UNITED STATES (1951) and culminating with the incitement standard set forth in BRANDENBURG V. OHIO (1969), was widely understood to be largely restricted to attempted governmental interference with individual or otherwise nongovernmentally-sponsored acts of political,

moral, social, religious, and ideological expression. The only questions raised were ones about the degree of the protection afforded to such acts, as with, for example, the debates about "CLEAR AND PRESENT DANGER" in *Schenck* and the "gravity of the evil discounted by its improbability" standard in *Dennis*. The 1969 Supreme Court decision in *Brandenburg*, which set forth the current (and extremely stringent) test for restrictions on the advocacy of unlawful conduct, can best be seen as the culmination of an era in which the primary focus was on the degree of protection.

In an intriguing inversion of the expected order of analysis, it is only recently that the focus has turned away from the degree of protection and toward the scope of coverage. This focus on coverage can be divided into two categories, the first being the nature of the behavior and the second being the nature of the restriction.

As to the nature of the behavior, consider first the question of so-called COMMERCIAL SPEECH, or, more precisely, the question whether pure commercial advertisements, such as the typical advertisement for a product which describes the product and urges consumers to buy it, fall within the coverage of the First Amendment. The Court first answered this question in the affirmative in VIRGINIA STATE BOARD OF PHARMACY V. VIRGINIA CONSUMERS COUNCIL (1976) and has continued, even in the wake of intense criticism, to hold ever since, as in *Rubin v. Coors Brewing Co.* (1995) and *44 Liquormart, Inc. v. Rhode Island* (1996). And if commercial advertising is covered by the First Amendment, does this entail the conclusion that something like the registration provisions of the federal SECURITIES LAWS, which condition lawful publication of a written offer to sell securities—"speech" in the literal sense of that word—upon prior approval by a government agency based on the agency's determination that the speech is neither false nor misleading, represent an unconstitutional PRIOR RESTRAINT? Thus, the decision to expand the coverage of the First Amendment into areas hitherto thought to have nothing whatsoever to do with the First Amendment implicates questions about the extent of the protection to be available within the expanded coverage. Not implausibly, it is often argued, as Justice LEWIS F. POWELL, JR., did in a commercial speech case, *Ohralik v. Ohio State Bar Association* (1978), that continually expanding the coverage of the First Amendment risks diluting the strength of its protection.

Similar issues arise in the context of criminal solicitation. In the United States, it is well-accepted after *Brandenburg* that, for example, speaking to a large crowd about the moral necessity of disobeying conscription under the SELECTIVE SERVICE ACTS is a central free speech case. But if the size of the audience is reduced, the nature of the crime is changed, and the explicit advocacy subjugated to the provision of information, plans, or instructions, is the conclusion the same? To take a different example, if one person tells three others in a private room that the combination to the company president's safe is 37 left, 14 right, 22 left, the case looks far less like one in which free speech analysis is even relevant. And if this kind of situation is thought even to raise free speech concerns (it is, after all, the verbal transmittal of information desired by the recipient), is there then a risk that this dilutes First Amendment protection and trivializes the ideological core of the idea of freedom of speech?

As a final example, consider the employer who repeatedly makes sexually suggestive remarks to one of his employees. Is the application of WORKPLACE HARASSMENT law in this context subject to free speech constraints, or is this a context, as the Court has obliquely suggested by refusing even to mention free speech concerns in *Harris v. Forklift Systems, Inc.* (1993) (a verbal harassment case in which free speech issues had been briefed and argued), which is no more related to the First Amendment than are the registration provisions of the Securities Act of 1933? The employer in this case is, literally, speaking, and thus to hold the employer legally liable because of his conduct would appear to some to be a restriction on the employer's First Amendment rights. But, on the other hand, the closed environment of the workplace, the one-on-one nature of the speech, the typical lack of anything resembling ideological or political fact or argument, and the frequent similarity between unwanted verbal sexual advances and unwanted sexual touching have led others, including, it appears, the Court, to concluded that a large number of sexual harassment cases, even ones involving mostly or solely verbal conduct, still do not raise important free speech issues, and are thus uncovered by the First Amendment.

Similarly difficult questions about the boundaries of the First Amendment are presented when the issue is not about the nature of the behavior, as in the previous examples, but about the nature (rather than the degree) of the restriction. With respect to the nature of the restriction, in the traditional free speech case the state seeks to restrict the speech of someone, like Clarence Brandenburg or *The New York Times* or the Philip Morris Corporation or the flag desecrator in *United States v. Eichman* (1990), who wishes to communicate largely with his, her, or its own resources, and on his, her, or its own time. In numerous other contexts, however, this model does not reflect the issues that with increasing frequency are characterized in free speech or "censorship" terms.

Consider, for example, the issue of government funding for the arts. Under one view, the decision by the government about which artistic endeavors to fund raises no free speech question at all. Thus, to take some recent examples, if government funding were withheld from the homoerotic photographs of Robert Mapplethorpe because of their sexually explicit content, or from the blasphemous art of Andres Serrano because it offended people's religious beliefs, or from an exhibition that featured disrespectful images of the American flag, the concept of free speech—the coverage of the First Amendment—would not be implicated because Mapplethorpe, Serrano, and the flag desecrators would remain free to say, publish, and photograph whatever they wished, including the offending works, as long as they did so without the financial support of the state. The abortion-counseling decision in RUST V. SULLIVAN (1991) would support this conclusion. In addition, the argument continues, funding for the arts inevitably involves choices about what to fund and what not to fund. The First Amendment would not require the government to fund bad art, or render unconstitutional a Nebraska program for funding Nebraska artists. As a result, it is said, the choices that are inevitably a part of the decision to fund or sponsor public art lie well outside of the coverage of the First Amendment.

There is an argument on the other side, however, which would distinguish permissible from impermissible refusals to fund on the basis of whether the refusal was based on the form of government viewpoint-discrimination, which is inimical to the First Amendment in a wide variety of contexts. An example is ROSENBERGER V. RECTOR AND VISITORS OF THE UNIVERSITY OF VIRGINIA (1995), involving state funding of college newspapers. Although government might choose not to fund bad art because of its "badness," or even possibly (as long as it was not a pretense for viewpoint discrimination) refuse to fund art dealing with the flag, it cannot, having decided to fund art dealing with the flag, fund art that treats the flag respectfully but not art treating the flag disrespectfully. This strikes at the core of the First Amendment, and thus presents a clearly covered First Amendment case, even though it is about how the state chooses to allocate its "own" resources.

Similar issues arise in the context of library book selection, where some would argue, again, that the entire enterprise is not covered by the First Amendment because the question is one about state expenditure of state resources and not about state restriction of private conduct. But others, as with the arts funding example, maintain that to remove a book, or to refuse to select a book, solely because of its point of view (as with some recent controversies involving challenges to books that were sympathetic to gay and lesbian lifestyles), is to bring in the First Amendment, which, as R. A. V. V. CITY OF ST. PAUL (1992) reminds us, is as concerned about viewpoint-based restrictions as it is about total prohibitions.

Most commonly, this variety of question about the coverage of the First Amendment comes up in the context of government employment. As with the other examples, one side of the argument maintains that no one is obliged to take government employment, and that for the state to restrict the speech of its employees, especially when they are in the very process of doing their job (as with teachers while actually teaching), is an inevitable part of the employer–employee relationship, and no part of the concept of freedom of speech. But on the other side is once again the argument against viewpoint-based restrictions, holding that it is one thing to tell a teacher that he or she must teach history and not mathematics (a much more permissible subject-matter distinction), and quite another, and one with serious First Amendment implications, to tell a teacher that he or she must teach one view of how to interpret a particular historical event to the exclusion of another.

In none of these cases is the existing legal DOCTRINE clear. With respect to teachers, for example, the courts appear to accept a fair amount of even viewpoint discrimination at the level of the primary and secondary schools, reasoning that the state may have a viewpoint, that the state may teach this viewpoint to its students, and that the state may compel its voluntary employees to serve as its agents in this task. At the college and university level, however, the doctrine is largely to the contrary, holding that both the free speech rights of the teachers and the First Amendment's commitment to the university classroom as an important forum for the MARKETPLACE OF IDEAS urge a moderately extensive amount of First Amendment– based judicial oversight. Similar distinctions apply to library book choices, where courts have been more willing to scrutinize removals than initial selections, as in BOARD OF EDUCATION V. PICO (1982), and arts funding, where a recent Supreme Court decision, *National Endowment for the Arts v. Finley* (1998), suggests that some of the most extreme forms of viewpoint discrimination might be subject to invalidation.

The larger issue raised by arts funding, by library book choices, and by restrictions on employee speech is again the question of the coverage of the First Amendment. Will cases like these be seen as instances of inevitable speech restriction and beyond the boundaries of the First Amendment, or will they instead be understood as recognizing that the First Amendment is relevant in previously untouched areas, and that the coverage of the First Amendment is becoming broader than historically understood. As with the expansion of coverage on the basis of the nature of the speech, the expansion of the coverage based on the context of the restriction is likely to be the dominant question of free speech in the decades to come, as courts and others wrestle with the question of the range of human conduct, obviously far less than the full universe of verbal, written, linguistic, and symbolic behavior, to which the First Amendment is even relevant. This is the question of coverage, and this is the question that unites the vast majority of the most important of current and likely future First Amendment controversies.

FREDERICK SCHAUER
(2000)

(SEE ALSO: *Anonymous Political Speech; Attorney Speech; Campaign Finance; Compelled Speech; Electoral Process and the First Amendment; Employee Speech Rights (Private); Free Speech and RICO; Libel and the First Amendment.*)

Bibliography

ALEXANDER, LAWRENCE A. 1989 Low Value Speech. *Northwestern University Law Review* 83:547–581.

ESTLUND, CYNTHIA L. 1990 Speech on Matters of Public Concern: The Perils of an Emerging First Amendment Category. *George Washington Law Review* 59:1–46.

—— 1997 The Architecture of the First Amendment and the Case of Workplace Harassment. *Notre Dame Law Review* 72:1361–1390.

GREENAWALT, R. KENT 1989 *Speech, Crime, and the Uses of Language.* New York: Oxford University Press.

LEFF, THOMAS P. 1995 The Arts: A Traditional Sphere of Free Expression?: First Amendment Implications of Government Funding to the Arts in the Aftermath of *Rust v. Sullivan. American University Law Review* 45:353–391.

SABRIN, AMY 1993 Thinking About Content: Can It Play an Appropriate Role in Government Funding of the Arts? *Yale Law Journal* 102:1209–1232.

SCHAUER, FREDERICK 1981 Categories and the First Amendment: A Play in Three Acts. *Vanderbilt Law Review* 34:265–305.

—— 1988 Commercial Speech and the Architecture of the First Amendment. *University of Cincinnati Law Review* 56:1181–1204.

—— 1988 Principles, Institutions and the First Amendment. *Harvard Law Review* 112:84–120.

SHIFFRIN, STEVEN H. 1983 The First Amendment and Economic Regulation: Away From a General Theory of the First Amendment. *Northwestern University Law Review* 78:1212–1257.

WILLIAMS, SUSAN H. 1991 Content Discrimination and the First Amendment. *University of Pennsylvania Law Review* 139:615–654.

FREEDOM OF SPEECH, LEGISLATOR'S

See: Legislative Immunity; Speech or Debate Clause

FREEDOM OF THE PRESS

The constitutional basis for freedom of the press in the United States is the FIRST AMENDMENT, which provides: "Congress shall make no law . . . abridging the FREEDOM OF SPEECH, or of the press, or the right of the people peaceably to assemble, and to petition the Government for a redress of grievances." In a constitutional interpretation the separate rights enumerated in the First Amendment are merged into a composite right to freedom of expression. Within this general system freedom of the press focuses on the right to publish. Originally concerned with the product of printing presses—newspapers, periodicals, books, pamphlets, and broadsides—the term "press" now includes the electronic media. In general the constitutional issues involving freedom of the press are similar to those pertaining to other aspects of freedom of expression. However, certain areas are of special interest to the press, particularly to the mass media.

Freedom of the press has its roots in English history. When printing presses were introduced into England at the end of the fifteenth century they were quickly brought under total official control. Through a series of royal proclamations, Parliamentary enactments, and Star Chamber decrees a rigid system of censorship was established. No material could be printed unless it was first approved by a state or ecclesiastical official. Further, no book could be imported or sold without a license; all printing presses were required to be registered; the number of master printers was limited; and sweeping powers to search for contraband printed matter were exercised. (See PRIOR RESTRAINT AND CENSORSHIP.)

In 1695, when the then current licensing law expired, it was not renewed and the system of advance censorship was abandoned. The laws against SEDITIOUS LIBEL remained in effect, however. Under the libel law any criticism of the government or its officials, or circulation of information that reflected adversely upon the government, regardless of truth or falsity, was punishable by severe criminal penalties. Sir WILLIAM BLACKSTONE, summarizing the English law as it existed when he published his *Commentaries* in 1769, put it in these terms: "The liberty of the press is indeed essential to the nature of a free state; but this consists in laying no *previous* restraints upon public actions, and not in freedom from censure for criminal matter when published. Every free man has an undoubted right to lay what sentiments he pleases before the public; to forbid this, is to destroy the freedom of the press; but if he publishes what is improper, mischievous or illegal, he must take the consequences of his own temerity."

Developments in the American colonies followed those in England. Censorship laws existed in some of the colonies well into the eighteenth century. Likewise, prosecutions for seditious libel were not uncommon. in both England and America, however, there was strong opposition to the seditious libel laws. Thus in the famous ZENGER'S CASE, where the publisher of a newspaper was prosecuted for printing satirical ballads reflecting upon the governor of New York and his council, the defense argued vigorously (but unsuccessfully) that truth should be a defense, and urged the jury (successfully) to give a general verdict of not guilty.

The law was in this state of flux when the First Amendment, with its guarantee of freedom of the press, was added to the Constitution in 1791. The specific intention of the Framers was never made explicit. It is generally agreed that the First Amendment was designed to make unconstitutional any system of advance censorship of the press, or "prior restraint," but its impact upon the law of seditious libel has been the subject of controversy. The latter issue was brought into sharp focus when the ALIEN AND SEDITION ACTS, which did include a modified seditious libel law, were enacted by Congress in 1798. Prosecutions under the Sedition Act were directed largely at editors of the press. The constitutionality was upheld by a number of trial judges, including some members of the Supreme Court sitting on circuit, but the issues never reached the Supreme Court. The lapse of the Alien and Sedition Acts after two years ended public attention to the problem for the time being.

For well over a century, although freedom of the press was at times not realized in practice, the constitutional issues did not come before the Supreme Court in any major decision. This situation changed abruptly after WORLD WAR I as the Court confronted a series of First Amendment problems. Two of these early cases were of paramount importance for freedom of the press. In NEAR V. MINNESOTA (1931) the Court considered the validity of the so-called Minnesota Gag Law. This statute provided that any person "engaged in the business" of regularly publishing or circulating an "obscene, lewd and lascivious" or a "malicious, scandalous and defamatory" newspaper or periodical was "guilty of a nuisance," and could be enjoined from further committing or maintaining such a nuisance. The Court held that the statutory scheme constituted a "prior restraint" and hence was invalid under the First Amendment. The Court thus established as a constitutional principle the doctrine that, with some narrow exceptions, the government could not censor or otherwise prohibit a publication in advance, even though the communication might be punishable after publication in a criminal or other proceeding. In a second decision, GROSJEAN V. AMERICAN PRESS CO. (1936), the Court struck down a Louisiana statute, passed to advance the political interest of Senator Huey Long, that imposed a two percent tax on the gross receipts of newspapers and periodicals with circulations in excess of 20,000 a week. The *Grosjean* decision assured the press that it could not be subjected to any burden, in the guise of ECONOMIC REGULATION, that was not imposed generally upon other enterprises.

In the years since *Near* and *Grosjean* an elaborate body of legal doctrine, interpreting and applying the First Amendment right to freedom of the press in a variety of situations, has emerged. Before we turn to a survey of this constitutional structure, two preliminary matters need to be considered.

First, the functions that freedom of the press performs in a democratic society are, in general, the same as those served by the system of freedom of expression as a whole. Freedom of the press enhances the opportunity to achieve individual fulfillment, advances knowledge and the search for understanding, is vital to the process of self-government, and facilitates social change by the peaceful interchange of ideas. More particularly the press has been conceived as playing a special role in informing the public and in monitoring the performance of government. Often referred to as the "fourth estate," or the fourth branch of government, an independent press is one of the principal institutions in our society that possesses the resources and the capacity to confront the government and other centers of established authority. This concept of a free press was forcefully set forth by Justice HUGO L. BLACK in his opinion in NEW YORK TIMES CO. V. UNITED STATES (1971) (the Pentagon Papers case): "In the First Amendment the Founding Fathers gave the free press the protection it must have to fulfill its essential role in our democracy. The press was to serve the governed, not the governors. The Government's power to censor the press was abolished so that the press would remain forever free to censure the Government. The press was protected so that it could bare the secrets of government and inform the people. Only a free and unrestrained press can effectively expose deception in government."

A second preliminary issue is whether the fact that the First Amendment specifically refers to freedom "of the press," in addition to "freedom of speech," means that the press is entitled to a special status, or special protection, different from that accorded other speakers. It has been suggested that the First Amendment should be so construed. Thus Justice POTTER STEWART has argued that the Framers of the Constitution intended to recognize "the organized press," that is, "the daily newspapers and other established news media," as "a fourth institution outside the Government," serving as "an additional check on the three official branches." As such an institution, he suggested, the press was entitled to enjoy not only "freedom of speech," available to all, but an additional right to "freedom of the press." Some commentators have echoed Justice Stewart's argument.

There are obvious drawbacks to according a special status to the "organized press." It is difficult to draw a line between "the press" and others seeking to communicate through the written or spoken word, such as scholars, pamphleteers, or publishers of "underground" newspapers. Nor are there persuasive reasons for affording the one greater advantages than the other. Any attempt to differentiate would merely tend to reduce the protection given the "nonorganized" publisher. In any event the Supreme Court has never accepted the distinction.

However, there are some situations where the capacities and functions of the "organized press" are taken into account. Thus where there are physical limitations on access to the sources of information, as where a courtroom has only a limited number of seats, or only a limited number of reporters can ride on the President's airplane, representatives of the "organized press" may legitimately be chosen to convey the news to the general public. Beyond this point, however, the rights of the "organized press" to freedom of expression are the same as those of any writer or speaker.

The constitutional issues that have been of most concern to the press fall into two major categories. One involves the constraints that may be placed upon the publication of material by the press. The other relates to the rights of the press in gathering information.

On the whole the press has won its battle against the law of seditious libel. The Sedition Act of 1798 has never been revived. In NEW YORK TIMES CO. V. SULLIVAN (1964) the Supreme Court, declaring that the Sedition Act violated the central meaning of the First Amendment, said: "Although the Sedition Act was never tested in this Court, the attack upon its validity has carried the day in the court of history." Many states still retain criminal libel laws upon the books, but they have been so limited by the Supreme Court as to be largely inoperative. Even vigorous attacks upon the courts for their conduct in pending cases, traditionally a sensitive matter, are not punishable unless they present a CLEAR AND PRESENT DANGER to the administration of justice. (See CONTEMPT POWER.) Only the civil libel laws impose restrictions. The result is that the press is free to criticize the government, its policies, and its officials, no matter how harsh, vituperative, or unfair such criticism may be. Likewise it is free to publish information about governmental matters, even though incorrect, subject only to civil liability for false statements knowingly or recklessly made.

The extent to which the press can be prevented from

publishing material claimed to be injurious to NATIONAL SECURITY has become a matter of controversy in recent years. The issues are crucial to the operation of a democratic system. Clearly there are some areas, particularly those relating to tactical military operations, where government secrecy is justified. On the other hand, the process of self-government cannot go on unless the public is fully informed about matters pending decision. Moreover, the very concept of "national security," or "national defense," is virtually open-ended, capable of covering a vast area of crucial information. Hence any constitutional doctrine allowing the government to restrict the flow of information alleged to harm national security would be virtually without limits. In addition, claims of danger to national security can be, and have been, employed to hide incompetence, mistaken judgments, and even corruption on the part of government officials in power.

For these reasons no general statutory ban on the publication of material deemed to have an adverse effect upon national security has ever been enacted by Congress. Laws directed at traditional espionage do, of course, exist. And Congress has passed legislation, thus far untested, instituting controls in certain very narrow areas. Thus the Intelligence Identities Protection Act (1982) forbids disclosure of any information that identifies an individual as the covert agent of an agency engaged in foreign intelligence. Beyond this, however, statutory controls on freedom of the press in the national security area have never been attempted. Even during wartime, censorship of press reporting on information pertaining to military operations has taken place only on a voluntary basis.

The constitutional authority of the government to restrict the publication of national security information was considered by the Supreme Court in the Pentagon Papers case. There the government sought an INJUNCTION against the *New York Times* and the *Washington Post* to prevent the publication of a government-prepared history of United States involvement in the Vietnam War. The documents had been classified as secret but were furnished to the newspapers by a former government employee who had copied them. The government contended that publication of the Pentagon Papers would result in "grave and irreparable injury" to the United States.

The Supreme Court ruled, 6–3, that the attempt at prior restraint could not stand, concluding that the government had not met "the heavy burden of showing justification for the imposition of such a restraint." Several theories of the right of the government to prohibit the publication of national security information emerged, none of which commanded a majority of the Court. At one end of the spectrum Justices Black and WILLIAM O. DOUGLAS thought that the government possessed no power to "make laws enjoining publication of current news and

abridging freedom of the press in the name of "national security." Justice WILLIAM J. BRENNAN held the same view, except that he would have allowed the government to stop publication of information that "must inevitably, directly and immediately cause the occurrence of an event kindred to imperiling the safety of a transport already at sea." Justices Stewart and BYRON WHITE believed that a prior restraint was permissible if the government could demonstrate "direct, immediate, and irreparable damage to our Nation or its people," a showing they concluded had not been made in the case before them. Justice THURGOOD MARSHALL, not passing on the First Amendment issues, took the position that, in the absence of express statutory authority, the government had no power to invoke the JURISDICTION OF THE FEDERAL COURTS to prevent the publication of national security information. At the other end of the spectrum Chief Justice WARREN E. BURGER and Justices JOHN M. HARLAN and HARRY L. BLACKMUN, the dissenters, urged that the function of the judiciary in reviewing the actions of the executive branch in the area of FOREIGN AFFAIRS should be narrowly restricted and that in such situations the Court should not attempt "to redetermine for itself the probable impact of disclosure on national security."

The result in the Pentagon Papers case was a significant victory for the press. Had the decision gone the other way the road would have been open for the government to prevent publication of any material when it could plausibly assert that national security was significantly injured. Yet the failure of the Court to agree upon a constitutional doctrine to govern in national security cases left the press vulnerable in future situations. Moreover, the issues were limited to an effort by the government to impose a prior restraint. The Justices did not address the question whether, if appropriate legislation were enacted, a criminal penalty or other subsequent punishment for publication of national security information would be valid.

In two subsequent cases the Supreme Court revealed some reluctance to restrict the executive branch in its efforts to control the publication of information relating to foreign intelligence. In SNEPP V. UNITED STATES (1980) the Court upheld an injunction to enforce an agreement, which the Central Intelligence Agency required each of its employees to sign, that the employee would not publish any information or material relating to the agency, either during or after employment, without the advance approval of the agency. The Court treated the issue primarily as one of private contract law; it dealt with First Amendment questions only in a footnote, saying that the government has "a compelling interest in protecting both the secrecy of information important to our national security and the appearance of confidentiality so essential to effective operation of our foreign intelligence service." Likewise in

HAIG V. AGEE (1981) the Court upheld the action of the secretary of state in revoking the passport of a former CIA employee traveling abroad, on the grounds that he was causing "serious damage to the national security [and] foreign policy of the United States" by exposing the names of undercover CIA officers and agents. The constitutional RIGHT TO TRAVEL abroad, said the majority opinion, is "subordinate to national security and foreign policy considerations," adding that [m]atters intimately related to foreign policy and national security are rarely proper subjects for judicial intervention." Unless these later decisions are limited to their somewhat unusual facts, the right of the press to publish national security information that the government wishes to keep secret could be sharply curtailed.

Civil libel laws have also been a matter of paramount concern to the press. For many years it was assumed that the First Amendment was not intended to restrict the right of any person, under COMMON LAW or statute, to bring a suit for damages to reputation arising out of false and defamatory statements. In its well-known OBITER DICTUM in CHAPLINSKY V. NEW HAMPSHIRE (1942) the Supreme Court had declared that there were "certain well-defined and narrowly limited classes of speech," including the "libelous," which had never been thought to raise any constitutional problem.

In time it became clear, however, that libel laws could be used to impair freedom of the press and other First Amendment rights. In 1964 the issue came before the Supreme Court in New York Times Co. v. Sullivan. In that case the commissioner of public affairs in Montgomery, Alabama, sued the New York Times for publication of an advertisement, paid for by a New York group called the Committee to Defend Martin Luther King, which criticized certain actions of the police in dealing with CIVIL RIGHTS activity in Montgomery. Some of the statements in the advertisement were not factually correct. The Alabama state courts, after a jury trial, awarded the police commissioner $500,000 in damages. The majority opinion of the Court, stating that "libel can claim no talismanic immunity from constitutional limitations," went on to say: "Thus we consider this case against the background of a profound national commitment to the principle that debate on public issues should be uninhibited, robust, and wide-open, and that it may well include vehement, caustic, and sometimes unpleasantly sharp attacks on government and public officials." The Court ruled that public officials could recover damages in a libel action only if they could prove that a false and defamatory statement was made with "actual malice," that is, "with knowledge that it was false or with reckless disregard of whether it was false or not." Three Justices would have gone further and given the press full protection against libel suits regardless of proof of actual malice.

The "actual malice" rule for reconciling First Amendment rights with the libel laws was extended in 1967 to suits brought by "public figures," and in 1971 to all suits involving matters "of public or general interest." At this point it appeared that, although a majority of the Supreme Court had not gone the full distance, the press did have substantial protection against harassing libel suits. Weaknesses in the press position, however, soon developed. In 1974 the Court, changing directions, held that, apart from cases involving "public officials" and "public figures," libel laws would be deemed to conform to First Amendment standards so long as they did not impose liability in the absence of negligence. Moreover, the Court greatly narrowed the definition of "public figure," holding in one case that a person convicted of contempt of court for refusing to appear before a GRAND JURY investigating espionage was not a "public figure." In addition, juries in some cases began to award large sums in damages, legal expenses skyrocketed, and the costs in time and money of defending libel suits, even where the defense was successful, often became a heavy burden. By the same token, persons or organizations without substantial resources found it difficult to finance libel actions.

Efforts to dispose of unjustified libel suits at an early stage by motions to dismiss received a setback from the Supreme Court in HERBERT V. LANDO (1979). Lieutenant Colonel Anthony Herbert brought a libel suit against Columbia Broadcasting System because of a program on "60 Minutes" which suggested that Herbert had falsely accused his superior officers of covering up war crimes. Conceding he was a "public figure" and had to show "actual malice," Herbert sought in DISCOVERY proceedings to inquire into the mental states and editorial processes of the CBS officials who were responsible for the program. The Court held that, despite the CHILLING EFFECT of such probing and the resulting protraction of libel proceedings, the right to make such inquiries was inherent in the "actual malice" rule. The result of the Herbert case has been to diminish substantially the value to the press of the "actual malice" doctrine.

Because of these considerations, sections of the press as well as some commentators have urged that libel laws are incompatible with the First Amendment and should be abolished, at least where matters of public interest are under discussion. The courts, however, have shown no disposition to follow this course. The solution most in accord with First Amendment principles would be to provide for a right of reply by the person aggrieved. Yet this poses other difficulties. The press argues, with considerable justification, that it would be impossible for the government to supervise and enforce an effective right of reply system without sacrificing the independence of the media in the process. Federal Communication Commission regulations now grant a limited right of reply where "personal attacks" are made over radio or television and, because of the pervasive governmental controls already in place, such regulation probably does not appreciably reduce existing freedoms of the electronic media. But any broad extension to the printed press or to other forms of communication would almost certainly be seriously inhibiting. Indeed in MIAMI HERALD PUBLISHING CO. V. TORNILLO (1974) the Supreme Court unanimously invalidated a state statute requiring a newspaper to grant equal space for a political candidate attacked in its columns to reply. Moreover, practical difficulties, such as finding a suitable forum, would greatly limit the effectiveness of any attempt to substitute a right of reply for an action for damages. Thus the tension between the libel laws and freedom of the press is likely to continue.

A similar tension exists between freedom of the press and the RIGHT OF PRIVACY. Common law and statutory actions for invasion of privacy are permitted in most states. Moreover, the Supreme Court has recognized a constitutional right of privacy, running against the government, which would seem to impose restrictions upon disclosure to the press of certain information in the government's possession. The Supreme Court has held that the publication of material already in the public domain, such as the name of a rape victim which is available from public records, cannot be prohibited. However, it has never ruled upon the broad issue whether publication of information that is true but is alleged to invade the privacy of an individual can under some circumstances be restricted. The press has expressed concern over the possibility that the right of privacy might be used to curtail its freedom to publish. If the right of privacy is not narrowly limited— and there is presently no agreement upon the scope of the right—the chilling effect upon the press could be substantial. Nevertheless, in view of the current power of the press and the relative weakness of persons seeking to preserve privacy, any danger to the independence of the press from recognition of the right of privacy would seem to be remote.

Another conflict between freedom of the press and rights of the individual arises over the publication of news relating to criminal proceedings. The administration of justice is, of course, a matter of great public concern, and the role of the press in informing the public about such matters is crucial to the maintenance of a fair and effective system of justice. In most cases no conflict arises. On the other hand press reporting of occasional sensational crimes can be of such a nature as to prejudice the right of an accused to a FAIR TRIAL guaranteed by the DUE PROCESS clause and the Sixth Amendment. (See FREE PRESS/FAIR TRIAL.)

A number of remedies are available to the courts by which fairness in criminal proceedings can be assured without imposing restrictions upon the conduct of the press. These include change of VENUE, postponement of the trial, careful selection of jurors to weed out those likely to be prejudiced by the publicity, warning instructions to the jury, sequestration of witnesses and jurors, and, as a last resort, reversing a conviction and ordering a new trial. By and large the courts have found the use of these devices adequate. In some cases, however, trial courts have issued "gag" orders prohibiting the press from printing news about crimes or excluding the press from courtrooms.

In NEBRASKA PRESS ASSOCIATION V. STUART (1976) the Supreme Court dealt at some length with the "gag order" device. The majority opinion pointed out that the trial judge's order constituted a prior restraint, "the most serious and least tolerable infringement on First Amendment rights," but declined to hold that the press was entitled to absolute protection against all restrictive orders. The issue, the Court ruled, was whether in each case the newspaper publicity created a serious and likely danger to the fairness of the trial. And that issue in turn depended upon what was shown with respect to "(a) the nature and extent of pretrial news coverage; (b) whether other measures would be likely to mitigate the effects of unrestrained pretrial publicity; and (c) how effectively a restraining order would operate to prevent the threatened danger." The Court's ruling thus left the issue open to separate decision in each instance. The conditions laid down by the Court for issuance of a restrictive order, however, afford little room for use of that device except under rare circumstances. Three Justices urged that a prior restraint upon publication in this situation should never be allowed.

The exclusion of the press from courtrooms in criminal cases has also received the attention of the Supreme Court. Initially the Court rejected the contention that the Sixth Amendment's guarantee of a PUBLIC TRIAL entitled the press and the public to attend criminal trials, holding that the right involved was meant for the benefit of the defendant alone. Subsequently, however, in RICHMOND NEWSPAPERS, INC. V. VIRGINIA (1980) the Court recognized that the First Amendment extended some protection against exclusion from criminal trials. The Court again refused to hold that the First Amendment right was absolute, but it did not spell out the nature of any exceptions. Because it is always possible in a criminal trial for the judge to sequester the jury, few occasions for closing trials are likely to arise. On the other hand, the right of the press to attend pretrial hearings, where opportunity for sequestration does not exist, was left uncertain.

For many years the press has urged the courts to permit the use of radio, television, and photographic equipment in courtrooms. The courts have been reluctant to allow such forms of reporting. And in 1964 the Supreme Court overturned the conviction of Billie Sol Estes, accused of a notorious swindle, on the grounds that the broadcasting of parts of the trial by radio and television had been conducted in such a manner as to deprive him of a fair trial. Recently the courts have been more willing to open the courtroom to the electronic media and many of them have done so. The movement received the sanction of the Supreme Court in CHANDLER V. FLORIDA (1981) when an experimental program in Florida, which allowed broadcast and photographic coverage of trials subject to certain guidelines and under the control of the trial judge, was upheld by a unanimous vote.

The right of the press to gather news, as distinct from its right to publish the news, raises somewhat different issues. Freedom of the press implies in some degree a right to obtain information free of governmental interference. Indeed the Supreme Court in BRANZBURG V. HAYES (1972) expressly recognized that news-gathering did "qualify for First Amendment protection," saying that "without some protection for seeking out the news, freedom of the press could be eviscerated." But the limits of the constitutional right are difficult to define and remain undeveloped. The issue has arisen in three principal areas: REPORTER'S PRIVILEGE, the application of the FOURTH AMENDMENT to the press, and the right of the press to obtain information from the government.

The press has consistently asserted a right to refuse to disclose the sources of information obtained under a pledge of confidentiality—a claim known as "reporters' privilege." From the point of view of the press the right to honor a commitment to secrecy is essential to much reporting, particularly investigative reporting into organized crime, government corruption, and similar sensitive areas. On the other hand, under certain circumstances the need to obtain evidence in the possession of a reporter is also pressing, particularly where the information is necessary for defense in a criminal prosecution or to prove malice in a libel suit. Over the years the courts have generally refused to recognize the reporters' privilege, but they have attempted to avoid open conflict with the press. Reporters nevertheless continued to urge their claim, often to the point of going to jail for CONTEMPT OF COURT. A number of states have passed legislation recognizing the privilege in whole or in part, but the courts have tended to construe such statutes in a grudging manner, sometimes invoking constitutional objections.

The question whether reporters could invoke the privilege as a constitutional right under the First Amendment came before the Supreme Court in the *Branzburg* case. The reporters, who had refused to appear before grand juries, did not assert an absolute privilege but claimed they should not be compelled to give testimony unless the government demonstrated substantial grounds for believing they possessed essential information not available from other sources. The Court, in a 5–4 decision, rejected their claims. The majority opinion said that reporters had no greater claims to refuse testimony than other citizens. However, Justice LEWIS F. POWELL, whose vote was necessary to make the majority, expressed a more qualified position in a CONCURRING OPINION: "if the newsman . . . has reason to believe that his testimony implicates confidential source relationships without a legitimate need of law enforcement," the court should strike the "balance of these vital constitutional and societal interests on a case-by-case basis." In practice the courts appear to have accepted the Powell formula. Thus, although reporters cannot count on substantial constitutional protection the courts still prefer to avoid direct confrontation with the press tradition that reporters will not reveal confidential sources.

The First Amendment right to freedom of the press and the Fourth Amendment right to be secure from unreasonable SEARCHES AND SEIZURES have historically been closely linked. It was the GENERAL WARRANTS, used in America to obtain evidence of customs violations (and in England to find seditious publications), that in large part prompted the framing of the Fourth Amendment. At times the Supreme Court has recognized that Fourth Amendment protection extends with particular rigor to governmental intrusions affecting First Amendment rights. In the much discussed case of ZURCHER V. STANFORD DAILY (1978), however, the Court displayed less sympathy for the traditional position. The issue was whether the police could search the offices of a student newspaper for evidence of criminal offenses growing out of a student demonstration, or whether they should be confined to the issuance of a SUBPOENA requiring the newspaper to produce what evidence it had. Despite the vulnerability of the press to police searches tht could result in the ransacking of their news rooms, the Court by a 5–3 vote approved the warrant procedure. The press greeted the decision with strong criticism, mixed with alarm.

The third major issue with respect to operations of the press relates to the right of the press to obtain information from the government. The constitutional basis for such a claim grows out of the broader doctrine of the RIGHT TO KNOW. For many years the Supreme Court has recognized that the First Amendment embraces not only a right to communicate but also a right to receive communications. (See LISTENERS' RIGHTS.) The press has insisted that this feature of the First Amendment includes a right to have access to information in the possession of the government. Because a major purpose of the First Amendment is to facilitate the process of self-government, a strong constitutional argument can be advanced that, apart from a limited area of necessary secrecy, all material relating to operations of the government should be made available to the public. The press urged this position in a series of cases where it sought access to prisons in order to interview inmates and report on conditions inside. The Supreme Court, however, was not receptive. In rejecting the press proposals four of the Justices expressly declared in *Houchins v. KQED* (1978) that "the First and Fourteenth Amendments do not guarantee the public a right of access to information generated or controlled by government."

In 1980, in the Richmond Newspapers case, the Supreme Court shifted its position. In ruling that the press had a First Amendment right to attend criminal trials the majority relied heavily upon the right-to-know doctrine. Moreover, the concurring Justices were plainly willing to carry the right-to-know concept beyond the confines of the particular case before them. As Justice JOHN PAUL STEVENS correctly observed, the decision constituted "a watershed case": "never before has [the Court] squarely held that the acquisition of newsworthy material is entitled to any constitutional protection whatsoever." The full scope of the right to obtain information from the government remains to be seen. The development, however, is potentially one of great significance for the press.

Taken as a whole, freedom of the press in the United States rests upon a relatively firm constitutional footing. The press has not been granted any special status in the First Amendment's structure, but its general right to publish material, regardless of potential impacts on government operations or other features of the national life, has been accepted. There are some weaknesses in the position of the press. The law with respect to publication of national security information is obscure and, in its present form, poses some threat to press freedoms. The press is also vulnerable to libel suits, as the protections thought to have been afforded by the "actual malice" rule have not been altogether realized. Likewise the courts have been reluctant to assist the press in its news-gathering activities. From an overall view, however, constitutional developments have left the press in a position where it is largely free to carry out the functions and promote the values sought by the Framers of the First Amendment.

THOMAS I. EMERSON
(1986)

Bibliography

ANDERSON, DAVID A.   1983   The Origins of the Press Clause. *University of California at Los Angeles Law Review* 30:455–537.

BARRON, JEROME A.   1973   *Freedom of the Press for Whom?* Bloomington: Indiana University Press.

LEVY, LEONARD W., ed.   1966   *Freedom of the Press from Zenger to Jefferson.* Indianapolis: Bobbs-Merrill.

LOFTON, JOHN   1980   *The Press as Guardian of the First Amendment.* Columbia: University of South Carolina Press.

NELSON, HAROLD L., ed.   1967   *Freedom of the Press from Hamilton to the Warren Court.* Indianapolis: Bobbs-Merrill.

SCHMIDT, BENNO C., JR.   1976   *Freedom of the Press vs. Public Access.* New York: Praeger.

SIEBERT, FREDRICK SEATON   1952   *Freedom of the Press in England 1476–1776.* Urbana: University of Illinois Press.

SYMPOSIUM   1975   First Amendment and the Media. *Hastings Law Journal* 26:631–821.

FREEDOM OF THE PRESS
(Update 1)

The FIRST AMENDMENT's guarantee of freedom of the press is vitalized, as is FREEDOM OF SPEECH, by the synergy among the justifications for the protection of freedom of expression: (1) the marketplace of ideas is the best way of ascertaining truth; (2) full discussion of options is necessary to maintain a self-governing polity; (3) choice of both the means and the content of conveying one's messages is inherent to the notion of individual self-expression; and (4) free discussion is necessary as a check on governmental power by providing information for a resisting citizenry. The justifications have been translated into a set of DOCTRINES that preclude the following in declining order of absoluteness: government licensing the printed press; prepublication censorship; demands that certain information be published; and with tightly circumscribed exceptions, civil or criminal liability for what is published. The right to publish is thus highly protected, but the right to gather news, although essential to the operation of freedom of the press, has proved difficult to implement by judicial decision.

Licensing the printed media, as Great Britain required before its Glorious Revolution, has never been seriously suggested. Occasionally, Congress has debated a specific wartime or national security preclearance censorship provision, but none has been adopted; and if adopted, it would almost certainly have been successfully challenged. When Minnesota did appear to have enacted a limited preclearance scheme with its so-called gag law, the Supreme Court held it UNCONSTITUTIONAL in NEAR V. MINNESOTA EX REL. OLSON (1931).

MIAMI HERALD PUBLISHING COMPANY V. TORNILLO (1974), invalidating a right-to-reply law, suggests that a newspaper may never be required to publish or be punished for not publishing an item it wishes to exclude. Tornillo, a candidate for the Florida legislature, had been savaged by a pair of editorials in the *Miami Herald* just before the election. He demanded that the *Herald* print his responses as required by a state law regulating electoral debates. The Court, however, unanimously held the law unconstitutional, reasoning that it would "chill" the newspaper's willingness to enunciate its views and that it intruded into editorial choice. The latter rationale sweeps broadly enough to assure autonomy in deciding what to exclude.

The contested areas of freedom of the press involve attempts by the press to acquire information and attempts by the state to punish publication of certain sensitive information. Under very limited circumstances, government may successfully block publication by an INJUNCTION remedy. Under broader, but still limited circumstances both civil and criminal remedies may be allowable.

Near analogized the Minnesota gag law, which placed a newspaper under a permanent injunction banning future "malicious, scandalous and defamatory" publication, to the traditional common law PRIOR RESTRAINT created by preclearance licensing. Because a barebones guarantee of freedom of the press was a ban on prior restraints, the Minnesota gag law was unconstitutional—the first statute ever found to violate the First Amendment. *Near* did not go all the way and ban all prior restraints. Thus, in *Near's* most famous passage, the Court implied that national security might well be a ground for a prior restraint: "No one would question but that a government [during actual war] might prevent actual obstruction to its recruiting service or the publication of the sailing dates of troops and transports or the number and location of troops." Subsequently, it has been assumed that if a prior restraint were ever appropriate, national security would be the justification. Nevertheless, in NEW YORK TIMES V. UNITED STATES (1971), its most publicized national security case, the Supreme Court concluded that the government had not met its BURDEN OF PROOF to prevent publication of the *Pentagon Papers*, which described top secret decision making involving the VIETNAM WAR. The modern reality of copying machines and computer disks has made injunctive prior restraints obsolete because the materials will always show up somewhere else and any injunction will be futile to prevent disclosure—facts not yet reflected in the doctrine.

Despite upholding the press in every single case involving PRIVACY AND THE FIRST AMENDMENT and in other noncopyright contexts where the press has published truthful information noncoercively obtained from governmental sources, the Court has avoided sweeping rules and always assumed that somewhere lies a situation where the press ought not publish. Again, national security heads the list, and the Court has recognized the enforceability of contracts that forbid publication without approval of the Central Intelligence Agency; it would undoubtedly sustain the federal prohibition on disclosing the identities of intelligence agents as part of a pattern of activities intended to expose covert action. Beyond national security, the protection of sensitive private information of nonpublic fig-

ures is the next most likely candidate for a limitation on publication, although any such limitation will have to be carefully circumscribed. Thus, in *Florida Star v. B.J.F.* (1989), a civil privacy case, the Court set aside an award of DAMAGES for negligent publication of a rape victim's name because the paper had lawfully obtained the information through governmental disclosure. The Court recognized, as it had previously, that the state is in the best position to protect against disclosure through careful internal procedures.

Florida Star may usefully be contrasted with *Seattle Times v. Rhinehart* (1984), where the Court held that a trial court can forbid publication of information acquired by the press in state-mandated DISCOVERY, unless the information actually comes out in the litigation. *Rhinehart's* balance demonstrates that there are some circumstances where it is too unfair to allow the press to publish (without sanction) information that it has. One may extrapolate from *Rhinehart* that, if the press were to break into property and pillage files (or plant bugs) and later to publish, then the publication could also be penalized.

But these examples of coercive acquisition of information are a far cry from the issue ducked ever since the *Pentagon Papers Cases* (1971): what if the press should publish information unlawfully taken by a third party (as federal law forbids)? Here, outcomes of the Court's decisions, rather than the reasons offered, appear to preclude sanctions in cases where the press does not coercively acquire the information, while leaving the potential deterrent of criminal penalties hanging as a last resort.

A similar outcome prevails in cases of efforts of the press to obtain information. Constitutional rhetoric surrounding the importance of information to a self-governing citizenry supports a right of the press to obtain the information necessary for self-governance, but this rhetoric also leaves no principled stopping places. As a result, the Court has stated that news gathering is part of freedom of the press, but has also found implementation of such a right to be largely beyond its skills. When BRANZBURG V. HAYES (1972) raised the claim of a reporter's privilege not to disclose sources, the Court rejected it, although in OBITER DICTA it stated that orders designed to "disrupt a reporter's relationship with news sources would have no justification." Despite fears of the press, government generally has not abused its limited right to require disclosure.

The Court initially rejected claims of the press of access to prisons and pretrial hearings, but in RICHMOND NEWSPAPERS V. VIRGINIA (1980), it held that the press and public have a right to watch criminal trials. Although the press acted as if *Richmond Newspapers* might convert the First Amendment into a freedom of information sunshine law, it is not. This decision opens courtroom doors, but not those of GRAND JURIES or the other branches of government.

The least satisfying area of the Court's JURISPRUDENCE on freedom of the press is the one where the Court has been the most active: the constitutionalization of the law of LIBEL in the wake of NEW YORK TIMES V. SULLIVAN (1964). Despite this decision's promise to balance successfully the interests of reputation against the CHILLING EFFECT that civil liability imposes on the press, over the years the constitutional law of defamation has become an ever more intricate maze of rules that in operation protect neither reputation, the press, nor the public's interest in knowing accurate information.

Although the best-known feature of current libel law may be its division of defamed plaintiffs into two classes, PUBLIC FIGURES and private figures, with the former having to meet the *New York Times* actual-malice standard—this distinction has had little impact on litigation. The reason is that private figures also need to show actual malice if they are to recover punitive damages—the financial key to their attorneys' taking their cases on contingent fees. At trial, the current constitutional rules attempt to minimize jury discretion. According to *Milkovich v. Lorain Journal* (1990), the plaintiff bears the burden of proving falsity, and those statements that "cannot reasonably be interpreted as stating actual facts" are fully protected. There is also strict appellate supervision of the evidence, something unmatched in any other area of law.

The intricate structure of First Amendment libel law has been widely criticized. In operation, the overwhelming number of libel suits are disposed of before trial; in such a case, the plaintiff is never granted an opportunity to show that the defamatory statements were false. If the case goes to a jury, the odds shift heavily to the plaintiff, although the damage awards are likely to be set aside either by the trial judge or the appellate court. It is the rarest of plaintiffs who successfully hurdles all the rules designed to protect the press. As a result, the rules do not provide the public with an opportunity to know the truth about injured plaintiffs; the law underprotects reputation; and in all likelihood, individuals are deterred from entering the public arena where, rightly or wrongly, they are often perceived as fair game.

Nevertheless, current law also fails to serve the interests of the press. A wholly unanticipated aspect of *New York Times* was the way it turned the libel trial away from what the defendant said about the plaintiff to scrutiny of how the press put the story together. When the trial focuses on the practices, care, motives, and views of the press—especially when, as is likely for a case reaching trial, the story is false—the dynamics of the case invite punishment of the press. A good trial lawyer will be able to paint the dispute as a contest between good and evil, and the evidence necessary to prove reckless disregard of the truth leaves no doubt as to which side is evil. In the 1980s, the average jury award in cases where reckless disregard was found exceeded $2 million.

It does not reduce the chill on newspapers to learn that few plaintiffs get to keep their awards and that the average successful plaintiff receives a mere $20,000. There seems to be a damages explosion in tort verdicts generally, and newspapers know catastrophe can arrive with just one huge verdict. An example was the $9 million judgment against the *Alton (Illinois) Evening Telegraph,* which sent the paper to bankruptcy court (although a subsequent settlement allowed the 38,000-circulation paper to stay in business). What makes defamation a special tort is that the injury that plaintiffs suffer seems far less severe than that suffered by a physically injured tort plaintiff. Large jury verdicts, both for punitive damages and those for emotional pain and suffering, thus seem designed more to punish than to compensate.

The operation of *New York Times* has thus produced a strange landscape. Issues of truth and falsity rarely surface, and reputations are not cleared for the vast majority of plaintiffs. For those few that get to a jury, however, trying the press can lead to a large, albeit momentary, windfall. The possibility of that windfall, coupled with the necessary legal fees to avoid it, maintains a chilling effect, even though appellate supervision typically cuts the verdicts to size. Libel law, having been wholly remade in the wake of *New York Times*, needs to be rethought again. It is not that the Court has misunderstood what to balance; rather, its balance systematically undermines all the values it attempts to protect.

A free press is essential in a democracy, and the Court's doctrines have never lost sight of this. Typically, press cases parallel speech cases, but one area where the Court has split the two is taxation. To protect the press, the Court has struck down press taxes that are unique to the press or treat different parts of the press differently. Whatever the imperfections of the law of freedom of the press, few areas of constitutional law have achieved a more coherent whole than freedom of the press. Even an "outrageous" parody of the Reverend Jerry Falwell in HUSTLER MAGAZINE V. FALWELL (1988), found by a jury to have inflicted extreme emotional distress, received the unanimous protection of a Court certain that freewheeling caustic discussion must be a central object of constitutional protection if we are to have a free and therefore secure press.

L. A. POWE, JR.
(1992)

Bibliography

ANDERSON, DAVID A. 1975 The Issue Is Control of Press Power. *Texas Law Review* 54:271–282.

POWE, LUCAS A., JR. 1991 *The Fourth Estate and the Constitution: Freedom of Press in America.* Berkeley: University of California Press.

SMOLLA, RODNEY A. 1986 *Suing the Press.* New York: Oxford University Press.

SYMPOSIUM 1977 Nebraska Press Association v. Stuart. *Stanford Law Review* 29:383–624.

FREEDOM OF THE PRESS
(Update 2)

The FIRST AMENDMENT sets forth the press clause in the same breath that announces the FREEDOM OF SPEECH. The Supreme Court generally has rejected the notion that these provisions have separate and independent meanings, especially when asked to give the press a privileged status reflecting its unique role in facilitating informed self-governance. Although the press may not have a preferred position in the First Amendment matrix, it nonetheless has a status distinguishable from speech and is governed by a body of principles reflecting this distinction.

Freedom of the press, in its modern sense, is not a function of a uniform principle governing all communications media. As new communications technologies have evolved, First Amendment analysis has focused on the unique characteristics and perils that each medium possesses and creates. As the Court initially put it in *Joseph Burstyn, Inc. v. Wilson* (1952), a given medium is not "necessarily subject to the precise rules governing any other particular method of expression. Each method tends to present its own peculiar problems." This decision and other rulings over the last half of the twentieth century reflect the view of Justice ROBERT H. JACKSON that "[t]he moving picture screen, the radio, the newspaper, the handbill, the sound truck and the street corner orator have differing natures, values, abuses and dangers. Each . . . is a law unto itself."

Within this medium-specific constitutional framework, the editorial freedom of publishers is most protected. Striking down a right of reply statute governing newspapers, in MIAMI HERALD PUBLISHING CO. V. TORNILLO (1974), the Court found it inconsistent "with First Amendment guarantees of a free press as they have evolved to this time." A similar law governing BROADCASTING had been upheld in RED LION BROADCASTING CO. V. FCC (1969). Broadcasting was distinguished on grounds that the medium uses a scarce resource to disseminate its signals. Because there are more persons wanting to broadcast than frequencies to allocate, the Court found it "idle to posit an unabridgeable First Amendment right to broadcast comparable to the right of every individual to speak, write, or publish."

The wisdom of medium-specific regulation increasingly is challenged by growth in technology. With print and electronic media crossing into each other's domains, trading upon the same methods of distribution, and blurring distinctions of form, conventional constitutional thinking confronts an era of rapidly changing circumstance. The phenomenon of convergence—as televisions, telephones, and computers create networked possibilities for processing and transmitting voice, video, and data—presents particular risks to the established analytical order. Legal developments over the past decade have reflected a limited awareness of this reality. Following decades of criticism, the Federal Communications Commission (FCC) in 1987 abandoned the scarcity premise that had been the basis for much content regulation in broadcasting including the FAIRNESS DOCTRINE. Reasoning "that the role of the electronic press in our society is the same as that of the printed press," the FCC concluded "that full First Amendment protections against content regulation should apply to the electronic and the printed press."

Administrative repudiation of the scarcity premise has not prefaced constitutional redirection. In METRO BROADCASTING, INC. V. FCC (1990), the Court reaffirmed the scarcity premise in upholding minority preferences in the broadcast licensing process. Although the AFFIRMATIVE ACTION aspects of *Metro Broadcasting* were overruled a few years later, the Court has continued to reference the scarcity premise in broadcasting. Kindred concepts have extended to other electronic media. In TURNER BROADCASTING SYSTEM, INC. V. FCC (1997), the Court upheld a federal law requiring cable television operators to carry the signals of local broadcasters. Accepting Congress's concern that cable operators might use their economic power to the detriment of local broadcasting's viability, the Court in an earlier decision had stressed their "gatekeeping" function in selecting the programs they disseminate. Transcending the notion of scarcity and its derivatives, as a constitutional reference point for broadcasting in particular, is what the *Turner* Court cites as a "history of extensive regulation of the . . . medium." Assuming that the future of media is defined by convergence, this premise heralds a broad spectrum First Amendment competition between traditions of editorial freedom and regulation.

"MUST CARRY" LAWS, like fairness obligations, represent an official content diversification scheme. Such methods exist within a regulatory world also populated by medium-specific content restrictive regimens. In FEDERAL COMMUNICATIONS COMMISSION V. PACIFICA FOUNDATION (1978), the Court upheld the FCC's power to regulate the broadcast of "patently offensive sexual and excretory language." The prohibition was justified on grounds that broadcasting was a pervasive and intrusive medium easily accessible to children. Although indecency regulation has expanded in the field of broadcasting, it generally has not extended into other media contexts. Because cable television typically provides viewers with greater control over programming, through subscription or blocking technology, the transferability of the *Pacifica* premise has been limited. Likewise, in *Sable Communications of California, Inc. v. FCC* (1989), the Court invalidated a congressional prohibition of DIAL-A-PORN services. Because consumers of these services have to take affirmative steps to obtain them, the Court distinguished indecent telephone communications from broadcast signals that may take a person "by surprise." Safeguards in the form of access codes, credit card payment, and scrambling rules, moreover, minimize the problem of easy availability to children.

Reviewing "the vast democratic fora of the Internet," the Court in *Reno v. American Civil Liberties Union* (1997) identified a multidimensional medium characterized by "traditional print and news services, . . . audio, video, and still images, as well as interactive, real-time dialogue." Against this backdrop, the Court determined that "our cases provide no basis for qualifying the level of First Amendment scrutiny that should be applied to this medium." Even as it acknowledged the phenomenon of convergence, interactivity, and choice in the INTERNET context, the Court reaffirmed its investment in medium specific analysis. Rather than responding to a general media universe comprising interacting and complementary parts, First Amendment principle remains a function of microcosmic form and perspective.

With media evolving toward common attributes and capabilities, constitutional attention to unique characteristics is not without peril. To the extent that communications technology affords expanding opportunities for interactivity and choice, it redefines a mass media society accustomed to editorial centralization and one-way information flow. Insofar as technology enables consumers to avoid what offends them, individual choice may achieve the results of official control without taxing the interests of expressive pluralism. Within this context of change, regulatory intervention to facilitate diversity (or shield from its excesses) seems more likely to be justified on the basis of habit and custom rather than reason. Because methodologies of electronic communications tend to be the least constitutionally protected, even as they have emerged as the dominant media, it is not yet clear whether a First Amendment model based on market liberty or managed care will prevail. At stake as the republic progresses into its third century, however, is whether freedom of the press ultimately accounts for original notions of autonomous judgment or more recent traditions of authoritative selection.

DONALD E. LIVELY
(2000)

Bibliography

BLANCHARD, MARGARET A. 1992 The American Urge to Censor: Freedom of Expression Versus the Desire to Sanitize Society—from Anthony Comstock to 2 Live Crew. *William and Mary Law Review* 33:741–851.

DE SOLA POOL, ITHIEL 1983 *Technologies of Freedom*. Cambridge, Mass.: Harvard University Press.

EMORD, JONATHAN W. 1991 *Freedom, Technology, and the First Amendment*. San Francisco, Calif.: Pacific Research Institute for Public Policy.

FERRIS, CHARLES D. and KIRKLAND JAMES A. 1985 Fairness—The Broadcaster's Hippocratic Oath. *Catholic University Law Review* 34:605–623.

FOWLER, MARK S. and BRENNER, DANIEL L. 1982 A Marketplace Approach to Broadcast Regulation. *Texas Law Review* 60:207–257.

HAMMOND, ALLEN S., IV 1992 Regulating Broadband Communication Networks. *Yale Journal on Regulation* 9:181–235.

LIVELY, DONALD E. 1994 The Information Highway: A First Amendment Roadmap. *Boston College Law Review* 35:1067–1101.

LIVELY, DONALD E.; HAMMOND, ALLEN S., IV; MORANT, BLAKE D.; and WEAVER, RUSSELL L. 1997 *Communications Law*. Cincinnati, Ohio: Anderson Publishing Co.

POWE, LUCAS A., JR., 1987 *American Broadcasting and the First Amendment*. Berkeley: University of California Press.

FREE EXERCISE OF RELIGION

See: Religious Liberty

FREEMAN v. HEWITT
329 U.S. 249 (1946)

Justice FELIX FRANKFURTER, for a 6–3 Supreme Court, here voided an Indiana tax levied on proceeds realized from the sale of securities in another state. Frankfurter struck down the tax as a greater burden than police regulations on INTERSTATE COMMERCE. Justice WILLIAM O. DOUGLAS, dissenting, denied the existence of any interstate commerce.

DAVID GORDON
(1986)

FREEPORT DOCTRINE

During the LINCOLN-DOUGLAS DEBATES of 1858, Senator STEPHEN A. DOUGLAS attacked ABRAHAM LINCOLN and the Republicans for their unwillingness to accept the Supreme Court's decision in DRED SCOTT V. SANDFORD (1857), which held that Congress could not proscribe SLAVERY in federal territories. But at the same time, Douglas and the Northern Democrats contended that the issue of slavery was to be decided by the people who lived in each territory, a position for which Douglas appropriated the name POPULAR SOVEREIGNTY. At Freeport, Lincoln asked Douglas: "Can the people of a United States territory, in any lawful way, . . . exclude slavery from its limits prior to the formation of a state constitution?"

Douglas's reply is known as the "Freeport Doctrine." It was that "slavery cannot exist a day or an hour anywhere, unless it is supported by local police regulation." In other words, a territorial legislature could exclude slavery by "unfriendly legislation" or simply by failing to pass the laws necessary to enforce slaveholding. The Freeport Doctrine appeared intended to neutralize the *Dred Scott* decision, and it effectively cut Douglas off from the slaveholding interests and divided the Democratic party.

DENNIS J. MAHONEY
(1986)

Bibliography

JAFFA, HARRY V. 1959 *Crisis of the House Divided: An Interpretation of the Issues in the Lincoln-Douglas Debates.* Garden City, N.Y.: Doubleday.

FREE PRESS/FAIR TRIAL

Although press coverage has challenged the fairness and dignity of criminal proceedings throughout American history, intensive consideration of free press/fair trial issues by the Supreme Court has mainly been a product of recent decades. The first free press/fair trial issue to receive significant attention was the extent of press freedom from judges' attempts to hold editors and authors in contempt for criticizing or pressuring judicial conduct in criminal proceedings. The next category of decisions to receive attention, reversals of convictions to protect defendants from pretrial publicity, began rather gingerly in 1959, but in the years following the 1964 Warren Commission Report the Supreme Court reversed convictions more readily and dealt in considerable detail with the appropriate treatment of the interests of both the press and defendants when those interests were potentially in conflict. More recently, the Court has considered whether the press can be enjoined from publishing prejudicial material, and whether the press can be excluded from judicial proceedings.

In view of the large number of free press/fair trial decisions handed down over the years by the Supreme Court, this particular corner of the law of FREEDOM OF THE PRESS is probably the best developed of any, and offers a particularly instructive model of how the Supreme Court seeks to accommodate colliding interests of constitutional

dimension. Overall, the Court has sought a balance that respects Justice HUGO L. BLACK'S OBITER DICTUM in the seminal case of BRIDGES V. CALIFORNIA (1941) that "free speech and fair trial are two of the most cherished policies of our civilization, and it would be a trying task to choose between them."

In one of our history's pivotal FIRST AMENDMENT cases, the Supreme Court in 1941 sharply restricted the power of state judges to hold persons in contempt for publishing material that attacked or attempted to influence judicial decisions. By a 5–4 vote in *Bridges* the Supreme Court struck down two contempt citations, one against a newspaper based on an editorial that stated that a judge would "make a serious mistake" if he granted probation to two labor "goons," the second against a union leader who had sent a public telegram to the secretary of labor criticizing a judge's decision against his union and threatening to strike if the decision was enforced. Black's majority opinion held that the First Amendment protected these expressions unless they created a CLEAR AND PRESENT DANGER of interfering with judicial impartiality. From the start, this test as applied to contempt by publication has been virtually impossible to satisfy. Black insisted that "the substantive evil must be extremely serious and the degree of imminence extremely high before utterances can be punished," and, in order to remove predictions about the likelihood of interference from the ken of lower courts, the Court reinforced the strictness of this standard by using an apparently IRREBUTTABLE PRESUMPTION that judges would not be swayed by adverse commentary. "[T]he law of contempt," wrote Justice WILLIAM O. DOUGLAS in *Craig v. Harney* (1947), echoing a position taken in *Bridges,* "is not made for the protection of judges who may be sensitive to the winds of public opinion. Judges are supposed to be men of fortitude, able to thrive in a hardy climate." Under these decisions, it seems doubtful that anything short of a direct and credible physical threat against a judge would justify punishment for contempt.

For general First Amendment theory and more specifically for the rights of the press in free press/fair trial contexts, the chief significance of the contempt cases is the emergence of a positive conception of protected expression under the First Amendment. As Black put it in *Bridges,* "it is a prized American privilege to speak one's mind, although not always with perfect good taste, on all public questions." Drawing upon the decisions in NEAR V. MINNESOTA (1931) and DE JONGE V. OREGON (1937), which stressed the Madisonian conception of free expression as essential to political democracy, opinions in the contempt cases shifted the clear and present danger rule toward a promise of constitutional immunity for criticism of government. The contempt cases are thus the primary doctrinal bridge between the Court's unsympathetic approach to political dissent during and after WORLD WAR I and the grand conception of NEW YORK TIMES CO. V. SULLIVAN (1964) that the central meaning of the First Amendment is "the right of free discussion of the stewardship of public officials." Beyond this, the contempt cases make it clear that protecting expressions about judges and courts is itself a core function of the First Amendment. Douglas put it this way in *Craig*, in words that have echoed in later free press-fair trial cases: "A trial is a public event. What transpires in the court room is public property. . . . There is no special perquisite of the judiciary which enables it, as distinguished from other institutions of democratic government, to suppress, edit, or censor events which transpire in proceedings before it."

Although the contempt cases focused on the rights of the press and others who sought to publicize information about trials, the next set of free press-fair trial cases, without dealing with the right to publish, looked with a sympathetic eye toward defendants who might have been convicted because of prejudice caused by such publications. Although individual Justices had objected bitterly to the prejudicial effects of media coverage on jurors, not until 1959 did the Supreme Court reverse a federal conviction because of prejudicial publicity. The first reversal of a state court conviction followed two years later in IRVIN V. DOWD (1961), where 268 of 430 prospective jurors said during their VOIR DIRE examination that they had a fixed belief in the defendant's guilt, and 370 entertained some opinion of guilt. News media had made the trial a "cause célébre of this small community," the Court noted, as the press had reported the defendant's prior criminal record, offers to plead guilty, confessions, and a flood of other prejudicial items.

In 1963, the special problems of television were introduced into the pretrial publicity fray by *Rideau v. Louisiana*, producing another reversal by the Supreme Court of a state conviction. A jailed murder suspect was filmed in the act of answering various questions and of confessing to the local sheriff, and the film was televised repeatedly in the community that tried and convicted him. The Supreme Court held that "[a]ny subsequent court proceedings in a community so pervasively exposed to such a spectacle could be but a hollow formality." Two years later, in ESTES V. TEXAS (1965), a narrowly divided Court held that, at least in a notorious case, the presence of television in the courtroom could generate pressures that added up to a denial of due process.

In the mid-1960s the Court took a more categorical and more aggressive stance against prejudicial publicity. The shift was consistent with the WARREN COURT's growing impatience toward ad hoc evaluations of fairness in its review of state criminal cases. This period of heightened concern

for the defendant was triggered by the disgraceful media circus that surrounded the murder trial of Dr. Sam Sheppard. Before Sheppard's trial, most of the print and broadcast media in the Cleveland area joined in an intense publicity barrage proclaiming Sheppard's guilt. During the trial, journalists swarmed over the courtroom in a manner that impressed upon everyone the spectacular notoriety of the case. "The fact is," wrote Justice TOM C. CLARK in his most memorable opinion for the Court, "that bedlam reigned at the courthouse during the trial and newsmen took over practically the entire courtroom, hounding most of the participants in the trial, especially Sheppard." The deluge of publicity outside the courtroom, and the disruptive behavior of journalists inside, combined to make the trial a "Roman holiday' for the news media" that "inflamed and prejudiced the public."

In *Sheppard v. Maxwell* (1966) Clark adumbrated the techniques by which trial judges may control prejudicial publicity and disruptions of the judicial process by the press. The opinion is a virtual manual for trial judges, suggesting proper procedures initially by listing the particular errors in the case: that Sheppard was not granted a continuance or a change of VENUE, that the jury was not sequestered, that the judge merely requested jurors not to follow media commentary on the case rather than directing them not to, that the judge failed "to insulate" the jurors from reporters and photographers, and that reporters invaded the space within the bar of the courtroom reserved for counsel, created distractions and commotion, and hounded people throughout the courthouse.

But the *Sheppard* opinion went beyond these essentially traditional judicial methods for coping with publicity and the press. The Court identified the trial judge's "fundamental error" as his view that he "lacked power to control the publicity about the trial" and insisted that "the cure lies in those remedial measures that will prevent the prejudice at its inception." Specifically, Clark admonished trial judges to insulate witnesses from press interviews, to "impos[e] control over the statements made to the news media by counsel, witnesses, and especially the Coroner and police officers," and to "proscrib[e] extrajudicial statements by any lawyer, party, witness, or court official which divulged prejudicial matters. . . ."

Sheppard left open the central question whether the courts could impose direct restrictions on the press by INJUNCTIONS that would bar publications that might prejudice an accused. In NEBRASKA PRESS ASSOCIATION V. STUART (1976) the Supreme Court, unanimous as to result though divided in rationale, answered this question with a seemingly definitive No. The Nebraska state courts had ordered the press and broadcasters not to publish confessions or other information prejudicial to an accused in a pending murder prosecution. Some of the information covered by the injunction had been revealed in an open, public preliminary hearing, and the Supreme Court made clear that a state could in no event bar the publication of matters disclosed in open judicial proceedings. As to other information barred from publication by the state courts, Chief Justice WARREN E. BURGER's majority opinion went by a curious and circuitous route to the conclusion that the impact of prejudicial publicity on prospective jurors was "of necessity speculative, dealing ... with factors unknown and unknowable." Thus, the adverse effect on the fairness of the subsequent criminal proceeding "was not demonstrated with the degree of certainty our cases on PRIOR RESTRAINT require." Burger's opinion made much of the fact that the state court had not determined explicitly that the protections against prejudicial publicity set out in *Sheppard* would not suffice to guarantee fairness, as if trial court findings to this effect might make a difference in judging the validity of a prior restraint against publication. And Burger said again and again that he was dealing with a particular case and not laying down a general rule. But because Burger termed the evils of prejudicial publicity "of necessity speculative," and viewed the prior restraint precedents as requiring a degree of certainty about the evils of expression before a prior restraint should be tolerated, his opinion for the Court seems to be, in the guise of a narrow and particularistic holding, a categorical rejection of prior restraints on pretrial publicity. Lower courts have read the decision as an absolute bar to judicial injunctions against the press forbidding the publication of possibly prejudicial matters about pending criminal proceedings.

Beyond its rejection of prior restraints against the press to control pretrial publicity, the *Nebraska Press Association* decision emphatically affirmed all the methods of control set out in *Sheppard,* including the validity of judicial orders of silence directed to parties, lawyers, witnesses, court officers, and the like not to reveal information about pending cases to the press. Such orders, indeed, have flourished in the lower courts since the *Nebraska Press Association* decision.

The free press/fair trial conundrum has also presented the Supreme Court with the only occasion it has accepted to shed light on the very murky question whether the First Amendment protects the right to gather information, as against the right to publish or refuse to publish. No doubt in response to the Supreme Court's rejection of direct controls on press publication, either by injunctions or by the CONTEMPT POWER, several lower courts excluded news reporters and the public from preliminary hearings and even from trials themselves to prevent the press from gathering information whose publication might be prejudicial to current or later judicial proceedings. Initially, in GANNETT CO. V. DE PASQUALE (1979), reviewing a closing of a preliminary

hearing dealing with the suppression of EVIDENCE, the Supreme Court found no guarantee in the Sixth Amendment of public and press presence. The decision produced an outcry against secret judicial proceedings, and only a year later, in one of the most precipitous and awkward reversals in its history, the Court held in RICHMOND NEWSPAPERS V. VIRGINIA (1980) that the First Amendment barred excluding the public and the press from criminal trials except where special considerations calling for secrecy, such as privacy or national security, obtained. The decision marks the first and only occasion to date in which the Court has recognized a First Amendment right of access for purposes of news gathering, and the Court was careful to limit its holding by resting on the long tradition of open judicial proceedings in English and American law. One year later, in *Chandler v. Florida* (1981), the Court held that televising a criminal trial was not invariably a denial of due process, thus removing *Estes* as an absolute bar to television in the courtroom.

The pattern of constitutional law formed by the free press/fair trial decisions has several striking aspects. While direct judicial controls on the right of publication have been firmly rejected, the courts have proclaimed extensive power to gag sources of information. (See GAG ORDERS.) Participants in the process can be restrained from talking, but the press cannot be restrained from publishing. However, the broad power to impose secrecy on sources does not go so far as to justify closing judicial proceedings, absent unusual circumstances. The interests of freedom of expression and control over information to enhance the fairness of criminal trials are accommodated not by creating balanced principles of general application but rather by letting each interest reign supreme in competing aspects of the problem. Moreover, the principles fashioned in the cases tend to be sweeping, as if the Supreme Court were acting with special confidence in fashioning First Amendment standards to govern the familiar ground of the judicial process. And in dealing with its own bailiwick, the judicial process, the Supreme Court has acted not defensively but with a powerful commitment to freedom of expression.

BENNO C. SCHMIDT, JR.
(1986)

Bibliography

FRIENDLY, ALFRED and GOLDFARB, RONALD 1967 *Crime and Publicity.* New York: Twentieth Century Fund.
JAFFE, LOUIS 1965 Trial by Newspaper. *New York University Law Review* 40:504–524.
LEWIS, ANTHONY 1980 A Public Right to Know about Public Institutions: The First Amendment as Sword. *Supreme Court Law Review* 1980:1–25.
SCHMIDT, BENNO C., JR. 1977 Nebraska Press Association: An

Expansion of Freedom and Contraction of Theory. *Stanford Law Review* 29:431–476.

TAYLOR, TELFORD 1969 *Two Studies in Constitutional Interpretation.* Evanston, Ill.: Northwestern University Press.

FREE PRESS/FAIR TRIAL
(Update)

The Supreme Court has firmly established a FIRST AMENDMENT right of access to criminal proceedings. In *Press-Enterprise Co. v. Superior Court* (1986), the Court held that a "presumption of openness" in criminal trials extends to aspects of the trial beyond the actual testimony of witnesses. All trial matters, such as the jury selection (VOIR DIRE) process, are presumptively open. The media can be excluded only if the trial court specifically finds compelling reasons to close the trial and finds that less-restrictive alternatives cannot safeguard the defendant's right to a FAIR TRIAL.

Since 1984 the Court has defined the scope of the media's right of access. In *Waller v. Georgia* (1984), the Court expanded the right of access to pretrial evidentiary hearings, although it did so on the basis of the defendant's Sixth Amendment right to an open trial. In *Press-Enterprise*, the Court concluded that the media have a qualified First Amendment right of access to pretrial proceedings that can be overcome only by "an overriding interest based on findings that closure is essential to preserve higher values and is narrowly tailored to serve that interest." Therefore, courts must decide case-by-case whether any portion of a criminal proceeding can and should be closed. Laws that automatically close proceedings, such as the Massachusetts law in GLOBE NEWSPAPER COMPANY V. SUPERIOR COURT (1982) excluding the press from hearing the testimony of young victims of sex crimes, are constitutionally infirm.

Although the media's general right to attend and report on court proceedings has been secured, courts do possess limited power to restrict press access to information outside the courtroom door. Not only do courts retain the power to issue GAG ORDERS directed at parties, attorneys, and witnesses in a case, but attorneys are now subject to professional disciplinary action if they make extrajudicial statements that have a "substantial likelihood of materially prejudicing an adjudicative proceeding." The Court upheld the constitutionality of such orders in *Gentile v. State Bar of Nevada* (1991). The Court also held in *Seattle Times v. Rhinehart* (1984) that courts may limit the media's access to information by sealing information under a protective order.

Difficult issues still facing the courts include the use of cameras inside the courtroom and whether the press's right of access also applies in civil cases. The Court has never found that the press has a constitutional right to use cameras in the courtroom. However, in CHANDLER V. FLORIDA (1981), the Court held that televising trials is constitutionally permissible. Thus, it is left to the discretion of legislatures and trial judges to decide whether to permit the televising of trials. Courts typically will balance the interest of the public in viewing the proceedings against the possible disruption of the proceedings from televised coverage. Another major concern for courts is the possible effect of camera coverage on unsequestered jurors. The televised trials of high-publicity cases, including the 1994 murder trial of football star O.J. Simpson, has caused many courts to reconsider their willingness to allow cameras in the courtroom.

Traditionally, issues involving press access to trials have focused on the media's coverage of criminal proceedings. The Court has never explicitly ruled on whether the same rights of access apply to civil proceedings. The First Amendment would seem to safeguard such access. Historically, the press has had access to civil, as well as criminal, proceedings. Even more importantly, the critical role of the press in allowing the public to scrutinize the performance of its governmental institutions and officials applies with equal force to civil trials. The free press, rather than being an obstacle to a fair trial, is one of the means by which a fair trial can be ensured.

LAURIE L. LEVENSON
(2000)

(SEE ALSO: *Freedom of the Press.*)

Bibliography

BARBER, SUSANNA 1987 *News Cameras in the Courtroom: A Free Press–Fair Trial Debate.* Norwood, N.J.: Ablex Publishing Corp.

FREEDMAN, WARREN 1988 *Press and Media Access to the Criminal Courtroom.* New York: Quorum Books.

UELMEN, GERALD F. 1997 Leaks, Gags, and Shields: Taking Responsibility. *Santa Clara Law Review* 37:943–979.

FREE SPEECH AND RICO

In 1970, Congress enacted the ORGANIZED CRIME CONTROL ACT, Title IX of which is known as the RACKETEER INFLUENCED AND CORRUPT ORGANIZATIONS ACT (RICO). RICO is enforced through criminal prosecutions and through private civil suits in which treble damages and awards of counsel fees are authorized. Organized crime, that is, groups such as the Mafia, gave rise to RICO, but it applies to conduct engaged in by "any person." For this reason, individuals have challenged RICO as a threat to FREEDOM OF SPEECH. Objections are made to its VAGUENESS, to its application to certain conduct, and to its administration by the courts.

Standards of guilt must be ascertainable, and yet vagueness is a question of degree. A statute is not vague merely because it is difficult to determine whether marginal or hypothetical cases fall within its terms; typically, too, a statute is judged "as applied" to the defendant's conduct. Only free speech challenges are "facial," that is, tested by looking to the text of the statute. Because RICO specifies "OBSCENITY" and "extortion" within its prohibited conduct, RICO implicates free speech. RICO's application to obscenity was upheld in 1989 in *Fort Wayne Books, Inc. v. Indiana*. The Supreme Court found that because the term "obscenity" itself was not vague, RICO was not vague. Because RICO requires a "pattern" of "obscenity" violations in connection with an "enterprise," "RICO is inherently *less* vague than obscenity [by itself]." According to the Court, any "obscenity" prosecution induces self- censorship, but RICO's enhanced sanctions, by themselves, do not implicate vagueness concerns.

RICO's application to extortion was challenged in 1994 in *National Organizations For Women, Inc. v. Scheidler*. ANTI-ABORTION MOVEMENT demonstrators argued that because RICO's legislative history indicated that Congress narrowed it in 1970 to avoid its application to antiwar protests it was improper to apply it to similar demonstrations today; courts, they argued, were turning "extortion" under RICO into "coercion." For example, the gay activists in 1988 who entered St. Patrick's Cathedral in New York City sought not the church's building, but a change in the church's policy. This raised the possibility that Dr. MARTIN LUTHER KING, JR., the CIVIL RIGHTS advocate, could be equated with John Gotti, the Mafia don. Unfortunately, the Court held in *Scheidler* that this legislative history argument was inconclusive, so no per se objection existed to using RICO against political demonstrators. The Court did not reach the "extortion" argument. Courts, therefore, continue to use the "extortion/coercion" theory to attack political demonstrations where the protestor's conduct goes beyond picketing. Instead of a minor trespass, the conduct is escalated into "racketeering."

Sadly, RICO litigation today is also conducted contrary to the earlier free speech teachings of the Court in *Watts v. United States* (1969) and *NAACP v. Claiborne Hardware Co.* (1982). In *Watts*, the Court distinguished between "true threats" and "political hyperbole." An antidraft protestor in 1966 who "threatened" to shoot President LYNDON B. JOHNSON was found not guilty of threatening the President; his remarks were found to be "crude and offensive" but reflecting "political opposition," not "criminal intent." That distinction is ignored today when anti-abortion groups publish posters identifying abortionists as "war criminals." Here, too, there is a CHILL-ING EFFECT on free speech.

Similarly, in *Claiborne Hardware Co.*, the Court held that where violent and nonviolent conduct were mixed in a civil rights BOYCOTT, the nonviolent conduct was free speech and could not be made the basis of suit. Only damage caused by unprotected conduct could be remedied, and individual liability had to be based on individual, not group, conduct unless the individual joined the group with the intent to further its unlawful objectives. To protect free speech, the Court required pleading, instructions, and jury verdicts to separate protected from unprotected activity.

Nevertheless, when Scheidler was tried in 1998, the jury assessed $85,926 for the security costs of clinics for anti-abortion demonstrations. Scheidler was not connected by the court to any conspiracy to murder or commit arson. The jury was, however, permitted to make generic findings and return its verdict in a lump sum, despite *Clairborne*; it was not required to apportion the costs between Scheidler's protected and unprotected conduct, nor between his conduct and that of others who might murder doctors or burn clinics. Similarly, in *Northeastern Women's Center v. McMonagle* (1989), an earlier decision of a federal appellate court, although $887 of injury was done by an unidentified party to equipment during a SIT-IN, all of the defendants, who had engaged in picketing over nine years, were held liable under RICO for treble damages ($2,661) and $65,000 in attorney's fees. Such indiscriminate jury verdicts and awards of disproportionate legal fees chill free speech.

Heavy-handed litigation under RICO against protest movements was not what Congress had in mind in 1970. If this kind of litigation is to be allowed, it ought to be conducted with a scrupulous concern for free speech. If not, RICO threatens free speech.

G. ROBERT BLAKEY
(2000)

Bibliography

BLAKEY, G. ROBERT and RODDY, KEVIN P.   1996   Reflections on *Reves v. Ernst & Young. American Criminal Law Review* 33: 1345, 1657–1675.

LaFAVE, WAYNE and SCOTT, AUSTIN   1986   *Criminal Law*, 2nd ed. St. Paul, Minn.: West Publishing Co.

FREE SPEECH, MURDER MANUALS, AND INSTRUCTION OF VIOLENCE

The FIRST AMENDMENT guarantee of FREEDOM OF SPEECH is perhaps tested most severely when speech either advocates or instructs how to commit violent, illegal action. Even where speech does not do so directly, but merely has the potential to induce such illegality through suggestive words or images, juries are being asked to punish that speech by awarding substantial judgments in civil damages lawsuits. For their part, some trial and appellate court judges are increasingly treating such speech as conduct—balancing the perceived social value of the speech against its perceived potential for causing harm. In the wake of a rash of tragic high school shootings across the United States that have killed or injured dozens of students and teachers, coupled with recent multimillion-dollar jury verdicts and settlements in high-profile cases, the pressure to bring and permit such litigation seems likely to increase.

In its 1919 decision in SCHENCK V. UNITED STATES, the Supreme Court considered whether one could be criminally punished for advocating resistance to military conscription. The Court held that "[t]he question in every case is whether the words used are used in such circumstances and are of such a nature as to create a clear and present danger that they will bring about the substantive evils that Congress has a right to prevent. It is a question of proximity and degree."

Fifty years later, in BRANDENBURG V. OHIO (1969), the Court announced a more restrictive reformulation of *Schenck's* CLEAR AND PRESENT DANGER standard: "[T]he constitutional guarantees . . . do not permit a State to forbid or proscribe advocacy of the use of force or of law violation except where such advocacy is directed to inciting or producing imminent lawless action and is likely to incite or produce such action." The *Brandenburg* Court found that an Ohio statute prohibiting advocacy of crime and terrorism was unconstitutional because it failed to "refine the statute's bald definition of the crime in terms of mere advocacy not distinguished from incitement to imminent lawless action."

Unfortunately, lower courts have frequently failed to follow the Supreme Court's *Brandenburg* edict. In cases involving speech urging tax evasion, courts have declined to protect speech that merely advocates or instructs how to commit unlawful conduct. Federal courts have also failed to protect speech advocating or instructing commission of a variety of other illegal acts, including the manufacture of the drug PCP and creation of an explosive device. In none of these cases, however, was it clearly shown that the speech was either intended to or likely to cause imminent lawlessness.

In *Rice v. Paladin Enterprises, Inc.* (1997), the U.S. Court of Appeals for the Fourth Circuit held that a book publisher could be liable for publishing speech that described how to be a contract killer. The court emphasized that the government had a COMPELLING STATE INTEREST "in preventing the particular conduct at issue" and that a jury could find that the only communicative value of the speech was the "indisputably illegitimate one of training persons how to murder and to engage in the business of murder for hire." The decision purported to distinguish *Brandenburg* on the grounds that it protected only the "abstract teaching of the moral propriety or even moral

necessity for resort to lawlessness, or its equivalent," but not speech that instructs how to commit crimes.

Relying directly on *Rice*, the Louisiana Court of Appeal permitted discovery to proceed in *Byers v. Edmondson* (1998), a lawsuit claiming that the shooting of a convenience store clerk was inspired by the motion picture "Natural Born Killers." The Louisiana court's ruling—issued just weeks after the Supreme Court denied review of *Rice*—accepted plaintiffs' claims that "the film falls into the incitement to imminent lawless activity exception."

In truth, *Brandenburg* does not sanction any balancing of the perceived social value of speech against that speech's potential for harm. Indeed, doing so would appear to violate the First Amendment's fundamental proscription against content-based restrictions on speech articulated, for example, in the Supreme Court's opinion in R. A. V. V. CITY OF ST. PAUL (1992).

Although perceived social value is a factor that has been considered in the context of defining categorically unprotected speech, such as OBSCENITY, it should have no bearing on the protection of speech advocating or instructing how to commit illegal action. Rather, courts should adhere to the *Brandenburg* formulation by considering only whether speech is intended to and is likely to cause imminent lawlessness.

The wave of high school violence that has gripped America at the close of the 1990s has already begun to inspire litigation that will further test judicial fealty to *Brandenburg*. The parents of three students killed during a Paducah, Kentucky, high school shooting spree filed a $130 million lawsuit against two Internet websites, several computer game companies, and the makers and distributors of the 1995 movie "The Basketball Diaries." Moreover, for better or worse, *Rice* will not be the crucible in which the *Brandenburg* principles are tested. Rather than risk a trial just weeks after the massacre that left fifteen dead at Columbine High School in Littleton, Colorado, the defendant publisher reportedly agreed to a multimillion-dollar settlement and the removal of its book from the market.

DOUGLAS E. MIRELL
ROBERT N. TREIMAN
(2000)

FREUND, ERNST
(1864–1932)

Ernst Freund, professor of law at the University of Chicago, is best remembered today for his huge and immensely influential *Police Power: Public Policy and Constitutional Rights* (1904), the first systematic exposition of its subject. POLICE POWER, said Freund, was the "power of promoting the public welfare by restraining and regulating the use of liberty and property." Because Freund saw the power "not as a fixed quantity, but as the expression of social, economic, and political conditions," he praised that elasticity which helped adapt the law to changing circumstances. This endorsement, along with only minimal approval of laissez-faire doctrines such as FREEDOM OF CONTRACT, helped provide support for the Progressive movement. His views strongly contrasted with those of CHRISTOPHER TIEDEMAN, a vigorous and authoritative exponent of laissez-faire who decried the use of the police power. In *Standards of American Legislation* (1917), Freund attempted to formulate positive principles to guide legislators and to give DUE PROCESS OF LAW a more definite meaning.

DAVID GORDON
(1986)

FREUND, PAUL A.
(1908–1992)

Paul A. Freund was the leading constitutional scholar in the United States in the generation following WORLD WAR II. Born in St. Louis in 1908, he graduated from Washington University and the Harvard Law School, where he was president of the Harvard Law Review. In the 1930s, he was successively law clerk to Justice LOUIS D. BRANDEIS of the Supreme Court, attorney for various government agencies, and then a lawyer in the office of the SOLICITOR GENERAL for ten years, with a brief stint in the middle of his service as a faculty member at Harvard Law School. Returning to Harvard in 1946, he quickly established himself as a constitutional scholar in a remarkable series of essays on a wide variety of constitutional law subjects. He remained at Harvard for the rest of his life, declining an offer from President JOHN F. KENNEDY to become Solicitor General and, many people thought, thereby forfeiting his chance of appointment to the Supreme Court.

Although FELIX FRANKFURTER was Freund's teacher and mentor, Freund more resembled BENJAMIN N. CARDOZO in both personality and constitutional philosophy. Like Cardozo, Freund was a shy bachelor, who had a zest for learning in all fields of human knowledge, and a photographic memory for stories and apt quotation that made him a popular speaker on all occasions. Like Cardozo, Freund sought to understand and accommodate the contending principles in all legal disputes. Freund taught that "[i]f the first requisite of a constitutional judge is that he be a philosopher, the second requisite is that he be not too philosophical. Success in the undertaking requires absorption in the facts rather than deduction from large and rigidly held abstractions. . . . In the familiar phrase, judgment

from speculation should yield to judgment from experience."

Freund was no less eloquent in his vision of law: "in a larger sense all law resembles art, for the mission of each is to impose a measure of order on the disorder of experience without stifling the underlying diversity, spontaneity, and disarray. . . . In neither discipline will the craftsman succeed unless he sees that proportion and balance are both essential, that order and disorder are both virtues when held in a proper tension . . . new vistas give a false light unless there are cross-lights. There are, I am afraid, no absolutes in law or art except intelligence."

Freund's wit, grace, and style made him one of the foremost essayists of his time on subjects legal and nonlegal, but particularly on topics of constitutional law. He was a commanding presence and taught the virtues of tolerance, accommodation, and learning for its own sake to a whole generation of students, lawyers, and judges.

ANDREW L. KAUFMAN
(2000)

Bibliography

FREUND, PAUL A. 1961 *The Supreme Court of the United States.* Cleveland, Ohio: World Publishing Co.
—— 1968 *On Law and Justice.* Cambridge, Mass.: Harvard University Press.

FRIENDLY, HENRY J.
(1903–1986)

Henry J. Friendly was among the greatest federal judges of the twentieth century. After graduating from Harvard Law School (where he was president of the *Harvard Law Review*) and clerking for Justice LOUIS D. BRANDEIS, Friendly entered private practice in New York City, where he had a distinguished career. Appointed to the UNITED STATES COURT OF APPEALS for the Second Circuit in 1959 by President DWIGHT D. EISENHOWER, Judge Friendly served on the court for twenty-seven years until his death.

Judge Friendly's unquestioned brilliance, his towering intellect, and his unrelenting concern with the facts are reflected in his judicial opinions in almost every area of the law. His contributions to ADMINISTRATIVE LAW and federal jurisdiction, two areas in which he took a special interest, are unsurpassed in their analytical power and insight. In addition, Judge Friendly's opinions on SECURITIES LAW and CRIMINAL PROCEDURE are widely regarded as unequaled in their thoughtfulness, craft, and scholarship. Perhaps Judge Friendly's extraordinary ability for deft analysis of legally and factually complex issues was most impressively displayed in the series of comprehensive opinions he wrote during the 1970s for the Special Railroad Court. This court was established to handle the litigation arising over the congressionally directed reorganization of the eastern railroads, many of which were in bankruptcy reorganization.

In addition to his prolific output of judicial opinions, Judge Friendly wrote a number of influential law review articles as well as a short book on federal jurisdiction. He was also active in the American Law Institute. Perhaps the unique combination of talents that Judge Friendly possessed are most succinctly captured by the thought that he was considered to be a lawyer's lawyer, a scholar's scholar, and a judge's judge.

WALTER HELLERSTEIN
(1992)

Bibliography

SYMPOSIUM 1984 In Honor of Henry J. Friendly. *University of Pennsylvania Law Review* 133:1–77.

FRIES' REBELLION

In 1798 Congress levied a tax on houses, land, and slaves, to finance a possible war with France. There was considerable resistance to the tax and, in February 1799, an armed band led by John Fries rescued tax resisters from the United States marshal at Bethlehem, Pennsylvania. President JOHN ADAMS ordered the army and militia to suppress the uprising.

Fries and his followers were arrested and some seventy-two insurrectionists were tried for various offenses relating to the incident. Fries and two companions were tried before Justice SAMUEL CHASE and Judge RICHARD PETERS and were convicted of TREASON, the prosecution arguing that armed resistance to the enforcement of federal law amounted to levying war against the United States. President Adams, against the advice of his cabinet, subsequently granted a general pardon to all participants in the "rebellion."

DENNIS J. MAHONEY
(1986)

FRISBY v. SCHULTZ
487 U.S. 474 (1988)

In response to anti-abortion protesters picketing the home of a local abortionist, a Wisconsin town passed an ordinance forbidding picketing "before or about the residence . . . of any individual." The Court held in a 6–3 vote that the ordinance did not on its face violate the FIRST AMENDMENT. Writing for five members of the majority, Justice SANDRA DAY O'CONNOR narrowly construed the law

as applying only to picketing directed at a particular home. The law served a significant government interest, according to O'Connor, because it sought to protect the sanctity of the home from unwanted—and inescapable—intrusions. O'Connor noted that "[t]he First Amendment permits the government to prohibit offensive speech as intrusive when the 'captive' audience cannot avoid the objectionable speech. . . . [Here] [t]he resident is figuratively, and perhaps literally, trapped within the home, and because of the unique and subtle impact of such picketing is left with no ready means of avoiding the unwanted speech."

The dissenters sympathized with the intent of the law, but found that its language suffered from OVERBREADTH.

JOHN G. WEST, JR.
(1992)

FROHWERK v. UNITED STATES
249 U.S. 204 (1919)

In the second major test of the wartime ESPIONAGE ACT to reach the Supreme Court, the Justices unanimously affirmed the conviction of the publisher of a pro-German publication for conspiring to obstruct military recruitment through publication of antidraft articles. Justice OLIVER WENDELL HOLMES invoked the CLEAR AND PRESENT DANGER test. "We do not lose our right to condemn either measures or men because the Country is at war," he wrote, "But . . . it is impossible to say that it might not have been found that the circulation of the paper was in quarters where a little breath would be enough to kindle a flame. . . ." Holmes and his brethren declined to inquire themselves into the degree or probability of the danger represented by the publication.

MICHAEL E. PARRISH
(1986)

FRONTIERO v. RICHARDSON
411 U.S. 677 (1973)

In *Reed v. Reed* (1971) a unanimous Supreme Court had invalidated a state law preferring the appointment of men, rather than women, as administrators of decedents' estates. The Court had used the rhetoric of the RATIONAL BASIS standard of review but had in fact employed a more rigorous standard of JUDICIAL REVIEW. Conceding the rationality of eliminating one type of contest between would-be administrators, the Court had concluded that the preference for men was an "arbitrary legislative choice" that denied women the EQUAL PROTECTION OF THE LAW.

In *Frontiero*, two years later, the Court came within one

vote of radically restructuring the constitutional doctrine governing SEX DISCRIMINATION. Under federal law, a woman member of the armed forces could claim her husband as a "dependent" entitled to certain benefits only if he was, in fact, dependent on her for more than half his support; a serviceman could claim "dependent" status for his wife irrespective of actual dependency. Eight Justices agreed that this discrimination violated the Fifth Amendment's equal protection guarantee, but they divided 4–4 as to their reasoning.

Justice WILLIAM J. BRENNAN, for four Justices, concluded that sex, like race, was a SUSPECT CLASSIFICATION demanding STRICT SCRUTINY of its justifications. Four other Justices merely rested on the precedent of *Reed*. Justice LEWIS F. POWELL, writing for three of them, added that it would be inappropriate for the Court to hold that gender was a suspect classification while debate over ratification of the EQUAL RIGHTS AMENDMENT was still pending. Justice WILLIAM H. REHNQUIST dissented.

The confusion in the wake of *Frontiero* ended three years later, in CRAIG V. BOREN (1976), when the Justices compromised on an intermediate STANDARD OF REVIEW.

KENNETH L. KARST
(1986)

FROTHINGHAM v. MELLON
MASSACHUSETTS v. MELLON
262 U.S. 447 (1923)

In the SHEPPARD-TOWNER MATERNITY ACT of 1921, a predecessor of modern FEDERAL GRANTS-IN-AID, Congress authorized federal funding of state programs "to reduce maternal and infant mortality." These companion cases involved suits to halt federal expenditures under the act, challenging it as a deprivation of property without DUE PROCESS OF LAW and a violation of the TENTH AMENDMENT. Justice GEORGE SUTHERLAND, for a unanimous Supreme Court, dismissed the *Massachusetts* case for failing to present a justiciable controversy. The state's suit in its own behalf presented a POLITICAL QUESTION calling on the Court to adjudicate "abstract questions of political power," not rights of property or even "quasi-sovereign rights actually invaded or threatened." The state was under no obligation to accept federal monies. The state also lacked STANDING to represent its citizens, who were also citizens of the United States.

Frothingham's due process argument relied on the premise that spending under the act would increase her tax liability. Sutherland concluded that she, too, lacked standing to sue. Any personal interest in federal tax monies "is comparatively minute and indeterminable; and the effect upon future taxation, of any payment out of the funds, so remote, fluctuating and uncertain, that no basis is afforded for an appeal." Because Frothingham could not demonstrate direct injury, her suit must fail. An OBITER DICTUM implying the constitutionality of grants-in-aid was the Court's only pronouncement on such programs until approved in STEWARD MACHINE COMPANY V. DAVIS (1937).

DAVID GORDON
(1986)

FRUIT OF THE POISONOUS TREE

No DOCTRINE in constitutional CRIMINAL PROCEDURE has created more confusion than the disarmingly simple proposition that when the state has violated FUNDAMENTAL RIGHTS, it may receive no benefit from the violation. The "poisonous tree" is the violation, an illegal search for instance, in which the key to a safe deposit is found. Clearly under the EXCLUSIONARY RULE the government may not use as EVIDENCE the discovery of the key; but neither may it use whatever incriminating items are in the safe deposit box. These are the "fruits."

The existence of a "poisonous tree," however, does not mean that all that is discovered after the tree sprouts is automatically a "fruit." The issue in its classic though grammatically inelegant formulation is: "whether, granting establishment of the primary illegality, [the evidence] has been come at by exploitation of that illegality or instead by means sufficiently distinguishable to be purged of the primary taint" (WONG SUN V. UNITED STATES, 1963). Many exceptions to the fruits doctrine have evolved from these words and have been variously named by courts and commentators, although the basic question is always how far from the tree the fruit has fallen.

The exception used most often is "attenuation": too much has intervened between the primary illegality and the gathering of the fruit. In *Wong Sun* itself, a confession made after an illegal ARREST was found not to be a fruit because of the passage of time between the arrest and confession, during which the accused was free on BAIL. Another exception is labeled "independent source"; the idea is that although the evidence could have been a fruit, it was actually uncovered by means distinguishable from the primary illegality. Closely allied to the independent source exception is that of "inevitable discovery," which the Supreme Court endorsed in NIX V. WILLIAMS (1984). Although the body of the deceased was discovered through a blatant violation of the defendant's Sixth Amendment RIGHT TO COUNSEL, the Court held that it would have been found through other proper investigative techniques that the police were employing at the time that the primary illegality was committed. The burden is on the government to show that the discovery would have been "inevitable." Finally, while refusing to establish an across-the-board rule that eyewitness testimony could never be a fruit, the Supreme Court has indicated that the free will of a witness expressed in the desire to testify would, in virtually every case, attenuate the taint, even when the witness would never have been found without the primary illegality.

As can be seen from the number and nature of the exceptions, the fruit of the poisonous tree doctrine is subject to much interpretation. For instance, in *Harrison v. United States* (1968) the Court held that the defendant's testimony at trial was a fruit of illegally obtained confessions introduced into evidence. Two years later, in *Mc-Mann v. Richardson* (1970), the Court found that a guilty plea entered after an arguably illegal confession was not induced by the prospect of the admission of the confessions. These cases can be reconciled by applying the attenuation exception—the defendant's decision to plead guilty was an intervening event that dissipated the poison. But this is hardly a satisfying distinction.

The case that most strikingly reveals the difficulties with the fruits doctrine and is also the key to future interpretation is *United States v. Crews* (1980). In connection with his illegal arrest, the police obtained Crews's photograph which would not otherwise have been available. They showed it in an array of pictures to the victims who made an immediate identification. Next, Crews was placed in a fair LINEUP where the victims also identified him. The first question was whether testimony about the pretrial identifications was fruit; this was easily resolved because the prosecution conceded that it was. The harder issue was whether the victim's identification at trial of Crews must be suppressed. In the metaphoric language that seizes courts when dealing with this doctrine, the Court concluded that: "At trial, [the victim] retrieved the [mental image of her assailant], compared it to the figure of the defendant, and positively identified him as the robber. No part of this process was affected by respondent's illegal arrest. . . . [T]he toxin in this case was injected only after the evidentiary bud had blossomed; the fruit served at trial was not poisoned."

The Court in *Crews* went on to say that there could be cases where the victim's in-court identification was a result of the primary illegality—in other words, that the photograph and lineup identifications had led to the ability to point to the defendant at trial. In finding that this was not such a case the Court implicitly emphasized that the analysis of whether evidence is the fruit of the poisonous tree will continue in a case-by-case, highly pragmatic, and utterly unpredictable vein.

BARBARA ALLEN BABCOCK
(1986)

Bibliography

LaFave, Wayne R. 1978 *Search and Seizure: A Treatise on the Fourth Amendment.* Vol. 3:621–681. St. Paul, Minn.: West Publishing Co.

FUGITIVE FROM JUSTICE

The second clause of Article IV, section 2, of the Constitution provides that a person charged with a crime in one state, who has fled to another to escape justice, "shall, on demand of the executive authority of the state from which he fled, be delivered up. . . ." The clause makes rendition (or extradition) of fugitives from justice a duty of state officials.

Although extradition of escaped felons from one political JURISDICTION to another was long recognized as an obligation of comity in international law, the process is not automatic. Between sovereign nations, extradition normally occurs only when there is a treaty providing for it. Permanent extradition arrangements were not common before the nineteenth century.

Among the earliest standing arrangements for extradition of accused criminals was the one embodied in the articles of the New England Confederation (1643), which provided for the surrender of a fugitive to the colony from which he had fled when demand was made by two magistrates of that colony. Interstate extradition has been from the first, therefore, a feature of American FEDERALISM. The ARTICLES OF CONFEDERATION contained a provision identical to that in the Constitution. The Constitution's fugitive from justice clause was proposed in the CONSTITUTIONAL CONVENTION as part of the New Jersey Plan and was given its present form by the committee of detail.

EDMUND RANDOLPH, the first attorney general, issued an opinion that the fugitive from justice clause was not self-executing, that is, the Constitution did not specify what official was to render fugitives or establish enforcible procedures. Congress therefore, in 1793, passed a law imposing the duty of rendition on state governors.

The first test of the clause in the Supreme Court was in *Kentucky v. Dennison* (1861). The governor of Ohio had refused to honor Kentucky's demand that he render a fugitive wanted in Kentucky for aiding the escape of a slave. Chief Justice ROGER B. TANEY, for the Court, rejected Ohio's contention that the crime in question was not one contemplated by the Framers of the Constitution as within the scope of the clause; the clause extends to any act defined as a crime in the place where it was committed. The Court held that rendition of a fugitive was a MINISTERIAL ACT, one which a state governor has a duty to perform and not one over which he has any discretion. However, the Court also held that there was no power in the federal courts to compel compliance with the duty. Subsequently, governors have occasionally refused, for various reasons, to deliver fugitives to the states in which they were wanted.

Fugitives' careers are complicated by other factors. In 1934, Congress made it a federal crime to travel in INTERSTATE COMMERCE with the intent to avoid prosecution or confinement. The federal crime must be tried in the state from which the fugitive fled, and one practical effect of the statute is to return fugitives to the states in which they are wanted, facilitating arrest on state charges. Interstate rendition has also been facilitated by INTERSTATE COMPACTS and by adoption in most states of the Uniform Criminal Extradition Act.

DENNIS J. MAHONEY
(1986)

FUGITIVE SLAVERY

The problem of runaways plagued American slave societies since the seventeenth century and was not solved until the abolition of SLAVERY itself during the CIVIL WAR. Statutes of the colonial period dealing with indentured servants and slaves contained extensive provisions providing for punishment of runaways. Those relating to black slaves became increasingly severe over time, culminating in various eighteenth-century provisions permitting death, whipping, branding, outlawry, castration, dismemberment, and ear-slitting for runaways and compensation by the colony to masters of "outlying" slaves who were killed.

Provisions for interjurisdictional rendition of fugitives began with the fugitive-servant provisions of the New England Confederation (1643), but until 1787 rendition was a matter of comity between the colonies/states. The NORTHWEST ORDINANCE (1787) contained a fugitive slave/servant clause. The Constitution contained a clause providing that a "Person held to Service or Labour" shall not be freed when he absconds into another state, "but shall be delivered up." The use of the passive voice and the location of the clause in Article IV blurred responsibility for its enforcement, which caused protracted constitutional controversies in the 1840s and 1850s.

In 1793, Congress enacted the first Fugitive Slave Act, which provided that any slave holder or his "agent or attorney" could seize an alleged runaway, take him before a federal judge or local magistrate, prove title to the slave by affidavit or oral testimony, and get a certificate of rendition entitling him to take the slave back to the master's domicile. The constitutionality of the statute was repeatedly upheld by eminent authority: implicitly in JOSEPH STORY's *Commentaries on the Constitution of the United States* (1833); explicitly by Chief Justice William Tilghman of the Pennsylvania Supreme Court in *Wright v. Deacon*

(1819) and Chief Justice Isaac Parker of the Massachusetts Supreme Judicial Court in *Commonwealth v. Griffin* (1823). Early abolitionist societies worked to prevent free blacks from being kidnapped through the instrumentality of the 1793 act and provided counsel to alleged fugitives. Abolitionists challenged the statute on the grounds that Congress exceeded its powers in forcing state officials to participate in federal rendition proceedings, in permitting rendition from TERRITORIES as well as states, and in interfering with the rights of the states to protect their free citizens.

Before 1843, a few states enacted PERSONAL LIBERTY LAWS that provided various procedural safeguards, such as HABEAS CORPUS or TRIAL BY JURY, to alleged fugitives. The slave states resented these and challenged their constitutionality in PRIGG V. PENNSYLVANIA (1842). Speaking for a majority of the Court, Justice Joseph Story held that: the fugitive slave clause of the Constitution was an essential compromise necessary to ratification of the Constitution by the southern states; the 1793 act was constitutional; the master had a right of recapture of a runaway slave, derived either from the COMMON LAW or from the fugitive slave clause; and the Pennsylvania personal liberty law was unconstitutional because it infringed on masters' rights protected by the federal statute. In an OBITER DICTUM, Story stated that the federal government could not constitutionally oblige state officials to participate in enforcement of the act.

Insubstantial as this suggestion was, northern states after 1842 enacted new personal liberty laws prohibiting state officials from participating in enforcement of the federal statute and prohibiting the use of state facilities such as jails for detaining runaways. Abolitionists then mounted a more sophisticated, wide-ranging attack on the constitutionality of the 1793 statute, alleging that it violated the Fifth Amendment's DUE PROCESS clause and the FOURTH AMENDMENT'S SEARCHES AND SEIZURES clause.

Congress, as part of the COMPROMISE OF 1850, enacted a new Fugitive Slave Act, which was an extension of the 1793 Act, not a replacement for it. It contained these novel features: owners and agents were authorized to seize alleged fugitives with or without legal process; certificates of rendition could be granted by federal commissioners as well as federal judges; any adult male could be drafted into a posse to assist in capture and rendition; obstruction of the act was punishable by a fine of $1,000; the commissioner's fee was $5 if he determined that the black was not a runaway, but $10 if he awarded the certificate of rendition, prompting an abolitionist's remark that the statute set the price of a Carolina Negro at $1,000 and a Yankee soul at $5.

Residents of the free states objected vehemently to the new statute. Throughout the 1850s, dramatic rescues and recaptures of runaways provided real-life drama to accompany the sensational success of the serialized, book, and stage versions of *Uncle Tom's Cabin*, with its melodramatic runaway scene. Federal authorities and northern conservatives responded to abolitionist challenges and to rescues of fugitives by affirming the constitutionality of the 1850 Act (Chief Justice LEMUEL SHAW of the Massachusetts Supreme Judicial Court in *In re Sims*, 1851) and by demanding that resistance to enforcement of the measure be prosecuted as treason. Two efforts at doing so, however (resulting from the Jerry rescue, Syracuse, New York, 1851, and the Oberlin-Wellington rescue, northern Ohio, 1858), ended in inglorious failure for the prosecution. In general, however, the northern states attempted to comply with the statute, and most blacks seized as fugitives under the act were sent into slavery.

In a dictum in ABLEMAN V. BOOTH (1859) Chief Justice ROGER B. TANEY declared the 1850 statute constitutional, but the question was soon to be mooted. After the outbreak of the Civil War, the policies of some Union commanders discouraged the return of runaways who fled behind Union lines. Congress partially repealed the Fugitive Slave Acts in 1862 and then fully in 1864. The whole issue, and the fugitive slave clause of the Constitution, became dead letters with the abolition of slavery in 1864–1865.

WILLIAM M. WIECEK
(1986)

Bibliography

CAMPBELL, STANLEY W. 1968 *The Slave Catchers: Enforcement of the Fugitive Slave Law, 1850–1860.* Chapel Hill: University of North Carolina Press.
DUMOND, DWIGHT L. 1961 *Antislavery: The Crusade for Freedom in America.* Ann Arbor: University of Michigan Press.
HYMAN, HAROLD M. and WIECEK, WILLIAM M. 1982 *Equal Justice under Law: Constitutional Development, 1835–1875.* New York: Harper & Row.

FULL EMPLOYMENT ACT
60 Stat. 23 (1946)

Despite the post-WORLD WAR II desire to shake off wartime economic controls, Congress passed a Full Employment Act in February 1946, establishing a new concept of the relation of the government to the national economy. The measure declared officially that it was the responsibility of the national government to insure effective operation of the country's economic system and maintain maximum employment, production, and purchasing power. Through a newly created three-person Presidential Council of Economic Advisors, the nation's economic patterns were stud-

ied and analyzed with the government responsible for evolving new controls essential to the nation's economic security. These included: tax rates designed to produce a predetermined deficit or surplus based on whether the administration sought to stimulate or cool off the economy; controlling the ease or tightness of credit; raising or lowering public spending levels; and maintaining wage and price guidelines. Such use of deficit financing, public works, and economic controls might alleviate the negative effects of the business cycle and avoid another major economic depression.

The measure was a constitutional landmark. It formally rejected the concept that the government's main role in the economic sphere was negative: to maintain a free enterprise system by preserving, through laws and court decisions, a hands-off policy toward American economic activities.

PAUL L. MURPHY
(1986)

Bibliography

BAILEY, STEPHEN K. 1950 *Congress Makes a Law: The Story Behind the Employment Act of 1946.* New York: Columbia University Press.

FULLER, MELVILLE W.
(1833–1910)

Melville Weston Fuller, eighth Chief Justice of the United States, was appointed by GROVER CLEVELAND in 1888 and presided over the Court until his death on July 4, 1910. Fuller's twenty-two-year tenure as Chief Justice, the longest during the Court's second century, spanned one of the most significant periods of constitutional development in American history. Fuller and his associates circumscribed the rights of state criminal defendants under the FOURTEENTH AMENDMENT, established an inferior legal status for residents of the new overseas colonies, articulated the infamous SEPARATE BUT EQUAL DOCTRINE, and devised a spate of other juristic strategies for avoiding interventions on behalf of black petitioners in the fields of education and VOTING RIGHTS. At the same time the FULLER COURT made so many new departures in decisions affecting the economic order that one scholar has described its work as "the new judicialism." Fuller and his colleagues invalidated the federal income tax, emasculated the Interstate Commerce Commission, put the Court's imprimatur on the labor INJUNCTION, construed the commerce clause so that the SHERMAN ANTITRUST ACT frustrated the activities of labor unions yet failed to impede the fusion of manufacturing corporations, and elaborated the concept of SUBSTANTIVE

DUE PROCESS as a guarantor of VESTED RIGHTS and LIBERTY OF CONTRACT.

The vast bulk of the Fuller Court's work in constitutional law reflected the Chief Justice's constitutional understanding, the contours of which had been firmly fixed before Fuller came to the bench. Beginning in 1856, when he left his native Maine and settled in Chicago, Fuller was an active stump speaker and essayist for the Illinois Democratic party; he styled himself a disciple of Thomas Hart Benton and STEPHEN A. DOUGLAS long after both were dead. Fuller spoke often in favor of free trade, hard money, and equal opportunity in the market. "Paternalism, with its constant intermeddling with individual freedom," he wrote in 1880, "has no place in a system which rests for its strength upon the self-reliant energies of the people." But Fuller's version of the equal rights creed had no place for blacks. An exponent of a conservative naturalism that stressed the importance of homogeneous communities and local autonomy in American public life, Fuller believed that union and republican liberty were possible only if the federal government acquiesced in local racial arrangements on the same ground that it acquiesced in state laws regulating the status of women. He objected to the EMANCIPATION PROCLAMATION on the ground that it was "predicated upon the idea that the President may annul the constitutions and laws of sovereign states." He claimed that the THIRTEENTH AMENDMENT and Fourteenth Amendment protected only the "common rights" of individuals against discriminatory classification. And he never ceased to insist that Congress's powers to regulate persons or property were limited, derivable only from specific grants and not from any assumption of an underlying national SOVEREIGNTY. Fuller's longest, most plaintive dissents came in the INSULAR CASES (1901), where he denied Congress's power to levy tariffs on the products of colonial possessions, and in CHAMPION V. AMES (1903), where he contended that Congress could not exercise police powers on the pretense of regulating commerce.

Fuller did not grapple with the Court's role in the American system of government following his appointment as Chief Justice. For Fuller, as for Benton, Douglas, and Cleveland, the Constitution was more than a text that allocated specific powers and secured particular rights against government. The Constitution was significant above all as the repository of values so integral to the existence of republicanism that any public official who failed to protect and defend them was guilty of a breach of trust. Consequently, Fuller conceptualized the judicial function in terms of duty rather than in terms of role; his approach to judging was instinctive rather than ratiocinative. Since he had long associated the Constitution with the Democratic party's mid-nineteenth-century dogmas, Fuller impulsively enforced those dogmas as the law of the land. It

was no accident that JAMES BRADLEY THAYER published his path-breaking assessment of "The Origins and Scope of the American Doctrine of Constitutional Law" five years after Fuller's appointment or that a school of jurisprudence dedicated to "judicial self-restraint" grew increasingly large and vocal during his tenure. Other critics accused his Court of aiding the rich and powerful at the expense of the poor and helpless in the name of judicial neutrality. But Fuller neither replied to them nor sought to persuade others to do so. He simply hoped it would always be said of him, as he said of Cleveland in a 1909 eulogy, that "he trod unswervingly the path of duty, undeterred by doubts, single-minded and straight-forward."

The Chief Justice's constitutional understanding may have been "single-minded and straight-forward," but the Fuller era abounds with anomalies all the same. First there is the matter of Fuller's reputation. Until EARL WARREN's day, no Court was subjected to more strident criticism for a more sustained period of time than Fuller's. Yet when Fuller died the press concurred that none of his predecessors had been so successful in earning the respect and confidence of the country. Even THEODORE ROOSEVELT's *Outlook* conceded that Fuller was "perhaps the most popular" though "not the strongest or most famous Chief Justice." Perceptions of Fuller's capacity for judicial leadership were equally anomalous. The Chief Justice voted with the majority in virtually every leading case decided during his tenure. If STEPHEN J. FIELD is to be believed, moreover, Fuller was effective in setting the tenor of conference discussion. "Field told me on the bench this morning," Fuller informed his wife in 1891, "that in the conference I was almost invariably right. He said I was remarkably quick in seizing the best point." Yet contemporary observers invariably described him as a weak Chief Justice who neither led his Court nor exerted a substantial influence on its outlook.

The greatest anomaly of the Fuller era was the doctrinal structure of "the new judicialism." When Fuller contemplated the future of the republic in a centennial address on GEORGE WASHINGTON, two fears loomed especially large. One was that "the drift toward the exertion of the national will" might ultimately result in "consolidation," which in turn would impair the "vital importance" of the states and undermine self-government by extending the sphere of legislative authority to such a degree that the people no longer controlled it. The other was "the drift . . . towards increased interference by the State in the attempt to alleviate inequality of conditions." Fuller admitted that "[s]o long as that interference is . . . protective only," it was not only legitimate but necessary. "But," he added, "the rights to life, to use one's faculties in all lawful ways, and to acquire and enjoy property, are morally fundamental rights antecedent to constitutions, which do not create, but secure and protect them." It was imperative, he said, that Americans never grow "unmindful of the fact that it is the duty of the people to support the government and not of the government to support the people." Each of these concerns soon reappeared as major premises in the Court's construction of Congress's COMMERCE POWER and in its articulation of the liberty of contract protected by the Fifth and Fourteenth Amendments. But the Chief Justice directed a cacophonous band, not an orchestra. Decisions which, in Fuller's view, were consistent with one another looked antithetical to other observers because different Justices expressed the Court's opinions in different language.

Fuller regarded the liberty of contract doctrine as a juristic device for distinguishing between "paternalism," which he thought was unconstitutional, and legislation that "is protective only." Thus the maximum hours law for miners at issue in HOLDEN V. HARDY (1898) was valid because it protected the health and safety of workers employed in an inherently dangerous occupation. But the maximum hours law for bakery workers invalidated in LOCHNER V. NEW YORK (1905) and the ERDMAN ACT of Congress prohibiting discrimination against union members were unconstitutional because neither statute was "protective only." In Fuller's view, government had no authority to redress inequalities in the bargaining relation. "The employer and the employee have equality of right," JOHN MARSHALL HARLAN explained for the Court in *Adair v. United States* (1908), "and any legislation that disturbs that equality is an arbitrary interference with liberty of contract, which no government can legally justify in a free land." Yet in *Holden* HENRY BROWN spoke at length about the inequality of bargaining power between employees and employers; he also implied that the worker's inability to contract for fair terms provided a legitimate rationale for government intervention. Although Brown apparently retreated from that position when he joined the *Lochner* majority seven years later, the language he used in *Holden* was never expressly disapproved.

The disparity between Fuller's constitutional understanding and the language used by colleagues in opinions he assigned was even more pronounced in the commerce field. Speaking for the Court in UNITED STATES V. E. C. KNIGHT CO. (1895), Fuller held that the Sherman Act could not be constitutionally construed to require the dissolution of manufacturing corporations when the transactions deemed unlawful in the government's complaint involved neither interstate transportation nor interstate sales. "Commerce succeeds to manufacturing," he explained, "and is not part of it." Underlying this distinction were three assumptions which Fuller elaborated with varying degrees of clarity. Congress could not regulate manufacturing combinations under the commerce clause, he said,

for if that were permitted there was nothing to prevent Congress from regulating "every branch of human activity." Fuller also contended that that line between manufacturing and commerce was readily ascertainable. In a spate of recent dormant commerce clause decisions the Court had invalidated state tax laws and police regulations that burdened interstate transactions yet had sustained such legislation when it burdened the production process. With the exception of state laws that burdened commerce "indirectly" and might therefore be sustained under the rule of COOLEY V. BOARD OF WARDENS (1851), then, Congress could regulate only what the states could not and vice versa. Finally, Fuller made it clear that when manufacturing firms made "contracts to buy, sell, or exchange goods to be transported among the several states," the federal government had a duty to intervene under the Sherman Act if those contracts, or agreements pursuant to them, were in restraint of trade. In *Robbins v. Shelby County Taxing District* (1887), a leading dormant commerce clause case, the Court had held that "the negotiation of sales of goods which are in another state . . . is INTERSTATE COMMERCE."

Fuller believed that his construction of Congress's powers under the Sherman Act had two important virtues. It forestalled "consolidation" and it was easy to apply. Congress could certainly reach the agreement at issue in *Addyston Pipe & Steel Co. v. United States* (1899), for there a pool had been devised to allocate the interstate distribution of goods among the cooperating firms. And in LOEWE V. LAWLOR (1908) the hatter's union had not only gone on strike, thus disrupting the production process, but had engaged in a secondary boycott to prevent the sale of hats in interstate commerce. SWIFT & CO. V. UNITED STATES (1905) posed equally simple issues for Fuller. Some thirty firms had agreed to refrain from bidding against one another when livestock was auctioned prior to its delivery for slaughter at the Chicago packinghouses. Clearly, as the Court explained, "the subject-matter [was] sales and the very point of the combination . . . to restrain and monopolize commerce among the states in respect to such sales." But Fuller had designated OLIVER WENDELL HOLMES to speak for the Court in *Swift*, and Holmes had a great deal more to say. Holmes remarked that "commerce among the States is not a technical legal conception, but a practical one, drawn from the course of business." He spoke metaphorically about a current of commerce, suggesting that local production and interstate marketing were not distinct processes so much as parts of a single, undifferentiated process. (See STREAM OF COMMERCE DOCTRINE.) And he cast a pall of doubt on the idea, implicit in Fuller's *Knight* opinion, "that the rule which marks the point at which State taxation or regulation becomes permissible necessarily is beyond the scope of interference by Congress in cases where such interference is deemed necessary for the protection of commerce among the States."

Each of the anomalies of the Fuller years is attributable to the personality of the Chief Justice and his conception of the office. Fuller was a self-effacing, amiable man who was gracious and courteous, even deferential, to his colleagues. He made every effort to secure harmonious relations among the Justices. Fuller inaugurated the custom, still followed today, that each Justice greet and shake hands with every other Justice each morning. And he used his authority to assign opinions when in the majority not to enhance his own reputation or to elaborate favorite doctrines but to cultivate the good will of his associates. The opinion in a leading case ordinarily went to the colleague who, in Fuller's judgment, was most likely to want to speak for the Court. Cases involving questions of JURISDICTION and practice or mundane matters of private law Fuller kept to himself. Thus he let Field deliver the Court's opinions in *Georgia Banking & Railroad Co. v. Smith* (1889), a rate regulation case, and *Chae Chan Ping v. United States* (1889), the Chinese Exclusion Case. Both controversies raised issues of enormous importance to Field; for that very reason Fuller's predecessor had been disinclined to permit Field to address them for the Court.

Fuller also assumed that Brown would consider *Holden* a plum, for he had recently addressed the American Bar Association on the labor question. RUFUS PECKHAM had earned the right to speak for the majority in *Lochner* by dissenting without opinion in every previous case involving legislative regulation of the labor contract. The *Adair* decision provided Fuller with an opportunity to elaborate his own liberty of contract views in a systematic fashion, but he gave the opinion to Harlan instead. Harlan had dissented in *Lochner* on the grounds that the Court had no authority to reject the legislature's reasonable claim that long hours affected the health and safety of bakery workers. In *Adair* the government advanced no such claim and Harlan's opinion barely noticed the Court's prior liberty of contract rulings. Holmes was the logical choice for *Swift*, for the opinion would show Roosevelt that the administration had drawn spurious conclusions about Holmes's antitrust views from NORTHERN SECURITIES CO. V. UNITED STATES (1904).

The Chief Justice's obsession with courtesy also accounts for the striking differences between his own views and the Court's language in opinions which he assigned. He stubbornly defended his convictions in conference and, if necessary, in dissent. But once he had voted with the majority and had authorized an associate to speak for the Court, Fuller never criticized the work produced by a colleague. Good will among the Justices might be lost forever because of a single quarrel; incongruities of DOCTRINE could always be repaired later. Fuller let it be known that forthright yet polite concurring opinions were preferable to postconference haggling over doctrine, and silent acquiescence in the opinion of the Court was more preferable still. Fuller's own behavior set high standards for his associates; he wrote only seven concurring opinions in twenty-two years.

Underlying Fuller's management of the Court was a belief that the Chief Justice's primary duty was to convey to the public the impression that in the Court, more than in any other institution of government, reason triumphed over partisanship and statesmanship prevailed over pettiness. Fuller's success in achieving that goal while rarely speaking for the Court in landmark cases accounts for misperceptions of his capacity for intellectual leadership and for his great popularity despite persistent criticism of his Court's work. But Fuller's winning personality and the apparent anomalies it produced should not overshadow the relationship between his convictions and the new principles of law his Court articulated. Not since JOHN MARSHALL's day had the constitutional understanding of the Chief Justice been more at odds with that of voters and party leaders for such a prolonged period of time. Nevertheless, Fuller presided over a Court that made fundamentally new departures in constitutional interpretation which, in the main, incorporated the values he had imbibed during the party battles of a bygone era in American public life. Although Fuller hoped that eulogists would compare him with Cleveland, it might be more appropriate to analogize his career with that of another charming nineteenth-century Democrat. Like MARTIN VAN BUREN, he rowed to his objectives with muffled oars.

CHARLES W. MCCURDY
(1986)

Bibliography

FULLER, MELVILLE 1890 Address in Commemoration of the Inauguration of George Washington as First President of the United States, Delivered Before the Two Houses of Congress, December 11, 1889. New York: Banks & Brothers.

KING, WILLARD L. 1950 *Melville Weston Fuller: Chief Justice of the United States, 1888–1910.* Chicago: University of Chicago Press.

PAUL, ARNOLD M. 1959 *Conservative Crisis and the Rule of Law: Attitudes of Bar and Bench, 1887–1895.* Ithaca, N.Y.: Cornell University Press.

FULLER COURT
(1888–1910)

MELVILLE W. FULLER was Chief Justice of the United States from 1888 to 1910. Lawyers and historians know the period, and its significance for constitutional law, but do not generally identify it with Fuller's name—and for good reason. He was no leader. Fuller discharged his administrative duties effectively, and in "good humor," to borrow a phrase from OLIVER WENDELL HOLMES, one of his admirers, but he was not an important source of the ideas and vision that shaped the work of the Court.

The year of Fuller's appointment, 1888, was nonetheless an important date in the life of the Court because it marked the beginning of a period of rapid turnover. From 1888 to 1895 there were a considerable number of vacancies, and the two Presidents then in office, GROVER CLEVELAND, a Democrat, and BENJAMIN HARRISON, a Republican—whose politics were conservative and largely indistinguishable—appointed six of the Justices. One was Fuller himself. At the time of his appointment he was a respected Chicago lawyer and, perhaps more significantly, a friend of Cleveland's. The others were DAVID J. BREWER, a federal circuit judge in Kansas; HENRY BILLINGS BROWN, a federal district judge in Detroit; RUFUS PECKHAM, a judge on the New York Court of Appeals; GEORGE SHIRAS, a lawyer from Pittsburgh; and EDWARD D. WHITE, a senator from Louisiana. (LUCIUS Q. C. LAMAR and HOWELL JACKSON were also appointed during this period, but served for relatively short periods.) The intellectual leaders of this group of six were Brewer and Peckham. They appeared in their written opinions as the most powerful and most eloquent, and the Chief Justice usually turned to one or the other to write for the Court in the major cases.

In constructing their majorities, Brewer and Peckham could usually count on the support of STEPHEN J. FIELD (Brewer's uncle), who earlier had achieved his fame by protesting various forms of government regulation in the SLAUGHTERHOUSE CASES and the GRANGER CASES. In the late 1890s Field was replaced by JOSEPH MCKENNA, who was chosen by WILLIAM MCKINLEY, a President who continued in the conservative tradition of Cleveland and Harrison. Another ally of this Cleveland-Harrison group, though perhaps not so steadfast as Field or McKenna, was HORACE GRAY. Gray was appointed in 1881 by President CHESTER A. ARTHUR and served until 1902.

As a result of these appointments, the Court over which Fuller presided was perhaps one of the most homogeneous in the history of the Supreme Court. Even more striking, its composition did not significantly change for most of Fuller's tenure. Fuller died in July 1910, just months after Brewer and Peckham. It was almost as though he could not go on without them. Brown resigned in 1906 and Shiras in 1903, but their replacements—WILLIAM H. MOODY and WILLIAM R. DAY—did not radically alter the balance of power. The only important break with the past came when THEODORE ROOSEVELT appointed Oliver Wendell Holmes, Jr., to replace Gray.

At the time of his appointment, Holmes was the Chief Justice of the Supreme Judicial Court of Massachusetts and had already written a number of the classics of American jurisprudence. Brown described Holmes's appointment as a "topping off." On the Court, however, Holmes played a different role, for he had no taste for either the method of analysis or general philosophical outlook of the Cleveland-Harrison appointees. His stance was fully captured by his quip in LOCHNER V. NEW YORK (1905) that "The FOURTEENTH AMENDMENT does not enact Mr. Herbert Spencer's Social Statics." In this remark Holmes was finally vindicated in 1937 with the constitutional triumph of the New Deal, but in the early 1900s he spoke mostly for himself, at least on the bench, and had no appreciable impact on the course of decisions. No other Justice joined his *Lochner* dissent.

The other significant presence on the Court at the turn of the century was JOHN MARSHALL HARLAN. He was originally appointed by President RUTHERFORD B. HAYES in 1877 and served until 1911. He is greatly admired today for his views on the rights of the newly freed slaves and on the power of the national government. But, like Holmes, Harlan suffered the fate of a prophet: He was a loner. He had his own agenda, and though he sometimes spoke for the Cleveland-Harrison group, Harlan seemed most comfortable playing the role of "the great dissenter."

At the turn of the century, as in many other periods of our history, the Court was principally concerned with the excesses of democracy and the danger of tyranny of the majority. In one instance, the people in Chicago took to the streets and, through a mass strike, tied up the rail system of the nation and threatened the public order. President Cleveland responded by sending the army, and the judiciary helped by issuing an INJUNCTION. In IN RE DEBS (1895) Brewer, writing for a unanimous Court, upheld the contempt conviction of the leader of the union, and legitimated the use of the federal injunctive power to prevent forcible obstructions of INTERSTATE COMMERCE. For the most part, however, the people fought their battles in the legislative halls, and presented the Court with a number of statutes regulating economic relationships. The question posed time and time again was whether these exercises of state power were consistent with the limitations the Constitution imposed upon popular majorities. Sometimes the question was answered in the affirmative, but the Court over which Fuller presided is largely remembered for its negative responses. It stands as a monument to the idea of limited government.

The most important such response consists of POLLOCK V. FARMERS' LOAN & TRUST CO. when, in the spring of 1895, the Court invalidated the first federal income tax enacted in peacetime. The statute impose . . . percent tax on all annual incomes above $4,000, and it was estimated that, due to the exemption, the tax actually fell on less than 2 percent of the population, the wealthy few who resided in a few northeastern states. The tax was denounced by JOSEPH CHOATE, in arguments before the Supreme Court, as an incident in the "communistic march," but the Court chose not to base its decision on a rule that would protect the wealthy few from redistribution. The Court instead largely relied upon that provision of the Constitution linking REPRESENTATION and taxation and requiring the apportionment among the states according to population of all DIRECT TAXES.

The Constitution identified a POLL TAX as an example of a direct tax. It was also assumed by all that a real estate tax would be another example of a direct tax, and the Court first decided that a tax upon the income from real estate is a direct tax. This ruling resulted in the invalidation of the statute as applied to rents (since the tax was not apportioned according to population), but on all other issues the Court was evenly divided, 4–4. The ninth justice, Howell Jackson, was sick at the time. A second argument was held and then the Court continued along the path it had started. Just as a tax on income from real property was deemed a direct tax, so was the tax on income from personal property (such as dividends). This still left unresolved the question whether a tax on wages was a direct tax, but the majority held that the portions of the statute taxing rents and dividends were not severable and that as a result the whole statute would fall. As Fuller reasoned, writing for the majority, if the provision on wages were severable, and it alone sustained, the statute would be transformed, for "what was intended as a tax on capital would remain in substance a tax on occupations and labors."

A decision of the Court invalidating the work of a coordinate branch of government is always problematic. *Pollock* seemed especially so, however, because the Court was sharply divided (5–4), and even more so because one of the Justices (whose identity is still unknown) seems to have switched sides after the reargument. The Justice who did not participate the first time (Jackson) voted to uphold the statute, yet the side he joined lost. It was no surprise, therefore, that *Pollock*, like *Debs*, became an issue in the presidential campaign of 1896, when William Jennings Bryan—a sponsor of the income tax in Congress—wrested control of the Democratic Party from the traditional, conservative elements and fused it with the emerging populist movement. Bryan lost the election, but remained the leader of the party for the next decade or so, during which the political elements critical of the Court grew in number and persuasiveness. By 1913 a constitutional amendment—the first since Reconstruction—

was adopted. The SIXTEENTH AMENDMENT did not directly confront the egalitarian issue, any more than did the Court, but simply declared that an income tax did not have to be apportioned.

The Court's first encounter with the SHERMAN ACT of 1890 was negative and thus bore some resemblance to *Pollock*. In UNITED STATES V. E. C. KNIGHT COMPANY, also announced in 1895, just months before *Debs* and *Pollock*, the Court refused to read the Sherman Act to bar the acquisition of a sugar refinery even though it resulted in a firm that controlled 98 percent of the market and aptly was described (by Harlan in dissent) as a "stupendous combination." The Court reasoned that manufacturing was not within the reach of Congress's power over "commerce." The difference with *Pollock*, however, lay in the fact that this decision (written by Fuller) was in accord with long-standing interpretations of the COMMERCE CLAUSE, which equated "commerce" with the transportation of goods and services across state lines. And this decision was not denounced by the populists; they had no desire whatsoever to have the federal government assume jurisdiction over productive activities such as agriculture. In any event, by the end of Fuller's Chief Justiceship, *E. C. Knight* was in effect eradicated by the Court itself. The Court fully indicated that it was prepared to apply the act to manufacturing enterprises, provided the challenged conduct impeded or affected the flow of goods across state lines.

In the late 1890s, almost immediately after *E. C. Knight,* the Court, speaking through Peckham, applied the Sherman Act to prohibit open price-fixing arrangements by a number of railroads. There was little issue in these cases about the reach of the commerce power, because they involved transportation, but the Court was sharply divided over an issue that was presented by these early antitrust cases, namely, whether such an interference with what was then perceived as ordinary or accepted business practices (supposedly aimed at preventing "ruinous competition") was an abridgment of FREEDOM OF CONTRACT. At first the argument about freedom of contract was presented as a constitutional defense of the application of the Sherman Act, wholly based on the DUE PROCESS clause, but starting with Brewer's separate concurrence in UNITED STATES V. NORTHERN SECURITIES COMPANY (1903) and then again in White's opinions for a near-unanimous Court in the STANDARD OIL COMPANY V. UNITED STATES (1911) and UNITED STATES V. AMERICAN TOBACCO COMPANY (1911), the liberty issue dissolved into a question of statutory interpretation. The Sherman Act was read to prohibit not all but only "unreasonable" restraints of trade, and if a business practice was "unreasonable," then it was, almost by definition, the proper subject of government regulation.

In the late 1890s and early 1900s, antitrust sentiments were the principal cause of the growing Progressive movement. While populists extolled cooperative activity, progressives tried to use the legislative power to preserve the market and the liberties that it implied. They condemned activities (such as mergers or price fixing) that stemmed from the ruthless pursuit of self-interest but that, if carried to their logical extreme, would destroy the social mechanism that both legitimates and is supposed to control such self-interested activity. Progressives were also concerned, however, with stopping certain practices that did not threaten the existence of the market, but rather offended some standard of "fairness" or "decency" that had a wholly independent source. And they used the legislative power for this end.

The Justices were not unmoved by the moralistic concerns that fueled the progressives, but they were also determined—as they had been in *Pollock*—to make certain that the majorities were not using the legislative power to redistribute wealth or power in their favor. In some instances the Court allowed redistributive measures that benefited some group that was especially disadvantaged and thus could be deemed a ward of the state. On that theory, the Court, in a unanimous opinion by Brewer, upheld in MULLER V. OREGON (1908) a statute creating a sixty-hour maximum work week for women employed in factories or laundries. More generally, however, the Court voiced the same fears that had animated *Pollock* and insisted that there be a "direct" connection between the legislative rule and an acceptable (that is, nonredistributive) end such as health. The statute at issue in *Lochner v. New York*, for example, was defended on the ground that a work week for bakers in excess of sixty hours would endanger their health. Justice Peckham's opinion for the majority acknowledged that there might be some connection between a maximum work week and health, but suspected redistributive purposes and argued that if, in the case of bakers, this connection with health were deemed sufficient—that is, direct—the same could be said for virtually every occupation or profession: "No trade, no occupation, no mode of earning one's living, could escape this all-pervading power."

Just as it was fearful of state intervention to control the terms of employment, the Court was also wary of legislation regulating consumer prices—a practice initiated by the Granger movement of the 1870s but continued by the populists and progressives in the 1890s and the early 1900s. In this instance the Court feared that the customers would enrich themselves at the expense of the investors. The danger was, as Brewer formulated it, one of legalized theft. In contrast to cases like *Lochner*, however, the Court took up this issue with a viable and highly visible precedent on the books, namely, *Munn v. Illinois* (1877). Some

consideration was given to OVERRULING the decision (there was no limit to the daring of some of the Justices), but the Court finally settled upon a more modest strategy—of cabining *Munn*.

For one thing, the *Munn* formula for determining which industries would be regulated—a formula that allowed the state to reach "any industry AFFECTED WITH A PUBLIC INTEREST"—was narrowed. In *Budd v. New York* (1892) the Court upheld the power of the legislature to regulate the rates of grain operators, but placed no reliance on the *Munn* public interest formula. Instead, it stressed the presence of monopoly power and the place of the grain operation in the transportation system. Second, the Court began to surround the rate-settling power with procedural guarantees. Legislatures were now delegating the power of setting prices to administrative bodies, such as railroad commissions, and the Court, in *Chicago, Milwaukee & St. Paul Railway Co. v. Minnesota*, (1890), required agencies of that type to afford investors a full, quasi-judicial hearing prior to setting rates. Finally, the Court ended the tradition of judicial deference initiated by *Munn* by authorizing judicial review of the rate actually set. The purpose was to insure against confiscation and to this end Brewer articulated in REAGAN V. FARMERS' LOAN & TRUST (1894) a right of FAIR RETURN ON FAIR VALUE. In that case the rate was set so low as to deny the investors any return at all. In the next case, SMYTH V. AMES (1898), there was some return to the investors, but the Court simply concluded that the rate was "too low."

Reagan v. Farmers' Loan & Trust and *Smyth v. Ames* were both unanimous and thrust the federal judiciary into the business of policing state rate regulations. A particularly momentous and divisive exercise of this supervisory jurisdiction occurred when a federal judge in Minnesota enjoined the attorney general of that state from enforcing a state statute that set maximum railroad rates. The attorney general disobeyed the injunction and was held in criminal contempt. Peckham wrote the opinion for the Court in EX PARTE YOUNG (1908) affirming the contempt conviction, and in doing so, constructed a theory that, notwithstanding the ELEVENTH AMENDMENT, provided access to the federal EQUITY courts to test the constitutionality of state statutes—an avenue of recourse that was to become critical for the CIVIL RIGHTS movement of the 1960s. Ironically, Harlan, who, by dissenting in the CIVIL RIGHTS CASES (1883) and in PLESSY V. FERGUSON (1896), had already earned for himself an honored place in the history of civil rights, bitterly dissented in *Ex parte Young*, because, he argued, the Court was opening the doors of federal courts to test the validity of all state statutes.

The confrontations between the Court and political branches in economic matters such as antitrust, maximum hours, and rate regulation were considerable—*Northern*

Securities, *Lochner*, and *Ex Parte Young* were important public events of their day. Some of these decisions were denounced by political forces, particularly by the Progressive movement, which had begun to dominate national politics. Roosevelt made his disappointment with Holmes's performance in *Northern Securities* well known ("I could carve out of a banana a judge with more backbone than that"—a comment that seems only to have either amused or pleased Holmes) and finished his presidency in 1908 with a speech to Congress sharply critical of the Court. By 1912 the Supreme Court and its work were once again the subject of debate in a presidential election, as it had been in the election of 1896. It was as though the body politic was scoring the Court over which Fuller had presided for the past twenty years. Now the critical voices were more respected and covered a wider political spectrum than in 1896, but the results were mixed.

In the 1912 election the Democratic candidate, Woodrow Wilson, beat the incumbent WILLIAM HOWARD TAFT, who was generally seen as the defender, indeed the embodiment, of the judicial power. On the other hand, Wilson was less critical of the Court than Roosevelt, who ran as a Progressive. The legislation of this period also was two-sided. The CLAYTON ACT of 1914, for example, exempted labor from antitrust legislation (thus reversing the *Danbury Hatters* decision of 1908), and also imposed procedural limits on the use of the labor injunction (thus revising *Debs*), but it did not in fact have as critical an edge as the Sixteenth Amendment of 1913. The Clayton Act did not repudiate the idea of the labor injunction altogether nor did it repudiate the rule of reason in antitrust cases. Similarly, although Congress reacted in 1910 to *Ex Parte Young*, it did so only in a trivial, near-cosmetic way, by requiring three judges (as opposed to one) to issue an injunction against the enforcement of state statutes.

In attempting to construct limits on the power of the political branches, and to guard against the tyranny of the majority as it did in *Pollock*, *Ex Parte Young*, and *Lochner*, the Court assumed an activist posture. The Justices were prepared to use their power to frustrate what appeared popular sentiments. The activist posture was, however, mostly confined to economic reforms—redistributing income, regulating prices, controlling the terms of employment—as though the constitutional conception of liberty were structured by an overriding commitment to capitalism and the market. This characterization of their work, voiced in a critical spirit in their day and in ours, is strengthened when a view is taken of the Justices' overall receptiveness to the antitrust program of the progressives, and even more when account is taken of the pattern of decisions outside the economic domain, respecting human rights as opposed to property rights. The Justices were passive about human rights—by and large willing to let majorities have their way.

A particularly striking instance of this passivity consists of their reaction to the treatment of Chinese residents. Ever since the Civil War the Chinese were by statute denied the right to become naturalized citizens, but in the late 1880s and the early 1900s their situation worsened. The doors of the nation were closed to any further IMMIGRATION, and Congress (in the Geary Act of 1892) created an oppressive regime for those who had previously been admitted. Chinese residents were required to carry passes, and failure to have the passes subjected them to DEPORTATION proceedings that were to be conducted by commissioners (rather than judges or juries) and that put them to the task of producing "at least one credible white witness." YICK WO V. HOPKINS (1886), which invalidated, on EQUAL PROTECTION grounds, a San Francisco laundry ordinance that had disadvantaged the Chinese, was already on the books. But neither it nor the passionate dissent of Brewer ("In view of this enactment of the highest legislative body of the foremost Christian nation, may not the thoughtful Chinese disciple of Confucius fairly ask, why do they send missionaries here?") was of much avail. The Court sustained the Geary Act in *Fong Yue Ting v. United States* (1893) in virtually all its particulars.

A few years later the Court held in UNITED STATES V. WONG KIM ARK (1898) that Chinese children born here were, by virtue of the FOURTEENTH AMENDMENT, citizens of the United States. But this decision sharply divided the Court, despite the straightforward language of the amendment ("All persons born . . . in the United States and subject to the jurisdiction thereof are citizens of the United States"), and did not materially improve the quality of the process the Chinese received. There was, by virtue of *Wong Kim Ark*, a chance that a Chinese person whom the government was trying to deport was a natural born citizen, yet the Court did not even require that this claim of CITIZENSHIP be tried by a judge. Holmes wrote the opinion in these cases, *United States v. Sing Tuck* (1904) and *United States v. Ju Toy* (1905), and once again Brewer, now joined by Peckham, dissented with an intensity equal to that he had exhibited in *Fong Yue Ting*.

The same spirit of acquiescence was manifest in the cases involving the civil rights of blacks, though here it was Harlan who kept the nation's conscience. In *Plessy v. Ferguson* (1896) the Court upheld a Louisiana statute requiring racial SEGREGATION of rail cars; Harlan dissented and, borrowing a line from Plessy's lawyer, Albion Tourgee, insisted that "our Constitution is colorblind." In HODGES V. UNITED STATES (1906) the Court dismissed a federal INDICTMENT against a group of white citizens in Arkansas who forced a mill owner to discharge the blacks who had been hired. Brewer, for the majority, said that the power of the federal government under the Civil War–Reconstruction amendments (and thus under the criminal statute in question) extended only to acts by state officials. He reaffirmed the principle of the CIVIL RIGHTS CASES of 1883 by which the Court effectively ceded to the states exclusive jurisdiction to govern the treatment of one citizen by another. In *Hodges,* Harlan, the Union general from Kentucky, replayed his dissent in the *Civil Rights* cases, and denounced this principle as a fundamental distortion of the Thirteenth and Fourteenth Amendments. And in BEREA COLLEGE V. KENTUCKY (1908) the Court, over Harlan's dissent, upheld a state law that prohibited a private educational corporation from conducting its educational programs on an integrated basis.

Berea College was also written by Brewer. He was mindful of the contrast with a case such as *Lochner,* where the judicial power had been used to the utmost to protect the contractual freedom of worker and employer. Accordingly, Brewer stressed the fact that this law was applicable only to CORPORATIONS, which, to pick up a theme he had previously articulated in his concurring opinion in *Northern Securities,* were merely artificial entities created by government, not entitled to the same degree of protection as natural persons. He specifically left open the question of the validity of a similar statute if it regulated the conduct of natural persons. Harlan, in an equally equivocal dissent, said that a different result might follow if the statute regulated public rather than private education. In fact, the distorting impact of public subsidies upon the articulation of civil rights had been implicitly acknowledged some years earlier in *Cumming v. Board of Education* (1899). In that case Harlan dismissed a challenge by black parents to a decision of a local county, which ran its schools on a segregated basis, to close the only black high school and to send the black students out of the county for their education.

In the 1890s and early 1900s blacks, through one scheme or another, were disenfranchised on a grand scale. The FIFTEENTH AMENDMENT was reduced to a nullity, as Jim Crow was becoming more firmly entrenched. On several occasions, the Court was presented with challenges to these electoral practices, yet it was unable to respond with the energy that it had summoned in *Pollock* or *Lochner* or *Reagan* or, even more to the point, *Debs.* Holmes, the spokesman in these early VOTING RIGHTS cases, saw judicial relief as nothing but an "empty form": "[R]elief from a great political wrong, if done, as alleged, by the people of a State and the State itself, must be given by them or by the legislative and political department of the government of the United States." Harlan dissented, as might be expected, but so did Brewer. They realized that, because the disenfranchisement was the work of state officials, something more was at issue than the allocation of power between states and nation approved in the *Civil Rights*

Cases. What was at issue, according to Brewer and Harlan, was nothing less than the integrity of the judicial power and the duty of the judiciary, to borrow a line from *Debs,* to do whatever it could to fulfill the promise of the Constitution.

The principal issue before the Court at the turn of the century was democracy and, more specifically, the determination of what limits should be placed on popular majorities. As was evident in the civil rights cases, however, the Court was also asked to allocate power between the states and the national government. The FEDERALISM issue arose in many contexts, including antitrust, labor, and rate regulation, but the one in which it proved most troublesome was PROHIBITION. By the late 1880s the prohibition movement was an active force in the states, and Fuller began his Chief Justiceship with a set of constitutional decisions that were unstable. In MUGLER V. KANSAS (1887) the Court had held that prohibition was within the STATE POLICE POWER, yet, just weeks before Chief Justice MORRISON R. WAITE's death, the Court in *Bowman v. Iowa* (1888) had also held that the states were without power to prohibit the importation of liquor from other states. The Court seemed to take away in one decision what it gave in the other. Fuller confronted this problem early on in LEISY V. HARDIN (1890), and in probably his most lasting contribution to constitutional law, fashioned an odd response. First, he announced that the commerce clause barred the states from prohibiting the sale of imported liquor (as well as its actual importation). Second, he invited Congress to intervene, and to authorize states to pass laws that would prohibit out-of-state liquor. Congress quickly responded to this invitation, and in the Wilson Act of 1890 authorized states to enact measures aimed at erecting walls to out-of-state liquor.

The state laws in question in *Leisy v. Hardin* were invalidated on the theory that they sought to regulate a matter that required nationwide uniformity. When it came to judging the congressional response, Fuller found the requisite uniformity since it was Congress that had spoken (even though it did no more than allow the states to choose) and on that theory, in *In re Rahrer* (1891), upheld the Wilson Act. In 1898, however, after some change in the composition of the Court and after the responsibility of speaking on this issue had shifted to one of the new appointees, Edward White, a sharply divided Court cut back on the Wilson Act. *Rhodes v. Iowa* (1890) held that the Wilson Act authorized a ban on sales of imported liquor within the state but not a ban on the importation itself. White insisted that any other construction would raise grave constitutional doubts as to the validity of the Wilson Act. Fuller joined White's opinion.

Over the next decade, mail order business in out-of-state liquor grew. The conflict between the Court and the prohibition movement escalated. Then in 1913 Congress, as part of the same era that saw the Sixteenth Amendment and the Clayton Act, passed the WEBB-KENYON ACT to remove any ambiguity over what it sought to accomplish in the Wilson Act. Congress allowed states to bar both the sale and the importation of out-of-state liquor. After considerable struggle and deliberation, the Webb-Kenyon Act was upheld in an opinion by White (then Chief Justice) on the theory (if that is what it can be called) that "liquor is different." For all other goods, the common market was deemed a constitutional necessity.

The federalism issue has recurred throughout the entire history of the Supreme Court. The Court over which Fuller presided did, however, confront one issue pertaining to structure of government that was unique to the times: colonialism. The issue arose from the "splendid little war," as Secretary of State John Hay called the Spanish American War of 1898, which left the United States with two former Spanish colonies, PUERTO RICO and the Philippines. (Much earlier the United States had purchased Alaska, and in the late 1890s it had also taken possession of Hawaii.) The assumption was that the United States would hold these territories as territories, for an indefinite period, and perhaps ultimately build a colonial empire along the European model. The question posed for the Supreme Court—not just by the litigants but by the nation at large—was whether colonialism was a constitutionally permissible strategy for the United States. Technically, the case involved a challenge to a statute imposing a tariff on goods (sugar) imported from Puerto Rico into the states. The Constitution bars Congress from imposing duties on the importation of goods from one state to another, and so the issue was whether a territory was to be treated the same as a state, or, as phrased in the language of the day, whether the Constitution followed the flag.

Three positions emerged in a series of decisions beginning in 1901 known as the INSULAR CASES. The first, most in keeping with the position of the Court in *Pollock* and the other economic cases, proclaimed the idea of limited government. The government of the United States was formed and established by the Constitution, and thus it was impossible to conceive of a separation of Constitution and government. This was the position taken by Brewer, Peckham, Fuller, and Harlan. At the opposite end of the spectrum was the so-called annexation position. It proclaimed the separation of Constitution and flag, and generally left the government unrestricted in its activities in the territories; whatever restrictions there were flowed from natural law or from a small group of provisions of the Constitution deemed essential (the tariff provision was not one). This position was most congenial to the government and yet at odds with the general jurisprudence of the Court. Only Justice Brown subscribed to it.

The remaining four Justices, in an opinion written by White, put forth what was called the incorporation theory.

It tried to chart a middle course, as appeared to be White's trade. It made the Constitution fully applicable to a territory, but only after that territory was incorporated into the United States. (Prior to incorporation the government would be subject only to the restraints of natural law.) Justice White's opinion also made it clear that the decision to incorporate a territory resided in Congress. In the case before it the Court decided that the territory was not incorporated, but White also acknowledged that incorporation could be done by implication and, even more to the point, he reserved for the judiciary the power to determine whether that act of incorporation had taken place.

Ultimately incorporation was adopted as the position of the Court. But this did not occur until 1905, after an insurrection in the Phillipines and other developments in the world (such as the Boer War) had made the idea of a colonial empire seem less attractive, and the danger of further imperial acquisitions seemed to have waned. In fact, incorporation became majority doctrine in *Rassmussen v. United States* (1905) in which the Court held that Alaska had been *implicitly* incorporated and that the United States was bound by the BILL OF RIGHTS in its governance of that territory. The outcome in this case affirmed the idea of limited government and JUDICIAL SUPREMACY, the hallmarks of this Court, and made it possible for Fuller, and perhaps even more significantly, for Brewer and Peckham, to abandon their absolutist position and to support the middle-of-the-road theory of White— perhaps a sign of what was to come in 1910, when Fuller died and Taft, who had once served as the commissioner in the Philippines, replaced him with White.

OWEN M. FISS
(1986)

Bibliography

DUKER, WILLIAM 1980 Mr. Justice Rufus W. Peckham: The Police Power and the Individual in a Changing World. *Brigham Young University Law Review* 1980:47–67.
——— 1980 Mr. Justice Rufus W. Peckham and the Case of *Ex Parte Young:* Lochnerizing *Munn v. Illinois. Brigham Young University Law Review* 1980:539–558.
GOODWYN, LAWRENCE 1976 *Democratic Promise: The Populist Movement in America.* New York: Oxford University Press.
KING, WILLARD 1967 *Melville Weston Fuller, Chief Justice of the United States, 1888–1910.* Chicago: University of Chicago Press.
KOLKO, GABRIEL 1963 *The Triumph of Conservatism: A Reinterpretation of American History 1900–1916.* New York: Free Press.
PAUL, ARNOLD 1960 *Conservative Crisis and the Rule of Law: Attitudes of Bar and Bench 1887–1895.* Ithaca, N.Y.: Cornell University Press.
PIERCE, CARL 1972 A Vacancy on the Supreme Court: The Politics of Judicial Appointment, 1893–1894. *Tennessee Law Review* 39:555–612.

ROCHE, JOHN   1974   *Sentenced to Life.* New York: Macmillan.

ROGAT, YOSAL   1963   The Judge as Spectator. *University of Chicago Law Review* 31:231–278.

THORELLI, HANS   1954   *The Federal Antitrust Policy: Origination of an American Tradition.* Baltimore: Johns Hopkins University Press.

TWISS, BENJAMIN   1942   *Lawyers and the Constitution: How Laissez Faire Came to the Supreme Court.* Princeton, N.J.: Princeton University Press.

WESTIN, ALAN   1953   The Supreme Court, the Populist Movement and the Campaign of 1896. *Journal of Politics* 15:3–41.

——— 1958   Stephen J. Field and the Headnote to *O'Neil v. Vermont:* A Snapshot of the Fuller Court at Work. *Yale Law Journal* 67:363–383.

WOODWARD, C. VANN   1966   *The Strange Career of Jim Crow,* rev. ed. New York: Oxford University Press.

FULL FAITH AND CREDIT

The full faith and credit clause of the Constitution (Article IV, section 1) provides that: "Full Faith and Credit shall be given in each State to the public Acts, Records and judicial Proceedings of every other State. And the Congress may by general Laws prescribe the Manner in which such Acts, Records and Proceedings shall be proved, and the Effect thereof."

The first sentence of the clause closely tracked language contained in Article IV of the ARTICLES OF CONFEDERATION, the precursor of our present Constitution. The second sentence, which authorizes Congress to enact implementing legislation, was new. "Faith and credit" was a familiar term in English law where it had been used on occasion for some centuries to describe the respect owed to judgments and other public records. Its precise meaning, however, was obscure; it was not clear whether it was concerned only with the admission of public records, including judgments, into evidence or whether it was intended to deal likewise with the effect as RES JUDICATA to which a judgment was entitled. There is similar uncertainty with respect to the meaning which the term was intended to bear in the Articles of Confederation.

The subject of full faith and credit evoked little discussion in the CONSTITUTIONAL CONVENTION, and it seems unlikely that there was any general understanding among the delegates of what the clause was designed to accomplish. In any event, Congress was quick to exercise its power to pass implementing legislation. The initial statute was enacted in 1790 by the First Congress. It provided for the manner of authenticating the acts of the legislatures and of the records and judicial proceedings of the several states and concluded that "the said records and judicial proceedings shall have such faith and credit given to them in every court of the United States, as they have by law or usage in the courts of the State from whence the said records are or shall be taken." The second congressional act, that of 1804, extended the scope of full faith and credit by requiring that the same measure of respect should be given to the records and judicial proceedings of the TERRITORIES of the United States and of the countries subject to its JURISDICTION.

Judicial decisions have now made clear many things that the full faith and credit clause and its implementing statutes left uncertain. The Supreme Court has decided that, provided the requirements of jurisdiction, NOTICE, and opportunity to be heard have been satisfied, a judgment rendered in one state, territory, or possession of the United States shall in general be given the same res judicata effect that it has in the state of its rendition. Exceptions to this rule, if any there be, are few indeed. A state cannot, for example, deny effect to a judgment on the ground that the underlying claim was contrary to its public policy. Initially, some might have wondered whether Congress was empowered to extend the protection of full faith and credit to the records and judicial proceedings of territories and possessions of the United States. The full faith and credit clause itself gives no such authority, but the Supreme Court has held that this is to be found in those provisions of the Constitution that afford the United States with JUDICIAL POWER (Article III), authorize LEGISLATION that is NECESSARY AND PROPER to execute the powers entrusted to the federal government (Article II, section 8), and provide that the Constitution and the laws and treaties of the United States shall be the supreme law of the land (Article VI). Neither the clause nor the implementing statute refer to judgments of the federal courts. The Supreme Court has filled this gap by holding that these judgments are entitled to the same respect that is owed to state judgments.

A sharp distinction must be drawn between the recognition and the enforcement of judgments. With respect to recognition, the Supreme Court has held, as has already been said, that a judgment must be given the same res judicata effect that it enjoys under the law of the state of its rendition. On the other hand, the method of enforcing a judgment is determined by the law of the state where enforcement is sought. It is therefore for this latter law to determine whether a new action in the nature of debt must be brought on the judgment or whether it can be enforced by means of a registration procedure.

Full faith and credit is not owed to the judgments of foreign countries. Each state of the United States determines for itself the measure of respect that such judgments are to receive in its courts. Perhaps because of their experience in giving full faith and credit to federal and sister state judgments, American courts are extremely liberal, perhaps the most liberal in the world, in giving respect to the judgments of other countries.

The intentions of the original Framers may have been obscure. But the Supreme Court has said that the full faith and credit clause should become "a nationally unifying force" by establishing "throughout the federal system the salutory principle of the COMMON LAW that a litigation once pursued to judgment shall be as conclusive of the rights of the parties in every other court as in that where the judgment was rendered."

It will have been noted that whereas the full faith and credit clause speaks of "public Acts, Records and judicial Proceedings," the implementing statutes of 1790 and 1804 required only that full faith and credit be given to records and judicial proceedings. No definite information is available on why public acts were omitted, but it can be surmised that this omission was deliberate and stemmed from the realization that the circumstances, if any, in which one state should be required to apply another's law presented considerations infinitely more complex than those involving the recognition and enforcement of judgments. (See CHOICE OF LAW.) After some years, the Supreme Court held that the clause was self-executing and that there were limited circumstances in which a state was required to apply another's laws. By and large, the Supreme Court has now withdrawn from its earlier opinions and today the command of full faith and credit with respect to public acts is slight indeed. The Supreme Court has, however, held that full faith and credit imposes limitations upon the power of a state to refuse on public policy grounds to entertain suit on a claim arising under the law of a sister state. It can be expected that in due course restrictions will likewise be placed upon a state's power to dismiss a suit on the ground that the claim involved is one for a penalty.

The implementing statute remained substantially unchanged from 1804 to 1948. In the latter year, it was amended as part of a general revision of Title 28 of the United States Code. This revision was not intended to make controversial substantive changes in the law. Nevertheless, the implementing statute was amended to require that full faith and credit be given not only to records and judicial proceedings, as had been the case heretofore, but to acts as well. It seems improbable that this change in wording will lead to any substantial change in the law. No such change was presumably intended by the revisers, and, to date, the amendment has not influenced the decisions of the courts. But, taken literally, the statute, as now worded, requires the same measure of respect for statutes that it does for judgments. There is always the possibility that at some time in the future the courts will seize upon this new language to make substantial changes in what is owed under full faith and credit to the statutes of sister states and of United States territories and possessions.

WILLIS L. M. REESE
(1986)

Bibliography

AMERICAN LAW INSTITUTE 1971 *Restatement of the Law: Conflict of Laws, Second.* Chap. 5, pages 271–348. St. Paul, Minn.: American Law Institute Publishers.
NADELMANN, KURT 1957 Full Faith and Credit to Judgments and Public Acts. *Michigan Law Review* 56:33–88.
WHITTEN, RALPH U. 1981 The Constitutional Limitations on State-Court Jurisdiction: An Historical-Interpretative Reexamination of the Full Faith and Credit and Due Process Clauses. *Creighton Law Review* 14:499–606.

FULL FAITH AND CREDIT
(Update)

Until recently, four propositions regarding the full faith and credit clause were beyond doubt. First, a judgment consistent with DUE PROCESS rendered by any state or federal court was entitled to recognition in any other American court; indeed, this rule was so strong it could be said to be an "Iron Law." Second, the full faith and credit clause did not require state courts to recognize the judgments of foreign courts, leaving that issue a matter of state law. Third, statutes of other states were not entitled to full faith and credit despite the plain and contrary language of both the constitutional provision itself and the general federal implementing statute. Finally, state courts did not have to enforce sister-state judgments subject to modification, such as alimony and child custody and support judgments. Although each of the propositions remains true, there has been some movement in each area.

First, the Iron Law of full faith and credit remains secure. The Supreme Court has indicated, however, that it will not look fondly upon attempts to bind strangers (nonparties) to the first litigation.

Second, many a recent state decision has refused to recognize a foreign judgment even though rendered by an impeccably fair tribunal, such as a British court, when the judgment contradicts basic American notions of public policy. Most notable have been cases seeking to enforce large awards in defamation actions entered without the significant substantive and procedural safeguards American courts provide defendants in such cases. The United States has engaged in lengthy discussions with many other countries concerning an international convention on mutual recognition of judgments. Such a convention would cause dramatic changes. At the least, enforcement of foreign judgments will be a matter for federal, not state, law. Further, American courts might be called upon to enforce judgments they find repugnant, and, conversely, deny recognition to judgments they find congenial.

Third, a few prominent scholars have suggested that the full faith and credit clause requires recognition of the statutory law of other states. Although the Supreme Court seems unlikely to adopt this interpretation, the topic was much discussed when Congress passed the Defense of Marriage Act (DOMA). This law expressly permitted a state to disregard any state rule authorizing SAME-SEX MARRIAGE. Although DOMA was redundant under existing law, which also permits nonrecognition by one state of the statutes of other states, it gave ammunition to both camps in the larger debate. Nevertheless, the practical difficulties of working out which of two or more competing statutes is entitled to full faith and credit—a difficulty confirmed by the Court's fruitless attempts to do so during the first four decades of this century—suggest that statutory law will long remain immune from the mandate of recognition under the full faith and credit clause.

Finally, Congress has decided to use its LEGISLATIVE POWERS to implement the full faith and credit clause to help enforce orders in child custody and support cases. This bundle of LEGISLATION is remarkable for several reasons. It represents the first specific legislation implementing the full faith and credit clause in our history. Second, it runs counter to the principle that the federal government should have nothing to do with family law. Finally, the legislation overcame the strong tradition that the full faith and credit clause did not require enforcement of modifiable orders.

The success of the family law legislation, as well as the proposed covention on recognition of foreign judgments, may lead to further congressional efforts, by full faith and credit legislation, to address problems caused by our federal system of government.

WILLIAM L. REYNOLDS
WILLIAM M. RICHMAN
(2000)

Bibliography

LAYCOCK, DOUGLAS 1992 Equal Citizens of Equal and Teritorial States: The Constitutional Foundations of Choice of Law. *Columbia Law Review* 92:249–337.

REYNOLDS, WILLIAM 1994 The Iron Law of Full Faith and Credit. *Maryland Law Review* 53:412–449.

FULLILOVE v. KLUTZNICK
448 U.S. 448 (1980)

The Supreme Court's fragmentation in REGENTS OF UNIVERSITY OF CALIFORNIA V. BAKKE (1978) left open the question of the constitutionality of government-imposed RACIAL QUOTAS or preferences. The following year, in UNITED STEELWORKERS V. WEBER, the Court held that a voluntary AFFIRMATIVE ACTION plan, calling for a racial quota in hiring by a private employer and approved by a union, did not violate Title VII of the CIVIL RIGHTS OF 1964. *Ful-lilove* reopened *Bakke*'s question: Can government impose a racial quota to remedy the effects of past discrimination?

Congress, in a public works statute aimed at reducing unemployment, provided that ten percent of the funds distributed to each state should be set aside for contracts with "minority business enterprises" (MBE). An MBE was defined as a business at least half owned by persons who are "Negroes, Spanish-speaking, Orientals, Indians, Eskimos and Aleuts." Nonminority contractors challenged this limitation as a denial of the Fifth Amendment's guarantee of EQUAL PROTECTION, as recognized in BOLLING V. SHARPE (1954) and later cases.

The Supreme Court held, 6–3, that the MBE limitation was valid. Three Justices, speaking through Chief Justice WARREN E. BURGER, paid great deference to Congress's judgment that the racial quota was a "limited and properly tailored remedy to cure the effects of past RACIAL DISCRIMINATION." Emphasizing the flexibility provided for the law's administration, they said that the funds could be limited to MBEs that were in fact disadvantaged because of race. The other three majority Justices, speaking through Justice THURGOOD MARSHALL, took the position they had taken in *Bakke*, concluding that the racial quota was "substantially related to . . . the important and congressionally articulated goal of remedying the present effects of past racial discrimination."

Justice POTTER STEWART, joined by Justice WILLIAM H. REHNQUIST, dissented; they would forbid any statutory racial classification, allowing race-conscious remedies only in cases of proven illegal discrimination. Justice JOHN PAUL STEVENS was not prepared to take so absolute a position but dissented here because Congress had not sufficiently articulated the reasons for its racial quota and tailored its program to those reasons.

KENNETH L. KARST
(1986)

FUNDAMENTAL INTERESTS

The idea that some interests are fundamental, and thus deserving of a greater measure of constitutional protection than is given to other interests, is an old one. Justice BUSHROD WASHINGTON, sitting on circuit in CORFIELD V. CORYELL (1823), held that the PRIVILEGES AND IMMUNITIES clause of Article IV of the Constitution protected out-of-staters against discriminatory state legislation touching only those privileges that were "in their very nature, fundamental; which belong, of right, to the citizens of all free governments." Washington's list of such interests was limited but significant: free passage through a state; HABEAS CORPUS; the right to sue in state courts; the right to hold and dispose of property; freedom from discriminatory taxation.

Although the *Corfield* doctrine suggested an active role for the federal judiciary in protecting NATURAL RIGHTS against state interference—at least on behalf of citizens of other states—the doctrine was not embraced by the full Supreme Court during Washington's lifetime. If some hoped that the FOURTEENTH AMENDMENT's privileges and immunities clause would breathe new life into the fundamental rights theory, those hopes were disappointed in the SLAUGHTERHOUSE CASES (1873). Rejecting the theory as propounded in two eloquent dissenting opinions, the Court again refused to find any special federal constitutional protection against state invasions of preferred rights.

Within a generation, however, the Court had identified a cluster of preferred rights of property and the FREEDOM OF CONTRACT, to be defended against various forms of ECONOMIC REGULATION. The Court did not use the language of fundamental interests; for doctrinal support it avoided both privileges and immunities clauses, relying instead on a theory of SUBSTANTIVE DUE PROCESS. When this doctrinal development played out in the late 1930s, the Court abandoned its STRICT SCRUTINY of business regulation in favor of a STANDARD OF REVIEW demanding no more than a RATIONAL BASIS for legislative judgments.

Even as the Court adopted its new permissive attitude toward economic regulation, it was laying the groundwork for another round of protections of preferred rights. (See UNITED STATES V. CAROLENE PRODUCTS CO.; SKINNER V. OKLAHOMA.) When the WARREN COURT set about its expansion of the reach of EQUAL PROTECTION doctrine, it not only followed these precedents but also revived the rhetoric of fundamental interests. A state law discriminating against the exercise of such an interest, the Court held, must be justified as necessary for achieving a COMPELLING STATE INTEREST.

The Warren Court hinted strongly that it would expand the list of fundamental interests demanding strict judicial scrutiny to include all manner of claims to equality. In fact, the Court's holdings placed only a limited number of interests in the "fundamental" category: VOTING RIGHTS and related interests in the electoral process; some limited rights of ACCESS TO THE COURTS; and rights relating to marriage, the family, and other intimate relationships. Even so modest a doctrinal development evoked the strong dissent of Justice JOHN MARSHALL HARLAN: "I know of nothing which entitles this Court to pick out particular human activities, characterize them as "fundamental,' and give them added protection under an unusually stringent equal protection test."

The BURGER COURT, making Harlan's lament its theme song, called a halt to the expansion of fundamental interests occasioning strict judicial scrutiny under the equal protection clause. However, in cases touching marriage and other close personal relationships, the Court continued to promote the notion of fundamental liberties deserving of special protection—now on a substantive due process theory. (See ABORTION AND THE CONSTITUTION; ILLEGITIMACY; FREEDOM OF INTIMATE ASSOCIATION.) The notion of natural rights as part of our constitutional law is deeply ingrained. Our modern doctrines about fundamental rights are novel only in the particular interests they have termed fundamental.

KENNETH L. KARST
(1986)

Bibliography

TRIBE, LAURENCE H. 1978 *American Constitutional Law.* Chaps. 8, 11, 15, and 16. Mineola, N.Y.: Foundation Press. 000 002

FUNDAMENTALISTS AND THE CONSTITUTION

See: Religious Fundamentalism

FUNDAMENTAL LAW
(History)

The institution of a written CONSTITUTION as fundamental law superior to and limiting ordinary statutory law and government, which we now take for granted, was distinctively American. The concept of fundamental law embodied in a written constitution was one of the most influential and radical ideas to emerge from the AMERICAN REVOLUTION. It involved a break with the recent English past.

The notion of fundamental law has had a continuing history in Western political thought. Mid-seventeenth century Englishmen anticipated the use of a written constitution as the foundation of government, but the half-hearted experiment did not last. Fundamental law remained an ill-defined and vague term then, standing for the customary constitution as distinguished from revolutionary change. Parliamentarians accused Charles I and James II of attempting by arbitrary acts to subvert the fundamental laws of the realm, especially the traditional rights of liberty and property. Although interest in fundamental law declined in the eighteenth century, the concept never lost its attractiveness for the English. However, the growing acceptance of the omnipotence of Parliament made the idea of a single written instrument creating and limiting the government decidedly obsolete, because no restraints existed on parliamentary power, and for that reason Americans would finally repudiate the unwritten English constitution as less than the embodiment of truly fundamental law.

Reformist ideas about law, current in early seventeenth-century England, influenced the settlers of early America in the creation of their legal systems. The colonists developed a conception of the sources and nature of law that was much more expansive than the traditionally narrow conception of the English COMMON LAW. This broad approach reflected the fundamentally altered state of many aspects of law in the New World. Leaders of the American colonies also assimilated new currents in political thought which led to the conclusion that fundamental or natural law lay behind the civil law of every nation. Fundamental law became equated in their minds with natural law or the law of nature. Many residents of the New World regarded their charters from the crown as a fundamental source for their basic rights as Englishmen.

The revolutionary ferment of the 1760s and 1770s in the American colonies produced the idea of a written constitution embodying fundamental law. Americans regarded as unconstitutional several of Parliament's statutes governing America. In 1761 JAMES OTIS argued that WRITS OF ASSISTANCE were "against the fundamental Principles of Law." Like the English a century earlier, Americans gravitated toward an understanding of a constitution as something antecedent and paramount to all branches of government, including even their legislative representatives. Fundamental law controlled statutory law. A 1760 *Letter to the People of Pennsylvania* noted the relevance to forming a plan of government of "the fundamental laws and rules of the constitution, which ought never to be infringed. . . ." Writing against the authority of Parliament over the colonies in 1774, JOHN ADAMS regarded New Englanders as deriving their laws "not from parliament, not from common law, but from the law of nature and the compact made with the king in our charter. . . . English liberties are but certain rights of nature, reserved to the citizen by the English constitution, which rights cleaved to our ancestors when they crossed the Atlantic. . . ."

The process of state constitution-making that began in 1776 led to eleven written constitutions by 1780, but the basic and largely unchanging nature of such documents was not fully recognized in practice in the first decade, mainly because the first constitutions granted predominant power to the legislatures. Criticisms of excessive legislative activity in the 1780s led to general acceptance of the idea that constitutions should serve as fundamental laws to control legislatures. THOMAS JEFFERSON eagerly sought a Virginia constitution that the legislature could not easily change.

The American states gradually came to regard their written constitutions as fundamental or HIGHER LAWS superior to ordinary legislative acts—which meant restrictions on legislative power, because ordinary courts of law eventually implemented the written constitutions through a process of JUDICIAL REVIEW. The argument in favor of the innovative practice of judicial review was that fundamental laws were predominant. Thus the CONSTITUTIONAL CONVENTION that met in Philadelphia in 1787 accepted the notion that a legislature could not change a constitution without the calling of a special constitutional convention. The recognition of the new federal Constitution as a fundamental law required the calling of special ratifying conventions to avoid disputes about its legitimacy. This process of creating fundamental law through constitution-making was the source of the basic appeal of the American Revolution to continental Europeans.

DAVID H. FLAHERTY
(1986)

Bibliography
GOUGH, J. W. (1955) 1971 *Fundamental Law in English Constitutional History.* Oxford: Clarendon Press.
MELLETT, CHARLES F. (1933) 1966 *Fundamental Law and the American Revolution 1760–1776.* New York: Octagon.
WOOD, GORDON S. 1969 *The Creation of the American Republic, 1776–1787.* Chapel Hill: University of North Carolina Press.

FUNDAMENTAL LAW AND THE SUPREME COURT

The DECLARATION OF INDEPENDENCE explicitly invoked the concept of natural justice—a HIGHER LAW, timeless and universal—as a defense against tyranny. By the late eighteenth century there had evolved a conviction that the essence of this fundamental law could at one stroke be captured in a document that would endure for ages to come. Of the original state constitutions several were declared in force without constituent ratification and some made no provision for amendment. By the time of the federal CONSTITUTIONAL CONVENTION OF 1787, these extreme forms of immutability had given way. Article V provided a formalized process of constitutional amendment, while Article VII conditioned adoption on ratification by state conventions. But the concept of written constitutions as the embodiment of fundamental law was central to the federal Constitution and to later state constitutions.

The issue whether fundamental law had other appropriate functions in the American constitutional scheme arose early among Justices of the Supreme Court of the United States, and remains critical at the Constitution's bicentenary. Debate opened in CALDER V. BULL (1798). The Connecticut legislature had set aside a court decree refusing to probate a will, granting a new hearing at which the will was admitted. Denied relief in the state courts, the disappointed heir appealed to the Supreme Court. Outraged at the destruction of the heir's expectancy, Justice SAMUEL CHASE declared "it is against all reason and justice, for a people to intrust a legislature with such powers, and therefore, it cannot be presumed that they have done it." In Chase's view, the fundamental law could not tolerate "a law that takes property from A and gives it to B," even in the absence of constitutional prohibition. Justice JAMES IREDELL challenged this claim of extraconstitutional power to nullify legislation, insisting that if legislation is within constitutional limits "the Court cannot pronounce it to be void, merely because it is, in their judgment, contrary to the principles of natural justice."

Iredell's logic prevailed in *Calder* but in the long run could not hold the line. Chief Justice JOHN MARSHALL hedged on the question in FLETCHER V. PECK (1810), declaring that Georgia's attempt to revoke fraudulent land grants was void "either by general principles which are common to our free institutions, or by the particular provisions of the constitution of the United States...." Similarly, Justice JOSEPH STORY rested the Court's opinion in TERRETT V. TAYLOR (1815) upon several grounds, among them "the principles of natural justice" and "the spirit and letter of the [federal] constitution...." LOAN ASSOCIATION V. TOPEKA (1874), although decided following ratification of the FOURTEENTH AMENDMENT, was grounded by Justice SAMUEL F. MILLER on extraconstitutional principles founded in fundamental law. The taking from A (by taxation) in aid of B (bridge manufacturer not a public utility) was stricken as an "unauthorized invasion of private right." In contrast, DRED SCOTT V. SANDFORD (1857) and *Hepburn v. Griswold* (1869) invalidated congressional "takings" under the Fifth Amendment's due process clause.

At the turn of the century the issue of extraconstitutional adjudication intensified with an OBITER DICTUM in ALLGEYER V. LOUISIANA (1897). With LOCHNER V. NEW YORK (1905) and *Adair v. United States* (1908), the majority of the court opened a period in which much economic and social legislation was held unconstitutional, ostensibly under the due process clauses. However, the basis given was violation of FREEDOM OF CONTRACT, for which there was no constitutional warrant. Justice OLIVER WENDELL HOLMES, in his celebrated *Lochner* dissent, insisted that the Fourteenth Amendment, properly construed, should accord with "fundamental principles as they have been understood by the traditions of our people and our law." Yet to him that amendment correctly embraced condemnation of governmental expropriation of property from A for B's benefit, as he made clear in *Pennsylvania Coal Co. v. Mahon* (1922). Justice LOUIS D. BRANDEIS there dissented, but he later invoked the identical principle under both due process clauses: the Fifth Amendment clause in *Wright v.*

Vinton Branch of Mountain Trust Bank (1937) upholding a revised moratorium law, and the Fourteenth Amendment clause in *Thompson v. Consolidated Gas Utilities Corp.* (1937). In the latter he declared, "Our law reports present no more glaring instance of the taking of one man's property and giving it to another."

The *Lochner-Adair* venture into noninterpretive constitutionalism was rejected by a split vote in NEBBIA V. NEW YORK (1934), followed by unanimity in *Lincoln Federal Labor Union v. Northwestern Iron & Metal Co.* (1949). Yet only two years after categorical repudiation in FERGUSON V. SCRUPA (1963), the seductive appeal of the philosophy of *Lochner* and its progeny was back, this time in the service of noneconomic interests. In GRISWOLD V. CONNECTICUT (1965) the due process clause was used to invalidate an anticontraception law; in HARPER V. VIRGINIA BOARD OF ELECTIONS (1966) the EQUAL PROTECTION clause provided the basis for invalidating the POLL TAX as a condition for exercise of VOTING RIGHTS. In both cases the majority sought to ground decision in constitutional provisions, but Justice HUGO L. BLACK, unpersuaded, accused the Court of invoking "the old 'natural-law-due-process formula,'" which, he declared, "is no less dangerous when used to enforce this Court's views about personal rights than those about economic rights." ROE V. WADE (1973), insulating from governmental intervention a woman's decision to have an abortion during the first trimester of pregnancy, rested upon a doctrine of "personhood" demonstrably beyond the ambit of constitutional text, context, or structure. Reaffirmed in AKRON V. AKRON CENTER FOR REPRODUCTIVE HEALTH, INC. (1983) out of respect for STARE DECISIS, *Roe* highlights the Supreme Court's continuing temptation to give constitutional force to extraconstitutional values it finds lying in the recesses of unwritten fundamental law.

FRANK R. STRONG
(1986)

Bibliography

GREY, THOMAS 1978 Origins of the Unwritten Constitution: Fundamental Law in American Revolutionary Thought. *Stanford Law Review* 30:843–893.

HAND, LEARNED 1960 *The Spirit of Liberty*, 3rd ed. New York: Knopf.

PERRY, MICHAEL 1982 *The Constitution, the Courts, and Human Rights*, chap. 4. Columbus: Ohio State University Press.

FUNDAMENTAL LAWS OF WEST NEW JERSEY

See: New Jersey Colonial Charters

FUNDAMENTAL ORDERS OF CONNECTICUT
(January 14, 1639)

Historians almost invariably refer to this document as a CONSTITUTION, indeed as the first written constitution of the modern world. It was very probably a statute enacted by a provisional legislative body representing the freemen of three towns meeting in Hartford. It was not, however, an ordinary statute, because it described a frame of government, though the statute lacked any explicit provision for amendment. The assembly or "general court" which enacted it, derived its powers from it but could and did alter it.

THOMAS HOOKER, the founder of Hartford and the leading divine of the colony, was probably the principal author of the document. In a 1638 sermon he had declared that the foundation of authority in both state and church was the free consent of the people expressed in a covenant or SOCIAL COMPACT; the people, according to Hooker, had power to appoint officers for their governance and "to set the bounds and limitations of the power and place unto which they call them." But the Fundamental Orders did not impose such limitations or reserve any rights that the government could not abridge.

The preamble stated that the inhabitants of the towns joined together to become "one Public State or Commonwealth" to preserve their churches and be governed according to laws made and administered by the officers described in the document. The people, "all that are admitted inhabitants," chose an assembly or "general court" which in turn annually elected a governor and magistrates, who together exercised the judicial power. The document empowered the general court to make laws, impose taxes, dispose of lands, and admit freemen and deputies from other towns. The general court, "the supreme power of the Commonwealth," consisted of the governor, magistrates, and deputies, who were guaranteed "liberty of speech," probably the progenitor of the SPEECH OR DEBATE CLAUSE in Article I, section 6, of the Constitution.

LEONARD W. LEVY
(1986)

Bibliography

ANDREWS, CHARLES MCLEAN 1936 *The Colonial Period of American History.* Vol. 2, pages 94–113. New Haven, Conn.: Yale University Press.

FUNDAMENTAL RIGHTS

Inherent in the Anglo-Saxon heritage of DUE PROCESS OF LAW, the concept of fundamental rights defies facile analysis. Yet it constitutes one of those basic features of democracy that are the test of its presence. As defined by Justice FELIX FRANKFURTER, dissenting in *Solesbee v. Balkcom* (1950), it embraces "a system of rights based on moral principles so deeply embedded in the traditions and feelings of our people as to be deemed fundamental to a civilized society. ..." The Justice whom Frankfurter succeeded on the high bench, BENJAMIN N. CARDOZO, had spoken in *Snyder v. Massachusetts* (1934) of "principles of justice so rooted in the traditions and conscience of our people as to be deemed fundamental." Three years later, in PALKO V. CONNECTICUT, Cardozo articulated fundamental rights as "implicit in the concept of ORDERED LIBERTY." Because these rights are "fundamental," they have been accorded special protection by the judiciary, which has thus viewed them as PREFERRED FREEDOMS that command particularly STRICT SCRUTINY of their infringement by legislative or executive action. In other words, to pass judicial muster, laws or ordinances affecting fundamental rights must demonstrate a more or less "compelling need," whereas those affecting lesser rights need only be clothed with a RATIONAL BASIS justifying the legislative or executive action at issue.

But which among our rights fall on the "fundamental" and which on the "nonfundamental" side of constitutional protection? The Supreme Court commenced to endeavor to draw a dichotomous line in the turn-of-the-century INSULAR CASES: on the "fundamental" side now fell such rights as those present in the FIRST AMENDMENT (religion, FREEDOMS OF SPEECH, PRESS, ASSEMBLY, and PETITION); on the other side, styled "formal rights," fell such "procedural" rights or guarantees as those embedded in the FOURTH, FIFTH, SIXTH, SEVENTH, and EIGHTH AMENDMENTS, including, for example, TRIAL BY JURY. Justice Cardozo reconfirmed the dichotomy with his *Palko* division, adding to the roster of "fundamental" rights those of assigned counsel to INDIGENT defendants in major criminal trials and the general right to a FAIR TRIAL. He relegated other procedural rights to the nonfundamental sphere, noting that "justice would not perish" in the absence of such "formal rights" at the state level.

Cardozo's dichotomy did not apply to the federal BILL OF RIGHTS, which was wholly enforceable against federal abridgment or denial by the terms of its specific provisions. He used it instead to explain which provisions of the Bill of Rights were, and which were not, made applicable to the states by the FOURTEENTH AMENDMENT. While the "formal" rights, as he explained, do have "value and importance ... they are not of the essence of a scheme of ordered liberty. To abolish them is not to violate a principle of justice so rooted in the traditions and conscience of our people as to be deemed fundamental. ... Few would be so narrow as to maintain that a fair and enlightened system of justice would be impossible without them." This dichotomy stood until the 1960s when, through acceleration of the process known as INCORPORATION or "absorption," most of the enumerated safeguards in the Bill of Rights were made applicable to the states by judicial decisions. The Supreme Court's rationale for these decisions was its expanding view of the nature and reach of "fundamental" rights. In practical affect, the incorporation doctrine no longer draws an appreciable distinction between "formal" and "fundamental" rights.

Yet concurrently the WARREN COURT gave new life to the notion that certain fundamental rights should be protected by heightened judicial scrutiny of laws limiting them. This development built on Justice HARLAN FISKE STONE's famed formulation in UNITED STATES V. CAROLENE PRODUCTS CO. (1938). Voting rights and rights concerning marriage, procreation, and family relationships were identified as "fundamental" and clothed with special judicial protection. The Warren Court's other chief category of occasions for strict scrutiny of legislation—that of SUSPECT CLASSIFICATIONS—can also be seen in a similar light. If race is a suspect classification, surely the reason is that no interest in civil society is more fundamental than being treated as a full-fledged member of the community.

In effect, although all but a few of the enumerated rights in the Constitution and its amendments are now regarded as *fundamental,* and thus fully entitled to thorough judicial protection and scrutiny, the Court has embraced a hierarchical or "tiered" formulation. Some fundamental rights thus remain preferred. To what extent that arrangement will stand the test of time and experience will depend chiefly upon the judiciary's perception.

HENRY J. ABRAHAM
(1986)

Bibliography

ABRHAM, HENRY J. 1987 *Freedom and the Court: Civil Rights and Liberties in the United States,* 5th ed. New York: Oxford University Press.

CORTNER, RICHARD C. 1981 *The Supreme Court and the Second Bill of Rights.* Madison: University of Wisconsin Press.

GUNTHER, GERALD 1972 The Supreme Court: 1971 Term; In Search of Evolving Doctrines on a Changing Court: A Model for a Newer Equal Protection. *Harvard Law Review* 86:1–48.

FURMAN v. GEORGIA

See: Capital Punishment Cases of 1972

FURNEAUX, PHILIP
(1726–1783)

Philip Furneaux, an English dissenter minister, in 1770 published a volume criticizing WILLIAM BLACKSTONE's exposition of the laws of toleration. Furneaux opposed all restraints on the expression of religious or irreligious opinions. He flatly rejected the BAD TENDENCY TEST, proposing in its place punishment of overt acts only. His book of 1770 was republished in Philadelphia in 1773 under the title *The Palladium of Conscience.* Furneaux influenced THOMAS JEFFERSON and the writing of the Virginia Statute of Religious Freedom.

LEONARD W. LEVY
(1986)

G

GAG ORDER

"Gag order" is the press's pejorative term for a judicial order forbidding public comment, usually about a pending criminal case. Judges issue the order in an effort to prevent publicity that might make it impossible for a criminal defendant to receive a fair trial by an impartial jury. The orders came into use as a result of criticism by the American Bar Association (ABA) and others of press coverage of notorious cases such as the 1932 kidnap-murder of Charles Lindbergh's baby, the murder trial of Dr. Sam Sheppard in 1954, and the assassination of President JOHN F. KENNEDY in 1963. Each of those cases generated a torrent of publicity, much of it prejudicial to the accused's right to a fair trial.

The Supreme Court first discussed gag orders in *Sheppard v. Maxwell* (1966), when it reversed Sheppard's conviction on the ground that he had been denied DUE PROCESS OF LAW. Although the decision turned on the trial judge's failure to control "the carnival atmosphere at trial" rather than prejudicial pretrial publicity, the Court went out of its way to suggest that the judge "should have made some effort to control the release of leads, information, and gossip to the press by police officers, witnesses, and the counsel for both sides."

This *obiter dictum* finally made pretrial publicity a constitutional, rather than merely ethical, issue. In 1968 an ABA committee promulgated new "Standards on Fair Trial and Free Press," endorsing prohibitions against release of information by lawyers and law enforcement officers. Gag orders then came into widespread use, usually over the vehement opposition of the press.

The ABA report distinguished between gag orders directed at lawyers and other trial participants and those directed at the press itself. It did not endorse the latter, fearing that restrictions on the press would violate the FIRST AMENDMENT. This distinction is still widely observed, even though gag orders against lawyers operate as prior restraints on speech just as surely as those against the press.

The constitutionality of gag orders reached the Supreme Court in NEBRASKA PRESS ASSOCIATION V. STUART (1976). In a multiple murder case a state trial judge had forbidden the local press to publish confessions or "other information strongly implicative of the accused as the perpetrator of the slayings." The Supreme Court treated the order as a prior restraint on publication, and held it unconstitutional because there was no showing that less drastic alternatives, such as postponement or sequestration of jurors, would have been insufficient to protect the defendant's right to a fair trial. The Court also doubted the efficacy of the order, because of difficulties in controlling publicity by media beyond the trial judge's jurisdiction and by word of mouth within the community.

The *Stuart* opinion stopped short of saying that all gag orders against the press are unconstitutional, but three members of the Court would have said so, and two others doubted that such orders could ever be justified. Since *Stuart*, gag orders against the press have been rare. The Court reserved judgment on orders against trial participants, however, and these continue to be issued with some frequency. The lower courts generally have upheld narrowly drawn restrictions against lawyers and defendants when judges have determined that they are necessary to prevent a "reasonable likelihood" or "a serious and imminent threat" of interference with a fair trial.

DAVID A. ANDERSON
(1986)

(SEE ALSO: *Free Press/Fair Trial.*)

Bibliography

BARRON, JEROME A. and DIENES, C. THOMAS 1979 *Handbook of Free Speech and Free Press.* Boston: Little, Brown.

HALLAM, OSCAR 1940 Some Object Lessons on Publicity in Criminal Trials. *Minnesota Law Review* 24:454–508.

PORTMAN, SHELDON 1977 The Defense of Fair Trial from *Sheppard* to *Nebraska Press Association:* Benign Neglect to Affirmative Action and Beyond. *Stanford Law Review* 29:393–410.

GAG RULE

See: Civil Liberties and the Antislavery Controversy; Freedom of Petition; Slavery and the Constitution

GALLAGHER v. CROWN KOSHER SUPER MARKET

See: Sunday Closing Laws

GALLATIN, ALBERT
(1761–1849)

Born in Geneva, Switzerland, Albert Gallatin came to America in 1780 and settled in western Pennsylvania. He opposed RATIFICATION OF THE CONSTITUTION because he thought the union too consolidated and the presidency too monarchial. In 1788–1789, as a delegate to the Pennsylvania state CONSTITUTIONAL CONVENTION, Gallatin spoke out for virtually universal suffrage and for popular election of United States senators.

Gallatin served three terms in the Pennsylvania Assembly (1790–1792), where he was leader of the Republican minority. He there advocated public education and INTERNAL IMPROVEMENTS. In 1792 he was secretary of a convention called to denounce ALEXANDER HAMILTON's federal whiskey excise, and he drafted a petition to Congress against the excise; but two years later he publicly opposed the violence of the WHISKEY REBELLION.

Elected to the United States Senate in 1793, Gallatin was denied his seat on the grounds that he had not been a citizen for the requisite nine years. From 1795 until 1801 he served in the House of Representatives, the last four years as Republican floor leader; he rigorously opposed the ALIEN AND SEDITION ACTS.

As secretary of the treasury under Presidents THOMAS JEFFERSON and JAMES MADISON (1801–1814) Gallatin attempted to reorganize public finance on a Republican basis by abolishing both the national debt and all internal taxes and supporting the government by revenue from the tariff and sale of public lands. That design was ultimately frustrated by the War of 1812. During his tenure at the Treasury, Gallatin introduced more efficient statistical accountability and began the practice of issuing annual reports to Congress of revenues and expenditures.

In 1814 Gallatin helped negotiate peace with Great Britain. He continued his diplomatic career as minister to France (1816–1823) and to Britain (1826–1827). He later became a bank president and devoted his leisure to the study of American Indian languages.

DENNIS J. MAHONEY
(1986)

GALLOWAY, JOSEPH
(1731–1803)

A conservative political leader, Joseph Galloway long sought compromise with England. At the FIRST CONTINENTAL CONGRESS (1774) he proposed establishment of an "inferior and distinct" branch of Parliament in America. A president-general, chosen by the king, would preside over a "grand council," execute its acts (to which he must assent), and direct all matters concerning more than one colony. Approval by both this council and Parliament would be required for all "general acts," but each colony would retain its own government. Galloway's plan lost by one vote. Although he opposed a parliamentary tax and defended the colonies' right to govern themselves, he accepted parliamentary supremacy and understood English attempts to have the colonies share in the cost of their defense. Galloway's loyalism doomed him to exile after Philadelphia's capture by American forces in 1778.

DAVID GORDON
(1986)

Bibliography

WERNER, RAYMOND C. 1931 Joseph Galloway. In *Dictionary of American Biography.* New York: Scribner's.

GANNETT CO., INC. v. DEPASQUALE
443 U.S. 368 (1978)

In *Gannett* the trial judge excluded the public, including the press, from a pretrial hearing involving evidence of an involuntary confession in a highly publicized murder case. The Supreme Court rejected arguments that the Sixth Amendment provided a constitutional public right to attend criminal trials. Reasoning that the constitutional guarantee of a public trial is designed to benefit the defendant, not the public, the Court concluded that where the litigants agree to close a pretrial proceeding to protect the defendant's right to a FAIR TRIAL, the Constitution does not require that it remain open to the public. The Court declined to address the corollary issue whether the FIRST AMENDMENT created a right of access to the press to attend criminal trials—a question later answered affirmatively in RICHMOND NEWSPAPERS, INC. V. VIRGINIA (1980).

Justice LEWIS F. POWELL, concurring, conceded that the press had an interest, protected by the First Amendment, in being present at the pretrial hearing, but said that this interest should be balanced against the defendant's right to a fair trial. The order excluding the press from attending the pretrial hearing in *Gannett* was distinguished from the GAG ORDER in NEBRASKA PRESS ASSOCIATION V. STUART (1976) because the press was merely excluded from one source of information; it was not told what it might or might not publish.

Justice HARRY A. BLACKMUN, joined by Justices WILLIAM J. BRENNAN, BYRON R. WHITE, and THURGOOD MARSHALL, also framed the issue as one of access to the judicial proceeding, not one of prior restraint on the press. Blackmun, upon a lengthy historical examination, concluded that the criminally accused did not have a right to compel a private pretrial proceeding or trial. Only in certain circumstances, with appropriate procedural safeguards, might a court give effect to the accused's attempts to waive the right to a public trial.

KIM MCLANE WARDLAW
(1986)

(SEE ALSO: *Free Press/Fair Trial.*)

GARCIA v. SAN ANTONIO METROPOLITAN TRANSIT AUTHORITY
469 U.S. 528 (1985)

In NATIONAL LEAGUE OF CITIES V. USERY (1976) a 5–4 majority of the Supreme Court sought to establish a new doctrinal foundation for the concept of STATES' RIGHTS. Overruling its eight-year-old PRECEDENT in *Maryland v. Wirtz* (1968), the Court held unconstitutional the application of the wage and hour provisions of the federal FAIR LABOR STANDARDS ACT to state and local government employees in areas of "traditional governmental functions" such as police and fire protection. After eight more years,

Garcia followed *Wirtz* and overruled *Usery*—again by 5–4 vote. Justice HARRY A. BLACKMUN, whose change of vote produced this second about-face, wrote the OPINION OF THE COURT.

Lower court decisions following *Usery*, said Justice Blackmun, had failed to establish any principle for determining which governmental functions were "traditional" and essential to state sovereignty, and thus immune from impairment by congressional regulations. Justice Blackmun did not mention his own contribution to the confusion, first in his *Usery* concurrence, which suggested that the reach of Congress's power depended on the importance of the national interests at stake, and later in his votes to uphold congressional power in cases only doubtfully distinguishable from *Usery*, such as *Federal Regulatory Commission v. Mississippi* (1982) and EQUAL EMPLOYMENT OPPORTUNITY COMMISSION V. WYOMING (1983). The reasoning in those opinions—heatedly disputed by the four *Garcia* dissenters—had sapped *Usery*'s strength as a precedent by making the states pass through a doctrinal labyrinth before *Usery* could be applied.

The aspect of the *Garcia* opinion that drew the most fire, from within the Court and from the outside, was its announcement of the Court's virtual abdication from JUDICIAL REVIEW of acts of Congress challenged as invasions of state SOVEREIGNTY. The principal remedy for such potential abuses of congressional power, said Justice Blackmun, is not judicial but political. The constitutional structure assures the states a significant role in the selection of the national government; the influence of the states was demonstrated in the federal government's financial aid to the states and in the numerous exemptions for state activities provided in congressional regulations. The Court's abdication was not complete; Justice Blackmun acknowledged that some "affirmative limits . . . on federal action affecting the States" may remain. Yet he explicitly left to another day the specification of what those limits might be.

Justice LEWIS F. POWELL wrote the main opinion for the four dissenters. He began with a lament for the demise of STARE DECISIS—which he had not mourned when *Usery* overruled *Wirtz*. The *Usery* principle had been "reiterated consistently over the past eight years," he said—not mentioning that those same opinions uniformly had sustained congressional regulations against challenges founded on *Usery*. Justice Powell argued that the majority had abandoned the FEDERALISM envisioned by the Framers, leaving the states' role to "the grace of elected federal officials." In any event, he contended, the "political safeguards of federalism" are not what they used to be. Congressional regulatory techniques have changed, increasingly displacing or commandeering the states' sovereign functions. Furthermore, although the people of the states are represented in the federal government, the state governments as institutions are apt to have little influence on national decision making, in comparison with nationwide interest groups.

Some of the dissenters left no doubt that they expect the *Usery* principle to return when members of the *Garcia* majority are replaced by new Justices more attuned to the symbolism of states' rights. But symbolism may be all that is left of that once vital principle, whatever the future may hold for the *Garcia* precedent. First, Congress can dragoon the state into its regulatory schemes as it did in HODEL V. VIRGINIA SURFACE MINING AND RECLAMATION ASSOCIATION (1981): regulating private conduct directly, but allowing a state to opt out of the federal regulation by adopting its own law under federal guidelines. Furthermore, if Congress wants to buy state sovereignty, it will find willing sellers. By placing conditions on FEDERAL GRANTS-IN-AID—which now amount to about one-fifth of state budgets—Congress can achieve through the spending power virtually anything it might achieve by direct regulation. Even if *Garcia* should be overruled and *Usery* reinstated, Congress can offer subsidies that are vital to local transit authorities or police departments, conditioned on promises to pay transit and police employees the federal minimum wage. The passion of the Justices on both sides may indicate that in these cases the symbolism is what counts.

KENNETH L. KARST
(1986)

Bibliography

FIELD, MARTHA A. 1985 *Garcia v. San Antonio Metropolitan Transit Authority:* The Demise of a Misguided Doctrine. *Harvard Law Review* 99:84–118.

VAN ALSTYNE, WILLIAM W. 1985 The Second Death of Federalism. *Michigan Law Review* 83:1709–1733.

GARFIELD, JAMES A.
(1831–1881)

A CIVIL WAR general, James Abram Garfield served in Congress from 1863 until 1881, when he became President of the United States. In Congress Garfield was a skilled parliamentarian and self-taught expert on finance. After 1868 he was one of the most powerful Republicans in Congress, and served as minority leader from 1876 until 1880. In a period of pervasive corruption Garfield remained relatively untainted. In 1876 he helped frame the legislation that led to the COMPROMISE OF 1877 that settled the disputed presidential election. He served on the electoral commission, supporting President Rutherford B. Hayes on every issue. In 1880 the Ohio legislature chose him for

the United States SENATE, for a term beginning in 1881. However, that summer he became a compromise candidate for the presidency, after the Republican convention deadlocked. As President, Garfield attempted to root out corruption in the Post Office Department and the notorious New York customs house. Garfield's insistence that he, as President, should make all appointments, regardless of long-standing notions of senatorial privilege, led ROSCOE CONKLING of New York to resign from the Senate. In July 1881 Garfield was shot and killed by a disappointed office seeker who shouted that he was a party "stalwart" and that now CHESTER A. ARTHUR would be President. In the wake of this tragedy Arthur continued Garfield's investigation of the Post Office and secured the passage of the first civil service reform law, the PENDLETON ACT.

PAUL FINKELMAN
(1986)

Bibliography

PESKIN, ALAN 1978 *Garfield.* Kent, Ohio: Kent State University Press.

GARLAND, AUGUSTUS H.
(1832–1899)

Augustus Hill Garland, a WHIG lawyer, opposed SECESSION in 1861 but represented Arkansas in the Confederate Congress throughout the CIVIL WAR. He won readmission to the federal bar in *Ex parte Garland* (1867), one of the TEST OATH CASES; but the same year the United States Senate, to which he had been elected, denied him his seat. He served as governor of Arkansas (1874–1876) and United States senator (1877–1885) before becoming President GROVER CLEVELAND's attorney general (1885–1889). He was later a prominent lawyer practicing in Washington, D.C. He was co-author of a treatise on federal court JURISDICTION.

DENNIS J. MAHONEY
(1986)

GARLAND, EX PARTE

See: Test Oath Cases

GARRISON, WILLIAM LLOYD
(1805–1879)

William Lloyd Garrison edited America's leading abolitionist newspaper, *The Liberator* (1831–1865), and helped found the New England Anti-Slavery Society (1831) and the American Anti-Slavery Society (1833; president,

1843–1865). Garrison believed pacifism, nonresistance, and moral suasion could end SLAVERY. He argued that the Constitution supported slavery and was "a covenant with death and an agreement with Hell." Thus, he refused to vote or voluntarily support civil government, and after 1843 Garrison and his followers advocated a peaceful dissolution of the Union under the slogan "No Union with Slaveholders." More moderate abolitionists rejected Garrison's analysis of the Constitution, his opposition to antislavery political candidates and parties, and his extreme tactics, such as publicly burning the Constitution and declaring "So perish all compromises with tyranny." Despite his disunionist beliefs, he ultimately gave tacit support to ABRAHAM LINCOLN and the Union during the CIVIL WAR.

PAUL FINKELMAN
(1986)

Bibliography
THOMAS, JOHN L. 1963 *The Liberator.* Boston: Little, Brown.

GARRITY v. NEW JERSEY
385 U.S. 493 (1967)

Justice WILLIAM O. DOUGLAS, for a 6–3 majority, ruled that coercion had tainted confessions exacted from police officers suspected of fixing traffic tickets, when they were made to choose between exercising their RIGHT AGAINST SELF-INCRIMINATION and retaining their jobs. The dissenters argued that the state could require police officers to assist in detecting unlawful activities, that the officers' confessions were not involuntary, and that their constitutional right was not burdened.

LEONARD W. LEVY
(1986)

GAULT, IN RE
387 U.S. 1 (1967)

In re Gault is the Supreme Court's most important landmark concerning juveniles, both because of its specific requirements for delinquency proceedings and because of its unequivocal declaration of the broad principle that young persons, as individuals, have constitutional rights of their own. Rejecting the informality that had long characterized state juvenile courts, the Supreme Court held that DUE PROCESS OF LAW required four procedural safeguards in the adjudicatory (or guilt-determining) phase of delinquency proceedings: adequate written NOTICE to the juvenile and his parents of the specific charges; notification of the RIGHT TO COUNSEL, with appointed counsel for those who lack the means to retain a lawyer; the right of

CONFRONTATION and cross-examination of witnesses; and the notification of the RIGHT AGAINST SELF-INCRIMINATION. For the first time the Supreme Court declared boldly, in a seminal opinion by Justice ABE FORTAS, that "whatever may be their precise impact, neither the FOURTEENTH AMENDMENT nor the Bill of Rights is for adults alone."

The facts of the case dramatically suggested the risks of procedural informality and "unbridled discretion," which the Court saw as a poor substitute for "principle and procedure." Fifteen-year-old Gerald Gault was found to be a delinquent and was committed for up to six years to the Arizona Industrial School for an offense that would have subjected an adult to a small fine and no more than two months' imprisonment. Neither Gerald nor his parents were ever served with a petition that disclosed the factual basis of the juvenile court proceedings. It was claimed that Gerald and a friend had made an obscene telephone call to a neighbor who never appeared in the proceedings. Although the judge subsequently reported that Gerald had made some sort of admission to him, no transcript was made of what was said at either of Gerald's two appearances before the judge, nor was Gerald offered counsel.

Although a few states had anticipated the Court's rulings in *Gault* by adopting new juvenile justice acts that provided greater safeguards, procedural informality had characterized most juvenile courts since their creation around 1900. This was typically justified on two interrelated grounds. First, the goal of JUVENILE PROCEEDINGS was said to be treatment and rehabilitation, not punishment or deterrence. Second, investigation, diagnosis, and treatment required individualized determinations of what was best for each particular child. Legalistic formalities were seen as inconsistent and counterproductive in a benevolent and paternalistic institution committed to the rehabilitative ideal. State courts had refused to impose safeguards that "restrict the state when it seeks to deprive a person of his liberty," typically with conclusory statements that minors had no interest in liberty (because they would be subject in all events to parental control) or that delinquency proceedings were civil, rather than criminal, because their purpose was not punitive.

Gault rejected these traditional justifications. Pointing to various empirical studies, the *Gault* majority challenged the rehabilitative effectiveness of the juvenile justice system by suggesting that juvenile crime had increased since the establishment of the juvenile courts; questioned the value of procedural informality as a means to shape desirable attitudes about justice in the young people caught up by the system; and disparaged the significance, in terms of loss of liberty, of the difference between detention in a "home" or "school" after a finding of delinquency and incarceration after conviction of a crime. The strength of much of the social science evidence cited by the Court has been subsequently challenged, but the Court's willingness to attach substantial weight to the interest of a young person in avoiding the serious practical consequences of an erroneous determination of delinquency is certainly justified.

The Court did not suggest in *Gault* or in its subsequent decisions that the Constitution requires the state to treat a juvenile accused of delinquency in all respects like an adult accused of a similar act. The Court has extended other procedural safeguards to juveniles in delinquency proceedings—in IN RE WINSHIP (1970) it required proof beyond a REASONABLE DOUBT, for example, and in *Breed v. Jones* (1975) it held that the prohibition against DOUBLE JEOPARDY applied—but it has refused, as in MCKEIVER V. PENNSYLVANIA (1971), to require TRIAL BY JURY in delinquency proceedings. Although the traditional goals of the juvenile courts do not justify the absence of certain safeguards, *Gault* and its progeny suggest that the Constitution does not require abolition of the separate juvenile court system with some distinctive procedural features. Nor does *Gault* require the states to impose identical sanctions on minors and adults after a determination that a criminal statute has been violated. Indeed, by emphasizing that the procedural requirements extended only to the adjudicatory phase, and not to the dispositional phase, of delinquency proceedings, the Court in *Gault* argued that its decision did not threaten the emphasis juvenile courts have traditionally claimed to place on individualized treatment and rehabilitation.

ROBERT H. MNOOKIN
(1986)

(SEE ALSO: *Children's Rights.*)

Bibliography

STAPLETON, W. VAUGHAN and TEITELBAUM, LEE E.   1972   *In Defense of Youth: A Study of the Role of Counsel in American Juvenile Courts.* New York: Russell Sage Foundation.

GELBARD v. UNITED STATES
408 U.S. 41 (1972)

The Supreme Court held that a witness who refuses to answer a GRAND JURY question derived from illegal electronic surveillance may not be held in CONTEMPT. Title III of the OMNIBUS CRIME CONTROL AND SAFE STREETS ACT excludes from grand jury proceedings any EVIDENCE obtained from illegal surveillance and a witness need not answer a question based on such information.

HERMAN SCHWARTZ
(1986)

GELPCKE v. DUBUQUE
1 Wallace 175 (1864)

In his introduction to the 1864 reports of the Supreme Court, John Wallace, the Supreme Court reporter, remarked that in *Gelpcke* the Court imposed "high moral duties . . . upon a whole community seeking apparently to violate them." The community was Dubuque, Iowa, which attempted to enhance its property values by issuing municipal bonds, backed by local taxes, to promote railroad development that would put Dubuque on the map. Dubuque acted on authority granted by the Iowa legislature, although the state constitution prevented the legislature from investing in private railroads, as Dubuque did, and from increasing the state's indebtedness as much as the legislature authorized the city to increase its indebtedness. Responding to railroad shenanigans and the objections of taxpayers, Dubuque repudiated its debt, and the Iowa Supreme Court held that the legislature had violated the state constitution when authorizing Dubuque to issue the bonds.

Bondholders, seeking federal relief against default, persuaded the Supreme Court to rule that a contract once valid under state law cannot have its validity or obligation impaired by the subsequent action of a state court. Justice NOAH H. SWAYNE, speaking for all but Justice SAMUEL F. MILLER, who dissented, refused to accept the state supreme court's ruling on a matter of state constitutional law. Swayne took the high ground by declaring, "We shall never immolate truth, justice, and the law, because a state tribunal has erected the altar and decreed the sacrifice." However, the ground of decision was not clear, and the Supreme Court construed a state judicial decision as a "law," contrary to conventional usage.

Justice OLIVER WENDELL HOLMES later remarked that the decision in *Gelpcke* took the Court a good while to explain. In fact, the explanation subsequently provided by the Court was that the state judicial decision had violated the CONTRACT CLAUSE. However construed, *Gelpcke* was a means of the Supreme Court's expansion of its JURISDICTION, either under the doctrine of SWIFT V. TYSON (1842) or under the contract clause, which had previously applied only to statutes, not judicial decisions. And the Court established a basis for curbing municipal repudiation of debts and protecting municipal bondholders.

LEONARD W. LEVY
(1986)

GENDER DISCRIMINATION

See: Sex Discrimination

GENDER RIGHTS

Strictly speaking, there can be no distinct class of gender rights under the Constitution, but only the same rights for all persons, or all citizens, regardless of sex. The Constitution secures rights only of individuals, not of groups, and makes no distinction between men and women.

No nouns or adjectives denote sex in the Constitution except for the use of the word "male" in the FOURTEENTH AMENDMENT, in a provision no longer operative, which never provided any positive authority for SEX DISCRIMINATION.

There are, to be sure, many masculine pronouns in the text, but they have always been understood to be genderless; to hold that these pronouns refer only to men would mean, unless the Constitution is amended, that women are ineligible to serve in the Congress or the presidency, that a female FUGITIVE FROM JUSTICE fleeing to another state need not "be delivered up" (Article IV, section 2), and that accused women do not have the RIGHT TO COUNSEL—absurdities that have not been indulged in by courts or responsible scholars.

The only mention of sex is in the NINETEENTH AMENDMENT, forbidding denial of the right of citizens to vote "on account of sex," but its ratification did not require any change in the text of the Constitution. If the EQUAL RIGHTS AMENDMENT, forbidding denial of "equality of rights . . . on account of sex," had been ratified, the same would have been true: nothing already in the text of the Constitution would have been altered, because there is in it no positive authorization for denial of the right to vote, or of any other right, "on account of sex."

There is another indication that no distinction between men and women is intended in the Constitution. For purposes of determining representation, "the whole number of persons" is to be counted (Article I, section 2, as amended by the Fourteenth Amendment, section 2)— that is, females and males equally. This contrasts strikingly with similar provisions in other documents of the time; for example, the NORTHWEST ORDINANCE of 1787 provides that only "male inhabitants" be counted for purposes of representation.

The fact that there has never been any constitutional justification for denying rights or privileges to any person or citizen on account of sex has not prevented legislatures and courts from discriminating against women. Judicial discrimination often relied on sources and doctrines extraneous to the Constitution and, ironically, was frequently expressed in terms of protective concern for the well-being of women. In BRADWELL V. ILLINOIS (1873), Justice JOSEPH P. BRADLEY gave classic form to the pronouncement that the denial of a woman's right was for her own good: "The civil law as well as nature herself has always recognized a wide difference in the respective spheres and destinies of man and woman. Man is, or should be, women's protector and defender. The natural and proper timidity and delicacy which belongs to the female sex evidently unfits it for many of the occupations of civil life."

To justify his denial that women have the same constitutional right as men "to engage in any and every profession, occupation, or employment," Justice Bradley cited "the civil law," "nature herself," "the divine ordinance," "the nature of things," "the law of the Creator," and, finally, "the general constitution of things"—but not the Constitution of the United States.

Well past the middle of the twentieth century, this combination of protective concern, extraneous doctrines, and silence about the text of the Constitution served as the foundation of sex discrimination in many areas, including employment, PROPERTY RIGHTS, jury duty, voting, pensions, EDUCATION, and WELFARE BENEFITS. The decisive turn around finally began in the courts in *Reed v. Reed* (1971) and FRONTIERO V. RICHARDSON (1973). But the correction of centuries of denying women their rights does not establish gender rights, which, like all other group rights, lacks constitutional justification.

In the series of cases since Reed, the Supreme Court sought for the appropriately strict "level of judicial scrutiny of legislation" under the Fourteenth Amendment's equal protection clause. The effort to afford EQUAL PROTECTION OF THE LAWS is a belated acknowledgment that there is no affirmative basis in the Constitution, and never was, for treating the rights of one person differently from the rights of others on account of sex.

ROBERT A. GOLDWIN
(1992)

(SEE ALSO: *Woman Suffrage; Women in Constitutional History.*)

Bibliography

GOLDWIN, ROBERT A. 1990 *Why Blacks, Women, and Jews Are Not Mentioned in the Constitution.* Washington, D.C.: Aei Press.
WORTMAN, MARLENE STEIN 1985 *Women in American Law.* Vol. 1. New York: Holmes and Meier.

GENERAL LAWS AND LIBERTIES OF MASSACHUSETTS

See: Massachusetts General Laws and Liberties

GENERAL WARRANT

General warrants command either apprehension for unstated causes or the arrest, search, or seizure of unspecified persons, places, or objects. Since the *Five Knights Case* (1628) English courts have consistently disallowed the first category of warrant, although its use survived a century later. The general warrant of the second sort, which allowed its bearer to search wherever or seize whomever or whatever he wished, was more common. It existed by the early fourteenth century and found ever growing applications. The Star Chamber and "High Commission" of the Tudor-Stuart period used such warrants vigorously to suffocate political and religious dissent. By the middle of the eighteenth century, general warrants were or had also been used to combat vagrancy, regulate publications, impress persons into the army and navy, pursue felons, collect taxes, and find stolen merchandise. A close relative, the WRIT OF ASSISTANCE, allowed customs officers to search all houses in which they suspected concealed contraband.

Beginning with the WILKES CASES (1763–1770), British courts undermined the use of general SEARCH WARRANTS by secretaries of state. Although they were widely used in colonial and revolutionary America, eight state constitutions of 1776–1784 forbade them, as does the FOURTH AMENDMENT to the federal Constitution.

WILLIAM CUDDIHY
(1986)

Bibliography

CUDDIHY, WILLIAM and HARDY, B. CARMON 1980 A Man's House Was Not His Castle: Origins of the Fourth Amendment to the United States Constitution. *William and Mary Quarterly* 37: 371–400.

GENERAL WELFARE CLAUSE

With no enforceable power to tax under the ARTICLES OF CONFEDERATION, Congress "requisitioned" funds from the states each of which then decided how and whether to raise its share of the confederation's needs. Uneven responses brought resentment among the states and frequent frustration of congressional policies. Dissatisfaction with this system was a leading cause of the failure of the Articles. As a remedy, the CONSTITUTIONAL CONVENTION proposed to empower the new Congress to "lay and collect Taxes, Duties, IMPOSTS, and EXCISES, to pay the Debt and provide for the common Defense and general welfare of the United States." Some ANTI-FEDERALISTS said this language defeated the principle of ENUMERATED POWERS because it could be read to authorize action for the common defense and general welfare by any legislative means whatever. JAMES MADISON disclaimed this interpretation in THE FEDERALIST #41, saying that the general welfare clause conferred power to tax and spend only for purposes indi-

cated by the enumerated powers that followed in Article I, section 8. Congress could tax and spend for armies and navies, for example, but not for purposes reserved to the states.

Later, during conflicts with the Jeffersonians over national economic policy, ALEXANDER HAMILTON argued that the enumerated powers did not exhaust the concept of "the general welfare" and that Congress could tax and spend for purposes beyond the enumerated powers, so long as it acted in the general interest. Constitutional history has thus produced three theories of the general welfare clause: as the Anti-Federalists charged, that Congress could claim unrestricted power to act in the general interest; that Congress could tax and spend only for purposes indicated by the enumerated powers, as Madison claimed; and that Congress could tax and spend for purposes beyond the enumerated powers, as Hamilton claimed. In OBITER DICTUM, the Supreme Court adopted the Hamiltonian theory in UNITED STATES V. BUTLER (1936).

In *Butler*, the court voided a federal tax as part of an unconstitutional scheme to use the spending power to invade powers reserved to the states. After first declaring that Congress could tax and spend for purposes beyond the enumerated powers, the Court then ignored the Hamiltonian theory by holding the act unconstitutional as an attempt to invade an area (agricultural production) beyond Congress's enumerated powers. Later decisions that were friendlier to the NEW DEAL effectively reversed this holding and rescued the Hamiltonian theory. The Court enlarged the scope of the COMMERCE CLAUSE by affirming Congress's authority directly to regulate any social or economic activity with an "effect" upon INTERSTATE COMMERCE, regardless of Congress's motives relative to the reserved powers of the states. (See UNITED STATES V. DARBY LUMBER COMPANY, 1941; IMPLIED POWERS.) In SONZINSKY V. UNITED STATES (1937) the Court refused to scrutinize Congress's motives for taxing socially harmful activities so long as the tax produced some revenue. And in STEWARD MACHINE COMPANY V. DAVIS (1937) the Court upheld the taxing scheme that was the foundation of the Social Security system, irrespective of any other enumerated power of Congress.

Such decisions eliminated doubts about the Court's acceptance of the Hamiltonian theory, and the era following WORLD WAR II saw a great increase in federal regulatory taxes and subsidies conditioned on conformity with policies (such as racial integration) which some state and local governments otherwise would more actively have opposed. The Hamiltonian theory has also supported federal regulatory taxes on narcotics, gambling, and other morally injurious practices. (See UNITED STATES V. KAHRIGER.) No development has had a more corrosive effect on the old idea that some concerns lay beyond the reach of Congress.

Given the broad regulatory uses of the TAXING AND SPENDING POWERS, the triumph of Hamilton's theory vindicated the Anti-Federalists' predictions of what the general welfare clause eventually would become.

SOTIRIOS A. BARBER
(1986)

(SEE ALSO: *National Police Power.*)

Bibliography

BARBER, SOTIRIOS A. 1984 *On What the Constitution Means.* Baltimore: Johns Hopkins University Press.

GENETIC PRIVACY

See: DNA Testing and Genetic Privacy

GEORGIA v. STANTON

See: *Mississippi v. Johnson*

GERENDE v. BOARD OF SUPERVISORS OF ELECTIONS
341 U.S. 56 (1951)

A Maryland statute barred from public employment or office anyone who belonged to a "subversive" organization. In this unanimous PER CURIAM OPINION, the VINSON COURT sustained the law upon an understanding that the term "subversive" was limited to those somehow engaged in the attempt to overthrow the government by force or violence. The Court assumed that an affidavit negating such activity would satisfy the state's LOYALTY OATH required of those running for office.

MICHAEL E. PARRISH
(1986)

GERRY, ELBRIDGE
(1744–1814)

A Massachusetts merchant, Elbridge Gerry was particularly active in Revolutionary politics and served as a delegate to the Second Continental Congress. He signed the DECLARATION OF INDEPENDENCE as an early and vigorous supporter of separation from a government and people that he believed had become "corrupt and totally destitute of Virtue."

Gerry devoted most of his life to public service. He represented Massachusetts in Congress from 1779 to 1785, signing the ARTICLES OF CONFEDERATION. As a Mas-

sachusetts delegate to the CONSTITUTIONAL CONVENTION OF 1787, Gerry was, at the outset, a moderate nationalist who favored a strong central government although emphasizing the need for certain "federal features." Gerry opposed democracy—"the evils we experience flow from the excess of democracy"—and he often supported his own business interests. Indeed, he early recognized the need for congressional power "competent to the protection of" FOREIGN COMMERCE in order for Congress to "command reciprocal advantages in trade." A firm believer in republicanism, Gerry insisted on the need for a SEPARATION OF POWERS and the inclusion of additional checks on the national government. He chaired the committee that formulated the GREAT COMPROMISE and helped secure its adoption. The absence of a BILL OF RIGHTS, however, and the concentration of power in the federal government led Gerry to oppose RATIFICATION OF THE CONSTITUTION.

Elected to Congress in 1789, he served for four years as a strong supporter of ALEXANDER HAMILTON's financial program. Gerry retired from Congress in 1793 and was elected Republican governor of Massachusetts in 1810 and 1811. He so opposed the idea of legitimate opposition that his second term saw the passage of a bill radically redistricting the state to assure the Republicans greater representation in the state legislature than their actual strength justified. This political technique was satirized in a cartoon showing one oddly shaped district in the form of a salamander, hence the name GERRYMANDER. JAMES MADISON selected Gerry as his vice-presidential running mate in 1812, and until his death in 1814 Gerry championed Madison's administration.

DAVID GORDON
(1986)

Bibliography

BILLIAS, GEORGE A. 1976 *Elbridge Gerry, Founding Father and Republican Statesman.* New York: McGraw-Hill.

GERRYMANDER

A gerrymander is a political district drawn to advantage some and disadvantage others: candidates, parties, or interest groups. The name comes from a particularly spectacular partisan apportionment engineered by ELBRIDGE GERRY in 1812. Technically, any winner-take-all district can be called a gerrymander, for district lines inevitably favor some against others. But common usage limits the term to districts deemed unnatural in form or unfair in intent or effect. The Supreme Court boldly and unanimously attacked a blatant racial gerrymander in GOMILLION V. LIGHTFOOT (1960), but it has been almost uniformly acquiescent since then.

Gomillion voided an "uncouth, 28-sided figure" surgically excluding almost all of the blacks in Tuskegee, Alabama, from voting in the city while retaining every white. It cleared the way for BAKER V. CARR (1962) and the REAPPORTIONMENT revolution. But, apart from a few cases of municipal expansion challenged under the VOTING RIGHTS ACT OF 1965, the Court has never since been able or willing to find "cognizable discrimination" in gerrymandering cases.

The leading cases, *Wright v. Rockefeller* (1964) and UNITED JEWISH ORGANIZATIONS V. CAREY (1977), both involved packing of New York black and Puerto Rican voters into what dissenting Justice WILLIAM O. DOUGLAS (in *Wright*) called a "racial borough." Its packed nonwhite majority, if unpacked and spread to adjacent districts, might have formed two or three nonwhite majorities.

But it is difficult to tell clearly what packing does to a group's power, because "wasted" surplus votes in good years can be badly needed in bad years. In *Wright* the black plaintiffs wanted more "effective" black votes through dispersion, while the black incumbent, siding with the defendants, argued for strength through concentration: better one safe seat than two marginal ones. The baffled Court claimed it could find "no evidence of racial discrimination" in the obvious gerrymander, but the Court's real lack was simple rules for making sense of the evidence it had.

It is also impossible to equalize everyone's effective REPRESENTATION, short of ordering proportional representation, which could be a cure worse than the disease. In *UJO v. Carey* the United States attorney general had found the ethnically packed district discriminatory under the Voting Rights Act and ordered the state to create two more districts with nonwhite majority quotas. To do so, the state had to dismember a Hasidic Jewish community, which objected to the explicit RACIAL QUOTAS as a violation of the FOURTEENTH and FIFTEENTH AMENDMENTS. But the Court, ignoring the constitutional attack, argued that the racial quotas served the purposes of the Voting Rights Act by enhancing the black vote and did not involve "cognizable discrimination" against the Jews, who, as "whites in Kings County," might be submerged in their own districts but would have vicarious "fair representation" by white representatives of other districts.

Only in a few cases under the Voting Rights Act, with its heavy statutory burden on the state to prove nondiscrimination, has the Court intervened against racial gerrymandering since *Gomillion*. In constitutional terms, partisan and incumbent-favoring gerrymanders are deemed tolerable, perhaps because political districting is indeed a "mathematical quagmire" ill-suited for resolution with simple rules. The Court all but announced its retreat in *Gaffney v. Cummings* (1973).

Gerrymandering, largely unregulated, has flourished in reapportionment years. Theoretically, it could give the dominant party a manifold advantage over a numerically equal rival. In practice, it gives a thirty to forty percent advantage to the dominant party in seats per vote, often rewarding a minority of votes with a majority of seats.

Once it was hoped that objective standards—of compactness, contiguity, or competitiveness—or impartial judges or commissioners would curb gerrymandering. But standards have been largely ineffectual and judges and commissioners overwhelmingly partisan. A few states have limited partisan gerrymanders with bipartisan commissions, and roughly half the states have found protection through the happenstance of divided, two-party control of the elected branches. Ironically, despite *Gomillion* and the reapportionment revolution, the chief protection against gerrymandering has not come from courts but from the "weak" SEPARATION OF POWERS, and multiplication of competing factions—that court intervention was supposed to supplant.

WARD E. Y. ELLIOTT
(1986)

Bibliography

DIXON, ROBERT G. 1968 *Democratic Representation*. New York: Oxford University Press.
ELLIOTT, WARD E. Y. 1975 *The Rise of Guardian Democracy: The Supreme Court's Role in Voting Rights Disputes, 1845–1969*. Cambridge, Mass.: Harvard University Press.
SICKELS, ROBERT J. 1966 "Dragons, Bacon Strips, and Dumbbells—Who's Afraid of Reapportionment?" *Yale Law Journal* 75:1300–1308.

GERRYMANDER
(Update)

By the mid-1980s the focus of attention in racial gerrymandering controversies had shifted from the FOURTEENTH AMENDMENT to the VOTING RIGHTS ACT OF 1965, which Congress had amended in 1982 to assist minority-group plaintiffs. In *Thornburgh v. Gingles* (1986) the Supreme Court laid down guidelines for application of the revised Section 2 of the act.

While constitutional controversy over racial gerrymandering was subsiding, the issue of partisan gerrymandering was nearing its climax. In *Davis v. Bandemer* (1986) a 6–3 majority held that attacks on partisan gerrymanders under the EQUAL PROTECTION clause were justiciable, but only two Justices voted to strike down the districting plan that was being challenged by Indiana Democrats.

Justice BYRON R. WHITE's plurality opinion for the four Justices who believed the question was justiciable but that the Indiana plan was constitutional has received divergent interpretations. In one common view, the opinion is simply confused or self-contradictory. Others have read it to mean that plans yielding a legislative seat distribution sharply disproportionate to the statewide partisan vote will be struck down.

In *Davis*, the Republican National Committee supported the Indiana Democrats in an AMICUS CURIAE brief, while the Democratic congressional delegation from California supported the Indiana Republicans. This apparent display of political disinterestedness might have been influenced by the pending Republican challenge to the California congressional districting plan on similar grounds. After *Davis*, a lower court dismissed the California case, interpreting White's opinion in *Davis* to require pervasive discrimination against the plaintiff group beyond the gerrymander that is being challenged. Under this interpretation, major-party gerrymandering claims would rarely if ever be successful. The Supreme Court refused to review the California dismissal in *Badham v. Eu* (1988).

After much sound and fury, the prospects for judicial invalidation of partisan gerrymanders may have been no greater at the end of the 1980s than at the beginning.

DANIEL H. LOWENSTEIN
(1992)

Bibliography

GROFMAN, BERNARD, ed. 1990 *Political Gerrymandering and the Courts*. New York: Agathon Press.
SYMPOSIUM 1985 Gerrymandering and the Courts. *UCLA Law Review* 33:1–281.

GERTZ v. ROBERT WELCH, INC.
418 U.S. 323 (1974)

In this major case on LIBEL AND THE FIRST AMENDMENT, the Supreme Court in an opinion by Justice LEWIS F. POWELL held, 5–4, that the rule of NEW YORK TIMES V. SULLIVAN (1964) did not apply when the party seeking damages for libel is not a public official or a public figure. *New York Times* had applied the rule of "actual malice": the First Amendment bars a public official from recovering damages for a defamatory falsehood relating to his conduct in office unless he proves that the publisher or broadcaster made the statement knowing it to be false or "with reckless disregard of whether it was false or not." The Court had extended that rule in 1967 to PUBLIC FIGURES. In *Rosenbloom v. Metromedia, Inc.* (1971) a plurality ruled that if the defamation concerned a public issue the actual malice rule extended also to private individuals, who were not public figures. In *Gertz* the Court, abandoning that rule, held that a private plantiff had to prove actual malice only if seeking punitive damages; the FIRST AMENDMENT did not

require him to produce such proof merely to recover actual damages for injury to reputation.

Powell reasoned that public officers and public figures had a far greater opportunity to counteract false statements than private persons. Moreover, an official or a candidate for public office knowingly exposes himself to close public scrutiny and criticism, just as public figures knowingly invite attention and comment. The communications media cannot, however, assume that private persons similarly expose themselves to defamation. Powell declared that they "are not only more vulnerable to injury than public officials and public figures; they are also more deserving of recovery." Their only effective redress is resort to a state's libel laws. So long as a state does not permit the press or a broadcaster to be held liable without fault and applies the actual malice rule to requests for punitive damages, the Court held that the First Amendment requires a "less demanding showing than that required by *New York Times*" and that the states may decide for themselves the appropriate standard of liability for media defendants who defame private persons.

Each of the dissenting Justices wrote a separate opinion. The dissents covered a wide spectrum from greater concern for the defamed party to alarm about the majority's supposedly constrictive interpretation of the First Amendment. Chief Justice WARREN E. BURGER worried that the party libeled in this case was a lawyer who ought not to be invidiously identified with his client. Justice WILLIAM O. DOUGLAS thought all libel laws to be unconstitutional. Justice WILLIAM J. BRENNAN preferred the actual malice test to be applied to private individuals in matters of public concern. Justice BYRON R. WHITE, opposing the Court's restriction of the COMMON LAW of libels, condemned the nationalization of so large a part of libel law.

LEONARD W. LEVY
(1986)

GIBBONS v. OGDEN
9 Wheaton 1 (1824)

Chief Justice JOHN MARSHALL's great disquisition on the COMMERCE CLAUSE in this case is the most influential in our history. *Gibbons* liberated the steamship business and much of American INTERSTATE COMMERCE from the grip of state-created monopolies. More important, Marshall laid the doctrinal basis for the national regulation of the economy that occurred generations later, though at the time his opinion buttressed laissez-faire. He composed that opinion as if statecraft in the interpretation of a constitutional clause could decide whether the United States remained just a federal union or became a nation. The New York act, which the Court voided in *Gibbons*, had closed the ports of the state to steamships not owned or licensed by a monopoly chartered by the state. Other states retaliated in kind. The attorney general of the United States told the *Gibbons* Court that the country faced a commercial "civil war."

The decision produced immediate and dramatic results. Within two weeks, a newspaper jubilantly reported: "Yesterday the Steamboat *United States*, Capt. Bunker, from New Haven, entered New York in triumph, with streamers flying, and a large company of passengers exulting in the decision of the United States Supreme Court against the New York monopoly. She fired a salute which was loudly returned by huzzas from the wharves." Senator MARTIN VAN BUREN (Democrat, New York), who had recently advocated curbing the Court, declared that even those states whose laws had been nullified, including his own, "have submitted to their fate," and the Court now justly attracted "idolatry," its Chief respected as "the ablest Judge now sitting upon any judicial bench in the world." For a Court that had been under vitriolic congressional and state attack, *Gibbons* wedded a novel popularity to its nationalism.

One of the ablest judges who ever sat on an American court, JAMES KENT of New York, whose opinion Marshall repudiated, grumbled in the pages of his *Commentaries on American Law* (1826) that Marshall's "language was too general and comprehensive for the case." Kent was right. The Court held the state act unconstitutional for conflicting with an act of Congress, making Marshall's enduring treatise on the commerce clause unnecessary for the disposition of the case. The conflict between the two statutes, Marshall said, "decides the cause." Kent was also right in stating that "it never occurred to anyone," least of all to the Congress that had passed the Coastal Licensing Act of 1793, which Marshall used to decide the case, that the act could justify national supremacy over state regulations respecting "internal waters or commerce." The act of 1793 had been intended to discriminate against foreign vessels in the American coastal trade by offering preferential tonnage duties to vessels of American registry. Marshall's construction of the statute conformed to his usual tactic of finding narrow grounds for decision after making a grand exposition. He announced "propositions which may have been thought axioms." He "assume[d] nothing," he said, because of the magnitude of the question, the distinction of the judge (Kent) whose opinion he scrapped, and the able arguments, which he rejected, by Thomas Emmett and Thomas Oakely, covering over 125 pages in the report of the case.

Except for the arguments of counsel, the Court had little for guidance. It had never before decided a commerce clause case, and the clause itself is general: "Congress shall have power to regulate commerce with foreign nations and among the several states. . . ." The power to regulate what would later be called "interstate commerce" appears in the same clause touching FOREIGN COMMERCE, the regulation of which is necessarily exclusive, beyond state control. But the clause does not negate state regulatory authority over interstate commerce, and the framers of the Constitution had rejected proposals for a sole or EXCLUSIVE POWER in Congress. Interstate commerce could be, as counsel for the monopoly contended, a subject of CONCURRENT POWER. Marshall had previously acknowledged that although the Constitution vested in Congress bankruptcy and tax powers, the states retained similar powers. THE FEDERALIST #32 recognized the principle of concurrent powers but offered no assistance on the commerce clause. Congress had scarcely used the commerce power except for the EMBARGO ACTS, which had not come before the Supreme Court. Those acts had interpreted the power to "regulate" as a power to prohibit, but they concerned commerce with foreign nations and were an instrument of foreign policy.

Prior to *Gibbons* the prevailing view on the interstate commerce power was narrow and crossed party lines. Kent, a Federalist, differed little from the Jeffersonians. JAMES MADISON, for example, when vetoing a congressional appropriation for INTERNAL IMPROVEMENTS, had declared in 1817 that "the power to regulate commerce among the several states cannot include a power to construct roads and canals, and to improve the navigation of water courses." In 1821, when JAMES MONROE had vetoed the CUMBERLAND ROAD BILL, whose objective was to extend national authority to turnpikes within the states, he had virtually reduced the commerce power to the enactment of duties and imports, adding that goods and vessels are the only SUBJECTS OF COMMERCE that Congress can regulate. "Commerce," in common usage at the time of *Gibbons*, meant trade in the buying and selling of commodities, not navigation or the transportation of passengers for hire. That was the business of Mr. Gibbons, who operated a steamship in defiance of the monopoly, between Elizabethtown, New Jersey, and New York City, in direct competition with Ogden, a licensee of the monopoly. Had Gibbons operated under sail, he would not have violated New York law; as it was, the state condemned his vessel to fines and forfeiture.

In *Gibbons*, then, the Court confronted a stunted concept of commerce, a STRICT CONSTRUCTION of the commerce power, and an opinion bearing Kent's authority that New York had regulated only "internal" commerce. Kent had also held that the commerce power was a concurrent one and that the test for the constitutionality of a state act should be practical: could the state and national laws co-exist without conflicting in their operation? Marshall "assumed nothing" and in his step-by-step "axioms" repudiated any argument based on such premises.

He began with a definition of "commerce." It comprehended navigation as well as buying and selling, because "it is intercourse." This sweeping definition prompted a disgruntled states-rightist to remark, "I shall soon expect to learn that our fornication laws are unconstitutional." That same definition later constitutionally supported an undreamed of expansion of congressional power over the life of the nation's economy. Having defined commerce as every species of commercial intercourse, Marshall, still all-embracing, defined "commerce among the several states" to mean commerce intermingled with or concerning two or more states. Such commerce "cannot stop at the external boundary line of each State, but may be introduced into the interior"—and wherever it went, the power of the United States followed. Marshall did not dispute Kent's view that the "completely internal commerce" of a state (what we call INTRASTATE COMMERCE) is reserved for state governance. But that governance extended only to such commerce as was completely within one state, did not "affect" other states, "and with which it is not necessary to interfere, for the purpose of executing some of the general powers of the [United States] government." Marshall's breath-taking exposition of the national commerce power foreshadowed the STREAM OF COMMERCE DOCTRINE and the SHREVEPORT DOCTRINE of the next century. "If Congress has the power to regulate it," he added, "that power must be exercised whenever the subject exists. If it exists within the States . . . then the power of Congress may be exercised within a State."

Having so defined the reach of the commerce power, Marshall, parsing the clause, defined the power to "regulate" as the power "to prescribe the rule by which commerce is to be governed." It is a power that "may be exercised to its utmost extent, and acknowledges no limitations. . . ." In COHENS V. VIRGINIA (1821) he had said that the United States form, for most purposes, one nation: "In war, we are one people. In making peace, we are one people. In all commercial regulations, we are one and the same people," and the government managing that people's interests was the government of the Union. In *Gibbons* he added that because the "sovereignty of Congress" is plenary as to its objects, "the power over commerce with foreign nations, and among the several states, is vested in Congress as absolutely as it would be in a single government. . . ." Were that true, the commerce power would be as exclusive as the TREATY POWER or WAR POWERS and could not be shared concurrently with the states.

Marshall expressly denied that the states possessed a concurrent commerce power; yet he did not expressly declare that Congress possessed an exclusive commerce power, which would prevent the states from exercising a commerce power even in the absence of congressional legislation. That was DANIEL WEBSTER' s argument in *Gibbons*, against the monopoly, and Marshall found "great force" in it. Notwithstanding the ambiguity in Marshall's opinion, he implicitly adopted Webster's argument by repeatedly rejecting the theory of concurrent commerce powers. He conceded, however, that the states can reach and regulate some of the same subjects of commerce as Congress, but only by the exercise of powers distinct from an interstate commerce power. Referring to the mass of state regulatory legislation that encompassed inspection laws, health laws, turnpike laws, ferry laws, "etc.," Marshall labeled them the state's "system of police," later called the POLICE POWER. But his jurisprudence-by-label did not distinguish interstate from intrastate commerce powers. Having declared that Congress might regulate a state's "internal" commerce to effectuate a national policy, he allowed the state police power to operate on subjects of interstate commerce, in subordination, of course, to the principle of national supremacy. (See WILLSON V. BLACKBIRD CREEK MARSH CO.)

Following his treatise on the commerce clause, Marshall turned to the dispositive question whether the New York monopoly act conflicted with an act of Congress. The pertinent act of 1793 referred to American vessels employed in the "coasting trade." It made no exception for steamships or for vessels that merely transported passengers. The New York act was therefore "in direct collision" with the act of Congress by prohibiting Gibbons's steamship from carrying passengers in and out of the state's ports without a license from the monopoly.

Justice WILLIAM JOHNSON, although an appointee of THOMAS JEFFERSON, was even more nationalistic than Marshall. Webster later boasted that Marshall had taken to his argument as a baby to its mother's milk, but the remark better suited Johnson. Concurring separately, he declared that the commerce clause vested a power in Congress that "must be exclusive." He would have voided the state monopoly act even in the absence of the Federal Coastal Licensing Act: "I cannot overcome the conviction, that if the licensing act was repealed tomorrow, the rights of the appellant to a reversal of the decision complained of, would be as strong as it is under this license." Johnson distinguished the police power laws that operated on subjects of interstate commerce; their "different purposes," he claimed, made all the difference. In fact, the purpose underlying the monopoly act was the legitimate state purpose of encouraging new inventions.

In a case of first impression, neither Marshall nor Johnson could lay down DOCTRINES that settled all conflicts between state and national powers relating to commerce. Not until 1851 did the Court, after much groping, seize upon the doctrine of SELECTIVE EXCLUSIVENESS, which seemed at the time like a litmus paper test. (See COOLEY V. BOARD OF PORT WARDENS OF PHILADELPHIA.) Yet *Gibbons* anticipated doctrines concerning the breadth of congressional power that emerged in the next century and still govern. Marshall was as prescient as human ability allows. The Court today cannot construe the commerce clause except in certain state regulation cases without being influenced by Marshall's treatise on it. "At the beginning," Justice ROBERT JACKSON declared in WICKARD V. FILBURN (1941), "Chief Justice Marshall described the federal commerce power with a breadth never exceeded."

LEONARD W. LEVY
(1986)

Bibliography

BAXTER, MAURICE G.   1972   *The Steamboat Monopoly: Gibbons v. Ogden, 1824.* New York: Knopf.

BEVERIDGE, ALBERT J.   1916–1919   *The Life of John Marshall.* 4 vols. Vol. IV:397–460. Boston: Houghton Mifflin.

FRANKFURTER, FELIX   1937   *The Commerce Clause under Marshall, Taney and Waite.* Pages 1–45. Chapel Hill: University of North Carolina Press.

GIBONEY v.
EMPIRE STORAGE & ICE CO.
336 U.S. 490 (1949)

Speaking through Justice HUGO L. BLACK, the Supreme Court unanimously sustained an INJUNCTION issued by a Missouri court against labor pickets who attempted to pressure a supplier of ice not to deal with nonunion peddlers. The pickets claimed that the injunction violated their right to FREEDOM OF SPEECH and also conflicted with THORNHILL V. ALABAMA (1940), where the Justices had protected peaceful PICKETING. The Court rejected these arguments, by pointing out that the dominant purpose of the picketing here was to induce a violation of state law forbidding agreements in RESTRAINT OF TRADE. The FIRST AMENDMENT, Black noted, does not protect speech used as part of conduct that violates a valid state criminal statute.

MICHAEL E. PARRISH
(1986)

GIBSON, JOHN BANNISTER
(1780–1853)

John Bannister Gibson was a Pennsylvania judge for forty years, thirty-seven of which were spent on the state su-

preme court. Born in 1780, he studied at Dickinson College and was admitted to the bar in 1803. After a brief legislative experience, the governor appointed him to the Court of Common Pleas in 1813 and three years later elevated him to the state's highest court. In 1827, Gibson became chief justice, a position he retained until 1851 when a constitutional change inaugurated a rotation system. He spent the remaining two years of his life as an associate justice.

Gibson's views on judicial power form the bedrock of his reputation. In particular, his dissent in EAKIN V. RAUB (1825) presented the most important response to JOHN MARSHALL's opinion in MARBURY V. MADISON (1803). Gibson insisted that without specific constitutional authorization, the judiciary had no power to nullify legislative acts. His permissive view of legislative power complemented the "commonwealth idea." For example, he held that state-created monopolies were not constitutionally prohibited and, furthermore, that they were "useful institutions" (*Case of "The Philadelphia and Trenton Railroad Company,"* 1840).

Legislative interference with the judicial process resulted in the only exception to Gibson's temporizing course. The Pennsylvania legislature traditionally had exercised EQUITY powers through private acts. But after the courts were granted substantially complete equity jurisdiction in 1836, Gibson and his colleagues struck down attempts by the legislature to maintain their own practice. When the legislature ordered a new trial in a simple trespass action, Gibson ruled that "the power to order new trials is judicial; but the power of the legislature is not judicial" (*De Chastellux v. Fairchild*, 1850).

Gibson's views of judicial power were eclipsed by the judicial activism of the post-CIVIL WAR era. But subsequent demands for judicial restraint in the twentieth century resulted in renewed interest in Gibson and respect for his ideas. ROSCOE POUND ranked him among the ten leading American jurists, and MORRIS R. COHEN praised him as one of the "great creative minds" in American law.

STANLEY I. KUTLER
(1986)

Bibliography

KUTLER, STANLEY I.   1965   John Bannister Gibson: Judicial Restraint and the "Positive State." *Journal of Public Law* 14: 181–197.

GIBSON v. FLORIDA LEGISLATIVE
INVESTIGATION COMMISSION
372 U.S. 539 (1963)

The committee ordered the president of the Miami branch of the NAACP to produce his membership records and refer to them when the committee asked whether specific individuals, suspected of being communists, were NAACP members. Earlier committee attempts to expose the NAACP's entire membership list showed that the communist issue was a screen behind which the state sought to use publicity to weaken a group engaged in activities aimed at racial equality and DESEGREGATION.

The Supreme Court, 5–4, held that Gibson's conviction for contempt for refusal to produce the records infringed the FREEDOM OF ASSOCIATION, which protected associational privacy. The Court, in an opinion by Justice ARTHUR GOLDBERG, was prepared to balance the state interest in legislative investigation against this FIRST AMENDMENT interest, but it held that such an infringement could be constitutional only if "the state convincingly show[s] a substantial relation between the information sought and a subject of overriding and COMPELLING STATE INTEREST," and that Florida had not done so in this instance. Accordingly Gibson's conviction was invalidated.

Gibson and its predecessor, *Bates v. Little Rock* (1960), must be read in conjunction with the BALANCING TEST applied to a congressional investigation into communist activity in BARENBLATT V. UNITED STATES (1959). The later cases may be read narrowly to distinguish *Barenblatt* and provide greater constitutional protection from investigative exposure only for "groups which themselves are neither engaged in subversive or other illegal . . . activities nor demonstrated to have any substantial connections with such activities." Alternatively, *Bates* and *Gibson* can be seen to modify the balancing test of *Barenblatt* to a "preferred position" balancing in which the government must show a compelling interest before it can invade associational privacy.

MARTIN SHAPIRO
(1986)

GIDEON v. WAINWRIGHT
372 U.S. 335 (1963)

From time to time in constitutional history an obscure individual becomes the symbol of a great movement in legal doctrine. Character and circumstance illuminate a new understanding of the Constitution. So it was in the case of Clarence Earl Gideon.

Gideon was a drifter and petty thief who had served four prison terms when, in 1961, he was charged with breaking and entering the Bay Harbor Poolroom in Panama City, Florida, and stealing a pint of wine and some coins from a cigarette machine. At the age of fifty he had the look of defeat: a gaunt wrinkled face, white hair, a trembling voice. But inside there was still passion—a con-

cern for justice that approached obsession. Through it, in a manner of speaking, Gideon changed the Constitution.

When he went to trial in the Circuit Court of Bay County, Florida, on August 4, 1961, he asked the judge to appoint a lawyer for him because he was too poor to hire one himself. The judge said he was sorry but he could not do that, because the laws of Florida called for appointment of counsel only when a defendant was charged with a capital offense. Gideon said: "The United States Supreme Court says I am entitled to be represented by counsel." When the Florida courts rejected that claim, he went on to the Supreme Court. From prison he submitted a petition, handwritten in pencil, arguing that Florida had ignored a rule laid down by the Supreme Court: "that all citizens tried for a felony crime should have aid of counsel."

Gideon was wrong. The rule applied by the Supreme Court at that time was in fact exactly the opposite. The Constitution, it had held, did *not* guarantee free counsel to all felony defendants unable to retain their own. That was the outcome—the bitterly debated outcome—of a line of cases on the right to counsel.

The Supreme Court first dealt with the issue in 1932, in the Scottsboro Case, *Powell v. Alabama*. Due process of law required at least a "hearing," Justice GEORGE H. SUTHERLAND said, and the presence of counsel was "fundamental" to a meaningful hearing.

But Sutherland said that the Court was not deciding whether poor defendants had a right to free counsel in all circumstances, beyond the aggravated ones of this case: a capital charge, tried in haste and under public pressure.

In JOHNSON V. ZERBST (1938) the Court read the Sixth Amendment to require the appointment of counsel for all indigent *federal* criminal defendants. But in BETTS V. BRADY (1942), when considering the right of poor *state* defendants to free counsel in noncapital cases, the Court came out the other way. Justice OWEN J. ROBERTS said that "the states should not be straitjacketed" by a uniform constitutional rule. Only when particular circumstances showed that want of counsel denied FUNDAMENTAL FAIRNESS, he said, were such convictions invalid.

For twenty years the rule of *Betts v. Brady* applied. Counsel was said to be required only when a defendant suffered from "special circumstances" of disability: illiteracy, youth, mental illness, the complexity of the charges. But during that period criticism of the case mounted. No one could tell, it was said, when the Constitution required counsel. More and more often, too, the Supreme Court found "special circumstances" to require counsel.

That was the situation when Clarence Earl Gideon's petition reached the Court. The Justices seized on the occasion to think again about the Constitution and the right to counsel. Granting review, the Court ordered counsel to discuss: "Should this Court's holding in *Betts v. Brady* be reconsidered?" And then it appointed to represent Gideon, who had had no lawyer at his trial, one of the ablest lawyers in Washington, ABE FORTAS—later to sit on the Supreme Court himself.

On March 18, 1963, the Court overruled *Betts v. Brady*. Justice HUGO L. BLACK, who had dissented in *Betts*, wrote the opinion of the Court: a rare vindication of past dissent. He quoted Justice Sutherland's words on every man's need for the guiding hand of counsel at every step of the proceeding against him. "The right of one charged with crime to counsel may not be deemed fundamental and essential to fair trials in some countries," Justice Black said, "but it is in ours."

The decision in *Gideon v. Wainwright* was an important victory for one side in a general philosophical debate on the Court about whether constitutional protections should apply with the same vigor to state as to federal action: a victory for Justice Black over Justice Felix Frankfurter's more deferential view of state power. But on this particular issue changing ideas of due process would have led Justice Frankfurter in 1963 to impose a universal rule; retired and ill, he told a friend that he would have voted to overrule Betts. The case thus showed how time may bring a new consensus on the meaning of the Constitution.

And, not least, the *Gideon* case showed that the courts still respond to individuals in a society where most institutions of government seem remote and unresponsive. The least influential of men, riding a wave of legal history, persuaded the Supreme Court to reexamine a premise of justice. The case in fact represented more than an abstract principle. It was a victory for Clarence Earl Gideon. After the Supreme Court decision he was tried again in Bay County, Florida, this time with a lawyer—and the jury acquitted him. Gideon stayed out of prison until he died, on January 18, 1972.

ANTHONY LEWIS
(1986)

Bibliography

LEWIS, ANTHONY   1964   *Gideon's Trumpet*. New York: Random House.

GILES, WILLIAM B.
(1762–1830)

Virginia ANTI-FEDERALIST William Branch Giles served in six of the first seven Congresses and opposed the policies of ALEXANDER HAMILTON, especially the BANK OF THE UNITED STATES (1791). He opposed the ALIEN AND SEDITION ACTS, endorsed the VIRGINIA AND KENTUCKY RESOLUTIONS, and advocated repeal of the JUDICIARY ACT OF 1801. As a Jeffer-

sonian leader in the Senate (1804–1815) he voted to convict Justice SAMUEL CHASE, arguing that "if the judges of the Supreme Court should . . . declare an act of Congress unconstitutional, . . . it was the undoubted right of the House of Representatives to impeach them, and of the Senate to remove them." After the acquittal of AARON BURR (1807), Giles, at President THOMAS JEFFERSON's behest, introduced a bill to expand the definition of TREASON. In his declining years Giles was an outspoken champion of STATES' RIGHTS.

DENNIS J. MAHONEY
(1986)

GILMAN, NICHOLAS
(1755–1814)

Nicholas Gilman represented New Hampshire at the CONSTITUTIONAL CONVENTION OF 1787 and signed the Constitution. Gilman was not an active participant in the deliberations or committee work of the Convention. He later served in Congress, first as a Federalist, later as a Republican.

DENNIS J. MAHONEY
(1986)

GINSBERG v. NEW YORK
390 U.S. 629 (1968)

In *Ginsberg* the Supreme Court upheld the validity under the FIRST AMENDMENT and FOURTEENTH AMENDMENT of a New York criminal statute that prohibited the sale to persons under seventeen years of age of sexually explicit printed materials that would not be obscene for adults. Drawing upon the criteria suggested in ROTH V. UNITED STATES (1957) and MEMOIRS V. MASSACHUSETTS (1966), the New York statute broadly defined sexually explicit descriptions or representations as "harmful to minors" when the material: "(i) predominantly appeals to the prurient, shameful or morbid interest of minors, and (ii) is patently offensive to prevailing standards in the adult community as a whole with respect to what is suitable material for minors, and (iii) is utterly without redeeming social importance for minors." Convicted for selling two "girlie" magazines to a sixteen-year-old, Ginsberg claimed that the statute was unconstitutional because the state was without the power to deny persons younger than seventeen access to materials that were not obscene for adults. Justice WILLIAM J. BRENNAN, for the 6–3 majority, rejected this challenge by introducing the concept of "variable obscenity." According to the majority, the New York statute had "simply adjust[ed] the definition of OBSCENITY to social realities by permitting the appeal of this type of material to be assessed in terms of the sexual interests . . . of such minors."

Although the decision rests on the legitimacy of protecting children from harm, the Court found it unnecessary to decide whether persons under seventeen were caused harm by exposure to materials proscribed by the statute. After suggesting that scientific studies neither proved nor disproved a causal connection, the majority held that it was "not irrational" for the New York legislature to find that "exposure to material condemned by the statute is harmful to minors."

To what extent does a minor's own First Amendment rights constrain the state's power to limit a minor's access to written or pictorial materials? Because of the nature of Ginsberg's challenge to the statute, the Court did not concern itself with the question whether a minor might have the constitutional right to buy "girlie" magazines. In ERZNOZNIK V. JACKSONVILLE (1975) the Court later indicated that while the First Amendment rights of minors are not coextensive with those of adults, "minors are entitled to a significant measure of First Amendment protection" and that under the *Ginsberg* variable obscenity standard "all nudity" in films "cannot be deemed as obscene even as to minors."

ROBERT H. MNOOKIN
(1986)

(SEE ALSO: *Children's Rights.*)

GINSBURG, RUTH BADER
(1933–   )

In 1960, Justice FELIX FRANKFURTER declined to offer a clerkship to recent law graduate Ruth Bader Ginsburg, explaining that the candidate was impressive but he was not "ready to hire a woman." Thirty-three years later, on August 10, 1993, Ginsburg took the oath of office as an Associate Justice of the Supreme Court. Ginsburg's legal career not only spanned this period of transformation, however; her work also catalyzed the change in women's employment opportunities. As a Columbia Law School professor and as director of the Women's Rights Project of the AMERICAN CIVIL LIBERTIES UNION (ACLU), she selected, briefed, and argued a series of constitutional challenges to laws that discriminated between men and women. Through these cases, often brought on behalf of male plaintiffs, Ginsburg sought to demonstrate that laws based on invalid stereotypes injured both women and men. Working incrementally, from the least controversial cases to the more challenging, Ginsburg persuaded the courts to establish gender equality in a range of public

opportunities. As a Court of Appeals judge, and later as a Justice of the Supreme Court, Ginsburg has demonstrated many of the same qualities that marked her pathbreaking work as a litigator. She has manifested a strong commitment to gender equality, marking cases from sexual harassment to equal educational opportunity with her distinctive, liberal feminist vision. But she has also reflected the pragmatic, incrementalist strategy that distinguished her as a litigator. She has often decided cases narrowly, and she has sometimes urged procedural grounds as a basis for building consensus or deferring controversial choices.

Ruth Bader was born March 15, 1933, in the Flatbush section of Brooklyn. Her father, Nathan Bader, owned small clothing stores. Her mother, Celia Bader, whom Justice Ginsburg describes as a formative influence, died of cancer the day before her daughter's graduation from James Madison High School. Ginsburg attended Cornell University, where she graduated with high honors and was elected to Phi Beta Kappa. At Cornell, she met Martin Ginsburg, whom she married shortly after her graduation in 1954. The Ginsburgs then moved to Fort Sill, Oklahoma, where Martin Ginsburg served in the U.S. Army, and Ruth Ginsburg gave birth to their first child, Jane. (A second child, James, was born a decade later.) In 1956 the Ginsburgs moved to Cambridge, Massachusetts, where both were enrolled at Harvard Law School. At the time that the Justice was a first-year student, there were only nine women in a class of over five hundred students. Their presence was viewed not only as atypical, but as problematic. Dean Erwin Griswold, entertaining the women students at a dinner at his home, asked each to explain in turn how she justified taking a position in the class that would otherwise have gone to a man. Despite these pressures, Ginsburg excelled at her studies, and earned a place on the Harvard Law Review. She enjoyed comparable success at Columbia, to which she transferred when her husband took a job in New York City. Notwithstanding these achievements, she was not offered a single job on graduation. "Many firms were just beginning to hire Jews," Ginsburg has explained, "and to be a woman, a Jew and a mother to boot was an impediment . . . but motherhood was the major impediment. The fear was I would not be able to devote my full mind and time to a law job." Through the determined effort of her academic mentors, she obtained a clerkship with Judge Edmund Palmieri, of the U.S. District Court for the Southern District of New York, who resolved to hire her only after securing the agreement of a recent male law graduate that he would leave his law firm position to assume the clerkship if Ginsburg did not "work out."

Following her clerkship, Ginsburg joined the Columbia Project on International Civil Procedure. In 1963 she was offered a teaching position at Rutgers Law School, only the second woman ever to be hired there. Despite the fact that the Equal Pay Act became law that same year, the dean explained to Ginsburg that, particularly given the state university's limited resources, "it was only fair to pay [her] modestly, because [her] husband had a very good job." She was later part of a large class of women faculty members who filed an Equal Pay Act claim against Rutgers and received a large salary increase in settlement of that claim. During her time at Rutgers, Ginsburg began to take on cases referred by the New Jersey affiliate of the ACLU. These cases, which involved facial inequalities in educational and employment opportunity for women, encouraged Ginsburg to develop and teach one of the first seminars on Women and the Law. At the same time, Ginsburg was invited to write the brief for *Reed v. Reed* (1971), the first successful constitutional challenge to any law mandating SEX DISCRIMINATION. Following this victory, Ginsburg became the director of the ACLU's Women's Rights Project, which orchestrated a series of constitutional challenges to official denials of equal opportunity to women. In 1972, she also assumed a tenured professorship at Columbia Law School.

Between 1972 and her appointment to the Court of Appeals in 1980, Ginsburg designed and implemented a strategic assault on state and federal LEGISLATION that distinguished between men and women. The challenge she faced was substantial, given that many of these legal distinctions were thought to reflect salutary protections for female frailty, and given that her judicial audience— the federal courts—consisted almost entirely of men. The approach she developed to address these difficulties was twofold. First, Ginsburg sought to demonstrate that laws thought to respond to basic, sex-based differences were actually grounded in flawed and injurious stereotypes. To make this point she arrived at the bold stroke of bringing cases involving male plaintiffs. The male plaintiffs, as Professor David Cole has explained, were more likely to elicit the sympathy of the all-male Court, both because the Justices would find it easier to identify with them, and because the harms they suffered as a result of the stereotypic legislation were more concrete. This strategy may be illustrated with the case of FRONTIERO V. RICHARDSON (1973), one of the earliest cases brought by Ginsburg and the Women's Rights Project. *Frontiero* challenged two statutes that provided servicemen with automatic dependency benefits, while servicewomen received benefits only if they demonstrated that their spouses depended on them for more than half of their support. Sharon Frontiero, the servicewoman whose benefits were in question, suffered the dignitary harm of the government's presumptive refusal to treat her as the family breadwinner. Joseph Frontiero, her spouse, however, suffered the more concrete

denial of housing and medical benefits. Ginsburg believed that by focusing the Court first on the tangible disadvantage gender classifications created for male plaintiffs, she could ultimately lead them to recognize the dignitary damage done to their female spouses.

The second distinguishing characteristic of Ginsburg's strategy was its careful incrementalism. Her cases moved in a series of gradations from the most straightforward to the most ambitious, and in each case she used the legal premises established in the previous case to build a slightly larger analytic edifice. For example, Ginsburg used the Court's ambiguous invocation of RATIONAL BASIS scrutiny in *Reed*, to argue for a clarifying standard in *Frontiero;* and she used a plurality's endorsement of STRICT SCRUTINY in *Frontiero* to argue for heightened, or intermediate, scrutiny in *Weinberger v. Wiesenfeld* (1975), a strategy that bore fruit the next year in CRAIG V. BOREN (1976), in which Ginsburg wrote a brief AMICUS CURIAE. Ginsburg's incrementalism could be conceptual as well. *Reed,* which concerned a state legislative preference for male estate administrators, reflected a facial assumption of female inferiority; the differential treatment was not justified by reference to any motive of protection. Yet after her success in *Reed*, Ginsburg could move on to *Frontiero,* in which the statutory classification, while also injurious, could be justified by reference to a desire to protect women in their dependent familial roles. Ginsburg scrutinized potential cases closely for the optimal sequential effect, often telling colleagues that it was "not yet time" for a particular case. These strategic choices produced an impressive record of change: not only did Ginsburg persuade the Court to embrace intermediate scrutiny for gender classifications, but she also persuaded the Court to invalidate disparate treatment of men and women, in areas from "mothers' insurance benefits" (*Weinberger v. Wiesenfeld,* 1975) to JURY SERVICE (*Edwards v. Healy,* TAYLOR V. LOUISIANA, 1974).

After President JIMMY CARTER appointed Ginsburg to the U.S. Court of Appeals for the District of Columbia Circuit in 1980, she continued to define and extend the DOCTRINE of gender equality. Yet her record was, in some respects, less progressive than her supporters had expected. She ruled against the RIGHT OF PRIVACY claim of a discharged gay serviceman in *Dronenberg v. Zech* (1984) and developed a reputation as a conservative on criminal defense issues. Ginsburg also displayed a surprising tendency toward judicial restraint: she favored narrower, factually contained rulings, and in several contexts voted, as in *Randall v. Meese* (1988), to resolve controversial cases on procedural grounds. Her public statements about the judicial role also perplexed some longtime supporters. In a speech delivered shortly before her nomination to the Supreme Court, Ginsburg described ROE V. WADE (1973) as having exacerbated the ABORTION conflict by injecting a broad judicial holding into a controversy that was beginning to be resolved by state legislatures. Her position remained pro-choice: she argued that a right to reproductive choice might better have been grounded in the EQUAL PROTECTION clause than in the right of privacy, so as to comprehend the rights of indigent women. Yet she also opined that a narrower ruling, simply striking down the Texas abortion statute, might have proved less divisive than the detailed opinion that emerged.

Commentators divided over how to interpret Ginsburg's record on the Court of Appeals. Some ascribed her more restrictive opinions to the limitations imposed by PRECEDENT; others concluded that her commitment to gender equality was simply a departure from a more substantively, and jurisprudentially, conservative bent. Her performance since her appointment to the Supreme Court in 1993 suggests that precedent may have constrained her on the Court of Appeals: notwithstanding her opinion in *Dronenberg*, she voted with the majority in striking down the Colorado state constitutional amendment that prevented the state or its subdivisions from legislating against discrimination on the basis of SEXUAL ORIENTATION in ROMER V. EVANS (1996). Yet Ginsburg's emerging record on the Supreme Court reflects ongoing tensions that continue to absorb of the judiciary.

Ginsburg has remained a resourceful champion of gender equality. Her opinion in UNITED STATES V. VIRGINIA (1996), reflecting the careful historicism and liberal feminist vision that animated her briefs, is to date the best example of this commitment. Ginsburg's opinion for the 7–1 majority not only edged the Court closer to strict scrutiny by demanding an "exceedingly persuasive justification" for sex-based classifications; it also established a right of educational access on behalf of a group of women whose taste for "adversative" military training was far from typical. Yet the typicality of these women, according to Ginsburg, was not the point. Generalizations about women, be they flattering or stereotypical, are precisely what the FOURTEENTH AMENDMENT proscribes. Women willing to endure the rigors of this method should not be prevented from doing so because of their gender, but should have the same opportunity to make authentic, if idiosyncratic, choices as do men. With this interpretation, Ginsburg's portrait of woman as an equal, autonomous chooser reached its fullest stage of elaboration.

Yet Ginsburg has also reflected a kind of judicial particularism that contrasts with the more ambitious intervention of WARREN COURT liberals, such as Justices WILLIAM J. BRENNAN, JR., and THURGOOD MARSHALL. She has continued to resolve many cases on narrow, fact-specific grounds: even *United States v. Virginia* does not proceed beyond declaring the unconstitutionality of this particular, SINGLE-SEX SCHOOL. She has also resolved some controversial cases on purely procedural grounds: in *Arizonans for Official English v. Arizona* (1997), the long-awaited challenge to Arizona's controversial "OFFICIAL ENGLISH" LAW, her MAJORITY OPINION dismissed the case on grounds of MOOTNESS.

This particularism, however, may reflect less tension with Ginsburg's earlier record than some analysts suggest. Ginsburg has always displayed an acute awareness of factual particularity and the importance of context. Her alertness to the sensibilities of an all-male Court; her understanding of the relations between the successive cases she brought to the Court; and her sensitivity to the "right time" to bring a particular case are all examples of this sensibility. This kind of awareness makes narrow decisions prudent; and procedural grounds—to a former professor of civil procedure—reflect a promising form of narrowness. There may also be a larger jurisprudential concern at play: part of the context that Ginsburg so carefully observes is the institution of which she is a part.

Ginsburg has publicly stated her concern to maintain the legitimacy of the Court, and the larger federal court system. She has warned that this legitimacy may be taxed by overreaching, or by unseemly discord among its members. One solution may be found in the avoidance of unnecessary controversy, and of fruitless antagonism among the Justices. Ginsburg has counseled against writing separately, particularly in divisive terms. The "effective judge," she wrote in 1992, "speaks in a 'moderate and restrained' voice, engaging in dialogue with, not a diatribe against, co-equal departments of government, state authorities, and even her own colleagues." She has also sought to preserve harmony by seeking common ground. Justices should continually ask, Ginsburg recently stated, "Is this conflict really necessary? Perhaps there is a ground, maybe a procedural ground, on which everyone can agree, so that the decision can be unanimous, saving the larger question for another day." Thus it may be today, as it was during her career as an advocate, that Ginsburg's activism is shaped by its emergence in a particular political and institutional context. That context was once the solipsistic paternalism of a male judiciary; it is now the embattled legitimacy of the Supreme Court.

KATHRYN ABRAMS
(2000)

Bibliography

COLE, DAVID 1984 Strategies of Difference: Litigating for Women's Rights in a Man's World. *Law and Inequality* 2:33–96.

GILLMAN, ELIZABETH and MICHELETTI, JOSEPH 1993 Justice Ruth Bader Ginsburg. *Seton Hall Constitutional Law Journal* 3:657–663.

GINSBURG, RUTH BADER 1975 Gender and the Constitution. *University of Cincinnati Law Review* 44:1–42.

——— 1992 Speaking in a Judicial Voice. *New York University Law Review* 67:1185–1209.

——— 1997 Remarks on Women's Progress in the Legal Profession in the United States. *Tulsa Law Journal* 33:13–21.

HALBERSTAM, MALVINA 1998 Ruth Bader Ginsburg: The First Jewish Woman on the United States Supreme Court. *Cardozo Law Review* 19:1441–1454.

MARKOWITZ, DEBORAH L. 1992 In Pursuit of Equality: One Woman's Work to Change the Law. *Women's Rights Law Reporter* 14:335–359.

ROSEN, JEFFREY 1997 The New Look of Liberalism on the Court. *New York Times Magazine*, October 5, p. 60.

GINZBURG v. UNITED STATES

See: *Memoirs v. Massachusetts*

GIROUARD v. UNITED STATES
328 U.S. 61 (1946)

An applicant for United States CITIZENSHIP declared that he could take the oath of allegiance ("support and defend the Constitution and laws of the United States against all enemies . . .") only with the reservation that he would not serve in the military in a combatant role.

The Court, speaking through Justice WILLIAM O. DOUGLAS, held that despite UNITED STATES V. SCHWIMMER (1929), *United States v. MacIntosh* (1931), and *United States v. Bland* (1931), Girouard met the requirements for NATURALIZATION. Justice Douglas argued that Congress had not specifically insisted upon willingness to perform combatant service. Chief Justice HARLAN F. STONE dissented, joined by Justices STANLEY F. REED and FELIX FRANKFURTER.

This case established the eligibility of CONSCIENTIOUS OBJECTORS to be naturalized as citizens of the United States.

RICHARD E. MORGAN
(1986)

GITLOW v. NEW YORK
268 U.S. 652 (1925)

Gitlow was convicted under a state statute proscribing advocacy of the overthrow of government by force. In a paper called *The Revolutionary Age*, he had published "The Left Wing Manifesto," denouncing moderate socialism and prescribing "Communist revolution." There was no evidence of any effect resulting from the publication. Rejecting the CLEAR AND PRESENT DANGER test which OLIVER WENDELL HOLMES and LOUIS D. BRANDEIS reasserted in their dissent, Justice EDWARD SANFORD for the Court upheld the statute. Enunciating what subsequently came to be called the remote BAD TENDENCY TEST, Sanford declared that the state might "suppress the threatened danger in its incipiency." "It cannot reasonably be required to defer the adoption of measures for its own . . . safety until the revolutionary utterances lead to actual disturbances of the public peace or imminent and immediate danger of its own destruction."

Unwilling to reverse its decision in SCHENCK V. UNITED STATES (1919), the Court limited the clear and present danger test enunciated there to the situation in which a speaker is prosecuted under a statute prohibiting acts and making no reference to language. Under such a statute the legislature has made no judgment of its own as to the danger of any speech, and the unlawfulness of the speech must necessarily depend on whether "its natural tendency and probable effect was to bring about the substantive evil" that the legislature had proscribed. In short, Sanford sought to confine the danger test to its origin in the law of attempts and to strip it of its imminence aspect. He argued that where a legislature itself had determined that a certain category of speech constituted a danger of substantive evil, "every presumption [was] to be indulged in favor of the validity" of such an exercise of the police power.

The PREFERRED FREEDOMS doctrine that became central to the speech cases of the next two decades was largely directed toward undermining the *Gitlow* position that state statutes regulating speech ought to be subject to no more demanding constitutional standards than the reasonableness test applied to state economic regulation.

The *Gitlow* formula was rejected in the 1930s, but the Court returned to some of its reasoning in the 1950s, particularly to the notion that where revolutionary speech is involved, government need not wait until "the spark . . . has enkindled the flame or blazed into the conflagration." Such reasoning, bolstered by the *Gitlow* distinction between advocacy and abstract, academic teaching informed the DENNIS V. UNITED STATES (1951) and YATES V. UNITED STATES (1951) decisions that upheld the Smith Act, a federal statute in part modeled on the New York criminal anarchy statute sustained in *Gitlow*.

The Court's language in *Gitlow* was equivocal, and it provided no rationale. Indeed, *Gitlow* is most often cited today for its dictum, "incorporating" FIRST AMENDMENT free speech guarantees into the DUE PROCESS clause of the FOURTEENTH AMENDMENT, thus rendering the Amendment applicable to the states as well as to Congress. (See INCORPORATION DOCTRINE.)

Holmes's *Gitlow* dissent did not address the question so troublesome to believers in judicial self-restraint: why should courts not defer to the legislature's judgment that a particular kind of speech is too dangerous to tolerate when, in applying the due process clause, they do defer to other legislative judgments? He did attack the majority's distinction between lawful abstract teaching and unlawful INCITEMENT in language that has become famous:

> Every idea is an incitement. It offers itself for belief and if believed it is acted on unless some other belief outweighs it. . . . The only difference between the expression of an opinion and an incitement in the narrower sense is the speaker's enthusiasm for the result. . . . If in the long run the beliefs expressed in proletarian dictatorship are destined to be accepted by the dominant forces of the community, the only meaning of free speech is that they should be given their chance and have their way.

MARTIN SHAPIRO
(1986)

Bibliography

CHAFEE, ZECHARIAH 1941 *Free Speech in the United States.* Cambridge, Mass.: Harvard University Press.

GLIDDEN v. ZDANOK

See: Claims Court; Legislative Court

GLOBAL MARKETS AND THE CONSTITUTION

See: Multinational Corporations, Global Markets, and the Constitution

GLOBE NEWSPAPER COMPANY v. SUPERIOR COURT
457 U.S. 596 (1982)

Writing for a 7–2 Court, Justice WILLIAM J. BRENNAN sweepingly broadened the right of the public and press to attend criminal trials. On FIRST AMENDMENT grounds the Court held unconstitutional a state act intended to protect the juvenile victims of sex crimes by closing the trial proceedings. The exclusion of the press and public rested chiefly on the state's interest in safeguarding those victims from additional trauma and humiliation by not requiring them to testify in open court. The Supreme Court did not find that interest adequately compelling to warrant a mandatory closure rule. The decision created an anomalous condition of law: states can close trials to protect juvenile rapists but not to protect their victims. Chief Justice WARREN E. BURGER and Justice WILLIAM H. REHNQUIST dissented.

LEONARD W. LEVY
(1986)

GLONA v. AMERICAN GUARANTEE & LIABILITY INSURANCE CO.

See: *Levy v. Louisiana*

GODCHARLES v. WIGEMAN

See: *Millett v. People of Illinois*

GODFREY v. GEORGIA
446 U.S. 420 (1980)

This is another case in which the Supreme Court reversed a death sentence because it was imposed under the state's standardless discretion: death for murder "outrageously or wantonly vile, or inhuman." Justice POTTER STEWART for a PLURALITY ruled that those words lacked objectivity and provided no principled basis for distinguishing the few cases in which death is imposed from the many in which it is not. Georgia's standard therefore placed no restraint on arbitrary and capricious infliction of the ultimate penalty. Two Justices argued that the death penalty is always CRUEL AND UNUSUAL. Three found Georgia's standard unobjectionable.

LEONARD W. LEVY
(1986)

GOESAERT v. CLEARY
335 U.S. 464 (1948)

Goesaert typified the Court's SEX DISCRIMINATION decisions in the century between BRADWELL V. ILLINOIS (1873) and the 1970s. Michigan denied a woman a bartender's license unless she were "the wife or daughter of the male owner" of a licensed establishment. The Supreme Court, 6–3, rejected an EQUAL PROTECTION attack on this limitation. For the majority, Justice FELIX FRANKFURTER applied a RATIONAL BASIS standard of review: the legislature might rationally have believed that the presence of a barmaid's husband or father would help avoid "moral or social problems." Thus the Court could not "give ear to the suggestion that the real impulse behind this legislation was the unchivalrous desire of male bartenders to try to monopolize the calling."

Justice WILEY B. RUTLEDGE, for the dissenters, argued that the law failed to serve these protective ends, because unrelated, nonowner males might be present in some cases, and related male owners might be absent.

KENNETH L. KARST
(1986)

GOLDBERG, ARTHUR J.
(1908–1990)

Arthur Joseph Goldberg's tenure on the Supreme Court was a brief chapter in a long and distinguished career. He served fewer than three years, from October 1, 1962, until he resigned on July 25, 1965, to become the United States ambassador to the United Nations. Goldberg consistently voted with the WARREN COURT majority on CIVIL LIBERTIES and CRIMINAL PROCEDURE issues, although three terms as the Court's junior Justice scarcely gave him enough time to develop a distinctive voice on the major constitutional questions of that active period.

When Goldberg came to the Court, the unanimity of the earlier Warren years had begun to erode. The Court was struggling to give specific content to the broad principles established in the landmark rulings of the 1950s and early 1960s. Goldberg's appointment to replace FELIX FRANKFURTER allowed the flowering of the liberal JUDICIAL ACTIVISM for which the Warren Court is best remembered. Frequently his vote helped to create a bare majority for a FIRST AMENDMENT claim or for the rights of a criminal defendant.

ESCOBEDO V. ILLINOIS (1964), Justice Goldberg's best known opinion for the Court, was such a case. A year before, in GIDEON V. WAINWRIGHT, the Court had ruled unanimously that the state was required to provide counsel for an indigent defendant accused of a serious crime. The question in *Escobedo* was at what stage in the process from arrest through INDICTMENT the Sixth Amendment RIGHT TO COUNSEL attached. Voting 5–4, the Court overturned the murder conviction of a man whose request to consult a lawyer during interrogation by the police had been denied. In his opinion, Goldberg wrote: "The fact that many confessions are obtained during this period points up its critical nature as a "stage when legal aid and advice' are surely needed. The right to counsel would indeed be hollow if it began at a period when few confessions were obtained." Escobedo thus pried open the door for MIRANDA V. ARIZONA (1966).

Goldberg's opinions for the Court also contributed to the growth of the First Amendment's protection of the freedoms of expression and association. COX V. LOUISIANA (1965) promoted the development of the concept of the "public forum." GIBSON V. FLORIDA LEGISLATIVE INVESTIGATION COMMITTEE (1963) remains a major precedent for protecting the privacy of political association. And APTHEKER V. SECRETARY OF STATE (1964) struck down a section of the Subversive Activities Control Act of 1950, which denied passports to members of various communist organizations. The law, Goldberg wrote for the Court, "sweeps too widely and too indiscriminately across the liberty guaranteed in the Fifth Amendment." *Aptheker* was an important stop in the elaboration of the First Amendment doctrine of OVERBREADTH. Goldberg also wrote the opinion for the Court in *Kennedy v. Mendoza-Martinez* (1963), striking down a federal law that automatically revoked the CITIZENSHIP of anyone who left the country during a time of war or national emergency in order to evade the draft.

Goldberg's area of professional expertise was labor law, and he was widely regarded as the nation's most eminent labor lawyer. But because he joined the Court directly from eighteen months as secretary of labor in the cabinet of President JOHN F. KENNEDY, he excused himself from participation in many of the labor cases that reached the Court during his tenure.

Goldberg was born in Chicago on August 8, 1908, and received his law degree from Northwestern University in 1929. He built a labor law practice in Chicago before moving to Washington, D.C., in 1948 to serve as general counsel to both the Congress of Industrial Organizations (CIO) and the United Steelworkers. He was instrumental in the 1957 merger of organized labor's two factions, the CIO and the American Federation of Labor (AFL), and continued to play a key role in AFL-CIO affairs until he joined the Kennedy cabinet in 1961. His appointment to the Supreme Court followed the next year.

In 1965, President LYNDON B. JOHNSON persuaded him to leave the Court to fill the United Nations post made vacant by the death of Ambassador Adlai Stevenson. He resigned his ambassadorship in 1968 and practiced law briefly in New York, where he ran unsuccessfully for governor on the Democratic ticket in 1970. He then returned to Washington, where he continued to practice law and to speak out on civil liberties issues.

LINDA GREENHOUSE
(1986)

Bibliography

CARMEN, IRA H.   1966   One Civil Libertarian among Many: The Case of Mr. Justice Goldberg. *Michigan Law Review* 65:301–336.

FRIEDMAN, STEPHEN J.   1969   Arthur J. Goldberg. In Leon Friedman and Fred L. Israel, eds., *The Justices of the United States Supreme Court 1789–1969*. New York: Chelsea House.

GOLDBERG v. KELLY
397 U.S. 254 (1970)

Residents of New York receiving WELFARE BENEFITS brought suit challenging the state's procedures authorizing termination of a beneficiary's benefits without a prior hearing on his or her eligibility. The Supreme Court, 6–3, held that these procedures denied PROCEDURAL DUE PROCESS.

For the majority, Justice WILLIAM J. BRENNAN rejected the state's argument that because welfare benefits were a "privilege" and not a "right," their termination could not deprive a beneficiary of "property" within the meaning of the due process clause. Those benefits, said Brennan, were "a matter of statutory entitlement for persons qualified to receive them" and thus qualified as "property" interests whose termination must satisfy the requirements of due process.

These requirements included an evidentiary hearing prior to the termination of welfare benefits, including timely notice of the reasons for the proposed termination, the right to retain counsel, opportunity to confront any adverse witnesses, and opportunity to present the beneficiary's own evidence. The procedural safeguards thus required approximated those available in judicial proceedings; the Court underscored the point by insisting on an impartial decision maker who would "state the reasons for his determination and indicate the evidence he relied on."

Goldberg was the leading decision extending the guarantees of procedural due process in civil proceedings beyond the protection of traditional COMMON LAW property interests to "entitlements" defined by statute, administrative regulation, or contract. It was aptly called the beginning of a "procedural due process revolution." By the mid-1970s, however, the counterrevolution had begun. (See BISHOP V. WOOD; PAUL V. DAVIS; MATHEWS V. ELDRIDGE.)

KENNETH L. KARST
(1986)

GOLD CLAUSE CASES

Norman v. Baltimore & Ohio Railroad Co.
294 U.S. 240 (1935)

Nortz v. United States
294 U.S. 317 (1935)

Perry v. United States
294 U.S. 330 (1935)

The decisions in these cases were virtually the only Supreme Court opinions upholding congressional NEW DEAL legislation before the judicial "revolution" of 1937. The Depression had caused an emergency in which contracts calling for payment in gold, rather than paper, "obstruct[ed] the power of Congress." So declaring, Congress passed the JOINT RESOLUTION of June 5, 1933, which asserted its regulatory power over gold as an item that "affect[ed] the public interest." Such gold clauses were "against public policy," and henceforth debtors could legally discharge their obligations in any other legal tender.

Creditors resisted this action because, in conjunction with earlier legislation that had reduced the gold value of the dollar, it effectively devalued debts by allowing paper to be substituted for gold. Even though these suits involved relatively small amounts, they represented one hundred billion dollars in outstanding gold obligations (three-fourths of which were private debts) at a time when the Treasury had only some four billion dollars in gold reserves.

In *Norman v. Baltimore & Ohio Railroad Company*, the plaintiffs sought to enforce payment of $38.10 in currency, the equivalent of the value of the gold ($22.50) specified in the contract, a sixty-nine percent markup. Chief Justice CHARLES EVANS HUGHES, for a 5–4 Court, reviewed the MONETARY POWER and, resting on *Knox v. Lee* (1871), insisted on the government's power to void any private OBLIGATION OF CONTRACTS that interfered with the exercise of Congress's power to regulate currency. The majority said that requiring debtors to pay sixty-nine percent more in currency to match the gold value of their debts would cause "dislocation of the domestic economy." The majority opinion, while reaching perhaps the only possible satisfactory result for the stability of the economy, was, in the conventional constitutional wisdom of the time, tenuous. In a spiteful dissent, Justice JAMES MCREYNOLDS attacked Hughes's purely pragmatic approach as a monstrous miscarriage of justice. Delivering his opinion orally, he exclaimed, "This is Nero at his worst. The Constitution is gone!"

In cases involving public obligations, the majority rested on sturdier constitutional ground. In accordance with the EMERGENCY BANK ACT, E. C. Nortz had surrendered his gold certificates after the government refused his demand for payment in gold. He sued for the difference between the currency he received and the value of the gold, over $64,000. Hughes, writing in *Nortz v. United States*, declared that gold certificates were only one form of currency and were thus replaceable by any other valid currency. Because Nortz suffered only "nominal" damages, his suit failed. In so deciding, the Court avoided the question whether gold certificates amounted to a contract with the government. In *Perry v. United States*, however, an 8–1 Court admitted that a government Liberty bond was a contractual obligation. Insofar as the joint resolution abrogated gold clauses in public contracts, it must be unconstitutional. A 5–4 majority quickly moved to destroy the force of this concession, however. Because the rise in gold prices which formed the basis of Perry's suit resulted from government manipulation of monetary values, payment in excess of a simple dollar-for-dollar exchange would constitute "unjust enrichment." Perry, like Nortz, had sustained only minimal damages and his suit likewise failed.

As McReynolds's dissent aptly noted, the majority was more concerned with economic and political consequences than constitutional precedent. ROBERT H. JACKSON, later on the Court himself, wrote that "in the guise of private law suits involving a few dollars, the whole American economy was haled before the Supreme Court." In these cases, by theoretically destroying thousands of obligations, the Court sustained Congress's exercise of the monetary power—a course it found itself unable to follow when later confronted by other major New Deal legislation.

DAVID GORDON
(1986)

Bibliography

DAWSON, JOHN P. 1935 Gold Clause Decisions. *Michigan Law Review* 33:647–684.

GOLDFARB v. VIRGINIA STATE BAR
421 U.S. 773 (1975)

By extending antitrust liability to the legal profession, this decision afforded consumers further protection against illegal business practices. The minimum fee schedule of the Fairfax County Bar Association, enforced by the Virginia State Bar, fixed the lowest charge for title searches at one percent of the value of the property involved. A unanimous eight-member Supreme Court, led by Chief Justice WARREN E. BURGER, sustaining a CLASS ACTION against the state and county bars, found violations of the price-fixing provisions of the SHERMAN ANTITRUST ACT as well as restraint of INTERSTATE COMMERCE.

DAVID GORDON
(1986)

GOLDMAN v. WEINBERGER
475 U.S. 503 (1986)

Goldman, an orthodox Jew and ordained rabbi, was forbidden from wearing a yarmulke while on duty as an Air Force officer. The prohibition was pursuant to an Air Force regulation enjoining the wearing of headgear indoors "except by armed security police." Goldman sued, claiming that the prohibition violated his FIRST AMENDMENT right to the free exercise of religion. The Supreme Court disagreed, 5–4.

Writing for the majority, Justice WILLIAM H. REHNQUIST declined to require a government showing of either a COMPELLING STATE INTEREST or a RATIONAL BASIS to justify the yarmulke prohibition. Rehnquist argued that the military must be accorded wide-ranging deference by the courts in order to carry out its mission; hence he refused to second-guess the Air Force's "professional judgment" about how to maintain a uniform dress code. Rehnquist used similar reasoning a year later to uphold the power of prison authorities to restrict the free-exercise rights of prisoners in O' LONE V. ESTATE OF SHABAZZ (1987).

Justices WILLIAM J. BRENNAN, HARRY A. BLACKMUN, and SANDRA DAY O'CONNOR each filed separate dissents. All three believed that the Court should have attempted to weigh Goldman's free-exercise rights against the government interest at stake; they further agreed that the government interest should give way in this case because the military had made no attempt to show a reasonable basis for the regulation as applied to Goldman. They noted, in particular, that Goldman had been allowed to wear his yarmulke by the Air Force for almost four years before the practice was challenged.

JOHN G. WEST, JR.
(1992)

(SEE ALSO: *Armed Forces; Employment Division, Department of Human Resources of Oregon v. Smith.*)

GOLD RESERVE ACT
48 Stat. 337 (1934)

Following the Gold Content Rider of mid-1933, the government sought to stabilize the gold value of the dollar in an effort to raise prices. Congress, fulfilling a request from President FRANKLIN D. ROOSEVELT, passed the Gold Reserve Act on January 30, 1934, under its MONETARY POWER and extended broad authority to establish a sound currency system. The act called in all gold and gold certificates in circulation, with specified exceptions, and granted the Treasury title to all monetary gold. The act also established an Exchange Stabilization Fund with which the secretary of the treasury was empowered to deal in gold in international markets to preserve a favorable balance of exchange and support the dollar. Congress also granted the President authority to regulate the gold content of the dollar. Further sections dealt with silver coinage and retroactively approved actions taken under authority of the EMERGENCY BANK ACT.

On January 31, Roosevelt reduced the gold content of the dollar to just under sixty percent of its former value. By mid-year the absence of circulating gold necessitated a congressional joint resolution abrogating clauses in private contracts and government bonds that called for payment in gold; the Supreme Court sustained this action in the GOLD CLAUSE CASES (1935).

DAVID GORDON
(1986)

GOLDWATER v. CARTER
444 U.S. 285 (1979)

Members of Congress sued the President for declaratory and injunctive relief, claiming he had exceeded his powers in terminating a treaty with the Republic of China (Taiwan) without any congressional participation. Without briefing or ORAL ARGUMENT, a fragmented Supreme Court held, 6–3, that the case was not justiciable. Justice WILLIAM H. REHNQUIST, for four Justices, concluded that the case presented a POLITICAL QUESTION. Justice LEWIS F. POWELL rejected this argument but concluded that the case lacked ripeness because the President and Congress had not reached an impasse. Justice THURGOOD MARSHALL concurred in the result. Justice WILLIAM J. BRENNAN would have affirmed the court of appeals's decision upholding the President's action, and the other dissenting Justices would have set the case for full argument.

KENNETH L. KARST
(1986)

GOMILLION v. LIGHTFOOT
364 U.S. 339 (1960)

Alabama redrew the boundaries of the city of Tuskegee in "an uncouth twenty-eight-sided figure" that excluded from the city all but a handful of black voters while excluding no whites. The lower federal courts refused to grant any relief from this racial GERRYMANDER, concluding on the basis of COLEGROVE V. GREEN (1946) that municipal boundaries, like legislative districting, presented only POLITICAL QUESTIONS that lacked JUSTICIABILITY.

The Supreme Court unanimously held the case justiciable, and eight Justices, speaking through Justice FELIX FRANKFURTER, concluded that the gerrymander violated the FIFTEENTH AMENDMENT. The effect of the law was so clear as to demonstrate a purpose to deprive blacks of their vote for city officials. Justice CHARLES E. WHITTAKER concurred, on the basis of the EQUAL PROTECTION clause of the FOURTEENTH AMENDMENT.

The door which *Gomillion* pried open was flung wide in BAKER V. CARR (1962), when the Court held that the malapportionment of state legislative districts presented a justiciable controversy under the equal protection clause.

KENNETH L. KARST
(1986)

GOMPERS v. BUCK'S STOVE & RANGE COMPANY
221 U.S. 418 (1911)

In a decision that presaged the CLAYTON ACT, a unanimous Supreme Court held that an advertisement encouraging a SECONDARY BOYCOTT was unlawful and not protected by the FREEDOM OF SPEECH or of the PRESS. To support a local affiliate, the American Federation of Labor had run a notice in its magazine, the *American Federationist,* which transformed a local dispute into a national boycott by including the firm in a "We Don't Patronize" list. Prompted by a local strike, the company obtained an INJUNCTION prohibiting the AFL, its officers, and the local from obstructing sales or furthering any boycott, including use of the firm's name on the "We Don't Patronize" list. When Samuel Gompers and other union leaders ignored the injunction, they were jailed for contempt. Their APPEAL to the Court maintained that they could lawfully ignore the injunction because it abridged their rights of free speech and press.

Speaking for the Court, Justice JOSEPH R. LAMAR dismissed the free speech claim. Publication might provide a means of continuing an illegal boycott because the printing of words in an unlawful conspiracy might foster actions, thereby "exceeding any possible right of speech which a single individual might have." The resultant "verbal acts" would necessarily be subject to injunction. In this case, the publicity destroyed business and illegally restrained commerce. Here Lamar introduced the analogy of a SHERMAN ANTITRUST ACT violation, an analogy that has misled many authorities to believe that the case found such a violation—which it did not, for the company had not sought such relief. Declaring that the decision in LOEWE V. LAWLOR (1908) extended to any unlawful method of restraint, Lamar asserted that a failure to "hold that the restraint of trade under the Sherman anti-trust act, or on general principles of law, could be enjoined . . . would be to render the law impotent." This was no more than an analogy. Because the boycott constituted an illegal conspiracy, the Court had the power and the duty to sustain the injunction.

With the effectiveness of the boycott reduced by this decision, labor turned to politics to influence elections and legislation. In a well-intentioned, if ambiguous, attempt to eliminate the confusion over labor's rights and obligations under the Sherman Act, Congress passed the Clayton Act in 1914. Section 20 of this act, ostensibly addressed to the *Gompers* issue, prohibited the issuance of injunctions restraining unions from maintaining secondary boycotts or "from recommending, advising, or persuading others by peaceful and lawful means so to do." Although the Court would virtually divest this section of meaning in DUPLEX PRINTING PRESS COMPANY V. DEERING (1921), Congress had the last word, passing the NORRIS-LAGUARDIA ACT in 1932.

DAVID GORDON
(1986)

Bibliography

BERMAN, EDWARD (1930) 1969 *Labor and the Sherman Act.* New York: Russell & Russell.

GONG LUM v. RICE
275 U.S. 78 (1927)

Classifying a youngster of Chinese ancestry as "colored," thereby compelling her to attend a black school, did not deny her EQUAL PROTECTION under the FOURTEENTH AMENDMENT. By so ruling, a unanimous Supreme Court upheld a Mississippi decision. The Court declined to consider the issue at length; citing ROBERTS V. BOSTON (Massachusetts, 1850) and PLESSY V. FERGUSON (1896), the Court concluded that PRECEDENT had clearly established a state's right to settle such issues of racial SEGREGATION without "intervention of the federal courts."

DAVID GORDON
(1986)

GOOD BEHAVIOR

Until the late seventeenth century, royal judges held their offices "during the king's good pleasure." After the Glorious Revolution (1688–1689), judges in England (but not in the colonies) were appointed "during good behavior." This was a crucial step toward insuring the independence of the judiciary. The phrase was used in several revolutionary state constitutions, and the CONSTITUTIONAL CONVENTION OF 1787 unanimously adopted it to define the tenure of federal judges. ALEXANDER HAMILTON, in THE FEDERALIST, defended such tenure on the grounds that judicial independence is as necessary in a republic as in a monarchy.

It is by no means certain that a judge deviates from "good behavior" only when he commits "high crimes and misdemeanors"; however, the Constitution provides for no means of removal except IMPEACHMENT.

DENNIS J. MAHONEY
(1986)

GOOD FAITH EXCEPTION

The good faith exception to the EXCLUSIONARY RULE created to enforce the FOURTH AMENDMENT allows prosecutorial use of illegally seized EVIDENCE if the police made the seizure in good faith reliance on the validity of a SEARCH WARRANT, even though an appellate court later finds that the warrant was unconstitutionally issued. As Justice BYRON R. WHITE for the Supreme Court stated the doctrine in UNITED STATES V. LEON (1984), the Court "modified" the exclusionary rule "so as not to bar the use in the prosecution's case-in-chief of evidence seized on a search warrant issued by a detached and neutral magistrate but ultimately found to be unsupported by PROBABLE CAUSE."

Those who support the good faith exception claim that it does not prevent either the Fourth Amendment or the exclusionary rule from achieving its intended functions. They see the exclusionary rule as a judicially created remedy designed to deter violations of the amendment; and they stress that the substantial costs exacted by the rule often outweigh its benefits. By excluding genuine evidence from the truth-finding process, the rule allows guilty persons to escape punishment and offends basic concepts of criminal justice. These costs can be justified only if the rule deters police misconduct. Advocates of the good faith exception assert, too, that the rule does not lower the probable cause standard and that it loses its deterrent capability when the officer has acted on a good faith belief that he was executing a warrant properly issued by a neutral magistrate and based on probable cause.

Opponents of the exception defend the exclusionary rule as inherent in the Fourth Amendment, preventing law enforcement officials from making any use of evidence obtained through their misconduct or misjudgment. Opponents claim that the amendment itself, not just the rule, makes convictions difficult. They stress that empirical studies show that the social cost of the exclusionary rule in lost prosecutions and acquittals has been exaggerated, and they argue that the rule improves police work by giving real effect to requirements to which law enforcement officials must conform. The good faith exception, on the other hand, places a premium on police ignorance of the law. Although they concede that no individual officer is likely to be deterred from unconstitutional conduct by exclusion of evidence seized in reliance on a defective warrant, the opponents argue that a good faith exception weakens the rule's influence toward a systemic or institutional compliance with the Fourth Amendment. They point out, too, that an objectively reasonable reliance on an UNREASONABLE SEARCH or on a warrant lacking probable cause is *impossible*, because no search and seizure can simultaneously be reasonable and unreasonable. The warrant requirement lies at the heart of the amendment, they contend; and the good faith exception erodes the requirement of probable cause. The Framers of the amendment sought to condition search and seizure on probable cause. They were primarily concerned with illegal warrants— GENERAL WARRANTS and WRITS OF ASSISTANCE. The exception admits illegally seized evidence and in so doing implicates the integrity of the judicial process. The exclusionary rule exists to deter violations of the amendment by all law enforcement agencies, the courts included.

Proponents of the good faith exception regard the courts, including the magistrates who issue warrants, as independent of, not part of, law enforcement agencies. Proponents and opponents of the exception, and of the exclusionary rule, argue from different premises and rarely confront each other's arguments.

LEONARD W. LEVY
(1986)

Bibliography

KAMISAR, YALE 1984 Gates, "Probable Cause," "Good Faith," and Beyond. *Iowa Law Review* 69:551–615.

GOODNOW, FRANK J.
(1859–1939)

Frank Johnson Goodnow, founding president of the American Political Science Association (1903–1905), professor at Columbia University (1891–1912) and subsequently president of Johns Hopkins University (1914–1929), was one of the leading proponents of PROGRESSIVE CONSTITUTIONAL THOUGHT. Rejecting the traditional doctrine of SEPARATION OF POWERS, he urged a new separation of political decision making from public administration. In *Social Reform and the Constitution* (1911) he condemned the STRICT CONSTRUCTION of the Constitution that blocked implementation of progressive reforms. He advocated a flexible CONSTITUTIONALISM that would reflect the pace of social change.

DENNIS J. MAHONEY
(1986)

Bibliography

MAHONEY, DENNIS J. 1984 A New Political Science for a World Made Wholly New: The Doctrine of Progress and the Emergence of American Political Science. Ph.D. dissertation, Claremont Graduate School.

GORDON, THOMAS

See: Cato's Letters

GORHAM, NATHANIEL
(1738–1796)

Nathaniel Gorham, a prominent businessman and political leader, signed the Constitution as a representative of Massachusetts. One of the handful of most active delegates to the CONSTITUTIONAL CONVENTION OF 1787, Gorham presided over the Committee of the Whole, served on several committees, including the Committee on Detail, and spoke frequently. He was a supporter of strong national government.

DENNIS J. MAHONEY
(1986)

GOSS v. LOPEZ
419 U.S. 565 (1975)

Ohio law authorized a public school principal to suspend a misbehaving student for up to ten days, without a hearing. A 5–4 Supreme Court held that this law violated a student's right to PROCEDURAL DUE PROCESS. For the majority, Justice BYRON R. WHITE found a "PROPERTY" interest in the state's statute setting out a student's "entitlement" to attend school, and a "liberty" interest in the loss of reputation attending suspension for misconduct. While trivial school discipline might not require any hearing, a ten-day suspension demanded notice of the charges against the student, and, if the charges were denied, an explanation of the EVIDENCE and an opportunity to present his or her story. Justice LEWIS F. POWELL, a former school board president, led the dissenters. The statute authorizing suspension gave only a conditional entitlement to attend school—as Justice WILLIAM H. REHNQUIST had argued in ARNETT V. KENNEDY (1974)—and the injury to reputation was not serious enough to invade a "liberty" interest. Thus, Powell argued, the school discipline here did "not assume constitutional dimensions."

KENNETH L. KARST
(1986)

GOUDY, WILLIAM CHARLES
(1824–1893)

The leader of the Chicago bar, William Goudy was a creative constitutional lawyer and railroad counsel who argued many cases before the Supreme Court. He familiarized the Court with the relationship of laissez-faire tenets and constitutional limitations on STATE POLICE POWER. In *Munn v. Illinois* (see GRANGER CASES), WABASH, ST. LOUIS, AND PACIFIC RAILROAD V. ILLINOIS (1886), and CHICAGO, MILWAUKEE, AND ST. PAUL RAILROAD V. MINNESOTA (1890), he advanced SUBSTANTIVE DUE PROCESS of law in the context of arguments, stressing that the right to property included its unfettered use as well as its title and possession. State regulation of rates, by reducing profits, constituted a TAKING OF PROPERTY without JUST COMPENSATION and a denial of due process, according to Goudy.

LEONARD W. LEVY
(1986)

Bibliography
TWISS, BENJAMIN 1942 *Lawyers and the Constitution.* Pages 76–84. Princeton, N.J.: Princeton University Press.

GOVERNMENT AID TO RELIGIOUS INSTITUTIONS

Constitutionality of governmental aid to religious institutions, generally, though not exclusively, in the form of financial subsidies, is most often challenged under the FIRST AMENDMENT's ban on laws respecting an ESTABLISHMENT OF RELIGION. When the purpose of the subsidy is to finance obviously religious activities, such as the erection or repairing of a church building, UNCONSTITUTIONALITY is generally recognized. In large measure the purpose of the establishment clause was to forbid such grants, as is indicated by the Court's opinion and Justice WILEY RUTLEDGE's dissenting opinion in EVERSON V. BOARD OF EDUCATION (1947). On the other hand, where the funds are used for what would generally be considered secular activities, such as maintaining hospitals or providing meals for pupils in church-related (often called parochial) schools, constitutional validity is fairly unanimously assumed.

Constitutional controversy revolves largely around governmental financing of church-related schools that combine the inculcation of religious doctrines and beliefs with what is generally considered the teaching of secular subjects, substantially, though not necessarily entirely, as they are taught in public schools.

In *Everson*, the Court upheld as a valid exercise of the POLICE POWER a state statute financing bus transportation to parochial schools, on the ground that the legislative purpose was not to aid religion by financing the operations of the schools but to help insure the safety of children going to or returning from them. A law having the former purpose would violate the establishment clause, which forbids government to set up a church, aid one or more religions, or prefer one religion over others. "No tax in any amount, large or small," the Court said, "can be levied to support any religious activities or institutions, whatever they may be called, or whatever form they may adopt to teach or practice religion."

The *Everson*, or "no-aid," interpretation of the establishment clause as applied to governmental financing of religious schools next reached the Supreme Court in the case of BOARD OF EDUCATION V. ALLEN (1968). There the Court upheld a New York statute providing for the loan to pupils attending nonpublic schools of secular textbooks authorized for use in public schools. The Court concluded that the statute did not impermissibly aid religious schools within the meaning of *Everson*, nor did it violate the establishment clause ban on laws lacking a secular legislative purpose or having a primary effect that either advances or inhibits religion, as that clause had been interpreted in ABINGTON SCHOOL DISTRICT V. SCHEMPP (1963). In upholding the New York law, the Court recognized that the police power rationale of *Everson* was not readily applicable to textbook laws, but it adjudged that the processes of secular and religious training are not so intertwined that secular textbooks furnished to students by the public are in fact instrumental in the teaching of religion.

It is fairly obvious that the *Allen* rationale could be used to justify state aid to religious schools considerably more extensive than mere financing of transportation or provision of secular textbooks. It could, for example, justify state financing of supplies other than textbooks, costs of maintenance and repair of parochial school premises, and, most important, salaries of instructors who teach the nonreligious subjects, which constitute the major part of the parochial school curriculum.

That this extension was intended by Justice BYRON R. WHITE, the author of the *Allen* opinion, is indicated by the fact that he thereafter dissented in all the decisions barring aid to church-related schools. The first of these decisions came in the companion cases of LEMON V. KURTZMAN and *Earley v. DiCenso* (1973). In *Lemon*, Pennsylvania purchased the services of religious schools in providing secular education to their pupils. In *DiCenso*, Rhode Island paid fifteen percent of the salaries of religious school teachers who taught only secular subjects.

A year earlier, in WALZ V. TAX COMMISSION (1970), the Court had expanded the purpose-effect test by adding a third dimension: a statute violated the establishment clause if it fostered excessive governmental entanglement with religion. The statutes involved in *Lemon* and *DiCenso* violated the clause, the Court held, because in order to insure that the teachers did not inject religion into their secular classes or allow religious values to affect the content of secular instruction, it was necessary to subject the teachers to comprehensive, discriminating, and continuing state surveillance, which would constitute forbidden entanglement of church and state.

In other cases the Court held unconstitutional laws enacted to reimburse religious schools for the cost of preparing, conducting, and grading teacher-prepared tests, of maintaining and repairing school buildings, of transporting students on field trips to museums and concerts as part of secular courses, and of purchasing instructional materials and equipment susceptible of diversion to religious use. The Court also held unconstitutional state tuition assistance to the parents of parochial school pupils, whether by direct grant or through state income tax benefits.

On the other hand, the Court has upheld the constitutionality of reimbursement for noninstructional health and welfare services supplied to parochial school pupils, such as meals, medical and dental care, and diagnostic services relating to speech, hearing, and psychological problems. In COMMITTEE FOR PUBLIC EDUCATION AND RELIGIOUS LIBERTY V. REGAN (1980) the Court allowed reimbursement for the expense of administering state-prepared and mandated objective examinations.

The Court has manifested a considerably more tolerant approach in cases challenging governmental aid to church-related institutions of higher education. While the purpose-effect-entanglement test is in principle equally applicable, the Court held that where a grant is used to finance facilities in colleges and universities used only for secular instruction, the primary effect of the law is not to advance religion. As for entanglement, religion does not necessarily so permeate the secular education provided by church-related colleges nor so seep into the use of their facilities as to require a ruling that in all cases excessive surveillance would be necessary to assure that the facilities were not used for religious purposes. The Court also gave consideration to the skepticism of college students, the nature of college and postgraduate courses, the high degree of academic freedom characterizing many church-related colleges, and their nonlocal constituencies. For all these reasons, in TILTON V. RICHARDSON (1973) the Court sanctioned substantial governmental financing of church-related institutions of higher education.

In *Walz v. Tax Commission* the Court upheld the constitutionality of tax exemption accorded to property used exclusively for worship or other religious purposes. Exemption, it held, does not entail sponsorship of religion and involves even less entanglement than nonexemption, since it does not require the government to examine the affairs of the church and audit its books or records. The longevity of exemption, dating as it does from the time the Republic was founded, constitutes strong evidence of its constitutionality.

The Court, in *Walz*, did not hold that the free exercise clause would be violated if exemption were disallowed (although it was urged to do so in the AMICUS CURIAE brief submitted by the National Council of Churches). Nor, on the other hand, did it decide to the contrary. As of the present, therefore, it seems that governments, federal or state, have the constitutional option of granting or denying exemption.

LEO PFEFFER
(1986)

(SEE ALSO: *Separation of Church and State.*)

Bibliography

MORGAN, RICHARD E.   1972   *The Supreme Court and Religion.* New York: Free Press.
PFEFFER, LEO   1967   *Church, State and Freedom.* Rev. ed. Boston: Beacon Press.
———   1975   *God, Caesar and the Constitution.* Boston: Beacon Press.
TRIBE, LAURENCE   1978   *American Constitutional Law.* Chap. 14. Mineola, N.Y.: Foundation Press.

GOVERNMENT AID TO RELIGIOUS INSTITUTIONS
(Update 1)

A theme of equality has dominated recent Supreme Court decisions in the area of church-state relations. This may be seen most dramatically in the shrunken protection for RELIGIOUS LIBERTY under the Court's peyote ruling in EMPLOYMENT DIVISION, DEPARTMENT OF HUMAN RESOURCES OF OREGON V. SMITH (1990), which held that the free-exercise clause of the FIRST AMENDMENT affords no religious exemption from a neutral law that regulates conduct even though that law imposes a substantial burden on religious practice. Similarly, on the subject of RELIGION IN PUBLIC SCHOOLS, the Court held in BOARD OF EDUCATION OF WESTSIDE COMMUNITY SCHOOLS V. MERGENS (1990) that the First Amendment's ban on laws respecting an ESTABLISHMENT OF RELIGION permits student religious groups in secondary schools to meet for religious purposes (including prayer) on school premises during noninstructional time as long as other non-curriculum-related student groups are allowed to do so. This theme of neutral treatment of religious and secular groups has been prominent in regard to the subject of governmental aid as well.

It has long been the rule that a government subsidy to religious institutions violates the ESTABLISHMENT CLAUSE when the subsidy's purpose or primary effect is to finance religious (rather than secular) activities. The decision in BOWEN V. KENDRICK (1988) affirmed this proposition and also revealed the present Court's inclination to give a generous interpretation to the term "secular" activities. The case upheld the constitutionality of Congress's granting funds to a variety of public and private agencies (including religious organizations) to provide counseling for prevention of adolescent sexual relations and to promote adoption as an alternative to ABORTION. Whereas this program may be fairly characterized as having a "secular" purpose (even though it coincides with the approach of certain prominent religious groups), there appears to be a substantial danger that the program's primary effect will be to further religious precepts when religiously employed counselors deal with a subject so closely and inextricably tied to religious doctrine.

Substantial constitutional controversy continues to revolve around government financing of church-related schools that combine the inculcation of religious doctrines with the teaching of secular subjects substantially, although not necessarily entirely, as they are taught in public schools. Most forms of public aid for parochial schools, even to support secular courses, have been held to violate the establishment clause, particularly when the aid has been provided directly to the schools themselves rather than to the parents. The Court has usually reasoned that although the aid had a secular (in contrast to a religious) purpose, it was still invalid. The Court's analysis of the problem began with a critical premise: The mission of church-related elementary and secondary schools is to teach religion, and all subjects either are, or carry the potential of being, permeated with religion. Therefore, if the government funds any subjects in these schools, the primary effect will be to aid religion unless public officials monitor the situation to see to it that those courses are not infused with religious doctrine. However, if public officials engage in adequate surveillance, there will be excessive entanglement between government and religion—the image being government spies regularly in parochial school classrooms.

Although no holding of the Supreme Court has overturned this approach, the separate opinion of Justices ANTHONY M. KENNEDY and ANTONIN SCALIA in *Bowen v. Kendrick* reasons that the fact that the assistance goes directly to the schools is not important. Rather, these Justices believe that the use to which the aid is put is crucial. This opinion strongly suggests that a majority of the Court would no longer invalidate most forms of aid to the schools themselves as long as there were adequate controls to assure that the funds were not spent for religious purposes. This is a sound precept. If governmental assistance to parochial schools does not exceed the value of the secular educational service the schools render, then there is no use of tax-raised funds to aid religion and thus no threat of this historic danger to religious liberty.

Tax relief—either exemptions for property used exclusively for worship or other religious purposes, or income tax deductions for parents who send their children to parochial schools—had been held not to violate the establishment clause as long as the benefits extended beyond religion-related recipients. For example, the Court had upheld property-tax exemptions for educational and charitable institutions and tax deductions for school expenses to all parents of school children. By the same token, in TEXAS MONTHLY, INC. V. BULLOCK (1989) the Court invalidated a state sales-tax exemption for books and magazines that "teach" or are "sacred" to religious faith. Because the

exemption was for religious purposes only and not the broad-based type of tax relief provided in the earlier cases, the Court held that this governmental aid violated the establishment clause.

In the mid-1980s, probably the most important uncertainty regarding governmental assistance to parochial schools concerned VOUCHERS. Although the decision in WITTERS V. WASHINGTON DEPARTMENT OF SERVICES FOR THE BLIND (1986) involved only a special type of voucher and did not speak to the constitutionality of school vouchers generally, its rationale goes a long way to sustaining their validity. The case upheld a state program giving visually handicapped persons a voucher (although it was not called that) for use in vocational schools for the blind. Witters was studying religion at a Christian college "in order to equip himself for a career as a pastor, missionary or youth director." A majority of the Court, even before Justices Kennedy and Scalia had been appointed, agreed that "state programs that are wholly neutral in offering educational assistance to a class defined without reference to religion do not violate the [establishment clause], because any aid to religion results from the private choices of individual beneficiaries." The state's money, however, was plainly being spent for religious purposes. If the government, whether through a voucher or a direct grant to parochial schools, is financing not only the value of secular education in those schools, but also all or part of the cost of religious education, the support is an expenditure of compulsorily raised tax funds for religious purposes and should be held to violate the establishment clause.

JESSE H. CHOPER
(1992)

Bibliography

CHOPER, JESSE H.   1987   The Establishment Clause and Aid to Parochial Schools—An Update. *California Law Review* 75: 5–14.

CORD, ROBERT L.   1982   *Separation of Church and State: Historical Fact and Current Fiction.* New York: Lambeth Press.

GOVERNMENT AID TO RELIGIOUS INSTITUTIONS
(Update 2)

The 1990s witnessed the slow demise of the three-pronged LEMON TEST articulated by the Supreme Court in LEMON V. KURTZMAN (1971) and the ascendancy of the neutrality principle for determining whether government aid to a religious institution violates the ESTABLISHMENT CLAUSE. This doctrinal change has occurred along two fronts, one involving FREEDOM OF SPEECH challenges to government refusals to aid religious expressive activities, and the other involving challenges to government programs that benefit religious as well as secular institutions.

In LAMB'S CHAPEL V. CENTER MORICHES UNION FREE SCHOOL DISTRICT (1993), the Court held that public school officials had violated the free speech clause of the FIRST AMENDMENT when they refused to allow a religious group (wanting to show a film) the same access to the school gym granted to secular groups. According to the Court, providing equal access to school facilities after- hours does not amount to government advancement of religion, and therefore there was no compelling justification for this kind of viewpoint discrimination. Extending this rationale to government funding decisions in ROSENBERGER V. RECTORS & VISITORS OF THE UNIVERSITY OF VIRGINIA (1995), the Court held that a public university may not deny a religious group equal access to subsidies for student publications.

In cases decided during the 1990s involving challenges to government aid to religious institutions, the Court has ignored or significantly modified the 1970s-era *Lemon* test. In *Zobrest v. Catalina Foothills School District* (1993), the Court ruled that a government-paid sign language interpreter may assist a deaf student attending classes at a Roman Catholic high school. The Court reasoned that because the program provided interpreters to students on a religiously neutral basis, the interpreter's presence in the religious school was the "result of the private decision of individual parents" and "[could] not be attributed to state decision-making." Although the Court in *Zobrest* did not cite the *Lemon* test, its holding clearly conflicted with prior decisions under *Lemon* that had forbidden PUBLIC EMPLOYEES from providing educational services on the grounds of a religious school.

In AGOSTINI V. FELTON (1997), the only modern decision to expressly OVERRULE a *Lemon*-period PRECEDENT, the Court reversed its earlier holding in AGUILAR V. FELTON (1985) invalidating the use of federal funds to pay for remedial education provided by public school teachers on the grounds of parochial schools. Relying on *Zobrest*, the Court rejected the idea that government employees may never provide educational assistance on religious school grounds. The question, according to the Court, was whether the aid was provided on a religiously neutral basis and whether the program so entangled church and state as to have the effect of inhibiting religion. Writing for the Court, Justice SANDRA DAY O'CONNOR concluded that the funds were religiously neutral and that government oversight of the program would be no more intrusive than the oversight private religious schools already are subject to under state law. The innovation of *Agostini* was O'Connor's revision of the *Lemon* test. According to O'Connor, the no-entanglement prong of the *Lemon* test is best assessed as one aspect of the inquiry into whether or not a government program has a primary effect of advancing or inhibiting religion, and not as a separate requirement.

Agostini did not directly consider whether the state may include religious schools in government-funded school voucher programs. Nevertheless, the combined effect of recent religious expression and government funding cases seem to permit, if not require, equal participation by a religious school in a properly structured voucher program. In fact, in WITTERS V. WASHINGTON DEPARTMENT OF SERVICES FOR THE BLIND (1986), the Court upheld a voucher-like "college choice" program, on the ground that the program was religiously neutral and the aid arrived at the institution by way of private choice, not government direction. After *Agostini*, it seems but a small step to apply this rationale to uphold elementary and high school voucher programs. The issue the Court soon must face is whether the government may exclude religious institutions from general benefits programs when the establishment clause no longer stands as a barrier to their equal participation.

KURT T. LASH
(2000)

(SEE ALSO: *Establishment of Religion; Religion in Public Schools; Religious Liberty; Separation of Church and State; School Choice.*)

GOVERNMENT AS PROPRIETOR

Constitutional litigants in disparate contexts have sought to characterize particular government acts as proprietary, rather than sovereign, in order to substitute for the constitutional standards otherwise applicable to government something like those applicable to private proprietors. Government at any level—local, state, or federal—not only may regulate and tax (the most coercive and quintessentially sovereign exercises of power), but may borrow, spend, buy or sell goods and services, build and operate offices or mass transit, manage property of many kinds, and employ workers. Our constitutional regime sharply differentiates between government and private spheres. When government acts in capacities that resemble the proprietary activities of private owners, managers, and employers, suggestions of modified constitutional analysis may be inevitable. Sometimes the litigant who suggests such a modification seeks to enlarge government power by skirting the constitutional limitations that normally bind federal or state sovereigns, but not private proprietors, in their treatment of individuals; the courts have grappled with this problem through the STATE ACTION doctrine. Sometimes the objective is to dislodge SOVEREIGN IMMUNITY in its various forms and render government accountable to individuals or to subject it to regulation and taxation by superior sovereigns, just as other individuals are. As a double-edged sword that can cut down either constitutional obligation or constitutional immunity, the proprietary analogy is potentially a formidable and versatile tool.

This analogy's checkered past includes adoption, and later rejection, in some constitutional contexts and continuing influence in various forms in others. Courts that reject the government-proprietor distinction make two main arguments: first, it is impossible to draw a sensible line between government's proprietary and sovereign activities, and second, there is questionable legitimacy in drawing such a line in order to discount the value of using proprietary means to accomplish democratically chosen ends. The government-proprietor distinction's frequent recurrence and continued influence rests, in the strongest version, on the superficial appeal of the private analogy or, in a weaker version, on factors sometimes associated with the difference between proprietary and regulatory conduct. Proprietary activity sometimes may implicate other constitutional values to a lesser degree than does more "sovereign" activity: it may interfere less with individual freedom or other values such as interstate harmony; it may provide additional legitimate justifications for governmental policy; or, by analogy to the lesser constitutional protection afforded private COMMERCIAL SPEECH and activity than is afforded political speech and activity, sovereign immunity may be deemed less important for government's proprietary than for its "sovereign" behavior. But the proprietary designation is often too inexact a shorthand for these relevant elements of constitutional analysis. Furthermore, as a determinative or even very strong factor, the proprietary designation too readily slights other important considerations that sometimes should temper or overwhelm it. The designation's mixed success is partially attributable to the fact that it is far too broad and insensitive a constitutional measure and partially to the fact that stronger principles often obviate any value it might otherwise have.

Other drawbacks further limit the utility of treating government as if it were a private business. The government as proprietor may be analogous to a private proprietor, but it differs in its motivations and responsibilities. It is still government, subject to political as well as commercial or proprietary influences and to constitutional restraints inapplicable to private actors.

Imprecise and multiple meanings also limit the usefulness of the proprietary designation. Acting as an owner may differ from one kind of property to another and may differ from acting as a business, a consumer, or an employer. Not only are there varying kinds and gradations of proprietary activity, but the line between regulatory or other sovereign activity and proprietary activity is often blurred. The difference between management policy with respect to government property, business, or employees and regulation of the citizenry at large is a matter of degree, not kind.

Perhaps most fundamentally, in each kind of constitutional controversy, claims of proprietary prerogative or liability encounter varying responses depending on the perceived nature and strength of the countervailing constitutional values. According to PUBLIC FORUM analysis, people free to speak at home may be prevented from speaking at will in government offices—an example of a proprietary justification for limiting the locations of FREEDOM OF SPEECH—yet may not be prevented from speaking in parks or on street corners. Proprietary prerogatives of government thus may affect FIRST AMENDMENT free speech analysis with respect to some but not all publicly owned property. Nor may a government business discriminate on an invidious basis, such as by race or political viewpoint, any more than it may so discriminate in a tax or regulatory capacity. These antidiscrimination restrictions on government behavior are so strong that they may apply fully whether government behaves in a sovereign or proprietary capacity.

The idea of government as proprietor thus has not worked as a categorical concept of overarching importance. It must be understood by reference to the particular kind of proprietary activity involved, the reasons why that activity is thought relevant to solving the specific constitutional controversy, the nature and strength of the constitutional values with which the activity competes, and the practical consequences of the concept. A survey of relevant constitutional controversies reveals this complexity. The controversies include intergovernmental claims by municipalities that their proprietary acts, just like those of private parties, are constitutionally protected from state interference; claims by states of constitutional immunity from control by Congress or the federal courts; state claims of freedom to prefer their own citizens over residents of other states with respect to proprietary policies; and claims by government at all levels that the constitutional rights of individuals may be more circumscribed on government property than on private property. Each set of controversies has its own story.

The simplest story is the unsuccessful attempt of LOCAL GOVERNMENT to carve out a proprietary-rights exception from the principle that each state's power over its political subdivisions generally is unrestricted by the federal Constitution. The Supreme Court easily rejected municipal claims that constitutional provisions like those prohibiting impairment of the OBLIGATIONS OF CONTRACTS or the TAKING OF PROPERTY without JUST COMPENSATION should limit state interference, not only with private contracts and property, but with city contracts and property used in the city's proprietary activities. Even with respect to contract and PROPERTY RIGHTS that the state had originally granted to a private business, that the business then assigned to a city, the Court refused in *City of Trenton v. New Jersey* (1923) to adopt a proprietor-sovereign distinction that would impose on the states constitutional obligations toward the "proprietary" acts of their constituent governments. Originally a judge-made distinction designed to circumvent the sovereign immunity doctrine of COMMON LAW and hold municipalities liable for tortious injuries caused by their proprietary conduct, the proprietor-sovereign distinction lacked a principled basis or definable content and would not be transferred to this area of constitutional law.

The proprietary notion had already been adopted in disputes about the extent of Congress's power to tax state activities, however, though it was ultimately rejected for some of the same reasons in this very different context. Congress expanded its tax programs at the turn of the century just as state trading activity increased. The Supreme Court, in cases like *South Carolina v. United States* (1905), sustained federal taxes on state-sold liquor and other commodities by holding that the constitutional DOCTRINE of INTERGOVERNMENTAL TAX IMMUNITY, which otherwise prohibited federal taxation of state operations, did not extend to state proprietary operations. This proprietary exception was designed to preserve common federal-revenue sources and, possibly, in this area of strong constitutional protection for private enterprise (LOCHNER V. NEW YORK also was decided in 1905), to equalize the competitive positions of state and private business. But by 1947, in *New York v. United States*, the Court, in sustaining a federal tax on state-bottled water, adopted new standards that were more generous to congressional authority and expressly rejected "limitations upon the taxing power of Congress derived from such untenable criteria as "proprietary' against "governmental' activities of the States."

Congress's power to regulate, rather than tax, state operations has followed a different story line. Even if some form of state tax immunity might be important to preserve, *United States v. California* (1936) established for forty years that, when Congress exercised a plenary regulatory power like the power to regulate INTERSTATE COMMERCE, there was no need to distinguish between sovereign and proprietary operations because both were subject to federal regulation. Federal safety, price control, and labor regulations could be applied to state operations because, as the Court said in *Maryland v. Wirtz* (1968), "the Federal Government, when acting within a delegated power, may override countervailing state interests whether these be described as "governmental' or "proprietary."

The overruling of the *Wirtz* decision, by a 5–4 vote, in NATIONAL LEAGUE OF CITIES V. USERY (1976) did backtrack and protect certain state operations from federal regula-

tory as well as taxing power. Ostensibly, the boundary was not drawn according to whether a state operation was governmental or proprietary, but by whether it was an "integral" or "traditional" government function. However, this formulation led to distinguishing between impermissible federal labor regulation of state police and fire-department employees and permissible labor regulation of the employees of state-owned railroads. The state as employer would sometimes be immune, but not with respect to employees providing services like those the private sector traditionally provided.

The *Usery* case was soon itself overruled, however, by the 5–4 decision in GARCIA V. SAN ANTONIO METROPOLITAN TRANSIT AUTHORITY (1985), which held that, at least with respect to congressional regulation—if not possibly taxation—the states must rely on their political influence in Congress, not on judicial enforcement of the Constitution, for protection against burdensome congressional interference with state operations. By withdrawing from the task of defining any core of state SOVEREIGNTY, the *Garcia* decision again obviated the need to draw a government-proprietor or similar distinction. The Court had now concluded that such distinctions were not only "unworkable in practice," but "unsound in principle" because they wrongly devalued an important principle of federalism—each state's lawful and democratically selected means of carrying out its legitimate policy objectives should be equally respected, however unconventional the choice of means might be.

The complete rejection of the proprietor-sovereign distinction in virtually all hierarchical intergovernmental disputes—whether invoked by municipalities claiming more constitutional protection from state control for proprietary than for governmental activities or by states conversely claiming more constitutional immunity from Congress for governmental than for proprietary activities—so far has not been replicated outside the constitutional clashes between superior and subordinate levels of government. Yet, doctrinal turbulence and perennial dissatisfaction with reliance on proprietary notions remain.

The tale of changing Supreme Court responses to state policies that give preference to their residents in the distribution of "proprietary" commercial benefits is a major example. To further political and economic union, the PRIVILEGES AND IMMUNITIES clause of Article IV, Section 2, generally prohibits each state from discriminating against citizens of other states, and the DORMANT COMMERCE CLAUSE prohibits state discrimination against interstate business. However, each state's primary obligation to serve its own residents necessitates some resident preference. Various proprietary concepts have been employed to mediate the Constitution's interstate-equality demands and its conflicting recognition of state sovereignty.

Under the privileges and immunities clause, no state, absent substantial justification, may limit nonresident access to private-sector commercial opportunities more severely than it limits resident access. Beginning in the nineteenth century, however, the Court permitted resident preference regarding commercial exploitation of state-owned natural resources. The Court concluded that government property owners, like private owners, generally may be selective in sharing what they own with whom they wish. This proprietary escape hatch from the regulatory nondiscrimination rule was criticized as "a fiction," but not fully abandoned, in TOOMER V. WITSELL (1948), just a year after the decision in *New York v. United States* had discarded the proprietor-sovereign distinction as a standard for demarcating the line between federal taxing authority and state tax immunity. *Toomer* rejected South Carolina's attempt to justify charging nonresidents 100 times more than it charged its own residents for a license to shrimp in state coastal waters; the Court called the state's claim to "own" the shrimp and the sea extravagant. Since then, even true state resource ownership does not render the privileges and immunities clause wholly inapplicable. Although ownership is "often the crucial factor" in evaluating the constitutionality of discriminatory resource distribution, the Court in HICKLIN V. ORBECK (1978) limited resident preference to the state's direct proprietary dealings and disallowed conditional policies requiring those in the immediate proprietary relationship to prefer residents in "downstream" relationships.

The proprietary idea followed a similar but not identical course in dormant-commerce-clause jurisprudence. At the end of the nineteenth century, the Court carved a generous proprietary exception from the usual rule that a state may not prevent the shipment of local goods to other states. In *Geer v. Connecticut* (1896), for example, it allowed a complete ban of shipping game birds out of state; the Court applied the fictitious theory that the state owned the wildlife within its borders and thus could control its disposition, even after the birds lawfully had been reduced to private possession. *Geer* was eventually overruled a year after *Hicklin* in *Hughes v. Oklahoma* (1979), which applied the same dormant-commerce-clause standards applicable to regulation of private goods to the regulation of wildlife. At a minimum, *Hughes* limited the proprietary justification to instances of actual, not pretended, state ownership.

Moving in the other direction, several decisions in the last two decades have allowed states to discriminate against interstate commerce on the basis of a different kind of proprietary prerogative—that of the state acting as a commercial buyer or seller, rather than just as owner of property. Whether favoring in-state suppliers for government purchases, as in *Hughes v. Alexandria Scrap Corp.* (1976), or preferring in-state customers when demand for state-manufactured goods exceeds supply, as in *Reeves v. Stake* (1980), states have been exempted from the normal dormant-commerce-clause antidiscrimination limits when acting as "market participants" rather than as regulators of private buyers or sellers in the interstate market. The Court's position articulated in *United Building and Construction Trades Council v. Mayor and Council of the City of Camden* (1984) is that the grant to Congress of the power to regulate interstate commerce serves only as an "implied restraint upon state regulatory powers." Thus, the nonregulatory activities of the states are not subject to dormant-commerce-clause scrutiny—a rationale that assumes a ready distinction between state regulatory and proprietary activity. Even so, the Court sought to limit the state-as-trader exception in two ways. First, as with proprietary prerogatives under the privileges and immunities clause, the market-participant doctrine allows local favoritism only in the state's dealings with its direct trading partners and disallows requiring those partners to favor residents in their independent economic relationships with others. Second, the Court in the *Camden* case held that discriminatory state market participation, which is free from dormant-commerce-clause restraints, is not wholly exempt from privileges-and-immunities-clause analysis. The latter provision directly restrains state action in the interests of interstate harmony, whether regulatory or not. Both these attempts to confine the damage that might be done by a wholesale lifting of interstate equality obligations for state proprietary activity are familiar symptoms of the beguiling but dubious use of proprietary justifications.

Several elements in the history of proprietary adjustments to interstate equality doctrine also appear in the history of proprietary adjustments to free-speech doctrine. The general question is whether government has power to deny the right to communicate on public property what freely may be communicated on private property. In the late nineteenth century era, when the Supreme Court forcefully protected private property from government intrusion and state property from nonresident demands of equal access, the excessive attribution of plenary control to property ownership prevailed. In *Davis v. Massachusetts* (1897) the Court affirmed a ruling by OLIVER WENDELL HOLMES, JR., then a state judge, that "[f]or the legislature absolutely or conditionally to forbid public speaking in a highway or public park is no more an infringement of rights of a member of the public than for the owner of a private house to forbid it in the house." By the late 1930s, however, as the Court found constitutional room for extensive government regulation of private property, it also found government's proprietary claims insufficient to justify complete denial of public communication in streets and parks. The power associated with property, governmental or private, would not categorically overwhelm other important considerations.

Neither was ownership always irrelevant. What ensued, with frequent division within the Court, was the development of public-forum doctrine, which sometimes distinguishes among different kinds of public property to determine what rights of access private speakers may enjoy. The core First Amendment principle that government may not discriminate against viewpoints it dislikes is so strong that it applies to all public property. Moreover, quintessential public forums like streets and parks cannot be completely closed to speech, even though banning all access would be viewpoint neutral. Yet, the Court remains excessively influenced by proprietary prerogatives. Rather than directly weighing the particular property-management interests of government against the First Amendment importance of speaker access to the particular public location, the Court has permitted government to deny access altogether—at least when the denial is not viewpoint selective—to other forms of public property, ranging from prison grounds to schools to offices to military bases, even where the speech would not interfere with the property's intended purpose. In the leading case of PERRY EDUCATION ASSOCIATION V. PERRY LOCAL EDUCATORS ASSOCIATION (1983) the Court said, "The existence of a right of access to public property and the standard by which limitations upon such a right must be evaluated differ depending on the character of the property at issue." In that and other cases where access claims have been denied, the Court has hearkened back to Justice HUGO L. BLACK's statement for the majority in the jail-grounds case of ADDERLEY V. FLORIDA (1966): "The State, no less than a private owner of property, has power to preserve the property under its control for the use to which it is lawfully dedicated." The Court's deference to government's proprietary prerogatives thus depends not on property ownership alone, but at least formally, on distinctions among different kinds of public property.

If the fact of ownership is sometimes still weighed too heavily in public-forum doctrine generally, that weight may be even more excessive when, as with the market-participant exception to dormant-commerce-clause doctrine, government property is used in a commercial setting. Normally, if the government, with respect to public property that could be closed to all, voluntarily makes it available for speech on some subjects, it cannot deny access to speakers on other subjects. In *Lehman v. Shaker Heights* (1974), however, the Court allowed a city that sold space on its buses for commercial and public-service advertising to refuse to sell space for political and public-issue advertising. Putting aside First Amendment norms of equal treatment of subject matter in the "voluntary" public forum, four Justices emphasized that the city was "engaged in commerce" and acting "in a proprietary capacity."

Some deference to government's proprietary powers in managing its property, its business dealings, or its PUBLIC EMPLOYEES is undoubtedly appropriate, at least so long as those powers are not exercised for invidiously selective reasons. The Court's opinion in RUTAN V. REPUBLICAN PARTY OF ILLINOIS (1990) is a recent example of the limits of such deference; *Rutan* invalidated government personnel decisions based on political patronage over the dissent of three Justices, who complained that government should be less restricted as employer than as lawmaker. The extent to which proprietary interests permit regulation that otherwise would violate the individual rights of the general populace should, and sometimes (if not often enough) does, depend on additional considerations, such as the importance of the competing constitutional right and its claim to affirmative public support, including the availability of alternative opportunities to exercise that right and the degree to which government monopolizes those opportunities. These considerations surely support the Court's willingness to override proprietary prerogatives in favor of free speech in the streets, parks, and other traditional areas of popular assembly. (Although the recent 5–4 decision in *United States v. Kokinda* upheld a postal regulation barring solicitation on postal property as applied to soliciting political contributions on a sidewalk separating a post office from its parking lot, only four Justices relied on proprietary justifications for the exclusion; even they agreed that the "Government, even when acting in its proprietary capacity, does not enjoy absolute freedom from First Amendment constraints, as does a private business.") Having safeguarded these public locales, perhaps the Court is more comfortable in approving limits on access rights in others.

In determining whether government has left too little room for individual liberty, however, the proprietary idea is too indirect and blunt an instrument, just as it is too imprecise a measure in determining whether state autonomy should be protected against congressional regulation and in determining whether a state's preferences for its own residents will threaten interstate harmony. The government-proprietor distinction's complete rejection in some spheres and its resilience and mutations in others counsel us to acknowledge its intuitive appeal, but to beware excessive reliance on its seductive power.

JONATHAN D. VARAT
(1992)

Bibliography

GILLEN, TERESA 1985 A Proposed Model of the Sovereign-Proprietary Distinction. *University of Pennsylvania Law Review* 133:661–684.

KREIMER, SETH F. 1984 Allocational Sanctions: The Problem of Negative Rights in a Positive State. *University of Pennsylvania Law Review* 132:1293, 1314–1324.

LINDE, HANS 1964 Justice Douglas on Freedom in the Welfare State: Constitutional Rights in the Public Sector. *Washington Law Review* 39:4–46.

—— 1965 Constitutional Rights in the Public Sector: Justice Douglas on Liberty in the Welfare State. *Washington Law Review* 40:10–77.

POST, ROBERT C. 1987 Between Governance and Management: The History and Theory of the Public Forum. *UCLA Law Review* 34:1713–1835.

VARAT, JONATHAN D. 1981 State "Citizenship" and Interstate Equality. *University of Chicago Law Review* 48:487–572.

WELLS, MICHAEL and HELLERSTEIN, WALTER 1980 The Governmental-Proprietary Distinction in Constitutional Law. *Virginia Law Review* 66:1073–1141.

GOVERNMENT INSTRUMENTALITY

Government instrumentalities are agencies, including government-owned corporations, created by Congress or the state legislatures to carry out public functions or purposes. Since MCCULLOCH V. MARYLAND (1819) the doctrine of INTERGOVERNMENTAL IMMUNITY has precluded the state and federal governments from directly taxing one another's governmental instrumentalities.

DENNIS J. MAHONEY
(1986)

GOVERNMENT REGULATION OF THE ECONOMY

See: Economic Regulation

GOVERNMENT SECRECY

The FIRST AMENDMENT guarantees of FREEDOM OF SPEECH and FREEDOM OF THE PRESS are essential to democratic rule because they protect the right to communicate and receive information needed for self-government. Self-government might seem to require that "the public and the press" also enjoy "rights of access to information about the operation of their government," as Justice JOHN PAUL STEVENS stated in RICHMOND NEWSPAPERS V. VIRGINIA (1980). Yet, despite its broad protection of speech and the press, the Constitution imposes meager limits on government secrecy. Judicial recognition of a RIGHT TO KNOW generally has been limited to the right to learn what others may choose to disclose and not a right to know what the government elects to conceal.

The most prominent right of access to an official event recognized by the Supreme Court is the right to attend criminal trials and proceedings. Even here, however, early signs were inauspicious. In GANNETT CO., INC. V. DEPASQUALE (1979) a newspaper relied on the Sixth Amendment to require a judge to open pretrial hearings over objections from the accused and prosecutor. The Sixth Amendment guarantees "the accused . . . the right to [a] public trial." The Court rejected the newspaper's argument on the ground that the amendment gave *the public* no "right . . . to insist upon a public trial."

A year later, after much criticism, a fragmented Court found such a right in the First Amendment. In *Richmond Newspapers* the trial judge had closed a murder trial at the defendant's request. Chief Justice WARREN E. BURGER, writing for himself and Justices BYRON R. WHITE and John Paul Stevens, acknowledged that the First Amendment did not explicitly mention a right of access to governmental functions. But he found a right to attend criminal trials "implicit in the guarantees of the First Amendment." He emphasized that other "unarticulated rights" had been found implicit in the Constitution, including the right of association, the RIGHT OF PRIVACY, and the RIGHT TO TRAVEL. The CHIEF JUSTICE also cited the NINTH AMENDMENT, which he said was adopted "to allay . . . fears . . . that expressing certain guarantees could be read as excluding others."

Justice WILLIAM J. BRENNAN (joined by Justice THURGOOD MARSHALL) took a broader view of the right to government information, as did Justice Stevens in a separate opinion. For Justice Brennan, the First Amendment had "a *structural* role to play in securing and fostering our republican system of self-government. Implicit in this structural role is [the] assumption that valuable public debate . . . must be informed." His structural analysis extended to "governmental information" generally, not only criminal trials, with the "privilege of access . . . subject to a degree of restraint dictated by the nature of the information and countervailing interests in security or confidentiality." Justice WILLIAM H. REHNQUIST alone dissented.

The Court has since relied on the First Amendment to invalidate a law that excluded the press and public during the trial testimony of a minor alleged to be the victim of a sexual offense in GLOBE NEWSPAPER COMPANY V. SUPERIOR COURT (1982); to overturn a trial court's secret examination of prospective jurors in *Press-Enterprise Co. v. Superior Court* (1984); and to uphold public access to a pretrial hearing at which the prosecution must prove the existence of PROBABLE CAUSE to bring a defendant to trial in *Press-Enterprise Co. v. Superior Court* (1986). In each case, the Court said that the interest in public access could be outweighed in particular cases by demonstrated need for exclusion.

Beyond criminal proceedings, the argument for public access to government information has fared poorly. After suggesting in BRANZBURG V. HAYES (1972) that "news gathering is not without its First Amendment protections," the Court has recognized almost none. In *Houchins v. KQED, Inc.* (1978) the Court said that the Constitution accords the press no greater rights than it gives the public generally. But some members of the Court, notably Justice Stevens, have argued that the press should nonetheless receive greater access "to insure that the citizens are fully informed regarding matters of public interest and importance." The seven Justices participating in *Houchins* could not agree on a majority opinion, but a combination of views granted the press more frequent visits to a local jail than the public enjoyed and the right to bring recording equipment, which the public could not. But journalists had no right to enter a problem area of the jail or to interview randomly encountered inmates.

The Supreme Court has not recognized a First Amendment right of access to civil trials, although individual Justices have supported one, as have lower courts. A right of access in criminal matters is easier to uphold for two reasons. First, the Sixth Amendment, although not the source of an access right, already contemplates constitutional limits on societal efforts to close criminal proceedings. No equivalent limit exists for civil matters. Second, when the Constitution was adopted, "criminal trials both here and in England had long been presumptively open," as Chief Justice Burger pointed out in *Richmond Newspapers*.

A right of access to fiscal information would seem to reside in the accounts clause of the Constitution, which provides that "a regular Statement and Account of the Receipts and Expenditures of all public Money shall be published from time to time." Even if this provision does guarantee fiscal information, it is not clear who might be able to enforce it. In *United States v. Richardson* (1974) a taxpayer challenged the government's failure to disclose the CIA budget. The Court refused to address the merits of the challenge because the taxpayer lacked STANDING to assert it. Taxpayer status did not confer a right to sue.

Judicial and congressional SUBPOENAS would seem one way to require the executive branch of government to produce information. But a constitutional EXECUTIVE PRIVILEGE of uncertain dimension will sometimes entitle the President and other executive officers to maintain the secrecy of their communications by resisting such subpoenas. UNITED STATES V. NIXON (1974) recognized a qualified executive privilege, but declined to apply it to protect the President's Watergate tapes.

FREEDOM OF INFORMATION ACTS afford the single best route around official secrecy. These acts, which exist at the federal level and in many states, guarantee access to a great deal of information. However, the guarantee is legislatively, not constitutionally, created.

STEPHEN GILLERS
(1992)

Bibliography

BRENNAN, WILLIAM J. 1979 Address. *Rutgers Law Review* 32: 173–183.
LEWIS, ANTHONY 1980 A Public Right to Know About Public Institutions: The First Amendment as a Sword. *Supreme Court Review* 1980:1–25.

GOVERNMENT SPEECH

FIRST AMENDMENT commentary has emphasized the danger of government as censor; thus lavish attention has been given to whether government can prevent Nazis from marching in Skokie, Illinois, Communists from advocating revolution, pornographers from selling their wares, or eccentrics from yelling fire in crowded theaters. Much less attention has been paid to the role of government as speaker; yet, one need only notice the ready access of government officials to the mass media, the constant stream of legislative and executive reports and publications, and the massive system of direct grants and indirect subsidies to the communications process (including federal financing of elections) to recognize that speech financed or controlled by government plays an enormous role in the marketplace of ideas. Sometimes the government speaks as government; sometimes it subsidizes speech without purporting to claim that the resulting message is its own. The term "government speech," therefore, includes all forms of state-supported communications: official government messages; statements of public officials at publicly subsidized press conferences; artistic, scientific, or political subsidies; even the classroom communications of public school teachers.

Basic assumptions of First Amendment law are sharply modified when governments speak. A basic canon of First Amendment law is that content distinctions are suspect. Indeed, in POLICE DEPARTMENT OF CHICAGO V. MOSLEY (1972) the Court insisted that government could not deviate " 'from the neutrality of time, place and circumstances into a concern about content.' This is never permitted." When governments speak, however, content distinctions are the norm. Government does not speak at random; it makes editorial judgments; it decides that some content is appropriate for the occasion and other content is not. The public museum curator makes content distinctions in selecting exhibits; the librarian, in selecting books; the public official, in composing press releases. If government could not make content distinctions, it could not speak effectively.

The government speech problem is to determine the constitutional limits, if any, on the editorial decisions of government. BUCKLEY V. VALEO (1976) squarely presented the issue. Certain minor party candidates argued that their exclusion from the system of public financing of presidential elections violated the First Amendment and the DUE PROCESS CLAUSE of the Fifth Amendment. The Court briskly dismissed the relevance of the First Amendment challenge on the ground that a subsidy "furthers, not abridges, pertinent First Amendment values." This cryptic response has prompted criticism on the ground that it ignores the equality values in the First Amendment. One wonders, for example, how the Court would have reacted if the Congress had funded Democrats but not Republicans. Nonetheless, the Court did consider an equality claim grounded in Fifth Amendment due process, and concluded that the financing scheme was in "furtherance of sufficiently important government interests and has not unfairly or unnecessarily burdened the political opportunity of any party or candidate."

Buckley is important for two reasons. First, it affirms that government subsidies for speech enhance First Amendment values, recognizing that our "statute books are replete with laws providing financial assistance to the exercise of free speech, such as aid to public broadcasting and other forms of educational media . . . and preferential postal rates and antitrust exceptions for newspapers." Second, it seems to recognize that political subsidies are subject to constitutional limits under the equality principle, if not under the principle of free speech.

The First Amendment issues given short shrift in *Buckley* were fully aired in BOARD OF EDUCATION V. PICO (1982). Students alleged that the school board had removed nine books from school libraries because "particular passages in the books offended their social, political and moral tastes and not because the books, taken as a whole, were lacking educational value." The case produced seven different opinions and no clear resolution of the First Amendment issues. Over the dissent of four Justices, the Court ruled that the students' complaint could survive a summary judgment motion. Four of the Justices in the majority stated that if the allegations of the complaint were vindicated, the First Amendment barred the board's action. The fifth Justice, BYRON R. WHITE, thought that because of unresolved questions of fact the case should proceed to trial; he maintained, however, that discussion of the First Amendment issues was premature.

Most of the eight Justices who did discuss the issues expressed three important notes of agreement. First, they agreed that a major and appropriate purpose of government speech in the public schools is to transmit community values "promoting respect for authority and traditional values be they social, moral, or political." There was substantial disagreement, however, about the relevance of this purpose to book selections for a school library. Second, the Justices agreed that local authorities had wide latitude in making content decisions about library materials. Finally, most agreed that discretion could not be employed in a "narrowly partisan or political manner," such as removing all books written by Republicans. Beyond these agreements, however, the Justices struggled over differences between libraries and classrooms, between lower and higher levels of education, between acquiring books and removing books. *Pico* stands for little more than the proposition that government's broad discretion in subsidizing speech is not entirely unfettered by the First Amendment.

Perhaps the most serious challenges of government speech have surrounded government spending to influence the outcome of election campaigns. In many lower court cases, taxpayers have challenged the constitutionality of spending by cities or administrative agencies to influence the outcome of initiative campaigns. Lower courts have frequently avoided constitutional issues, concluding that state law does not authorize the city or administrative agency to spend the money. At least one question is implicitly resolved by these decisions, however, namely, that cities and administrative agencies do not have First Amendment rights against the state, at least none comparable to the rights of individuals or business corporations. The decisions have left open the question of the extent to which the Constitution permits governments to use their treasuries to help one side in an election campaign.

The establishment clause unquestionably prohibits some forms of religious government speech, and the EQUAL PROTECTION clause presumably prohibits some forms of racially discriminatory government speech. It remains to be seen what other limits the First Amendment or the equal protection clause may place on government's massive role in subsidizing speech.

STEVEN SHIFFRIN
(1986)

Bibliography

SHIFFRIN, STEVEN 1983 Government Speech. *UCLA Law Review* 27:565–655.
YUDOF, MARK 1983 *When Government Speaks: Politics, Law,*

and Government Expression in America. Berkeley and Los Angeles: University of California Press.

GOVERNMENT WRONGS

In his *Commentaries on the Law of England* (1765), WILLIAM BLACKSTONE articulated what he took to be the fundamental principle governing legal redress against the Crown: "The King can do no wrong." This maxim, which Bracton had reported in the thirteenth century, was for Blackstone and for the legal historians who followed him an implication of the royal prerogative signifying that the Crown could not be brought to account judicially without its consent. Even in Bracton's time, however, the Crown had established remedies for many wrongs committed by royal officers. The maxim, then, probably meant not that the king was above the law but that he would not ordinarily suffer wrong to be done to his subjects by his officers without remedy.

Prior to the AMERICAN REVOLUTION the law in England, as summarized in *Lane v. Cotton* (1701), recognized the personal liability of individual officers for negligent wrongs committed in the course of their duties, but denied governmental liability for negligence. The American Constitution, however, established political and legal principles that were radically different from those that prevailed in English public law. State-law principles also reflected certain departures from the English model. This discussion focuses on tort claims, not contractual disputes. The discussion will distinguish between state and federal government wrongs, between immunity doctrine in the state courts and in the federal courts, and between actions asserting DAMAGE CLAIMS and suits for injunctive relief.

In CHISHOLM V. GEORGIA (1793) the Supreme Court upheld state government liability, ruling that Article III conferred federal court jurisdiction over COMMON LAW actions against states initiated by citizens of other states. In an OBITER DICTUM, however, the Court stated that Article III immunized the United States from suit, a position affirmed in later cases. The *Chisholm* ruling on state liability aroused a firestorm of political protest, culminating in the adoption of the ELEVENTH AMENDMENT, which was understood to bar any federal court action against a state, even one claiming a constitutional violation.

The JURISPRUDENCE relating to the states' Eleventh Amendment immunity soon became quite complex and remains so. For example, in *Hans v. Louisiana* (1890) the immunity was extended to suits brought against states by their own citizens, contrary to Article III's text, and to suits that were effectively, though not nominally, against states. In EX PARTE YOUNG (1908), however, the Court created

what proved to be a transformative exception to the immunity. There, the Court permitted the federal courts to grant injunctive relief against state officials in their individual capacities if their actions, although valid under state law, violated the Constitution. From this seed, the CIVIL RIGHTS revolution in the courts would grow.

The most far-reaching federal-law limitation on states and local government wrongs, SECTION 1983, TITLE 42, U.S. CODE, authorizes courts to grant monetary or injunctive relief against "any person who, under color of [state or local] law," deprives the plaintiff of rights secured by federal law. Enacted in 1871 to implement the newly ratified FOURTEENTH AMENDMENT, it was of little significance until the Court, in *Monroe v. Pape* (1961), interpreted the statute to cover official wrongs that were authorized by state law. Only two years after the decision, section 1983 litigation had increased by more than sixty percent. Subsequently decisions expanded this remedy even further. In 1976 Congress authorized the award of attorneys' fees to successful plaintiffs in section 1983 cases.

Today, the main limitations on section 1983 liability are the following: A LOCAL GOVERNMENT is not liable for its officials' wrongs unless the illegal actions reflect an "official policy or custom"; punitive damages may be awarded against individual officials but ordinarily not against governments; comprehensive regulatory schemes may override section 1983's remedy; simple negligence is not actionable; and, most important, certain immunities may protect governments and officials from actions for damages and other retrospective relief. These immunities are absolute as to judicial, legislative, and prosecutorial actions, and are qualified (protecting an official who acts in good faith) as to administrative actions.

Each state has established its own regime of liability and immunity law for its officials' wrongs. These regimes usually center on statutory waivers of SOVEREIGN IMMUNITY. In interpreting these statutes, state courts often distinguish between "discretionary" and "governmental" decisions, which are absolutely immune, and "ministerial" and "proprietary" decisions, which are not. These state-law regimes are largely unaffected by the Constitution, although they may provide remedies under state law for federal-law violations.

Wrongs committed by federal officials are subject to three different remedies under federal law: (1) the Federal Tort Claims Act of 1946 (FTCA); (2) the "Bivens action" and (3) direct JUDICIAL REVIEW OF ADMINISTRATIVE ACTION under the Administrative Procedure Act of 1946 or particular review provisions in statutes.

The FTCA is a limited waiver of the United States's sovereign immunity derived, as noted above, from judicial interpretations of Article III. It creates a damage remedy for federal officials' negligence and for certain intentional torts of "investigative or law enforcement officers" so long as the conduct is tortious under the applicable state law. The FTCA substitutes governmental for official liability; although it confers no immunities, it creates some broad exceptions. The two most important ones deny liability for most intentional torts, and for "any claim . . . based upon the exercise or performance or the failure to exercise a discretionary function or duty . . . whether or not the discretion involved be abused." Neither a jury trial nor punitive damages is available under the FTCA.

The eponymous *Bivens* action, from BIVENS V. SIX UNKNOWN NAMED AGENTS (1971), is a judicially created remedy against individual federal officials (not the government) for violations of certain constitutional rights; the Court has specifically extended it to FOURTH AMENDMENT, Fifth Amendment EQUAL PROTECTION, and Eighth Amendment rights. In *Bivens* actions, the FTCA exceptions do not apply, but the official may claim an absolute or qualified immunity (depending on the nature of the act). Punitive damages and jury trials are permitted.

The Administrative Procedure Act authorizes JUDICIAL REVIEW of the decisions of almost all federal agencies at the instance of one who is aggrieved by an agency action and seeks injunctive, mandatory, or declaratory relief. The only important exceptions are cases in which a statute precludes judicial review, as in *Block v. Community Nutrition Institute* (1984), or in which the agency action "is committed to agency discretion by law," as in *Heckler v. Chaney* (1985).

The legal structure for remedying governmental wrongs, especially at the federal level, is formidable. That structure, however, displays some problematic features. First, certain doctrines limit victims' redress. These include the Eleventh Amendment immunity; the Court's rejection, in MONELL V. DEPARTMENT OF SOCIAL SERVICES OF NEW YORK CITY (1978), of local governments' vicarious liability for their employees' section 1983 violations; and the limitations on liability, damages, and fee-shifting under the FTCA. Such doctrines, by effectively confining many victims to a remedy against an individual official, may defeat both the compensation and deterrence goals of the law. Individual officials are unlikely to be able to pay substantial damages. They are also likely to be poorly situated to alter the bureaucratic policies or practices that may have caused their wrongdoing and may cause more of it in the future. In addition, doctrines about STANDING, RIPENESS, and irreparable harm have sometimes been used to restrict access to injunctive relief against governmental wrongdoing of a more or less systematic nature. An example is *City of Los Angeles v. Lyons* (1983).

Second, this focus on the liability of individual officials, some of whom will be neither legally represented nor indemnified by the governments that employ them, creates incentives for the officials to adopt self-protective strategies of inaction, delay, formalism, and change in the character of their decisions. The circumstances in which many low-level officials work also provide ample opportunity to pursue such incentives. Although these strategies may succeed in minimizing the officials' personal exposure to liability, they tend to undermine the officials' functions and impose wasteful costs on the public.

A remedial structure that limited the liability of individual officials for damages, transferring remedial responsibility to the governmental entities that employed them, would strike a better balance among the competing social interests. Those interests are to deter official wrongdoing, maintain vigorous decision making, compensate victims of illegality, respect the distinctive institutional competences of different decision makers, and accomplish these ends at a tolerable public cost.

PETER H. SCHUCK
(1992)

Bibliography

NAHMOD, SHELDON   1986   *Civil Rights and Civil Liberties Litigation: The Law of Section 1983.* Colorado Springs, Colo.: Shepard'sMcGraw-Hill.

SCHUCK, PETER   1983   *Suing Government: Citizen Remedies for Official Wrongs.* New Haven, Conn.: Yale University Press.

GRACE v. UNITED STATES
461 U.S. 171 (1983)

A federal statute forbids display of any flag or device designed to "bring into public notice any party, organization, or movement" in the United States Supreme Court building or on its grounds. The Supreme Court held this statute invalid, on FIRST AMENDMENT grounds, as applied to lone individuals engaging in expressive activity on the sidewalk adjoining the Court's building. The Court did not address the law's validity as applied to the building or the grounds inside the sidewalk, or to parades or demonstrations on the sidewalk.

KENNETH L. KARST
(1986)

GRAHAM v. RICHARDSON
403 U.S. 365 (1971)

Arizona denied certain WELFARE BENEFITS to ALIENS who had not lived in the country fifteen years. Pennsylvania denied similar benefits to all aliens. The Supreme Court unanimously held these restrictions unconstitutional.

Justice HARRY A. BLACKMUN, for the Court, said that alienage, like race, was a SUSPECT CLASSIFICATION, demanding STRICT SCRUTINY by the Court of its justification. The state argued that its "special public interest" in aiding its own citizens justified discriminating against aliens, but the Court, citing TAKAHASHI V. FISH AND GAME COMMISSION (1948), rejected the argument. The discrimination thus denied aliens the EQUAL PROTECTION OF THE LAWS.

Again citing *Takahashi*, the Court concluded that the two state laws invaded the province of Congress to regulate aliens, encroaching on an area of "exclusive federal power." Justice JOHN MARSHALL HARLAN concurred only as to this FEDERALISM ground, refusing to join in the equal protection ground.

KENNETH L. KARST
(1986)

GRAMM-RUDMAN-HOLLINGS ACT
99 Stat. 1037 (1985)

The Balanced Budget and Emergency Deficit Control Act of 1985 is better known by the names of its three principal Senate sponsors, Phil Gramm (Republican, Texas), Warren B. Rudman (Republican, New Hampshire), and Ernest Hollings (Democrat, South Carolina). Attached as a rider to the bill that raised the national debt ceiling to $2 trillion, theact amended the CONGRESSIONAL BUDGET AND IMPOUNDMENT CONTROL ACT OF 1974. Under the Gramm-Rudman-Hollings Act the maximum budget deficit for fiscal year 1986 was set at $180 billion, and maximum deficits were set for the next four fiscal years, with deficits to be completely eliminated beginning in fiscal year 1991. To enforce the deficit limitation, the act established an automatic mechanism according to which the OFFICE OF MANAGEMENT AND BUDGET (an executive agency) and the Congressional Budget Office (a congressional agency) were required annually to report their estimates of the deficit to the comptroller general (the head of the General Accounting Office, another congressional agency), who was to average the two estimates and report the result to the President. The President would be required to issue an executive order "sequestering" appropriated funds to the extent that the estimated deficit exceeded the deficit authorized by the act. Other provisions of the act divided the sequestration equally between defense appropriations and nondefense domestic programs and exempted from sequestration funds appropriated for Social Security, interest payments on the national debt (the total of previous deficits), and certain other programs.

The constitutionality of some aspects of the act was questioned even before the act was passed by Congress; and President RONALD REAGAN alluded to outstanding con-stitutional questions even as he signed the act into law. Indeed, the act contained provisions facilitating JUDICIAL REVIEW. It authorized members of Congress to file suit challenging the constitutionality of the act, it provided for challenges to be heard by a special three-judge federal court with direct appeal to the Supreme Court, and it set up an expedited process at each level of the judiciary.

Within hours of President Reagan's signing the act, Representative Michael Synar (Democrat, Oklahoma) filed suit charging that Congress, in the act, unconstitutionally delegated its power to control federal spending and that, even if the DELEGATION OF POWER were constitutional, delegation to the comptroller general, who serves at the pleasure of Congress, was unconstitutional. The latter argument was based on the modern understanding of SEPARATION OF POWERS, exemplified by the Supreme Court's decision in IMMIGRATION AND NATURALIZATION SERVICE V. CHADHA (1983). Should Synar's suit prevail, the deficit limits would be left intact, but the automatic enforcement provisions would be eliminated and imposition of spending controls to meet the limits would depend on the ability of members of Congress to agree to a JOINT RESOLUTION reducing spending. In early 1986, a three-judge federal court in the District of Columbia heard Synar's suit and held that the automatic provisions of the act, insofar as they delegated authority other than to executive branch officials, were unconstitutional.

DENNIS J. MAHONEY
(1986)

GRANDFATHER CLAUSE

This expression, born of legislative skulduggery, has survived to serve more acceptable purposes. A number of southern states, seeking to circumvent the FIFTEENTH AMENDMENT's prohibition against RACIAL DISCRIMINATION in the field of VOTING RIGHTS, adopted LITERACY TESTS for voter eligibility. These provisions standing alone would have disqualified not only most black registrants but also a large number of whites. Under a typical exception, however, an illiterate might be registered if he had been eligible to vote before some date in 1865 or 1866, or if he were the descendant of a person eligible at that time. The Supreme Court, in GUINN V. UNITED STATES (1915) and *Lane v. Wilson* (1939), held such grandfather clauses invalid.

More recently, the same term has described any legislative exception relieving from regulation a person who has been engaging in a certain practice for a period of time. A new ZONING law, for example, might limit LAND USE in one zone to single-family residences, but contain a grandfather clause allowing the continuation of businesses or apartment houses already operating there. In part, such an exception is designed to avoid constitutional problems that arguably might arise in its absence. (See TAKING OF PROPERTY; VESTED RIGHTS; SUBSTANTIVE DUE PROCESS.) But the exception itself may be challenged as unconstitutional. In NEW ORLEANS V. DUKES (1976), the city had prohibited the sale of food from pushcarts in the French Quarter, but had exempted pushcart vendors who had been operating there more than eight years. The Supreme Court unanimously upheld this grandfather clause against an EQUAL PROTECTION attack. Quite properly, the Court omitted mention of *Lane v. Wilson;* it did say, however, that in cases of ECONOMIC REGULATION, "only the INVIDIOUS DISCRIMINATION" was invalid.

KENNETH L. KARST
(1986)

Bibliography

SCHMIDT, BENNO C., JR.   1982   Principle and Prejudice: The Supreme Court and Race in the Progressive Era. Part 3: Black Disfranchisement from the KKK to the Grandfather Clause. *Columbia Law Review* 82:835–905.

GRAND JURY

Historians date the grand jury to King Henry II's Assize of Clarendon in 1166. That ancient ancestor was markedly different from its American descendants. The Grand Assize, as it was known, was comprised of local gentry, relying on personal knowledge and local rumor to report alleged cases of misconduct. Today's grand jury—surviving in America, but since 1933 abolished in England—normally considers events and people unknown to the grand jurors, who receive fairly formal testimony and other EVIDENCE, presented by prosecutors to decide whether or not alleged wrongdoers ought to be indicted.

Between 1166 and 1791, when the American BILL OF RIGHTS was adopted, the grand jury had come to be viewed as a safeguard for the people rather than an investigative arm of the executive. This is reflected in the portion of the Fifth Amendment that says: "No person shall be held to answer for a capital, or otherwise infamous crime, unless on a PRESENTMENT or INDICTMENT of a Grand Jury, except in cases arising in the land or naval forces, or in the Militia, when in actual service in time of War or public danger."

This means that nobody outside the armed forces may be put to trial for a serious federal crime unless a grand jury has heard enough evidence to satisfy it that there is PROBABLE CAUSE (enough evidence on the prosecution side, largely or wholly ignoring what the defendant may show, to make it reasonable) to issue an indictment. The good sense of the safeguard is the realization that "merely" being brought to trial can be an agonizing, expensive, destructive experience. In this light, the grand jury stands as a shield against arbitrary or wicked or careless prosecutors bringing people to trial on insufficient or improper grounds.

In modern times, this role as bulwark retains an exceedingly limited reality. As a practical matter, grand juries, especially in the busy urban settings where they do the bulk of their work, function largely as the investigative and indicting arms of prosecutorial officials. There could be no other feasible or acceptable way for them to operate. The detection of crime, the decision to investigate, the judgment as to where prosecution resources should be invested are no longer, if they ever were, subjects suitable for amateur, part-time management. Inevitably, then, grand jurors work almost entirely under the guidance and effective control of prosecutors. They consider cases brought to them by the government's lawyers. They tend almost always to indict when they are advised to indict, and not otherwise.

Although this quality of "rubber stamp" is markedly unlike the constitutional ideal, there is no agreeable alternative if we are to keep the grand jury as a body of lay citizens. The grand jury is a potent instrument for invading PRIVACY, threatening reputations, and cutting a swath of terror and anxiety if it proceeds without a prudent awareness of its impact and a deep sense of its duty to be fair and discreet. In the hands of untrained people, it would be an engine of destruction. Such considerations might point in the end to abolishing the grand jury altogether. But while and wherever it survives, the leadership role of professionals is probably desirable as well as inevitable.

The passive character of the grand jury should not, however, be overstated. In strict law, the grand jury is an agency of the court rather than of the prosecution. A judge of the court is required to instruct the jurors concerning their powers and responsibilities. A judge should be available to answer questions and give guidance as the group proceeds with its work. Properly performed, these judicial directions can promote some measure of the independent judgment and common-sense wisdom that grand jurors are in principle expected to supply. Grand jurors do in fact decline now and again to return indictments sought by the prosecution. In far fewer cases "runaway" grand juries may contrive to investigate and indict people whom the prosecutors, for reasons that may be good or bad, do not deem suitable targets. These occurrences are, however, rare indeed, and usually happen in circumstances of local disarray and political upset.

In its normal functioning, the grand jury operates as a peculiar variant of the familiar Anglo-American judicial process—in some measure aping courtroom procedures but differing in fundamental respects. The similarity consists mainly in the types of evidence and, partially, in the mode of presentation. Grand juries hear witnesses under oath, proceeding by question and answer in something close to the style of the courtroom, with a prosecuting attorney doing most or all of the interrogation. Similarly, the grand jurors are given documents or other things as "exhibits" to assist in the attempted reconstruction, or partial reconstruction, of the events under inquiry. A critical difference from the courtroom is the one-sidedness of the presentation. In a system that prides itself on being "adversarial"—as distinguished from the so-called inquisitorial system of the European continent and many other countries—the grand jury is more purely inquisitorial and nonadversarial than almost any other criminal law agency anywhere. Subject to some variations among the states, the norm is that only one side, the prosecution, is heard. There is no opposing lawyer to object to questions or answers on grounds of relevance, fairness, privilege, or anything else. Nobody impartial presides; there are no disputes to umpire. In some places a potential defendant may be allowed on request to appear and present evidence that may persuade the grand jurors not to indict. More commonly, the prospective target will be heard only upon being summoned (and duly warned about the RIGHT AGAINST SELF-INCRIMINATION) by the prosecution.

The EX PARTE character of the proceeding means, in most states and in the federal courts, that the trial rules of evidence are not applicable. These rules require for effective operation the presence of an opposing lawyer to object and a judicial officer to rule on objections as the evidentiary record is being made. Free (or deprived) of all that, the grand jury may receive, and base indictments upon, hearsay or other evidence that would be excluded on objection in a trial.

Still more thoroughly ex parte, the grand jury's proceedings, until an indictment is published, are almost totally secret. This aspect accounts for a good part of what is perceived (and not infrequently functions) as fearsome and threatening in the grand jury. The concealed tribunal is by its nature more likely than the open courtroom to be a place where corners are cut and abuses are perpetrated, ranging from the tricking and bullying of witnesses to the misleading of the grand jurors themselves. Still, the received doctrine thought to justify the secrecy retains considerable vitality. As they were summarized in 1958 by the Supreme Court, the reasons are:

(1) To prevent the escape of those whose indictment may be contemplated; (2) to insure the utmost freedom to the grand jury in its deliberations, and to prevent persons subject to indictment or their friends from importuning the grand jurors; (3) to prevent subornation of perjury or tampering with the witnesses who may testify before [the] grand jury and later appear at the trial of those indicted

by it; (4) to encourage free and untrammeled disclosures by persons who have information with respect to the commission of crimes; (5) to protect [the] innocent accused who is exonerated from disclosure of the fact that he has been under investigation, and from the expense of standing trial where there was no probability of guilt. [*United States v. Procter & Gamble Company*, 356 U.S. 677, 681 n. 6 (1958).]

Granting these salutary concerns, the concealed proceedings of grand juries are pregnant with grave possibilities of abuse, too often realized in the work of insensitive or malevolent prosecutors. As mentioned, witnesses in the grand jury room face dangers of abuse, oppression, harassment, and entrapment. Judge LEARNED HAND, never tender in enforcing the criminal law, noted this familiar problem in *United States v. Remington* (2d Cir. 1953) where he thought decent bounds had been overstepped: "Save for torture, it would be hard to find a more effective tool of tyranny than the power of unlimited and unchecked ex parte examination."

A grand jury has the power to compel witnesses to testify. (See IMMUNITY GRANTS; BRANZBURG V. HAYES.) The plight of a grand jury witness is aggravated by the standard rule, in federal and most state courts, barring lawyers from accompanying witnesses to the grand jury room. Abstruse questions of privilege, the ever present dangers of later perjury prosecutions, and problems of relevance or other evidentiary objections must be discerned by the lay witness and somehow handled on the spot or made the subject of hurried consultation with counsel outside the grand jury room, an ungainly procedure that often has witnesses trotting back and forth between lawyer and grand jurors during hours or days of interrogation.

Among other grievances evoked by grand juries is the superficially paradoxical complaint against failures of secrecy. The grand jury "leak" is a familiar and pernicious phenomenon, scarring reputations and threatening the right to a FAIR TRIAL. The problems of preventing and sanctioning leaks remain among the unresolved doubts concerning the grand jury's net worth as an institution. Probably all these criticisms have helped persuade the Supreme Court not to extend the INCORPORATION DOCTRINE, applying the "right" to indictment by grand jury to state felony prosecutions. (See HURTADO V. CALIFORNIA.)

These unresolved doubts are subjects of ongoing debate. Many distinguished jurists and scholars argue that the grand jury has outlived its usefulness and should be abolished. That is a tall order at the federal level, where it would require amendment of the Fifth Amendment (which would be the first change in any portion of the Bill of Rights since its adoption). On the other hand, over half the states have dispensed with the requirement of grand jury indictment, permitting felonies to be prosecuted by INFORMATION (a written accusation by the prosecutor), and that trend seems likely to continue.

Still, at the federal level and in at least a number of states, total abolition seems highly improbable through at least the remainder of the twentieth century. In this setting, grand jury reform is a recurrently lively topic. Among the proposals (and changes already effected in some states) are provisions that would allow counsel to accompany witnesses before the grand jury; require closer control and supervision by judges; prescribe more detailed accounting by prosecutors and records of grand jury proceedings; better advise and protect prospective defendants; and confine the abuses of leaks and prejudicial publicity by prosecutorial staffs. The prospects for sound reform are greatest when citizens outside the legal profession take an informed interest in the problems.

MARVIN E. FRANKEL
(1986)

Bibliography

DASH, SAMUEL   1972   The Indicting Grand Jury: A Critical Stage. *American Criminal Law Review* 10:807–828.

FRANKEL, MARVIN E. and NAFTALIS, GARY P.   1975   *The Grand Jury.* New York: Hill & Wang.

NOTE   1961   The Grand Jury as an Investigatory Body. *Harvard Law Review* 74:590–605.

YOUNGER, RICHARD D.   1963   *The People's Panel: The Grand Jury in the United States.* Providence, R.I.: Brown University Press.

GRAND JURY
(Update)

The grand jury clause of the Fifth Amendment is an anomaly. It gives constitutional stature to a secret inquisitorial process that is quite at odds with the open adversarial character of the remainder of the federal judicial system. The clause preserves the institution of the grand jury without placing it clearly within any of the three branches of the federal government. The federal grand jury, like its English progenitor, has two conflicting functions. The guarantee of review by a grand jury was included in the Fifth Amendment because the grand jury serves as a shield or buffer protecting individuals against baseless or malicious charges. But the grand jury also has another side: it serves as an investigatory agency that ferrets out crime.

Since the original publication of this encyclopedia in 1986 the Supreme Court has decided six grand jury cases. Four involved prosecutorial errors or abuses that could impair the grand jury's ability to shield individuals from unfounded charges. In each case, the question was the availability of a judicial remedy. The other two cases considered the ramifications of grand jury secrecy.

The issue of remedies for abuse of the grand jury reached the Supreme Court because of the lower courts' increasing willingness to invalidate federal INDICTMENTS if the government committed errors at the grand jury phase. Until the mid-1970s, federal courts showed little inclination to police the grand jury process to ensure that it fulfilled its constitutional function of protecting the accused against unfounded criminal charges. In *Costello v. United States* (1956) the Supreme Court held that the federal grand jury was to operate, like its English progenitor, free of technical rules of evidence and procedure. Under the influence of *Costello*, the lower federal courts typically refused to consider claims of error or abuse in the grand jury process. Beginning in the mid-1970s, some lower courts became increasingly willing to review grand jury proceedings and consider claims of abuse, with the understanding that the indictment might be dismissed if the claims were well founded. Grand jury litigation was attractive to the defense because, even if the indictment was not dismissed, the review process offered an opportunity for discovery otherwise precluded by jury secrecy.

Three of the Supreme Court's recent decisions rebuffed the lower courts' efforts to ensure that the grand jury fulfilled its protective function. In the first of the three decisions, *United States v. Mechanik* (1986), the Court held that any error that had occurred at the grand jury stage was harmless in light of the jury's guilty verdict. The Court stated that the federal rule limiting the persons who could be present during grand jury sessions was designed to protect against the danger of charges not supported by PROBABLE CAUSE. The trial jury's guilty verdict established that there was proof beyond a REASONABLE DOUBT of the defendant's guilt and thus any violation of the procedural rule at the grand jury phase was harmless. Reversal of a conviction entails significant social costs. A retrial burdens witnesses, victims, the prosecution, and the courts. If the prosecution is unable to retry the defendant after the first conviction is reversed, the social cost is even greater. These costs are not justified, the Court concluded, where an error at the grand jury stage had no effect on the outcome of the trial.

Although *Mechanik* was criticized as an open invitation to prosecutors to disregard grand jury procedures, it left open two possible avenues of JUDICIAL REVIEW and relief. First, some lower courts held that *Mechanik* did not limit the federal courts' supervisory powers. This interpretation left the courts free to grant relief from grand jury abuse, even in the absence of demonstrable prejudice in the exercise of supervisory power. Second, several circuits permitted defendants to bring interlocutory appeals seeking review of unfavorable pretrial rulings on grand jury issues under the collateral order doctrine, on the theory that the issues would be mooted by the verdict.

The Supreme Court eventually resolved both of these issues, again rebuffing the lower courts' efforts to police the grand jury process. In *Bank of Nova Scotia v. United States* (1988), the Court applied the HARMLESS ERROR rule announced in *Mechanik* to supervisory power rulings. *Mechanik* and *Bank of Nova Scotia* increased the pressure on the appellate courts to grant interlocutory review on claims of grand jury abuse, and the Supreme Court was forced to turn next to the issue of interlocutory appeals. In *Midland Asphalt Corp. v. United States* (1989), the Court concluded that interlocutory review would be available on claims of grand jury abuse only when the defendant alleged a defect so fundamental that it caused the grand jury not to be a grand jury or the indictment not to be an indictment.

Taken together, *Mechanik*, *Bank of Nova Scotia*, and *Midland Asphalt* demonstrate the Supreme Court's unwillingness to subject the grand jury's internal proceedings to judicial review. *Midland Asphalt* holds that interlocutory appeal ordinarily is not permitted if the trial judge denies relief on a grand jury claim before trial. *Mechanik* and *Bank of Nova Scotia* hold that if the defendant is convicted and appeals, the jury's guilty verdict moots any error in the grand jury process. Relief is theoretically available in the district court before trial, but given grand jury secrecy, the defendant will seldom have sufficient information about the grand jury process at this point to make the necessary showing of government error and resulting prejudice. These decisions reflect a firm consensus on the Court. Eight members of the Court joined the opinion in *Bank of Nova Scotia*, and the opinion in *Midland Asphalt* was unanimous. Given the limited resources available to the CRIMINAL JUSTICE SYSTEM, the Court is simply unwilling to divert judicial resources to a preliminary trial of the grand jury process, particularly when there is no indication that the outcome of a case will change. The Court's decisions avoid not only the cost of reversals in cases where there has been a serious abuse of the grand jury but also the cost of extensive judicial review (with the resultant breach in grand jury secrecy) in all cases.

The Supreme Court did reverse one conviction because of an error at the grand jury stage in a case involving what the Court called the "special problem of racial discrimination." In *Vasquez v. Hillery* (1986) the Court held that racial discrimination in the selection of the grand jury required the reversal of a twenty-year-old murder conviction, even if the state could not reprosecute so long after the original conviction. In a striking contrast to *Mechanik*, which was decided during the same term, the Court rejected the argument that the discrimination at the grand

jury phase was harmless error in light of the jury's guilty verdict after a fair trial. Emphasizing that racial discrimination strikes at the fundamental values of the criminal justice system, the Court concluded that the remedy of dismissing the indictment and reversing the resulting conviction was not disproportionate. Although the constitutional prohibition against racial discrimination was the driving force behind this decision, it is worth noting that claims of racial discrimination at the selection stage (unlike the claims in *Mechanik*, *Bank of Nova Scotia*, and *Midland Asphalt*) can be adjudicated without any breach of grand jury secrecy. Traditionally secrecy is required only after the grand jury has been impaneled.

The Court also decided two cases involving facets of grand jury secrecy. *United States v. John Doe, Inc. I* (1987) dealt with the question of when the government can use materials collected in a grand jury investigation. *Doe* effectively cut back on an earlier decision that held grand jury secrecy prohibits prosecutors from disclosing grand jury evidence to other government lawyers for use in civil proceedings unless the prosecutors obtain a court order based upon a showing of particularized need. This rule ensured that prosecutors had no incentive to misuse the grand jury for civil discovery and decreased the likelihood that grand jury secrecy will be breached. *Doe* gave the grand jury secrecy rule a narrow interpretation, allowing prosecutors conducting grand jury proceedings freely to disclose grand jury materials to civil division attorneys with whom they were consulting about the desirability of filing a civil suit. Permitting informal disclosure without judicial supervision facilitated the government's determination whether to proceed civilly or criminally without duplicative investigations by civil attorneys.

The Court also recognized that the FIRST AMENDMENT places limits on the principle of grand jury secrecy. *Butterworth v. Smith* (1990) held that the Florida rule prohibiting a witness from ever diclosing his own testimony violates the First Amendment. The Court found that the state's interests were not sufficient to justify a permanent ban on a reporter's right to make a truthful statement of information that he gathered on his own before he was called to testify. Although neither the federal rules nor those in the majority of states would have prohibited disclosure under those circumstances, fourteen other states have secrecy rules like Florida's. The Court did not question the validity of the more narrowly drawn federal and state secrecy rules.

SARA SUN BEALE
(1992)

Bibliography

ARNELLA, PETER 1980 Reforming the Federal Grand Jury and the State Preliminary Hearing to Prevent Conviction Without Adjudication. *Michigan Law Review* 78:463–585.

BEALE, SARA SUN and BRYSON, WILLIAM C.　1986　and Supp. 1990 *Grand Jury Law and Practice*. Wilmette, Ill.: Callaghan.

NOTE [ARFAA, CHRISTOPHER M.] 1988 *Mechanikal* Applications of the Harmless Error Rule in Cases of Prosecutorial Grand Jury Misconduct. *Duke Law Journal* 1988:1242–1271.

GRAND RAPIDS SCHOOL DISTRICT v. BALL

See: *Aguilar v. Felton*

GRANGER CASES
(1877)

Munn v. Illinois, 94 U.S. 113

Chicago, Burlington & Quincy Railroad Co. v. Iowa, 94 U.S. 155

Peik v. Chicago & Northwestern Railway Co., 94 U.S. 164

Chicago, Milwaukee & St. Paul Railroad Co. v. Ackley, 94 U.S. 179

Winona and St. Peter Railroad Co. v. Blake, 94 U.S. 180

Stone v. Wisconsin, 94 U.S. 181

The *Granger Cases*, decided on March 1, 1877, included *Munn v. Illinois*, in which state regulation of grain warehouse and elevator rates and practices was challenged, and five railroad cases in which the companies attacked the validity of state legislatures' imposition of fixed maximum rates. In these decisions, the Supreme Court upheld the state regulations. Conservative, pro-business voices—and Justice STEPHEN J. FIELD, in vigorous dissent in *Munn*—regarded the decisions as a catastrophic surrender of DUE PROCESS values in law and a mortal blow to entrepreneurial liberty. They left legislatures, Field contended, with an unfettered power over private PROPERTY RIGHTS of business firms. To the Court's majority, speaking through Chief Justice MORRISON R. WAITE, however, the issue of state regulation's legitimacy must turn on the difference in nature between business that was purely private and business that was AFFECTED WITH A PUBLIC INTEREST, hence peculiarly subject to regulation.

Laws for the regulation of railroads and grain warehouses, enacted in Illinois, Wisconsin, Iowa, and Minnesota during the period 1871–1874, were at issue in the 1877 decisions. Until recent years, historians and students of constitutional law have tended to accept the view that the Grange and other farm organizations provided the political muscle in the midwestern reform movements that produced those laws. Indeed, it was customary to regard the legislation as radical, antibusiness, and anti-private property in intent and content. Recent research (particularly the work of historian George L. Miller) has shown, however, that there was no general antagonism between agrarian and business interests in the debates over the regulatory laws. Instead, reform was sought by coalitions, in a pattern of intrastate sectionalism; farmers lined up with commercial interests in some sections that favored regulation, and similar interests joined against regulation in other sections. The division of views depended much more upon calculations of local advantage and disadvantage from regulation than upon political ideology, "agrarian" or otherwise, or even upon political party alignments.

Contrary to another view long held by scholars, the Granger laws did not lack legislative precedent. The charters of early railway companies typically had carried maximum rate provisions and other features that bespoke the state's interest in the efficient provision of transport services. And in the 1850s several states (notably New York and Ohio) had prohibited local discrimination in railroad rate-making and had levied special taxes on railroad companies to offset the effects of rail competition on state-owned canals. The Granger laws may be seen as an extension of a regulatory tradition well established in American railway law.

Still another common error of interpretation concerns the doctrinal basis of the "affectation" doctrine as employed in Waite's majority opinion in *Munn*. The concept of "business affected with a public interest," according to a long-standard view, was a surprising resort to a forgotten antiquity of English COMMON LAW—a concept reintroduced into American law after a lapse of nearly two centuries. In fact, the concept of affectation was well known in American riparian and ADMIRALTY law; and equally familiar was the jurist from whose writings Waite drew the affectation concept for use in *Munn*, for Lord Chief Justice Matthew Hale's tracts on common law had been cited in scores of important American cases in riparian and EMINENT DOMAIN law.

The Court's majority in the *Granger Cases* rejected the contention of railroad counsel that if state legislatures were permitted to mandate fixed, maximum rates, the result would be to deprive business of fair profits, and thus to produce effective "confiscation" of private property. The majority also rejected the view that the EQUAL PROTECTION and due process clauses of the Fourteenth Amendment warranted judicial review of the fairness of rates. Such regulatory power was subject to abuse, Waite conceded, but this was "no argument against its existence. For protection against abuses by legislatures the people must resort to the polls, not to the courts."

Thus the *Granger Cases* decisions held back, at least for a time, the conservative efforts to make the Fourteenth Amendment a fortress for VESTED RIGHTS against the STATE POLICE POWER. The decisions were also of enduring importance in constitutional development for their elaborate formulation of the "affectation with a public interest" doctrine. Relying upon the advice of his colleague Justice JOSEPH P. BRADLEY, who was learned in the English law of common carriers and in admiralty law, Waite explored in his opinion the legitimate reach of the police power in regulation of business. He concluded that modern railroad companies and warehouses played a role in commerce that was analogous to the role played by ferry operators and others who in the seventeenth century had exercised a "virtual monopoly" of vital commercial services, hence were held subject to regulations not ordinarily imposed on other businesses. Thus the Court indicated, by implication at least, that businesses not so affected with a special public interest could not be regulated.

Not long after publication of the decisions, Waite wrote privately: "The great difficulty in the future will be to establish the boundary between that which is private, and that in which the public has an interest. The Elevators furnished an extreme case, and there was no difficulty in determining on which side of the line they properly belonged." This proved an accurate forecast of the Court's future travails, until in *Nebbia v. New York* (1934) the Court finally abandoned the "affectation" doctrine, holding that *all* businesses were subject to state regulation under the police power.

Within fifteen years after the *Granger Cases*, moreover, the Court had begun to invoke both the COMMERCE CLAUSE and the Fourteenth Amendment to strike down state regulations of interstate railroad operations and to review both procedural and substantive aspects of state regulation of business. The drive to establish a new constitutional foundation for vested rights, in sum, for many years relegated the *Granger Cases'* support of a broad legislative discretion to the status of a doctrinal relic.

HARRY N. SCHEIBER
(1986)

Bibliography

FAIRMAN, CHARLES 1953 "The So-Called Granger Cases, Lord Hale, and Justice Bradley." *Stanford Law Review* 5:587–679.

MAGRATH, C. PETER 1963 *Morrison R. Waite: The Triumph of Character*. New York: Macmillan.

MILLER, GEORGE L. 1971 *Railroads and the Granger Laws*. Madison: University of Wisconsin Press.

SCHEIBER, HARRY N. 1971 The Road to *Munn*: Eminent Domain and the Concept of Public Purpose in the State Courts. *Perspectives in American History* 5:327–402.

GRANT, ULYSSES SIMPSON
(1822–1885)

Next to President ABRAHAM LINCOLN, Ulysses S. Grant was the most important individual in the struggle to maintain the Union and the RECONSTRUCTION of the nation in the CIVIL WAR period. A West Point graduate, Grant left the military in 1854 but returned as a colonel in the Illinois Volunteers in 1861. By 1864 Grant had risen to become America's first lieutenant general since Washington, and commander of all Union forces. Throughout the war Grant understood that victory was synonymous with preserving the Union and the Constitution. He developed strategies that devastated the South, because he believed that only a decisive defeat of the Confederacy, with a military abolition of SLAVERY and an unconditional surrender of southern troops, would remove SECESSION from the American constitutional vocabulary.

In 1866 Grant became America's first full general, and he gradually challenged ANDREW JOHNSON's leadership. Grant accepted an interim appointment as secretary of war, in defiance of the TENURE OF OFFICE ACT, but he relinquished the post to EDWIN M. STANTON, paving the way for Johnson's IMPEACHMENT. As President (1869–1877), Grant supported the FIFTEENTH AMENDMENT (1870), the Ku Klux Klan Act (1871), the Civil Rights Act of 1875, and the creation of a Department of Justice and SOLICITOR GENERAL's office to help enforce these new measures. However, after 1872 Grant gave little support to the freedmen and their white allies. He dismissed his aggressively integrationist attorney general, Amos Akerman, and in 1875–1876 he refused to send federal troops to protect black voters.

Three of Grant's Supreme Court nominees were never confirmed while a fourth, Edwin Stanton, died before he could take office. Apart from JOSEPH BRADLEY, Grant's successful Court appointments to the Court, WILLIAM STRONG, WARD HUNT, and MORRISON WAITE, were lackluster. Grant's administration was scandal-ridden. His secretary of war was impeached and avoided conviction only through resignation.

PAUL FINKELMAN
(1986)

Bibliography

MCFEELY, WILLIAM S. 1981 *Grant: A Biography*. New York: Norton.

GRANTS-IN-AID

See: Federal Grants-in-Aid

GRAVEL v. UNITED STATES
408 U.S. 606 (1972)

In the midst of efforts by the United States government to enjoin publication of the classified Pentagon Papers (see NEW YORK TIMES CO. V. UNITED STATES), Senator Mike Gravel (Democrat, Alaska) held a "meeting" of his subcommittee, read extensively from the papers, and placed their entire text in the record. In this case a federal GRAND JURY sought to question Gravel's aide concerning the senator's action and the subsequent private publication of the papers. The Supreme Court, in an opinion by Justice BYRON R. WHITE and over four dissents, confirmed that reading the papers in subcommittee was protected by the SPEECH OR DEBATE CLAUSE. The clause also extended its protection to congressional aides acting as alter egos to members of Congress. But *Gravel* held that dissemination of the papers to a private publisher was not a legislative act, and thus was not protected by the speech or debate clause. Therefore, Gravel's aide could be questioned about the private publication of the papers.

THEODORE EISENBERG
(1986)

GRAVES v. NEW YORK EX REL. O'KEEFE
306 U.S. 466 (1939)

For practical purposes the decision in *Graves* by a 7–2 Supreme Court toppled an elaborate structure of INTERGOVERNMENTAL TAX IMMUNITIES, which the Justices had erected from assumptions about the federal system. The right of self-preservation immunized the United States and the states from taxation by competing governments within the system. Obviously the United States cannot tax the Commonwealth of Massachusetts or the state capitol in Sacramento, California, any more than the states can tax a congressional investigation. From a sensible assumption first advanced in MCCULLOCH V. MARYLAND (1819) protecting a national instrumentality from state taxation, the Court made progressively sillier decisions that hampered the TAXING POWER of the state and national governments and allowed many commercial activities to escape taxation. COLLECTOR V. DAY (1871) made the salaries of state judges exempt from federal income taxes. In time the Court held unconstitutional a federal tax on the income of a private corporation leasing state land, and a federal sales tax on a motorcycle sold by a private corporation to city police.

By 1939 the Court had already begun to retrench its doctrines of reciprocal tax immunities enjoyed by "government" instrumentalities. In *Graves*, Justice HARLAN FISKE STONE faced the question whether a state tax on the salary of an employee of a federal instrumentality created by Congress violated the principles of national supremacy. Stone observed that the tax was imposed on an employee's salary, not on the instrumentality itself. Because the Constitution did not mandate tax immunity and such immunity should attach only to a government instrumentality, the Court not only sustained the tax but also overruled *Day* and several related cases. A state may tax the income of officers or employees of the national government, and vice versa. In *New York v. United States* (1946), the Court upheld a national tax on soft drinks bottled by the state. To the extent that government functions cannot be be taxed by another government the core doctrine from *McCulloch* endures.

LEONARD W. LEVY
(1986)

GRAY, HORACE
(1828–1902)

Horace Gray, Jr., reporter of the Supreme Judicial Court of Massachusetts (1854–1861) and Associate Justice (1864–1873) and Chief Justice (1873–1881) of the same court, was appointed to the United States Supreme Court in 1882 and served until his death twenty years later. Anglo-American legal history was his forte; he was the nation's leading judicial exponent of Harvard-style "legal science" during the second half of the nineteenth century. Like Dean Christopher Columbus Langdell, his Harvard classmate and lifelong friend, Gray viewed the law neither as the changing product of specific historical struggles nor as an imperfect reflection of "the spirit of the age" but rather as an array of immanent principles firmly rooted in a vibrant COMMON LAW tradition. Consequently he insisted on a radical separation of law from politics, linking the former with reason and the latter with will and power. According to John Chipman Gray, his commitment to these central concepts of "legal science" was complete yet unreflexive. "My brother's historical knowledge was confined to a knowledge of legal precedents," he wrote in 1902. "In this sphere he was not only learned, but his treatment of historical matter was strong and broad: but, outside of that, he made and had no pretensions. He was neither a philosophical historian nor a political economist."

Gray's understanding of Anglo-American legal history produced an idiosyncratic style of judging with significant implications for CONSTITUTIONAL INTERPRETATION. His treatise-like opinions were bereft of appeals to public policy or social advantage; because he assumed that the validity of legal rules was unrelated to particular historical contexts, Gray was virtually immune to both historicist and functionalist arguments against the constitutionality of legislation. In *Wabash, St. Louis & Pacific Railway v. Illinois*, (1886), *Robbins v. Shelby County Taxing District* (1887), and LEISY V. HARDIN (1890), for example, he dissented when the majority invoked national market imperatives to invalidate state police regulations and tax laws of a sort that had never before run afoul of the COMMERCE CLAUSE. Gray also resisted the majority's contraction of what he regarded as venerable SOVEREIGN IMMUNITY doctrines in *United States v. Lee* (1882) and the *Virginia Coupon Cases* (1885).

Gray's metahistorical approach to judging was especially apparent in Fourteenth Amendment cases. In *Head v. Amoskeag Manufacturing Company* (1884) and *Wurts v. Hoagland* (1885) he conceded that mill acts and drainage laws invariably disturbed valuable rights of property. In each case, however, Gray provided a lengthy digest of statutes to demonstrate that the several states had authorized compulsory flooding or drainage of property for one hundred years or more. It was simply too late, then, for the Court to suggest that such legislation took property either for private use or without JUST COMPENSATION in violation of the DUE PROCESS clause. Similar considerations prompted Gray's dissent in the landmark SUBSTANTIVE DUE PROCESS case of CHICAGO, MILWAUKEE & ST. PAUL RAILWAY V. MINNESOTA (1890). And in *Budd v. New York* (1892), where the Court upheld a New York statute fixing rates of charge for grain storage, he supplied the majority's spokesman with a long memorandum "showing that the prices of necessary articles were controlled by the legislature, in England and America, at the time of the adoption of the State and National Constitutions." His authorities included Hening's statutes of colonial Virginia and a 1709 act of Parliament regulating coal prices.

Gray voted with the majority in every case involving the rights of racial minorities decided during his tenure on the Court. Yet his route to the results often differed substantially from that of his colleagues. If Gray had been assigned PLESSY V. FERGUSON (1896), for example, he would no doubt have supplied a thorough digest of state legislation, as well as acts of Congress pertaining to the DISTRICT OF COLUMBIA, in an attempt to show that racial classifications in "social" contexts had been just as common in American law after ratification of the FOURTEENTH AMENDMENT as before. Legal history, not the conservative sociology that figured so prominently in HENRY B. BROWN's opinion or the natural justice to which JOHN MARSHALL HARLAN appealed in dissent, shaped Gray's construction of minority rights. Thus his associates were not surprised by his opinion in UNITED STATES V. WONG KIM ARK (1898), confirming the CITIZENSHIP claim of a Chinese child born in the United States, even though he had also spoken for the Court in *Elk v. Wilkins* (1884), denying the same claim

when filed by an American Indian who had left a government reservation and renounced all privileges of tribal membership. In Gray's view, the anomalous status of Indians as wards of the nation had already been fixed by nine decades of administrative usage. But the status of persons born of unnaturalizable ALIENS was a new question in American law. Consequently he assumed that *Wong Kim Ark* could be decided only after an examination of all the juridical authorities on birthright citizenship running back to CALVIN'S CASE (1608).

It is ironic that Gray is best known as the probable "vacillating Justice" in POLLOCK V. FARMER'S LOAN & TRUST CO. (1895). We shall never know for certain whether he changed his vote on the validity of the income tax following the second hearing; but, as EDWARD S. CORWIN observed, "the surprising thing would be not that Gray was the last Justice to line up against the act, but that he should have done so at all." Gray's extraordinarily BROAD CONSTRUCTION of Congress's IMPLIED POWERS in *United States v. Jones* (1883), *Juilliard v. Greenman* (1884), and *Fong Yue Ting v. United States* (1893) underscored his constitutional nationalism. Yet he set a face of flint to HOWELL E. JACKSON's claim, in dissent, that *Pollock* was "the most disastrous blow ever struck at the constitutional power of Congress." It is equally astonishing that a self-conscious practitioner of historical method concurred in an opinion that, as Corwin put it, "played ducks and drakes with the precedents." The unkind verdict of modern scholarship is that even Gray, a jurist for whom the separation of law and politics ordinarily served as the very touchstone for judging, succumbed in *Pollock* to the reactionary impulse that gripped the legal profession at large during the turbulent 1890s.

CHARLES W. MCCURDY
(1986)

Bibliography

CORWIN, EDWARD S. 1938 *Court over Constitution*. Princeton, N.J.: Princeton University Press.
FILLER, LOUIS 1969 Horace Gray. Pages 1379–1389 in Leon Friedman and Fred L. Israel, eds., *The Justices of the United States Supreme Court, 1789–1969: Their Lives and Major Opinions*. New York: Chelsea House.

GRAY v. SANDERS
372 U.S. 368 (1963)

Gray, along with WESBERRY V. SANDERS (1964), was a waystation between BAKER V. CARR (1962) (legislative districting presents a justiciable controversy) and REYNOLDS V. SIMS (1964) (the ONE PERSON, ONE VOTE principle governs the issue). In *Gray*, the Supreme Court, 8–1, invalidated

Georgia's "county unit system," which weighed rural votes more heavily than urban votes in PRIMARY ELECTIONS for statewide offices. The state, said Justice WILLIAM O. DOUGLAS, was the electoral unit; within that unit, EQUAL PROTECTION demanded the principle of one person, one vote. Justice JOHN MARSHALL HARLAN dissented, drawing an analogy to the ELECTORAL COLLEGE.

KENNETH L. KARST
(1986)

GREAT ATLANTIC & PACIFIC TEA CO. v. COTTRELL
424 U.S. 366 (1976)

Mississippi allowed the resale of milk from another state only if that state reciprocally accepted Mississippi milk. A. & P. stores were refused a permit to sell Louisiana milk in Mississippi, even though Louisiana milk satisfied all Mississippi quality standards, because Louisiana had not entered a reciprocity agreement with Mississippi. Citing DEAN MILK CO. V. MADISON (1951), the Supreme Court, 8–0, held that the Mississippi law was an unconstitutional STATE REGULATION OF COMMERCE. The law severely burdened INTERSTATE COMMERCE without significantly promoting public health objectives; sales of Louisiana milk would have been allowed in the state if Louisiana had signed a reciprocity agreement. Mississippi could not "use the threat of economic isolation" to force other states into such agreements.

KENNETH L. KARST
(1986)

GREAT COMPROMISE

The defeat of the NEW JERSEY PLAN provoked the fiercest battle at the CONSTITUTIONAL CONVENTION OF 1787. Small-state nationalists believed that they could not obtain ratification of any constitution that put their states at the political mercy of the large ones. The struggle focused on representation in the bicameral Congress. Small-state delegates, seeking compromise, would accept representation in the lower house based on population, but as to the upper house they would not retreat from the principle of state equality. ROGER SHERMAN of Connecticut declared that he would agree to two houses with "proportional representation in one of them, provided each State have an equal voice in the other." WILLIAM S. JOHNSON of Connecticut explained that in one house "the people ought to be represented, in the other, the States." State representation was essential to a Union "partly national, partly federal,"

declared OLIVER ELLSWORTH of Connecticut. But the stubbornness of the large state faction resulted in a 5–5 tie vote on what would later be called the "Connecticut Compromise." Its initial defeat brought the convention, in Sherman's words, "to a full stop," and the convention stood at the brink of failure. Concessions were politically necessary. A special committee shrewdly recommended the compromise urged by Connecticut. That recommendation carried by the slimmest majority, averting a breakup of the convention. The principle of state equality having been won, small-state nationalists then supported a motion allowing members of the Senate to vote as individuals, although LUTHER MARTIN objected that individual voting violated "the idea of the *States* being represented."

LEONARD W. LEVY
(1986)

Bibliography

BRANT, IRVING 1950 *James Madison: Father of the Constitution, 1787–1800.* Pages 79–100. Indianapolis: Bobbs-Merrill.

GREEN v. BIDDLE
8 Wheaton 1 (1823)

This case extended the CONTRACT CLAUSE to INTERSTATE COMPACTS, the obligation of which a state may not impair. The Supreme Court, in an opinion by Justice JOSEPH STORY, voided Kentucky acts that failed to protect property rights guaranteed by that state's compact with Virginia, entered into when Kentucky became an independent state. On reargument, Senator HENRY CLAY defended the state. His Kentucky colleague, Senator Richard Johnson, inveighing against judicial "despotism" and "oligarchy," demanded repeal of section 25 of the JUDICIARY ACT OF 1789, proposed packing the Court, and sought a restriction of JUDICIAL REVIEW. Justice BUSHROD WASHINGTON, grounding the Court's second opinion in the contract clause, declared that "we hold ourselves answerable to God, our consciences and our country . . . be the consequences of the decision what they may." Kentucky passed state-sovereignty resolves, but congressional measures to limit judicial review and to repeal section 25 failed, because the Court's enemies were unable to unite behind one bill. Nevertheless hostility to the Court, further aggravated by OSBORN V. BANK OF THE UNITED STATES (1824), remained intense.

LEONARD W. LEVY
(1986)

GREEN v. COUNTY SCHOOL BOARD OF NEW KENT COUNTY
391 U.S. 430 (1968)

In states where racial segregation of school children had been commanded or authorized by law, the process of DE-SEGREGATION following BROWN V. BOARD OF EDUCATION (1954–1955) was impeded by officials' tactics of delay and evasion. One such tactic was the "freedom of choice" plan, which allowed pupils to select their schools. This "freedom" was often restricted by the fear of black parents that sending their children to formerly white schools would be followed by the loss of a job, or by violence and harassment directed at them or their children. In *Green*, the Supreme Court held that a rural Virginia county's "freedom of choice" plan was an insufficient remedy for segregation.

The Court took note of the practical restrictions on the freedom of black parents but did not rest decision on that ground. Instead the Court adopted a doctrinal position that reshaped the course of school desegregation. Justice WILLIAM J. BRENNAN, writing for a unanimous Court, reinterpreted *Brown II* (1955) to require "the dismantling of well-entrenched dual [segregated] systems." A school board had an affirmative duty "to come forward with a plan that . . . promises realistically to work *now*." A "freedom of choice" plan might possibly suffice, but where other alternatives were "more promising" the board must use them. The Court left no doubt that it had in mind the actual integration of black and white children as the index of success in dismantling a dual system.

In a small rural county with no residential segregation, integration would be easily achieved through geographical attendance zones and neighborhood schools. The question remained whether the Court would similarly insist on integrative results in large cities where housing was segregated. That question was answered affirmatively, three years after *Green*. (See SWANN V. CHARLOTTE-MECKLENBURG BOARD OF EDUCATION; SCHOOL BUSING.)

KENNETH L. KARST
(1986)

GREEN v. OKLAHOMA

See: Capital Punishment Cases of 1976

GREGG v. GEORGIA

See: Capital Punishment Cases of 1976

GREGORY v. ASHCROFT
501 U.S. 452 (1991)

In GARCÍA V. SAN ANTONIO METROPOLITAN TRANSIT AUTHORITY (1985), the Supreme Court eschewed its previous effort to insulate substantive enclaves of state activity from congressional regulation as "unsound in principle and unworkable in practice." According to the Court, state sovereign interests "are more properly protected by procedural safeguards inherent in the structure of the federal system than by judicially created limitations on federal power."

The Court supplemented the Constitution's inherent procedural safeguards in *Gregory v. Ashcroft*, by deploying a clear statement rule to protect states from congressional regulation. After outlining the advantages purportedly preserved by our constitutional regime of "dual sovereignty," the Court announced that it would interpret federal statutes not to regulate state governmental functions unless Congress makes its intent to do so "unmistakably clear in the language of the statute." The Court then construed the Age Discrimination in Employment Act not to override Missouri's mandatory retirement age for state judges.

The clear statement rule is controversial because it neither reflects an objective inquiry into LEGISLATIVE INTENT, nor is grounded in constitutional text, history, or structure. In this respect, *Gregory* may support further process-based FEDERALISM doctrines that are not constitutionally compelled, but nevertheless reasonably balance the competing values of national authority and state autonomy.

EVAN H. CAMINKER
(2000)

(SEE ALSO: *Age Discrimination Act; Statutory Interpretation*.)

GRIER, ROBERT C.
(1794–1870)

The SENATE on August 4, 1846, unanimously confirmed Robert Cooper Grier as the thirty-third Justice of the Supreme Court. President JAMES K. POLK nominated Grier because of his STATES' RIGHTS Democratic principles, his position on the FUGITIVE SLAVERY issue, and his familiarity through thirteen years of previous judicial experience with Pennsylvania's unique law of real property. The bar of Pennsylvania thought the last of these particularly important since Grier's duties included presiding over the Third Circuit which included Pennsylvania.

Grier embraced the concept of dual SOVEREIGNTY. He believed that the inherent state police powers included the power to curb the flow of liquor for purposes of public health and morality. (See LICENSE CASES.) Yet Grier also believed that the states could not interfere in areas of responsibility granted by the COMMERCE CLAUSE to the Congress. Thus, he sided with the narrow majority in the PASSENGER CASES (1849) in striking down taxes levied by two states on ship masters bringing immigrants to the United States.

Grier contributed significantly to the constitutional law of CORPORATIONS and PATENTS. He formulated an important legal fiction in *Marshall v. Baltimore and Ohio Railroad* (1853) by holding that for purposes of establishing federal JURISDICTION federal judges could assume that corporate officers resided in the state of incorporation. The decision aided litigants seeking access to federal courts and prevented a corporation from electing officers in the state of a complaining party in order to avoid a suit in federal court.

Because of his experience with patent litigation in the Third Circuit, Grier spoke for the Court in several important patent cases. He wrote the opinions in *Seymour v. McCormick* (1854) and *McCormick v. Talbot* (1858), which involved the exclusivity of Cyrus McCormick's patent on the reaper. In the 1864 case of *Burr v. Duryee*, the most important patent decision to that time, Grier, writing for the Court, held that the patent clause protected inventors of machinery but did not extend to scientific principles. The decision guaranteed accessibility to technical information in a rapidly expanding economy while protecting manufacturers in recovering the costs of developing new machinery.

Grier staunchly enforced the fugitive slave acts. He regularly charged circuit court juries to find for the rights of masters, even when it meant a hostile public reaction. Contrary to the position of Justice JOSEPH STORY in PRIGG V. PENNSYLVANIA (1842), Grier employed the dual sovereignty theory (in *Moore v. Illinois*, 1852) to assert that state and national governments shared a CONCURRENT POWER of rendition over fugitive slaves so long as the states did not interfere with the performance of federal officers.

Grier compromised his dual sovereignty principles in DRED SCOTT V. SANDFORD (1857). He initially opposed any decision that addressed the issues, and he urged his colleagues to adopt the rule of STRADER V. GRAHAM (1851) that the laws of the state in which a slave resided should prevail. President JAMES BUCHANAN, at the urging of Justice JOHN CATRON, wrote Grier urging him to add bisectional unity to a forceful resolution by the Court of the SLAVERY controversy. Grier succumbed, although he did so equivocally. His one-paragraph opinion concurred in Chief Justice ROGER B. TANEY's holding that the MISSOURI COMPROMISE was unconstitutional and in Justice SAMUEL NELSON's

position that the laws of Missouri established Dred Scott's legal status.

Grier's participation in the *Scott* case faded before his loyal unionism. His most notable constitutional contribution while a member of the Court came during the PRIZE CASES (1863). The owners of vessels and cargoes seized as prizes at the beginning of the CIVIL WAR argued that President ABRAHAM LINCOLN had imposed an unconstitutional blockade of southern ports, because Congress had not declared war. Grier spoke for a 5–4 majority in holding that Lincoln had acted constitutionally when confronted with hostilities of sizable proportions. The Justice circumvented the constitutional issues of presidential ursurpation and the definition of the conflict by stressing the President's inherent obligation to preserve the Union.

Grier tarnished his reputation by lingering on the Court after senility had taken its toll. The crisis came when the Justices considered the constitutionality of the Legal Tender Acts. In conference Grier voted in favor of the acts in *Hepburn v. Griswold* (1870), but when the Justices moved to consider the next case involving the same issue Grier's mind wandered. He switched his vote. (See LEGAL TENDER CASES.) With the prodding of Justice STEPHEN J. FIELD, Grier submitted his resignation in December 1869 and left the Court the following February. Six months later he died at his home in Philadelphia.

KERMIT L. HALL
(1986)

Bibliography

GATELL, FRANK O.   1969   Robert C. Grier. Pages 873–892 in Leon Friedman and Fred L. Israel, eds., *The Justices of the United States Supreme Court, 1789–1969: Their Lives and Major Opinions.* New York: Chelsea House.

GRIFFIN v. BRECKENRIDGE
403 U.S. 88 (1971)

This decision provided a generous construction of section 1985(3) of Title 42 of the United States Code and of Congress's power to reach private deprivations of CIVIL RIGHTS. Casting aside some constitutional considerations that had led to a more constricted reading of section 1985(3) in *Collins v. Hardyman* (1951), and effectively overruling UNITED STATES V. HARRIS (1883), the Court, in an opinion by Justice POTTER STEWART, concluded that section 1985(3) provides a cause of action against private conspiracies to violate constitutional rights. To avoid the "constitutional shoals that would lie in the path of interpreting 1985(3) as a general federal tort law," the Court required that the conspiracy be the product of some racial or other class-based animus.

THEODORE EISENBERG
(1986)

GRIFFIN v. CALIFORNIA
380 U.S. 609 (1965)

Overruling *Adamson v. California* (1947) without saying so, the Court, speaking through Justice WILLIAM O. DOUGLAS, held that state laws allowing adverse comment on the failure of a criminal defendant to take the stand and deny or explain evidence of which he had knowledge violated his RIGHT AGAINST SELF-INCRIMINATION. A jury acting on its own might infer what it wished, said Douglas, but what it infers "when the court solemnizes the silence of the accused into evidence against him is quite another thing" and imposes a penalty on the exercise of a constitutional right. Two dissenters argued that adverse comment on the right to silence did not compel the accused to be a witness against himself.

LEONARD W. LEVY
(1986)

GRIFFIN v. COUNTY SCHOOL BOARD OF PRINCE EDWARD COUNTY
377 U.S. 218 (1964)

Griffin, one of the school segregation cases decided with BROWN v. BOARD OF EDUCATION (1954–1955), arose in Prince Edward County, Virginia. In 1956 Virginia adopted legislation aimed at closing mixed-race schools and providing state aid to private schools. The state courts held much of this "massive resistance" legislation unconstitutional in 1959. The legislature responded by making compulsory school attendance a matter of local option and by authorizing TUITION GRANTS and property tax credits to help support private schools.

Meanwhile, the federal district court in *Griffin* had ordered the commencement of DESEGREGATION in the 1959–1960 year. The county school commissioners refused to levy school taxes for the year, and in the fall of 1959 the public schools of Prince Edward County remained closed. Private schools for white children were established, taking advantage of the state's financial aid. The *Griffin* plaintiffs challenged the constitutionality of this new response to *Brown*, and the case returned to the Supreme Court.

In an opinion by Justice HUGO L. BLACK, the Court held that closing the schools denied EQUAL PROTECTION to black pupils in the county. The Court acknowledged that no general equal protection principle required a state to treat all counties alike. However, the only reason for different treatment of this county's children was to ensure the continuation of racial segregation—an unconstitutional objective. (See LEGISLATION.)

Only the question of remedy divided the Court. All the Justices agreed that the TUITION GRANTS and tax credits should be enjoined while the public schools remained closed. (A federal court of appeals later enjoined them, irrespective of the closure of the public schools.) But the majority went further, authorizing the district court to order county officials to open the schools and, if necessary, to levy taxes to support them: "the time for mere "deliberate speed' has run out." Justices TOM C. CLARK and JOHN MARSHALL HARLAN briefly noted their disagreement with the holding that the federal courts had power to order the opening of the county's schools.

Griffin's doctrinal importance is twofold. It is an early suggestion of the state's affirmative obligation to equalize educational opportunity, and it is an early example of federal court intervention deep in the processes of local government. (See INSTITUTIONAL LITIGATION.) In practical terms, the episode also provides a sad example of "white flight." (See DESEGREGATION.) The county's public schools opened, but they were populated almost entirely by black pupils. A whites-only private school flourished, even without the aid of the state's money. Today, while it is true that such "segregation academies" cannot lawfully exclude applicants on account of race (see RUNYON V. MCCRARY), it is also true that their tuition fees are beyond the reach of most black families. When middle-class white children withdraw from desegregated schools—in Chicago and Los Angeles as well as Prince Edward County—the result is segregation by economic status and the likely continuation of continued racial segregation.

KENNETH L. KARST
(1986)

GRIFFIN v. ILLINOIS
351 U.S. 12 (1956)

Griffin was the first decision giving constitutional status to an INDIGENT person's claim to invalidate an economic barrier to his or her ACCESS TO THE COURTS.

Illinois normally required persons appealing from their criminal convictions to provide trial transcripts to the appellate courts. The state supplied free transcripts to INDIGENTS appealing in capital cases, but not in other cases. The Supreme Court held, 5–4, that the state must furnish a free transcript to an appellant in a noncapital case.

The opinion of Justice HUGO L. BLACK, for four Justices, rested on both due process and EQUAL PROTECTION grounds, asserting the state's constitutional obligation to provide "equal justice for poor and rich." Justice FELIX FRANKFURTER, concurring, emphasized the irrationality of the capitalnoncapital distinction. The dissenters found this distinction reasonable and argued that the state had no affirmative duty to alleviate the consequences of economic inequality.

Griffin, along with DOUGLAS V. CALIFORNIA (1963), raised expectations that the equal protection clause would be interpreted as a broad guarantee against WEALTH DISCRIMINATION, but these decisions are seen today as standing for a more modest proposition: that the right to state criminal appeals must not be foreclosed to the poor because of their poverty. (See ROSS V. MOFFITT.)

KENNETH L. KARST
(1986)

GRIFFITHS, IN RE

See: *Sugarman v. Dougall*

GRIGGS v. DUKE POWER CO.
401 U.S. 924 (1971)

Although subject to narrower interpretations, *Griggs* is viewed as establishing that employment selection criteria that disqualify blacks at higher rates than whites may violate Title VII of the CIVIL RIGHTS ACT OF 1964 even if the selection criteria are not chosen for discriminatory purposes. *Griggs* opened the door to vast numbers of Title VII actions seeking to establish violations through statistical analysis of the relative effect of employment criteria on minorities. *Griggs*'s emphasis on effects also influenced non-Title VII cases. Until WASHINGTON V. DAVIS (1976) was decided, many courts and analysts relied in part on *Griggs* to interpret the EQUAL PROTECTION clause to prohibit unequal effects. Even after *Davis, Griggs*'s effects test continued to influence litigation under Title VI of the Civil Rights Act of 1964, Title VIII of the CIVIL RIGHTS ACT OF 1968, and other provisions.

THEODORE EISENBERG
(1986)

(SEE ALSO: *Legislation.*)

GRIMAUD, UNITED STATES v.
220 U.S. 506 (1911)

In 1905, Congress authorized the secretary of agriculture to administer public lands set aside as forest reservations. Varying local conditions had made congressional regulation impractical, so the act designated him to make regulations respecting the use of these lands, violation of which would constitute a criminal offense. A federal district court judge held the act unconstitutional on the grounds that it constituted a delegation of legislative power to the executive and that it empowered the secretary to define federal crimes.

Justice JOSEPH R. LAMAR, speaking for a unanimous Supreme Court, sustained the act. The Court validated the delegation of broad discretion because "the authority to make administrative rules is not a delegation of legislative power." Even the imposition of criminal penalties did not render the regulations legislative. When a statute prescribes the penalty for a violation of administrative regulations, Congress—not the administrative officer—fixes the penalty. The notion, nurtured by this and other cases, that legislative DELEGATION OF POWER had become unimportant received a shock when the Court revived it in 1935 to strike down portions of the NATIONAL INDUSTRIAL RECOVERY ACT. (See PANAMA REFINING COMPANY V. RYAN.)

DAVID GORDON
(1986)

GRISWOLD, ERWIN N.
(1904–1994)

Erwin N. Griswold had a notable career as the dean of the Harvard Law School, SOLICITOR GENERAL of the United States, and a leading tax practitioner. Born in 1904, he was graduated from Oberlin College and from Harvard Law School, where he was president of the Harvard Law Review. Griswold served as an attorney in the Solicitor General's Office for five years, arguing many cases in the Courts of Appeals and the Supreme Court. Invited to join the Harvard Law faculty in 1934, he remained until 1967, serving as dean from 1946–1967. With his powerful, somewhat brusque personality, he was nevertheless a fairminded man, and he was heavily responsible for reinvigorating the Harvard Law School after WORLD WAR II. He also managed to find time to argue many cases in the Supreme Court, mostly tax matters.

Griswold resigned as dean in 1967 when appointed Solicitor General by President LYNDON B. JOHNSON, and he continued in that increasingly difficult role under President RICHARD M. NIXON until 1973. As Solicitor General, Griswold argued the government's losing position in the *Pentagon Papers* case, NEW YORK TIMES V. UNITED STATES (1971), and its winning position in both the DRAFT CARD BURNING case UNITED STATES V. O'BRIEN (1968) and the DESEGREGATION case SWANN V. CHARLOTTE-MECKLENBURG BOARD OF EDUCATION (1971), in which the use of large-scale

SCHOOL BUSING to remedy intentional segregation was first approved by the Court. He then went into private practice in Washington, D.C., where he continued an active appellate practice until his death in 1994.

In the 1950s, when Senator Joseph McCarthy was leading his anti-Communist crusade, Griswold, himself a Republican, made a major contribution to constitutional law in a series of lectures in which he defended the RIGHT AGAINST SELF-INCRIMINATION as an important part of our constitutional liberties. While at Harvard Law School, he also served the cause of racial justice by appearing as an expert witness for THURGOOD MARSHALL in CIVIL RIGHTS cases and by becoming an effective and energetic member of the United States Commission on Civil Rights. Griswold played a leading role in American law for sixty years as public and private practitioner, teacher, scholar, and legal educator.

ANDREW L. KAUFMAN
(2000)

Bibliography

GRISWOLD, ERWIN N. 1955 *The 5th Amendment Today.* Cambridge, Mass.: Harvard University Press.

GRISWOLD v. CONNECTICUT
381 U.S. 479 (1965)

Seen in the perspective of the development of constitutional doctrine, *Griswold* stands among the most influential Supreme Court decisions of the latter part of the twentieth century. A full understanding of its effect on the constitutional future requires a look at *Griswold's* antecedents. Even seen narrowly, *Griswold* was something of a culmination. The BIRTH CONTROL movement had made two previous unsuccessful attempts to get the Court to invalidate Connecticut's law forbidding use of contraceptive devices. In *Tileston v. Ullman* (1943) a doctor was held to lack STANDING to assert his patients' constitutional claims, and in *Poe v. Ullman* (1961), when a doctor and his patients sued in their own rights, the Court again dismissed—this time on jurisdictional grounds that could charitably be called ingenuous. *Griswold* proved to be the charm; operators of a birth control clinic had been prosecuted for aiding married couples to violate the law, furnishing them advice and contraceptive devices. The Supreme Court held the law invalid, 7–2.

Griswold fanned into flames a doctrinal issue that had smoldered in the Supreme Court for nearly two centuries: the question whether the Constitution protects NATURAL RIGHTS OR FUNDAMENTAL INTERESTS beyond those specifically mentioned in its text. (See CALDER V. BULL; FUNDAMENTAL LAW AND THE SUPREME COURT; HIGHER LAW.) In

the modern era, that question of CONSTITUTIONAL INTERPRETATION had focused on Justice HUGO L. BLACK's argument that the FOURTEENTH AMENDMENT fully incorporated the specific guarantees of the BILL OF RIGHTS and made them applicable to the states. Black's dissent in *Adamson v. California* (1947) had scorned the competing view, limiting the content of the Fourteenth Amendment DUE PROCESS to the fundamentals of ORDERED LIBERTY. This "natural-law-due-process formula," said Black, not only allowed judges to fail to protect rights specifically covered by the Constitution but also permitted them "to roam at large in the broad expanses of policy and morals," trespassing on the legislative domain. In *Adamson* Justice FRANK MURPHY had also dissented; accepting the INCORPORATION DOCTRINE, Murphy argued that other "fundamental" rights, beyond the specific guarantees of the Bill of Rights, were also protected by due process. *Griswold* offered a test of the Black and Murphy views.

Justice WILLIAM O. DOUGLAS, who had agreed with Black in *Adamson*, recognized that the Connecticut birth control law violated no specific guarantee of the Bill of Rights. A number of other guarantees, however, protected various aspects of PRIVACY, and all of them had "penumbras, formed by emanations from those guarantees that [helped] give them life and substance." The *Griswold* case concerned "a relationship lying within the zone of privacy created by several fundamental constitutional guarantees." The NINTH AMENDMENT recognized the existence of other rights outside those specifically mentioned in the Bill of Rights, and the right of marital privacy itself was "older than the Bill of Rights." Enforcement of Connecticut's law would involve intolerable state intrusion into the marital bedroom. The law was invalid in application to married couples, and the birth control clinic operators could not be punished for aiding its violation.

In form, this "penumbras" theory was tied to the specifics of the Bill of Rights; in fact, it embraced the Murphy contention. Justices JOHN MARSHALL HARLAN and BYRON R. WHITE, concurring, candidly rested on SUBSTANTIVE DUE PROCESS grounds. Justice Black, dissenting, expressed distaste for the Connecticut law but could find nothing specific in the Constitution to prevent the state from forbidding the furnishing or the use of contraceptives. He chided the majority for using natural law to "keep the Constitution in tune with the times"—a function that lay beyond the Court's power or duty.

Griswold served as an important precedent eight years later when the Court held, in ROE V. WADE (1973), that the new constitutional right of privacy included a woman's right to have an abortion. (See REPRODUCTIVE AUTONOMY.) The *Roe* opinion, abandoning the shadows of *Griswold's* penumbras, located the right of privacy in the "liberty" protected by Fourteenth Amendment due process. *Gris-*

wold thus provided a bridge from the Murphy view in *Adamson* to the Court's modern revival of substantive due process. Underscoring this transition, later decisions such as EISENSTADT V. BAIRD (1972) and CAREY V. POPULATION SERVICES INTERNATIONAL (1977) have made plain that *Griswold* protected not only marital privacy but also the marital relationship—and, indeed, a FREEDOM OF INTIMATE ASSOCIATION extending to unmarried persons. If substantive due process is a vital part of today's constitutional protections of personal liberty, much of the credit goes to the *Griswold* decision and to Justice Douglas.

KENNETH L. KARST
(1986)

Bibliography

Kauper, Paul G. 1965 Penumbras, Peripheries, Emanations, Things Fundamental and Things Forgotten: The Griswold Case. *Michigan Law Review* 64:235–258.

GROSJEAN v. AMERICAN PRESS CO., INC.
297 U.S. 233 (1936)

In this unique case the Court unanimously held unconstitutional, as abridgments of the FREEDOM OF THE PRESS, any "taxes on knowledge"—a phrase, from British history, used to designate any punitive or discriminatory tax imposed on publications for the purpose of limiting their circulation. Louisiana, under the influence of Governor Huey Long, exacted a license tax (two percent of gross receipts) on newspapers with a circulation exceeding 20,000 copies weekly. By no coincidence the tax fell on thirteen publications, twelve of which were critics of Long's regime, and missed the many smaller papers that supported him. The large publishers sued to enjoin enforcement of the license tax and won a permanent INJUNCTION.

Justice GEORGE SUTHERLAND, writing for the Court, reviewed the history of taxes on knowledge, concluding that mere exemption from PRIOR RESTRAINT was too narrow a view of the freedom of the press protected by the FIRST and FOURTEENTH AMENDMENTS. In addition to immunity from censorship, that freedom barred any government action that might prevent the discussion of public matters. Sutherland declared that publishers were subject to the ordinary forms of taxation, but the tax here was an extraordinary one with a long British history, known to the framers of the First Amendment, of trammeling the press as a vital source of public information. Similarly, Louisiana's use of the tax showed it to be a deliberate device to fetter a selected group of newspapers. To allow a free press to be fettered, Sutherland said, "is to fetter ourselves." De-

ciding that the tax abridged the freedom of the press made unnecessary a determination whether it also denied the EQUAL PROTECTION OF THE LAWS. In subsequent cases the Court sustained nondiscriminatory taxes on publishers but extended the principle of *Grosjean* to strike down taxes inhibiting RELIGIOUS LIBERTY.

LEONARD W. LEVY
(1986)

GROSSCUP, PETER S.
(1852–1921)

Peter Stenger Grosscup served nineteen years in the lower federal courts, the last twelve (1899–1911) on the Seventh Circuit Court of Appeals. Controversy dogged his judicial career. He preached the inevitability of industrial consolidation and the need for reasonable regulation of capital and LABOR. The judge's numerous critics within the Progressive movement charged that his conception of reasonableness merely disguised a probusiness bias.

Grosscup in 1894 gained national attention during the violent confrontation between Eugene V. Debs's American Railway Union and the Pullman Palace Car Company. The judge's sympathies were clear. Grosscup issued an INJUNCTION ordering the strikers to cease disruption of INTERSTATE COMMERCE and the mails. Grosscup, describing the strikers to a federal GRAND JURY, observed that "neither the torch of the incendiary, or the weapon of the insurrectionist, nor the inflamed tongue of him who incites to fire and sword is the instrument to bring about reform."

Grosscup's pronouncements in favor of reasonable regulation clashed with his advocacy of the abolition of the SHERMAN ANTITRUST ACT and his evanescent enforcement record. In *United States v. Swift & Co.* (1903) he did hold that since the commerce power included intercourse brought about by sale or exchange, application of the Sherman Act to outlaw price fixing by the Beef Trust was constitutional. However, in *Standard Oil Co. of Indiana v. United States* (1908), he spoke for a unanimous circuit court in reversing a district court fine of $29,240,000 against an oil company valued at $1,000,000. Grosscup testily wrote that the holding company—which could have afforded to pay—had not been on trial. The judge responded with mocking indifference to President THEODORE ROOSEVELT's sharp denunciation of the opinion.

Grosscup was publicly perceived as a tool of the corporations. His involvement as a shareholder and director of several businesses further undermined his judicial credibility. After resigning under pressure, Grosscup successfully defied his critics to prove misconduct.

KERMIT L. HALL
(1986)

Bibliography

VANCE, JOHN T. 1964 Peter Stenger Grosscup. *Dictionary of American Biography*, Vol. 4:21–22. New York: Scribner's.

GROSSMAN, EX PARTE
267 U.S. 87 (1925)

This OPINION, elucidating the scope of the PARDONING POWER, declared executive discretion absolute in the matter. The President had commuted Grossman's sentence, but a court ordered him reimprisoned to serve a sentence for contempt. The Supreme Court, recurring to history, rejected arguments that extension of the pardoning power to criminal contempts would violate judicial independence or the SEPARATION OF POWERS: "Whoever is to make [the pardoning power] useful must have full discretion to exercise it."

DAVID GORDON
(1986)

GROSSO v. UNITED STATES

See: *Marchetti v. United States*

GROUNDS OF OPINION

The grounds of OPINION are the stated reasons given by a court or a judge for the DECISION (or dissent) in a case. The grounds are the principles, precedents, and logical steps relied upon to support the conclusion. In the opinion of the Court, the grounds are the RATIO DECIDENDI, as opposed to the OBITER DICTA. In CONCURRING and DISSENTING OPINIONS, the grounds are, correspondingly, the points necessary to establish the desired result.

DENNIS J. MAHONEY
(1986)

GROUP CONFLICT AND THE CONSTITUTION

See: National Unity, Group Conflict, and the Constitution

GROUP LIBEL

Group libel statutes pose uniquely difficult issues, for they produce a clash between two constitutional commitments: to equality and to FREEDOM OF SPEECH. Such laws impose punishments on the defamation of racial, ethnic, or religious groups. Group libel statutes were first enacted following WORLD WAR II. It was widely believed that the Nazis had come to power in Germany by means of systematic calumny of their opponents and of Jews and other groups that might serve as scapegoats. Group libel statutes were enacted to afford remedies for defamation, to prevent breaches of the peace, and ultimately to protect democracy against totalitarianism. On the other hand, as the Supreme Court stated in NEW YORK TIMES CO. V. SULLIVAN (1964), the FIRST AMENDMENT manifests "a profound national commitment to the principle that debate on public issues should be uninhibited, robust and wide-open." Group libel statutes test that commitment.

The Court purported to settle the question in BEAUHARNAIS V. ILLINOIS (1952). A deeply divided Court upheld an Illinois group libel statute by resort to constitutional premises that have been substantially eroded by subsequent decisions. Although the continuing force of *Beauharnais* as a precedent is subject to serious doubt, it has not been overruled and was cited by the Court with seeming approval in *New York v. Ferber* (1982).

Beauharnais had been convicted for circulating a leaflet calling on officials in Chicago "to halt the further encroachment, harassment and invasion of white people, their property, neighborhoods, and persons, by the Negro." Calling upon white people to unite, Beauharnais's leaflet counseled that "if persuasion and the need to prevent the white race from becoming mongrelized by the Negro will not unite us, then the . . . rapes, robberies, knives, guns and marijuana of the Negro surely will."

One of the dissenting Justices, WILLIAM O. DOUGLAS, found it an easy case. In his view, if the "plain command of the First Amendment was to be overridden, the state was required to show that "the peril of speech" was "clear and present."

Justice FELIX FRANKFURTER, writing for the Court's majority, found it unnecessary to consider any CLEAR AND PRESENT DANGER test; libel, he said, is beneath First Amendment protection. Given the history of racial violence in Illinois, he argued, the legislature was not "without reason" in concluding that expressions like Beauharnais's had contributed to the violence and should be curbed.

In dissent, Justice HUGO L. BLACK challenged the Court's equation of group libel and ordinary libel. He suggested that the limited scope of libel assured that it applied to "nothing more than purely private feuds." The move from libel to group libel, he declared, was a move "to punish discussion of matters of public concern" and "a corresponding invasion of the area dedicated to free expression by the First Amendment."

Although Justice Black's characterization of the law of libel exaggerated its limits, constitutional developments since *Beauharnais* strongly support his general perspective. In *New York Times Co. v. Sullivan* the Court ruled that despite prior history, fresh assessment of the First Amendment yielded the conclusion that some libel was indeed within the scope of First Amendment protection. In a trail of decisions from *Sullivan* to GERTZ V. ROBERT WELCH, INC. (1974), the Court concluded that the First Amendment afforded some protection for a broad range of defamatory material. The driving force behind this constitutionalization of the tort of defamation was *Sullivan's* recognition of the First Amendment's commitment to uninhibited debate; moreover, the profound First Amendment importance of expression on public issues has been echoed in many subsequent opinions.

Sullivan and its successor decisions undermine the premises of *Beauharnais*. No Justice today could write an opinion saying that because libel is beneath First Amendment protection, so is group libel. First, most libel is clearly entitled to some measure of First Amendment protection. Second, putting group libel aside, if some libel remains entirely outside the First Amendment's scope, it would be speech of a private or commercial character. Justice Black's point that the move from libel to group libel is a move from the private sphere to the public sphere describes today's doctrine more accurately than it described the doctrine of 1952.

Another reason to doubt *Beauharnais's* continuing vitality is the Court's statement in *Gertz v. Robert Welch, Inc.* that "under our Constitution, there is no such thing as a false idea." That expression has generally been interpreted to mean that opinions are immune from any imposition of liability based on their asserted falsity. Although the line between fact and opinion is hard to draw, and although some group libel contains false assertions of fact, the sting of most group libel comes from unverifiable opinions. For example, what evidence could have proved the "truth" of Beauharnais's pejorative comments about black Americans? A separate issue is whether it is desirable for American trials to be conducted about the truth or falsity of various pejorative statements about ethnic groups. In the case of religious groups, the legal resolution of such questions could pose serious issues under the religion clauses of the First Amendment.

If group libel statutes are to find constitutional refuge, the necessary constitutional principles will have to be found beyond the defamation decisions. A growing body of opinions resonate with the theme of *Paris Adult Theatre v. Slaton* (1973) pronouncing the right to maintain "a decent society." From *Young v. American-Mini Theatres, Inc.* (1976) to FEDERAL COMMUNICATIONS COMMISSION V. PACIFICA FOUNDATION (1978) and a series of dissents in decisions involving FIGHTING WORDS, there is support for arguments based on concepts of civility, decency, and dignity. Whether or not these arguments succeed in validating group libel statutes, the conflict between public morality and freedom of speech will persist as an abiding theme of constitutional law.

STEVEN SHIFFRIN
(1986)

Bibliography

ARKES, HADLEY 1974 Civility and the Restriction of Speech: Rediscovering the Defamation of Groups. *Supreme Court Review* 1974:281–335.
KALVEN, HARRY, JR. 1965 *The Negro and the First Amendment.* Columbus: Ohio State University Press.

GROUPS AND THE CONSTITUTION

ALEXIS DE TOCQUEVILLE famously observed, "Americans of all ages, all stations in life, and all types of dispositions are forever forming associations." Yet CONSTITUTIONAL THEORY hardly has begun to connect to reality in which individual identities are anchored within myriad associations, both voluntary and involuntary.

Judges, lawyers, and scholars have constructed quite different standards regarding the relationship between groups and the Constitution at varying moments in American history. No unified general theory of FREEDOM OF ASSOCIATION seems possible today. Yet there remains a need for careful, nuanced consideration of the constitutional position of groups in the United States. In some instances, an association is thought to merit greater protection and more expansive rights than would be afforded any single individual; in other situations, an association may merit substantially less protection and have rights more constricted than would a single individual. Often, associations are said to merit precisely the same rights any single individual would enjoy.

Prevailing opinion maintains that the Constitution protects no explicit independent freedom of association. This theory—largely derived from a binary approach within the central paradigm of individual and the state—considers groups of people as sums divisible into their parts. Even leading FIRST AMENDMENT scholars such as Thomas I. Emerson, for example, argued that it "is impossible to construct a meaningful constitutional limitation on government power based upon a generalized notion of the right to form or join an association." In those respects in which associations are unique, Emerson would allow additional governmental regulation.

In some cases, however, individuals are persecuted precisely because of their membership in groups. Some groups, moreover, have been punished for their very existence. Guilt by association periodically has dominated our legal landscape. In tense times, judges tend to acquiesce in restricting the rights of individuals because of their memberships—volitional or nonvolitional—in particular associations. In *New York ex rel. Bryant v. Zimmerman* (1926), for example, the Supreme Court upheld the conviction of a Ku Klux Klan officer based solely on the group's failure to disclose its membership list. As late as 1961, the Court reiterated a theory of restricted associational rights regarding membership in the Communist Party. Perhaps the most striking "guilt by association" decision, however, was KOREMATSU V. UNITED STATES (1944), which upheld the internment of Japanese Americans during WORLD WAR II. The Court deferred to revocation of constitutional rights because race positioned thousands of people as members of an identifiable, feared group.

In contrast to *Korematsu*, the Court occasionally has extended group rights that are decidedly more protective than the rights afforded to any individual. In a number of situations, members of groups are legally protected though a lone individual engaged in the same activity might not be: for example, members of groups who parade, report the news, engage in certain LABOR activities and boycotts, and gain protection from deportation because of persecution in their home countries. In NAACP V. ALABAMA (1958), Justice JOHN MARSHALL HARLAN's OPINION FOR THE COURT described a First Amendment right of association and protected the NAACP from one of the attempts by Southern states to obtain membership lists in order to punish activists in the CIVIL RIGHTS MOVEMENT. In *NAACP v. Claiborne Hardware Co.* (1982), Justice JOHN PAUL STEVENS's MAJORITY OPINION echoed Harlan's freedom of association approach. *Claiborne Hardware* insulated a local NAACP chapter from a huge fine imposed by a state court for organizing and enforcing a long BOYCOTT of white merchants in Port Arthur, Mississippi.

The Court also has recognized some First Amendment rights of business associations in the form of CORPORATIONS. *Consolidated Edison Company v. Public Service Commission* (1980), for example, categorized the huge power company as a private party protected in COMMERCIAL SPEECH communications via enclosures in its utility bills. Newspapers seek profits, Justice LEWIS F. POWELL, JR., reasoned for the majority, so other profit-seeking corporations also should be entitled to express themselves.

Nonetheless, recent Court decisions tend to limit special associational rights either to the FREEDOM OF INTIMATE ASSOCIATION or to "the freedom of individuals to associate for the purpose of engaging in protected speech or religious activities," as described in *Board of Directors of Rotary Club International v. Rotary Club of Duarte* (1987). Rights surrounding intimate association are derived primarily from RIGHT OF PRIVACY and SUBSTANTIVE DUE PROCESS sources. The other main freedom of association source is

anchored in the First Amendment. By deriving two different associational rights from other constitutional rights, the Court often seems to render freedom of association nearly otiose.

A few notable exceptions to this limiting approach have breathed new life into associational rights, albeit in a scattered and inconsistent way. In *Roberts v. United States Jaycees* (1984), *Federal Election Commission v. Massachusetts Citizens For Life* (1987), and AUSTIN V. MICHIGAN CHAMBER OF COMMERCE (1990), for example, the Court suggested that the group quality of the claimed right made a constitutional difference in striking the balance under the First Amendment. The communicative purposes of the association as well as the type of communication involved are key factors. Yet in BOB JONES UNIVERSITY V. UNITED STATES (1983), *Regan v. Taxation With Representation of Washington, Inc.* (1983), and CORNELIUS V. NAACP LEGAL DEFENSE AND EDUCATIONAL FUND, INC. (1985), the Court deferred to the discretion of government agencies in deciding whether to recognize associations' First Amendment claims.

Some argue that, primarily through the First and the FOURTEENTH AMENDMENTS the Constitution entails direct protection for those concerned enough to assemble together. This right, whether or not linked explicitly to other constitutional protections, might provide guarantees for groups who would speak, write, petition, or pray against orthodoxy. Such an associational right would not always trump competing claims, of course—no constitutional right ever does—but it would establish a rebuttable presumption to be overcome only by a conflicting and COMPELLING STATE INTEREST. Another claim, akin to that made in the famous Footnote 4 of UNITED STATES V. CAROLENE PRODUCTS (1938), asserts that for marginalized or endangered groups—"DISCRETE AND INSULAR MINORITIES" — there ought to be more careful constitutional scrutiny of actions that intrude upon or discriminate against such groups as groups. Yet the Court recently has insisted, albeit inconsistently, that even EQUAL PROTECTION claims are limited to individuals.

As a matter of contemporary constitutional DOCTRINE groups generally are treated—with notable exceptions such as heterosexual couples, explicitly political associations, and the NAACP—as if they are simply conglomerations of individuals that accurately reflect the sums of their individual parts. Certainly no unified general theory of freedom of association seems possible today, if it ever could have been.

AVIAM SOIFER
(2000)

(SEE ALSO: *Asian Americans and the Constitution; Japanese American Cases.*)

Bibliography

EMERSON, THOMAS I. 1964 Freedom of Association and Freedom of Expression. *Yale Law Journal* 74:1–35.

GARET, RONALD A. 1983 Communality and Existence: The Rights of Groups. *Southern California Law Review* 56:1001–1075.

SOIFER, AVIAM 1995 *Law and the Company We Keep.* Cambridge, Mass.: Harvard University Press.

GROVES v. SLAUGHTER
15 Peters 449 (1841)

Groves was the only case to come before the United States Supreme Court involving the relative powers of the state and federal governments over the interstate slave trade. Mississippi's Constitution forbade the importation of slaves for sale. In suit on a defaulted note given for an imported slave, the Court majority, speaking through Justice SMITH THOMPSON, held that the state constitutional provision was not self-executing and was unenforceable without legislation implementing it. Concurring opinions revealed a wide divergence of opinion among the justices on slavery-related questions. Justice JOHN MCLEAN asserted that slaves were essentially persons, not property. Chief Justice ROGER B. TANEY insisted that state power over blacks, slave or free, was exclusive and superseded any exercise of federal power under the slave-trade or COMMERCE CLAUSE. Justice HENRY BALDWIN denied that states could exclude the slave trade.

WILLIAM M. WIECEK
(1986)

GROVEY v. TOWNSEND
295 U.S. 45 (1935)

Following the DECISION in NIXON V. CONDON (1932), the Texas state convention of the Democratic party adopted a rule limiting voting in PRIMARY ELECTIONS to whites. Grovey, a black, was refused a primary ballot and sued for DAMAGES. The Supreme Court unanimously held that the party's rule did not amount to STATE ACTION under the FOURTEENTH or FIFTEENTH AMENDMENT and thus violated no constitutional rights. Grovey was merely denied membership in a private organization. The Court distinguished *Nixon v. Condon* as a case in which the party's executive committee had acted under state authorization. Only nine years later, in SMITH V. ALLWRIGHT (1944), the Court overruled *Grovey.*

KENNETH L. KARST
(1986)

GUARANTEE CLAUSE

Article IV, section 4, of the Constitution provides that "The United States shall guarantee to every State in this Union a REPUBLICAN FORM OF GOVERNMENT. ...." Anticipated between 1781 and 1787 in various state and federal legislative requirements that territorrial governments be republican ideology in the Confederation era. At a minimum, it prohibited regression to monarchial and aristocratic government, but it also incorporated the principles of POPULAR SOVEREIGNTY, representative government, majority rule, SEPARATION OF POWERS, and federal supremacy.

The guarantee clause was first invoked under circumstances JAMES MADISON anticipated in THE FEDERALIST #43: to suppress an insurrectionary challenge to the authority of one of the states (Dorr's Rebellion, Rhode Island, 1842). Then, and in the earlier WHISKEY REBELLION (western Pennsylvania, 1794), it took on a repressive character as a bulwark of extant institutions, affirming GEORGE WASHINGTON's insistence in his Farewell Address (1796) that "the constitution which at any time exists till changed by . . . the whole people is sacredly obligatory upon all."

In the first significant judicial interpretation of the clause, LUTHER V. BORDEN (1849), Chief Justice ROGER B. TANEY declined to overturn the Rhode Island government established in the aftermath of the Dorr Rebellion. Taney held that the determination of whether a state government was republican rested exclusively with Congress, whose action was binding on the courts. In this case, Taney invoked the POLITICAL QUESTION doctrine, asserting that the issue presented "belonged to the political power and not to the judicial."

The guarantee clause figured prominently in debates on reconstruction of the Union during and after the Civil War. Democrats opposed to effective Reconstruction measures relied on a conservative interpretation of the clause as securing extant, nonmonarchical governments; they extolled self-government but limited it to whites. Republicans rejected the static, backward-looking, and racist implications of the Democratic view. Echoing earlier abolitionist contentions that slavery was incompatible with republican government, Republicans fashioned Reconstruction · policies (including military Reconstruction, federal guarantees of blacks' CIVIL RIGHTS, and enfranchisement) that were conceptually derived from Taney's assertion of the exclusive power of Congress to assure republican government in the states. Chief Justice SALMON P. CHASE validated the Republican uses of the clause in TEXAS V. WHITE (1869).

The clause has played a less prominent role in public affairs during the twentieth century. The Supreme Court rejected a conservative interpretation of the clause that would have invalidated the initiative and referendum (*Pa-*

cific States Telephone and Telegraph Co. v. Oregon, 1912). Together with the political question doctrine, the clause became linked with the concept of JUSTICIABILITY (a characteristic of cases requisite to their resolution by judicial tribunals). But the majority opinion of Justice WILLIAM J. BRENNAN in BAKER V. CARR (1962) restricted the scope of the political question doctrine, thus creating the possibility of future judicial, as well as congressional, reliance on the clause to evaluate the republican character of state institutions.

WILLIAM M. WIECEK
(1986)

Bibliography

WIECEK, WILLIAM M. 1972 *The Guarantee Clause of the U.S. Constitution.* Ithaca, N.Y.: Cornell University Press.

GUARANTEE CLAUSE
(Update)

The Constitution declares that "The United States shall guarantee to every State in this Union a Republican Form of Government" (Article IV, section 4). This guarantee clause has a rich political history, having been wielded as a potent legal and rhetorical weapon by various government reformers since the Constitution's framing. For example, ABOLITIONISTS in the early nineteenth century invoked the republican guarantee when urging extension of the concept of United States CITIZENSHIP, and later the franchise, to once-enslaved persons; and suffragists in the mid-nineteenth and early twentieth centuries invoked the republican guarantee when urging extension of the franchise to women. The guarantee clause proved an ineffective weapon in federal court litigation, however, because the courts generally steered clear of what they considered to be quintessentially political battles. In a series of cases stretching from the mid-1800s, starting with LUTHER V. BORDEN (1849), through the mid-1900s, the Supreme Court held that the questions whether a state government is republican in form, or which of two competing governments may properly claim the title, lack JUSTICIABILITY in federal court under the POLITICAL QUESTION DOCTRINE. State courts generally followed suit. From the perspective of judicially enforceable rights, therefore, the guarantee clause has long lain dormant. While occasionally a potent political weapon, the clause has not been deployed successfully as a legal one.

Recently, however, the guarantee clause has received renewed attention from both scholars and courts. Political theorists have revived the Founding Era's focus on ideals of REPUBLICANISM, and this revival in turn has spurred legal scholars to focus once again on the legal content of the clause. And in NEW YORK V. UNITED STATES (1992), the Supreme Court teasingly suggested that "perhaps not all claims under the guarantee clause present nonjusticiable political questions," though it found the particular legislative scheme under challenge in that case not to violate the clause.

Most of the recent legal scholarship considers whether the INITIATIVE and REFERENDUM forms of DIRECT DEMOCRACY used by states are consistent with the republican government guarantee. Modern scholars generally agree that the clause historically was designed to protect democratic states from both monarchy and mob rule. Some scholars argue that a REPUBLICAN FORM OF GOVERNMENT entails governance through elected agents. The concept of direct democracy was anathema to the Framers, they argue, and should be considered unconstitutional today. In contrast, other scholars argue that the Framers considered state government to be republican in form so long as the people ultimately retained SOVEREIGNTY, whether they exercised their sovereignty directly or through elected agents. In other words, they argue, the Framers used the terms "democracy" and "republican government" as synonyms. For these latter scholars, widespread governance through plebiscites is not constitutionally infirm. Given the zeal with which numerous states have recently employed direct democracy techniques to resolve deeply controversial matters, it is unsurprising that the current debate among legal scholars as to the validity of those techniques is vigorous indeed. As yet, however, courts have not engaged in this debate. Federal courts still reject guarantee clause challenges to initiatives and referenda as nonjusticiable, and state courts either do so as well, or reject such challenges on the merits.

EVAN H. CAMINKER
(2000)

(SEE ALSO: *Voting Rights.*)

Bibliography

LINDE, HANS A. 1989 When Is Initiative Lawmaking Not "Republican Government"? *Hastings Constitutional Law Quarterly* 17:159–173.

SYMPOSIUM 1994 Guaranteeing a Republican Form of Government. *University of Colorado Law Review* 65:709–946.

GUEST, UNITED STATES v.
383 U.S. 745 (1966)

This case raised important questions about Congress's power to enforce the FOURTEENTH AMENDMENT and about the scope of section 241 of Title 18 of the United States Code, a federal criminal CIVIL RIGHTS statute deriving from section 6 of the FORCE ACT of 1870. Section 241 outlaws conspiracies to interfere with rights or privileges secured by the Constitution or laws of the United States. A group of whites allegedly murdered Lemuel A. Penn, a black Army officer, while he was driving through Georgia on his way to Washington, D.C. Two of the whites were charged with murder and acquitted by a state court jury. They and others then were indicted under section 241 for conspiracy to deprive blacks of specified constitutional rights by shooting, beating, and otherwise harassing them and by making false criminal accusations causing the blacks to be arrested. The rights allegedly deprived included the right to use state facilities free of RACIAL DISCRIMINATION and the RIGHT TO TRAVEL freely throughout the United States. The Supreme Court held that the alleged conduct constituted a crime under section 241, punishable by Congress under the Fourteenth Amendment.

Guest's principal significance stems from two separate opinions, joined by a total of six Justices, that addressed the question whether the Fourteenth Amendment empowers Congress to outlaw private racially discriminatory behavior. In an opinion concurring in part and dissenting in part, Justice WILLIAM J. BRENNAN, joined by Chief Justice EARL WARREN and Justice WILLIAM O. DOUGLAS, stated that section 5 of the Fourteenth Amendment grants Congress authority to punish individuals, public or private, who interfere with the right to equal use of state facilities. Justice TOM C. CLARK, in a concurring opinion joined by Justices HUGO L. BLACK and ABE FORTAS, in effect agreed with the portion of Justice Brennan's opinion relating to Congress's power. Justice Clark's opinion stated that there could be no doubt about Congress's power to punish all public and private conspiracies that interfere with Fourteenth Amendment rights, "with or without STATE ACTION."

Guest also raised the question whether, in light of the state action doctrine, the defendants, all private persons, were legally capable of depriving others of Fourteenth Amendment rights within the meaning of section 241. Justice POTTER STEWART's opinion for the Court, which, as to this point, Justice Clark's opinion expressly endorsed, avoided the issue by construing the INDICTMENT's allegation that the conspiracy was accomplished in part by "causing the arrest of Negroes by means of false reports that such Negroes had committed criminal acts" to be an allegation of state involvement. Justice Brennan read Justice Stewart's opinion to mean that a conspiracy by private persons to interfere with Fourteenth Amendment rights was not a conspiracy to interfere with a right secured by the Constitution within the meaning of section 241. Justice Brennan rejected this interpretation, arguing that private persons could deprive blacks of rights "secured" by the Constitution "even though only govern-

mental interferences with the exercise of that right are prohibited by the Constitution itself."

Other aspects of *Guest* generated less disagreement among the Justices. The case revived a question addressed in SCREWS V. UNITED STATES (1945) when the Court interpreted section 242 (a remnant of the CIVIL RIGHTS ACT OF 1866). Sections 241 and 242 define proscribed behavior as conduct violating constitutional rights. Since constitutional standards change, defendants argued that the sections were unconstitutionally vague. As in *Screws*, the Court construed the statute to require a specific intent to violate constitutional rights and, therefore, found section 241 not unconstitutionally vague. And the Court found the right to travel throughout the United States to be a basic constitutional right that, like freedom from INVOLUNTARY SERVITUDE, is protected even as against private interference. Only Justice JOHN MARSHALL HARLAN dissented from the HOLDING that the right to travel is protected against private interference.

Both the suggestion by six Justices (through the Brennan and Clark opinions) concerning Congress's power under section 5 of the Fourteenth Amendment and Justice Brennan's views about the scope of section 241 are difficult to reconcile with important nineteenth-century decisions. In UNITED STATES V. CRUIKSHANK (1876), one of the first cases construing Reconstruction-era civil rights legislation, indictments charging violations of section 6 of the FORCE ACT of 1870 were ordered dismissed in part on the ground that Fourteenth Amendment rights could not be violated by private citizens. In UNITED STATES V. HARRIS (1883) the Court held unconstitutional a civil rights statute that punished private conspiracies to interfere with rights of equality. The provision struck down in *Harris*, which stemmed from section 2 of the Civil Rights Act of 1871, was so similar to section 241 that, until *Guest*, it seemed unlikely that section 241 could be applied to private conspiracies to interfere with rights of equality. And *Guest*'s expansive view of Congress's Fourteenth Amendment powers is difficult to reconcile with the Court's decision in the CIVIL RIGHTS CASES (1883).

Guest thus represents a shift in attitude toward Congress's Fourteenth Amendment power to reach private discrimination. But *Guest* also is part of a larger shift in attitude toward the Civil War amendments. In KATZENBACH V. MORGAN (1966) and SOUTH CAROLINA V. KATZENBACH (1966), cases decided during the same term as *Guest*, the Court for the first time found Congress to have broad powers to interpret and define the content of the Fourteenth and FIFTEENTH AMENDMENTS.

Guest's generous attitude toward Congress's power has had less influence than might have been expected. Prior to *Guest*, HEART OF ATLANTA MOTEL, INC. V. UNITED STATES

(1964) and KATZENBACH V. MCCLUNG (1964) already had found Congress to have broad power under the COMMERCE CLAUSE to reach discrimination in facilities affecting INTERSTATE COMMERCE. In JONES V. ALFRED H. MAYER CO. (1968), the Court found Congress to have broad THIRTEENTH AMENDMENT powers to reach private discrimination in all areas. *Jones* and the Commerce Clause cases rendered moot much of the question about Congress's Fourteenth Amendment powers. GRIFFIN V. BRECKENRIDGE (1971), where the Court again faced the question of Congress's power to reach private discriminatory conspiracies, underscores *Guest's* modest influence. *Griffin* involved a civil statute, section 1985(3), that is similar to section 241. By the time of *Griffin*, however, the Court could rely on Congress's Thirteenth Amendment powers to sustain legislation proscribing private racial conspiracies. *Guest's* possible implications will be realized only in cases, if any, to which Congress's Thirteenth Amendment and commerce clause powers are inapplicable.

THEODORE EISENBERG
(1986)

Bibliography

COX, ARCHIBALD 1966 Foreword: Constitutional Adjudication and the Promotion of Human Rights. *Harvard Law Review* 80:91–122.
NOTE 1967 Fourteenth Amendment Congressional Power to Legislate Against Private Discrimination: The *Guest* Case. *Cornell Law Quarterly* 52:586–599.
——— 1974 Federal Power to Regulate Private Discrimination: The Revival of the Enforcement Clauses of the Reconstruction Era Amendments. *Columbia Law Review* 74:449–527.
TRIBE, LAURENCE H. 1978 *American Constitutional Law.* Pages 273–275. Mineola, N.Y.: Foundation Press

GUFFEY-SNYDER ACT

See: Bituminous Coal Act; *Carter v. Carter Coal Co.*

GUILT BY ASSOCIATION

The United States Supreme Court frequently proclaims that guilt by association has no place in our constitutional system (for example, *Schneiderman v. United States*, 1943; WIEMAN V. UPDEGRAFF, 1952). Sanctions imposed for membership in a group are said to be characteristic of primitive cultures, or elements of the early COMMON LAW long since eliminated with prohibitions against such punishments as attaint and forfeiture.

In 1920, CHARLES EVANS HUGHES made what is probably still the most famous statement attacking guilt by association as inconsistent with our individualistic legal norms. In protesting the action of the New York Assembly, which had suspended five elected members because they were members of the Socialist Party, Hughes argued: "It is the essence of the institutions of liberty that it be recognized that guilt is personal and cannot be attributed to the holding of opinion or of mere intent in the absence of overt acts."

Other Justices frequently quoted or paraphrased this argument by Hughes, made between the two periods Hughes served on the Court, in decisions invalidating deportations, employment dismissals, and denials of licenses, as well as in criminal prosecutions. It is obvious, however, that frequently ascription of guilt by association is permitted. For example, members of a CRIMINAL CONSPIRACY may be found guilty for actions by their co-conspirators based entirely on their association in the conspiracy. The Supreme Court recognized the potential for abuse in criminal conspiracy in *Krulewitch v. United States* (1949), but convictions of coconspirators still may be upheld without proof of their direct knowledge or participation in the range of crimes committed by other members of the conspiracy.

There are also striking examples of the Court's condoning of government action based on the presumption of guilt by association in constitutional law. These include the JAPANESE AMERICAN CASES (1943–1944), which upheld the internment of West Coast residents of Japanese ancestry during WORLD WAR II, and numerous decisions during the 1950s, such as AMERICAN COMMUNICATIONS ASSOCIATION V. DOUDS (1950) and BARENBLATT V. UNITED STATES (1959), which allowed sanctions for membership in communist organizations.

Despite reiteration of the unacceptability of punishment premised upon guilt by association, judgments about individuals based upon their membership in groups frequently—perhaps even necessarily—are made in a bureaucratized world in which personal knowledge of others seems increasingly elusive. Nevertheless, the assignment of individual guilt premised on one's associations remains anathema. It is still thought to be an important premise of constitutional law that the government may not use a gross shorthand such as guilt by association to stigmatize or to punish citizens.

Constitutional safeguards derived primarily from the FIRST AMENDMENT and the DUE PROCESS clauses are said to surround FREEDOM OF ASSOCIATION. When the government employs the technique of guilt by association, it endangers this freedom, which the Court proclaimed in DEJONGE V. OREGON (1937) to be among the most fundamental of constitutional protections. Guilt by association also is inconsistent with basic premises of individual responsibility, which lie close to the core of much of America's legal culture.

AVIAM SOIFER
(1986)

Bibliography

EMERSON, THOMAS I. 1970 *The System of Freedom of Expression.* Pages 105–110, 126–129, 161–204, 235–241. New York: Random House.

O'BRIAN, JOHN L. 1948 Loyalty Tests and Guilt by Association. *Harvard Law Review* 61:592–611.

GUINN v. UNITED STATES
238 U.S. 347 (1915)

In an 8–0 DECISION, the Supreme Court sustained the conviction of two Oklahoma election officials of conspiracy to deprive blacks of their VOTING RIGHTS. In an opinion by Chief Justice EDWARD D. WHITE, the court held that a state constitutional amendment enacting a GRANDFATHER CLAUSE, which exempted from the literacy test the descendants of persons who had been entitled to vote before 1866, violated the FIFTEENTH AMENDMENT, and that officials could be prosecuted for attempting to enforce it. In a COMPANION CASE (*Myers v. Anderson*) the Court held that Maryland officials were liable for civil DAMAGES for enforcing that state's grandfather clause.

DENNIS J. MAHONEY
(1986)

GULF OF TONKIN RESOLUTION
73 Stat. 384 (1964)
84 Stat. 2053 (1971) (repeal)

One criticism of American participation in the VIETNAM WAR was based on the Constitution: half a million troops had been committed to combat without a DECLARATION OF WAR by Congress. In 1964 President LYNDON B. JOHNSON reported that North Vietnamese boats had attacked United States naval vessels in the Gulf of Tonkin. Accepting the truth of these reports, Congress adopted a resolution supporting the President in "taking all necessary measures to repel any armed attack against the forces of the United States and to prevent further aggression." The resolution further approved the use of armed force to defend other nations that had signed the Southeast Asia treaty. Massive escalation of the American involvement in South Vietnam soon followed; the President cited this resolution and successive appropriations measures as evidence of congressional ratification of his actions.

In 1971 Congress repealed the Gulf of Tonkin Resolution. President RICHARD M. NIXON did not oppose the repeal; he asserted that his power as COMMANDER-IN-CHIEF of the armed forces authorized continuation of American participation. After the American troops were withdrawn in 1973, Congress reasserted its authority, adopting the WAR POWERS RESOLUTION over Nixon's VETO.

KENNETH L. KARST
(1986)

GULF WAR

On August 2, 1990 Iraq invaded and conquered the neighboring state of Kuwait. President GEORGE H. W. BUSH announced U.S. policy regarding the invasion and marshaled diplomatic efforts focused in the UNITED NATIONS (UN) to oppose it. The UN Security Council quickly condemned the invasion, demanded that Iraq withdraw, and imposed mandatory economic and diplomatic sanctions to coerce Iraqi compliance with UN demands. Over the next four months the United States created and led a coalition of allied forces to counter the Iraqi aggression. In November 1990 the United States deployed over 500,000 troops, including naval and air forces, to Saudi Arabia and the adjacent region. On November 29, 1990 the UN Security Council issued an ultimatum to Iraq to withdraw, which Iraq did not heed. The U.S.-led coalition forces counterattacked starting on January 17, 1991 with air strikes. Ground operations began February 24, and within four days the Iraqi forces had been expelled from Kuwait.

The President formulated U.S. policy and conducted diplomacy, including voting in the UN Security Council, pursuant to his constitutional FOREIGN AFFAIRS powers. He imposed economic sanctions against Iraq pursuant to delegated LEGISLATIVE POWERS under the International Emergency Economic Powers Act and the UN Participation Act. The President deployed U.S. ARMED FORCES to the Gulf region on the basis of his foreign relations and COMMANDER-IN-CHIEF powers. Existing LEGISLATION authorized, and appropriated funds for, those forces. The President complied with the consultation and reporting requirements of the WAR POWERS ACTS.

Congress had adjourned after the invasion of Kuwait and after the initial deployment of U.S. forces. When Congress reconvened each house passed a resolution supporting the President's policy, and Congress provided supplemental funds for the armed forces. It also passed the Iraq Sanctions Act of 1990 approving economic sanctions. However, the major troop deployment was made after the mid-term election in November. At that time Congress had adjourned "sine die" and its leaders seemed reluctant to reconvene the session to consider the decision of whether to continue to rely on economic sanctions to pressure Iraq to withdraw or to vote for war. Under pressure from public opinion, the press, and opponents of military action, however, the congressional leadership reconvened Congress and, after a thorough debate, Congress authorized U.S. participation in the war that was soon to follow. The President had steadfastly maintained that he had the requisite legal authority to use military force to expel Iraq from Kuwait on the basis of EXECUTIVE POWER. Nevertheless, after some discussion, Bush wrote the congressional leaders a letter requesting a JOINT RESOLUTION. As a result the claim of presidential WAR POWERS was not tested. In the end the President had ample legislative support for all the actions taken up to and including the war itself.

Congressional action in the Gulf War situation, coupled with its authorization of U.S. participation in the VIETNAM WAR, goes far toward diluting the importance of the KOREAN WAR precedent for supporting a presidential war power to initiate major military actions without specific congressional authorization.

PHILLIP R. TRIMBLE
(2000)

Bibliography

GLENNON, MICHAEL J. 1991 The Gulf War and the Constitution. *Foreign Affairs* 70:84–101.

HENKIN, LOUIS; GLENNON, MICHAEL J.; and RODGERS, WILLIAM D., eds. 1990 *Foreign Affairs and the U.S. Constitution.* Ardsley-on-Hudson, N.Y.: Transnational Publishers.

GUN CONTROL

"Gun control" is a constitutional issue because of the SECOND AMENDMENT: "A well regulated Militia, being necessary to the security of a free State, the right of the people to keep and bear Arms, shall not be infringed." Does this rather oddly phrased language place genuine constraints on the ability of government to regulate firearms? Those who favor vigorous control, including outright prohibition of the private ownership of handguns and other weapons, argue that the preamble to the amendment clearly rejects what has come to be called the "individual rights" view; instead, it limits any constitutional protection to members of an official militia, as organized (and regulated) by state governments. So long as Congress makes no effort to limit a state's right to place guns in the hands of its official militia, then the regulation of ordinary private citizens presents no problem. Opponents of gun control, on the other hand, read the amendment far more broadly, arguing that it protects the general public, all of whom were viewed by eighteenth-century theorists as members of the "general militia" (as distinguished from the "select militia" con-

trolled by the state), and all with a right to keep and bear arms.

One should note that most argument about the meaning of the Second Amendment assumes that it applies to all governments. Yet the Supreme Court held, in a number of late-nineteenth-century cases, that it limited only the national government and did not extend to the states at all. In spite of the "INCORPORATION" of much of the BILL OF RIGHTS to the states through the FOURTEENTH AMENDMENT, the Court has certainly done nothing to suggest that the Second Amendment has been incorporated.

One might, then, argue that the Second Amendment, especially if construed in light of the likely aims of its original proponents in 1789, was designed to limit drastically the ability of a feared and mistrusted national government to limit the rights of members of the citizen-militia to keep and bear arms. But, just as the FIRST AMENDMENT notoriously limited only Congress while leaving states free to impair the FREEDOM OF SPEECH or to establish a religion, the states could be read as continuing to possess almost plenary power to regulate firearms however they wish. Not surprisingly, devotees of firearms, such as the National Rifle Association (NRA), are among the strongest proponents of incorporating the Second Amendment to apply it against the states. Indeed, there is evidence that the members of Congress who proposed the Fourteenth Amendment did assume that the "right to bear arms" would be extended to newly freed blacks who were facing violent repression from the Ku Klux Klan.

If one offers a limited interpretation of the Second Amendment, there are obviously no real barriers to regulation, by Congress or by states. But what if one accepts a view closer to the NRA's? Does that necessarily invalidate all governmental control of firearms? The answer most certainly is no.

One begins by noting the resistance among constitutional interpreters to almost any notion of exceptionless limits on governmental power. Whatever the linguisitic forms of, say, the First Amendment or the CONTRACT CLAUSE in Article I, section 10, both of which seem absoutely to limit the ability to infringe the freedom of speech or press or to impair the obligation of contracts, the Court has developed the COMPELLING STATE INTEREST doctrine (in regard to the First Amendment) that allows restriction when the reasons are good enough. Similarly, no serious person suggests that the Second Amendment would ever disallow even "compellingly" supported regulation. It is inconceivable, practically speaking, that even a far more "pro-gun" Court would refuse to limit access to guns by children or by convicted felons (who can, after all, be denied the FUNDAMENTAL RIGHT to vote). Nor can one imagine a Court's holding that what have come to be known as weapons of mass destruction are protected—and for good reason, even if one takes the Second Amendment with utmost seriousness. After all, the most plausible explanation of the amendment's presence in the Constitution is the desire to allow ordinary citizens to "keep and bear arms" in case there is a need to use them against a corrupt or tyrannical government. (No one reads the amendment as actually protecting the use of arms. As a practical matter, one must win the struggle, as did the American revolutionaries in 1776, to escape punishment. Rather, the idea is that knowledge that the citizenry was armed and might resort to their use would serve to limit tyrannical propensities on the part of government.) The least plausible rationale for the amendment would be one that protected private tyrants who, for example, would be able to threaten mass destruction if the populace did not accede to their wishes. This suggests that the reach of the amendment could be legitimately confined to relatively low-level weapons whose practical power would depend on the joining together of many members of the community in rebellion against the presumptively tyrannical government.

It should be obvious that this rationale, even if faithful to the historical evidence, is shocking to many Americans. Thus most opponents of gun control emphasize far more the potential utility of firearms as a defense against criminals than the possible usefulness as a way of overthrowing the state. Ironically, though, the very word "militia," which can be used to justify a strong notion of Second Amendment liberties, itself suggests that the more palatable, at least to contemporary Americans, anticriminal argument as an attack on regulation of guns, probably has less constitutional warrant, at least from the perspective of ORIGINAL INTENT, than the more extreme argument emphasizing governmental tyranny.

SANFORD LEVINSON
(2000)

(SEE ALSO: *Militia, Modern; Right of Revolution.*)

Bibliography

AMAR, AKHIL REED   1998   *The Bill of Rights.* New Haven, Conn.: Yale University Press.

COTTROL, ROBERT J., ed.   1994   *Gun Control and the Constitution: Sources and Explorations on the Second Amendment.* New York: Garland Publishing Company.

NISBET, LEE, ed.   1990   *The Gun Control Debate.* Buffalo, N.Y.: Prometheus Books.

GUTHRIE, WILLIAM D.
(1859–1935)

A corporation lawyer and professor of law at Columbia (1913–1922), William D. Guthrie was one of several prominent attorneys who successfully challenged the federal income tax in POLLOCK V. FARMERS' LOAN & TRUST COMPANY (1895). His most famous appearance before the Supreme Court, however, came in a losing cause: CHAMPION V. AMES (1903). In that case, he advocated a doctrine EDWARD S. CORWIN would later call DUAL FEDERALISM (and which the Supreme Court itself would adopt in HAMMER V. DAGENHART, 1918). Drawing on his *Lectures on the Fourteenth Article of Amendment to the Constitution* (1898), Guthrie argued that the suppression of lotteries did not fall under the national commerce power because no commerce was involved. Such regulation belonged solely to the STATE POLICE POWER, to which Guthrie accorded great deference. He also favored the RULE OF REASON in ANTITRUST cases (though he was unable to convince the Court to accept it in UNITED STATES V. TRANS-MISSOURI FREIGHT ASSOCIATION, 1897) and he vigorously opposed the SIXTEENTH AMENDMENT on dual federalism grounds.

DAVID GORDON
(1986)

H

HABEAS CORPUS

(Latin: "You shall have the body.") Habeas corpus is the most celebrated of Anglo-American judicial procedures. It has been called the "Great Writ of Liberty" and hailed as a crucial bulwark of a free society. Compared to many encomia, Justice FELIX FRANKFURTER's praise in BROWN V. ALLEN (1953) is measured:

> The uniqueness of habeas corpus in the procedural armory of our law cannot be too often emphasized. It differs from all other remedies in that it is available to bring into question the legality of a person's restraint and to require justification for such detention. Of course this does not mean that prison doors may readily be opened. It does mean that explanation may be exacted why they should remain closed. It is not the boasting of empty rhetoric that has treated the writ of *habeas corpus* as the basic safeguard of freedom in the Anglo-American world. "The great writ of habeas corpus has been for centuries esteemed the best and only sufficient defence of personal freedom." Mr. Chief Justice [SALMON P.] CHASE, writing for the Court, in *Ex parte Yerger*, 8 Wall. 85, 95. Its history and function in our legal system and the unavailability of the writ in totalitarian societies are naturally enough regarded as one of the decisively differentiating factors between our democracy and totalitarian governments.

Though even this rhetoric may be a bit overdone, it nonetheless reflects the importance that has come to be attached to habeas corpus. It is a symbol of freedom, as well as an instrument. What is significant in the rhetoric is not the degree of exaggeration but rather the extent of truth.

Habeas corpus is accorded a special place in the Constitution. Article I, section 9, of the basic document, included even before the BILL OF RIGHTS was appended, contains the following provision: "The privilege of the Writ of Habeas Corpus shall not be suspended, unless when in Cases of Rebellion or Invasion the public Safety may require it."

This text of course presumes an understanding of what habeas corpus is. Technically, it is simply a writ, or court order, commanding a person who holds another in custody to demonstrate to the court legal justification for that restraint of personal liberty. The name "habeas corpus" derives from the opening words of the ancient COMMON LAW writ that commanded the recipient to "have the body" of the prisoner present at the court, there to be subject to such disposition as the court should order. A writ of habeas corpus, even one directed to an official custodian, can be obtained routinely by the prisoner or by someone on his behalf. As at common law, the writ that starts proceedings also defines the nature of those proceedings (and lends its name to them and, sometimes, to the final order granting relief). Thus, habeas corpus not only requires the custodian promptly to produce the prisoner in court but also precipitates an inquiry into the justification for the restraint and may result in an order commanding release.

The writ itself is no more than a procedural device that sets in motion a judicial inquiry. Yet the importance attached to habeas corpus necessarily posits that a court will not accept a simple showing of official authority as sufficient justification for imprisonment. Otherwise, the constitutional provision would indeed be much ado about nothing. "The privilege of the Writ" would hardly be worth guaranteeing if it did not invoke substantial criteria for what are sufficient legal grounds for depriving a person of liberty.

The principle that even an order of the king was not itself sufficient basis had been established in England before the time of our Constitution. In *Darnel's Case* (1627), during the struggle for parliamentary supremacy, a custodian's return to a writ of habeas corpus asserted that the prisoner was held by "special command" of the king, and the court accepted this as sufficient justification. This case precipitated three House of Commons resolutions and a PETITION OF RIGHT, assented to by the king, declaring habeas corpus available to examine the underlying cause of a detention and, if no legitimate cause be shown, to order the prisoner released. But even these actions did not resolve the matter. Finally, two HABEAS CORPUS ACTS, of 1641 and 1679, together established habeas corpus as an effective remedy looking beyond formal authority to examine the sufficiency of the actual cause for holding a prisoner.

Although the Habeas Corpus Acts did not extend to the American colonies, the principle that the sovereign had to show just cause for imprisoning an individual was carried over to the colonies. After the Revolution, the underlying principle was implicitly incorporated in the constitutional provision guaranteeing the regular availability of habeas corpus against suspension by the new central national government.

The broad assumptions underlying the Great Writ have been well articulated by HENRY HART. Speaking in the particular context of PROCEDURAL DUE PROCESS for ALIENS, but with general implications, he wrote of:

> the great and generating principle . . . that the Constitution always applies when a court is sitting with JURISDICTION in habeas corpus. For then the Court has always to inquire, not only whether the statutes have observed, but whether the petitioner before it has been "deprived of life, liberty, or property, without due process of law," or injured in any other way in violation of the FUNDAMENTAL LAW. . . .
>
> That principle forbids a CONSTITUTIONAL COURT with JURISDICTION in habeas corpus from ever accepting as an adequate return to the writ the mere statement that what has been done is authorized by act of Congress. The inquiry remains, if MARBURY V. MADISON still stands, whether the act of Congress is consistent with the fundamental law. Only upon such a principle could the Court reject, as it surely would, a return to the writ which informed it that the applicant for admission [to the United States] lay stretched upon a rack with pins driven in behind his fingernails pursuant to authority duly conferred by statute in order to secure the information necessary to determine his admissibility. The same principle which would justify rejection of this return imposes responsibility to inquire into the adequacy of other returns [Hart, 1953: 1393–1394].

It hardly requires demonstration that an executive directive can provide no more justification than an act of Congress. In fact the Supreme Court very early held in *Ex parte Bollman and Swartwout* (1807) that a President's order was not itself a sufficient basis for a return to a writ of habeas corpus.

The purpose of the habeas corpus clause of Article I, section 9, is to assure availability of the writ, but the provision clearly allows its suspension when necessary in the event of rebellion or invasion. The power to suspend the writ has been rarely invoked. Suspensions were proclaimed during the CIVIL WAR; in 1871, to combat the Ku Klux Klan in North Carolina; in 1905, in the Philippines; and in Hawaii during WORLD WAR II. Furthermore, two of these suspensions were limited by the Supreme Court. In the first case, EX PARTE MILLIGAN (1866), the Supreme Court held that the writ was not suspended in states (e.g., Indiana) where the public safety was not threatened by the Civil War. In the last case, DUNCAN V. KAHANAMOKU (1946), the Supreme Court held that the writ was not suspended in Hawaii eight months after the attack on Pearl Harbor because the public safety was no longer threatened by invasion.

The point is not the rarity with which the power to suspend the writ of habeas corpus has been invoked in this country's history. That can be seen as a function of the relative stability and insulation that the nation has enjoyed. Rather, the significant point is the basic acceptance of the proposition that the courts remain open in habeas corpus proceedings to consider the validity of an attempted suspension of the writ and, if they find it invalid, to examine the validity of the detention. This position has not always been respected by the immediately affected executive or military authorities, and such holdings by the Supreme Court have been handed down after immediate hostilities have ended. Nevertheless, the ultimate verdict of history has upheld the courts' position. The existence of those Supreme Court precedents, and their acceptance and perceived vindication by history, help bolster the likelihood of similar judicial action in response to future emergencies.

The habeas corpus writ described by Article I is not necessarily one issued by a federal court. The Constitution posits the existence of state courts as the basic courts of the nation; it does not require the creation of lower federal courts at all. Thus, the suspension clause was designed to protect habeas corpus in state courts from impairment by the new national government.

The clause may nonetheless have reflected a wider sense of moral duty. The first Congress, in establishing a system of lower federal courts, gave federal judges the power to issue the writ on behalf of prisoners held "under or by colour of the authority of the United States." The federal courts have always retained that habeas corpus jurisdiction, and it has since been much expanded.

Perhaps the most dramatic example of the use of habeas corpus occurred in *Ex parte Milligan*. Milligan, a civilian living in Indiana, was sentenced to death by a court-martial during the Civil War though the local GRAND JURY had refused to indict him. The Supreme Court held that courts-martial do not have jurisdiction to try civilians so long as the civilian courts are open. The Court further held that the writ of habeas corpus was not suspended, despite the general language of a statute purporting to suspend the writ during the Civil War, because the public safety was not threatened in Indiana.

Habeas corpus also provided an effective remedy for challenging an extraordinary extension of military power during World War II. The government relocated Japanese Americans away from their homes on the West Coast to detention camps inland. Although the Supreme Court in *Korematsu v. United States* (1944) held the relocation to be constitutional, the Court on the same day held in a habeas corpus case, *Ex parte Endo* (1944), that the government was not authorized to confine Japanese Americans in the camps against their will. (See JAPANESE AMERICAN CASES, 1943–1944.)

Nor is the availability of habeas corpus to challenge extraordinary military actions limited to American citizens or residents. Even German saboteurs, landed in this country by submarine, were permitted during wartime to challenge the power of a special military commission over them. Though the Court rejected that challenge in EX PARTE QUIRIN (1942), the exercise of military power was drawn into question and examined; the Court denied relief on the merits, holding that the asserted jurisdiction was constitutional.

Habeas corpus is not restricted to testing major or extraordinary extensions of power. Particularly in the last few decades, the writ has provided a means by which federal courts have regularly controlled the reach and exercise of fairly commonplace court-martial jurisdiction. For example, in United States ex rel. *Toth v. Quarles* (1955), military police arrested an ex-serviceman in Pennsylvania and flew him to Korea to stand trial in a court-martial on charges related to his time in service. (See MILITARY JUSTICE AND THE CONSTITUTION.) A writ of habeas corpus issued, Toth was returned to the United States, and the civilian court that had issued the writ ordered him released on the ground that he was a civilian not subject to military jurisdiction. More generally and more routinely, habeas proceedings have provided the means to define and enforce constitutional boundaries determining which persons and events may be tried without civilian courts and their procedures. Habeas corpus is a residual font of authority to ensure that the Constitution is not violated whenever individuals are imprisoned.

Indeed, habeas corpus proceedings are not limited to the enforcement of constitutional rights; they also open for scrutiny other issues of basic legal authority. For example, the writ has been used as a means to invoke JUDICIAL REVIEW of individual administrative orders for military CONSCRIPTION or alien DEPORTATION. The issues raised have included questions of statutory authority and the existence of a basis in fact for the official order. Most significant, the federal courts were unwilling to take general language precluding judicial review as barring habeas corpus; habeas corpus proceedings were held to be available even though the applicable statutes expressly provided that the administrative action should be final. Here again that position, insisting on the primacy of habeas corpus, was subsequently vindicated, and indeed, ratified by Congress in statutory revisions. Whether the Constitution entitles an individual to judicial review of military draft or IMMIGRATION orders still has not been authoritatively resolved. One of the strengths of habeas corpus, however, is that it permitted that issue to be finessed. The availability of *habeas corpus* facilitated avoidance of an ultimate confrontation—which might well have resulted in a rejection of the constitutional claim—while securing reaffirmation of the principle that government is subject to the RULE OF LAW as applied in the ordinary courts.

Our focus to this point has been on the writ from a federal court directed to a federal officer or custodian. The matter becomes more complex when the issues involve the relationships between federal and state governments. Seizure of one government's agents by the other, and their release from resulting custody, can be crucial factors in a struggle for political power. It is no accident, then, that the writ has been involved—and had evolved—in jurisdictional battles within or among governments. This involvement was evident, as mentioned earlier, in the battle for parliamentary supremacy over the crown in Britain. The writ has also played an important role in the changing relationships of federal and state governments in this country, and has in turn been shaped by these evolving relationships.

When the first Congress gave the lower federal courts power to issue the writ, it limited the power to federal prisoners and, even as to them, did not provide for exclusive jurisdiction. The state courts, then, had CONCURRENT JURISDICTION to issue habeas corpus for federal prisoners and exclusive *habeas* jurisdiction for state prisoners. The succeeding centuries have witnessed a huge expansion of federal power, including a shift of much power from the states to the central government. As the power of the federal government grew, the federal courts gradually gained the power to issue writs of habeas corpus for state prisoners. At the same time, the power of state courts to issue habeas corpus for federal prisoners has narrowed and today is practically extinguished.

As with many American legal institutions the conflict

over slavery figured prominently in the development. The Fugitive Slave Act of 1850, which was enacted as part of the COMPROMISE OF 1850, increased federal power at the expense of the states. Enforcement of the act, which required return of escaped slaves to their owners, met strong resistance in Northern states. State courts would order the arrest of federal officers who attempted to enforce the act and would issue writs of habeas corpus to release individuals charged with violating the act. The federal officers were not helpless, however. Although the federal courts did not have general power to issue writs of habeas corpus for state prisoners, they had been empowered to release state prisoners imprisoned for actions taken pursuant to federal law. Congress had granted this power in 1833 in response to South Carolina's threat to arrest anyone who attempted to collect the federal tariff. The federal courts exercised the power in the 1850s and 1860s to release federal agents arrested for enforcing the Fugitive Slave Act. (See FUGITIVE SLAVERY.)

A more intractable problem was posed by state court writs of habeas corpus releasing individuals convicted in federal court of violating the Fugitive Slave Act. The Supreme Court resolved this problem in ABLEMAN V. BOOTH (1859), holding that state courts did not have the power to release prisoners held pursuant to proceedings in federal court. Otherwise, the laws of the United States could be rendered unenforceable in states whose courts were in opposition. After the Civil War, the Supreme Court went further and held in *Tarble's Case* (1872) that state courts could not issue habeas corpus to release someone held under authority, or color of authority, of the federal government. A state court may only require the federal officer to inform it of the authority for a prisoner's detention; all further questions as to actions under color of federal authority are to be resolved in the federal courts. Habeas corpus cannot be entirely barred, but so long as the writ is available from the federal courts, state courts are effectively precluded from issuing habeas corpus on behalf of persons held in custody by the federal government.

The power of federal courts to issue habeas corpus for state prisoners followed the opposite course. The JUDICIARY ACT OF 1789 did not give the federal courts any such power and, until after the Civil War, these courts were granted it only in a limited number of circumstances. An example was the release of those seized for enforcing federal law, mentioned earlier. The HABEAS CORPUS ACT OF 1867, however, was general, giving federal courts power to issue the writ "in all cases where any person may be restrained of his or her liberty in violation of the constitution, or of any treaty or law of the United States. . . ." Jurisdiction in essentially these terms continues to the present day.

The precise objectives of the 1867 act were never defined. The act aimed generally at extending the effectiveness of federal authority, particularly against resistance in the former slave states. Its terms extended to prisoners in state custody as to all other persons. Until well into the twentieth century, its thrust was principally against restraints without (or before) trial. Among other reasons, the federal Constitution had not yet been construed to impose any significant requirements for state criminal proceedings. In more recent times, federal habeas corpus has become a forum for challenging state criminal convictions on constitutional grounds. In terms of volume, this is the federal writ's principal use today.

This pattern evolved only sporadically, and only after a number of limiting concepts had been loosened. The first of these was a principle of long standing that habeas corpus was available to persons imprisoned under authority of a court, particularly following criminal trial and conviction, only on the grounds that the court had no jurisdiction to try him. If that court had jurisdiction, all challenges, including constitutional ones, were to be raised there. Trial court decisions were to be reviewable, if at all, by higher courts, not by COLLATERAL ATTACK in other courts of the same level. It was often stated that habeas corpus was not to serve as a substitute for appeal.

The formal doctrine that the habeas corpus court would not look beyond whether the holding or convicting court had jurisdiction prevailed until near the middle of the twentieth century. Nevertheless, the scope of federal habeas corpus grew substantially even before that time. The concept of "lack of jurisdiction" is not inelastic, and the Supreme Court gradually expanded the meaning of that term to include constitutional violations that might be said to preclude a fair trial.

The first step in this expansion of the meaning of the issue of jurisdiction was to allow habeas corpus relief for a prisoner convicted of violating an unconstitutional law. Unconstitutional laws were null and void, it could be rationalized; thus the state court was without jurisdiction because *no* law authorized the conviction. The next step was to issue habeas corpus to remedy constitutional violations so gross as effectively to deprive the prisoner of a real trial. Such violations were held to be so fundamental that a court, proceeding in those circumstances, lost jurisdiction. Examples included mob-dominated trials and denial to defendants of opportunity to be heard. Reliance on the concept of lack of jurisdiction became more and more attenuated until, in *Waley v. Johnston* (1942), the Supreme Court explicitly abandoned that formal concept as linch-pin. From that time forward, the Court focused on more realistic considerations: whether the constitutional claims being asserted could not have been presented effectively in the original court that tried the case or on direct review of the conviction.

The concerns over the proper "deference" to be accorded by the habeas corpus court to the court that originally tried and convicted a prisoner arose even where both courts were federal. When federal habeas corpus was being sought by a state-convicted prisoner, these concerns were reinforced by further considerations of mutual respect and comity between state and federal systems. In response to these considerations, there developed early two substantial limits on the availability of federal habeas corpus for state prisoners: if the state courts had fully and fairly litigated the prisoner's claim, or if the prisoner failed to exhaust all state remedies, federal habeas corpus would not lie.

The requirement that state remedies be exhausted was established in *Ex parte Royall* (1886). To meet it, the prisoner must first press his claims to be free based on federal law, through the state courts. Thus, the prisoner must appeal his conviction or must seek state habeas corpus or other available postconviction remedy. (See EXHAUSTION OF REMEDIES.) Under the Constitution's SUPREMACY CLAUSE, state courts are required to follow and apply federal constitutional law. Principles of comity—essentially respect for the state courts' responsibility and ability to reach a correct decision—were seen to require that state courts be allowed an opportunity to correct their own errors before federal habeas corpus could be issued. The general exhaustion requirement is now codified in the statute governing habeas corpus.

In view of the exhaustion requirement, it may seem ironic that for many years presentation of the federal claim in state proceedings might mean that it could not thereafter be considered in federal habeas corpus. Federal collateral attack was barred if the state courts had sufficiently considered and passed upon the prisoner's constitutional claim. This is not so perverse as might first appear. Habeas corpus, as a collateral remedy, was to deal with serious constitutional problems involving circumstances outside the record or cognizance of the state courts. It would also serve where appellate consideration was unavailable or ineffective. If the state courts had adjudicated the federal constitutional contention adversely to the prisoner, on full and fair consideration and with effective appellate review, the remedy for error was to seek review in the United States Supreme Court. This was another aspect of the principle that habeas corpus was not to do service as an appeal.

The soundness of this reasoning depends, of course, upon Supreme Court reviews being available and effective. But whatever may once have been true, by the middle of the twentieth century that premise had clearly become unreliable. The Court's docket had grown to the point that it could pass on the merits of no more than a sixth of the cases in which its review was sought. The percentage has become even smaller in recent years. Moreover, even when available, appellate review in particular cases may be innately limited in significant respects because it must be conducted on the basis of a "cold" written record. Tones, attitudes, inflections of voice, and other subtle factors may exert powerful influences on outcomes and yet not be evident on the record. Beyond that, in many criminal proceedings an adequate written record may not even be produced. The significance of these factors in limiting the utility of Supreme Court review is greatly heightened when the applicable federal law is developing rapidly, and particularly if state judges are hostile to or less than entirely sympathetic with the direction of that development. Both of these conditions existed in the 1930s and 1940s and both intensified in the period following World War II, when the Supreme Court greatly expanded the procedural requirements imposed by federal constitutional law in state criminal prosecutions. Many requirements that previously governed only federal CRIMINAL PROCEDURE were "incorporated" into the FOURTEENTH AMENDMENT and made applicable in state trials. (See INCORPORATION DOCTRINE.) Moreover, and surely of no less import, the Supreme Court was also expansively construing the EQUAL PROTECTION CLAUSE of the Fourteenth Amendment to heighten prohibitions against RACIAL DISCRIMINATION. That attitude enhanced federal scrutiny of jury selection and other elements of state criminal proceedings. Particularly in the early stages of the development of these growing constitutional demands, there was reason to believe that many state judges might be less than fully sympathetic, if not directly hostile, to these new federal principles and DOCTRINES.

Under these conditions, direct appellate review by the Supreme Court could not alone provide reliable and effective enforcement of federal constitutional guarantees in the state courts. Indeed, any tendency toward heel-dragging or resistance might well be encouraged by the knowledge that the statistical probability of federal appellate review was very low. Moreover, by diverting Supreme Court energy to enforcement of earlier holdings, resistance might effectively retard further development of the new doctrines.

Habeas corpus from federal courts probing the validity of state convictions could offer an alternative mode for securing effective enforcement of the new constitutional rights. Federal judges generally could be relied upon to be more in tune with Supreme Court developments than their state counterparts. Because the entire federal judiciary would be involved, case-load capacity would be much more equal to the task. Moreover, because trial-type hearings were possible, habeas corpus had the further advantage that the federal courts need not be dependent upon the state court record. These gains could, of course, be achieved only by abandoning the rule that barred consideration on federal habeas corpus of contentions that had been adjudicated previously in the state courts. The Supreme Court took that step in 1953 in *Brown v. Allen.*

Brown v. Allen represented a major extension of the functions of habeas corpus. Its holding, allowing federal reconsideration of issues previously considered fully by state courts, also effectively opened wide the range of constitutional contentions that could serve as sufficient grounds for seeking federal habeas corpus. From that point forward, it was clear that at the very least any constitutional claim that could be said to raise any significant issue of trial fairness would be open to consideration. That expansion of the scope of habeas corpus serves important ends, but it has significant costs.

One of these costs is the adverse reaction of many state judges. The result of *Brown v. Allen* is that federal courts on habeas corpus may reexamine a state prisoner's constitutional challenges to his conviction after a state court has considered and rejected those same challenges. Because the prisoner must exhaust his state remedies before federal habeas corpus, normally the federal constitutional claims have been pressed not only at the state trial but throughout the state court system, including the state supreme court. The upshot of the new role of federal habeas corpus, then, is that a single federal district judge routinely may review the determination of the highest court of a state and, if he disagrees with it, overturn the conviction that the collegial, multimember court had upheld.

People and state officials in general, and state supreme court justices in particular, long since have become accustomed to review by the Supreme Court of the United States. Whatever may have been thought in their time of the challenges raised and rejected in MARTIN V. HUNTER'S LESSEE (1816) and COHENS V. VIRGINIA (1821), the higher authority of the Supreme Court in matters of federal law has been fully accepted. There has not been a corresponding acceptance of the habeas corpus authority of lower federal court judges. That federal judges may be more in accord with developing Supreme Court doctrines, though offered as justification, does not palliate the felt insult. On the contrary, if state judges are hostile to those developments, that fact exacerbates it. If the state court justices see themselves as entirely in accord with the Supreme Court's developing doctrines, the routine reexamination by a single district judge may still be offensive, to some perhaps even more so. On occasion, state courts have even openly refused to pass upon a constitutional claim on the grounds that a federal judge would pass on it anyway. On balance, the expansion of federal habeas corpus jurisdiction has almost certainly enhanced even state court enforcement of federal constitutional rights, but the felt slight to status and the consequent resentment are real.

At least as important as the resentment of state judges is the concern that the wide availability of federal habeas corpus may dilute the deterrent effect of the criminal law. Part of this concern grows out of the belief that deterrence is enhanced by certainty of punishment and that the expansion of federal habeas corpus increases the possibility that a conviction may be overturned. Certainly, the availability of federal habeas corpus, after the full range of state court remedies, does mean that the finality of a conviction is greatly delayed, even when the conviction is ultimately upheld. Moreover, the knowledge that the ultimate decision can always be greatly delayed itself diminishes any general sense in the community that punishment may be swift or certain.

When the conviction is overturned years after the trial and even longer after the alleged crime, these effects are exacerbated. Although the usual habeas corpus remedy is to order release only if the prisoner is not retried and convicted within a reasonable time, retrial after considerable delay may be practically impossible: witnesses may have died or disappeared; memories inevitably fade; other evidence may be lost. In those instances a reversal on procedural grounds amounts to a full release.

In fact, the proportion of habeas corpus proceedings that result in any victory for the prisoner is exceedingly small. But the effect of those few cases may be far greater than their number, particularly if a case was notorious in the community. Each such incident attracts attention and presumably lessens the deterrent effect of the criminal law. It may also be important that each raises questions for the citizenry at large who are already fearful about the capacity of the system to cope with crime.

Finally, the rehabilitative functions of the penal system may be affected. It has been suggested that demonstration of society's deep concern for fair procedure is useful, and even that channeling prisoners' efforts into litigation may be helpful. But it is more likely that the indefinite stringing-out of a conclusion is counterproductive. As Justice LEWIS F. POWELL, concurring in SCHNECKLOTH V. BUSTAMONTE (1973), wrote: "No effective judicial system can afford to concede the continuing theoretical possibility that there is error in every trial and that every incarceration is unfounded. At some point the law must convey to those in custody that a wrong has been committed, that consequent punishment has been imposed, that one should no longer look back with the view to resurrecting every imaginable basis for further litigation but rather should look forward to rehabilitation and to becoming a constructive citizen."

The concerns expressed are real and significant, but they can be accommodated only by restricting the scope of federal habeas corpus. That in turn involves a judgment as to the necessity of having federal judges routinely available to consider particular claims of constitutional violations. Every constitutional claim is important. But the issue here is not whether a constitutional right shall be declared, or whether rights so declared shall be binding on state courts and subject to review and enforcement by the federal Supreme Court. The issue is whether there should be an additional, collateral channel for routine re-examination of every state court rejection of every constitutional claim asserted in a criminal proceeding.

While perhaps in theory all constitutional rights are equal, there are differences among them. For one thing, there may be substantial differences in the justifications for, and consequences of, seeking thoroughgoing enforcement of particular rights in every case where they may be colorably claimed. The Supreme Court has recognized as much in holding that some newly established constitutional rights should be given full retroactive effect (applying to all habeas corpus cases regardless of when the original conviction was obtained) and others should not. In at least one sense it is fair to characterize these decisions as holding some constitutional rights to be more fundamental than others.

Furthermore, constitutional rights serve different sets of purposes. Most procedural requirements in criminal prosecutions are designed to minimize the likelihood of an erroneous conviction, for example, the RIGHT TO COUNSEL or the right to confront prosecution witnesses. (See CONFRONTATION.) Others are designed to protect personal privacy or dignity at trial or in the society; among these are the rules against UNREASONABLE SEARCHES or seizures, and the RIGHT AGAINST SELF-INCRIMINATION. Finally, there may be relevant distinctions between rights and remedies. Thus, the rule excluding evidence obtained by prohibited police actions may be viewed as a means to deter official misconduct rather than an independent right.

These distinctions may be highly relevant in determining the appropriate scope of federal habeas corpus in re-examining state court convictions. Consider, for example, the EXCLUSIONARY RULE that evidence obtained by an unconstitutional search may not be used in a criminal prosecution. State convictions obtained after such evidence has been introduced are invalid and subject to reversal on direct Supreme Court review. (See MAPP V. OHIO, 1961). But if in a particular case the state courts should decide that the search was legal, how important is it that the decision be reviewable on federal habeas corpus—even assuming that the state decision might be wrong and yet not important enough to warrant Supreme Court attention? Illegally seized evidence does not mean actually unreliable evidence; in fact, such evidence is generally highly probative (for example, the drugs themselves in a prosecution for possession or sale of narcotics). The ban on unreasonable searches and the exclusionary rule do not protect

against convicting the wrong person; they aim to protect individual privacy and control police conduct. Thus the sole purpose of extending habeas corpus to encompass the exclusionary rule would be to enhance the rule's deterrent effect. But that enhancement would be only marginal, *i.e.*, only to the extent of whatever additional disincentive might be generated by the extra possibility of a conviction, upheld by the state courts, being overturned years later on federal habeas corpus. At the same time, any such gain could be only obtained at the cost of the side effects of habeas corpus already described, including particularly the problems involved in releasing individuals who have been proven to have violated the law.

The Supreme Court has vacillated on precisely this issue. After many years in which federal habeas corpus was held to encompass claims under the exclusionary rule, the Court in STONE V. POWELL (1976) decided that it would not be available to review decisions of SEARCH AND SEIZURE issues reached after full consideration.

That decision stirred much debate. Perhaps as a result of the prominent role of lawyers and judicial review in interpreting the Constitution, there is a tendency to focus attention on the borderlines of case law development. That perspective can be misleading. What is more important than the decision to exclude search and seizure issues is the scope of federal habeas corpus for state prisoners that remains available. Constitutional claims need not be related to ultimate accuracy of conviction in order to be included. Moreover, despite strong suggestions from respected sources that the prisoner's factual innocence ought to be a major element in the availability of habeas corpus relief, the Court has not adopted that position. By any measure, the range of constitutional claims that may be raised and relitigated in federal habeas corpus is far greater than those few precluded—and then only after full and fair state consideration.

Similarly, much of the legal writing concerning habeas corpus today deals with its use to challenge criminal convictions. It is sometimes even suggested that Congress could not constitutionally restrict the scope of that kind of habeas corpus. Related to this, but more generally, it is argued that the provision of Article I, section 9, against the suspension of the privilege of habeas corpus should now be interpreted as prohibiting Congress from suspending or limiting federal habeas corpus—including habeas corpus for state convicted prisoners. The argument generally acknowledges that this was not the original intention of the suspension clause. It contends, rather, that in view of subsequent developments and present conditions, the original purpose now calls for extending it to cover habeas corpus from federal courts.

While these arguments, and the general issue of federal habeas corpus for persons held under state court convictions, are important, too exclusive a focus on them risks distorted perspective. Far more significant than the existence of these arguments, or their validity, is their currently academic nature. Despite strenuous objections to the jurisdiction, Congress has not significantly restricted the scope of federal habeas corpus for state prisoners. Moreover, it does not derogate from the importance of this use of habeas corpus to point out that at base the availability of the Great Writ to challenge executive or military actions or other imprisonments without semblance of judicial process is far more vital to the maintenance of liberty. Even the most ardent advocates of collateral attack on judicial convictions are not likely to disagree.

It is surely a measure of the state of liberty in the United States that so much can be taken for granted. Habeas corpus for extraordinary assertions of executive, military, or other nonjudicial authority comes to the fore only rarely—and that is a measure of freedom's health in the nation. Yet it is that general freedom from that kind of arbitrary authority that is most crucial. Habeas corpus has helped to secure that freedom in the past, and its continuing availability helps secure it continually. It is true that liberty is most prevalent when habeas corpus is needed least. It is also true that the effectiveness of the remedy of habeas corpus is dependent upon the substantive criteria that come into play. Yet the existence of the Great Writ, indeed precisely in its taken-for-granted quality, plays a major role in supporting and reinforcing the conditions of freedom.

PAUL J. MISHKIN
(1986)

Bibliography

BATOR, PAUL M. et al. 1973 Supplement 1981 Chaps. I, IV, and X in *Hart & Wechsler's The Federal Courts and the Federal System*, 2nd ed. Mineola, N.Y.: Foundation Press.

CHAFEE, ZECHARIAH, JR. 1952 *How Human Rights Got into the Constitution*. Pages 51–74. Boston: Boston University Press.

COVER, ROBERT M. and ALEINIKOFF, T. ALEXANDER 1977 Dialectical Federalism: Habeas Corpus and the Court. *Yale Law Journal* 86:1035–1102.

DUKER, WILLIAM F. 1980 *A Constitutional History of Habeas Corpus*. Westport, Conn.: Greenwood Press.

FRIENDLY, HENRY J. 1970 Is Innocence Irrelevant? Collateral Attack on Criminal Judgments. *University of Chicago Law Review* 38:142–172.

HART, HENRY M. 1953 The Power of Congress to Limit the Jurisdiction of the Federal Courts: An Exercise in Dialectic. *Harvard Law Review* 66:1362–1402.

NOTE 1970 Developments in the Law—Federal Habeas Corpus. *Harvard Law Review* 83:1038–1280.

OAKS, DALLIN H. 1966 Legal History in the High Court—Habeas Corpus. *Michigan Law Review* 64:451–472.

HABEAS CORPUS
(Update 1)

A federal court is empowered to grant a writ of habeas corpus to any individual who is held in custody by federal or state government in violation of the Constitution of the United States. Although state courts also can provide habeas corpus relief to those in state custody, the most important contemporary use of habeas corpus is as a vehicle for federal court review of state court criminal convictions. After almost 200 years of habeas corpus litigation in the United States, including more than a century under the RECONSTRUCTION statutes that made federal court relief available to state prisoners, the scope of habeas corpus remains controversial.

Conservatives view habeas corpus as a means for guilty people to escape punishment. They seek to limit the availability of the writ, arguing that habeas corpus undermines the finality of criminal convictions and creates friction between federal and state courts. Liberals, in contrast, see federal habeas corpus review as an essential protection to assure that no person whose constitutional rights have been violated—whether factually innocent or guilty—is imprisoned.

The debate over the scope of habeas corpus review implicates major underlying disputes in constitutional law. For example, federal district court review of state court criminal convictions raises questions of FEDERALISM, along with the question of whether state judiciaries can be trusted to protect federal constitutional rights. Moreover, disagreements about the availability of habeas corpus reflect different views about the value of the constitutional rules governing CRIMINAL PROCEDURE. Those who oppose Supreme Court protections for criminal defendants (such as the EXCLUSIONARY RULE and MIRANDA RULE warnings) seek to limit their enforcement by narrowing the scope of habeas corpus review.

Not surprisingly, the Supreme Court frequently splits along ideological lines in ruling on habeas corpus issues. The WARREN COURT's expansion of habeas corpus relief was halted by the BURGER COURT, which adopted substantial new restrictions on federal court habeas review. Most recently, the REHNQUIST COURT has announced important additional limits on the matters that can be raised in federal habeas corpus proceedings. Three restrictions are particularly significant.

First, a petitioner is allowed to present in federal habeas corpus only those matters that were argued in the proceedings that led to his or her conviction, unless the individual can demonstrate cause for the failure to raise the objection and prejudice from the asserted constitutional violation. Under the Warren Court decision in FAY V. NOIA (1963), an individual could present a constitutional issue on habeas corpus, even if not argued earlier, unless it could be demonstrated that the person "deliberately bypassed" the earlier opportunity to litigate the matter. But the Burger Court expressly overruled this standard, which presumptively allowed issues to be presented in federal court, and instead held that new matters could be raised only if there was "cause" for the earlier default and "prejudice" arising from it.

In recent years, the Court has made it clear that the "cause and prejudice" standard is a difficult one to meet. In *Murray v. Carrier* (1986) the Supreme Court summarized the circumstances under which an individual has sufficient cause to raise a new matter on habeas corpus. The Court explained that there was sufficient cause to permit a federal habeas petition to raise a new matter only if defense counsel could not reasonably have known of a legal or factual issue, if the government's attorney interfered with the presentation of the issue, or if there was ineffective assistance of counsel. Each of these proofs of cause is hard to accomplish, and the difficulty reflects the Court's expressly stated view that federal habeas corpus relief has significant costs and should be limited. The Court, however, has said, in *Smith v. Murray* (1986), that individuals who can demonstrate that they are probably innocent of the crime for which they were convicted should be able to secure relief, regardless of the reason for the earlier procedural default.

Although several Supreme Court opinions define "cause," the Court has found fewer occasions to clarify the meaning of "prejudice." The Court indicated in *United States v. Frady* (1982) that a petitioner can meet this requirement only by demonstrating that the constitutional violations caused "actual and substantial disadvantage" that infected the "entire trial with errors of constitutional dimension."

Second, the Supreme Court has restricted the ability of individuals to relitigate on habeas corpus issues that were raised and decided in state court. In BROWN V. ALLEN (1953) the Court ruled that individuals claiming to be held in custody in violation of the United States Constitution could present their claims in federal court even if those claims had been fully and fairly litigated in the state court. But in STONE V. POWELL (1976) the Burger Court limited this PRECEDENT, holding that a petitioner could not relitigate the claim that a state court improperly had admitted evidence that was the product of an illegal search or seizure, provided that the state court had offered a full and fair opportunity for a hearing on the issue. The Court emphasized that exclusionary rule claims do not relate to the

accuracy of the fact-finding process. Furthermore, the Court said, state judges could be trusted to protect the FOURTH AMENDMENT.

The Court refused to extend *Stone v. Powell* to challenges to racial discrimination in GRAND JURY selection (*Rose v. Mitchell*, 1979), to BURDEN OF PROOF issues (*Jackson v. Virginia*, 1979), or to claims of ineffective assistance of counsel based on the failure to object to admission of evidence (*Kimmelman v. Morrison*, 1986). But in the 1989 case of *Duckworth v. Eagan*, two Justices, SANDRA DAY O'CONNOR and ANTONIN SCALIA, stated that they would apply *Stone* to bar habeas corpus review of claims of Fifth Amendment violations because of improper administration of *Miranda* warnings. In light of the evident desire of the conservative majority on the Court to constrict the availability of habeas corpus, the O'Connor-Scalia position may come to command a majority of the Court.

Finally, in *Teague v. Lane* (1989) the Supreme Court restricted the power of a federal court in habeas corpus to recognize new constitutional rights. Until *Teague*, federal courts considered habeas corpus petitions alleging constitutional violations, regardless of whether the court would be recognizing a new right that would not be applied retroactively in other cases. But in *Teague*, the Court held that habeas petitions may raise only claims to rights that are "dictated" by precedent, except where the recognition of a new right would have retroactive effect. Because few newly recognized criminal procedure rights are given retroactive application, *Teague* will effectively prevent federal habeas petitioners from presenting claims, except as to rights that have been established previously.

These three sets of restrictions on federal habeas corpus reflect the Supreme Court's desire to limit the procedural protections available to criminal defendants. But these decisions are disturbing for those who believe that a federal forum should be available to those convicted through violations of federal constitutional rights. Moreover, given a conservative Court that sees the costs of habeas corpus as generally outweighing its benefits given legislative pressures for federal statutes limiting habeas corpus review, further restrictions seem likely.

ERWIN CHEMERINSKY
(1992)

(SEE ALSO: *Procedural Due Process of Law, Criminal.*)

Bibliography

FRIEDMAN, BARRY 1988 A Tale of Two Habeas. *Minnesota Law Review* 73:247–347.
YACKLE, LARRY 1985 Explaining Habeas Corpus. *New York University Law Review* 60:991–1060.

HABEAS CORPUS
(Update 2)

The latin phrase "habeas corpus," literally translated as "produce the body," refers to a procedure in which persons held in custody by either the federal or state government may challenge their incarceration and/or sentence as unlawful. The person raising the challenge asks (or "petitions") a court to examine whether the custody or sentence is lawful. The relief sought—whether it be outright release, a new trial, or a change in the sentence—is in the form of a court order (or "writ").

Although Article I, section 9 of the Constitution refers to "[t]he privilege of the Writ of Habeas Corpus," it nowhere defines this right nor explains what circumstances will justify a court in granting a writ. Thus, the power of a federal court to issue a habeas corpus writ has always been defined by statute.

The first habeas corpus statute, the JUDICIARY ACT OF 1789, permitted federal courts to issue writs only with respect to federal prisoners. In the HABEAS CORPUS ACT OF 1867, Congress first provided that federal courts could also issue writs with respect to state prisoners who were "restrained in violation of the constitution, or of any treaty or law of the United States. . . ." In 1966, Congress enacted a habeas corpus statute using language virtually identical to that used in the 1867 act.

During the 1960s, the liberal WARREN COURT issued a series of rulings that greatly expanded the constitutional rights of criminal defendants. In a parallel development, the court also expanded the power of the federal courts to remedy unconstitutional state court convictions by granting habeas corpus relief. The combination of developments had an immediate practical consequence; state prisoners increasingly began to seek relief in federal court for violations of their constitutional rights.

This trend was perhaps most evident in CAPITAL PUNISHMENT cases. In 1976, the Supreme Court ruled that capital punishment was constitutional. In the decades since this ruling, habeas corpus became an extremely effective tool used by defense lawyers to prevent their clients from being executed.

With the expansion of rights in the 1960s, and with the increasing number of capital cases in the background, there was a reaction against the increasing use of habeas corpus to upset state court convictions. Many conservative jurists and scholars argued that grants of habeas relief imposed significant burdens on the CRIMINAL JUSTICE SYSTEM and caused tensions between state and federal courts. A state conviction upheld by the state supreme court could be overturned by a single federal judge who finds a constitutional violation. This power undercuts the concept of finality in state court proceedings. Conservatives argue that such a system breeds frustration among victims of crime and contempt for the criminal justice system. They claim that state judges are every bit as competent as federal judges to determine whether the federal Constitution has been violated, and that determinations made in state court should be respected by federal judges. Those advocating this view place a heavy emphasis on the finality of state court convictions as well as fostering COMITY between state and federal courts.

Moderate and liberal scholars have a distinctly different emphasis. They point out that the state judges who initially assess constitutional violations are, in many cases, locally elected officials. In criminal cases generally, and capital cases specifically, community tensions often run high. Frequently, a ruling in a defendant's favor, particularly in a high-profile capital case, could be extremely unpopular and have devastating consequences on the career of a popularly elected official.

In *Harris v. Alabama* (1995), Supreme Court Justice JOHN PAUL STEVENS examined statistics showing the startling frequency with which elected judges rule in favor of the state in capital cases. Stevens concluded that "[n]ot surprisingly, given the political pressures they face, judges are far more likely than juries to impose the death penalty." Because federal judges have lifetime tenure, their livelihood does not depend on maintaining the favor of an electorate. These judges, the argument goes, have a greater freedom to make decisions that may be unpopular. Those advocating this view are more concerned with the validity of a conviction in a particular case than with the more abstract notions of finality of state court convictions and comity between state and federal courts.

In light of these starkly different views of habeas corpus, it is not surprising that the conservative BURGER COURT and REHNQUIST COURT have reversed many rulings of the Warren Court and scaled back the power of federal courts to grant habeas relief. It is also not surprising that the debate over the appropriate role of habeas corpus has continued not only in the judicial branch, but in the legislative branch as well.

For many years conservative members of Congress sought to enact LEGISLATION that would curtail the ability of federal courts to grant habeas relief to persons in state custody. With the election of a Republican-controlled Congress in 1994, conservatives finally had an opportunity to pass this legislation. Motivated largely by concern over the increasing number of capital convictions found to be unconstitutional by federal courts throughout the country, Congress enacted the ANTITERRORISM AND EFFECTIVE DEATH PENALTY ACT OF 1996.

The act represents a massive revision of habeas corpus law. Although the act contains many new provisions—

most of which have yet to be interpreted—two of its provisions stand out as stark departures from longstanding practice.

Initially, and for the first time ever, the new act imposes a time limit within which a prisoner must seek habeas corpus relief. Under the old law, there was no formal time limit, only equitable principles regarding delay. Federal courts took a flexible approach to the issue. If a prisoner showed a serious violation of his constitutional rights, relief could be granted years later so long as the delay was not unreasonable and did not prejudice the state in its ability to respond to the claimed constitutional violation.

The new act jettisons this flexible approach and imposes a strict one-year time limit within which prisoners must seek relief. In the typical case, the one-year time period begins to run from the date the state conviction is final on appeal. This provision—mainly fueled by concern over delays in capital cases—applies to both noncapital and capital cases. Thus, in cases where a state conviction is final on appeal, the prisoner must either seek relief within one year or potentially forfeit the right to seek relief. Moreover, because the vast majority of prisoners are indigent (and because there is no right to have a lawyer appointed to determine whether habeas relief is warranted), most prisoners with meritorious claims will forfeit their rights without even knowing they had any.

The second major change fashioned by the 1996 act appears to be an extraordinary departure from existing practice. At least as early as BROWN V. ALLEN (1953), the Court had recognized that in deciding whether habeas relief was appropriate, federal courts were required to make an independent inquiry into the constitutionality of a particular conviction or sentence. The fact that a state court had passed on the question, and found no constitutional violation, was irrelevant. If the federal courts found that there was a constitutional violation, relief was appropriate.

Some lower courts have held that the new act alters this longstanding practice as well. According to this view, the new act requires federal courts to defer to the conclusions of state judges. Thus, even when a conviction is marred by a constitutional violation, relief is no longer permissible in most cases unless the state court's decision to the contrary was unreasonable. In other words, the new statute requires that state convictions be affirmed even though the state courts incorrectly concluded there were no constitutional violations, so long as the state courts were at least close.

As these provisions show, the new act reflects an approach to habeas corpus which exalts the finality of state court convictions and seeks to minimize the tension between state and federal courts. The cost of this approach is extreme; the act explicitly eliminates any remedy for many individuals who have convictions and sentences that

are plainly unconstitutional. Whether this is merely the latest and most politically expedient balance of the conflicting concerns that have been at the heart of the habeas debate for decades, or a lasting alteration of the habeas corpus landscape, remains to be seen.

CLIFF GARDNER
(2000)

Bibliography

GARDNER, CLIFF 1997 Litigating Habeas Cases Under the Antiterrorism and Effective Death Penalty Act of 1996: Retroactivity and Statutes of Limitations Questions. *California Criminal Defense Practice Reporter* 1997:441–446.

LIEBMAN, JAMES S. 1988 *Federal Habeas Corpus Practice and Procedure.* Chap. 2. Charlottesville, Virginia: Michie Co.

NOTE 1997 Rewriting the Great Writ: Standards of Review for Habeas Corpus Under The New 28 U.S.C. § 2254. *Harvard Law Review* 110:1868–1885.

YACKLE, LARRY W. 1996 A Primer on the New Habeas Corpus Statute. *Buffalo Law Review* 44:381–449.

HABEAS CORPUS ACT OF 1679
31 Charles II c.2 (1679)

The right to the writ of HABEAS CORPUS, as ZECHARIAH CHAFEE, Jr., said, is "the most important human rights provision in the Constitution" (Article I, section 9) because it safeguards personal liberty, without which other liberties cannot be exercised. This act of Parliament created no new right; the writ was already about a century old as a mechanism by which a prisoner could test in court the legality of his imprisonment. But crown officers knew a variety of stratagems that hamstrung the writ. This statute, which runs on and on in dull detail without a word about the liberty of the subject or any high-sounding principle, sought to seal off every means of circumventing the writ. It is a technical instruction manual—how and what to do in any situation—to make the writ enforceable as a practical remedy for illegal imprisonment. It imposed steep penalties on every officer of government, from the local jailor to the lord high chancellor for breach, evasion, or delay. The only loophole in the statute, a failure to prohibit excessive BAIL, was plugged in 1689 by the BILL OF RIGHTS. Although the statute did not extend to the colonies, it provided a model, and Americans regarded the great writ as a fundamental right protected by COMMON LAW and gave it constitutional status.

LEONARD W. LEVY
(1986)

Bibliography

PERRY, RICHARD L., ed. 1959 *Sources of Our Liberties.* Pages 189–203. New York: American Bar Foundation.

HABEAS CORPUS ACT OF 1863
12 Stat. 755 (1863)

Justice, before the CIVIL WAR and RECONSTRUCTION, was overwhelmingly state justice. Under the Constitution's Article III, implemented in the JUDICIARY ACT OF 1789, few litigants qualified for federal JURISDICTION. The 1863 Habeas Corpus law lessened this imbalance at least for federal officials who, enforcing EXECUTIVE ORDERS or statutes, were defendants in state courts. After legitimizing ABRAHAM LINCOLN'S HABEAS CORPUS suspensions since 1861 and authorizing future suspensions, Congress, in the Habeas Corpus Act, indemnified federal officials who had been found guilty in state courts of wrongs against civilians. Further, the law authorized a federal officer facing a state court proceeding to remove the case to a federal court. United States attorneys would act for the defendant if the state proceeding were prejudiced against him and if the defendant had been carrying out orders in a proper manner. Though federal proceedings were to flow from state rules, blacks could testify even adversely to whites, and all court officers and jurors were sworn to the TEST OATH. In extending these protections to its officials, the nation bridged, for them at least, ancient interstices in the dual system of courts. Congress exacted a price from the executive, however, by requiring relevant Cabinet department heads to report to federal judges on civilians arrested by soldiers for allegedly violating draft, internal security, emancipation, or trade-control policies. In the HABEAS CORPUS ACT of 1867, Congress further expanded the classes of protected persons who could resort to federal justice.

HAROLD M. HYMAN
(1986)

Bibliography

DUKER, WILLIAM F. 1980 *A Constitutional History of Habeas Corpus.* Pages 126–224. Westport, Conn.: Greenwood Press.

HABEAS CORPUS ACT OF 1867
14 Stat. 385 (1867)

This act, whose intent one expert has called "unusually murky," fundamentally amended the HABEAS CORPUS provisions of the JUDICIARY ACT OF 1789. Where that act limited availability of the writ to those persons jailed under federal authority, the new act applied "in all cases where any person may be restrained of his or her liberty in violation of the constitution, or of any treaty or law of the United States." Section 1 vested power to issue the writ in all United States courts and judges, established procedures, and authorized APPEALS from inferior courts to CIRCUIT COURTS and to the Supreme Court. A writ could issue

at any point in state court proceedings, halting them until the federal habeas corpus action ended. The second section made available WRITS OF ERROR from the Supreme Court in specified instances.

The act gave the Supreme Court JURISDICTION over the appeal of a Mississippi editor who challenged the constitutionality of military reconstruction, but in 1868 Congress withdrew the provisions establishing the Supreme Court's APPELLATE JURISDICTION, and in EX PARTE MCCARDLE (1869) the Court declined to hear the editor's case. The Court nevertheless asserted authority on another statutory basis in *Ex parte Yerger* (1869), and Congress restored the Court's power to hear habeas corpus appeals in 1885.

The federal courts' statutory authority to grant writs of habeas corpus to state prisoners unconstitutionally held in custody continues to this day.

DAVID GORDON
(1986)

HAGUE v. CONGRESS OF INDUSTRIAL ORGANIZATIONS
307 U.S. 496 (1939)

In separate opinions yielding no majority, over two dissents, and with only seven Justices participating, the Court enjoined enforcement of a local ordinance used to harass labor organizers. Justices OWEN ROBERTS and HUGO L. BLACK and Chief Justice CHARLES EVANS HUGHES deemed the right to organize under and discuss the WAGNER (NATIONAL LABOR RELATIONS) ACT a privilege or immunity of national CITIZENSHIP. Justices HARLAN FISKE STONE and STANLEY F. REED held it a right protected by the FIRST AMENDMENT. Justice Stone's separate opinion, which suggested that SECTION 1983's jurisdictional counterpart authorized federal courts to hear actions involving personal liberty but not to hear actions involving property rights, influenced subsequent CIVIL RIGHTS cases. Some courts accepted the distinction and applied the dichotomy to section 1983 itself. *Lynch v. Household Finance Corp.* (1972) discredited the distinction.

THEODORE EISENBERG
(1986)

HAIG v. AGEE
453 U.S. 280 (1981)

Philip Agee, a former employee of the Central Intelligence Agency (CIA) who was familiar with its covert intelligence gathering, revealed the identities of its agents and sources, disrupting the intelligence operations of the United States, and exposing CIA operatives to assassination. The secretary of state revoked Agee's passport because his activities abroad damaged national security. Agee objected that revocation of his passport violated his constitutional FREEDOM OF SPEECH, and PROCEDURAL DUE PROCESS. An 8–2 SUPREME COURT found his claims meritless, because his freedom to travel abroad was subordinate to national security considerations, his disclosures obstructed intelligence operations and therefore were unprotected by the FIRST AMENDMENT, and his right to due process was satisfied by the opportunity for a prompt hearing after revocation. The dissenters did not rely on constitutional grounds.

LEONARD W. LEVY
(1986)

HAINES, CHARLES G.
(1879–1948)

Charles Grove Haines was an eminent scholar of American constitutional history who taught political science at the University of California, Los Angeles. In 1939 he was president of the American Political Science Association. His major books continue to be among the best on their subjects. His *Revival of Natural Law Concepts* (1930) is a comparative study of theories of FUNDAMENTAL LAW. *The American Doctrine of Judicial Supremacy* (revised edition, 1932) is the finest book on the history of JUDICIAL REVIEW from the standpoint of a critic of the institution. His *Role of the Supreme Court in American Government and Politics* (volume I, 1944; volume II, posthumous and coauthored by Forest Sherwood, 1957), covering the period 1789 to 1864, is a trenchant history from the viewpoint of a Jeffersonian democrat.

LEONARD W. LEVY
(1986)

HALL v. DECUIR
95 U.S. 485 (1877)

In 1870 the operator of a steamboat regularly traveling between New Orleans, Louisiana, and Vicksburg, Mississippi, refused a black woman accommodation in the cabin reserved for whites. He thereby violated a Louisiana statute, adopted during the period of MILITARY RECONSTRUCTION, which prohibited RACIAL DISCRIMINATION by common carriers operating within the state. Speaking for the Court, Chief Justice MORRISON R. WAITE sought to avoid the "great inconvenience and unnecessary hardship" which might arise if all states bordering the Mississippi River were to enact divergent and conflicting laws. Waite stressed the importance of uniform regulations and struck down the

state act as a "direct burden upon INTERSTATE COMMERCE" in violation of Article I, section 8. Nearly seventy years later, in MORGAN V. VIRGINIA (1946), the Supreme Court struck down a law requiring racial SEGREGATION on buses, on a similar commerce ground. Neither opinion discussed the EQUAL PROTECTION clause.

DAVID GORDON
(1986)

HAMILTON, ALEXANDER
(1755–1804)

Alexander Hamilton, American statesman, member of the Constitutional Convention (1787), coauthor of THE FEDERALIST, first secretary of the Treasury (1789–1795), and leading member of the Federalist party in New York, was born on the island of Nevis in the British West Indies. He came to New York in 1773 and enrolled in King's College; he served with distinction in the Revolutionary War, from 1777 to 1781 as GEORGE WASHINGTON's aide-de-camp. Hamilton was a leading member of the New York bar before and after he served in President Washington's cabinet.

During the prelude to independence, Hamilton participated in the pamphlet controversies between American Whigs and supporters of Britain. His most important pamphlet, "The Farmer Refuted" (1775), expressed a conventional natural rights philosophy. He asserted that "nature has distributed an equality of rights to every man." He also upheld the right to resort to first principles above and beyond the "common forms of municipal law." He subscribed to the theory of government as a social compact between ruler and ruled (a model used by WILLIAM BLACKSTONE rather than JOHN LOCKE) and, like JOHN ADAMS and THOMAS JEFFERSON, argued that the British king was "King of America, by virtue of a compact between us and the King of Great Britain."

Hamilton, who by origin was not rooted in any one of the thirteen states, became an early and perhaps the most outspoken advocate of a stronger and more centralized government for the United States. In 1780 he developed a far-reaching program of constitutional reform. First, he pleaded for a vast increase in the power of Congress and asked for a convention for the purpose of framing a confederation, to give Congress complete sovereignty in all matters relating to war, peace, trade, finance, and the management of FOREIGN AFFAIRS. Second, he called for a more efficient organization of the executive tasks of Congress. Individuals were better suited than boards of administration (with the possible exception of trade matters), because responsibility was then less diffused; "men of the first pretentions" would be more attracted to these tasks if offered individual responsibility. Hamilton developed his plea for strengthening Congress in "The Continental-ist" (1781–1782) in which he revealed his future political program by pointing to the need "to create in the interior of each state a mass of influence in favour of the Foederal Government." As a delegate from New York to Congress (1782–1783), Hamilton criticized the ARTICLES OF CONFEDERATION. Only in September 1786 did he succeed having the Annapolis Convention endorse his resolution for calling a convention to meet in Philadelphia in May 1787 "to devise such further provisions as shall appear to them necessary to render the constitution of the Foederal Government adequate to the exigencies of the Union."

Hamilton took a strong stand during that period against New York state legislation discriminating against Loyalists. His "Letters of Phocion" (1784) defended individual rights and the rule of law against "arbitrary acts of legislature," as well as the supremacy of the state constitution over acts of the legislature. As counsel for the defense in the New York case of RUTGERS V. WADDINGTON (1784) Hamilton argued that the New York Trespass Act (1783), which enabled people who had fled New York when British forces occupied the city to recover damages from persons who had held their premises during the occupation, was incompatible with higher law—that of the law of nations, of the peace treaty, and of commands of Congress. The Court did not accept the argument for JUDICIAL REVIEW, but followed another of Hamilton's arguments: that the legislature could not have meant to violate the law of nations.

At the CONSTITUTIONAL CONVENTION OF 1787, Hamilton was somewhat an outsider for two reasons. First, the other two members of the New York delegation, JOHN LANSING and ROBERT YATES, opposed a stronger central government. Second, Hamilton's views, presented to the Convention in a five-hour speech on June 18, were extreme on two counts: he advocated the abolition of states as states, favoring a system that would leave them only subordinate jurisdiction; and he advocated tenure during GOOD BEHAVIOR both for members of the Senate and for the chief executive. He admitted that in his private opinion the British government was "the best in the world." Hamilton's constitutional proposals reflected the idea of "mixed government": the lower house of Congress should be elected on the basis of democratic manhood suffrage, yet the Senate and the President ought to be elected by electors with high property qualifications. A chief reason for Hamilton's "high-toned" constitutional ideas was that "he was much discouraged by the amazing extent of Country"; he feared disruptive tendencies, originating particularly from the larger and more powerful states.

Could his constitutional proposals influenced by the British model still be termed republican? Hamilton held that the standards of republican government were re-spected as long as "power, mediately, or immediately, is derived from the consent of the people," or as long as all magistrates were appointed by "the people, or a process of election originating with the people." Against later charges of "monarchism," Hamilton replied that his plan submitted at Philadelphia was conformable "with the strict theory of a Government purely republican; the essential criteria of which are that the principal organs of the Executive and Legislative departments be elected by the people and hold their offices by a responsible and temporary or defeasible tenure."

Though Hamilton absented himself during much of the Convention's work, he signed the Constitution on September 17, 1787, as the only member from New York, indicating that he saw only an alternative between anarchy, on the one hand, and "the chance of good to be expected from the plan," on the other.

During the struggle for ratification of the Constitution (1787–1788), Hamilton's two major achievements were the publication of *The Federalist* essays and his part in the New York ratifying convention at Poughkeepsie. He organized and coordinated publication of *The Federalist*, which appeared over the signature of "Publius" from late October 1787, to late May 1788. Of the eighty-five essays, Hamilton wrote fifty-one. In them he developed several major themes, some of which also recurred in his speeches in the New York Ratifying Convention.

Hamilton proved the utility of the union to America's political prosperity chiefly by painting a somber picture of international rivalry, ever ready to exploit dissensions among the states; he raised the specter of a disrupted Confederation, of war between the states, and of the rise of partial confederations, the most likely and most dangerous contingency being the formation of a northern and a southern confederacy. Hamilton then demonstrated the insufficiency of the Confederation to preserve the union by pointing to the necessity that the federal government, to be effective, "carry its agency to the persons of the citizens." He envisaged a broad scope for the powers granted to the federal government. The powers needed to provide for the common defense of the members of the Union "ought to exist without limitation." A vast scope for the federal power to regulate commerce and to provide for the financial needs of the Union, and the maxim that "every POWER ought to be in proportion to its OBJECT," foreshadowed Hamilton's later constructions of the Constitution while he directed the Treasury. The Constitution ought to allow a capacity "to provide for future contingencies," which were illimitable.

Hamilton's most important contribution to the analysis of institutions and procedures is his discussion of the executive branch in *The Federalist* #67–77. Believing that efficient administration was the very core of good government, he supported an individual executive who would be less likely than a plural executive "to conceal faults, and destroy responsibility." The office of chief magistrate, if not shackled by brief duration or restrictions on reeligibility, might attract men imbued with "the love of fame, the ruling passion of the noblest minds" (#72).

Hamilton's analysis of the federal judiciary is best known for the justification of judicial review in *The Federalist* #78. There Hamilton tried to refute the argument presented by the Anti-Federalist "Brutus" that judicial review implied JUDICIAL SUPREMACY. Hamilton invoked the superiority of the will of the people as declared in the Constitution and the duty of the judges to be governed by that will. A constitution "is in fact, and must be regarded by the judges as fundamental law." His statement in *The Federalist* #81 "that the Constitution ought to be the standard of construction for the laws, and that wherever there is an evident opposition, the laws ought to give place to the Constitution" is similarly significant.

Hamilton argued against a federal bill of rights in *The Federalist* #84. His main point that bills of rights were not needed in constitutions founded upon the power of the people is rhetorical; it is contradicted by his own admission that the Constitution as drafted did in fact contain a rudimentary bill of rights, including provisions on habeas corpus, the prohibition of BILLS OF ATTAINDER and EX POST FACTO laws and the guarantee of TRIAL BY JURY in criminal cases.

The office of secretary of the Treasury, coveted by Hamilton more than any other, afforded him the opportunity to initiate policies for strengthening the public support, and particularly the support of the moneyed community, for the federal government. He considered leadership not only as compatible with, but incumbent on, executive office, and once spoke of the "executive impulse." He seems to have considered his office as that of a prime minister on the British model. Hamilton's major effort and achievement was the establishment of public credit for the new federal government. His measures included funding the foreign and domestic debt at par, assumption of the revolutionary state debts, creation of the Bank of the United States, and levying of federal excise taxes; his most important policy papers were his Report on Public Credit (January 1790) and his Report on the National Bank (December 1790). As a program for the future, Hamilton, in the Report on Manufactures (1791), envisaged protective tariffs, aid for agriculture, and INTERNAL IMPROVEMENTS. Increasingly, his policies encountered and provoked opposition from Thomas Jefferson, JAMES MADISON, and the Republican party forming around them.

There were two great constitutional issues on which Hamilton spoke out during his membership in Washington's cabinet: the constitutionality of the proposed Bank of the United States (1791), and the constitutionality of the President's PROCLAMATION OF NEUTRALITY (1793). In the dispute on the bank, both Attorney General EDMUND RANDOLPH and Secretary of State Jefferson denied that the United States had the power to incorporate a bank, this power not being enumerated in the catalogue of powers granted to Congress by the Constitution. Hamilton, in his "Opinion on the Constitutionality of an Act to Establish a Bank," developed the theory of IMPLIED POWERS granted by the Constitution, arguing that implied powers as well as express powers were in fact delegated by the Constitution; he also asserted the existence of such resulting powers as those resulting from the conquest of neighboring territory. Grants of power included means to attain a specified end, the criterion of constitutionality being met if the end was specified in the Constitution. To attain the objective of the "effectual administration of the finances of the United States," there was no "parsimony of power." Also, Hamilton argued that the NECESSARY AND PROPER CLAUSE ought to be construed "to give a liberal latitude to the exercise of specified powers" rather than construing the word "necessary" restrictively, as had Jefferson. These arguments were later adopted by the Supreme Court in MCCULLOCH V. MARYLAND (1819), and still guide the interpretation of Congress's legislative powers.

Hamilton's second major constitutional pronouncement concerned the power of the executive to issue a declaration of neutrality. In the first of his "Pacificus" articles justifying the President's action against Jeffersonian criticism, he presented an extremely broad construction of Article II. The grant of "executive power" (singular) as opposed to the "powers" (plural) granted to Congress meant a general grant of power; the enumeration of specific powers of the executive was merely demonstrative, "intended by way of greater caution." Hamilton also argued that the executive conducted the nation's foreign policy and that his duty obligated him to execute the laws including the law of nations.

During the years after his retirement from the Treasury, Hamilton, as leading Federalist politician, yet without federal office except for a brief spell as Inspector of the Army (1798–1800), on several occasions commented on constitutional matters.

Controversy over JAY'S TREATY (1794) involved constitutional issues between the executive and the House of Representatives. Was the President bound to submit papers pertaining to the treaty negotiations to the legislature? Did the treaty power, jointly exercised by President and Senate, oblige the legislature to appropriate the needed funds without any liberty of exercising legislative discretion? Hamilton denied any obligation on the part of the President to transmit papers, arguing that such a transmittal would "tend to destroy" the confidence of foreign governments in the "prudence and delicacy" of the government. He further argued that a treaty could obligate the legislature to appropriate funds.

Representing the federal government in HYLTON V. UNITED STATES (1796), his only appearance as counsel before the Supreme Court, Hamilton argued that a federal tax on carriages (levied by Congress in 1794 on Hamilton's recommendation) was an excise rather than a direct tax, and so did not have to be apportioned among the states according to the census. Hamilton argued that as an excise the tax was constitutional, and the Court upheld his view.

In 1796 Hamilton was approached for a legal opinion on the Yazoo land grant affair in Georgia. An act of the Georgia legislature had repealed an earlier act providing for the sale of vast tracts of land, the repeal having been prompted by charges of fraud in the original transaction and a political changeover in the legislature. Hamilton argued that Article I, section 10, of the Constitution, prohibiting the states from passing any law "impairing the obligation of contracts," applied not merely to contracts between individuals but to contracts between states and individuals as well, and that a land grant was a contract covered by the contract clause. Hamilton's views became the basis of the Supreme Court's decision in FLETCHER V. PECK (1810).

When New York State election results in the spring of 1800 made it virtually certain that the state legislature would elect presidential electors favoring Jefferson as President, Hamilton suggested that Governor JOHN JAY call the outgoing legislature into special session to elect anti-Jefferson electors. Hamilton believed that it "is easy to sacrifice the substantial interests of society by a strict adherence to ordinary rules." Jay rejected this proposal, which shows Hamilton's readiness to neglect, in cases he considered extraordinary crises or emergencies, "ordinary rules." Hamilton approved, incidentally, the LOUISIANA PURCHASE.

Although not technically concerning the Constitution, Hamilton's defense of freedom of the press in PEOPLE V. CROSWELL (1804) deserves notice. Hamilton was counsel for the appellant before the high court of New York, the appellant having been convicted of LIBEL for publishing an anti-Jefferson piece. Hamilton's two main points, based on the successful plea of Andrew Hamilton in ZENGER'S CASE (1735), were that truth of an alleged libel should be admitted as evidence and that juries, in libel cases, ought to decide both on fact and on law. The Court divided and thus the conviction was allowed to stand, though no sentence was passed. State legislation to give effect to Hamilton's points was enacted soon afterward.

Hamilton's understanding of the federal Constitution was informed by his vision of the United States as one nation rather than thirteen states, and also by his conviction that the United States constituted one nation among many nations in a state of permanent rivalry. In his interpretation of the Constitution, three points stand out: the broad construction of federal powers as opposed to state powers; the broad construction of executive powers; and the doctrine of judicial review.

GERALD STOURZH
(1986)

Bibliography

COOKE, JACOB ERNEST 1982 *Alexander Hamilton*. New York: Scribner's.

GOEBEL, JULIUS, JR., et al., eds. 1964–1980 *The Law Practice of Alexander Hamilton: Documents and Commentaries*. 4 Vols. New York: Columbia University Press.

MITCHELL, BROADUS 1957–1962 *Alexander Hamilton*. 2 Vols. New York: Macmillan.

ROSSITER, CLINTON 1964 *Alexander Hamilton and the Constitution*. New York: Harcourt, Brace.

STOURZH, GERALD 1970 *Alexander Hamilton and the Idea of Republican Government*. Stanford: Stanford University Press.

SYRETT, HAROLD E. et al., eds. 1961–1978 *The Papers of Alexander Hamilton*. 26 Vols. New York: Columbia University Press.

HAMILTON, ANDREW

See: Zenger's Case

HAMILTON, WALTON HALE
(1881–1958)

Although Walton Hale Hamilton never formally studied law, he became an influential member of the faculty of Yale Law School and one of the nation's leading experts on government regulation of the economy. Hamilton's many books discussing the relationship between the government and the economic order include *Prices and Price Policies* (1938), *The Patterns of Competition* (1940), *Patents and Free Trade* (1941), and *The Politics of Industry* (1957). In these and other works, Hamilton criticized as unrealistic the traditional view of the American economy as a self-regulating free market; he pointed out that the government is deeply enmeshed in the economy, often at the urgent request of the private sector. Hamilton's most substantial contribution to constitutional scholarship, *The Power to Govern*, written with Douglass Adair (1937), followed naturally from his other interests. Exploring the intellectual background of the framing of the Constitution, Hamilton and Adair focused on the meaning of the word "commerce"; they concluded that the Framers intended to grant the national government broad powers through the Constitution's COMMERCE CLAUSE to regulate all forms of economic activity resulting in transactions across state lines, thus implicitly supporting the constitutionality of NEW DEAL federal regulation.

RICHARD B. BERNSTEIN
(1986)

HAMILTON v. BOARD OF REGENTS OF THE UNIVERSITY OF CALIFORNIA
292 U.S. 245 (1934)

This case raised the problem of CONSCIENTIOUS OBJECTION to military service in a state context. California required that male freshman and sophomore state university students enroll in a course of military science. Hamilton, a religious objector, argued that this requirement violated the liberty guaranteed him by the FOURTEENTH AMENDMENT. Justice PIERCE BUTLER spoke for a unanimous Supreme Court, and concluded that nothing in the Constitution relieved a conscientious objector from the obligation to bear arms.

RICHARD E. MORGAN
(1986)

HAMMER v. DAGENHART
247 U.S. 251 (1918)

From 1903 to 1918, the Supreme Court consistently had approved NATIONAL POLICE POWER regulations enacted under the COMMERCE CLAUSE. But in *Hammer v. Dagenhart*, the Court deviated from this tradition and invalidated the KEATING-OWEN CHILD LABOR ACT, which prohibited the interstate shipment of goods produced by child labor. The Court's restrictive DOCTRINE nevertheless proved vulnerable and the decision itself eventually was overruled.

In CHAMPION V. AMES (1903) the Justices had sustained a congressional prohibition against the interstate shipment of lottery tickets. The ruling actually was quite narrow, holding that such tickets were proper SUBJECTS OF COMMERCE and that Congress could prevent the "pollution" of INTERSTATE COMMERCE. A more general, expansive doctrine seemed to emerge as the Court soon approved similar regulations of the interstate flow of adulterated foods and impure drugs, prostitutes, prize fight films, and liquor. The Court abruptly deviated from this course in the child labor case, perhaps signaling a reaction against some of the Progressive era's social reforms and the Court's prior tendency toward liberal nationalism.

Justice WILLIAM R. DAY, speaking for a 5–4 majority, maintained at the outset that in each of the other cases the Court had acknowledged that the "use of interstate transportation was necessary to the accomplishment of harmful results." But the child labor regulations, Day held, were different because the goods shipped were of themselves harmless in contrast with lottery tickets, impure foods, prize fight films, and liquor. It was an unsound distinction, but one perhaps anticipated by Justice JOHN MARSHALL HARLAN's remarks in the *Lottery Case* that the Court would not allow Congress arbitrarily to exclude every article from interstate commerce.

The Court refuted any suggestions that congressional authority extended to prevent unfair competition among the states, thus enabling it to ignore any discussion of the evils or deleterious effects of child labor. This argument was grounded in the majority's revival of rigid notions of dual federalism. Production, Day said, as he resurrected an older, dubious, and arbitrary distinction, was not commerce; the regulation of production was reserved by the TENTH AMENDMENT to the states. "If it were otherwise," Day noted, "all manufacture intended for interstate shipment would be brought under federal control to the practical exclusion of the authority of the States, a result certainly not contemplated by the . . . Constitution." The regulation of child labor, he maintained, not only exceeded congressional authority but also invaded the proper sphere of local power. To allow such a measure, Day concluded, would end "all freedom of commerce," eliminate state control over local matters, and thereby destroy the federal system.

In dissent, Justice OLIVER WENDELL HOLMES uttered his oft-quoted remark that "if there is any matter upon which civilized countries have agreed—far more unanimously than they have with regard to intoxicants and some other matters over which this country is now emotionally aroused—it is the evil of premature and excessive child labor." But Holmes offered more than his customary philosophical discourse on judicial restraint. Congress plainly had the power to regulate interstate shipments, and its motives of doing so were no less legitimate here than they had been in the regulations.

Whether "evil precedes or follows the transportation" was irrelevant, Holmes said; once states transported their goods across their boundaries, they were "no longer within their rights."

The *Hammer* decision did not significantly diminish the Court's willingness or ability to sustain congressional police regulations under the commerce clause. The ruling revealed that the Court seemed less concerned with the evils of child labor than Congress and was more interested in maintaining the purity of the federal system. In BAILEY V. DREXEL FURNITURE (1922), the Justices invalidated a congressional attempt to regulate child labor by using the TAXING POWER, again despite ample precedents justifying national power. But three years later, Chief Justice WIL- LIAM HOWARD TAFT, who had written the child labor tax opinion, reverted to the Court's earlier POLICE POWER decisions and broadly approved the National Motor Vehicle Act (1919) which made the transportation of stolen automobiles across state lines a federal crime. In *Brooks v. United States* (1925), Taft agreed that Congress could forbid the use of interstate commerce "as an agency to promote immorality, dishonesty or the spread of any evil or harm of other States from the State of origin." *Hammer v. Dagenhart* marred an otherwise consistent pattern in the precedents, but Taft quickly disposed of it by reiterating the distinction that the products of child labor were not harmful. Yet his 1925 opinion refuted such doctrine as he demonstrated that a perceived evil required national action and the question of harmfulness was secondary.

Throughout the 1920s, the Supreme Court, following Taft's strong views, generally approved an ever expanding scope to the commerce clause. There was some retreat during the bitter constitutional struggle over the New Deal, but it proved temporary. After 1937, a number of decisions reaffirmed a broad nationalistic view of the commerce power. Finally, in 1941, the Court specifically overruled *Hammer*. Justice HARLAN FISKE STONE, in UNITED STATES V. DARBY, rebuked the earlier decision as "novel," "unsupported," "a departure," and "exhausted" as a precedent.

The most poignant historical commentary on *Hammer* came from the supposed victor, Reuben Dagenhart, whose father had sued in order to sustain his "freedom" to allow his fourteen-year-old boy to work in a textile mill. Six years later, Reuben, a 105-pound man, recalled that his victory had earned him a soft drink, some automobile rides from his employer, and a salary of one dollar a day; he had also lost his education and his health.

STANLEY I. KUTLER
(1986)

Bibliography
WOOD, STEPHEN 1968 *Constitutional Politics in the Progressive Era: Child Labor and the Law.* Chicago: University of Chicago Press.

HAMPTON v. MOW SUN WONG
426 U.S. 88 (1976)

In this case the Supreme Court declined to extend to federal government action the constitutional limits it had imposed on the states' discrimination against ALIENS. The Court recognized that "overriding national interests" might justify a limitation of employment in the federal civil service to citizens—as required by the Civil Service Commission (CSC) here—despite the invalidity of a parallel state law. (See SUGARMAN V. DOUGALL.) But the interests identified by CSC were insufficient: some of them could be asserted only by the President or Congress; others, within CSC's purview, were after-the-fact rationalizations that had not been considered before the regulation was adopted. The regulation thus violated the Fifth Amendment's guarantee of DUE PROCESS OF LAW; that amendment's EQUAL PROTECTION component need not be reached. The vote was 5–4.

Shortly after the Court's decision in *Hampton*, President GERALD R. FORD issued an order embracing the policy of the invalidated CSC rule.

KENNETH L. KARST
(1986)

HAMPTON & CO. v. UNITED STATES
276 U.S. 394 (1928)

In *J. W. Hampton, Jr., & Co. v. United States*, a unanimous Supreme Court, speaking through Chief Justice WILLIAM HOWARD TAFT, upheld Congress's DELEGATION OF POWER to the President to adjust tariffs in order to protect American business. The delegation was not improper because the law provided an intelligible standard to which tariffs had to conform. The Court also sustained the protective tariff itself, holding that, because its effect was to raise revenue, Congress's motive in enacting it was irrelevant.

DENNIS J. MAHONEY
(1986)

HAND, AUGUSTUS N.
(1868–1954)

Born in upstate New York to a prominent legal family, Augustus Noble ("Gus") Hand, after graduating from Harvard College and Harvard Law School, practiced law in New York City from 1897 to 1914. President WOODROW WILSON appointed him in 1914 to the UNITED STATES DISTRICT COURT for the Southern District of New York. A defendant in a trial over which Hand presided described him as a judge of such integrity and impartiality that he could have sustained the dignity of the law in a hurricane. In 1927 President CALVIN COOLIDGE, deferring to the acclaim of the bench and bar, promoted Hand, a Democrat, to the UNITED STATES COURT OF APPEALS, Second Circuit, where he joined his famous cousin, LEARNED HAND.

No appellate judge was more austere than Gus Hand, who commanded the respect and influenced the votes of his brethren for a quarter of a century. He preferred judicial self-restraint to JUDICIAL ACTIVISM. A moderate, he once declared that the ignorance of conservatives hardly exceeded the intolerance of liberals obsessed with change. The ardent crusaders who administered NEW DEAL agencies, he declared, should be left to "fry in their own fat" until Congress reformed them.

Hand dissented rarely and cultivated a passionless style, though he could be eloquent. His opinions tended to favor prosecutors in cases involving the rights of the criminally accused and the government in cases involving subversive activities. For example, he sustained the summary contempt conviction of the lawyers who defended the Communist party leaders tried under the SMITH ACT, even though the trial judge who convicted the lawyers gave them no hearing and waited until the trial's end, months after their contemptuous acts. Hand upheld the SEPARATE BUT EQUAL DOCTRINE and ruled that the Army's racially based quota system during WORLD WAR II did not violate the SELECTIVE SERVICE ACT. But he championed RELIGIOUS LIBERTY and extended the benefits of conscientious objection to persons who founded their claims on philosophical and political considerations as well as purely religious ones. "A mighty oak has fallen," said one of his colleagues on his death.

LEONARD W. LEVY
(1986)

Bibliography

SCHICK, MARVIN 1970 *Learned Hand's Court*. Baltimore: Johns Hopkins University Press.

HAND, LEARNED
(1872–1961)

Learned Hand is widely viewed, with OLIVER WENDELL HOLMES, LOUIS D. BRANDEIS, and BENJAMIN N. CARDOZO, as among the leading American judges of the twentieth century. His influence on constitutional law stems more from his extrajudicial advocacy of judicial restraint and his modest, yet creative, performance on lower federal courts in fifty-two years of judging than from the relatively few constitutional rulings among his nearly 3,000 decisions.

Christened Billings Learned Hand, the son and grandson of upstate New York lawyers and judges, Hand dropped the Billings after graduating from Harvard Law School in 1896. Hand surrendered to family pressures in turning to law rather than pursuing his interest in philosophy engendered by his Harvard College teachers, including William James, Josiah Royce, and George Santayana. In six years of practice in Albany and seven in New York City, he performed competently but considered himself inadequate. But the young lawyer's associations with New York City intellectuals and reformers prompted President WILLIAM HOWARD TAFT to name the thirty-seven-year-old Hand to the federal trial bench in 1909. President CALVIN COOLIDGE elevated him to the Court of Appeals for the Second Circuit in 1924, where Hand served for the rest of his life.

Hand's persistent belief in judicial restraint antedated his appointment to the bench. He had been strongly influenced by JAMES BRADLEY THAYER at Harvard Law School. His major publication before the judgeship was an article attacking LOCHNER V. NEW YORK (1905). His deepseated skepticism and allergy to absolutes, as well as his devotion to democratic policymaking and his unwillingness to be ruled by a bevy of Platonic Guardians, made him disdainful of judges ready to pour subjective philosophies into vague constitutional phrases. He was unwilling to suppress his hostility to JUDICIAL ACTIVISM, developed in the era of the Nine Old Men and its use of SUBSTANTIVE DUE PROCESS to strike down ECONOMIC REGULATION, in the post-1937 years, when the philosophy of HARLAN FISKE STONE's footnote to UNITED STATES V. CAROLENE PRODUCTS COMPANY (1937), with its preference for personal rather than economic rights, gained ascendancy.

In his early years as a federal judge, Hand participated widely in extrajudicial activities. He was a member of the group that founded *The New Republic* magazine, and he helped draft THEODORE ROOSEVELT's Bull Moose platform in 1912. Indeed, he was so devoted to the Progressive cause that he permitted his name to be entered as that party's candidate for the New York Court of Appeals in 1913.

After WORLD WAR I, Hand decided that his position precluded extrajudicial involvements in controversial issues. But he had frequent occasion to continue airing his views of the judicial role in papers and addresses, many of which are collected in *The Spirit of Liberty* (1952). Hand's Holmes Lectures, delivered at Harvard three years before his death and published under the title *The Bill of Rights*, were an extreme restatement of Hand's hostility to the *Lochner* interventionist philosophy. The lectures even questioned the judicial enforceability of vague BILL OF RIGHTS provisions.

Hand's judicial reputation rests mainly on his craftsmanlike performance in operating creatively within the confines set by the political branches. His strength is best revealed in the way he handled many small cases in private law and statutory interpretation. He probed deeply to discover underlying questions, rejecting glib formulations and striving for orderly sense amidst the chaos of received legal wisdoms. Although constitutional issues seldom came before his court, he touched upon a wide range of them, from favoring strong enforcement of FOURTH AMENDMENT guarantees in *United States v. Rabinowitz* (1949) to offering innovative views on defining OBSCENITY in *United States v. Kennerley* (1913).

Hand's most important judicial contributions dealt with political speech under the FIRST AMENDMENT. His most enduring impact stems from his controversial decision in MASSES PUBLISHING CO. V. PATTEN (1917). The ruling, overturned on appeal, protected the mailing of antiwar materials in the midst of national hostility to dissent. Hand's approach shielded all speech falling short of direct INCITEMENT TO UNLAWFUL CONDUCT. Two years later, the Supreme Court, in its first confrontation with the problem, refused to go so far as Hand had. Instead, SCHENCK V. UNITED STATES (1919) launched the CLEAR AND PRESENT DANGER test, under which the protection of speech turned on guesses about its probable impact. In a rare disagreement with his one judicial idol, Oliver Wendell Holmes, Hand criticized Holmes's approach, in ABRAMS V. UNITED STATES (1919) as well as *Schenck,* as an inadequate bulwark against majoritarian passions. With the Supreme Court adhering to Holmes's standard for decades, Hand assumed that his *Masses* approach had failed. But in 1969, Hand's incitement test, combined with the best elements of Holmes's approach, became the modern standard for First Amendment protection, in BRANDENBURG V. OHIO (1969).

Hand is equally well known for recasting and, many believe, diluting the clear and present danger test by affirming convictions of the Communist leaders in UNITED STATES V. DENNIS (1950). This ruling reflected not only Hand's mounting skepticism about judicial protection of fundamental rights but also his consistent obedience to Supreme Court pronouncements. In affirming the *Dennis* convictions, Chief Justice FRED M. VINSON'S PLURALITY OPINION adopted Hand's reformulation as the proper criterion. Hand, however, remained convinced even in the 1950s that his *Masses* approach offered better protection to dissenters.

The distinctive traits of Hand's model of judging—open-mindedness, impartiality, skepticism, restless probing—came naturally to him. Those traits were ingredients of his personality by the time Hand became a judge. Philosopher and humanist as well as judge, Hand remained intellectually engaged, ever ready to reexamine his own assumptions.

Hand's unmatched capacity to behave according to the model of the modest judge was not wholly a conscious deduction from the theory of judicial restraint instilled by Thayer and confirmed by Hand's early experiences. It was at least as much a product of Hand's temper and personality. The doubting, open-minded human being could not help but act that way as a judge. Hand's major legacy, to

constitutional law as well as to all other areas of the law, lies in his demonstration that detached and open-minded judging is within human reach.

GERALD GUNTHER
(1986)

Bibliography

HAND, LEARNED   (1952) 1960   *The Spirit of Liberty: Papers and Addresses,* ed. Irving Dilliard. New York: Knopf.
——— 1958   *The Bill of Rights.* Cambridge, Mass.: Harvard University Press.
SHANKS, HERSHEL, ed.   1968   *The Art and Craft of Judging.* New York: Macmillan.

HARASSMENT

See: Sex Discrimination; Workplace Harassment and the First Amendment

HARDING, WARREN G.
(1865–1923)

Warren Gamaliel Harding, twenty-ninth President of the United States, served one of the shortest presidential terms, from his inauguration on March 4, 1921, until his death on August 2, 1923. An Ohio newspaperman and politician, and a United States senator (1915–1921), Harding was nominated as a compromise candidate at the deadlocked 1920 Republican party convention and won a landslide victory over his Democratic opponent, James Cox.

Harding's policies flowed from an understanding of the American Constitution very different from that of his predecessor, WOODROW WILSON. His economic policy consisted of tax reduction, economy in government, a higher tariff, and various measures to aid agriculture in its recovery from the postwar depression. His foreign policy consisted of opposition to American participation in the League of Nations (but support for membership in the World Court), reduction of armaments, and refusal to forgive war debts owed to the United States or its citizens.

Harding's presidency was marred by scandals, which were exposed fully only after his death and in which he was not personally implicated. Despite his brief tenure as President, Harding appointed four Supreme Court Justices: WILLIAM HOWARD TAFT, PIERCE BUTLER, GEORGE H. SUTHERLAND, and EDWARD T. SANFORD.

THOMAS B. SILVER
(1986)

Bibliography

MURRAY, ROBERT K.   1969   *The Harding Era: Warren G. Harding and His Administration.* Minneapolis: University of Minnesota Press.

HARLAN, JOHN MARSHALL
(1833–1911)

Among the Justices of the Supreme Court, few have provoked more diverse reactions from colleagues, contemporaries, and later generations than the first Justice John Marshall Harlan. Despite a distinguished tenure of over thirty-three years (1877–1911), during which he participated in many cases of constitutional significance and established himself as one of the most productive, independent, and voluble members of the Court, both jurists and historians were inclined to hold Harlan in low esteem from his death in 1911 to the middle of the twentieth century. But two signal events in 1954—the Court's implicit adoption of Harlan's famous solitary dissent in PLESSY V. FERGUSON (1896) in its decision of the public school SEGREGATION cases, BROWN V. BOARD OF EDUCATION and BOLLING V. SHARPE, and President DWIGHT D. EISENHOWER's appointment of his distinguished grandson and namesake to the highest bench—prompted historians to reevaluate the first Justice Harlan. No longer belittled and neglected, Harlan now began to be recast as a great dissenter who had foretold many of the most fundamental developments in later constitutional interpretation: the virtually complete INCORPORATION of the BILL OF RIGHTS into the FOURTEENTH AMENDMENT; the inherent inequality of racial segregation; and the plenary power of Congress under the COMMERCE CLAUSE. How can one account for the wide disparity between the traditional and revisionist interpretations of Mr. Justice Harlan?

Harlan was born in 1833 in Kentucky, the son of a two-term WHIG member of the United States House of Representatives. A stern Presbyterian, young Harlan grew up during the worsening estrangement of the South and the Union. Kentucky, as a border state, was sharply divided. Harlan was graduated from Centre College, and, at twenty, completed his law courses at Transylvania University and was admitted to the Kentucky bar.

Harlan participated actively as a moderate in the political struggles that racked the country on the eve of the CIVIL WAR. In 1859 he ran for Congress, but was narrowly defeated. A traditional southern gentleman and conservative, he refused to join the Republican party or to support ABRAHAM LINCOLN's 1860 campaign. He supported the Constitutional Union party which sought the peaceful preservation of the status quo.

After the attack on Fort Sumter, Kentucky declined to furnish troops. Harlan volunteered to fight on the northern side and, in the fall of 1861, organized the Tenth Kentucky Volunteer Infantry. Harlan rose rapidly to the rank of colonel and served as acting commander of a brigade until he resigned his military commission in 1863 upon the death of his father.

Shortly after returning to civilian life, Harlan campaigned for the Constitutional Union party and was elected attorney general of Kentucky, a post he held until 1867. Harlan stumped for General George McClellan in the presidential election of 1864, bitterly criticizing the Lincoln administration. He opposed the THIRTEENTH AMENDMENT and continued to hold slaves until forced to free them.

In 1867, however, Harlan changed his party affiliation, becoming the unsuccessful Republican gubernatorial candidate. As a southern slaveholder and Whig he had long sought to support both SLAVERY and a strong national government—a position that grew increasingly difficult in the political environment of *antebellum* Kentucky, where supporters of slavery based their political programs on opposition to the federal government. In the end Harlan resolved his dilemma in favor of the national government. Contending that he would rather be right than consistent, Harlan publicly repudiated his views favoring slavery and defended the civil war amendments as necessary to the reconstruction of the Union. A second try for the Kentucky governorship in 1871 also ended in failure.

At the national level, Harlan supported ULYSSES S. GRANT in the presidential election of 1868 and had attained sufficient prominence by 1872 to have been proposed as a vice-presidential candidate. Four years later Harlan led the Kentucky delegation to the Republican convention. When it became apparent that his friend, Benjamin Bristow, could not win, Harlan threw the Kentucky delegation's support to RUTHERFORD B. HAYES, enabling Hayes narrowly to defeat James G. Blaine and obtain the nomination.

On October 16, 1877, President Hayes nominated Harlan to the Supreme Court, an appointment that was widely regarded as a payment for political services rendered. Until five days before his death on October 15, 1911, for almost thirty-four years, Harlan served on the Court. With the exception of JOHN MARSHALL and JOSEPH STORY, none of its members up to that time had taken part in so many decisions that ultimately so crucially affected the future of American constitutionalism.

Harlan served on the Supreme Court during a period of rapid social and economic change. Although the era of RECONSTRUCTION had passed, the effect of the postwar amendments on the federal system remained a topic of bitter constitutional dispute. The Court was also increasingly obliged to rule on constitutional challenges to the validity of state and federal statutes purporting to regulate the economy in the public interest.

Harlan brought to the Court two fundamental convictions drawn from his upbringing and early experiences in Kentucky politics. He believed in a strong national government, especially in the spheres of commerce and economic development. Hence Harlan would view federal laws regulating the economy much more favorably than similar state initiatives. Second, he would ardently support the rights of blacks, although he had developed that posture only late in his political career. While Harlan never wavered in his judicial support for black rights and a strong national economy, the political implications of his Whig principles varied widely during his judicial tenure. When he came to the Court in 1877 Harlan quickly established himself as its foremost defender of private contracts against state regulation since Marshall. Indeed, throughout his long career Harlan closely scrutinized any state law that impinged on private property rights. He often voted to invalidate such statutes under the contract, JUST COMPENSATION, or EQUAL PROTECTION clauses.

After the passage of the INTERSTATE COMMERCE ACT of 1877 and the SHERMAN ANTITRUST ACT of 1890, however, Harlan came to look quite favorably upon national, as opposed to state, regulation of the economy. Harlan's Whig philosophy explains much of his apparent inconsistency in decisions concerning private property rights. Harlan generally upheld national ECONOMIC REGULATION, but often voted to strike down state economic regulations that discriminated against interstate commerce without furthering significantly an important state interest under the POLICE POWER.

During his thirty-four years on the Court, Harlan articulated a broad body of constitutional principles respecting both governmental powers and individual rights. A convinced believer in legislative authority and judgment, he abhorred and denounced what he viewed as "judicial legislation" and advocated a straightforward application of the law as set forth in the Constitution and legislative enactments. But when it came to determining the provisions of a given law, his view was unique: "It is not the words of the law but the internal sense of it that makes the law: the letter is the body; the sense and reason of the law is the soul" (CIVIL RIGHTS CASES, 1883).

Justice Harlan lifted the practice of employing LEGISLATIVE INTENT as a guide to the sound construction of the law to the level of a philosophical principle. In addition, he, above all others, had an all but religious reverence for the Constitution as the fundamental instrument of the ideals of American democracy. A fervent Marshall disciple, he viewed the Court as the ultimate guardian of the Constitution. Harlan also adhered to Marshall's views on the proper distribution of powers within the federal system.

With respect to congressional power under the INTERSTATE COMMERCE clause, Harlan was a liberal national constitutionalist, with an almost slavish devotion to Chief Justice Marshall's opinions in general, and GIBBONS V. OGDEN (1824) in particular. Harlan displayed his broad interpretation of the commerce power most forcefully in opinions construing the Interstate Commerce Act of 1887 and the Sherman Antitrust Act of 1890. He dissented in *Texas & Pacific Railroad Co. v. Interstate Commerce Commission* (1896) and INTERSTATE COMMERCE COMMISSION V. ALABAMA MIDLAND RAILWAY CO. (1897) when the Court interpreted the Interstate Commerce Act as not granting the commission the power either to void discriminatory railroad rates or to set nondiscriminatory rates itself. Harlan believed that these decisions went far "to make that commission a useless body for all practical purposes, and to defeat many of the important objectives designed to be accomplished by the various enactments of Congress relating to interstate commerce. . . ." Congress eventually agreed, amending the Interstate Commerce Act to give the commission the powers for which Harlan had contended in his dissents.

When the Court emasculated the Sherman Antitrust Act, Justice Harlan, again in dissent, registered his strong advocacy of congressional power and the spirit of the law. In UNITED STATES V. E. C. KNIGHT CO. (1895) the Court narrowly interpreted the Sherman Act as applying to monopolies in interstate commerce but not to intrastate monopolies in manufacture of goods; it also stated that Congress lacked power under the commerce clause to regulate manufacturing. In the majority's view, "Commerce succeeds to manufacture, and is not a part of it." Yet Harlan insisted that the statute applied because the goods, although manufactured in one state, entered into interstate commerce. Four decades later, in the WAGNER ACT CASES (1937), Harlan's expansive view of congressional power under the commerce clause would become the generally accepted view.

Although Harlan held to a broad interpretation of national power under the commerce clause, he nonetheless supported some positive uses of STATE POLICE POWER that affected interstate commerce. He believed that, although a state might not—under the guise of inspection laws—discriminate against meat imported from out of state (MINNESOTA V. BARBER, 1890), it might require certain passenger stops of interstate railroad trains unless Congress had superseded local laws. Indeed, Harlan thought that state power should prevail if the statute in question affected interstate commerce "only incidentally" and furthered an important state interest under the police power—as was the case with state laws prohibiting the importation or sale of intoxicating liquor (BOWMAN V. CHICAGO & NORTHWESTERN RAILWAY, 1888). Whether agreeing or dissenting, however, Harlan consistently stood for the freedom of commerce and the rights of citizens of other states. While he upheld state enactments genuinely aiming to protect the public morals, safety, health, or convenience, he strongly expressed his disapproval of those that appeared to have been enacted for the ulterior purpose of discriminating against commerce from other states.

Although fervently opposed to Justice STEPHEN J. FIELD'S NATURAL RIGHTS philosophy, Harlan strongly defended the Bill of Rights and, in spite of his border state origin, became a vigorous and eloquent advocate of a nationalistic interpretation of the Thirteenth, Fourteenth, and FIFTEENTH AMENDMENTS. Harlan's most celebrated CIVIL RIGHTS dissent, *Plessy v. Ferguson* (1896), became law in the unanimous Warren Court holding in *Brown v. Board of Education* (1954). It was in *Plessy,* dissenting alone from the Court's decision upholding a Louisiana "Jim Crow" train-segregation statute under the SEPARATE BUT EQUAL doctrine, that Harlan had warned: "The thin disguise of "equal' accommodations . . . will not mislead anyone, nor atone for the wrong this day done. . . ."

However, it was his dissent in the CIVIL RIGHTS CASES (1883) that Harlan considered as his most notable. There the majority ruled that Congress lacked power under the Fourteenth Amendment to protect blacks against private discrimination; Harlan, in contrast, argued that Congress could prohibit discrimination "by individuals or CORPORATIONS exercising public functions or authority, against any citizen because of his race or previous condition of servitude."

In these and other cases involving racial discrimination, Harlan demonstrated his belief that the Thirteenth Amendment meant more than the mere prohibition of one person's owning another as property. He urged that the framers of the Thirteenth, Fourteenth, and Fifteenth Amendments could not have expected the very states that had held blacks in bondage willingly to protect their new civil rights. Harlan thus championed congressional authority to define and regulate the entire body of civil rights of citizens.

Although Justice Harlan's dissents in racial segregation cases have received widespread attention, some of the most critical questions presented to the Court during his tenure centered on what later came to be termed the INCORPORATION DOCTRINE. Harlan joined the Court after a pattern of decisions had been set. Alone, except for Field, among Justices of his time, Harlan viewed the due process clause of the Fourteenth Amendment as encompassing at least the first eight amendments of the Bill of Rights (for example, HURTADO V. CALIFORNIA, 1884), a stand for which he was still severely castigated more than sixty years later by Justice FELIX FRANKFURTER, in *Adamson v. California* (1947). The process of "selective incorporation" of Bill of Rights guarantees, which was nearly complete by the end of the Warren Court, vindicated Justice Harlan's position in practice, if not in theory.

Interestingly, the emphasis accorded Harlan's famous dissents in civil rights cases concerning life and liberty interests resulted in a widespread neglect of his staunch defense of property rights. In CONTRACT CLAUSE cases involving states' attempts either to void or alter their obligations to bondholders, or to amend corporate charters without express reservation of the right to do so, Harlan strongly asserted the contractual rights of the individual. Under the equal protection clause Harlan voted to strike down state laws that imposed special contractual duties on corporations without imposing similar obligations on individuals.

More significant, Harlan wrote the opinion in Chicago, *Burlington Quincy Railroad Co. v. Chicago* (1898), frequently cited as the first "incorporation" of a Bill of Rights provision, the Fifth Amendment's just compensation clause, into the Fourteenth Amendment's due process clause. The famous rate case of SMYTH V. AMES (1898) provided an indication of how far Harlan would go in striking down, under SUBSTANTIVE DUE PROCESS principles, an exercise of state police power. Speaking for the Court, he voided a Nebraska statute that pegged intrastate freight rates, on the grounds that the rates were so low as to deprive railroads of property without due process of law. A public utility, asserted Harlan, has a judicially enforceable constitutional right to a "reasonable return" upon the "fair value" of its operating assets. (See FAIR RETURN ON FAIR VALUE.)

Harlan's constitutional doctrines evoked diverse reactions from contemporaries and later generations: patronization, neglect, disdain, and praise. His colleague and friend, Justice DAVID J. BREWER, described Harlan as a simple man who "retired at eight, with one hand on the Constitution and the other on the Bible, safe and happy in perfect faith in justice and righteousness." Justice OLIVER WENDELL HOLMES patronized him in private as "old Harlan . . . the last of the tobacco-spitting judges." Contemporaneous observers of the Court viewed Harlan as a militant dissenter who was inflexible on civil rights.

How could Harlan's contemporaries and historians in the first half of the twentieth century have held him in such low esteem when the prophetic nature of his many dissents appears so obvious today? Part of the answer is that traditional and revisionist interpreters of Justice Harlan have employed widely different analytical perspectives. Viewed narrowly in comparison with his contemporaries, Harlan was simply an "eccentric exception" on the Court. Many of his most famous dissents were solos. His constitutional doctrines were often "out of tune with the times."

Harlan's eccentricity, however, was principled. In a letter of 1870 Harlan described his conception of the proper role of a Justice as that of "an independent man, with an opportunity to make a *record* that will be remembered long after he is gone." Throughout his tenure on the Court Harlan was constantly concerned with broad questions of the public interest; consequently his opinions often contained extraneous matter, referring to circumstances with no direct bearing on the case at hand.

When the Court in POLLOCK V. FARMERS' LOAN & TRUST COMPANY (1895) decided that a tax on the income from land and personal property constituted DIRECT TAXATION and thereby held unconstitutional the recently enacted Federal Income Tax Act, Harlan vehemently dissented. He correctly warned that the Court's decision would make a constitutional amendment necessary for the imposition of the income tax. Harlan's contemporaries, however, saw his denunciation of judicial legislation and his appeals to practical considerations as ignorance of the principles of legal argumentation.

Recent admirers have perhaps too strongly emphasized Harlan's opinion on civil rights and CIVIL LIBERTIES, recasting him as a Jeffersonian Democrat. Although he strongly defended the Bill of Rights against STATE ACTION and private action clothed in public functions, Harlan viewed himself as a staunch adherent to the views of John Marshall and rejected THOMAS JEFFERSON's states' rights views. Moreover, Harlan was one of the most vigorous defenders of individual property rights ever to sit on the Court, as his opinion in *Adair v. United States* (1908) illustrated. His STRICT CONSTRUCTION of the contract and just compensation clauses and his adherence to substantive property protections under the due process clause have been soundly rejected by subsequent Courts.

The composite figure emerging from history is that of a Southern gentlemen of the nineteenth century—absolute confidence in the correctness of his own views; a firm belief that human beings could clearly discern between right and wrong; and an inability to understand, once he had made this distinction, how any reasonable man could disagree with him. An ardent disciple of Chief Justice Marshall's views of the proper judicial role and the nature of the federal system, Harlan was an egalitarian when confronted with questions of civil rights.

But today's distinction between property and liberty interests, with enhanced judicial solicitude for the latter, found no place in Harlan's constitutional philosophy. This antebellum slaveholder applied substantive due process equally to liberty and property interests.

Although Harlan's legacy thus contains elements out of tune with contemporary constitutional fashion, many of his dissents presaged what our nation would become in the second half of the twentieth century. Succeeding generations owe a great debt to this solitary dissenter. Because his philosophy contained a touch of immortality, he will be numbered among the great Justices of the Supreme Court (and he was so voted as one of but twelve "greats" in a 1970 study).

HENRY J. ABRHAM
(1986)

Bibliography

ABRAHAM, HENRY J. 1955 John Marshall Harlan: A Justice Neglected. *Virginia Law Review* 41:871–891.
CLARK, FLOYD B. 1915 *The Constitutional Doctrines of John Marshall Harlan*. Baltimore: Johns Hopkins University Press.
FRIEDMAN, LEON and ISRAEL, FRED L. 1969 Pages 1281–1295 in *The Justices of the United States Supreme Court, 1789–1969*. New York: Chelsea House.
WATT, RICHARD F. and ORLIKOFF, RICHARD M. 1953 The Coming Vindication of Mr. Justice Harlan. *Illinois Law Journal* 44:13–40.
WESTIN, ALAN F. 1958 The First Justice Harlan: A Self-Portrait from his Private Papers. *Kentucky Law Journal* 46:321–357.
WHITE, G. EDWARD 1975 John Marshall Harlan I: The Precursor. *American Journal of Legal History* 19:1–21.

HARLAN, JOHN MARSHALL
(1899–1971)

John Marshall Harlan, grandson of the Justice of the same name, served as Associate Justice of the United States Supreme Court from 1955 to 1971. Educated principally at Princeton and Oxford, he enjoyed a highly successful career as a New York trial lawyer, with intervals for military service and in various public positions. Immediately prior to his appointment to the Supreme Court he served briefly on the United States Court of Appeals for the Second Circuit. His work on the Supreme Court was marked by rigorous intellectual honesty, unflagging industry, and an uncommon dedication to judicial craftsmanship. No Justice sought more earnestly to evaluate fairly every relevant fact and authority, and none labored more carefully to decide, not policies or causes, but actual and concrete cases. In the "measured" assessment of Judge Henry Friendly, no other Justice has "so consistently maintained a high quality of performance" or has enjoyed "so nearly uniform respect."

Influenced in his first years on the Court by FELIX FRANKFURTER, Harlan ultimately developed a constitutional philosophy distinctly his own. He combined dignity with an attractive modesty, personal qualities that were reflected in his conception of the judicial function. In REYNOLDS V. SIMS (1964) he emphasized that the Constitution required a "diffusion of governmental authority" within which the Court was assigned a "high" but "limited" function. Rigidly nonpolitical after his appointment to the bench, he believed that the Court could effectively perform its "limited" constitutional role only by studiously respecting the powers variously entrusted to the states, Congress, or the federal executive. He denied that courts are entitled to promote or compel reform whenever others fail to act, and warned that judges should not seek solutions to every social ill in the Constitution.

More than any Justice in recent years, Harlan regarded FEDERALISM as an important limitation upon the Court's authority. He believed, with Justice LOUIS D. BRANDEIS, that the states could serve as laboratories for the solution of social and political issues, and he willingly afforded them freedom to seek such solutions. In FAY V. NOIA (1963), MIRANDA V. ARIZONA (1966), and other cases he resisted the Court's imposition of federal standards upon the conduct of state criminal proceedings, arguing in *Fay* that the federal system would "exist in substance as well as form" only if the states were permitted, within the limits of FUNDAMENTAL FAIRNESS, to devise their own procedures. In HARPER V. VIRGINIA BOARD OF ELECTIONS (1966) he dissented from the Court's invalidation of a state's use of a POLL TAX as a condition on voting, despite his obvious doubts as to the law's wisdom, in part because the issue should be left for decision by the state itself. In ROTH V. UNITED STATES (1957) he urged that the states be permitted greater leeway than the federal government to control "borderline" PORNOGRAPHY because the risks of nationwide censorship were "far greater." Because the Court could not devise clear rules for regulating OBSCENITY, he saw "no overwhelming danger" if the states were given room to seek their own answers.

Harlan's federalism did not, however, prevent him in appropriate cases from denying the constitutionality of state legislation. In *Poe v. Ullman* (1961) he wrote one of the most important of his opinions, dissenting from the Court's refusal to decide a challenge to a Connecticut statute prohibiting the use of contraceptive devices. Observing that the statute intruded upon "the most intimate details of the marital relation" in order to enforce "a moral judgment," Harlan declared marital privacy to be a "most fundamental" right, any invasion of which requires STRICT SCRUTINY. He defined DUE PROCESS in terms of evolving national traditions and the balance between "liberty and the demands of organized society," and concluded on that basis that the statute was unconstitutional. Four years later, in GRISWOLD V. CONNECTICUT (1965), a majority of the Court reached the same result.

One of the issues most revealing of Harlan's constitutional outlook was the INCORPORATION DOCTRINE, by which large portions of the BILL OF RIGHTS have been held applicable to the states through "incorporation" in the FOURTEENTH AMENDMENT. Harlan vigorously resisted both the "total" incorporation theory advanced by Justice HUGO L. BLACK and the "selective" version adopted by other Justices. In POINTER V. TEXAS (1965), DUNCAN V. LOUISIANA (1968), and other cases he argued that the doctrine lacks historical basis and creates a "constitutional straitjacket" that risks preventing the states from responding to the nation's "increasing experience and evolving conscience." He preferred to test state LEGISLATION and procedures by a standard of fundamental fairness derived from the due process clause of the Fourteenth Amendment, whose generality affords room for future constitutional development. Indeed, in *Griswold* he expressed the fear that the incorporation doctrine might "restrict" the reach of the due process clause, limiting the Court's review of future state actions.

Due process formed the heart of Harlan's constitutional outlook, and two cases illustrate both the breadth of his conception and the restraint with which he employed it. In BODDIE V. CONNECTICUT (1971) Harlan held for the Court that filing and service fees imposed by the state upon persons seeking divorce were denials of due process when applied to INDIGENTS. Carefully avoiding reliance upon the EQUAL PROTECTION clause, whose scope and implications he evidently distrusted, he held that as a matter of fundamental fairness a state could not preempt the right to dissolve marriages unless all its citizens were afforded access to the mechanism prescribed for that purpose. The opinion provoked Justice Black in dissent to reiterate that Harlan's conception of due process permitted judges to determine constitutionality merely by their "sense of fairness." Quoting *Williams v. North Carolina* (1945), Black added that due process afforded judges "a blank sheet of paper" on which to order constitutional change.

The deaths of the two close friends prevented Harlan and Black from continuing their debate after *Boddie*, but part of Harlan's response may be inferred from IN RE GAULT (1967), in which the Court first addressed the constitutional issues presented by state systems of juvenile justice. Such systems often imposed penalties similar to those in criminal cases without the accompanying procedural protections. Harlan's concurring opinion emphasized the novelty of the questions, and urged caution in imposing detailed constitutional requirements. He feared that the hasty adoption of rigid standards might "hamper enlightened development," and found room in the spacious contours of due process to impose only selected procedural requirements. Harlan's caution illustrated his conviction, previously expressed in *Poe v. Ullman*, that the discretion afforded judges by the due process clause must be exercised with "judgment and restraint."

Harlan also made significant contributions to the development of FIRST AMENDMENT principles. In COHEN V. CALIFORNIA (1971) he wrote the opinion for a divided Court overturning the conviction of a man wearing a jacket bearing an antidraft expletive in the halls of a Los Angeles courthouse. Although the protest's form was "distasteful," Harlan explained that "fundamental societal values" are implicated even in "crude" exercises of First Amendment rights. In GINZBURG V. UNITED STATES (1966), he dissented from the affirmance of a federal obscenity conviction in which the Court held that evidence of "commercial exploitation" could tip the balance toward a determination that a publication was obscene. Harlan responded that the Court, by "judicial improvisation," had created a new and impermissibly vague statutory standard, under which "pandering" could justify the censorship of otherwise protected materials. In contrast to his less rigid attitude toward state obscenity prosecutions, he argued that the federal government should be permitted to ban from the mails only hard-core pornography.

The concern for privacy interests expressed in *Poe v. Ullman* was also reflected in Harlan's First Amendment opinions. In NAACP V. ALABAMA (1958) he wrote the Court's opinion overturning an order holding the NAACP in civil contempt for failing to reveal the names of its members and agents in Alabama. He found that such disclosures had previously resulted in threats and reprisals, and explained the "vital relationship" between organizational privacy and freedom of association. Because the contempt order would adversely affect the NAACP's ability to foster beliefs it was constitutionally entitled to advocate, the association's privacy interests overrode the state's regulatory goals. In *Time, Inc. v. Hill* (1967) he argued that where private individuals had by misadventure become involuntary subjects of publicity, the state could constitutionally require the press to conduct a reasonable investigation and to limit itself to fair comment upon the facts. The denial of such state authority, he contended, would create a "severe risk of irremediable harm" to those who had not sought public exposure and were "powerless to protect themselves against it."

Harlan's contributions to constitutional law are not fully measured by the opinions he wrote or conclusions he reached. Time and again, his prodding compelled the Court to revise or reconsider its first assessment of a fact or an issue, drawing from others a higher quality of performance than they might otherwise have achieved. No Justice labored more earnestly to act with care and fairness, and none adhered to a more rigorous standard of judicial integrity. His reassuring example of craftsmanship and rectitude meant much in a period of rapid constitutional change, when the Court and its members were frequently the subject of hostility or question.

CHARLES LISTER
(1986)

Bibliography

DORSEN, NORMAN 1969 John Marshall Harlan. Pages 2803–2820 in Leon Friedman and Fred L. Israel, eds., *The Justices of the United States Supreme Court 1789–1969*. New York: Chelsea House.

FRIENDLY, HENRY J. 1971 Mr. Justice Harlan, as Seen by a Friend and Judge of an Inferior Court. *Harvard Law Review* 85:382–389.

SHAPIRO, DAVID L. 1969 *The Evolution of a Judicial Philosophy: Selected Opinions and Papers of Justice John M. Harlan.* Cambridge, Mass.: Harvard University Press.

HARLOW v. FITZGERALD

See: *Nixon v. Fitzgerald*

HARMLESS ERROR

Not all denials of a defendant's federal constitutional rights compel reversal of a conviction. The Supreme Court announced in *Chapman v. California* (1967) as a matter of federal constitutional law that, in criminal proceedings, if the beneficiary of the error can prove beyond a REASONABLE DOUBT that the error in no way contributed to the result, the case need not be reversed. This standard applies to state as well as federal proceedings and state rules requiring only a lesser showing of the harmlessness of error are not controlling when federal constitutional error has been shown.

Although the Supreme Court's standard is stricter than that of many state courts (which may adhere to a lesser standard than reasonable doubt or even in some cases shift the BURDEN OF PROOF to the victim of the error), it nevertheless falls short of a per se rule requiring automatic reversal for all violations of federal constitutional rights. Thus, for example, where EVIDENCE obtained through an UNREASONABLE SEARCH in violation of the FOURTH AMENDMENT is improperly admitted into a trial, reversal of a guilty verdict is not always required. The Supreme Court has stated that certain kinds of violations do, indeed, require automatic reversal—such as coerced confessions or unconstitutionally obtained guilty pleas—but these kinds of violation are few in number.

Chapman itself concerned a prosecutor's comments to the jury upon the defendants' failure to testify, in violation of defendants' Fifth Amendment RIGHT AGAINST SELF-INCRIMINATION, and cases involving harmless error doctrine may arise from any part of the Constitution. The bulk of the decided cases, though, have involved application of the EXCLUSIONARY RULE to evidence unconstitutionally seized.

Where illegally obtained evidence is the sole or primary basis for a conviction, of course, the conviction must be reversed. On the other hand, where independent, admissible evidence of defendant's guilt is overwhelming, or illegally obtained evidence is noninflammatory and merely cumulative, reversal is not required. But such a finding will often involve difficult determinations. First, which evidence is actually admissible, and which is a fruit of the federal constitutional error? Second, since the prosecutor in introducing the tainted evidence has represented that it tended to prove guilt, the Supreme Court may look carefully at later claims that the evidence was in fact harmless.

The Court has not yet definitively settled the issue of whether a federal constitutional error can be cured through the trial judge's instructions to the jury. *Chapman* suggests that such instructions may render the error harmless, if they are shown beyond a reasonable doubt to have prevented the error from affecting the jury's verdict. But none of the cases decided by the Court since *Chapman* has found this standard to have been met.

JOHN KAPLAN
(1986)

Bibliography

SALZBURG, STEPHEN A. 1984 *American Criminal Procedure*, 2nd ed. St. Paul, Minn.: West Publishing Co.

HARMLESS ERROR
(Update)

When an appellate court finds that a criminal defendant's constitutional rights were violated at trial, it must then decide whether to reverse the defendant's conviction. In a case where the appellate court has little reason to believe that the constitutional error contributed to the jury's decision to convict, the court will conclude that the constitutional error was "harmless" and will affirm the defendant's conviction.

Often the appellate court's inquiry will focus on whether the government offered the jury overwhelming evidence of the defendant's guilt; whether the constitutional violation was likely to inflame or prejudice the jury; whether erroneously admitted evidence was merely duplicative of other properly admitted evidence; and whether the trial judge was able to dissipate the likely effect of the error on the jury through curative instructions.

A tiny category of constitutional errors are not subject to harmless error analysis but instead trigger automatic reversal. These include the complete denial of the Sixth Amendment RIGHT TO COUNSEL; the denial of the defendant's right to represent himself at trial; the denial of a PUBLIC TRIAL; the giving of an inaccurate instruction to the jury on the standard of proof beyond a reasonable doubt; the denial of an impartial factfinder; and the racially discriminatory selection of jurors. In *Arizona v. Fulminante* (1991), the Supreme Court explained that these constitutional violations are structural errors, basic defects in the trial framework which can be presumed to make the trial unfair. The Court distinguished this small group of structural errors from what it called "trial errors," the vast number of other constitutional violations that can occur during the presentation of the case to the jury. Because an appellate court can assess the likely impact of trial errors on the jury's assessment of the case, automatic reversal is not necessary, and harmless error analysis will apply.

ERIC L. MULLER
(2000)

Bibliography

EDWARDS, HARRY T. 1995 To Err Is Human, But Not Always Harmless: When Should Legal Error Be Tolerated? *New York University Law Review* 70:1167–1228.
TRAYNOR, ROGER J. 1970 *The Riddle of Harmless Error.* Columbus: Ohio State University Press.

HARPER v. VIRGINIA BOARD OF ELECTIONS
383 U.S. 663 (1966)

Harper epitomizes the WARREN COURT's expansion of the reach of the EQUAL PROTECTION clause of the FOURTEENTH AMENDMENT. Virginia levied an annual $1.50 POLL TAX on residents over twenty-one, and conditioned voter registration on payment of accrued poll taxes. The Supreme Court, 6–3, overruled BREEDLOVE V. SUTTLES (1937), holding that the condition on registration denied the equal protection of the laws.

The *Harper* opinion, by Justice WILLIAM O. DOUGLAS, played an important part in crystallizing equal protection DOCTRINE by justifying heightened levels of judicial scrutiny. The Court did not quite hold that wealth or indigency was a SUSPECT CLASSIFICATION, saying only that "lines drawn on the basis of wealth of property, like those of race, are traditionally disfavored." It did say, following REYNOLDS V. SIMS (1964), that voting was a FUNDAMENTAL INTEREST, requiring STRICT SCRUTINY of its restriction. The poll tax by itself might be constitutionally unobjectionable; wealth as a condition on voting, however, not only failed the test of strict scrutiny; it was a "capricious or irrelevant factor."

For Justice HUGO L. BLACK, dissenting, *Harper* represented a relapse into judicial subjectivism through a variation on the "natural-law-due-process" formula he had decried in *Adamson v. California* (1947). The Virginia scheme was not arbitrary; it might increase revenues or ensure an interested electorate. The Court should not substitute its judgment for the Virginia legislature's. Justice JOHN MARSHALL HARLAN also dissented, joined by Justice POTTER STEWART. Harlan, who shared Black's views, added that it was arguable that "people with some property have a deeper stake in community affairs, and are consequently more responsible, more educated, more knowledgeable, more worthy of confidence, than those without means." That this belief was not his own did not matter; it was arguable, and that was all the RATIONAL BASIS standard demanded.

Commentators saw in *Harper* and other contemporary decisions a major shift away from the tradition of minimal judicial scrutiny of laws challenged under the equal protection clause. Invasions of interests of great importance, or discrimination against disadvantaged groups, appeared to call for judicial scrutiny more demanding than that required by the relaxed rational basis standard. Soon the Court found a formula for two levels of review: rational basis for most "social and economic" legislation, and strict scrutiny for laws invading fundamental interests or employing suspect classifications.

The Court has not pursued *Harper's* suggestion that WEALTH DISCRIMINATION is suspect. VOTING RIGHTS, however, are firmly established as interests whose invasion demands strict scrutiny. Implicitly, as in cases involving ALIENS or ILLEGITIMACY, and explicitly, as in cases on SEX DISCRIMINATION, the Court has transformed its two levels of judicial scrutiny into a sliding-scale approach that is interest balancing by another name: the more important the interest invaded, or the more "suspect" the classification, the more the state must justify its legislation. In broad outline this development was portended in *Harper*, which exemplified not only Warren Court egalitarianism but also Justice Douglas's doctrinal leadership.

KENNETH L. KARST
(1986)

Bibliography

KARST, KENNETH L. 1969 Invidious Discrimination: Justice Douglas and the Return of the "Natural-Law-Due-Process Formula." *UCLA Law Review* 16:716–750.

HARRIS, UNITED STATES v.
106 U.S. 629 (1883)

Harris, like UNITED STATES V. CRUIKSHANK (1876), involved a federal prosecution under a general conspiracy statute, and like *Cruikshank* it was a victory for the Ku Klux Klan. The Supreme Court had gutted the *Cruikshank* statute but allowed it to survive; the *Harris* statute, though similar, did not survive. Section two of the FORCE ACT OF 1871 made it a federal crime, punishable by fine and up to six years in prison, for two or more persons to conspire for the purpose of depriving anyone of the EQUAL PROTECTION OF THE LAWS or hindering lawful authorities from securing equal protection for others. The United States prosecuted Harris who, at the head of an armed lynch mob, had bro-

ken into a Tennessee jail and captured four black prisoners, despite the efforts of the sheriff to protect them. The mob had beaten the four, killing one. Could the United States try them under the act of 1871? With Justice JOHN MARSHALL HARLAN dissenting silently, the Court held, in an opinion by Justice WILLIAM WOODS, that the act of Congress was unconstitutional. Woods declared that the FOURTEENTH AMENDMENT merely authorized Congress to take remedial measures against STATE ACTION that violated the amendment; it applied only to acts of the states, not to acts of private individuals. The THIRTEENTH AMENDMENT did not apply to the acts of private individuals, but this statute could apply to conspiracies by whites against whites, a subject having nothing to do with SLAVERY. The statute, therefore, had no constitutional basis.

LEONARD W. LEVY
(1986)

HARRIS v. MCRAE
448 U.S. 297 (1980)

A 5–4 Supreme Court here sustained a series of restrictions on congressional appropriations for the Medicaid program. The restrictions went beyond the law sustained in MAHER V. ROE (1977) by refusing funding even for medically necessary abortions.

Justice POTTER STEWART's opinion for the Court relied heavily on *Maher* in rejecting claims based on the SUBSTANTIVE DUE PROCESS right of PRIVACY and on the EQUAL PROTECTION clause. A woman's right to be free from governmental interference with her decision to have an abortion did not imply a right to have government subsidize that decision. Equal protection demanded only a RATIONAL BASIS for the law's discrimination between therapeutic abortions and other medical necessities, and such a basis was found in the protection of potential life. Justice Stewart also rejected a claim that the law amounted to an ESTABLISHMENT OF RELIGION. Opposition to abortion might be a tenet of some religions, but the establishment clause did not forbid governmental action merely because it coincided with religious views.

The *Maher* dissenters were joined in *McRae* by Justice JOHN PAUL STEVENS, who had joined the *Maher* majority. The cases were different, he argued; here an indigent woman was denied a medically necessary abortion for lack of funds, at the same time that the government was funding other medically necessary services. ROE V. WADE (1973), allowing a state to forbid abortions in the later stages of pregnancy, had excepted abortions necessary to preserve pregnant women's lives or health. The government could not create exclusions from an aid program, Justice Stevens argued, solely to promote a governmental interest (preservation of potential life) that was "constitutionally subordinate to the individual interest that the entire program was designed to protect."

KENNETH L. KARST
(1986)

(SEE ALSO: *Abortion and the Constitution; Reproductive Autonomy*.)

HARRIS v. NEW YORK
401 U.S. 222 (1971)

This case is significant as a limitation on MIRANDA V. ARIZONA (1966). Harris sold narcotics to undercover police officers. The police failed to inform him, after his arrest, that he had a RIGHT TO COUNSEL during a custodial POLICE INTERROGATION and they ignored his request for an attorney. Harris eventually admitted that he had acted as an intermediary, buying heroin for the undercover agent, but he denied selling it to the agent. During the trial Harris contradicted the statement that he had made during interrogation; the judge overruled defense objections that the custodial statement was inadmissible under the MIRANDA RULES because it was made involuntarily and in violation of his rights. The judge instructed the jury that although the statement was unavailable as EVIDENCE OF GUILT, they might consider it in assessing Harris's credibility as a witness.

The Supreme Court, 5–4, upheld Harris's conviction. *Miranda* dissenters JOHN MARSHALL HARLAN, BYRON R. WHITE, and POTTER J. STEWART along with Justice HARRY A. BLACKMUN joined in Chief Justice WARREN E. BURGER's opinion holding that testimony secured without the necessary warnings could nevertheless be used to impeach contradictory testimony at trial. Burger flatly asserted that Harris made "no claim that the unwarned statements were coerced or involuntary"—a statement clearly controverted by the record. Burger also dismissed, as OBITER DICTUM, the assertion in *Miranda* that all such statements were inadmissible for any purpose. The majority relied heavily on *Walder v. United States* (1954), in which evidence secured in an UNREASONABLE SEARCH was admitted to impeach testimony although the EXCLUSIONARY RULE would have prohibited its use as evidence of guilt.

Justice WILLIAM J. BRENNAN, dissenting, said that *Miranda* prohibited the use of any statements obtained in violation of its guarantees and denied the contention that that was obiter dictum. Brennan also distinguished *Walder*: the statement there had no connection to the crime with which the defendant had been charged; in *Harris* the defendant's statements related directly to the crime. Moreover, the evidence there could have been used

to assess credibility; here the jury could have misused it as evidence of guilt because the statement provided information about the crime charged.

DAVID GORDON
(1986)

Bibliography
LEVY, LEONARD W. 1974 *Against the Law: The Nixon Court and Criminal Justice.* New York: Harper & Row.

HARRIS v. UNITED STATES

See: Search Incident to Arrest

HARRISON, BENJAMIN
(1833–1901)

One of a series of "caretaker" Presidents in the last quarter of the nineteenth century, Benjamin Harrison exercised only minimal influence on constitutional issues during his administration from 1889 to 1893. Though Harrison favored civil service reform and a reduction in the labor workday, and opposed southern disenfranchisement of blacks, his philosophy of the executive function limited his actions. Harrison believed his duty lay solely in enforcing the public will, as expressed by Congress.

Although he had called for federal antitrust action in his first message to Congress, claiming that trusts "are dangerous conspiracies against the public good, and should be made the subject of prohibitory and even penal legislation," Harrison's only contribution to the SHERMAN ANTITRUST ACT, passed during his term, was his signature. His administration, moreover, was rather indifferent to the act; of seven cases instituted by the government, only two resulted in a government victory and none was pressed to the Supreme Court. Harrison appointed four Justices to the Court: DAVID J. BREWER, HENRY B. BROWN, GEORGE SHIRAS, and HOWELL E. JACKSON, all conservatives. These appointments indicated Harrison's desire to secure property interests and vested rights against the assaults of reformers.

DAVID GORDON
(1986)

Bibliography
VOLWILER, ALBERT T. 1932 Harrison, Benjamin. In *Dictionary of American Biography*, Vol. 8, pp. 331–335. New York: Scribner's.

HARRISON ACT
38 Stat. 785 (1914)

Congress passed this act at the behest of the Treasury Department to implement the 1912 Hague Convention banning narcotics trafficking. As with other legislation of the period, the act reflected a belief in the necessity of federal regulation to curb social evils. Although most such acts relied on the COMMERCE CLAUSE, Congress here used the TAXING POWER to establish a complex network of national drug control.

The act required all manufacturers and dealers in certain narcotics to register with the government and to pay a $1 annual license tax. The act also mandated the use of federal forms to complete transactions and ordered these forms kept for two years, accessible to federal inspection. Sale or shipment of specified drugs in INTERSTATE COMMERCE—even their possession by an unregistered person—was illegal. The act exempted physicians and other professionals from filing the federal forms but required them to maintain separate records. A 5–4 Supreme Court sustained the act in UNITED STATES V. DOREMUS (1919). Justice WILLIAM R. DAY asserted Congress's complete discretion to levy taxes, subject merely to the constitutional requirement of geographical uniformity.

DAVID GORDON
(1986)

HART, HENRY M., JR.
(1904–1969)

At Harvard Law School, Henry Hart was a disciple of FELIX FRANKFURTER. After a clerkship with Justice LOUIS D. BRANDEIS, Hart returned to Harvard as a member of the law faculty, where he remained—with an interruption during WORLD WAR II—all his life.

Hart was one of a handful of the most authoritative academic lawyers of his time. He was, above all, a teacher; his most important scholarship is embodied in two books designed for law school courses. In *The Federal Courts and the Federal System* (1953), co-authored with Herbert Wechsler, Hart introduced students to a conception of the functions of the federal judiciary that still dominates the thinking of courts and commentators. In *The Legal Process* (1958), co-authored with Albert Sacks, Hart expounded a view of the role of courts in lawmaking focused on "reasoned elaboration" of principle. For a generation that view was so influential that today's critics speak of a "legal process school" as the focus for their attack.

For Hart, reason was "the life of the law." His intellectual integrity was legendary. Nor was the integrity merely intellectual. He was a decent man, as generous and humane in personal dealings as he was formidable in print. During his last illness, he continued to meet his classes until he was physically unable to get to the classroom. To the end, he taught everyone around him.

KENNETH L. KARST
(1986)

Bibliography
HART, HENRY M., JR.   1971   *Southern California Law Review* 44: i-x, 305–498.

HARTFORD CONVENTION
(December 15, 1814–January 5, 1815)

The Hartford Convention, called by the Federalists of the Massachusetts legislature, consisted of delegates chosen by the legislatures of Massachusetts, Connecticut, and Rhode Island. The delegates sought to promote the interests and policies of the New England Federalists, who vehemently opposed the War of 1812. Although secessionist sentiment flourished among extremists, moderates—those who opposed a separate New England confederacy and civil war—controlled the convention. The fact that it was held showed a respect for the Constitution, however perverse. Despite the convention's endorsement of theories of state NULLIFICATION and INTERPOSITION similar to those of the VIRGINIA AND KENTUCKY RESOLUTIONS of 1798–1799, the delegates unanimously advocated amendments to the Constitution as a means of curtailing federal powers. After a manifesto assailing the war, American foreign policy, national control of state militias, and the admission of western states, the convention proposed that congressional REPRESENTATION and federal taxation be based on the number of free persons only; embargoes be restricted to sixty days; Congress be prevented from declaring war, restricting foreign trade, or admitting new states except by a two-thirds majority; federal offices be restricted to native-born citizens; and the President be restricted to one term.

The convention had the misfortune of meeting while events were making it irrelevant. As three delegates left for Washington to present its proposals for constitutional amendments, the news arrived of ANDREW JACKSON's victory at New Orleans, and when the delegates arrived in Washington, the town celebrated peace reports from Ghent. President JAMES MADISON excoriated the convention as a "rebel Parliament" that had engaged in a treasonable conspiracy, and the public ridiculed it. It accomplished nothing, left a bitter heritage, and enhanced the respectability of the doctrine of interposition.

LEONARD W. LEVY
(1986)

Bibliography

BANNER, JAMES M., JR. 1970 *To the Hartford Convention.* New York: Knopf.

HASTIE, WILLIAM HENRY
(1904–1976)

William Henry Hastie was the first black federal judge. He studied law at Harvard Law School, where he was elected to the *Harvard Law Review.* After graduation in 1930 he pursued a career that included service to the national government, the Howard Law School, and the NAACP.

Hastie in 1939 took the chair of that CIVIL RIGHTS organization's National Legal Committee, a post he used to influence the course of civil rights litigation. He argued successfully with THURGOOD MARSHALL in SMITH V. ALLWRIGHT (1941) that a Texas all-white PRIMARY ELECTION law violated the Fifteenth Amendment. He also joined with Marshall five years later in arguing MORGAN V. VIRGINIA. They persuaded the Court that a Virginia law imposing SEGREGATION on interstate buses unconstitutionally burdened the uniform flow of commerce. *Smith* and *Morgan* were critical victories in the NAACP's attack on the South's dual system of race relations: the former leveled a barrier to black voting; the latter marked the first victory in a transportation case.

Following appointment as judge of the Third Circuit in 1949, Hastie had few judicial opportunities to advance the cause of civil rights. Scarcely two dozen of his 486 opinions dealt with civil rights, and these reveal a commitment to constitutional law rooted in principle and judicial restraint. In *Lynch v. Torquato* (1965) Hastie declined to expand the STATE ACTION theories he had advanced in *Smith.* He held that the EQUAL PROTECTION clause of the FOURTEENTH AMENDMENT did not embrace the management of the internal affairs of the Democratic party. In an article he spurned AFFIRMATIVE ACTION programs that used "race alone as a determinant of eligibility or qualification."

William Hastie stood in the front rank of civil rights leaders. Notably, a strong sense of Madisonian constitutionalism balanced his commitment to legal activism.

KERMIT L. HALL
(1986)

Bibliography

RUSCH, JONATHON J. 1978 William H. Hastie and the Vindication of Civil Rights. *Howard Law Journal* 21:749–820.

HATCH ACT
53 Stat. 1147 (1939); 54 Stat. 767 (1940)

The Hatch Act prohibits most federal employees from engaging in any of a broad range of partisan political activities. It was adopted in 1939, but its antecedents go back well into the nineteenth century. The act has twice been challenged on FIRST AMENDMENT, VAGUENESS, and OVERBREADTH grounds, and has twice been upheld: *Civil Service Commission v. National Association of Letter Carriers* (1973) and *United Public Workers v. Mitchell* (1947). Similar state legislation was upheld in BROADRICK V. OKLAHOMA (1973).

Although public employee organizations are among the most formidable lobbies in Congress and state legislatures, laws like the Hatch Act severely restrict the individual employee's political activities. These restrictions have been justified as assuring impartiality in public service, preventing the incumbent party from constructing a political machine, and preventing coercion of public employees.

The Hatch Act cases contrast sharply with later BURGER COURT decisions such as BUCKLEY V. VALEO (1976), protecting unlimited campaign spending, and FIRST NATIONAL BANK OF BOSTON V. BELLOTTI (1978), protecting corporate spending in ballot measure campaigns.

These decisions, in combination with the Hatch Act cases, suggest that, in the Burger Court's view, no liberty may be sacrificed to prevent unfair grasping of power by the use of concentrated wealth, but a great deal of liberty may be sacrificed to prevent unfair grasping of power by a mass-based device such as political patronage.

DANIEL H. LOWENSTEIN
(1986)

Bibliography

COMMISSION ON POLITICAL ACTIVITY OF GOVERNMENT PERSONNEL 1968 *A Commission Report.*
ROSE, HENRY 1962 A Critical Look at the Hatch Act. *Harvard Law Review* 75:510–526.

HATE CRIMES

A hate crime is a crime committed as an act of prejudice against the person or PROPERTY of a victim as a result of that victim's real or perceived membership in a particular group. Although "hate crime" is the popular term used in connection with bias-motivated violence, "bias crime" is a more accurate label. Not every crime that is motivated by hatred for the victim is a bias crime. Hate-based violence is a bias crime only when this hatred is connected with antipathy for a group, such as a racial or ethnic group, or for an individual because of membership in that group. Some statutes define this bias in terms of actual animus. Others look to discriminatory selection of the victim on the basis of membership in the group. Bias crimes can arise out of mixed motivation where the perpetrator of a violent crime is motivated to commit the crime by a number of different factors, bias among them. To constitute a bias crime, the bias motivation must be a substantial motivation for the perpetrator's criminal conduct. The requirement can be put as a question: but for the ethnicity of the victim, would this crime have been committed?

Bias crime statutes in the United States encompass crimes that are motivated by the race, color, ethnicity, national origin, or religion of the victim. Many statutes reach SEXUAL ORIENTATION or gender as well, and some include other categories such as age or disability. Bias crime laws may either create a specific crime of bias- motivated violence or raise the penalty of a crime when it is committed with bias motivation.

The justification for bias crime laws turns primarily on the manner in which bias crimes differ from other crimes. Bias crimes cause greater harm than parallel crimes—those crimes that lack a prejudicial motivation but are otherwise identical to the bias crime. The harm is greater on three levels: harm to the individual victim, harm to victim's group or community, and harm to the society at large.

Bias crimes generally have a more harmful emotional and psychological impact on the individual victim. The victim of a bias crime is not attacked for a random reason (as is the person injured during a shooting spree in a public place), nor is he attacked for an impersonal reason (as is the victim of a mugging for money). He is attacked for a specific, personal reason, such as, for example, his race. Moreover, the bias crime victim cannot reasonably minimize the risks of future attacks, for he is unable to change the characteristic that made him a victim. The heightened sense of vulnerability caused by bias crimes is beyond that normally found in crime victims. Studies have suggested that the victims of bias crimes tend to experience psychological symptoms such as depression or withdrawal, as well as anxiety, feelings of helplessness, and a profound sense of isolation.

The impact of bias crimes reaches beyond the harm done to the immediate victim or victims of the criminal behavior. There is a more widespread impact on the target community—the community that shares the race, religion or ethnicity of the victim. Members of the target community of a bias crime may experience that crime in a manner that has no equivalent in the public response to a parallel crime. Not only does the reaction of the target community go beyond mere sympathy with the immediate bias crime victim, it exceeds empathy as well. Members of the target community of a bias crime perceive the crime as if it were an attack on themselves directly and individually.

Finally, the impact of bias crimes may spread beyond the immediate victims and the target community to the general society. This effect includes a large array of harms

from the very concrete to the most abstract. On the most mundane level—but by no means least damaging—the isolation effects discussed above have a cumulative effect throughout a community. Bias crimes cause an even broader injury to the general community because they violate not only society's general concern for the security of its members and their property but also the shared values of equality among its citizens and harmony in a heterogeneous society. A bias crime is therefore a profound violation of the egalitarian ideal and the antidiscrimination principle that have become fundamental not only to the American legal system but to American culture as well.

The enhanced punishment of bias motivated violence raises two sets of constitutional questions. The first questions, which apply to bias crime laws generally, concern the FIRST AMENDMENT right of FREEDOM OF SPEECH. The second set of questions, which apply only to federal bias crime laws, concern questions of FEDERALISM and the constitutional authority for such LEGISLATION.

The free expression challenges to hate crime laws were the subject of a flurry of judicial activity bracketed by the Supreme Court decisions in R. A. V. V. CITY OF ST. PAUL (1992), which struck down a municipal cross-burning ordinance, and WISCONSIN V. MITCHELL (1993), which upheld a state law that provided for increased penalties for bias crimes. Among courts and scholars alike, three general positions have emerged concerning the consonance of bias crime laws with principles of free expression. One position argues that the enhanced punishment of bias-motivated crimes is an unconstitutional punishment of thought because the increased punishment is due solely to the defendant's expression of a conviction or viewpoint of which the community disapproves. A second position permits the enhanced punishment of bias crimes based on a view that bias motivations and hate speech are unprotected by the First Amendment. Ironically, these two opposing positions share a common premise: that proscription of bias crimes involves regulation of expression and is therefore either impermissible or requiring of justification.

The third position, which appears to be that of the Supreme Court, distinguishes between hate speech and bias crimes, protecting the former but permitting the enhanced punishment of the latter. This has been understood in two related ways. One approach is to distinguish between speech and conduct—the premise of the decision in *Wisconsin v. Mitchell.* An alternative approach focuses on the actor's state of mind, and distinguishes behavior that is intended to communicate from behavior that is intended to cause harm to a targeted victim. Each approach protects some measure of hate speech and allows for the enhanced punishment of bias crimes.

The federalism challenges to the constitutionality of a federal bias crime law arise from the fact that the vast majority of bias crimes are state law crimes. The question of constitutional authority for a federal bias crime law is especially acute in the aftermath of UNITED STATES V. LÓPEZ (1995), in which the Court struck down the Federal Gun-Free School Zones Act, holding that, because the act neither regulated a commercial activity nor contained a requirement that the firearm possession be connected to INTERSTATE COMMERCE, it exceeded Congress's authority under the COMMERCE CLAUSE. It is partially for this reason that, at the time of this writing, there is no pure federal bias crimes statute. Nevertheless, bias motivation is an element of certain federal CIVIL RIGHTS crimes, and in 1994 Congress directed the U.S. Sentencing Commission to promulgate guidelines enhancing the penalties for any federal crimes in which there is racial, religious, or ethnic motivation. These statutes, however, cover only a small range of cases involving bias motivation.

The commerce clause, which has been used as constitutional authority for ANTIDISCRIMINATION LEGISLATION or for laws barring discrimination in PUBLIC ACCOMMODATIONS, housing, and EMPLOYMENT, is a potential source for constitutional authority for a federal bias crime law. The more promising source for such authority lies in the post–CIVIL WAR constitutional amendments. Congress has expressly relied, in part, on the FOURTEENTH AMENDMENT and the FIFTEENTH AMENDMENT as authority for the federalization of bias motivated deprivation of rights individuals hold under state law. Not every bias crime, however, deprives the victim of the ability to exercise some right under state law. It may be that the THIRTEENTH AMENDMENT provides broad constitutional authority for a federal bias crime law. In a series of cases— most notably JONES V. ALFRED H. MAYER CO. (1968), and RUNYON V. MCCRARY (1976)—the Supreme Court articulated a theory of the Thirteenth Amendment as a source of broad proscription of all BADGES OF SERVITUDE, empowering Congress to make any rational determination as to what conduct constitutes a badge or incident of SLAVERY and to ban it, whether from public or private sources. Moreover, the abolition of slavery in the Thirteenth Amendment, although immediately addressed to the enslavement of African Americans, has been understood to apply beyond the context of race to include religious and ethnic groups as well. As a matter of constitutional authority, Congress may enact a federal bias crime law so long as it is rational to determine that bias motivated violence is as much a "badge" or "incident" of slavery as is discrimination in contractual or property matters, a determination that would appear to have ample support.

FREDERICK M. LAWRENCE
(2000)

(SEE ALSO: *Hate Speech*.)

Bibliography

JACOBS, JAMES B. and POTTER, KIMBERLY 1998 *Hate Crimes: Criminal Law and Identity Politics.* New York: Oxford University Press.

KELLY, ROBERT J., ed. 1991 *Bias Crime: American Law Enforcement and Legal Responses.* Chicago: University of Illinois.

LAWRENCE, FREDERICK M. 1999 *Punishing Hate: Bias Crimes Under American Law.* Cambridge, Mass.: Harvard University Press.

LEVIN, JACK and MCDEVITT, JACK 1993 *Hate Crimes: The Rising Tide of Bigotry and Bloodshed.* New York: Plenum Press.

WANG, LU-IN 1997 *Hate Crimes Law.* St. Paul, Minn.: Clark, Boardman & Callaghan.

HATE SPEECH

Hate speech is usually thought to include communications of animosity or disparagement of an individual or a group on account of a group characteristic such as race, color, national origin, sex, disability, religion, or SEXUAL ORIENTATION. Hate speech takes many forms. Examples include Ku Klux Klan cross-burnings directed at racial or religious minorities; obscene phone calls threatening violence against women; epithets shouted at gay marchers; published diatribes against marginalized racial or immigrant groups; defacement of places of worship; and harassment of an interracial couple because of race. Some would define hate speech even more broadly, to include an expression that race or another characteristic "marks a person as suspect in morals or ability." Such a definition would encompass communications as broad and diverse as stereotypical descriptions of other groups; descriptions of women as suited for domestic life but not leadership positions; abstract advocacy of SEGREGATION; "jokes" stereotyping minorities; or, in sum, any communication that tends toward the stigmatization or marginalization of any individual or group on account of one of the mentioned characteristics.

Although few FIRST AMENDMENT advocates would argue that hate speech is worthy in itself, many oppose government regulation. Their reasons range from the necessity of wide latitude for FREEDOM OF SPEECH in a democratic society, to preserving the MARKETPLACE OF IDEAS and the free exchange of unpopular ideas, to a fear that repressing one idea or means of expressing that idea leads inevitably to repressing others (the "slippery slope"). In contrast, other scholars, some of whom have been instrumental in developing CRITICAL RACE THEORY in the late 1980s and 1990s, have emphasized that our history of segregation and RACIAL DISCRIMINATION make expressions of race hatred different, in that they tend to maintain subordinated peoples in a subordinated status. Some FEMINIST THEORY scholars, notably Catherine MacKinnon, have contended that PORNOGRAPHY is a form of hate speech that at once oppresses and justifies the oppression of women. These scholars' arguments have provoked widespread debate among legal scholars.

To be sure, the courts have allowed much regulation of hate speech. The government can constitutionally ban targeted vilification of others on the basis of race, color, national origin, sex, or religion, where the expressions undermine others' equal enjoyment of rights to housing and employment. For example, the federal Fair Housing Act prohibits threats or intimidations directed at an interracial couple to discourage them from renting in one's neighborhood. A state can also punish verbal harassment designed to prevent others from exercising constitutional rights such as VOTING, or threats of violence that may have a racial or gender component to them. Moreover, a state can regulate expressions that are likely to incite others to imminent criminality, or even ban so-called FIGHTING WORDS, those expressions likely to lead to immediate responsive violence.

However, the mode the government chooses to regulate such expressions is critical. If the government targets expression because it does not like the content of the expression, the permissible arenas of regulation are extremely limited. Courts have repeatedly struck down regulations that targeted the racial or sexual character of speech, but have permitted other regulations whose effect might be the same but whose provisions focused more carefully on the secondary characteristics of expression, such as its effects, time, place, or manner. A general prohibition against cross-burnings would be invalid, while a prohibition against burning combustible materials in a forest during fire season would be constitutional, even as applied to cross burners. A regulation that prohibited parades at midnight in residential communities, or even one that banned picketing targeted at a single house, would be valid, but a regulation that banned marches by neo-Nazis in Jewish neighborhoods would be invalid.

Another example demonstrates the Supreme Court's hostility toward governmental regulations targeting hate speech because of the particular message conveyed. In cases arising prior to the 1990s the Court had indicated that government could ban fighting words; that is, those likely to incite others to engage in responsive violence. The City of St. Paul, Minnesota sought to use this DOCTRINE to defend an ordinance that, in effect, banned only racist fighting words. St. Paul argued that its law simply regulated a subcategory of regulable fighting words. However, in R. A. V. V. CITY OF ST. PAUL (1992), the Court disagreed, holding that St. Paul could not single out for special prohibition those fighting words the content of which was "racist."

Mere offensiveness of hateful language is never sufficient, as a constitutional matter, to warrant regulation of the expression. Even reprehensible diatribes against other racial or immigrant groups cannot constitutionally be forbidden unless the speech provokes imminent violence, or threatens or harasses specific persons. For example, a Ku Klux Klan cross-burning conducted away from minority neighborhoods or even a Nazi march through a Jewish neighborhood cannot constitutionally be forbidden to prevent the message from being heard. Both, however, might be punished under a properly drafted regulation prohibiting racially or ethnically motivated targeted threats against the homes of others.

On the other hand, the Court has approved other regulations of hate speech that focused on modes of regulation other than its racist or sexist content. As R. A. V. itself recognized, the Court has allowed the government to regulate much speech on the basis of its content. OBSCENITY, fighting words, and threats of violence can be regulated, but R. A. V. means the Court is unwilling to permit states to prohibit only racist obscenity, racist fighting words, or racist threats of violence.

The point of R. A. V. is not that hate speech may not be regulated. Rather, when regulations focus on the content of speech, targeting its racist or sexist character, for example, the Court has determined that the risk of suppressing free speech is too great. A permissible regulation must aim at a target that is different from the mere racist content of the expression. For example, in addition to CIVIL RIGHTS laws that protect housing rights, the Court has allowed regulation of sexually themed speech constituting WORKPLACE HARASSMENT on grounds that such speech is part of a broader regulatory regime attacking EMPLOYMENT DISCRIMINATION. In R. A. V. itself, where a white teenager had burned a cross on the lawn of an African American family's home, the Court emphasized that the conduct itself could have been punished under a trespass or criminal mischief statute. It is also likely that the conduct could have been punished under a statute that prohibited threats of violence. And, in WISCONSIN V. MITCHELL (1993), the Court allowed a state to give extra punishment for common crimes where those crimes were motivated by racial animosity, rejecting arguments that the criminal's thought processes were inevitably punished by such statutes. Decisions such as these suggest that in order to meet the Court's First Amendment tests, hate speech regulations must be drawn in ways that target their impact on one's enjoyment of common civil rights or CIVIL LIBERTIES rather than on their offensive content.

JOHN T. NOCKLEBY
(2000)

(SEE ALSO: *Hate Crimes*.)

Bibliography

KARST, KENNETH L. 1990 Boundaries and Reasons: Freedom of Expression and the Subordination of Groups. *University of Illinois Law Review* 1990:95–149.

MACKINNON, CATHERINE 1993 *Only Words.* Cambridge, Mass.: Harvard University Press.

MASSARO, TONI 1991 Equality and Freedom of Expression: The Hate Speech Dilemma. *William and Mary Law Review* 32:211–265.

MATSUDA, MARI J.; LAWRENCE, CHARLES R., III; DELGADO, RICHARD; and CRENSHAW, KIMBERLÉ WILLIAMS 1993 *Words that Wound: Critical Race Theory, Assaultive Speech, and the First Amendment.* Boulder, Colo.: Westview Press.

NOCKLEBY, JOHN T. 1994 Hate Speech in Context: The Case of Verbal Threats. *Buffalo Law Review* 42:653–713.

POST, ROBERT C. 1991 Racist Speech, Democracy, and the First Amendment. *William and Mary Law Review* 32:267–327.

HAUPT v. UNITED STATES
330 U.S. 1 (1947)

Herbert Haupt, a German American, infiltrated into the United States during WORLD WAR II from a German submarine as part of a Nazi plot to sabotage American war industry. His father, Hans Max Haupt, allowed him to stay at the latter's home, bought a car for him, and helped him to get a job in a factory where Norden bomb sights were manufactured. There were at least two witnesses to each of these three acts, and on the basis of that testimony Hans Haupt was convicted of TREASON.

The Supreme Court sustained Haupt's conviction in an 8–1 decision. In an opinion by Justice ROBERT H. JACKSON, the Court held that the overt acts testified to met the test laid down in CRAMER V. UNITED STATES (1945): each constituted the actual giving of aid and comfort to an enemy spy. Unlike Anthony Cramer's public meetings with the saboteurs, Hans Haupt's "harboring and sheltering" of his son were of direct support to the enemy mission.

DENNIS J. MAHONEY
(1986)

(SEE ALSO: *Quirin, Ex Parte.*)

HAWAII v. MANKICHI

See: Insular Cases

HAWAIIAN SOVEREIGNTY

See: Native Hawaiian Sovereignty Movements

HAWAII HOUSING AUTHORITY v. MIDKIFF
467 U.S. 229 (1984)

The system of feudal land tenure developed under the Hawaiian monarchy had modern consequences. Seventy-two landowners owned forty-seven percent of the land in the state, and the federal and state governments owned forty-nine percent; only four percent of the land was left for other owners. The Hawaii legislature, finding that this system distorted the land market, in 1967 adopted a land reform act. The law authorized use of the state's EMINENT DOMAIN power to condemn residential plots and to transfer ownership to existing tenants. Landowners challenged the law as authorizing TAKINGS OF PROPERTY for private benefit rather than PUBLIC USE. The Supreme Court unanimously rejected this argument, upholding the law's validity. The legislature's purpose to relieve perceived evils of land concentration was legitimately public, and the courts' inquiry need extend no further. Apart from issues of JUST COMPENSATION, the taking of property has virtually ceased to present a judicial question.

KENNETH L. KARST
(1986)

HAYBURN'S CASE
2 Dallas 409 (1792)

Hayburn's Case was regarded in its time and has been regarded by many historians since as the first case in which a federal court held an act of Congress unconstitutional. Congress in 1791 directed the CIRCUIT COURTS to rule on the validity of pension claims made by disabled Revolutionary War veterans; the findings of the courts were to be reviewable by the secretary of war and by Congress. The circuit court in New York, presided over by Chief Justice JOHN JAY, and the circuit court in North Carolina, presided over by Justice JAMES IREDELL, addressed letters to President GEORGE WASHINGTON explaining why they could not execute the act in their judicial capacities but that out of respect for Congress they would serve voluntarily as pension commissioners.

In the Pennsylvania circuit, Justices JAMES WILSON and JOHN BLAIR, confronted by a petition from one Hayburn, decided not to rule on his petition, and they also explained themselves in a letter to the President. They would have violated the Constitution to have ruled on the petition, they said, because the business directed by the act was not of a judicial nature and did not come within the JUDICIAL POWER OF THE UNITED STATES established by Article III. They objected to the statute because it empowered officers of the legislative and executive branches to review court actions, contrary to the principle of SEPARATION OF POWERS and judicial independence.

Hayburn's Case thus presented no suit, no controversy between parties, and, technically, no "case," and none of the courts rendered judicial decisions; they reported to the President their refusal to decide judicially. (See CASES AND CONTROVERSIES.) Some congressmen thought that *Hayburn's Case* was "the first instance in which a Court of Justice had declared a law of Congress to be unconstitutional," and the same opinion was delightedly trumpeted in anti-administration newspapers, which praised a precedent that they hoped would lead to judicial voiding of Hamiltonian legislation. The "case" reported in 2 Dallas 409 involved a motion for a WRIT OF MANDAMUS to compel the circuit court to grant a pension to Hayburn, but the court held the case over, and Congress revised the statute, providing a different procedure for the relief of pension-seeking veterans.

LEONARD W. LEVY
(1986)

HAYES, RUTHERFORD B.
(1822–1893)

An Ohio lawyer and CIVIL WAR general, Rutherford Birchard Hayes briefly served in Congress and was thrice elected Governor. A compromise Republican presidential candidate in 1876, Hayes received a minority of the popular vote and probably should not have been elected. However, the electoral vote was uncertain because of disputed results in South Carolina, Florida, Louisiana, and Oregon. Claims of vote fraud and threats of civil war led to a crisis which was resolved by the COMPROMISE OF 1876 which gave the election to Hayes on the condition that federal troops would be removed from the South. During his Presidency the rights of the freedmen were severely undermined as Reconstruction came to an end.

PAUL FINKELMAN
(1986)

Bibliography
DAVISON, KENNETH E. 1972 *The Presidency of Rutherford B. Hayes.* Westport, Conn.: Greenwood Press.

HAYNE, ROBERT YOUNG
(1791–1839)

As a United States senator from South Carolina, Robert Young Hayne debated DANIEL WEBSTER of Massachusetts in the famous Webster-Hayne Debate of 1830. The debate began over a bill to slow down the sale of western lands but developed into a heated discussion over slavery, the nature of the Union, and the relationship between the states and the federal government. Hayne argued for the right of states to nullify federal laws. After the debate—which most contemporaries and historians agree was won by Webster—Hayne was a key participant in the South Carolina NULLIFICATION Convention of 1833. The Convention asserted that the federal tariffs of 1828 and 1832 were unconstitutional and null and void in South Carolina. Hayne was then elected governor of the state. In his inaugural address he asserted "we will STAND OR FALL WITH CAROLINA." As governor he organized troops to defend South Carolina's SOVEREIGNTY from the federal government, but he ultimately accepted a compromise that peacefully ended the "Nullification Crisis."

PAUL FINKELMAN
(1986)

Bibliography
JERVEY, THEODORE D. (1909) 1970 *Robert Y. Hayne and His Times.* New York: DaCapo Press.

HAYNES v. UNITED STATES

See: *Marchetti v. United States*

HAYNES v. WASHINGTON
373 U.S. 503 (1963)

This was the last of many confessions cases, prior to ESCOBEDO V. ILLINOIS (1964), in which the Supreme Court decided the voluntariness of a confession by a DUE PROCESS standard. In 1944 the Court had held that due process was violated if the police obtained a confession by continuous interogation while the prisoner was held incommunicado in an inherently coercive situation. Thereafter, however, the Court frequently had deferred to a determination of voluntariness by state courts. *Haynes* was the first case since 1944 in which the Court revived the standard of inherent coerciveness where the facts showed incommunicado detention and the prisoner was not allowed to call his lawyer. The case foreshadowed *Escobedo* and MIRANDA V. ARIZONA (1966).

LEONARD W. LEVY
(1986)

HAYS, ARTHUR GARFIELD
(1881–1954)

A leading defense counsel for and later director of the AMERICAN CIVIL LIBERTIES UNION, Arthur Garfield Hays devoted his career to protecting CIVIL LIBERTIES and FREEDOM OF SPEECH. Two of his books, *Let Freedom Ring* (1928) and *Trial by Prejudice* (1933), recount his participation in the Scottsboro cases (see NORRIS V. ALABAMA), the Scopes anti-evolution trial in Tennessee with Clarence Darrow (see TENNESSEE V. SCOPES), and on behalf of Sacco and Vanzetti (see COMMONWEALTH V. SACCO AND VANZETTI). Hays maintained a laissez-faire attitude toward government regulation of business and vigorously championed democracy, positions he elucidated in *Democracy Works* (1939).

DAVID GORDON
(1986)

HAZELWOOD SCHOOL DISTRICT v. KUHLMEIER
484 U.S. 260 (1988)

In TINKER V. DES MOINES INDEPENDENT SCHOOL DISTRICT (1969) the Supreme Court held that school officials could not interfere with students' speech unless that speech threatened substantial disorder, a material disruption of the educational program, or invasion of the rights of others. The *Kuhlmeier* decision continues the erosion of *Tinker* that had begun in the BETHEL SCHOOL DISTRICT V. FRASER (1986).

A journalism class in a Missouri public high school wrote and edited the school newspaper. The school's principal, after reviewing proofs, ordered the deletion of two of the paper's projected six pages to avoid publication of two articles: one detailing the experiences of three pregnant students and another on students' feelings about their parents' divorces. The first story, the principal said, was inappropriate for the school's younger students; the second contained derogatory comments by a named student about her father. With no notice to the student writers or editors, the paper was printed with the offending pages deleted. Three of the students brought suit against school officials, seeking a DECLARATORY JUDGMENT that the censorship violated their FIRST AMENDMENT rights. They lost in the federal district court, but prevailed in the court of appeals on the theory of the *Tinker* decision. The Supreme Court reversed, 5–3.

Justice BYRON R. WHITE, for the Court, first concluded that the paper was not a PUBLIC FORUM because its pages had not been opened up to students generally or to any other segment of the general public. He distinguished *Tinker* in two main ways. First, the school could legitimately seek to inculcate the community's values, and thus could act to avoid the inference that it endorsed the conduct that led to student pregnancy. Second, the principal's control over the school paper was a series of decisions about the educational content of the journalism curriculum, and

courts must pay deference to educators in such matters. Thus, the proper STANDARD OF REVIEW was not STRICT SCRUTINY but one of "reasonableness"—a standard satisfied by the principal's decision.

For the three dissenters, Justice WILLIAM J. BRENNAN, argued that the majority's "reasonableness" test effectively abandoned the much more demanding standards of *Tinker*. Surely some members of the *Kuhlmeier* majority would be satisfied to paint *Tinker* into a corner where its value as a PRECEDENT would be severely limited. Whether the Court will complete this process of doctrinal retrenchment remains to be seen.

KENNETH L. KARST
(1992)

HEALTH INSURANCE FOR THE AGED ACT (MEDICARE)
79 Stat. 286 (1965)

The 1965 amendment of the SOCIAL SECURITY ACT establishing a system of health insurance operated by the Social Security Administration culminated thirty years of controversy over the proper role of the federal government in relation to medical care. Medicare provided hospital insurance and a variety of medical benefits for citizens sixty-five years or older. The act was designed to meet the serious problem of providing care for those who faced old age fearful of the financial ravages of illness.

Medicare's two insurance programs operated differently. The Hospital Benefit program automatically covered anyone over sixty-five with no "needs" test. It paid for hospitalization, nursing home care, home visits, and diagnostic services. It was financed by compulsory contributions from the protected persons and their employers and provided benefits as a matter of entitlement. The Supplementary Medical Insurance section created a voluntary individual program subsidized and administered by the government, using private insurance companies to assist in its administration.

Medicare influenced the entire pattern of medical care in the United States. With government financing a growing share of total health care expenditures, its power and role within the American health care system expanded proportionately. Not only administrators but also doctors and nurses adjusted their conduct to comply with newly mandated rules and procedures.

PAUL L. MURPHY
(1986)

Bibliography

FEDER, JUDITH 1977 *Medicare: The Politics of Federal Hospital Insurance.* Lexington, Mass.: Lexington Books.

HEARING

See: Fair Hearing

HEARSAY RULE

The hearsay rule is a nonconstitutional rule of EVIDENCE which obtains in one form or another in every JURISDICTION in the country. The rule provides that in the absence of explicit exceptions to the contrary, hearsay evidence of a matter in dispute is inadmissible as proof of the matter. Although jurisdictions define "hearsay" in different ways, the various definitions reflect a common principle: evidence that derives its relevance in a case from the belief of a person who is not present in court—and thus not under oath and not subject to cross-examination regarding his credibility—is of questionable probative value.

The Constitution does not explicitly refer to the hearsay rule or implicitly constitutionalize the hearsay rule in civil or criminal cases generally; but it does contain two provisions that share common purposes with the hearsay rule. The TREASON clause of Article III, section 3, prohibits a conviction for treason "unless on the testimony of two witnesses to the same overt act, or on a confession in open court." In CRAMER V. UNITED STATES (1945) the Supreme Court construed this clause to require the federal government to produce witnesses who possessed direct evidence—as opposed to circumstantial evidence—of the same overt act. Although *Cramer* itself did not involve hearsay evidence, its reasoning applies as well to hearsay evidence of overt acts, because hearsay evidence is itself a kind of circumstantial evidence.

The other provision of the Constitution that bears on the hearsay rule is the Sixth Amendment's CONFRONTATION clause, which entitles the accused in a criminal case "to be confronted with the witnesses against him." In contrast to the hearsay rule, the confrontation clause does not treat hearsay evidence as presumptively inadmissible against the accused, and it does not treat traditional exceptions to the hearsay rule as automatically admissible. Nevertheless, the confrontation clause addresses the questionable nature of hearsay evidence by requiring the state to produce at trial the hearsay declarants whose statements it uses against the accused, when it appears that the declarants are available to testify in person and that the defendant could reasonably be expected to wish to examine them in person at the time their hearsay statements are introduced into evidence.

PETER WESTEN
(1986)

(SEE ALSO: *Compulsory Process, Right to.*)

Bibliography
MCCORMICK, CHARLES 1972 *Evidence*, 2nd ed. Pages 579–756. St. Paul, Minn.: West Publishing Co.

HEART OF ATLANTA MOTEL v. UNITED STATES
379 U.S. 241 (1964)
KATZENBACH v. MCCLUNG
379 U.S. 294 (1964)

In these cases the Supreme Court unanimously upheld the portion of the CIVIL RIGHTS ACT OF 1964 forbidding RACIAL DISCRIMINATION by hotels, restaurants, theaters, and other PUBLIC ACCOMMODATIONS.

Congressional debates had discussed the appropriate source of congressional power to prohibit private racial discrimination. The COMMERCE CLAUSE was proposed as a safe foundation for the bill; since 1937 the Supreme Court had upheld every congressional regulation of commerce that came before it. Because Congress obviously was seeking to promote racial equality, some thought the commerce clause approach "artificial" and thus "demeaning." They argued for reliance on the power of Congress to enforce the FOURTEENTH AMENDMENT. That amendment's STATE ACTION limitation, however, seemed to obstruct reaching private discrimination. As enacted, the 1964 act's public accommodations provisions were limited to establishments whose operations "affect commerce" or whose racial discrimination is "supported by state action."

The Supreme Court moved swiftly, accelerating decision in these two cases. The majority relied on the commerce power, validating the act in application not only to a large whites-only motel that mainly served out-of-state guests but also to a restaurant with no similar connection to interstate travel. The latter case, *McClung*, illustrates how far the commerce power has been stretched in recent years to allow Congress to legislate on matters of national concern. The restaurant mainly served a local clientele; it served blacks, but only at a take-out counter. Almost half the food used by the restaurant had come from other states, but even the Court recognized that this fact was trivial. More persuasive was the fact, fully documented in congressional hearings, that discrimination in public accommodations severely hindered interstate travel by blacks. Justices WILLIAM O. DOUGLAS and ARTHUR J. GOLDBERG, concurring, argued that both the commerce clause and the Fourteenth Amendment empowered Congress to impose these regulations.

In retrospect the pre-enactment debate over which power Congress should assert seems unimportant, in either institutional or doctrinal terms. Congress need not, after all, specify which of its powers it is using. And the Supreme Court has not needed to explore the full reach of Congress's Fourteenth Amendment power, because in JONES V. ALFRED H. MAYER CO. (1968) it held that the THIRTEENTH AMENDMENT empowered Congress to prohibit private racial discrimination. (See BADGES OF SERVITUDE.)

KENNETH L. KARST
(1986)

HEATH v. ALABAMA
474 U.S. 82 (1985)

By the same act, Heath committed crimes in two states. Men whom he hired kidnapped his wife in one state and killed her in another. He pleaded guilty in one state to avoid CAPITAL PUNISHMENT, and he received a life sentence. However, the other state tried him for essentially the same offense, convicted him, and sentenced him to death. Heath claimed that the second trial exposed him to DOUBLE JEOPARDY in violation of the clause of the Fifth Amendment, applicable to the states via the INCORPORATION DOCTRINE.

In many cases, the Court had held that a state and the federal government may prosecute the same act if it was a crime under the laws of each. Never had the Court previously decided whether two states could prosecute the same act.

Justice SANDRA DAY O'CONNOR, for a 7–2 Court, declared that although the Fifth Amendment's double-jeopardy clause protects against successive prosecutions for the same act, if that act breached the laws of two states, it constituted distinct offenses for double-jeopardy purposes. The "dual sovereignty" rule in such cases meant that each affronted sovereign had criminal JURISDICTION. The states are as sovereign toward each other as each is toward the United States. In a sense, the case created no new law because the double-jeopardy clause had never previously barred different jurisdictions from trying the same person for the same act. Nevertheless, Justices WILLIAM J. BRENNAN and THURGOOD MARSHALL sharply dissented.

LEONARD W. LEVY
(1992)

HEFFRON v. INTERNATIONAL SOCIETY FOR KRISHNA CONSCIOUSNESS, INC.
452 U.S. 640 (1981)

One rule governing the Minnesota State Fair allows the sale or distribution of literature, or the solicitation of funds, only at fixed booths. The International Society for Krishna Consciousness (ISKCON) sued in a state court challenging this rule's validity on its face and as applied. ISKCON contended that the rule violated its FIRST AMENDMENT rights of FREEDOM OF SPEECH and RELIGIOUS LIBERTY. The Minnesota Supreme Court held the law invalid as applied to ISKCON, saying that the state authorities had not shown that exempting ISKCON from the rule would significantly interfere with crowd control at the fair.

The Supreme Court reversed, upholding the rule on its face and as applied to distribution (5–4) and to sales and solicitation (9–0). Justice BYRON R. WHITE wrote for the Court. He concluded that the rule, which made no distinctions based on speech content and allowed no discretion to the licensing authorities, was valid as a regulation of the time, place, and manner of speech. The fair was a PUBLIC FORUM, but differed significantly from a public street. Considerations of safety and crowd control amounted to substantial state interests, justifying the rule restricting sales, distribution, and solicitation to booths. Exempting ISKCON would require exempting all applicants. Other less restrictive means for achieving those interests, such as penalizing disorder or limiting the number of solicitors, were unlikely to deal with the problems posed by large numbers of solicitors roaming the fairgrounds.

Justice WILLIAM J. BRENNAN's partial dissent, joined by two other Justices, argued that the rule was invalid in application to ISKCON's proposed distribution of literature. Such distribution, he argued, was no more disruptive than the making of speeches, or face-to-face proselytizing, both of which were permitted. Justice HARRY A. BLACKMUN also dissented as to the distribution of literature.

KENNETH L. KARST
(1986)

HELVERING v. DAVIS
301 U.S. 619 (1937)

Plaintiff, a stockholder of an affected CORPORATION, challenged Titles II and VIII of the 1935 SOCIAL SECURITY ACT. Title II creates the old age benefits program, popularly known as "social security," and Title VIII contains the funding mechanism for that program. Under Title VIII, an employer must take a payroll deduction from each employee's wages and pay it, together with an equal amount directly from the employer, to the treasury.

Plaintiff's primary argument was that Congress lacked constitutional power to levy a tax for the purpose of providing old age benefits. Justice BENJAMIN N. CARDOZO, writing an opinion in which six other Justices joined, resoundingly rejected the argument that Congress had transgressed the TENTH AMENDMENT reservation to the states of powers not delegated to the federal government. Only Justices JAMES C. MCREYNOLDS and PIERCE BUTLER dissented. The majority classified the old age benefits program as a legitimate exercise of Congress's power "to lay and collect taxes ... to ... provide ... for the GENERAL WELFARE of the United States." The Court adopted a fluid definition of the general welfare. "Nor is the concept of the general welfare static. Needs that were narrow or parochial a century ago may be interwoven in our day with the well-being of a nation." The Court then examined the effects on older workers of the "purge of nation-wide calamity that began in 1929" and concluded that the problem was national in scope, acute in severity, and intractable without concerted federal effort. State governments were deficient in economic resources and reluctant to finance social programs that would place them at comparative economic disadvantage with competitor states: industry would flee the new taxes and INDIGENTS would flock to any state that provided the new social benefits. (Justice Cardozo's analysis proved prescient. In the 1960s and 1970s a number of socially progressive northeastern and western states experienced these twin problems when they far exceeded national benefit norms in the federal-state cooperative programs of Aid to Families with Dependent Children and Medicaid.) Having determined that the purpose of Title II was well within the scope of the "general welfare" clause, the Court sustained the Title VIII funding provisions.

In its broad, though imprecise, reading of the term "general welfare," *Helvering v. Davis*, even more than its companion case, STEWARD MACHINE CO. V. DAVIS (1937), rejects the view that Congress, in exercising its power to tax for the general welfare, is required by the Tenth Amendment to eschew regulation of matters historically controlled by the states. In so doing, it repudiates that vein of case law, exemplified by UNITED STATES V. BUTLER (1936), that treats the Tenth Amendment as a limitation on the federal TAXING AND SPENDING POWER. Though *Butler* is factually distinguishable, the analysis used by Justice Cardozo in *Steward Machine Co.* and *Helvering v. Davis* would surely have sustained the agricultural price support provisions struck down in *Butler* a year earlier.

GRACE GANZ BLUMBERG
(1986)

won fame and popularity with a series of resolutions opposing the STAMP ACT as an unconstitutional imposition of TAXATION WITHOUT REPRESENTATION. A flamboyant and persuasive orator, Henry became the leader of the radical patriot faction in Virginia. As a delegate to the FIRST CONTINENTAL CONGRESS Henry favored both issuance of a declaration of grievances and formation of the ASSOCIATION. At home, he successfully urged the arming of the militia and served briefly as commander-in-chief of Virginia's forces. He was a member of the convention that, in 1776, adopted the VIRGINIA DECLARATION OF RIGHTS AND CONSTITUTION and instructed the state's congressional delegation to call for a DECLARATION OF INDEPENDENCE. Henry was himself a delegate to Congress but resigned in June 1776 when he was elected first governor of Virginia. In 1776 Governor Henry supported a BILL OF ATTAINDER (written by THOMAS JEFFERSON) against a notorious Tory brigand. When Jefferson and JAMES MADISON proposed to end the ESTABLISHMENT OF RELIGION in Virginia, Henry countered with a plan for general assessment to support all Christian churches and teachers.

Although Henry was a longtime self-proclaimed nationalist and had often called for enlargement of the powers of Congress under the ARTICLES OF CONFEDERATION, he declined appointment as a delegate to the CONSTITUTIONAL CONVENTION OF 1787. In the Virginia state convention of 1788 he was the leader of the anti-Federalists and spoke and voted against RATIFICATION OF THE CONSTITUTION. He argued that the document lacked a BILL OF RIGHTS and infringed on state SOVEREIGNTY, and he warned that the new federal Congress might someday abolish SLAVERY.

Henry later converted to the Federalist cause; in 1795 President GEORGE WASHINGTON offered to make Henry secretary of state, but Henry declined. In the 1796 case of WARE V. HYLTON Henry appeared with JOHN MARSHALL as counsel for Virginians who claimed that, the Treaty of Paris notwithstanding, state law precluded their obligation to repay debts due to British subjects. That same year Henry turned down Washington's offer of appointment as Chief Justice of the United States. Like SAMUEL ADAMS of Massachusetts, Henry proved better suited to making a revolution than to erecting a stable constitutional order.

DENNIS J. MAHONEY
(1986)

HENRY, PATRICK
(1736–1799)

Unsuccessful as a merchant, Patrick Henry turned to the law. He was admitted to the Virginia bar in 1760 and rose rapidly to prominence and prosperity. In 1765 Henry was elected to the House of Burgesses and, in his first term,

HEPBURN ACT
34 Stat. 584 (1906)

A string of adverse decisions by the Supreme Court left the Interstate Commerce Commission (ICC) with few effective powers. Abuses abounded despite the ELKINS ACT of 1903, and in December 1905 THEODORE ROOSEVELT reiterated his earlier calls for corrective legislation. The resulting bill, which met significant opposition only in the Senate, expressly vested the ICC with the power to prescribe "reasonable" maximum rail rates only after current rates and practices had been condemned in a hearing. The bill, which became law on June 29, 1906, nonetheless failed to establish any standards for those rates, thus leaving the Court to apply the FAIR RETURN rule of SMYTH V. AMES (1898). Rates initiated by the ICC were subject to narrow JUDICIAL REVIEW; new rates became effective upon issuance unless challenged in the CIRCUIT COURTS and successfully enjoined, in which case they took effect only when sustained by the courts. The "commodities clause," which forbade carriers from transporting goods produced by railroads or in which they had an interest, was primarily addressed to rail lines serving mining interests. Additional provisions, effective immediately, shifted the burden of APPEALS to the carriers, not the commission. Congress followed this with the MANN-ELKINS ACT in 1910, further supporting the commission.

DAVID GORDON
(1986)

(SEE ALSO: *Interstate Commerce Commission v. Illinois Central Railroad.*)

Bibliography

SHARFMAN, ISAIAH L. 1931–1937 *The Interstate Commerce Commission*, 4 vols. New York: Commonwealth Fund.

HERBERT v. LANDO
441 U.S. 153 (1979)

In *Herbert v. Lando* a majority of the Supreme Court soundly rejected the argument that the constitutional protections afforded journalists should be expanded to bar inquiry into the editorial processes of the press in libel actions. Anthony Herbert, a Vietnam veteran, received widespread media attention when he accused his superior officers of covering up atrocities and other war crimes. Herbert sued for libel when CBS broadcast a report and *The Atlantic Monthly* published an article, both by Barry Lando, about Herbert and his accusations. Herbert conceded that he was a PUBLIC FIGURE required by NEW YORK TIMES V. SULLIVAN (1964) to prove that the media defendants acted with "actual malice." During pretrial discovery, Lando refused to answer questions on the ground that the FIRST AMENDMENT precluded inquiry into the state of mind of those who edit, produce, or publish, and into the editorial process.

The Court recognized that the FIRST AMENDMENT affords substantial protection to media defendants in libel actions, citing specifically the *Sullivan* requirement that public figures and officials must prove knowing or reckless untruth. The Court noted, however, that the Framers did not abolish civil or criminal liability for defamation when adopting the First Amendment. It reasoned that upholding a constitutional privilege that barred inquiry into facts relating directly to the central issue of the defendant's state of mind would effectively deprive plaintiffs of the very evidence necessary to prove their case. That result would substantially eliminate recovery by plaintiffs who were public figures or public officials.

Justice LEWIS F. POWELL separately elaborated upon the majority's admonition that in supervising discovery in libel actions, trial judges should exercise appropriate controls to prevent abuse, noting the courts' duty to consider First Amendment interests along with plaintiffs' private interest. Justice WILLIAM J. BRENNAN, dissenting in part, asserted that the First Amendment provided a qualified editorial privilege which would yield once the plaintiff demonstrated a *prima facie* defamatory falsehood. Separately dissenting, Justice POTTER J. STEWART argued that inquiry into the editorial process is irrelevant, and Justice THURGOOD MARSHALL rejected the majority's balance of the competing First Amendment and private interests.

KIM MCLANE WARDLAW
(1986)

(SEE ALSO: *Balancing Test; Evidence; Freedom of the Press.*)

HERNDON v. LOWRY
301 U.S. 242 (1937)

Herndon was a black organizer convicted of attempting to incite insurrection in violation of a state law. Herndon had sought to induce others to join the Communist party. At the time the party was seeking to organize southern blacks and calling for separate black states in the South. While only indirectly adopting the CLEAR AND PRESENT DANGER test, the Court refused to apply the BAD TENDENCY TEST of GITLOW V. NEW YORK (1925) and stressed the absence of any immediate threat of insurrection. In an opinion by Justice OWEN ROBERTS, a 5–4 Court held (1) that the evidence presented failed "to establish an attempt to incite others to insurrection" even at some indefinite future time; and (2) that the statute was unconstitutionally vague as applied and contrued because "every person who attacks existing conditions, who agitates for a change in the form of government, must take the risk that if a jury should be of opinion he ought to have foreseen that his utterances might contribute in any measure to some future forcible resistance to the existing government he may be convicted of the offense of inciting insurrection." The VAGUENESS

DOCTRINE invoked was not specifically articulated as a FIRST AMENDMENT standard; instead, the general criminal standard of "a sufficiently ascertainable standard of guilt" was applied.

The state supreme court believed that a conviction would be justified if the defendant intended that insurrection "should happen at any time within which he might reasonably expect his influence to continue to be directly operative in causing such action by those whom he sought to induce. . . ." This formula, which the Supreme Court found constitutionally infirm, must be compared with its own of the 1950s upholding convictions for conspiracy to advocate overthrow of the government where the intention was that of an organized group to bring about overthrow "as speedily as circumstances would permit."

MARTIN SHAPIRO
(1986)

HICKLIN v. ORBECK
437 U.S. 518 (1978)

A unanimous court, speaking through Justice WILLIAM J. BRENNAN, held unconstitutional an Alaska law requiring private firms working on oil and gas leases or pipelines to give preference in hiring to Alaska residents. By discriminating against nonresidents, the "Alaska Hire" law violated the PRIVILEGES AND IMMUNITIES clause of Article IV of the Constitution.

DENNIS J. MAHONEY
(1986)

HIGHER LAW

Americans have never been hesitant to argue that if a law is bad it must be unconstitutional. When no written constitutional provision suggests an interpretation that undermines the law under attack, American lawyers have often looked to the ancient tradition of unwritten higher law for support.

It is worth distinguishing two kinds of unwritten higher law. The first is natural law, conceived by the ancient Stoics as, in Cicero's words, "right reason, harmonious, diffused among all, constant, eternal." The Stoic conception was integrated with Christian theology by the medieval scholastics, and later was reformulated in a secular and individualistic direction by the NATURAL RIGHTS theorists of the Enlightenment. In this latter form, the natural law tradition provided the intellectual background for the American colonists' assertion of "certain inalienable rights" in the DECLARATION OF INDEPENDENCE.

The second kind of unwritten higher law, which we may call FUNDAMENTAL LAW, derives from those conventional and largely unquestioned values and practices that need be neither constant, eternal, nor dictated by reason. The members of a society may see their fundamentals as contingent, peculiar to themselves, and mutable—though, because fundamental, not easily or quickly mutable. On the other hand, those who see their own society's basic conventions as the only possible ones do not accept, perhaps cannot even understand, the distinction between "natural" and "fundamental" law.

In the practice of legal argument either natural or fundamental law can have priority, with the other regarded as ancillary. Thus one can argue that a principle is legally binding because it comports with right reason, as is incidentally confirmed by its acceptance in society; or one can reverse the priorities, leaving reason to confirm what convention and tradition primarily establish. Until about the mid-nineteenth century, American lawyers alternated between these rhetorical strategies, but since the Civil War the fundamental law strand has predominated.

The American idea of fundamental law derived originally from the seventeenth-century English habit of conducting political disputes in terms of an "ancient constitution," unwritten and believed (like the COMMON LAW itself) to be of "immemorial antiquity." Sir EDWARD COKE exemplified this habit when he merged natural with traditional law and both with English common law, and then asserted judicial authority to override legislation in the name of this powerful conglomerate. His declaration in BONHAM'S CASE (1608) that "when an Act of Parliament is against common right and reason . . . the common law will control it, and adjudge such act to be void" supplied a significant argument in the American colonists' struggle with Parliament between 1761 and 1776.

During the prerevolutionary period, the Americans argued for limitations on Parliament's authority over them on the basis of this same conglomerate of reason, common law, and constitutional tradition. Only when they broke with the English crown altogether in 1776—an avowedly revolutionary step—was their justification purely in terms of natural right.

With independence, the new states enacted popularly ratified written constitutions, a process later repeated in the adoption of the federal Constitution. The question then arose whether the new constitutions subsumed the older idea of unwritten constitutional law based on reason or tradition. The classic debate on this question was the exchange of OBITER DICTA between Justices JAMES IREDELL and SAMUEL CHASE of the Supreme Court in CALDER V. BULL (1798). Iredell argued that a law consistent with the applicable written constitutions was immune from further JUDICIAL REVIEW; because the "ablest and the purest minds differ" concerning the requirements of natural justice, judges should assume no special authority to enforce so indeterminate a standard. Chase insisted that "certain vital principles in our free Republican governments" would invalidate inconsistent legislation whether the principle were enacted or not; thus a law that took the property of A and gave it to B could not stand, even if the applicable written constitution did not explicitly protect private property.

Chase's dictum followed the tenor of the NINTH AMENDMENT to the federal Constitution (1791): "The enumeration in the Constitution, of certain rights, shall not be construed to deny or disparage others retained by the people." But the Ninth Amendment does not settle the Chase-Iredell dispute, as it might if it said explicitly whether the unenumerated and retained rights have enforceable constitutional status.

During the first years of the republic, a number of state courts, as in *Ham v. McClaws* (South Carolina, 1789), anticipated Chase by invoking unenacted constitutional law to invalidate legislation. On the other hand, the most influential discussions of judicial review during the early federal period—ALEXANDER HAMILTON'S THE FEDERALIST #78 (1787) and JOHN MARSHALL's opinion in MARBURY V. MADISON (1803)—echoed Iredell's view in basing power solely on the judicial authority to construe the written constitution, itself conceived as the expressed will of a fully sovereign people.

On the whole, judicial practice before 1830, particularly in the state courts but in a few federal cases as well, adopted Chase's view while also invoking his natural-law language with its appeal to "general principles of republican government." Marshall himself, in FLETCHER V. PECK (1810), ambiguously justified invalidation of a Georgia statute "either by general principles which are common to our free institutions, or by the particular provisions of the constitution of the United States." The particular provision in question was the CONTRACT CLAUSE, which Marshall heroically stretched to fit the case, perhaps out of reluctance to rest decision solely on "general principles." In a few later cases, such as TERRETT V. TAYLOR (1815), the Supreme Court did invalidate state legislation without reference to constitutional text.

Even during their heyday before 1830, the "general principles" of the unwritten constitution were never regarded as federal constitutional law, binding on the states under the SUPREMACY CLAUSE. Because they did not count as "the Constitution or laws of the United States," unwritten general principles would not support appeal to the Supreme Court from the decision of a state court; federal courts invoked these principles against state legislatures only when acting as substitute state courts under DIVERSITY OF CITIZENSHIP JURISDICTION.

In their content, the unwritten "general principles" ap-

plied during this period were largely confined to the protection of traditional vested property rights against retroactive infringement. As such, they were equally well supported by common law tradition and by contemporary ideas of natural justice.

From about 1830 on, judicial assertion of pure unwritten constitutional law became less common, perhaps because of its conflict with Jacksonian ideas of popular sovereignty. The process of stretching the language of vague constitutional provisions to encompass notions of natural or traditional justice continued, however, and there began a historic shift in the favored vague provision from the federal contract clause to the clauses of state constitutions guaranteeing the LAW OF THE LAND and DUE PROCESS OF LAW—phrases that began to be construed to mean more than their originally understood sense as guarantees of customary common law procedures. Thus was born the concept bearing the oxymoronic name of SUBSTANTIVE DUE PROCESS, which ever since has been the main vehicle for the implementation of higher law notions in American constitutional law.

A leading case in this development was *Taylor v. Porter* (New York, 1843), which incorporated in "due process" the prohibition, earlier invoked by Chase as an unwritten general principle, against the state's taking the property of the worthy A only to give it to the undeserving B. In these early substantive due process decisions the language of immutable natural law mixed indiscriminately with talk of historically based common law and tradition; there was no felt conflict between the two rhetorical strands.

By contrast, the discourses of natural justice and of customary practice did conflict in the great constitutional debates over SLAVERY that occurred, largely outside the courts, during the period 1830–1860. Proslavery forces occasionally argued that the natural right of property protected the owners of human as of other chattels. Indeed, in the most notorious of constitutional slavery cases, DRED SCOTT V. SANDFORD (1857), Chief Justice ROGER B. TANEY held that congressional prohibition of SLAVERY IN THE TERRITORIES violated slaveholders' property rights guaranteed by the Fifth Amendment's due process clause. But the legal defenders of slavery did not generally have to rely on unwritten higher law; they could point to the positive guarantees the slave states had insisted on inserting in the federal Constitution.

On the other hand, antislavery lawyers had almost no basis for legal argument except the increasingly widespread conviction that slavery was intolerably unjust. With positive law and custom against them, they tried to translate natural law directly into constitutional doctrine. To this end, they invoked the PRIVILEGES AND IMMUNITIES clause of Article IV; the "liberty" protected by substantive due process; and the proclamation of human equality in the Declaration of Independence, for which they claimed constitutional status. More radical abolitionists opposed these efforts to accommodate the Constitution, the "covenant with Hell," to the antislavery cause; on the other hand, the pre-Civil War courts found the antislavery constitutional arguments unacceptable because too radical. But abolitionist constitutional theory triumphed in larger arenas; it became part of the political program of the Republican party, and thus part of the world view of the politicians who led the war against slavery and afterward framed the Reconstruction amendments.

The language of section 1 of the FOURTEENTH AMENDMENT (1868) directly echoes the old triad of antislavery constitutional arguments in its guarantees of due process, EQUAL PROTECTION OF THE LAW, and the privileges and immunities of national citizenship. These general clauses have ever since provided the main textual basis for the continuation of the higher law tradition in constitutional law.

In the SLAUGHTERHOUSE CASE (1874) the Supreme Court at first by a 5–4 vote rejected the argument that the new amendment constitutionally bound the states to the whole array of unenumerated rights. But by the end of the century, the courts had accepted the arguments of commentators, chief among whom was THOMAS M. COOLEY (*Constitutional Limitations*, 1868), that due process prohibited all legislative intrusions upon basic liberties and property rights that did not reasonably promote the limited ends of public health, safety, or morals. Of the protected liberties, the dearest to the courts of this period was FREEDOM OF CONTRACT, and in a series of decisions epitomized by LOCHNER V. NEW YORK (1905) the courts invalidated economic regulatory laws on the grounds that they unreasonably constrained the terms on which adults could contract with each other.

In developing this doctrine, courts and commentators sometimes echoed the old language of natural law, but the more characteristic note of this aggressive laissez-faire constitutionalism was struck by Justice RUFUS PECKHAM, who condemned a price regulation law as a throwback to the past that ignored "the more correct ideas which an increase of civilization and a fuller knowledge of the fundamental laws of political economy . . . have given us today" (*Budd v. State*, New York, 1889). The notion of evolution had taken hold, and it not only supported the doctrines of Social Darwinism but also promoted the idea that fundamental legal principles evolved—a progress that the courts should accommodate by developing the law of the due process clause through a "gradual process of judicial inclusion and exclusion" (*Davidson v. New Orleans*, 1878). Tradition continued to play a role as well; thus the courts invalidated much new legislation regulat-

ing the price charged for goods while accepting old usury laws that regulated the price charged for the use of money, and generally tolerating public regulation of those businesses that had traditionally been treated as AFFECTED WITH A PUBLIC INTEREST.

The legal supporters of Progressive politics fiercely attacked "liberty of contract" and its associated doctrines in the name of popular sovereignty, which they argued required repudiation of the very idea of unwritten constitutional law. When laissez-faire constitutionalism was finally put to rest in the mid-1930s under the combined influence of FRANKLIN D. ROOSEVELT's court-packing plan and more long-run historical forces, it appeared that the higher law tradition might finally have come to the end of its long influence on American constitutionalism.

Only if higher law is given its narrower sense derived from classic natural law has this come to pass. The New Deal and post-New Deal courts found a new active role in the program of correcting for legislative failures sketched by the famous footnote four of the opinion in UNITED STATES V. CAROLENE PRODUCTS (1938). They promoted racial equality and electoral reform while protecting political dissidents, religious deviants, and criminal defendants, a role that reached its peak during the years of the WARREN COURT (1953–1969). The doctrinal vehicles for these projects have been the gradual incorporation within due process of the specific guarantees of the BILL OF RIGHTS and above all the evolutionary interpretation of the equal protection clause as a vehicle of fundamental law.

One of the most effective promoters of these developments, Justice HUGO L. BLACK (1937–1971), did wholly repudiate any invocation of higher law in their support; his characteristic stance was a rigorously exclusive appeal to constitutional text as a source of doctrine. While Justice Black's colleagues did not share his strict constructionist views, they too generally avoided invoking notions of natural or universal human rights, often resting decision on imaginative readings of original intent. Frequently, however, the Justices have openly construed vague constitutional language in light of an evolving fundamental law specific to American history and culture. During these years the Court has said that "notions of what constitutes equal treatment . . . do change" (HARPER V. VIRGINIA BOARD OF ELECTIONS, 1966); that due process requires states to institute criminal procedures that are "fundamental" in the sense of "necessary to an Anglo-American regime of ordered liberty" (DUNCAN V. LOUISIANA, 1968); and that the prohibition of CRUEL AND UNUSUAL PUNISHMENT is to be construed in the light of "those evolving standards of decency that mark the progress of a maturing society" (*Furman v. Georgia*, 1972).

Its association with laissez-faire constitutionalism had discredited substantive due process as a doctrinal tool during the generation following the New Deal, but beginning with GRISWOLD V. CONNECTICUT (1965) the Court moved toward reviving the use of this old rubric for the protection of substantive liberties. The role once held by "liberty of contract" was now taken by the RIGHT OF PRIVACY, a misleading name for what was at its core a constitutional protection for freedom of REPRODUCTIVE CHOICE, surrounded by a periphery of other doctrines limiting governmental power to regulate the FAMILY. The privacy decisions openly used as precedents substantive due process cases decided before the New Deal. Like those earlier decisions, the privacy cases avoided reference to universal right or natural law in support of their doctrines, with a plurality of Justices stating in MOORE V. EAST CLEVELAND (1977) that "the Constitution protects the sanctity of the family precisely because the institution of the family is deeply rooted in this Nation's history and tradition."

The natural law strand of argument, though much muted in this century, has never entirely disappeared from American constitutional rhetoric. Justice WILLIAM O. DOUGLAS was at times inclined to argue in this vein; before the *Griswold* decision he supported constitutional protection for marriage and procreation on the grounds that they were, as he said in SKINNER V. OKLAHOMA (1945), "basic CIVIL RIGHTS of man." Since the 1970s a number of constitutional commentators have argued for the use of "the methods of moral philosophy" in constitutional decision, referring to philosophical theories that claim universality for their results, and in this sense directly descend from classic natural law approaches. Whether there will be a revival of natural law discourse in constitutional doctrine remains an open question. On the other hand, the broader tradition of an unwritten higher law of the Constitution, encompassing both fundamental and natural law, seems by now too firmly entrenched to be dislodged.

THOMAS C. GREY
(1986)

Bibliography

CORWIN, EDWARD S. (1928–1929) 1955 *The "Higher Law" Background of American Constitutional Law.* Ithaca, N.Y.: Cornell University Press.
——— 1948 *Liberty Against Government.* Baton Rouge: Louisiana State University Press.
GRAHAM, HOWARD JAY 1968 *Everyman's Constitution.* Madison: State Historical Society of Wisconsin.
HAINES, CHARLES GROVE 1930 *The Revival of Natural Law Concepts.* Cambridge, Mass.: Harvard University Press.
TEN BROEK, JACOBUS (1951) 1965 *Equal under Law.* New York: Collier Books.
WRIGHT, BENJAMIN F., JR. 1931 *American Interpretations of Natural Law.* Cambridge, Mass.: Harvard University Press.

HILDRETH, RICHARD
(1807–1865)

A prolific pamphleteer, Richard Hildreth passionately opposed SLAVERY and took a Federalist or Whig stance on most issues. He was also a nationalist and an economic determinist who insisted on free competition. His *History of the United States* (1849–1852), ending in 1821, is meticulous in detail, scrupulously presenting each argument on major issues. His bias is nevertheless apparent in his championing of Federalist legislation; he minimized the effects of the ALIEN AND SEDITION ACTS, stressed the "virulence" of the VIRGINIA AND KENTUCKY RESOLUTIONS, and decried the repeal of the JUDICIARY ACT OF 1801. This six-volume study is still extraordinary for its realism and rejection of nineteenth-century romantic and heroic traditions.

DAVID GORDON
(1986)

HILLS v. GAUTREAUX
425 U.S. 284 (1976)

Two years after MILLIKEN V. BRADLEY (1974) rejected metropolitan relief for school DESEGREGATION absent a showing of a constitutional violation by both city and suburban districts or by state officials, the Supreme Court encountered a parallel issue in the field of housing discrimination. The United States Department of Housing and Urban Development (HUD) had aided a Chicago city agency in locating low-income housing sites for the purpose of maintaining residential SEGREGATION. HUD, citing *Milliken*, argued that relief should be limited to the city. However, the Court approved the district court's order, which had regulated HUD's conduct beyond Chicago's boundaries. No restructuring or displacement of local government would result here, the Court said.

KENNETH L. KARST
(1986)

HINES v. DAVIDOWITZ
312 U.S. 52 (1941)

Hines held that under the PREEMPTION doctrine, enforcement of a state alien registration law was barred by the federal ALIEN REGISTRATION ACT. Justice HUGO L. BLACK, for the Court, emphasized the broad power of Congress over ALIENS. Justice HARLAN FISKE STONE, for three dissenters, noted the absence of any conflict between state and federal laws or any express congressional prohibition of state regulation.

KENNETH L. KARST
(1986)

HIPOLITE EGG COMPANY v. UNITED STATES
220 U.S. 45 (1911)

A unanimous Supreme Court relied on the decision in CHAMPION V. AMES (1903) to sustain the PURE FOOD AND DRUG ACT's prohibition on the interstate transportation of adulterated food. Justice JOSEPH MCKENNA's opinion acknowledged few limits on congressional power over INTERSTATE COMMERCE, declaring that there was no trade "carried on between the states to which it does not extend," and that it was "subject to no limitations except those found in the Constitution." McKenna did not consider the purpose or intent of the act as the Court had previously done in *Champion* and would do so again in HOKE V. UNITED STATES (1913) and HAMMER V. DAGENHART (1918).

DAVID GORDON
(1986)

HIRABAYASHI v. UNITED STATES

See: Japanese American Cases

HISTORY IN CONSTITUTIONAL ARGUMENTATION

ALEXANDER HAMILTON, writing in THE FEDERALIST, declared: "Let experience, the least fallible guide of human opinions, be appealed to for an answer to these inquiries" about how best to frame a government. The Founders—the individuals who framed, debated, and ratified the Constitution—drew heavily from experience, both their own immediate past as well as the experience of governments long past. JAMES MADISON, for example, often cited the experience of ancient Greece. JAMES IREDELL turned to England under the Stuarts. Hamilton himself drew lessons from the fall of the Roman Republic. Just as the founding generation turned to the past when establishing the Constitution, many who seek to interpret the Constitution draw from its history, especially the experience of the Founders themselves.

The practice of using history in this interpretive sense dates back to the Constitution's earliest days. Historians tend to agree that the Founders initially had little desire for their own understandings of the Constitution to bind future generations. Yet many scholars also point out that this goal was increasingly honored more in theory than practice. Foes in constitutional disputes sought to bolster contending positions with what the authors of the document desired as early as the ratification debates. By the time President GEORGE WASHINGTON left office, arguments about the Constitution's meaning appealed to its history frequently—often with different Founders offering different accounts about the origins of the same provision. In one celebrated dispute, Hamilton and THOMAS JEFFERSON differed over whether history showed an original understanding that Congress have the power to charter a national bank. In another, Hamilton and Madison appealed to founding understandings in arguing radically different positions concerning presidential power in FOREIGN AFFAIRS.

The Supreme Court soon followed this lead. Faced with Jeffersonian appeals to ORIGINAL INTENT, Chief Justice JOHN MARSHALL responded in kind. When, for example, Marshall needed to refute the claim that the states established the Constitution in MCCULLOCH V. MARYLAND (1819), he turned to history. On his account, "the Convention which framed the constitution was indeed elected by the State legislatures. But the instrument, when it came from their hands, was a mere proposal, without obligation, or pretensions to it. This mode of proceeding was adopted; and by the Convention, by Congress, and by the State Legislatures, the instrument was submitted to the people. They acted upon it in the only manner in which they can act safely, effectively, and wisely, on such a subject, by assembling in Convention."

The Court has invoked history along similar lines, off and on, ever since. Chief Justice ROGER BROOKE TANEY in part justified the infamous result in DRED SCOTT V. SANDFORD (1857) by making the disputable assertion that no, even free, African American could have been considered part of "We the People of the United States" when the Constitution was first established. In more recent times history has continued to serve as a cornerstone in a number of significant opinions. In REYNOLDS V. UNITED STATES (1878), Chief Justice MORRISON R. WAITE relied on an 1802 letter Jefferson wrote to a group of Connecticut Baptists to conclude that the Framers meant for the FIRST AMENDMENT to create a "wall of separation" between church and state. At the same time the Justices have engaged in a continuing historical debate over the original understanding of RECONSTRUCTION and the FOURTEENTH AMENDMENT. Deploying history in a somewhat different fashion, Justice HARRY A. BLACKMUN's majority opinion in ROE V. WADE (1973) surveys ABORTION practices from contemporary America to the ancient Middle East.

In many ways the use of history in constitutional law has never been more central or controversial than today thanks to the ongoing debate over ORIGINALISM. This debate intensified during the 1980s when a number of advocates opposed to the perceived excesses of the WARREN COURT contended that judges should interpret the Constitution based primarily on the original views of those who wrote and ratified particular provisions. Champions of originalism, many of whom were associated with the administration of President RONALD REAGAN, included Attorney General Edwin Meese, Judge Robert Bork, and Justice ANTONIN SCALIA. After some initial hesitation, some more liberally inclined thinkers themselves responded in kind, asserting that more rigorous historical study often showed original understandings that were either more flexible or progressive than the original "originalists" contended. Leaders in this group include Bruce Ackerman in the academy and, to an extent, Justice DAVID H. SOUTER in the judiciary. Perhaps as never before, appeals to history now come from the political left as well as right, practitioners as well as academics, and even those who are not otherwise concerned with history in the first place.

Whether recent or longstanding, there have always been nearly as many reasons for using history as there have been persons using it. Among the most common, though least commonly stated, justifications for citing the past is simply that it appears to add authority, weight, and even "class" to what might otherwise be a mundane constitutional argument. The practice takes its most dubious form as "law office"—or more benignly, "forensic"—history, in which a lawyer or judge will "dress up" a preconceived conclusion with a few out-of-context quotations from celebrated historical figures.

Other justifications rely on good, or at least better, faith. The most obvious commitment to history comes from those who emphasize the Constitution's democratic foundations. For a wide array of thinkers, the keys to constitutional provisions lie with those who first established them. Since "We the People" ratify constitutional provisions and later generations govern themselves within the framework of that law, these later generations must follow the command of the "People" unless one of those generations successfully amends the Constitution and so acts as the "People" in its own right. Originalists take this claim the furthest in arguing that the historical understandings underlying constitutional provisions are dispositive.

Reliance on the past also figures heavily in those the-

ories that emphasize the Constitution's commitment to rights and justice. The history that these approaches invoke, however, is less the background to certain constitutional clauses than to ongoing traditions that shape our constitutional culture. Nowhere do accounts of our evolving traditions figure more prominently than in the Court's SUBSTANTIVE DUE PROCESS jurisprudence. It was partly in this context that the majority in *Roe* considered historical abortion practices relevant to modern case law.

Yet however much lawyers cite to history, they are less enthusiastic about learning it. Constitutional law is replete with historical assertions that are at best problematic or at worst just plain laughable. Among historians, the reputation of lawyerly use of history is dismal. More than a few scholars agree that this reputation is not unjustified. Most lawyers, judges, and even legal academics lack the perspective, time, patience, and knowledge of sources to pursue historical study well. Some commentators defend this result by asserting that historians, in their attempts to reconstruct the past, and lawyers, in their effort to use it to win arguments, simply pursue different types of history. Many in both camps would agree, however, that at some point those who draw from history for greater authority must provide accounts that are at least minimally accurate and credible.

One obvious—though not uncontroversial—solution for this state of affairs would be for lawyers to respect standards that genuine historians employ in studying the past, including relying on the work of historians themselves. One scholar recently suggested what such guidelines would mean for examining the framing era, or by extension other periods of constitutional change: (1) examine specific sources on point such as the records of the Federal Convention; (2) survey more general sources, including contemporary newspaper articles and correspondence; (3) explore the general intellectual setting of the period; and, perhaps most important; (4) understand the political experience and context of those establishing the constitutional norms. Following just these guidelines is time-consuming work, often too time-consuming to meet the demands of legal calendars. But if lawyers cannot follow these strictures themselves, at least they can rely on those who do. The legal community would improve its reliance on history by first relying on respected and relevant accounts of such noted historians as Gordon S. Wood and Eric Foner, among many others. While this modest reform is itself hard work, it is more efficient than reading through the hundreds of sources that historians themselves study and more rigorous than quoting snippets of *The Federalist* without context or corroboration.

The past generation's turn to history in constitutional law has arguably led to some improvement in the level of historical scholarship that lawyers, judges, and legal academics undertake. Only time will tell whether that level will ever become generally adequate. Until then, students wanting to learn about American history and tradition on its own terms should treat the accounts offered in legal writings with caution.

MARTIN S. FLAHERTY
(2000)

Bibliography

ACKERMAN, BRUCE 1991 *We The People: Foundations.* Cambridge, Mass.: Harvard University Press.
—— 1998 *We The People: Transformations.* Cambridge, Mass.: Harvard University Press.
BORK, ROBERT H. 1990 *The Tempting of America: The Political Seduction of the Law.* New York: Free Press.
FLAHERTY, MARTIN S. 1995 History "Lite" in Modern American Constitutionalism. *Columbia Law Review* 95:523–590.
KALMAN, LAURA 1986 *The Strange Career of Liberal Constitutionalism.* New Haven, Conn.: Yale University Press.
LEVY, LEONARD W. 1988 *Original Intent and the Framers' Constitution.* New York: Macmillan.
LOFGREN, CHARLES A. 1988 The Original Understanding of Original Intent? *Constitutional Commentary* 5:53–115.
NELSON, WILLIAM E. 1986 History and Neutrality in Constitutional Adjudication. *Virgina Law Review* 72:1237–1296.
POWELL, H. JEFFERSON 1985 The Original Understanding of Original Intent. *Harvard Law Review* 98:885–948.
RAKOVE, JACK N. 1996 *Original Meanings: Politics and Ideas in the Making of the Constitution.* New York: Knopf.
REID, JOHN PHILLIP 1993 Law and History. *Loyola Los Angeles Law Review* 27:193–224.
SYMPOSIUM 1997 Fidelity in Constitutional Theory. *Fordham Law Review* 65:1247–1854.
TREANOR, WILLIAM MICHAEL 1995 The Original Understanding of the Takings Clause and the Political Process. *Columbia Law Review* 95:782–887.

HITCHMAN COAL & COKE CO. v. MITCHELL
245 U.S. 229 (1917)

In this case a 6–3 Supreme Court approved use of an INJUNCTION to enforce YELLOW DOG CONTRACTS. The injunction prohibited the union from inducing breach of contract by communicating with employees or potential employees of the company. The majority emphasized that Hitchman had as much right to condition employment contracts on promises not to join a union as the workers had to decline job offers. Indeed, "this is a part of the constitutional right of personal liberty and private property" protected by SUBSTANTIVE DUE PROCESS of law. The Court thus held that these workers were not free because they had signed the yellow dog contracts.

Justice LOUIS D. BRANDEIS dissented, joined by Justices OLIVER WENDELL HOLMES and JOHN H. CLARKE. The union, they said, had merely sought promises to join, and the yellow dog contracts were not genuine contracts because they were not freely entered into by the workers. The Court's hostility to LABOR would not change until 1937. (See HUGHES COURT.)

DAVID GORDON
(1986)

H. L. v. MATHESON

See: Reproductive Autonomy

HODEL v. VIRGINIA SURFACE MINING AND RECLAMATION ASSOCIATION
452 U.S. 264 (1981)

The *Hodel* opinion provided a formula for interpreting the demands of NATIONAL LEAGUE OF CITIES V. USERY (1976). The Supreme Court unanimously upheld an act of Congress stringently regulating private stripmining operations, but providing for relaxation of the federal regulations when a state undertook to regulate the same activities according to standards set out in the act. Justice THURGOOD MARSHALL, for the Court, wrote that an act of Congress would not be held invalid under the *Usery* principle unless it satisfied three conditions: that the law regulated "the States as States"; that it addressed "matters that are indisputably "attributes of state SOVEREIGNTY"; and that it directly impaired the states' ability "to structure integral operations in areas of traditional governmental functions." In *Hodel* itself, the law failed the first part of the test, for it regulated only private parties. All three requirements were taken from the *Usery* opinion; in combination, they proved an insuperable hurdle to states seeking to rely on *Usery* to invalidate federal regulation of state activities, and ultimately led to the overruling of *Usery* in GARCIA V. SAN ANTONIO METROPOLITAN TRANSIT AUTHORITY (1985). Justice WILLIAM H. REHNQUIST, who concurred only in the judgment, wrote separately to decry the majority's assumptions concerning the breadth of Congress's commerce power.

KENNETH L. KARST
(1986)

HODGES v. UNITED STATES
203 U.S. 1 (1906)

Black laborers had agreed to work for a lumber firm. Hodges and the other white defendants, all private citizens, ordered the blacks to stop working, assaulted them, and violently drove them from their workplace. The defendants were indicted for violating federal CIVIL RIGHTS laws. In a decision reconfirming much of the CIVIL RIGHTS CASES (1883) opinion, the Supreme Court indicated that the federal prosecution could not be supported under the FOURTEENTH or FIFTEENTH AMENDMENTS because those amendments restrict only STATE ACTION. The THIRTEENTH AMENDMENT did not support a federal prosecution because group violence against blacks was not the equivalent of reducing them to SLAVERY. In JONES V. ALFRED H. MAYER CO. (1968) and GRIFFIN V. BRECKENRIDGE (1971) the Court adopted a more generous attitude towards Congress's Thirteenth Amendment power to prohibit private discrimination.

THEODORE EISENBERG
(1986)

HODGSON v. MINNESOTA
OHIO v. AKRON CENTER FOR
REPRODUCTIVE HEALTH
497 U.S. 417 (1990)

Minnesota and Ohio adopted laws requiring that parents be notified before abortions were performed on minors. By shifting 5–4 votes, the Supreme Court struck down one version of Minnesota's law and upheld another. The Court upheld the Ohio law, 6–3. Four Justices thought all the laws were valid, and three thought they were all invalid; the swing votes were Justices SANDRA DAY O'CONNOR and JOHN PAUL STEVENS.

Minnesota required notification to both of a minor's biological parents before she could have an abortion. A majority concluded that this law "[did] not reasonably further any legitimate state interest." This formulation avoided the question whether a restriction on the right to have an ABORTION must pass the test of STRICT SCRUTINY, as ROE V. WADE (1973) had held. Whatever the rhetoric, the effective STANDARD OF REVIEW was a demanding one. Justice Stevens, for the majority, acknowledged the state's interest in supporting parents' authority and counseling, but said that any such interest could be served by a one-parent notification rule. He also conceded that the state might wish to protect parents' interests in shaping their children's values, but said this interest could not "overcome the liberty interests of a minor acting with the consent of a single parent or court." Justice O'Connor, too, found this version of the Minnesota law "unreasonable," especially considering that only half the minors in the state lived with both biological parents.

The Minnesota legislature, anticipating that the Court might hold the statute invalid, had adopted a fall-back pro-

cedure: If a minor could convince a judge that she was mature enough to give her informed consent to an abortion or that an abortion without two-parent notification was in her best interests, the judge might dispense with that notification. This "judicial bypass" was enough to secure the approval of Justice O'Connor, and so was upheld, 5–4.

The Ohio law required notification of only one parent. Here Justices O'Connor and Stevens joined the four Justices who had considered both Minnesota laws valid. Justice ANTHONY M. KENNEDY wrote the principal opinion, most of which was joined by a majority of the Court. The dissenters in this case, who also dissented as to the Court's disposition of Minnesota's fall-back law, emphasized the severe costs of any parental notification requirement to a minor who dared not tell her parents she was pregnant and who was likely to find a judicial proceeding intimidating. As Justice THURGOOD MARSHALL said, those costs are not merely psychological; the fear of confronting parents may cause a young woman to delay an abortion, with attendant increases in risks to her health.

Justice ANTONIN SCALIA, who voted to uphold all three laws, took note of the way in which different majorities were pieced together in these cases and concluded that the reason lay in the lack of a principled way to distinguish the results when the Court persists in "this enterprise of devising an Abortion Code." Given the retirement from the Court of Justice WILLIAM J. BRENNAN, who formed part of the five-Justice majority that invalidated the first Minnesota law, the issue of parental notification seems sure to return to the Court. When it does so, some Justices seem prepared to avoid the complications identified by Justice Scalia in a single doctrinal stroke, sweeping abortion rights—and thus, in some states, abortions—into the back alley.

KENNETH L. KARST
(1992)

HODGSON AND THOMPSON v.
BOWERBANK
5 Cranch 303 (1809)

Hodgson is a constitutional trivium, of little doctrinal importance. Its interest today is captured in a question: Was *Hodgson* the one occasion between MARBURY V. MADISON (1803) and DRED SCOTT V. SANDFORD (1857) when the Supreme Court held an act of Congress unconstitutional? Various scholars have answered that question differently.

Article III of the Constitution does not explicitly authorize Congress to confer JURISDICTION on federal courts to decide a case in which one ALIEN sues another. The JUDICIARY ACT OF 1789, however, conferred such jurisdiction on the circuit court when "an alien is a party." In *Hodgson*, plaintiffs were British subjects; defendants' CITIZENSHIP was unknown. Chief Justice JOHN MARSHALL, responding to counsel's claim of jurisdiction, was quoted by the reporter, Cranch, as saying only this: "Turn to the article of the constitution of the United States, for the statute cannot extend the jurisdiction beyond the limits of the constitution."

Hodgson plainly holds that Congress cannot constitutionally confer federal court jurisdiction in the alien-versus-alien case. But was Marshall merely limiting the 1789 act's construction to avoid constitutional problems, or was he holding a part of the act's reach unconstitutional? Eighteen decades after the event, the debate goes on.

KENNETH L. KARST
(1986)

(SEE ALSO: *Unconstitutionality*.)

Bibliography

MAHONEY, DENNIS J. 1982 A Historical Note on *Hodgson v. Bowerbank*. *University of Chicago Law Review* 49:725–740.

HOFFA v. UNITED STATES
385 U.S. 293 (1966)

Information received from a secret government informer and used to obtain a conviction of James Hoffa, the Teamsters' union leader, did not constitute an illegal search, because the informer was an invited guest; did not violate the RIGHT AGAINST SELF-INCRIMINATION, because compulsion was absent; and did not abridge the RIGHT TO COUNSEL, because the information did not breach the confidential relationship between petitioner and counsel. Hoffa's conviction for jury bribery was sustained.

LEONARD W. LEVY
(1986)

HOKE v. UNITED STATES
227 U.S. 308 (1913)
CAMINETTI v. UNITED STATES
242 U.S. 470 (1917)

Opinions in CHAMPION V. AMES (1903) and HIPOLITE EGG CO. V. UNITED STATES (1911) laid the foundation for a unanimous decision sustaining the MANN ACT, which prohibited the interstate transportation of women for immoral purposes. Justice JOSEPH MCKENNA, generously construing the power over INTERSTATE COMMERCE, declared in *Hoke* that

Congress might exercise means that "may have the quality of police regulations." He denied that the Mann Act violated the TENTH AMENDMENT by usurping the STATE POLICE POWER. In *Caminetti*, the Court held that transportation was illegal under the act, even if not accompanied by financial gain: "To say the contrary would shock the common understanding of what constitutes an immoral purpose." These cases helped establish a broad basis for the growth of the NATIONAL POLICE POWER.

DAVID GORDON
(1986)

HOLDEN v. HARDY
169 U.S. 366 (1898)

Utah adopted a maximum hours law fixing an eight-hour day for miners. A mine owner, convicted for working his employees ten hours a day, claimed that the statute violated his FOURTEENTH AMENDMENT rights. For a 7–2 Supreme Court, Justice HENRY B. BROWN declared that the right to FREEDOM OF CONTRACT protected by SUBSTANTIVE DUE PROCESS of law is subject to legitimate POLICE POWER regulations intended to protect the public health. The Court sustained the statute as a reasonable exercise of the police power on the ground that mining is a dangerous occupation that requires an exception to freedom of contract. Brown realistically observed that employees are often induced by fear of discharge to obey management rules that might be detrimental to health. In such cases self-interest is an unsure guide, justifying legislative intervention. Had the Court adhered to this understanding, LOCHNER V. NEW YORK (1905) might have been stillborn.

LEONARD W. LEVY
(1986)

HOLDING

The holding of a court is the *ratio decidendi* or the ground(s) upon which it bases its DECISION of a case. The holding, includes all the court's declarations of law necessary to the decision of the case; other pronouncements are OBITER DICTA. The holding in a case establishes a precedent and may be generalized into a DOCTRINE. The term may also be used more narrowly to signify the court's resolution of any particular legal issue or question of constitutional interpretation presented in a case.

DENNIS J. MAHONEY
(1986)

HOLLAND v. ILLINOIS

See: *Batson v. Kentucky*

HOLMES, OLIVER WENDELL, JR.
(1841–1935)

When he was appointed to the Supreme Court in 1902, at the age of sixty-one, he was best known to the general public as the son of a famous poet and man of letters; when he retired, thirty years later, he had been called "the greatest of our age in the domain of jurisprudence, and one of the greatest of the ages." Oliver Wendell Holmes's thirty years on the Supreme Court unquestionably made his reputation, and yet those years, given the aspirations of Holmes's earlier career, were years in which his mood as a judge can best be described as resignation. He was not able to achieve anything like what he thought he could achieve as a judge; regularly he confessed his inability to do anything other than ratify "what the crowd wants." He wryly suggested that on his tombstone should be inscribed "here lies the supple tool of power," and he allegedly told JOHN W. DAVIS that "if my country wants to go to hell, I am here to help it." For these expressions of resignation he was called "distinguished," "mature," and "wise," the "completely adult jurist." The constitutional jurisprudence of Holmes could be called a jurisprudence of detachment, indifference, or even despair; yet it was a jurisprudence in which contemporary commentators reveled.

Holmes's career hardly began with his appointment to the Court. He had previously written *The Common Law*, a comprehensive theoretical organization of private law subjects, taught briefly at Harvard Law School, and served for twenty years as a justice on the Massachusetts Supreme Judicial Court. Although he had not considered many constitutional cases as a state court judge, he had a distinctive philosophy of judging. There was little difficulty in the transition from the Massachusetts court to the Supreme Court; Holmes simply integrated a new set of cases with his preexistent philosophy. That philosophy's chief postulate was that judicial decisions were inescapably policy choices, and that a judge was better off if he did not make his choices appear too openly based on the "sovereign prerogative" of his power.

Arriving at that postulate had been an unexpected process for Holmes. He was convinced, at the time he wrote *The Common Law* (1881), that private law could be arranged in a "philosophically continuous series." His lectures on torts, criminal law, property, and contracts stressed the ability of those subjects to be ordered by general principles and the desirability of having judges ground their decisions in broad predictive rules rather than deferring to the more idiosyncratic and less predictable verdicts of juries. Holmes had accepted a judgeship in part because he believed that he could implement this conception of private law. Academic life was "half-life," he later said, and judging gave him an opportunity to "have a share in the practical struggle of life."

In practice, however, Holmes found that the law resisted being arranged in regular, predictable patterns. Too many factors operated to create dissonance: the need for court majorities to congeal on the scope and language of a decision; the insignificance of many cases, which were best decided by routine adherence to precedent; the very difficult and treacherous policy choices truly significant cases posed, fostering caution and compromise among judges. The result, for Holmes, was that legal DOCTRINE developed not as a general progression toward a philosophically continuous series but rather as an uneven clustering of decisions around opposing "poles" that represented alternative policy judgments. "Two widely divergent cases" suggested "a general distinction," which initially was "a clear one." But "as new cases cluster[ed] around the opposite poles, and beg[a]n to approach each other," the distinction became "more difficult to trace." Eventually an "arbitrary . . . mathematical line" was drawn, based on considerations of policy.

Thus judging was ultimately an exercise in making policy choices, but since the choices were often arbitrary and judges had "a general duty not to change but to work out the principles already sanctioned by the practice of the past," bold declarations of general principles were going to be few and far between. Indeed in many cases whose resolution he thought to turn on "questions of degree," or "nice considerations," or line drawing, Holmes attempted, as a state court judge, to avoid decision. He delegated "questions of degree" to juries where possible; he relied on precedents even where he felt that they had ceased to have a functional justification; he adhered to the findings of trial judges; he resorted to "technicalities" to "determine the precise place of division." And on those relatively few occasions when he was asked to consider the impact of a legislature's involvement, Holmes tended to defer to legislative solutions, especially in close cases. "Most differences," he said in one case, were "only one[s] of degree," and "difference of degree is one of the distinctions by which the right of the legislature to exercise the STATE POLICE POWER is determined." Deference to the legislature was another means of avoiding judicial policy choices.

Holmes thus brought a curious, if consistent, theory of judging with him to the Supreme Court. Although his original aim as a legal scholar had been the derivation of general guiding principles in all areas of law, as a judge he had concluded that principles were not derived in a logical and continuous but in a random and arbitrary fashion, and that in hard cases, where principles competed, policy considerations dictated the outcome. Judges should be sensitive to the fact that cases did involve policy choices, but they should exercise great caution in making them. Hard cases, turning on "questions of degree" or "nice considerations" should be delegated to other lawmaking bodies, such as the jury and the legislature, that were closer to the "instinctive preferences and inarticulate convictions" of the community. What started out as a theory of bold, activist judicial declarations of principle had ended as a theory of deference to lawmakers who were more "at liberty to decide with sole reference . . . to convictions of policy and right." The creative jurist of *The Common Law* had become the apostle of judicial self-restraint.

In his first month on the Supreme Court Holmes wrote to his longtime correspondent Sir Frederick Pollock that he was "absorbed" with the "variety and novelty of the questions." And indeed Holmes's docket was strikingly different from that he had encountered as a Massachusetts state judge: more federal issues, a greater diversity of issues, and far more cases involving the constitutionality of legislative acts. But the new sets of cases did not require Holmes to modify his theory of judging; they merely emphasized his inclination to defer hard policy choices to others. As a Massachusetts state judge Holmes had found only one act of the Massachusetts legislature constitutionally invalid; as a Supreme Court justice he was to continue that pattern. His first opinion, *Otis v. Parker* (1902), sustained a California statute prohibiting sales of stock shares on margin on the ground that although the statute undoubtedly restricted freedom of exchange, that "general proposition" did not "take us far." The question was one of degree: how far could the legislature restrict that freedom? Since the statute's ostensible purpose, to protect persons from being taken advantage of in stock transactions, was arguably rational, Holmes's role was to defer to the legislative judgments.

Otis v. Parker set a pattern for Holmes's decisions in cases testing the constitutionality of economic regulations. Rarely did he find that questions posed by statutes were not ones of "degree"; rarely did he fail to uphold the legislative judgment. He believed that the New York legislature could regulate the hours of bakers (LOCHNER V. NEW YORK, 1905) even though he thought that hours and wages laws merely "shift[ed] the burden to a different point of incidence." He supported PROHIBITION and antitrust legislation notwithstanding his beliefs that "legislation to make people better" was futile and that the SHERMAN ACT was "damned nonsense." His position, in short, was that "when a State legislature has declared that in its opinion policy requires a certain measure, its actions should not be disturbed by the courts . . . unless they clearly see that there is no fair reason for the law."

Deference for Holmes did not mean absolute passivity. He thought Congress and the states had gone too far in convicting dissidents in a number of war-related speech cases, including ABRAMS V. UNITED STATES (1919) (the case in which he proposed the CLEAR AND PRESENT DANGER test), GITLOW V. NEW YORK (1924), and UNITED STATES V. SCHWIMMER (1928). He invalidated a Pennsylvania statute that regulated mining operations without adequate compensation in *Pennsylvania Coal Company v. Mahon* (1922). He did not think that Congress could constitutionally allow the postmaster general to deny "suspicious" persons access to the mails, and said so in two cases, *Milwaukee Socialist Democratic Publishing Co. v. Burleson* (1920) and *Leach v. Carlile Postmaster* (1921). And he struck down a Texas statute denying blacks eligibility to vote in primary elections in NIXON V. HERNDON (1922), declaring that "states may do a good deal of classifying that it is difficult to believe rational, but there are limits."

Holmes was called, especially in the 1920s, the "Great Dissenter," and some of his dissenting opinions were memorable for the pithiness of their language. In *Lochner v. New York* (1905), Holmes protested against the artificiality of the FREEDOM OF CONTRACT argument used by the majority by saying that "the FOURTEENTH AMENDMENT does not enact Mr. Herbert Spencer's *Social Statics.*" In *Abrams* he said that "the best test of truth is the power of the thought to get itself accepted in the competition of the market," and that "every year . . . we have to wager our salvation upon some prophecy based on imperfect knowledge." And in *Olmstead v. United States* (1928), he decried the use of WIRETAPPING by federal agents: "I think it a less evil that some criminals should escape than that the government should play an ignoble part."

Each of these dissents was subsequently adopted as a majority position by a later Court. Freedom of contract was repudiated as a constitutional doctrine in WEST COAST HOTEL V. PARRISH (1937); Holmes's theory of free speech was ratified by the Court in such decisions as HERNDON V. LOWRY (1937) and YATES V. UNITED STATES (1957); and KATZ V. UNITED STATES (1967) and BERGER V. NEW YORK (1967) overruled the majority decision in *Olmstead.* Despite the eventual triumph of Holmes's position in these cases and despite the rhetorical force of his dissents, "Great Dissenter" is a misnomer by any standard other than a literary one. Holmes did not write an exceptionally large number of dissents, given his long service on the Court, and his positions were not often vindicated.

Holmes's dissents also gave him the reputation among commentators as being a "liberal" justice. But for every Holmes decision protecting CIVIL LIBERTIES one could find a decision restricting them. The same Justice who declared in *Abrams v. United States* (1919) that "we should be eternally vigilant against attempts to check the expression of opinions" held for the Court in BUCK V. BELL (1927) that a state could sterilize mental defectives without their knowing consent. "It is better for all the world, if instead of waiting to execute degenerate offspring for crime, or to let them starve for their imbecility, society can prevent those who are manifestly unfit from continuing their kind," Holmes argued. "Three generations of imbeciles are enough."

Holmes supported the constitutionality of laws prohibiting child labor, defended the right of dissidents to speak, and resisted government efforts to wiretap bootleggers. At the same time he upheld the compulsory teaching of English in public schools, supported the rights of landowners in child trespasser cases, and helped develop a line of decisions giving virtually no constitutional protection to ALIENS. For a time critics ignored these latter cases and followed the *New York Times* in calling Holmes "the chief liberal of the supreme bench for twenty-nine years," but recent commentary has asserted that Holmes was "largely indifferent" to civil liberties.

Holmes's constitutional thought, then, resists ideological characterization and is notable principally for its limited interpretation of the power of JUDICIAL REVIEW. How thus does one explain Holmes's continued stature? In an age where JUDICIAL ACTIVISM, especially on behalf of minority rights, is a commonplace phenomenon, Holmes's interpretation of his office appears outmoded in its circumscription. In an age where the idea of rights against the state has gained in prominence, Holmes's decisions appear to tolerate altogether too much power in legislative majorities. Only in the speech cases does Holmes seem to recognize that the contribution of dissident minorities can prevent a society's attitudes from becoming provincial and stultifying. Elsewhere Holmes's jurisprudence stands for the proposition that the state, as agent of the majority, can do what it likes until some other majority seizes power. That hardly seems a posture inclined to elicit much contemporary applause.

Yet Holmes's reputation remains, on all the modern polls, among the highest of those Justices who have served on the Supreme Court. It is not likely to change for three reasons. First, in an era that was anxious to perpetuate the illusion that judicial decision making was somehow different from other kinds of official decision making, since judges merely "found" or "declared" law, Holmes demonstrated that judging was inescapably an exercise in policymaking. This insight was a breath of fresh air in a stale jurisprudential climate. Against the ponderous intonations of other judges that they were "making no laws, deciding no policy, [and] never entering into the domain of public action," Holmes offered the theory that they were doing all those things. American jurisprudence was never the same again.

Second, Holmes, as a sitting judge, followed through the implications of his insight. If judging was inevitably an exercise in policy choices, if all legal questions eventually became "questions of degree," then there was much to be said for judges' avoiding the arbitrary choice. Other institutions existed whose mandate for representing current community sentiment seemed clearer than the judiciary's; judging could be seen as an art of avoiding decision in cases whose resolution appeared to be the arbitrary drawing of a line. In a jurisprudential climate that was adjusting to the shock of realizing that judges were making law, Holmes's theory of avoidance seemed to make a great deal of sense. Federal judges were not popularly elected officials; if they made the process of lawmaking synonymous with their arbitrary intuitions, the notion of popularly elected government seemed threatened. The wisdom in Holmes's approach to judging seemed so apparent that it took the WARREN COURT to displace it.

These first two contributions of Holmes, however, can be seen as having a historical dimension. To be sure, seeing judges as policymakers was a significant insight, but it is now a commonplace; judicial deference was undoubtedly an influential theory, but it has now been substantially qualified. The enduring quality of Holmes appears to rest on his having a first-class mind and in his unique manner of expression: his style. No judge has been so quotable as Holmes; no judge has come closer to making opinion writing a form of literature. Paradoxically, Holmes's style, which is notable for its capacity to engage the reader's emotions in a manner that transcends time and place, can be seen as a style produced out of indifference. The approach of Holmes to his work as a judge was that of a person more interested in completing his assigned tasks than in anything else. Holmes would be assigned opinions at a Saturday conference and seek to complete them by the following Tuesday; his opinions are notable for their brevity and their assertiveness. The celebrated epigrams in Holmes's opinions were rarely essential to the case; they were efforts to increase the emotional content of opinions whose legal analysis was often cryptic.

Holmes's style of writing was of a piece with his general attitude toward judging. Since judging was essentially an effort in accommodating competing policies, the outcome of a given case was relatively insignificant. Just where the line was drawn or where a given case located itself in a "cluster" of related cases insignificant. One might as well, as a judge, announce one's decision as starkly and vividly as one could. A sense of the delicacy and ultimate insignificance of the process of deciding a case, then, fostered a vivid, emotion-laden, and declarative style.

Thus the legacy of Holmes's constitutional opinions is an unusual one. As contributions to the ordinary mine run of legal doctrine, they are largely insignificant. Their positions are often outmoded, their analyses attenuated, their guidelines for future cases inadequate. One feels, somehow, that Holmes has seen the clash of competing principles at stake in a constitutional law case, but has not probed very far. Once he discovered what was at issue, he either avoided decision or argued for one resolution in a blunt, assertive, and arbitrary manner. One cannot take a Holmes precedent and spin out the resolution of companion cases; one cannot go to Holmes to find the substantive bottomings of an area of law. Holmes's opinions are like a charismatic musical performance: one may be inspired in the viewing but one cannot do much with one's impressions later.

As literary expressions, however, Holmes's opinions probably surpass those of any other Justice. While it begs questions and assumes difficulties away to say that "a policeman may have a constitutional right to talk politics, but he has no constitutional right to be a policeman," the vivid contrast catches one's imagination. While "three generations of imbeciles are enough" was a misstatement of the facts in *Buck v. Bell* and represents an attitude toward mentally retarded persons one might find callous, it engages us, for better or worse. In phrases like these Holmes will continue to speak to subsequent generations; his constitutional opinions, and consequently his constitutional thought, will thus endure. It is ironic that Holmes bequeathed us those vivid phrases because he felt that a more painstaking, balanced approach to judging was futile. He thought of judging, as he thought of life, as "a job," and he got on with it.

G. EDWARD WHITE
(1986)

Bibliography

BURTON, DAVID 1980 *Oliver Wendell Holmes, Jr.* Boston: Twayne Publishers.

FRANKFURTER, FELIX 1938 *Mr. Justice Holmes and the Supreme Court.* Cambridge, Mass.: Harvard University Press.

HOWE, MARK DEWOLFE 1957 *Justice Oliver Wendell Holmes: The Shaping Years, 1841–1870.* Cambridge, Mass.: Harvard University Press.

—— 1963 *Justice Oliver Wendell Holmes: The Proving Years, 1870–1882.* Cambridge, Mass.: Harvard University Press.

KONEFSKY, SAMUEL J. 1956 *The Legacy of Holmes and Brandeis: A Study in the Influence of Ideas.* New York: Macmillan.

LERNER, MAX 1943 *The Mind and Faith of Justice Holmes.* Boston: Little, Brown.

ROGAT, YOSEL 1963 Mr. Justice Holmes: A Dissenting Opinion. *Stanford Law Review* 15:3–44, 254–308.

WHITE, G. EDWARD 1971 The Rise and Fall of Justice Holmes. *University of Chicago Law Review* 39:51–77.

—— 1982 The Integrity of Holmes' Jurisprudence. *Hofstra Law Review* 10:633–671.

HOLMES v. WALTON
(New Jersey, 1780)

Decided by the Supreme Court of New Jersey in 1780, this is the first alleged state precedent for JUDICIAL REVIEW. The case, which was unreported, is referred to in *State v. Parkhurst*, 4 Halsted 427, supposedly decided in 1802 but not reported until 1828, where the state court said that in *Holmes* a state act providing for trial by a six-man jury violated the state constitution. In fact, the act, which involved the seizure and forfeiture of goods traded with the enemy, provided for a TRIAL BY JURY. New Jersey employed six-man juries in cases of small amounts (under six pounds) from colonial times to 1844, twelve-man juries in all other cases. The property in *Holmes v. Walton* being valued at $27,000, Holmes had a right to a trial by a twelve-man jury. The trial judge having allowed him only a six-man jury, Holmes contended not that the seizure act was unconstitutional but that the trial judge denied him a twelve-man jury to which he was entitled under the seizure act as well as under the state constitution; the high court so held. The constitutionality of the seizure act was not at issue, and there was no opinion given in which the court discussed, even by OBITER DICTA, its power to void an act for UNCONSTITUTIONALITY. Soon after the decision of the case, which allowed Holmes a new trial by a jury of twelve members, disaffected citizens of the locality alleged in a petition to the state assembly that the high court of the state had held the seizure act unconstitutional. The legislature, however, supported the court by enacting in 1782 that in any suit exceeding six pounds trial by jury meant a jury of twelve. Somehow, a misleading view of the case originated in the 1780s and survived, making *Holmes v. Walton* a "precedent," however inauthentic, for judicial review.

LEONARD W. LEVY
(1986)

HOLMES AND FREE SPEECH

In the conventional mythology, Justice OLIVER WENDELL HOLMES, JR., is the judicial architect of the tradition of FREEDOM OF SPEECH in American constitutional law. According to that mythology, Holmes's formulation of the CLEAR AND PRESENT DANGER test for evaluating subversive speech in SCHENCK V. UNITED STATES (1919), coupled with his stirring dissent in ABRAMS V. UNITED STATES that same year, in which he claimed that "the theory of the Constitution" was that "the ultimate good desired is better reached by free trade in ideas," reoriented American thinking about the significance of the FIRST AMENDMENT in American culture. By the time Holmes retired from the

Supreme Court in 1932, the conventional account runs, a new generation of judges and legal commentators was ready to carry the libertarian torch that he had first lit.

As in all cases where a conventional mythology has endured, there are elements of accuracy in the standard account. The First Amendment was not generally taken to be a significant limitation on legislative restrictions of expression prior to WORLD WAR I. Holmes, together with Justice LOUIS D. BRANDEIS and several academic commentators, notably ZECHARIAH CHAFEE, JR., did carve out, and maintain, a more speech-protective position on freedom of expression issues than most judges of his time, including the majority of his colleagues on the Court. Holmes's capacity to write memorable, arresting paragraphs in his free speech opinions helped communicate, to many different American audiences, the political and philosophical justifications for protecting speech in a constitutional democracy. Finally, there is no doubt that by the time Holmes left the Court in 1932 his own free speech jurisprudence had evolved from a quite conventional posture that assumed a quite limited role for the First Amendment as a shield for unpopular expression, and no role at all for the DUE PROCESS clause of the FOURTEENTH AMENDMENT in that capacity, to a posture that can fairly be described as seeing a free speech issue lurking behind a great many legal bushes.

To understand the kernels of truth in the conventional mythology, however, is not to convert it to wisdom. The conventional account bristles with difficulties. The first difficulty is one of causal attribution. In *Patterson v. Colorado*, a 1907 case, Holmes wrote an opinion for the Court denying a free speech claim and intimating that the First or Fourteenth Amendment "liberties" of speech might be confined to protection against governmental "PRIOR RESTRAINTS" on expression. Similarly, in the 1915 case of *Fox v. Washington*, Holmes's opinion for the Court intimated that the "liberty" in the Fourteenth Amendment needed to be read narrowly and might not include protection of speech at all. In both cases criminal convictions of the speakers—one under a statute proscribing criticism of public officials and the other under a statute proscribing utterances that tended to cause breaches of the peace—were upheld under the conventional test: whether a particular expression had a "tendency" to encourage action that the state clearly had a right to prohibit.

Holmes's "clear and present" danger opinions in *Schenck* and *Abrams* appeared to be departures from the BAD TENDENCY TEST. But the former opinion was ambiguous in that respect. Although Holmes said in *Schenck* that "the question in every case" was whether a "clear and present danger" to the state followed from the expression being restricted, the speech of the defendants in *Schenck*—issuing circulars encouraging conscriptees in

World War I to resist the draft—had a "bad tendency" but did not necessarily pose a clear and present danger. Yet Holmes's opinion for the Court in *Schenck* upheld the conviction.

Holmes's opinion in *Abrams*, in contrast, would have overturned the convictions of persons who dropped leaflets calling for a general strike in the vicinity of factory workers employed in the munitions trade. Since World War I was still going on when the leaflets were distributed, the defendants—Russian immigrants sympathetic to the Bolshevik regime—were prosecuted under the 1918 SEDITION ACT for interfering with the war effort, and a general strike clearly would have impeded that effort. Holmes's dissent in *Abrams* was a clear departure from his position in *Schenck*, notwithstanding his rhetorical efforts to make the opinions appear consistent. He had changed his mind about speech issues and begun to adopt a more expansive reading of the protective scope of the First Amendment. Subsequently Holmes and some of his academic admirers, especially Chafee, FELIX FRANKFURTER, and HAROLD J. LASKI, would treat the *Schenck– Abrams* sequence as all of a piece and identify Holmes as the modern founder of a robust free speech jurisprudence. The truth was more complicated.

As World War I drew to a close Holmes began a series of discussions with a group of younger legal intellectuals, including Chafee, Frankfurter, Laski, and Judge LEARNED HAND, about the importance of freedom of expression as a means by which citizens in a democratic society could reach "the truth" about public issues and thereby become more informed participants in government. Being an elitist, and being skeptical about the philosophical integrity of universal principles, Holmes doubted whether majoritarian sentiment could be equated with wisdom, but at the same time recognized that majoritarianism was a bedrock principle of democracy. Although some of his younger colleagues believed that freedom of expression was part of a more general liberalization and democratization of American life, Holmes tended to believe that if most "subversive" talk was permitted to be uttered, its intellectual worthlessness would soon be apparent. Although Holmes talked about the First Amendment as protecting "free trade in ideas," he believed that the MARKETPLACE OF IDEAS would result in only those expressions that had some significant intellectual weight surviving. He was contemptuous of the substantive value of most of the "radical" expressions his free speech opinions came to protect, but he was not contemptuous of the value of freedom of expression in a modern democracy. The latter insight he had gleaned from his younger colleagues. Thus the first set of Holmes's contributions to free speech jurisprudence, the *Schenck–Abrams* sequence—which also included two other opinions, FROHWERK V. UNITED STATES (1919) and DEBS

V. UNITED STATES (1919) in which Holmes upheld convictions for "seditious speech," ignoring his own clear and present danger language—cannot accurately be described as the work of a pioneer. It was the work of a gifted intellectual absorbing the contributions of others and making them part of his consciousness.

The second difficulty with the conventional account is that it fails to advance an adequate characterization of the remainder of Holmes's free speech opinions in the years following *Abrams*. A close reading of those opinions, which included two more memorable dissents, in GITLOW V. NEW YORK (1925) and UNITED STATES V. SCHWIMMER (1929), reveals nothing like jurisprudential consistency. In a series of cases in the 1920s involving state efforts to restrict the teaching of foreign languages in public schools, Holmes dissented from Court opinions striking down those statutes as invasion of the Fourteenth Amendment "liberties" of teachers or scholars. In *Gitlow*, where a majority of the Court summarily extended the application of the First Amendment to the states through "INCORPORATION" of that provision in the due process clause of the Fourteenth Amendment, Holmes's dissent accepted that result only grudgingly. Yet in *Gitlow* Holmes dissented from an opinion upholding the conviction of a writer of an anarchist manifesto even though the legislature had determined in advance that calls for the overthrow of the capitalist system constituted a clear and present danger to the existence of the state.

Similarly in *Schwimmer* Holmes converted a deportation proceeding, in which the Immigration and Naturalization Service (INS) determined that those ALIENS unprepared to defend the United States in time of war should no longer be entitled to remain in the country, into a free speech case. Traditionally aliens had not been treated as having the same constitutional rights as those with CITIZENSHIP, and were eligible for deportation at the pleasure of the INS. Rosika Schwimmer, a pacifist who was ineligible for military service on age and gender grounds, declined to affirm that she would defend the United States, and the INS's effort to deport her, although doubtless punitive, was not a violation of any constitutional right. Holmes turned the case into an essay on "freedom for the thought we hate," but his comments had no legal significance for the case before the Court. Schwimmer could have been deported simply for failing to affirm allegiance, whatever her reason. Holmes took the occasion to juxtapose his contempt for the ideology of pacifism against his belief that pacifists should be allowed to speak freely, but Schwimmer was an alien pacifist.

Holmes's last decade of free speech opinions thus reduced itself to a series of vivid rhetorical expressions and a somewhat inconsistent voting record. But the very elo-

quence of those expressions, his great stature as a judge, and the enticing image of a nineteenth-century Brahmin voicing support for the "poor and puny" communications issued by marginalized dissidents has been too much for a long line of commentators, themselves enthusiastic about free speech, to resist. Consequently Holmes's judicial career will invariably be associated with the libertarian progression of twentieth-century free speech jurisprudence in America. One hopes the association will be seen as more nuanced than the conventional mythology suggests.

G. EDWARD WHITE
(2000)

Bibliography

GUNTHER, GERALD   1975   Learned Hand and the Origin of Modern First Amendment Doctrine. *Stanford Law Review* 27:719–773.

LEWIS, ANTHONY   1991   *Make No Law: The Sullivan Case and the First Amendment*. New York: Random House.

WHITE, G. EDWARD   1993   *Justice Oliver Wendell Holmes: Law and the Inner Self*. New York: Oxford University Press.

———   1996   The First Amendment Comes of Age. *Michigan Law Review* 95:299–392.

HOME BUILDING & LOAN ASSOCIATION v. BLAISDELL
290 U.S. 398 (1934)

This was the most important CONTRACT CLAUSE case since CHARLES RIVER BRIDGE V. WARREN BRIDGE CO. (1837). The great Depression of the 1930s, by wiping out jobs and savings and savaging the economy, threatened homeowners, farmers, shopkeepers, and others with the loss of their property through foreclosures on mortgages. The states responded by enacting debtors' relief legislation that postponed the obligations of mortgagors to meet payments. Minnesota's statute authorized a state court, on application from a debtor, to exempt property from final foreclosure for no more than two years, during which time the creditor must be paid a reasonable rental value fixed by the court and the debtor might refinance the mortgage. The Supreme Court's precedents seemed to require a decision that the contract clause was violated by the statute, which operated retroactively on mortgages contracted prior to its enactment and delayed enforcement of the mortgagee's contractual rights.

By a 5–4 vote the Court sustained the statute in an opinion by Chief Justice CHARLES EVANS HUGHES. The prohibition of the contract clause, he declared, "is not an absolute one and is not to be read with literal exactness like a mathematical formula." In times of acute economic distress the states might employ their RESERVED POLICE POWER, "notwithstanding interference with contract," to prevent immediate enforcement of obligations by a temporary and conditional restraint, in order to safeguard the vital public interest in private ownership. As Justice GEORGE SUTHERLAND, for the dissenters, trenchantly observed, the POLICE POWER, whether reserved or inalienable, had never previously justified impairing the OBLIGATION OF CONTRACT between private parties. Hughes, however, distinguished precedents such as BRONSON V. KINZIE (1843) by saying that they had not, as here, provided for securing the mortgagee the rental value of the property during the extended period. Although the statute affected contracts, it was addressed to a legitimate end of the police power and employed reasonable means to achieve it. The restraint and realism that characterized this opinion and that in NEBBIA V. NEW YORK (1934) of the same term did not dominate the Court's opinions during the next two critical terms, when it confronted NEW DEAL legislation. After *Blaisdell*, however, the contract clause lay almost dormant until the late 1970s.

LEONARD W. LEVY
(1986)

HOMELESSNESS AND THE CONSTITUTION

The federal Constitution does not expressly address the condition of homelessness. Nor does it expressly create a right to housing, in contrast to the constitutions of France, Spain, Sweden, and Belgium.

Numerous commentators argue that there is also no implicit right to shelter or housing in the Constitution, relying on *Lindsey v. Normet*, a 1972 Supreme Court case. *Lindsey*, however, held that there is no right to *adequate* housing under the Constitution; it did not consider whether there is a right to *some* form of housing or shelter. Many would argue against recognizing such a right under our Constitution, which is generally considered to create "negative" rather than "positive" rights. Others, however, frame economic rights in "negative" terms, as President FRANKLIN D. ROOSEVELT did with his concept of "freedom from want."

Regardless of the resolution of this underlying issue, the Constitution still affects homelessness and homeless people. Particularly over the past two decades, courts have addressed the federal constitutional rights of homeless persons in several key areas.

Numerous courts have held that begging is speech protected by the FIRST AMENDMENT. In *Loper v. New York City Police Department* (1993), the U.S. Court of Appeals for the Second Circuit noted that begging is generally "intertwined" with a social or political message indicating extreme poverty and the need for help. In contrast, in *Young v. New York City Transit Authority* (1990), the same court had held that begging in the subway could be prohibited. At least one scholar has argued that begging is COMMERCIAL SPEECH and thus due lesser constitutional protection. The weight of authority is that begging is political speech, and thus subject to the highest protection under our Constitution. Broad bans on peaceful begging in public spaces are likely to be unconstitutional; however, narrowly tailored, content-neutral limitations on time, place, and manner are generally upheld.

More recently, prohibitions on begging have more narrowly targeted "aggressive panhandling." Such laws may also raise First Amendment concerns if they are not sufficiently precise or neutral. Moreover, they may also raise concerns under the EQUAL PROTECTION clause to the extent they target aggressive begging but not other forms of aggressive solicitation or speech.

Laws that criminalize sleeping or carrying out other "necessary life activities" in public places may also be unconstitutional as applied to homeless people. In *Pottinger v. Miami* (1992), a federal district court held that where there are insufficient shelter beds compared to the numbers of homeless people in a city, a law that makes it a crime to sleep—or to conduct other harmless, necessary life activities, such as eating or bathing—in any public area essentially punishes the involuntary "status" of homelessness and thus is CRUEL AND UNUSUAL PUNISHMENT in violation of the Eighth Amendment. Alternatively stated, such a law impermissibly punishes involuntary conduct. However, in *Joyce v. City of San Francisco* (1994), a federal district court reasoned that homelessness is not an immutable characteristic of the person and thus not properly a personal status in the Eighth Amendment sense. At least one commentator has argued that the constitutionality of such a law is fact-dependent: in the absence of sufficient indoor resources, there is no alternative to conducting necessary life activities in public and involuntary conduct—or status—is impermissibly punished.

Some courts have also upheld RIGHT TO TRAVEL challenges to such laws, reasoning that they effectively preclude homeless persons from remaining in the city or state that applies them; others have rejected such challenges, holding that the right to travel is not implicated in the absence of differential treatment of residents and nonresidents. In *Streetwatch v. National Railroad Passenger Corp.* (1995), a federal district court in New York held that policies prohibiting the presence of homeless people in a quasi-public place—a transportation station—infringe their "fundamental freedom of movement" in violation of the DUE PROCESS clause. Furthermore, laws prohibiting loitering or vagrancy, which may be disproportionately enforced to "sweep" homeless people out of public areas, may be subject to constitutional challenge for VAGUENESS.

Homeless people enjoy some RIGHT OF PRIVACY under the FOURTH AMENDMENT. Generally, shelters are akin to homes for Fourth Amendment purposes; they cannot be entered and subjected to WARRANTLESS SEARCHES. Similarly, homeless people's PROPERTY, placed or wrapped in such a way as to suggest it is not abandoned, may be protected even if it is left in a public place. The criterion in these cases—as generally in Fourth Amendment analysis—is whether there is a reasonable expectation of privacy. As noted in the leading case on this issue, the Connecticut Supreme Court's *State v. Mooney* (1991), the circumstances of homeless persons must be taken into account in making this judgment.

Several courts have considered homeless persons' VOTING RIGHTS. In *Pitts v. Black* (1984), a federal district court held that under the equal protection clause, the lack of a traditional street address cannot be a basis for depriving a homeless person of his or her fundamental right to vote. As long as there is some identifiable location to which a homeless person regularly returns—be it a shelter, park bench, or street corner—that is sufficient to establish residency within a particular district for voting purposes.

MARIA FOSCARINIS
(2000)

Bibliography

ADES, PAUL   1989   Comment: The Unconstitutionality of "AntiHomeless" Laws. *California Law Review* 77:595–628.

AVRAMOV, DRAGANA   1996   *The Invisible Hand of the Housing Market: A Study of the Effects of Changes in the Housing Market on Homelessness in the European Union.* Brussels: FEANTSA (The European Federation of National Organizations Working with the Homeless).

BENNETT, SUSAN D.   1995   "No Relief but on the Terms of Coming into the House"—Controlled Spaces, Invisible Disentitlements, and Homelessness in an Urban Shelter System. *Yale Law Journal* 104:2157–2212.

ELLICKSON, ROBERT C.   1996   Controlling Chronic Misconduct in City Spaces: Of Panhandlers, Skid Rows, and Public-Space Zoning. *Yale Law Journal* 105:1165–1248.

FOSCARINIS, MARIA   1996   Downward Spiral: Homelessness and Its Criminalization. *Yale Law and Policy Review* 14:1–63.

GARRETT, BETH D. and DANIELS, WES   1993   Law and the Homeless: An Annotated Bibliography. *Law Library Journal* 85: 463–529.

HERSHKOFF, HELEN and COHEN, ADAM   1991   Begging to Differ: The First Amendment and the Right to Beg. *Harvard Law Review* 104:896–916.

NATIONAL LAW CENTER ON HOMELESSNESS & POVERTY   1999   *Out of Sight—Out of Mind? A Report on Anti-Homeless Laws, Litigation and Alternatives in 50 U.S. Cities.* Washington, D.C.: National Law Center on Homelessness & Poverty.

ROISMAN, FLORENCE W.   1991   Establishing a Right to Housing. *Clearinghouse Review* 25:203–227.

SIMON, HARRY   1995   The Criminalization of Homelessness in Santa Ana, California: A Case Study. *Clearinghouse Review* 29:725–729.

STONER, MADELEINE R.   1995   *The Civil Rights of Homeless People.* New York: Aldine de Gruyter.

WALDRON, JEREMY   1991   Homelessness and the Issue of Freedom. *UCLA Law Review* 39:295–324.

HOMESTEAD ACT
12 Stat. 392 (1862)

The Homestead Act provided for distribution of public land to settlers who would live on the land and improve it. As enacted in 1862, the act provided for allocation of a quarter section (160 acres) to a homesteader who lived on it for five years and paid a ten dollar fee. The act was sponsored by Speaker of the House Galusha A. Grow (Republican of Pennsylvania), and its passage culminated more than a decade's efforts.

The act bespoke a national commitment to the farmer-freeholder as the prototypical American citizen. The system it established was designed, among other things, to solve the problem of SLAVERY IN THE TERRITORIES by insuring a permanent antislavery majority there; and, for that reason, earlier proposals for a homestead bill were supported by the Liberty and Free Soil parties. The homestead program populated the Midwest and plains with hundreds of thousands of independent farmers, and allowed rapid conversion of wilderness TERRITORIES into STATES.

The act was repealed in 1910, a victim of fraud and inefficiency, as well as of an antipathy during the Progressive era toward distribution of public land. In a little less than half a century, over 100 million acres had been distributed under the act.

DENNIS J. MAHONEY
(1986)

HOMOSEXUALITY

See: *Bowers v. Hardwick*; Same-Sex Marriage; Sexual Discrimination; Sexual Orientation; Sexual Preference and the Constitution

HOMOSEXUALS' RIGHTS

See: Sexual Preference and the Constitution

HOOD & SONS v. UNITED STATES

See: *Wrightwood Dairy Co., United States v.*

HOOKER, THOMAS
(1586–1647)

To escape persecution for his Puritan beliefs, Thomas Hooker fled England in 1633 and settled in Newton, Massachusetts, as its Congregational minister. In 1636 he led most of his congregation to a new settlement at Hartford, thus becoming a founder of Connecticut.

A leader among Puritan clergy, Hooker wrote a major defense of New England Congregationalism and extended his theological convictions into politics. Adopting his flexible stand on formal church affiliation, Connecticut refused to limit the franchise to church members.

In 1639 Hooker's preference for explicit covenants probably prompted Connecticut's leaders to organize the colony's government by drawing up a SOCIAL COMPACT, regarded by some historians as the first written American CONSTITUTION, known as the FUNDAMENTAL ORDERS. This document mirrored Hooker's beliefs that civil government should be a covenant between citizens for the promotion of peace and unity; that political authority should reflect the free choice of the people; that rulers were responsible to those they ruled; that the people, as the source of government's existence, had the right not only to choose magistrates but specifically to limit their powers; and that magistrates should consult with the people on issues involving the common good and heed popular judgment in such matters.

THOMAS CURRY
(1986)

Bibliography

MILLER, PERRY 1956 *Errand into the Wilderness.* Pages 16–47. Cambridge, Mass.: Harvard University Press.

HOOVER, HERBERT C.
(1874–1964)

Born in Iowa and trained as a mining engineer at Stanford University, Herbert Clark Hoover initially became involved in politics as chairman of the Commission for Relief in Belgium and of the United States Food Administration Board during WORLD WAR I. After the war, President WOODROW WILSON made Hoover director of European economic relief, and in 1921 President WARREN G. HARDING appointed him secretary of commerce.

Hoover was elected President of the United States on the Republican ticket in 1928. Seven months after his inauguration, the stock market collapsed as the depression that had gripped Europe since the end of the war reached America as well. In the face of the economic crisis Hoover clung to his conservative constitutional principles. He advocated private, voluntary action to spur recovery and expanded relief programs at the state level. He resisted federal government intervention until the election year 1932, when he proposed the Reconstruction Finance Corporation.

Hoover's nominations to the Supreme Court were a mixed lot. He appointed former Justice CHARLES EVANS HUGHES to be Chief Justice in 1930. His nomination of conservative Judge John J. Parker of North Carolina to be an Associate Justice was narrowly rejected by the Senate, but two other appointments were confirmed: moderate OWEN J. ROBERTS of Pennsylvania in 1930 and liberal BENJAMIN N. CARDOZO of New York in 1932.

After FRANKLIN D. ROOSEVELT defeated him in the 1932 election, Hoover retired from public office, but remained influential within the Republican party. He was recalled to public service after WORLD WAR II to direct food relief programs in Europe, and he served as chairman of two Commissions on the Organization of the Executive Branch. The Hoover Commission Reports of 1949 and 1955 led to greater efficiency in the executive branch, mostly through regrouping of functions and agencies.

DENNIS J. MAHONEY
(1986)

Bibliography

NASH, GEORGE H. 1983 *The Life of Herbert Hoover.* New York: Norton.

HOOVER, J. EDGAR
(1895–1972)

From his graduation from George Washington University Law School in 1917 until his death in 1972, John Edgar Hoover was continuously employed by the United States Department of Justice. He started as a file reviewer, but in 1919 Hoover became special assistant to Attorney General A. MITCHELL PALMER, with oversight responsibility for the DEPORTATION cases arising out of the PALMER RAIDS. In 1921 Hoover was assigned to the department's Bureau of Investigations, and in 1924 he became its director.

Over the next decade, Hoover transformed his small bureau into a national police agency. As federal criminal law expanded, the bureau expanded with it, acquiring a reputation for professionalism, competence, and efficiency. By the time it was renamed the FEDERAL BUREAU OF INVESTIGATION (FBI) in 1935, the bureau had established a national fingerprint file, a crime laboratory, and a training academy. The FBI's dual mandate was to investigate violations of federal law and to serve as a domestic, civilian counterintelligence agency. The bureau's success in tracking down bootleggers, gangsters, kidnappers, and spies became legendary.

The FBI was largely Hoover's personal creation, and he ran it autocratically. Although formally supervised by the ATTORNEY GENERAL, Hoover operated with a great deal of independence, gained by tenure, public success, and, reputedly, maintenance of secret dossiers concerning his political superiors. Hoover used the FBI to conduct personal feuds, like that with MARTIN LUTHER KING, JR., and to publicize his own brand of anticommunism. In the end, his apparent indifference to CIVIL LIBERTIES compromised the very professionalism he had worked to instill in the FBI.

DENNIS J. MAHONEY
(1986)

Bibliography

DE TOLEDANO, RALPH 1973 *J. Edgar Hoover: The Man in His Times.* New Rochelle, N.Y.: Arlington House.

HOPWOOD v. TEXAS
78 F.3d 932 (5th Cir. 1996)

Lawyers and policymakers have long looked to Justice LEWIS F. POWELL, JR.'s, solo opinion in REGENTS OF THE UNIVERSITY OF CALIFORNIA V. BAKKE (1978) as a guide to creating and administering AFFIRMATIVE ACTION programs. The continuing import of Powell's opinion was questioned by the U.S. Court of Appeals for the Fifth Circuit in *Hopwood v. Texas*, where the court invalidated the University of Texas School of Law's affirmative action program and declared that Powell's "lonely opinion" was not binding PRECEDENT.

The law school adopted separate, segregated evaluation processes for white applicants on the one hand, and African American and Mexican American applicants on the other. Under this system, the law school admitted African American and Mexican American applicants with lower Law School Aptitude Test scores and college grade point averages than white applicants. Four rejected European American students brought suit against the law school, claiming the evaluation practices amounted to RACIAL DISCRIMINATION in violation of the FOURTEENTH AMENDMENT that could not be justified under STRICT SCRUTINY.

The law school defended its program in part as necessary to insure a diverse student body—a goal Powell had characterized in *Bakke* as a COMPELLING STATE INTEREST. The Fifth Circuit rejected the diversity argument, noting that Powell's opinion was not joined by other Justices and that subsequent Supreme Court opinions held that race-

based affirmative action could only be justified to remedy prior discrimination by the relevant state entity. (The one exception, METRO BROADCASTING, INC. V. FCC (1990), was judged under a lower STANDARD OF REVIEW subsequently held to be inappropriate by the Court.) Although the law school offered a remedial justification for its program, the Fifth Circuit ruled that there was no record evidence of discrimination against the preferred minority groups by the law school to warrant a remedy.

The Supreme Court declined to hear the case, with two Justices noting that the case had become moot. Nevertheless, *Hopwood* became a symbol both of the mounting hostility to race-based affirmative action in the 1990s and of the JUDICIAL ACTIVISM of conservative judges appointed to the federal bench by Republican Presidents RONALD REAGAN and GEORGE H. W. BUSH.

ADAM WINKLER
(2000)

HOSTILE AUDIENCE

Nothing is more antagonistic to the FREEDOM OF SPEECH than a mob shouting a speaker into silence. For state officials to suppress speech merely because the audience is offended by the speaker's message is a violation of the FIRST AMENDMENT. Although some lower courts have experimented with the notion of a heckler's First Amendment right, there is no place in our constitutional order for what HARRY KALVEN called the "heckler veto." The duty of the police, when the audience is hostile, is to protect the speaker so long as that is reasonably possible. Similarly, the potential hostility of an audience—even its potential violence—will not justify denying a license to meet or parade in a PUBLIC FORUM.

When police protection is inadequate, however, and audience hostility poses an immediate threat of violence, the police may constitutionally order a speaker to stop, even though the speech does not amount to INCITEMENT TO UNLAWFUL CONDUCT, and is otherwise protected by the First Amendment. The Supreme Court so held in FEINER V. NEW YORK (1951), a case involving no more than "some pushing, shoving and milling around" in an audience hostile to a speaker in a park. The principle retains vitality, although *Feiner* itself, on its facts, seems an insecure precedent.

The constitutionality of police action requiring someone to stop addressing a hostile audience depends on one form of the CLEAR AND PRESENT DANGER test: the police may not stop the speaker unless the threat of violence is immediate and police resources are inadequate to contain the threatened harm. Thus, if the speaker refuses to stop and is charged with BREACH OF THE PEACE, the court must look beyond the arresting officers' good faith—a point emphasized by the Supreme Court in *Feiner*—to the objective likelihood of violence. Appellate courts, too, in reviewing convictions in such cases, must closely examine lower courts' findings of fact. An important difference between *Feiner* and *Edwards v. South Carolina* (1963), where the Court reversed breach of peace convictions of civil rights demonstrators facing a hostile audience, lay in the *Edwards* Court's willingness to scrutinize the record and reject the state courts' findings of danger.

KENNETH L. KARST
(1986)

Bibliography

KALVEN, HARRY, JR. 1965 *The Negro and the First Amendment.* Pages 139–145. Columbus: Ohio State University Press.

HOT PURSUIT

See: Exigent Circumstances Search

HOUSE COMMITTEE ON UN-AMERICAN ACTIVITIES

In 1938, because of a growing fear of Nazi and communist activity in the United States, conservative congressmen secured passage of a House Resolution creating a Special Committee on Un-American Activities (HUAC). Under publicity-conscious Texas congressman MARTIN DIES, the Committee set out to expose left-wing groups and individuals whom it considered security risks. After five renewals, by overwhelming votes, the group was made into an unprecedented standing committee of the House in 1945. From then until the mid-1950s, the Committee became a sounding board for ex-radicals, publicity seekers, and critics of the NEW DEAL and the Truman administration. It identified the following tasks for itself: to expose and ferret out communists and their sympathizers in the federal government; to show how communists had won control over vital trade unions; and to investigate communist influences in the press, religious and educational organizations, and the movie industry. The sensational Alger Hiss-Whittaker Chambers hearings, in connection with turning over security information, and the resultant perjury conviction of Hiss, a former New Deal official, added to the Committee's prestige. By 1948, the Committee sponsored legislation against the Communist party, pushing the MUNDT-NIXON BILL.

The activities of HUAC, however, raised important constitutional questions. The Committee's constant probing into political behavior and belief led critics to charge that such forced exposure abridged FREEDOM OF SPEECH and association, and punished citizens for their opinions. Also questioned was the legitimacy of its "exposure for its own sake" approach, when action did not seem to relate to legitimate legislative purpose, and when legislative "trials" violated many aspects of DUE PROCESS including the right to be tried in a court under the protection of constitutional guarantees.

The Supreme Court ultimately dealt with both questions, with contradictory and changing results. In three cases (*Emspack v. United States*, 1955; *Quinn v. United States*, 1955; and WATKINS V. UNITED STATES, 1957) the Court narrowly interpreted the statutory authority for punishing recalcitrant witnesses, and questioned forced exposure of views and activities in light of the FIRST AMENDMENT. Facing sharp criticism, the Court retreated in the cases of BARENBLATT V. UNITED STATES (1958), *Wilkinson v. United States* (1961), and *Braden v. United States* (1961), only to move back again to a more critical position as the 1960s progressed—from 1961 to 1966 reversing almost every contempt conviction which came to it from the Committee. By mid-1966, conservative legislators were condemning the "unseemly spectacles" HUAC chronically elicited. Thus, in 1969, it was rechristened the Internal Security Committee, and although its procedures were modified somewhat in this new form, the committee was eventually abolished by the House in 1975.

PAUL L. MURPHY
(1986)

Bibliography

GOODMAN, WALTER 1968 *The Committee: The Extraordinary Career of the House Committee on Un-American Activities.* New York: Farrar, Straus.

HOUSE OF REPRESENTATIVES

The House of Representatives was born of compromise at the CONSTITUTIONAL CONVENTION OF 1787. Early during the Convention, the VIRGINIA PLAN, favored by the larger states, proposed a bicameral legislature in which states would be represented on the basis of wealth or population. New Jersey and other small states balked at this plan and proposed maintaining a unicameral legislature in which each state would have equal representation. The present structure of Congress was accepted as the heart of the GREAT COMPROMISE. In the SENATE each state was guaranteed equal representation, while in the House, representation was to be determined by each state's population, excluding Indians but including three-fifths of the slave population.

The compromise served dual purposes: it resolved a major conflict between the delegates, and it created one of the CHECKS AND BALANCES within the Congress to guard against the flawed legislation that might come from a uni-cameral legislature. The House of Representatives was planned to reflect populist attitudes in society.

Article I, section 2, of the Constitution establishes the structure of the House. Members are chosen every second year. By law, this occurs the Tuesday after the first Monday in November in even-numbered calendar years. The frequency of elections was expected to make House members particularly responsive to shifting political climates. The Framers believed this influence would be balanced by requiring legislation to be passed by the Senate and House together. Senators are elected for six-year terms, with a third of the seats contested in each biennial election. The two-year term in the House was a compromise between those favoring annual elections and others, including JAMES MADISON, who favored elections once every third year. Subsequent attempts to set House terms at four years have failed. Opponents of such plans believe that having all congressional elections coincide with presidential elections would make House candidates unduly vulnerable to the effects of coattail politics. There is no limit to the number of terms a representative or senator may serve.

The Constitution requires that representatives be chosen by "the People of the several States," as opposed to the indirect election of the President and Vice-President by the ELECTORAL COLLEGE, and the original plan called for election of senators by the state legislatures. The SEVENTEENTH AMENDMENT now requires direct election of senators. The precise method of direct election is not constitutionally determined. Until 1842, some states allowed voters to select a slate of at-large representatives, making it possible for voters to select every representative from a given state. Congress forbade this practice, mandating the use of congressional districts—that is, equally apportioned subdivisions within the states. Each district sends one representative to the House.

Congressional districts have been the subject of continuous controversy. Districts are drawn by the state legislatures, and the political parties in control of the individual legislatures often GERRYMANDER boundary lines, creating oddly shaped districts that benefit the fortunes of the majority party. The federal courts have been loath to intervene in these disputes, although the issue does not fall squarely into the category of the unreviewable POLITICAL QUESTION, and the Supreme Court has hinted that an extreme partisan gerrymander might be unconstitutional.

The Court has been far more strict in requiring that state legislatures draw district lines to achieve population equality among the several districts within a given state. This principle, first set forth in WESBERRY V. SANDERS (1964), has been consistently reaffirmed.

Anyone who can vote in an election for "the most numerous Branch of the State Legislature" can vote for members of the House of Representatives. Early in the country's history, VOTING RIGHTS were limited to white males and were often linked to property holdings. As a result, voter eligibility varied from state to state. The scope of suffrage has broadened over time, through the adoption of the FIFTEENTH AMENDMENT (vote for former slaves), the NINETEENTH AMENDMENT (vote for women), the TWENTY-FOURTH AMENDMENT (abolition of poll taxes), the VOTING RIGHTS ACT OF 1965, and the TWENTY-SIXTH AMENDMENT (vote for all citizens eighteen or older). Indians are also now eligible to vote and are counted for purposes of apportionment.

Article I, section 2, requires that representatives be at least twenty-five years old, U.S. citizens for at least seven years, and citizens of the states they represent. Although not constitutionally required, political practice in the United States requires House members to reside in the districts they represent. This practice is not common to all national legislatures, most notably the British House of Commons.

Under Article I, section 5, the House and the Senate are the judges of the qualifications of their members, as well as the final arbiters of contested elections. On ten occasions, elected candidates have failed to meet constitutional requirements for House membership. Prior to 1969, both chambers occasionally refused to seat victorious candidates who were thought unacceptable for moral or political reasons. The Supreme Court limited Congress's ability to make such judgments in POWELL V. MCCORMACK (1969). The Court ruled that the House could not refuse to seat Adam Clayton Powell, Jr., on the basis of his being held in contempt of court. So long as an elected candidate meets the constitutional requirements of age, CITIZENSHIP, and residence, the member's chamber must seat him or her, although members may be censured or expelled for violating internal chamber rules. Article I grants each chamber of Congress the power to establish and enforce internal rules.

The number of House seats allotted to each state is determined by the decennial census. Article I, section 2, paragraph 3, sets forth the original apportionment scheme. The apportioning mechanism remains, but the size of the House has increased with the growth of the country. The House was initially designed to seat 65 members, each representing not less than 30,000 countable constituents. During the twentieth century, allowing the maximum membership under the Constitution would have produced an unwieldly body of several thousand members, Congress has permanently capped the size of the House at 435 voting members. In the 1980s, members from all but the smallest states represented an average of approximately 520,000 constituents.

When a vacancy occurs in the House of Representatives

because of death or other circumstances, the governor of the state with the vacant seat calls a special election. Vacant Senate seats are filled by gubernatorial appointment. The special-election requirement reaffirms the constitutional principle that representatives are the elected national officals most directly tied to their constituents. In practice, when vacancies occur in the second year of a congressional term, seats often remain vacant until the next general election.

Article I, section 2, paragraph 5, provides for the election of the Speaker of the House and other officers. The Speaker is actually chosen by the majority-party caucus and then formally elected by the House. House rules dictate the specific functions of the Speaker and other officers, and by Act of Congress the Speaker is second in the line of PRESIDENTIAL SUCCESSION, behind the Vice-President. The Speaker is not constitutionally required to be a member of the House, although political practice has limited the Speaker's office to senior House members from the majority party.

Few specific powers are granted exclusively to the House of Representatives. In the event that no presidential candidate receives a majority of Electoral College votes, representatives, voting in state delegations with one vote per state, choose the President from among the three candidates with the greatest number of electoral votes. This process, set forth in Article II, section 1, and modified by the TWELFTH AMENDMENT, has been used only following the elections of 1800 and 1824.

The House has the sole constitutional power to impeach officers of the United States. When impeaching a federal officer, the House brings formal charges of high crimes or misdemeanors against the accused. Following a vote to impeach by the House, the Senate may vote to convict the officer by a two-thirds majority. The House has impeached only one President, ANDREW JOHNSON, in 1868. The Senate failed to convict him by a single vote. A dozen federal judges have been formally impeached, and four convicted. In July 1974 the House Committee on the Judiciary initiated IMPEACHMENT hearings against President RICHARD M. NIXON and recommended his impeachment on three counts. Nixon resigned following his court-ordered release of the Watergate tapes, and the House dropped its proceedings.

The final power held exclusively by the House is the "power of the purse." The Constitution requires that all bills to raise federal revenues originate in the House. The larger states at the Constitutional Convention insisted on linking taxation and representation, believing that the direct and frequent election of the representatives would cause them to proceed with caution in proposing tax measures. In fact, the Senate can propose revenue measures through the process of amending bills from the House.

The adoption of the Seventeenth Amendment has diluted much of the original concern regarding taxation and direct representation.

ROBERT F. DRINAN, S.J.
(1992)

Bibliography

CONGRESSIONAL QUARTERLY 1982. *Powers of Congress*, 2nd ed. Washington, D.C.: Congressional Quarterly.

CORWIN, EDWARD SAMUEL 1985 *Corwin and Peltason's Understanding the Constitution*, 10th ed. New York: Holt, Rinehart & Winston.

GALLOWAY, GEORGE B. 1976 *History of the House of Representatives*, 2nd ed. New York: Thomas Y. Crowell.

HINCKLEY, BARBARA 1987 *Stability and Change in Congress*, 4th ed. San Francisco: Harper & Row.

HOUSTON, CHARLES H.
(1895–1950)

Charles H. Houston was the foremost black CIVIL RIGHTS lawyer before THURGOOD MARSHALL. He was a member of the faculty of Howard Law School and from 1932 to 1935 served as dean. He obtained accreditation and respect for the institution, which trained many civil rights lawyers. From 1935 to 1940 Houston was special counsel for the National Association for the Advancement of Colored People (NAACP). Although he returned to private practice thereafter, he remained active with the NAACP and other civil rights organizations. Marshall later called him "The First Mr. Civil Rights." Houston was of counsel in NIXON V. CONDON (1932), arguing against the white primary, and he assisted in the defense of the Scottsboro Boys. He argued and won MISSOURI EX REL. GAINES V. CANADA (1938), which forced the state to open its law school to black students. He also won from the Supreme Court decisions prohibiting discrimination against black railroad employees. Perhaps his most difficult and greatest victory came in HURD V. HODGE (1948), in which the Court accepted his arguments that the CIVIL RIGHTS ACT OF 1866 outlawed the judicial enforcement of RESTRICTIVE COVENANTS by the courts of the DISTRICT OF COLUMBIA, and that even in the absence of the congressional act, the enforcement of such covenants would violate the public policy of the United States.

LEONARD W. LEVY
(1986)

Bibliography

MCNEIL, GENNA RAE 1982 *Charles Hamilton Houston and the Struggle for Civil Rights*. Philadelphia: University of Pennsylvania Press.

HOUSTON, EAST & WEST TEXAS RAILWAY CO. v. UNITED STATES
(Shreveport Rate Case)
234 U.S. 342 (1914)

To relieve a competitive inequality in rail rates, the Interstate Commerce Commission (ICC) ordered the Texas Railroad Commission to raise intrastate rates to equal interstate rates. Shreveport, Louisiana, to east Texas rates, set by the ICC, were higher than west Texas to east Texas rates, fixed by the states, thereby placing INTERSTATE COMMERCE at a competitive disadvantage. With only Justices HORACE LURTON and MAHLON PITNEY dissenting, Justice CHARLES EVANS HUGHES relied on the INTERSTATE COMMERCE ACT and the COMMERCE CLAUSE in upholding the ICC order. Hughes distinguished the MINNESOTA RATE CASES (1913) as neither involving an attempt at federal regulation nor adversely affecting or burdening interstate commerce. Emphasizing Congress's "complete and paramount" power over interstate commerce, he announced the SHREVEPORT DOCTRINE: "Wherever the interstate and intrastate transactions of carriers are so related that the government of the one involves the control of the other, it is Congress and not the state, that is entitled to prescribe the final and dominant rule."

DAVID GORDON
(1986)

HOWARD, JACOB M.
(1805–1871)

Jacob Merritt Howard was an abolitionist, a champion of CIVIL RIGHTS, and a leading northern politician whose constitutional legacy derived from his advocacy of Radical Republicanism. Born and educated in New England, Howard moved to Detroit where, after admission to the bar, he began his political career as a WHIG. In 1854 he helped found the Republican party and framed its resolutions.

In 1862 he became a United States senator, and for a decade he remained in the vanguard of the Radical Republican wing of his party. He advocated black VOTING RIGHTS, served influentially during the CIVIL WAR on both the SENATE JUDICIARY COMMITTEE and the Committee on Military Affairs, and vigorously supported the FREEDMEN'S BUREAU ACT and the CIVIL RIGHTS ACT OF 1866. Howard was a coauthor of the THIRTEENTH AMENDMENT and, as a ranking Senate Republican on the powerful JOINT COMMITTEE ON RECONSTRUCTION, chaperoned the approval by the Senate of the FOURTEENTH AMENDMENT.

LEONARD W. LEVY
(1986)

HOWE, MARK DEWOLFE
(1902–1966)

Mark DeWolfe Howe began his legal career as a clerk to Justice OLIVER WENDELL HOLMES, and throughout his life Holmes was the focus of much of Howe's most valuable scholarly work. While professor of law at Harvard Law School, Howe prepared definitive editions of Holmes's correspondence with Sir Frederick Pollock (1941) and HAROLD J. LASKI (1953), his CIVIL WAR diary and letters (1947), his *Speeches* (1962), and *The Common Law* (1963). Although Howe never lived to complete his biography of Holmes, the two volumes he did publish (1957, 1963) are unparalleled for their illumination of Holmes's intellectual life up to his appointment to the Massachusetts Supreme Judicial Court. A pioneer in the field of American legal history, Howe specialized in the history of freedom of religion. In his last published book, *The Garden and the Wilderness* (1965), Howe criticized the Supreme Court's reading of the history of religion in America, pointing out that the "wall of separation" between church and state was based as much on evangelical theory as Jeffersonian rationalism; Howe suggested that the Constitution recognized a *de facto* ESTABLISHMENT OF RELIGION in American society. An activist as well as a scholar, Howe worked tirelessly for the NAACP LEGAL DEFENSE & EDUCATIONAL FUND, both as a teacher and as a litigator.

RICHARD B. BERNSTEIN
(1986)

H. P. HOOD & SONS v. UNITED STATES

See: *Wrightwood Dairy Co., United States v.*

HUDGENS v. NATIONAL LABOR RELATIONS BOARD
424 U.S. 507 (1976)

In terminating its experiment with extending MARSH V. ALABAMA (1946) to privately owned SHOPPING CENTERS, the Supreme Court, 7–2, announced in *Hudgens* that the refusal of owners to permit union picketing did not constitute STATE ACTION and thus did not violate the FIRST AMENDMENT, even though the private property was "open to the public." That vast shopping plazas, which are central features of American culture, are not required by the First Amendment to grant FREEDOM OF SPEECH is a highly significant feature of contemporary constitutional law.

MARTIN SHAPIRO
(1986)

HUDSON v. PALMER

See: Prisoners' Rights

HUDSON AND GOODWIN, UNITED STATES v.

See: Federal Common Law of Crimes

HUGHES, CHARLES EVANS
(1862–1948)

The only child of a Baptist minister and a strong-willed, doting mother who hoped their son would become a man of the cloth, Charles Evans Hughes compiled a record of public service unparalleled for its diversity and achievement by any other member of the Supreme Court with the exception of WILLIAM HOWARD TAFT. In addition to pursuing a lucrative career at the bar, Hughes taught law at Cornell, served as a two-term governor of New York, was secretary of state under two Presidents during the 1920s, and served as associate Justice and Chief Justice of the United States. By the narrowest of margins, he lost the electoral votes of California in 1916 and thus the presidency to the incumbent, WOODROW WILSON. Hughes was a man of imposing countenance and intellectual abilities, who left an indelible mark upon the nation's politics, diplomacy, and law.

First appointed to the Court as associate justice by President William Howard Taft, Hughes brought to the bench the social and intellectual outlook of many American progressives, those morally earnest men and women from the urban middle class who wished to purge the nation's politics of corruption, infuse the business world with greater efficiency and concern for the public welfare, and minister to the needs of the poor in the great cities. In an earlier era, such people had found an outlet for their moral energies in religion. By the turn of the twentieth century, they practiced a social gospel and undertook a "search for order" through secular careers in law, medicine, public administration, journalism, engineering, and social welfare.

"We are under a Constitution," Governor Hughes remarked shortly before his appointment to the bench, "but the Constitution is what the judges say it is, and the judiciary is the safeguard of our liberty and of our property under the Constitution." This statement reflected the ambivalence of many progressives about the nation's fundamental charter of government and its judicial expositers on the Supreme Court. On the one hand, Hughes and other progressives clearly recognized that constitutional decision-making was a subjective process, strongly influenced by the temper of the times and by the social biases and objectives of individual jurists. The Constitution, they believed, was flexible enough to accommodate the growing demands for reform that sprang from the manifold desires of businessmen, consumers, farmers, and industrial workers who wished to use government to promote economic security in an increasingly complex, interdependent capitalist economy. Like other progressives, Hughes saw government, both state and federal, as a positive instrument of human welfare that could discipline unruly economic forces, promote moral uplift, and guarantee domestic social peace by protecting the citizen from the worst vicissitudes of the marketplace.

At the same time, Hughes and other middle-class reformers had a morbid fear of socialism and resisted endowing government with excessive power over persons and property. They wanted social change under the rule of law, in conformity with American traditions of individualism, and directed by a disinterested elite of lawyers, administrators, and other experts of enlightened social progress.

By the time Hughes took his seat on the nation's highest court, the Justices had grappled inconclusively for almost five decades with the question of the reach of the constitutional power of the states and the national government to regulate economic activity. One group of Justices, influenced by the Jacksonian legacy of entrepreneurial individualism, equality, and STATES' RIGHTS, had combined an expansive reading of the FOURTEENTH AMENDMENT'S DUE PROCESS clause and a narrow interpretation of the COMMERCE CLAUSE and the TAXING AND SPENDING POWER in order to restrict both state and federal regulation of private economic decision making. Another group of Justices, heirs to the radical Republican tradition of moral reform and positive government, had been more receptive to governmental efforts at ECONOMIC REGULATION and redistribution.

Hughes placed his considerable intellectual resources on the side of the economic nationalists and those who refused to read the due process clause as a mechanical limitation upon state regulation of economic affairs. In *Miller v. Wilson* (1915), for example, he wrote for a unanimous bench to sustain California's eight-hour law for women in selected occupations against a challenge that the law violated FREEDOM OF CONTRACT. The liberty protected by the due process clause, he noted, included freedom from arbitrary restraint, but not immunity from regulations designed to protect public health, morals, and welfare.

More significant, he joined the dissenters in COPPAGE V. KANSAS (1915), where six members of the Court, speaking through Justice MAHLON PITNEY, invalidated a Kansas law prohibiting YELLOW DOG CONTRACTS on the ground that the regulation deprived employers of their contractual liberty. Hughes endorsed the dissent by Justice WILLIAM R. DAY which argued that the law attempted only to protect the right of individual workers to join labor unions if they so pleased and represented a legitimate exercise of the STATE POLICE POWER, ", not to require one man to employ another against his will, but to put limitations upon the sacrifice of rights which one may exact from another as a condition of employment."

Hughes's views on the federal commerce power were equally generous during this period. He wrote the two leading opinions of the era supporting the authority of Congress and the Interstate Commerce Commission (ICC) to regulate both interstate railroad rates and purely intrastate rates that undermined the efficiency of the nation's transportation network. In the Minnesota Rates Cases (1913) he upheld the particular exercise of rate-making by the state, although he and the majority affirmed that the power of Congress "could not be denied or thwarted by the commingling of interstate and intrastate operations" of the railroad. A year later, in the landmark Shreveport Case, *Houston, East & West Texas Railway Company v. United States*, (1914), he spoke for all but two Justices in sustaining an order of the ICC that effectively required an increase in intrastate rates in order to bring them into line with those fixed by the commission for interstate carriers over the same territory. The power of Congress to regulate interstate commerce, he wrote, was "complete and paramount"; Congress could "prevent the common instrumentality of interstate and intrastate commercial intercourse from being used in their intrastate operations to the injury of interstate commerce."

Most progressives displayed little sympathy for the plight of either American blacks or the foreign immigrants who entered the country in large numbers during the decades before WORLD WAR I. Hughes was a striking exception to the usual pattern of collaboration with the forces of racial and ethnic intolerance. He began to speak out in these years against various forms of oppression and bigotry and to lay the foundation for many of his subsequent opinions on CIVIL RIGHTS during the 1930s.

In *McCabe v. Atchison, Topeka & Santa Fe Railroad* (1914), Hughes led a five-Justice majority in striking down a state law that authorized intrastate railroads to provide dining and sleeping cars only for members of the white race. The state and the carriers argued that the statute was reasonable in light of the limited economic demand by black passengers for such services, a point of view that also appealed to Justice OLIVER WENDELL HOLMES. Hughes, however, flatly condemned the law as a violation of the Fourteenth Amendment's EQUAL PROTECTION clause. With support from all but one of the Justices, he also overturned, in *Truax v. Raich* (1915), an Arizona law that had limited the employment of ALIENS in the state's principal industries to twenty percent of all workers in firms with five or more employees. Discrimination against such inhabitants "because of their race or nationality," he declared, "clearly falls under the condemnation of the FUNDAMENTAL LAW."

His most impressive effort in this regard came in the famous debt peonage case, BAILEY V. ALABAMA (1911), where he both invalidated the state's draconian statute and gained a notable rhetorical victory over Justice Holmes. Under the Alabama law, as under similar ones in force throughout the South, a person's failure to perform a labor contract without just cause and without paying back money advanced was prima facie evidence of intent to defraud, punishable by fine or imprisonment. The accused, furthermore, could not rebut the presumption with testimony "as to his uncommunicated motives, purposes, or intention." Hughes condemned this "convenient instrument for . . . coercion" as a violation of both the THIRTEENTH AMENDMENT and the Anti-Peonage Act of 1867.

With a few exceptions, the progressives also displayed more concern for the suppression of crime than for the rights of the accused. The due process clause had seldom been invoked successfully against questionable methods of law enforcement and CRIMINAL PROCEDURE on the state level. In this field, too, Hughes attempted to break new ground that anticipated the jurisprudence of a later era. One case in point is FRANK V. MANGUM (1915), arising out of the notorious Leo Frank trial in Georgia. A young Jewish defendant had been convicted of murder and sentenced to death with a mob shouting outside the courtroom, "Hang the Jew, or we'll hang you." Frank and his lawyers had not been present during the reading of the verdict, because the trial judge could not guarantee their safety in the event of an acquittal.

Despite this evidence of intimidation, the Georgia Supreme Court upheld the conviction and sentence; a federal district judge refused Frank's petition for HABEAS CORPUS, which raised a host of due process challenges; and a majority of the Supreme Court affirmed that decision. Hughes joined a powerful dissent written by Holmes, which chastised the majority for its reasoning and called upon the Justices to "declare lynch law as little valid when practiced by a regularly drawn jury as when administered by one elected by a mob intent on death."

Hughes's initial appointment to the Court, following in the wake of his progressive achievements as governor of New York, had been received with almost unanimous acclaim. However, his nomination as Chief Justice by President HERBERT HOOVER in 1930 sparked furious debate. Twenty-six senators, led by the redoubtable GEORGE NORRIS of Nebraska, voted against his confirmation. Many of them believed, as Norris did, that the former Justice's profitable law practice during the 1920s had turned him into a pliant tool of the "powerful combinations in the political and financial world" and therefore rendered him incapable of fairly deciding the "contests between organized wealth and the ordinary citizen." Events proved Norris to be half right.

Beginning in 1930, Hughes was called upon to pilot the Court through the years of social and economic crisis spawned by the financial collapse of 1929 and the Great Depression. These were the most turbulent years in the Court's history since the decade before the CIVIL WAR and the economic crisis of the 1890s—two earlier occasions when the Justices had attempted to hold back the tide of popular revolt against the status quo.

Under Hughes's leadership, the Court majority became aggressively liberal with respect to the protection of CIVIL LIBERTIES and civil rights, often building upon the doctrinal structure erected by the Chief Justice himself during the Progressive Era. In STROMBERG V. CALIFORNIA (1931), NEAR V. MINNESOTA (1931), and DEJONGE V. OREGON (1937) Hughes's distinguished opinions significantly enlarged the scope of FIRST AMENDMENT rights protected against state abridgment via the due process clause. He personally drove the first judicial nail into the coffin of the SEPARATE BUT EQUAL doctrine with his opinion in MISSOURI EX REL. GAINES V. CANADA (1938), holding that a state university's refusal to admit a qualified black resident to its law school constituted a denial of equal protection. He endorsed Justice GEORGE H. SUTHERLAND's opinion in the initial Scottsboro case, POWELL V. ALABAMA (1932), and wrote the second one, NORRIS V. ALABAMA (1935), himself. Both opinions tightened the Supreme Court's supervision over state criminal trials involving the poor and members of racial minorities.

Hughes contributed to Justice HARLAN F. STONE's famous fourth footnote in UNITED STATES V. CAROLENE PRODUCTS COMPANY (1938), where the latter suggested that the Court had a special role to play in defending PREFERRED FREEDOMS, including FREEDOM OF THE PRESS, and VOTING RIGHTS, from legislative abridgment and also to protect DISCRETE AND INSULAR MINORITIES from the tyranny of the majority. Under Hughes, finally, the Court broadened the reach of habeas corpus to attack constitutionally defective state criminal convictions, and greatly expanded the IN FORMA PAUPERIS docket which permitted INDIGENT defendants to seek Supreme Court review of their convictions. By any yardstick, Hughes as Chief Justice compiled a civil liberties record of impressive range and impact.

The Hughes who regularly cast his vote on the libertarian side in cases touching civil liberties and civil rights during the 1930s also voted in 1935 and 1936 against many of the social and economic reforms sponsored by the FRANKLIN D. ROOSEVELT administration and state govern-

ments in their efforts to cope with the economic crisis of the decade. It is this side of his performance as Chief Justice that has fueled the most controversy—and puzzlement, too, considering Hughes's toleration for many of the early anti-Depression nostrums of both the NEW DEAL and the individual states. It was Hughes, after all, who wrote for the five-Justice majority in HOME BUILDING & LOAN ASSOCIATION V. BLAISDELL (1934), upholding a far-reaching mortgage moratorium law that many observers found to be in flat violation of the Constitution's CONTRACT CLAUSE. He also wrote for the narrow majority in the GOLD CLAUSE CASES, where the Justices sustained the New Deal's monetary experiments over the protests of Justice JAMES C. MCREYNOLDS who declared, "This is Nero at his worst. The Constitution is gone."

The Chief Justice sided as well with Justice OWEN J. ROBERTS' views in NEBBIA V. NEW YORK (1934), which expanded the sphere of business activities subject to state regulation, and he spoke out forcefully against the crabbed interpretation of the federal commerce power in RAILROAD RETIREMENT BOARD V. ALTON RAILROAD COMPANY (1935), where five Justices voted to strike down a mandatory pension plan for railway workers. In 1935 and 1936, however, Hughes began to vote more consistently with Roberts and the Court's four conservatives—Justices McReynolds, PIERCE BUTLER, WILLIS VAN DEVANTER, and Sutherland—against the New Deal and various state reform programs.

Six months later, in the aftermath of Roosevelt's crushing reelection victory and his threats to reorganize the federal judiciary, the Court reversed gears once again when a bare majority of the Justices—including Hughes and Roberts—sustained a minimum wage law in WEST COAST HOTEL COMPANY V. PARRISH (1937) and the New Deal's major labor law in the WAGNER ACT CASES (1937). Hughes wrote both landmark opinions, the first laying to rest "liberty of contract" and the second affording Congress ample latitude to regulate labor-management conflicts under the commerce clause.

Various explanations have been advanced since the 1930s to explain both Hughes's alignment with the conservatives and his eventual return to the progressive fold in 1937. Hughes justified his behavior during the first period by casting blame upon the New Deal's lawyers, who, he complained, wrote vague, unconstitutional statutes. This thesis has some credibility with respect to the controversial NATIONAL INDUSTRIAL RECOVERY ACT which the Court invalidated in SCHECHTER POULTRY CORPORATION V. UNITED STATES (1935), but none at all when one reflects upon the care with which very good lawyers wrote both the AGRICULTURAL ADJUSTMENT ACT and the Guffey Bituminous Coal Act. (See CARTER V. CARTER COAL CO.) Others have suggested that Hughes voted with Roberts and the four conservatives on several occasions in 1935 and 1936 in order to avoid narrow 5–4 decisions that might damage the Court's reputation for constitutional sagacity. But this hypothesis does not explain why he found 5–4 decisions in favor of the New Deal any less injurious to the Court in 1937.

A more plausible explanation may be that Hughes regarded many New Deal regulatory programs and some on the state level as dangerously radical, both to the inherited constitutional system and to the social order, because of their redistributive implications. Other old progressives also fought the New Deal for similar reasons after 1935. Those who resisted the leftward drift of the administration in 1935 hoped that the electorate would repudiate Roosevelt's course of action in the 1936 referendum, but Roosevelt's landslide victory left them with few alternatives but capitulation to the popular will. In bowing to the election returns, Hughes became the leader of the Court's progressive wing once again, salvaged the basic power of JUDICIAL REVIEW, and at the same time administered a fatal blow to the President's misconceived reorganization bill. It was a stunning triumph for the Chief Justice.

Hughes accomplished this feat without serious damage to his intellectual integrity. The Justice who wrote *Miller v. Wilson* in 1915 did not find it too difficult to sustain minimum wage legislation two decades later. And the ideas expressed in *NLRB v. Jones & Laughlin* (1937) had already been given initial shape in the *Minnesota Rates Cases* and the Shreveport Case. For a Justice as brilliant and as crafty as Hughes, leading the constitutional revolution in 1937 was as easy as resisting it a year before, but the latter course assured his place in history.

MICHAEL E. PARRISH
(1986)

(SEE ALSO: *Constitutional History, 1933–1945.*)

Bibliography

FREUND, PAUL A. 1967 Charles Evan Hughes. *Harvard Law Review* 81:34–48.
HENDEL, SAMUEL 1951 *Charles Evans Hughes and the Supreme Court.* New York: Russell & Russell.
PUSEY, MERLO J. 1951 *Charles Evans Hughes.* 2 Vols. New York: Harper & Row.

HUGHES COURT
(1930–1941)

The years in which Chief Justice CHARLES EVANS HUGHES presided over the Supreme Court of the United States, 1930–1941, are notable for the skillful accomplishment of a revolution in CONSTITUTIONAL INTERPRETATION. The use of the DUE PROCESS clauses of the Fifth Amendment and FOURTEENTH AMENDMENT to protect FREEDOM OF CONTRACT and economic Darwinism against government regulation yielded to legislative supremacy and judicial self-restraint. The prevailing limits on the regulatory powers of Congress under the COMMERCE CLAUSE were swept away. The Hamiltonian view that Congress has power to spend money for any purpose associated with the general welfare was solidified by judicial approval. The Court acquiesced in the delegation of vast lawmaking power to administrative agencies. The groundwork was laid for expanding the constitutionally guaranteed FREEDOM OF SPEECH and freedom of the press.

Change was all about the Hughes Court. Of the eight Justices who flanked Hughes when he took his seat as Chief Justice, seven left the Court before he retired. The Court moved across the street from the cozy, old Senate Chamber in the Capitol to the gleaming white marble palace and ornate conference room used today. Profounder changes were occurring in the social, economic, and political conditions that give rise to constitutional litigation, that shape the briefs and arguments of counsel, and that the Court's decisions must address.

The preceding era had been marked by the rise to dominance of large-scale business and financial enterprise. Vast aggregations of men and women and material wealth were needed to develop America's resources, to harness the power unleashed by science and technology, and to capture the efficiencies of mass production for mass markets. Unlocking America's agricultural and industrial wealth made for higher standards of living and an extremely mobile society. With the gains had come corruption, hardships, injustices, and pressure for political action; but in the general prosperity of the 1920s the costs were too often ignored.

Yet the farmers were left behind and too much of the wealth was committed to speculation in corporate securities. The bursting of the latter bubble in November 1929 heralded an economic depression of unprecedented length and depth. Ninety percent of the market value of stock in industrial corporations was wiped out in three years. Twenty-five percent of the land in Mississippi was auctioned off in mortgage foreclosure sales. Factory payrolls were cut in half. One out of every four persons seeking employment was without work. The Depression destroyed people's faith in the industrial magnates and financiers, even in the ethic of individual self-reliance. The stability of American institutions seemed uncertain.

The election of FRANKLIN D. ROOSEVELT as President of the United States brought a new, more active political philosophy to government. Government, Roosevelt asserted, should seek to prevent the abuse of superior economic power, to temper the conflicts, and to work out the accommodations and adjustments that a simpler age had supposed could safely be left to individual ability and the free play of economic forces. Government should also meet the basic need for jobs and, in the case of those who could not work, for food, clothing, and shelter. For the most part these responsibilities must be met by the federal government, which alone was capable of dealing with an economy national in scope and complexity.

Roosevelt's "NEW DEAL" not only provided money and jobs for the worst victims of the Depression; it enacted the legislation and established the government agencies upon which national economic policies would rest for at least half a century: the Agricultural Adjustment Acts, the WAGNER NATIONAL LABOR RELATIONS ACT, the Fair Labor Standards Act, the Social Security Act, and the Securities and Exchange Act.

JUDICIAL REVIEW permits those who lose battles in the executive and legislative branches to carry the war to the courts. Earlier in the century many courts, including the Supreme Court, had clung to the vision of small government, economic laissez-faire, and unbounded opportunity for self-reliant individuals. Judges had thus struck down as violations of the due process clauses of the Fifth and Fourteenth Amendments many measures now generally accepted as basic to a modern industrial and urban society: MAXIMUM HOURS AND MINIMUM WAGE LAWS, laws forbidding industrial homework, and laws protecting the organization of labor unions. The critical question for the Supreme Court in the Hughes era would be whether the Court would persevere or change the course of American constitutional law.

The response of Justices WILLIS VAN DEVANTER, JAMES C. MCREYNOLDS, GEORGE SUTHERLAND, and PIERCE BUTLER was predictable: they would vote to preserve the old regime of limited federal government and economic laissez-faire. Three Justices—LOUIS D. BRANDEIS, HARLAN F. STONE, and BENJAMIN N. CARDOZO—could be expected to eschew the use of judicial power to protect economic liberty, and might not condemn broader congressional interpretation of the commerce clause. The balance rested in the hands of Chief Justice HUGHES and Justice OWEN J. ROBERTS.

At first the Court challenged the New Deal. The National Recovery Administration sought to halt the downward spiral in wages and prices by stimulating the negotiation of industry-by-industry and market-by-market codes of "fair competition" fixing minimum prices and wages and outlawing "destructive" competitive practices. In SCHECHTER POULTRY CORPORATION V. UNITED STATES (1935) the Court held the underlying legislation unconstitutional. The major New Deal measure for dealing with the plight of the farmers was held unconstitutional in UNITED STATES V. BUTLER (1936) as "a statutory plan to regulate and control agricultural production, a matter beyond the powers delegated to the federal government." CARTER

V. CARTER COAL COMPANY (1936) held that, because production was a purely local activity, Congress lacked power to legislate concerning the wages and hours of bituminous coal miners. In MOREHEAD V. NEW YORK EX REL. TIPALDO (1936) the four conservative Justices, joined by Justice Roberts, reaffirmed the 1923 decision in *Adkins v. Children's Memorial Hospital* invalidating a law fixing minimum wages for women. These opinions seemed to presage invalidation of such other fundamental New Deal measures as the National Labor Relations Act, a proposed federal wage and hour law, and even the Social Security Act.

President Roosevelt responded with strong criticism. The *Schechter* ruling, he said, was evidence that the Court was still living "in the horse and buggy age." On February 5, 1937, the President sent a special message to Congress urging enactment of a bill to create one new judgeship for every federal judge over the age of seventy who railed to retire. The message spoke of the heavy burden under which the courts—particularly the Supreme Court—were laboring, of the "delicate subject" of "aged or infirm judges," and of the need for "a constant infusion of new blood in the courts." No one doubted Roosevelt's true purpose. Six of the nine Supreme Court Justices were more than seventy years old. Six new Justices would ensure a majority ready to uphold the constitutionality of New Deal legislation. A month later the President addressed the nation more candidly, acknowledging that he hoped "to bring to the decision of social and economic problems younger men who have had personal experience and contact with modern facts and circumstances under which average men have to live and work."

Despite overwhelming popular support for New Deal legislation and despite the President's landslide reelection only a few months earlier, the Court-packing plan was defeated. The President's disingenuous explanation was vulnerable to factual criticism. Justice Brandeis, widely known as a progressive dissenter from his colleagues' conservative philosophy, joined Chief Justice Hughes in a letter to the Senate Judiciary Committee demonstrating that the Court was fully abreast of its docket and would be less efficient if converted into a body of fifteen Justices. Much of the political opposition came from conservative strongholds, but the current ran deeper. The American people had a well-nigh religious attachment to CONSTITUTIONALISM and the Supreme Court. They intuitively realized that packing the Court in order to reverse the course of its decisions would destroy its independence and erode the essence of constitutionalism. Yet no explanation is complete without recalling the contemporary quip: "A switch in time saves nine." The final defeat of the Court-packing plan came after a critical turning in the Court's own interpretation of constitutional limitations.

The shift first became manifest in WEST COAST HOTEL

COMPANY V. PARRISH (1937), a 5–4 decision upholding the constitutionality of a state statute authorizing a board to set minimum wages for women. The Chief Justice's opinion overruled the *Adkins* case and markedly loosened the standards of SUBSTANTIVE DUE PROCESS that had previously constricted regulation of contractual relations. To the old STATE POLICE POWER doctrine confining the permissible objectives of government to health, safety, and morals, the Chief Justice added broadly the "welfare of the people" and "the interests of the community." Where the old opinions declared as an abstract truth that "The employer and the employee have equality of right and any legislation that disturbs the equality is an arbitrary interference with liberty of contract," the new majority more realistically asserted that a legislature may consider the "relatively weak bargaining power of women" and may "adopt measures to reduce the evils of the "sweating system." There were also hints of greater judicial deference to legislative judgments: "regulation which is reasonable in relation to its subject and is adopted in the interests of the community is due process."

The *West Coast Hotel* case inaugurated a line of decisions sustaining every challenged economic regulation enacted by a state legislature or by the Congress. General minimum wage and maximum hour laws, price regulations, and labor relations acts—all were upheld. Even prior to Hughes's retirement, the trend was intensified by the normal replacement of all but one of the Justices who had sat with Hughes on his first day as Chief Justice. The philosophy of judicial self-restraint gradually became dominant on the Court, in the laws, and throughout the legal profession.

The troublesome problems of constitutional interpretation often call for striking a balance between the opposing ideals of democratic self-government and judicial particularization of majestic but general and undefined constitutional limitations. The philosophy of legislative supremacy and judicial self-restraint that came to dominate constitutional interpretation in the time of the Hughes Court was often asserted and widely accepted as broadly applicable to all constitutional adjudication except the enforcement of clear and specific commands. The Hughes Court thus set the stage for the central constitutional debate of the next major era in constitutional history. As claims to judicial protection of CIVIL LIBERTIES and CIVIL RIGHTS became the focus of attention, JUDICIAL ACTIVISM would be revived by substituting STRICT SCRUTINY for judicial deference in many areas of PREFERRED FREEDOMS and FUNDAMENTAL RIGHTS. Many of the new judicial activists would be liberals or progressives of the same stripe that had pressed for democratic self-government in the days when their political power confronted conservative dominance of the courts. But the opinions of the Hughes Court still mark the end of effective constitutional challenges to legislative regulation of economic activity.

The Hughes Court broke new ground in interpretation of the commerce clause only a few months after the minimum wage decision. In *National Labor Relations Board v. Jones & Laughlin Steel Corporation* (1937) the Labor Board, under authority delegated by the Wagner Act, had ordered Jones & Laughlin to reinstate four employees discharged from production and maintenance jobs in a basic steel mill because of their union activity. Both Jones & Laughlin's anti-union activities and the order for reinstatement were beyond the reach of federal power as delimited by the old line between production and interstate movement. The lower court had so decided. Led by Chief Justice Hughes, a bare majority of the Supreme Court Justices reversed that decision. Rejecting the old conceptualism that had asked whether the regulated activity had a "legal or logical connection to interstate commerce," the Court appraised the relation by "a practical judgment drawn from experience." Congress could reasonably conclude that an employer's anti-union activities and refusal to bargain collectively might result in strikes, and that a strike at a basic steel mill drawing its raw materials from, and shipping its products to, many states might in fact affect the movement of INTERSTATE COMMERCE. (See WAGNER ACT CASES.)

The *Jones & Laughlin* opinion appeared to retain some judicially enforceable constitutional check upon the congressional power under the commerce clause: "Undoubtedly the scope of this power must be considered in the light of our dual system of government and may not be extended so far as to embrace effects upon interstate commerce so indirect and remote that to embrace them, in view of our complex society, would effectually obliterate the distinction between what is national and what is local and create a completely centralized government." But the check proved illusory. The quoted admonition, while operable as a political principle guiding congressional judgment, yields no rule of law capable of judicial administration. Once the distinctions between interstate movement and production and between "direct" and "indirect" effects upon interstate commerce are rejected, the number of links in the chain of cause and effect becomes irrelevant. Federal power would reach to the local machine shop that repaired the chain saws that cut the trees that yielded the pulp wood that yielded the pulp that made the paper bought by the publisher to print the newspaper that circulated in interstate commerce. The size of the particular establishment or transaction also became irrelevant, for the cumulative effect of many small local activities might have a major impact upon interstate commerce. The new judicial deference, moreover, called for leaving such questions to Congress.

A second doctrinal development accelerated the trend. The Fair Labor Standards Act of 1938 required employers to pay workers engaged in the production of goods for shipment in interstate commerce no less than a specified minimum wage. The act also forbade shipping in interstate commerce any goods produced by workers who had not received the minimum wage. Congress claimed the power to exclude from the pipeline of interstate commerce things that would, in its judgment, do harm in the receiving state. Goods produced at substandard wages and shipped in interstate commerce might depress wages paid in the receiving states, and also in other producing states. The theory had been applied as early as 1903 to uphold a congressional law forbidding the interstate shipment of lottery tickets, but in 1918, under the doctrine barring federal regulation of production, the Court had struck down an act of Congress barring the interstate shipment of goods made with child labor. Having rejected that doctrine in the Labor Board Cases, the Hughes Court readily upheld the constitutionality of the Fair Labor Standards Act upon the theory of the lottery cases. The direct prohibition against paying less than the specified minimum wage was also upheld as a necessary and proper means of preventing goods made under substandard conditions from moving in interstate commerce and doing harm in other states. Years later similar reasoning supported broader decisions upholding the power of Congress to regulate or prohibit the local possession or use of firearms and other articles that have moved in interstate commerce.

Much more than legal logic lay behind the Hughes Court's recognition of virtually unlimited congressional power under the commerce clause. The markets of major firms had become nationwide. A complex and interconnected national economy made widely separated localities interdependent. A century earlier layoffs at the iron foundry in Saugus, Massachusetts, would have had scant visible effect in other states. During the Great Depression no one could miss the fact that layoffs at the steel mills in Pittsburgh, Pennsylvania, reduced the demand for clothing and so caused more layoffs at the textile mills in Charlotte, North Carolina, and Fall River, Massachusetts. Even as the Hughes Court deliberated the Labor Board Cases, a strike at a General Motors automobile assembly plant in Michigan was injuring automobile sales agencies in cities and towns throughout the United States.

The states were incapable of dealing with many of the evils accompanying industrialization. Many states were smaller and less powerful than the giant public utilities and industrial corporations. Massachusetts might forbid the employment of child labor, or fix a minimum wage if the due process clause permitted, but the cost of such measures was the flight of Massachusetts industries to North Carolina or South Carolina. New York might seek to ensure the welfare of its dairy farmers by setting minimum prices that handlers should pay for milk, only to watch the handlers turn to Vermont farmers who could sell at lower prices. The commerce clause barred the states from erecting protective barriers against out-of-state competition.

A shift in intellectual mode was also important. The rise of LEGAL REALISM stimulated by publication of OLIVER WENDELL HOLMES's *The Common Law* in 1881 had made it increasingly difficult for courts to find guidance in such abstractions as the equality of right between employer and employee or in such rhetorical questions as "What possible legal or logical connection is there between an employee's membership in a labor organization and the carrying on of interstate commerce?" The harsh facts of the Depression made both impossible.

The proper division of regulatory activity between the nation and the states is and may always be a much debated question of constitutional dimension. Today the question is nonetheless almost exclusively political. The Hughes Court yielded the final word to Congress.

The enormous expansion of the federal establishment that began in the 1930s and continued for half a century finds a second constitutional source in the power that Article I, section 8, grants to Congress: "to lay and collect taxes . . . and provide for the common defense and general welfare of the United States." Here, too, the key judicial precedents of the modern era are decisions of the Hughes Court.

The scope of the TAXING AND SPENDING POWER had been disputed from the beginning. Jeffersonian localists argued that the words "general welfare" encompassed only the purposes expressly and somewhat more specifically stated later in Article I. Spending for INTERNAL IMPROVEMENTS gradually became accepted practice in the political branches, but the Supreme Court had had no occasion to adjudicate the issue of constitutional power because no litigant could show that he or she had suffered the kind of particular injury that would sustain a cause of action.

The Roosevelt administration not only spent federal funds on an unprecedented scale in order to relieve unemployment; it also broke new ground in using subsidies to shape the conduct of both state governments and private persons. The Agricultural Adjustment Act of 1933 levied a tax upon processors in order to pay subsidies to farmers who would agree to reduce the acreage sown to crops. The aim was to stabilize the prices of agricultural commodities. Linking the subsidy payments to the processing tax gave the processors STANDING to challenge the tax on the ground that the payments exceeded the limits of the federal spending power. In *United States v. Butler* (1936) the Hughes Court held the act unconstitutional because conditioning the farmer's allotments upon the reduction of his planted acreage made the whole "a statutory plan to regulate and control agricultural production, a matter beyond the power delegated to the federal government."

The decision was a prime target of President Roosevelt's criticism. It aroused fears that the Hughes Court would also invalidate the Social Security Act, a key New Deal measure establishing systems of unemployment and old age and survivors insurance. The title of the act dealing with unemployment levied a federal payroll tax upon all employers of eight or more individuals but gave a credit of up to 90 percent of the federal tax for employer contributions to a state employment fund meeting federal standards specified in the act. Very few states had previously established unemployment insurance, but the act's combination of pressure and inducement proved effective. The combination was attacked as a coercive, unconstitutional invasion of the realm reserved exclusively to the states by the TENTH AMENDMENT, which, if generalized, would enable federal authorities to induce, if not indeed compel, state enactments for any purpose within the realm of state power, and generally to control state administration of state laws. In STEWARD MACHINE COMPANY V. DAVIS (1937) the five-Justice majority answered that offering a choice or even a temptation is not coercion. Spending to relieve the needs of the army of unemployed in a nationwide depression serves the general welfare, the majority continued; the spending power knows no other limitation.

In later decades congressional spending programs would grow in size, spreading from agriculture and social insurance to such areas as housing, highway construction, education, medical care, and local LAW ENFORCEMENT. Many FEDERAL GRANTS-IN-AID to both state and private institutions are conditioned upon observance of federal standards. The balance to be struck between federal standards and state autonomy is sharply debated, but in this area, as under the commerce clause, the question is now almost exclusively left to political discretion as a result of the decisions of the Hughes Court.

Questions concerning the DELEGATION OF POWER gave rise to the fourth major area of constitutional law shaped by the Hughes Court. Congress makes the laws, it is said; the executive carries out the laws; and the judiciary interprets the laws and resolves controversies between executive and legislative officials. Never quite true, this old and simple division of functions proved largely incompatible with the new role established for federal government by the Roosevelt administration. Much law, however denominated, would have to be made by executive departments or new administrative agencies authorized by Congress, such as the Securities and Exchange Commission and the Civil Aeronautics Board. Under the traditional division the

new arrangements were subject to attack as unconstitutional attempts to delegate to other agencies part of the legislative power that Congress alone can exercise.

The flow of decisions in the Hughes Court upon this question paralleled the course taken under the due process, commerce, and spending clauses. At first the majority seemed disposed to resist the new political order as in PANAMA REFINING COMPANY V. RYAN (1935) and *Schechter Poultry Corporation v. United States* (1935). Later decisions, however, reversed the initial trend. UNITED STATES V. ROCK ROYAL COOPERATIVE, Inc., (1939) is illustrative. The AGRICULTURAL MARKETING AGREEMENT ACT gave the secretary of agriculture broad authority to regulate the marketing of eight agricultural commodities, including milk, with a view to reestablishing the purchasing power of farmers at the level in a base period, usually 1909–1914. In the case of milk, however, if the secretary found the prices so determined to be unreasonable, he was authorized to fix producer prices at a level that would reflect pertinent economic conditions in local milk markets, provide an adequate supply of wholesome milk, and be in the public interest. The purported standards were numerous and broad enough to impose no significant limit upon the secretary's decisions. Nevertheless, the Court upheld the delegation. It was enough that Congress had limited the secretary's power to specified commodities, had specifically contemplated price regulation, and had provided standards by which the secretary's judgment was to be guided after hearing interested parties. The decision set the pattern for all subsequent legislative draftsmen and judicial determinations.

The contributions of the Hughes Court to the law of the FIRST AMENDMENT were less definitive than in the areas of the commerce clause, economic due process, the spending power, and delegation; but they were not less important. The Hughes Court infused the First Amendment with a new and broader vitality that still drives the expansion of the constitutional protection available to both individual speakers and institutional press.

Apart from the WORLD WAR I prosecution of pacifists and socialists for speeches and pamphlets alleged to interfere with the production of munitions or conscription for the armed forces, federal law posed few threats to freedom of expression. State laws were more restrictive. The illiberal decisions of the 1920s sustaining the prosecution of leftists under state CRIMINAL SYNDICALISM LAWS assumed that the First Amendment's guarantees against congressional abridgment of freedom of expression are, by virtue of the Fourteenth Amendment, equally applicable to the states. These OBITER DICTA encouraged constitutional attack upon state statutes, municipal ordinances, and judge-made doctrines restricting political and religious expression. In this area Chief Justice Hughes and Justice Roberts quickly allied themselves with the three Justices of established liberal reputation.

Two early opinions highlight the protection that the First and Fourteenth Amendments afford the press against previous restraints. NEAR V. MINNESOTA (1931) was decided upon appeal from a state court's injunction forbidding further publication of *The Saturday Press*, a weekly newspaper, upon the ground that it was "largely devoted to malicious, scandalous and defamatory articles." The newspaper had charged Minneapolis officials with serious offenses in tolerating gambling, bootlegging, and racketeering; the articles were scurrilous and anti-Semitic in tone and content. The decree was authorized by a Minnesota statute. Minnesota had experienced a rash of similar scandal sheets, some of whose publishers were believed to use their journals for blackmail. In an opinion by Chief Justice Hughes, the Supreme Court held that the injunction against publication was an infringement upon the liberty of the press guaranteed by the Fourteenth Amendment regardless of whether the charges were true or false. For any wrong the publisher had committed or might commit, public and private redress might be available; but this PRIOR RESTRAINT was inconsistent with the constitutional liberty.

The law's strong set against previous restraints was underscored a few years later by GROSJEAN V. AMERICAN PRESS COMPANY (1936), where a review of history led the Hughes Court to conclude that the First and Fourteenth Amendments bar not only censorship but also taxes that single out the press and are thus calculated to limit the circulation of information.

The chief danger to freedom or expression by the poor, the unorthodox, and the unpopular lies in state statutes and municipal ordinances that give local authorities wide discretion in preserving the peace and public order. Such laws not only invite suppression of unorthodox ideas by discriminatory enforcement but they also encourage self-censorship in hope of avoiding official interference. The Hughes Court laid the foundations for current constitutional doctrines narrowing the opportunities for abuse.

LOVELL V. CITY OF GRIFFIN (1938) introduced the doctrine that a law requiring a license for the use of the streets or parks for the distribution of leaflets, speeches, parades, or other forms of expression must, explicitly or by prior judicial interpretation, confine the licensing authority to considerations of traffic management, crowd control, or other physical inconvenience or menace to the public. From there it was only a short step to holding in CANTWELL V. CONNECTICUT (1941) that a man may not be punished for words or a street DEMONSTRATION, however offensive to the audience, under a broad, general rubric that invites reprisal for the expression of unorthodox views instead of requiring a narrow judgment concerning the risk of im-

mediate violence. THORNHILL V. ALABAMA (1941), once important for the ruling that peaceful PICKETING in a labor dispute is a form of expression protected by the First Amendment, also introduced the then novel and still controversial doctrine that an individual convicted under a law drawn so broadly as to cover both expression subject to regulation and constitutionally protected expression may challenge the constitutionality of the statute "on its face" even though his own conduct would not be constitutionally protected against punishment under narrower legislation. (See OVERBREADTH DOCTRINE.)

Supreme Court Justices and other constitutionalists still debate the theoretical question how far the First and Fourteenth Amendments secure individuals a right to some PUBLIC FORUM for the purposes of expression. The Hughes Court's decision in HAGUE V. CONGRESS OF INDUSTRIAL ORGANIZATIONS (1939) recognized such a right to the use of streets, parks, and like public places traditionally open for purposes of assembly, communication, and discussion of public questions: "Such use of the streets and public places has, from ancient times, been a part of the privileges, immunities, rights and liberties of citizens. The privilege . . . to use the streets and parks for communication of views on national questions may be regulated in the interest of all; . . . but must not in the guise of regulation be abridged or denied." On this ground *Schneider v. State* (1939) invalidated four city ordinances banning the use of the streets to hand out leaflets. Against this background later Justices would wrestle with the constitutional problems raised by restrictions upon house-to-house canvassing and the use of other government properties for the purpose of expression.

The Hughes Court presided over a revolution in constitutional interpretation. Many conservatives were convinced that in joining the liberal Justices, the Chief Justice and Justice Roberts unconscionably distorted the law to suit the winds of politics. Yet while the revolution is plain, the ground-breaking decisions did appreciably less violence than some reforming decisions of the later WARREN COURT and BURGER COURT to the ideal of a coherent, growing, yet continuing body of law binding the judges as well as the litigants. Doubtless the presence of two competing lines of authority in the Court's earlier decisions often made it easier for the Hughes Court to perform this part of the judicial function. Liberty of contract had never been absolute. The Court had previously sustained, in special contexts, the power of Congress to regulate local activities affecting interstate commerce. Acceptance of the Hughes Court's changes was also the easier because the Hughes Court was diminishing judicial interference with legislative innovations whereas the Warren and Burger Courts pressed far-reaching reforms without legislative support and sometimes against the will expressed by the people's elected representatives. That the old structure and powers of government should be shaped to industrialization, urbanization, and a national economy seemed more inevitable than that public schools should be integrated by busing, that prayer and Bible-reading should be banned from the public schools, or that abortion should be made a matter of personal choice. Yet even when the differences are acknowledged, much of the success of the Hughes Court in managing its revolution in constitutional interpretation seems attributable to the Chief Justice's belief in the value of a coherent, though changing, body of law, to his character, and to his talents combining the perception and sagacity drawn from an earlier, active political life with his extraordinary legal craftsmanship, earlier fine-honed as an Associate Justice.

ARCHIBALD COX
(1986)

Bibliography

ALSOP, JOSEPH and CATLEDGE, TURNER   1938   *The 168 Days.* Garden City, N.Y.: Doubleday.

JACKSON, ROBERT H.   1941   *The Struggle for Judicial Supremacy.* New York: Knopf.

MURPHY, PAUL   1972   *The Constitution in Crisis Times 1918–1969* New York: Harper & Row.

PUSEY, MERLO J.   1951   *Charles Evans Hughes.* New York: Macmillan.

STERN, ROBERT L.   1946   The Commerce Clause and the National Economy, 1933–1946. *Harvard Law Review* 59:645–693.

SWINDLER, WILLIAM F.   1970   *Court and Constitution in the Twentieth Century,* Part I. Indianapolis: Bobbs-Merrill.

HUMPHREY, HUBERT H.
(1911–1978)

Hubert Horatio Humphrey was the latest in a line of distinguished United States senators whose influence has exceeded that of many Presidents. He served as senator from Minnesota from 1948 to 1964 and from 1972 to his death, during which time he wrote over forty acts of Congress and coauthored considerably more than twice that many on subjects as diverse as children's nutrition, aid to education, nuclear disarmament, full employment, solar energy, and medicare. He led the anticommunist liberal wing of the Democratic party and cofounded its political organ, Americans for Democratic Action, whose constitution barred membership by communists and Fascists. In 1954 Humphrey wrote the COMMUNIST CONTROL ACT; his original version would have made it a crime to be a member of the party. He never spoke against Senator Joseph R. McCarthy in the Senate. Otherwise he was the quintessential liberal, involved in nearly every achievement and failure of Amer-

ican liberalism from the close of WORLD WAR II until his untimely death. He believed that government existed to serve people, the more service to the larger number of people the better.

Humphrey's finest hours were devoted to CIVIL RIGHTS. In 1948 he became a national celebrity by leading a successful fight for a strong civil rights plank in his party's platform, provoking a walkout of intransigent Southerners who formed the Dixiecrat party. In 1964, when he was party whip, he was floor manager of the battle for the passage of the CIVIL RIGHTS ACT of that year.

As thirty-eighth vice-president, Humphrey was the most unflaggingly active of any in our history. When he was his party's nominee for President in 1968, he lost the election by half a million votes because his strong support of the VIETNAM WAR cost him the allegiance of antiwar voters, and because his civil rights record cost him southern votes that went to a third party candidate.

The pell-mell, all-directions-at-once character of the Great Society mirrored Humphrey as well as President LYNDON B. JOHNSON. Humphrey was not only an effective legislator. He was probably the gabbiest, most exuberant, open-hearted person in American public life.

LEONARD W. LEVY
(1986)

Bibliography

SOLBERG, CARL   1984   *Hubert Humphrey: A Biography.* New York: Norton.

HUMPHREY'S EXECUTOR v. UNITED STATES
295 U.S. 602 (1935)

This decision probably more than any other contributed to President FRANKLIN D. ROOSEVELT's animus against the Supreme Court. As Attorney General ROBERT H. JACKSON wrote, the opinion of the unanimous Court by Justice GEORGE SUTHERLAND gave the impression "that the President had flouted the Constitution, rather than that the Court had simply changed its mind within the past ten years." In MYERS V. UNITED STATES (1926) a 6–3 Court had sustained the removal power of the President in a case involving a postmaster. Sutherland had joined the opinion of the Court, including its OBITER DICTUM that the removal power extended even to members of independent REGULATORY COMMISSIONS. Roosevelt, relying on *Myers,* removed from the Federal Trade Commission (FTC) William Humphrey, who had been reappointed for a six-year term in 1931. The FEDERAL TRADE COMMISSION ACT provided for removal for cause, including inefficiency or malfeasance.

Humphrey was a blatantly probusiness, antiadministration official who thwarted the objectives of the FTC. After he died, his executor sued for Humphrey's back pay, raising the question whether a member of an administrative tribunal created by Congress to implement legislative policies can be removed as if he were a member of the executive department. Ruling against the removal power, Sutherland distinguished *Myers*, overruled the dictum, and failed to mention that Roosevelt had acted in good faith when he relied on *Myers*. Liberal Justices joined Sutherland for the reason given privately by Justice LOUIS D. BRANDEIS: if a Huey Long were President and the administration's argument prevailed, the commissions would become compliant agents of the executive.

Despite the Court's unanimity, its strict reliance on a simplistic SEPARATION OF POWERS theory ignored the fact that the administrative agencies, however mixed their powers, were executive agencies and Congress acknowledged that fact. Moreover, had Roosevelt chosen to remove Humphrey for cause, the Court would not likely have challenged his judgment. The Court followed *Humphrey* in *Wiener v. United States* (1958), ruling that President DWIGHT D. EISENHOWER could not remove a member of a quasi-judicial agency without cause.

LEONARD W. LEVY
(1986)

HUNT, WARD
(1810–1886)

Ward Hunt, a New York judge, was appointed to the Supreme Court by ULYSSES S. GRANT in late 1872; seven years later, although permanently incapacitated by a stroke, he refused to resign until Congress passed a special retirement act in 1882. His judicial contributions were largely unexceptional and insignificant. He consistently sided with the WAITE COURT majority in supporting bondholders' claims, upholding state regulation under traditional POLICE POWER doctrines, and denying claims for racial equality under the FOURTEENTH AMENDMENT.

Hunt also upheld claims of immunity from federal taxation for states or their instrumentalities. (See INTERGOVERNMENTAL IMMUNITY.) Earlier, in COLLECTOR V. DAY (1871), the Court had exempted state judges from the federal income tax. In one of his first opinions, Hunt treated municipally financed railroads as state agencies and as similarly exempt. "Their operation," he said in *United States v. Railroad Co.* (1873), "may be impeded and may be destroyed, if any interference is permitted." A few years later he dissented from the nationalistic holding in PENSACOLA TELEGRAPH CO. V. WESTERN UNION TELEGRAPH CO. (1877), in which the majority held that states could not

interfere with telegraph lines established under federal law. Hunt, however, insisted that federal authority extended only to lands in the public domain.

Hunt usually followed his colleagues in ruling against claims advancing Negro rights. But in UNITED STATES V. REESE (1876) he alone dissented to support the constitutionality of the FORCE ACT (1870) which was designed to implement the FIFTEENTH AMENDMENT. Hunt interpreted the amendment as guaranteeing "the right to vote in its broadest terms" for all citizens, an all elections, state as well as federal. The majority had refused to sanction federal interference against acts of individual state officers who had refused on their own account to allow blacks to vote. For Hunt, it was obvious that such individual acts were tantamount to state action and subject to federal restraint. The word "state" in the Fifteenth Amendment, he maintained, included "the acts of all those who proceed under [a state's] ... authority." The *Reese* decision reflected the growing national consensus for sectional reconciliation which inevitably meant abandonment of national protection for the freedmen's CIVIL RIGHTS. Hunt acknowledged this mood and he recognized that the majority's decision "brings to an impotent conclusion the vigorous amendments on the subject of slavery." Yet he silently acquiesced later that term in the further emasculation of the Force Act in UNITED STATES V. CRUIKSHANK (1876).

Hunt's fleeting concern for guaranteeing black suffrage did not extend to women. On circuit in 1873, he presided at the trial of SUSAN B. ANTHONY, who had voted in the 1872 presidential election in New York despite a state constitutional requirement limiting the franchise to men. Anthony claimed that the state denied her the PRIVILEGES AND IMMUNITIES guaranteed under the Fourteenth Amendment. Hunt flatly denied the argument. He invoked the reasoning of the recent SLAUGHTERHOUSE CASES (1873) and held that such regulations, however unjust, were under the absolute domain of the state. Hunt directed a guilty verdict, refused to poll the jury, and fined Anthony $100. The sentence was not enforced, and there was no APPEAL to the Supreme Court.

Hunt was a hard-working able craftsman during his brief career on the Court (1873–1882) but he had little apparent influence on his brethren or on constitutional law.

STANLEY I. KUTLER
(1986)

Bibliography

FAIRMAN, CHARLES 1971 *Reconstruction and Reunion, 1864–1888*. Volume 6 of the *Oliver Wendell Holmes Devise History of the Supreme Court of the United States*. New York: Macmillan.

MAGRATH, C. PETER 1963 *Morrison R. Waite: The Triumph of Character.* New York: Macmillan.

HUNTER v. ERICKSON
393 U.S. 385 (1969)

In a perverse application of the EQUAL PROTECTION clause, an 8–1 Supreme Court struck down an amendment to the Akron, Ohio, city charter subjecting any council-passed OPEN HOUSING LAW to a REFERENDUM before it could take effect and requiring a referendum on an open housing law previously enacted.

Six Justices, speaking through BYRON R. WHITE, found in the referendum requirement an "explicitly racial classification," although they conceded that it drew "no distinctions among racial and religious groups." The majority argued that the charter amendment, by making open housing laws harder to enact, "disadvantaged those who would benefit" from such laws—and presumed that the potential beneficiaries were the members of ethnic and religious minorities. The FOURTEENTH AMENDMENT was held to protect minorities against barriers to enactment of favorable legislation.

Justice HUGO L. BLACK dissented, contending that referenda were part of the democratic political process and that advocates of particular types of legislation were not constitutionally disadvantaged merely because they might lose an election.

DENNIS J. MAHONEY
(1986)

HURD v. HODGE

See: *Shelley v. Kraemer*

HURLEY v. IRISH-AMERICAN GAY, LESBIAN, AND BISEXUAL GROUP OF BOSTON
515 U.S. 557 (1995)

The City of Boston authorized the South Boston Allied War Veterans Council to organize the annual St. Patrick's Day Parade. The Council refused a place in the parade to the Irish-American Gay, Lesbian, and Bisexual Group of Boston (GLIB), an organization formed for the purpose of expressing its members' pride in their Irish heritage as openly gay, lesbian, and bisexual individuals. GLIB filed suit claiming that this refusal violated a Massachusetts law prohibiting discrimination on account of SEXUAL ORIENTATION in places of PUBLIC ACCOMMODATION. The state courts sustained this claim, but the Supreme Court, in a unanimous opinion by Justice DAVID H. SOUTER, held that the application of the statute in this context violated the FIRST AMENDMENT rights of the council.

The Court explained that, because "every participating unit affects the message conveyed by the private organizers," the application of the statute in this situation effectively required the council "to alter the expressive content" of its parade. The Court declared that "this use of the State's power" violates "the fundamental rule" that "a speaker has the autonomy to choose the content of his own message." Thus, if the council "objects," for example, to GLIB's implicit assertion that homosexuals and bisexuals are entitled to full and equal "social acceptance," it has a right "not to propound" this message.

The Court distinguished PRUNEYARD SHOPPING CENTER V. ROBINS (1980), in which the Court had held that a state could constitutionally require the owner of a private shopping center to permit individuals to circulate petitions on the grounds of the shopping center. The Court explained that, unlike the council, the owner of a shopping center (1) is "running 'a business establishment that is open to the public,'" and (2) could more easily "'expressly disavow any connection with the message by simply posting signs in the areas where the speakers or handbillers stand.'"

GEOFFREY R. STONE
(2000)

(SEE ALSO: *Compelled Speech; Freedom of Speech; Freedom of Assembly and Association.*)

HURON PORTLAND CEMENT COMPANY v. DETROIT
362 U.S. 440 (1960)

In a case involving a major COMMERCE CLAUSE issue, a 7–2 Supreme Court sustained Detroit's Smoke Abatement Code. That city sued a Michigan manufacturer operating ships in INTERSTATE COMMERCE for violating its air pollution regulations. The manufacturer stressed its adherence to congressional regulations, claiming that Detroit could not impose stricter standards. Justice POTTER STEWART's opinion, devoted primarily to rejecting claims that federal laws had preempted the field, accorded a high priority to the STATE POLICE POWER. Exercise of that power must stand unless clearly discriminatory or violative of national uniformity, and nothing "suggest[s] the existence of any . . . competing or conflicting local regulations."

DAVID GORDON
(1986)

HURST, J. WILLARD
(1911–1997)

James Willard Hurst was perhaps the outstanding twentieth-century figure in American legal historiography. Educated at the Harvard Law School, Hurst clerked for Justice LOUIS D. BRANDEIS on the U.S. Supreme Court, and then joined the faculty of the University of Wisconsin Law School in 1937, where he remained until his retirement.

In a series of path-breaking works, Hurst virtually created the field of American legal history. The little work done on the subject before he began to produce his own work had been written from the "internal" (lawyer's) standpoint—it was concerned with DOCTRINES and case law almost exclusively, and had few points of contact with mainstream historical writing. Hence, *The Growth of American Law: The Law Makers* (1950) was a revolutionary book. It announced that the "most creative, driving, and powerful pressures upon our law emerged from the social setting"; and in chapters on the legislature, the courts, the bar, and the executive branch, proceeded to flesh out and illustrate this thesis through an examination of the institutions that actually made law in the United States.

In *Law and the Conditions of Freedom in the Nineteenth-Century United States* (1956), originally a series of lectures at Northwestern University, Hurst described nineteenth-century American law as essentially developmental—as animated by the desire to "release . . . individual creative energy," stimulating the economy and establishing a vigorous market system. Americans, in other words, used law instrumentally, to further agreed-upon or dominant goals, mostly economic. In his most elaborate work, *Law and Economic Growth* (1964), Hurst produced an exhaustive and fine-grained case study to illustrate his general approach, using the legal history of one industry (lumber) in one state (Wisconsin), in the period 1835–1915. Later works included *A Legal History of Money in the United States* (1973) and *Law and Markets in United States History* (1982).

Hurst was the founder of what came to be called the Wisconsin school of legal history. He influenced a whole generation of younger historians. He directed and inspired a series of monographic studies of Wisconsin law in the nineteenth century—an emphasis on the state and local, and on everyday processes of law, which helped to cement the relationship between legal history and the emerging fields of economic and social history.

Hurst himself was a member of the NEW DEAL generation; he deplored what he saw as aimlessness and drift in public life and public policy in the generations before the New Deal. His scholarly work, however, though strikingly original, was exceptionally rigorous and meticulous. It influenced not only legal historians, but also scholars in other fields who studied the relationship of law and society.

LAWRENCE M. FRIEDMAN
(2000)

Bibliography

HURST, J. WILLARD 1950 *The Growth of American Law: The Law Makers.* Boston: Little, Brown.
—— 1956 *Law and the Conditions of Freedom in the Nineteenth-Century United States.* Madison: University of Wisconsin Press.
—— 1964 *Law and Economic Growth: The Legal History of the Lumber Industry in Wisconsin, 1836–1915.* Cambridge, Mass.: The Belknap Press of Harvard University Press.
—— 1970 *The Legitimacy of the Business Corporation in the Law of the United States, 1780–1970.* Charlottesville: University Press of Virginia.

HURTADO v. CALIFORNIA
110 U.S. 516 (1884)

DUE PROCESS OF LAW reached a watershed in *Hurtado.* For centuries due process had stood for a cluster of specific procedures associated especially with TRIAL BY JURY. Sir EDWARD COKE, for example, explicitly associated due process with INDICTMENT by GRAND JURY. The BILL OF RIGHTS enumerated many of the rights that the concept of due process spaciously accommodated. The FOURTEENTH AMENDMENT's due process clause was copied verbatim from the Fifth Amendment, where the same clause sat cheek-by-jowl with a number of specific guarantees that due process had embodied as a COMMON LAW concept. The framers of the Fifth Amendment had added the due process clause as an additional assurance, a rhetorical flourish, and a genuflection toward the traditions of MAGNA CARTA. In *Hurtado,* the Supreme Court began to whittle away at the conventional meanings of PROCEDURAL DUE PROCESS and did not pause until MOORE V. DEMPSEY (1923).

California tried and convicted Hurtado on an INFORMATION for murder, filed by his prosecutor. He claimed that because the state had denied him indictment by grand jury, it had violated the due process clause of the Fourteenth Amendment. The Court, sustaining the conviction, 7–1, rejected Hurtado's claim on the ground that "any legal proceeding" that protects "liberty and justice" is due process. Justice STANLEY MATTHEWS, for the Court, reasoned that the Constitution, having been framed for an undefined and expanding future, must recognize new procedures. To hold otherwise, he said, would render the Constitution "incapable of progress and improvement. It would be to stamp upon our jurisprudence the unchange-ableness attributed to the Medes and the Persians. . . ." Matthews also argued that no part of the Constitution was superfluous; the fact that the Fifth Amendment included both a guarantee of grand jury proceedings in federal prosecutions and the guarantee of due process showed that the latter did not mean the former.

Justice JOHN MARSHALL HARLAN, dissenting, had history on his side when he found grand jury proceedings to be an indispensable requisite of due process, but whether history should have disposed of the question is a different issue. Harlan did not think that prosecuting individuals for their lives by information inaugurated a new era of progress in the constitutional law of CRIMINAL PROCEDURE. The Court's inexorable logic, he asserted, as if asserting the unthinkable, would lead to the conclusion that due process did not even guarantee the traditional trial by jury. Later cases justified his fears. (See MAXWELL V. DOW.)

LEONARD W. LEVY
(1986)

HUSTLER MAGAZINE AND LARRY FLYNT v. JERRY FALWELL
485 U.S. 46 (1988)

On first glance, this appears to be a case in which the FIRST AMENDMENT ran amok because the Supreme Court extended its constitutional protection to a malevolent and disgusting LIBEL that in no way expressed an opinion or an idea. *Hustler Magazine*, which caters to prurient interests, published a parody of an advertisement in which Jerry Falwell, a nationally syndicated television preacher and head of a political organization called The Moral Majority, was purportedly interviewed. By innuendo, the parody suggested that his first experience with sexual intercourse was with his mother in an outhouse when he was drunk. At the bottom of the page in small print was a disclaimer, "ad parody—not to be taken seriously."

Falwell sued for DAMAGES, claiming libel and the intentional infliction of emotional distress. A jury found for him on the issue of emotional distress but against him on the libel claim because the parody could not reasonably be understood to describe actual facts. *Hustler* appealed the verdict on the emotional distress issue, arguing that the "actual malice" standard of NEW YORK TIMES V. SULLIVAN (1964) must be met before one could recover for emotional distress. The Fourth Circuit sustained the verdict on ground that the *Sullivan* standard had been met because *Hustler* acted recklessly. Unanimously, the Supreme Court sustained *Hustler* in an opinion by Chief Justice WILLIAM H. REHNQUIST.

His opinion makes little sense unless one understands that the dispositive fact was the trial jury's refusal to find that *Hustler* had libeled Falwell. One might think that if the parody was not believable, it was false, and if it was false and recklessly published with malice, the *Sullivan* standard had been met; but the Court took as decisive the jury's finding that *Hustler* had not published a libel because no one would reasonably believe the parody described a fact. Accordingly, the question before the Court was not whether Falwell's reputation had been maliciously and recklessly libeled. Rather, the question was whether his emotional distress overcame a First Amendment protection for offensive speech calculated to inflict psychological injury, "even when that speech could not reasonably have been interpreted as stating actual facts about the public figure involved."

In response to this question, Rhenquist discoursed on the importance of the First Amendment to the free flow of "ideas and opinions" and the need for "robust debate" concerning PUBLIC FIGURES involved in important public issues. One might read this section of the opinion as a parody of the Court's great free-speech opinions, for nothing in *Hustler*'s alleged interview with Falwell related to any public issues or reflected the expresison of ideas or opinions. The interview reflected slime and sleaze.

More persuasive was Rehnquist's argument that to hold that public figures or public officials might recover damages for the infliction of emotional distress might mean that "political cartoonists and satirists would be subjected to damages awards without any showing that their work falsely defamed its subject." Nevertheless, Thomas Nast's depictions of the Tweed Ring or Herblock's of Richard Nixon seem wholly different from *Hustler*'s of Falwell; *Hustler* carried no ring of truth and addressed no issues other than, broadly speaking, Falwell's moral character. The outrageousness of the allegation against him places it apart from traditional political cartooning and satire, but the Court was unable to make distinctions. It relied on the *Sullivan* standard by concluding that a public figure victimized by a publication inflicting emotional injury could not recover damages without showing false facts published with actual malice.

Justice BYRON R. WHITE in an inch of space, separately concurring, noted that as he saw the case, the *Sullivan* precedent was irrelevant because the jury found that the *Hustler* parody contained no assertion of fact. That being so, one may conclude that the Court correctly decided that the First Amendment barred Falwell from recovering damages on the sole ground that he had suffered emotional distress.

LEONARD W. LEVY
(1992)

HUTCHINSON, THOMAS
(1711–1780)

Thomas Hutchinson, described by his biographer, Bernard Bailyn, as "the most distinguished, as well as the most loyal, colonial-born official of his time," was the leading exponent of "Tory" constitutional theory at the outbreak of the AMERICAN REVOLUTION. Hutchinson was not a political theorist, however, but a practical politician who turned to theory in order to justify his actions.

Hutchinson was the leader of the wealthy, interrelated clique that ruled Massachusetts in the eighteenth century. Although he was born in Boston, his loyalty was always to the ministry in England, and he defended his policies by appealing to the most extreme doctrines of royal and parliamentary supremacy. During his career he held every important office in the colony, and at one point (in 1763) he was simultaneously lieutenant governor, chief justice of the Supreme Court, president of the Council, and judge of probate.

In 1761 Hutchinson, as Chief Justice, presided over the PAXTON'S CASE, in which the Superior Court was asked to issue GENERAL WARRANTS to authorize searches by customs officials. He personally opposed the use of WRITS OF ASSISTANCE and as lieutenant governor had argued against their issuance on the governor's authority, but as a judge Hutchinson rejected the argument of JAMES OTIS that such writs were illegal under the COMMON LAW. It was sufficient that writs of assistance were valid in English law and that Parliament had, by statute, authorized their use in the colonies, and so the writs were issued.

Hutchinson became acting governor of Massachusetts in 1769 and governor in 1771. He was temperamentally unsuited for the position in so critical a time. When the policies he pursued became so unpopular that the Assembly would not appropriate money to pay his salary, Hutchinson secured for himself a special salary paid by the British crown. To insure that the courts would remain loyal to the British government he arranged that the judges' salaries, too, should be paid by the crown. These moves, which rendered the executive and judicial powers independent of the legislature and of the citizens, enraged public opinion.

Responding defiantly, Hutchinson summoned the General Court and, on January 6, 1773, delivered an address that spelled out his understanding of the principles of Anglo-American constitutionalism. The British Empire and Massachusetts's place in it, he argued, required the absolute and indivisible SOVEREIGNTY of the king-in-Parliament. The power of the British Parliament was unlimited and illimitable, but, since Parliament represented all British subjects, both in Britain and in the colonies, that power would necessarily be used benignly and humanely. As the

American colonies were too weak to survive without British protection, the freedom of Americans depended upon their acceptance of absolute parliamentary authority. Hutchinson refused to concede the possibility that the General Court of Massachusetts exercised a separate legislative authority. "No line," he argued, "can be drawn between the supreme authority of Parliament and the total independence of the colonies."

If Hutchinson expected the address to quell criticism he was seriously mistaken. The effect was rather to enhance the standing of the most radical leaders of the opposition. The task of preparing the Assembly's response fell to SAMUEL ADAMS, the leader of the popular party and Hutchinson's chief rival. The Assembly adopted a resolution accepting, for argument's sake, Hutchinson's position that there could be no middle ground between absolute parliamentary authority and colonial autonomy. But the conclusion drawn was the opposite of Hutchinson's. The Assembly claimed that Massachusetts was a realm separate from Britain, sharing a common executive—the king—but with its own legislature. Only the General Court, and not Parliament, could legislate for Massachusetts.

Hutchinson was only reluctantly an enemy of his fellow colonists. He opposed many of the measures adopted by the British government, including the Sugar Act and the STAMP ACT. But Hutchinson's objections were prudential, not constitutional. He never doubted Parliament's right to legislate for the colonies, however disastrous the exercise of that right, or his own duty to obey and enforce such legislation.

After being forced in 1774 to flee to England, Hutchinson endured the six years until his death as a lonely pensioner of the crown. His career had a deep, if negative, influence on American constitutional thought: it was proof of the evils of plural office-holding and of an executive not dependent on the people's representatives for his pay. His outspoken insistence on the indivisibility of sovereignty helped to impel the formation of American theories of FEDERALISM.

DENNIS J. MAHONEY
(1986)

Bibliography

BAILYN, BERNARD 1974 *The Ordeal of Thomas Hutchinson.* Cambridge, Mass.: Harvard University Press.

HUTCHINSON, THOMAS 1936 *History of the Colony of Massachusetts Bay.* Cambridge, Mass.: Harvard University Press.

HUTCHINSON v. PROXMIRE
443 U.S. 111 (1979)

This decision reaffirmed a line first drawn in GRAVEL V. UNITED STATES (1972) between official and unofficial communications by members of Congress. Senator William Proxmire gave one Dr. Hutchinson a "Golden Fleece" award for what Proxmire considered to be wasteful government-sponsored research conducted by Dr. Hutchinson. Proxmire publicized the award through a press release and a newsletter to constituents. Under the Supreme Court's interpretation of the SPEECH OR DEBATE CLAUSE, members of Congress are absolutely immune from suit only for legislative acts. In *Hutchinson*, the Court found that Proxmire's communications were not "essential to the deliberations of the Senate" and, therefore, were not legislative acts protected from libel actions by the speech or debate clause.

THEODORE EISENBERG
(1986)

HYDE AMENDMENT

Beginning in 1976, Congress adopted a series of measures (amendments to appropriation bills, and JOINT RESOLUTIONS) prohibiting the use of any federal funds in the Medicaid program to pay for the costs of ABORTIONS. These provisions were known collectively as the "Hyde Amendment," after their original sponsor, Representative Henry J. Hyde of Illinois.

All versions of the amendment contained exceptions permitting federal funding of an abortion when the woman's pregnancy endangered her life. Some of them also permitted funding of abortions when pregnancies resulted from rape or incest. One version included still another exception when two physicians determined that "severe and long-lasting physical health damage to the mother would result" from a full-term pregnancy.

The Medicaid program was designed to provide federal financial assistance to states that reimbursed needy persons for medical treatment. Funds were provided for reimbursing the expenses of childbirth—at an average cost per recipient around nine times the cost of abortions. Some states continued to provide funds for needy women's abortions. In other states, the effect of the Hyde Amendment was to deny to poor women the financial assistance they needed to exercise the constitutional right recognized in ROE V. WADE (1973): to decide whether to terminate their pregnancies. Critics argued that the amendment was an unconstitutional WEALTH DISCRIMINATION, but the Supreme Court upheld its validity, 5–4, in HARRIS V. MCRAE (1980).

KENNETH L. KARST
(1986)

Bibliography

PERRY, MICHAEL J. 1980 Why the Supreme Court Was Plainly Wrong in the Hyde Amendment Case: A Brief Comment on *Harris v. McRae. Stanford Law Review* 32:1113–1128.

HYLTON v. UNITED STATES
3 Dallas 171 (1796)

The first case in which the Supreme Court passed on the constitutionality of an act of Congress, *Hylton* stands for the principle that the only DIRECT TAXES are taxes on land and CAPITATION TAXES. The Constitution provides that no capitation "or other direct tax" be imposed except in proportion to the population of the states, but that "all duties, IMPOSTS and EXCISES" be levied uniformly, that is, at the same rate. Congress imposed a uniform tax of $16 on all carriages (horse-drawn coaches), despite protests that the tax should have been apportioned among the states according to the census. When Congress levied a direct tax it fixed the total amount of money it intended to raise, so that in a state with ten percent of the nation's population, the parties taxed (carriage-owners) would have paid ten percent of the total. Thus, if a tax on carriages were a direct tax, the amount raised in two states of equal population would be the same, but if one state had twice as many carriages as the other, the tax rate in that state would be twice as great. The contention in this case was that the carriage tax was unconstitutional because it was a direct tax uniformly levied.

The case seems to have been contrived to obtain a Court ruling on the constitutionality of Congress's tax program. To meet the requirement that federal JURISDICTION attached only if the amount in litigation came to $2,000, Hylton deposed that he owned 125 carriages for his private use, each of which was subject to a $16 tax; if he lost the case, however, his debt would be discharged by paying just $16. The United States paid his counsel, ALEXANDER HAMILTON, who defended the tax program he had sponsored as secretary of the treasury. Notwithstanding the farcical aspects of the case, its significance cannot be overestimated: if a tax on carriages were indirect and therefore could be uniform, Congress would have the utmost flexibility in determining its tax policies. As Justice SAMUEL CHASE said, "The great object of the Constitution was to give Congress a power to lay taxes adequate to the exigencies of government." Justice WILLIAM PATERSON, having been a member of the CONSTITUTIONAL CONVENTION OF 1787, explained why the rule of apportionment applied only to capitation and land taxes, making all other taxes indirect taxes. The judgment of the Court was unanimous.

LEONARD W. LEVY
(1986)

ILLEGAL ALIENS

See: Alien; Immigration and Alienage

ILLEGAL IMMIGRATION REFORM AND IMMIGRANT RESPONSIBILITY ACT
110 Stat. 3009 (1996)

The Illegal Immigration Reform and Immigrant Responsibility Act of 1996 adopted major new restrictions in both substantive immigration law and immigration procedure and raised numerous constitutional questions. PROCEDURAL DUE PROCESS issues arose from its authorization of "expedited removal" of unadmitted ALIENS by individual immigration inspectors after rudimentary hearings and without administrative or JUDICIAL REVIEW. The act's limitations on judicial review of decisions ordering removal of permanent residents have been challenged as violating ARTICLE III and the prohibition in Article I, section 9 against suspending HABEAS CORPUS. Its provisions imposing mandatory detention of aliens pending removal proceedings implicated not only personal liberty but also rights to humane conditions of confinement. Together with the Personal Responsibility and Work Opportunity Reconciliation Act of 1996, the statute denied many government benefits to lawful residents, and authorized the states to do so in a manner that was questionable under prior EQUAL PROTECTION doctrines concerning IMMIGRATION AND ALIENAGE.

GERALD L. NEUMAN
(2000)

Bibliography
SYMPOSIUM 1997 Lady Liberty's Doorstep: Status and Implications of American Immigration Law. *Connecticut Law Review* 29:1395–1711.

ILLEGITIMACY

The Anglo-American law of illegitimacy derives from two interrelated purposes of our institutional progenitors. First, imposing the legal disabilities of illegitimacy on a child was seen as a punishment of the parents for their sin. More importantly, the law of legitimacy supported a system of male control over economic resources. The chief effect of the principle of bastardy-as-punishment was to disable illegitimate children from making claims against their deceased fathers' estates. Similarly, formal marriage was the only basis for a woman's claim to inherit from the man who fathered her children. Thus the punishment was reserved for unmarried women and their children. Unmarried fathers, far from being punished, were strengthened in their power to control the transmission of wealth and status. As the Supreme Court began to recognize in two 1968 decisions, these themes are modern as well as medieval.

The cases were LEVY V. LOUISIANA and *Glona v. American Guarantee & Liability Insurance Co.* On EQUAL PROTECTION grounds, the Court invalidated provisions of Louisiana's wrongful death statute that allowed damages to a surviving child for the death of a parent, and vice versa, only in cases of legitimate parentage. From that time forward, most of the Court's decisions on illegitimacy have dealt with laws regulating inheritance by illegitimate children (especially from their fathers), and laws restricting the right to death damages or benefits in cases of illegitimacy. Both in their results and in their doctrinal explanations, these decisions have pursued a crooked path.

Much of the early doctrinal uncertainty surrounded the question of the appropriate STANDARD OF REVIEW. *Levy* and *Glona* purported to apply the RATIONAL BASIS standard, but in fact they represented a more demanding judicial scrutiny. There were good reasons for categorizing illegitimacy as a SUSPECT CLASSIFICATION that would demand STRICT SCRUTINY of the state's asserted justifications. As the Court has said more than once, it is "illogical and unjust" to burden innocent children because their parents have not married. The status of illegitimacy is out of the child's control. Illegitimates have suffered historic disadvantage. The status has been the centuries-old source of stigma; such legislative classifications are apt to be the result of habit, prejudice, and stereotype rather than serious attention to public needs. After a series of cases characterized by doctrinal instability, in *Mathews v. Lucas* (1976) the Court rejected the assimilation of illegitimacy to the suspect classifications category. The Court did remark, however, that its standard of review in such cases was "not a toothless one."

Part of the reason for the tortuous doctrinal path from *Levy* and *Glona* to *Mathews v. Lucas* was that the Justices were closely divided on the general issue of the Court's approach to illegitimacy as a legislative classification; in these circumstances, trifling factual distinctions tended to affect the decisions of cases. Even after *Mathews v. Lucas* this pattern continued, as TRIMBLE V. GORDON (1977) and LALLI V. LALLI (1978) illustrate—although the Court has identified a verbal formula for its standard of review: An illegitimacy classification must be "substantially related to a permissible state interest." As Justice LEWIS F. POWELL said for a plurality in *Lalli*, the Court's concern for the plight of illegitimates must be measured against a state's interest in "the just and orderly disposition of property at death." A seventeenth century probate lawyer would not be surprised to learn that the justice and order emerging from *Lalli* offered protection for a father's estate against the claims of illegitimate children, even though paternity had been established beyond question.

The Supreme Court has invoked its intermediate standard of review to invalidate state laws imposing severe time restrictions on suits to establish paternity and compel fathers to support children born outside marriage. But if *Lalli* validated an ancient tradition of domination through control over the transmission of wealth and status, *Parham v. Hughes* (1978), just four months later, validated the tradition of the illegitimacy relation as punishment for sin. An illegitimate child and his mother were killed in an automobile accident. State law would have allowed only the mother to sue for wrongful death damages, if she had survived. Given the mother's death, the father would have been entitled to bring the suit if he had formally legitimated the child. Although he had not undertaken formal legitimation proceedings, the father had signed the child's birth certificate, and had supported the child and visited him regularly; the child had taken the father's name. The Court upheld the state's denial of a right to sue, 6–3.

The state court in *Parham* had said the law was a means of "promoting a legitimate family unit" and "setting a standard of morality." The *Parham* dissenters, focusing on SEX DISCRIMINATION, faulted the state for doing its promoting and standard-setting selectively, along lines defined by gender. The decision also intruded seriously on the FREEDOM OF INTIMATE ASSOCIATION. The father-son relationship was complete in every sense but the formal one. Four members of the majority said it was all right, nevertheless, for the state to "express its 'condemnation of irresponsible liaisons beyond the bounds of marriage'" by denying the father the right to damages for the death of his son. In other words, the father should be ashamed of himself.

In *Glona*, the Court had rejected precisely this sort of reasoning. The fact that the legislature was "dealing with sin," the Court said, could not justify so arbitrary a discrimination as the denial of wrongful death damages. *Glona* had involved the claim of a mother, and mothers of illegitimate children have been the historic victims of a system of illegitimacy in a way that fathers have not. But *Parham* involved a man who not only sired a child but was a father to him. What had been protected in *Glona* was not merely the damages claim of a mother, but the status of the intimate relationship between a mother and her son. The *Parham* law's arbitrariness lay in its assumption that significant incidents of the parent-child relationship should be denied because of the absence of a formal marriage. Seen in this light, the law's discrimination demands some substantial justification for its invasion of the freedom of intimate association. *Glona* teaches that the required justification is not to be found in the state's wish to punish "sin." The Supreme Court plainly is not yet prepared to hold that the status of illegitimacy is itself constitutionally defective. When that day arrives, however, *Glona* will serve as a precedent.

KENNETH L. KARST
(1986)

(SEE ALSO: *Nonmarital Children*.)

Bibliography

PERRY, MICHAEL J. 1979 Modern Equal Protection: A Conceptualization and Reappraisal. *Columbia Law Review* 79:1023–1084.
WALLACH, ALETA and TENOSO, PATRICIA 1974 A Vindication of

the Rights of Unmarried Mothers and Their Children: An Analysis of the Institution of Illegitimacy, Equal Protection, and the Uniform Parentage Act. *University of Kansas Law Review* 23:23–90.

ILLINOIS v. GATES
462 U.S. 213 (1983)

This decision revived pre-WARREN COURT law of the FOURTH AMENDMENT concerning SEARCH WARRANTS issued on IN-FORMANTS' TIPS. Justice WILLIAM H. REHNQUIST for a six-member majority declared, "we . . . abandon the "two pronged test' established by our decisions in *Aguilar* and *Spinelli*. In its place we reaffirm the totality of circum-stances analysis that traditionally had informed PROBABLE CAUSE determination." In AGUILAR V. TEXAS (1962) the Court had developed a test to govern a magistrate's prob-able cause hearing to determine whether a warrant should issue. Although HEARSAY information (an informer's tip not reflecting the personal knowledge of the police) may un-derlie an officer's affadavit for a warrant, the officer must also explain his belief that the informant is trustworthy or that his information is reliable. SPINELLI V. UNITED STATES (1969) made the magistrate's hearing a mini-trial con-trolled by strict rules of EVIDENCE; the Court insisted on a degree of corroboration that proved the truthfulness of a tip apart from any evidence that might subsequently verify it. In effect the Court had escalated the constitutional re-quirement of probable cause to reasonably certain cause in order to insure that a magistrate could evaluate all facts and allegations for himself. *Aguilar-Spinelli* meant that al-though the police secured a warrant based on a tip and their search uncovered evidence of crime, that evidence could be suppressed and a conviction set aside if a court later decided that the magistrate should not have issued the warrant. In *Illinois v. Gates* Rehnquist recalled that probable cause is founded on practical, nontechnical con-siderations and that magistrates should apply flexible stan-dards based on all circumstances rather than on a rigid set of rules. Justice WILLIAM J. BRENNAN, dissenting, declared that the majority opinion reflected "an overly permissive attitude towards police practices" contrary to Fourth Amendment rights.

LEONARD W. LEVY
(1986)

ILLINOIS v. PERKINS
496 U.S. 292 (1990)

An eight-member majority of the Supreme Court held that the RIGHT AGAINST SELF-INCRIMINATION is not abridged when prisoners incriminate themselves in statements vol-untarily made to a cellmate who is an undercover officer. Justice ANTHONY M. KENNEDY for the Court reasoned that the officer posing as a prisoner did not have to give *Mi-randa* warnings before asking questions that sought in-criminating responses because Perkins, although in custody, was not in a coercive situation when he boasted to his cellmate about a murder. He spoke freely to a fellow inmate. He was tricked, but the MIRANDA RULES prohibit coercion, not deception. Any statement freely made with-out compelling influences is admissible in evidence. The Court also held that because the prisoner had not yet been charged for the crime that was the subject of the inter-rogation, the RIGHT TO COUNSEL had not yet come into play. Therefore, the prisoner suffered no violation of his Sixth Amendment right. Justice WILLIAM J. BRENNAN who con-curred separately, agreed completely on the Fifth Amend-ment issue, but believed that the police deception raised a question of DUE PROCESS OF LAW.

Justice THURGOOD MARSHALL, the lone dissenter, con-tended that because the prisoner was in custody, the in-terrogation should not have occurred without Miranda warnings. He believed that the Court had carved out of *Miranda* an undercover-agent exception.

LEONARD W. LEVY
(1992)

(SEE ALSO: *Miranda v. Arizona; Police Interrogation and Confes-sions.*)

ILLINOIS v. RODRIGUEZ
497 U.S. 177 (1990)

This is another in a growing list of recent decisions that circumscribe the protections of the FOURTH AMENDMENT. In this case, a woman who made a criminal complaint against Rodriguez accompanied police to his apartment where they might arrest him. She had a key, claimed to be a cotenant, and consented to their entrance. IN PLAIN VIEW, they found EVIDENCE of his possession of illegal drugs, and a state court convicted him for the narcotics violation. The facts showed that the woman was no longer a cotenant and possessed the key without Rodriguez's knowledge. The Court held that even if the police receive permission to search a home from one who does not have authority to grant consent, the SEARCH AND SEIZURE is reasonable if the police act in the good-faith belief that they have received consent from one entitled to give it.

The liberal trio of Justices, led by THURGOOD MARSHALL, dissented from Justice ANTONIN SCALIA's opinion for a six-member majority. Marshall asserted that THIRD-PARTY CON-SENT must be more than "reasonable"; it must be based on actual authority to give consent because one possesses a legitimate expectation of privacy in the home. Absent a voluntary limitation on one's expectation of privacy, the police should not be able to dispense with the Fourth Amendment's requirement of a SEARCH WARRANT. The majority had extended the exceptions to the warrant requirement by broadening the concept of a CONSENT SEARCH.

LEONARD W. LEVY
(1992)

IMBLER v. PACHTMAN
424 U.S. 409 (1976)

Imbler established prosecutorial immunity from suit under SECTION 1983, TITLE 42, UNITED STATES CODE, for activities that are integral parts of the judicial process. *Imbler* left open the question whether prosecutors may be civilly liable for administrative or investigative activities. Justice LEWIS F. POWELL, writing for the Supreme Court, indicated in OBITER DICTUM that judges and prosecutors are subject to criminal prosecution for willful deprivations of constitutional rights.

THEODORE EISENBERG
(1986)

IMMIGRATION AND ALIENAGE

The ambivalence that characterizes today's national policies toward immigration had antecedents in the colonial era. Although the DECLARATION OF INDEPENDENCE complained that the king and Privy Council had tried "to prevent the population of these states," many of the colonies had resisted Roman Catholic immigration, and in 1776 some of them still resounded with expressions of nativist resentment against populations that were non-English. The nation is justly proud of its tradition as a refuge for the oppressed and persecuted. Yet American immigration policy, from colonial times to our own, has been dictated by the "native" majorities' perceptions of self-interest. The perceived need for settlers and workers hangs in precarious balance against the suspicions and hostilities that flow out of cultural differences. Congress decides how the balance shall be struck; in the field of immigration, constitutional law has placed few limits on governmental power.

For almost a century, Congress took little part in the regulation of immigration. Even the ALIEN AND SEDITION ACTS (1798), for all their spirit of partisan nativism, were not conceived as immigration restrictions. An early minimal state regulation of the immigration process survived challenge under the COMMERCE CLAUSE in MAYOR OF NEW YORK V. MILN (1837), but more severe state regulations were held invalid in the PASSENGER CASES (1849). Direct state limits on immigration were held unconstitutional in *Henderson v. New York* (1875), the same year in which Congress adopted the first direct national restriction, forbidding immigration by convicts and prostitutes.

By 1875, Congress's constitutional power to control immigration had come to be seen as one aspect of its power to regulate foreign commerce. Later, the Supreme Court articulated a more sweeping doctrine: the power of the national government to control FOREIGN AFFAIRS was inherent in the idea of nationhood and did not need explicit recognition in the Constitution. That doctrine eventually found its fullest expression in UNITED STATES V. CURTISS-WRIGHT EXPORT CORP. (1936), but it had surfaced half a century earlier in the context of immigration. In CHAE CHAN PING V. UNITED STATES (1889) the Court announced that if Congress "considers the presence of foreigners of a different race in this country, who will not assimilate with us, to be dangerous to its peace and security, . . . its determination is conclusive upon the judiciary." Having cast itself in an acquiescent role, the Court in *Nishimura Eiku v. United States* (1892) justified nearly absolute congressional power over immigration as "inherent in SOVEREIGNTY." An exceedingly inscrutable image of a national community now formally protected Congress's immigration decisions from effective constitutional challenge.

The law upheld in the *Chae Chan Ping* decision was the CHINESE EXCLUSION ACT of 1882. In the years since 1850, some 300,000 Chinese had come to the Pacific Coast, most of them responding to active recruitment of labor for mines and railroad construction in the American West. By the 1860s Chinese had come to compose about nine percent of California's population, and an anti-Chinese crusade was in full cry, fueled by racism and fear. After a long campaign, the Chinese Exclusion Act suspended immigration from China for ten years, made the Chinese ineligible for CITIZENSHIP—not even the strongest congressional supporters of unrestricted immigration could conceive of the Chinese as permanent members of the community—and imposed other restrictions on them.

Although the act was accompanied by unashamedly sinophobic rhetoric, it was ostensibly passed to protect citizen workers. So, too, was the federal legislation of 1882 that added new categories of prohibited immigrants—lunatics, idiots, and persons likely to become public charges—and went on to impose a head tax of fifty cents on each immigrant who entered the United States. Similar justifications were offered for the acts of 1885 and 1887, prohibiting payment for an immigrant's transportation to the United States in return for a promise of labor. This series of laws in the 1880s imposed the first severe restrictions on immigration in the nation's history.

The Supreme Court upheld the head tax, in the *Head Money Cases* (1884), on the basis of Congress's power to regulate foreign commerce—a theory broad enough to sustain the whole series of enactments. However, all the laws were ineffective by design. Congress left border inspections and collection of the head tax to state agencies, which largely ignored the laws. The contract labor laws exempted both skilled workers and domestics, along with foreigners residing temporarily in the country and "coincidentally" working here. The practical effect was to permit a continued disregard for the border and a deepening disrespect for the law, especially among Mexican laborers and the employers who recruited them.

From the 1880s on, a steady trickle of minor immigration restrictions issued from Congress. Paupers and polygamists were excluded, and then epileptics, professional beggars, and anarchists or persons believing in the violent overthrow of the government—the latter provisions a reaction to the assassination of President WILLIAM MCKINLEY. Not surprisingly, the next major immigration restrictions accompanied a new surge of nativism associated with a wave of immigration from eastern and southern Europe that began in the 1890s, encouraged by the demand for workers in a growing industrial economy. This nativist impulse was accelerated by WORLD WAR I and reached a climax in the Red Scare of 1919–1920. Congress adopted a LITERACY TEST for immigrants in 1917, and in the early 1920s set in place a system of immigration quotas based on national origins. The quotas restricted the ethnic proportions of immigration to the ethnic proportions of the nation's population before 1890—that is, before the arrival of large numbers of eastern and southern Europeans. The quota system reflected some of the most respected "scientific" thought of the Progressive era; the racism that produced the Chinese Exclusion Act had broadened into Anglo-Saxonism, which extended its hostility and its assumptions of superiority beyond race to ethnicity.

The constitutionality of racial and ethnic restrictions on immigration was taken for granted in the 1920s. The *Chae Chan Ping* opinion had placed the whole matter outside the reach of substantive constitutional guarantees such as the EQUAL PROTECTION OF THE LAWS. To say the very least, however, this position is in tension with the Supreme Court's modern treatment of RACIAL DISCRIMINATION. Yet no recent decision has reexamined the premises of *Chae Chan Ping*, and the Court's opinions continue to refer, as in *Fiallo v. Bell* (1977), to "the limited scope of judicial inquiry in immigration litigation." Nonetheless, the modern constitutional climate in race cases seems to have contributed to the abandonment, in 1965, of the national origins quota system. In its place Congress has adopted a single worldwide annual ceiling on immigration, with a system of preferences designed to protect the interests of citizens and of aliens who are already documented residents.

The substantive problem of squaring the nation's constitutional commitment to equal protection with the tradition of judicial deference to Congress on immigration matters has a procedural counterpart. The *Nishimura Eiku* decision held that the DUE PROCESS clause of the Fifth Amendment imposed no limits on the power of Congress to govern procedures for entry into the United States. A few years later, in *Wong Wing v. United States* (1896), the Supreme Court did hold that due process forbade enforcement of the immigration laws by sentencing aliens to hard labor. In the modern era, *Landon v. Plascencia* (1982) has recognized due process rights of a resident alien who was seeking readmission after a short trip to Mexico. But such constitutional limitations are rare; the judicial protection of aliens in the exclusion process mainly has taken the form of interpretations of the immigration statutes.

A notable recent example is *Jean v. Nelson* (1985), in which the Court confronted the practice of long-term detention, without parole, of Haitian aliens who had been taken into custody as they attempted to enter the country without permission. The detention was challenged as unconstitutional discrimination based on race or national origin. Rather than decide that issue, the Court approved a REMAND of the case to determine whether immigration officials were observing the statutes and regulations, which, in the Court's interpretation, required individualized parole decisions without such discrimination. *Jean* appears to reflect an increasing judicial reluctance to keep the exclusion process unfettered by due process considerations. It also strongly suggests that if the Congress were to revive explicit racial exclusions, the PRECEDENT of *Chae Chan Ping* would not prevent judicial examination of their constitutionality.

The interpretation of the United States Constitution concerning immigration has always been influenced by widely shared attitudes concerning the constitution of American society. Today's issues of immigration policy focus on the use of "temporary" workers from other countries. Central to this theme is the story of Mexican labor migration. After 1882 Mexican and Japanese workers, along with immigrants from eastern and southern Europe, were recruited to help fill the void left by the exclusion of the Chinese. When Japanese immigration was effectively closed in 1907, employers in the Southwest intensified the recruitment of Mexicans. Assisted by statutory exemptions and waivers, many employers grew rich on the backs of immigrants who were poor and powerless. When poor whites competed for menial jobs, however—as after the crash of 1929—hundreds of thousands of Mexican workers were deported.

The pattern is repeated, from WORLD WAR II through the 1942–1964 Bracero Program (admitting temporary workers) and beyond, in a cycle that has not yet ended: Mexican workers are recruited when they serve the needs of domestic employers, and expelled when their usefulness seems to decline. They fill jobs as needed, and at a low wage, but they are not to be allowed to burden local communities. The Bracero Program amounted to an official (but unacknowledged) program of undocumented Mexican migration. At a time when the Border Patrol might have made a real difference in curbing undocumented entry—and thus restricting American growers from employing undocumented workers—the agency's budget was cut. Since 1952, Congress has exempted employers from liability for employing undocumented workers.

The result of all these developments is that the cheapest labor in the United States has become almost exclusively the province of undocumented workers. An entrenched migratory culture now supplies workers from Mexico and other countries to fill low-paying and socially undesirable jobs. If recruitment has become unnecessary, effective enforcement of formal immigration law has become virtually impossible. Very large numbers of undocumented workers are here to stay—and, predictably, America's long-standing ambivalence toward immigration is translated into a paradox of constitutional law. On the one hand, government is to be given the widest powers to seek out and deport undocumented workers, including such far-reaching methods as BORDER SEARCHES and the factory sweeps approved in *Immigration and Naturalization Service v. Delgado* (1984). On the other hand, PLYLER V. DOE (1982), holding it unconstitutional for Texas to deny free public education to children of the undocumented, almost certainly rested on the premise that most of those children are going to remain part of the American community, whether or not Texas chooses to educate them. The *Plyler* decision is one of major potential importance for the definition of the boundaries of that community, and for the recognition and fulfillment of the national community's concrete responsibilities to all its members.

GERALD P. LÓPEZ
KENNETH L. KARST
(1986)

Bibliography

GORDON, CHARLES and ROSENFELD, HARRY N. 1985 *Immigration Law and Procedure*, Rev. ed. Vol. 1. New York: Matthew Bender.
LOPEZ, GERALD P. 1981 Undocumented Mexican Migration: In Search of a Just Immigration Law and Policy. *UCLA Law Review* 28:615–714.

NOTE 1983 Developments in the Law—Immigration and the Rights of Aliens. *Harvard Law Review* 96:1286–1465.

IMMIGRATION AND ALIENAGE
(Update 1)

Federal regulation of immigration did not begin until late in the nineteenth century, and the current code of complex admissions categories and limitations is wholly a product of the twentieth century. The first significant tests of congressional authority to exclude and deport noncitizens came in CHAE CHAN PING V. UNITED STATES (1889) and *Fong Yue Ting v. United States* (1893), cases challenging federal immigration law that barred the entry of Chinese laborers, notably the CHINESE EXCLUSION ACT OF 1882. Although the Constitution includes no express provision authorizing the enactment of immigration laws, the Supreme Court held that such a power inhered in the notion of SOVEREIGNTY and was closely associated with exercise of the FOREIGN AFFAIRS power of the United States. It also ruled that congressional decisions as to which classes of aliens should be entitled to enter and remain in the United States are largely beyond judicial scrutiny.

Modern cases reaffirm that the Constitution provides virtually no limit on Congress's power to define the substantive grounds of exclusion and DEPORTATION. It is also well established that removal of aliens from the United States is not "punishment" in a constitutional sense, and therefore, prohibitions against CRUEL AND UNUSUAL PUNISHMENT, EX POST FACTO LAWS, and BILLS OF ATTAINDER are not deemed to apply to regulations of immigration. Nor does the due process clause of the Constitution offer protection to ALIENS applying for initial admission to the United States. Such an alien, the Court stated most recently in *Landon v. Plasencia* (1982), requests a "privilege" and has "no constitutional rights regarding his application" for admission.

It is a dramatic overstatement, however, to conclude that noncitizens in the United States have no constitutional rights. Aliens are generally afforded the constitutional rights extended to citizens (although they are not eligible for federal elective office and do not come within the protection of constitutional provisions prohibiting discrimination in voting). An alien arrested for a crime is entitled to the various protections of the FOURTH AMENDMENT, Fifth Amendment, Sixth Amendment, and Eighth Amendment; an alien may assert FIRST AMENDMENT rights in a situation in which such claims may be made by citizens. In the important case of *Wong Wing v. United States* (1896), the Court invalidated a provision of the 1892 immigration statute providing for the imprisonment at hard labor of any Chinese laborer determined by executive branch officials to be in the United States illegally. Distinguishing this provision from immigration regulations that bar entry or mandate removal of aliens—which are virtually immune from judicial scrutiny—the Court held that such "infamous punishment" could not be imposed without a judicial trial.

Even within the immigration context, the Court has ruled that DUE PROCESS applies to proceedings aimed at removing an alien who has entered the United States. Similar protections must be afforded permanent resident aliens seeking to reenter the United States after a trip outside the country.

Furthermore, the Supreme Court has adopted interpretations of the immigration code that temper the harsher aspects of its constitutional doctrine. "Because deportation is a drastic measure and at times the equivalent of banishment or exile," the Court stated in *Fong Haw Tan v. Phelan* (1948), ambiguities in deportation grounds should be resolved in an alien's favor. In *Jean v. Nelson* (1985), the Court held that federal statutes do not authorize immigration officials to discriminate on the basis of race or national origin in deciding whether to release aliens from detention prior to a determination of their right to enter the United States.

While the current constitutional doctrine may be described in fairly short order, it is harder to provide a coherent theoretical justification for the case law. The cases may reflect the existence of two conflicting norms. One, based on a theory of membership in a national community, views immigration as a privilege extended to guests whose invitation may be revoked at any time for any reason; the other, grounded in a notion of fundamental human rights, protects all individuals within the United States, irrespective of their status.

Those two norms seem to underlie the Court's bifurcated approach to federal and state laws that discriminate on the basis of alienage. In YICK WO V. HOPKINS (1886), the Supreme Court held that a local ordinance invidiously applied against Chinese aliens violated the FOURTEENTH AMENDMENT. While *Yick Wo* may be read as a case primarily condemning racial prejudice, later cases make clear that state classifications drawn on the basis of alienage will be subjected to searching judicial scrutiny. Discriminatory state legislation is deemed suspect for two reasons. First, because immigration regulation is characterized as an exclusive federal power, state laws that burden aliens conflict with federal policy. Second, as announced by the Supreme Court in GRAHAM V. RICHARDSON (1971), aliens constitute a "discrete and insular minority for whom heightened judicial solicitude is appropriate." Since *Graham*, which struck down laws disqualifying aliens from state WELFARE BENEFITS, scores of state laws excluding aliens from public benefit programs and economic opportunities in the private sphere have been invalidated. Supreme Court opinions have sustained Fourteenth Amendment challenges to law prohibiting aliens from receiving state scholarships and from serving as lawyers, civil engineers, state civil servants, and notaries public.

In PLYLER V. DOE (1982), the Court held that the EQUAL PROTECTION clause protects undocumented aliens in the United States against some forms of state discrimination. The Court invalidated a Texas statute that authorized local school districts to exclude undocumented alien children from school. Although the Court eschewed STRICT SCRUTINY—concluding that EDUCATION was not a FUNDAMENTAL RIGHT protected by the Constitution and that laws discriminating against undocumented aliens were not based on a SUSPECT CLASSIFICATION—it nonetheless appeared to apply a standard more strict than the traditional RATIONAL BASIS test. Important to the Court were the nature of the interest burdened and the consequences of denying an education to children, many of whom were likely to remain resident in the United States. The Court also noted that no federal policy authorized the exclusion of children from local schools.

Not all state classifications that discriminate against aliens have fallen. CITIZENSHIP is viewed as a legitimate qualification for those jobs or functions deemed to be closely linked with the exercise of a state's sovereign power. According to Justice BYRON R. WHITE, writing for the Court in *Cabell v. Chavez-Salido* (1982), "exclusion of aliens from basic governmental processes is not a deficiency in the democratic system but a necessary consequence of the community's process of self-definition." Aliens may therefore be excluded from voting, eligibility for elective office, and jury service. The "political function" exception has also been applied where the linkage to usual conceptions of citizenship seems more attenuated. The Court has upheld state laws prohibiting aliens from serving as police officers, public school teachers, and probation officers. In these cases, the Court does not apply the strict scrutiny test. Rather, it deems the presence of the governmental function as warranting application of a rational basis test.

Federal statutes that draw distinctions based on alienage have been judged by a very lenient constitutional standard. In *Fiallo v. Bell* (1977), the Court refused to invalidate a section of the Immigration and Nationality Act that permitted children born out of wedlock to enter the United States based on their relationship with their natural mother but did not accord a similar entitlement to nonmarital children seeking to enter based on their relationship with their natural father. Noting that "Congress regularly makes rules that would be unacceptable if applied to citizens," the Court refused to apply heightened scrutiny to the statutory provision, despite its alleged "double-barreled" discrimination based on sex and illegitimacy.

Outside the immigration context, the Court has likewise demonstrated great restraint in its review of federal legislation regulating aliens. *Mathews v. Diaz* (1976) upheld a provision of the federal Medicare program that denied eligibility to permanent resident aliens unless they had resided in the United States for five years. The Court rejected the claim that the strict scrutiny applied to discriminatory state laws should control, reasoning that given congressional power to regulate immigration, federal laws may classify on the basis of alienage for noninvidious reasons. In *Diaz* the five-year RESIDENCE REQUIREMENT was not irrational, for "Congress may decide that as the alien's tie grows stronger, so does the strength of his claim to an equal share" in "the bounty that a conscientious sovereign makes available to its own citizens and some of its guests." And although the Court held in HAMPTON V. MOW SUN WONG (1976) that a regulation excluding aliens from the federal civil service was beyond the authority of the Civil Service Commission, lower courts subsequently sustained a presidential order reimposing the exclusion.

Despite its constitutional authority to limit federal programs to citizens, Congress has generally made available to permanent resident aliens those benefits and opportunities provided to citizens. Such practice may indicate a political norm that membership in the American community arises from entry as a permanent resident alien rather than through NATURALIZATION several years later.

T. ALEXANDER ALEINIKOFF
(1992)

Bibliography

ALEINIKOFF, T. ALEXANDER 1989 Federal Regulation of Aliens and the Constitution. *American Journal of International Law* 83:862–871.

LEGOMSKY, STEPHEN H. 1984 Immigration Law and the Principle of Plenary Congressional Power. *Supreme Court Review* 1984:255–307.

MARTIN, DAVID A. 1983 Due Process and Membership in the National Community: Political Asylum and Beyond. *University of Pittsburgh Law Review* 44:165–235.

ROSENBERG, GERALD M. 1977 The Protection of Aliens from Discriminatory Treatment by the National Government. *Supreme Court Review* 1977:275–339.

SCHUCK, PETER H. 1984 The Transformation of Immigration Law. *Columbia Law Review* 84:1–90.

IMMIGRATION AND ALIENAGE
(Update 2)

The Constitution's silences about immigration and the rights of ALIENS leave great room for interpretation and contestation. The text does not confer an express immigration power on the federal government. Before the CIVIL WAR, states often attempted to regulate immigration, directing their POLICE POWER against the poor, the sick, criminals, and free blacks. After 1875, the Supreme Court began to deny the states' authority, relying variously on Congress's FOREIGN COMMERCE power, its NATURALIZATION power, and IMPLIED POWERS of national SOVEREIGNTY in FOREIGN AFFAIRS. The Court's focus on a linkage to foreign affairs has contributed to extreme judicial deference to congressional determinations of substantive immigration policy, even where the constitutional rights of aliens or of citizens are affected.

The BILL OF RIGHTS makes no explicit reference to citizens, noncitizens, or CITIZENSHIP and terms like "person" and "accused" in the Fifth and Sixth Amendments presumably include aliens as well. In the debates over the Alien Act of 1798, some FEDERALISTS sought to reserve rights to citizens as the exclusive parties to the constitutional compact. Their Jeffersonian opponents' position, which emphasized the mutuality between subjection to the law and legal rights, has prevailed. Ambiguities remain, however, regarding rights of aliens against extraterritorial government action, and some judges and advocates have sought to reopen the question of the rights of aliens unlawfully present in the United States. In *United States v. Verdugo-Urquídez* (1990), a majority of the Court held that the FOURTH AMENDMENT did not limit the federal government's power to search the home in Mexico of a nonresident alien. The opinions reflect several different theories about the reach of constitutional rights. Portions of Chief Justice WILLIAM H. REHNQUIST's opinion invoked the Fourth Amendment's reference to "the people," a category that he viewed as including lawfully resident aliens, but not aliens outside the United States, and possibly not unlawfully resident aliens. Justice ANTHONY M. KENNEDY's crucial CONCURRING OPINION rejected this textual argument, and adopted instead a flexible DUE PROCESS approach to determining aliens' extraterritorial rights. The DISSENTING OPINIONS of Justices WILLIAM J. BRENNAN, JR., and HARRY A. BLACKMUN favored extension of the mutuality approach. The fact that the case involved EXTRATERRITORIAL government action deserves repetition; it is well settled, for example, that aliens outside the United States enjoy constitutional protection for their PROPERTY inside the United States.

Earlier predictions that permanent resident aliens were acquiring full social membership or that U.S. citizenship was suffering devaluation required revision after 1996 when Congress passed the ILLEGAL IMMIGRATION REFORM AND IMMIGRANT RESPONSIBILITY ACT. Congress reinvigorated the historical policy against migration of the poor, and drew sharp distinctions between citizens and aliens in eligibility for many government benefits. Congress also authorized the states to draw similar distinctions in their own benefit programs, in a manner that challenged prior Court cases such as GRAHAM V. RICHARDSON (1971). These changes in benefit policy, and the anti-immigrant atmosphere against which they were enacted, prompted enormous increases in the demand for naturalization. It may be debated in what sense these events restored the value of citizenship.

GERALD L. NEUMAN
(2000)

Bibliography

HING, BILL ONG   1998   Don't Give Me Your Tired, Your Poor: Conflicted Immigrant Stories and Welfare Reform. *Harvard Civil Rights–Civil Liberties Law Review* 33:159–182.

NEUMAN, GERALD L.   1996   *Strangers to the Constitution: Immigrants, Borders, and Fundamental Law.* Princeton, N.J.: Princeton University Press.

SCHUCK, PETER H.   1997   The Re-Evaluation of American Citizenship. *Georgetown Immigration Law Journal* 12:1–34.

IMMIGRATION AND NATURALIZATION SERVICE v. CHADHA
462 U.S. 919 (1983)

Immigration and Naturalization Service v. Chadha cast serious doubt on the use of the LEGISLATIVE VETO, a device by which Congress seeks to retain control over the use of DELEGATED POWERS. *Chadha* involved a provision in the IMMIGRATION AND NATIONALITY ACT that permitted either house of Congress, by resolution, to overturn orders of the attorney general suspending DEPORTATION of ALIENS.

The Supreme Court held, 7–2, that congressional review of such cases was legislative in character, and was therefore subject to the provisions of Article I requiring the concurrence of both houses and an opportunity for the President to exercise his VETO POWER before the resolution can have the force of law. The majority opinion, by Chief Justice WARREN E. BURGER, declared that the one-house legislative veto violated the constitutional principles of SEPARATION OF POWERS and BICAMERALISM.

Justice BYRON R. WHITE, dissenting, ascribed to the decision much greater scope than did the majority. White asserted that the *Chadha* decision effectively invalidated every legislative veto provision in federal law. A majority in future cases, however, may choose not to apply the *Chadha* rationale to two-house legislative vetoes or to legislative vetoes of agency actions that are clearly legislative rather than executive or quasi-judicial. It would be curious indeed if administrative agencies promulgating regulations with the force of law were freed from congressional

oversight by a Court intent on preserving the separation of powers and bicameralism.

DENNIS J. MAHONEY
(1986)

IMMIGRATION AND NATURALIZATION SERVICE v. LOPEZ-MENDOZA

See: Deportation

IMMIGRATION REFORM AND CONTROL ACT
100 Stat. 3359 (1986)

The major innovation in the lengthy Immigration Reform and Control Act of 1986 was the adoption of employer sanctions penalizing businesses that hired or continued to employ ALIENS who were not legally authorized to work. On a symbolic level the statute corrected a policy that had condoned utilization of illegal workers while threatening those workers with deportation. The statute nonetheless impaired the enforceability of employer sanctions by prohibiting the development of a national identity card, in order to protect the RIGHT OF PRIVACY of citizens. The statute accompanied its new enforcement regime by an amnesty ("legalization") for undocumented aliens who were already residing in the United States. More than two million aliens, most of whom were Mexicans, achieved lawful resident status through this program. Ambivalence toward these former illegal aliens contributed to debates in the 1990s on IMMIGRATION AND ALIENAGE.

GERALD L. NEUMAN
(2000)

Bibliography

U.S. COMMISSION ON IMMIGRATION REFORM   1994   *U.S. Immigration Policy: Restoring Credibility.* Washington, D.C.: U.S. Commission on Immigration Reform.

CALAVITA, KITTY   1990   Employer Sanctions Violations: Toward a Dialectical Model of White-Collar Crime. *Law and Society Review* 24:1041–1069.

IMMUNITY

See: Executive Immunity; Immunity of Public Officials; Judicial Immunity; Legislative Immunity; Presidential Immunity; Sovereign Immunity; State Immunity from Federal Law

IMMUNITY GRANT (SELF-INCRIMINATION)

"No person," the Fifth Amendment unequivocally states, "shall be . . . compelled in any criminal case to be a witness against himself. . . ." It does not add, "unless such person cannot be prosecuted or punished as a result of his testimony," and it does not refer to self-incrimination. Yet, if the government wants EVIDENCE concerning a crime, it can compel a witness to testify by granting immunity from prosecution. In law, such immunity means that the witness cannot incriminate himself and therefore has suffered no violation of his RIGHT AGAINST SELF-INCRIMINATION. The common sense of the matter is that to "incriminate" means to implicate criminally; in law, however, it means exposure to prosecution or penalties. The law indulges the fiction that when one receives a grant of immunity, removing him from criminal jeopardy, the right not to be a witness against oneself is not violated. If the witness cannot be prosecuted, the penalties do not exist for him, so that his testimony can be compelled without forcing him to incriminate himself or "be a witness against himself."

The first immunity statute in Anglo-American jurisprudence was probably the one enacted by Connecticut in 1698. That act specified that witnesses in criminal cases must give sworn evidence, on pain of punishment for refusal, "always provided that no person required to give testimonie as aforesaid shall be punished for what he doth confesse against himself when under oath." Similarly, an act that Parliament passed against gambling in 1710, which some colonies copied, guaranteed that gamblers who confessed their crimes and returned their winnings should be "acquitted, indemnified [immunized] and discharged from any further or other Punishment, Forfeiture, or Penalty which he or they may have incurred by the playing for or winning such Money. . . ." New York in 1758 obtained the king's pardon for certain ship captains in order to compel their testimony against the ships' owners. Although the pardons had eliminated the perils of the criminal law for the captains, they persisted in their claim that the law could not force them to declare anything that might incriminate them. A court fined them for contempt, on grounds that the recalcitrant captains no longer faced criminal jeopardy by giving evidence against themselves.

In modern language these colonial precedents illustrate grants of "transactional" immunity, an absolute guarantee that in return for evidence, the compelled person will not under any circumstances be prosecuted for the transaction or criminal episode concerning which he gives testimony. Absolute or transactional immunity was the price paid by the law for exacting information that would otherwise be actionable criminally. The paradox remained: one could be compelled to be a witness against oneself, but from the law's perspective the immunized witness would stand to the offense as if he had never committed it, or had received AMNESTY or a pardon despite having committed it.

Congress enacted its first immunity statute in 1857, granting freedom from prosecution for any acts or transactions to which a witness offered testimony in an investigation. Reacting against the immunity "baths" that enabled corrupt officials to escape from criminal liability by offering immunized testimony, Congress in 1862 supplanted the act of 1857 with one that offered only "use" immunity. Use immunity guarantees only that the compelled testimony will not be used in a criminal prosecution, but prosecution is possible if based on evidence independent from or unrelated to the compelled testimony. Under a grant of use immunity one might confess to a crime secure in the knowledge that his confession could not be used against him; however, if the prosecution had other evidence to prove his guilt, he might be prosecuted. By 1887 Congress extended the standard of use immunity from congressional investigations to all federal proceedings.

Until 1972 the Supreme Court demanded transactional rather than use immunity as the sole basis for displacing the Fifth Amendment right to remain silent. In COUNSEL-MAN V. HITCHCOCK (1892) the Court unanimously held unconstitutional a congressional act offering use immunity because use immunity was "not co-extensive with the constitutional provision." The compelled testimony might provide leads to evidence that the prosecution might not otherwise possess. To supplant the constitutional guarantee, an immunity statute must provide "complete protection" from all criminal perils; "in view of the constitutional provision, a statutory enactment, to be valid, must afford absolute immunity against future prosecution for the offense to which the question relates." Congress responded with a statute safeguarding against prosecution, forfeiture, or penalty for any transaction about which one might be compelled to testify. In BROWN V. WALKER (1896) the Court held that transactional immunity "operates as a pardon for the offense to which it relates," thus satisfying the constitutional guarantee. In effect the Court permitted what it had declared was impossible: congressional amendment of the Constitution. By a statute that served as a "substitute," Congress altered the guarantee that no one can be compelled to be a witness against himself criminally.

Until 1970 there were over fifty federal immunity statutes conforming with *Brown's* transactional immunity standard, which the Court reendorsed in ULLMANN V. UNITED STATES (1956). When the Court scrapped its TWO SOVEREIGNTIES RULE in *Murphy v. Waterfront Commission* (1964), it held that absent an immunity grant, a state witness could not be compelled to testify unless his testimony "and its fruits" could not be used by the federal government. *Murphy* was a technical relaxation of the transactional immunity standard, as ALBERTSON V. SUBVERSIVE ACTIVITIES CONTROL BOARD (1965) proved, because a unanimous Court reconfirmed the transactional immunity standard.

Through the ORGANIZED CRIME CONTROL ACT of 1970, Congress made use immunity and derivative-use immunity the standard for all federal grants of immunity, and most states copied the new standard. No compelled testimony or its "fruits" (information directly or indirectly derived from such testimony) could be used against a witness criminally, except to prove perjury. In KASTIGAR V. UNITED STATES (1972) the Court relied on *Murphy,* ignored or distorted all other precedents, and upheld the narrow standard as coextensive with the Fifth Amendment, which it is not. One who relies on his right to remain silent forces the state to rely wholly on its own evidence to convict him. By remaining silent he gives the state no way to use his testimony, however indirectly. When he is compelled to be a witness against himself, his admissions assist the state's investigation against him. The burden of proving that the state's evidence derives from sources wholly independent of the compelled testimony lies upon the prosecution. But use immunity permits compulsion without removing criminality.

In *New Jersey v. Portash* (1979) the Court held that a defendant's immunized grand jury testimony could not be introduced to impeach his testimony at his trial. Whether the state may introduce immunized testimony to prove perjury has not been decided. In *Portash,* however, the Court conceded, "Testimony given in response to a grant of legislative immunity is the essence of coerced testimony." The essence of the Fifth Amendment's provision is that testimony against oneself cannot be coerced. Any grant of immunity that compels testimony compels one to be a witness against himself—except, of course, that it is "impossible," as the Court said in *Counselman,* for the constitutional guarantee to mean what it says.

LEONARD W. LEVY
(1986)

Bibliography
LEVY, LEONARD W. 1974 *Against the Law: The Nixon Court and Criminal Justice.* Pages 165–187. New York: Harper & Row.

IMMUNITY OF GOVERNMENT OFFICIALS

See: Executive Immunity; Immunity of Public Officials; Judicial Immunity; Legislative Immunity; Presidential Immunity; Sovereign Immunity

IMMUNITY OF PUBLIC OFFICIALS

State and federal officials enjoy traditional immunity from state-law tort claims. These traditional immunities are more readily available for the discretionary functions of officials than for their ministerial functions. The post-1950s growth of constitutionally-based CIVIL RIGHTS actions created forms of public official liability not contemplated by the immunities. A federal body of official immunity DOCTRINE developed simultaneously with the new civil rights actions.

Federal immunity of public officials can be absolute or qualified. Both kinds of immunity shield officials from liability to disgruntled constituents, and thus promote fearless decisionmaking. Allowing immunity defenses implicitly rejects a literal interpretation of SECTION 1983, TITLE 42, U.S. CODE, which states that "every person . . . shall be liable" if they cause a deprivation of federal rights.

Absolute immunity shields legislative, judicial, and prosecutorial officials from liability even if they maliciously violate constitutional rights. Under the SPEECH OR DEBATE CLAUSE, members of Congress have absolute immunity from civil or criminal actions based on legislative acts. Under TENNEY V. BRANDHOVE (1951) and *Bogan v. Scott-Harriss* (1998), the legislative acts of state and local legislators are absolutely immune from federal civil rights actions. The Supreme Court endorsed absolute JUDICIAL IMMUNITY for judicial acts in *Randall v. Brigham* (1869), reaffirmed it in PIERSON V. RAY (1967) and STUMP V. SPARKMAN (1978), but denied it in cases seeking injunctive relief in *Pulliam v. Allen* (1984). The Federal Courts Improvement Act of 1996 narrowed *Pulliam's* exception to cases in which declaratory relief is unavailable or has preceded injunctive relief. Absolute prosecutorial immunity has its recent origins in IMBLER V. PACHTMAN (1976). Prosecutors, however, are not absolutely immune for making false statements of fact in seeking an arrest warrant, *Kalina v. Fletcher* (1997); for conduct at a press conference, *Buckley v. Fitzsimmons* (1993); or for legal advice to the police during pretrial investigation, *Burns v. Reed* (1991). In LAKE COUNTRY ESTATES V. TAHOE REGIONAL PLANNING AGENCY (1979) and BUTZ V. ECONOMOU (1978), the Court extended absolute legislative, judicial, and prosecutorial immunity to officials, such as federal ADMINISTRATIVE LAW judges, who perform functions similar to absolutely immune officials but who are not traditional legislators, judges, or prosecutors.

Only NIXON V. FITZGERALD (1982) has granted an executive official, the President, absolute immunity for official actions. CLINTON V. JONES (1997) holds that the President has no immunity while in office from civil-damages litigation arising out of events that occurred before the President took office.

Qualified immunity from civil rights liability has its origins in COMMON LAW immunities of officials, especially police officers. Immunity at common law, however, is no longer a prerequisite to qualified immunity. Under *Harlow v. Fitzgerald* (1982), an official enjoys qualified immunity from damages actions whenever a reasonable official would believe his act to be constitutional, whether or not the act is in fact constitutional. To shelter officials further from the discovery and trial process, denials of qualified immunity are immediately appealable, *Mitchell v. Forsyth* (1985), and multiple appeals of a denial are possible, *Behrens v. Pelletier* (1996). Officials may assert a qualified immunity defense whether or not they are eligible for absolute immunity.

THEODORE EISENBERG
(2000)

Bibliography

EISENBERG, THEODORE   1996   *Civil Rights Legislation*, 4th ed. Charlottesville, Virginia: Michie.

IMPEACHMENT

The English Parliament devised impeachment for the removal of ministers of the Crown, the House of Commons serving as prosecutor of charges that the House of Lords adjudged. This, ALEXANDER HAMILTON wrote, was the "model" of the American proceeding—the HOUSE OF REPRESENTATIVES files and prosecutes charges and the SENATE is the trial tribunal. The Framers of the Constitution also adopted the English grounds for removal, "TREASON, bribery, or other high crimes and MISDEMEANORS." They defined "treason" narrowly; "bribery" was a COMMON LAW term of familiar meaning; but the scope of "other high crimes and misdemeanors" remains a subject of continuing debate. Some would confine those terms to indictable crimes. At the other pole, Congressman GERALD FORD, in proposing the impeachment of Justice WILLIAM O. DOUGLAS in 1970, asserted that an impeachable offense is whatever the House, with the concurrence of the Senate, "considers [it] to be." The historical facts indicate, however, that an impeachable offense need not be indictable, but that such offenses have their limits, for which we must look to the English practice the terms expressed.

Advocates of the indictable crime interpretation point to the criminal terminology, for example, "high crimes and misdemeanors." Article III, section 2, of the Constitution provides, "The trial of all Crimes, except in cases of Impeachment, shall be by Jury"; Article II, section 2, confers a power to grant pardons "except in Cases of Impeachment," and pardons relieve from punishment for a crime. In England the House of Lords combined removal and punishment in the impeachment proceeding. But Article I, section 3, clause 7, made an important departure: "Judgment in cases of impeachment shall not extend further than to removal from office, and disqualification to hold and enjoy any [federal] office . . . but the party convicted shall nevertheless be liable and subject to INDICTMENT, trial, judgment and punishment, according to law." The separation of removal from criminal prosecution meant that political passions could no longer sweep an accused to his death, but that he would be tried by a jury of his peers.

In the North Carolina Ratification Convention, JAMES IREDELL explained that if the President "commits any misdemeanor in office, he is impeachable, removable from office. . . . If he commits any crime, he is punishable by the laws of his country," distinguishing an impeachable "misdemeanor" (which has a common law connotation of misconduct in office) from an indictable crime. Hamilton likewise distinguished between "removal from office" and "actual punishment in cases which admit of it," indicating that some impeachable offenses were not criminal. As will appear, some impeachable offenses were not and still are not punishable crimes; nor does the absence of fine and imprisonment, the customary criminal sanctions, comport with the view that impeachment is a criminal proceeding. The doctrine of DOUBLE JEOPARDY also conduces to this conclusion. Although double jeopardy at the framing of the Constitution referred to jeopardy of life, as the Fifth Amendment attests, Congress speedily made treason punishable by death. Impeachment for treason could not, therefore, be regarded as criminal without raising a bar to indictment. Such thinking was carried over to all impeachments by JAMES WILSON: because they "are founded on different principles . . . directed to different objects . . . the trial and punishment of an offense on impeachment, is no bar to a trial of the same offense at common law." Justice JOSEPH STORY deduced from the separation between removal and indictment that "a second trial for the same offense" would not be barred by double jeopardy. Thus double jeopardy requires impeachment to be read in noncriminal terms.

The Sixth Amendment furnishes further confirmation. Earlier Article III, section 2, clause 3, expressly exempted impeachment from the "Trial of all Crimes" by jury. With that exemption before them, the draftsmen of the Sixth Amendment required TRIAL BY JURY in "all criminal prosecutions," thereby canceling the former exception. Since the later Amendment controls, it must be concluded either that the Founders felt no need to exempt impeachment from the Sixth Amendment because they did not consider it a "criminal prosecution" or that jury trial is required if impeachment be in fact a "criminal" prosecution. The latter conclusion is inadmissible. Perhaps the use of criminal terminology is attributable to the fact that words like "offenses," "convict," and "high crimes" had been employed in the English impeachments, and the Framers, engaged in hammering out a charter of government that required major political compromises, could not pause to coin a fresh and different vocabulary for every detail.

Treason and bribery, in contradistinction to crimes against the individual such as murder and robbery, are crimes against the State—political crimes. James Wilson, a chief architect of the Constitution, observed that "impeachments are confined to political characters, to political crimes and misdemeanors." And Justice Story added that they are designed "to secure the state against gross official misdemeanors." By association with "treason, bribery," the phrase "other high crimes and misdemeanors" likewise may be deemed to refer to "political" offenses. "High crimes and misdemeanors" meant "and *high* misdemeanors," not as a matter of grammatical construction but of historical usage. "High misdemeanors" are first met in a 1386 impeachment, long before there was such a crime as a "misdemeanor." At that time FELONIES were coupled with TRESPASSES, private as distinguished from political offenses. It was not until well into the sixteenth century that "misdemeanors" replaced "trespasses" in the general criminal law; and in England "high misdemeanors" remained a term peculiar to impeachment and did not find its way into ordinary criminal law, as is true of American law but for a very few statutory "high misdemeanors." Explaining "high misdemeanors," Sir WILLIAM BLACKSTONE stated that the "first and principal is the *maladministration* of such high officers as are in the public trust and employment. This is usually punished by the method of parliamentary impeachment," which proceeded not under the common law but under the *lex parliamentaria*, the "laws and course of parliament."

Though this arguably left Parliament free to fashion political offenses ad hoc, the Framers took a more restricted view. English impeachments proceeded largely for neglect of duty, abuse of power, betrayal of trust, corruption; and early state constitutions likewise provided for removal for misconduct in office, maladministration, corruption. In the Convention there were proposals for removal upon malpractice, neglect of duty, betrayal of trust, corruption, malversation (misconduct in office). Throughout, the focus was on machinery for removal rather than punishment for misconduct. When the impeachment provision came to the floor of the Convention, it employed "treason or bribery." GEORGE MASON protested that the narrow definition of treason would not reach "many great and dangerous offenses," among them "attempts to subvert the Constitution," which lay at the root of the leading English precedent. He therefore suggested the addition of "maladministration," but Madison objected that "so vague a term will be equivalent to a tenure during the pleasure of the Senate," whereupon Mason substituted "other high crimes and misdemeanors." Some two weeks earlier RUFUS KING had identified treason "agst. particular States" as "high misdemeanors"; a week before, "high misdemeanor" had been replaced in the extradition provision because it had "a technical meaning too limited." These facts show, first, that "other high crimes and misdemeanors" referred to "high misdemeanors," and second, that the terms were chosen precisely because they were "limited and technical" and would not leave the accused at the "pleasure of the Senate." As with other common law terms employed by the Framers, they expected them to have the meaning ascribed to them under English practice.

Justice Story stated that for the meaning of "high crimes and misdemeanors" resort must be had "to parliamentary practice" or "the whole subject must be left to the arbitrary discretion of the Senate," a "despotism" "incompatible" with "the genius of our institutions," and, it may be added, with the legislative history of the provision. Were impeachment restricted to common law crimes it would founder because there are no FEDERAL COMMON LAW crimes; all federal crimes are creatures of statute. Early on Congress enacted statutes that made treason and bribery crimes; a few statutes made certain minor acts criminal "high misdemeanors." But no statute declared "abuse of power," "neglect of duty," or "subversion of the Constitution" to be criminal, yet the Founders unquestionably regarded these as impeachable offenses. Except for treason and bribery, the "silence of the statute book," said Story, would render the power of impeachment "a complete nullity" and enable the most serious offender to escape removal. It is preferable to regard such silence as a continuing construction by Congress that its impeachment powers are not dependent on a statutory proscription and definition of impeachable offenses, particularly because most of its impeachment proceedings have involved nonindictable offenses. In extrajudicial statements, Chief Justice WILLIAM HOWARD TAFT and Justice CHARLES EVANS HUGHES recognized that such offenses were embraced by "high crimes and misdemeanors."

Another much debated issue is whether impeachment constitutes the sole means for removal of judges. Long before there was mention of impeachment of Justices in the Convention, it conditioned judicial tenure on "GOOD BEHAVIOR." This wording was not, as has been urged, "used simply to describe a life term," but a technical phrase of established meaning: "as long as he shall behave himself well." Hamilton noted that "good behavior tenure" was a "defeasible tenure," copied from the British model. At common law an appointment conditioned on "good behavior" was forfeited on nonperformance of the condition, that is, it terminated on misbehavior. Given a lapse from "good behavior," WILLIAM MURRAY (Lord Mansfield) observed, there must be power to remove the officer lest the formula be impotent. The remedy, Blackstone wrote, was by writ of *scire facias* determinable by the judiciary. Attempts by the Crown to remove a couple of high court judges who enjoyed "good behavior" tenure, Sir John Walter, Chief Baron of the Exchequer, and Sir John Archer, a Justice of Common Pleas, met insistence on removal by *scire facias*. This view was endorsed by Chief Justice Holt, Lord Chancellor Erskine, the future Lord Justice Denman, William Holdsworth, and CHARLES MCILWAIN. When the Framers employed a common law term, they expected it would be given its accepted meaning, as is shown by their redefinition of treason to avoid historic excesses, by JOHN DICKINSON's caution that if EX POST FACTO were to be expanded beyond the Blackstonian association with criminal cases it "would require some further provision," and by assurances in the Virginia Ratification Convention that reference to "trial by jury" included all its attributes, including the right to challenge jurors.

The Framers conceived impeachment as a remedy for misconduct by the President, and throughout the Convention such was its almost exclusive focus. Hamilton explained that "the true light in which it ought to be regarded" is as "a bridle in the hands of the legislative body upon the executive servants of the government." Consequently the Framers placed the provision for impeachment of the President in Article II, the Executive article. Almost at the last minute they amplified it by the addition of the "Vice President, and all civil officers," suggesting it was to apply to officers of the Executive department. The interpretive canon that each provision of an instrument should, if possible, be given effect counsels recognition of judicial removal for breaches of "good behavior," particularly because the standards of "high crimes and misdemeanors" differ from those of "good behavior," so that to insist that impeachment is the sole means for removal of judges is to leave some judicial "misbehavior" beyond remedy.

A number of utterances may seem to require the exclusivity of impeachment; for example, Hamilton stated in THE FEDERALIST #79 that impeachment "is the only provision" for removal of judges found in the Constitution and "consistent with the necessary independence of judges." Yet he had said in *The Federalist* #78 that "the standard of good behavior" is an "excellent barrier . . . to the encroachments and oppression of the representative body"; independence from Congress, not from judges, was the aim. Hamilton recognized that the "standard of good behavior" created a "defeasible tenure," a tenure terminated by breach of "good behavior." So too, the debate in the First Congress respecting the President's power to remove his subordinates contains tangential references to the protection from removal (chiefly by the President) that "good behavior" tenure afforded judges. Removal of his subordinates by the President made a breach in the "exclusivity" of impeachment, notwithstanding the fact that they squarely fit within "all civil officers" of Article II. It is easier to recognize an "exception" from exclusivity for the forfeiture that was an established concomitant of "good behavior," thus giving effect to that separate provision, than to make an exception for Executive subordinates.

What the First Congress did do with respect to judges further undermines reliance upon such dicta. By the Act of 1790 it provided that upon conviction in court for bribery a judge shall "forever be disqualified to hold an office." Since the impeachment clause provides both for removal and disqualification upon impeachment and conviction, the Act represents a construction that the clause does not exclude other means of disqualification. As with "disqualification," so with "removal," for the two stand on a par in the impeachment clause. The action of the First Congress, whose constitutional constructions carry great weight, when it dealt with judges thus speaks against reliance upon passing remarks in a debate that did not involve their removal. The several remarks, moreover, do not meet the test laid down by Chief Justice JOHN MARSHALL, showing that had "this particular case been suggested"—that is, judicial removal of judges for "misbehavior"—"the language would have been so varied as to exclude it." Well aware of the perils posed to judges by "the gusts of faction which might prevail" in Congress, the Founders were little likely to jettison the time-honored nonpolitical removal trial of judges by the courts in favor of a factional proceeding in Congress. Impeachment could be reserved for the grave situation in which the judiciary neglects to cleanse its own house, exactly as impeachment remains available for removal of a wrongdoing subordinate or "favorite" whom the President fails to remove.

JAMES BRYCE observed that impeachment is so heavy a "piece of artillery" as to "be unfit for ordinary use." The Founders repeatedly stressed that impeachment was meant only for "great injuries"; like Solicitor General, later Lord Chancellor Somers, they were aware that "impeachment ought to be like Goliath's sword, kept in the temple, and used but on great occasions." Hamilton too referred in *The Federalist* #70 to the "awful discretion" of the impeachment tribunal to doom "to infamy the . . . most distinguished characters of the community." Such views do not square with the insistence that the wheels of the nation must grind to a halt so that Congress can oust a venal district judge. Congress is in fact reluctant to undertake the ouster of such judges even, said Senator William McAdoo, "in cases of flagrant misconduct," because an impeachment proceeding draws the Congress away for weeks from weightier tasks. That situation, he stated, constitutes "a standing invitation for judges to abuse their authority with impunity and without fear of removal." To insist that impeachment is the sole means of removal of judges is in practical effect to immunize grave misconduct. In the almost two hundred years since adoption of the Constitution hundreds of complaints have resulted in fifty-five investigations, followed in some cases by censure or resignation. But only nine judges have been impeached and only four convicted and removed.

Some regard the acquittal of Justice SAMUEL P. CHASE in 1805 as a triumph of justice over heated political partisanship. Others view his impeachment as a natural reaction to the gross partisanship of the Federalist judiciary, given to intemperate attacks upon the Republican opposition in harangues to the GRAND JURY, which might be regarded as an "abuse of power" for political ends. Of Chase's trial of James Callender for alleged violations of the ALIEN AND SEDITIONS ACTS, EDWARD S. CORWIN, said that Chase came to the case "with the evident disposition to play the hanging judge," and there is evidence that he prejudged the case. Callendar was entitled under the canons of his time to a trial free of "the tyrannical partiality of judges," and Chase was under statutory oath to administer justice impartially. Most students of the era consider that conviction failed of a two-thirds vote because the inept, acid-tongued manager of the impeachment, JOHN RANDOLPH, had alienated many Republicans as well as Federalists.

The *cause célèbre* is the impeachment of President ANDREW JOHNSON in 1868, essentially, as Justice SAMUEL F. MILLER foresaw, "for standing in the way of certain political purposes of the majority in Congress," but ostensibly for discharging his secretary of war, EDWIN M. STANTON, whom Congress had attempted to rivet in place by the TENURE OF OFFICE ACT. Critics of Johnson have noted Stanton's "defective loyalty," his conferences with Republican leaders behind Johnson's back respecting measures that divided Congress from the President. Finally Johnson removed him, presenting the issue whether a President who considered a statute to be an unconstitutional invasion of his prerogative to remove a disloyal subordinate—Stanton himself had advised Johnson that the statute was unconstitutional—and who felt that it was his constitutional duty to exercise his independent judgment, was impeachable. Such differences were contemplated as part of the CHECKS AND BALANCES of the Constitution.

The tone of the proceedings was sounded in BENJAMIN BUTLER's opening statement: "You are bound by no law," "you are a law unto yourselves." THADDEUS STEVENS asserted that Johnson was "standing at bay, surrounded by a cordon of living men, each with the ax of an executioner

uplifted for his just punishment." Stevens dared the Senators who had voted for the Tenure of Office Act four times now to vote for acquittal "on the ground of its UNCONSTITUTIONALITY," condemning backsliders to the "gibbet of everlasting obloquy." Senator CHARLES SUMNER dismissed "the quibbles of lawyers" in a trial that "is a battle with slavery." One of the impeachment articles charged that on his "Swing Around the Circle" before the 1866 elections, Johnson attempted to bring Congress into ridicule, disgrace, and contempt. But as Senator John Sherman pointed out, members of Congress themselves had resorted to grossly abusive epithets, so that Johnson was not to be blamed for responding in kind. FREEDOM OF SPEECH, Senator James Patterson cautioned, was not solely for Congress. Current revulsion against Johnson does not overcome the verdict of Samuel Eliot Morison and Eric McKitrick that the impeachment was a "disgraceful episode," "a great act of ill-directed passion." Johnson's conviction failed by one vote. Whatever his faults, Johnson was entitled to a FAIR TRIAL, and that, the record amply discloses, was denied to him. Had Johnson been convicted, a revisionist historian wrote, it would have established a precedent "for the removal of any President refusing persistently to cooperate with Congress."

The failure of that impeachment led another revisionist historian to prophesy in 1973 that impeachment would never again be employed to remove a President. Shortly thereafter the House Judiciary Committee instituted an investigation whether President RICHARD M. NIXON participated in the WATERGATE conspiracy to obstruct justice. Once more the proceedings evidenced that impeachments are swayed by political affiliations; with a few notable exceptions, a Republican phalanx opposed impeachment until the judicially compelled disclosure of the "White House tapes" revealed that Nixon was a participant in the conspiracy. When he learned as a result of that disclosure that he could not count on more than ten votes in the Senate, he resigned from the presidency. In accepting a pardon from his successor, President GERALD FORD stated, he acknowledged his guilt. Fortunate it was for America that the Founders provided "Goliath's sword" for "great occasions."

RAOUL BERGER
(1986)

(SEE ALSO: *Articles of Impeachment of Andrew Johnson; Articles of Impeachment of Richard M. Nixon.*)

Bibliography

BERGER, RAOUL 1973 *Impeachment.* Pages 313–322. Cambridge, Mass.: Harvard University Press.
——— 1979 "Chilling Judicial Independence": A Judicial Scarecrow. *Cornell Law Quarterly* 64:822–854.

KAUFMAN, IRVING 1979 Chilling Judicial Independence. *Yale Law Journal* 88:681–716.

KURLAND, PHILIP 1974 Watergate, Impeachment and the Constitution. *Mississippi Law Review* 45:531–600.

IMPEACHMENT
(Update)

The power of impeachment is Congress's ultimate constitutional check against misconduct by executive and judicial branch officers of the United States. Article II, section 4 of the Constitution provides a single standard governing impeachment and removal of all such officers: "The President, Vice President and all civil Officers of the United States, shall be removed from Office on Impeachment for, and Conviction of, Treason, Bribery, or other high Crimes and Misdemeanors." Article I of the Constitution gives to the U.S. HOUSE OF REPRESENTATIVES "the sole Power of Impeachment," meaning the power to charge an officer with having committed such an offense, and to the U.S. SENATE "the sole Power to try all Impeachments." The Senate's power to try impeachments is subject to just three procedural limitations: When sitting as a court of impeachment, the senators "shall be on Oath or Affirmation"; when the President of the United States is tried, the CHIEF JUSTICE (rather than the Vice President) is the presiding officer of the Senate; and a two-thirds majority of senators is necessary to convict the accused. Article I further specifies that judgment in cases of impeachment "shall not extend further than to removal from Office, and disqualification to hold and enjoy any Office of honor, trust, or profit under the United States," but that "the Party convicted shall nevertheless be liable and subject to Indictment, Trial, Judgment and Punishment, according to Law."

The Constitution's impeachment provisions have produced much scholarly and political debate, especially in recent years by virtue of President WILLIAM J. CLINTON's impeachment, trial, and acquittal in 1998 and 1999. (See ARTICLES OF IMPEACHMENT OF WILLIAM J. CLINTON.) The most important question is the meaning of the term "high Crimes and Misdemeanors" for which officials may be impeached and removed. The best answer, confirmed by recent and perennial debates over the point, is that the term simply does not have a clear, fixed, or determinate meaning, and that application of this general standard was deliberately committed to the judgment of Congress in making the decision whether to impeach (by the House) and convict (by the Senate).

As ALEXANDER HAMILTON wrote in FEDERALIST No. 65 in explaining the justification for vesting the impeachment power in Congress rather than in the courts or some other body, "the nature of the proceeding" is such that it "can never be tied down by such strict rules, either in the delineation of the offence by the prosecutors, or in the construction of it by the Judges, as in common cases serve to limit the discretion of courts in favor of personal security." Rather, the Constitution recognizes "[t]he awful discretion, which a court of impeachments must have, to doom to honor or to infamy. . . ." The Supreme Court has apparently endorsed this view, ruling unanimously in NIXON V. UNITED STATES (1993), involving the impeachment of federal judge Walter Nixon, that the Constitution's assignment of "sole Power" to impeach and try to the House and Senate, respectively, constitutes a textual commitment of virtually all impeachment questions to the judgment of these bodies, where the Constitution does not provide clear answers to the contrary.

Congress's constitutional power to interpret and apply the "high Crimes and Misdemeanors" standard is broad, but not limitless. Certain guidelines are clear from history or implicit in the structure of the Constitution as a whole. First, it is clear that misconduct need not be a crime in the ordinary sense of the term in order to justify impeachment and removal, but may include "political crimes" in the sense of perceived offenses against the Constitution or the People—such as violation of one's oath of office or breach of a public trust. Hamilton in *Federalist* No. 65, for example, said that proper grounds for impeachment and removal included "offenses which proceed from the misconduct of public men, or in other words from the abuse or violation of some public trust." Such offenses, Hamilton wrote, constitute "injuries done immediately to the society itself."

At the same time, however, it is implicit in our constitutional structure of separate, independent legislative, executive, and judicial branches that impeachment must be more than simply a policy vote of "no confidence" in the executive, leading to the fall of an administration (akin to parliamentary systems of government) or, in the case of judges, attempted removal from office because of disapproval of a judge's rulings made in good faith. The narrow impeachment–acquittal of President ANDREW JOHNSON by a RECONSTRUCTION Congress strongly opposed to Johnson's policies, but with flimsy charges of "high Crimes and Misdemeanors," has been taken by many as a precedent against impeachment even for strongly felt reasons of policy believed to be of vital concern to the future of the nation. The impeachment–acquittal of Justice SAMUEL CHASE, early in our nation's history, similarly has been taken by many as a precedent against impeachment of judges merely because of disagreement (however intense and perhaps justified) with their judgments and demeanor.

While conduct need not be a crime in order to constitute an impeachable offense, it is clear that criminal acts in the ordinary sense of the term may themselves be "high

Crimes and Misdemeanors" sufficient to warrant removal from office, if Congress judges them to be serious enough offenses. The misconduct need not be a felony—high "Misdemeanors" fall within the standard—but the commission of felonies is a classic case in which the Constitution contemplates, and Congress's practice over the centuries confirms, that federal officers should be impeached and removed. (Moreover, Congress is not bound by the "proof beyond a reasonable doubt" standard that applies in a criminal prosecution in which an individual may be imprisoned or fined if found guilty; indeed, Congress has impeached and removed a federal judge, Alcee Hastings, who had been *acquitted* of essentially the same charges in a federal criminal prosecution.)

Thus, federal judges have been removed for bribery (Judge Hastings, in 1989), tax evasion (Judge Harry Claiborne, in 1986), and giving false testimony before a federal GRAND JURY (Judge Nixon, in 1989). President RICHARD M. NIXON resigned in 1974 rather than face near-certain impeachment (and probable conviction) for obstruction of justice. President Clinton was impeached for perjury and obstruction of justice, both serious federal felonies carrying substantial prison terms, but acquitted largely on the basis of votes of senators of his own party who concluded either that the charges were not proved or that such misconduct, even if proved, did not constitute "high Crimes and Misdemeanors."

Once again, as the Clinton case confirms, the question of what is sufficiently "high" criminal misconduct—sufficiently serious, important, weighty—is committed to the "awful discretion" (in Hamilton's terms) of Congress. Congress may exercise that judgment well or badly and need not be consistent or principled in its decisions. It seems highly likely, for example, that Congress in 1974 would have judged obstruction of justice to be an impeachable offense in the case of President Nixon (a scholarly report of the House Judiciary Committee indeed had so concluded), but many senators in 1999 concluded that it was not such an offense in the case of President Clinton.

One possible ground for distinguishing the Clinton and Nixon cases, advanced by Clinton's defenders (including numerous academics), is that Clinton's misconduct was of a "private" nature rather than an abuse of his office and that "private" crimes are not included within the meaning of "high Crimes and Misdemeanors." There must exist a nexus, the argument goes, between the criminal act and the official's public office. The text of the Constitution does not support this distinction, however, and Hamilton's argument that the impeachment power characteristically is directed at breaches of a public trust does not imply that the power may not be exercised to remove an official for crimes for which any citizen guilty of such offense might well be sent to prison. "Bribery," identified by the Constitution as an offense warranting removal from office, need not involve any use of a judge's or executive officer's official capacity. Other private-capacity corrupt conduct, like tax evasion, has served as a basis for impeachment and removal of federal judges (for example, Judge Claiborne in 1986). Clinton's prosecutors, and the fifty senators who voted to convict him, additionally maintained that there is no such thing as "private" perjury or obstruction of justice; that such crimes committed by the chief law enforcement officer of the nation do relate to the performance of his duties; that perjury is strongly akin to "Bribery," which is explicitly a ground for removal; and that Clinton's misconduct in any event involved a violation of his oath of office and a breach of trust with the People. On this account, the commission of serious crimes is itself a breach of the public trust.

There is a further flaw with the nexus-to-office limitation. Taken seriously, it would require the absurdity of permitting a federal officer to remain in office following commission of a "private" first-degree murder if that homicide was unrelated to the performance of his or her office. In an attempt to avoid this problem, a letter signed by law professors sympathetic to President Clinton argued that private criminal conduct does not warrant impeachment unless the crime is a "heinous" one. Again, however, the "heinous" standard does not appear in the Constitution, nor is it mentioned in the Framers' discussions and debates over impeachment. The standard chosen was "high" crimes and misdemeanors. It has been plausibly argued that "high" in this context denotes the rank or office of the alleged miscreant, but the better answer is that it creates a general standard of seriousness or importance (as judged by Congress). A crime can be serious without being "heinous." The Constitution clearly imposes no separate "heinousness" limitation on the impeachment power.

A final argument advanced during the Clinton case was that, for purposes of impeachment, the President should be held to a lower standard of conduct than federal judges and other federal officers; that is, that the "height" of "high" crimes needs to be higher in the case of the President before Congress is constitutionally justified in removing him from office. There is no basis for this argument in the text of the Constitution. Article III's provision that judges serve "during good behavior" is a description of judges' tenure (for life), not a substitute for Article II's statement of the impeachment–removal standard applicable to "all civil officers of the United States," a term that embraces Article III judges. While removal of a sitting President is obviously a more serious matter than removal of a single federal judge, this political reality does not alter the meaning of the Constitution's terms. Nor does the claim that removal of a President would "upset" the result of a national election change the Constitution's standard. Presidential impeachment will nearly always seek to remove an elected leader; the Framers, in creating an impeachment standard that explicitly mentions the President and Vice President, obviously contemplated such a possibility.

Though the Constitution does not require it, a practical necessity for removal of the President is that he *both* has committed serious offenses *and* lost popular political support, extending to members of his own POLITICAL PARTY in the Senate. Experience has shown that the two- thirds majority requirement makes it extremely difficult to convict a sitting President, regardless of the merits of the charges. As the acquittal of President Johnson shows, even large partisan majorities strongly opposed to an unpopular President on policy grounds encounter principled defections of senators opposed to a removal that is based on constitutionally dubious grounds. Conversely, as the acquittal of President Clinton shows, a popular President retaining the unified support of senators of his own party may avoid removal from office even when few (in either party) doubt that he has committed serious criminal offenses. (President Nixon resigned, rather than face impeachment, once it became clear that he had lost the support even of his own political party.)

A related issue that arose in the Clinton impeachment is whether Congress has the power to punish presidential misconduct by "censure." Censure, in the form of a resolution of disapproval (without further penalty), is neither mentioned in nor expressly prohibited by the Constitution. Whatever its propriety, censure is a remedy outside the impeachment process. The Constitution prescribes that conviction carries a mandatory penalty of removal from office (Article II, section 4), and a discretionary penalty of disqualification from future office (Article I, section 3), but forbids Congress from imposing any "further" punishment—presumably including supposedly "lesser" punishments like fines—with the clarification that the party convicted is nonetheless subject to criminal prosecution in the courts. A "censure" consisting of mere words may or may not be thought meaningful punishment, but in any event such expression could be accomplished outside the impeachment process as a matter of collective speech of senators and representatives, and thus is permissible. (Congress has no analogous power to fine or otherwise punish a President outside the impeachment process.)

The proviso that "the Party convicted shall, nevertheless, be subject to Indictment, Trial, Judgment and Punishment, according to Law" has been thought by many to imply that the President must be removed from office before he may be indicted. But if this is so, it must be because of some other constitutional provision, not the punishment proviso, which in form merely holds that Congress's judgment is separate from and not preclusive of criminal prosecution. The proviso does not dictate that impeachment precede indictment; prosecution has preceded impeachment in the case of several removed federal judges. It is probably the case that the Framers *expected*, in the case of the President at least, that removal would precede prosecution, for the simple reason that federal prosecutors are subordinates of the President within the executive branch and might be expected not to indict the Chief Executive. State prosecutions of a sitting President or other federal officer, although also theoretically possible, may not be practically enforceable without federal judicial or congressional approval (through impeachment). But where an "INDEPENDENT COUNSEL" serves as federal prosecutor acting on behalf of the executive branch (an arrangement constitutionally dubious in its own right, but upheld by the Supreme Court in 1988 in the case of *Morrison v. Olson*), or where a federal prosecutor is not otherwise countermanded by the President, the Constitution would not seem to bar those stages of a criminal case—indictment, trial, entry of judgment—that do not effect the equivalent of removal of a President from office (arrest, imprisonment). Removal is the exclusive province of impeachment. But otherwise the President is not above the requirements and burdens of the law that apply to any other citizen, taking into account the needs of the nation, as the Supreme Court has twice held, unanimously, in different contexts: UNITED STATES V. NIXON (1974) (the President is not immune to subpoenas for evidence in a federal criminal case) and CLINTON V. JONES (1997) (the President is not immune from private civil litigation concerning his personal conduct).

It has been suggested that the Article I, section 3 mandate of removal upon conviction for "high Crimes and Misdemeanors" does not necessarily imply that Congress lacks power to impeach and, in the Senate's *discretion*, remove or impose some lesser punishment (like censure) for perceived *lesser* offenses. Otherwise, the argument goes, what mechanism would have existed (prior to adoption of the TWENTY-FIFTH AMENDMENT in 1967) for removing an incapacitated or incompetent President? The argument has some serious problems, however. First, it imports into the word "impeachment" a broader power than appears supported by the language of the various clauses of the Constitution, and one that would seem inconsistent with other structural provisions of the Constitution. For example, Congress could, under this view, remove a President for vetoing a law more readily than it could override his veto—which requires a two-thirds majority of both houses, not just the Senate. Such a power tends too much toward creating a quasi-parliamentary regime at odds with the Framers' design. Had such a sweeping discretionary power been intended, it seems probable it would have been set forth far more clearly, especially given the extensive treatment of impeachment in fact contained in the Constitution's terms. Moreover, the breadth of the term "high Crimes and Misdemeanors" is already such as to permit impeachment—but, importantly, require removal upon conviction—for virtually any serious misconduct, including noncriminal misconduct, that Congress judges sufficiently serious to warrant such a remedy. At the same time, the mandatory punishment of removal deters unserious impeachments and creation by Congress of graduated penalties for perceived lesser political offenses, sapping the independence of the executive branch from Congress.

Finally, the apparent point-of-departure for this argument—the problem of presidential incapacity—is exactly the reason the Twenty-Fifth Amendment was adopted. The amendment filled a gap that was indeed left open by the impeachment power, and for which We the People felt further provision was needed. This highlights what should be a constitutional truism: The Constitution is not perfect and does not perfectly anticipate and address all of today's problems. But that does not mean that the Constitution's impeachment clauses (or any other clauses) should be distorted to suit the perceived needs of the moment. If the need for constitutional change is sufficiently great, the amendment process exists to address it.

Indeed, with respect to the power of impeachment, one can detect an embarrassing glitch that begs for a remedy: While the Chief Justice, rather than the Vice President, serves as presiding officer of the Senate when the President is tried (to remove obvious conflict-of-interest problems), no such substitution is prescribed in the case when the Vice President is put on trial, leaving open the prospect that the Vice President could preside at his own impeachment trial!

While imperfect in theory and even less perfect in practice, the Constitution's impeachment provisions provide a vital constitutional check against lawlessness and misconduct by executive and judicial officers—if Congress is prepared to employ that check in a serious manner. THOMAS JEFFERSON bemoaned the impeachment power as exercised in his day as a mere "scarecrow." But Jefferson's remark, as with the trials of Presidents Johnson and Clinton, simply highlights the fact that the application of the constitutional power of impeachment depends on the judgment of Congress and thus, for good or for ill, on the politics of the moment.

MICHAEL STOKES PAULSEN
(2000)

Bibliography

BERGER, RAOUL   1973   *Impeachment: The Constitutional Problems*. Cambridge, Mass.: Harvard University Press.

BLACK, CHARLES LUND   1974   *Impeachment: A Handbook*. New Haven, Conn.: Yale University Press.

GERHARDT, MICHAEL J.   1996   *The Federal Impeachment Process: A Constitutional and Historical Analysis*. Princeton, N.J.: Princeton University Press.

HAMILTON, ALEXANDER; JAY, JOHN; and MADISON, JAMES   1982   *The Federalist Papers*, Nos. 65 and 66. New York: Bantam Books.

PAULSEN, MICHAEL STOKES   1997   Someone Should Have Told Spiro Agnew. *Constitutional Commentary* 14:245–246.

———   1999   *Nixon Now: The Courts and the Presidency After Twenty-Five Years*. *Minnesota Law Review* 83:1337–1404.

REHNQUIST, WILLIAM H.   1992   *Grand Inquests: The Historic Impeachments of Justice Samuel Chase and President Andrew Johnson*. New York: Wm. Morrow.

U.S. CONGRESS   1974   *Constitutional Grounds for Presidential Impeachment*. Report prepared by the Staff of the Impeachment Inquiry of the House. 93rd Congress, 2nd Session. Committee Print.

———   1999   Committee on the Judiciary: Impeachment. [Documentation of the House Judiciary Committee hearings and of the House management of the impeachment trial of President William Jefferson Clinton.] <http://www.house.gov/judiciary/icreport.htm>.

———   1999   Impeachment of President William Jefferson Clinton. Senate Document 106-3. <http://www.access.gpo.gov/congress/senate/sd106-3.html>.

———   1999   Independent Counsel's Report to the United States House of Representatives. House Document 105-310. <http://www.access.gpo.gov/congress/icreport>.

IMPLIED CONSTITUTIONAL RIGHTS OF ACTION

One may seek judicial vindication of federal constitutional rights in at least three ways. Constitutional protections may be used as a shield against governmental misbehavior, as for example, when one relies on the Sixth Amendment guarantee of the RIGHT TO COUNSEL to contest a criminal prosecution. Second, one may rely on a constitutional right to enjoin allegedly unconstitutional behavior such as enforcement of an unconstitutional statute. Third, an aggrieved party may seek monetary compensation for past violations of constitutional rights. When invoked without express stautory authorization, the second and third techniques depend upon inferring the existence of implied rights of action to vindicate constitutional rights.

There is disagreement over whether, prior to EX PARTE YOUNG (1908), the offensive assertion of a federal right without a corresponding state-created right was sufficient to invoke a federal court's injunctive power. *Young*, which endorsed a federal INJUNCTION against enforcement of an allegedly unconstitutional state law, became the leading case to suggest that a federal cause of action for injunctive relief was implied merely from the existence of a constitutional right. This result has been a cornerstone of modern litigation contesting statutes and other government behavior. In later years, the Court interpreted SECTION 1983, TITLE 42, UNITED STATES CODE, to supply statutory support for both equitable and monetary relief in constitutional actions against state officials.

By 1971, in light of *Young* and section 1983, only the existence of implied damages actions against federal officials remained open to question. *Bell v. Hood* (1946) suggested that federal courts have JURISDICTION to consider whether alleged Fifth and FOURTH AMENDMENT violations by federal officials give rise to a cause of action for damages but it did not address the question of the cause of action's existence. In BIVENS V. SIX UNKNOWN NAMED AGENTS OF THE FEDERAL BUREAU OF NARCOTICS (1971), however, the Court held that an implied damages action exists for Fourth Amendment violations. DAVIS V. PASSMAN (1979) held that a damages action was implied in the EQUAL PROTECTION guarantee that has been found in the Fifth Amendment and constituted the Court's first extension of *Bivens* beyond Fourth Amendment claims. *Carlson v. Green* (1980), in which plaintiffs were allowed to bring an implied action under the Eighth Amendment, confirmed that *Bivens*-type actions are available under many constitutional provisions. Significantly, the Court has not held that such actions exist against state officials, a holding that would render superfluous much of its section 1983 jurisprudence.

Bivens, *Davis*, and *Carlson* suggested that Congress has an important role to play in determining the availability and scope of implied damages actions. The Court has left open the possibility of not inferring an implied damages action when defendants demonstrate "special factors counselling hesitation in the absence of affirmative action by Congress," or when, as in *Bush v. Lucas* (1983), Congress provides an effective alternative remedy. But *Davis* and *Carlson v. Green* indicated that the Court does not readily detect a congressional desire to foreclose *Bivens* actions. In *Davis*, Congress had declined to extend federal employment discrimination laws to preclude the behavior for which the Court inferred an implied private right of action. *Carlson* held that the existence of a remedy against the United States under the FEDERAL TORT CLAIMS ACT did not foreclose a *Bivens* action against individual officers alleged to have violated the Constitution.

THEODORE EISENBERG
(1986)

Bibliography

DELLINGER, WALTER E. 1972 Of Rights and Remedies: The Constitution as a Sword. *Harvard Law Review* 85:1532–1564.

HART, HENRY M., JR. 1954 The Relations between State and Federal Law. *Columbia Law Review* 54:489–542.

IMPLIED POWERS

"Loose and irresponsible use of adjectives colors . . . much legal discussion. . . . "Inherent' powers, "implied' powers, "incidental' powers are used, often interchangeably and without fixed ascertainable meanings." Justice ROBERT H. JACKSON's remark in YOUNGSTOWN SHEET & TUBE COMPANY V. SAWYER (1952) was correct. The vocabulary of "implied powers" is frequently used indiscriminately with other terms. It is associated with not less than six quite different usages.

The original use of "implied powers" was to contrast, rather than to explain, the powers that would vest in the United States. The national government would not automatically possess all the customary attributes of SOVEREIGNTY, but only those expressly provided. As to these, JAMES MADISON declared (in THE FEDERALIST #45): "The powers delegated by the proposed Constitution to the Federal Government, are few and defined. Those which are to remain in the State Governments are numerous and indefinite." Writing for a unanimous Supreme Court in 1804, Chief Justice JOHN MARSHALL, in *United States v. Fisher,* agreed that there were no implied-at-large national powers: "[I]t has been truly said, that under a constitution conferring specific powers, the power contended for must be granted, or it cannot be exercised." And more than a century later, Justice DAVID BREWER in *Kansas v. Colorado* (1907) confirmed the conventional wisdom: "[T]he proposition that there are legislative powers [not] expressed in the grant of powers, is in direct conflict with the doctrine that this is a government of ENUMERATED POWERS."

In this original sense, then, it may be said that the Constitution does not imply a government of general legislative, executive, and judicial powers; it establishes a government of limited, express, enumerated powers alone.

In 1936, in UNITED STATES V. CURTISS-WRIGHT EXPORT CORPORATION, Justice GEORGE SUTHERLAND, in an OBITER DICTUM for the Supreme Court, suggested that the national government need not rely upon any express power to sustain an assertion of executive authority prohibiting American companies from foreign trade which (in the President's view) might compromise the nation's neutral status at international law. Sutherland observed that the United States, as a nation within an international community of sovereign national states possessed "powers of external sovereignty" *apart* from any one or any combination of the Constitution's limited list of powers respecting foreign relations. Accordingly, Sutherland declared: "The broad statement that the federal government can exercise no powers except those specifically enumerated in the Constitution, and such implied powers as are necessary and proper to carry into effect the enumerated powers, is categorically true only in respect of our internal affairs." Such an extraconstitutional power may informally be described as one derived from the status of being a sovereign nation or as implied by the fact of national sovereignty.

The soundness of this view has been seriously questioned, however, and in fact its acceptance has not been necessary to the outcome of any case. Rather, its principal positive law use has been as a reference in support of very broad interpretations of the several provisions in the Constitution which expressly enumerate executive and congressional powers respecting FOREIGN AFFAIRS. It has also been relied upon to uphold extremely permissive DELE-GATIONS OF POWER by Congress to permit the President to determine conditions of trade between American companies and foreign countries, or conditions of American travel and activity abroad.

Not inconsistent with the general view that any claim of implied-at-large national powers is precluded by the text and presuppositions of the Constitution, such specific powers as are conferred by the Constitution have been deemed to carry with them exceedingly wide-ranging implications. Partly this results merely from the doctrine of BROAD CONSTRUCTION that every specific grant of power is to be deferentially interpreted, rather than narrowly construed. For instance, the power vested in Congress to "regulate" commerce among the several states might have been interpreted quite narrowly, in keeping with the principal objectives of enabling Congress to provide for a nationwide free trade zone, as against the tendency of some states to enact discriminatory taxes, and other self-favoring economic barriers. Instead, the power was construed in no such qualified fashion. The power to regulate commerce among the several states is "the power to prescribe the rule by which such commerce shall be governed," which therefore includes the power to limit or to forbid outright such commerce among the states as Congress sees fit to disallow. The result has been that to this extent, the express power to regulate commerce among the states gives to Congress a limited NATIONAL POLICE POWER.

Beyond adopting an attitude of permissive construction respecting each enumerated power, however, the Supreme Court took an additional significant step. It accepted the view that acts of Congress not themselves direct exercises of conferred powers would be deemed authorized by the Constitution if they facilitated the exercise of one or more express powers. An act of Congress establishing a national bank under a corporate charter granted by Congress, vesting authority in its directors to set up branch banks with general banking prerogatives, may arguably facilitate borrowing on the credit of the United States, paying debts incurred by the United States, regulating some aspects of commerce among states, and

serving as a place of deposit for funds to meet military payrolls. Each of these *uses* is itself identified as an express, enumerated power vested in Congress although the act establishing such an incorporated national bank may itself not be regarded as legislation that borrows money, pays debts, etc. Nevertheless, insofar as provision for such a bank might usefully serve as an instrument by means of which several expressly enumerated powers could be carried into execution, the Supreme Court unanimously concluded that the congressional power to furnish such a bank was "implied" "incidentally" in those enumerated powers. The opinion by Chief Justice Marshall in MCCULLOCH V. MARYLAND (1819) is crowded with the repeated use of both terms. In tandem with the principle of generous construction, this view of "implied" incidental powers has had a profound influence in assuring to Congress an immense latitude of legislative discretion despite the conventional wisdom that the national government is one of specific, enumerated powers alone. Laws not probably within even a latitudinarian construction of specific grants of power, but nonetheless instrumentally relatable to such grants, are thus deemed to be adequately "implied" by those grants as incidents of grants.

A contemporary example is furnished by WICKARD V. FIL-BURN (1942). Though some of the "commerce" regulated by the act upheld in that case was not commerce at all (because it was not offered for trade, but was used solely for the farmer's personal consumption), and although the activity regulated was entirely local (growing and consuming wheat on one's own farm), insofar as the regulation of these local matters was nonetheless instrumentally relatable to an act fixing the volume of wheat permitted to be grown for purposes of interstate sale, the power to include local growing and consumption, as part of the larger regulation, was deemed to be implied by the express power to regulate commerce among the several states. The imaginative capacity of Congress to relate the aggregate interstate effects of local activity, thus bringing it within a uniform and integrated national economic policy, has made the principle of incidental implied power at least as important as the principle of broad construction in respect to enumerated national power. Indeed, the combination of the two doctrines has led Justice WILLIAM H. REHNQUIST, in HODEL V. VIRGINIA SURFACE MINING (1981), to suggest: "It is illuminating for purposes of reflection, if not for argument, to note that one of the greatest "fictions" of our federal system is that the Congress exercises only those powers delegated to it, while the remainder are reserved to the States or to the people. The manner in which this Court has construed the COMMERCE CLAUSE amply illustrates the extent of this fiction." However that may be, the notion that express powers imply an authority to undertake action instrumentally relatable to the use of those powers, albeit action not itself an exercise of any express power, has given to the national government a flexibility and discretion that it would not otherwise possess.

The bank case (*McCulloch*) and the wheat quota case (*Wickard*) are examples of implied powers incidental to *specific* enumerated powers. Each involved acts of Congress establishing an enterprise or furnishing a regulation instrumentally related to one or another express power. Different from this kind of "incidental implied power," but resting on much the same sort of constitutional justification, are implied powers common to each of the three branches of the national government. These powers, sometimes called INHERENT POWERS, are deemed to be implied as reasonably necessary to each department's capacity to discharge effectively its enumerated responsibilities. Because they are regarded as effecting that capacity generally (and not merely in respect to one or another specific enumerated power alone), however, they are generically implied, incidental powers.

A prominent example is the unenumerated (but implied) power of each house of Congress to hold legislative hearings, to subpoena witnesses, and otherwise to compel the submission of information thought useful in determining whether acts of Congress on particular subjects need to be adopted, repealed, or modified. The power to conduct LEGISLATIVE INVESTIGATIONS, nowhere expressly conferred, is deemed to be implied as a reasonable incident of the legislative function. Similarly, a power of federal courts to maintain order in adjudicative proceedings, independent of any act of Congress providing such a power (pursuant to the NECESSARY AND PROPER CLAUSE), rests on the same ground. And although never challenged, presumably the power of the Supreme Court to exclude all but its own members from its private conferences in which discussion is held and votes are taken on pending cases is an example.

A qualified power of EXECUTIVE PRIVILEGE, enabling the President to interdict discovery of advice, memoranda, and other internal executive communications is conceded by the Supreme Court to be implied as an incident of executive necessity and power. The principle common to these several examples was illustrated in a remark by ALEXANDER HAMILTON, in *The Federalist* #74, commenting briefly upon the express power vested in the President by Article II, authorizing the President to "require the opinion in writing of the principal officer in each of the executive departments upon any subject relating to the duties of their respective offices." As to this express provision, Hamilton suggested, "I consider [it] a mere redundancy in the plan; as the right for which it provides would result of itself from the office." And so, undoubtedly, it would, especially as the Supreme Court was subsequently to hold

that the President has an implied power to dismiss any executive subordinate at will, though no express clause so provides, and the clause respecting appointment of such officers requires the consent of the Senate.

One may phrase the matter variously, as power "resulting" from the establishment of the executive, legislative, and judicial branches, or as powers "incidental" to their designated powers. The point is the same: instrumental powers deemed reasonably necessary generally to each department's independent capacity to exercise its express, vested powers are treated as generically implied by Articles I, II, and III.

As noted in *McCulloch* an act of Congress establishing a national bank in corporate form may be useful as a means of carrying into execution the several specific fiscal powers of the United States. Equally, a regulation of local commerce may be necessary to keep a regulation of INTERSTATE COMMERCE from frustration. In either case the Court has upheld such exercise of congressional power when instrumentally relatable to the exercise of an express, enumerated power. In neither case, however, is it necessary in fact to describe the power to adopt such instrumentally relatable laws as "implied" power. Rather, all such laws are themselves specifically and expressly authorized by an *enumerated* grant of enabling power vested in Congress: "Congress shall have power to make all laws necessary and proper to carry into execution the foregoing powers, and all other powers vested in the government of the United States or any officer or department thereof." This clause, located at the end of the enumerated powers of Congress in Article I, section 8, is known as the "necessary and proper" clause. Originally, in anticipation of its elasticizing effects, it was known as "the sweeping clause," vesting in Congress discretion to carry into effect its own enumerated powers, and those of the executive and judiciary as well, by means of its own choosing. Consistent with that background, and consistent also with the general doctrine of generous (or loose) construction, the sweeping clause has been construed by the Supreme Court very liberally: "necessary and proper" are regarded as synonymous with "reasonable." Thus, whatever acts of Congress may reasonably relate to a regulation of commerce among the several states are authorized by this clause. Likewise, whatever acts of Congress may reasonably relate to the conduct of the JUDICIAL POWER OF THE UNITED STATES, or the conduct of the executive powers (as described in Article II), as an aid to those departments to carry into execution the executive or judicial powers, are authorized by this clause.

Because of this interpretation of the sweeping clause, it is not clear why the Supreme Court developed the notion of incidental *implied* powers. From one point of view, the latter doctrine is both redundant, because it duplicates a power *already* provided in the Constitution, and illogical because insofar as there is a clause expressly providing for such an instrumental power vested in Congress, to speak of such a power as "implied" rather than as "express" makes little sense. Had there been no necessary and proper clause, the innovation of a doctrine of implied power, incidental to enumerated powers, might be rested on the felt necessity of rendering the national government equal to ultimate growth and needs of the nation. But insofar as the necessary and proper clause was itself construed to provide for such flexibility, no need remained to be filled by the additional innovation of "implied, incidental" power. The doctrine of generous construction (respecting the scope of enumerated power) and the necessary and proper clause (itself generously construed), would in combination grant a vast instrumental latitude to Congress in respect both to its own powers and to those of the executive and the judiciary.

One consequence of this partial redundancy is that there is no particular consistency in the pattern of Supreme Court decisions respecting unsuccessfully challenged acts of Congress. Sometimes they are sustained as but implied incidents of one or more enumerated substantive powers. And sometimes, as happened in *McCulloch*, they are sustained on both grounds at the same time.

Were it not for a related problem, the question whether an exertion of national power not within an express enumerated power (but nonetheless instrumentally relatable to such a power) properly rests on the necessary and proper clause, or instead merely represents an implied power instrumentally incidental to an express power, would be merely academic. But, unfortunately, it is not always so. The necessary and proper clause vests its power in Congress. It implies, by doing so, that if Congress believes it appropriate to facilitate the executive and judicial enumerated powers, it may do so by enacting legislation helpful, albeit not indispensable, to those departments. Merely "helpful" instrumental powers assertable by the executive or by the judiciary will depend, therefore, on whether Congress has, by law, acting pursuant to the necessary and proper clause, provided for them. Correspondingly, the absence of any such act of Congress providing for such incidental executive or judicial powers would be a sufficient basis for a successful challenge to any such unaided assertions of executive or judicial power.

On the other hand, if the mere enumeration of executive and judicial powers (in Articles II and III) are themselves deemed to imply incidentally helpful (but not indispensable) ancillary powers, then the absence of a supportive act of Congress is not fatal to such claims. Thus, in this instance, it does make a difference to resolve the relationship between the necessary and proper clause (addressed solely to what Congress may provide) and the doctrine of implied, incidental powers.

Interestingly, two centuries into the positive law history of the Constitution, this particular question has not been addressed by the Supreme Court. Rather, an uneasy accommodation has been made. Each department of government has been regarded by the Court as possessing a range of incidental powers implied by its express powers, and such assertions of authority have been generally upheld. Nonetheless, insofar as Congress has legislated affirmatively, and by statute has found that such an assertion of incidental executive (or judicial) authority is *not* necessary or proper, the tendency of the Supreme Court is to defer to the authoritative judgment of Congress and, correspondingly, rule against the assertion of "implied" incidental executive power.

The pragmatic accommodation of the doctrine of implied incidental powers and the necessary and proper clause, therefore, has been to treat Congress as *primus inter pares*. Each department of the national government has separate enumerated powers of its own, not subject to abridgment by either of the other two departments. In addition, each may assert implied incidental powers, instrumentally relatable to its enumerated powers albeit not literally within those enumerated powers as even generously construed. But a specific determination by Congress with respect to this latter class of powers is regarded as virtually conclusive of the subject. If the act of Congress confirms such power, it is virtually certain to be sustained. If the act of Congress either expressly or implicitly denies the appropriateness of such incidental executive or judicial power, then that determination also is likely to govern. The case best known for this view is *Youngstown Sheet & Tube Co. v. Sawyer.*

The Constitution enumerates express WAR POWERS and express powers enabling Congress to insure each state against domestic violence. Curiously, however, it has no express clauses directed to the internal security of the national government. Nevertheless, the authority to provide for laws punishing attempts of violent overthrow has been sustained as an implied power of self-preservation. Depending upon how deeply such laws may affect certain freedoms to criticize the government or to bring about fundamental changes in its composition by peaceful means, these acts of Congress may be vulnerable to challenge under the FIRST AMENDMENT or other provisions of the Constitution. Nevertheless, a considerable implied power of self-preservation is deemed to vest in Congress, essentially on the common-sense inference that its express enumerated powers imply a residual existence of the government possessing those powers and thus, of necessity, a power of self-preservation. The Sedition Act of 1798 (see ALIEN AND SEDITION ACTS) was sustained in the lower federal courts partly on this rationale.

Less frequently drawn into litigation, but presumably resting on similar grounds, is the implied power of Congress to provide for incidents of national status. The adoption of a national flag rests on no particular enumerated power. Rather, like other acts of Congress identifying symbols of national status, it is but an implied incident of an expressly established government—of the United States of America.

In sum, the phrase "implied powers" houses a half-dozen quite discrete meanings. They are bound together by but one common element, namely the obviousness of contrast with express powers. Beyond that, however, they speak to distinct (and not always completely reconcilable) propositions. One is an implied residual sovereign power of national self-preservation and the incidental power to adopt ordinary insignia of nationhood. In addition, there are implied powers peculiar to each of the three branches of the national government, incidental to the exercise of all enumerated powers expressly vested in each branch. Such generic implied powers apart, there are also implied cognate powers incidental to each expressly enumerated power, extending the reach of those enumerated powers even beyond what might otherwise be their scope under a doctrine of loose or generous construction. Then, too, although the usage seems inept in reference to an *enumerated* general enabling power, the necessary and proper clause of the Constitution has often been used to anchor the textual source of extensive, instrumental powers. And last, there is also the claim of implied, extraconstitutional power in respect to the external sovereign relations of the United States, standing over and apart from the several enumerations of power provided by the Constitution.

The solidness of the foundations respecting these several varieties of implied powers are not all of a piece, that is, quite plainly they are not all of equally convincing legitimacy. Rather, they but illustrate in still one more way how two centuries of history have operated to show what has followed from Chief Justice Marshall's observation that it is a Constitution we are expounding.

WILLIAM W. VAN ALSTYNE
(1986)

Bibliography

GUNTHER, GERALD, ed. 1969 *John Marshall's Defense of McCulloch v. Maryland.* Stanford, Calif.: Stanford University Press.

HENKIN, LOUIS 1972 *Foreign Affairs and the Constitution.* St. Paul, Minn.: West Publishing Co.

VAN ALSTYNE, WILLIAM W. 1976 The Role of Congress in Determining Incidental Powers of the President and of the Federal Courts: The Horizontal Effect of the Sweeping Clause. *Law & Contemporary Problems* 1976:102–134.

IMPORT-EXPORT CLAUSE

The Constitution provides: "No State shall . . . lay any Imposts or Duties on Imports or Exports, except what may be absolutely necessary for executing its inspection Laws." It also prohibits the federal government from placing any tax or duty on exports.

The limitation on state taxation of imports came before the Supreme Court in BROWN V. MARYLAND (1827). Chief Justice JOHN MARSHALL pointed out that the clear intention of the Framers was to prohibit the states from levying customs duties. Only Congress was to have this power. He recognized, however, that state power to raise revenues would be unduly restricted if goods that had come from another country could never be subject to taxation along with other goods within the state. He resolved the dilemma by holding that imported goods should be free from state taxation until they have been incorporated into the mass of property in the state. Such incorporation would take place when the importer sold the goods or when he took them out of the original package in which they were imported. Hence was born the ORIGINAL PACKAGE DOCTRINE, which survived as the measure for state taxation of imports until MICHELIN TIRE CORP. V. WAGES (1976).

In *Michelin* the Supreme Court held that the intention of the Framers was only to prevent the states from imposing special taxes on imports. Hence, it concluded that imported goods could, as soon as they came to rest in the taxing state, be subject to nondiscriminatory state property taxes.

The Supreme Court has long held that goods become exports—and thus free from either state or federal taxes—when they have actually commenced the journey to another country. Once the journey has commenced or they have been committed to a common carrier for transport abroad, they may not be taxed.

Application of the import-export clause to those businesses that transport or otherwise handle goods in FOREIGN COMMERCE has posed a separate problem. Recently the Court has held that nondiscriminatory taxes apportioned to cover only values within the taxing state may be imposed upon the instrumentalities of foreign commerce or the business of engaging in such commerce. Thus, in *Department of Revenue of Washington v. Association of Washington Stevedoring Companies* (1978), it upheld a Washington tax on the privilege of engaging in business activities measured by gross receipts as applied to a stevedoring company that confined its activities to the loading and unloading in Washington ports of ships engaged in foreign commerce.

In general, the rules governing state taxation of INTERSTATE COMMERCE now seem to apply to imports and exports.

EDWARD L. BARRETT, JR.
(1986)

(SEE ALSO: *State Taxation of Commerce.*)

Bibliography

HELLERSTEIN, WALTER 1977 Michelin Tire Corp. v. Wages: Enhanced State Power to Tax Imports. *Supreme Court Review* 1977:99–123.

IMPOST

In its broadest sense the term "impost" refers to any tax or tribute levied by authority. By usage it has come to have the narrower meaning of a tax or duty imposed on imports. The Supreme Court has recently stated that "imposts and duties" as used in the Constitution "are essentially taxes on the commercial privilege of bringing goods into a country."

EDWARD L. BARRETT, JR.
(1986)

(SEE ALSO: *Excise Tax; Import-Export Clause; Michelin Tire Company v. Administrator of Wages; State Taxation of Commerce.*)

IMPOUNDMENT OF FUNDS

Presidents from time to time, and especially beginning with the regime of FRANKLIN D. ROOSEVELT, have asserted a right not to execute the laws or parts thereof, by a decision to "impound" the funds provided by Congress for the effectuation of the law. In effect, this would be an exercise of an item VETO POWER. There is no warrant in the Constitution for the exercise of the power of impoundment. The history of the veto provision in the CONSTITUTIONAL CONVENTION OF 1787 makes clear that the Founders were wary of any veto authority, no less one that would allow the President to rewrite the laws of Congress to suit his predilections. Instead, the Constitution clearly requires that the President "take Care that the Laws be faithfully executed." Only if the provisions of Article II vesting the "executive power" are read to create implicit authority in the President to do as he pleases—what Arthur Schlesinger, Jr., calls a "plebiscitary" presidency—

can the impoundment authority be deemed a constitutional one.

This is not to say that a President may not be authorized to exercise the impoundment power. But that authority must derive from legislation and not from the Constitution. Where Congress has mandated the expenditure of funds in support of a legislative program, the President has no choice but to effectuate Congress's will. But legislation may explicitly create discretion in the executive branch as to whether programs are to be carried out in whole or in part. And the courts have suggested that legislation may imply that such presidential power exists. Arguments have also been made that certain general statutes such as those ordering the executive to choose the most economic means of enforcement of the laws, or putting ceilings on the national debt, create a legislative warrant for presidential impoundment. There is little merit in the proposals that these statutes create a general statutory authority for the President to pick and choose among congressional programs.

The President has a veto power. If it is used successfully, the congressional program need not be effected for it is not the law. If the veto be used unsuccessfully, however, it is clear that Congress has mandated the program and it is Congress's will, not the President's, that makes the law of the land. Although there is no item veto, no restriction exists on the veto message explaining that the veto was invoked in response to a particular item in the legislation. If Congress overrides the veto, it will be clear that the portion found objectionable by the President was found desirable by the Congress.

After particularly egregious efforts by President RICHARD M. NIXON to throttle congressional legislation through "impoundment," the CONGRESSIONAL BUDGET AND IMPOUNDMENT CONTROL ACT was enacted (1974). This statute requires the President to inform Congress if he proposes to rescind or defer appropriations. There can be no rescission unless Congress acting through both houses concurs within forty-five days. A deferral can be invalidated by a resolution of disapproval by one house but is valid unless disapproved. The statute is thorny with constitutional issues, but both the legislators and the executive seem willing to accept it as an appropriate accommodation of their respective interests.

The question whether a President may refuse to enforce a law that he deems unconstitutional is not really an "impoundment" question. That issue was mooted but not resolved in the IMPEACHMENT and trial of President ANDREW JOHNSON. Clearly the President can challenge or refuse to defend in the courts any legislation he finds unconstitutional.

PHILIP B. KURLAND
(1986)

Bibliography

FISHER, LOUIS 1972 *President and Congress: Power and Policy.* New York: Free Press.

GENERAL ACCOUNTING OFFICE 1977 *Review of the Impoundment Control Act of 1974.* Washington, D.C.: Government Printing Office.

INALIENABLE POLICE POWER

THOMAS COOLEY, writing on the STATE POLICE POWER in 1868, concluded that the CONTRACT CLAUSE did not permit a state "under pretense of regulation, [to] take from the CORPORATION any of the essential rights and privileges which the charter confers." Constitutional law changed quickly. In BOSTON BEER CO. V. MASSACHUSETTS (1878), when holding that the RESERVED POLICE POWER allowed a state to revoke the charter of a brewery company, the Supreme Court declared that even in the absence of a reserved power to revoke, the revocation would be valid: the legislature cannot contract away or otherwise alienate the sovereign power to protect the lives, health, safety, or morals of its citizens. A legislature can, however, alienate its tax powers, as NEW JERSEY V. WILSON (1812) and PIQUA BRANCH BANK V. KNOOP (1854) demonstrated. As the Court frequently explained, the tax power is a right of government that the contract clause does not protect; it protects property rights only. That distinction scarcely explains why the power of EMINENT DOMAIN, a government right, cannot be contracted away. Nevertheless, the inalienable police power proved to be an effective rationale for supporting a variety of regulatory legislation against contract clause claims.

In NORTHWESTERN FERTILIZING COMPANY V. HYDE PARK (1878) the Court upheld as a protection of public health an ordinance forcing the removal of a fertilizer plant. In STONE V. MISSISSIPPI (1880) the Court sustained a state act revoking the charter of a lottery company; the contract clause could not limit a power to protect public morality from gambling. Within a few years the Court upheld one state act revoking a monopoly of the slaughterhouse business and another establishing a commission to fix the rates of a railroad company whose charter expressly authorized it to fix its own rates. In the rate case, STONE V. FARMERS' LOAN AND TRUST COMPANY (1886), the fact that the state had not reserved a power to alter or amend the charter made the defeat of the contract clause claim seem kindred to a victory for the inalienable police power. The unreliability of the contract clause, especially in rate cases, led shortly to the acceptance of SUBSTANTIVE DUE PROCESS OF LAW to defeat the police power.

That the inalienable police power was not limited to cases of public health, safety, or morality is shown by the unanimous opinion in *Chicago and Alton Railroad v. Tranbarger* (1915), sustaining a state requirement that railroads construct roadbeds that prevent water damage to private property. Justice MAHLON PITNEY for the Court declared that all contract and property rights are held subject to the exercise of a police power that "is inalienable even by express grant" and is not limited by either the contract clause or the DUE PROCESS clause. Pitney added that the power embraced regulations promoting "public convenience or the GENERAL WELFARE and prosperity" as well as the "public health, morals, or safety." Protection of the "general welfare and prosperity" figured prominently in the Court's decision in HOME BUILDING AND LOAN ASSOCIATION V. BLAISDELL (1934). In that case the Court referred to the reserved police power but meant the inalienable police power.

LEONARD W. LEVY
(1986)

Bibliography

WRIGHT, BENJAMIN F. 1938 *The Contract Clause of the Constitution.* Pages 195–213. Cambridge, Mass.: Harvard University Press.

INCIDENTAL BURDENS ON CONSTITUTIONAL RIGHTS

Government actions may interfere with individual rights in two principal ways. First, government may disadvantage a person because that person exercised a right. A law that by its terms prohibits the "burning of an American flag as a statement of political protest" is an example of a law directed at a right in this way. Second, the government may enforce a law that is not directed at an individual right but has the incidental effect of burdening a right in the particular case. The application of a law prohibiting "the lighting of a public fire," to an act of politically motivated flag burning is an example of such an incidental burden. The Supreme Court has held that most constitutional rights are protected against direct burdens but not against incidental ones. Thus, in the above examples, the law directed at flag burning would be unconstitutional, while the application of the fire prohibition to the flag burner would be constitutional, so long as the law was not being used as a pretext for punishing unpopular expression. Similarly, a law using race as an express criterion is presumptively unconstitutional, while a facially neutral law that has a disparate impact on a racial group will be upheld if it was adopted for a nondiscriminatory purpose.

From the perspective of an individual right-holder, there may be little difference between direct and incidental burdens on constitutional rights. In each case, some government policy infringes the right. However, to say that incidental burdens always raise the same constitutional concerns as targeted ones would open the floodgates of litigation, because every law can, under various circumstances, impose incidental burdens on rights. User fees for government services often have a disparate racial impact, and taxation of all CORPORATIONS increases the marginal cost of doing business for those corporations that run newspapers, thereby burdening FREEDOM OF THE PRESS. To avoid subjecting nearly all laws to searching constitutional scrutiny, the courts must either ignore incidental burdens entirely or find some way to identify some relatively small subset of incidental burdens that pose the gravest dangers. For the most part, the Court has chosen the former course. As a comparison of speech and religion cases illustrates, however, this strategy presents problems.

As a formal matter, in FREEDOM OF SPEECH cases, the Court treats some incidental burdens as constitutionally significant. In practice, however, the Court only gives serious scrutiny to direct content-based burdens on speech, which are presumptively invalid. For example, in *Simon & Schuster, Inc. v. Members of The New York State Crime Victims Board* (1991), the Court invalidated as content-based New York's "Son-of-Sam" law, which required publishers of accounts of crimes committed by their authors to set aside the royalties of those authors for a victim compensation fund.

Content-neutral laws target the noncommunicative element of communicative activity. For example, in KOVACS V. COOPER (1949), the Court upheld an ordinance prohibiting sound trucks because the ordinance aimed to control noise, regardless of the message conveyed. The Court has said that content-neutral laws will be upheld if they serve important interests unrelated to the suppression of ideas and burden no more expression than necessary. Although this test sounds forbidding in principle, in practice the courts have upheld virtually every regulation subject to it.

The Court's interpretation of the free exercise of religion clause makes explicit what is implicit in the speech cases: incidental burdens do not raise constitutional difficulties. In EMPLOYMENT DIVISION, DEPARTMENT OF HUMAN RESOURCES OF OREGON V. SMITH (1990), the Court rejected the claim that Native Americans who used peyote as part of a religious ritual had a free exercise right to an exemption from the state's prohibition on drug use. The Court held that the free exercise clause is essentially an antidiscrimination principle. It proscribes laws that target religious practices as such, but does not reach generally applicable laws that impose incidental burdens on religion.

It is easier to justify the Court's treatment of incidental burdens on speech than its treatment of incidental burdens on religion. A person who wishes to communicate a message may choose from a variety of means of expression, so that laws imposing incidental burdens on speech may be upheld while leaving open adequate alternative means of expression. The medium is not the message. By contrast, religious obligations do not ordinarily admit of alternatives. Thus, the *Smith* decision was widely viewed as unduly harsh to members of minority religions whose practices the legislative process often burdens indirectly.

MICHAEL C. DORF
(2000)

Bibliography

ALEXANDER, LARRY A. 1993 Trouble on Track Two: Incidental Regulations of Speech and Free Speech Theory. *Hastings Law Journal* 44:921–962.

DORF, MICHAEL C. 1996 Incidental Burdens on Fundamental Rights. *Harvard Law Review* 109:1175–1251.

EISGRUBER, CHRISTOPHER L. and SAGER, LAWRENCE G. 1994 The Vulnerability of Conscience: The Constitutional Basis for Protecting Religious Conduct. *University of Chicago Law Review* 61:1245–1315.

MCCONNELL, MICHAEL W. 1990 Free Exercise Revisionism and the *Smith* Decision. *University of Chicago Law Review* 57: 1109–1153.

SCHAUER, FREDERICK 1985 Cuban Cigars, Cuban Books, and the Problem of Incidental Restrictions on Communications. *William & Mary Law Review* 26:779–791.

STONE, GEOFFREY R. 1987 Content-Neutral Restrictions. *University of Chicago Law Review* 54:46–118.

TRIBE, LAURENCE H. 1988 *American Constitutional Law*, 2nd ed. Mineola, N.Y.: Foundation Press.

INCITEMENT TO UNLAWFUL CONDUCT

Incitement to unlawful conduct raises a central and difficult issue about the proper boundaries of freedom of expression and of the FIRST AMENDMENT. Many of the Supreme Court's most important FREEDOM OF SPEECH decisions have involved some form of incitement. Though the term incitement sometimes refers to emotionally charged appeals to immediate action, the word is most often used to cover any urging that others commit illegal acts.

The basic problem about incitement is fairly simple, involving a tension between a criminal law perspective and a free speech perspective. Any society seeks to minimize the number of crimes that are committed. Some people commit crimes because others urge them to do so. Although the person who actually commits a crime may usually seem more to blame than someone who encourages him, on other occasions the inciter, because of greater authority, intelligence, or firmness of purpose, may actually be more responsible for what happens than the person who is the instrument of his designs. In any event, because the person who successfully urges another to commit a crime bears some responsibility and because effective restrictions on incitement are likely to reduce the amount of crime to some degree, sound reasons exist for punishing those who incite.

Anglo-American criminal law, like the law of other traditions, has reflected this view. In 1628, EDWARD COKE wrote that "all those that incite . . . any other" to commit a FELONY are guilty of a crime; and, at least by 1801, unsuccessful incitement was recognized as an offense in England. Modern American criminal law generally treats the successful inciter on a par with the person who performs the criminal act; the unsuccessful inciter is guilty of criminal solicitation, treated as a lesser crime than the one he has tried to incite.

From the free speech perspective, the problem of incitement takes on a different appearance. A basic premise of a liberal society is that people should be allowed to express their views, especially their political views. Some important political views support illegal actions against actual or possible governments. Indeed, one aspect of the political tradition of the United States is that revolutionary overthrow of existing political authority is sometimes justified. Other views deem certain illegal acts justified even when the government is acceptable. Were all encouragements of illegal activity suppressed, an important slice of political and social opinions would be silenced. Further, in the practical administration of such suppression some opinions that did not quite amount to encouragement would be proceeded against and persons would be inhibited from saying things that could possibly be construed as encouragements to commit crimes. Thus, wide restrictions on incitement have been thought to imperil free expression, particularly when statutes penalizing incitement have been specifically directed to "subversive" political ideologies.

The tension between criminal law enforcement and freedom of expression is addressed by both legislatures and courts. Legislatures must initially decide what is a reasonable, and constitutionally permissible, accommodation of the conflicting values. When convictions are challenged, courts must decide whether the statutes that legislatures have adopted and their applications to particular situations pass constitutional muster.

Most states have statutes that make solicitation of a crime illegal. These laws are drawn to protect speech interests to a significant extent. To be convicted of solicitation, one must actually encourage the commission of a specific crime. Therefore, many kinds of statements, such as disinterested advice that committing a crime like draft evasion would be morally justified, approval of present lawbreaking in general, or urging people to prepare themselves for unspecified future revolutionary acts, are beyond the reach of ordinary solicitation statutes.

One convenient way to conceptualize the First Amendment problems about incitement is to ask whether any communications that do amount to ordinary criminal solicitation are constitutionally protected and whether other communications that encourage criminal acts but fall short of criminal solicitation lack constitutional protection.

All major Supreme Court cases on the subject have involved political expression of one kind or another and have arisen under statutes directed at specific kinds of speech. Some of the cases have involved CRIMINAL CONSPIRACY charges, but because the conspiracy has been to incite or advocate, the constitutionality of punishing communications has been the crucial issue. In SCHENCK V. UNITED STATES (1919) the Court sustained a conviction under the 1917 ESPIONAGE ACT, which made criminal attempts to obstruct enlistment. The leaflet that Schenck had helped to publish had urged young men to assert their rights to oppose the draft. Writing the majority opinion that found no constitutional bar to the conviction, Justice OLIVER WENDELL HOLMES penned the famous CLEAR AND PRESENT DANGER test: "The question in every case is whether the words used are used in such circumstances and are of such a nature as to create a clear and present danger that they will bring about the substantive evils that Congress has a right to prevent." Much was unclear about this test as originally formulated and as subsequently developed, but the results in *Schenck* and companion cases show that the Court then did not conceive the standard as providing great protection for speech. During the 1920s, while the majority of Justices ceased using the test, eloquent dissents by Holmes and LOUIS D. BRANDEIS forged it into a principle that was protective of speech, requiring a danger that was both substantial and close in time in order to justify suppressing communication. Even these later opinions, however, did not indicate with clarity whether the test applied to ordinary criminal solicitation or whether an intent to create a clear and present danger would be sufficient for criminal punishment.

During the 1920s, the majority of the Supreme Court was willing to affirm convictions for expression, so long as the expression fell within a statutory prohibition and the statutory prohibition was reasonable. Thus, in GITLOW V. NEW YORK (1925) the Court upheld a conviction under a criminal anarchy statute that forbade teaching the propriety of illegally overthrowing organized government. The Court concluded that the legislature could reasonably anticipate that speech of this type carried the danger of a "revolutionary spark" kindling a fire. The standard applied in *Gitlow* and similar cases would permit suppression of virtually any type of speech that a legislature might consider to create a danger of illegal activity, a category far broader than ordinary criminal solicitation.

In the 1930s the Supreme Court began to render decisions more protective of speech, and in HERNDON V. LOWRY (1937) the Court reversed a conviction for attempting to incite insurrection, when the evidence failed to show that the defendant, a Communist party organizer, had actually urged revolutionary violence. The majority in *Herndon* referred to the clear and present danger test with approval. In a series of subsequent decisions, that test was employed as an all-purpose standard for First Amendment cases.

In 1951, the Supreme Court reviewed the convictions of eleven leading communists in DENNIS V. UNITED STATES. The defendants had violated the Smith Act by conspiring to advocate the forcible overthrow of the United States government. As in *Gitlow*, the expressions involved (typical communist rhetoric) fell short of inciting to any specific crime. The plurality opinion, representing the views of four Justices, accepted clear and present danger as the appropriate standard, but interpreted the test so that the gravity of the evil was discounted by its improbability. In practice, this formulation meant that if the evil were very great, such as overthrow of the government, communication creating a danger of that evil might be suppressed even though the evil would not occur in the near future and had only a small likelihood that it would ever occur. The dissenters and civil libertarian observers protested that this interpretation undermined the main point of "clear and present" danger. *Dennis* is now viewed by many as a regrettable product of unwarranted fears of successful communist subversion. In subsequent cases, the Court emphasized that the Smith Act reached only advocacy of illegal action, not advocacy of doctrine. In the years since *Dennis* only one conviction under the act has passed this stringent test.

The modern constitutional standard for incitement cases arose out of the conviction of a Ku Klux Klan leader for violating a broad CRIMINAL SYNDICALISM statute, not unlike the statute involved in *Gitlow*. Unsurprisingly, the Court said in BRANDENBURG V. OHIO (1969) that the broad statute was unconstitutional. But it went on to fashion a highly restrictive version of clear and present danger: that a state may not "forbid or proscribe advocacy of the use of force or of law violation except where such advocacy is directed to inciting or producing imminent lawless action and is likely to incite or produce such action." This test requires lawless action that is likely, imminent, and intended by the speaker. Only rarely could such a test possibly be met by speech that does not amount to criminal solicitation, and under this test both solicitation of crimes in the distant future and solicitation unlikely to be acted upon are constitutionally protected. In *Brandenburg*,

however, the Court had directly in mind public advocacy; it is unlikely that this stringent test also applies to private solicitations of crime that are made for personal gain. The present law provides significant constitutional protection for political incitements, but how far beyond political speech this protection may extend remains uncertain.

KENT GREENAWALT
(1986)

Bibliography

AMERICAN LAW INSTITUTE 1985 *Model Penal Code*, Section 5.02 and Commentary. St. Paul, Minn.: West Publishing Co.

GREENAWALT, KENT 1980 Speech and Crime. *American Bar Foundation Research Journal* 1980:647–785.

LINDE, HANS A. 1970 "Clear and Present Danger" Reexamined: Dissonance in the Brandenburg Concerto. *Stanford Law Review* 22:1163–1186.

INCOME TAX CASES

See: *Pollock v. Farmers' Loan & Trust Company*

INCORPORATION DOCTRINE

According to the incorporation doctrine the FOURTEENTH AMENDMENT incorporates or absorbs the BILL OF RIGHTS, making its guarantees applicable to the states. Whether the Bill of Rights applied to the states, restricting their powers as it did those of the national government, was a question that arose in connection with the framing and ratification of the Fourteenth Amendment. Before 1868 nothing in the Constitution of the United States prevented a state from imprisoning religious heretics or political dissenters, or from abolishing TRIAL BY JURY, or from torturing suspects to extort confessions of guilt. The Bill of Rights limited only the United States, not the states. JAMES MADISON, who framed the amendments that became the Bill of Rights, had included one providing that "no State shall violate the equal rights of conscience, of the FREEDOM OF THE PRESS, or the trial by jury in criminal cases." The Senate defeated that proposal. History, therefore, was on the side of the Supreme Court when it unanimously decided in BARRON V. BALTIMORE (1833) that "the fifth amendment must be understood as restraining the power of the general government, not as applicable to the States," and said that the other amendments composing the Bill of Rights were equally inapplicable to the States.

Thus, a double standard existed in the nation. The Bill of Rights commanded the national government to refrain from enacting certain laws and to respect certain procedures, but it left the states free to do as they wished in relation to the same matters. State constitutions and COM-

MON LAW practices, rather than the Constitution of the United States, were the sources of restraints on the states with respect to the subjects of the Bill of Rights.

Whether the Fourteenth Amendment was intended to alter this situation is a matter on which the historical record is complex, confusing, and probably inconclusive. Even if history spoke with a loud, clear, and decisive voice, however, it ought not necessarily control judgment on the question whether the Supreme Court should interpret the amendment as incorporating the Bill of Rights. Whatever the framers of the Fourteenth intended, they did not possess ultimate wisdom as to the meaning of their words for subsequent generations. Moreover, the PRIVILEGES AND IMMUNITIES, due process, and EQUAL PROTECTION clauses of section 1 of the amendment are written in language that blocks fixed meanings. Its text must be read as revelations of general purposes that were to be achieved or as expressions of imperishable principles that are comprehensive in character. The principles and purposes, not their framers' original technical understanding, are what was intended to endure. We cannot avoid the influence of history but are not constitutionally obligated to obey history which is merely a guide. The task of CONSTITUTIONAL INTERPRETATION is one of statecraft: to read the text in the light of changing needs in accordance with the noblest ideals of a democratic society.

The Court has, in fact, proved to be adept at reading into the Constitution the policy values that meet its approval, and its freedom to do so is virtually legislative in scope. Regrettably in its first Fourteenth Amendment decision, in the SLAUGHTERHOUSE CASES (1873), the Court unnecessarily emasculated the privileges and immunities clause by ruling that it protected only the privileges and immunities of national CITIZENSHIP but not the privileges and immunities of state citizenship, which included "nearly every CIVIL RIGHT for the establishment and protection of which organized government is instituted." Among the rights deriving from state, not national, citizenship were those referred to by the Bill of Rights as well as other "fundamental" rights. Justice STEPHEN J. FIELD, dissenting, rightly said that the majority's interpretation had rendered the clause "a vain and idle enactment, which accomplished nothing. . . ." The privileges and immunities clause was central to the incorporation issue because to the extent that any of the framers of the amendment intended incorporation, they relied principally on that clause. Notwithstanding the amendment, *Barron v. Baltimore* remained controlling law. The Court simply opposed the revolution in the federal system which the amendment's text suggested. The privileges and immunities of national citizenship after *Slaughterhouse* were those that Congress or the Court could have protected,

under the SUPREMACY CLAUSE, with or without the new amendment.

In HURTADO V. CALIFORNIA (1884) the Court initiated a long line of decisions that eroded the traditional procedures associated with due process of law. *Hurtado* was not an incorporation case, because the question it posed was not whether the Fourteenth Amendment incorporated the clause of the Fifth guaranteeing INDICTMENT by GRAND JURY but whether the concept of due process necessarily required indictment in a capital case. In cases arising after *Hurtado*, counsel argued that even if the concept of due process did not mean indictment, or freedom from CRUEL AND UNUSUAL PUNISHMENT, or trial by a twelve-member jury, or the RIGHT AGAINST SELF-INCRIMINATION, the provisions of the Bill of Rights applied to the states through the Fourteenth Amendment; that is, the amendment incorporated them either by the privileges and immunities clause, or by the due process clause's protection of "liberty." In *O'Neil v. Vermont* (1892), that argument was accepted for the first time by three Justices, dissenting; however, only one of them, JOHN MARSHALL HARLAN, steadfastly adhered to it in MAXWELL V. DOW (1900) and TWINING V. NEW JERSEY (1908), when all other Justices rejected it. Harlan, dissenting in *Patterson v. Colorado* (1907), stated "that the privilege of free speech and a free press belong to every citizen of the United States, constitute essential parts of every man's liberty, and are protected against violation by that clause of the Fourteenth Amendment forbidding a state to deprive any person of his liberty without due process of law." The Court casually adopted that view in OBITER DICTUM in GITLOW V. NEW YORK (1925).

Before *Gitlow* the Court had done a good deal of property-minded, not liberty-minded, incorporating. As early as *Hepburn v. Griswold* (1870), it had read the protection of the CONTRACT CLAUSE into the Fifth Amendment's due process clause as a limitation on the powers of Congress, a viewpoint repeated in the SINKING FUND CASES (1879). The Court in 1894 had incorporated the Fifth's JUST COMPENSATION clause into the Fourteenth's due process clause and in 1897 it had incorporated the same clause into the Fourteenth's equal protection clause. In the same decade the Court had accepted SUBSTANTIVE DUE PROCESS, incorporating within the Fourteenth a variety of doctrines that secured property, particularly corporate property, against "unreasonable" rate regulations and reformist labor legislation. By 1915, however, PROCEDURAL DUE PROCESS for persons accused of crime had so shriveled in meaning that Justice OLIVER WENDELL HOLMES, dissenting, was forced to say that "mob law does not become due process of law by securing the assent of a terrorized jury."

The word "liberty" in the due process clause had absorbed all FIRST AMENDMENT guarantees by the time of the decision in EVERSON V. BOARD OF EDUCATION (1947). Incorporation developed much more slowly in the field of criminal justice. POWELL V. ALABAMA (1932) applied to the states the SIXTH AMENDMENT'S RIGHT TO COUNSEL in capital cases, as a "necessary requisite of due process of law." The Court reached a watershed, however, in PALKO V. CONNECTICUT (1937), where it refused to incorporate the ban on DOUBLE JEOPARDY. Justice BENJAMIN N. CARDOZO sought to provide a "rationalizing principle" to explain the selective or piecemeal incorporation process. He repudiated the notion that the Fourteenth Amendment embraced the entire Bill of Rights, because the rights it guaranteed fell into two categories. Some were of such a nature that liberty and justice could not exist if they were sacrificed. These had been brought "within the Fourteenth Amendment by a process of absorption" because they were "of the very essence of a scheme of ORDERED LIBERTY." In short, they were "fundamental," like the concept of due process. Other rights, however, were not essential to a "fair and enlightened system of justice." First Amendment rights were "the indispensable condition" of nearly every other form of freedom, but jury trials, indictments, immunity against compulsory self-incrimination, and double jeopardy "might be lost, and justice still be done."

The difficulty with *Palko*'s rationalizing scheme was that it was subjective. It offered no principle explaining why some rights were fundamental or essential to ordered liberty and others were not; it measured all rights against some abstract or idealized system, rather than the Anglo-American accusatory system of criminal justice. Selective incorporation also completely lacked historical justification. And it was logically flawed. The Court read the substantive content of the First Amendment into the "liberty" of the due process clause, but that clause permitted the abridgment of liberty with due process of law. On the other hand, selective incorporation, as contrasted with total incorporation, allowed the Court to decide constitutional issues as they arose on a case-by-case basis, and allowed, too, the exclusion from the incorporation doctrine of some rights whose incorporation would wreak havoc in state systems of justice. Grand jury indictment for all felonies and trials by twelve-member juries in civil suits involving more than twenty dollars are among Bill of Rights guarantees that would have that result, if incorporated.

In *Adamson v. California* (1947) a 5–4 Court rejected the total incorporation theory advanced by the dissenters led by Justice HUGO L. BLACK. Black lambasted the majority's due process standards as grossly subjective; he argued that only the Justices' personal idiosyncrasies could give content to "canons of decency" and "fundamental justice." Black believed that both history and objectivity required

resort to the "specifics" of the Bill of Rights. Justices FRANK MURPHY and WILEY RUTLEDGE would have gone further. They accepted total incorporation but observed that due process might require invalidating some state practices "despite the absence of a specific provision in the Bill of Rights." Justice FELIX FRANKFURTER, replying to Black, denied the subjectivity charge and turned it against the dissenters. Murphy's total-incorporation-"plus" was subjective; total incorporation impractically fastened the entire Bill of Rights, with impedimenta, on the states along with the accretions each right had gathered in the United States courts. Selective incorporation on the basis of individual Justices' preferences meant "a merely subjective test" in determining which rights were in and which were out.

Frankfurter also made a logical point long familiar in constitutional jurisprudence. The due process clause of the Fourteenth, which was the vehicle for incorporation, having been copied from the identical clause of the Fifth, could not mean one thing in the latter and something very different in the former. The Fifth itself included a variety of clauses. To incorporate them into the Fourteenth would mean that those clauses of the Fifth and in the remainder of the Bill of Rights were redundant, or the due process clause, if signifying all the rest, was meaningless or superfluous. The answer to Frankfurter and to those still holding his view is historical, not logical. The history of due process shows that it did mean trial by jury and a cluster of traditional rights of accused persons that the Bill of Rights separately specified. Its framers were in many respects careless draftsmen. They enumerated particular rights associated with due process and then added the due process clause partly for political reasons and partly as a rhetorical flourish—a reinforced guarantee and a genuflection toward traditional usage going back to medieval reenactments of MAGNA CARTA.

Numerous cases of the 1950s showed that the majority's reliance on the concept of due process rather than the "specifics" of the Bill of Rights made for unpredictable and unconvincing results. For that reason the Court resumed selective incorporation in the 1960s, beginning with MAPP V. OHIO (1961) and ending with *Benton v. Maryland* (1969). The Warren Court's "revolution in criminal justice" applied against the states the rights of the Fourth through Eighth Amendments, excepting only indictment, twelve-member civil juries, and bail. IN RE WINSHIP (1970) even held that proof of crime beyond a REASONABLE DOUBT, though not a specific provision of the Bill of Rights, was essential to due process, and various decisions have suggested the Court's readiness to extend to the states the Eighth Amendment's provision against excessive bail.

The specifics of the Bill of Rights, however, have proved

to offer only an illusion of objectivity, because its most important clauses, including all that have been incorporated, are inherently ambiguous. Indeed, the only truly specific clauses are the ones that have not been incorporated—indictment by grand jury and civil trials by twelve-member juries. The "specific" injunctions of the Bill of Rights do not exclude exceptions, nor are they self-defining. What is "an ESTABLISHMENT OF RELIGION" and what, given libels, pornography, and perjury, is "the freedom of speech" or "of the press"? These freedoms cannot be abridged, but what is an abridgment? Freedom of religion may not be prohibited; may freedom of religion be abridged by a regulation short of prohibition? What is an "UNREASONABLE" SEARCH, "PROBABLE" CAUSE, or "excessive" bail? What punishment is "cruel and unusual"? Is it really true that a person cannot be compelled to be a witness against himself in a criminal case and that the Sixth Amendment extends to "all" criminal prosecutions? What is a "criminal prosecution," a "SPEEDY" TRIAL, or an "impartial" jury? Ambiguity cannot be strictly construed. Neutral principles and specifics turn out to be subjective or provoke subjectivity. Moreover, applying to the states the federal standard does not always turn out as expected. After DUNCAN V. LOUISIANA (1968) extended the trial by jury clause of the Sixth Amendment to the states, the Court decided that a criminal jury of less than twelve (but not less than six) would not violate the Fourteenth Amendment, nor would a non-unanimous jury decision. (See JURY SIZE.) Examples can be multiplied to show that the incorporation doctrine has scarcely diminished the need for judgment and that judgment tends to be personal in character.

On the whole, however, the Court has abolished the double standard by nationalizing the Bill of Rights. The results have been mixed. More than ever justice tends to travel on leaden feet. Swift and certain punishment has always been about as effective a deterrent to crime as our criminal justice system can provide, and the prolongation of the criminal process from arrest to final appeal, which is one result of the incorporation doctrine, adds to the congestion of prosecutorial caseloads and court dockets. However, the fundamental problem is the staggering rise in the number of crimes committed, not the decisions of the Court. Even when the police used truncheons to beat suspects into confessions and searched and seized almost at will, they did not reduce the crime rate. In the long run a democratic society is probably hurt more by lawless conduct on the part of law-enforcement agencies than by the impediments of the incorporation doctrine. In the First Amendment field, the incorporation doctrine has few critics, however vigorously particular First Amendment decisions may be criticized.

LEONARD W. LEVY
(1986)

Bibliography

ABRAHAM, HENRY J. 1977 *Freedom and the Court*, 3rd ed. Pages 33–105. New York: Oxford University Press.

CORTNER, RICHARD C. 1981 *The Supreme Court and the Second Bill of Rights: The Fourteenth Amendment and the Nationalization of Civil Liberties.* Madison: University of Wisconsin Press.

FRIENDLY, HENRY J. 1967 *Benchmarks.* Pages 235–265. Chicago: University of Chicago Press.

HENKIN, LOUIS 1963 "Selective Incorporation" in the Fourteenth Amendment. *Yale Law Journal* 73:74–88.

NORTH, ARTHUR A. 1966 *The Supreme Court: Judicial Process and Judicial Politics.* Pages 65–133. New York: Appleton-Century-Crofts.

INCORPORATION DOCTRINE AND ORIGINAL INTENT

Scholars have variously concluded that the FOURTEENTH AMENDMENT was intended to require the states to obey all, some, or none of the guarantees of the federal BILL OF RIGHTS. To understand the relationship of the Fourteenth Amendment to the Bill of Rights requires examining history leading up to the 1866 framing of the Fourteenth Amendment.

In 1833 the Supreme Court ruled in BARRON V. CITY OF BALTIMORE that the guarantees of the Bill of Rights did not limit state and local governments. Confronted with abolitionist literature and fearing slave revolts, in the 1830s southern states made it a crime to criticize SLAVERY.

On the eve of the CIVIL WAR, two southern states prosecuted their citizens for disseminating an antislavery book. Republicans had used an abridged version of the same book as a campaign document. In the LINCOLN-DOUGLAS DEBATES both ABRAHAM LINCOLN and STEVEN DOUGLAS recognized that Republicans could not campaign in the South. To protect slavery, federal, territorial, and state governments violated other basic liberties as well.

In the 1857 case of DRED SCOTT V. SANFORD, Chief Justice ROGER BROOKE TANEY said blacks (even free blacks) belonged to a degraded class when the Constitution was written, could not be citizens of the United States, and were entitled to none of the rights, privileges, and immunities secured by the Constitution to citizens, including rights in the Bill of Rights.

Concern for CIVIL LIBERTIES became part of the ideology of the REPUBLICAN PARTY. The Republican campaign slogan in 1856 was "Free Speech, Free Labor, Free Soil, and Fremont."

Leading Republicans adhered to an unorthodox, antislavery legal philosophy. Although the Supreme Court had suggested that blacks could not be citizens of the United States, Republicans insisted that free blacks were citizens.

Leading Republicans also thought, contrary to Supreme Court decisions, that the Bill of Rights protected American citizens against state violation of their liberties. From 1864 to 1866 these views were expressed by Republican conservatives, moderates, and radicals.

When Congress met in 1866, the defeated southern states sought readmission to the Union and to Congress. Southern states and localities had passed BLACK CODES restricting for blacks many FUNDAMENTAL RIGHTS accorded to whites, including freedom to move, to own property, to contract, to bear arms, to preach, and to assemble. Congress appointed the Joint Committee on RECONSTRUCTION to consider the condition of the southern states and to consider whether further conditions should be required before their readmission.

To deal with the Black Codes, Congress passed the CIVIL RIGHTS ACT OF 1866. It provided that persons born in the United States were citizens and gave such citizens the same rights to contract, to own property, to give evidence, and "to full and equal benefit of laws and proceedings for the security of person and property as enjoyed by white citizens." Because leading Republicans accepted the idea that the Bill of Rights liberties limited the states even before the passage of the Fourteenth Amendment, they could read "the full and equal benefit of laws . . . for the security of person and property" to include Bill of Rights liberties.

Democrats, along with President ANDREW JOHNSON, denied the power of the federal government to pass the Civil Rights Act. Republicans insisted that the power to pass the act could be found in the THIRTEENTH AMENDMENT, which abolished slavery; in the original PRIVILEGES AND IMMUNITIES clause of Article IV, section 2; and, in the view of several leading Republicans, in the DUE PROCESS clause of the Fifth Amendment.

Although most Republicans thought Congress had the power to pass the Civil Rights Act, Congressman JOHN A. BINGHAM, later principal drafter of the Fourteenth Amendment's first section, argued that a constitutional amendment was required. Bingham and James Wilson, chairman of the House Judiciary Committee, understood the Civil Rights Act as an attempt to enforce the guarantees of the Bill of Rights.

The final version of Section 1 of the Fourteenth Amendment provided that all persons born in the United States and subject to its jurisdiction were citizens and that no state should make or enforce any law abridging the privileges and immunities of citizens of the United States or deny due process or EQUAL PROTECTION to any person. Bingham explained that the amendment provided the power "to protect by national law the privileges and immunities of all citizens of the Republic and the inborn rights of every person within its jurisdiction whenever the same shall be abridged or denied by the unconstitutional acts of any State."

Senator JACOB M. HOWARD presented the amendment to the Senate on behalf of the joint committee. He explained that court decisions had held that the rights in the Bill of Rights did not limit the states. The privileges and immunities of citizens of the United States, Howard said, included the rights in the Bill of Rights. "The great object of the first section of this amendment is, therefore, to restrain the power of the States and compel them at all times to respect these great fundamental guaranties."

Both in Congress and in the election campaign of 1866, discussion of Section 1 was brief. Republicans said variously that the amendment would ensure that the rights of citizens of the United States would not be abridged by any state; that it would protect the rights of American citizens; that it would protect constitutional rights, including free speech and the right to bear arms; or that it embodied the Civil Rights Act or its principles. Suggestions that the amendment was identical to the Civil Rights Act imply that the act incorporated the due process guarantee and that guarantees of the Bill of Rights limited the states prior to the ratification of the Fourteenth Amendment.

Many state ratification debates were not recorded. Often Republicans said nothing at all, being content to wait and vote. In Pennsylvania, Republicans said the amendment was necessary to secure freedom, including FREEDOM OF SPEECH; was needed to protect citizens in all their constitutional rights; and embodied both the principles of the Civil Rights Act and the inalienable rights to life and liberty referred to in the DECLARATION OF INDEPENDENCE. Radicals in Massachusetts insisted that the amendment was useless because it provided for things already secured by the Constitution, including black CITIZENSHIP and protection of Bill of Rights guarantees against state action.

In Congress and in the campaign of 1866, except for statements by Bingham and Howard, there were few extended discussions, and often none at all, of the legal meaning of Section 1. Discussions of application of one or more Bill of Rights liberties to the states under Section 1 of the Fourteenth Amendment were similarly brief. Republicans concentrated their attention on different questions—on the merits of the contest between President Andrew Johnson and Congress, on the readmission of southern states, and on broad statements of political principle. Still, in 1866 many Republicans indicated that Section 1 would protect particular Bill of Rights liberties, and none explicitly said that it would leave the states free to deny their citizens privileges set out in the Bill of Rights.

MICHAEL KENT CURTIS
(1992)

(SEE ALSO: *Freedom of Assembly and Association; Freedom of Contract; Freedom of the Press; Incorporation Doctrine; Property Rights; Second Amendment.*)

Bibliography

BERGER, RAOUL 1989 *The Fourteenth Amendment and the Bill of Rights.* Norman: University of Oklahoma Press.

CURTIS, MICHAEL KENT 1986 *No State Shall Abridge: The Fourteenth Amendment and the Bill of Rights.* Durham, N.C.: Duke University Press.

GRAHAM, HOWARD 1968 *Everyman's Constitution.* Madison: State Historical Society of Wisconsin.

HYMAN, HAROLD and WIECEK, WILLIAM 1982 *Equal Justice Under Law.* New York: Harper & Row.

TEN BROEK, JACOBUS 1965 *Equal Under Law.* New York: Macmillan.

WIECEK, WILLIAM 1977 *The Sources of Anti-Slavery Constitutionalism in America, 1760–1848.* Ithaca, N.Y.: Cornell University Press.

INCORPORATION OF TERRITORIES

Incorporation is the process of formally making a territory part of the United States. Even before the Constitution was written, the United States exercised SOVEREIGNTY over lands not part of any state; but those TERRITORIES were to be organized and prepared for statehood. In the late nineteenth century the United States began to acquire territory outside North America, most of which appeared unsuited for statehood. The Constitution contains no provision for governing a colonial empire, but Congress, under Article IV, section 3, made rules and regulations respecting overseas possessions and dependencies. In the INSULAR CASES (1901–1911) the Supreme Court formulated a DOCTRINE to define the constitutional status of the territories. Those which Congress, expressly or implicitly, intends to make part of the United States are deemed to be incorporated. The people of incorporated territories are United States citizens with all the rights guaranteed by the Constitution. Absent such congressional intent, territories are unincorporated. The residents of unincorporated territories enjoy protection of fundamental NATURAL RIGHTS but not of rights merely procedural or formal—although Congress may, at its discretion, extend United States CITIZENSHIP and full CIVIL RIGHTS to the people of unincorporated territories. There are currently no incorporated territories.

DENNIS J. MAHONEY
(1986)

INDEPENDENT COUNSEL

In 1978, Congress established a permanent framework for dealing with allegations that a senior official of the federal government had committed federal crimes. The fundamental element of the new process is the selection of a special officer with the sole responsibility of investigating the allegations. The special selection of a person from outside the government frees the person from the institutional and personal restraints that might affect the judgment and objectivity of a regular Justice Department prosecutor called upon to investigate his governmental superiors or colleagues.

As originally enacted as part of the Ethics in Government Act of 1978, this officer was called a SPECIAL PROSECUTOR. Congress later changed the officer's title to "independent counsel" in order to diffuse criticism that appointment of an official called a "special prosecutor" prejudged the outcome of the investigation. The original title seemed to suggest that the offense being investigated was special and that prosecution was probable or necessary. The title "independent counsel" signifies that the official's responsibility is to be more neutral and dispassionate.

Before Congress acted in 1978 to provide a permanent mechanism for appointing an independent counsel, the decision whether to take any unusual steps to respond to reports of high-level corruption was left to an unpredictable combination of public notoriety and political integrity. For example, in order to deal with reports of massive corruption in the WARREN HARDING administration concerning the sale of the Teapot Dome petroleum reserves, Congress enacted a special statute authorizing the President, with Senate confirmation, to appoint "special counsel" to investigate and prosecute criminal violations relating to the leases on oil lands in former naval reserves. The incumbent ATTORNEY GENERAL, Harry Daugherty, lacked public trust, since he himself faced separate criminal allegations. President CALVIN COOLIDGE appointed a former Ohio senator and a private lawyer from Pennsylvania (later a Supreme Court Justice) to serve as special counsel. Among those prosecuted was the former secretary of the interior, Albert B. Fall, who was convicted of bribery and sentenced to prison.

During the administration of HARRY S. TRUMAN, public pressure forced Attorney General J. Howard McGrath to appoint a highly respected former New York City official to serve as his "special assistant" to investigate widespread corruption in federal tax cases. The special assistant, however, had no statutory mandate. When he tried to press his investigation by seeking information from high-level Justice Department officials, including the attorney general himself, Attorney General McGrath fired him. President Truman immediately fired the attorney general, but did not see to the appointment of any replacement special prosecutor. Not until a new administration took over did the allegations yield prosecutions and convictions, including the convictions of the former assistant attorney general in charge of the Tax Division and of President Truman's own appointments secretary.

Then came WATERGATE. Shortly after the beginning of President RICHARD M. NIXON's second term, allegations surfaced that his senior aides in his reelection committee, the White House, and the Justice Department had been personally involved in planning a burglary at the offices of the Democratic National Committee during the 1972 presidential campaign or had helped to cover up the guilt of the conspirators. Public skepticism about a Justice Department investigation led the new attorney general, Elliot Richardson, to appoint a Harvard Law School professor, Archibald Cox, as the "Watergate special prosecutor." When Cox insisted on subpoenaing tape recordings that President Nixon had made in his White House office and refused to yield voluntarily, the President fired him.

The public firestorm that followed Cox's firing and Richardson's resignation forced the President to agree to the appointment of a new special prosecutor, Leon Jaworski, whose authority was derived from newly issued Justice Department regulations that the President pledged to respect. Those regulations guaranteed that the special prosecutor would not be removed except for "gross impropriety" or other special cause. In UNITED STATES V. NIXON (1974), the Supreme Court upheld the constitutional authority of the Special Prosecutor to press another subpoena directed to the President, despite the President's objection that it invaded his constitutional right to invoke executive privilege. The Court concluded that the Justice Department regulations to which the President had agreed and which remained in effect provided the special prosecutor with autonomy to pursue the investigation, regardless of the President's wishes.

During the JIMMY CARTER administration, Attorney General Griffin Bell appointed an official outside the Justice Department to serve as his "special counsel" to investigate allegations concerning the financial interests of the President and his brother.

The 1978 legislation goes well beyond any of the prior approaches. It requires the attorney general to apply to a special court to appoint a special prosecutor (or independent counsel) whenever preliminary inquiry into allegations against the President or other senior government officials specified in the statute leads the attorney general to conclude that there are "reasonable grounds" for further investigation. The court then must appoint an independent counsel from outside the government. That counsel becomes vested with all of the investigative and prosecutorial authority that the attorney general and his subordinates would otherwise have. In exercising his judgment, the independent counsel is not subject to supervision or direction by the attorney general or even the President. The statute protects the independent counsel's autonomy by specifying that he may be removed only by the attorney general personally and only for "good cause." The statute also makes the removal decision subject to JUDICIAL REVIEW.

In the first ten years of experience under the statute, there were more than thirty instances in which the statute came into play and at least eight special prosecutors or independent counsels were formally appointed. In *Morrison v. Olson* (1988) the Supreme Court upheld the constitutionality of the independent-counsel provisions. Their constitutionality had been challenged by the target of an investigation, a former assistant attorney general. The Justice Department itself joined in urging the Court to strike down the statute as an invasion of the President's constitutional prerogatives. The constitutional attack rested on two basic arguments: first, that the provisions for court appointment and protected tenure violated the President's right to appoint and remove all senior "officers" of the government and, second, that the independent counsel's autonomy invaded the prerogatives assigned to the President under the SEPARATION OF POWERS, particularly the responsiblity for enforcing federal law.

The Court ruled, however, that an independent counsel is only an "inferior officer" within the meaning of the APPOINTMENTS CLAUSE of Article II of the Constitution, so that Congress may vest the appointment power in a court. The Court reasoned that the narrowness of the investigative charter and other statutory constraints put an independent counsel into the "inferior officer" status.

The Court also rejected the more fundamental objection that the independent-counsel mechanism violates the Constitution's separation of powers. The Court agreed that investigation and prosecution of federal crimes is essentially an executive-branch function, but concluded that the attorney general's role in the initial decision to apply for appointment of an independent counsel and his power to remove the counsel "for good cause" provide adequate executive-branch control over the assertion of these powers. The Court also concluded that Congress' solution to a difficult problem of assuring public confidence in the integrity of the criminal process satisfies the constitutional separation of powers because neither the legislature nor the judiciary had "aggrandized" its powers at the expense of the executive branch.

Although the Court's decision settles the constitutional question, doubts about the wisdom of the statute remain. An independent counsel lacks either an electoral base or public accountability. The appointment to investigate a particular set of allegations, with virtually no limit on the resources that can be devoted to the investigation, may tend to distort, rather than protect, the fair and objective judgment that the statutory mechanism is supposed to promote. This special charter may also lead to relentlessly intensive and sweeping investigations that subject government officials to substantially more onerous treatment than an "ordinary" criminal suspect would receive at the hands of a full-time, professional prosecutor.

PHILIP A. LACOVARA
(1992)

Bibliography

BAKER, HOWARD H. 1975 The Proposed Judicially Appointed Independent Office of Public Attorney: Some Constitutional Objections and an Alternative. *Southwestern Law Journal* 29: 671–683.

CUMMINGS, HOMER S. and MCFARLAND, CARL 1937 *Federal Justice: Chapters in the History of Justice and the Federal Executive*. New York: Macmillan.

HUSTON, LUTHER A. 1967 *The Department of Justice*. New York: Praeger.

—— 1968 *Roles of the Attorney General of the United States*. Washington, D.C.: American Enterprise Institute.

JACOBY, JOAN E. 1980 *The American Prosecutor: A Search for Identity*. Indianapolis: Lexington Books.

TIEFER, CHARLES 1983 The Constitutionality of Independent Officers as Checks on Abuses of Executive Power. *Boston University Law Review* 63:59–103.

INDEPENDENT COUNSEL
(Update)

By the end of the 1990s, the institution of the independent counsel had come to dominate political and legal events in a manner that its drafters could not have imagined. By 1998, independent counsel investigations had produced the second IMPEACHMENT and trial of a President in American history, the resignation and punishment of cabinet secretaries, and the judicial restriction of PRESIDENTIAL POWERS that had undergone little challenge during the Cold War (with the ever-applicable exception of President RICHARD M. NIXON). The activities and conduct of independent counsels also triggered vociferous reactions, including political attacks on individual counsels and their method of appointment, proposals to eliminate or alter the independent counsel law, and criticisms that the ATTORNEY GENERAL of the United States had appointed either too many or not enough counsels. Recovering from the strains of scandal and investigation, Congress let lapse the Independent Counsel law in 1999.

Independent counsels became the top political and legal story of the scandal-besieged administration of President WILLIAM J. CLINTON. Six independent counsels were appointed to investigate Clinton and various cabinet secretaries and advisers. Most notably, Kenneth G. Starr's inquiry into whether Clinton had committed fraud and obstruction of justice in regard to his investment (before he became President) in the Whitewater development deal mushroomed into an investigation of the President's sexual relationships and conduct. Starr came under unprecedented political attack as he examined whether the President had committed perjury and obstruction of justice in attempting to conceal his intimate relationship with a White House intern, Monica S. Lewinsky, from a federal court in a sexual harassment suit. In the course of the Starr investigation, which was vigorously contested by the President's government and private lawyers, the federal courts were confronted with several disputes concerning privilege, including executive immunity from suit, EXECUTIVE PRIVILEGE, attorney–client privilege, and a newly claimed one, U.S. Secret Service protective privilege. Allowing Starr's inquiries to go forward, the courts ruled against the administration on all of these claims, with the exception of attorney–client privilege.

Starr provided evidence to the U.S. HOUSE OF REPRESENTATIVES, under a special provision of the 1978 Independent Counsel Act, that the President had committed "high crimes and misdemeanors." In the course of the House's remarkable deliberations, Starr appeared as a witness to justify his investigatory tactics, which had included efforts to place a recording device on Lewinsky. The House even provided the President's lawyers, who had criticized the independent counsel's ethics, methods, and goals, with the opportunity to question Starr. Nonetheless, the House impeached Clinton by a close vote in late 1998, and the U.S. SENATE conducted an unsuccessful removal trial in 1999.

Although the constitutionality of the counsel's freedom from presidential control was settled by the Supreme Court in *Morrison v. Olson* (1988), many raised doubts about the policies behind the law. Chief among them was the ease with which independent counsels were appointed. Under the statute, a relatively low threshold of proof could trigger the Attorney General's duty to seek the appointment of an independent counsel. The Attorney General could not inquire into whether, for example, the target of the investigation had the requisite mens rea to commit the crime. The low standard of proof led to a proliferation of counsels, with no required showing that U.S. Department of Justice officials were politically or institutionally incapable of conducting these investigations. The statute might profitably have been limited to investigations of only the President, Vice President, and the Attorney General, where the threat of a conflict of interest would be greatest. Criticizing the unreviewable nature of the Attorney General's decisions, others pointed to Clinton administration Attorney General Janet Reno's failure to seek a counsel for the 1996 Clinton campaign fundraising scandals as a ground for even broadening the statute's reach where those officials are involved.

INDICTMENT 1361

Many were in agreement, however, that the institutional freedom of the independent counsel required reform. Without budgetary or resource constraints, investigations had continued for many years and involved large sums of money that no regular federal prosecutor could expend. The investigation into the IRAN–CONTRA AFFAIR lasted for seven years and cost taxpayers almost $50 million; the Clinton Whitewater inquiry will last at least six years and cost even more. Without responsibility to any superior, independent counsels could pursue individuals and violations that normally would not receive Justice Department attention. Indeed, the statutory duty of the counsel was to pursue the issues over which he had JURISDICTION, rather than to make judgments about what crimes to pursue in light of overall prosecutorial resources.

Congress revisited these issues in 1999 when the Ethics in Government Act came up for its periodic re-authorization. One oft-mentioned approach to address these problems would have folded the independent counsel into the Justice Department's Office of Public Integrity, which already operates with substantial autonomy. Other proposals urged that Congress subject counsels to the same budgetary, time, and resource restraints that apply to other U.S. Attorneys. It should be noted, however, that even during the WATERGATE scandals, the federal justice system proved itself able to investigate and prosecute criminal wrongdoing at the highest levels without the assistance of an independent counsel. After twenty years of investigating counsels and presidential scandal, Congress concluded not to renew the law and that the time had come to end an ill-conceived experiment in creating independent operators with the powers of investigation and prosecution.

JOHN YOO
(2000)

Bibliography

CARTER, STEPHAN L. 1988 The Independent Counsel Mess. *Harvard Law Review* 102:105–141.

EASTLAND, TERRY 1989 *Ethics, Politics, and the Independent Counsel: Executive Power, Executive Vice.* Washington, D.C.: National Legal Center.

HARRIGER, KATY J. 1992 *Independent Justice: The Federal Special Prosecutor in American Politics.* Lawrence: University of Kansas Press.

O'SULLIVAN, JULIE 1996 The Independent Counsel Statute: Bad Law, Bad Policy. *American Criminal Law Review* 33: 463–509.

ROZELL, MARK 1994 *Executive Privilege: The Dilemma of Secrecy and Democratic Accountability.* Baltimore, Md.: Johns Hopkins Press.

SYMPOSIUM 1998 The Independent Counsel Act: From Watergate to Whitewater and Beyond. *Georgetown Law Journal* 86:2011–2443.

INDEPENDENT STATE GROUNDS

See: Adequate State Grounds

INDIANS

See: American Indians and the Constitution; Tribal Economic Development and the Constitution

INDICTMENT

An indictment is a formal written accusation charging an individual with a crime. An indictment is issued by a GRAND JURY when, in its view, there is PROBABLE CAUSE to believe that an individual has committed a crime.

Indictments generally arise in two ways. Most commonly, a prosecutor will submit a bill of indictment to the grand jury alleging specific criminal activity by an individual. If the grand jury believes the allegations, the grand jurors will endorse the bill of indictment with the words "a true bill" and thereby officially indict the accused individual. The grand jury can also decide that the accused should not be prosecuted, in which case the bill of indictment will be marked "no true bill" and be dismissed.

An indictment can also originate from a grand jury as a result of the grand jury's own information or as a result of an investigation conducted by a special or investigative grand jury. This type of indictment often arises in cases involving organized crime or political corruption after a secret, lengthy grand jury investigation.

Grand jurors need not be unanimous to indict. The federal grand jury, for example, consists of between sixteen and twenty-three persons, twelve of whom must concur to indict.

The indictment process had its origin in the English grand jury system. Indictments were designed, as the Supreme Court said in *Costello v. United States* (1956), to provide "a fair method for instituting criminal proceedings against persons believed to have committed crimes." Indictment by a grand jury was historically seen as a way of ensuring that citizens were protected against unfounded criminal prosecutions; however, there is now considerable debate as to whether indictment actually fulfills its protective function. Indictments are also designed to inform accused individuals of the charges against them so that they may adequately prepare their defense.

Under the Fifth Amendment an individual has a right to a grand jury indictment in all federal FELONY prosecutions. The Supreme Court, however, held in HURTADO V. CALIFORNIA (1884) that grand jury indictments are not constitutionally required in state criminal prosecutions. Nevertheless, some states, pursuant to their state constitutions, require grand jury indictments in all felony prosecutions.

One recurring question about indictments has been whether they can be based on EVIDENCE that would be inadmissible at trial. The Supreme Court held in CALANDRA V. UNITED STATES (1974) that "an indictment valid on its face is not subject to challenge on the ground that the grand jury acted on the basis of inadequate or incompetent evidence." Indictments can be based even on evidence obtained illegally, which must therefore be excluded at trial.

Furthermore, a grand jury indictment can be based on HEARSAY evidence and other types of evidence that would not be admissible at trial. These decisions rest on the historical view of the grand jury as being a lay body with broad investigative powers that should not be restrained by technical rules of evidence. In addition, the Supreme Court has observed that an indictment is only a formal charge, not an adjudication of guilt or innocence. "In a trial on the merits, defendants are entitled to a strict observance of all the rules designed to bring about a fair verdict," the Court said in *Costello*, so defendants are not prejudiced by indictments based on inadmissible evidence. The prosecutor, therefore, is permitted to find some admissible evidence to support the indictment between the time it comes from the grand jury and the time of trial.

CHARLES H. WHITEBREAD
(1986)

Bibliography

FRANKEL, MARVIN E. 1977 *The Grand Jury: An Institution on Trial*. New York: Hill & Wang.

INDIGENT

An indigent is a person too poor to provide for certain basic needs. It would be unconstitutional for a state or the national government deliberately to deny benefits or impose burdens on the basis of a person's indigency. To this extent, today's law fulfills Justice ROBERT H. JACKSON's prescription, concurring in EDWARDS V. CALIFORNIA (1941): "The mere state of being without funds is a neutral fact—constitutionally an irrelevance, like race, creed, or color." In a market economy, however, indigency is anything but an irrelevance; unrelieved, it bars access to virtually everything money can buy. Unsurprisingly, therefore, the Supreme Court has found in the Constitution affirmative obligations on government to supply to indigents certain benefits that they cannot afford to buy for themselves. These obligations are few in number; the very idea of a

market economy implies de facto WEALTH DISCRIMINATION in the sense of differential access to goods and services, and in no sense has the Court declared capitalism unconstitutional. (See FREEDOM OF CONTRACT.)

The first focus for the Court's egalitarian concerns for relieving the poor from consequences of their poverty was the criminal process. In cases such as GRIFFIN V. ILLINOIS (1956) and DOUGLAS V. CALIFORNIA (1963), one doctrinal vehicle was the EQUAL PROTECTION clause. But the goal of "equal justice for poor and rich, weak and powerful alike" contained no easily discernible place to stop, and it was always clear that the Court would not require the states to make unlimited funds available so that all accused persons could match the spending of the very rich on their criminal defense. The alternative to the equality principle was insistence on minimum standards of criminal justice for everyone, and the Court's post-1950 decisions tightening those standards—not merely in areas such as the RIGHT TO COUNSEL or the setting of BAIL but throughout the criminal process—can be seen in this egalitarian light, reflecting a recognition that the criminal justice system generally bears most heavily on the poor.

A similar approach, setting minimum standards of justice, had characterized the Court's treatment of claims by the poor to access to civil courts and administrative hearings. PROCEDURAL DUE PROCESS, not equal protection, provides the doctrinal foundation for this development. A concern for hardship to the poor surely played an important role in decisions such as BODDIE V. CONNECTICUT (1971) (access to divorce courts for persons unable to afford filing fees), *Sniadach v. Family Finance Corp.* (1969) (prior hearings prerequisite for prejudgment garnishment), and GOLDBERG V. KELLY (1970) (prior hearings prerequisite for termination of WELFARE BENEFITS). But just as the Court has stopped far short of a general principle of equal access to criminal justice, so it has refused to make equality the guiding principle for its decisions on access to civil justice; in LASSITER V. DEPARTMENT OF SOCIAL SERVICES (1981) the Court denied the existence of a right to state-appointed counsel in proceedings to terminate parental rights.

The one area where the equality principle has guided the Supreme Court's treatment of poverty is the electoral process. The development began with HARPER V. VIRGINIA STATE BOARD OF ELECTIONS (1966), which invalidated a POLL TAX as a condition on voting in a state election. Property qualifications to vote, too, were invalidated, except in the elections of special-purpose districts. Not only VOTING RIGHTS but also rights of access to the ballot were secured against financial barriers that would disqualify the poor.

The early 1970s marked a turning point in the constitutional protection of indigents against the consequences of their poverty. Since that time, the Court has drawn one line after another constricting the expansion of either equal protection or due process doctrines to impose on government further affirmative obligations to relieve the burdens of poverty—even when those burdens affect the quality of an indigent's relations with government itself.

KENNETH L. KARST
(1986)

Bibliography

BRUDNO, BARBARA 1976 *Poverty, Inequality, and the Law.* St. Paul, Minn.: West Publishing Co.

INDIRECT TAXES

See: Direct and Indirect Taxes

INFAMY

Our legal system depends upon the reliability of a person's word—his oath as an officer, his promise as a contractor, his testimony as a witness. Under the COMMON LAW, conviction of certain crimes so diminished a person's credibility that he permanently forfeited certain of his CIVIL RIGHTS, his oath was of no legal value, and he was incompetent to testify in court. Infamy, as this is called, resulted from conviction of FELONY, or a crime involving willful falsehood. The Fifth Amendment requires PRESENTMENT or INDICTMENT by a GRAND JURY before a person may be tried in federal court for an infamous crime.

In modern political rhetoric, the term "infamy" often means general harm done to a person's reputation, especially as a result of LEGISLATIVE INVESTIGATIONS or other governmental action.

DENNIS J. MAHONEY
(1986)

INFLUENCE OF THE AMERICAN CONSTITUTION ABROAD

It can easily be argued that America's most important export has been the Constitution of the United States. It was the first single-document CONSTITUTION. It is the longest-lived. And in only two centuries, virtually every nation has come to accept the inevitability and value of having a constitution. This fact transcends differences of culture, history, and legal heritage. The United States Constitution is perceived as the fundamental point of reference, even by regimes whose philosophical outlook is antidemocratic. Furthermore, nearly every nation has accepted the "Phila-

delphia formula"—either internally or universally—as the means by which an effective constitution can best be produced.

The international impact of the U.S. Constitution is an ongoing reality: most of the world's constitutions have been written in the last forty years, and constitutions are rewritten and revised all the time. The Constitution of the United States continues to be the guiding pattern, and a wellspring of inspiration and innovation. The fundamental idea behind the U.S. Constitution was the belief that the people of a nation comprise the constituent power. The founders of this country, conceiving of the people as the sovereign, asserted that the people themselves could formulate and promulgate a constitution. The idea of a constitutional convention was the natural expression of this concept, for it literally embodied the SOVEREIGNTY of the people.

Universally influential also have been the American ratification and amending processes. For it was these that gave the U.S. Constitution—and all subsequent constitutions—the essential characteristic of permanence. Prior to the creation of such machinery, any law could be superseded by another law. Now it is no longer possible. A method had been created for public approbation of the work of the constitution-makers before the constitution could come into effect. And a method had been created for constitutional change to be effected by that public. Every constitution has since copied or been guided by those formulations. Indeed, the very nature of maintaining permanent written constitutions depends upon the creation of these political devices.

The federal structure—the essential product of the U.S. Constitution—innovated a means by which local and central power could be reconciled. The underlying assumption was that the citizenry, and not the government, is sovereign and is the source of derived power. Thus was established a basis for maintaining national unity, and it has been widely adapted.

Australia, Canada, West Germany, Switzerland, Yugoslavia, and, most recently, Nigeria boast of adherence to American concepts in the creation of their own federal structure and so to a lesser extent do Argentina, Brazil, Mexico, and Venezuela.

The United States was the first nation to have an elected head of state called a president. It was a constitutionally created president, described by HAROLD J. LASKI as "both more and less than a king; both more and less than a prime minister." Today more than half the world's nations have presidents as their chief executives, some with even more constitutional power than the American president (France, South Africa), many with only nominal ceremonial powers (India, Zimbabwe).

The American Constitution formalized the concepts required to make such a system work: the SEPARATION OF POWERS and the system of CHECKS AND BALANCES. The result balances leadership and minimizes abuse, encourages stability and obviates tyranny.

It is now universally understood—as it was by a vocal American citizenry that backed the BILL OF RIGHTS 200 years ago—that fundamental freedoms cannot be guaranteed merely by good intentions. The ratifiers of the U.S. Constitution taught that there could be no fundamental law of the land without a separate section listing individual rights. With the adoption of the Canadian Charter of Rights and Freedoms in 1982, the United Kingdom is the only major nation without a constitutional Bill of Rights, although such has been proposed. The belief that liberties require an explicit statement in order to assure their protection animates political endeavors and constitutionalism throughout the world today.

The sheer longevity of America's constitutional experiment illuminates with each passing year a great, yet hidden strength of the U.S. Constitution: It is a device for assuring national dialogue and conflict resolution. The legislative branch, the executive, and especially the judiciary are more than divisions of government. They are America's ongoing constitutional convention. And as much as anything, this aspect of their identities explains why the American constitutional model remains so attractive and thought-provoking at its bicentennial.

Any study of the international influence of the U.S. Constitution must take into account the fact that this influence is both historic and ongoing. And it should consider how American guidelines, practices, and innovations have been improved on by other nations. But more would be accomplished than just a study of the past. A new understanding would be achieved, of what is fundamental to the American Constitution and what is ephemeral, of what is exportable, and even universally applicable.

So pervasive has been the influence of the Constitution of the United States that most nations have followed its lead by adopting one-document constitutions of their own. Beginning in 1791 with Poland and France, the American concept of a constitution to create government speedily became the norm.

Although some nations are under martial rule or have a transitional government with their constitutions in suspension, all but the United Kingdom, New Zealand, and Israel are committed to the concept and principle of the one-document constitution and all have such a document in some stage of preparation or have one in place. Significantly, the act of constitutional suspension has become the most extreme political act of modern government. What makes this American-influenced constitutional universality so historically significant is its short duration on the world stage.

What has made the U.S. Constitution so admired and so imitated? It was not the establishment of a supreme LAW OF THE LAND; that was no innovation. Plato taught in *The Laws* that "some body of law should exist on a permanent basis, on a superior plane—neither subject to individual tyranny nor to raw majority democracy." Historian K. C. Wheare noted that "from the earliest times . . . people had thought it proper or necessary to write down in a document the fundamental principles upon which their government for the future should be established and conducted."

Nor was it the theory of LIMITED GOVERNMENT that intrigued foreign statesmen. Even the notions of establishing a republic or electing a president or the radical concept of POPULAR SOVEREIGNTY were already commonplace—at least in theory. The philosophers of the Enlightenment and their forebears all had written on such subjects and were familiar with each other's works. And there had already existed such governmental documents as the 1579 Act of Union of the United Provinces of the Netherlands, but until the American experience no one had thought of calling their documents "constitutions."

The written constitution is an American innovation. Its genesis can be traced to THOMAS HOOKER'S FUNDAMENTAL ORDERS OF CONNECTICUT (1639) which was the first to create a state or governmental entity. This prefigured the state constitutions of Virginia and Pennsylvania, which in turn influenced the French Declaration of the Rights of Man. The U.S. Constitution, however, was the document that influenced and continues to influence foreign constitution-makers. For since that date nationhood was to be achieved via a constitution.

The primary reason for the great influence of the U.S. Constitution abroad is that it institutionalized government based on the sovereignty of the people. Americans also created the machinery to translate constitutional philosophy into constitutional reality. Their main device was the CONSTITUTIONAL CONVENTION or constituent assembly. This device has been the most significant and most followed precedent in constitutional development. For in this way a nation can be formed and gets its "supreme law of the land" (save in those instances where the former colonial power grants independence and bestows a constitution for independence). The constituent assembly institutionalized democracy. It legitimized revolution, enabling men to do what they had not yet been able to do peacefully and legally—to alter or abolish government and institute new governments deriving their authority from the consent of the governed.

By following the United States model, all constitution

writers after 1787 could legitimize their revolutions, their independence, their nationhood. In his study of Latin American political institutions, Jacques Lambert wrote: "Here . . . was the worthy model of a constitution that repudiated monarchy and clearly proclaimed the principle of political freedom. . . . The Constitution of the United States lent authority the cloak of democratic respectability. A few countries very shortly adopted constitutions directly inspired by it—Venezuela in 1811, Mexico in 1824, the Central American Federation in 1825, and Argentina in 1826."

Just by being the first, the U.S. Constitution inevitably influenced constitutions abroad. It was the only available national model for the 1791 constitution-makers of Poland who copied its preamble and its impeachment provisions, and in their famous Article V provided Europe's first statement of popular sovereignty.

Another reason for the widespread influence of the United States Constitution abroad is that constitutions are largely written by lawyers, and lawyering normally involves the search for source and precedent. Lawyers have dominated the constituent assemblies and constitutional conventions abroad. The lawyer constitutionalists of America were also proselytizers. They shared the gospel so often proclaimed by THOMAS JEFFERSON. "We feel," he wrote, "that we are acting under obligations not confined to the limits of our own society. It is impossible not to be sensible that we are acting for all mankind."

This message has been well received, starting with France and the men who made the French Revolution. The fact that the constitution consisted of lawyers' ideas contributed to their ready transmittal. Lawyers were popular; the Dantons and Robespierres had sided with the people in their revolt against authority. Jacques Vincent de la Croix, a lawyer, offered a course on the Constitution of the United States at the Lycée de Paris, an institution of free higher education established in 1787. This pattern has continued. The lawyer has been the commoner charged with teaching constitutionalism and translating the needs and aspirations of the people into a legal document. Every constitutional lawyer in the world knows about the U.S. Constitution.

The lawyers who wrote the American constitutions also wrote about them. JOHN ADAMS, author of the MASSACHUSETTS CONSTITUTION and prime "inventor" of the concept of a constitutional convention, could not be in Philadelphia in 1787 as he was then envoy to England. But his *Defence of the Constitutions of Government of the United States of America* was one of the most influential works on constitutionalism, at home and abroad.

Even more influential was THE FEDERALIST, almost immediately translated into French, German, and Spanish to provide constitutional guidelines for a dozen or more nations in Europe and Latin America. Now translated into more than twenty languages, *The Federalist* is still taught in constitutional law classes abroad and new translations are still being published.

The records of the 1848 German constitutional assembly at Frankfurt contain references not only to the U.S. Constitution and *The Federalist* but also to the constitutional commentaries of Justice JOSEPH STORY and Chancellor JAMES KENT. Modern examples abound, with copious references in India's 1947 Constituent Assembly Debates, and, more recently, in the commentaries on the Nigerian Constitution of 1979.

The tradition of the American participant, counsel, or consultant in foreign constitution-making dates from the service of THOMAS PAINE as a member of the 1791 French constitutional assembly. Lawrence Ward Beer wrote of the American role in constitution-making in Asia: "A basic context for American influence has been the *consultation* of American experts on constitutionalism and law during the process of drawing up, applying, interpreting, or amending a national constitution. Concretely, the views of individual American judges and legal scholars have been solicited during visits by Asian constitutionalists to America; American legal literature (including judicial precedent) has been studied, and many Americans have been directly involved in Asian constitution-making."

And the tradition continues. Americans have influenced the writing of constitutions for nations throughout the world, including Liberia, China, Ethiopia, Nigeria, Zimbabwe, Bangladesh, and Peru. ALEXIS DE TOCQUEVILLE was the best known of the foreigners who came to study United States government and who returned home as advocates of the American system. His *Democracy in America*, published in French editions in 1835 and 1840, heightened interest in the United States constitutional system both in Europe and in Latin America.

But Tocqueville was preceded by scores of other Europeans who were attracted by the hope and promise of the new world, most notably Thaddeus Kosciusko, who was later to lead the struggle for democracy in Poland. And Tocqueville was followed by many thousands of scholars in law, government, history, and political science who likewise transported American constitutional ideology. Current manifestations of this development are apparent in the 1982 constitutions of Canada and Honduras and the 1983 constitution of El Salvador.

The United States, a great colonizer, has offered a solution to colonialism. As pointed out by HENRY STEELE COMMAGER:

No Old World nation had known what to do with colonies except to exploit them for the benefit of the mother country. The new United States was born the largest nation in the Western world and was, from the beginning and throughout the 19th century, a great colonizing power with a hinterland that stretched westward to the Mississippi and, eventually, to the Pacific. [And thence beyond the mainland to Alaska and Hawaii.] By the simple device of transforming colonies into states, and admitting these states into the union on the basis of absolute equality with the original states, the Founding Fathers taught the world a lesson which it has learned only slowly and painfully down to our own day.

This constitutional concept has been studied and followed in France, Portugal, Spain, Yugoslavia, and the Soviet Union, to provide a few examples, but not always with successful results. Algeria is no longer part of Metropolitan France, but French Guiana, Guadeloupe, Martinique, Reunion, and Saint Pierre and Miquelon are. Angola is no longer an integral part of Portugal, but Madeira and the Azores are.

Another reason for the influence of the American Constitution abroad is rooted in military conquest. Although the influence of the Philadelphia experience had been felt in Baden, Bavaria, Frankfurt, and Wrttemberg before there was a unified Germany, a more general reception of American style constitutionalism attended the preparation of the post-World War II 1949 Basic Law of the Federal Republic. Similarly, the "MacArthur Constitution" influenced—to use an understatement of the greatest order—Japan's 1947 constitution.

Under United States military authority following the Spanish American War, Cuba's 1901 constitution bears obvious American imprints. And so does the 1904 constitution of Panama, which in Article 136 gave the United States authority to intervene to establish "constitutional order." Haiti's 1918 constitution, putatively the work of then Assistant Secretary of the Navy FRANKLIN D. ROOSEVELT, was based on compromises between existing government forums and the ideologies of the American military forces which had occupied the country since 1915.

American influence was also significant in the preparation of the South Vietnam Constitution of 1967. The Vietnamese actually copied more from the United States model than was appropriate for a nation with a French legal tradition. (The preamble to the North Vietnamese Constitution had been taken directly from Lincoln's Gettysburg Address.)

Most pervasive has been the influence of the U.S. Constitution upon its former colony, the Republic of the Philippines. Under American sovereignty from 1896 until its independence in 1946, the Philippines were given a commonwealth constitution in 1935 which remained virtually unchanged until 1973. And on the eve of the American constitutional bicentennial there was a significant move-

ment to call a new constitutional convention in Manila. A new constitutional structure will predictably once again follow the Philadelphia model.

ALBERT P. BLAUSTEIN
(1986)

Bibliography

BEER, LAWRENCE W. 1979 *Constitutionalism in Asia: Asian Views of the American Influence.* Berkeley: University of California Press.

BLAUSTEIN, ALBERT P. 1984 The United States Constitution: A Model in Nation Building. *National Forum* 64:14–17.

BLAUSTEIN, ALBERT P. and FLANZ, GISBERT H., eds. 1971 *Constitutions of the Countries of the World.* 20 Vols. looseleaf, updated quarterly. Dobbs Ferry, N.Y.: Oceana.

CAPPELLETTI, MAURO 1971 *Judicial Review in the Contemporary World.* Indianapolis: Bobbs-Merrill.

COMMAGER, HENRY STEELE 1977 *The Empire of Reason: How Europe Imagined and America Realized the Enlightenment.* Garden City, N.Y.: Anchor PressDoubleday.

HAWGOOD, JOHN A. 1939 *Modern Constitutions Since 1787.* New York: Macmillan.

HENDERSON, DAN FENNO, ed. 1968 The Constitution of Japan: Its First Twenty Years, 1947–67. Seattle: University of Washington Press.

PALMER, R. R. 1959 *The Age of the Democratic Revolution: A Political History of Europe and America, 1760–1800.* 2 Vols. Princeton, N.J.: Princeton University Press.

STARCK, CHRISTIAN, ed. 1983 *Main Principles of the German Basic Law.* Baden-Baden: Nomos.

INFLUENCE OF THE AMERICAN CONSTITUTION ABROAD
(Update)

As Americans began their third century living under the constitutional system ordained by the Philadelphia Constitution, much of the world was undergoing constitutional transformation. The collapse of communism spawned constitutional reform in many parts of the former Soviet empire. The end of apartheid brought a new constitution to South Africa, while in many parts of Africa, Latin America, and elsewhere there were stirrings of democracy and constitutional change.

The Framers of the U.S. Constitution would have appreciated and understood these changes. From the beginning of the modern constitutional era, the American model has been a centerpiece in changing the face of constitutionalism around the world. The VIRGINIA DECLARATION OF RIGHTS (1776) profoundly influenced France's *Declaration of Rights of Man and the Citizen* (1789), and the early American state constitutions were invoked in the National Assembly's 1791 debates on the first French Constitution.

Nineteenth-century reformers looked to American precedents. At the Frankfurt National Assembly in 1849, German delegates spoke of the "instructive example of America." In Latin America, Juan Bautista Alberdi, father of Argentina's 1853 Constitution, drew heavily from American ideas, including the Constitution of California, in hopes that Argentina might replicate the economic success of the United States.

The most famous examples of direct American constitutional influence in the twentieth century are drawn, paradoxically, from colonialism and military conquest. The constitutional arrangements designed in the 1930s to carry the Philippines to independence closely tracked the American system. After WORLD WAR II, the military government of General Douglas MacArthur had a direct hand in the drafting of a new constitution for Japan, while the assembly that drafted Germany's Basic Law of 1949 (elected, like the delegates of 1787, by the constituent polities) was constrained to produce a constitution that was federal, republican, democratic, and protective of FUNDAMENTAL RIGHTS.

If one traces the relative influence of the American Constitution over the past two centuries and beyond, one finds that influence to have been most immediate and obvious in the early years. That was the period, after all, when there were few competing constitutional models to be had (for the Poles of 1791, for example). As time passed, however, and more countries entered the modern age of constitution-making, the constitutional path became wider and more varied. Especially in the twentieth century, alternative assumptions about the nature of state and society began to feature more conspicuously in constitution-making; for example, positive rights were prominent in such constitutions as those of Mexico in 1917 and Germany in 1919.

Today constitution-making is above all an eclectic exercise. Drafters borrow freely from other countries, the United States but one among them. In post-communist Central and Eastern Europe, for example, one finds the powerful pull of Western European models, partly because of the hope of new democracies to join regional arrangements such as the North Atlantic Treaty Organization (NATO) and the European Union. International and regional norms, such as United Nations conventions, the European Convention on Human Rights, and the expectations of the Organization on Security and Cooperation in Europe, are also influential.

No matter how attractive its broad principles, the American constitutional experience has obvious limitations as a model for foreign constitution-makers. The U.S. Constitution was written in the eighteenth century, long before the age of the modern administrative state. Moreover, it is by design an incomplete document, in that one cannot understand the American constitutional system without knowing about the state constitutions. Also, a full picture of American constitutionalism requires dealing with the extensive judicial gloss accumulated over the years. With the constitutions of most countries being of relatively recent origin, models such as those of Germany (1949) and France (1958) become especially attractive to a constitutional drafter.

Many factors bear on the relative influence of the American Constitution abroad. Among them are the forces of history, culture, and tradition. For example, the felt need to reinforce a sense of national identity in a country with significant minorities may lead to rejection of FEDERALISM in favor of a unitary state. Similarly, the identification of a nation with a historically dominant religion, as in Eastern Europe, often leads constitution-makers to eschew SEPARATION OF CHURCH AND STATE.

Other factors are at work. Countries with a civil law system are more likely to produce long, detailed constitutions, while COMMON LAW countries may be more inclined to allow constitutional law's details to take shape in the courts. Countries with a recent history of one-party or military rule may be drawn to code-like constitutions in an effort to cure the mistakes of the past in the constitution's text. The American example of treating the constitution as the place where fundamental principles are spelled out is often lost when drafters, as in Brazil in 1988, lose sight of the distinction between a constitution and a code of laws.

The enduring influence of the American Constitution does not turn, however, on whether the text of a country's constitution may be thought to resemble in its details that of the United States. The American constitutional experience remains even today the ultimate example of success in self-government. It still offers a stirring example of balancing democracy and accountable government against constitutional limitations.

Among America's most pervasive and influential exports is JUDICIAL REVIEW. The example set by Chief Justice JOHN MARSHALL in MARBURY V. MADISON (1803) has spread around the world. After Canada's adoption in 1982 of the Charter of Rights and Freedoms, that country's Supreme Court said that to look to a constitution's "larger objects" comports with the "classical principles of American constitutional construction" articulated by Marshall in MCCULLOCH V. MARYLAND (1819). One finds conspicuous examples of decisions of the U.S. Supreme Court being relied on even in countries of strikingly different cultural traditions, such as India. Justice WILLIAM J. BRENNAN, JR., may have been on the losing side in the Court's CAPITAL PUNISHMENT cases, but his opinions have had powerful influence in high court decisions of such countries as South Africa and Zimbabwe.

On the surface a particular country's constitutional arrangements may seem to bear little resemblance to those of the United States. Where post-communist countries in Central and Eastern Europe, for example, opt for judicial review, they inevitably look to a European model, especially to Germany's Constitutional Court. Yet it is through such intermediate models as that of Germany that American ideas, such as the principle of *Marbury*, become domesticated. The American Constitution's influence is nonetheless important when it takes a form shaped by local tastes. In the family tree of modern world constitutionalism, America's experience remains a respected and influential figure.

A. E. DICK HOWARD
(2000)

Bibliography

BILLIAS, GEORGE ATHAN, ed. 1990 *American Constitutionalism Abroad: Selected Essays in Comparative Constitutional History.* New York: Greenwood Press.

HENKIN, LOUIS and ROSENTHAL, ALBERT J., eds. 1989 *Constitutionalism and Rights: The Influence of the United States Constitution Abroad.* New York: Columbia University Press.

HOWARD, A. E. DICK, ed. 1993 *Constitution Making in Eastern Europe.* Washington, D.C.: Woodrow Wilson Center Press.

LESTER, ANTHONY 1988 The Overseas Trade in the American Bill of Rights. *Columbia Law Review* 88:541–561.

LUDWIKOWSKI, RETT R. 1996 *Constitution-Making in the Region of Former Soviet Dominance.* Durham N.C.: Duke University Press.

PERRY, BARBARA A. 1992 Constitutional Johnny Appleseeds: American Consultants and the Drafting of Foreign Constitutions. *Albany Law Review* 55:767–791.

INFORMANT'S TIP

A police officer's own observations may not be required to establish PROBABLE CAUSE for an ARREST WARRANT or SEARCH WARRANT (or for an arrest without warrant). Probable cause may be established by an informant's tip, even if it is hearsay, if there is adequate basis to credit his word. The Supreme Court has, however, been troubled by the criteria necessary to determine an informant's truthfulness.

DRAPER V. UNITED STATES (1959) was the first case to hold that an informant's word, when corroborated, was sufficient to establish probable cause; the informant had previously proved reliable, and his story was later substantially verified by the officer's own observations. AGUILAR V. TEXAS (1964) established a "two-pronged" test, amplified in SPINELLI V. UNITED STATES (1969) and generally followed until 1983: the affidavit (or the officer's personal testimony) must make clear to the magistrate, first, some of the underlying circumstances from which the *informant*

concluded that criminal activity was afoot (such as personal observation of the suspect's action), and second, some of the circumstances from which the *officer* concluded that the informant was telling the truth (for example, his previous record of reliability). Failure fully to satisfy either "prong" could be remedied by substituting highly detailed information (even of a nonsuspicious nature) demonstrating that the informant's statement was based neither on rumor nor on the suspect's bad reputation.

In ILLINOIS V. GATES (1983) the Court abandoned the *Aguilar-Spinelli* test in favor of a much looser "totality of the circumstances" approach, which would permit "a balanced assessment of the relative weight of all the various indicia of reliability." Thus, said the Court, the report of an informant who had previously been usually reliable would be acceptable even if it did not explain the basis of his knowledge.

The need to corroborate an informant's statement and demonstrate his reliability arises when the informant has a criminal past; his veracity is naturally suspect. The word of a law enforcement officer who provides information to another officer or that of an honest private citizen without ulterior motive requires no such corroboration according to the decision in *Ventresca v. United States* (1965). Uncorroborated anonymous tips to the police are worthless for establishing probable cause.

In order to prevent reprisals and maintain the future effectiveness of informants, the Court denied in MCCRAY V. ILLINOIS (1967) that a defendant has the right to demand the identity of a government informant at a suppression hearing on the question of probable cause. The accuracy of statements, including those of informants, in affidavits for warrants can be challenged at a hearing if the defendant offers proof that the affiant lied or acted with "reckless disregard for the truth" in statements pertinent to the establishment of probable cause. The warrant's legality will not be affected by an informant's misrepresentation, however, if the officer had no reason to doubt the truth of the informant's statement.

JACOB W. LANDYNSKI
(1986)

Bibliography

LAFAVE, WAYNE R. 1978 *Search and Seizure: A Treatise on the Fourth Amendment.* Vol. 1:489–586. St. Paul, Minn.: West Publishing Co.

IN FORMA PAUPERIS

(Latin: "In the manner of a poor person.") To insure that ACCESS TO THE COURTS is not barred by inability to pay the costs of litigation, poor persons may have fees and some procedural requirements waived and counsel appointed at public expense. In the federal courts this privilege is granted by law to anyone swearing he is without means.

More than half the petitions received by the Supreme Court are filed *in forma pauperis,* often by prisoners seeking review of criminal convictions or of denials of HABEAS CORPUS petitions on constitutional grounds. Probably the most famous case to arise in this way was GIDEON V. WAINWRIGHT (1963).

DENNIS J. MAHONEY
(1986)

INFORMATION

An information is a formal written accusation against a person for a criminal offense presented under oath by a public officer, usually a prosecutor. An information is used to charge an individual with criminal activity in cases where an INDICTMENT by a GRAND JURY is unnecessary or is waived by the accused. Like an indictment, the filing of an information results in the commencement of a formal prosecution. Thus, the information must be clear and specific in order to give adequate notice to the accused of the charges against him and permit him to prepare his defense.

Most states permit prosecution by information or indictment at the option of the prosecutor. In these states, it is rare for a prosecutor not to use an information because it is easier and less time-consuming than an indictment. Grand jury indictments will be used in these jurisdictions only when the prosecutor wants to use the investigative powers of the grand jury. In other states, indictments are required in all FELONY cases or in all capital cases. However, even in these states, informations are used in MISDEMEANOR cases and in felony cases where the accused has waived his right to a grand jury indictment.

In federal misdemeanor cases, prosecutors have the option under the FEDERAL RULES OF CRIMINAL PROCEDURE to proceed by indictment or information. In federal felony cases, accused individuals have the right to insist on prosecution by indictment, but this right can be waived in all but capital cases.

Most jurisdictions limit the prosecutor's discretion to file an information. Generally, the prosecutor cannot file an information unless the accused has had a preliminary hearing before a magistrate. This requirement is designed to weed out groundless charges, thereby relieving an accused of the burden of preparing a defense. However, the effectiveness of this limitation on prosecutorial abuse in filing informations is undercut in several ways. First, in most jurisdictions, a finding of no PROBABLE CAUSE by one

magistrate at a preliminary hearing does not preclude presenting the case to another magistrate. Thus, a prosecutor can "shop around" for a magistrate who will find the requisite probable cause and enable the prosecutor to file an information.

In addition, in filing an information, the prosecutor is not always bound by the findings of the magistrate at the preliminary hearing. Some states permit the prosecutor to charge the accused in the information only with the crimes for which the magistrate decided there was probable cause. In other states, the information can charge the offense for which the accused was bound over at the preliminary hearing and any other offenses supported by the EVIDENCE at the preliminary hearing.

Another problem with using the preliminary hearing as a check on the prosecutor's decision to file an information is that the prosecutor often dominates the magistrate's hearing. Furthermore, in *Gerstein v. Pugh* (1975), the Supreme Court implied that the federal Constitution does not require a preliminary judicial hearing to determine whether there is probable cause for the prosecutor to file an information.

CHARLES H. WHITEBREAD
(1986)

Bibliography

AMERICAN BAR ASSOCIATION, SECTION OF CRIMINAL JUSTICE 1977 *Policy on the Grand Jury.* Washington, D.C.: ABA Section of Criminal Justice.

INGERSOLL, JARED
(1749–1822)

Jared Ingersoll represented Pennsylvania at the CONSTITUTIONAL CONVENTION OF 1787 and signed the Constitution. Although reputed the best trial lawyer in Philadelphia, he was not a frequent speaker at the convention. He unenthusiastically described the plan proposed by the convention as "all things considered, most eligible."

DENNIS J. MAHONEY
(1986)

INGRAHAM v. WRIGHT
430 U.S. 651 (1977)

Two Florida junior high school students, disciplined by severe paddling, sued school officials for damages and injunctive relief, claiming that the paddling constituted CRUEL AND UNUSUAL PUNISHMENT. They also claimed that they had been deprived of their right to a prior hearing in violation of their PROCEDURAL DUE PROCESS rights. The lower federal courts denied relief, and the Supreme Court affirmed, 5–4.

For the majority, Justice LEWIS F. POWELL, a former school board president, concluded that the guarantee against cruel and unusual punishment was limited to cases of punishment for criminal offenses and thus had no application to paddling as a means of school discipline. The openness of public schools provided a safeguard against abusive punishments of the kind that might be visited on prisoners. COMMON LAW restraints on the privilege of school officials to administer corporal punishment were sufficient to prevent excesses. As for due process, Powell conceded that the paddling had implicated a "liberty" interest, but he concluded that due process required no hearing, in view of the availability of common law remedies or damages.

For the dissenters, Justice BYRON R. WHITE argued that it was anomalous to conclude that some punishments are "cruel and unusual" when inflicted on convicts but raise no such problem when they are inflicted on children for breaches of school discipline. The relevant inquiry, White argued, was not the label of criminal punishment but the purpose to punish. While some spanking might be permissible in public schools, the majority was wrong in saying "that corporal punishment in the public schools, no matter how barbaric, inhumane, or severe, is never limited by the Eighth Amendment." Here the record showed not just spanking but severe beatings. Furthermore, the risk of erroneous punishment—a crucial aspect of the due process calculus established in MATHEWS V. ELDRIDGE (1976)—demanded at least some informal discussion between student and disciplinarian before paddling was administered. The common law damages remedy offered no redress for punishments mistakenly administered in good faith and obviously could not undo the infliction of pain.

Ingraham seems an unstable precedent. Constitutional law, following social practice, has increasingly insisted that children be treated as persons, as members of the community deserving of respect. (See CHILDREN'S RIGHTS.) The due process right to a hearing rests partly on the premise that the dignity of being heard, before the state takes away one's liberty or property, is one of the differences between being a participating citizen and being an object of administration. The *Ingraham* majority, unmoved by such concerns, reflected nostalgia for a day when children were seen and not heard.

KENNETH L. KARST
(1986)

INHERENT POWERS

In theory the Constitution establishes the institutions of the national government and vests those institutions with

their responsibilities. Such a government is one of delegated powers. Some of these powers are expressed, others are implied. But all powers of the government—expressed and implied—are delegated powers originating in deliberate acts of the sovereign people. This theory cannot successfully deny that the Constitution may in fact succumb to "necessity," or prove inadequate in contingencies beyond human foresight and control. Nor does it deny that the document's terms (like "due process" and "executive power") are open to construction in light of broader ideas and needs. It simply means that to be lawful, a move of the government must fall within a range permitted by arguable interpretations of constitutional language and tradition.

Constitutional theory can admit a notion of "inherent power" in a sense of IMPLIED POWER as in inherent powers of executive privilege and removal of certain administrative appointees. But constitutional theory cannot admit the doctrine of "inherent power" that finds governmental powers beyond those that have been delegated expressly or by implication on the argument that a government must have certain powers before it can be considered a real government. This strong sense of inherent power is the subject here.

A doctrine of inherent power is frequently asserted in connection with a right to national self-preservation, which, as an inherent power, would differ from implied powers, like an implied power of national defense. Looked upon as an implied but still delegated power, a power of national defense can be derived from such expressed constitutional provisions as authorizing Congress to raise, support, and govern military and naval forces, and to declare war. Questions about the scope of an implied power of national defense would have to be answered in ways that would retain its status as part of a greater whole. A constitutionally derived power of national defense would be consistent with the SEPARATION OF POWERS, individual rights, and other provisions, or arguable interpretations thereof. By contrast, inherent powers need not be consistent with other constitutional provisions; asserting them does not require the interpretive adjustments needed to make something fit into a greater whole. A power to suspend elections and declare a dictatorship during a foreign invasion might become a practical necessity, but it could not be considered an implied power of national defense because no plausible interpretation of the Constitution could make room for such a power.

Appeals to inherent power should be distinguished from appeals to HIGHER LAW to which the Constitution might be open. The latter provide arguments for interpreting the Constitution in certain ways. The former propose reasons that might justify violating or suspending the Constitution. Historically, the former usually invoke considerations of "necessity" or "self-preservation" as reasons for ignoring the separation of powers and the BILL OF RIGHTS. These considerations have surfaced in decisions to put innocent Americans in war-time concentration camps and to deny that the government has an obligation to treat ALIENS fairly. They have been used to rationalize congressional abdications of responsibility, especially in FOREIGN AFFAIRS. They therefore imply the supremacy of material safety over constitutional ideals and structures, even over the Constitution itself as a product of deliberative reason.

A strong doctrine of inherent power may have seemed necessary to constitutional theory as a way to circumvent artificially narrow conceptions of national power originating largely in a STATES' RIGHTS parochialism. But this is no longer the problem it used to be. Understanding national powers in terms of the broad ends to which they point— national defense, for example,—reduces the need for a doctrine of inherent power—unless precisely what is sought is justification for ignoring the Constitution.

SOTIRIOS A. BARBER
(1986)

(SEE ALSO: *Constitutional Reason of State; Delegation of Power; Enumerated Powers; Necessary and Proper Clause; Tenth Amendment.*)

Bibliography
HENKIN, LOUIS 1972 *Foreign Affairs and the Constitution.* Mineola, N.Y.: Foundation Press.
LOFGREN, CHARLES A. 1973 United States v. Curtiss-Wright Export Corp.: An Historical Reassessment. *Yale Law Journal* 83: 1–32.

INITIATIVE

Initiative is the practice by which legislation may be proposed and voted on directly by the people (rather than their representatives). Its adoption was an important element of the Progressive era political reform movement. Of some twenty states that now use the initiative all but Alaska adopted it before 1919. Initiative makes possible enactment of legislation that contravenes the class interest of politicians—such as tax reduction and limitation on public expenditure.

Restrictions on the initiative process, such as a requirement for an extraordinary majority to enact housing legislation, have been held to violate the EQUAL PROTECTION clause of the FOURTEENTH AMENDMENT when the Justices were convinced that the intent was to disadvantage racial minorities.

Although the people of a state may reserve a portion of the legislative power, they may not, by initiative, directly exercise powers (for example, RATIFICATION OF AMEND-

MENTS) conferred on the state legislatures by the federal Constitution.

DENNIS J. MAHONEY
(1986)

INITIATIVE
(Update)

Lawmaking by popular votes on initiatives or REFERENDA is a constitutional feature of the individual states rather than the United States. After a century in which some form of direct lawmaking by voters spread to about half the states, however, its legal status under the U.S. Constitution has not been finally settled. This results from the Supreme Court's choice of premises for reviewing the processes as well as the substance of state laws.

Lawmaking by popular vote on measures initiated or referred by signed petitions is a legacy of the late-nineteenth-century Populist and PROGRESSIVE political movements, along with the direct election of U.S. senators, WOMAN SUFFRAGE, local "home rule," and voter RECALL of elected officials. Combining democratic ideology with resentment against the domination of elected governments by large business and financial interests, the initiative and referendum gained wide acceptance during the first two decades of the twentieth century, especially in the western states. In the early and influential form added to the Oregon Constitution in 1902, the "people reserve to themselves the initiative power" to propose and to enact or reject laws and constitutional amendments, as well as "the referendum power" to approve or reject legislative acts upon the petition of a percentage of voters. Later amendments further "reserved" the same powers to the voters of municipalities and local districts. This local lawmaking must be distinguished from initiatives for state-wide laws and constitutional amendments.

Opponents argued against direct lawmaking on the ground that it contradicted the U.S. Constitution's guarantee of a REPUBLICAN FORM OF GOVERNMENT in each state, and the Oregon Supreme Court seized the first opportunity to defend this innovation. In *Kadderly v. City of Portland* (1903), the court cited the definition of JAMES MADISON, written in THE FEDERALIST, of a republican government as one administered by elected representatives. Noting that Oregon continued to have a legislature, a governor, and courts, the court sustained the initiative and referendum in principle, before either had been used, on grounds that they left the legislature free to enact, change, or repeal the laws, and that the courts still could test their constitutional validity. *Kadderly* became the leading PRECEDENT in other states that adopted the initiative and referendum.

When the Pacific Telephone & Telegraph Company in

1908 challenged an initiated tax measure under the GUARANTEE CLAUSE, the Oregon court rejected this claim with a simple reference to its *Kadderly* opinion. The U.S. Supreme Court, in *Pacific Telephone & Telegraph Co. v. Oregon* (1912), dismissed the company's WRIT OF ERROR for lack of federal JURISDICTION, holding that the guarantee of republican government was the responsibility of Congress rather than of the Court. This left standing the Oregon court's decision in the case. Since *Pacific Telephone*, the status of initiative lawmaking and other state practices under the guarantee clause has been deemed to lack JUSTICIABILITY in the federal courts, though not necessarily in state courts, which are bound by the SUPREMACY CLAUSE to apply the Constitution in their states. Nevertheless, many state courts have assumed that they cannot decide claims under the guarantee clause.

Because direct legislation is designed to reflect popular desires (what Madison knew as "interests" and "passions"), the initiative or referendum often are less sensitive than legislatures to the concerns of identifiable minority groups. Examples are an Oregon initiative aimed at closing parochial schools, invalidated as a denial of DUE PROCESS in PIERCE V. SOCIETY OF SISTERS (1925); a California constitutional amendment against laws forbidding housing discrimination; Washington initiatives concerning SCHOOL BUSING and requiring plebiscites on ordinances against housing discrimination; and a Colorado constitutional amendment against equal rights laws for homosexuals. In the latter two cases, the Court invalidated the requirements under the EQUAL PROTECTION clause for depriving identifiable minorities of equal opportunities to gain favorable laws.

Late-twentieth-century experience showed new problems with unbounded statewide initiative powers. Sponsors turned to drafting measures as constitutional amendments in order to place them beyond the reach of the legislature and state courts, essentially excluding government altogether, contrary to the premise on which the *Kadderly* opinion had held the system compatible with republican government. Following California's lead, many amendments limited state and local fiscal powers, especially PROPERTY taxes, while others forced spending increases on state pensions, prisons, and mandatory prison sentences. Other measures abandoned century-old state guarantees in the law enforcement process under the guise of "victims' rights" amendments.

Moreover, sponsors increasingly relied on paid workers rather than citizen volunteers for the required signatures on petitions, after the Court held in *Meyer v. Grant* (1988) that the FIRST AMENDMENT prevents prohibition of this practice. The First Amendment also prohibits requiring petition circulators to be registered voters under *Buckley v. American Constitutional Law Foundation, Inc.* (1999), and protects campaign spending for and against ballot measures under FIRST NATIONAL BANK OF BOSTON V. BELLOTTI (1978). Begun as a progressive reaction against the political power of money, initiatives and referenda in time drew larger campaign expenditures than elections for any state office.

At the end of its first century, academic critics began to question the very premise of direct lawmaking—its democratic credentials—because it allows a fraction of all voters to make public law in private, for personal reasons, without any obligation to represent or to account to others for their votes. Nonetheless, initiated laws are accorded special deference in political rhetoric, and sometimes in state lawmaking requirements. Initiatives can force change in political structures, like TERM LIMITS and CAMPAIGN FINANCING, that elected officials will not make. Voters are unlikely to abandon the system where it exists.

HANS A. LINDE
(2000)

(SEE ALSO: *Direct Democracy.*)

Bibliography

LINDE, HANS A. 1993 When Initiative Lawmaking Is Not "Republican Government": The Campaign Against Homosexuality. *Oregan Law Review* 72:19–45.

MAGLEBY, DAVID 1984 *Direct Legislation.* Baltimore, Maryland: Johns Hopkins University Press.

SYMPOSIUM 1994 Guaranteeing a Republican Form of Government. *University of Colorado Law Review* 65:709–946
——— 1998 Redirected Democracy: An Evaluation of the Initiative Process. *Willamette Law Review* 34:391–773

INJUNCTION

In use long before the Constitution, the injunction in the twentieth century came to play one of its most important roles as the enforcer of constitutional and CIVIL RIGHTS. Precisely because it is effective, flexible, and open-ended, the injunction has drawn opposition, and constitutional cases have often included fierce battles over whether the injunction ought to be used as a remedy. These battles have resulted in some complex judicially imposed limitations on the use of injunctions in public law cases.

The injunction rests on a simple idea: that a court may order someone to perform or to cease some action. However simple the idea, it was not a usual feature of the earliest English COMMON LAW. Although it is inaccurate to say that early common law never commanded the performance of an action, by the sixteenth century its typical judgment simply decreed that A, having won the suit, was entitled to "take" some sum of money from B. If B did not cooperate, A could often gain the assistance of the sheriff, but B was subject to no direct order to do anything.

By contrast to the common law courts, the Court of

Chancery administered a system of remedies that came to be called EQUITY, vindicated by an order directing someone to do or cease doing something. At an early stage only the imagination of the Chancellor, who presided over the court, limited the precise nature of such orders. Equity has never lost this tradition of flexibility and discretion, but as Chancery developed a sense of precedent, the occasions for such orders began to seem standardized. For example, a court might require a defendant to perform a trust, to convey land, to carry out a contract, or to pay money owed to a business partner. Some orders, typically those forbidding an action (for example, requiring a party to halt a lawsuit or to cease polluting a stream), came to be called injunctions, though the term "injunctive relief" is often used broadly to refer to direct judicial orders of many sorts. Such equitable remedies always remained relatively discretionary: Chancery would not, for example, enter an injunction in all cases; the litigant seeking such an order first had to convince that court that his remedy at law (i.e., from the common law courts) would be "inadequate," a deceptively simple term that over five centuries has taken on some surprising baggage. Because of this requirement a litigant can have a valid legal right for which, however, he cannot obtain injunctive relief.

In America before the civil rights era the injunction saw its most controversial use in labor disputes in which courts, acting on the view that union organizing and strikes were either common law torts or violations of antitrust statutes, frequently enjoined strikes or PICKETING by workers. Such actions engendered great bitterness and led to Congress's withdrawing from federal courts JURISDICTION to enter an injunction in any labor dispute. (See NORRIS-LAGUARDIA ACT.) That withdrawal in turn has bolstered arguments in favor of occasional proposals to withdraw injunctive jurisdiction in other areas in which courts were enforcing unpopular decisions.

In the late twentieth century the injunction has had its most prominent career not as a remedy in tort, contract, and property disputes but as a vindicator of civil rights. That new role flowed largely from EX PARTE YOUNG (1908), which held that although SOVEREIGN IMMUNITY might bar a damage action against a state, it did not bar injunctive relief against a state official acting unconstitutionally. This development meant that even if there was no remedy for past unlawful action, an injunction could halt continuation of that activity. Until the birth of the modern civil rights damage action with MONROE V. PAPE (1961) and the CIVIL RIGHTS ACTS of the 1960s, the injunction served as a primary tool for the enforcement of civil and constitutional rights.

Because the injunction is open-ended, it has the potential for use in a wide variety of contexts. Not only can simple acts be required or forbidden but, more important, elaborate public institutions can be restructured. Probably the most noteworthy and certainly the most controversial use of injunctive relief came in the years following BROWN V. BOARD OF EDUCATION (1954) as the courts ordered school systems to end racial SEGREGATION. Drawing on their experience in complex antitrust and BANKRUPTCY cases, the courts employed the injunction as a tool for the reorganization of the schools. In the case of recalcitrant systems, such desegregation decrees sometimes called forth elaborate and detailed orders concerning the assignment of students and teachers, the curriculum, and other details of the schools' operation. Such orders often engendered resistance and involved the courts in the conduct of the schools over a number of years in particularly intractable cases. Courts have also ordered injunctive relief in INSTITUTIONAL LITIGATION involving PRISONERS' RIGHTS and the rights of mental patients.

Part of what makes the injunction such a powerful and controversial tool is the enforcement power that stands behind it. One disobeying an injunction is subject to CONTEMPT penalties—with the threat of indefinite imprisonment and mounting fines until one obeys the order. Perhaps because the injunction carries with it such a formidable arsenal for enforcement, the Supreme Court has enunciated a series of restrictions on the use of injunctive relief in favor of litigants wishing to challenge official action. Thus a federal court may abstain from deciding the constitutionality of a state practice until the state courts have had an opportunity to clarify the law or practice in question, as in *Railroad Commission of Texas v. Pullman Co.* (1941). Moreover, even if the law or practice is clear, a federal court should refrain from adjudicating the constitutionality of a state statute if the challenger of the statute will have an adequate opportunity to present that challenge in pending litigation to which the state is a party (YOUNGER V. HARRIS, 1971). Both the so-called *Pullman* and *Younger* ABSTENTION doctrines have complexities not hinted at in these summaries; they testify to the power of the injunction and its centrality in much modern constitutional litigation.

STEPHEN C. YEAZELL
(1986)

Bibliography

FISS, OWEN   1978   *The Civil Rights Injunction.* Bloomington: Indiana University Press.
FRANKFURTER, FELIX and GREENE, NATHAN   1930   *The Labor Injunction.* New York: Macmillan.

IN PERSONAM

(Latin: "Against the person.") A legal action or case is *in personam* if it is directed against a particular individual to enforce an obligation. Cases in EQUITY proceed *in personam.*

DENNIS J. MAHONEY
(1986)

IN RE

(Latin: "In the matter [of]. . . .") This is a way of titling a case that presents a question to be decided or an action to be taken in the absence of adversary parties.

DENNIS J. MAHONEY
(1986)

IN RE . . .

See under name of party

IN REM

(Latin: "Against the thing.") A legal action or case is *in rem* if it undertakes to establish the title to or status of a thing with respect to all persons.

DENNIS J. MAHONEY

INSTITUTIONAL LITIGATION

"Institutional litigation" refers to cases in which the courts, responding to allegations that conditions in some institutions violate the Constitution or CIVIL RIGHTS statutes, become involved in supervising the institutions in question. Loosely used, the term might describe any number of lawsuits, ranging from an assertion of discriminatory employment practices in a CORPORATION to an attack by inmates on the conditions at a state prison. What such apparently diverse cases have in common is the possibility that if the plaintiffs convince the court that a violation of the law has occurred and if the institution proves recalcitrant in remedying the violation, the court may become involved in detailed supervision of the institution over long periods. Though details of such complex suits naturally vary widely, it is the combination of continuous judicial scrutiny and detailed substantive involvement that has characterized institutional litigation.

Laws such as those forbidding discrimination in employment apply to both public and private institutions. Many constitutional provisions, however, guarantee rights only against the government and most institutions to which individuals are involuntarily committed are run by the government. Consequently most of the institutions involved have been public: prisons, mental hospitals, school systems, and the like. Moreover, though the Constitution

binds both state and federal courts, the latter tribunals have played the most active role in vindicating constitutional rights. The typical institutional case therefore has involved a federal district court supervising the conduct of a state institution, a setting that has raised constitutional concerns beyond those of the particular substantive law of the case.

From a wide perspective one can trace the roots of institutional litigation to earlier classes of cases: nineteenth-century EQUITY receiverships, bankruptcy reorganizations, antitrust decrees requiring the restructuring of a large industry, even to the efforts of fifteenth-century English chancellors to enforce the duties of trustees to establish and supervise the religious and charitable institutions endowed in a will. Modern institutional cases also have more recent origins in the efforts of the federal judiciary to desegregate schools in the 1950s and 1960s. Resistance to simple desegregation decrees forced federal courts to become involved in many details of local school administration. As some school boards adjusted their strategies for resistance, courts delved deeper into school board practices, to the point of displacing some traditional school board functions. In GRIFFIN V. SCHOOL BOARD OF PRINCE EDWARD COUNTY (1964) the Supreme Court even suggested that a federal court could order taxes imposed to raise funds to finance a public school system that officials had closed to avoid desegregation.

At about the same time courts were articulating other constitutional rights, including constitutional limitations on prison and mental hospital conditions. In cases such as *Wyatt v. Stickney* (1971) and *Holt v. Sarver* (1969) lower federal courts combined the procedural aggressiveness of the school desegregation cases with the newly developed constitutional rights, enforcing their decrees against recalcitrant officials with INJUNCTIONS backed by the force of the contempt power. In dozens of institutional cases in the 1970s these same forces triggered widespread court-ordered institutional reform that covered such details of institutional life as cell size, visiting hours, telephone privileges, hygiene, and disciplinary procedures.

Describing institutional litigation and tracing its origins are easier than isolating, much less resolving, the controversies that surround it. Nearly all the issues that arise in public discourse about a federal system and an independent judiciary eventually appear in some discussion of institutional litigation. Perhaps the most central of these issues are questions about the relationship of institutional litigation to (1) the nature of litigation; (2) the judicial capacity to run institutions; (3) the power of the purse; and (4) FEDERALISM.

Some view institutional cases as a form of litigation previously unknown to Anglo-American jurisprudence. In the contrasted traditional vision of litigation, a lawsuit involves two parties who present an isolatable set of facts to a court, which issues a JUDGMENT; the losing party complies with the court's decree, and judicial involvement with the case ends. To the extent that this statement of traditional litigation is accurate, institutional litigation involves a substantial departure. In institutional litigation the set of facts presented to the court often constitutes all of the physical, psychological, and social conditions within the institution. Such widespread allegations prevent the court from addressing any single dispute which, when resolved, will restore the parties to a proper relationship. In several institutional cases, no matter how many disputes the court resolves, additional issues arise with respect to implementation of and compliance with previous orders.

The frequency with which institutional litigation requires courts to address some aspect of institutional life highlights the second central issue—judicial capacity to supervise large public institutions. By training, judges are neither wardens nor hospital administrators. Some critics question whether judges should substitute their judgment about institutional life for that of professional administrators appointed by elected officials. Courts often try to compensate for their inexperience by appointing SPECIAL MASTERS and expert advisory panels and by seeking the views of the defendant administrators. But these tactics may raise further questions about institutional litigation's departure from traditional ideas about litigation. Yet, once a court has concluded that institutional life is constitutionally deficient because of the acts of the regular administrators, it is difficult for courts simply to defer to the judgment of those same persons found to be responsible for the unconstitutional conditions.

In many cases, however, institutional conditions are constitutionally deficient less because of the acts of administrators than because the state has allocated insufficient funds to institutional budgets. Even willing administrators experience difficulty in upgrading conditions at some institutions. A new prison building may be necessary or more staff may need to be hired. When institutional reform may be accomplished only through expenditures of substantial sums, a new issue arises: may courts order the allocation of public funds against the wishes of legislators who presumably reflect their constituents' wishes?

For many observers, this fiscal confrontation reveals the least palatable aspect of institutional litigation—the antimajoritarian judicial usurpation of legislative and executive authority. Courts, self-conscious about express allocative decision making, sometimes disavow authority to order funds raised to carry out institutional reform. And, despite *Griffin's* OBITER DICTUM about imposing taxes, there is doubt about how far courts may and ought to go in ordering funds raised to satisfy their orders. Yet it is also a commonplace for courts to state that lack of funds is no

excuse for failure to comply with the Constitution. Since any public law decision may have important fiscal effects, perhaps institutional cases have been unjustifiably isolated from the rest of the public litigation on this issue. Indeed, if one assumes that, put to the choice between releasing inmates and rectifying the conditions of their institutional confinement, the public and their elected officials would choose the latter, judicially decreed funding may be more in accord with the majority's wishes than any other course of action.

Ironically, institutional cases flourished during the 1970s, while the Supreme Court was emphasizing that federal courts should not interfere with traditional state or local functions. In RIZZO V. GOODE (1976) and O'SHEA V. LITTLETON (1974) the Court rejected systemic attacks on, respectively, a police department and a city's system of criminal justice. In YOUNGER V. HARRIS (1971) and its progeny the Court established prohibitions on federal court interference with state adjudicative proceedings. As a doctrinal matter, the issues in most institutional cases proved distinguishable from the issues in *Rizzo*, *O'Shea*, and *Younger*. Nevertheless the Court's federalism theme could have been viewed as requiring curtailment of judicial receptivity to institutional litigation. Yet during this period of growing deference to states, the lower federal courts, without Supreme Court disapproval, continued to hear and resolve institutional cases.

THEODORE EISENBERG
STEPHEN C. YEAZELL
(1986)

Bibliography

CHAYES, ABRAM 1976 The Role of the Judge in Public Law Litigation. *Harvard Law Review* 89:1281–1316.
DIVER, COLIN S. 1979 The Judge as Political Powerbroker: Superintending Structural Change in Public Institutions. *Virginia Law Review* 65:43–106.
EISENBERG, THEODORE and YEAZELL, STEPHEN C. 1980 The Ordinary and the Extraordinary in Institutional Litigation. *Harvard Law Review* 93:465–517.
FISS, OWEN M. 1979 The Supreme Court 1978 Term, Foreword: The Forms of Justice. *Harvard Law Review* 93:1–58.

INSULAR CASES

Originally applied to three cases decided in 1901, the term "insular cases" has come to denominate a series of cases decided in the early twentieth century defining the place of overseas TERRITORIES in the American constitutional system. Following the acquisition of PUERTO RICO, the Philippines, Hawaii, and various other island possessions, the Supreme Court was called upon to decide whether, or to what extent, in William Jennings Bryan's phrase, "the Constitution follows the flag." From the insular cases emerged the DOCTRINE of INCORPORATION OF TERRITORIES.

The first three insular cases (*DeLima v. Bidwell, Dooley v. United States, Downes v. Bidwell*) were argued together and decided in 1901. They raised the question whether Puerto Rico was part of the United States within the meaning of the "uniformity clause" for purposes of levying customs duties. In *DeLima* and *Dooley*, the Court held that from the Treaty of Paris (1899), by which Spain ceded Puerto Rico to the United States, until the Foraker Act (1900), by which Congress organized the territorial government, the collection of duties on goods moving between the United States and Puerto Rico was unconstitutional. In the far more important *Downes* case, the court upheld collection of duties after passage of the Foraker Act. The apparent meaning of the three cases was that the constitutional status of overseas possessions is for Congress to determine, but constitutional protection is to be assumed in the absence of congressional action. The Justices divided into three schools of thought: four Justices, led by Chief Justice MELVILLE W. FULLER and Justice JOHN MARSHALL HARLAN, contended that the Constitution applied automatically and completely to any territory under United States SOVEREIGNTY; Justice HENRY B. BROWN, who wrote the lead opinion in all three cases, believed that Congress, under Article IV, section 3, enjoyed plenary power over the territories and could extend to them all, any part, or none of the Constitution, at its discretion; and four Justices, led by Justice EDWARD D. WHITE, argued that the Constitution applied fully to the territories only after positive action by the Congress to incorporate them into the United States.

In 1903 and 1904 the Court decided four cases dealing with CRIMINAL PROCEDURE in Hawaii, Puerto Rico, and the Philippines (*Hawaii v. Mankichi, Crowley v. United States, Kepner v. United States, Dorr v. United States*). The Court made a distinction between fundamental or NATURAL RIGHTS, which are constitutionally protected everywhere, and rights merely procedural or remedial, peculiar to Anglo-American jurisprudence, which do not apply in the territories—at least "until Congress shall see fit to incorporate the . . . territory into the United States." In the former category was protection against DOUBLE JEOPARDY; in the latter were INDICTMENT by GRAND JURY, TRIAL BY JURY, and JURY UNANIMITY. *Dorr* (1904) was the first case in which the incorporation of territories doctrine received the formal assent of a majority of the Court.

In the 1905 case of *Rasmussen v. United States*, the Court unanimously held the jury trial guarantee of the SIXTH AMENDMENT applicable to Alaska. White, writing for himself and six colleagues, demonstrated that Congress had explicitly incorporated Alaska into the United States

and thus had brought its residents under complete constitutional protection. Harlan and Brown, in separate CONCURRING OPINIONS, each reiterated his original position on the Constitution and the territories.

In *Trono v. United States* (1905) and *Dowdell v. United States* (1911), the Court sustained Philippine criminal convictions obtained through indigenous procedures which would have violated the Sixth Amendment had the Philippines been incorporated territory. But in WEEMS V. UNITED STATES (1910), the Court ruled that since Congress had extended the protection against CRUEL AND UNUSUAL PUNISHMENT to the Philippines, the protection was identical to that enjoyed by mainlanders under the Eighth Amendment.

The most forceful and consistent opposition to the incorporation doctrine came from Justice Harlan. He argued that all of Congress's power flows from the Constitution, and therefore Congress is bound in its every action by that document's limitations and guarantees. The "occult" doctrine of the insular cases, he said, permitted Congress, contrary to the spirit and genius of the Constitution, to erect a colonial empire and exercise absolute dominion over dependent peoples.

In *Board of Public Utilities Commissioners v. Ynchausti* (1920), White, by then Chief Justice, was able to report the Court's unanimous acceptance of the incorporation of territories doctrine; and in *Balzac v. Porto Rico* (1922), Chief Justice WILLIAM HOWARD TAFT, for a unanimous Court, applied it as the settled law governing the status of territories.

DENNIS J. MAHONEY
(1986)

Bibliography

BLOOM, JOHN PORTER, ed. 1973 *The American Territorial System.* Athens: Ohio University Press.

COUDERT, FREDERICK R. 1926 The Evolution of the Doctrine of Territorial Incorporation. *Columbia Law Review* 66:823–850.

FUSTER, JAIME B. 1974 Origins of the Doctrine of Territorial Incorporation and Its Implications Regarding the Power of the Commonwealth of Puerto Rico to Regulate Interstate Commerce. *Revista Juridica de la Universidad de Puerto Rico* 43:259–294.

SEMONCHE, JOHN E. 1978 *Charting the Future: The Supreme Court Responds to a Changing Society, 1890–1920.* Chaps 5 and 6. Westport, Conn.: Greenwood Press.

INTEGRATION

See: Desegregation; Segregation

INTEGRATION OF THE FEDERAL GOVERNMENT

See: Executive Orders 9980 and 9981

INTELLECTUAL PROPERTY LAW AND THE FIRST AMENDMENT

COPYRIGHT law, trademark law, right of publicity law, and trade secret law are all speech restrictions. They restrict what people may say or write or perform. They do so based on the content of the speech. And they cover not just literal copying, but also the creation of new works. Saying that these laws protect PROPERTY RIGHTS cannot resolve the problem; the question still remains: To what extent may the government protect intellectual property rights by restricting speech?

The Supreme Court, in *Harper & Row Publishers v. Nation Enterprises* (1985), held that copyright law is a permissible speech restriction, essentially carving out a new exception to FIRST AMENDMENT protection: Speech that copies another's expression, and that is not a fair use, is unprotected by the First Amendment against a copyright infringement claim. Nonetheless, the Court suggested that these conditions—that copyright law restricts only the copying of expression and not of ideas or facts, and that copyright law provides a safe harbor for certain fair uses such as criticism or news reporting or parody— may be constitutionally required. Laws that restrict dissemination of facts, such as tort causes of action for misappropriation of news or statutes restricting copying of fact databases, might be unconstitutional.

Even given copyright law's substantive constitutionality, the First Amendment should impose the usual procedural safeguards on copyright litigation (and other intellectual property litigation). The PRIOR RESTRAINT doctrine, for instance, may bar preliminary injunctions in many copyright cases. The independent appellate review doctrine described in *Bose Corp. v. Consumer Reports* (1984) might require de novo review of findings of substantial similarity of expression. The rules related to strict liability, PUNITIVE DAMAGES, quantum of proof, and burden of proof might likewise in some measure affect copyright law. Most of these claims have not been seriously explored by courts.

Most trademark infringement cases involve commercial advertising that is allegedly likely to confuse. Restricting this advertising poses little constitutional difficulty, because FREEDOM OF SPEECH law allows restriction on misleading COMMERCIAL SPEECH. Nonetheless, some trademark cases, especially those involving uses that are not primarily advertising—for instance, book parodies that borrow the books' titles or cover layouts—do pose First Amendment problems. Lower courts are split about the extent to which the First Amendment provides a defense in these situations.

The relatively new state and federal trademark dilution statutes raise more serious First Amendment questions, because they restrict commercial uses of trademarks even when there is no likelihood of consumer confusion, and thus fall outside the doctrine that misleading commercial speech may be restricted. Courts have not yet had much occasion to confront this question. *San Francisco Arts & Athletics, Inc. v. United States Olympic Committee* (1987), which involved a specialized antidilution statute, suggests that such laws would probably be upheld; but the Court's recent, more speech-protective commercial speech jurisprudence makes the matter unclear.

The right of publicity gives people the exclusive ability to control use in commerce of their names, likenesses, voices, and other attributes that may remind the public of them. Lower courts have generally carved out exceptions, on First Amendment grounds, for news reporting, biography, fiction, and similar uses, even though these works are often sold for money; but courts have generally upheld the right of publicity as applied to commercial advertising and to merchandising (posters, busts, T-shirts, and the like).

It is not clear whether the right of publicity is always constitutional even when so narrowed. Even commercial advertising is usually entitled to considerable constitutional protection, and posters, busts, and T-shirts are as protected as movies or books or any other works that are commercially sold. Banning the unauthorized sales of, say, busts of MARTIN LUTHER KING, JR.—as one court did— poses considerable First Amendment difficulties. Nonetheless, outside the context of merchandising that constitutes a parody, lower courts have generally rejected free speech arguments in advertising and merchandising cases.

The Court's only right of publicity case, *Zacchini v. Scripps-Howard Broadcasting* (1977), sheds little light on this subject. *Zacchini* upheld an unusual sort of right of publicity—a performer's right to prevent rebroadcasts of his entire performance—and said little about the much more common name/likeness/voice/identity claims.

Many trade-secret claims can probably be upheld on the grounds that they merely enforce a confidentiality contract, something that COHEN V. COWLES MEDIA (1991) holds is constitutional. On the other hand, when the defendant is not bound by a contract—for instance, a media organization to which the information was leaked— the First Amendment may pose serious obstacles to imposing liability, and even more serious obstacles to injunctions. The Court has not fully confronted the matter, though one

Justice, granting a stay in *CBS, Inc. v. Davis* (1994), rejected on prior restraint grounds a request for an injunction against revealing trade secrets.

EUGENE VOLOKH
(2000)

Bibliography

LEMLEY, MARK and VOLOKH, EUGENE 1998 Freedom of Speech and Injunctions in Intellectual Property Cases. *Duke Law Journal* 48:147–242.

VOLOKH, EUGENE and McDONNELL, BRETT 1998 Freedom of Speech and Independent Judgment Review in Copyright Cases. *Yale Law Journal* 107:2431–2470.

INTEREST GROUP LITIGATION

Interest group litigation is sponsored by organizations whose attorneys typically are less interested in specific legal claims than in the constitutional principles that a litigation represents. In contrast, most court cases are pursued for the benefit of the parties directly involved.

In seeking their clients' immediate interests private attorneys sometimes invoke constitutional arguments, but these are incidental to the specific claims of the parties. A sponsored case, however, is often pursued in the name of a litigant even though it is initiated, financed, and supported by an organization seeking its own constitutional goals. INTEREST GROUPS are particularly attracted to cases involving constitutional principles because the judicial decisions emerging from such cases are relatively insulated from subsequent attacks by legislators and other public officials.

It is arguable, of course, that group-supported litigation has always been in existence. For example, following the WAGNER (NATIONAL LABOR RELATIONS) ACT and other NEW DEAL legislation, litigation was managed, or otherwise assisted, by LABOR unions, trade associations, stockholder groups, and other business interests. However, the social and economic ferment of the 1960s and 1970s brought interest group litigation into sharper focus. The CIVIL RIGHTS MOVEMENT and the VIETNAM conflict not only produced federal legislation but also stimulated new constitutional demands by litigious organizations representing women, welfare recipients, consumers, and persons resisting military service.

The strategies and tactics of interest group litigants are heavily influenced by SOCIOLOGICAL JURISPRUDENCE and LEGAL REALISM. These philosophies hold that judges, especially Supreme Court Justices, decide controversial cases by choosing among conflicting goals and policies. Such judges do not reach results or write opinions merely by construing statutes, analogizing cases, or analyzing DOCTRINES. Instead, inquiries into judicial decision making have focused on the ways litigation is influenced by the timing of cases and the quality of the constitutional arguments reaching the appellate courts.

Prototypes of interest group litigation are the cases managed by the United States Department of Justice and similar state agencies. Their attorneys select the appropriate government cases to be appealed, and by confessing error or by compromising cases brought against the government, they seek to inhibit the establishment of unfavorable precedents. Also, a federal Legal Service Corporation, independent of the Department of Justice, has become one of the principal sources for funding and supporting litigation aimed at social and economic reform. Consumers, poor people, prisoners, and other low-resource persons have been represented by government-subsidized attorneys in suits against federal and state agencies and private organizations. Besides managing their own cases, government agencies promote private interest group litigation by reimbursing attorneys who participate and intervene for them in administrative proceedings and in court cases involving ADMINISTRATIVE LAW.

Although strategically less favorably situated than government attorneys, those representing private interest groups are also in a position to choose cases for APPEAL and to control the flow of argument in the higher courts. Unlike government litigation, however, the legal requirements for participation in private law suits sometimes prevent an organization from suing on its own, in behalf of its members, or for a similarly situated class of people. This problem has been partially alleviated by Supreme Court decisions liberalizing rules of legal STANDING to permit lawsuits by environmentalists, taxpayers, and other special interests.

Litigation activity by interest groups is visible in constitutional civil cases as well as in the criminal *cause célèbre*. In some of these cases attorneys representing factions of social movements vie for litigation sponsorship. The extensive publicity often connected with such cases, the constitutional issues perceived to be intertwined in the conflict, and the opportunities for fund-raising sometimes result in interest group controversies. For example, in several church-state cases attorneys representing different organizations have quarreled over the management of litigation. In the "Scottsboro" case, involving blacks accused of rape, attorneys representing civil rights organizations and those representing a communist-sponsored legal defense organization disagreed about the use of trial publicity.

Ideological differences among lawyers are occasionally reflected in varying conceptions of litigation strategy. Some attorneys emphasize the importance of a complete trial record raising all possible legal issues while others concentrate on the constitutional issues.

An alternative approach to a single TEST CASE is a litigation program aimed at accumulating a series of favorable decisions changing constitutional law. An incremental approach emphasizes narrow factual issues and specific claims, and groups with large legal staffs and cooperating attorneys are strategically positioned to conduct litigation in this way. Litigation programs of this kind have achieved changes in the constitutional doctrine governing racial CRIMINAL PROCEDURE, selective service, religion, and employment.

In politically tinged criminal cases the less provident and unpopular groups are not likely to use incremental litigation; they usually face immediate problems of securing relief for organization leaders and raising money for their causes. For example, in the 1950s when large numbers of cases involving congressional investigations of communism reached the Supreme Court, the lion's share was controlled by lawyers who depended on individual financial contributions to sustain their legal work.

When litigation is controlled by interest groups, constitutional issues are likely to be advanced and developed at the trial level. The "perfecting of a trial record" also gives the adversaries an opportunity to debate broader issues that are likely to be considered on appeal.

The development of a "good" trial record facilitates the preparation of appellate briefs interlaced with statistical and authoritative bibliographical references to social and economic facts supporting particular constitutional arguments. This technique was first used in the early-twentieth-century social legislation cases, and it has been used to illuminate fields ranging from racial equality to abortion. Similar forms of extralegal argument are found in complex court cases involving PUBLIC UTILITY REGULATION and other economic matters. (See BRANDEIS BRIEF.)

Besides expanding the scope of their arguments, interest group attorneys have become increasingly adept at coordinating litigation by discouraging the appeal of inconsistent cases or those with less developed records. They have also been successful in getting publication of sympathetic views in legal, scholarly, and popular journals. Networks of attorneys and other observers have also emerged to monitor court decisions and keep central clearinghouses informed about promising court cases.

Sometimes the immediate concerns of the litigants may conflict with those of the sponsoring interest group. A litigant's claim may be compromised or settled. Legal issues advanced by the parties may be formulated so as to avoid the constitutional issues raised by the sponsor. Also, the trial and appellate preparation may be a labor of love, or the work-product of an attorney who jealously guards his professional prerogatives.

A failure to control a litigation does not necessarily mean that an interest group lacks influence. When the issues defined in court are narrow, or the litigant's attorney has failed to develop the case's constitutional implications, an interest group attorney can still participate as AMICUS CURIAE (friend of the court). Nowhere has this phenomenon been more visible than in the medical school admission case, REGENTS OF THE UNIVERSITY OF CALIFORNIA V. BAKKE (1978). In this case fifty-seven organizations submitted amicus curiae briefs to the Supreme Court. Although some interest group attorneys will refrain from submitting such briefs when a client's attorney adequately has argued the constitutional issues, the filing of such a brief does serve the political function of announcing the group's support for a constitutional argument. Amicus curiae participation usually requires the consent of both parties or the approval of the court, and the influence of either briefs or ORAL ARGUMENTS as amicus remains debatable.

Even though interest group litigation is growing, part of the increase is attributable to government legal services and private foundation philanthropy. If government support is curtailed and private foundations are subjected to closer tax scrutiny, individual contributions and voluntary legal services will be called upon to fill the gap. Such a decline in government support seems likely since some judges and political leaders have expressed concern about government-sponsored litigation directed against public officials. They also criticize lawyers who represent causes rather than clients and overburden the judicial process. Other factors affecting the growth of interest group litigation are the strictness of enforcement of traditional restrictions on the scope of law suits (see INSTITUTIONAL LITIGATION) and the rules governing the award of attorneys' fees to interest group attorneys.

Finally, no description of interest group litigation would be complete without noting that many highly publicized civil cases and "showcase" criminal trials as well as ordinary law cases are financed and carried forward without the participation of organized interest groups. The constitutional and policy arguments advanced by attorneys in these cases, in many instances, are just as likely to advance the development of legal and constitutional doctrine.

NATHAN HAKMAN
(1986)

(SEE ALSO: *Groups and the Constitution.*)

Bibliography

COUNCIL FOR PUBLIC INTEREST LAW 1976 *Balancing the Scales of Justice: Financing Public Interest Law in America.* Washington, D.C.: Council on Public Interest Law.

HAKMAN, NATHAN 1966 Lobbying the Supreme Court: An Appraisal of "Political Science Folklore." *Fordham Law Review* 35:15–50.

——— 1972 Political Trials in the Legal Order: A Political Scientist's Perspective. *Journal of Public Law* 21:73–126.

KIRCHHEIMER, OTTO 1961 *Political Justice: The Use of Legal Procedure for Political Ends.* Princeton, N.J.: Princeton University Press.

VOSE, CLEMENT E. 1972 *Constitutional Change: Amendment Politics and Supreme Court Litigation Since 1900.* Lexington, Mass.: D. C. Heath.

WEISBROD, BURTON A.; HANDLER, JOEL F., and KOMESAR, NEIL K. 1978 *Public Interest Law: An Economical and Institutional Analysis.* Berkeley: University of California Press.

INTEREST GROUPS

Interest groups, or groups of people who try to use the power of government to advance their own interests, have played an important part in the development of both constitutional law and CONSTITUTIONAL THEORY.

CHARLES A. BEARD argued that a particular array of interest groups lay behind the support for and opposition to the Constitution in 1787–1789. Examining the property holdings of supporters and opponents, Beard argued that debtors and owners of real property opposed the Constitution, while personalty interests, especially creditors whose property consisted largely of promises to repay loans, supported it. Beard's specific conclusions have been rejected by later scholars, who have found more complex patterns of property holding than Beard's argument required. Even if the specific argument is rejected, however, consistent patterns of support and opposition based on interests can be found. Constitutional provisions like the ban on state impairments of the OBLIGATION OF CONTRACTS and the prohibition of state issuance of money are best explained by the fact that the supporters of the Constitution feared that they would be outvoted in state legislatures on important issues related to debt and might be able to defend their interests better in the national Congress. Similarly, the likelihood that the new government would be able to resolve controversies over ownership of the undeveloped lands to the west meant that speculators who had purchased western lands were inclined to support the Constitution. Many of the Constitution's compromises over SLAVERY resulted from the sort of interest-group bargaining that characterizes politics. At the same time, the action of interest groups alone seems insufficient to account for the RATIFICATION OF THE CONSTITUTION. Because too many people with too many conflicting interests supported ratification, interest alone cannot explain the adoption of the document. In the end, the Constitution was ratified because of the interaction between interest-group support and conviction that the new government promised to be better as a matter of principle than the Confederation.

Supporters of the new Constitution were alert to the problems that interest groups posed for good government. The central theme in THE FEDERALIST is probably the necessity of designing a government to "curb the influence of faction." *The Federalist*'s notion of "faction" is not precisely the same as modern ideas about interest groups, for "factions" included groups brought together by a common "passion" as well as those acting to advance a common "interest." Nonetheless, the arguments in *The Federalist* about the evils of faction capture many modern concerns about the problems interest groups pose for government. For *The Federalist*, factions must be checked because they are motivated by passions or interests "adverse to the rights of other citizens or to the permanent and aggregate interests of the community"—what we would today call the public interest. This remains true, even if the faction amounts to a majority; even a majority can invade the interests of others, and more controversially, even a majority can act in ways that fail to advance the public interest, conceived of as something different from the interests of a majority.

According to *The Federalist* the new government was well suited to check the influence of faction. Its federal structure allowed the government to extend over a rather large territory. By extending the geographic scope of government, the Constitution made it more difficult for individual factions to gain control of the government. Because the nation would be large, it was unlikely that any single faction or interest group would be represented in sufficient numbers throughout the country to gain control of the machinery of the national government. Even if different factions attempted to put together a coalition, the size of the nation would make coordination of their plans difficult. In addition, the SEPARATION OF POWERS in the national government meant that interest groups would have to mobilize their political forces for a long time and in a number of forums before they could control the government. DIRECT ELECTIONS for the HOUSE OF REPRESENTATIVES might register factional concerns every two years, but gaining control of the SENATE, elected by the people indirectly acting through their state legislatures, would be more difficult. In the initial conception, the ELECTORAL COLLEGE, which was to select the President, was another constraint on the ability of interest groups to control the government. The life-tenured judiciary, too, could stand in the way of factional control, invalidating legislation that contravened constitutional provisions designed to limit faction, such as the CONTRACT CLAUSE.

As a theoretical matter *The Federalist*'s defense of the new government as a means of checking the influence of interest groups is quite powerful. Yet it has some limitations. The structures of the government of a territorially extended republic might be sufficient to protect against the influence of interest groups, but on *The Federalist's* theory as here summarized, it is difficult to understand why the national government would be able to adopt programs that were truly in the national interest. Moreover, modern developments have undermined the cogency of *The Federalist's* arguments. The rise of national political parties makes it somewhat easier for interest groups scattered throughout the nation to coordinate their programs. The direct election of members of the Senate and the elimination of the electoral college as a body that seriously deliberates about who the President should be have limited the power of those institutions to stand up to factional influence.

Modern constitutional law deals with interest groups in two ways. Where the interest groups are organized around economic concerns, in recent years the Supreme Court has never found their ability to secure government aid conclusively unconstitutional. WILLIAMSON V. LEE OPTICAL COMPANY (1955) is typical. The Court upheld a statute requiring that consumers purchase duplicate lenses for their glasses only with a prescription from an eye doctor. The statute obviously was the result of lobbying pressure from eye doctors facing competition from opticians who lacked medical training. According to the Court, the statute was constitutional because the state legislature might have believed that requiring a new prescription was helpful in assuring that consumers would get glasses whose prescriptions suited their needs. As most commentators have recognized, this explanation is extremely weak. In general, the Court's approach to constitutional claims by or against economic interest groups, framed as violations of the DUE PROCESS or EQUAL PROTECTION clauses, leaves the matter entirely to the legislature. In that sense, factions are now allowed to control the government.

Some areas of JUDICIAL REVIEW dealing with economic matters remain of interest. In enforcing the restrictions that the COMMERCE CLAUSE places on STATE REGULATION OF COMMERCE, the Court has sometimes been sensitive to the role that local interest groups play in securing restrictionist legislation. In *Washington State Apple Advertising Commission v. Hunt* (1977), the Supreme Court invalidated a statute requiring that apples be repackaged in ways that concealed from purchasers the fact—which they might be interested in learning—that some of the apples came from Washington, where particularly good apples are grown. The Court noted in passing that the statute had been adopted at the behest of North Carolina's apple growers, whose apples were less attractive to consumers. In other cases, however, the Court has not been so concerned about the interest group politics that lies behind

legislation. *Exxon Corp. v. Governor of Maryland* (1978) upheld a statute, designed to aid corner gas station owners, prohibiting national gasoline producers from owning retail gas stations in the state.

In addition, the Constitution bars governments from TAKINGS OF PROPERTY without JUST COMPENSATION and from impairing the obligation of contracts. In extreme cases, the Supreme Court has been willing to invalidate laws that seem to it to be the product of pure interest-group motivation rather than of sincere consideration of the public interest. In UNITED STATES TRUST CO. OF NEW YORK V. NEW JERSEY (1977), the Court invoked the contract clause to invalidate a New Jersey statute that diverted revenue from tolls on automobiles, which were by contract supposed to be used to pay off road-building bonds, instead using them to support mass transit. In *Nollan v. California Coastal Commission* (1987), the Court invalidated a California statute that had been interpreted to allow an owner of a beachfront residence to expand his house only if he allowed the public to walk across the beach in front of the house. The New Jersey statute might be seen as the result of interest-group lobbying by mass transit commuters, who might be easier to organize than the holders of the road-building bonds, while the California law might be seen as imposing costs on isolated individual owners in the service of the interests of a majority faction.

The significance of these decisions, though, should not be exaggerated; they are controversial, in part because in both there does seem to be a genuine public interest promoted by each of the statutes the Court invalidated. In general, where economic interests are involved, the Court tolerates a great deal of interest-group legislation, even if there seems to be little "public interest" justification for the legislation, although the Court most often does require that the state offer a public interest justification, no matter how weak, for what it does.

Interest groups play another role in modern constitutional law. In UNITED STATES V. CAROLENE PRODUCTS CO. (1938), Justice HARLAN FISKE STONE suggested that laws adversely affecting DISCRETE AND INSULAR MINORITIES would have to be strongly justified to be constitutional. Such minorities might be thought of as a type of interest group, which because of its position in the society is unable to attain political power commensurate with its numbers. Their political opportunities might be blocked by a history of discrimination against them, which might lead members of the groups to believe that attempting to secure government assistance is futile or might demonstrate that a majority consistently undervalues the interests of the minority.

The idea that the courts should be alert to protect these minorities gains much of its force from the experience of blacks in the period before BROWN V. BOARD OF EDUCATION

(1954, 1955) and the VOTING RIGHTS ACT OF 1965. Other candidates for inclusion in the group of DISCRETE AND INSULAR MINORITIES are women, nonmarital children, and the poor. But the Supreme Court has been reluctant to expand the group of protected minorities. In CITY OF CLEBURNE V. CLEBURNE LIVING CENTER (1985), the Court refused to give the mentally retarded formal inclusion in the group, noting that many legislatures had acted to promote the interests of the mentally retarded and that, were they to be treated as a special group, many other groups with "perhaps immutable disabilities" and unable to "mandate the desired legislative responses" (e.g., the aging, the disabled, and the mentally ill) might "claim some degree of prejudice."

The Court has not expanded the list of discrete and insular minorities because it believes that with respect to most groups, the ordinary operation of politics allows any interest group to participate in the process of bargaining and trading votes that leads coalitions to achieve their goals. In many ways, that is the image of politics offered in *The Federalist*, and if the political process works in that way, the Court's reluctance is well founded. Yet Stone's insight regarding the imperfections of the political process suggests that on occasion interest groups might be unable to secure legislative action no matter how hard they try. Recent theories of the political process offered by students of "public choice" indicate, however, that the difficulty may not be that minority interest groups cannot get their way, but rather that majority groups, those that wish to advance the public interest, might find themselves defeated by well-organized interest groups: the members of the smaller interest groups are likely to have more at stake, and are therefore more likely to organize effectively, than the members of the majority, each of whom has so little at stake that none will make any effort to oppose legislation that imposes substantial costs on the group as a whole.

Public choice theories of the Constitution reinvigorate *The Federalist*'s concern that factions or interest groups might control the government and lead to the adoption of legislation that impairs the public interest. If those theories accurately describe the contemporary scene, however, they show that neither judicial review nor the structures of government on which *The Federalist* relied have been sufficient to curb the influence of faction.

MARK TUSHNET
(1992)

(SEE ALSO: *Economic Analysis; Mental Illness and the Constitution; Mental Retardation and the Constitution; Political Philosophy of the Constitution*.)

Bibliography

BEARD, CHARLES 1913 *An Economic Interpretation of the Constitution*. New York: Macmillan.

OLSEN, MANCUR 1965 *The Logic of Collective Action*. Cambridge, Mass.: Harvard University Press.
SUSTEIN, CASS 1985 Interest Groups in American Public Law. *Stanford Law Review* 38:29–87.

INTERGOVERNMENTAL IMMUNITY

Intergovernmental immunities are exemptions of the state and national governments from attempts to interfere with each other's governmental operations. Thus, one government may claim immunity from the other's regulations and taxes. Though immunity claims may invoke specific provisions such as the TENTH AMENDMENT, they reflect deeper assumptions about the institutional structure envisioned by the Constitution as a whole. Immunity problems originate in the tension between the nation's need to acknowledge the supremacy of federal policies while respecting a tradition of indestructible states. Governmental structures are not ends in themselves in constitutional theory; their ultimate status depends on their efficacy in securing what THE FEDERALIST #45 called "the solid happiness of the people." Implying ends, institutions also imply powers. (See NECESSARY AND PROPER CLAUSE.) Grant the supremacy of national powers over state powers, and the erosion of state institutions follows eventually despite talk of indestructible states. Conversely, protection for state institutions will eventually defeat national power in some respects, talk of federal supremacy notwithstanding. On balance, judicial resolutions of this tension have favored national supremacy.

Immunity claims usually occur in the areas of taxation, regulation, and litigation. Most of the latter involve state claims of immunity from suits by private parties in federal court under the ELEVENTH AMENDMENT. The amendment, however, does not extend immunity that would be considered inconsistent with the Constitution's general plan of government, including the principle of national supremacy. The amendment grants no immunity from suits by other states and the national government. It is not a barrier to Supreme Court review of state court decisions involving federal law. Nor does the amendment bar private plaintiffs seeking federal court injunctions to enforce Congress's CIVIL RIGHTS laws or federal constitutional rights. In *Parden v. Terminal Railway* (1964) the Court declined to exclude state-owned railroads from a congressional act authorizing employees' suits for negligence. The Court reasoned that the state had effectively waived immunity by engaging in activity subject to congressional regulation. Though later decisions gave this doctrine of "constructive waiver" a STATES' RIGHTS twist by requiring clear statements of congressional intent, the Court still assumes that

Congress can lift state immunity as necessary for national objectives.

The doctrine that one government cannot tax the instrumentalities of the other is sometimes credited to the OBITER DICTUM in MCCULLOCH V. MARYLAND that power to tax is power to destroy. Chief Justice JOHN MARSHALL made this remark in the course of voiding a state tax on the Second Bank of the United States; he was not seeking to protect the states against Congress. But future Courts transformed Marshall's doctrine of federal immunity into a dual-federalist or states' rights doctrine of reciprocal immunity. In COLLECTOR V. DAY (1871) a Court grown fearful of RECONSTRUCTION voided a CIVIL WAR federal income tax on the salary of a Massachusetts judge, arguing that if immunity was necessary to preserve the federal government, the same held for the states. Laissez-faire Justices later expanded the immunity doctrine to protect both governments. Items held immune to state taxation included the income of lessees of federal oil lands, sales of gasoline to the national government, and royalties from a federal patent. Fewer decisions went against Congress, but the Court did void some federal taxes, including taxes on income from municipal bonds, profits of state oil leases, and motorcycle sales to a municipal police department.

This pattern of decision ended in the late 1930s as the HUGHES COURT began overruling the most important of the earlier decisions, including those conferring tax immunity on the incomes of governmental officials and contractors. Some tax immunity remains, however. On a theory that combines the principle of national supremacy with the argument that states' interests receive more representation in Congress than national interests receive in state legislatures, the modern Court recognizes a narrower tax immunity for the states than for the national government. Dicta identify state property, state revenues, and traditionally essential state activities as immune to federal taxation. These dicta did not prevent a recent decision upholding a federal registration on state police helicopters. As for federal tax immunity, Congress can confer it on federal contractors and others. Where Congress has not done so, the Court recognizes immunity from state taxation only when the tax legally falls on the federal government itself or its closely connected agencies and instrumentalities. This rule offers no protection to a federal government contractor even where, by contract, the economic impact of a state tax is passed on to the government. The Court continues to invalidate state taxes that discriminate against entities doing business with the federal government or that manifest hostility to federal policy.

Although the SUPREMACY CLAUSE protects federal officials and agencies from state attempts to control the performance of their duties, federal personnel are subject to state laws that do not conflict with federal policies. Indeed, under the federal Assimilative Crimes Act, state criminal law applies to persons on federal enclaves where Congress has not provided otherwise. Examples of state regulations held in conflict with federal policies include attempts to regulate liquor sales and milk prices on military bases and to inspect fertilizer distributed in a national soil conservation program. Until 1985 states were immune from direct federal attempts to interfere in the performance of "functions essential to [the states'] separate and independent existence." The Court failed to give a formula for identifying these essential functions, but they included decisions on where to locate a state capital and the hours and wages of certain state employees. (See NATIONAL LEAGUE OF CITIES V. USERY.) The Court permitted federal regulation of such "nonessential" state functions as state liquor, timber, and railroad operations and it declined to apply the *Usery* rationale against federal policies affecting state agencies in the areas of civil rights, environmental regulation, and energy policy. The Court overruled *Usery* in 1985 and all but eliminated direct regulatory immunity for the states. (See GARCIA V. SAN ANTONIO METROPOLITAN TRANSIT AUTHORITY.) Massive, though indirect, federal regulatory control of state policy continues through conditional FEDERAL GRANTS-IN-AID to the states. (See GENERAL WELFARE CLAUSE.)

SOTIRIOS A. BARBER
(1986)

Bibliography

POWELL, THOMAS REED 1940 Intergovernmental Tax Immunities. *George Washington Law Review* 8:1213–1220.
TRIBE, LAURENCE H. 1978 *American Constitutional Law.* Pages 131–143. Mineola, N.Y.: Foundation Press.

INTERGOVERNMENTAL TAX IMMUNITIES

To what extent should the federal government be able to collect taxes from the states? To what extent should the states be able to collect taxes from the federal government? The Supreme Court has struggled with these questions for over 170 years.

In 1819, in MCCULLOCH V. MARYLAND, the Court held that a state tax on the operations of a bank created by the United States was in violation of the SUPREMACY CLAUSE of the Constitution. Speaking for the Court, Chief Justice JOHN MARSHALL asserted that "the power to tax is the power to destroy" and stated "that the states have no power, by taxation or otherwise, to retard, impede, burden, or in any manner control the operations of the constitutional laws enacted by Congress to carry into the execution the powers vested in the general government." This same logic was used in WESTON V. CITY COUNCIL OF CHARLESTON (1829) to hold that a city tax imposed on stocks and bonds generally could not be applied to bonds issued by the federal government and in *Dobbins v. Commissioners of Erie County* (1842) to hold that states could not tax the salaries of federal employees.

In COLLECTOR V. DAY (1871) the Court took a major step and held the federal income tax could not be applied to the salaries of state officials. It said the immunity was reciprocal and that the exemption from taxation of the federal government by the states and the states by the federal government "rests upon necessary implication, and is upheld by the great law of self-preservation."

For over half a century the Court applied the intergovernmental immunity doctrine to permit large numbers of private taxpayers to escape federal and state taxes on the ground that the tax burden would be passed on to the federal or state governments. For example, in *Indian Motorcycle Co. v. United States* (1931) the Court held invalid a tax imposed by the United States on the sale of a motorcycle to a city for use in its police force. The Court said that the state and federal governments were equally exempt from taxes by the other. "This principle is implied from the independence of the national and state governments within their respective spheres and from the provisions of the Constitution which look to the maintenance of the dual system." The only exception to this broad doctrine recognized by the Court was that the federal government could impose taxes on state enterprises which departed from usual government functions and engaged in businesses of a private nature, such as running a railroad or selling mineral water.

In the late 1930s, the Court began a process of dismantling the tax immunity doctrine. In GRAVES V. NEW YORK EX REL. O'KEEFE (1939), the Court upheld the imposition of a state income tax on the salary of a federal official, saying, "So much of the burden of a non-discriminatory general tax upon the incomes of employees of a government, state or national, as may be passed on economically to that government through the effect of the tax on the price level of labor or materials, is but the normal incident of the organization within the same territory of two governments, each possessing the taxing power." And, in *Alabama v. King & Boozer* (1941) the Court upheld a state sales tax imposed on a government contractor, even though the financial burden of the tax was entirely passed on to the federal government through a cost-plus contract.

Over the past half-century the Court has reduced the tax immunity doctrine to a very narrow scope. Private parties doing business with the federal government or leasing government property, even for completing a government contract, may be subjected to state taxation. In *United States v. New Mexico* (1982) the Court upheld the right of a state to tax fixed fees paid by the United States to private contractors in return for managing government installations, saying that "tax immunity is appropriate in only one circumstance: when the levy falls on the United States itself, or on an agency or instrumentality so closely connected to the Government that the two cannot realistically be viewed as separate entities." The only limit on the states is that they cannot impose taxes that discriminate against the United States. Thus, in *Davis v. Michigan Department of Treasury* (1989), a state was not permitted to tax the pensions received by federal retirees when it exempted state employees from the same tax.

The immunity of the states is even narrower. The Court assumes that the states themselves or their property cannot be directly subjected to federal taxation, but even here there is an exception permitting the application of non-discriminatory federal taxes directly to some kinds of state enterprises. Recently, in *South Carolina v. Baker* (1988), the Court said the intergovernmental tax immunity doctrine had been "thoroughly repudiated" and held that the federal government could impose its income tax on the income received from state and local bonds. The federal tax was limited in this case to income from bonds issued in bearer form, but the Court said it could apply to all such bonds if Congress so provided.

Under the supremacy clause the federal government has one additional power: it can expand or retract its immunity from state taxation, permitting states to tax what the Court otherwise would forbid or denying the states the right to tax what the Court would otherwise permit.

The intergovernmental tax immunity doctrine now has so little vitality that it should not interfere with any reasonable, nondiscriminatory taxation by either state or federal governments. Yet attempts to use it persist. In 1989 the Supreme Court had cases in which it held that a state could tax an oil company on profits from producing oil on an Indian reservation; that a state could tax BANKRUPTCY liquidation sales by a bankruptcy trustee; and that a tax on pensions of federal retirees was invalid when it exempted state employees from the same tax.

EDWARD L. BARRETT
(1992)

(SEE ALSO: *Federalism, Contemporary Practice of; Federalism, History of; Federalism, Theory of; Federalism and Shared Powers.*)

Bibliography

ROTUNDA, RONALD D. 1986 Intergovernmental Tax Immunity and Tax-Free Municipals After *Garcia. University of Colorado Law Review* 57:849–869.

INTERLOCUTORY

The term means temporary, not final, provisional. An interlocutory order is one entered by a court before it renders FINAL JUDGMENT—for example, a preliminary INJUNCTION, to preserve conditions during trial.

KENNETH L. KARST
(1986)

INTERNAL COMMERCE

See: Intrastate Commerce

INTERNAL IMPROVEMENTS

"Internal Improvements" was the name given to large public works programs in the first half of the nineteenth century. State governments engaged in planning, subsidizing, building, and in some instances owning and operating roads, bridges, canals, and railroads. Most had ambitious programs. None was more successful than New York's Erie Canal. Completed in 1825, it had profound effects on American economic development.

Federal support for internal improvements commenced in 1806 when Congress appropriated money for construction of the Cumberland, or National, Road. The policy was not then a serious constitutional issue, although President THOMAS JEFFERSON, proposing a major program, called for a constitutional amendment to place it beyond cavil. It became a serious constitutional issue after the War of 1812. A federal program was advocated on several grounds: to bind the Union together, to lower the cost of transportation, to effect the "home market" of the American System. Henry Clay and others found constitutional warrant for federal assistance in the powers to establish post roads, to provide for the common defense and GENERAL WELFARE, and to regulate INTERSTATE COMMERCE. In 1817 Congress passed the Bonus Bill to create a permanent fund for internal improvements from the bonus paid by the Bank of the United States for its charter and future dividends on government-owned Bank stock. Surprisingly, President JAMES MADISON, in a return to STRICT CONSTRUCTION principles, vetoed the bill and called for an amendment. His successor, JAMES MONROE, at first took the same position. In 1822, however, he conceded the unlimited power of Congress to appropriate money for improvements of national character, though not to build or operate them. Two years later he approved the General Survey Bill, which offered substantial government assistance. Many projects, the greatest of which was the Chesapeake and Ohio Canal, were launched under federal auspices. The movement was then brought to a virtual halt by President ANDREW JACKSON's veto of the MAYSVILLE ROAD BILL in 1830. He, too, asserted strict construction principles and repeated the call, knowing it to be futile, for a constitutional amendment.

MERRILL D. PETERSON
(1986)

Bibliography

GOODRICH, CARTER 1960 *Government Promotion of American Canals and Railroads, 1800–1890.* New York: Columbia University Press.
HARRISON, JOSEPH HOPSON 1954 The Internal Improvements Issue in the Politics of the Union, 1783–1825. Ph.D., diss., University of Virginia.

INTERNAL SECURITY ACT
64 Stat. 987 (1950)

The Internal Security Act, or McCarran Act, of 1950 was a massive and complex conglomeration of varied security measures as well as many features of the MUNDT-NIXON BILL and an Emergency Detention Bill, which had been introduced, unsuccessfully, earlier in 1950. Passed over President HARRY S. TRUMAN's veto in September, shortly after the outbreak of hostilities in Korea, the measure went beyond the Truman loyalty program for government employees and attempted to limit the operation of subversive groups in all areas of American life. It also sought to shift the authority for security matters to congressional leadership.

The measure, the most severe since the SEDITION ACT of 1918, was composed of two parts. Title I, known as the Subversive Activities Control Act, required communist organizations to register with the attorney general and furnish complete membership lists and financial statements. Although membership and office holding in a communist organization was not, by the act, a crime, the measure did make it illegal knowingly to conspire to perform any act that would "substantially contribute" to the establishment of a totalitarian dictatorship in the United States. It also forbade employment of communists in defense plants and granting them passports. Finally it established a bipartisan SUBVERSIVE ACTIVITIES CONTROL BOARD to assist the attorney general in exposing subversive organizations. In ALBERTSON V. SUBVERSIVE ACTIVITIES CONTROL BOARD (1965), the Court held the compulsory registration provisions unconstitutional. (See MARCHETTI V. UNITED STATES, 1968.)

Title II provided that when the President declared an internal security emergency, the attorney general was to apprehend persons who were likely to engage in, or conspire with others to engage in, acts of espionage or sabotage and intern them "in such places of detention as may be prescribing by the Attorney General." Congress subsequently authorized funds for special camps for such purposes. (See PREVENTIVE DETENTION.) Other provisions denied entrance to the country to ALIENS who were members of communist organizations or who "advocate[d] the economic, international, and governmental doctrines of any other form of totalitarianism." Naturalized citizens joining communist organizations within five years of acquiring CITIZENSHIP were liable to have it revoked.

The courts subsequently held invalid the passport, registration, and employment sections of the act. Section 103, establishing detention centers for suspected subversives, was repealed in September 1971.

PAUL L. MURPHY
(1986)

Bibliography

HARPER, ALAN 1969 *The Politics of Loyalty: The White House and the Communist Issue, 1946–1952.* Westport, Conn.: Greenwood Press.

INTERNATIONAL EMERGENCY ECONOMIC POWERS ACT
91 Stat. 1625 (1977)

This act grants the President limited economic powers "to deal with any unusual and extraordinary threat . . . to the national security, foreign policy, or economy of the United States" which arises "in whole or substantial part outside the United States" and which is declared by the President to constitute "a national emergency." The primary purpose of the act, however, was to restrict the Trading With the Enemy Act of 1917, under which the President had come to enjoy large discretionary power during times of declared emergency.

The 1977 act limits the authority created by declaration of a national emergency to an instant threat only and removes the President's authority to exercise during peacetime certain economic powers available in time of war. It also obligates the President to "consult" with Congress, if possible, prior to the declaration of a national emergency, to report on the circumstances said to necessitate the extraordinary measures, and to report to Congress every six months on the exercise of powers under the act.

Although the act permits the termination of a declared national emergency by concurrent resolution of Congress, the decision in IMMIGRATION AND NATURALIZATION SERVICE v. CHADHA (1983), declaring the use of the LEGISLATIVE VETO unconstitutional, places this restraint in doubt. In sum, however much Congress may have intended to restrict presidential EMERGENCY POWERS over international

economic transactions, the actual extent of the change is uncertain.

BURNS H. WESTON
(1986)

(SEE ALSO: *Dames & Moore v. Regan; Foreign Affairs; War Powers; War Powers Acts.*)

Bibliography

HENKIN, LOUIS 1972 *Foreign Affairs and the Constitution.* Pages 118–123. Mineola, N.Y.: Foundation Press.
NOTE 1978 Presidential Emergency Powers Related to International Economic Transactions: Congressional Recognition of Customary Authority. *Vanderbilt Journal of Transnational Law,* 11:515–534.

INTERNATIONAL HUMAN RIGHTS

The Constitution includes, notably and famously, guarantees for individual rights. Indeed, other elements of U.S. "constitutionalism"—POPULAR SOVEREIGNTY, the RULE OF LAW, limited government of ENUMERATED POWERS, SEPARATION OF POWERS, and FEDERALISM—might also be seen as designed to safeguard individual rights and liberties. Americans have enjoyed the protections of the Constitution for more than two hundred years, and their constitutional rights have flourished particularly since WORLD WAR II.

The second half of the twentieth century has seen the birth and growth of "international human rights" as a universal ideology with an agreed catalog of rights, an ideology that the United States has supported and joined. The international human rights movement has engendered an international law of human rights and international institutions to induce compliance with that law.

International human rights relate to the Constitution in different ways. In substantial measure international human rights were inspired by the Constitution and by American life under the Constitution. To the extent that the international law of human rights is provided for in TREATIES to which the United States is party, it is law for and in the United States. Like other customary international law, customary international law of human rights is law of the land in the United States. In several additional contexts, the international law of human rights is given effect in courts in the United States, supplementing safeguards for individual rights under the Constitution, treaties, and laws. Although U.S. constitutional rights and international human rights are intimately related, they differ in their theory and sources, in their scope and content, in the means of their implementation, and in their contribution to individual well-being.

The Constitution, established at the end of the eighteenth century, reflects the ideology articulated in the American DECLARATION OF INDEPENDENCE and in early state constitutions, an ideology rooted in inherent, individual, NATURAL RIGHTS. Natural rights of individuals were translated into the "sovereignty of the people," government with the consent of the governed, and rights retained by the individual even against government. The commitment to rights was reflected in several guarantees in the original Constitution, for example, the right to TRIAL BY JURY and the privilege of HABEAS CORPUS. It was confirmed and elaborated by constitutional amendment in the BILL OF RIGHTS and in subsequent amendments, notably the THIRTEENTH, FOURTEENTH, FIFTEENTH, NINETEENTH, and TWENTY-FIFTH. Thanks to JUDICIAL REVIEW, U.S. constitutional rights have been elaborated by the Supreme Court in a rich constitutional jurisprudence and implemented by acts of Congress. International human rights were born during World War II and confirmed at Nuremberg and in the UNITED NATIONS CHARTER. International human rights have been developed in subsequent international instruments, notably in the Universal Declaration of Human Rights, and in covenants and conventions that derive from it.

Indisputably, the international human rights movement, and international human rights law, drew heavily on the Constitution as it had developed during 150 years. But the Constitution was not the only source of, or influence on, international human rights. And differences in their birth-dates, their political contexts, and their biographies have produced two related but different systems of law and institutions.

Constitutional rights and international human rights differ in their sources and in their theoretical foundations. The Constitution derives from English political and legal tradition back to MAGNA CARTA, and from the English COMMON LAW as modified by occasional acts of Parliament. The theory of the Constitution reflects the writings of JOHN LOCKE and of the European Enlightenment, restated in the bills of rights of early state constitutions and succinctly and eloquently articulated in the American Declaration of Independence.

The international human rights ideology is the product of the international political system during and after World War II. Its principal instruments—the Universal Declaration of Human Rights and the two International Covenants—were produced by international political bodies in the post-war world, were eclectic in their sources, were designed for universal application, and strove for universal acceptance. By then, "natural law" and "natural rights" had long been discredited ("anarchical fallacies," Jeremy Bentham characterized them), and had suffered the onslaughts of "positivism"; the liberal state had been threatened by varieties of socialism and every-

where was transmuting, in some measure, into the WELFARE STATE. In influential countries, republican elitist government was moving steadily toward representative parliamentary democracy based on popular sovereignty and universal suffrage. The Universal Declaration of Human Rights (unlike the American Declaration of Independence) contains no reference to "the Creator" and no hint of natural rights (which would have been unacceptable to the U.S.S.R. with its atheist, socialist, positivist ideology). Indeed, the Universal Declaration of Human Rights eschews theory. Instead, it links human rights to one fundamental value, "human dignity," and justifies human rights by their aim and purpose: recognition of human rights is declared to be "the foundation of freedom, justice and peace in the world."

The Constitution guarantees the rights explicitly articulated in the Constitution, in the Bill of Rights, and in later amendments. No rights are protected unless rooted in constitutional text (as interpreted). Although the NINTH AMENDMENT declares that "[t]he enumeration in the Constitution, of certain rights, shall not be construed to deny or disparage others retained by the people," no rights have been recognized and held to be specifically protected by implication of the Ninth Amendment (or of the TENTH AMENDMENT, as rights reserved to "the people"). But the U.S. Supreme Court has interpreted the different provisions broadly, giving some of them (notably the "liberty" and the "DUE PROCESS" required by the Fifth and Fourteenth Amendments) meaning probably not anticipated by their authors.

International human rights also claim their principal foundation in various texts, but some international human rights are based in customary international law. Though its normative character is still debated, the Universal Declaration of Human Rights is recognized as an authoritative catalog of human rights, much of which has become customary law. And other rights not explicitly mentioned in the text—such as freedom from genocide, extralegal killing, systematic RACIAL DISCRIMINATION, prolonged arbitrary detention—when practiced as state policy are protected by customary international law even if not set forth in any authoritative text to which the violating state has adhered.

For the rest, international human rights are protected against state violation if the state has undertaken to honor them in a binding covenant or convention. Unlike the Constitution, which protects rights only against STATE ACTION (or, exceptionally, against private imposition of SLAVERY), the international obligation "to respect and ensure" rights implies an obligation on the state to protect the enumerated rights against private action as well.

In sum, U.S. constitutional rights at the end of the twentieth century, though rooted in a few authoritative provisions in the Constitution, have to be distilled from hundreds of volumes of interpretation by the Supreme Court. In contrast, except for a few principles recognized as binding by customary law, the international law of human rights is rooted largely in international texts hammered out by governments. The texts are interpreted occasionally by the monitoring committees created by various treaties, but that jurisprudence is small and its authority disputed. Only the commission and court created by the European Convention on Human Rights (replaced in 1998 by a new, enlarged court), and, to an extent also, the parallel bodies established under the Inter American convention, have contributed significant interpretive jurisprudence.

The Constitution, it was said, protects not the rights of man but the rights of gentlemen. These were rights that the former colonists had enjoyed under British law, such as freedom from UNREASONABLE SEARCH and seizure and the right to trial by jury, and protections for life, liberty, and PROPERTY against deprivation without due process of law. The Bill of Rights also guaranteed rights its authors valued because they had been denied under British rule: hence the right to bear arms provided by the SECOND AMENDMENT and the right not to have troops quartered in private homes in time of peace provided by the THIRD AMENDMENT. But the Bill of Rights was not intended to be a complete declaration of rights, leaving many safeguards to be provided by state constitutions or by state or federal law. On the other hand, international human rights could not incorporate or rely on any existing body of law or on any domestic legal system (such as the English common law); the Universal Declaration, therefore, is a more explicit, more complete, catalog of rights.

International human rights include rights that in the United States were not explicitly guaranteed by the Constitution but which were later inferred by interpretation— for example, the FREEDOM OF ASSOCIATION, the presumption of innocence, and the RIGHT TO TRAVEL. Similar (or related) rights expressed in different terms in the Constitution or in international instruments may imply different protections: the Universal Declaration protects against torture and inhuman or degrading treatment or punishment; and explicitly, at least, the Constitution protects only against torture, and only if it is used to compel testimony or as CRUEL AND UNUSUAL PUNISHMENT for crime. International human rights include a right to a nationality: the Constitution has been held to protect only U.S. CITIZENSHIP, and only against involuntary termination. In an ambiguous provision, the Universal Declaration recognizes a right to "seek and to enjoy asylum from persecution"—a provision that has no American constitutional parallel. Both the Constitution and the Universal Declaration guarantee RELIGIOUS LIBERTY, but International Human Rights norms do not accord protection against an ESTABLISHMENT OF RELIGION.

The Universal Declaration and the International Covenant on Civil and Political Rights provide for universal suffrage. The Constitution protects VOTING RIGHTS against INVIDIOUS DISCRIMINATION in voting on grounds of race, gender, or age; not until the 1960s was the Constitution interpreted to safeguard the right to vote and provide, in effect, for universal suffrage.

The Universal Declaration and the covenants depart radically from U.S. constitutional jurisprudence in that they guarantee what have come to be described as "economic and social rights"—WELFARE RIGHTS such as social security, the right to work and leisure, a right to education, and a right to an adequate standard of living. In the United States some welfare rights are provided by law but they are not required by the Constitution, and inequalities in welfare assistance have been held not to deny the guarantee of EQUAL PROTECTION OF THE LAWS.

The Constitution has been held not to prohibit CAPITAL PUNISHMENT, and "life" is protected only to the extent implied in "due process of law," procedural and substantive. International human rights instruments have imposed some limitations on capital punishment, and international conventions requiring complete abolition have continued to gain adherents. The Constitution guarantees the right to an ABORTION (subject to some limitations); international human rights laws tend to be silent on the subject though the American Convention on Human Rights requires parties to protect the right to life, "in general, from the moment of conception." The International Covenant on Civil and Political Rights requires states to prohibit war propaganda and HATE SPEECH in circumstances where such expression might enjoy constitutional protection in the United States.

The Constitution protects rights against violation but does not provide, or explicitly require, remedies for violations. The courts exercise JUDICIAL REVIEW and invalidate state or federal laws that violate constitutional rights, but that protects only against future violation and provides no remedy for the past. Congress is authorized, but not required, to legislate remedies for violations of rights. In fact, Congress has enacted CIVIL RIGHTS laws to afford remedies for violation of rights, and in some cases the courts have created remedies on their own authority. In contrast, the International Covenant on Civil and Political Rights explicitly calls on participating states to adopt laws and take all necessary steps to give effect to the rights recognized in the covenant. "Each State Party . . . undertakes: To ensure that any person whose rights or freedoms . . . are violated shall have an effective remedy . . . [and] [t]o ensure that the competent authorities shall enforce such remedies. . . ."

Indirectly, the Constitution has provided support for international human rights, as applied both in the United States and abroad. The Constitution declares treaties to be the supreme law of the land. The United States has adhered to several human rights treaties, notably—as of 1999—the International Covenant on Civil and Political Rights, the Convention on Racial Discrimination, the Convention against Genocide, and the Convention against Torture. Ratifications by the United States have been subject to reservations, understandings, and declarations, but, subject to such qualification, international human rights obligations are law in the United States. The international customary law of human rights is also law in the United States.

The Constitution has contributed to international human rights by the powers it has conferred upon Congress, including, for example, power to impose sanctions against countries that are guilty of gross violations of human rights and the power to confer JURISDICTION on U.S. courts to provide remedies, in some circumstances, for violations of human rights in foreign countries.

The U.S. constitutional system and international human rights continue to influence each other. U.S. constitutional jurisprudence is invoked by international bodies, in particular by the European and the Inter American human rights courts. U.S. courts are only beginning to look at the growing jurisprudence in the judgments of foreign constitutional courts or of international human rights courts. But the heavy emphasis on equality and nondiscrimination in international human rights instruments has doubtless influenced U.S. interpretations of constitutional norms of flexible outline and contributed to expanding the scope of equal protection of the laws, for example, to end SEGREGATION.

Neither U.S. constitutional jurisprudence nor international human rights promises radical change in the years ahead. The Constitution is not likely to be amended, or radically reinterpreted, in respects that are of acute international interest; for example, the right to an abortion. International human rights are likely to maintain their movement toward the abolition of capital punishment, but there is no sign of any move toward abolition in U.S. constitutional jurisprudence. The differences between U.S. constitutional jurisprudence and international human rights in respect of FREEDOM OF SPEECH (including hate speech) seem likely to persist. Economic and social, welfare-state entitlements in the United States will not acquire constitutional character, though such benefits are likely to continue to be provided, subject to political forces and financial restraints.

The Constitution retains an older vision of human rights in the liberal state, rights of liberty and property; international human rights are contemporary and multicultural, marrying rights in the liberal state to those of the welfare state. Where the Constitution maintains a stronger commitment to freedom, including freedom of expression, international human rights are more sympathetic to competing claims of public interest—outlawing war propaganda and hate speech. Yet, ideally, the Constitution and international human rights support each other in pursuit of a clearer vision of human dignity.

LOUIS HENKIN
(2000)

Bibliography

HENKIN, LOUIS 1958 *Arms Control and Inspection in American Law.* New York: Columbia University Press.

—— 1978 *The Rights of Man Today.* Boulder, Colo.: Westview Press.

—— 1979 *How Nations Behave: Law and Foreign Policy,* 2nd ed. New York: Published for the Council on Foreign Relations by Columbia University Press.

—— 1990 *Constitutionalism, Democracy, and Foreign Affairs.* New York: Columbia University Press.

—— 1995 *International Law: Politics and Values.* Norwell, Mass.: Kluwer Academic Publishers.

—— 1996 *The Age of Rights.* New York: Columbia University Press.

—— 1996 *Foreign Affairs and the Constitution,* 2nd ed. New York: Oxford University Press.

HENKIN, LOUIS and HARGROVE, JOHN LAWRENCE, eds. 1994 *Human Rights: An Agenda for the Next Century.* Washington, D.C.: American Society of International Law.

INTERNATIONAL LAW AND FEDERAL–STATE RELATIONS

One of the principal purposes of the Constitution was to create a national government with power over FOREIGN AFFAIRS. As JAMES MADISON wrote in FEDERALIST No. 42, "If we are to be one nation in any respect, it clearly ought to be in respect to other nations." Thus, the Constitution gives the President the power to make TREATIES with the approval of two-thirds of the U.S. SENATE and explicitly denies that power to the states. It gives Congress the power to regulate FOREIGN COMMERCE and to define and punish offenses against the law of nations. Moreover, the SUPREMACY CLAUSE makes not just acts of Congress but treaties "the Supreme Law of the Land."

The power of the federal government to PREEMPT state law by entering a treaty is broader than its power under the COMMERCE CLAUSE. In MISSOURI V. HOLLAND (1920), the Supreme Court upheld an act of Congress implementing a treaty with Canada on the hunting of migratory birds despite the fact that similar LEGISLATION had twice been struck down for exceeding Congress's commerce power. Concerned that the federal government might use treaties on INTERNATIONAL HUMAN RIGHTS to dismantle SEGREGATION, proponents of STATES' RIGHTS led by Senator John Bricker of Ohio tried unsuccessfully in the 1950s to reverse *Holland* with a constitutional amendment providing that "[a] treaty shall become effective in the United States only through legislation which would be valid in the absence of a treaty."

EXECUTIVE AGREEMENTS are not mentioned in the supremacy clause, but the Court ruled that the President may preempt state law by entering such agreements in UNITED STATES V. BELMONT (1937) and UNITED STATES V. PINK (1942), both of which upheld the Litvinov agreement recognizing the Soviet Union and disposing of claims between the two countries.

Until 1938, customary international law was applied by state and federal courts alike as part of the general COMMON LAW without regard to its state or federal character. The Court declared in *The Paquete Habana* (1900): "International law is part of our law, and must be ascertained and administered by the courts of justice . . . as often as questions of right depending upon it are duly presented for their determination." The Court's pronouncement in ERIE RAILROAD V. TOMPKINS (1938) that "[t]here is no federal general common law" cast some doubt on the status of customary international law. Professor Philip Jessup soon argued, however, that *Erie* should not apply to international law, which should continue to be viewed as FEDERAL COMMON LAW. In *Banco Nacional de Cuba v. Sabbatino* (1964) the Court endorsed Jessup's position, firmly establishing customary international law's status as federal common law. Because customary international law is federal law, it preempts inconsistent state law just as a treaty or statute would.

Even in the absence of a treaty, executive agreement, or rule of customary international law, federal courts have found state laws to be preempted under the DORMANT COMMERCE CLAUSE or where they intrude on the federal government's foreign relations power. In *Japan Line v. County of Los Angeles* (1979), the Court struck down a California tax on foreign-owned containers under the commerce clause because it prevented the federal government from "speaking with one voice" in international trade; and in *Zschernig v. Miller* (1968) the Court invalidated an Oregon statute denying inheritance to residents of communist countries as an unconstitutional "intrusion by the State into the field of foreign affairs which the Constitution entrusts to the President and the Congress." Moves by state and local governments in the 1980s to oppose apartheid by divesting from South Africa were sometimes upheld, but a Massachusetts law that imposed sanctions against companies that did business in Burma was struck down by a DISTRICT COURT in 1998 as contrary to *Zschernig*.

While the Constitution and Supreme Court decisions give the federal government nearly complete power over international law and foreign relations, the federal government has tended to exercise that power in ways that are quite deferential—indeed, too deferential—to state SOVEREIGNTY. In order to avoid imposing obligations on the states (and head off the proposed Bricker Amendment), the administration of President DWIGHT D. EISENHOWER promised not to accede to international human rights conventions. When the United States finally did ratify treaties like the Genocide Convention, the Torture Convention, and the International Covenant on Civil and Political Rights, it declared them not to be "self-executing," so that they would grant no legally enforceable rights in the absence of implementing legislation passed by Congress. When implementing the General Agreement on Tariffs and Trade (GATT) and the NORTH AMERICAN FREE TRADE AGREEMENT (NAFTA), Congress provided that only the federal government, and not private parties, could bring suit challenging state laws as inconsistent with GATT or NAFTA. And in 1998, the executive branch sided with Virginia in *Breard v. Greene*, arguing successfully to the Court that Virginia's failure to notify a criminal defendant of his right under the Vienna Convention on Consular Relations to speak with a consular official should not constitute grounds for staying his execution.

ALEXANDER HAMILTON observed in *Federalist* No. 80 that "[t]he Union will undoubtedly be answerable to foreign powers for the conduct of its members." The unfortunate practice of the federal government, particularly in the 1980s and 1990s, has been to give the states a license to violate the international obligations of the United States, violations for which the federal government bears responsibility under international law.

WILLIAM S. DODGE
(2000)

Bibliography

BILDER, RICHARD B.   1989   The Role of States and Cities in Foreign Affairs. *American Journal of International Law* 83: 821–831.

BRADLEY, CURTIS A. and GOLDSMITH, JACK L.   1997   Customary International Law as Federal Common Law: A Critique of the Modern Position. *Harvard Law Review* 110:815–876.

BRILMAYER, LEA   1994   Federalism, State Authority, and the Preemptive Power of International Law. *Supreme Court Review* 1994:295–243.

HENKIN, LOUIS   1995   U.S. Ratification of Human Rights Conventions: The Ghost of Senator Bricker. *American Journal of International Law* 89:341–351.

———   1996   *Foreign Affairs and the United States Constitution*, 2nd ed. Oxford, England: Clarendon Press.

JESSUP, PHILIP   1939   The Doctrine of *Erie Railroad v. Tompkins* Applied to International Law. *American Journal of International Law* 33:740–743.

KOH, HAROLD HONGJU   1998   Is International Law Really State Law? *Harvard Law Review* 111:1824–1861.

INTERNATIONAL SOCIETY FOR KRISHNA CONSCIOUSNESS v. LEE
505 U.S. 672 (1992)

The Port Authority of New York and New Jersey, which owns and operates three major airports in the New York City area, adopted a regulation forbidding within the airport terminals the solicitation of money and the sale or distribution of any merchandise, "including . . . brochures, pamphlets, books or any other printed or written material." In a bewildering array of opinions, the Supreme Court upheld the ban on solicitation, but held that the ban on the sale or distribution of literature violates the FIRST AMENDMENT.

Chief Justice WILLIAM H. REHNQUIST delivered the opinion of the Court on the issue of solicitation. The Court explained that airport terminals are not PUBLIC FORUMS because they have not been used "time out of mind" for expressive purposes and have not "been intentionally opened by their operators to such activity." This being so, the Court held that the prohibition on solicitation "need only satisfy a requirement of reasonableness," a standard the Court held was easily met because of "the disruptive effect" that solicitation might have on "the normal flow of traffic" within the terminals.

In an opinion by Justice ANTHONY M. KENNEDY, four Justices disagreed with the Court's conclusion that the terminals were not public forums, arguing that "in these days an airport is one of the few government-owned spaces where people have extended contact with other members of the public" and that "the recent history of airports" demonstrates that some "expressive activity is quite compatible with the uses of major airports."

On the issue of sale or distribution of literature, Justice SANDRA DAY O'CONNOR concluded that, even though airport terminals are not public forums, the regulation was "unreasonable" because "leafleting does not necessarily entail the same kinds of problems presented by face-to-face solicitation." She therefore joined the four Justices who had argued that airport terminals are public forums to form a 5–4 majority to invalidate this part of the regulation.

GEOFFREY R. STONE
(2000)

INTERNET AND FREEDOM OF SPEECH

The Internet is a worldwide network of networks that allows individuals to communicate in ways previously unimaginable. The two most popular forms of communication on the Internet are electronic mail and the World Wide Web. Through electronic mail, an individual can send a message—traditionally text but increasingly multimedia—to another individual, group of individuals, or to public forums. Through the World Wide Web, an individual can browse millions of pages of multimedia content that individuals, businesses, and other institutions have made available for public access. Individuals can also publish their own thoughts, complete orders and forms, and engage in commercial transactions.

The physical technology of the Internet comprises communication lines (imagine them as telephone lines), routers (specially designated computers that send packets of information to their proper addresses), and computers (which send, receive, and process the information transmitted). No single person or entity owns all this equipment. And no single national or international body governs the Internet. To understand this decentralized network, it is best to view the Internet as physical hardware, owned by myriad persons, both public and private, who all speak the same language of information exchange. That language, or protocol, is called TCP/IP (Transmission Control Protocol/Internet Protocol).

As individuals harness the Internet to expand their ability to speak and listen, they sometimes do so in harmful ways. Examples include anonymous defamation, e-mail death threats, and PORNOGRAPHY accessible to children. When the state responds, it confronts the FREEDOM OF SPEECH guarantee of the FIRST AMENDMENT. But the scope of constitutionally protected freedom of expression differs among various communication technologies. As Justice ROBERT H. JACKSON wrote in KOVACS V. COOPER (1949), "[t]he moving picture screen, the radio, the newspaper, the handbill, the sound truck and the street corner orator have differing natures, values, abuses and dangers. Each, in my view, is a law unto itself."

The First Amendment has been most protective of the printing press; it has been least protective of television and radio BROADCASTING on the grounds of spectrum scarcity and intrusiveness. In RED LION BROADCASTING CO. V. FCC (1969), the Supreme Court upheld the Federal Communication Commission's FAIRNESS DOCTRINE, which required a broadcast licensee to grant a right of reply to any individual or group that was personally attacked, and to any political candidate editorialized against. Although this requirement would not be tolerated in newsprint, as would be made clear in MIAMI HERALD PUBLISHING CO. V. TORNILLO (1974), it was accepted in broadcasting. The principal justification was that broadcasting employs the electromagnetic spectrum, which is a scarce resource, subject to easy interference by competing users. The use of this spectrum must therefore be licensed by the state and managed to ensure that the public receive "suitable access to social, political, esthetic, moral, and other ideas and experiences."

In addition to scarcity, the Court has emphasized the intrusiveness and pervasiveness of broadcasting. For example, in FEDERAL COMMUNICATIONS COMMISSION V. PACIFICA FOUNDATION (1978), the Court upheld regulations that channeled profanity on the radio to those hours when children were not likely to listen. According to the Court, the broadcast media had a "uniquely pervasive presence" in our lives, in which airwaves confronted us not only in public but also in the privacy of the home. Further, such broadcasting was uniquely accessible to children. These characteristics required tolerating more regulation.

Thus, traditional print and broadcasting mark the two extremes on an axis of First Amendment protection. The central question for governing any new communication technology has been its placement on that axis. Recently, the Court has struggled with the proper positioning of telephone communications in the context of DIAL-A-PORN, as well as cable systems in the context of "MUST CARRY" LAWS (which force cable operators to carry certain speakers). The Internet's place on that axis was addressed for the first time in *American Civil Liberties Union v. Reno* (1997).

As part of the Telecommunications Act of 1996, Congress enacted the COMMUNICATIONS DECENCY ACT. This act criminalized the knowing transmission of "obscene or indecent" messages to any minor through a telecommunications device. It also prohibited the knowing sending or displaying to a minor, through an interactive computer service, of any message "patently offensive as measured by contemporary community standards."

The Court rejected the broadcasting analogy. First, the spectrum scarcity rationale simply did not apply to the Internet, which "provides relatively unlimited, low-cost capacity for communication of all kinds." Second, information on the Internet was not so "invasive" as broadcast information. In contrast to broadcast profanity, which might shock an unexpecting listener changing radio stations, indecent content on the Internet does not generally arrive unexpectedly on one's computer screen. Instead, it must be more actively sought out. Finally, the Internet lacked the history of extensive government regulation that broadcasting had, and the Court was uninterested in starting one now. Having rejected the broadcasting analogy, the Court applied the rigorous standard for regulating the content of traditional print. Under this STRICT SCRUTINY, the indecency provisions were struck down as unconstitutional.

JERRY KANG
(2000)

Bibliography

THORNE, JOHN; HUBER, PETER W.; and KELLOGG, MICHAEL K.   1995 *Federal Broadband Law.* Boston: Little, Brown.

INTERPOSITION

State governments have occasionally declared that acts of Congress are unconstitutional and have sought to "interpose" their authority between their citizens and the national government. This interposition has taken several forms, from refusals to cooperate with federal administration to the purported NULLIFICATION of federal acts, SECESSION, and even armed rebellion. JAMES MADISON and THOMAS JEFFERSON lent their prestige to the general notion of interposition when they wrote, respectively, the VIRGINIA AND KENTUCKY RESOLUTIONS in opposition to the ALIEN AND SEDITION ACTS of 1798. New England Federalists claimed powers of interposition in opposition to trade embargoes and the federal use of state militias during the War of 1812. Acting on the state sovereignty theory of JOHN C. CALHOUN in 1832, South Carolina declared two tariff acts "null, void, and no law." Antislavery legislatures enacted PERSONAL LIBERTY LAWS to obstruct federal fugitive slave laws. Long after the CIVIL WAR, southern legislatures attempted "massive resistance" to school DESEGREGATION. And in 1970 Massachusetts sought to prohibit the conscription of its citizens for the VIETNAM WAR.

Although these and other attempts express no single constitutional philosophy, interposition is usually associated with the theory that the sole basis of the Union is the written Constitution, not a common culture or other integrative forces; that the people who created the Constitution were members of separate and still sovereign states, not a national community; and that the Constitution is a mere contract among the states for establishing a general government with but few, well-defined objectives. From these premises it was supposed to follow that individual states could interpose to protect their reserved powers. To Calhoun and his followers in the 1830s interposition included nullifying federal laws and, in extreme cases, secession. The nullificationists cited the Virginia and Kentucky Resolutions and presented their position as consistent with the Constitution. Madison, then in his eighties, bitterly opposed and sought to disclaim paternity of any nullificationist theory. He insisted that his original version of interposition sanctioned no more than nonbinding state expression of constitutional opinion as steps toward arousing the public or amending the Constitution. This kind of interposition was fully consistent with national supremacy, the divisibility of sovereignty between nation and states, and a perpetual union. The nullificationists, said Madison, were asserting a RIGHT OF REVOLUTION, not a constitutional right.

Scholars point out that an extended constitutional debate would hardly have been necessary in the 1790s if all that Madison had then contemplated was a state's right to express and invite other states to express nonbinding opinions. But, Madison's candor aside, his final version of interposition need not have been toothless. The history of interposition shows that the states' role in the AMENDING PROCESS gives even the nonbinding opinions of a small number of states a special potential for awakening public interest in constitutional questions and undermining the perceived legitimacy of national policy. Practiced with sufficient regularity by enough states, the tamest kind of interposition might have had a strong influence on the pace and direction of constitutional change.

SOTIRIOS A. BARBER
(1986)

(SEE ALSO: *Theories of the Union.*)

Bibliography

CORWIN, EDWARD S.   1912   National Power and State Interposition. *Michigan Law Review* 10:535–551.
KILPATRICK, JAMES JACKSON   1957   *The Sovereign States: Notes of a Citizen of Virginia.* Chicago: Henry Regnery Co.

INTERPRETIVISM

The rationale that JOHN MARSHALL provided for constitutional review in MARBURY V. MADISON (1803) declared that the Constitution is law and that the courts as courts of law are obliged to apply its dictates, even when the consequence is invalidation of a duly enacted statute. JUDICIAL REVIEW has, of course, evolved into a major pillar of the American governmental system, but exercise of the power has never ceased to arouse controversy. Marshall used several examples of clear violations of explicit constitutional language to bolster the case for judicial review, but such easy cases seldom get to court. In cases that typically do get to court, the constitutional language leaves room for doubt and debate, and the consequent clash between democratic decision making and judicial choice has been a focal point of an ongoing national concern about judicial review.

The contemporary phase of the national soul-searching about judicial review can be traced to a period of JUDICIAL ACTIVISM that began with the Supreme Court's 1954 decision in BROWN V. BOARD OF EDUCATION, holding that racial SEGREGATION in public schools is a violation of the EQUAL PROTECTION clause of the FOURTEENTH AMENDMENT. Starting with *Brown,* the Supreme Court, under the leadership of EARL WARREN, tackled a broad range of controversial social issues in the name of the Constitution. Much legislation was struck down, and Warren himself and the WARREN COURT became familiar targets in political debate in 1950s and 1960s. Despite the controversy, the Court did not really approach center stage of the nation's politics

until 1973, when, under the leadership of WARREN E. BURGER, it held in ROE V. WADE that a woman's interest in decisions about ABORTION was constitutionally protected from most state criminal laws and many forms of state regulation. *Brown* had led the way to a rough social consensus in opposition to racial segregation, but *Roe*'s resolution of the abortion issue proved much less prescient. Abortion became the most divisive public issue in the United States in the late twentieth century, and the Supreme Court found itself the object of a great deal of attention in the ensuing political controversy.

Before *Roe,* opponents of the Court's activism had not found much common theoretical ground for their concern. *Roe,* like *Brown,* was decided under the Fourteenth Amendment, but the abortion issue, unlike the racial segregation issue in *Brown,* was rather remote from the problems that had originally inspired the amendment. This fact helped stimulate an academic literature questioning the Court's activism on the ground of its disregard of the ORIGINAL INTENT behind constitutional provisions. These critics urged that constitutional language and original intentions were the preeminent sources on which courts were permitted to draw for guidance in CONSTITUTIONAL INTERPRETATION. This general approach was dubbed "interpretivism," and the neologism stuck, as did the even uglier NONINTERPRETIVISM to mean an insistence that the courts could legitimately be guided in constitutional decisions by values of the culture not fairly traceable to constitutional language or to original intentions.

The dispute between interpretivists and noninterpretivists found its way into political discourse, especially during the presidency of RONALD REAGAN, when Attorney General Edwin Meese railed against judicial activism and called for a return to a "jurisprudence of original intention." The dispute achieved an unusual degree of public visibility in 1987 when President Reagan nominated Robert Bork to succeed LEWIS F. POWELL for a seat on the Supreme Court. Powell had been a swing vote on a Court closely divided on a variety of issues, and the identity of his successor drew unusual attention from various interested groups. Bork had aligned himself with the interpretivist position, first in academic writings and later in speeches he gave while serving as a judge on the United States Court of Appeals for the District of Columbia Circuit. He viewed noninterpretivism as rampant among judges and scholars and as an illegitimate intrusion by the courts into both LEGISLATIVE POWER and EXECUTIVE PREROGATIVE. On that ground, Bork had expressed doubt about such decisions as GRISWOLD V. CONNECTICUT (1965), protecting access to BIRTH CONTROL devices against state prohibition. This and other positions on constitutional law that Bork viewed as matters of interpretivist principle became points of contention in the televised hearings on his nomination and surely contributed to his defeat in the Senate.

In addition to being ugly, the terms "interpretivism" and "noninterpretivism" were never terribly apt, for both sides purported to "interpret" the constitution. Gradually the synonymous and more descriptive (though perhaps not much less ugly) terms ORIGINALISM and "nonoriginalism" gained currency in the 1980s. Terminology aside, the distinction between interpretivism and noninterpretivism proved elusive under close examination. The most extreme form of interpretivism insisted that constitutional questions must be referred to an almost mechanical process of application of constitutional language and original intentions. In this strong form, interpretivism would surely defang the activist tiger, but commentators quickly exposed weaknesses in any pretense of interpretivism to answer constitutional questions by resorting to constitutional language and intention alone. Many of the criticisms suggested difficulties in softer versions of interpretivism as well.

Perhaps the most obvious problem is with the inadequacy of the historical record for so many key constitutional provisions. Lawyers and judges are not trained in historical research, and even if they were, they would find that history itself requires interpretation that necessarily draws on the cultural framework, and hence the values, of the inquirer. But those interpretive difficulties are substantially compounded by the sparseness of the historical record in the case of the original Constitution and many of the amendments. Reports of the debates in the state conventions called to ratify the original Constitution are particularly sketchy. In some cases, the official reports are virtually nonexistent, and newspaper or other informal reports that have survived are suspect or even demonstrably inaccurate.

This historical problem plays on another—the conceptual difficulty of combining intentions of the individual actors in enactment of constitutional provisions into an authorative corporate intention. The Confederation Congress, the CONSTITUTIONAL CONVENTION OF 1787, and the several state ratifying conventions all played important roles in the original Constitution. But there is no consensus about the right way to sum the individual states of mind of the participants for any one body, let alone for all the relevant bodies combined. In the case of the original Constitution, for instance, we usually recur to the intentions of the Framers at the Constitutional Convention, who did not have a formal role in the adoption of the document, and ignore the intentions of the delegates to the state ratifying conventions, who did. This is done without any particular theoretical justification. Just suggestive of the many questions that any thoroughgoing response to the summing problem would have to address are whether the mental frameworks of persons who voted against the Constitution or some provision of it are to be counted, whether views of sponsors of language count more than views of others with equal votes, and whether ratifying conventions after the required nine initial ratifications matter.

In practice, of course, we do rely comfortably on explanations by participants expressed contemporaneously with the enactment process. The dominant source in the case of the original Constitution is THE FEDERALIST. The essays of *The Federalist* are attractive for a variety of reasons, but most especially because of JAMES MADISON's authorship of so many of them and because they represent an intellectual tour de force that provides a compelling rationale for the Constitution. But those are hardly answers to the historical difficulty or to the summing problem. Indeed, *The Federalist* was produced after the Convention and as advocacy, rather than as a faithful reflection of the contemporaneous intentions of the Constitution's draftsmen. As such, *The Federalist* may well have been influential for members of the ratifying conventions in ways it could not have been for members of the Constitutional Convention. Ironically, *The Federalist* may thus provide evidence of intention—albeit strictly circumstantial evidence—for a group that is largely ignored in the literature about original intentions, while not providing much evidence at all for the group with which, because of Madison's central role at the Convention, they are more commonly associated.

It is interesting that the summing and historical problems have caused so little anguish. We have not seemed disabled by the lack of a summing algorithm or by the lack of historical evidence. This is probably so because we appreciate intuitively that all those states of mind were important as inputs to the real product of the constitutional process, the language of the document itself, about which there is no doubt at all. Intentions, in contrast, are suggestive guides to interpretation, helpful because language does not apply itself, because the views of those involved in the process are likely to provide useful perspectives, and because we have come to learn that the views of some—Madison and ALEXANDER HAMILTON in particular—contain special insight and special wisdom about the American constitutional system. The usefulness of what can be learned about original intentions is surely not unrelated to their historic association with the enactment of the Constitution, but their usefulness is not logically bound up with that association. And we need neither summing formulas nor definitive evidence to make use of the ideas those intentions provide.

Other critics of interpretivism have emphasized the ambiguity of what in an individual's mental framework is meant by his "intentions." Ronald Dworkin, for example, has pointed out that there may be a distinction between the hopes and the expectations of a constitutional draftsman. And these two may be different from what the draftsman fears his language may come to mean. A further difficulty of this sort is in specifying the level of generality at which the authoritative intentions are taken to be held. Lawmakers, for instance, will typically have had exemplary instances in mind of things that would be fostered or forbidden by the law. The language they enact, however, will usually be expressed generally rather than as a list of specific goals or specific evils. The framers of the Fourteenth Amendment, for instance, clearly assumed that specific discriminatory statutes of the southern states, known collectively as the BLACK CODES, would be forbidden by the amendment, while the constitutional language they chose is exceedingly general. When the language is that general, it would be strange indeed to confine the reach of the amendment to the exemplary instances, or even to matters closely analogous to those exemplary instances. Nor would it likely be faithful to any probable reconstruction of original intentions. The generality of the language suggests that many of those involved must have had more general norms in mind in addition to the exemplary instances. Thus, even if the historical evidence is plentiful and the summing problem somehow overcome, the interpreter must at a minimum mediate between levels of generality at which intentions almost surely were simultaneously held.

A further difficulty lies in the role of PRECEDENT in an interpretivist scheme. The animating force behind the interpretivist approach is a desire for stability and certainty in constitutional law that requires the taming of judicial activism. Original intentions are assumed to be an unchanging lodestar providing both stability and certainty. But what then happens if there has been an earlier decision that now appears mistaken by original-intention lights? The earlier decision will have induced reliance and will for a time at least have defined the "law" on the question. If that decision must be overruled on the basis of persuasive new historical data—to say nothing of a new judgment about the import of old data—the goals of stability and certainty are not served, but undermined. In addition, it is not clear how one would approach the role of precedent in original-intention terms. This is really part of a larger problem that Paul Brest has referred to as the problem of "interpretive intention." It is perfectly possible for someone involved in constitution making to believe that a given problem will be resolved one way under language he votes to enact but that precedential developments, a change in external circumstances, or even a change of heart by judges might appropriately lead to a different result. It is perfectly possible, that is, for constitution makers to appreciate that they are setting in motion a decisional process, grounded in a desire to eradicate certain bad things or foster certain good ones, but not inextricably tied to any list of what is forbidden or desired. In that case, the intender's substantive and interpretive intentions can well suggest opposed results. If we somehow had access to the full complexity of original intention, we might resolve the conflict, but not necessarily in any way that would provide stability and certainty in the law. This problem of interpretive intention is particularly acute in a system like the American one, where long tradition antedating the Constitution requires courts to defer significantly to prior decisions. In such a context, it seems quite likely that constitution makers took for granted that STARE DECISIS would have its due in constitutional law.

Interpretivist responses to these criticisms were complex and varied. While some interpretivists clung to a vision of original intentions that virtually applied themselves, most acknowledged that generally stated constitutional language had to leave room for judgment and hence choice by the courts. Some interpretivists, for instance, acknowledged that the intentions the judges were to apply were appropriately conceived at a level of substantial generality. Others embraced a role for precedent in constitutional law. Still others saw room for arguments from changed circumstances or from aspects of the constitutional system that did not come neatly packaged in a clause or an amendment. But the more these extratextual and extraintentional considerations are allowed to intrude, the more blurred becomes the line between the opposed interpretivist and noninterpretivist camps.

This is not to say that either side relented or that there was no difference between the two. Noninterpretivism had no unified approach to interpretation to offer. Some noninterpretivists advanced moral and POLITICAL PHILOSOPHY as the appropriate source for constitutional values when constitutional language ran out. Others urged judges to search for answers in conventional morality. Some saw judges as striving for a sort of global coherence in the law, while others urged adherence to precedent in more restricted domains. They were united only in their disdain for the oversimplified view of interpretation advanced by interpretivists, but the lack of any coherent noninterpretivist program reinforced the interpretivist view that noninterpretivism invited judicial tyranny.

As the debate proceeded, it became increasingly apparent that what was really at issue was the appropriate degree of judicial activism in a constitutional democracy, that interpretivism represented an appealing if ultimately unpersuasive theoretical grounding for the position that judges are constitutionally bound to exercise the judicial veto in only the clearest of cases. Despite protestations to the contrary, the two sides differed more in how clear the case had to be than in the type of evidence that could be considered. Differences over the role of original intentions were thus really ones of attitude and degree rather than anything more fundamental. It was interesting that, aside from Robert Bork, few judges joined the fray, and when they did, they seldom did so in the language of interpretivism and noninterpretivism. As the 1980s drew to a close, it appeared that political conservatives had largely prevailed in their campaign for a constrained judiciary. After ANTHONY M. KENNEDY succeeded to Lewis Powell's seat on the Court, Chief Justice WILLIAM H. REHNQUIST presided over a Supreme Court majority that articulated a philosophy of "judicial restraint" in constitutional review, but it was not a majority that did so under the banner of interpretivism.

ROBERT W. BENNETT
(1992)

(SEE ALSO: *Bork Nomination; Judicial Activism and Judicial Restraint; Ratifier Intent.*)

Bibliography

BENNETT, ROBERT W. 1984 Objectivity in Constitutional Law. *University of Pennsylvania Law Review* 132:445–496.
BREST, PAUL 1980 The Misconceived Quest for Original Understanding. *Boston University Law Review* 60:204–238.
DWORKIN, RONALD 1981 The Forum of Principle. *New York University Law Review* 56:469–518.
MONOGHAN, HENRY P. 1981 Our Perfect Constitution. *New York University Law Review* 56:353–396.

INTERSTATE COMITY

See: Full Faith and Credit; Privileges and Immunities

INTERSTATE COMMERCE

The term "interstate commerce" does not appear in the Constitution. Nor do the few debates in the CONSTITUTIONAL CONVENTION OF 1787 over the wording of the COMMERCE CLAUSE offer much help in discerning what the Framers meant by granting Congress the power to regulate commerce "among the several states." The absence of expressed specific intent led WILLIAM W. CROSSKEY to examine contemporary usage and to theorize that the national power over commerce was intended to be virtually exclusive and to include not only interstate commerce but INTRASTATE COMMERCE as well. One of the Framers' intentions was to eliminate the destructive conflicts between contradictory state practices under the Confederation government. Chief Justice JOHN MARSHALL so assumed when he defined the term in GIBBONS V. OGDEN (1824), a case that has guided interpretation to this day. Interstate

commerce, he wrote, is that "which concerns more states than one" and it even extends "to those internal concerns which affect the states generally." In the nineteenth century the clause was more often applied as a restriction on state powers than as a positive grant of national power, and as EDWARD S. CORWIN remarked, "the word "commerce,' as designating the thing to be protected against State interference, long came to dominate the clause, while the potential word "regulate' remained in the background." In *Houston, East & West Texas Railway v. United States*, (1914), the Court expanded the reach of congressional power by permitting federal regulation of purely intrastate commerce because, in the railroad case before it, the two were inextricably linked.

The scope of the commerce clause has encouraged the Court to devise a number of tests throughout its history to determine limits to the term, the best known of which is the STREAM OF COMMERCE DOCTRINE. (See also SELECTIVE EXCLUSIVENESS, EFFECTS ON COMMERCE, and SHREVEPORT DOCTRINE). The Supreme Court has thus held that "interstate commerce" means both movement that crosses state lines and movement that does not but that adversely affects interstate commerce. It includes tangible items as well as intangible ones. In *Gibbons*, Marshall defined it as "commercial intercourse," but even this expansive reading has been widened. *Caminetti v. United States* (1917) is only one of many cases in which the Court decided that no commercial motive need be present. Moreover, movement itself is not essential; in WICKARD V. FILBURN (1942), Justice ROBERT H. JACKSON disdained semantic formulas and declared that agricultural PRODUCTION affects interstate commerce. Such a broad view of the commerce power has allowed Congress to regulate not only traditional SUBJECTS OF COMMERCE but also criminal activity, professional sports, antitrust cases, and RACIAL DISCRIMINATION.

DAVID GORDON
(1986)

Bibliography

STERN, ROBERT L. 1955 The Scope of the Phrase *Interstate Commerce. American Bar Association Journal* 41:823–826, 871–874.

INTERSTATE COMMERCE ACT
24 Stat. 379 (1887)

This act, which initiated federal authority in ECONOMIC REGULATION, created an administrative commission to wield federal power. Congress's approach, in Isaiah Sharfman's words, was "tentative and experimental" because doubts existed whether the government could so act. The legislation nevertheless marked a first attempt to organize an increasingly chaotic field.

Until the 1870s railroads had been free to expand and operate, essentially unregulated, yet encouraged by land grants and public subsidies. As speculation, rate discrimination, and other abuses increased, popular opinion grew correspondingly negative. State legislatures, especially in the Midwest, began setting maximum rail rates and establishing commissions to maintain their reasonableness. Although the Supreme Court sustained such regulation in the GRANGER CASES (1877), it soon retrenched and, in *Wabash, St. Louis & Pacific Railway v. Illinois*, (1886) the Court asserted the states' inability to regulate rates even partly interstate. The Court thus created a vacuum—the states could not regulate and Congress had not regulated.

Compromise legislation finally passed Congress in 1887, the outcome of over 150 bills in nearly twenty years. The act applied to "any common carrier or carriers engaged in the [interstate or foreign] transportation of passengers or property," and specifically exempted INTRASTATE COMMERCE. Reiterating the COMMON LAW, the act ordered all charges to be "reasonable and just." The act created the INTERSTATE COMMERCE COMMISSION (ICC), empowered it to set aside unjust rates, but neglected to give it the power to replace them with new ones. The ICC also had authority to investigate complaints; significantly, an individual need not demonstrate direct damage to file a complaint. Several sections forbade devices such as rebates, pooling, and LONG HAUL-SHORT HAUL DISCRIMINATION. The act also required publication of rate schedules, rendering the carriers liable for injuries sustained as a result of any violations. Courts were to consider ICC findings *prima facie* EVIDENCE but commission orders became effective immediately *only* if voluntarily obeyed. Carriers took advantage of this loophole to APPEAL virtually every order, leaving them free to disregard the ICC until a court sustained it. Demanding to hear cases *de novo*, the courts implicitly invited the carriers to withhold evidence from the ICC; courts reversed ICC orders regularly on both legal and policy grounds. As Sharfman noted, the commission's powers were thus "restricted in scope and feeble in effect." In 1897 the Supreme Court dealt the ICC two stunning blows. Even though the act had not expressly granted the ICC rate-setting authority, the commission had assumed the power. In INTERSTATE COMMERCE COMMISSION V. CINCINNATI, NEW ORLEANS & TEXAS PACIFIC RAILWAY, the Court denied the commission this power. *ICC v. Alabama Midland Railway Co.* (1897) rendered the long haul-short haul clause a dead letter.

In part because of the judicial evisceration of the act, Congress amended it nearly a dozen times by 1925. Among the most important supplementary legislation were the ELKINS ACT, the HEPBURN ACT, and the MANN-

ELKINS ACT. The Supreme Court endorsed Congress's efforts in several cases, culminating in INTERSTATE COMMERCE COMMISSION V. ILLINOIS CENTRAL RAILROAD (1910).

DAVID GORDON
(1986)

Bibliography

HOOGENBOOM, ARI and OLIVE 1976 *A History of the ICC: From Panacea to Palliative.* New York: W. W. Norton.

SHARFMAN, ISAIAH L. 1931 *The Interstate Commerce Commission.* Vol. I. New York: Commonwealth Fund.

INTERSTATE COMMERCE COMMISSION

See: Regulatory Agencies

INTERSTATE COMMERCE COMMISSION v. ALABAMA MIDLAND RAILWAY COMPANY

See: *Interstate Commerce Commission v. Cincinnati, New Orleans & Texas Pacific Railway*

INTERSTATE COMMERCE COMMISSION v. CINCINNATI, NEW ORLEANS & TEXAS PACIFIC RAILWAY
167 U.S. 479 (1897)

INTERSTATE COMMERCE COMMISSION v. ALABAMA MIDLAND RAILWAY COMPANY
168 U.S. 144 (1897)

As one of Justice JOHN MARSHALL HARLAN's dissents in these cases declared, these decisions stripped the Interstate Commerce Commission (ICC) "of authority to do anything of an effective character." The ICC succeeded in only one APPEAL to the Supreme Court between 1897 and 1906. The INTERSTATE COMMERCE ACT required "reasonable and just" rates and, although it gave the commission the right to set aside unreasonable rates, it did not expressly grant them power to revise rates. The ICC had operated for a decade on the assumption that it had had such power; without it, the statute's injunction to provide reasonable rates could hardly be accomplished. In *ICC v. Cincinnati, New Orleans & Texas Pacific Railway* (1897) the Court majority insisted that if the act's framers had intended to grant them such powers, they "would have said so." The act provided no explicit authority, however, and the extent of the power militated against "such a grant . . . by mere implication." If the commission exercised such rate-making powers, it would have been making law and it had only the power to "execute and enforce, not to legislate." Such a quasi-legislative DELEGATION OF POWER could not yet secure approval from the Court; denied power to set rates, the commission now had only the right (of questionable use) to void unreasonable rates. Justice Harlan dissented from that decision as well as from Justice GEORGE SHIRAS's opinion in *ICC v. Alabama Midland Railway Company* (1897), decided a few months later. That case nearly destroyed the LONG HAUL-SHORT HAUL provision in the act as well as the commission's fact-finding authority. Despite unequivocal language declaring the ICC findings of fact to be conclusive and binding on courts, Shiras decided that the clause empowering CIRCUIT COURTS to hear appeals necessarily implied a right of the courts to reexamine all the facts; they could not overrule the commission in both law and fact. By not presenting all EVIDENCE until an appeal, the railroads could and soon did mock ICC orders. These decisions severely restricted the commission's usefulness; not until the HEPBURN ACT of 1906 and the MANN-ELKINS ACT of 1910 would Congress move to revive the commission.

DAVID GORDON
(1986)

INTERSTATE COMMERCE COMMISSION v. ILLINOIS CENTRAL RAILROAD
215 U.S. 452 (1910)

The HEPBURN ACT of 1906 and a decision by the Supreme Court the following year began reviving the Interstate Commerce Commission (ICC) after a series of devastating decisions. The Court had denied the commission the power to revise rates in INTERSTATE COMMERCE COMMISSION V. CINCINNATI, NEW ORLEANS & TEXAS PACIFIC RAILWAY (1897), and had struck hard at the provision of the INTERSTATE COMMERCE ACT outlawing LONG HAUL-SHORT HAUL DISCRIMINATION in *Interstate Commerce Commission v. Alabama Midland Railway Co.* (1897). The Court reversed ICC orders on both legal and policy grounds at an astonishing rate, and the commission spent nearly the first twenty years of its existence fighting Court-imposed obstacles.

The Interstate Commerce Act had declared that ICC findings were to be considered *prima facie* evidence but until 1907 the Court, in fact, reviewed all evidence *de novo*, thereby allowing the railroads to present previously withheld EVIDENCE on APPEAL. This practice discredited the commission and put the Court in the business of rate regulation. In *Illinois Central Railroad Company v. Interstate Commerce Commission* (1907), the Court declared that it would no longer reexamine the facts of a case on appeal; the commission was a responsible tribunal and its findings of fact would be accorded "probative force."

Because of the passage of the MANN-ELKINS ACT and a favorable 8–1 decision in *Interstate Commerce Commission v. Illinois Central Railroad,* 1910 was a good year for the ICC. In this case the Court indicated its willingness to support the commission, laying down its guidelines for the determination of the validity of ICC orders. The Justices expected to continue to review commission orders, but solely in reference to constitutional issues, statutory construction of "the scope of the delegated authority" under which the ICC issued the order, and the practical "substance" of the order. Nevertheless, the Court henceforth specifically refused "under the guise of exerting judicial power, [to] usurp merely administrative functions by setting aside a lawful administrative order upon our conception as to whether the administrative power has been wisely exercised. Power to make the order and not the mere expediency or wisdom of having made it is the question."

DAVID GORDON
(1986)

INTERSTATE COMPACT

The Constitution, in Article I, section 10, recognizes the right of the states to enter into compacts and agreements with one another, but provides that the right shall not be exercised without the consent of Congress. In this respect, the Constitution continued the practice that had obtained under the ARTICLES OF CONFEDERATION. The right to enter into compacts and agreements is, as the Supreme Court said in *Hinderlider v. La Plata Company* (1938), the survival under the Constitution of "the age-old treaty-making power of independent sovereign nations."

Before 1921, most interstate compacts involved two (or at most three) states, and were either about boundaries or about boundary streams. One notable exception was the Chesapeake and Ohio Canal Compact (1825), involving Virginia, Maryland, Pennsylvania, and the District of Columbia, providing for joint incorporation of the canal company and mutual acceptance of legislation in its favor. Another was the Virginia-West Virginia Compact (1862) by which seceding Virginia agreed to the creation of West Virginia from part of its territory while the latter assumed part of the state debt.

The modern era of interstate compacts began with the New York Port Authority Compact (1921) and the Colorado River Compact (1923). The former created a single commission, jointly appointed by New York and New Jersey, to administer the Port of New York and the surrounding area. The latter was the first true multistate compact, allocating irrigation water among six states drained by the Colorado.

The success of these two agreements led politicians and scholars to see in interstate compacts a great potential for solving multistate problems without national legislation. FELIX FRANKFURTER and JAMES M. LANDIS, in an influential article published in 1925, advocated "imaginative adaptation" of the device to reach a multitude of subjects they deemed beyond the scope of congressional power under the Constitution, such as the generation and distribution of electricity. Buoyed by this public optimism, states proposed open-membership compacts on subjects such as WORKERS' COMPENSATION and child labor. Experience, however, demonstrated that interstate compacts were not a panacea for the ills of FEDERALISM, and, although the number negotiated steadily increased, after the 1930s compacts were confined to more narrowly interstate matters. This is true even of compacts to which all the states are parties, such as the Interstate Compact for Supervision of Parolees and Probationers.

Compacts between states are somewhat more binding than treaties between sovereign nations, because the states are subject to the CONTRACT CLAUSE, and, within the limits of the ELEVENTH AMENDMENT, the obligations imposed by interstate compacts are enforceable in federal courts.

On its face, the Constitution seems to require congressional consent to all interstate compacts and agreements. However, in *Virginia v. Tennessee* (1893) the Supreme Court held that a boundary agreement of 1802 had received Congress's consent through acquiescence because, although it never voted to approve the agreement, Congress followed its terms in such matters as establishing judicial districts. The court reasoned that only compacts touching on the powers of the national government or substantially affecting intergovernmental relationships within the federal system required explicit congressional approval. On the other hand, Congress may veto *any* compact or agreement, even if the states would have been fully competent to act in the absence of the compact.

When explicit approval is required, it may be given either before or after the compact is negotiated by the states. But the failure of Congress to enact a resolution of consent is not equivalent to a denial of consent: it may signify no more than that Congress believes its explicit consent to a particular compact is unnecessary.

DENNIS J. MAHONEY
(1986)

Bibliography

FRANKFURTER, FELIX and LANDIS, JAMES M.   1925   "The Compact Clause of the Constitution—A Study in Interstate Adjustments." *Yale Law Journal* 34:685–729.

ZIMMERMAN, FREDERICK L. and WENDELL, MITCHELL   1951   *The Interstate Compact Since 1925*. Chicago: Council of State Governments.

——— 1976   *The Law and Use of Interstate Compacts*. Chicago: Council of State Governments.

INTIMATE ASSOCIATION

See: Freedom of Intimate Association

INTOLERABLE ACTS

See: First Continental Congress, Declarations and Resolves of

INTRASTATE COMMERCE

The CONSTITUTIONAL CONVENTION OF 1787, by listing among Congress's enumerated powers the power to regulate commerce "among the several states" as well as with Indian tribes and foreign countries, appeared to reserve for regulation by each state its own domestic commerce. Indeed, notwithstanding Chief Justice JOHN MARSHALL's dictum that commerce does not stop at the state line but penetrates into the interior, for most of American constitutional history Congress respected and the Supreme Court enforced that division of power over commerce. After WICKARD V. FILBURN (1938), the distinction between intrastate and INTERSTATE COMMERCE effectively ceased to have any significance in constitutional law.

DAVID GORDON
(1986)

INVALID ON ITS FACE

Legislation may be unconstitutional as applied to all, some, or none of the behavior it addresses. Usually, affected parties challenge a law's constitutionality only as applied to their own behavior. Occasionally, they claim a law is constitutionally invalid on its face—and therefore unenforceable against anyone, including them—because it would be unconstitutional ever to apply it. A penal law is invalid on its face, for example, when it so vaguely describes the conduct outlawed that it cannot give fair warning to anyone, or when every act the law prohibits is constitutionally protected. A challenge to such a law would present no STANDING problem. Sometimes, however, a litigant will assert that, regardless of whether a law is constitutional as applied to him it should be held invalid on its face because its coverage includes unconstitutional regulation of others.

Normally a federal court will deny standing to raise

such a facial challenge when the law constitutionally regulates the would-be challenger, for the court perceives the claim as a request to go beyond the case before it. Responding to the request would require the court to decide what other situations the law governs—frequently an unresolved question of statutory interpretation—and then to decide whether some of the law's unapplied coverage would be unconstitutional. If the court should conclude that part of the law is invalid and part valid, it would have to decide whether the legislative framers would want the valid part to stand separately or the whole law to fall. Finally, if the law is constitutional as applied to the litigant, but would be unconstitutional in hypothetical application to others, the court may still have to decide whether to hold the law facially invalid despite a legislative desire to have the law's valid applications stand.

Formidable considerations militate against judicial rulings that laws are facially invalid. JUDICIAL REVIEW originates in the need to apply constitutional law to decide the case before the court, and a corollary principle requires courts to refrain from deciding hypothetical questions. When a court focuses only on the situation before it, it minimizes the need for unnecessary decisions of issues of both statutory and constitutional interpretation, and avoids considering other possible applications of the law in a factual vacuum. Finally, a conclusion of facial invalidity would prevent the valid enforcement of the law against a party whom the legislature intended to regulate. Normally, then, the Supreme Court denies a litigant STANDING to assert the unconstitutionality of legislation as it would be applied to others, except when the most compelling reasons are present.

The reason most often found compelling is the need to protect the freedom of expression of persons not before the court whom the law might inhibit. That was the rationale, for example, of THORNHILL V. ALABAMA (1940). Specifically, the FIRST AMENDMENT doctrines of OVERBREADTH and VAGUENESS sometimes permit one whose conduct the law constitutionally could reach to escape punishment, arguing that the law is invalid on its face because its seeming application to others discourages their protected expression. Intense controversy surrounds these facial challenges, however, largely because of differing perceptions of how inhibiting such laws really are. In areas involving other fundamental freedoms, such as the RIGHT TO TRAVEL, facial challenges have occasionally been successful, as in APTHEKER V. SECRETARY OF STATE (1964), again to protect persons who are never likely to be before a court from having their liberty circumscribed by the seeming applicability of an unconstitutional regulation.

A court will hold a law invalid on its face only in a case of necessity: where the law's very existence may affect the exercise of cherished liberties by nonparties lacking opportunity or willingness to challenge them, and where the

inhibiting feature of the law cannot easily be cured by statutory interpretation. Absent such conditions federal courts will not, at the request of one whose behavior may constitutionally be regulated, decide how a law might apply and whether the law's potential application to other situations warrants holding it invalid on its face. The degree to which the Supreme Court permits facial challenges to legislation directly reflects the Justices' collective perception of the Court's institutional role in enforcing the Constitution. Narrow views of that role incline the Court to restrict facial challenges; a broader view commends it to entertain and encourage such a challenge in the interest of assuring the constitutional governance of society beyond the immediate case.

JONATHAN D. VARAT
(1986)

INVASION OF PRIVACY

See: Right of Privacy

INVERSE CONDEMNATION

The course of action which a property owner may pursue against a governmental defendant to recover the JUST COMPENSATION guaranteed by the Fifth and FOURTEENTH AMENDMENTS when the defendant, without initiating an eminent domain proceeding, "takes" private property is called "inverse condemnation."

The elements of a compensable TAKING OF PROPERTY can occur under many different circumstances. An action to establish inverse condemnation is clearly proper when a governmental entity has destroyed, confiscated, or substantially abridged some right or privilege in the plaintiff's property or when the normal operation of governmental facilities results in a destructive interference with the use of the plaintiff's property by third persons, as by jet aircraft noise. Excessive regulation, resulting in an effective prohibition of substantially all use and value of the interest regulated, may also constitute a taking.

The most intractable issue in inverse condemnation litigation currently relates to regulatory takings. Although government may carry out many types of programs that adversely affect economic values without its actions constituting a taking, in some contexts POLICE POWER regulations may be so restrictive in character as to constitute a compensable taking, as in *Pennsylvania Coal Co. v. Mahon* (1922). However, no "set formula" has been developed for determining when a legislative measure has adversely affected property interests to that degree. The relative magnitude of the loss sustained by the property owner is relevant but not controlling. Factors suggestive of a taking, however, include the extent to which the government's actions have impaired legitimate investment-backed expectations of the owner and the fact that the regulation has resulted in an uncompensated acquisition of resources by the public entity. (See PENN CENTRAL TRANSPORTATION CO. V. NEW YORK CITY.) Factors often relied upon to negate a taking include the existence of widely shared compensating benefits resulting from the restrictions and the reflecting in the regulation of a rational legislative choice between mutually incompatible private interests.

Inverse condemnation jurisprudence is also complicated by uncertainty, so far not resolved by the Supreme Court, as to the scope of the relief available for regulatory takings. In many cases, for example, *Pennsylvania Coal Co.*, the taking rationale has been invoked to invalidate excessive regulatory action; in others, an award of monetary compensation has been granted. In *San Diego Gas & Electric Co. v. City of San Diego* (1981), four Justices, with a supporting dictum from a fifth, intimated that when a taking is enjoined, compensation for interim losses sustained by the property owner should be granted. And when overriding public interest so requires, governmental action that effects a taking may even be declared valid, subject to the payment of just compensation to those persons whose property has thereby been taken. (See DAMES & MOORE V. REGAN.)

Some commentators have argued, and a few courts have held, that the exclusive remedy for a regulatory taking is invalidation of the offending measure. These decisions generally reflect judicial reluctance to impose onerous burdens that could interfere with orderly fiscal planning by governmental agencies engaged in regulatory functions. They appear to be based on the questionable assumption that invalidation will necessarily be less disruptive to the achievement of public objectives than payment of compensation. As Justice WILLIAM J. BRENNAN suggested in *San Diego Gas & Electric Co.*, a more appropriate remedial posture would permit the governmental entity to choose whether to repeal the offensive regulation with payment of compensation for temporary losses or to retain it in force with payment of full compensation.

ARVO VAN ALSTYNE
(1986)

Bibliography

MICHELMAN, FRANK I. 1967 Property, Utility, and Fairness: Commentaries on the Ethical Foundations of "Just Compensation Law." *Harvard Law Review* 80:1165–1258.
SAX, JOSEPH L. 1973 Takings and the Police Power. *Yale Law Journal* 74:36–76.

INVESTIGATIVE POWER

See: Legislative Investigation

INVIDIOUS DISCRIMINATION

Justice WILLIAM O. DOUGLAS led the Supreme Court's modern expansion of the guarantee of EQUAL PROTECTION OF THE LAWS. As early as 1942, in SKINNER V. OKLAHOMA, Douglas used the term "invidious discrimination" to differentiate state-imposed inequalities demanding strict judicial scrutiny from other discriminations (particularly economic regulations) that were valid so long as they had a RATIONAL BASIS. The word "invidious," which suggests a tendency to provoke envy or resentment, is an appropriate label for governmental discriminations imposing the stigma of caste, especially RACIAL DISCRIMINATIONS. Fittingly, Douglas used the same label in LEVY V. LOUISIANA (1968) to describe discrimination based on the status of ILLEGITIMACY.

In HARPER V. VIRGINIA STATE BOARD OF ELECTIONS (1966), Douglas termed "invidious" the state's use of a POLL TAX as a condition on voting. As a WEALTH DISCRIMINATION case, *Harper* fit the dictionary definition of "invidious." In another view, however, *Harper* required STRICT SCRUTINY because the state impaired the FUNDAMENTAL INTEREST in voting. In this perspective, "individious discrimination" broadens into a label for the Court's ultimate conclusion on the issue of an equal protection violation. For Justice Douglas, either use of the term was acceptable.

In more recent racial discrimination decisions, the Court has turned the dictionary meaning of "invidious" upside down, using it to denote not the tendency of a discrimination to provoke ill will, but the malevolent purpose of government officials. In WASHINGTON V. DAVIS (1976), for example, the Court held that a law's racially selective impact did not demand strict scrutiny, absent a showing of "invidious discriminatory purpose." The language of constitutional doctrine, like the language of diplomacy, stands ready to serve causes both fair and foul.

KENNETH L. KARST
(1986)

Bibliography

KARST, KENNETH L. 1969 Invidious Discrimination: Justice Douglas and the Return of the "Natural-Law-Due-Process Formula." *UCLA Law Review* 16:716–750.

INVOLUNTARY SERVITUDE

See: Peonage; Slavery and the Constitution

IRAN-CONTRA AFFAIR

The Iran-Contra hearings by a joint committee of both houses of Congress (the Senate Committee on Secret Military Assistance to Iran and the Nicaraguan Opposition and the House of Representatives Select Committee to

Investigate Covert Arms Transactions with Iran) were but one more episode in the almost constant twentieth-century battle between the presidency—not necessarily the President, but the executive branch and particularly the officials of the White House—and Congress for power over FOREIGN AFFAIRS assigned by the Constitution to the national government. Iran-Contra, like WATERGATE and the Steel Seizure Controversy, stands out among the few instances in which Congress mounted a successful, albeit short-lived, challenge to a thrust for power by the White House.

Following the debacle of the VIETNAM WAR, initiated by President JOHN F. KENNEDY and carried on disastrously by Presidents LYNDON B. JOHNSON and RICHARD M. NIXON without a specific congressional declaration of war, the United States found itself chastened, but not necessarily enlightened, by the experience. A large but by no means unanimous portion of the population wished to continue the fight against communism wherever it could be found, but preferably on foreign soil and, if necessary, without the endorsement of Congress. If American lives were wasted by unsuccessful military adventures in Korea and Vietnam, eventually bringing peace without honor, perhaps clandestine support of anticommunist guerrillas, in Central America with the approval of Congress could bring us honor without peace. After many years of unrestrained but unsuccessful activity in which American matériel and largess were profligately expended, along with the lives of the residents, Congress decided to call a halt to at least some of its clandestine support for insurgent forces below America's southern border, absent congressional approval. And when Congress discovered—it was an all but open secret—that secret operations in the foreign affairs apparatus of the White House were providing the wherewithal for much of the military resistance in Central America, in defiance of congressional law, a hearing was called to establish who, what, why, and when. As in Watergate, the hearings were politically dangerous because they came so close to involving the President himself in illegality. Unlike the case of Watergate, however, the President—in this instance, RONALD REAGAN—seemed more guilty of nonfeasance than malfeasance, as an investigation by a committee that the President had appointed, with former Senator John Tower as chairman, seemed to indicate in its report.

Fundamentally, the obligation of the President and his aides to abide by the terms of the laws enacted by Congress are not to be gainsaid. According to Article II, section 3, of the Constitution, the President "shall take care that the Laws be faithfully executed." Occasionally, the question may legitimately arise whether in fact that language rightfully cabins the chief executive in the circumstances and there is a conflict between the two branches,

which becomes a question of constitutional dimensions. Usually, the contesting sides reach a peaceful understanding. Sometimes the issue has to be resolved by the courts, as was the case when President HARRY S. TRUMAN seized the steel mills or when the executive branch froze the assets of the Iranian government without congressional authorization. Sometimes the controversy reaches the forum of a congressional hearing, as was the case with Watergate and again with the Iran-Contra controversy.

Prior to WORLD WAR I, the United States was governed by what Woodrow Wilson could label "congressional government" in his 1913 book of that title, which did not mean that Congress did not succumb to strong presidential leadership, such as ABRAHAM LINCOLN's, in times of crisis. During and after WORLD WAR II, government in the United States became the eponymous "presidential dictatorship" of CLINTON ROSSITER's 1985 volume, with Congress usually subordinated to the will expressed by the President. Since the KOREAN WAR, there has been a further realignment of power, again described by an astute critic's title, Arthur Schlesinger's *The Imperial Presidency* (1973), this time marking not a shift between Congress and the President but a development within the presidency of an unelected, politically irresponsible BUREAUCRACY.

It may well be that a congressional investigation of alleged wrongdoing at the level of the White House serves its function when it is called to the public's attention, when the wrongdoing that has taken place is brought to an end, and when some of the principal responsible presidential subordinates are subjected to criminal processes in the United States courts or otherwise chastised. Clearly the intent of the Framers was to fix the responsibility on the President for the conduct of his office. But we live now in more perilous times. If the continued threat of serious malefaction is to be eliminated, the price of the IMPEACHMENT process to determine whether the chief executive has erred is nevertheless too destabilizing in times of crisis for the nation to pay for such hearings. The national government was paralyzed for months in the Watergate crisis. Thus, the Iran-Contra affair may not have afforded as satisfying a resolution of the questions first raised by Senator Howard Baker: "What did the President know? And when did he know it?" But the Constitution's interests were served, and the nation's interests were protected.

The Iran-Contra hearings, however consequential in theory, were a contest for constitutional power between President and Congress, and were generally regarded by the American public as entertainment rather than enlightenment. It was as if some of Hollywood's second-rate script writers had concocted a "B" version of the Watergate hearings. Everyone was covering up for a generally beloved and pathetically inept President, who could not remember what had occurred in his meetings with his national security staff. There was a handsome Marine veteran wrapped in the flag and dedicated to the extermination of communists and communism by means in or out of the Constitution's limits. There was his beauteous secretary devoted to her boss, who helped destroy and remove secret documents. There were professional spies, cabinet officers locked out of the deliberations, national security chiefs, past and present. There were strange and sinister-looking Middle Eastern arms merchants. And there was a Rasputin figure, who, fortunately for the goals of the hearings, had died before his evidence could be secured. If the purpose of the Iran-Contra hearings were to prove that congressional hearings about the conduct of the presidential office can be a futile and useless CHECK AND BALANCE of one branch of the government on the other, the hearings succeeded beyond a peradventure of doubt. They also proved what "every schoolboy knew," that the American government had been secretly negotiating with Iran for the release of American prisoners and that it was supplying weapons to the Contra forces in Nicaragua—the first, in contradiction of the Reagan administration's own frequently announced policy; the second, at least without and likely in contradiction of congressional mandate. This is not the way American government is supposed to work.

After the hearings, many of the witnesses were indicted and some pleaded guilty to various offenses while others were found guilty. None of the major figures received heavy sentences. Lt. Col. Oliver North, the popular hero of the tale, was sentenced to 1200 hours of community service and fined $150,000 on three felony counts of willfully obstructing the congressional investigation, but his conviction was reversed—ironically, on civil liberties grounds. Robert McFarlane, former national security adviser to the President, pleaded guilty to four misdemeanor counts of assisting in secret efforts illegally to aid the Contras. He received two years probation, a $20,000 fine and 200 hours of community service. Admiral John M. Poindexter, Reagan's national security adviser and North's superior, did get six months on five counts of conspiracy.

PHILIP B. KURLAND
(1992)

(SEE ALSO: *Constitutional History, 1980–1989.*)

Bibliography

COHEN, WILLIAN and MITCHELL, GEORGE 1988 *Men of Zeal.* New York: Viking.
JOINT HEARINGS ON THE IRAN-CONTRA INVESTIGATION. 1987–1988 Washington D.C.: U.S. Government Printing Office.
REPORT OF THE JOINT CONGRESSIONAL COMMITTEE INVESTIGATING THE IRAN-CONTRA AFFAIR 1988 Washington, D.C.: U.S. Government Printing Office.

IREDELL, JAMES
(1751–1799)

James Iredell was one of the most active and important members of the United States Supreme Court during the 1790s. Although he was a strong nationalist and vigorous advocate of judicial power, he also was a political realist who understood, in a way that his contemporaries on the High Court did not, the widespread distrust of centralized government and an independent judiciary that existed in America following the AMERICAN REVOLUTION.

Iredell was the eldest son of a well-connected but financially troubled merchant from Bristol, England. When his father suffered a paralytic stroke, his mother's family, in 1768, arranged for him to become comptroller of the customs in Edenton, North Carolina. While performing his duties, Iredell studied law with Samuel Johnston, a leading member of the North Carolina bar, whose sister he married in 1773. Although he remained in the service of the king until the spring of 1776, his real sympathies were with the colonists, and after independence he became a firm supporter of the patriot cause. Following the break with England he served on a committee to revise old laws and draft new legislation to make government in North Carolina compatible with republicanism. He also helped create a judiciary system for the state, and reluctantly accepted an appointment as a Superior Court judge, a position from which he resigned after six months because he disliked riding circuit. In 1779 he was appointed attorney general of North Carolina.

In the sharp struggle that took place over the writing of a state constitution, Iredell sided with the more moderate and conservative Whigs who favored as few changes as possible from the old colonial form of government and wanted to see an independent judiciary, a strong executive, and property qualifications for voting. And in the political struggle of the 1780s, Iredell aligned himself with those who favored the enforcement of contracts, opposed debtor relief legislation, and defended the rights of Tories as protected by the Paris Peace Treaty of 1783. He denounced a number of laws adopted in the mid-1780s to confiscate Loyalist property, and in "An Address to the Public" in 1786 expressed his belief in the need for limitations upon the authority of the legislature: "I have no doubt but that the power of the Assembly is limited, and defined by the Constitution. It is the creature of the Constitution." Iredell further elaborated on how unbridled legislative authority could be checked in an August 26, 1787, letter to RICHARD DOBBS SPAIGHT, a delegate to the CONSTITUTIONAL CONVENTION, which contained one of the earliest and clearest theoretical expressions of the doctrine of JUDICIAL REVIEW: "I confess it has ever been my opinion that an act inconsistent with the Constitution was void; and that the judges consistently with their duties, could not carry it into effect. The Constitution appears to me to be a fundamental law, limiting the powers of the legislative, and with which every exercise of those powers must, necessarily, be compared."

Iredell was a warm proponent of the adoption of the United States Constitution in 1787–1788, even though the opposition to it was particularly intense in North Carolina. In fact, North Carolina at first refused to ratify the Constitution, and did not accept the new government until November 1789, eight months after it had begun operations. During the course of the debate over ratification Iredell published a pamphlet entitled "Answers to Mr. [George] Mason's Objections to the New Constitution," which attracted national attention. In February 1790, President GEORGE WASHINGTON, recognizing Iredell to be a firm friend of the central government, appointed him to the United States Supreme Court.

Although Iredell continually complained about the hardships entailed in riding circuit, he performed his duties conscientiously and participated in almost all the important cases of the 1790s. Despite the fact that his various decisions were knowledgeable in the law, intelligent, and forcefully presented, it is not easy to classify Iredell according to the political and intellectual currents of his day. To be sure, as a Federalist he supported ALEXANDER HAMILTON's financial program, JAY'S TREATY, and the ALIEN AND SEDITION ACTS. Moreover, his opinions in *Penhallow v. Doane's Administrators* (1795) and HYLTON V. UNITED STATES (1796) had strong nationalist implications, and in CALDER V. BULL (1798) he reiterated his belief in judicial review. He also argued in behalf of an independent judiciary by taking strong exception to an attempt by Congress to require the Justices of the United States Supreme Court to serve as pension commissioners. But Iredell's experiences with North Carolina politics made him not only aware of but also sensitive to the jealousy of the states for their rights and the popular hostility that existed toward the federal judiciary. He thus dissented when the Supreme Court ruled against the state of Georgia in a suit brought by a citizen of South Carolina in CHISHOLM V. GEORGIA (1793). Iredell argued that the decision would be viewed as a dangerous assault upon the sovereignty of the states. His fears were well founded, for the protests against the decision were so widespread and intense that the ELEVENTH AMENDMENT to the Constitution was quickly adopted to deny jurisdiction to the federal courts in suits brought against a state by the citizens of another state or by foreigners. He also dissented in WARE V. HYLTON (1796) when the High Court declared invalid a Virginia statute of 1777 sequestering pre-Revolutionary debts of British creditors. Although ultimately upheld and enforced, the decision, as

Iredell recognized, was the source of much popular dissatisfaction.

RICHARD E. ELLIS
(1986)

Bibliography

GOEBEL, JULIUS, JR. 1971 *History of the United States Supreme Court: Antecedents and Beginnings to 1801.* New York: Macmillan.

MCREE, GRIFFITH J., ed. 1857 *Life and Correspondence of James Iredell.* New York: D. Appleton.

IRREBUTTABLE PRESUMPTION

Virtually any statutory classification can be seen as an irrebuttable presumption. A law forbidding automobile driving by anyone under sixteen may be described as a conclusive presumption that younger persons are unfit to drive—a presumption that is not universally true. The irrebuttable presumptions DOCTRINE was never applied to strike down an age classification, but its reasoning would have served: the law arguably denied PROCEDURAL DUE PROCESS by denying an individualized hearing on the fitness to drive of a person under sixteen. For a brief season in the mid-1970s, the Supreme Court was fond of this sort of analysis, but the infatuation soon ended.

The doctrine was foreshadowed in Chief Justice HARLAN FISKE STONE's concurrence in SKINNER V. OKLAHOMA (1942), which invalidated an Oklahoma law requiring the STERILIZATION of three-time felons. The Court rested on the EQUAL PROTECTION clause, but Stone argued that the law denied due process by denying a hearing on the inheritability of the defendant's criminal traits. He might have called the law an irrebuttable presumption of the inheritability of criminal traits of three-time felons. We can speculate that Stone thought the sterilization law was an irrational deprivation of liberty, but he was disinclined to revive SUBSTANTIVE DUE PROCESS so soon after the Court had tried to lay that doctrine to rest.

When, a generation later, the Court explicitly invoked the irrebuttable presumptions theory, one contributing factor surely was a similar wish to avoid resting decision on another theory. In the mid-1970s the Court was struggling with the question whether sex, like race, should be characterized as a SUSPECT CLASSIFICATION for purposes of equal protection analysis. (See FRONTIERO V. RICHARDSON, 1973.) In two cases, the Court avoided that issue by resorting to irrebuttable presumptions analysis. *Stanley v. Illinois* (1972) invalidated a law providing that the children of an unwed father became wards of the state upon the death of the mother. The law was attacked on SEX DISCRIMINATION grounds, but the Court escaped that issue, holding that the law violated due process by denying Stanley an individualized hearing on his fitness as a parent. Similarly, in CLEVELAND BOARD OF EDUCATION V. LAFLEUR (1974), a school board insisted that a pregnant teacher take maternity leave of several months before the expected birth of her child, and the Court avoided the sex discrimination issue by calling the law an irrebuttable presumption of unfitness to teach during the months of mandatory leave. The denial of a teacher's right to a hearing on her individual fitness was held to deny procedural due process.

The Court's strongest articulation of the irrebuttable presumptions doctrine came in VLANDIS V. KLINE (1973), which invalidated a state law conclusively presuming that a person who was a nonresident upon entering a state college remained a nonresident (for tuition purposes) throughout his college career. It violated due process to deny resident tuition rates on the basis of this presumption which was "not necessarily or universally true."

The irrebuttable presumptions doctrine was severely criticized both within and outside the Court. It was accurately seen as an equal protection or substantive due process doctrine in disguise, demanding the strictest sort of STRICT SCRUTINY of the necessity of legislative classifications. The Court plainly could not invalidate all classifications resting on factual assumptions "not necessarily or universally true." By 1975, the Court had had enough. In *Weinberger v. Salfi* (1975) the Court considered an antifraud provision of the SOCIAL SECURITY ACT allowing death benefits to a surviving spouse only when the couple had been married nine months before the decedent's death. A widow claimed benefits even though she had been married a shorter time, noting that her husband had died of a sudden, unexpected heart attack. The law was an excellent candidate for irrebuttable presumptions reasoning, but the Court blandly upheld it on grounds of administrative convenience. The whole doctrinal development had run its course in four terms of court.

KENNETH L. KARST
(1986)

Bibliography

NOTE   1974   The Irrebuttable Presumption Doctrine in the Supreme Court. *Harvard Law Review* 87:1534–1556.

IRVIN v. DOWD
366 U.S. 717 (1961)

The Supreme Court ordered a new trial for a convicted mass murderer in Indiana on the ground that extensive pretrial coverage of the case by newspapers and radio had made it impossible for him to receive a FAIR TRIAL, even after one change of VENUE to a nearby county. In his opinion for the Court, Justice TOM C. CLARK noted that two-thirds of the jurors had been familiar with the facts of the case and believed Irvin to be guilty of the crimes. Justice FELIX FRANKFURTER used this occasion for one of his patented denunciations of overzealous reporting in criminal cases.

MICHAEL E. PARRISH
(1986)

IRVINE v. CALIFORNIA
347 U.S. 128 (1954)

California police installed a listening device in a bedroom. Although this action violated fundamental constitutional principles protecting personal security, the Supreme Court held that under WOLF V. COLORADO (1949) the unconstitutionally obtained EVIDENCE could be used; the bedroom microphone did not sufficiently "shock the conscience," under ROCHIN V. CALIFORNIA (1952), to warrant exclusion.

HERMAN SCHWARTZ
(1986)

ISLAND TREES BOARD OF EDUCATION v. PICO

See: *Board of Education v. Pico*

ITEM VETO

See: Line-Item Veto

JACKSON, ANDREW
(1767–1845)

Andrew Jackson, the seventh President of the United States, was the son of Irish immigrant parents who had settled in the South Carolina backcountry. Drifting to North Carolina after the Revolutionary war, he read enough law to gain admission to the bar. When only twenty-one he was appointed prosecuting attorney for the Western District at Nashville. There he built a flourishing practice, married, and became a leading planter-aristocrat. In 1796 he was elected a delegate to the CONSTITUTIONAL CONVENTION of Tennessee, then was chosen the new state's first representative in Congress. His service there was brief and undistinguished; it was followed by appointment to the Tennessee Superior Court, where he sat for six years, retiring in 1804. In the factional brawls of Tennessee politics Jackson won a reputation for hot-blooded courage. He killed an adversary in a celebrated duel and barely escaped with his own life in another.

Jackson rose to national fame during the War of 1812. It was mainly an Indian war on the southwest frontier. As major general of the Tennessee militia, Jackson defeated the Creeks and then imposed a humiliating treaty. In 1814 he was commissioned major general in the United States Army and was entrusted with the defense of the Gulf country from Mobile to New Orleans. He defeated the British in the Battle of New Orleans, the last and the greatest victory of the war; and although it occurred after the peace treaty was signed, the victory made Jackson a national hero. Criticized by a local citizen for refusing to lift martial law after the battle, Jackson arrested him; and when a federal judge, Dominick Hall, issued a writ of HA-BEAS CORPUS for the citizen, Jackson arrested the judge as well. Upon his release Judge Hall hauled the errant general into court. Jackson pleaded "the law of necessity" in his defense and got off with a thousand dollar fine. He paid, yet bristled at the alleged injustice until finally, in 1844 a Democratic Congress returned the fine with interest.

Jackson had a more serious scrape with the law in 1818. In command of an army ordered to suppress Indian disturbances along the Spanish border, he invaded Florida, executed two British subjects for stirring up the Seminoles, and captured Pensacola together with other Spanish posts. President JAMES MONROE disavowed the general's conquest, said it was unauthorized, and ordered surrender of the posts. Two cabinet officers wished to punish Jackson. Not only had he violated orders, he had violated the Constitution by making war on Spain, a power reserved to Congress. When Congress convened, a sensational month-long debate occurred in the House of Representatives on resolutions condemning Jackson for his behavior and recommending legislation to prohibit invasion of foreign territory without the consent of Congress except in direct pursuit of a defeated enemy. The resolutions failed. Jackson insisted he had acted within the broad confines of his orders. Monroe, while admitting none of this, conceded that Jackson had acted honorably on his own responsibility.

In 1822 the Tennessee legislature nominated Jackson for President. At first no one took the nomination seriously; it was obviously a stratagem of the General's political friends to avail themselves of his popularity in order to regain control of the state government. But the candidacy of "the military hero" caught fire in 1824. Jackson

Bibliography

SCHIFFMAN, IRVING   1970   Escaping the Shroud of Anonymity: Justice Howell Edmunds Jackson and the Income Tax Case. *Tennessee Law Review* 37:334–348.

JACKSON, ROBERT H.
(1892–1954)

The orderly, middle-class world of Jamestown, New York, the economic calamity of the Great Depression, and the horrors of Nazi Germany—these were the crucial experiences that shaped the jurisprudence of Robert Houghwout Jackson, the only Supreme Court Justice to serve both as SOLICITOR GENERAL and ATTORNEY GENERAL of the United States, and the last to learn his law initially through the old-fashioned apprentice method.

Appointed to the Court by FRANKLIN D. ROOSEVELT in 1941 and facing the most important constitutional issues of the post-Depression era—the scope of federal economic management and the nationalization of the BILL OF RIGHTS—Jackson helped to accelerate the former but resisted the latter. In alliance with his close friend and colleague FELIX FRANKFURTER, he often found himself locked in combat between 1941 and 1954 with Justices HUGO L. BLACK and WILLIAM O. DOUGLAS, the ideological leaders of the Court's liberal block.

Few Justices in the Court's history articulated a more robust version of economic nationalism than Justice Jackson who, despite his small-town heritage and solicitude for independent entrepreneurship, supported consistently the expansion of federal ECONOMIC REGULATION and the growth of an integrated national marketplace, which soon became dominated by giant CORPORATIONS. Jackson wrote a sweeping validation of congressional authority under the COMMERCE CLAUSE in WICKARD V. FILBURN (1942), and he also used that provision absent federal law in *H. P. Hood & Sons v. DuMond* (1949) to strike down state regulations that insulated local economic activities from the rigors of interstate competition.

The crisis of the Great Depression convinced Jackson of the dangers of both *laissez-faire* and economic Balkanization. His later confrontation with Nazism when he served as chief American prosecutor at Nuremberg persuaded him of the dangers posed to human freedom by the growth of a monolithic police state. His firm commitment to economic nationalism never wavered, except near the end of his life in situations where the federal government began to employ the COMMERCE CLAUSE in an effort to regulate more than traditional economic activities. A year before his death, for example, Jackson narrowly construed a federal anticrime statute, voting to sustain the dismissal of INDICTMENTS for failure to register as dealers in gambling machines in *United States v. Five Gambling Devices* (1953). In the course of making their arrests in the case, FBI agents had stormed into a Tennessee country club and seized slot machines that were not shown to have been transported in interstate commerce. Jackson read into the statute a requirement of such a showing.

Jackson's fears of expanded federal police controls became so pronounced that he resisted efforts to attack RACIAL DISCRIMINATION by means of the criminal and civil provisions of the Reconstruction-era CIVIL RIGHTS ACTS, especially where these efforts threatened to undermine the autonomy of local law enforcement officials, such as SCREWS V. UNITED STATES (1945) and *Collins v. Hardyman* (1951). He also opposed federal judicial intervention under the FOURTEENTH AMENDMENT to correct local abuses in the administration of criminal justice. Although he interpreted the FOURTH AMENDMENT strictly as to federal SEARCHES AND SEIZURES, as in his dissent in BRINEGAR V. UNITED STATES (1949), he refused to extend the EXCLUSIONARY RULE to state criminal prosecutions, and he exhibited broad toleration for local police practices that shocked other members of the Court. "Local excesses or invasions of liberty," he wrote, "are more amenable to political correction," a point of view which no doubt surprised Mississippi Negroes and many state criminal suspects who endured the third degree. Even Frankfurter broke with Jackson on these issues, for example, in IRVINE V. CALIFORNIA (1954).

Jackson's small-town roots and his fear of mass-based political movements such as Nazism colored his views of other CIVIL LIBERTIES issues as well. He often defended the lone individual against the repressive machinery of the state, but he thoroughly distrusted people in groups, especially well-organized, zealous minorities who threatened to disrupt what Jackson regarded as the community's peace, stability, and proper order. The Constitution, he believed, prohibited West Virginia officials from imposing a mandatory flag salute observance on the children of Jehovah's Witnesses. (See FLAG SALUTE CASES.) The federal government, likewise, could not convict without a finding of criminal intent, condemn for TREASON without substantial proof, or hold a hapless ALIEN indefinitely on Ellis Island without charging him with a specific crime. "This man, who seems to have led a life of unrelieved insignificance," he wrote angrily, in SHAUGHNESSY V. UNITED STATES EX REL. MEZEI (1953) (dissenting opinion), "must have been astonished to find himself suddenly putting the Government of the United States in such fear that it was afraid to tell him why it was afraid of him. . . . No one can make me believe that we are that far gone."

Yet Jackson did not believe that the Constitution gave cadres of Jehovah's Witnesses the right to distribute their religious literature in defiance of local ordinances prohibiting house-to-house canvassing and ringing doorbells. "I doubt if only the slothfully ignorant wish repose in their homes," he wrote sarcastically in *Martin v. City of Struthers* (1943), responding to Justice Black's opinion upholding the Witnesses' claim, "or that the forefathers intended to open the door to such forced "enlightenment' as we have here." A similar loathing for collective political behavior informed his attitude toward the Communist party which, like the Nazi organizations condemned at Nuremberg, he equated with a conspiracy against the social order in a concurring opinion in *Dennis v. United States* (1951).

Jackson's belief in the fragility of the political system also made him a conservative on most FREEDOM OF SPEECH issues, witness his dissenting opinion in KUNZ V. NEW YORK (1950). He objected, for instance, to the specific law upheld in the famous Illinois GROUP LIBEL case, BEAUHARNAIS V. ILLINOIS (1952), but he acknowledged the state's "commendable desire to reduce sinister abuses of our freedom of expression—abuses which I have had occasion to learn can tear society apart, brutalize its dominant elements, and persecute, even to extermination, its minorities."

Witty, combative, and gifted with an eloquent prose style, Jackson remained a person of many paradoxes: the rugged individualist who helped to fashion the New Deal's welfare state; the two-fisted prosecutor who wished to be the disinterested judge; and the economic nationalist who distrusted the growth of centralized, bureaucratic authority.

MICHAEL E. PARRISH
(1986)

Bibliography

GERHART, EUGENE C. 1958 *America's Advocate: Robert H. Jackson.* Indianapolis: Bobbs-Merrill.

JAFFE, LOUIS L. 1955 Mr. Justice Jackson. *Harvard Law Review* 68:940–998.

WHITE, G. EDWARD 1976 The Dilemmas of Robert Jackson. Pages 230–250 in White, *The American Judicial Tradition: Profiles of Leading American Judges.* New York: Oxford University Press.

JACKSON v. GEORGIA

See: Capital Punishment Cases of 1972

JACKSON v. METROPOLITAN EDISON CO.
419 U.S. 345 (1974)

In the WARREN COURT years, the STATE ACTION doctrine was progressively weakened as a limitation on the FOURTEENTH AMENDMENT; more and more "private" conduct fell under the Amendment's reach. The *Jackson* decision illustrates how the BURGER COURT called a halt to this trend, limiting the substantive scope of the Amendment by giving new life to the state action limitation.

Metropolitan Edison turned off Jackson's supply of electricity, asserting that she had not paid her bill. She sued for damages and injunctive relief under federal CIVIL RIGHTS laws, claiming PROCEDURAL DUE PROCESS rights to NOTICE, hearing, and an opportunity to pay any amounts due the company. The lower courts denied relief, holding that the company's conduct did not amount to state action. The Supreme Court affirmed, 6–3, in an opinion by Justice WILLIAM H. REHNQUIST, systematically rejecting a series of arguments supporting the contention that state action was present in the case.

The fact of state regulation was held insufficient to constitute state action. As in MOOSE LODGE NO. 107 V. IRVIS (1972), there was no showing of a "close nexus" between the company's no-hearing policy and the state. The approval by the state's public utilities commission of the company's tariff, stating the right to terminate service for nonpayment, was held insufficient to demonstrate explicit state approval of the no-hearing policy. Where *Moose Lodge* had relied on the absence of a monopoly under a state liquor license, *Jackson* characterized *Moose Lodge* as a near-monopoly case and said there was no showing of a connection between the utility's monopoly status and its no-hearing policy. Finally, the Court rejected the notion that Metropolitan Edison was performing a "public function" by supplying electricity, saying there had been no delegation to the company of a power "traditionally associated with sovereignty." The latter comment looked forward to the Court's decision in FLAGG BROS., INC. V. BROOKS (1978).

Justice WILLIAM J. BRENNAN dissented without reaching the merits. Justices WILLIAM O. DOUGLAS and THURGOOD MARSHALL dissented on the merits, pointing out how the majority was departing from the teaching of the Warren Court—something that Justice Rehnquist likely did not need to have explained. *Jackson* did more than reverse currents in the various individual streams of state action DOCTRINE (public functions, monopolies, state encouragement). By taking up each of these arguments separately and rejecting them one by one, the Court also implicitly abandoned the approach of BURTON V. WILMINGTON PARKING AUTHORITY (1961), which had called for determining state action questions by looking at the totality of circumstances in a particular case.

KENNETH L. KARST
(1986)

JACKSONIANISM

The election of ANDREW JACKSON to the presidency in 1828 was only the second time since the adoption of the Constitution that the "out" party came to power. The first occurred in 1800 with the election of THOMAS JEFFERSON, who at that time opted for a course of action that stressed moderation and reconciliation. Jefferson revised several of the government's policies and changed many of its personnel, but he refused to go along with any assault on the Constitution itself or on major FEDERALIST enactments. If anything, through the LOUISIANA PURCHASE TREATY and the EMBARGO ACTS of 1807–1809, he increased the powers of the national government. Jackson took a very different approach. He favored amendment of the Constitution and other policies to make the central government more amenable to popular control. Jackson also championed a strict interpretation of the Constitution and the decentralization of authority, stressing the close links between the will of the people, majority rule, and STATES' RIGHTS. He also was critical of the broad powers of interpretation that the Supreme Court had arrogated to itself over the preceding quarter-century.

Although the campaign of 1828 was particularly scurrilous, with much of it centered on the candidates' personalities, it also involved fundamental constitutional and even ideological considerations. Jackson's opponent, JOHN QUINCY ADAMS, had organized his whole administration and run for reelection on a platform of the AMERICAN SYSTEM— a federal program of INTERNAL IMPROVEMENTS, a high protective tariff, and the second BANK OF THE UNITED STATES— which was predicated upon a loose interpretation of the Constitution and the need for a strong and active national government. These views were a major issue in the election of 1828, and opposition to them explains much of the support Jackson received in the South, the Old West, and the Middle Atlantic states, from people who had strong emotional and ideological ties to ANTIFEDERALISM and Old Republicanism. This group—which included THOMAS HART BENTON, Amos Kendall, Silas Wright, Francis Preston Blair, NATHANIEL MACON, and Thomas Ritchie—was strongly committed to the view of the origin and nature of the Union that had been articulated in the VIRGINIA AND KENTUCKY RESOLUTIONS of 1798–1799. These resolutions viewed the Constitution as the product of a compact between the different states and asserted that the federal government was one of clearly defined and specifically delegated and limited powers. The resolutions denied that the Supreme Court was either the exclusive or final arbiter of constitutional questions and argued instead that the states should act as sentinels to watch over the activities of the federal government. They believed that these principles had been validated by Jefferson's election in 1800, but that they had been abandoned as the country pursued wealth and power between 1801 and 1828. Jackson's most avid supporters wanted him to reverse this development

and to return the country to plain republican principles, and they justified this by invoking the "Spirit of '98."

Jackson did not disappoint them. He began by advocating the principle of rotation of office for federal officeholders. This had been a popular constitutional concept in the 1780s and had found expression in the ARTICLES OF CONFEDERATION, the PENNSYLVANIA CONSTITUTION OF 1776, and a number of other STATE CONSTITUTIONS. The failure to include it in the United States Constitution had been a major concern of the Antifederalists, and Jackson's espousal of it in regard to presidential appointments was considered by his opponents to be a direct assault on the Constitution. Throughout his first administration Jackson also urged that the Constitution be amended to eliminate the ELECTORAL COLLEGE, limit the tenure of the President and vice-president to a single term of four or six years, provide for the popular election of senators and members of the federal judiciary, and give self-government to the DISTRICT OF COLUMBIA. He and most of his closest advisers also favored a repeal of section 25 of the JUDICIARY ACT OF 1789.

But these proposals were never endorsed by Congress, which was at odds with Jackson throughout most of his two terms in office. As a consequence, Jackson was forced to enunciate his views of the Constitution through his various annual addresses, veto messages, proclamations, policy decisions, and appointments. In these ways, Jackson made clear his opposition to a federal program of internal improvements on both constitutional and policy grounds. He also vetoed the bill to recharter the second Bank of the United States, in large part because its activities impinged on the rights of the states. Moreover, in exercising this veto and in implementing his policy toward AMERICAN INDIANS, he took direct issue with the nationalist claim that the Supreme Court was the exclusive or final arbiter in disputes between the federal and state governments. Jackson also appointed five Justices to the Supreme Court— JOHN MCLEAN, HENRY BALDWIN, JAMES M. WAYNE, PHILIP P. BARBOUR, and ROGER BROOKE TANEY as CHIEF JUSTICE—who were unsympathetic to the BROAD CONSTRUCTION and the nationalist decisions of the MARSHALL COURT.

Although deeply committed to the concept of states' rights, the Jacksonians had no sympathy for the doctrine of NULLIFICATION, promulgated by JOHN C. CALHOUN and South Carolina, who believed that the protective tariffs of 1828 and 1832 were unconstitutional and who were concerned with protecting the institution of SLAVERY from outside interference. The Jacksonians, for their part, advocated states' rights as a way of achieving majority rule, while the proslavery interests espoused the doctrine of states' rights as a way of protecting the interests of a minority. The difference can be seen most clearly in the two groups' positions on the issues of when and by whom the Constitution should be amended. The Jacksonians, consistent with their faith in majority rule, took upon themselves the burden of obtaining amendments to the Constitution in order to make the federal government more directly responsive to the will of the people and to limit and clarify the powers of the Supreme Court. Such a course would require the approval of two-thirds of both houses of Congress and three-quarters of the states. Historically, these have been difficult majorities to obtain, and the Jacksonians were never successful. Proslavery interests, on the other hand, argued during the nullification crisis that a single state had a right to nullify federal law and that, in the event of nullification, the law's proponents would have the responsibility of gaining the requisite majorities to alter the Constitution. This argument shifted in a decisive way the burden of obtaining the amendment.

Jacksonians also opposed Calhoun's version of the states' rights doctrine because they believed it threatened the existence of the Union. The right of states to secede from the Union had not traditionally been part of the concept of states' rights. The Jacksonian commitment to the rights of the states in no way precluded a belief that the Union was perpetual or that within its properly limited sphere of power (like the making of tariff laws) the federal government was supreme. The Jacksonians rejected the nullifiers' claim that SECESSION was a legal or constitutional right that could be peacefully exercised. Instead, they insisted it was only a natural or revolutionary right that had to be fought for and could be suppressed.

After Jackson left office, the Jacksonian interpretation of the Constitution dominated the administrations of three other Presidents. MARTIN VAN BUREN was a product of the Virginia-New York alliance that played such a dominant role in the politics of the early Republic and that had its roots in the strong Antifederalist tradition in both these states. As President, Van Buren was a strong advocate of states' rights, opposed a federal program of internal improvements, and implemented the independent treasury system, which divorced banking from the federal government. JAMES K. POLK was also a doctrinaire Jacksonian. He prevented the creation of a third Bank of the United States, reinstated the independent treasury system, and further circumscribed federal spending on internal improvements. FRANKLIN PIERCE also viewed the world from a Jacksonian perspective. He had a great respect for states' rights and opposed the federal government's involvement in the ECONOMY.

The Jacksonians were never proslavery in the sense that Calhoun and other southerners were, but they shared an antipathy to abolitionists, who wanted the federal government to move against the "peculiar institution." In fact, the Jacksonians never developed an effective position on the slavery question—a failure that, as much as anything else, explains the lack of success of two other Presidents who had roots in Jacksonianism, JAMES BUCHANAN and ANDREW JOHNSON.

Nonetheless, while the Jacksonian constitutional position did not lead to any basic changes in the Constitution itself and its orientation toward states' rights and strict interpretation was overturned by the extreme nationalist thrust of the CIVIL WAR, it did dominate much of American politics in the second third of the nineteenth century.

RICHARD E. ELLIS
(1992)

Bibliography

ELLIS, RICHARD E.   1987   The Union at Risk: Jacksonian Democracy, States' Rights, and the Nullification Crisis. New York: Oxford University Press.

REMINI, ROBERT V.   1988   The Legacy of Andrew Jackson: Essays on Democracy, Indian Removal, and Slavery. Baton Rouge: Louisiana State University Press.

VAN DEUSEN, GLYNDON G.   1959   The Jacksonian Era, 1828–1848. New York: Harper & Row.

JACKSON'S PROCLAMATION TO THE PEOPLE OF SOUTH CAROLINA
(December 10, 1832)

On November 24, 1832, a state convention adopted the SOUTH CAROLINA ORDINANCE OF NULLIFICATION declaring that the federal tariff acts of 1828 and 1832 were "null, void, and no law, nor binding upon this State, its officers or citizens." Sixteen days later President ANDREW JACKSON responded with a proclamation directed at the people of South Carolina, rather than at the state government. Jackson declared the NULLIFICATION ordinance "incompatible with the existence of the Union, contradicted expressly by the letter of the Constitution, unauthorized by its spirit, inconsistent with every principle on which it was founded, and destructive of the great object for which it was formed." After a detailed and withering analysis of the legality and constitutionality of the ordinance, Jackson turned to the question of SECESSION, which South Carolina threatened if the tariffs were enforced in that state. Jackson warned the people of South Carolina that "Disunion by armed force is TREASON " and that on their heads "may fall the punishment" for that crime. Congress subsequently modified the tariffs but also passed the FORCE ACT authorizing the use of military power to enforce federal laws. South Carolina then repealed its Nullification Ordinance, but in a final flurry of defiance passed an ordinance purporting to nullify the Force Act.

PAUL FINKELMAN
(1986)

Bibliography

FREEHLING, WILLIAM W.   1965   *Prelude to Civil War: The Nullification Controversy in South Carolina, 1816–1836.* New York: Harper & Row.

JACKSON'S VETO OF THE BANK OF THE UNITED STATES BILL
(July 10, 1832)

The first Bank of the United States was chartered in 1791 despite Jeffersonian opposition. In 1811 its charter expired, but in 1815 the bank was rechartered, with little opposition, as the Second Bank of the United States. The Supreme Court in MCCULLOCH V. MARYLAND (1819) upheld the constitutionality of the bank. In 1832 Congress extended the charter of the Second Bank. For a variety of reasons President ANDREW JACKSON opposed the extension. In his veto message Jackson asserted, more emphatically than previous Presidents, the necessity of exercising the presidential VETO POWER on constitutional grounds, rather than on grounds of policy or expediency. Jackson rejected *McCulloch,* arguing that "Mere PRECEDENT is a dangerous source of authority," which should not decide "questions of constitutional power except where the acquiescence of the people and the States can be considered as well settled." Furthermore, Jackson believed Supreme Court opinions "ought not to control the coordinate authorities of this Government." Rather, each branch of the government must "be guided by its own opinion of the Constitution" because a public official swears to support the Constitution "as he understands it, and not as it is understood by others." Jackson argued that the Bank was neither a necessary nor a proper subject for congressional legislation, and so he felt constitutionally obligated to veto the bill.

PAUL FINKELMAN
(1986)

Bibliography

REMINI, ROBERT V.   1967   *Andrew Jackson and the Bank War: A Study in the Growth of Presidential Power.* Norton Essays in American History. New York: Norton.

JACOBELLIS v. OHIO
378 U.S. 184 (1964)

The Supreme Court reversed Jacobellis's conviction for possessing and exhibiting an obscene motion picture, finding the movie not obscene under ROTH V. UNITED STATES (1957). Justice WILLIAM J. BRENNAN's plurality opinion announced two significant constitutional developments and presaged a third. First, in any case raising the issue whether a work was obscene, the Court would determine independently whether the material was constitutionally protected. Second, in judging the material's appeal to prurient interests against "contemporary community standards," courts were to apply a national standard, not the standards of the particular local community from which the case arose. Finally, purporting to apply standards based on *Roth* and foreshadowing his opinion in MEMOIRS V. MASSACHUSETTS (1965), Brennan noted that a work could not be proscribed unless it was "utterly' without social importance."

Jacobellis is best known, however, for Justice POTTER J. STEWART's concurring opinion. Contending that only hard-core pornography constitutionally could be proscribed, Stewart declined to define the material that term included, stating only, "I know it when I see it."

KIM MCLANE WARDLAW
(1986)

JACOBS, IN RE
98 N.Y. 98 (1885)

This exceptionally influential decision, cited hundreds of times by state and federal courts, reflected laissez-faire principles against government regulation of the economy. New York in 1884 enacted a statute to improve the public health by penalizing the manufacture of cigars on the same floor of tenement houses where people lived. Jacobs, a tenement occupant prosecuted under the statute, somehow retained WILLIAM M. EVARTS, "the Prince of the American Bar," whose powerful defense of free enterprise convinced the New York Court of Appeals to decide unanimously against the constitutionality of the regulation. Judge Robert Earl, drawing heavily on Evarts's argument, larded his opinion with polemics against state infringement on liberty and property conducted under the pretext of the POLICE POWER. The constitutional basis of the opinion is not clear because Earl stopped short of invoking the DOCTRINE OF FREEDOM OF CONTRACT, but the rhetoric of SUBSTANTIVE DUE PROCESS as a limitation on LEGISLATIVE POWER to regulate the economy stands out. "Under the mere guise of police regulations," Earl said, "personal rights and private property cannot be arbitrarily invaded," and JUDICIAL REVIEW determines whether the legislative power exceeded the limits. The court found that the state plainly had not passed a health law but had trampled personal liberty.

LEONARD W. LEVY
(1986)

JACOBSON v. MASSACHUSETTS
197 U.S. 11 (1905)

A Massachusetts statute required VACCINATION of a town's inhabitants when health authorities so ordered. For the Supreme Court, Justice JOHN MARSHALL HARLAN concluded the regulation was within the POLICE POWER of the commonwealth and violated no federal constitutional right.

The FIRST AMENDMENT was not then interpreted to apply to the states. Jacobson relied on the liberty guaranteed by the FOURTEENTH AMENDMENT'S DUE PROCESS clause, although his objection to vaccination was religious. Harlan concluded that SUBSTANTIVE DUE PROCESS implied no absolute right to control one's body. Justices DAVID BREWER and RUFUS PECKHAM dissented.

RICHARD E. MORGAN
(1986)

JAMES v. BOWMAN
190 U.S. 127 (1903)

A provision of the FORCE ACTS, passed to protect FIFTEENTH AMENDMENT guarantees, forbade bribery or intimidation to prevent the exercise of VOTING RIGHTS. Bowman, a private citizen, was indicted for preventing several blacks from voting in a Kentucky congressional election. Justice DAVID BREWER for a 6–2 Supreme Court, relying mainly on UNITED STATES V. REESE (1876), declared that the amendment applied to abridgments of the right to vote by the federal government or by a state on account of race; it did not reach private actions. A congressional measure purporting to punish "purely individual action," said Brewer, could not be sustained as an enforcement of the Fifteenth Amendment's prohibition against STATE ACTION abridging the right to vote on account of race. Further, the statute was not limited to RACIAL DISCRIMINATION denying the right to vote. Congress had not relied on its power under Article I to regulate federal elections.

DAVID GORDON
(1986)

JAMES v. VALTIERRA
402 U.S. 137 (1971)

The California state constitution required voter approval in a local REFERENDUM for the building of public low-rent housing projects. The Supreme Court, 5–3, sustained this requirement against an EQUAL PROTECTION attack.

Justice HUGO L. BLACK wrote for the majority. It was not the business of the courts to analyze governmental structures to see whether they disadvantaged one group or an-

other. In any case, advocates of low-rent housing had not been singled out for disadvantage; California required referenda for the adoption of a number of kinds of legislation. Black distinguished HUNTER V. ERICKSON (1969), which had struck down a similar referendum requirement imposed on fair housing laws. Here no RACIAL DISCRIMINATION was shown.

Justice THURGOOD MARSHALL, for the dissenters, argued that discrimination "between 'rich' and 'poor' as such" was forbidden, quoting Justice JOHN MARSHALL HARLAN'S dissent in DOUGLAS V. CALIFORNIA (1963). "[S]ingling out the poor to bear a burden not placed on any other class of citizens tramples the values that the FOURTEENTH AMENDMENT was designed to protect."

KENNETH L. KARST
(1986)

(SEE ALSO: *Indigent; Wealth Discrimination.*)

JAPANESE AMERICAN CASES
Hirabayashi v. United States
320 U.S. 81 (1943)
Korematsu v. United States
323 U.S. 214 (1944)
Ex parte Endo
323 U.S. 283 (1944)

For more than a month after the Japanese attack on Pearl Harbor in December 1941, no one of high authority in the armed services or elsewhere in the national government suggested seriously that persons of Japanese ancestry should be moved away from the West Coast. The Army's historian wrote that in February and March of 1942 the military estimates were that "there was no real threat of a Japanese invasion" of the area. Yet by March 1942 a program was fully underway to remove about 120,000 persons from their West Coast homes and jobs and place them in internment camps in the interior of the country. About 70,000 of these people were citizens of the United States; two out of every five people sent to the camps were under the age of fifteen or over fifty. All were imprisoned for an indefinite time without any individualized determination of grounds for suspicion of disloyalty, let alone charges of unlawful conduct, to be held in custody until their loyalty might be determined. (See PREVENTATIVE DETENTION.) The basis for their imprisonment was a single common trait—their Japanese ancestry.

The military services came to discover the "military necessity" of relocating the Japanese Americans in response to pressure from the West Coast congressional delegations and from other political leaders in the region—including, to his later regret, EARL WARREN, then attorney general of California. These politicians were responding, in turn, to a clamor from certain newspapers and labor unions, along with (as U.S. Attorney General FRANCIS BIDDLE later listed them) "the American Legion, the California Joint Immigration Committee, the Native Sons and Daughters of the Golden West, the Western Growers Protective Association, the California Farm Bureau Federation [and] the Chamber of Commerce of Los Angeles." The groups' campaign was aided by newspaper accounts of American military defeats and Japanese atrocities in the early days of the war, and by false reports of sabotage at Pearl Harbor. Anti-Asian racism, long a feature of California, now had a focus. In Hawaii, which *had* been attacked, no evacuation was proposed; persons of Japanese ancestry constituted almost one third of that territory's population. On the West Coast, Japanese Americans barely exceeded one percent of the population; thus, no political force resisted the mixture of fear, racism, and greed. "The Japanese race is an enemy race," said General John DeWitt in his official report to the War Department. Once the Army urged wholesale evacuation, the opposition of Biddle and the Justice Department was unavailing. President FRANKLIN D. ROOSEVELT sided with the Army, and the evacuation began.

The program, first established by EXECUTIVE ORDER 9066 and then partly ratified by Congress, called for three measures in "military areas"—that is, the entire West Coast. First, persons of Japanese descent were placed under curfew at home from 8:00 p.m. to 6:00 a.m. Second, they would be excluded from "military areas" upon military order. Third, they would be "relocated" in internment camps until their "loyalty" could be determined. The loyalty-determining process was leisurely; as late as the spring of 1945 some 70,000 persons remained in the camps.

The three parts of the program, all of which raised serious constitutional problems, were considered separately by the Supreme Court in three cases: *Hirabayashi v. United States* (1943), *Korematsu v. United States* (1944), and *Ex Parte Endo* (1944).

The *Hirabayashi* case offered the Court a chance to rule on the validity of both the curfew and the exclusion orders. A young American citizen was charged with violating the curfew and refusing to report to a control station to be evacuated from Seattle, where he lived. He was convicted on both counts, and sentenced to three months of imprisonment. In June 1943 the Supreme Court unanimously upheld the curfew violation conviction, and said that it need not consider the validity of the exclusion order, because the two sentences were to run concurrently.

Not until December 1944 did the Court reach the other parts of the evacuation program. In *Korematsu*, the Court divided 6–3 in upholding an order excluding an American

citizen from his home town, San Leandro, California. On the same day, the Court in *Endo* avoided deciding on the constitutional validity of internment. Instead, it concluded that the act of Congress ratifying the evacuation program had not authorized prolonged detention of a citizen whose loyalty was conceded. The Court assumed that some brief detention was implicitly authorized as an incident of an exclusion program aimed at preventing espionage and sabotage. Any further detention would have to rest on an assumption the Court was unwilling to make: that citizens were being detained because of their ancestry, in response to community hostility. Justice OWEN ROBERTS, concurring in the result, found congressional authority for internment in the appropriation of funds to operate the camps. Reaching the constitutional issues the majority had avoided, he concluded the Endo's detention violated "the guarantees of the BILL OF RIGHTS . . . and especially the guarantee of DUE PROCESS OF LAW."

The Japanese American cases have made two positive contributions to the development of egalitarian constitutional doctrine. The *Hirabayashi* and *Korematsu* opinions were links in a chain of precedent leading to the Supreme Court's recognition that the Fifth Amendment's due process clause contains a guarantee of equal protection as a substantive limit on the conduct of the national government. (See BOLLING V. SHARPE; EQUAL PROTECTION OF THE LAWS.) And *Korematsu* first announced the principle that legal restrictions on the civil rights of a racial group are "suspect." (See SUSPECT CLASSIFICATIONS.) Even so, these decisions deserve Eugene Rostow's epithet: "a disaster." The Supreme Court's evasion of issues, its refusal to examine the factual assumptions underlying the "military necessity" of evacuation—in short, its failures to perform as a court—are easier to forgive than to excuse. There is little comfort in the fact that the Court's *Hirabayashi* and *Korematsu* opinions were authored by Justices celebrated as civil libertarians.

Chief Justice HARLAN FISKE STONE wrote for a unanimous Court in *Hirabayashi*, approaching the validity of the curfew not so much as a question about the liberties of a citizen but as a question about congressional power. The WAR POWERS, of course, are far-reaching; they include, as Justices often repeat, "the power to wage war successfully." Thus, for Stone, the only issue before the Court was whether there was "a RATIONAL BASIS" for concluding that the curfew was necessary to protect the country against espionage and sabotage in aid of a threatened invasion. As to that necessity, the Chief Justice said: "We cannot close our eyes to the fact, demonstrated by experience, that in time of war residents having ethnic affiliations with an invading enemy may be a greater source of danger than those of a different ancestry." There was no effort to examine into the likelihood of invasion, or to specify what experience demonstrated the "fact" assumed. The one hard fact was that no sabotage or espionage had been committed by persons of Japanese ancestry at the time of the Hawaii attack or afterward. (California's Attorney General Warren had been equal to that challenge, however: " . . . that is the most ominous sign in our whole situation. It convinces me more than perhaps any other factor that the sabotage we are to get, the fifth column activities that we are to get, are timed just like Pearl Harbor was timed. . . .")

Another question remained: Why impose wholesale restrictions on persons of Japanese ancestry, when Germans and Italians were being investigated individually? Here the Court took refuge in a presumption: "We cannot say that the war-making branches of the Government did not have ground for believing that in a critical hour [disloyal] persons could not readily be isolated and separately dealt with. . . ." This is the classical language of "rational basis" review; government officials have made a factual determination, and a court "cannot say" they are mistaken. That standard of review serves well enough to test the reasonableness of a congressional conclusion that some type of activity substantially affects INTERSTATE COMMERCE. It is utterly inappropriate to test the justification for selectively imposing restrictions on a racial minority.

Justice HUGO L. BLACK began his opinion for the majority in Korematsu by recognizing this difference. Racial distinctions, he said, were "immediately suspect," and must be subjected to "the most rigid scrutiny." Following that pronouncement, however, all judicial scrutiny of the racial discrimination at hand was abandoned. The opinion simply quoted the "We cannot say" passage from the Hirabayashi opinion; stated, uncritically, the conclusions of the military authorities; observed that "war is an aggregation of hardships"; and—unkindest cut—concluded that "Citizenship has its responsibilities as well as its privileges."

Justice Roberts, dissenting, argued that Korematsu had been subjected to conflicting orders to leave the military area and to stay put, a plain due process violation. It was left to Justice FRANK MURPHY—in his finest hour—to expose the absence of imperial clothing. He demonstrated how the "military" judgment of the necessity for evacuation had departed from subjects in which Army officers were expert and had embarked on breathtaking sociological generalization: the Japanese American community were "a large, unassimilated, tightly knit racial group, bound to an enemy nation by strong ties of race, culture, custom and religion" (quoting General DeWitt).

Decades later, Peter Irons discovered in government archives irrefutable evidence that government officers had deliberately misled the Supreme Court on questions directly related to the claim of military necessity for the evacuations. In response to this evidence, in the mid-1980s federal district courts set aside the convictions of

Gordon Hirabayashi, Fred Korematsu, and Minoru Yasui (whose conviction had been affirmed along with Hirabayashi's).

Justice ROBERT H. JACKSON, dissenting in Korematsu, said, in effect: There is nothing courts can do to provide justice in this case, or in any case in which the military and the President are determined to take action in wartime; yet we should not lend our approval to this action, lest we create a precedent for similar extraconstitutional action in the future. Of all the oft-noted ironies of the Japanese American cases, this topsy-turvy prediction may be the most ironic of all. Korematsu as a judicial precedent has turned out to provide a strong doctrinal foundation for the Supreme Court's vigorous defense of racial equality in the years since mid-century. The disaster of the Japanese American cases was not doctrinal. It was instead the betrayal of justice there and then for Gordon Hirabayashi, Fred Korematsu, Minoru Yasui, and some 120,000 other individuals—and thus for us all.

KENNETH L. KARST
(1986)

(SEE ALSO: World War II.)

Bibliography
GRODZINS, MORTON 1949 Americans Betrayed: Politics and the Japanese Evacuation. Chicago: University of Chicago Press.
IRONS, PETER 1983 Justice at War. New York: Oxford University Press.
ROSTOW, EUGENE V. 1949 The Japanese American Cases—A Disaster. Yale Law Journal 54:489–533.

JAPANESE AMERICAN RELOCATION

See: Executive Order 9066 and Public Law 503

JAY, JOHN
(1745–1829)

John Jay was a major figure during the Revolutionary era. Born into one of colonial New York's leading families, he was aristocratic in appearance, well educated, and a hard worker with a precise and orderly mind. He graduated from King's College in 1764, was admitted to the bar four years later, and soon had a prosperous practice. He early took an interest in the constitutional debate between England and the American colonies; although uneasy about the radical implication of some of the resistance to imperial policies in the 1770s, he nevertheless was a firm patriot. He served as a member of the New York Committee of Correspondence and in the Provincial Congress, as well as in the first and second Continental Congresses in Philadelphia. In 1776 he returned to New York to help draft a state constitution (1777) and to become New York's first chief justice. His major interests, however, lay in the field of diplomacy: he became the United States Minister to Spain in 1779 and later joined BENJAMIN FRANKLIN and JOHN ADAMS in Paris to negotiate the treaty of 1783 that recognized American independence and formally ended the fighting with Great Britain.

Returning to the United States in 1784 Jay assumed the position of secretary of foreign affairs under the ARTICLES OF CONFEDERATION. Unhappy over the weakness of the central government during the 1780s, he sympathized with the movement to create a new constitution that would strengthen the power of the federal government over the states. Jay was not a member of the CONSTITUTIONAL CONVENTION OF 1787, but he strongly advocated adoption of the Constitution in the closely contested ratification struggle in New York the following year. Joining forces with ALEXANDER HAMILTON and JAMES MADISON, Jay contributed several pieces (#2-#5 and, after a bout with illness, #64) to THE FEDERALIST. In these essays Jay warned that failure to adopt the new government would probably lead to the dissolution of the Union and the creation of separate confederacies. He also stressed that only through the creation of a strong and energetic central government could the discord and jealousies of the various states be brought under control and the territorial integrity of the United States be protected from foreign encroachment.

Shortly after becoming President, GEORGE WASHINGTON appointed Jay the first Chief Justice of the United States, a position he held from 1789 to 1795. Two main themes ran through Jay's decisions. The first stressed the supremacy of the newly created national government. CHISHOLM V. GEORGIA (1793) involved the constitutional question of whether a state could be sued in a federal court by a citizen of a different state without its permission, thus limiting its SOVEREIGNTY. The question had been raised during the debate over ratification, and the supporters of the Constitution had given assurances that such suits would not be allowed. Nevertheless, under Jay's leadership the Court handed down an affirmative decision, couched in extremely nationalistic terms. Jay stressed the role of the people of the United States in the creation of the Union, and deemphasized the powers and sovereignty of the states. A very controversial decision, *Chisholm* was vitiated when reaction to it culminated in the adoption of the ELEVENTH AMENDMENT.

While riding circuit in 1793 Jay delivered a dissenting opinion in WARE V. HYLTON arguing that a Virginia statute sequestering prerevolutionary debts of British creditors was invalid because it had been nullified by the Treaty of Paris (1783) which specifically indicated that such debts would be honored. The case was appealed in 1796, and the Supreme Court, from which Jay had already resigned, adopted the former Chief Justice's reasoning and reversed the lower court's decision. In another important case, *Glass v. The Sloop Betsy* (1794), the Supreme Court overturned a Maryland District Court ruling that allowed French consuls in America to function as prize courts and dispose of prizes captured by French privateers. Writing for the Court, Jay concluded that United States sovereignty required that these cases be handled by American courts.

Jay's other major concern as Chief Justice was to protect the independence of the Supreme Court by insisting on a strict SEPARATION OF POWERS. He rejected various attempts to incorporate the Court into the activities of the legislative and executive branches. For example, when Congress passed an act that required the circuit courts to review the applications of military invalids for pensions, Jay, while riding circuit in New York, declared that "neither the Legislative nor Executive branch can constitutionally assign to the Judicial any duties but such as are properly judicial and to be performed in a judicial manner." This position was upheld a short time later by the United States Circuit Court of Pennsylvania, in what has become known as HAYBURN'S CASE (1792), when the constitutionality of the law was actually challenged. Jay also rejected occasional requests from the President and Secretary of the Treasury Alexander Hamilton for ADVISORY OPINIONS on controversial matters, arguing that the Supreme Court should render opinions only in actual lawsuits brought by contending parties.

Jay was never happy serving on the Court. He thought the circuit riding duties too arduous. He also believed the Court lacked "the energy, weight and dignity which are essential to its affording due support to the national government." Hoping to return to a more active political life, he was defeated in a bid to become governor of New York in 1792. In 1794, while still holding the position of Chief Justice, he went on a special diplomatic mission to try to resolve existing controversies with Great Britain. The result was the controversial but successful JAY'S TREATY. Resigning his post on the Court, Jay became governor of New York in 1795 for two terms. Following the Jeffersonian successes in 1800 he declined reappointment as Chief Justice of the United States Supreme Court and retired from public life.

RICHARD E. ELLIS
(1986)

Bibliography

MONAGHAN, FRANK   1935   *John Jay*. Indianapolis: Bobbs-Merrill.

MORRIS, RICHARD B.   1967   *John Jay, the Nation and the Court.* Boston: Boston University Press.

JAY BURNS BAKING COMPANY v. BRYAN

See: *Burns Baking Company v. Bryan*

JAY COURT

See: Supreme Court, 1789–1801

JAY'S TREATY
8 Stat. 116 (1795)

Although obligated by the treaty that ended the Revolutionary War to evacuate its military posts in the Northwest Territory, the British government held the posts, established new ones, and, in 1793, began a policy of encouraging Indian depredations against American settlers in the territory. At the same time, the British fleet, then at war with France, began seizing American ships that called at French ports.

In April 1794, President GEORGE WASHINGTON appointed Chief Justice JOHN JAY envoy extraordinary to Britain to negotiate for neutral shipping rights and evacuation of the Northwest Territory. The treaty Jay negotiated in London and signed in November 1794 provided for both; but it also made many concessions to the British, especially at the expense of Western settlers. Several questions were left to be decided by joint commissions, which would require appropriated funds for their operation.

The congressional debate on Jay's Treaty raised constitutional issues that endure to the present day. Republicans in the House of Representatives, led by ALBERT GALLATIN, objected to a treaty with the force of supreme law that required appropriation of money but from the making of which the House was excluded. They attempted to hold the TREATY POWER hostage to the spending power.

After the treaty was ratified, during the debate on the appropriation, Gallatin induced the House to request from the President documents related to the negotiations. Washington refused to comply, invoking EXECUTIVE PRIVILEGE in order that "the boundaries fixed by the Constitution between the different departments should be preserved."

DENNIS J. MAHONEY
(1986)

Bibliography

COMBS, JERALD A.   1970   *The Jay Treaty: Political Battleground of the Founding Fathers.* Berkeley: University of California Press.

JEFFERSON, THOMAS
(1743–1826)

Thomas Jefferson, statesman, philosopher, architect, champion of freedom and enlightenment, was United States minister to France when the federal CONSTITUTIONAL CONVENTION met in 1787. Long an advocate of a strengthened confederation, he applauded the convention and anxiously awaited the result of its deliberations. On seeing the roster of delegates, he exclaimed to his diplomatic colleague and friend JOHN ADAMS, "It is really an assembly of demigods." Jefferson soon made the Constitution the polestar of his politics, aligning its principles with those of aspiring American democracy, with momentous consequences for the future of the republic.

Educated for the law in his native Virginia, tutored by GEORGE WYTHE, young Jefferson was a keen student of the English constitution. Like a good Whig, he traced the venerable rights and liberties of Englishmen back to Saxon foundations. The degeneration under George III turned on the system of minsterial influence to corrupt the Parliament. This upset the balance of king, lords, and Commons upon which the freedom and order of the constitution depended; and it threatened, Jefferson came to believe, tyranny for America. He was thus led in his first published work, *A Summary View of the Rights of British America* (1774), to repudiate the political authority of the mother country over the colonies. When he penned the DECLARATION OF INDEPENDENCE two years later, he placed the American claim not in the prescriptive guarantees of the English constitution but on the Lockean ground of the NATURAL RIGHTS of man. In recoil from the treacheries of an unwritten constitution, he concluded with the mass of American patriots that a CONSTITUTION should be written; in this and other ways he sought to secure the supremacy of FUNDAMENTAL LAW over statutory law, which was the great failure of the English constitution. Finally, Jefferson entered upon the search for a new system of political balance consonant with American principles and capable of breaking the classic cycle of liberty, corruption, and tyranny, thereby ensuring the permanence of free government.

Jefferson's constitutional theory first found expression in the making of the VIRGINIA CONSTITUTION OF 1776. In June, while he was drafting the Declaration of Independence for Congress, Jefferson also drafted a plan of government for Virginia and sent it to the revolutionary convention meeting in Williamsburg. The work of framing a new government, he wrote, was "the whole object of the present controversy." In his mind, the relationship of one state paper to the other was that of theory to practice, principle to application. Endeavoring to reach all the great objects of public liberty in the constitution, he included a number of fundamental reforms in Virginia society and government. The constitution adopted at Williamsburg contained none of these reforms, however. Jefferson at once became its severest critic, not only because of its conservative character but also because it failed to meet the test of republican legitimacy. The "convention" that adopted it, as he observed, was the revolutionary successor of the House of Burgesses, elected in April to perform the ordinary business of government. It could not, therefore, frame a supreme law, a law binding on government itself. Jefferson was groping toward the conception of constituent SOVEREIGNTY, in which the government actually arises from "the consent of the governed" through the constitution-making authority of the people. Thus it was that he proposed a form of popular ratification of the constitution—a radical notion at that time. He also proposed, and included in his plan, a provision for amendment by the consent of the people in two-thirds of the counties. This proposal was unprecedented. Jefferson made the omission of any provision for constitutional change a leading count in his indictment of the Virginia frame of government.

Jefferson returned to Virginia in 1776, served his state as a legislative reformer, then as wartime governor, and reentered Congress in the fall of 1783. Turning his attention to the problems of the confederation, he followed his young friend JAMES MADISON in advocating the addition of new congressional powers to raise revenue and regulate FOREIGN COMMERCE. He persuaded Congress to try the provision of the ARTICLES OF CONFEDERATION for an interim executive in the form of a committee of the states, thereby overcoming the dilemma of a congress in perpetual session, which was one source of its debility, or virtual obliteration of the government of the United States. The plan promptly collapsed under trial. Congress seemed as incapable of exercising the powers it already had as it was of obtaining new powers from the states. Jefferson was no "strict constructionist" where the Articles were concerned. In the case of the LAND ORDINANCE OF 1784 for the government of the western territory, he prevailed upon Congress to adopt a bold nation-building measure without a stitch of constitutional authority.

Jefferson's congressional career ended in May 1784, when he was appointed minister plenipotentiary to join BENJAMIN FRANKLIN and John Adams, in Paris, on the commission to negotiate treaties of amity and commerce with European states. He had helped reformulate policy on this subject in Congress. The policy concerned trade, of course; but it also concerned the strength and character of the confederation. Although the front door to congressional commercial regulation was closed, the back door was open through the power of Congress to negotiate treaties. "The moment these treaties are concluded the JURISDICTION of Congress over the commerce of the states springs into existence, and that of particular states is suppressed," Jefferson wrote. Only in treating with foreign nations could the United States act as "one Nation," and so acting not only expand trade abroad but strengthen the bonds of union at home. Indeed, Jefferson asserted that the latter was his "primary object." His hopes were quickly disappointed, however. The European courts, with two or three exceptions, rebuffed the American overtures for freer trade; and as the various state legislatures undertook to regulate foreign trade, Jefferson's political objective was undermined. He reluctantly concluded with Madison and other nationalists that there was no alternative to the outright grant of commercial power to Congress. It was the logic of commercial policy, basically, that led Jefferson to support the federal convention.

Jefferson's position in France, where he had succeeded Franklin as minister, conditioned his response to the new constitution in opposite ways. On the one hand, he had seen the infant republic jeered, kicked, and scoffed at from London to Algiers, all respect for its government annihilated from the universal opinion of its feebleness and incompetence. He had been frustrated in commercial diplomacy even at Versailles; and he and Adams had gone begging to Dutch bankers to keep the confederation afloat. A stronger government, more national in character, with higher tone and energy, was therefore necessary to raise the country's reputation in Europe. On the other hand, Jefferson pondered the new constitution in Paris, where tyranny, not anarchy, was the problem, where the drama of the French Revolution had just begun, and where he had come to recognize the inestimable blessings of American liberty. Learning of SHAY'S REBELLION, which terrified Adams in London, Jefferson declared philosophically, "I like a little rebellion now and then. It is like a storm in the atmosphere." In this spirit, reading the convention's plan in November, he thought the delegates had overreacted to the insurrection in Massachusetts and set up "a kite to keep the hen yard in order." He was staggered, too, by the boldness of the work, a wholly new frame of government, when he had looked for reinvigorating amendments to the Articles.

But the more Jefferson studied the Constitution the more he liked it. He had two main objections. The perpetual reeligibility of the chief magistrate aroused monarchical fears in his mind. Most of the evils of European governments were traceable to their kings, he said; and an

American president reeligible every fourth year would soon become a king, albeit an elective one. The fears were little felt at home, however, chiefly because of the universal confidence in GEORGE WASHINGTON, whose election to the first office was a foregone conclusion. So, increasingly, Jefferson concentrated on his second objection, the omission of a BILL OF RIGHTS. In this, of course, he was supported by the mass of anti-Federalists. At first he unwittingly played into their game of using the demand for a bill of rights to delay or defeat RATIFICATION OF THE CONSTITUTION. His suggestion in a private letter that four states withhold their assent until the demand was met contributed to the initial rejection of the Constitution in North Carolina. Actually, Jefferson always wanted speedy adoption by the necessary nine states; and when he learned of the Massachusetts plan of unconditional ratification with recommended amendments, he backed this approach. Meanwhile, in a lengthy correspondence, he converted Madison, the Federalist leader, to the cause of a bill of rights. Acknowledging the inconveniences and imperfections of all such parchment guarantees and conceding the theoretical objection to denying powers that had not been granted, he nevertheless insisted "that a bill of rights is what the people are entitled to against every government on earth, general or particular, and what no just government should refuse, or rest on inference."

Jefferson returned from France in 1789 and became secretary of state in the Washington administration. Great issues of foreign and domestic policy, which struck to the bedrock of principle, soon brought him into conflict with treasury secretary ALEXANDER HAMILTON. The conflict symbolized the rising opposition, first in the government, then in the country at large, between two nascent POLITICAL PARTIES, Republican and Federalist. The Constitution itself became an issue in February 1791, on Hamilton's plan to incorporate a national bank. After Washington received the bank bill from Congress, where Madison had pointedly questioned its constitutionality, he asked the secretaries f or their opinions. Jefferson returned a brisk 2,200-word brief against the bill. No power to incorporate a bank had been delegated to Congress. None could be found among the ENUMERATED POWERS, nor could it be fairly inferred from either of the general clauses appealed to by the bank's advocates. The power of Congress to provide for the GENERAL WELFARE was only the power to lay taxes for that purpose; the NECESSARY AND PROPER CLAUSE, unless construed strictly, would "swallow up all the DELEGATED POWERS, and reduce the whole to one power." The bank bill, he concluded, would breach the limits of the Constitution, trample on the laws of the states, and open "a boundless field of power, no longer susceptible to definition." Washington, however, was persuaded by Hamilton's opinion founded on the doctrine of IMPLIED POWERS

and signed the bill. The issue of congressional power was reargued a year later on Hamilton's Report on Manufactures. No legislation resulted, but Jefferson told the President that on the principles of the report Congress could tax and spend without limit on the apology of aiding the general welfare. The deeper grounds of division involved matters of morals, interests, and politics; but because policies were debated in constitutional terms, the question of who was loyal to the Constitution—whether it was best served by strict or loose construction, by STATES' RIGHTS or national consolidation, whether it ought to be viewed as a superintending rule of political action or as a point of departure for vigorous statesmanship—became a major issue between the parties.

The general doctrine of states' rights had been present from the beginning of the controversy, but only in 1798, when Jefferson was vice-president, did it become firmly associated in his mind with the preservation of the Constitution, the Union, and republican liberty. (See UNION, THEORIES OF.), All were threatened, in his opinion, by the ALIEN AND SEDITION ACTS enacted during the war crisis with France. Under the pretense of saving the country from Jacobins and incendiaries, the Federalists, he believed, aimed by these laws to cripple or destroy the Republican party. Because of the danger of criminal prosecution, the delusion of public opinion, and Federalist control of the government, including the courts, the usual means of opposition were ineffectual; so Jefferson turned to the state legislatures as the point of protest and resistance. There was nothing novel in the proceeding. As early as 1790 the Virginia assembly had protested against the allegedly unconstitutional acts of the federal government; in fact, opposition of this kind had been contemplated, and approved, in THE FEDERALIST #28. But the resolutions secretly drafted by Jefferson, and adopted by the Kentucky legislature in November, offered an authoritative theory of "state interposition" that was destined to have great influence. (See VIRGINIA AND KENTUCKY RESOLUTIONS.) The Kentucky Resolutions set forth the theory of the Constitution as a compact among the states. Acts beyond the delegated powers were unconstitutional and void; and since the contracting parties had created no ultimate arbiter, each state had "an equal right to judge for itself, as well of infractions as of the mode and measure of redress." How far Jefferson meant to go was unclear. He called for NULLIFICATION of the oppressive laws; but rather than cause overt state defiance of federal authority, his aim was to arouse opposition opinion through the legislatures to force repeal of the laws. When this political strategy failed, he got Kentucky, as well as Virginia, to renew its protest in 1799, again to no avail. Nevertheless, Jefferson always believed that the Virginia and Kentucky Resolutions were crucial to "the revolution of 1800" that elevated him to the presidency. They had saved the party and the freedom of the political process upon which victory at the polls depended. To this extent, certainly, the resolutions strengthened principles of freedom and self-government under the Constitution. But in appealing to states' rights and state resistance—interposition or nullification or SECESSION—Jefferson struck a course potentially as dangerous to the Constitution and the Union as the odious laws were to civil and political liberty.

Jefferson entered the presidency pledged to return the government to the original principles of the Constitution. These principles included, first, the protection of the state governments in all their rights as the primary jurisdictions of domestic affairs; second, a frugal and simple administration of the federal government; and third, a sharp contradiction of executive power and influence, which had threatened to "monarchize" the Constitution. Such principles were likely to prove embarrassing to the President's leadership. The story of the administration became the story of how Jefferson escaped, evaded, or overcame the restraints of his own first principles in order to provide the strong leadership the country required.

Jefferson's first test concerned the judiciary. He had always favored an independent judiciary as the guardian of individual rights against legislative and executive tyranny. But in "the crisis of '98" the courts became the destroyers rather than the guardians of the liberties of the citizen. The power of this partisan judiciary had been increased by the JUDICIARY ACT OF 1801 passed in the waning hours of the Adams administration. The Federalists, Jefferson believed, had retired to the judiciary as a stronghold from which to assail his administration; and he promptly called for repeal of the Judiciary Act. This was done, although it involved the abolition of judgeships held on GOOD BEHAVIOR tenure. The case of MARBURY V. MADISON (1803) arose at the same time. It, too, was significant primarily in its political character, as a duel between the President and the new Chief Justice, JOHN MARSHALL. Jefferson, who disliked his Virginia cousin, objected to the decision not because the Court asserted the ultimate power to interpret the Constitution, for in fact it did not go that far, but because Marshall traveled out of the case, pretending to a JURISDICTION he then disclaimed, in order to slap the chief magistrate for violating constitutional rights.

With regard to JUDICIAL REVIEW, Jefferson consistently held to the theory of "tripartite balance," under which each of the coordinate branches of government had the equal right to decide questions of constitutionality for itself. This equality of decisional power was as necessary to maintaining the constitutional SEPARATION OF POWERS, in his view, as the doctrine of states' rights was to preserving the division of authority in the federal system. Under the theory he considered the Sedition Act, which had expired, unconstitutional from the beginning and pardoned those still suffering its penalties. The idea of governmental adaptation and change through construction of the Constitution was repugnant to Jefferson. Even more repugnant was the idea of vesting the ultimate authority of interpretation in a court whose members had no accountability to the people. But Jefferson, though he held the judiciary at bay, was unwilling to push his principles to conclusion and left the foundations of judicial power undisturbed for Marshall to build upon later.

Jefferson overcame the restraints of his whiggish view of executive power by capitalizing on his personal magnetism and influence as a party leader. In FOREIGN AFFAIRS, the principal field of the general government, he had generally taken a more expansive view. Yet the foreign affairs triumph of his administration, the LOUISIANA PURCHASE, became a constitutional crisis for him. While other Republicans easily discovered legal warrant for the treaty, he could not. It was "an act beyond the Constitution," and there was nothing for the President and Congress to do but "throw themselves on the country for doing them unauthorized, what we know they would have done for themselves had they been in a situation to do it." So he drafted a constitutional amendment—"an act of indemnity"—to sanction the treaty retroactively. "I had rather ask an enlargement of power from the nation," he wrote to a Virginia senator, "than to assume it by construction which would make our powers boundless. Our peculiar security is in the possession of a written Constitution. Let us not make it a blank paper by construction." Congress was less scrupulous, however, and when it declined to follow him, he acquiesced. A revolution in the Union perforce became a revolution in the Constitution as well. He found justification for other executive actions—in foreign affairs, in the suppression of the Burr Conspiracy—above and beyond the law. "It is," he wrote, "incumbent on those only who accept of great charges, to risk themselves on great occasions, when the safety of the nation, or some of its very high interests are at stake." In Jefferson's thinking, actions of this kind, which were exceptional and uncodified, were preferable to false and frivolous constructions of the Constitution, which permanently corrupted it. Yet he took little comfort from the theory of "higher obligation" in the case of the Louisiana Purchase.

In retirement at Monticello from 1809 until his death seventeen years later, Jefferson repeatedly confronted the problem of constitutional preservation and change. He knew there could be no preservation without change, no constructive change without preservation. He knew, as he wrote in again championing reform of the Virginia constitution, "that laws and institutions must go hand in hand with the progress of the human mind." And he did not hesitate to declare again his belief, formed in 1789 in the shadow of the Bastille, that each generation, representing a new constituent majority, should make its own constitution. Change should occur, fundamentally, by CONSTITUTIONAL CONVENTION. Next to that, it should occur by regular amendment. As President he had advocated the TWELFTH AMENDMENT, approved in 1804, and several others that were stillborn. Now, from Monticello, he advocated amendments authorizing federal INTERNAL IMPROVEMENTS, the direct election of the president, and the two-term limitation on the president. Nothing happened. Finally, not long before his death, he "despair[ed] of ever seeing another amendment to the Constitution," and observed, "Another general convention can alone relieve us." Thus in the nation, as in the state, he appealed to both lawmaking and constitution-making authorities to keep the fundamental law responsive to new conditions and new demands.

Jefferson continued to the end to reject constitutional change by construction or interpretation. In the wake of the Panic of 1819, which threw his affairs into hopeless disorder, he reacted sharply against the course of consolidation in the general government, above all the bold nationalism of the Supreme Court. "The judiciary of the United States is the subtle corps of sappers and miners constantly working under ground to undermine the foundations of our confederated fabric," he wrote in 1820. "They are construing our constitution from a coordination of a general and special government to a general and supreme one. This will lay all things at their feet." Only by combining the revolutionary theory of "constituent sovereignty" with the rule of "strict construction" would it be possible, Jefferson believed, to maintain constitutional government on the republican foundations of "the consent of the governed."

MERRILL D. PETERSON
(1986)

Bibliography

BOYD, JULIAN P., ed. 1950–1974 *The Papers of Thomas Jefferson.* 19 Vols. Princeton, N.J.: Princeton University Press.
LEVY, LEONARD W. 1963 *Jefferson and Civil Liberties: The Darker Side.* Cambridge, Mass.: Harvard University Press.
LIPSCOMB, A. A. and BERGH, A. E., eds. 1904 *The Writings of Thomas Jefferson.* 20 Vols. Washington, D.C.: Thomas Jefferson Memorial Association.
MALONE, DUMAS 1948–1982 *Jefferson and His Times.* 6 Vols. to date. Boston: Little, Brown.
PETERSON, MERRILL D. 1970 *Thomas Jefferson and the New Nation: A Biography.* New York: Oxford University Press.

JEFFERSONIANISM

THOMAS JEFFERSON wished to be remembered as the author of the DECLARATION OF INDEPENDENCE and as the founder of the University of Virginia, but history has credited him with much more. In the world of practical politics, Jefferson's achievements were legion—legal reformer, wartime governor of Virginia, author of the VIRGINIA STATUTE OF RELIGIOUS LIBERTY, draftsman of the great Ordinance of 1784, first secretary of state, leader of the "loyal opposition" in the administration of JOHN ADAMS, third President of the United States, purchaser of Louisiana, father of the Democratic party, and founder of the first political party system. In the world of ideas, Jefferson was the nation's premier advocate of political democracy, POPULAR SOVEREIGNTY, and a republican system of government. He was also a staunch advocate of public education, progressivism, and the RULE OF LAW both at home and abroad.

Somewhat less appreciated than these enduring contributions to the nation's history was Jefferson's role in the development of a theory of CONSTITUTIONALISM that, after two centuries, continues to inform the American commitment to constitutional government. Jefferson's first inaugural address (March 4, 1801), one of the nation's great state papers, provides a glimpse into part, though not all, of Jefferson's constitutional vision. Directing his remarks to the Washington community in the newly established seat of government in the DISTRICT OF COLUMBIA, Jefferson reflected upon those axioms of the American system that he prized above all. Referring to majoritarian rule as a "sacred principle," Jefferson reminded his listeners "that though the will of the majority is in all cases to prevail, that will to be rightful must be reasonable; that the minority possess their equal rights, which equal law must protect, and to violate would be oppression." In one of the most remarkable statements on the value of FREEDOM OF SPEECH in a free society, Jefferson declared, "If there be any among us who would wish to dissolve this Union or to change its republican form, let them stand undisturbed as monuments of the safety with which error of opinion may be tolerated where reason is left free to combat it." And with a single phrase, Jefferson identified the constitutional value whose full implementation has been the cornerstone of modern American constitutional JURISPRUDENCE: "Equal and exact justice to all . . . of whatever state or persuasion, religious or political."

The elements of Jeffersonian constitutionalism were these: the preservation of FUNDAMENTAL RIGHTS; the preeminence of the legislative branch in a government of separated powers; the integrity of the sovereign states in a federal union of shared and divided powers; strict adherence by Congress to those powers delegated to it in the written Constitution; RELIGIOUS LIBERTY as guaranteed by a regime in which church and state remained apart; and a recognition of the need for frequent constitutional change through the process of constitutional amendment. The fact that Jefferson himself, out of political necessity,

PETERSON, MERRILL D. 1962 *The Jeffersonian Image in the American Mind.* New York: Oxford University Press.

JENCKS ACT
71 Stat. 595 (1957)

In *Jencks v. United States*, in June 1957, the Supreme Court, speaking through Justice WILLIAM J. BRENNAN, reversed the conviction of a labor leader, Clinton E. Jencks, charged with perjury for falsely swearing he was not a communist. The five-man majority held that reports filed by FBI-paid informants alleging Jencks's participation in Communist party activities should have been available to his counsel when requested. The majority ruled that the prosecution must either disclose to the defense statements made by government witnesses or drop the case.

Justice TOM C. CLARK wrote a near-inflammatory dissent contending that unless Congress nullified the decision, "those intelligence agencies of our government engaged in law enforcement may as well close up shop." The decision, he warned, would result in a "Roman holiday" for criminals to "rummage" through secret files. Congress seized upon Clark's dissent and a Jencks Act was quickly passed, amending the United States Code. In sharply restricting the Court's decision, the measure provided that a defendant in a criminal case could, following testimony by a government witness, request disclosure of a pretrial statement made by that witness, so long as the statement was written and signed by the witness or was a transcription of an oral statement made at the time the statement was given. Other requested material was to be screened by the trial judge for relevance, with the judge given the right to delete unrelated matters. In subsequent challenges, raised in *Rosenberg v. United States* (1959) and *Palermo v. United States* (1959), the Justices upheld the law, carefully conforming to its provisions.

PAUL L. MURPHY
(1986)

Bibliography
NOTE 1958 The Jencks Legislation: Problems in Prospect. *Yale Law Journal* 67:674–699.

JENIFER, DANIEL OF ST. THOMAS
(1723–1790)

Daniel of St. Thomas Jenifer signed the Constitution as a Maryland delegate to the CONSTITUTIONAL CONVENTION OF 1787. The most national-minded of Maryland's delegates, he quarreled often with LUTHER MARTIN. His late arrival on

July 2 permitted approval of equal votes for the states in the SENATE.

DENNIS J. MAHONEY
(1986)

JENKINS v. ANDERSON
447 U.S. 231 (1980)

The Fifth Amendment allows a criminal defendant to remain silent during his trial and prevents the prosecution from commenting on his silence, in order to prevent the jury from drawing adverse inferences. In *Jenkins* the defendant surrendered to the police two weeks after killing a man and claimed that he had acted in self-defense. When he told that self-defense story at his trial, the prosecutor countered that he would have surrendered immediately had he killed in self-defense. After conviction the defendant, seeking HABEAS CORPUS relief, argued that the use of his prearrest silence violated his RIGHT AGAINST SELF-INCRIMINATION and fundamental fairness. The Supreme Court, like the federal courts below, denied relief. Justice LEWIS F. POWELL, for a 7–2 Court, ruled that the use of prearrest silence to impeach a defendant's credibility, if he testifies in his own defense, does not violate any constitutional rights. Powell's murky reasoning provoked Justices THURGOOD MARSHALL and WILLIAM J. BRENNAN, dissenting, to declare that a duty to incriminate oneself now replaced the right to remain silent. Powell had supported no such duty, but he rejected a "right to commit perjury," which no one claimed. His opinion weakened the right to remain silent.

LEONARD W. LEVY
(1986)

JENSEN, MERRILL
(1905–1980)

Author and editor of many books on American colonial and revolutionary history, Merrill Monroe Jensen is best known for his challenge of the traditional interpretation of the ARTICLES OF CONFEDERATION as an inadequate form of government whose weaknesses required that it be replaced by the Constitution of 1787. Jensen argued in his most influential books, *The Articles of Confederation* (1940) and *The New Nation* (1950), that the AMERICAN REVOLUTION was as much a political and social upheaval as the winning of independence from Great Britain and that the Articles of Confederation were the logical result of the democratic philosophy of the DECLARATION OF INDEPENDENCE and the state constitutions of the 1770s. Jensen also contended that the Articles' weaknesses were exaggerated both by the

Federalists of 1787–1788, who actually supported the Constitution as a check on the democratic tendencies of which the Articles were the clearest expression, and by most historians.

RICHARD B. BERNSTEIN
(1986)

JIM CROW LAWS

See: Segregation; Separate but Equal Doctrine

JIMMY SWAGGART MINISTRIES v. BOARD OF EQUALIZATION OF CALIFORNIA
493 U.S. 378 (1990)

In conjunction with its evangelistic activities in the state of California, Jimmy Swaggart Ministries sold religious books, tapes, records, and other merchandise. The group agreed to pay state sales tax on the nonreligious merchandise sold, but maintained that merchandise with specific religious content—such as Bibles, sermons, and Bible study manuals—were exempt from taxation on the basis of the FIRST AMENDMENT. The Supreme Court unanimously disagreed, holding that application of a sales tax to the religious merchandise did not violate either the free exercise clause or the excessive entanglement provision read into the ESTABLISHMENT CLAUSE by the LEMON TEST.

The Court distinguished the case from prior precedents that had invalidated the application of general licensing fees to those who sold and distributed religious materials door-to-door. In both MURDOCK V. PENNYSLVANIA (1943) and *Follett v. McCormick* (1944), the Court had objected to such licensing fees because they acted as a prior retraint on the free exercise of religion. In the same cases, however, the Court made clear that the First Amendment did not exempt religious groups from generally applicable taxes on income and property. The Court reaffirmed that principle here, noting that the tax under attack was a general levy on revenues raised from the sale of certain products. The Court acknowledged that in some cases a generally applicable tax of this sort might "effectively choke off an adherent's religious practices," but reserved for the future a determination on whether such a tax would violate the free exercise clause.

JOHN G. WEST, JR.
(1992)

(SEE ALSO: *Employment Division, Department of Human Resources of Oregon v. Smith; Texas Monthly, Inc. v. Bullock.*)

JOHNS, UNITED STATES v.
469 U.S. 478 (1985)

This case continued a trend of decisions by which the automobile exception to the FOURTH AMENDMENT's SEARCH WARRANT requirement expands without discernible limits. Warrantless AUTOMOBILE SEARCHES were first tolerated because a culprit might suddenly drive away with the evidence of his guilt before a warrant could be obtained. That possibility became the basis of holdings that if a vehicle can constitutionally be searched at the time it is found or stopped, it can be impounded and searched later; and if the vehicle can be searched, sealed containers found within may be opened and searched, too. In *Johns* the Court ruled that if officers unload the containers and store them, instead of searching them on the spot, three days later the containers may be opened without a warrant and any contraband that may be found can be introduced in EVIDENCE. Only Justices WILLIAM J. BRENNAN and THURGOOD MARSHALL dissented from the OPINION OF THE COURT by Justice SANDRA DAY O'CONNOR.

LEONARD W. LEVY
(1986)

(SEE ALSO: *Chambers v. Maroney; Ross, United States v.*)

JOHNSON, ANDREW
(1808–1875)

Born in 1808, Andrew Johnson became a Tennessee legislator in 1833, congressman in 1843, governor in 1853, United States senator in 1856, Tennessee's military governor in 1862, Vice-President of the United States in March 1865, and, on ABRAHAM LINCOLN's death in April 1865, President. Early in his career Johnson mixed STRICT CONSTRUCTION and STATES' RIGHTS views with an unusually warm nationalism, stern loyalty to the Democratic party (until the CIVIL WAR: Johnson returned to the Democratic allegiance in late 1866), and a remarkable devotion to white supremacy. By 1860 Johnson's sponsorship of homestead legislation (see HOMESTEAD ACT) and frontier-style campaign rhetoric had won him a reputation as a latter-day Jacksonian.

In the 1860–1861 winter, Johnson, the only slave-state senator who refused to follow his state into SECESSION, openly counseled Tennesseans against seceding. For his temerity he had to flee to Washington. In the SENATE, Johnson, achieving at last his homestead goal, won Republicans' appreciation also for supporting Lincoln's and Congress's policies on TEST OATHS, military arrests of civilians, confiscation, emancipation, and RECONSTRUCTION. Johnson insisted that the Constitution's WAR POWERS and

TREASON clauses authorized the nation, not to coerce a state, but to punish disloyal individuals directly. This believer in a fixed, state-on-top, race-ordered FEDERALISM in 1862 accepted from Lincoln assignment as Tennessee's military governor, a position unknown to the Constitution or statutes, supportable only from the most flexible contemporary ideas on national primacy under martial law.

As military governor, Johnson employed test oaths and troops against alleged pro-Confederates, sometimes purging unfriendly government officeholders and officials of private CORPORATIONS, to rebuild local and state governments. Johnson's policies helped the Republican-War Democratic "Union" coalition win Tennessee in 1864. That party named Johnson its vice-presidential candidate in order to attract the support of other Unionists in the reconquered South and border states, who seemed to be educable on race. Then, just as the Confederacy's collapse made Reconstruction an immediate concern, Johnson became President.

Although no specific Reconstruction statute constrained him, the 1861–1862 CONFISCATION ACTS, the 1862 test oath act, and the 1865 FREEDMEN'S BUREAU law limited and defined executive actions. Johnson arrogated to himself an unprecedented right to enforce them selectively or not at all in order to further his Reconstruction policy. (For a modern parallel, see IMPOUNDMENT OF FUNDS.)

That policy (announced May 29, 1865, for North Carolina and later for other states) he based on the war powers (but Johnson later insisted that the end of hostilities cut off this source of authority) and on the GUARANTEE CLAUSE: the same authorities Lincoln and Congress employed in wartime Reconstructions (later Johnson insisted that the guarantee clause did not justify a national interest in state residents' CIVIL RIGHTS). Without authority from statute, he appointed a provisional (that is, military) governor for every defeated state, who, with Army help, initiated elections for a CONSTITUTIONAL CONVENTION among qualified voters, including ex-rebels Johnson amnestied and pardoned. The convention was to renounce secession and ratify the THIRTEENTH AMENDMENT. Johnson secretly counseled his provisional governors to appoint officials who could swear to required test oaths and even, as Lincoln had advised publicly, to grant suffrage to token Negroes. But no states obeyed their creator; several only very reluctantly ratified the Thirteenth Amendment, balking at its enforcement clause.

In "reconstructing" thirteen states, Johnson had the largest federal patronage opportunity in American history, especially with respect to postal and tax officers, traditional nuclei of political parties. He filled these influential offices with pardoned ex-Confederates who could not subscribe to the required test oaths, exempting them from the stipulation, thus returning power to recent rebels.

Johnson canceled prosecutions under the confiscation laws and inhibited the work of the Freedmen's Bureau, thereby blighting blacks' prospects for a secure economic base. "Johnson" state and local officers, including judges, state attorneys, and police encouraged lawsuits against the Bureau and Army officers for alleged assaults and trespasses and for violating the BLACK CODES. Johnson did not protect his harassed military personnel under the HABEAS CORPUS ACT of 1863. In April 1866, he proclaimed that peace existed everywhere in the South and that all federal Reconstruction authority ended.

His policies made the security of blacks, white Unionists, and federal officials woefully uncertain and seriously distorted the Constitution's CHECKS AND BALANCES. Johnson insisted that Congress should admit delegates-elect from the Southern states, though conceding that Congress had independent authority (Article I, section 5, on CONGRESSIONAL MEMBERSHIP) to judge the qualifications of its members; he reiterated that the nation had no right to intervene in those states and assigned the Army to police them. Johnson unprecedentedly enlarged the VETO POWER. His stunning vetoes of bills on CIVIL RIGHTS, the Freedmen's Bureau, and military Reconstruction, among others, antagonized even congressmen sympathetic to his views. His vetoes invoked the decision in EX PARTE MILLIGAN (1866), paid tribute to the STATE POLICE POWER, and decried the centralized military despotism he claimed to discern in these bills. But Johnson appealed also to the lowest race views of the time. And he never dealt with the question, with which congressmen at least tried to grapple, of individuals' remedies when the states failed to treat them equally in civil and criminal relationships. The President's decision to campaign in the fall 1866 elections against the party that had elected him, his opposition to the FOURTEENTH AMENDMENT (public disapprobation by a President of a proposed amendment was itself unprecedented), and his intemperate attacks against leading congressmen further alienated many persons.

Johnson rejected the idea of an adaptable Constitution and of a federal duty to seek more decent race relations. There was no halfway house between the centralization he insisted was occurring and a total abandonment of any national interest in the rights of its citizens, who were also state citizens. Johnson's rigidity reflected his heightening racism and his yearning for an independent nomination for the presidency in 1868 from Democrats and the most conservative Republicans.

Johnson himself destroyed his presidential prospects. After obeying the TENURE OF OFFICE ACT by suspending (August 1867) Secretary of War EDWIN M. STANTON, Johnson decided, upon the Senate's nonconcurrence (February 1868), to violate that law. He ousted Stanton and named ULYSSES S. GRANT as interim secretary. Republican congressmen in 1867 had shied away from IMPEACHMENT but in February 1868 the HOUSE OF REPRESENTATIVES (128–74, 15 not voting) impeached Johnson for "high crimes and misdemeanors," an offense undefined in the few earlier American impeachments, especially as to whether the "high crimes" had to be criminally indictable (Article I, section 2; Article II, sections 2, 4; Article III, section 2). Contemporary legal scholar JOHN NORTON POMEROY held that indictability was not a prerequisite for impeachability, conviction, and removal from office. The impeachment committee's charges (Articles I-X) nevertheless stressed largely indictable offenses, including Johnson's obstructions of the military Reconstruction Tenure of Office, and Army Appropriations Acts. Article XI was a catch-all to attract senators who did not hold with indictability as a minimum for impeachability. (See ARTICLES OF IMPEACHMENT OF ANDREW JOHNSON.)

From February through May 1868 the President's able counsel HENRY STANBERY, by insisting on indictability as the test of impeachability, confused senators who formed the court in the impeachment trial. Johnson, at last restraining his intemperateness, now enforced the military reconstruction law and other statutes he had vetoed. He replaced Grant as secretary of war with John M. Schofield, who, though conservative on race, was trusted on Capitol Hill. The Republican majority, wedded to checks and balances, hesitated to subordinate the presidency by convicting and removing Johnson. The House "managers" of the trial harassed witnesses and journalists, outraging some Republican senators. And 1868 was an election year. Johnson, his hopes for a nomination destroyed, must leave office by March 1869. These factors combined to leave Johnson unconvicted by a single Senate vote, 35–19.

Johnson was not the victim of a Radical Republican conspiracy but was the architect of his own remarkably successful effort to thwart improvements in race equality. He won because he exploited men's lowest race fears, cloaking them in glorifications of states' rights. His return to Congress in 1875 as a Tennessee senator (he died later that year), when sentiment was rising even among Republicans to dump the Negro, symbolized his triumph.

HAROLD M. HYMAN
(1986)

Bibliography

BENEDICT, MICHAEL L. 1973 *The Impeachment and Trial of Andrew Johnson.* New York: Norton.
BERGER, RAOUL 1973 *Impeachment: Constitutional Problems.* Cambridge, Mass.: Harvard University Press.
SEFTON, JAMES 1980 *Andrew Johnson and the Uses of Constitutional Power.* Boston: Little, Brown.
TREFOUSSE, HANS L. 1975 *Impeachment of a President: Andrew Johnson, the Blacks, and Reconstruction.* Knoxville: University of Tennessee Press.

JOHNSON, LYNDON B.
(1908–1973)

Lyndon Baines Johnson was a strong President whose performance was tempered by an affectionate reverence for the constitutional system as a whole. He exploited the cumulative precedents for presidential leadership and authority in domestic, foreign, and military policy; protected presidential power against congressional intrusion while working with vigor to carry Congress with him; and turned the office over to his successor intact. Jointly with Congress, he extended federal power greatly in CIVIL RIGHTS, education, and welfare. He appointed the first black Supreme Court Justice, THURGOOD MARSHALL; but Johnson's attempt to assure liberal leadership beyond his term by the nomination of ABE FORTAS as Chief Justice failed when Fortas withdrew in 1968.

All this tells us little of how the American constitutional process actually operated in the turbulent, creative, and tragic days between November 22, 1963, and January 20, 1969. The agenda Lyndon Johnson confronted was unique. Aside from the urgent need to unify the nation and establish his legitimacy in the wake of JOHN F. KENNEDY's assassination, he faced simultaneous protracted crises at home and abroad: a crisis in race relations and a disintegrating position in Southeast Asia. WOODROW WILSON and FRANKLIN D. ROOSEVELT had also confronted both urgent domestic problems and war; but the course of events permitted them to be dealt with in sequence. Johnson faced them together and they stayed with him to the end.

By personality and conviction, Johnson was a man driven to grapple with problems. But he also carried into office a passionate moral vision of an American society of equal opportunity—a vision he proved capable of translating into LEGISLATION, above all in the fields of civil rights, education, and medical care. The CIVIL RIGHTS ACT OF 1964, the VOTING RIGHTS ACT OF 1965, and the Fair Housing and Federal Jury Reform Acts of 1968 were major results of his crusade for racial equality. The ELEMENTARY AND SECONDARY EDUCATION ACT and HEALTH INSURANCE FOR THE AGED ACT (MEDICARE) of 1965 were outstanding among dozens of acts passed in both fields. In carrying the religious constituencies on the Education Act, Johnson displayed skill bordering on wizardry. As proportions of gross national product, social welfare outlays of the federal government rose dramatically between 1964 and 1968 while national security outlays rose only slightly. This was possible because of an average real growth rate of 4.8 percent in the American economy.

Johnson had been a man of the Congress for some thirty years before assuming the presidency. No President ever came to responsibility with a deeper and more subtle working knowledge of the constitutional tensions between Congress and the President, and of the requirement of generating a partnership out of that tension, issue by issue. But Johnson knew from experience that, on domestic issues, a President's time for leading Congress and achieving major legislative results was short. From his first days as President, Johnson expected Congress would, in the end, mobilize to frustrate one of his initiatives and then progressively reduce or end his primacy. He was, therefore, determined to use his initial capital promptly. Although momentum slowed after mid-1965, Johnson proved capable of carrying Congress on significant domestic legislation virtually to the end of his term.

Johnson was opportunistic in the best sense. He exploited the Congress elected with him in November 1964; but he also channeled the powerful waves of popular feeling in the wake of the assassinations of John Kennedy, MARTIN LUTHER KING, JR., and ROBERT F. KENNEDY into support for his legislative program.

Johnson believed the presidency was the central repository of the nation's ideals and the energizing agent for change in the nation's policy. He understood the advantage a President enjoys relative to a fragmented Congress: the power to initiate. He brought into the White House every constructive idea he could mobilize from both private life and the bureaucracies, setting in motion some one hundred task forces, sixty within the government, forty made up of outside experts. Where possible, he also engaged members of Congress in the drafting of legislation at an early stage in the hope that their subsequent interest and support would be more energetic.

Johnson also understood that in domestic affairs there was little a President could constitutionally do on his own. His was primarily a license to persuade. He used the conventional levers of presidential influence in dealing with Congress. But his most effective instrument was his formidable power of persuasion, based on knowledge of individual members and a sensitive perception of the possibility of support from each on particular issues. He spent far more time with members of Congress than any President before or since—face to face, by telephone, or in group meetings at the White House.

Johnson judged that he had come to responsibility at a rare, transient interval of opportunity for social progress. Therefore, he used up his capital and achieved much. He left Washington with a sense of how much more he would have liked to have done; but he also realized that the nation was determined to pause and catch its breath rather than continue to plunge forward. Nevertheless, the pro-

grams initiated in Johnson's time continued to expand in the 1970s. As Ralph Ellison, the black novelist, said, Johnson will perhaps be recognized as "the greatest American President for the poor and for Negroes . . . a very great honor indeed."

But all did not go smoothly with the Great Society. In 1965, five days after the signing of the VOTING RIGHTS ACT, rioting broke out in Watts, and riots in urban ghettoes continued for three years. Despite vigorous and imaginative efforts, these problems proved relatively unyielding although violence subsided in 1968 as it became increasingly clear that the costs were primarily borne by the black community. Moreover, as new welfare programs moved from law to administration, resistance gradually built up both to their cost and to intrusions on state and local authority. Although significant modifications in the Great Society programs were made in the 1970s and 1980s, it seems unlikely that the basic extensions of public policy in civil rights, education, and welfare will be withdrawn.

Although Johnson led public opinion and drove Congress in domestic affairs, he conducted the war in Southeast Asia with a reserve that did not match the nation's desire for a prompt resolution of the conflict. Johnson's relations with the Congress on the VIETNAM WAR thus differed markedly from his approach on domestic policy. HARRY S. TRUMAN had decided, with the agreement of the congressional leadership, to resist the invasion of South Korea on the basis of his powers as COMMANDER-IN-CHIEF. Johnson preferred the precedents of the Middle East and Formosa Resolutions which he, when Democratic leader in the Senate, had recommended to DWIGHT D. EISENHOWER. He followed that course in the Tonkin Gulf Resolution in 1964. Despite later controversy over the resolution, the record of the Senate debate indicates that its members understood the solemn constitutional step they were taking. Johnson consulted the bipartisan leadership and received their unanimous support on July 27, 1965, before announcing the next day that he had ordered substantial forces to Vietnam—a decision which, at the time, had overwhelming popular as well as congressional support. The possibilities of a formal DECLARATION OF WAR or new congressional mandate were examined and rejected on the ground that they might have brought into effect possible secret military agreements between North Vietnam and other communist powers.

Johnson's determination to consult with and to carry the Congress in 1964 and 1965 was real. But he knew that legislative support at the initiation of hostilities would not prevent members of Congress, disciplined by changes in public opinion, from later opposing him. In the end, he was convinced, the primary responsibility under the Constitution in matters of war and peace rested with the President; and he accepted the implications of that judgment, including the possibility that support for his decision would fade and leave him, like some of his predecessors, lonely and beleaguered.

Johnson made his decision when the entrance of North Vietnamese regular units into South Vietnam had created a crisis, compounded by the Malaysian confrontation instigated by Indonesia with Chinese support. The choice before him was to accept defeat or to fight. He chose to fight because, in his view, the Southeast Asia Treaty (SEATO) reflected authentic United States interests in Asia; a failure to honor the treaty would weaken the credibility of American commitments elsewhere; and the outcome of withdrawal would not be peace but a wider war.

The strategy Johnson adopted was gradually to reduce communist military capabilities within South Vietnam; to use air power against the lines of supply; to impose direct costs on North Vietnam by attacks on selected targets in the Hanoi area; and to support the South Vietnamese in their efforts to create a strong military establishment and to build a viable economy and a democratic political system. His objective was to convince North Vietnam that the takeover of South Vietnam was beyond its military and political grasp and that the costs of continuing the effort were excessive. From the beginning to the end of his administration, Johnson was in virtually continuous diplomatic contact with the North Vietnamese. Protracted formal negotiations began in April 1968 in the wake of the Tet offensive, during which the communist cause suffered a severe military setback but gained ground in American public opinion.

Johnson's cautious strategy in Vietnam conformed to the views of neither the hawkish majority in American public opinion and the Congress, nor the dovish minority. Johnson realized that his conduct of the war was unpopular and that public support had eroded; the nation resisted a protracted engagement with limited objectives and mounting casualties. He nevertheless held to his strategy and resisted those who advocated decisive military action on the ground outside South Vietnam. As Commander-in-Chief, Johnson was determined to conduct the war in a way that minimized the chance of a large engagement with Chinese Communist or Soviet forces. The memory of Chinese Communist entrance into the KOREAN WAR may well have played an important part in Johnson's determination; and he knew that he would be judged in history, in part, on whether his assessment of the risks of a more decisive course of action was correct. Johnson's strategy may also have been affected by two other considerations: a determination to maintain the momentum of his domestic initiatives; and fear that an all-out mobilization might regenerate an undifferentiated anticommunism, with disruptive consequences for foreign policy and McCarthyite implications at home.

The tension between impatient public opinion and Johnson's cautious strategy led to a quasi-constitutional crisis in the early months of 1968. The bipartisan unity of the American foreign policy establishment, which began in 1940, ended, for a generation at least, in 1968. Johnson's distinguished outside advisers, who had been united in November 1967 in support of Johnson's Vietnam policy, were hopelessly divided four months later.

Many complex factors contributed to the schism, but in part it was the product of conflicting images. For Johnson and others who had foreseen the Tet offensive and acted to frustrate it, the communist military failure was apparent, and Johnson's March 31 bombing reduction and proposal to negotiate were designed to exploit a position of relative strength. For those to whom the offensive was a shock and a demonstration of the futility of the American effort, Johnson's negotiation initiative seemed an admission of defeat. Johnson's simultaneous announcement of his decision not to seek reelection may have strengthened the latter image in the public mind.

Thus, Johnson left to his successor a greatly improved military, political, and economic situation in Southeast Asia, a weary and discouraged majority of Americans, and a divided foreign policy establishment in addition to an ardent minority that had been advocating withdrawal from Vietnam for several years.

The antiwar crusaders challenged Johnson's assessment on multiple grounds, among them: the importance of American interests in Southeast Asia; the legality and morality of the war itself; and the belief that Vietnamese nationalism was overwhelmingly on the side of the communists. Johnson weighed carefully the antiwar views, but he remained convinced to the end of his life that his assessment of the issues at stake was correct. He was less sure that his cautious military strategy had been correct.

There was a great deal more to Johnson's foreign policy than the war in Southeast Asia. He stabilized NATO in the wake of French withdrawal from its unified military command; saw the Dominican Republic through a crisis in 1965 to a period of economic and social progress under democracy; and encouraged regional cohesion in Latin America, Africa, and Asia.

Like all American Presidents in the nuclear age, Johnson consciously bore an extraconstitutional responsibility to the human race to minimize the risk of nuclear war. He sought to normalize relations with the Soviet Union; he carried forward efforts to tame nuclear weapons through the Non-proliferation and Outer Space treaties; and he laid the foundation for strategic arms limitation talks.

But the central fact of his administration was the convergence of war and social revolution that resulted in an accelerated inflation rate and yielded four years of antiwar demonstrations and burning ghettoes against a backdrop of prosperity and social reform. Johnson was required, at the request of the governor of Michigan, to send regular Army units to suppress riots in Detroit in July 1967; and troops had to be deployed again in Washington, D.C., in April 1968 after the assassination of Martin Luther King, Jr.

In 1967, after reading the results of a poll assessing his presidency, Johnson said: "In this job you must set a standard for making decisions. Mine is: "What will my grandchildren think of my administration when I'm buried under the tree at the Ranch, in the family graveyard.' I believe they will be proud of two things: what I have done for the Negro and in Asia. But right now I've lost twenty points on the race issue, fifteen on Vietnam." As Lyndon Johnson's voice repeats many times each day on a tape played at the LBJ Library, ". . . it is for the people themselves and their posterity to decide."

W. W. ROSTOW
(1986)

Bibliography

BURNS, JAMES MCGREGOR   1968   *To Heal and to Build: The Programs of Lyndon B. Johnson.* New York: McGraw-Hill.

JOHNSON, LYNDON B.   1971   *The Vantage Point.* New York: Holt, Rinehart & Winston.

MCPHERSON, HARRY   1972   *A Political Education.* Boston: Little, Brown.

MUELLER, JOHN E.   1973   *War, Presidents and Public Opinion.* New York: Wiley.

REDFORD, EMMETTE S. and BLISSETT, MARLAN   1981   *Organizing the Executive Branch: The Johnson Presidency.* Chicago: University of Chicago Press.

ROSTOW, W. W.   1972   *The Diffusion of Power.* New York: Macmillan.

JOHNSON, REVERDY
(1796–1876)

A leading constitutional lawyer and Maryland Unionist, Reverdy Johnson argued numerous important Supreme Court cases, including *Seymour v. McCormick* (1854), DRED SCOTT V. SANDFORD (1857), and UNITED STATES V. CRUIKSHANK (1876). At President ABRAHAM LINCOLN's request Johnson published a rebuttal to Chief Justice ROGER B. TANEY's opinion in *Ex parte Merryman* (1861), in which Johnson argued that the President had authority to suspend HABEAS CORPUS. Johnson approved the use of Negro troops and as a senator (1854–1859; 1863–1868) voted for the THIRTEENTH AMENDMENT. However, Johnson broke with Lincoln over the suppression of civilians in Maryland and war aims. Johnson believed that the Confederate states had never been legally out of the Union, and thus once the rebellion was militarily suppressed, the states should be allowed to resume their antebellum status. Johnson opposed LOYALTY OATHS and was President AN-

DREW JOHNSON's leading SENATE supporter during the IMPEACHMENT trial.

PAUL FINKELMAN
(1986)

Bibliography

STEINER, BERNARD C.   1914   *Life of Reverdy Johnson.* Baltimore: Norman, Remington Co.

JOHNSON, THOMAS
(1732–1819)

Thomas Johnson served in Maryland's colonial House of Delegates and was a member of committees to instruct delegates to the STAMP ACT CONGRESS and to draft a protest against the TOWNSHEND ACTS. He sat in the Continental Congress but was absent when the DECLARATION OF INDEPENDENCE was signed. He was a member of the convention that drafted Maryland's revolutionary constitution (1776) and served as its first governor (1777–1779). Johnson served in Congress from 1781 to 1787 and was a judge of the special federal court to settle a boundary dispute between New York and Massachusetts. He supported RATIFICATION OF THE CONSTITUTION in the state convention of 1788.

His longtime friend, President GEORGE WASHINGTON, offered Johnson a district judgeship in 1789, but Johnson accepted instead the chief judgeship of the Maryland General Court. When JOHN RUTLEDGE resigned in 1791, Washington appointed Johnson to the Supreme Court.

Serving only fourteen months on the Court, Johnson took part in no major decision. He sat for a single term (during which the JAY COURT heard only four cases) and wrote a single short opinion. In 1793, plagued by illness and fatigued by circuit duty, he resigned and was replaced by WILLIAM PATERSON.

DENNIS J. MAHONEY
(1986)

JOHNSON, WILLIAM
(1771–1834)

Justice William Johnson of Charleston, South Carolina, was THOMAS JEFFERSON's first appointee to the Supreme Court. Johnson was the son of a blacksmith and revolutionary patriot. After attending Princeton and reading law with CHARLES COTESWORTH PINCKNEY, Johnson was elected to serve three terms in the state legislature as a member of the new Republican party. During his third term he became speaker of the House. In 1799, he was elected to the state's highest court, and on March 22, 1804, he was appointed to the Supreme Court, where he served until his death. Of all the fifteen Justices who sat on the MARSHALL COURT, Johnson was, at least to 1830, the most independent and vocal in advancing opinions different from those of Chief Justice JOHN MARSHALL. In treating the accountability of the members of the Court, the distribution of the national power among the three branches, the powers reserved to the states, and VESTED RIGHTS, Johnson often found himself in disagreement with the majority of the Marshall Court. At the time of his appointment, Johnson objected to Marshall's practice of rendering unaminous opinions. He felt that the judicial role required freedom of expression, and he fought to revive the practice of SERIATIM OPINIONS. "Few minds," he protested in a separate opinion in 1816, "are accustomed to the same habit of thinking. . . ." From his advent until 1822, Johnson wrote twelve of twenty-four CONCURRING OPINIONS and sixteen of thirty-two DISSENTING OPINIONS. Toward the end of his career, new Justices joined the Court who agreed with Johnson and frequently spoke out separately with him. Johnson succeeded in establishing the right to dissent, so important in later years.

Johnson also ran into conflict with other members of the Court concerning the allocation of power among the branches of the national government. Like the rest of the Marshall Court, he believed that a strong national government was vital to national unity, and he was willing to delegate broad powers to the government. However, he believed that Congress should be the chief recipient of these powers, and he was willing to construe more narrowly the powers of the judiciary and the President, as he did, for example, in *United States v. Hudson and Goodwin.* In relation to Congress, Johnson made assertions of broad power that surpassed even those of Marshall. For a unanimous Court, in *Anderson v. Dunn,* Johnson upheld Congress's LEGISLATIVE CONTEMPT POWER, and in so doing defended the legislative discretion. Every grant of congressional power draws with it "others, not expressed, but vital to its exercise; not substantive and independent, indeed, but auxiliary and subordinate." Johnson thought IMPLIED POWERS were essential to a responsive government that served the needs of the people. Securities against the abuse of discretion rested on accountability and appeals to the people. Individual liberty stood in little danger "where all power is derived from the people, and at the feet of the people, to be resumed again only at their will."

Johnson's conception of FEDERALISM was in many ways quite modern. In broadly construing powers of Congress, he looked on these less as limitations on the states than as means of strengthening national unity and improving the lot of individuals. In a separate opinion in GIBBONS V. OGDEN, Johnson wrote that where the language of the Constitution leaves room for interpretation, the judges should consult its overriding purpose: "to unite this mass of wealth and power for the protection of the humblest individual: his rights civil and political, his interests and prosperity, are the sole end; the rest are nothing but means." Chief among the means was "the independence and harmony of the states." As Justice Johnson knew from experience, some collisions between state and federal government was inevitable; the only remedy where two governments claimed power over the same individuals was a "frank and candid co-operation for the general good."

Finally, on the rights of property, Johnson showed somewhat less reverence than did the rest of the Court. Toward the end of his career, Johnson lost some of his esteem for a powerful judiciary enforcing property rights against the states, and he began to look to the states for economic and social regulation. In OGDEN V. SAUNDERS Johnson spoke for the majority. He argued that the CONTRACT CLAUSE did not prohibit "insolvent debtor laws" as applied to contracts made subsequent to the laws' enactment. In *Ogden* Johnson objected to construing that contract clause literally. He argued that contracts should receive a "relative, and not a positive interpretation: for the rights of all should be held and enjoyed to the good of the whole." Johnson seemed to foresee the notion of STATE POLICE POWERS when he insisted that the states had the power to regulate the "social exercise" of rights.

In winning tolerance for dissenting opinions and in contributing creatively and prophetically to the body of constitutional doctrine, William Johnson won a niche as an outstanding member of the early Court.

DONALD G. MORGAN
(1986)

Bibliography
MORGAN, DONALD G. 1954 *Justice William Johnson: The First Dissenter.* Columbia: University of South Carolina Press.

JOHNSON, WILLIAM SAMUEL
(1727–1819)

Dr. William Samuel Johnson signed the Constitution as a Connecticut delegate to the CONSTITUTIONAL CONVENTION OF 1787. A lawyer and educator, he had already served his state as a legislator and judge. Johnson, a conciliator respected by all delegates, formally proposed the Connecticut Compromise (GREAT COMPROMISE). He also proposed the words defining the extent of the JUDICIAL POWER OF THE UNITED STATES, inserting the key phrase, "all cases arising under *the Constitution and* laws of the United States," and he chaired the Committee on Style. Johnson helped keep the Convention from dissolving in the heat of factional dispute. He was later a United States senator (1789–1791).

DENNIS J. MAHONEY
(1986)

JOHNSON v. AVERY
393 U.S. 483 (1969)

In a 7–2 decision, the Supreme Court, through Justice ABE FORTAS, upheld the right of state prisoners to receive the assistance of fellow convicts in the preparation of writs. The Court overturned a Tennessee prison rule aimed at abolishing the "jailhouse lawyer" practice by which a few convicts, relatively skilled at writ-writing, achieved a position of power among the inmates. Because the rule might have the effect of denying the poor and illiterate the right of HABEAS CORPUS, Tennessee was ordered either to abolish the rule or to provide alternative legal assistance for prisoners wishing to seek postconviction review of their cases.

DENNIS J. MAHONEY
(1986)

JOHNSON v. LOUISIANA
406 U.S. 356 (1972)
APODACA v. OREGON
406 U.S. 404 (1972)

In DUNCAN V. LOUISIANA (1968) the Supreme Court declared that every criminal charge must be "confirmed by the unanimous suffrage of twelve jurors," and in WILLIAMS V. FLORIDA (1970) the Court found little reason to believe that a jury of six people functions differently from a jury of twelve "particularly if the requirement of unanimity is retained." Justice BYRON R. WHITE, the Court's spokesman in these cases, also wrote its opinion in *Johnson* and for a plurality of four Justices in *Apodaca;* he found nothing constitutionally defective in verdicts by a "heavy" majority vote and no constitutional mandate for verdicts by unanimous vote. The Court upheld the laws of two states that permitted verdicts of 9–3 and 10–2 respectively. These 1972 cases, according to the dissenters, diminished the BURDEN OF PROOF beyond REASONABLE DOUBT and made convictions possible by a preponderance of jurors.

For centuries the standard of proof of guilt beyond reasonable doubt was inextricably entwined with the principle of a unanimous verdict, creating a hedge against jury bias. The requirement of JURY UNANIMITY had meant that a single juror might veto all others, thwarting an overwhelming majority. Accordingly, Johnson contended that DUE PROCESS OF LAW, by embodying the standard of proof beyond a reasonable doubt, required unanimous verdicts and that three jurors who possessed such doubt in his case showed that his guilt was not proved beyond such doubt. White answered that no basis existed for believing that the majority jurors would refuse to listen to the doubts of the minority. Yet Johnson's jurors, who were "out" for less than twenty minutes, might have taken a poll before deliberating, and if nine had voted for a guilty verdict on the first ballot, they might have returned the verdict without the need of considering the minority's doubts. The dissenters saw the jury as an entity incapable of rendering a verdict by the undisputed standard of proof beyond a reasonable doubt if any juror remained unconvinced. The Court majority saw the jury as twelve individuals, nine of whom could decide the verdict if they were satisfied beyond a reasonable doubt, regardless of minority views.

If the prosecution's burden of proving guilt beyond a reasonable doubt does not change when a 9–3 verdict is permissible, verdicts returned by a nine-juror majority ought to be the same as those returned by unanimous juries of twelve. In fact, the 9–3 system yields a substantially higher conviction ratio and substantially fewer hung juries by which defendants avoid conviction, thus substantially lowering the prosecution's burden of proof.

Johnson also contended that Louisiana's complicated three-tier system of juries—unanimous verdicts of twelve in some cases, unanimous verdicts of five in others, and 9–3 verdicts in still others—denied him the EQUAL PROTECTION OF THE LAWS. In fact, the standard of proof varied with the crime, but White rejected the equal protection argument, claiming instead that Louisiana's three-tier scheme was "not invidious" because it was rational: it saved time and money. The Court hardly considered whether it diluted justice.

In *Apodaca*, the 10–2 verdict came under attack from an argument that the FOURTEENTH AMENDMENT extended to the states the same standard as prevailed in federal courts, where unanimity prevails. Four Justices, led by White, would have ruled that the SIXTH AMENDMENT does not require unanimous verdicts even in federal trials; four, led by Justice WILLIAM O. DOUGLAS, believed that because the amendment embodies the requirement of unanimous jury verdicts, no state can permit a majority verdict. LEWIS F. POWELL's opinion was decisive. He concurred with the Douglas wing to save the unanimous verdict in federal criminal trials and with the White wing to allow nonunanimous verdicts for states wanting them. In *Apodaca*, White contradictorily conceded that the reasonable doubt standard "has been rejected in *Johnson v. Louisiana*." Douglas proved, contrary to White, that the use of the nonunanimous jury altered the way the jury functioned, stacking it against the defendant. He interpreted the majority opinions as reflecting "a "law and order' judicial mood."

LEONARD W. LEVY
(1986)

(SEE ALSO: *Jury Size.*)

Bibliography

LEVY, LEONARD W. 1974 *Against the Law: The Nixon Court and Criminal Justice.* Pages 276–298. New York: Harper & Row.

JOHNSON v. TRANSPORTATION AGENCY
480 U.S. 616 (1987)

Paul Johnson sought promotion to the position of road dispatcher with the Transportation Agency of Santa Clara County, California; he was deemed the best-qualified applicant for the job by a board of interviewers and by the Road Operations Division Director, who normally would have made the promotion decision. But the agency's affirmative-action officer intervened, recommending to the agency director that a woman seeking the position be appointed instead. The agency director agreed, and the woman was selected over Johnson. Johnson subsequently filed a suit alleging SEX DISCRIMINATION, and a federal district court found gender to be "the determining factor" in the promotion. The Supreme Court nevertheless sustained the agency's action, 6–3.

Writing for the majority, Justice WILLIAM J. BRENNAN invoked the language of UNITED STEELWORKERS V. WEBER (1979) and argued that the agency's AFFIRMATIVE ACTION program was justified because it sought to correct a "manifest imbalance" that existed in job categories that had been "traditionally segregated" on the basis of gender. According to Brennan, the determination of whether a "manifest imbalance" exists usually rests on the disparity between the percentage of a protected group employed in specific job categories and the percentage of the protected group in the local labor force who are qualified to work in those categories. Precisely how high the disparity has to be before a "manifest imbalance" arises, Brennan did not say; but he did indicate that the requisite disparity was something less than that required in cases like WYGANT V. JACKSON BOARD OF EDUCATION (1986), where employees had to establish a prima facie case of discrimination against their employer.

Concurring, Justice JOHN PAUL STEVENS sought to push open the door to affirmative action still further. He implied that private employers should be able to discriminate in favor of "disadvantaged" racial and gender groups for a wide variety of reasons, including improving education, "averting racial tension over the allocation of jobs in a community," and "improving . . . services to black constituencies."

Justice SANDRA DAY O'CONNOR concurred in the Court's judgment, but on narrower grounds than the majority. She maintained that affirmative-action programs can be invoked only to remedy past discrimination. But her standard of proof for past discrimination was nearly the same as the majority's standard for "manifest imbalance": a statistical disparity between the percentage of an organization's employees who are members of a protected group and the percentage of the relevant labor pool that is made up of members of the group. Unlike Brennan, however, O'Connor did claim that the disparity must be enough to establish a prima facie case that past discrimination in fact occurred. In the present case this was a distinction without a difference, because O'Connor found that her standard had been met.

Writing for the dissenters, Justice ANTONIN SCALIA attacked the Court for converting "a statute designed to establish a color-blind and gender-blind workplace . . . into a powerful engine of racism and sexism. . . ." Scalia noted that although Brennan cited *Weber* as controlling, he had in fact dramatically extended *Weber* by redefining the meaning of the phrase "traditionally segregated job categories." In *Weber*, the phrase had "described skilled jobs from which employers and unions had systematically and intentionally excluded black workers. . . ." But in the present case, few women were employed in categories such as road maintenance workers because women themselves did not want the jobs. "There are, of course, those who believe that the social attitudes which cause women themselves to avoid certain jobs and to favor others are as nefarious as conscious, exclusionary discrimination. Whether or not that is so . . . the two phenomena are certainly distinct. And it is the alteration of social attitudes, rather than the elimination of discrimination, which today's decision approves as justification for state-enforced discrimination. This is an enormous expansion. . . ."

JOHN G. WEST, JR.
(1992)

Bibliography

UROFSKY, MELVIN I. 1991 *A Conflict of Rights: The Supreme Court and Affirmative Action.* New York: Scribners.

U.S. COMMISSION ON CIVIL RIGHTS 1987 *Toward an Understanding of Johnson.* Clearinghouse Publication 94. Washington, D.C.: U.S. Government Printing Office.

JOHNSON v. ZERBST
304 U.S. 458 (1938)

Defendants who neither sought nor were offered counsel were convicted in a federal court. The Supreme Court held that the SIXTH AMENDMENT requires counsel in all federal criminal proceedings unless the right is waived. This HOLDING is mainly of historical interest, but the case retains remarkable vitality and is often cited because of its definition of WAIVER. Starting with the proposition that there is "every reasonable presumption against "waiver," the Court declared: "A waiver is ordinarily an intelligent relinquishment or abandonment of a known right or privilege."

Johnson's strong suspicion of waiver of the RIGHT TO COUNSEL is reiterated in many decisions. In *Von Moltke v. Gillies* (1948) the Supreme Court established a duty of the trial judge "to investigate [waiver of counsel] as long and as thoroughly as the circumstances of the case before him demand." The Court has also said that waiver must affirmatively appear on the record and will not be presumed from a silent record.

Although the Court's definition of waiver applies to all FUNDAMENTAL RIGHTS, and although *Johnson* is cited in FOURTH AMENDMENT and Fifth Amendment cases, the definition has been rigorously applied only in the right to counsel context that spawned it.

BARBARA ALLEN BABCOCK
(1986)

JOINT ANTI-FASCIST REFUGEE COMMITTEE v. MCGRATH
341 U.S. 123 (1951)

Five members of the VINSON COURT dealt a setback to the HARRY S. TRUMAN administration's anticommunist crusade by condemning the procedures through which the ATTORNEY GENERAL of the United States listed certain organizations as "totalitarian, fascist, communist or subversive" under the President's Executive Order of 1947 creating a LOYALTY-SECURITY PROGRAM for all federal employees. Three organizations designated as "communist" by the attorney general complained that they had been stigmatized without an opportunity for a hearing at which they could rebut the government's presumption. Justice HAROLD H. BURTON concluded that the executive order did not permit the attorney general to make arbitrary, EX PARTE findings without a hearing. In separate concurring opinions, four Justices concluded that the President's order may have authorized such *ex parte* proceedings, but did so in violation of the DUE PROCESS clause. Justice HUGO L. BLACK also condemned the list as a violation of the FIRST AMENDMENT

and as a BILL OF ATTAINDER. Justice STANLEY F. REED, for three dissenters, said the attorney general's actions were appropriate "to guard the Nation from espionage, subversion and SEDITION."

MICHAEL E. PARRISH
(1986)

JOINT COMMITTEE ON RECONSTRUCTION

In December 1865, Congress by CONCURRENT RESOLUTION created the Joint Committee of Fifteen on Reconstruction to provide a deliberative body for consideration of RECONSTRUCTION policy, because Republicans refused to accept President ANDREW JOHNSON's "Restoration" as an accomplished fact. All legislation directly affecting Reconstruction was referred to it.

The majority report of the Joint Committee (1866), prepared by Senator WILLIAM P. FESSENDEN (Republican, Maine), rejected punitive theories of Reconstruction as "profitless abstractions" and repudiated the lenient policies of President Johnson and congressional Democrats. The Committee's Republican majority insisted that only Congress had final power to regularize the constitutional status of the seceded states. The Democratic minority report countered that the states were entitled to immediate readmission and self-government. The Joint Committee fashioned the FOURTEENTH AMENDMENT as a compendium of Republican Reconstruction objectives as of the summer of 1866: freedmen's CITIZENSHIP and voting, equality before the law and assurance of DUE PROCESS for freedmen, Confederate disfranchisement, repudiation of the Confederate war debt, denial of compensation for slaves, and confirmation of the Union debt. When the inadequacy of the Fourteenth Amendment as a comprehensive Reconstruction measure became apparent, Republican committee members drafted the first MILITARY RECONSTRUCTION ACT, which created legal machinery for beginning the process of congressional Reconstruction.

WILLIAM M. WIECEK
(1986)

Bibliography

KENDRICK, BENJAMIN B.   1914   *The Journal of the Joint Committee of Fifteen on Reconstruction.* New York: Columbia University Press.

JOINT RESOLUTIONS

Joint resolutions, unlike CONCURRENT RESOLUTIONS, have the force of law and require the signature of the President to be enacted. They are therefore subject to the VETO POWER. A joint resolution may be used when a permanent statutory enactment is inappropriate. Joint resolutions may be used to issue a DECLARATION OF WAR, to end a STATE OF WAR, to annex territory, or to extend the effective life of previously enacted legislation.

As part of the AMENDING PROCESS, joint resolutions are used to propose constitutional amendments. Such resolutions require a two-thirds vote in each house, but not the President's signature.

DENNIS J. MAHONEY
(1986)

JONES v. ALFRED H. MAYER CO.
392 U.S. 409 (1968)

This opinion contains important interpretations of a CIVIL RIGHTS statute and of Congress's power to prohibit private discrimination. Jones alleged that the defendants had refused to sell him a home because he was black. He brought an action under section 1982 of Title 42, United States Code, a remnant of the CIVIL RIGHTS ACT OF 1866, which states in part that all citizens shall have the same right as white citizens to purchase property.

Because Jones relied on a federal law to challenge private discrimination, and because the Supreme Court found that section 1982 encompassed Jones's claim, the case raised the question whether the Constitution grants Congress authority to outlaw private discrimination. The degree to which Congress may do so under the FOURTEENTH AMENDMENT has been a recurring unsettled question. (See UNITED STATES V. GUEST.) In *Jones*, Justice POTTER STEWART's opinion for the Court avoided that complex matter by sustaining section 1982's applicability to private behavior under Congress's THIRTEENTH AMENDMENT power to eliminate slavery. But even this HOLDING generated tension with the Court's nineteenth-century pronouncements on Congress's power to reach private discrimination.

In the CIVIL RIGHTS CASES (1883) the Court seemed to concede that the Thirteenth Amendment vests in Congress power to abolish all badges or incidents of slavery. (See BADGES OF SERVITUDE.) In that case, however, the Court viewed those badges or incidents narrowly and limited Congress's role in defining them. In striking down the CIVIL RIGHTS ACT OF 1875, a provision barring discrimination in PUBLIC ACCOMMODATIONS, the Court commented, "It would be running the slavery argument into the ground" to make it apply to every act of private discrimination in the field of public accommodations. In *Jones*, however, the Court acknowledged Congress's broad dis-

cretion not merely to eliminate the badges or incidents of slavery but also to define the practices constituting them.

Jones thus granted Congress virtually unlimited power to outlaw private RACIAL DISCRIMINATION. In later cases, *Jones* provided support for Congress's power to outlaw private racial discrimination in contractual relationships. Section 1981, another remnant of the Civil Rights Act of 1866, confers on all persons the same right "enjoyed by white citizens" to make and enforce contracts, to be parties or witnesses in lawsuits, and to be protected by law in person and property. RUNYON V. MCCRARY (1976) held section 1981 to prohibit the exclusion of blacks from private schools, and *Johnson v. Railway Express Agency, Inc.* (1974) held it to prohibit discrimination in employment.

As Justice JOHN MARSHALL HARLAN's dissent noted, *Jones*'s interpretation of section 1982 established it, more than a hundred years after its enactment, as a fair housing law discovered within months of passage of the CIVIL RIGHTS ACT OF 1868, which itself contained a detailed fair housing provision. (See OPEN HOUSING LAWS.) In finding that section 1982 reaches private discrimination not authorized by state law, *Jones* offers a questionable interpretation of the 1866 act's structure and manipulates legislative history. Whether a candid opinion could support *Jones*'s interpretation of section 1982 remains a subject of debate.

THEODORE EISENBERG
(1986)

Bibliography

CASPER, GERHARD 1968 *Jones v. Mayer:* Clio, Bemused and Confused Muse. *Supreme Court Review* 1968:89–132.
FAIRMAN, CHARLES 1971 Reconstruction and Reunion 1864–88: Part One. Volume 6 of The Oliver Wendell Holmes Devise History of the Supreme Court of the United States. New York: Macmillan.

JONES v. SECURITIES & EXCHANGE COMMISSION
298 U.S. 1 (1936)

Although unimportant as a matter of constitutional law, *Jones* has significance in constitutional history. The Court's decision and the tone of Justice GEORGE SUTHERLAND's opinion for the majority helped convince President FRANKLIN D. ROOSEVELT that the Court was prejudiced against the NEW DEAL. A Wall Street manipulator had withdrawn a securities offering on learning that the Securities and Exchange Commission was investigating his fraud. The commission had continued its investigation, raising the question whether it had exceeded its statuory authority. Sutherland called its action arbitrary, inquisitional, odious, and comparable to Star Chamber procedure. Justices BENJAMIN N. CARDOZO, LOUIS D. BRANDEIS, and HARLAN FISKE STONE answered Sutherland's charges and defended the commission. The opinion of the Court hardened Roosevelt's attitude toward it, culminating in his COURT-PACKING plan of 1937.

LEONARD W. LEVY
(1986)

JONES v. VAN ZANDT

See: Fugitive Slavery

JONES v. WOLF

See: Religious Liberty

JOSEPH BURSTYN, INC. v. WILSON

See: *Burstyn, Inc. v. Wilson*

JOURNALISTIC PRACTICES, TORT LIABILITY, AND THE FREEDOM OF THE PRESS

Two seemingly clear precepts come into sharp conflict when journalists are charged with wrongful acts in gathering news. On one hand, the media have never been held to be immune from the general civil and criminal laws that govern the rest of society. Thus, if a reporter pursuing a lead commits an assault or a trespass, or destroys the PROPERTY of another, the special nature of his or her mission creates no shield from general liability. When journalists sought to withhold from a GRAND JURY the identity of a confidential source, the Supreme Court rejected such requests for immunity; reporters, said the Court, must testify like other citizens, even though such a duty may inhibit or deter certain forms of newsgathering.

On the other hand, the FIRST AMENDMENT clearly confers on the press a special status, notably when it comes to printing or BROADCASTING the truth. Time and again the Court has barred civil and criminal sanctions against the media for publishing sensitive and confidential information like the name of a rape victim or of a juvenile offender. So long as the material was lawfully obtained, is accurate, and of public interest, whatever interest government may claim in enforcing secrecy must yield to the FREEDOM OF THE PRESS. Indeed, even where the material was obtained unlawfully—as with the Pentagon Papers—

the First Amendment bars government from imposing a PRIOR RESTRAINT in the interest of NATIONAL SECURITY.

The difficult cases arise between these relatively clear extremes. There the guiding principles become confused and contentious. When a tobacco company threatened in 1995 to sue CBS if the television network broadcast an interview with a former employee of the company, seasoned First Amendment lawyers were sharply at odds over the validity of such a suit.

The underlying tort claim—inducing a breach of contract—was a novel one that had never been tested against the media. Some experts argued that freedom of the press would bar such a damage claim, because a large award could severely inhibit expressive activity and freedom of communication. Other equally respected experts insisted that such a claim would be seen by the courts as part of the "generally applicable law" by which the media have always been held accountable. Because the particular case was settled, we still do not know how a court would have ruled on this novel issue.

The relatively few such cases that have been decided leave many uncertainties. On one hand, when a newspaper reporter promised confidentiality to a source, but her editors insisted on revealing that source in the resulting story, the source successfully sued the publisher for breach of promise in COHEN V. COWLES MEDIA CO. (1991). When a television network obtained damaging footage from a supermarket by posing two reporters as legitimate employees, the store owner recovered damages for the workers' alleged breach of a duty of loyalty and for the network's "unfair and deceptive trade practices" in FOOD LION, INC. V. AMERICAN BROADCASTING CO. (ABC) (1997).

On the other hand, a meat packer was unsuccessful in seeking to bar the broadcast of potentially damaging footage another network had obtained by getting a packing employee to carry a concealed camera into the freezer. In such cases, direct liability for causing tangible harm seems never to be in doubt. Of course the network must pay if the camera crew physically damages the freezer controls, or causes the contents to spoil while being filmed, or coerces or violates the privacy of a regular employee.

What remains uncertain and contentious is the degree to which collateral or indirect liability may also be imposed—for the intangible effects on consumer confidence of material obtained by trespass, for example, rather than for tangible harm inflicted by the trespasser's feet or hands.

Several possibly helpful principles emerge from these cases. For one, no matter how reprehensible the journalist's conduct may have been, it seems never likely to justify imposing a prior restraint against publication. That was the teaching of the Pentagon Papers case, NEW YORK TIMES CO. V. UNITED STATES (1971), where the fact that the materials had been taken in violation of trust seemed of virtually no importance to the Supreme Court.

Moreover, information that is both truthful and of public interest is likely to fare better when it comes to liability of any sort. The relative strength of the opposing interests—those of the media on one hand, and of the victim of wrongful media conduct on the other—are likely to help resolve otherwise close cases. On one side, favoring the media, there is the powerful interest of readers, listeners, and viewers in maximizing the flow of information. On the other side, there may be the interests of persons who are actual or potential victims of wrongful newsgathering practices. Both sets of interests may be considered and weighed in the process of striking a balance in cases that are inescapably close and difficult.

Finally, courts are likely to take into account the availability of less drastic alternative forms of regulation. Most clearly, if a victim of wrongful newsgathering could seek damages after publication, the always tenuous case against publication would be even weaker. Among various forms of postpublication relief, courts are likely to choose the one that least-severely affects or impairs the freedom of the press.

ROBERT M. O'NEIL
(2000)

Bibliography

O'NEIL, ROBERT M. 1996 Tainted Sources: First Amendment Rights and Journalistic Wrongs. *William and Mary Bill of Rights Journal* 4:1005–1025

SIMS, JOHN C. 1993 Triangulating the Boundaries of the Pentagon Papers Case. *William and Mary Bill of Rights Journal* 2:341–452.

JOURNALISTS AND THE SUPREME COURT

At the heart of the complex relationship between the Supreme Court and the journalists who cover it lies a contradiction. Due to its inherent inaccessibility, and to the fact that its members speak only through their written opinions without elaboration through news conferences or press releases, the Court, more than most other public institutions, depends on press coverage for public understanding of its work. Yet the Court fails to take a number of modest, relatively unobtrusive steps to achieve better, more accurate journalism about the Court.

The press therefore has a particularly heavy responsibility to provide comprehensive and accurate Court coverage. When it comes to learning about the Court's work, the public has few alternative channels of information available. Yet covering the Court is an afterthought for many news organizations that would not think of taking such a casual, almost haphazard approach to reporting about the White House or Congress.

Arguments and decisions in a handful of major cases each year attract a crowd of print and electronic journalists, but on most days when the Court is in session, the two rows of seats set aside in the courtroom for the press are empty, or nearly so. On days when the Court is not sitting, the number of journalists who spend time in the press room on the ground floor, reading briefs and petitions to prepare for upcoming cases, can usually be counted on the fingers of one hand.

The habits of these two institutions, the Court and the press, are mutually reinforcing. Neither pays due attention to the other. The result is journalism about the Court that is too often skimpy, imprecise, and lacking in context. That in itself is no doubt an improvement, however, from earlier decades, during which major developments at the Court could go entirely unreported.

In 1938, for example, the press missed the landmark ruling in ERIE RAILROAD CO. V. TOMPKINS, which revolutionized FEDERAL JURISDICTION by holding that there is no universal COMMON LAW and that federal courts are bound to apply state law in cases of DIVERSITY JURISDICTION. As Justice RUTH BADER GINSBURG recounted the incident to an audience at the Georgetown University Law Center, Justice HARLAN FISKE STONE let a week go by and then complained to Arthur Krock, the chief of *The New York Times* Washington Bureau, about the newspaper's failure to report on the decision. Mr. Krock soon produced an account of what he called a "transcendentally significant opinion" that had "generally eluded public notice."

In the media-saturated world in which the Court and the Washington press corps exist today, an omission of this sort would be most unlikely, because interested parties, served by public relations firms and aided by fax machines, would quickly bring a major ruling to the attention of the press. Today's lapses are likely to be of a more subtle variety, understating or overstating an opinion's significance or degree of conclusiveness. There is such a cacophony of voices responding to any important Court ruling, in fact, that reporters who are uncertain how to assess a decision often fall back on simply quoting the responses of the parties or outside experts, leaving readers to draw their own conclusions.

From a journalist's point of view, perhaps the most salient fact about covering the Court is the inaccessibility of the Justices themselves. Justices and reporters may encounter one another at social functions at the Court, or casually in the building's hallways. But the Justices are not available for off-the-record conversations about the Court's work. A reporter who finds an opinion ambiguous cannot call the author for an explanation.

must be obeyed." President JAMES MADISON, mindful of the repercussions of the case, chastised the state governor. "The Executive," he replied, "is not only unauthorized to prevent the execution of a decree sanctioned by the Supreme Court of the United States, but is expressly enjoined, by statute, to carry into effect any such decree, where opposition may be made to it."

The incipient rebellion immediately collapsed. The state withdrew its militia and appropriated the money to pay Olmstead. In the aftermath of the affair, the United States arrested and tried the commanding general of the state militia and eight of his officers for having obstructed the federal marshal. A federal jury convicted them in a trial before Justice BUSHROD WASHINGTON, who sentenced the defendants to fines and imprisonment, but the President pardoned them. Eleven state legislatures adopted resolutions condemning Pennsylvania's resistance to the federal courts. Every southern state rejected Pennsylvania's doctrines of STATES' RIGHTS. That northern state had also proposed the establishment of "an impartial tribunal" to settle disputes between "the general and state governments." The legislature of Virginia replied that "a tribunal is already provided by the Constitution of the United States, to wit: the Supreme Court, more eminently qualified . . . to decide the disputes aforesaid . . . than any other tribunal which could be erected." In a few years, however, Virginia would be playing Pennsylvania's tune. (See MARTIN V. HUNTER'S LESSEE, 1816.) The supremacy of the Supreme Court had by no means been established yet.

LEONARD W. LEVY
(1986)

Bibliography

HIGGINBOTHAM, SANFORD W. 1952 *The Keystone in the Democratic Arch: Pennsylvania Politics 1800–1816.* Pages 177–204. Harrisburg: Pennsylvania Historical and Museum Commission.

TREACY, KENNETH W. 1957 The Olmstead Case, 1778–1809. *Western Political Quarterly* 10:675–691.

WARREN, CHARLES 1923 *The Supreme Court in American History,* 3 vols. Vol. I:375–387. Boston: Little, Brown.

JUDGMENT

The judgment of a court is its conclusion or sentence of the law applied to the facts of a case. It is the court's final determination of the rights of the parties to the case. A judgment, once entered (unless successfully appealed), is conclusive as to the rights of the parties and ordinarily may not be challenged either in a future suit by the same parties or in a collateral proceeding. The judgment is essentially equivalent to the DECISION of the court. Judgments in EQUITY and admiralty cases are called "decrees"; judg-

ments in criminal and ecclesiastical cases are called "sentences."

DENNIS J. MAHONEY
(1986)

(SEE ALSO: *Final Judgment Rule; Habeas Corpus; Res Judicata.*)

JUDICIAL ACTIVISM AND JUDICIAL RESTRAINT

"Judicial activism" and "judicial restraint" are terms used to describe the assertiveness of judicial power. In no sense unique to the Supreme Court or to cases involving some construction of the Constitution, they are editorial summations of how different courts and different judges conduct themselves.

The user of these terms ("judicial activism" and "judicial restraint") presumes to locate the relative assertiveness of particular courts or individual judges between two theoretical extremes. The extreme model of judicial activism is of a court so intrusive and ubiquitous that it virtually dominates the institutions of government. The antithesis of such a model is a court that decides virtually nothing at all: it strains to find reasons why it lacks JURISDICTION; it avows deference to the superiority of other departments or agencies in construing the law; it finds endless reasons why the constitutionality of laws cannot be examined. It is a model of government virtually without useful recourse to courts as enforcers of constitutional limits.

The uses of "judicial activism" and "judicial restraint," however, are not entirely uniform. Often the terms are employed noncommittally, that is, merely as descriptive shorthand to identify some court or judge as more activist or more restrained than some other, or more than the same court formerly appeared to be. In this sense, the usage is neither commendatory nor condemnatory. Especially with reference to the Supreme Court, however, the terms are also used polemically. The user has a personal or professional view of the "right" role of the Court and, accordingly, commends or condemns the Court for conforming to or straying from that right role. Indeed, an enduring issue of American constitutional law has centered on this lively controversy of right role; procedurally and substantively, how activist or how restrained ought the Supreme Court to be in its use of the power of constitutional JUDICIAL REVIEW?

Ought that Court to confront the constitutionality of the laws as speedily as opportunity affords, the better to furnish authoritative guidance and settle political controversy in keeping with its unique competence and function as the chief constitutional court of the nation? Or ought it, rather, to eschew any unnecessary voluntarism, recognizing that all participants in government are as bound as the Court to observe the Constitution and that the very insularity of the Supreme Court from representative government is a powerful reason to avoid the appearance of constitutional arrogance or constitutional monopoly? In brief, what degree of strict necessity should the Supreme Court require as a condition of examining the substantive constitutionality of government acts or government practices?

Substantively, the issues of "proper" activism or proper restraint are similar. When the constitutionality of governmental action is considered, what predisposition, if any, ought the Supreme Court to bring to bear? Should it take a fairly strict view of the Constitution and, accordingly, hold against the constitutionality of each duly contested governmental act unless the consistency of that act with the Constitution can be demonstrated virtually to anyone's satisfaction? Or, to the contrary, recognizing its own fallibility and the shared obligation of Congress (and the President and every member of every state legislature) fully to respect the Constitution as much as judges are bound to respect it, should the Court hold against the constitutionality of what other departments of government have enacted only when virtually no reasonable person could conclude that the act in question is consistent with the Constitution?

Disputes respecting the Supreme Court's procedural judicial activism (or restraint) and substantive judicial activism (or restraint) are thus of recurring political interest. Most emphatically is this the case with regard to judicial review of the constitutionality of legislation, as distinct from nonconstitutional judicial review. For here, unlike activism on nonconstitutional issues (such as the interpretation of statutes), the consequences of an adverse holding on the merits are typically difficult to change. An act of Congress, held inapplicable to a given transaction, need only be approved in modified form to "reverse" the Supreme Court's impression. On the other hand, a holding that the statute did cover the transaction but in presuming to do so was unconstitutional is a much more nearly permanent boundary. It may be overcome only by extraordinary processes of amending the Constitution itself (a recourse successfully taken during two centuries only four times), or by a reconsideration and overruling by the Supreme Court itself (an eventuality that has occurred about 130 times). Thus, the special force of adjudication of constitutionality, being of the greatest consequence and least reversibility, has made the proper constitutional activism (or proper restraint) of the Supreme Court itself a central question.

An appraisal of the Supreme Court in these terms involves two problems: the activism (or restraint) with which the Court rations the judicial process in developing or in avoiding occasions to decide constitutional claims; and the activism (or restraint) of its STANDARDS OF REVIEW when it does decide such claims.

The Supreme Court's own description of its proper role in interpreting the Constitution is one of strict necessity and of last resort. In brief, the Court has repeatedly held that the Constitution itself precludes the Court from considering constitutional issues unless they are incidental to an actual CASE OR CONTROVERSY that meets very stringent demands imposed by Article III. In addition, the Court holds that prudence requires the complete avoidance of constitutional issues in any case in which the rights of the litigants can be resolved without reference to such an issue.

In 1982, in VALLEY FORGE CHRISTIAN SCHOOLS V. AMERICANS UNITED, Justice WILLIAM H. REHNQUIST recapitulated the Court's conventional wisdom. Forswearing any judicial power generally to furnish advice on the Constitution, and denying that the Supreme Court may extend its jurisdiction more freely merely because constitutional issues are at stake, he declared: "The constitutional power of federal courts cannot be defined, and indeed has no substance, without reference to the necessity to "adjudge the legal rights of litigants in actual controversies." Even when the stringent prerequisites of jurisdiction have been fully satisfied, moreover, "[t]he power to declare the rights of individuals and to measure the authority of governments, this Court said 90 years ago, "is legitimate only in the last resort, and as a necessity in the determination of real, earnest, and vital controversy." For emphasis, he added, "The federal courts were simply not constituted as ombudsmen of the general welfare. [Such a philosophy] has no place in our constitutional scheme."

In so declaring, Justice Rehnquist was relying substantially upon a similar position adopted by Chief Justice JOHN MARSHALL in MARBURY V. MADISON (1803). Explaining that the Court's determination of constitutional questions was but an incident of its duty to pass upon legal questions raised in the due course of litigation, in no respect different from its duty when some statutory issue or COMMON LAW question might likewise be presented in a case, Marshall had insisted: "The province of the Court is, solely, to decide on the rights of individuals," and not to presume any larger role.

Accordingly, though a constitutional issue may be present, if the dispute in which it arises does not otherwise meet conventionally strict standards of STANDING, RIPENESS, genuine adverseness of parties, or sufficient factual concreteness to meet the demands of a justiciable case or controversy as required by Article III, the felt urgency or gravity of the constitutional question can make no difference. In steering a wide course around the impropriety of deciding constitutional questions except as incidental to a genuine adversary proceeding, moreover, the Court has also declared that it will not entertain COLLUSIVE SUITS. As Marshall declared in *Marbury*, "it never was the thought that, by means of a friendly suit, a party beaten in the legislature could transfer to the courts an inquiry as to the constitutionality of a legislative act." Similarly, if during the course of genuine litigation the grievance has become moot in light of subsequent events, it must then be dismissed insofar as there remains no necessity to address the original issue.

When, moreover, all requisites of conventional, genuine litigation remain such that adjudication of the parties' rights is an unavoidable judicial duty, the Court has still insisted that it should determine whether the case can be disposed of without addressing any issue requiring it to render an interpretation of the Constitution itself. Accordingly (within the conventional wisdom), even with respect to disputes properly before it, well within its jurisdiction and prominently featuring a major, well-framed, well-contested constitutional question, the Supreme Court may still refuse to address that question. In his famous concurring opinion in ASHWANDER V. TENNESSEE VALLEY AUTHORITY (1936), Justice LOUIS D. BRANDEIS insisted that constitutional questions were to be decided only as a last resort: "When the validity of an act of Congress is drawn in question, and even if a serious doubt of constitutionality is raised, it is a cardinal principle that this Court will first ascertain whether a construction of the statute is fairly possible by which the question may be avoided." Indeed, Brandeis continued, the Court will not "pass upon a constitutional question although properly presented by the record, if there is also present some other ground upon which the case may be disposed of." Moreover, though there may be no other ground, if the constitutional question arises at the instance of a public official, "the challenge by a public official interested only in the performance of his official duty will not be entertained." Even when the issue is raised by a private litigant, his challenge to the constitutionality of a statute will not be heard "at the instance of one who has availed himself of its benefits."

Self-portrayals of the Court as a wholly reluctant constitutional tribunal that is not an oracle of constitutional proclamation but a court of law that will face constitutional questions only when a failure to do so would involve it as a tribunal in an unconstitutional oppression of a litigant go even further. A litigant may have much at stake, and nothing except his reliance upon some clause in the Constitution may remain to save him from jeopardy. Still, if the clause in the Constitution is deemed not to yield objective criteria adequate to guide its application by the Court, the Court may decline to attempt to fix any meaning for the clause on the basis that it is nonjusticiable. (See POLITICAL QUESTIONS.) Similarly, if the relief requested should require the Court to consider an order against the Congress itself, an order the Court cannot be confident would be obeyed and which it is without resources otherwise to enforce, it may refuse to consider the case. Identically, if an adjudication of the constitutional question, though otherwise imperative to the litigant's case, might involve conflict with the President respecting decisions already made, communicated to, and relied upon by other governments, the case may also be regarded as nonjusticiable.

In rough outline, then, these are the principal elements of the orthodoxy of extreme judicial restraint. Consistent with them, even when the Court does adjudicate a constitutional question, its decision is supposed to be "no broader than is required by the precise facts." Anything remotely resembling an advisory opinion or a gratuitous judicial utterance respecting the meaning of the Constitution is to be altogether avoided.

Although this combination of Article III requirements and policies has characterized a large part of the Court's history (most substantially when the constitutional questions involved acts of Congress or executive action), the Court's practice has not, in fact, been at all uniform. Collusive suits have sometimes been entertained, and the constitutional issues at once examined. Public officials sometimes have been deemed to have sufficient standing to press constitutional questions, though they have had no more than an official interest in the matter. Holdings on the Constitution occasionally have been rendered in far broader terms than essential to decide the case, often for the advisory guidance of other judges or for the benefit of state or local officials. When the constitutional issue seemed clear enough and strongly meritorious, parties placed in positions of advantage solely by force of the very condition of which they later complained on constitutional grounds have not always been estopped from securing a decision. On occasion when third parties would be unlikely or unable to raise a constitutional claim on their own behalf, moreover, other litigants deemed suitable to represent their claim have been allowed to proceed on the merits of the constitutional issues. And some utterly moot cases have been decided on the merits of their constitutional questions on the paradoxical explanation that unless the moot cases were treated as still lively, then conceivably the merits of the constitutional issues would forever elude judicial review. Indeed, the nation's most famous case, *Marbury v. Madison,* was in many respects an example of extreme procedural activism despite its disclaimer of strict necessity.

At issue in Marbury's case was the question of the Supreme Court's power to hear the case in the first instance, within its ORIGINAL JURISDICTION, rather than merely on appeal. The statute William Marbury relied upon to demonstrate his right to commence his action in the Supreme Court was altogether unclear as to whether it authorized his suit to begin in the Supreme Court. Avoidance of the necessity of examining the constitutionality of the statute was readily available merely by construing the statute as not providing for original jurisdiction: an interpretation thus making clear that Marbury had sued in the wrong court, resulting in his case's being dismissed for lack of (statutory) jurisdiction and obviating any need to say anything at all about the constitutionality of an act of Congress.

Rather than pursue that course, however, Chief Justice Marshall "actively" interpreted the act of Congress, that is, he interpreted it to draw into issue its very constitutionality and then promptly resolved that issue by holding the act unconstitutional. Beyond that, rather than be content to dismiss the case for lack of either statutory or constitutional jurisdiction, the Chief Justice also (and quite gratuitously) addressed every other question raised by the complaint, including Marbury's right to the public office he sought, the appropriateness of the remedy he asked for, the illegality of the secretary of state's refusal to give it to him, and the lack of immunity from such suits by the secretary of state. Each of these other issues was of substantial controversy. Several of them raised substantial constitutional questions. Marshall resolved all in an opinion most of which was purely advisory, that is, of no necessity in light of the ultimate holding, which was that the Court was (constitutionally) without power (jurisdiction) to address the merits of the case at all. Marshall addressed all these questions on the basis of a factual record supplied principally on affidavit of his own brother. Still, Marshall, far from recusing himself on that account or on account of his own participation as the secretary of state who failed to deliver Marbury's commission, fully participated in the case, voted, and wrote the opinion for the Court. In these many respects, the case of *Marbury v. Madison* was an extraordinary example of extreme procedural activism. Its resemblance to what the Court has otherwise said (as in the Brandeis *Ashwander* guidelines or the *Valley Forge* case) is purely ironic. Indeed, the unstable actual practices of the Court which has so often described its institutional role in constitutional adjudication as one of the utmost procedural restraint, while not uniformly adhering to that description, have contributed to the Court's great controversiality in American government.

As we have seen, procedural activism (and restraint) has consisted principally of two parts. The first part is the rigor or lack of rigor with which the Court has interpreted the limitation in Article III of the Constitution, according to which the use of the judicial power can operate solely on "cases and controversies." The second part is the extent to which the Court has also adopted a number of purely self-denying ordinances according to which it will decline to adjudicate the merits of a constitutional claim in any case in which a decision can be reached on some other ground.

In contrast, substantive activism (and restraint) has consisted principally of three parts, each reflecting the extent to which the Court has interpreted the Constitution either aggressively to invalidate actions taken by other departments of government, or diffidently to acquiesce in these actions. The first part pertains to the Court's substantive interpretations of the ENUMERATED and IMPLIED POWERS of the other departments of the national government, that is, the powers vested by Article I in Congress and the powers vested by Article II in the President. The second part pertains to the Court's interpretation of the Constitution as implicitly withdrawing from state governments a variety of powers not explicitly forbidden to them by the Constitution. And the third part pertains to the Court's interpretations of those clauses in the Constitution that impose positive restrictions on the national and the state governments, principally the provisions in Article I, sections 9 and 10, in the BILL OF RIGHTS, and in the FOURTEENTH AMENDMENT. Although there may be no a priori reason to separate the substantive activism and restraint of the Supreme Court into these three particular categories, it is nonetheless practically useful to do so: overall, the Court has responded to them quite distinctly. Indeed, in practice, despite very great differences among particular Justices, the general tendency has been to develop a constitutional jurisprudence of selective activism and selective restraint.

In respect to constitutional challenges to acts of Congress for consistency with Article I's enumeration of affirmative powers, the Court's standard of review has generally been one of extraordinary restraint. With the exception of the first three and a half decades of the twentieth century, the Court has largely deferred to Congress's own suppositions respecting the scope of its powers. During the first seventy-five years of the Constitution, for instance, only two acts of Congress were held not to square with the Constitution. During the most recent forty years (a period of intense and extremely far-reaching national legislation), again but two acts have been held to fail for want of enumerated or implied constitutional authorization. Indeed, even when the comparison is enlarged to include cases challenging acts of Congress not merely for want of enacting authority but rather because they were alleged to transgress specific prohibitions (for example, the FIRST AMENDMENT restriction that Congress shall make no law abridging the FREEDOM OF SPEECH), still the record overall is one of general diffidence and restraint. Over the entirety of the Court's history, scarcely more than 120 acts of Congress have been held invalid.

An influential rationale for such restraint toward acts of Congress was set forth in 1893, in an essay by JAMES BRADLEY THAYER that Justice FELIX FRANKFURTER subsequently identified as uniquely influential on his own thinking as a judicial conservative. Thayer admonished the judiciary to bear in mind that the executive and legislative departments of the national government were constitutionally equal to the judiciary, that they were equivalently bound by oath of office to respect the Constitution, and that each was a good deal more representative of the people than the life-tenured members of the Supreme Court. Accordingly, Thayer urged, the Court should test the acts of coordinate national departments solely according to a rule of "clear error." In brief, such acts were to be examined not to determine whether their constitutionality necessarily conformed to the particular interpretation which the judges themselves might independently have concluded was the most clearly correct interpretation of the Constitution. Rather, such acts should be sustained unless they depended on an interpretation of constitutional power that was itself manifestly unreasonable, that is, an interpretation *clearly* erroneous.

Thayer's rule provided a strong political rationale for extreme judicial deference in respect to enumerated and implied national powers. Of necessity, however, it also tended practically to the enlistment of the judiciary less as an independent guardian of the Constitution (at least in respect to the scope of enumerated and implied powers) than as an institution tending to validate claims of national authority against state perspectives on the proper boundaries of FEDERALISM. It is a thesis that has periodically attracted criticism on that account, but it does not stand as the sole explanation for the general restraint reflected in the Supreme Court's permissive construction of national legislative and executive powers. Rather, without necessarily assuming that Congress and the President possess a suitably reliable detachment to be the presumptive best judges of their respective powers, decades before the appearance of Thayer's essay the Supreme Court had already expressed a separate rationale: a judicial rule of BROAD CONSTRUCTION respecting enumerated national powers.

The most durable expression of that rule is reported in a famous OBITER DICTUM by Chief Justice John Marshall. In MCCULLOCH V. MARYLAND (1819), Marshall emphasized to his own colleagues, the federal judges: "We must never forget, that it is a *constitution* we are expounding." In full context, Marshall plainly meant that it was a Constitution for the future as well as for the present, for a nation then quite small and new but expected to become much more considerable. To meet these uncertain responsibilities, Congress would require flexibility and legislative latitude.

Thus, powers granted to it by the Constitution should be read generously.

The point was expanded upon more than a century later by Justice OLIVER WENDELL HOLMES, in MISSOURI V. HOLLAND (1920), defending the judiciary's predisposition to interpret the TREATY POWER very deferentially: "When we are dealing with words that also are a constituent act, like the Constitution of the United States, we must realize that they have called into life a being the development of which could not have been foreseen completely by the most gifted of its begetters. . . . [I]t has taken a century and has cost their successors much sweat and blood to prove that they created a nation." This rule of generous construction, like Thayer's rule of "clear error," tends to support a judicial policy of substantive interpretative restraint. And while not free of criticism on its own account (as federalism critics will tend to fault it as unfaithful to their view of the extent to which substantive legislative authority was meant to be reserved to the states), it is not contingent upon doubtful assumptions respecting the capacity of the President or of the Congress fairly to assess the scope of powers they are given by the Constitution. Arguably, it is as well that this policy of judicial restraint not be made to rest on such assumptions. Although reference to the early constitutional history of the United States tends to support Thayer's thesis (early members of Congress included many persons who had participated in the shaping of the Constitution and who frequently debated proposed legislation in terms of its consistency with that Constitution), two centuries of political change have weakened its suppositions considerably. Persons serving in Congress are far removed from the original debates over enumerated powers; the business of Congress is vastly greater than it once was; the electorate is itself vastly enlarged beyond the limited numbers of persons originally eligible to vote; and such attention as may be given within Congress to issues of constitutionality is understandably likely to be principally political in its preoccupations rather than cautious and detached. Thus, the Marshall rule of generous construction in respect to national powers, rather than the Thayer proposal (of yielding to not-unreasonable interpretations by Congress), tends more strongly to anchor the general policy of judicial restraint in this area. (When the issue had been one of conflict between Congress and the President, on the other hand, the Court has tended to defer to the position of Congress as first among equals.)

In contrast, there is less evidence of a consistent policy of substantive judicial restraint in the Supreme Court's examination of state laws and state acts. Here, to the contrary, the role of the Court has emphatically been significantly more activist, procedurally as well as substantively. The Court will more readily regard the review of governmental action as within the JUDICIAL POWER OF THE UNITED STATES in the litigation of state laws. A principal example is the ease with which state TAXPAYER SUITS impugning state laws on federal constitutional grounds will be deemed reviewable in the Supreme Court, when in most instances an equivalently situated federal taxpayer is deemed to have inadequate standing in respect to an act of Congress. In addition, the Court has interpreted the Constitution to create a judicial duty to determine the constitutionality of certain kinds of state laws, though the clauses relied upon do not themselves expressly confer such a judicial duty (or power) and speak, rather, solely of some preemptive power in Congress to determine the same matter. For instance, the COMMERCE CLAUSE provides merely that Congress shall have power to regulate commerce among the several states. But in the absence of congressional regulation, the Court has actively construed the clause as directing the federal courts themselves to determine, by their own criteria, whether state statutes so unreasonably or discriminatorily burden INTERSTATE COMMERCE that they should be deemed invalid by the courts as an unconstitutional trespass upon a field of regulation reserved to Congress.

Here also the rationales have differed, and indeed not every Supreme Court Justice has embraced either rationale. (Justice HUGO L. BLACK, for instance, preferring a constitutional jurisprudence of "literal" interpretation, generally declined to find any basis in the commerce clause for judicial intervention against state statutes.) In part, the substantive activism of the Court has been explained by a "political marketplace" calculus that is the obverse of Thayer's rule for deference to Congress. According to this view, as the state legislatures are not equal departments to the Supreme Court (in the sense that Congress is an equal department), and as national interests are not necessarily as well represented in state assemblies as state interests are said to be represented in Congress (insofar as members of Congress are all chosen from state-based constituencies), there are fewer built-in political safeguards in state legislatures than in Congress. To the extent of these differences, it is said that there is correspondingly less reason for courts to assume that state legislatures will have acted with appropriate sensitivity to federal constitutional questions and, accordingly, that there is more need for closer judicial attention to their acts. The sheer nonuniformity of state legislation may be of such felt distress to overriding needs for greater uniformity in a nation with an increasingly integrated economy that a larger measure of judicial activism in adjudicating the constitutional consistency of state legislation may be warranted in light of that fact. Something of this thought may lie behind Justice Holmes's view respecting the relative importance of constitutional review itself: "I do not think the United States would come to an end if we lost our power to declare an Act of Congress void. I do think the Union would be imperiled if we could not make that declaration as to the laws of the several states." Finally, more activist substantive review of state laws has been defended on the view that, assuming Congress itself may presume to substitute a uniform rule or otherwise forbid states to legislate in respect to certain matters, the frequency with which state statutes may be adopted and the resulting interference they may impose upon matters of national importance prior to any possibility of corrective congressional action require that the federal courts exercise an interim and activist responsibility of their own. In any event, this much is clear. In respect to substantive standards of constitutional review and challenges to state laws on grounds that they usurp national authority, the overall position of the Supreme Court has been that of an activist judiciary in umpiring the boundaries of federalism.

Finally, and most prominently within the last half-century, selective judicial activism has made its strongest appearance in the judicial review of either federal or state laws that, in the Court's view, bear adversely on one or more of the following three subjects: participation in the political process, specific personal rights enumerated in the Bill of Rights, and laws adversely affecting "DISCRETE AND INSULAR MINORITIES." The scope of these respective activist exceptions (to the general rule of procedural and substantive restraint) is still not entirely settled. Indeed, each is itself somewhat unstable. Nonetheless, the indication of more aggressive, judicially assertive constitutional intervention in all three areas was strongly suggested in a footnote to UNITED STATES V. CAROLENE PRODUCTS CO. (1938). There, the Court suggested that the conventional "presumption of constitutionality" would not obtain, and that "searching judicial inquiry" would be applied to the review of laws that, on their face, appeared "to be within a specific prohibition of the Constitution," or to "restrict those political processes which can ordinarily be expected to bring about the repeal of undesirable legislation," or to bear heavily on "discrete and insular minorities" suffering from prejudice likely to lead to their neglect in the legislative process.

In respect to the first of these categories, however, it is doubtful whether the standards applied by the Supreme Court should be defined as unconventionally activist at all. To the extent that a constitutional provision explicitly forbids a given kind of statute, its mere application by the Court scarcely seems exceptional. To the contrary, it would require an extreme version of "restraint" to do otherwise.

The second category (principally concerned with limitations on voting eligibility or with varieties of unfairness in REPRESENTATION) is differently reasoned. The Court has assumed generally that deference is ordinarily due the constitutional interpretations of legislative bodies because they are themselves representatives of the people (who have the greatest stake in the Constitution). But if the law in question itself abridges the representative character of the legislatures, it tends by that fact to undermine the entire foundation of judicial restraint in respect to all other legislative acts. As it tends thereby also to reduce the efficacy of the legislative process to repeal improvident legislation, such representation-reducing statutes ought to be severely questioned.

The third category (such legislation as bears adversely on insular and discrete minorities) has emerged as by far the most controversial and unstable example of modern judicial activism. Its theory of justification is one of rationing the activism of constitutional review inversely, again in keeping with the perceived "market failure" of representative government. And, up to a point, it is quite straightforward in keeping with that theory. Thus, when the numbers of a particular class are few and their financial resources insignificant, and when the class upon whom a law falls with great force is not well-connected but, to the contrary, seems left out of account in legislative processes (by prejudices entrenched within legislatures), the resulting market place failure of political power or ordinary empathy is felt to leave a gap to be filled by exceptional judicial solicitude.

The paradigm case for such activism is that of legislation adversely affecting blacks, when challenged on grounds of inconsistency with the EQUAL PROTECTION clause of the Fourteenth Amendment. On its face, the equal protection clause provides no special standards of justification that race-related legislation must satisfy that other kinds of adverse legislative classifications need not meet. Nonetheless, on quite sound historical grounds, race-related legislation was singled out for exceptional judicial activism by the WARREN COURT. Although many of the Warren Court decisions remain of enduring controversy, it is generally conceded that the Court's STRICT SCRUTINY of such race-based laws was itself consistent with the special preoccupation of the Fourteenth Amendment with that subject. Thus, as early as 1873, in the SLAUGHTERHOUSE CASES, the Court had observed: In the light of the history of [the THIRTEENTH, Fourteenth, and FIFTEENTH] AMENDMENTS, and the pervading purpose of them, [it] is not difficult to give a meaning to [the equal protection clause]. The existence of laws in the states where the newly emancipated negroes resided, which discriminated with gross injustice and hardship against them as a class,

was the evil to be remedied by this clause, and by it such laws are forbidden."

As this historical CIVIL WAR basis for that one exception was left behind, the Supreme Court plied an increasingly complicated sociology of political marketplace failure to explain an equivalent interventionism on a much broader front. Thus, gender-based laws, laws restricting ALIENS vis-à-vis citizens, and laws restricting minors vis-à-vis adults came also to be examined much more stringently under the equal protection clause than laws adversely affecting particular businesses, particular classes of property owners, certain groups of taxpayers, or others. The determination of "adequate representation" (whether direct or vicarious), the conjecture as to whether such legislative classifications were based on "stereotypes" rather than real differences, and ultimately the tentative extension of equal protection activism even to require a variety of state support for poor persons, produced unstable and largely unsustainable pluralities within the Supreme Court.

Indeed, the difficulties of selective activism in this area have been the principal object of contemporary criticism in American constitutional law. The most serious questions have been addressed to the apparent tendency of the Court to adjust its own interpretations of the Constitution not according simply to its own best understanding of that document, but rather according to its perceptions respecting the adequacy of representative government. Given the fact that far more cases compete for the opportunity to be determined by the Supreme Court than its own resources can permit it to hear, the Court might be expected to pursue a course of selective procedural activism according to which it would more readily entertain cases and more readily reach the merits of constitutional claims it should consider not to have been adequately considered elsewhere because of built-in weaknesses of representative government. On the other hand, it remains much more problematic why the Court should utilize its impressions respecting the adequacies of representative government twice over: once to determine which cases to review, and again to determine whether the Constitution has in fact been violated.

Descriptions of judicial activism and judicial restraint in constitutional adjudication are, of course, but partial truths. In two centuries of judicial review, superintended by more than one hundred Justices who have served on the Supreme Court and who have interpreted a Constitution highly ambiguous in much of its text, consistency has not been institutional but personal. Individual judges have maintained strongly diverse notions of the "proper" judicial role, and the political process of APPOINTMENT OF SUPREME COURT JUSTICES has itself had a great deal to do with the dominant perspectives of that role from time to time. Here, only the most prominent features of judicial activism and judicial restraint have been canvassed.

It is roughly accurate to summarize that in respect to interpreting the Constitution, procedurally the Supreme Court has usually exercised great restraint. Subject to some notable exceptions, it has eschewed addressing the constitutional consistency of acts of government to a dramatically greater degree of self-denial than it has exercised in confronting other kinds of legal issues seeking judicial resolution. Substantively, the Court has been predisposed to the national government in respect to the powers of that government: except for the early twentieth century, Thayer's law, requiring a showing of "clear error," has been the dominant motif. In respect to the states, on the other hand, the Court has been actively more interventionist, construing the Constitution to enforce its own notions of national interest in the absence of decisions by Congress. And, most controversially in recent decades, it has been unstably activist in deciding whether it will interpret the Constitution more as an egalitarian set of imperatives than as a document principally concerned with commerce, federalism, the SEPARATION OF POWERS, and the protection of explicitly protected liberties.

WILLIAM W. VAN ALSTYNE
(1986)

Bibliography

BICKEL, ALEXANDER M. 1962 *The Least Dangerous Branch: The Supreme Court at the Bar of Politics.* Indianapolis: Bobbs-Merrill.

ELY, JOHN H. 1980 *Democracy and Distrust: A Theory of Judicial Review.* Cambridge, Mass.: Harvard University Press.

JACKSON, ROBERT H. 1941 *The Struggle for Judicial Supremacy.* New York: Knopf.

THAYER, JAMES B. 1893 "The Origin and Scope of the American Doctrine of Constitutional Law." *Harvard Law Review* 7:129.

WECHSLER, HERBERT 1959 "Toward Neutral Principles of Constitutional Law." *Harvard Law Review* 73:1.

JUDICIAL ACTIVISM AND JUDICIAL RESTRAINT
(Update)

In contemporary constitutional rhetoric, "judicial activism" is almost always a term of opprobrium. Prospective Supreme Court nominees regularly disclaim activist inclinations, and political and academic critics of the Court regularly decry activist overreaching. Yet despite the term's salience, there is considerable confusion as to its precise meaning.

In a loose sense, the attack on judicial activism, and the defense of its cognate virtue, judicial restraint, rest on a distrust of judicial discretion and an insistence on RULE OF LAW values. On this view, judicial decisions are entitled to respect because they are legal, objective, impersonal, and apolitical. An "activist" judge risks bringing constitutional law into disrepute by using it as an excuse to implement merely personal or political values.

To be sure, most sophisticated contemporary students of constitutional law reject this dichotomy between the "personal" and "objective," at least in its simplest form. Although Justice OWEN J. ROBERTS once insisted that the task of Supreme Court Justices was simply to "lay the article of the Constitution which is invoked beside the statute which is challenged and to decide whether the latter squares with the former," there are few modern adherents to mechanical jurisprudence among observers of constitutional law. Yet, despite persistent and trenchant efforts to discredit the mechanical view, it retains a powerful hold on popular perceptions of the appropriate judicial function and, at least in diluted form, plays some role in most standard justifications for JUDICIAL REVIEW.

Moreover, perhaps paradoxically, the modern attack on the mechanical theory, as well as the theory itself, tends to buttress arguments for judicial restraint. For if it is indeed true that judges must inevitably insert their personal values into the task of constitutional review, as critics of the mechanical theory insist, then there is all the more reason to constrict sharply the occasions for this review. Restraint is especially important, these critics maintain, because policy decisions by judges, implemented under the guise of constitutional review, often have unintended and unfortunate consequences. It is claimed, for example, that the Court's invalidation of ABORTION laws in ROE V. WADE (1973) served only to obstruct an emerging, sensible compromise to the abortion dispute, and that the Court's condemnation of school SEGREGATION in BROWN V. BOARD OF EDUCATION (1954) did little or nothing to advance the cause of racial equality. Often these criticisms are linked to the claim that constitutional review is elitist and divisive. On this view, constitutional decisions unjustifiably reduce the space for democratic deliberation and needlessly bring to the fore contested and unresolvable issues of fundamental principle.

There are, then, a complex of powerful arguments that support judicial restraint. To some degree, however, these arguments conceal important fissures within the critique of activism. For example, it is not always clear whether critics of activism are referring to its procedural or substantive manifestations. Procedural restraint requires judges to limit the occasions for, and scope of, constitutional decisions. Among the tools that accomplish these objectives are DOCTRINES concerning STANDING, RIPENESS,

MOOTNESS, POLITICAL QUESTIONS, and AVOIDANCE of unnecessary constitutional exposition. In contrast, substantive restraint requires judges to interpret the substantive provisions of the Constitution narrowly. Familiar manifestations of this position include the insistence on no more than "mere rationality" for statutes challenged under the EQUAL PROTECTION clause, the rejection of SUBSTANTIVE DUE PROCESS, and the limitation of FREEDOM OF SPEECH protections to the kinds of political speech protected at the time of the Constitution's framing.

On some occasions, the procedural and substantive versions of restraint are in tension with each other. Sometimes, procedural restraint will prevent a Court from reaching the merits in circumstances where doing so might lead to greater substantive restraint. For example, in a 1986 decision, *Diamond v. Charles*, the Court rejected an appeal on standing grounds in circumstances where the appellant asked the Court to loosen substantive constitutional constraints on anti-abortion statutes.

Matters are made still more complicated by tensions internal to each version of restraint. Procedural devices like standing and political question can be used to avoid constitutional decisions, but they also increase the degree of judicial discretion. Many commentators have argued that these doctrines are not "principled" or firmly rooted in determinate constitutional doctrine and therefore allow courts great freedom to indulge personal, nonlegal preferences.

There are similar tensions internal to the substantive version of restraint. On one view, the argument against judicial activism pushes one toward some form of TEXTUALISM or ORIGINALISM. Only by tying constitutional doctrine closely to the text, or the ORIGINAL INTENT of the Framers, can judicial discretion be controlled. A second view holds that judges should be respectful of PRECEDENT, which makes their decisions more general and rule-like. Still a third view holds that judges ought to interpret the Constitution so as to maximize the space for political decisionmaking.

It should be apparent that these three views will often lead to different outcomes. For example, in a prior generation, both Justices HUGO L. BLACK and FELIX FRANKFURTER claimed to practice judicial restraint—Black, when he read the FIRST AMENDMENT free speech clause literally, resulting in the invalidation of many statutes; and Frankfurter, when he read it more loosely, so as to uphold many statutes. More recently, Justices WILLIAM J. BRENNAN, JR., and THURGOOD MARSHALL often accused their colleagues of "judicial activism" when they failed to follow prior precedent that the majority overruled or distinguished precisely because the precedent authorized more judicial intervention than the majority thought appropriate.

The upshot of this confusion is that almost everyone in contemporary constitutional debate can claim the mantle of judicial restraint, while almost no one need actually exercise much of it. The plain truth is that, despite all the rhetoric to the contrary, the modern Supreme Court lacks a single consistent proponent of judicial restraint. For example, the modern Court has embarked on an ambitious program of revitalizing FEDERALISM and SEPARATION OF POWERS limitations on the political branches; overseeing ELECTORAL DISTRICTING; protecting PROPERTY RIGHTS and the right to COMMERCIAL SPEECH; and invalidating AFFIRMATIVE ACTION programs. Critics of the Court complain that these decisions are "activist," but many of these critics would, themselves, like to make the Court more activist in the protection of reproductive and sexual freedom, racial minorities, and political dissidents.

All of this suggests that the real fault line in contemporary constitutional argument is not between activism and restraint, but between styles of activism. While conservative activists would make the Court active so as to keep the rest of government passive, thereby leaving more space for free markets and individual decisionmaking, liberal activists would make the Court active so as to require more aggressive programs of government regulation and redistribution. To a significant extent, rhetorical attacks on judicial activism have served only to distract attention from this central disagreement.

LOUIS MICHAEL SEIDMAN
(2000)

(SEE ALSO: *Constitutional Theory; Courts and Social Change.*)

Bibliography

BICKEL, ALEXANDER M. 1962 *The Least Dangerous Branch: The Supreme Court at the Bar of Politics.* Indianapolis, Ind.: Bobbs-Merrill.

BLASI, VINCENT 1983 The Rootless Activism of the Burger Court. Pages 198–217 in Vincent Blasi, ed., *The Burger Court: The Counter-Revolution That Wasn't.* New Haven, Conn.: Yale University Press.

BORK, ROBERT H. 1990 *The Tempting of America: The Political Seduction of the Law.* New York: Free Press.

DWORKIN, RONALD H. 1996 *Freedom's Law: The Moral Reading of the American Constitution.* Cambridge, Mass.: Harvard University Press.

GUNTHER, GERALD 1964 The Subtle Vices of the "Passive Virtues": A Comment on Principle and Expediency in Judicial Review. *Columbia Law Review* 64:1–25.

ROSENBERG, GERALD 1991 *The Hollow Hope: Can Courts Bring about Social Change?* Chicago: University of Chicago Press.

SUNSTEIN, CASS 1996 Foreword: Leaving Things Undecided. *Harvard Law Review* 110:4–101.

JUDICIAL APPOINTMENTS

See: Confirmation Process; Senate and Judicial Appointments

JUDICIAL CODE

The Judicial Code of the United States is an official collection and codification of laws governing the federal judiciary and federal court procedures. Codified as Title 28 of the United States Code, the Judicial Code is an exercise of the Article I power of Congress to make such laws as it deems NECESSARY AND PROPER for carrying into execution the broad and ill-defined powers vested in the judiciary by Article III of the Constitution.

The present code, enacted in 1948, is the lineal descendant of the original JUDICIARY ACT OF 1789, the judiciary portions of the REVISED STATUTES of 1877, and the Judicial Code of 1911. It is an effort by judicial, legislative, and legal experts to rearrange, update, and improve the many laws dealing with the federal judicial system. Additions and improvements are periodically made by Congress, and integrated into the structural scheme of the code. The code itself is divided into six main parts, with numerous subdivisions, each relating to a particular subject matter. Among the more important subjects covered by the code are: the organization, personnel, and administration of the federal courts, including the SUPREME COURT; the JURISDICTION conferred by Congress on these various courts, including the Supreme Court; provisions for determining the proper VENUE for instituting a case in a UNITED STATES DISTRICT COURT, and provisions governing the REMOVAL to a federal court of a case instituted in a state court; and the procedures to be followed in various kinds of federal court proceedings.

The 1948 revision and recodification have been both highly praised and highly criticized. Criticism has often been focused on the provisions dealing with the jurisdiction of the federal district courts, for it is the exercise of that jurisdiction that most directly affects the delicate and controversial federal-state court relationships. Concern for these relationships led the American Law Institute to undertake a major study of the Judicial Code, culminating in a 1968 proposal to revise substantial portions of the code. Specifically, the institute suggested major modifications and limitations respecting district courts' DIVERSITY-OF-CITIZENSHIP JURISDICTION, as well as clarifications of FEDERAL QUESTION JURISDICTION and ADMIRALTY AND MARITIME JURISDICTION, and changes as to venue and removal of actions from state courts. Some of the institute's proposals bore legislative fruit and influenced judicial thinking. But the major proposals have lain fallow, and in some respects they have been outmoded by the passage of time and the birth of new tensions in the JUDICIAL SYSTEM.

Controversy about some of the Judicial Code's provisions is endless, especially those that concern the scope and exercise of the diversity jurisdiction of the federal courts. Such controversy reflects the historic and perhaps unresolvable concern that, as Chief Justice EARL WARREN once said, "we achieve a proper jurisdictional balance between the Federal and State court systems, assigning to each system those cases most appropriate in the light of the basic principles of FEDERALISM."

EUGENE GRESSMAN
(1986)

Bibliography

CURRIE, DAVID P. 1968–1969 The Federal Courts and the American Law Institute. *University of Chicago Law Review* 36:1–49, 268–337.

WECHSLER, HERBERT 1948 Federal Jurisdiction and the Revision of the Judicial Code. *Law and Contemporary Problems* 13:216–243.

JUDICIAL COLLEGIALITY

"Collegiality" is defined by *Webster's Third New International Dictionary* (1993) as "the relationship of colleagues." "Colleagues" are "associate[s] or co-worker[s] typically in a profession or a civil or ecclesiastical office and often of similar rank or state." The derivation, common with "college," is the Latin *collegium*, although a purist might refer to the verb *legare*, meaning to send or choose a deputy.

For a court, collegiality consists in the relationship among equals in rank, and usually carries positive connotations of cooperativeness and joint efforts toward achieving appropriate aims, operations, and functioning of the court as an institution.

Thus, there may be collegiality among, say, trial judges, even though it does not necessarily extend to decision-making on particular cases. Trial judges have basically monarchial power over their own courtrooms, even though they may work with their colleagues, for example, in accomplishing trial court aims or fashioning trial court rules. At the same time, they may consult with their trial court colleagues on matters that do affect particular cases; for example, sentences, jury instructions, admissibility of particular evidence, or the like. But it is a collegiality of a different kind from that of appellate judges.

Appellate judges need collegiality in order to decide particular cases. Sitting generally in groups or panels of three or more—usually an odd number—a joint, one hopes cooperative, effort is needed to decide cases; to decide whether to hear arguments or to write opinions or summary orders, as well as how to write them; to fashion relief to the parties; to give guidance to the trial courts or to the bar or to the public; and, in a difficult or complex case, simply to reach a workable result. Three judges can sometimes approach a case with different viewpoints, resulting in different outcomes, yet needing resolution. Something has to give in such a situation, and "collegiality" is what helps bring about resolution.

It may be best to define "collegiality" in terms of what tends to promote it and what tends to discourage it. Means of promotion include friendship, civility, intellectual respect, consideration, dialogue and communication, good humor, and shared meals and events. Thus, personal elements, communications, socialization, and court ceremonies all tend to further collegiality. As former Chief Judge Jon O. Newman of the United States Court of Appeals for the Second Circuit put it recently, the term "collegiality" does not begin to capture "the subtle elements of respect, trust, cooperation, and accommodation that characterize members of a group court at work."

Discouraging collegiality follows from the contrary—geographic or social remoteness of the judges; the size of the court; or ill-feeling. One could add as examples of discouraging practices criticizing another's writing style; delegating opinion critiques to law clerks who are given free rein; or personalized attacks in opinions or memoranda on the motives or aims of other judges. But these examples are not inclusive.

Collegiality is an elusive concept. To borrow the description of obscenity of Justice POTTER J. STEWART in his CONCURRING OPINION in JACOBELLUS V. OHIO (1964), we know it when we see it, but to define it is almost impossible. We do know that, without collegiality, courts tend to become politicized, angry, or lacking in civility. Indeed, without it the independence of judges that we try to maintain may be undermined, as public and political criticism of the courts is promoted.

JAMES L. OAKES
(2000)

JUDICIAL CONFERENCE OF THE UNITED STATES

The Judicial Conference of the United States is a legacy of WILLIAM HOWARD TAFT's chief justiceship. Its establishment in 1922 constituted a part of the former President's broad campaign against progressives' demands for changes in the substance of then-prevailing federal law. Taft responded with a structural reform proposal: unprecedented administrative integration of a geographically dispersed court system manned by virtually autonomous

judges. Thus, the third branch as a whole would achieve enhanced independence coincident with, and protective of, the uniqueness of the essential judicial function.

The Judicial Conference remains the linchpin of national judicial administration. From its beginnings as an annual meeting of the presiding judges of the UNITED STATES COURTS OF APPEALS chaired by the CHIEF JUSTICE, the organization's membership has grown to include a representative from one of the UNITED STATES DISTRICT COURTS in each of the eleven numbered circuits and the District of Columbia and the chief judges of those circuits, the UNITED STATES COURT OF APPEALS FOR THE FEDERAL CIRCUIT, and the COURT OF INTERNATIONAL TRADE. Biennial meetings at Washington, held in executive session, are largely repositories for reports from an extensive committee system involving the participation of approximately two hundred federal judges. This system provides status differentiation among the more than 700-member federal judiciary, but more significantly responds to a work load spawned both by the brevity of conference sessions and by a voluminous and complex agenda associated with the growth of judicial business and personnel.

Further structural changes in the conference-related administrative organization originated in causes both within and without the third branch. Congress in 1939 established the Administrative Office of the United States Courts and provided for regional administrative units: circuit judicial councils and circuit judicial conferences. Chief Justice CHARLES EVANS HUGHES promoted the Administrative Office Act as a response to FRANKLIN D. ROOSEVELT's 1937 "COURT-PACKING" bill, perceived by conference members as threatening executive-branch domination of the judiciary.

The new act vastly increased the functions performed by the Judicial Conference and its committees. Although the director and deputy director are appointed by the Supreme Court, the Office acts under "the supervision and direction" of the conference. Consequently, housekeeping, personnel, and budgetary duties once performed by the ATTORNEY GENERAL AND DEPARTMENT OF JUSTICE now fall within the oversight of the conference. These and subsequent congressionally mandated duties, some of which affected the district judges, ignited trial judge demands for conference representation, achieved in 1957, and led to establishment in 1967 of the Federal Judicial Center. This research, development, education, and training arm of the courts is directed by a governing board whose members are appointed by the conference.

The Judicial Conference has from its inception promoted administrative centralization, a functional tendency enhanced by the information-gathering and supportive services available from the Administrative Office. Consonant with the 1922 act's charge "to promote uniformity of management procedures and expeditious conduct of court business," the conference formulates policies for allocating budgetary, personnel, and space resources. It similarly addresses administrative questions raised in areas such as legal defenders, bankruptcy, probation, magistrates, and rules of practice and procedure.

The Judicial Conference promulgates standards of judicial ethics. Its role in disciplining wayward judges received explicit congressional authorization in 1980. The Judicial Councils Reform and Judicial Conduct Act empowered the circuit judicial councils to certify intractable misbehavior problems to the conference for "appropriate action." Remedies include referral of such cases to the House Judiciary Committee upon finding "that consideration of IMPEACHMENT may be warranted," a procedure followed in three instances from 1986 through 1988.

The SEPARATION OF POWERS makes the federal judiciary dependent on Congress for support. Since Taft's chairmanship and later with congressional authorization, the Judicial Conference has developed and promoted legislative programs. Additional judgeships, appropriations, judicial salaries, court organization, jurisdiction, procedural rules, and impeachment recommendations have been among the proposals brought to Capitol Hill, usually by conference committee chairmen. Thus, judges do and must lobby Congress to obtain necessary resources. Yet, legislative liaison may embroil the judiciary in visible political conflict, as occurred when Chief Justice WARREN E. BURGER lobbied against portions of the 1978 BANKRUPTCY ACT.

The strategic position of the Judicial Conference, its policymaking functions, and its implementation responsibilities pose dilemmas. A quest by the conference for efficiency, uniformity, and equity has induced intrabranch policies favorable to development of "managerial" judges and has produced unavoidable tensions between centralized policymaking and individual court administration. Conference recommendations to Congress permit submission of proposals freighted with substantive public policy implications packaged in the wrappings of judicial administration, a characteristic that marked the struggle to divide the Fifth Circuit.

PETER GRAHAM FISH
(1992)

(SEE ALSO: *Progressive Constitutional Thought; Progressivism.*)

Bibliography

BARROW, DEBORAH J. and WALKER, G. THOMAS 1988 *A Court Divided: The Fifth Circuit Court of Appeals and the Politics of Judicial Reform.* New Haven, Conn.: Yale University Press.
FISH, PETER GRAHAM 1973 *The Politics of Federal Judicial Administration.* Princeton, N.J.: Princeton University Press.

JUDICIAL IMMUNITY

In *Randall v. Brigham* (1869) the Supreme Court endorsed the principle of judicial immunity. Under doctrine "as old as the law," Justice STEPHEN J. FIELD wrote for the Court, judges of courts of general jurisdiction are immune from suit for judicial acts "unless perhaps where the acts, in excess of JURISDICTION, are done maliciously or corruptly." In *Bradley v. Fisher* (1872) Justice Field, again writing for the Court, extended *Randall*'s standard for protecting judges to preclude liability for all judicial acts except "acts where no jurisdiction whatever" existed and illustrated the difference between acts "in excess of jurisdiction" and acts clearly without jurisdiction. A probate judge acts clearly without jurisdiction when he tries a criminal case. A judge who improperly holds an act to be a crime or sentences a defendant to more than the statutory maximum merely acts in excess of jurisdiction. *Bradley* also disavowed the suggestion in *Randall* that a malicious or corrupt motive might affect a judge's immunity.

The Civil War Amendments, ratified at about the time *Randall* and *Bradley* were decided, led many years later to a vast growth in individual constitutional protections. This development caused both a reexamination and an eventual reaffirmation of judicial immunity. Because actions against state officials for constitutional violations are brought under SECTION 1983, TITLE 42, UNITED STATES CODE, the scope of judicial immunity from suit for constitutional violations has been defined mainly in answer to the question whether judges may be sued under section 1983.

The unequivocal language of section 1983 led some lower courts to find judges subject to suit. In TENNEY V. BRANDHOVE (1951), however, the Supreme Court held that Congress did not intend section 1983 to overturn the traditional immunity of legislators from suit. Although judicial immunity was less firmly established at COMMON LAW than was legislative immunity, *Tenney* led courts to conclude that judges, like legislators, are immune from suit under section 1983. In PIERSON V. RAY (1967), with limited discussion of the issue, the Supreme Court adopted this view in holding a judge immune from suit for convicting defendants under a statute later found to be unconstitutional.

In STUMP V. SPARKMAN (1978) the Court reaffirmed the immunity in a case that presented extreme facts. Without a hearing and without NOTICE to the victim, the defendant judge had granted a mother's petition to have her daughter sterilized. Because granting the petition was found to be a judicial act and because no state law or decision expressly denied the judge authority to grant the petition, the judge was immune.

There are, however, some limits to judicial immunity.

In *Pulliam v. Allen* (1984) the Supreme Court held that state judges are not immune from section 1983 actions seeking injunctive relief or from awards of attorney's fees. In both O'SHEA V. LITTLETON (1974) and IMBLER V. PACHTMAN (1976) the Court suggested that judges are not immune from criminal prosecutions for violating constitutional rights.

A SEPARATION OF POWERS question lurks in the background of the judicial immunity DOCTRINE. Courts might well invalidate a federal statute that imposed liability on federal judges in what the courts believed to be inappropriate circumstances. Because the Court has been relatively generous in protecting its judicial colleagues from liability, and because most activity concerning judicial immunity involves actions against state judges under section 1983, the potential separation of powers issue goes largely unnoticed.

THEODORE EISENBERG
(1986)

Bibliography

NOTE 1969 Liability of Judicial Officers under Section 1983. *Yale Law Journal* 79:322–337.

JUDICIAL IMPEACHMENT

The Constitution is remarkably Delphic on the subject of judicial removal. Article III provides that judges shall hold office during "good Behavior," but leaves that term undefined and fails to indicate who is authorized to define it. Article II provides that the President, Vice-President, and "all civil officers of the United States" shall be subject to IMPEACHMENT and removal, but is silent on whether judges, for this purpose, are to be considered "civil officers." Nonetheless, it has been consistent practice to treat federal judges as removable by impeachment, and to equate "good Behavior," for all practical purposes, with such behavior as has not yet led to such removal.

With regard to federal judges, there have been fifty-eight documented impeachment investigations by the U.S. HOUSE OF REPRESENTATIVES, eleven impeachment trials conducted by the U.S. SENATE, and seven impeachment convictions—three during the 1980s—two of which prompted not only removal, but also disqualification from holding further federal office. A Senate conviction in a case of impeachment is final; in NIXON V. UNITED STATES (1993), the Court held that the POLITICAL QUESTION doctrine precludes JUDICIAL REVIEW. The constitutional ambiguities concerning judicial removal have prompted three recurring legal debates: May Congress or the executive discipline judges through any unilateral mechanism other than impeachment? Are sitting federal judges subject to criminal prosecution? And, may the federal judiciary itself discipline its members?

Both constitutional history and SEPARATION OF POWERS theory support a negative answer to the first question. The susceptibility of judges to executive removal was decried in the DECLARATION OF INDEPENDENCE, and the CONSTITUTIONAL CONVENTION debated and rejected the other political removal mechanism short of impeachment known to the former colonists—removal upon "legislative address" to the executive. Both ALEXANDER HAMILTON and Brutus described impeachment as the Constitution's sole judicial removal mechanism, although one applauded and one deplored the resulting degree of JUDICIAL INDEPENDENCE. Given that the Supreme Court, in *Bowsher v. Synar* (1986), held that Congress may participate in executive removals only through impeachment, it seems implausible that Congress has greater authority over judges.

Whether sitting judges may legitimately be prosecuted is less certain. Although no such prosecution had been brought prior to 1980, the U.S. Department of Justice launched five in the ensuing decade, all successful but none reaching the Supreme Court. Perhaps the strongest argument against such authority is that the vulnerability of sitting judges to criminal prosecution threatens judicial independence, and especially judicial evenhandedness in cases involving the government as party. Those lower courts that have thus far addressed the issue, however, have concluded that the importance of judicial integrity outweighs the potential harm.

In 1980, the Judicial Councils Reform and Judicial Conduct and Disability Act authorized a discipline process within the federal judiciary that may result in a variety of sanctions short of removal, including private or public reprimand or censure, the temporary nonassignment of cases, or a request for voluntary retirement. Congress avoided the most obvious separation of powers objections by stopping short of authorizing removals and by excluding Supreme Court Justices from the system's purview. In 1993, a commission charged by Congress to investigate the discipline and removal of judges concluded that the act did not represent an unconstitutional intrusion into judicial independence—an issue the Supreme Court has yet to address.

PETER M. SHANE
(2000)

Bibliography

GERHARDT, MICHAEL J. 1996 *The Federal Impeachment Process: A Constitutional and Historical Analysis.* Princeton, N.J.: Princeton University Press.
NATIONAL COMMISSION ON JUDICIAL DISCIPLINE AND REMOVAL 1993 *Research Papers of the National Commission on Ju-*

dicial Discipline and Removal, 2 vols. Washington, D.C.: U.S. Government Printing Office.

SIMON, MARIA 1994 Note: Bribery And Other Not So "Good Behavior": Criminal Prosecution as a Supplement to Impeachment of Federal Judges. *Columbia Law Review* 94:1617–1673.

SYMPOSIUM 1993 Disciplining the Federal Judiciary. *University of Pennsylvania Law Review* 142:1–430.

JUDICIAL INDEPENDENCE

Long recognized as one of the hallmarks of American constitutionalism, judicial independence takes several different forms, each of which is essential to good judging, but none of which is absolute.

One form—"party detachment"—concerns the relationship between the judge and the parties before the court and is rooted in the aspiration for impartiality. It requires that the judge not be related to these parties nor be in any way under their control or influence. Such a requirement guards against gross threats to impartiality, such as bribery and close kinship ties between judges and litigants, but many less blatant violations, such as cultural ties and ideological sympathy, cannot realistically be prevented. Judicial independence with respect to litigating parties is therefore an ideal that can be achieved only imperfectly.

A second form of judicial independence—"individual autonomy"—concerns the relationship between individual judges and other members of the judiciary. It demands that the judge be unconstrained by collegial and institutional pressures when deciding questions of fact and law. According to this rule, judicial decisions are matters of individual conscience and responsibility.

This aspect of judicial independence has its roots in broad cultural norms, largely of an individualist character, and is reinforced by the American practice of recruiting judges after they have had successful careers in practice or in politics. It is also reinforced by, and reflected in, the practice of having judges sign their own rulings and opinions. This practice requires judges to assume individual responsibility for legal decisions and thus fosters judicial accountability.

Like party detachment, individual autonomy is an ideal that is only partially realized. All judges are expected to adhere to the prior decisions of other judges through the doctrine of STARE DECISIS. Lower court judges are even more constrained: They are subject to appellate review and, more recently, bureaucratic control. For example, the Judicial Councils Reform Act of 1980 allows groups of federal circuit judges to bypass ordinary appellate procedures and form committees to investigate and impose sanctions on individual district court judges.

A third form of judicial independence—"political insularity"—is perhaps the most complex. It requires the judiciary to be independent from popularly controlled governmental institutions, in particular the executive and legislative branches. This form of independence overlaps with party detachment whenever one of the political branches is itself a party before the court, but it is a distinct requirement that encompasses a variety of other circumstances as well. Even when the parties before the court are purely private, the judge is expected to remain free from the influence or control of the political branches of government.

Political insularity is essential for the pursuit of justice, which requires courts to do what is right, not what is popular. This form of independence is also in keeping with SEPARATION OF POWERS doctrine, for it enables the judiciary to act as a countervailing force within the government, checking abuses of power by the legislature and the executive.

One important source of political insularity is Article III. It provides federal judges with life tenure and protection against diminution of pay. Another arises from the limits on the power of the legislature to overrule the courts. Because the federal judiciary is the authoritative interpreter of the Constitution, only an amendment can override a CONSTITUTIONAL INTERPRETATION, and the AMENDMENT PROCESS is a cumbersome one, requiring special majorities in each house of Congress and approval by three-fourths of the states.

Despite its importance, political insularity poses a certain dilemma for democratic theory: The more insulated the judiciary is from the popularly controlled governmental institutions, the more it is able to interfere with their policies and thereby frustrate the popular will. Accordingly, the demand for political insularity, perhaps even more so than party detachment and individual autonomy, is a qualified one. Indeed, the federal judiciary, long taken as one of the most independent of all judicial systems in the world, is best understood not as a fully insulated branch of government, but as one unit of an interdependent political system.

One of the primary constraints on the judiciary's political independence is the appointment process. In some countries, the judiciary is given authority to select its own members as a way of enhancing its political insularity. In the United States, the power to appoint federal judges is vested in the President, and this arrangement necessarily introduces an element of political control over the judiciary's composition. Presidents naturally will try to select judges whose concept of justice approximates their own and who are likely to further the policies of their administrations. The President is constrained by public expectations as to the qualifications of nominees, but even the

that including members of the Supreme Court in a revisory council "was quite foreign from the nature of the office," because it would not only "make them judges of the policy of public measures" but would also involve them in judging measures they had a direct hand in creating. Assigning ultimate legislative responsibility to the Congress apparently reflected the Framers' belief that, in popular forms of government, primary lawmaking responsibility should be lodged with the most representative branches of the government. In JAMES MADISON's words, "the people are the only legitimate fountain of power."

Justice FELIX FRANKFURTER expressed the same view in his concurring opinion in *American Federation of Labor v. American Sash and Door Co.* (1949). "Even where the social undesirability of a law may be convincingly urged," he said, "invalidation of the law by a court debilitates popular democratic government. . . . Such an assertion of JUDICIAL POWER deflects responsibility from those on whom in a democratic society it ultimately rests—the people." Frankfurter continued his brief for judicial restraint by arguing that because the powers exercised by the Supreme Court are "inherently oligarchic" they should "be exercised with rigorous self-restraint." The Court, Frankfurter laconically concluded, "is not saved from being oligarchic because it professes to act in the service of humane ends."

The modern Supreme Court is not so easily deterred as Frankfurter was by charges of oligarchy. Since the landmark BROWN V. BOARD OF EDUCATION decision in 1954, the Court has actively and overtly engaged in the kind of lawmaking and policymaking that in previous years was regarded as exclusively the province of the more political branches of government. William Swindler explained the Court's transition from judicial deference to judicial activisim in these terms: "If the freedom of government to act was the basic principle evolving from the Hughes-Stone decade, from 1937–1946, the next logical question—to be disposed of by the WARREN COURT—was the obligation created by the Constitution itself, to compel action in the face of inaction. This led in turn to the epochal decisions in *Brown v. Board of Education*, BAKER V. CARR, and GIDEON V. WAINWRIGHT."

Some scholars have argued that it was the identification of EQUAL PROTECTION rights as class rights and the attendant necessity of fashioning classwide remedies for class injuries that gave the real impetus to the Court's JUDICIAL ACTIVISM in the years immediately following *Brown*. The Court, in other words, effectively legislated under its newmolded EQUITY powers. (See INSTITUTIONAL LITIGATION.)

The Court's legislative role is usually justified in terms of its power of JUDICIAL REVIEW. But judicial review—even if it be regarded as a necessary inference from the fact of a written constitution—is not a part of the powers explic-

itly assigned to the Court by the Constitution. The Court made its boldest claim for the legitimacy of judicial legislation in COOPER V. AARON (1958). Justice WILLIAM J. BRENNAN, writing an opinion signed by all the members of the Court, outlined the basic constitutional argument for JUDICIAL SUPREMACY. Brennan recited "some basic constitutional propositions which are settled doctrine," and which were derived from Chief Justice JOHN MARSHALL's argument in MARBURY V. MADISON (1803). First is the proposition, contained in Article VI of the Constitution, that the Constitution is the supreme law of the land (see SUPREMACY CLAUSE); second is Marshall's statement that the Constitution is "the fundamental and paramount law of the nation"; third is Marshall's declaration that "[i]t is emphatically the province and duty of the judicial department to say what the law is." Justice Brennan concluded that *Marbury* therefore "declared the basic principle that the federal judiciary is supreme in the exposition of the law of the Constitution, and that principle has ever since been respected by this Court and the Country as a permanent and indispensable feature of our constitutional system. It follows that the interpretation of the FOURTEENTH AMENDMENT enunciated by this Court in the Brown Case is the supreme law of the land. . . ." The defect of Brennan's argument, of course, is that it confounds the Constitution with constitutional law.

Marshall did indeed say that the Constitution was "the fundamental and paramount law of the nation," and that any "ordinary legislative acts" "repugnant to the constitution" were necessarily void. But when Marshall wrote the famous line relied upon by Brennan that "it is emphatically the province and duty of the judicial department to say what the law is," he was referring not to the Constitution but to "ordinary legislative acts." In order to determine the law's conformity with the Constitution it is first necessary to know what the law is. And once the law is ascertained it is also necessary to determine whether the law is in conformity with the "paramount law" of the Constitution. This latter, of course, means that "in some cases" the Constitution itself "must be looked into by the judges" in order to determine the particular disposition of a case. But Marshall was clear that the ability of the Court to interpret the Constitution was incident to the necessity of deciding a law's conformity to the Constitution, and not a general warrant for CONSTITUTIONAL INTERPRETATION or judicial legislation. Marshall was emphatic in his pronouncement that "the province of the court is, solely, to decide on the rights of individuals."

"It is apparent," Marshall concluded, "that the framers of the constitution contemplated that instrument as a rule for the government of courts, as well as of the legislature." As he laconically noted in the peroration of his argument, "it is also not entirely unworthy of observation, that in declaring what shall be the supreme law of the land, the constitution itself is first mentioned; and not the laws of the United States generally, but those only which shall be made in pursuance of the constitution, have that rank." For Marshall, Brennan's assertion that the Court's decision in *Brown* was "the supreme law of the land" would indeed make "written constitutions absurd" because it would usurp the "original right" of the people to establish their government on "such principles" that must be "deemed fundamental" and "permanent." If the Supreme Court were indeed to sit as a "continuing constitutional convention," any written Constitution would certainly be superfluous since, under the circumstances there would be no "rule for the government of courts." After all, by parity of reasoning, if one were to accept Brennan's argument, it would also be necessary to hold that the Court's decision in DRED SCOTT V. SANDFORD (1857) was the supreme law of the land. But *Dred Scott* gave way because forces other than the Supreme Court decided that it was a decision not "pursuant" to the "fundamental and paramount law" of the nation. As John Agresto has cogently remarked; "If Congress can mistake the meaning of the text [of the Constitution], which is what the doctrine of judicial review asserts, so, of course, can the Court. And if it be said that it is more dangerous to have interpretive supremacy in the same body that directs the nation's public policy—that is, Congress—then (especially in this age of pervasive judicial direction of political and social life) an independent judicial interpretive power is equally fearsome for exactly the same reasons."

In SWANN V. CHARLOTTE-MECKLENBURG BOARD OF EDUCATION (1971) the Court was confronted with the question of the federal judiciary's equity powers under the equal protection clause of the Fourteenth Amendment. At issue was whether the Court could uphold SCHOOL BUSING as a "remedy for state-imposed segregation in violation of Brown I." As part of the CIVIL RIGHTS ACT OF 1964 the Congress had included in Title IV a provision that "nothing herein shall empower any official or court . . . to issue any order seeking to achieve a racial balance in any school by requiring the transportation of pupils or students from one school to another . . . or otherwise enlarge the existing power of the court to insure compliance with constitutional standards." Chief Justice WARREN E. BURGER, writing for a unanimous Court, remarked that on its face this section of Title IV is only "designed to foreclose any interpretation of the Act as expanding the *existing* powers of federal courts to enforce the Equal Protection Clause. There is no suggestion of an intention to restrict those powers or withdraw from courts their historic equitable remedial powers." According to Burger these equity powers flow directly from the Fourteenth Amendment—despite the fact that section 5 of the Amendment gives

Congress explicit enforcement authority, an authority that was mistakenly restricted by the Court in the SLAUGHTER-HOUSE CASES (1873) and the CIVIL RIGHTS CASES (1883).

A serious question arises, however, concerning Burger's claim that forced busing is one of the "historic" equity powers of the Court. It was never asserted as such by the Court prior to 1964, and as late as two years *after* the *Swann* decision it was still being described by Justice LEWIS F. POWELL as "a novel application of equitable power—not to mention a dubious extension of constitutional doctrine." Congress's response to *Swann*, the Equal Educational Opportunity and Transportation of Students Act of 1972, contained restrictions similar to those included in Title IV. These provisions suffered the same fate as the Title IV provisions, only now the Court was able to use *Swann* as authority for its ruling.

The *Swann* rationale derives equity powers directly from the Constitution. But the way in which the Court exercises its equity powers is indistinguishable from legislation. Thus, in effect, the Court now derives what is tantamount to legislative power from the Constitution. Because this power rests upon an interpretation of the Constitution, no act of Congress can overturn or modify the interpretation. Many scholars argue that if the Congress were to attempt to curtail the Court's power to order forced busing under the exceptions clause, the Court would be obligated, under the *Swann* reasoning, to declare such an attempt unconstitutional, because the Court's obligation to require busing as a remedy for equal protection violations is derived directly from the Constitution.

Judicial legislation incident to statutory interpretation is less controversial, for the Congress can overturn any constructions of the Court by repassing the legislation in a way that clarifies congressional intent. The interpretation of statutes necessarily involves the judiciary in legislation. In many instances the courts must engage in judicial legislation in order to say what the law is. In years past the Court's sense of judicial deference confined such judicial legislation to what Justice OLIVER WENDELL HOLMES called the "interstices" of the law. It was generally believed that the plain language of the statute should be the controlling factor in statutory construction and that extrinsic aids to construction such as legislative history should be used only where they were necessary to avoid a contradictory or absurd result.

The courts are not always the aggressive agents in the process of judicial legislation. In recent years courts have acted to fill the void created by Congress's abdication of legislative responsibility. Many statutes passed by Congress are deliberately vague and imprecise; indeed, the Congress in numerous instances charges administrative agencies and courts to supply the necessary details. This delegation of authority to administrative agencies with provisions for judicial oversight of the administrative process has contributed to the judiciary's increased participation in judicial legislation. This tendency was intensified by the Court's decision in IMMIGRATION AND NATURALIZATION SERVICE V. CHADHA (1983), holding the LEGISLATIVE VETO unconstitutional. Congress had for years used the single-house legislative veto as a device for overseeing the activities of administrative agencies. But, as Judge Carl McGowan has noted, "the question inevitably recurs as to whether judicial review is an adequate protection against the abdication by Congress of substantive policy making in favor of broad delegation of what may essentially be the power to make laws and not merely to administer them."

The volume of litigation calling for "legislation" on the part of the courts also increases in proportion with the liberalization of the rules of STANDING. In previous years the Court's stricter requirements for standing were merely a recognition that the province of the judiciary, in the words of John Marshall quoted earlier, "was solely to decide on the rights of individuals, not to inquire how the executive, or executive officers, perform duties in which they have a discretion." Liberalized rules of standing tend to produce what Court of Appeals Judge ATONIN SCALIA has called "an overjudicialization of the process of self-governance." Judge Scalia reminds us of the question posed by Justice Frankfurter—whether it is wise for a self-governing people to give itself over to the rule of an oligarchic judiciary. James Bradley Thayer wrote more than eighty-five years ago that "the exercise of [judicial review], even when unavoidable, is always attended with a serious evil, namely, that the correction of legislative mistakes comes from the outside, and the people thus lose the political experience, and the moral education and stimulus that comes from fighting the question out in the ordinary way, and correcting their own errors. The tendency of a common and easy resort to this great function, now lamentably too common, is to dwarf the political capacity of the people, and to deaden its sense of moral responsibility."

If, on the other hand, the processes of democracy are unsuited for protecting democratic ends—if, that is, in the words of Jesse Choper, it is necessary for the Supreme Court generally to act "contrary to the popular will" to promote "the precepts of democracy"—then the question whether the American people can be a self-governing people is indeed a serious one. It was once thought that constitutional majorities could rule safely in the interest of the whole of society—that constitutional government could avoid the formation of majority faction. Today many scholars—and often the Supreme Court itself—simply assume that the majority will always be a factious majority seeking to promote its own interest at the expense of the

interest of the minority. This requires that the judiciary intervene not only in the processes of democracy but also as the virtual representatives of the interest of those who are said to be permanently isolated from the majoritarian political process. If American politics is indeed incapable of forming nonfactious majorities—and America has never had such a monolithic majority—then the American people should give itself over honestly and openly to "government by judiciary," for if constitutional government is impossible, then so too is the possibility of self-governance.

EDWARD J. ERLER
(1986)

(SEE ALSO: *Judicial Policymaking; Judicial Review and Democracy.*)

Bibliography
AGRESTO, JOHN 1984 *The Supreme Court and Constitutional Democracy.* Ithaca, N.Y.: Cornell University Press.
ERLER, EDWARD J. 1985 Sowing the Wind: Judicial Oligarchy and the Legacy of *Brown v. Board of Education. Harvard Journal of Law and Public Policy* 8:399–426.
LEVY, LEONARD W. 1967 Judicial Review, History, and Democracy. Pages 1–42 in Leonard W. Levy, ed., *Judicial Review and the Supreme Court.* New York: Harper & Row.
SWINDLER, WILLIAM 1969 *Court and Constitution in the 20th Century.* Indianapolis: Bobbs-Merrill.

JUDICIAL POLICYMAKING

Judicial policymaking and related terms—JUDICIAL ACTIVISM, judicial creativity, and JUDICIAL LEGISLATION—emphasize that judges are not mere legal automatons who simply "discover" or "find" definite, preexisting principles and rules, as the declaratory or oracular conception of the judicial function insisted, but are often their makers. As Justice OLIVER WENDELL HOLMES remarked, they often exercise "the sovereign prerogative of choice," and they "can and do legislate." Indeed, that is why the Supreme Court has often been viewed as "a continuing constitutional convention."

Policymaking is deciding what is to be done by choosing among possible actions, methods, or principles for determining and guiding present and future actions or decisions. Courts, especially high appellate courts such as the SUPREME COURT, often make such choices, establishing new rules and principles, and thus are properly called policymakers. That was emphasized by CHARLES EVANS HUGHES's famous rhetorical exaggeration, "The Constitution is what the judges say it is," and by his remark that a federal statute finally means what the Court, as ultimate interpreter of congressional LEGISLATION, says it means.

The persistent "declaratory" conception of the judicial role, a view critics derided as MECHANICAL JURISPRUDENCE, and simplistic notions of the SEPARATION OF POWERS principle long obscured the reality of judicial policymaking. Today it is widely recognized that, as C. Herman Pritchett has explained, "judges are inevitably participants in the process of public policy formulation; that they do in fact "make law"; that in making law they are necessarily guided in part by their personal conceptions of justice and public policy; that written law requires interpretation which involves the making of choices; that the rule of STARE DECISIS is vulnerable because precedents are typically available to support both sides in a controversy."

As a system of social control, law must function largely through general propositions rather than through specific directives to particular persons. And that is especially true of the Constitution. The Framers did not minutely specify the national government's powers or the means for executing them: as Chief Justice JOHN MARSHALL said, the Constitution "is one of enumeration, rather than of definition." Many of its most important provisions are indeterminate and open-textured. They are not self-interpreting, and thus judges must read specific meanings into them and determine their applicability to particular situations, many of which their authors could not have anticipated.

Among the Constitution's many ambiguous, undefined, pregnant provisions are those concerning CRUEL AND UNUSUAL PUNISHMENT; DOUBLE JEOPARDY; DUE PROCESS OF LAW; EQUAL PROTECTION OF THE LAWS; ESTABLISHMENT OF RELIGION; excessive BAIL and fines; EX POST FACTO LAWS; FREEDOM OF SPEECH, press, assembly, and religion; life, liberty, and property; the power to regulate commerce among the several states; and unreasonable SEARCHES AND SEIZURES. Also undefined by the Constitution are such fundamental conceptions as JUDICIAL REVIEW, the RULE OF LAW, and the separation of powers. Small wonder, then, that Justice ROBERT H. JACKSON plaintively remarked that the Court must deal with materials nearly as enigmatic as the dreams of Pharaoh which Joseph had to interpret; or that Chief Justice EARL WARREN emphasized that the Constitution's words often have "an iceberg quality, containing beneath their surface simplicity submerged complexities which go to the very heart of our constitutional form of government."

Because the Constitution embodies in its ambiguous provisions both common and conflicting community ideals, the Supreme Court serves, as Edward H. Levi has said, as "a forum for the discussion of policy in the gap of ambiguity," which allows the infusion into constitutional law of new meanings and new ideas as situations and people's ideas change. That is the process which Justice FELIX FRANKFURTER described as "the evolution of social policy by way of judicial application of the Delphic provisions of the Constitution." Brief accounts of some notable Supreme Court decisions reveal their policymaking features.

Although the Constitution nowhere explicitly grants Congress the power to incorporate a national bank, the Supreme Court in MCCULLOCH V. MARYLAND (1819) held that power to be implied by the Constitution's NECESSARY AND PROPER CLAUSE. That clause empowers Congress, in executing its various enumerated powers, to make all laws for that purpose which are "necessary and proper." But those ambiguous words are not further defined by the Constitution.

In making its *McCulloch* decision, the Court chose between two historic, diametrically opposed interpretations. The narrow, STATES' RIGHTS, STRICT CONSTRUCTION, Jeffersonian interpretation of the clause was restrictive and limited Congress to legislation that was "absolutely necessary," that is, literally indispensable. The opposing interpretation, which the Court adopted, was the broad, nationalist, loose constructionist, Hamiltonian view that "necessary and proper" were equivalent to "convenient and useful" and thus were facilitative, not restrictive. The bank, declared the Court, was a convenient and useful means to legitimate ends and thus was constitutional.

Viewed broadly as the great implied powers case and the "fountainhead of national powers," *McCulloch* laid down the Hamiltonian doctrine as the authoritative rule of construction to be followed in interpreting Congress's various undefined powers. Subsequently, on that foundation, Congress erected vast superstructures of regulatory and social service legislation. The profound policy considerations underlying the Court's choices are highlighted by the contrast between Jefferson's warning that the dangerous Hamiltonian doctrine would give Congress a boundless field of undefined powers, and Chief Justice Marshall's emphasis upon the "pernicious, baneful," narrow construction which would make the national government's operations "difficult, hazardous, and expensive" and would reduce the Constitution to "a splendid bauble."

The RIGHT TO PRIVACY was recognized by the Supreme Court in GRISWOLD V. CONNECTICUT (1965). There, and in other cases, the Court variously discerned the "roots" of that right, which is not explicitly mentioned in the Constitution, in the FIRST, FOURTH, Fifth, NINTH, and FOURTEENTH AMENDMENTS and in "the penumbras of the BILL OF RIGHTS." Later, in ROE V. WADE (1973), the Court included a woman's right to an abortion in the right of privacy, and, in the detailed manner characteristic of legislation, divided the pregnancy term into three periods and prescribed specific rules governing each. Balancing a woman's interests against a state's interests during these three periods, the Court held that any decision regarding abortion during the first was solely at the discretion of the woman and her physician. But it further ruled that a state's interests in protecting maternal health, maintaining medical standards, and safeguarding potential human life—interests growing in substantiality as the pregnancy term extended—justified greater state regulation later. Thus, state regulations relating to maternal health and medical standards would be permissible in the second period, and more stringent state regulations, even extending to prohibition of abortion, would be permissible in the third period in the interest of safeguarding potential life.

The protests by dissenting Justices in the *Griswold* and *Roe* cases emphasized the judicial policymaking which those decisions revealed. The *Griswold* dissenters objected that no right of privacy could be found "in the Bill of Rights, in any other part of the Constitution, or in any case ever before decided by this Court." And dissenters in *Roe* complained that the Court's decision was "an improvident and extravagant exercise of the power of JUDICIAL REVIEW"; that the Court had fashioned "a new constitutional right for pregnant mothers"; and that the Court's "conscious weighing of competing factors" and its division of the pregnancy term into distinct periods were "far more appropriate to a legislative judgement than to a judicial one."

The Supreme Court's "REAPPORTIONMENT revolution" remedied long-standing discriminations against urban and metropolitan areas in favor of rural areas, by requiring states to reapportion their legislatures in conformity with the rule that legislative districts must be as nearly of equal population as is practicable.

That rule is not found in any constitutional provision specifically addressed to legislative apportionment, for none exists. It is a Court-created rule which clearly demonstrates the leeway for policymaking that open-ended constitutional provisions give the Court. Equal population, the Court said in WESBERRY V. SANDERS (1964), is required for congressional districts by "the command" of Article I, section 2, of the Constitution, that representatives "be chosen by the People" of the states; and is required for state legislative districts, the Court held in REYNOLDS V. SIMS (1964), by "the clear and strong command" of the FOURTEENTH AMENDMENT's equal protection clause, forbidding states to deny to any persons "the equal protection of the laws."

Courtesy may ascribe the Court's rule to CONSTITUTIONAL INTERPRETATION; but candor ascribes it to judicial policymaking. The dissenting Justices' objections in these cases made that clear. They included complaints that the Court had frozen one political theory of REPRESENTATION into the Constitution; had failed to exercise judicial self-restraint; had decided questions appropriate only for legislative judgment; had violated the separation of powers doctrine; and had excluded numerous important considerations other than population.

Supreme Court overruling decisions, in which it rejects its earlier positions for those later thought more fitting, often strikingly exemplify judicial policymaking. In MAPP V. OHIO (1961) the Court imposed upon state courts its judicially created EXCLUSIONARY RULE making illegally obtained evidence inadmissible in court. It overruled WOLF V. COLORADO (1949) which, in deference to state policies, had held an exclusionary rule not essential for due process of law.

Some overruling decisions illustrate "the victory of dissent," when earlier dissenting Justices' views in time became the law. Thus in GIDEON V. WAINWRIGHT (1963) the Court applied its rule that indigent defendants in all state felony trials must have court-appointed counsel. Overruling BETTS V. BRADY (1942), the Court adopted Justice Black's dissenting position from it, thus repudiating its *Betts* pronouncement that such appointment was "not a fundamental right, essential to a fair trial."

According to the Court in BARRON V. BALTIMORE (1833), the Bill of Rights—the first ten amendments—limits the national government but not the states. But the Court, by its INCORPORATION DOCTRINE, has read nearly all the specific guarantees of the Bill of Rights into the due process clause of the Fourteenth Amendment which provides simply that no state shall "deprive any person of life, liberty, or property, without due process of law." The incorporation has been called selective because the Court, proceeding case by case, has incorporated those guarantees which it considers "fundamental" and "of the very essence of a scheme of ORDERED LIBERTY."

Selective incorporation has involved two kinds of Supreme Court policymaking: adopting the FUNDAMENTAL RIGHTS standard for guiding incorporation, and making the separate decisions incorporating particular Bill of Rights guarantees. Thus the Court, applying its open-textured rule, has given specific meaning to "the vague contours" of the due process clause. And it has become "a perpetual censor" over state actions, invalidating those that violate fundamental rights and liberties.

Clearly the Supreme Court is more than just a legal body: the Justices are also "rulers," sharing in the quintessentially political function of authoritatively allocating values for the American polity. Representing a coordinate branch of the national government, they address their mandates variously to lawyers, litigants, federal and state legislative, executive, and judicial officials, and to broader concerned "publics." Concerning their role, no sharp line can be drawn between law and politics in the broad sense. They do not expound a prolix or rigid legal code, but rather a living Constitution "intended to be adapted to the various *crises* of human affairs," as Chief Justice Marshall said in the *McCulloch* case. And the Justices employ essentially COMMON LAW judicial techniques: they are inheritors indeed, but developers too—"weavers of the fabric of constitutional law"—as Chief Justice Hughes observed. The nature of the judicial process and the growth of the law are intertwined. The Constitution, itself the product of great policy choices, is both the abiding Great Charter of the American polity and the continual focus of clashing philosophies of law and politics among which the Supreme Court must choose: "We are very quiet there," said Justice Holmes plaintively, "but it is the quiet of a storm center, as we all know."

HOWARD E. DEAN
(1986)

Bibliography

CARDOZO, BENJAMIN N. 1921 *The Nature of the Judicial Process*. New Haven, Conn.: Yale University Press.

LEVI, EDWARD H. 1948 *An Introduction to Legal Reasoning*. Chicago: University of Chicago Press.

MILLER, ARTHUR SELWYN 1978 *The Supreme Court: Myth and Reality*. Westport, Conn.: Greenwood Press.

MURPHY, WALTER F. 1964 *Elements of Judicial Strategy*. Chicago: University of Chicago Press.

PRITCHETT, C. HERMAN 1969 The Development of Judicial Research. Pages 27–42 in Joel B. Grossman and Joseph Tanenhaus, eds., *Frontiers of Judicial Research*. New York: Wiley.

JUDICIAL POWER

"[T]he legislative, executive, and judicial powers, of every well constructed government," said JOHN MARSHALL in OSBORN V. BANK OF THE UNITED STATES (1824), "are co-extensive with each other; . . . [t]he executive department may constitutionally execute every law which the Legislature may constitutionally make, and the judicial department may receive from the legislature the power of construing every such law." The ARTICLES OF CONFEDERATION fell far short of this model. Not only was there no federal executive with authority to enforce congressional measures against individuals, but, apart from a cumbersome procedure for resolving interstate disputes, Congress was authorized to establish courts only for the trial of crimes committed at sea and for the determination of "appeals in all cases of captures." The remedy for these shortcomings was one of the major accomplishments of the Constitution adopted in 1789. As Article II gave the country a President with the obligation to "take care that the Laws be faithfully executed," Article III provided for a system of federal courts that more than satisfied Marshall's conditions for a "well constructed government."

Article III consists of three brief sections. The first describes the tribunals that are to exercise federal judicial power and prescribes the tenure and compensation of their judges. The second lists the types of disputes that may be entrusted to federal courts, specifies which of these matters are to be determined by the SUPREME COURT in the first instance, and guarantees TRIAL BY JURY in criminal cases. The third defines and limits the crime of TREASON.

"The judicial Power of the United States," Article III declares, "shall be vested in one Supreme Court, and in such inferior Courts as the Congress may from time to time ordain and establish." The text itself indicates that the Supreme Court was the only tribunal the Constitution required to be established, and the debates of the CONSTITUTIONAL CONVENTION demonstrate that the latter words embodied a deliberate compromise.

In fact, however, Congress created additional courts at the very beginning, in the JUDICIARY ACT OF 1789. Since 1911 the basic system has consisted of the UNITED STATES DISTRICT COURTS—at least one in every state—in which most cases are first tried; a number of regional appellate courts now called the UNITED STATES COURTS OF APPEALS; and the Supreme Court itself, which functions largely as a court of last resort. From time to time, moreover, Congress has created specialized courts with JURISDICTION to determine controversies involving relatively limited subjects. All this lies well within Congress's broad discretion under Article III to determine what lower courts to create and how to allocate judicial business among them. Specialization at the highest level, however, seems precluded; Congress can no more divide the powers of "one Supreme Court" among two or more bodies than abolish it altogether.

"The Judges, both of the supreme and inferior Courts," section 1 continues, "shall hold their Offices during GOOD BEHAVIOUR and shall, at stated Times, receive for their Services, a Compensation, which shall not be diminished during their Continuance in Office." Under the second section of Article II the judges have always been appointed by the President subject to Senate confirmation; under the fourth section of that article they may be removed from office on IMPEACHMENT and conviction of "Treason, Bribery, or other high Crimes and Misdemeanors." The central purpose of the tenure and salary provisions, as ALEXANDER HAMILTON explained in THE FEDERALIST #78, was to assure judicial independence.

The Supreme Court has repeatedly enforced the tenure and salary provisions. In EX PARTE MILLIGAN (1867), for example, the Court held even the Civil War no excuse for submitting civilians to military trials in states where the civil courts were open, and in *O'Donoghue v. United States* (1933), it held that the Great Depression did not justify reducing judicial salaries.

On a number of occasions, however, the Court has permitted matters within the judicial power to be determined by LEGISLATIVE COURTS whose judges do not possess tenure and salary guarantees. State courts may decide Article III cases, as the Framers of the Constitution clearly contemplated; the tenure and salary provisions do not apply to the TERRITORIES or to the DISTRICT OF COLUMBIA, where there is no SEPARATION OF POWERS requirement; Article III did not abolish the traditional COURT-MARTIAL for military offenses; federal magistrates may make initial decisions in Article III cases provided they are subject to unlimited reexamination by tenured judges.

Early in the twentieth century the Supreme Court appeared to give judicial blessing to the numerous quasi-judicial bodies that have grown up since the creation of the Interstate Commerce Commission in 1887, although scholars have debated heatedly whether there is any satisfactory way to distinguish them from the nontenured trial courts plainly forbidden by Article III. That these developments did not mean the effective end of the tenure and salary requirements, however, was made clear in 1982, when the Court in NORTHERN PIPE LINE CONSTRUCTION CO. V. MARATHON PIPE LINE CO. invalidated a statute empowering judges with temporary commissions to exercise virtually the entire jurisdiction of the district courts in BANKRUPTCY cases. Where to draw this line promises to be a continuing problem.

The power to be vested in federal courts is the "judicial power," and the various categories of matters that fall within this power are all described as CASES OR CONTROVERSIES—"Cases," for example, "arising under this Constitution," and "Controversies to which the United States shall be a Party." From the beginning the Supreme Court has taken this language as a limitation: federal courts may not resolve anything but "cases" and "controversies," and those terms embrace only judicial functions.

Thus, for example, when President GEORGE WASHINGTON asked the Justices for legal advice respecting the United States' neutrality during hostilities between England and France, they declined to act "extra-judicially"; and when Congress directed them to advise the war secretary concerning veterans' pensions, five Justices sitting on circuit refused, saying the authority conferred was "not of a judicial nature" (HAYBURN'S CASE, 1792). Washington's request for advice did not begin to resemble the ordinary lawsuit, but later decisions have invoked the "case" or "controversy" limitation to exclude federal court consideration of matters far less remote from the normal judicial function. The essential requirement, the Court has emphasized, is a live and actual dispute between adversary parties with a real stake in the outcome.

One dimension of this principle is the doctrine of RIPENESS or prematurity: the courts are not to give advice on the mere possibility that it might be of use in the future. Occasionally the Court has appeared to require a person to violate a law in order to test its constitutionality—causing one commentator to remark that "the only way to determine whether the subject is a mushroom or a toadstool, is to eat it." The DECLARATORY JUDGMENT ACT, passed to mitigate this hardship, has generally been applied to allow preenforcement challenges when the intentions of the parties are sufficiently firm, and it has been held consistent with the "Case" or "Controversy" requirement.

At the opposite end of the spectrum is the MOOTNESS doctrine, which ordinarily forbids litigation after death or other changed circumstances deprive the issue of any further impact on the parties. A series of debatable decisions essentially dating from *Moore v. Ogilvie* (1969), however, has relaxed the mootness doctrine especially in CLASS ACTIONS, so as to permit persons with no remaining interest to continue litigating issues deemed "capable of repetition, yet evading review."

The "case or controversy" requirement has also been held to forbid the decision of COLLUSIVE SUITS, and to preclude the courts from exercising the discretion of an administrator, as by reviewing de novo the decision to grant a broadcasting license. The most important remaining element of that requirement, however, is the constitutional dimension of the doctrine of STANDING to sue.

While standing has been aptly characterized as one of the most confused areas of federal law, its constitutional component was simply stated in *Warth v. Seldin* (1975): "[t]he Article III power exists only to redress or otherwise to protect against injury to the complaining party." Injury in this context is hardly self-defining, but it plainly requires something more than intellectual or emotional "interest in a problem." This principle puts under a serious cloud the periodic congressional attempts to authorize "any person" to obtain judicial relief against violations of environmental or other laws. On the other hand, other aspects of the standing doctrine are not of constitutional dimension and thus do not preclude Congress from conferring standing on anyone injured by governmental action.

One of the principal points of contention of the law of standing has been the right of federal taxpayers to challenge the constitutionality of federal spending programs. When a taxpayer attacked expenditures for maternal health on the ground that they exceeded the powers granted Congress by Article I, the Court in FROTHINGHAM V. MELLON (1923) found no standing: "the taxpayer's interest in the moneys of the treasury . . . is shared with millions of others, is comparatively minute and indeterminable, and the effect upon future taxation, of any payment out of the funds, so remote, fluctuating, and uncertain, that no basis is afforded for an appeal to the preventive powers of a court of EQUITY."

Although the apparent reference to equitable discretion made it uncertain that the Court was saying taxpayer suits were not "cases or controversies" within Article III, the remainder of the passage suggests that the taxpayer could not show the constitutionally required injury because it was uncertain that a victory would mean reduced taxes. Nevertheless, in FLAST V. COHEN (1968) the Court allowed a federal taxpayer to challenge expenditures for church-related education as an ESTABLISHMENT OF RELIGION in violation of the FIRST AMENDMENT. Unlike the taxpayer in *Frothingham,* who "was attempting to assert the States' interest in their legislative prerogatives," the plaintiff in *Flast* asserted "a federal taxpayer's interest in being free of taxing and spending in contravention of specific constitutional limitations," for one purpose of the establishment clause was to prevent taxation for religious ends. Whether the distinction was of constitutional scope the Court did not say; interestingly, the taxpayer opinions have tended to avoid entirely the traditional constitutional inquiry into the existence of an injury that will be redressed if the plaintiff's claim prevails.

Underlying the constitutional "case or controversy" limitation are a variety of policy concerns. The first group relates to reducing the risk of erroneous decisions. Concrete facts enable judges to understand the practical impact of their holdings; adverse parties help to assure that arguments on both sides will be considered; as argued by FELIX FRANKFURTER, "the ADVISORY OPINION deprives CONSTITUTIONAL INTERPRETATION of the judgment of the legislature upon facts." A second group of reasons focuses upon strengthening the Court's institutional position. Lawmaking by appointed judges is least difficult to reconcile with democratic principles when it is the inevitable by-product of the stock business of judging; the courts should not squander their power of moral suasion or multiply conflicts with other branches by deciding unnecessary legal questions. Third, and of considerable importance, is a concern for the separation of powers. The courts are not to exercise a general superintendence over the activities of the other branches.

The costs of the "case or controversy" limitation include the delay, uncertainty, and disruption incident to determining the constitutionality of legislation only in the course of subsequent litigation, and the danger that some legislative and executive actions may escape JUDICIAL REVIEW entirely. Whether the latter is cause for concern has much to do with one's perception of the function and importance of judicial review itself; it seems reasonable to expect that perception to influence the definition of a "case" or "controversy."

In addition to restricting federal courts to the decision of "cases" and "controversies" of a judicial nature, section 2 of Article III enumerates those categories of "cases" and "controversies" to which the "judicial Power shall extend." As the former limitation serves the interests of separating

federal powers, the latter serves those of FEDERALISM. In accord with the spirit of the TENTH AMENDMENT the Supreme Court has held that Congress may not give the federal courts jurisdiction over disputes of types not listed in Article III. John Marshall set the tone in cutting down to constitutional size a statute providing for jurisdiction over cases involving ALIENS in HODGSON V. BOWERBANK in 1809: "Turn to the article of the constitution of the United States, for the statutes cannot extend the jurisdiction beyond the limits of the constitution."

Article III's provision that federal judicial power "shall extend to" certain classes of cases and controversies has generally been taken to mean that it shall embrace nothing else. From the text alone one might think it even more plain that federal courts *must* be given jurisdiction over all the matters listed, for section 1 commands that the federal judicial power "shall be vested" in federal courts. Indeed, Justice JOSEPH STORY suggested just such an interpretation in MARTIN V. HUNTER'S LESSEE in 1816. This conclusion, however, was unnecessary to the decision, contrary to the understanding of the First Congress, and inconsistent with both earlier and later decisions of the Supreme Court.

Article III, in other words, has been read to mean only that Congress may confer jurisdiction over the enumerated cases, not that it must do so. This arguably unnatural construction has been defended by reference to the limited list of controversies over which the Supreme Court has original jurisdiction, the explicit congressional power to make exceptions to the Supreme Court's appellate authority, and the compromise at the Constitutional Convention permitting Congress not to establish inferior courts at all.

This is not to say, however, that Congress has unfettered authority to deny the courts jurisdiction, for all powers of Congress are subject to limitations found elsewhere in the Constitution. A statute depriving the courts of authority to determine cases filed by members of a particular racial group, for instance, would be of highly doubtful vitality under the modern interpretation of the Fifth Amendment DUE PROCESS clause, and one part of Marshall's reasoning in MARBURY V. MADISON (1803) supports an argument that closing all federal and state courts to free-speech claims would defeat the substantive right itself. Proposals to remove entire categories of constitutional litigation from the ken of one or more federal courts often follow controversial judicial decisions. Out of respect for the tradition of CHECKS AND BALANCES, however, such bills are seldom enacted; we have so far been spared the constitutional trauma of determining the extent to which they may validly be adopted.

The cases and controversies within federal judicial power fall into two categories: those in which jurisdiction is based upon the nature of the dispute and those in which it is based upon the identity of the parties. In the first category are three kinds of disputes: those "arising under this Constitution, the Laws of the United States, and Treaties made, or which shall be made, under their Authority"; those "of ADMIRALTY AND MARITIME Jurisdiction"; and those involving competing land claims "under Grants of different States." The provision last quoted is of minor importance; the second formed the staple business of the district courts throughout their early history; the first fulfills Marshall's condition for a "well constructed government" and is by any measure the most critical ingredient of federal jurisdiction today.

The provision for jurisdiction in cases arising under the Constitution and other federal laws has two essential purposes: to promote uniformity in the interpretation of federal law, and to assure the vindication of federal rights. The First Congress sought to accomplish the second of these goals by providing, in section 25 of the 1789 Judiciary Act, for Supreme Court review of state-court decisions denying federal rights; the additional uniformity attendant upon review of state decisions *upholding* federal claims was not provided until 1914. In sustaining section 25, the opinion in *Martin v. Hunter's Lessee* demonstrated the difficulty of achieving Article III's purpose without Supreme Court review of state courts: while plaintiffs might be authorized to file federal claims directly in federal courts and defendants to remove state court actions to federal courts on the basis of federal defenses, it was not easy to see how a state court opposing removal "could . . . be compelled to relinquish the jurisdiction" without some federal court reviewing the state court decision.

Conversely, although Congress failed to give federal trial courts general jurisdiction of federal question cases until 1875, Marshall made clear as early as 1824, in *Osborn v. Bank of the United States,* that it had power to do so. Supreme Court review alone was no more an adequate protection for federal rights, Marshall argued, than was exclusive reliance on litigation beginning in federal trial courts. As the latter would leave claimants without remedy against a recalcitrant state court, the former would give a state tribunal the critical power to shape the factual record beyond assurance of federal appellate correction.

The *Osborn* opinion also settled that jurisdiction of a federal trial court over a case arising under federal law was not defeated by the presence of additional issues dependent upon state law. In a companion case, indeed, the Court upheld jurisdiction over a suit by the national bank on notes whose validity and interpretation were understood to depend in substantial part upon nonfederal law: it was enough that the plaintiff derived its existence and its right to contract from the act of Congress incorporating it. The courts have not followed this broad approach, how-

ever, in determining whether FEDERAL QUESTION JURISDICTION lies under general *statutory* provisions; when the federal ingredient of a claim is remote from the actual controversy, as in a dispute over ownership of land whose title is remotely derived from a federal land grant, the district courts lack statutory jurisdiction.

In the contract dispute discussed in *Osborn,* federal and state law were bound together in the resolution of a single claim; in such a case, as HENRY HART and Herbert Wechsler said, "a federal trial court would . . . be unable to function as a court at all" if its jurisdiction did not extend to state as well as federal matters. In the interest of "judicial economy," however, as the Supreme Court put it in *United Mine Workers v. Gibbs* (1966), jurisdiction over a case arising under federal law embraces not only a plaintiff's federal claim but also any claims under state law based on the same facts. This so-called PENDENT JURISDICTION doctrine, however, is inapplicable when the Supreme Court reviews a state court decision. With one exception, in such a case the Court may review only federal and not state questions, as the Court held in *Murdock v. Memphis* (1875); for to reverse a state court in the interpretation of its own law would be a major incursion into state prerogatives not required by the purposes for which Supreme Court review was provided.

A corollary of the *Murdock* principle is that a state court decision respecting state law often precludes the Supreme Court from reviewing even federal questions in the same case. If a state court concludes, for example, that a state law offends both federal and state constitutions, the Supreme Court cannot reverse the state law holding; thus, however it may decide the federal issue, it cannot alter the outcome of the case. This independent and ADEQUATE STATE GROUND for the state court decision means there is no longer a live case or controversy between the parties over the federal question. In light of this relation between state and federal issues, *Martin* itself announced the sole exception to the *Murdock* rule: when the state court has interpreted state law in such a way as to frustrate the federal right itself—as by holding that a contract allegedly impaired in violation of the CONTRACT CLAUSE never existed—a complete absence of power to review the state question would mean the Court's authority to protect federal rights "may be evaded at pleasure."

"The most bigoted idolizers of state authority," wrote Alexander Hamilton in THE FEDERALIST #80, "have not thus far shown a disposition to deny the National Judiciary the cognizance of maritime causes"; for such cases "so generally depend upon the law of nations, and so commonly affect the rights of foreigners, that they fall within the considerations which are relative to the public peace." Jurisdiction over what Article III refers to as "Cases of admiralty, and maritime Jurisdiction" has been vested by statute in the district courts since 1789. Today federal admiralty jurisdiction extends, as the Court stated in another context in *The Daniel Ball* (1871), to all waters forming part of "a continued highway over which commerce is or may be carried on with other states or foreign countries."

Not everything occurring on navigable waters, however, is a proper subject of admiralty jurisdiction; in denying jurisdiction of claims arising out of an airplane crash in Lake Erie, the Supreme Court made clear that the case must "bear a significant relationship to traditional maritime activity . . . involving navigation and commerce on navigable waters." Conversely, the relation of an activity to maritime concerns may bring it within admiralty cognizance even if it occurs on land. Marine insurance contracts, for example, are within the jurisdiction although both made and to be performed on land. Similarly, the Court has acquiesced in Congress's provision for jurisdiction over land damage caused by vessels on navigable waters.

Because an additional purpose of federal judicial power over maritime cases is understood to have been to provide a uniform law to govern the shipping industry, the Supreme Court also held in *Southern Pacific Company v. Jensen* (1917) that Article III empowers the federal courts to develop a "general maritime law" binding even on state courts, and that Congress may supplement this law with statutes under its authority to adopt laws "necessary and proper" to the powers of the courts. Indeed the Court has held that this aspect of the judicial power, like the legislative authority conferred by the commerce clause of Article I, has an implicit limiting effect upon state law. Not only does state law that contradicts federal law yield under the SUPREMACY CLAUSE, but, as the Court said in rejecting the application of a state workers' compensation law to longshoremen in the case last cited, no state law is valid if it "interferes with the proper harmony and uniformity" of the general maritime law "in its international and interstate relations."

The remaining authorization of federal court jurisdiction protects parties whose fortunes the Framers were for various reasons unwilling to leave wholly at the mercy of state courts. Many of these categories involve government litigation: "Controversies to which the United States shall be a Party; . . . between two or more States; between a State and Citizens of another State, . . . and between a State, or the Citizens thereof, and foreign States, Citizens or Subjects." A federal forum for the national government itself protects against possible state hostility; federal jurisdiction over interstate conflicts provides not only a neutral forum but also a safeguard against what Hamilton in THE FEDERALIST #80 called "dissentions and private wars"; that "the union will undoubtedly be answerable to foreign powers, for the conduct of its members," was an additional reason for jurisdiction over disputes involving foreign countries as well as the related jurisdiction over "Cases affecting Ambassadors, other public Ministers and Consuls."

The most interesting issue concerning these provisions has been that of SOVEREIGN IMMUNITY. In CHISHOLM V. GEORGIA (1793), ignoring the assurances of prominent Framers like James Madison and Alexander Hamilton as well as the common law tradition that the king could not be sued without his consent, the Supreme Court relied largely on the text of Article III to hold that the power over "Controversies . . . between a State and Citizens of another State" included those in which the state was an unwilling defendant. Obviously, as the Justices pointed out, this was true of the parallel authority over "Controversies . . . between two or more States," and Justice JAMES WILSON added his understanding that the English tradition was a mere formality, since consent to sue was given as a matter of course.

Whether this decision was right or wrong as an original matter, within five years it was repudiated by adoption of the ELEVENTH AMENDMENT, which provides that "[t]he Judicial power of the United States shall not be construed to extend to any suit in law or equity, commenced or prosecuted against one of the United States by Citizens or Subjects of any Foreign State." Notably, the amendment does not mention admiralty cases, suits by foreign countries, suits against a state by its own citizens under federal law, or suits against the United States. Nevertheless the Supreme Court, taking the amendment as casting doubt on the reasoning underlying *Chisholm*, has denied jurisdiction in all of these instances. The best explanation has been that, although not excepted by the amendment, they are outside the power conferred by Article III itself. One state may still sue another, however, and the United States may sue a state. The Court has found such jurisdiction "essential to the peace of the Union" and "inherent in the constitutional plan." Why this is not equally true of a suit by a state against the United States has never been satisfactorily explained.

At least since the 1824 decision in *Osborn v. Bank of the United States*, however, both the Eleventh Amendment and its related immunities have been construed to allow certain actions against state or federal officers even though the effect of the litigation is the same as if the government itself had been named defendant. The theoretical explanation that the officer cannot be acting for the state when he does what the Constitution forbids is inconsistent with the substantive conclusion, often reached in the same cases, that his action is attributable to the state for purposes of the FOURTEENTH AMENDMENT. A more principled explanation is that suits against officers are necessary if the Constitution is to be enforced at all; the response is that those who wrote the amendment could not have intended to allow it to be reduced to a hollow shell.

In any event, the *Osborn* exception has not been held to embrace all suits against government officers. At one time it was said generally that an officer could be prevented from acting but could not be ordered to take affirmative action such as paying off a government obligation, for if he was not acting for the state he had no authority to reach into its treasury. The simplicity of this distinction was shattered, however, by opinions acknowledging the availability of a WRIT OF MANDAMUS to compel an officer to perform a nondiscretionary duty. The more recent formulation in EDELMAN V. JORDAN (1974), which essentially distinguishes between prospective and retrospective relief, seems difficult to reconcile with the language of the Constitution, with its apparent purposes, or with the fiction created to support the *Osborn* rule.

Even when the government is itself a party, it may consent to be sued, and the books are filled with a confusing and incomplete array of statutes allowing suits against the United States. Some judges and scholars have argued that suits against consenting states are inconsistent with the language of the amendment, which declares them outside the judicial power; the Court's persuasive explanation has been that, like venue and personal jurisdiction, immunity is a privilege waivable by the party it protects (*Clark v. Barnard*, 1883). More debatable was the Court's decision in *Parden v. Terminal Railway* (1964) that a state had "waived" its immunity by operating a railroad after passage of a federal statute making "every" interstate railway liable for injuries to its employees; in *Edelman v. Jordan*, retreating from this conclusion, the Court emphasized that "[c]onstructive consent is not a doctrine commonly associated with the surrender of constitutional rights." Still later, however, in FITZPATRICK V. BITZER (1976) the Court held that Congress had power to override a state's immunity in legislating to enforce the Fourteenth Amendment, although it has never suggested that that amendment allowed Congress to ignore other constitutional limitations, such as the BILL OF RIGHTS.

The two remaining categories of disputes within federal judicial power are "controversies . . . between Citizens of different States" and between state citizens and "Citizens or Subjects" of "foreign States." Once again the reasons for federal jurisdiction are generally said to be the avoidance of state-court bias and of interstate or international friction. In contrast not only to the admiralty cases but also to those between states, federal jurisdiction based solely on the diverse citizenship of the parties does not carry with it authority to make substantive law. Absent a federal statute, the Court held in ERIE RAILROAD V. TOMPKINS (1938), "the law to be applied . . . is the law of the State." Later cases such as *Textile Workers Union v. Lincoln Mills* (1957) have qualified the effect though not the principle of this decision by finding in silent statutes implicit authorization to the federal courts to make law. An occasional decision has upheld FEDERAL COMMON LAW, without the pretense of statutory authority, on matters mysteriously found to be "intrinsically federal"; an example was the Court's refusal in *Banco Nacional de Cuba v. Sabbatino* (1964) to look behind official acts of foreign governments. (See ACT OF STATE DOCTRINE.)

In early decisions the Supreme Court took a narrow view of what constituted a controversy between citizens of different states for purposes of the statute implementing this provision of Article III. More recently, however, the Court has generously interpreted the power of Congress to confer DIVERSITY JURISDICTION on the federal courts. And as early as the mid-nineteenth century, recognizing that corporations can be the beneficiaries or victims of state court prejudice without regard to the citizenship of those who compose them, the Court effectively began to treat corporations as citizens by employing the transparent fiction of conclusively presuming that the individuals whose citizenship was determinative were citizens of the state of incorporation.

The best known decision involving the diversity jurisdiction was DRED SCOTT V. SANDFORD (1857), in which three Justices took the position that a black American descended from slaves could never be a state citizen for diversity purposes because he could not be a citizen of the United States. Questionable enough at the time, this conclusion was repudiated by the Fourteenth Amendment's provision that all persons born in this country are citizens of the United States "and of the state wherein they reside." Nevertheless the courts have held that only American citizens are "Citizens of . . . States" within Article III, and conversely that only foreign nationals are "Citizens or Subjects" of "foreign States."

"In all Cases involving Ambassadors, other public Ministers and Consuls, and those in which a state shall be Party," Article III, section 2 provides, "the supreme Court shall have ORIGINAL JURISDICTION. In all the other Cases before mentioned, the supreme Court shall have APPELLATE JURISDICTION, both as to Law and Fact, with such Exceptions, and under such Regulations as the Congress shall make."

Original jurisdiction is the power to determine a dispute in the first instance; appellate jurisdiction, the power to review a decision already made. *Marbury v. Madison* (1803) held that Congress had no power to give the Supreme Court original jurisdiction of a case to which neither a diplomat nor a state was a party; a contrary result, Chief Justice Marshall argued, would make the constitutional distribution between original and appellate jurisdiction "mere surplusage." This reasoning is not especially convincing, and the converse is not true; in COHENS V. VIRGINIA in 1821 Marshall himself conceded that Congress could give the Court appellate jurisdiction over cases for which Article III provided original jurisdiction. *Cohens* also held that the Supreme Court had original authority not over all Article III cases in which a state happened to be a party but only over those "in which jurisdiction is given, because a state is a party," and thus not over a federal question case between a state and one of its own citizens. Inconsistently, however, the Court allowed the United States to sue a State in the Supreme Court in *United States v. Texas* (1892).

Marbury's implicit conclusion that the exceptions clause quoted above does not allow Congress to tamper with the original jurisdiction strongly suggests that the enumeration of original cases is a minimum as well as a maximum, and the Court has described as "extremely doubtful" the proposition that Congress may deprive it of original power over state or diplomat cases; yet the Court has concluded that it has discretion not to entertain cases within its original jurisdiction.

Unlike the original jurisdiction provision, that giving the Court appellate authority in "all the other" Article III cases contains an explicit escape valve: "with such Exceptions . . . as the Congress shall make." In THE FEDERALIST #81, Hamilton explained that this clause permitted Congress to limit review of facts decided by juries, but he did not say this was its sole objective. From the beginning Congress has denied the Court jurisdiction over entire classes of controversies within the constitutional reach of appellate power—such as federal criminal cases, most of which were excluded from appellate cognizance for many years even if constitutional issues were presented. The Court itself accepted this particular limitation as early as *United States v. More* (1805), without questioning its constitutionality. Moreover, when Congress repealed a statute under which a pending case attacking the Reconstruction Act had been filed, the Court in EX PARTE MCCARDLE (1869) meekly dismissed the case, observing that "the power to make exceptions to the appellate jurisdiction of this court is given by express words."

As the *McCardle* opinion noted, however, other avenues remained available for taking similar cases to the Supreme Court, and three years later the Court made clear in *United States v. Klein* (1872) that Congress could not under the guise of limiting jurisdiction effectively dictate the result of a case by directing dismissal if the Court should find for the plaintiff. Respected commentators have contended that the Supreme Court must retain appellate authority over certain constitutional questions, arguing that the exceptions clause cannot have been intended, in Henry Hart's words, to "destroy the essential

role of the Supreme Court in the constitutional plan." The persuasiveness of this position depends on one's perceptions of the function of judicial review. (See JUDICIAL SYSTEM.)

In order for the Court in *Marbury v. Madison* to dismiss an action that it found Congress had authorized, it had first to conclude that it had the right to refuse to obey an unconstitutional act of Congress. Marshall's argument that this power was "essentially attached to a written constitution" is contradicted by much European experience; and his assertion that choosing between the Constitution and a statute was an inescapable aspect of deciding cases begged the question, for the Constitution might have required the courts to accept Congress's determination that a statute was valid. For the same reason one may object to his reliance on Article VI's requirement that judges swear to support the Constitution: one does not offend that oath by enforcing an unconstitutional statute if that is what the Constitution requires.

The SUPREMACY CLAUSE of Article VI is no better support; the contrasting reference to "Treaties made, or which shall be made" in the same clause strongly suggests that the phrase "laws . . . which shall be made in Pursuance of" the Constitution, also invoked by Marshall, was meant to deny supremacy to acts adopted under the Articles of Confederation, not to those that were invalid. Most promising of the provisions brought forward in *Marbury* was Article III's extension of judicial power to "Cases . . . arising under this Constitution"; as Marshall said, it could scarcely have been "the intention of those who gave this power, to say that in using it the constitution should not be looked into." Yet even here the case is not airtight. For while Article III provides for jurisdiction in constitutional cases, it is Article VI that prescribes the force to be given the Constitution; and while the latter article plainly gives the Constitution precedence over conflicting *state* laws, it appears to place *federal* statutes on a par with the Constitution itself.

Nevertheless the *Marbury* decision should be regarded as neither a surprise nor a usurpation. Though Marshall did not say so, judicial review had a substantial history before *Marbury*, and despite occasional scholarly denials it seems clear that most of the Framers expected that the courts would refuse to enforce unconstitutional acts of Congress. Moreover, there is force to Marshall's argument that a denial of this power would effectively undermine the express written limitations on congressional power; the natural reluctance to assume that the Framers meant to leave the fox in charge of the chickens lends credence to the conclusion that judicial review is implicit in the power to decide constitutional cases or in the substantive constitutional limitations themselves.

In fact the *Marbury* opinion espouses two distinct theories of judicial review that have opposite implications for a number of related issues, some of which have been discussed above. If, as Marshall at one point seemed to suggest, judicial review is only an incidental by-product of the need to resolve pending cases, it is no cause for constitutional concern if Congress eliminates the Supreme Court's jurisdiction over First Amendment cases, or if no one has standing to attack a federal spending program. If, on the other hand, as argued elsewhere in *Marbury*, judicial review is essential to a plan of constitutional checks and balances, one may take a more restrictive view of Congress's power to make exceptions to the appellate jurisdiction, and perhaps a broader view of what constitutes a case or controversy as well.

Dissenting from the assertion of judicial authority over legislative reapportionment cases in BAKER V. CARR (1962), Justice Felix Frankfurter argued for a broad exception to judicial review of both federal and state actions: even unconstitutional acts could not be set aside if they presented POLITICAL QUESTIONS. Some have attempted to trace this notion to *Marbury* itself, where the Court did say that "[q]uestions in their nature political" were beyond judicial ken. The context suggests, however, that Marshall meant only that the Court would respect actions taken by other branches of government within their legitimate authority, and Louis Henkin has shown that most later decisions using "political question" language can be so explained.

The Court itself, however, spoke in *Baker* of a general "political question" doctrine preventing decision of the merits when, among other things, there was "a lack of judicially discoverable and manageable standards for resolving" a "political" issue. A number of lower courts relied on such a doctrine in refusing to decide the legality of the VIETNAM WAR. While the doctrine as so conceived appears at cross-purposes with the checks-and-balances aspect of *Marbury*, nothing in that decision bars a finding that a particular constitutional provision either gives absolute discretion to a nonjudicial branch (such as the power to recognize foreign governments) or makes an exception to Article III's grant of the judicial power itself (as, arguably, in the case of impeachment).

In most respects, then, Article III amply satisfies Marshall's conditions for a "well constructed government." Though the governmental immunities associated with the Eleventh Amendment may seem anachronistic today, unsympathetic judicial interpretation has blunted their interference with the enforcement of federal law. Decisions since the 1950s have generally rejected Justice Frankfurter's broad conception of the political question. Thus with rare exceptions the federal judiciary, as Marshall insisted, may be given authority to construe every federal law; and the extension of judicial power to controversies between citizens of different states means that the federal

courts may often be given power to apply state law as well. Though increased mobility has led to serious efforts to repeal the statutory basis for the diversity jurisdiction, it served an important function in the past and conceivably may become more important in the future. Moreover, the Framers were farsighted enough to assure federal judges the independence necessary to do their appointed job. The weakest point in the system is the arguable authority of Congress to take away all or a substantial part of the Supreme Court's appellate power in constitutional cases; for such an authority undermines other elements of the system of checks and balances that the Framers so carefully constructed.

DAVID P. CURRIE
(1986)

Bibliography

BICKEL, ALEXANDER 1962 *The Least Dangerous Branch*. Pages 111–199. Indianapolis: Bobbs-Merrill.

BORCHARD, EDWIN 1928 *Hearings on H.R. 5623 before the Subcommittee of the Senate Committee on the Judiciary*. 70th Cong., 1st Sess., pp. 75–76.

FARRAND, MAX, ed. 1911 *Records of the Federal Convention of 1787*. Vol. 1, pp. 119–129. New Haven, Conn.: Yale University Press.

HART, HENRY and WECHSLER, HERBERT 1973 *The Federal Courts and the Federal System*. Pages 309–418, 833–1103. Mineola, N.Y.: Foundation Press.

HENKIN, LOUIS 1976 Is There a "Political Question" Doctrine? *Yale Law Journal* 85:597–625.

JUDICIAL POWER AND LEGISLATIVE REMEDIES

Article III of the Constitution states that "[t]he judicial power of the United States, shall be vested in one Supreme Court, and in such inferior Courts as the Congress may from time to time ordain and establish." The Article itself fails to detail the nature and extent of the phrase "judicial Power." However, the Constitution, taken as a whole, is not so silent as to its meaning.

The Framers, borrowing from MONTESQUIEU the idea of SEPARATION OF POWERS, believed that each of the branches had to have a discrete role if the overall government was to avoid tyranny. Each branch was to have specific functions and tasks that would prevent the acquisition of too much power by any one branch. Montesquieu, writing in *The Spirit of the Laws*, stated that "there is no liberty, if the judiciary power be not separated from the legislative and executive. Were it joined with the legislative, the life and liberty of the subject would be exposed to arbitrary control; for the judge would be then the legislator. Were

JUDICIAL POWER AND LEGISLATIVE REMEDIES

it joined to the executive power, the judge might behave with violence and oppression."

The Constitution is more explicit in its explanation of legislative and executive powers. Article I, section 8, lists many of the specific powers to be exercised by Congress in carrying out its constitutional duties. Section 8 contains, among many duties, the power "to lay and collect Taxes, Duties, Imposts, and Excises . . . [t]o coin Money . . . [t]o establish Post Offices . . . [t]o raise and support Armies." Likewise, the executive powers described in Article II include the power to fill vacancies and to act as COMMANDER-IN-CHIEF of the ARMED FORCES.

Nevertheless, when one reviews the Constitution as a complete document and notes the placement of powers under specific articles, the power of the judiciary becomes something clear and distinct as well. That power is by nature a limited one. Publius wrote in THE FEDERALIST #78, "Whoever attentively considers the different departments of power must perceive, that in a government in which they are separated from each other, the judiciary, from the nature of its functions, will always be the least dangerous . . . [It] has no influence over either the sword or the purse, no direction either of the strength or of the wealth of society, and can take no active resolution whatever. It may truly be said to have neither Force nor Will, but merely judgment."

The debate concerning judicial power should not focus on JUDICIAL REVIEW. In fact, the question as to whether the Court should exercise judicial review is a moot one, at best. The writings of both *The Federalist* and the ANTI-FEDERALISTS assumed that the Court would rule on matters of law to determine whether statutory law complied with the standards of constitutionality.

The nature of judicial power, however, remains a subject of debate in the political arena because the Supreme Court continues to expand its role by directly implementing specific public-policy choices. In doing so, it has employed such constitutional provisions as EQUAL PROTECTION and DUE PROCESS in order to secure remedies in cases such as BROWN V. BOARD OF EDUCATION (1954), which effectively overturned the SEPARATE BUT EQUAL DOCTRINE of PLESSY V. FERGUSON (1896). More recently, courts have begun to propose remedies that encroach on the powers specifically delegated to the legislative branch. In some cases, courts have formulated the exact legislative programs by which wrongs will be righted. Two cases from the 1989 term illustrate the difference between legitimate exercise of judicial power and encroachment on legislative prerogatives.

In *Spallone v. United States* (1990) the Supreme Court reversed, by a 5–4 vote, the civil CONTEMPT charges and fines imposed by a UNITED STATES DISTRICT COURT on the city council members of Yonkers, New York. The city had been found in violation of Title VIII of the CIVIL RIGHT ACT OF 1968 and the equal protection clause of the FOURTEENTH AMENDMENT by "intentionally engag[ing] in a pattern and practice of housing discrimination." Chief Justice WILLIAM H. REHNQUIST, writing the majority opinion, framed the question narrowly, asking "whether it was a proper exercise of judicial power for the District Court to hold petitioners, four Yonkers city councilmembers, in contempt for refusing to vote in favor of legislation implementing a consent decree earlier approved by the city."

The Supreme Court, concluding that the district court lacked authority to impose the contempt fines against the individual members of the city council, upheld the contempt fines levied against the city. With the question framed so narrowly, the five-Justice majority explained that "[t]he imposition of sanctions on individual legislators is designed to cause them to vote, not with a view to the interest of their constituents or of the city, but with a view solely to their own personal interest." In so doing, the district court jeopardizes the legitimate exercise of deliberation by representative institutions accountable to a legitimate constituency and removes the legislative immunity that is essential to enable elected representatives to consider the common good of the community.

Although the mounting fines against the city (nearly one million dollars a day) had forced the council to vote in favor of the housing plan, the members of the council still could have decided that it was in the best interest of the city to go bankrupt, thereby defying the court. However, when the individual members of the council were forced to vote under threat of personal financial catastrophe, they were no longer able to represent the interest of the community. This point is of great consequence. A legislative body must have a will of its own while working collectively (and even if at time in conflict) with the courts toward the implementation of the Constitution and laws passed pursuant to it.

The second recent Supreme Court case concerning the limits of judicial power is MISSOURI V. JENKINS (1990). In this case, a unanimous Court agreed that a federal district court had exceeded its authority when, in fashioning a remedy for school desegregation, it ordered an increase in a school district's property tax levy, even though the increase exceeded the limits imposed by state law. The majority opinion by Justice BYRON R. WHITE, however, raises a serious question as to the limits of judicial authority. Justice White "agree[d] with the State that the tax increase contravened the principles of comity." But he went on to suggest that the district court, under the SUPREMACY CLAUSE of the Constitution, could order the school district to levy taxes at the rate needed to pay for the desegregation remedy.

In a CONCURRING OPINION by Justice ANTHONY M. KEN-

proper official character. In this character they have a negative on the laws. Join them with the Executive in the Revision and they will have a double negative."

Some scholars have argued, questionably, that judicial review was so normal a judicial function that it was taken for granted by the Framers. HENRY M. HART and Herbert Wechsler claimed to find clear support in the Convention debates: "The grant of judicial power was to include the power, where necessary in the decision of cases, to disregard state or federal statutes found to be unconstitutional. Despite the curiously persisting myth of usurpation, the Convention's understanding on this point emerges from its records with singular clarity." But with regard to original intent, EDWARD S. CORWIN's Senate testimony on the 1937 Court-packing plan still represents a fair summary of the state of the record. Corwin stated that the "people who say the framers intended [judicial review] are talking nonsense," but he added that "people who say they did not intend it are talking nonsense." As Leonard W. Levy commented after noting Corwin's assessment that there is "great uncertainty" on the issue: "A close textual and contextual examination of the evidence will not result in an improvement on these propositions."

Most important in the search for preconstitutional bases for judicial review authority is probably the late-eighteenth-century prevalence of general ideas conducive to the acceptance of the power asserted in *Marbury v. Madison.* The belief in written CONSTITUTIONS to assure LIMITED GOVERNMENT was hardly an American invention, but Americans had an unusually extensive experience with basic, HIGHER LAW documents of government, from royal charters to state constitutions and the Articles of Confederation. Yet it is possible to have constitutions without judicial review: to say that a government cannot exceed constitutional limits does not demonstrate who is to decide. It bears reiterating, then, that viewing a constitution as a species of "law" was the vital link between constitutionalism and judicial competence to decide constitutional issues. Moreover, the view that the Constitution was an act of the people rather than of the state governments helped provide an ideology congenial to Marshall's insistence that the courts could, in the name of the people, refuse to enforce the acts of the people's representatives.

Accepting the persuasiveness of Marshall's core argument is not tantamount to endorsing all of the alleged implications of judicial review that are pervasive in the late twentieth century. Marshall's stated view of the role of courts in constitutional cases was a relatively modest one; after nearly two centuries of exercise of judicial review by courts, and especially the Supreme Court, the scope and binding effect of judicial rulings are far broader. Most of Marshall's argument was largely defensive, designed to undergird judicial competence and authority to adjudicate

issues of constitutionality. He insisted that the Constitution is "a rule for the government of *courts* as well as the legislature" and concluded that "*courts,* as well as other departments, are bound by that instrument." Modern perceptions, by contrast, often view the courts as playing a superior or supreme role in CONSTITUTIONAL INTERPRETATION. Claims of JUDICIAL SUPREMACY and sometimes even exclusiveness are widespread in scholarly statements and popular understandings. The extent to which such impressions are justifiable continues to give rise to sharp controversy.

Marshall's claims about judicial competence and authority were closely tied to a tripartite theory of government reflecting the SEPARATION OF POWERS. He did not deny that other branches, including the President in the exercise of the veto power and Congress in enacting legislation, could and—under the oath to support the Constitution emphasized in *Marbury* itself—presumably must consider issues of constitutionality. Marshall's argument that courts *also* have competence to take the Constitution into account in their work was essentially a "me too" position. Modern variants on justifications for judicial review—and a number of statements from the modern Supreme Court itself—lend stronger support than anything in Marshall's reasoning to a "me superior" or even a "me only" view.

Nearly from the beginning, Presidents have taken issue with Supreme Court rulings. THOMAS JEFFERSON insisted that "nothing in the Constitution has given [the judges] a right to decide for the Executive, more than to the Executive to decide for them." And he argued that considering "the judges as the ultimate arbiters of all constitutional questions" was "a very dangerous doctrine indeed, and one which would place us under the despotism of an oligarchy." Similarly, ANDREW JACKSON insisted, in vetoing the bill to recharter the Bank of the United States in 1832, that MCCULLOCH V. MARYLAND (1819) did not preclude his action: "Mere precedent is a dangerous source of authority, and should not be regarded as deciding questions of constitutional power except where the acquiescence of the people and the States can be considered as well settled." Similar statements are found in the utterances of later Presidents, from Abraham Lincoln to FRANKLIN D. ROOSEVELT and beyond.

John Marshall was no doubt unhappy with the political statements of Jeffersonians and Jacksonians. Clearly, he would have preferred ready acceptance of his Court's glosses on the Constitution by all governmental officials and the entire nation. But nothing in the stances of the leaders of his day or since was in sharp conflict with anything in *Marbury v. Madison.* Jefferson, Jackson, and their successors did not deny the binding effect of the judges' constitutional rulings in the cases before them. But the

Presidents insisted on their right to disagree with the principles underlying the Court decision. As Lincoln said in the course of his debates with STEPHEN A. DOUGLAS, he did not propose that after Dred Scott had been held to be a slave by the Court—in DRED SCOTT V. SANDFORD (1857)—"we, as a mob, will decide him to be free." But, he added, "we nevertheless do oppose that decision as a political rule which shall be binding on the voter, to vote for nobody who thinks it wrong, which shall be binding on the members of Congress or the President to favor no measure that does not actually concur with the principles of that decision. [We] propose so resisting it as to have it reversed if we can, and a new judicial rule established upon this subject."

Does it follow that, if such presidential statements are consistent with *Marbury v. Madison*, the scheme sketched by Marshall in 1803 contemplated never-ending chaos—a state of chaos in which the political branches of the national government, and the states as well, might forever disagree with the principles of Supreme Court decisions, in which the only way to implement the Court's principles would be to bring the resisting parties to court in multiple lawsuits, in which no constitutional question would ever be settled? Not necessarily, and certainly not in American experience. Judicial review has not meant that the Supreme Court's reasoning ends all constitutional debate, but neither has it meant endless litigation and dispute over every constitutional issue. Yet the reasons for the growing role of the Supreme Court in settling constitutional issues rest less on any legal principle underlying judicial review than on considerations stemming from institutional arrangements and from prudence. The only arguable basis in *Marbury* itself for viewing the courts as the ultimate arbiters of constitutional issues is Marshall's ambiguous statement that it is "emphatically the province and duty of the judicial department to say what the law is." That statement establishes judicial competence, as noted; but its ambiguity also may provide the basis for arguments for a special judicial expertise in constitutional matters and for a de facto judicial supremacy. Marshall's statement is not so strong, however, as a similar one from Hamilton, in *The Federalist* #78: "The interpretation of laws is the proper and peculiar province of the courts."

The widely observable phenomenon that a Court interpretation of the Constitution has significance beyond the parties to a particular lawsuit rests on other, stronger bases. A central one is that, to the extent a disputed constitutional issue arises in a lawsuit, and to the extent that the Supreme Court is the highest court in the judicial hierarchy, a Supreme Court interpretation is final. Technically, it is final only with respect to the parties in the case, to be sure; but the Court gives general reasons in resolving specific controversies, and the Justices normally operate under a system of PRECEDENT and STARE DECISIS. Similarly situated parties not before the Court in the particular case ordinarily recognize that, other things being equal, the Court will adhere to precedent, will apply the same rule to them if litigation ensues, and accordingly choose not to engage in needless litigation.

Basically, then, the reason that the courts generally and the Supreme Court in particular wield such vast influence in Americans' understanding of their Constitution is that most constitutional issues can and do arise in lawsuits; and once they do, the courts, with the Supreme Court at the apex, do have the final say. As a result, most potential opponents of Court rulings follow the course implied in Lincoln's First Inaugural Address. Lincoln did not deny that Supreme Court decisions "must be binding in any case upon the parties to a suit as to the object of that suit" and "are also entitled to very high respect and consideration in all parallel cases by all other departments of the Government." He added: "And while it is obviously possible that such decision may be erroneous in any given case, still the evil effect following it, being limited to that particular case, with a chance that it may be overruled or never become a precedent for other cases, can better be borne than could the evil of a different practice." From that position, Herbert Wechsler's rhetorical question plausibly follows: When the chance that a judicial ruling "may be overruled and never become a precedent for other cases . . . has been exploited and has run its course, with reaffirmation rather than REVERSAL of decision, has not the time arrived when its acceptance is demanded, without insisting on repeated litigation? The answer here, it seems to me, must be affirmative, both as to a necessary implication of our constitutional tradition and to avoid the greater evils that will otherwise ensue." Wechsler's admonition, it should be noted, is one of prudence, not of any necessary legal mandate stemming from the *Marbury* rationale.

Beginning in the late twentieth century, however, the Supreme Court has repeatedly claimed a greater import for its exercises of judicial review than anything clearly set forth in *Marbury*. A major example came in one of the cases stemming from the school DESEGREGATION controversy, COOPER V. AARON (1958). The opinion in that case, signed by each of the Justices, provides the strongest judicial support for a view widely held by the public—that the Court is the ultimate, the supreme interpreter of the Constitution. Rejecting the premise of the actions of the legislature and of the governor of Arkansas in that case—that they were not bound by the ruling in BROWN V. BOARD OF EDUCATION (1954)—the Court purported to "recall some basic constitutional propositions which are settled doctrine." The Justices quoted Article VI and Marshall's "province and duty of the judicial department" passage in

Marbury and added: "This decision declared the basic principle that the federal judiciary is supreme in the exposition of the law of the Constitution. [It] follows that the interpretation of the Fourteenth Amendment enunciated by this Court in the *Brown* case is the supreme law of the land, and Article VI of the Constitution makes it of binding effect on the States. [Every] state legislator and executive and judicial officer is solemnly committed by oath taken pursuant to Article VI, 3, "to support this Constitution.""

Similar statements have surfaced in other controversial cases in recent years, especially in BAKER V. CARR (1962) (referring to the "responsibility of this Court as ultimate interpreter of the Constitution") and POWELL V. MCCOR-MACK (1969) ("[It] is the responsibility of this Court to act as the ultimate interpreter of the Constitution. *Marbury v. Madison*."). The Court in these cases was no doubt marshaling all possible rhetorical force in efforts to ward off actual or potential resistance from the states or from other branches of the federal government; but these broad modern assertions no doubt also reflect widespread popular understandings of the "ultimate" role of the Court, understandings bolstered by the nation's general acceptance of that role, despite frequent and continuing disagreements with particular decisions.

From the relatively modest assertions of the judicial review power in *Marbury v. Madison*, nearly two centuries of history have brought the Court increasingly close to the self-announced dominant role in constitutional interpretation it set forth in *Cooper v. Aaron*. That does not mean that Supreme Court interpretations are entitled to immunity from criticism, popular or academic. Nor does it signify the end of all political restraints on the Court, restraints stemming from the same Constitution that Marshall relied on in defending judicial review. Judges may be subjected to congressional IMPEACHMENT and Congress may arguably curtail the federal courts' JURISDICTION in constitutional cases. (See JUDICIAL SYSTEM.) But both weapons, though frequently brandished, have rarely been used. Moreover, the constitutional AMENDING PROCESS, albeit difficult to invoke, is available to overturn unpopular Court rulings. More significant, the composition of the Court as well as its size rest with the political branches, and the President's nominating role, together with the Senate's in confirmation, have been major safeguards against judges deviating too far from the national consensus. Despite these potential and actual checks, however, the Supreme Court's role in American government has outgrown both the view that it is the weakest branch and Marshall's own delineation of the judicial review power. What ALEXIS DE TOCQUEVILLE recognized over a century and a half ago has become ever more true since he wrote: "Scarcely any question arises in the United States which does not become, sooner or later, a subject of judicial debate."

Even though historical exercises of judicial review and popular acquiescence have largely stilled the outcries that the federal courts usurped the power to consider the constitutionality of legislation, the core arguments on behalf of the legitimacy of judicial review, summarized by Marshall in *Marbury v. Madison,* continue to generate controversial implications. Two especially important and recurrent modern debates involve arguments reaching back all the way to *Marbury.* The first issue is whether courts should strain to avoid decisions on controversial constitutional issues by invoking such devices as the PO-LITICAL QUESTION doctrine. The second issue concerns the proper sources of constitutional adjudication: Must courts limit themselves to "interpretation" of the Constitution, or are "noninterpretive" decisions also legitimate?

Courts confident about the legitimacy of judicial review may tend to exercise that power assertively; judges in doubt about the underpinnings of that authority may shrink from exercising the power to invalidate legislative acts and may indeed seek to escape altogether from rulings on the merits in constitutional cases. The connection between views of legitimacy and modern exercises (or nonexercises) of judicial review is illustrated by an exchange between LEARNED HAND and Herbert Wechsler. Hand insisted that there was "nothing in the United States Constitution that gave courts any authority to review the decisions of Congress" and that the text "gave no ground for inferring that the decisions of the Supreme Court [were] to be authoritative upon the Executive and the Legislature." He found the sole justification for judicial review in the practical need "to prevent the defeat of the venture at hand"—to keep constitutional government from foundering. Wechsler retorted: "I believe the power of the courts is grounded in the language of the Constitution and is not a mere interpolation."

These contending positions have contrasting implications. Thus, Hand concluded that "since this power is not a logical deduction from the structure of the Constitution but only a practical condition upon its successful operation, it need not be exercised whenever a court sees, or thinks it sees, an invasion of the Constitution. It is always a preliminary question how importantly the occasion demands an answer." Wechsler countered that there was no such broad discretion to decline constitutional adjudication in a case properly before a court: "For me, as for anyone who finds the judicial power anchored in the Constitution, there is no such escape from the judicial obligation; the duty cannot be attenuated in this way." (That "duty," he cautioned, was "not that of policing or advising legislatures or executives," but rather simply "to decide the litigated case [in] accordance with the law.")

It is true that courts do often abstain from deciding constitutional questions pressed upon them. There is no question about the legitimacy of that phenomenon to the extent that courts rely on nonconstitutional, narrower grounds of decision in disposing of a case. Nor is there any doubt that courts need not—and under the *Marbury* rationale may not—decide constitutional issues if they are not properly presented in a case because, for example, the litigation does not square with the CASE AND CONTROVERSY requirement of Article III. But twentieth-century courts have occasionally gone beyond such justifiable ABSTENTIONS to claim a more general and more questionable authority to resort to considerations of prudence in refusing to issue rulings on the merits even though a case falls within the contours of Article III and even though congressional statutes appear to confer obligatory jurisdiction on the courts.

Some commentators have defended judicial resort to the "passive virtues"; others have attacked such refusals to adjudicate as often unprincipled and illegitimate. The controversy about the political question doctrine is illustrative. To the extent that the doctrine rests on constitutional interpretation, as it does under its strand regarding what the Court in *Baker v. Carr* (1962) called "a textually demonstrable constitutional commitment of the issue to a coordinate political department," it is undoubtedly legitimate. But the courts have often gone beyond that concern to refuse adjudication on the ground of a lack of judicially "manageable standards" and on the basis of even broader, wholly prudential considerations as well. Wechsler argued that, in political question cases, "the only proper judgment that may lead to an abstention from decision is that the Constitution has committed the determination of the issues to another agency of government than the courts. [What] is involved is in itself an act of constitutional interpretation, to be made and judged by standards that should govern the interpretive process generally. That, I submit, is *toto caelo* [by all heaven] different from a broad discretion to abstain or intervene." ALEXANDER M. BICKEL strongly disagreed, insisting that "only by means of a play on words can the broad discretion that the courts have in fact exercised be turned into an act of constitutional interpretation." He saw the political question doctrine as something different from the interpretive process—"something greatly more flexible, something of prudence, not construction and not principle."

To the extent that the Supreme Court rests largely on discretionary, prudential concerns in refusing to adjudicate—as, for example, it appears to have done in holding federalistic restraints on congressional power largely nonjusticiable in GARCIA V. SAN ANTONIO METROPOLITAN TRANSIT AUTHORITY (1985)—it raises questions of legitimacy under *Marbury v. Madison*. Courts deriving their authority from a premise that the Constitution is law, as the *Marbury* argument does, are not authorized to resort to discretionary abstention devices not justified by law. As Marshall himself pointed out in COHENS V. VIRGINIA (1821): "We have no more right to decline the exercise of jurisdiction which is given, than to usurp that which is not given." But discretionary devices of self-limitation have become commonplace in judicial behavior, as a result of glosses articulated by modern judges rather than because of anything in the Constitution itself or in Marshall's reasoning. (See COMITY.)

There is a second modern issue, especially pervasive and controversial, in which the rationale of *Marbury v. Madison* affects debates about judicial review: Are the courts bound to limit themselves to "interpretations" of the Constitution in exercising judicial review? Marshall's reasoning in *Marbury* suggests that "noninterpretive" rulings are illegitimate. A justification that derives judicial review from the existence of a written constitution and from the premise that the Constitution is a species of law implies that the courts are confined by the Constitution in delineating constitutional norms. And courts indeed almost invariably purport to rest their constitutional rulings on "interpretations" of the basic document.

But modern academic commentary is sharply divided on this issue. Most scholars who insist on "interpretation" as the sole legitimate ingredient of constitutional rulings do not argue for a narrow, strict interpretation based solely on a literal reading of the constitutional text or a specific basis in the Framers' intent. But their "broad interpretivist" position does insist that constitutional rulings must rest on a clear nexus to—and plausible inference from—the Constitution's text, history, or structure. The "noninterpretivist" critics of that position emphasize the many opaque and open-ended phrases in the Constitution and the changing interpretations of these phrases over the years. They claim that the Court's behavior cannot be squared with even a broad interpretivist position and argue that the Court has always relied on extraconstitutional norms. These critics insist that "noninterpretivist" decision making is justified not only by the history of the Court's elaborations of such vague yet pervasive concepts as SUBSTANTIVE DUE PROCESS but also by the appropriate role of courts in American constitutional democracy. The noninterpretivist literature accordingly abounds with suggestions of sources courts might rely on in the search for fundamental, judicially enforceable values—sources that range from moral philosophy to contemporary political consensus and analogies to literary and scriptural analyses.

The interpretivist arguments that draw in part on Marshall's justification for judicial review have difficulty explaining the Court's performance in "reinterpreting" the Constitution in light of changing societal contexts. The noninterpretivist position has difficulty squaring its arguments with the *Marbury* view of the Constitution as a species of law. That position has difficulty as well in articulating limits on the legitimate ingredients of constitutional decision making that safeguard adequately against excessive judicial subjectivism—against the specter reflected in Learned Hand's fear of being "ruled by a bevy of Platonic Guardians." Whether constitutional decision making by judges can continue to contribute to the flexibility and durability of the Constitution without deteriorating into merely politicized and personalized rulings that risk subverting the legitimacy of constitutional government is the central and unresolved challenge confronting modern judicial review.

GERALD GUNTHER
(1986)

(SEE ALSO: *Interpretivism; Noninterpretivism.*)

Bibliography

BICKEL, ALEXANDER M. 1962 *The Least Dangerous Branch: The Supreme Court at the Bar of Politics.* Indianapolis: Bobbs-Merrill.

ELY, JOHN H. 1980 *Democracy and Distrust: A Theory of Judicial Review.* Cambridge, Mass.: Harvard University Press.

GREY, THOMAS 1975 Do We Have an Unwritten Constitution? *Stanford Law Review* 27:703–718.

GUNTHER, GERALD 1964 The Subtle Vices of the "Passive Virtues": A Comment on Principle and Expediency in Judicial Review. *Columbia Law Review* 64:1–25.

HAND, LEARNED 1958 *The Bill of Rights.* Cambridge, Mass.: Harvard University Press.

HART, HENRY M., JR. and WECHSLER, HERBERT 1973 Pages 1–241 in Paul Bator, Paul Mishkin, David Shapiro, and Herbert Wechsler, eds., *The Federal Courts and the Federal System,* 2nd ed. Mineola, N.Y.: Foundation Press.

LEVY, LEONARD W. 1967 Judicial Review, History, and Democracy: An Introduction. Pages 1–42 in Leonard W. Levy, ed., *Judicial Review and the Supreme Court: Selected Essays.* New York: Harper & Row.

McCLOSKEY, ROBERT G. 1960 *The American Supreme Court.* Chicago: University of Chicago Press.

McLAUGHLIN, ANDREW C. 1935 *A Constitutional History of the United States.* New York: Appleton-Century-Crofts.

PERRY, MICHAEL J. 1982 *The Constitution, the Courts, and Human Rights: An Inquiry into the Legitimacy of Constitutional Policymaking by the Judiciary.* New Haven, Conn.: Yale University Press.

WECHSLER, HERBERT 1961 *Principles, Politics, and Fundamental Law.* Cambridge, Mass.: Harvard University Press.

——— 1965 The Courts and the Constitution. *Columbia Law Review* 65:1001–1014.

JUDICIAL REVIEW AND DEMOCRACY

The American ideal of democracy lives in constant tension with the American ideal of JUDICIAL REVIEW in the service of individual liberties. It is a tension that sometimes erupts in crisis. THOMAS JEFFERSON planned a campaign of IMPEACHMENTS to rid the bench, and particularly the Supreme Court, of Federalist judges. The campaign collapsed when the impeachment of Associate Justice SAMUEL CHASE failed in the Senate. FRANKLIN D. ROOSEVELT, frustrated by a Court majority that repeatedly struck down New Deal economic measures, tried to "pack" the Court with additional Justices. That effort was defeated in Congress, though the attempt may have persuaded some Justices to alter their behavior. In recent years there have been movements in Congress to deprive federal courts of JURISDICTION over cases involving such matters as abortion, SCHOOL BUSING, and school prayer (see RELIGION IN PUBLIC SCHOOLS)—topics on which the Court's decisions have angered strong and articulate constituencies.

The problem is the resolution of what Robert Dahl called the Madisonian dilemma. The United States was founded as a Madisonian system, one that allows majorities to govern wide and important areas of life simply because they are majorities, but that also holds that individuals have some freedoms that must be exempt from majority control. The dilemma is that neither the majority nor the minority can be trusted to define the proper spheres of democratic authority and individual liberty.

It is not at all clear that the Founders envisaged a leading role for the judiciary in the resolution of this dilemma, for they thought of the third branch as relatively insignificant. Over time, however, Americans have come to assume that the definition of majority power and minority freedom is primarily the function of the judiciary, most particularly the function of the Supreme Court. This assumption places a great responsibility upon constitutional theory. America's basic method of policymaking is majoritarian. Thus, to justify exercise of a power to set at naught the considered decisions of elected representatives, judges must achieve, in ALEXANDER BICKEL's phrase, "a rigorous general accord between JUDICIAL SUPREMACY and democratic theory, so that the boundaries of the one could be described with some precision in terms of the other." At one time, an accord was based on the understanding that judges followed the intentions of the Framers and ratifiers of the Constitution, a legal document enacted by majorities, though subject to alteration only by supermajorities. A conflict between democracy and judicial review did not arise because the respective areas of each were specified and intended to be inviolate. Though this obedience to original intent was occasionally more pretense than reality, the accord was achieved in theory, and that theory stated an ideal to which courts were expected to conform. That is no longer so. Many judges and scholars now believe that the courts' obligations to intent are so highly generalized and remote that judges are in fact free to create the Constitution they think appropriate to today's society. The result is that the accord no longer stands even theoretically. The increasing perception that this is so raises the question of what elected officials can do to reclaim authority they regard as wrongfully taken by the judiciary.

There appear to be two possible responses to a judiciary that has overstepped the limits of its legitimate authority. One is political, the other intellectual. It seems tolerably clear that political responses are of limited usefulness, at least in the short run. Impeachment and COURT-PACKING, having failed in the past, are unlikely to be resorted to again. Amending the Constitution to correct judicial overreaching is such a difficult and laborious process (requiring either two-thirds of both houses of Congress or an application for a convention by the legislatures of two-thirds of the states, followed, in either case, by ratification by three-fourths of the states) that it is of little practical assistance. It is sometimes proposed that Congress deal with the problem by removing federal court jurisdiction, using the exceptions clause of Article III of the Constitution in the case of the Supreme Court. The constitutionality of this approach has been much debated, but, in any case, it will often prove not feasible. Removal of all federal court jurisdiction would not return final power either to Congress or to state legislatures but to fifty state court systems. Thus, as a practical matter, this device could not be used as to any subject where national uniformity of constitutional law is necessary or highly desirable. Moreover, jurisdiction removal does not vindicate democratic governance, for it merely shifts ultimate power to different groups of judges. Democratic responses to judicial excesses probably must come through the replacement of judges who die or retire with new judges of different views. But this is a slow and uncertain process, the accidents of mortality being what they are and prediction of what new judges will do being so perilous.

The fact is that there exist few, if any, usable and effective techniques by which federal courts can be kept within constitutional bounds. A Constitution that provides numerous CHECKS AND BALANCES between President and Congress provides little to curb a judiciary that expands its powers beyond the allowable meaning of the Constitution. Perhaps one reason is that the Framers, though many of them foresaw that the Supreme Court would review laws for constitutionality, had little experience with such a function. They did not remotely foresee what the power of judicial review was capable of becoming. Nor is it clear that an institutional check—such as Senator ROBERT LA FOLLETTE's proposal to amend the Constitution so that Congress could override a Supreme Court decision by a two-thirds majority—would be desirable. Congress is less likely than the Court to be versed in the Constitution. La

Follette's proposal could conceivably wreak as much or more damage to the Court's legitimate powers as it might accomplish in restraining its excesses. That must be reckoned at least a possibility with any of the institutional checks just discussed and is probably one of the reasons that they have rarely been used. In this sense, the Court's vulnerability is one of its most important protections.

If a political check on federal courts is unlikely to succeed, the only rein left is intellectual, the widespread acceptance of a theory of judicial review. After almost two centuries of constitutional adjudication, we appear to be further than ever from the possession of an adequate theory.

In the beginning, there was no controversy over theory. JOSEPH STORY, who was both an Associate Justice of the Supreme Court and the Dane Professor of Law at Harvard, could write in his *Commentaries on the Constitution of the United States*, published in 1833, that "I have not the ambition to be the author of any new plan of interpreting the theory of the Constitution, or of enlarging or narrowing its powers by ingenious subtleties and learned doubts." He thought that the job of constitutional judges was to interpret: "The first and fundamental rule in the interpretation of all instruments is, to construe them according to the sense of the terms and the intention of the parties."

The performance of the courts has not always conformed to this interpretivist ideal. In the last decade or so of the nineteenth century and the first third of the twentieth the Supreme Court assiduously protected economic liberties from federal and state regulation, often in ways that could not be reconciled with the Constitution. The case that stands as the symbol of that era of judicial adventurism is LOCHNER V. NEW YORK (1905), which struck down the state's law regulating maximum hours for bakers. That era ended when Franklin D. Roosevelt's appointments remade the Court, and *Lochner* is now generally regarded as discredited.

But, if the Court stopped defending economic liberties without constitutional justification in the mid-1930s, it began in the mid-1950s to make other decisions for which it offered little or no constitutional argument. It had been generally assumed that constitutional questions were to be answered on grounds of historical intent, but the Court began to make decisions that could hardly be, and were not, justified on that basis. Existing constitutional protections were expanded and new ones created. Sizable minorities on the Court indicated a willingness to go still further. The widespread perception that the judiciary was recreating the Constitution brought the tension between democracy and judicial review once more to a state of intellectual and political crisis.

Much of the new judicial power claimed cannot be derived from the text, structure, or history of the Constitution. Perhaps because of the increasing obviousness of this fact, legal scholars began to erect new theories of the judicial role. These constructs, which appear to be accepted by a majority of those who write about constitutional theory, go by the general name of noninterpretivism. They hold that mere interpretation of the Constitution may be impossible and is certainly inadequate. Judges are assigned not the task of defining the meanings and contours of values found in the historical Constitution but rather the function of creating new values and hence new rights for individuals against majorities. These new values are variously described as arising from "the evolving morality of our tradition," our "conventional morality" as discerned by "the method of philosophy," a "fusion of constitutional law and moral theory," or a HIGHER LAW of "unwritten NATURAL RIGHTS." One author has argued that, since "no defensible criteria" exist "to assess theories of judicial review," the judge should enforce his conception of the good. In all cases, these theories purport to empower judges to override majority will for extraconstitutional reasons.

Judges have articulated theories of their role no less removed from interpretation than those of the noninterpretivist academics. Writing for the Court in GRISWOLD V. CONNECTICUT (1965), Justice WILLIAM O. DOUGLAS created a constitutional RIGHT OF PRIVACY that invalidated the state's law against the use of contraceptives. He observed that many provisions of the BILL OF RIGHTS could be viewed as protections of aspects of personal privacy. These provisions were said to add up to a zone of constitutionally secured privacy that did not fall within any particular provision. The scope of this new right was not defined, but the Court has used the concept in a series of cases since, the most controversial being ROE V. WADE (1973). (See JUDICIAL ACTIVISM AND SELF RESTRAINT.)

A similar strategy for the creation of new rights was outlined by Justice WILLIAM J. BRENNAN in a 1985 address. He characterized the Constitution as being pervasively concerned with human dignity. From this, Justice Brennan drew a more general judicial function of enhancing human dignity, one not confined by the clauses in question and, indeed, capable of nullifying what those clauses reveal of the Framers' intentions. Thus, the address states that continued judicial tolerance of CAPITAL PUNISHMENT causes us to "fall short of the constitutional vision of human dignity." For that reason, Justice Brennan continues to vote that capital punishment violates the Constitution. The potency of this method of generalizing from particular clauses, and then applying the generalization instead of the clauses, may be seen in the fact that it leads to a declaration of the unconstitutionality of a punishment ex-

plicitly assumed to be available three times in the Fifth Amendment to the Constitution and once again, some seventy-seven years later, in the FOURTEENTH AMENDMENT. By conventional methods of interpretation, it would be impossible to use the Constitution to prohibits that which the Constitution explicitly assumes to be lawful.

Because noninterpretive philosophies have little hard intellectual structure, it is impossible to control them or to predict from any inner logic or principle what they may require. Though it is regularly denied that a return to the judicial function as exemplified in *Lochner v. New York* is underway or, which comes to the same thing, that decisions are rooted only in the judges' moral predilections, it is difficult to see what else can be involved once the function of searching for the Framers' intent is abandoned. When constitutional adjudication proceeds in a noninterpretive manner, the Court necessarily imposes new values upon the society. They are new in the sense that they cannot be derived by interpretation of the historical Constitution. Moreover, they must rest upon the moral predilections of the judge because the values come out of the moral view that most of us, by definition (since we voted democratically for a different result), do not accept.

This mode of adjudication makes impossible any general accord between judicial supremacy and democratic theory. Instead, it brings the two into head-on conflict. The Constitution specifies certain liberties and allocates all else to democratic processes. Noninterpretivism gives the judge power to invade the province of democracy whenever majority morality conflicts with his own. That is impossible to square either with democratic theory or the concept of law. Attempts have, nonetheless, been made to reconcile, or at least to mitigate, the contradiction. One line of argument is that any society requires a mixture of principle and expediency, that courts are better than legislatures at discerning and formulating principle, and hence may intervene when principle has been inadequately served by the legislative process. Even if one assumes that courts have superior institutional capacities in this respect, which is by no means clear, the conclusion does not follow. By placing certain subjects in the legislative arena, the Constitution holds that the tradeoff between principle and expediency we are entitled to is what the legislature provides. Courts have no mandate to impose a different result merely because they would arrive at a tradeoff that weighed principle more heavily or that took an altogether different value into account.

A different reconciliation of democracy and noninterpretive judicial review begins with the proposition that the Supreme Court is not really final because popular sentiment can in the long run cause it to be overturned. As we know from history, however, it may take decades to overturn a decision, so that it will be final for many people. Even then an overruling probably cannot be forced if a substantial minority ardently supports the result.

To the degree, then, that the Constitution is not treated as law to be interpreted in conventional fashion, the clash between democracy and judicial review is real. It is also serious. When the judiciary imposes upon democracy limits not to be found in the Constitution, it deprives Americans of a right that is found there, the right to make the laws to govern themselves. Moreover, as courts intervene more frequently to set aside majoritarian outcomes, they teach the lesson that democratic processes are suspect, essentially unprincipled and untrustworthy.

The main charge against a strictly interpretive approach to the Constitution is that the Framers' intentions cannot be known because they could not foresee the changed circumstances of our time. The argument proves too much. If it were true, the judge would be left without any law to apply, and there would be no basis for judicial review.

But that is not what is involved. From the text, the structure, and the history of the Constitution we can usually learn at least the core values the Framers intended to protect. Interpreting the Constitution means discerning the principle the Framers wanted to enact and applying it to today's circumstances. As John Hart Ely put it, interpretivism holds that "the work of the political branches is to be invalidated only in accord with an inference whose starting point, whose underlying premise, is fairly discoverable in the Constitution. That the complete inference will not be found there—because the situation is not likely to have been foreseen—is generally common ground."

This, of course, requires that constitutional DOCTRINE evolve over time. Most doctrine is merely the judge-made superstructure that implements basic constitutional principles, and, because circumstances change, the evolution of doctrine is inevitable. The FOURTH AMENDMENT was framed by men who did not foresee electronic surveillance, but judges may properly apply the central value of that amendment to electronic invasions of personal privacy. The difference between this method and that endorsed by Justices Douglas and Brennan lies in the level of generality employed. Adapting the Fourth Amendment requires the judge merely to recognize a new method of governmental search of one's property. The Justices, on the other hand, create a right so general that it effectively becomes a new clause of the Constitution, one that gives courts no guidance in its application. Modifying doctrine to preserve a value already embedded in the Constitution is an enterprise wholly different in nature from creating new values.

The debate over the legitimate role of the judiciary is likely to continue for some years. Noninterpretivists have not as yet presented an adequate theoretical justification for a judiciary that creates rather than interprets the Constitution. The task of interpretation is often complex and difficult, but it remains the only model of the judicial role that achieves an accord between democracy and judicial review.

ROBERT H. BORK
(1986)

Bibliography

AGRESTO, JOHN 1984 *The Supreme Court and Constitutional Democracy.* Ithaca, N.Y.: Cornell University Press.

BICKEL, ALEXANDER M. 1962 *The Least Dangerous Branch: The Supreme Court at the Bar of Politics.* Indianapolis: Bobbs-Merrill.

BORK, ROBERT H. 1985 Styles in Constitutional Theory. *South Texas Law Journal* 26:383–395.

CHOPER, JESSE 1980 *Judicial Review and the National Political Process.* Chicago: University of Chicago Press.

ELY, JOHN HART 1980 *Democracy and Distrust: A Theory of Judicial Review.* Cambridge, Mass.: Harvard University Press.

LEVY, LEONARD W., ed. 1967 *Judicial Review and the Supreme Court.* New York: Harper & Row.

JUDICIAL REVIEW OF ADMINISTRATIVE ACTS

To conform to basic SEPARATION OF POWERS precepts, JUDICIAL REVIEW of administrative actions must be limited yet effective. It must be limited to avoid entangling courts in policy decisions that belong to other branches; it must be effective to bind ADMINISTRATIVE AGENCIES to the RULE OF LAW. Many ADMINISTRATIVE LAW doctrines attempt to accommodate these two purposes. Often they do so by adapting COMMON LAW remedies against government to the American scheme of separated powers. This process began with MARBURY V. MADISON (1803), which announced that a court having jurisdiction could issue common law MANDAMUS against a cabinet officer. The Supreme Court emphasized the need to avoid judicial intrusion in the political discretion of executive officers, while conforming their decisions to the dictates of law.

Modern administrative agencies perform functions that are characteristic of all three constitutional branches: adjudication, rule-making, and execution. The legitimacy of these activities depends on the relationships between the agencies and the branches that the courts have defined. For example, *Crowell v. Benson* (1932) allowed agencies to exercise adjudicative authority only because judicial review could assure that agency decisions had adequate factual and legal support.

The delegation doctrine states that when Congress

grants LEGISLATIVE POWER to agencies it must provide intelligible standards to guide and confine agency discretion. Yet this dictrine is aspirational today: no congressional delegation to an agency has been invalidated for over fifty years. The delegation doctrine has been supplanted by a series of inquires into the legality of particular agency actions.

First, courts review the substantive conformity of agency actions with constitutional requisites, such as those in the BILL OF RIGHTS. Substantive constitutional criteria apply to statutes.

Second, courts review the fairness of agency procedures under DUE PROCESS and statutory guarantees. PROCEDURAL DUE PROCESS involves a two-stage inquiry that identifies the presence of an interest that constitutes "liberty" or "property," and then considers the individual and government interests at stake and the value of a more elaborate process. Statutory guarantees often flow from the generally applicable Administrative Procedure Act (1946), which defines the basic procedures of federal agencies for adjudication and rulemaking, and further defines the scope of judicial review of administrative acts. Such statutory procedures often are more elaborate than the minimal constitutional requisites.

Third, courts review the statutory interpretations that underlie administrative acts. Courts usually defer to agency interpretations of law that are consistent with ascertainable LEGISLATIVE INTENT and that are otherwise reasonable. The purpose of this doctrine is to give maximum scope to agency discretion within statutory bounds.

Fourth, courts review the factual basis for agency actions. Here they compare administrative explanations for decisions with materials in the administrative record and accept conclusions of fact and policy that are reasonable. The courts try to ensure that agencies have carefully considered the policy options before them and have inquired fully into the facts. Thus, ordinary rationality review is much more demanding in administrative law than it is under constitutional EQUAL PROTECTION or SUBSTANTIVE DUE PROCESS guarantees.

Any of several threshold considerations can prevent courts from reviewing the merits of administrative actions. STANDING to seek review is partly a constitutional doctrine. To present a "case" or "controversy" within the federal JUDICIAL POWER, parties must show that they are injured in fact by the government and that judicial relief will remedy the injury. In administrative cases, courts also require the parties challenging agency actions to be within the zone of interests affected by the governing statute. There are constitutional overtones in this latter test, because it denies review to persons so tangentially interested in a statute's administration that they are unlikely to present a concrete, sharply adversarial claim.

Parties must ordinarily exhaust their administrative remedies before seeking judicial review. Separation of powers considerations partly explain this doctrine, which enforces delegations of decision-making power to agencies. The courts make exceptions to this exhaustion requirement when the issues are ready for judicial review, delay would cause hardship to private parties, or agency autonomy would be unduly threatened by immediate judicial review.

Finally, not all administrative acts are reviewable. Statutes sometimes entirely preclude judicial review, subject to uncertain due process limitations. As in *Johnson v. Robinson* (1974), courts usually interpret statutes that preclude review to allow at least inquiries into the constitutionality of agency actions. In this way, the courts avoid deciding whether Congress can forbid all review of an administrative act for which review is otherwise appropriate. Courts do hold that certain agency functions are intrinsically unsuited for review, such as agency decisions not to undertake enforcement action. Here as elsewhere, courts attempt to control agencies only to an extent that is consistent with traditional notions of the limits of the JUDICIAL ROLE.

HAROLD H. BRUFF
(1992)

(SEE ALSO: *Cases and Controversies; Procedural Due Process, Civil.*)

Bibliography

DAVIS, KENNETH CULP 1978–1984 *Administrative Law Treatise,* 2nd ed., vols. 1–5. San Diego, Calif.: K. C. Davis.

PIERCE, RICHARD J., JR., et al. 1985 *Administrative Law and Process.* Mineola, N.Y.: Foundation Press.

JUDICIAL ROLE

Theories about the proper role of the Supreme Court have proliferated in recent decades. These theories have been too political in one sense and not political enough in another. They are too political in that they tend to be thinly veiled rationalizations of political preferences, valued less for their own sakes than for the results they entail in specific controversies. Today, knowing someone's attitude about the role of the Court, one can usually deduce his or her political positions, not so much on ECONOMIC REGULATION as on some divisive social questions.

To arrive at a consensus about JUDICIAL ACTIVISM, we need a political situation in which most groups feel that they have at least as much to gain as to lose by subscribing to an agreed conception of the Court's role. No such consensus exists. Today the country is divided over several major social issues: crime, PORNOGRAPHY, race, women's roles, homosexuality, and religion. Ever since the 1950s, social liberals have believed that on most of those issues they have everything to gain and little to lose by judicial intervention; conversely, social conservatives have usually had a stake in confining the Court's role. Each camp has fashioned jurisprudential theories that reflect its perceived stake in judicial activism or restraint. In this sense, the debate about the Court's role is basically political.

Yet the debate is usually couched in legal terms, and in this sense, it is excessively legalistic. Commentators usually do not directly discuss the appropriate role of the Court; instead, they argue about how to interpret the Constitution. Thus, proponents of judicial activism espouse loose-constructionist theories of interpretation, and advocates of judicial restraint usually defend a more literal adherence to the text and its original meaning.

This familiar argument has long since become repetitive and unenlightening. Worse still, it treats fundamental political questions as if they were analogous to disputes over the meanings of contracts. To analyze judicial governance solely in legal terms implies that objections to a broad judicial role can be fully met by a cogent legal response, such as an interpretation of a PRECEDENT, the NINTH AMENDMENT, or the EQUAL PROTECTION clause. Admittedly, such analyses are essential, and they may indeed solve the purely legal aspect of a constitutional problem. But fidelity to law is not the only constitutional virtue, for the Constitution is a political charter as well as a legal text. If judicial lawlessness were the sole issue, we could solve every problem with a constitutional amendment saying, "It shall be unconstitutional to treat any social problem unwisely; the Supreme Court may enforce this provision on its own motion." That would eliminate every legal ground for objecting to a large judicial role, and yet the political objections obviously would remain.

Legalism is popularly identified with a restrictive view of the Court's role, but as this hypothetical amendment illustrates, that assumption is only a half-truth. After the Justices sweep past the Maginot Line of ORIGINAL INTENT, legalism is as likely to justify judicial activism as restraint, offering no solid resistance to continual enlargement of JUDICIAL POWER. Legal training breeds indifference to trends; in most fields of law, lawyers ordinarily evaluate decisions as correct or incorrect, not as contributing to a tendency that should be evaluated as such. The law is expected to evolve and grow toward the limits of its logic; indeed, the very word "trend" connotes gradualism, a legal virtue. In COMMON LAW fields, that attitude is generally harmless. The doctrine of promissory estoppel, idling in a backwater of the law of contracts, does not affect our system of government, and even if it did, the legislature could change it. In constitutional law, by contrast, the Court's

role has enormous political implications; as in all politics, constitutional trends may be ominous well before the day of reckoning arrives.

In an effort to supplement narrow legal standards, some scholars have offered political objections to judicial activism. The most common of these objections may be called "the argument from democracy": America is a democracy, but the Court is not electorally accountable; therefore, excessive judicial activism is illegitimate, undermines public respect for the institution, and thus impairs its ability to perform its proper functions.

The argument from democracy, and the usual responses to it, are not narrowly legalistic, and their emphasis on democratic theory is explicitly political. Still, the search for criteria of democratic legitimacy has important similarities to conventional legal analysis: it focuses on individual decisions and doctrines, it asks whether each of them is correct (legitimate) or incorrect, and it seeks to answer that question by applying broad, consistent principles.

Without denying the value of such neolegalistic inquiries, it is important to emphasize that there is another way of looking at the Court's role, focusing less on individual decisions and more on trends and aggregates and recognizing that a decision may be justifiable from one point of view yet harmful from another. Conventional discussions of constitutional JURISPRUDENCE, with their legalistic tendency to label decisions as correct or incorrect, tend to obscure the fact that judicial governance, even when it is lawful and legitimate, exacts a price—not always an excessive or even a high price, but a price. For constitutional rights tend to diminish the role of self-government. This is not simply a question of lawfulness or legitimacy. When the Court enforces a constitutional right—even one fairly discoverable in text, traditions, and precedents—it reduces, however slightly, the responsibilities of politicians and reformers. Within the scope of legal expectations aroused by a specific right, they have less incentive to participate in politics. Within the scope of hopes aroused by the Court's general willingness to create rights, they may choose to forgo the onerous burden of self-government, waiting instead for an edict from Washington. Even if reformers lose in the Court, three or four dissents may nourish the hope that new Justices will solve the problem. To that extent, rights tend to relieve reformers of the tasks of CITIZENSHIP: studying public policy, creating reform commissions, drafting statutes, talking to bureaucrats and politicians, bargaining with opponents, persuading the uncommitted, and compromising. Likewise, judicially created rights sometimes enable politicians to avoid accountability to sharply divided constituencies.

Even as a legal issue, one open to creative solutions, a constitutional right is a problem that has been removed from the fifty states, with all their judges, to one Supreme Court. All other judges, though still free to interpret and suggest, cease to be ultimately responsible.

Admittedly, these hidden prices are nebulous and incalculable. No doubt the price of judicial governance is often low in individual cases, and even when it seems to be high, it may be worth paying. It may be offset by the beneficial effects of judicial intervention, for example, in opening up opportunities for an oppressed class (as in BROWN V. BOARD OF EDUCATION (1954)), in protecting FREEDOM OF SPEECH, or in purifying the electoral process. The essential point is that the citizenry should try to appraise the enlarged judicial role cumulatively—as it appraises the federal budget—and as a problem in government, not merely in law. In constitutional jurisprudence one should consider the destination, not just the next step of the journey. Do we want the Supreme Court to decide, case-by-case over the decades, just when and how the government may regulate sex, marriage, and privacy? To establish national standards for criminal punishment, fashioned case-by-case in litigation? To oversee regulation of the economy? Or provision of housing, under the aegis of a "constitutional right to shelter?" We generally discuss such questions as if they were discrete and legal. Yet they are more than that. They are political choices, most of which can be resolved either way in the long run by the accumulation of precedent, without violating the conventions of legal reasoning and the RULE OF LAW. It may sometimes take a more or less lawless decision to get the process started, but every kingdom begins as a usurpation. Given the leading role of precedent in legal analysis, judicial activism is ultimately self-legitimating.

Powell v. Texas (1967) exemplifies the difference between legal and political grounds for judicial restraint. In *Powell* the issue was whether it was CRUEL AND UNUSUAL PUNISHMENT for Texas to punish a chronic alcoholic for public drunkenness. The trial judge had found that chronic alcoholism is a disease whose symptoms include loss of will power and "a compulsion" to appear drunk in public. This being so, argued Powell's attorney, it would be unconstitutional to treat Powell as a criminal. By a 5–4 vote, the Court rejected this argument and upheld the conviction.

A proponent of STRICT CONSTRUCTION would presumably applaud this decision on the ground that it conformed to the original meaning of "cruel and unusual." But as precedents accumulate, such arguments often lose much or all of whatever cogency they originally possessed. The leading precedent in *Powell* was *Robinson v. California* (1962), in which the Court had reversed a conviction for the crime of being "addicted to the use of narcotics." The opinion in *Robinson* distinguished between punishing someone for an act and punishing him for a "status," the latter being unconstitutional. Some of the language of the opinion implied that the basic defect of a status crime is that a status (insanity or a disease, for example) is, or may be, involuntary. Arguably, therefore, the rationale of *Robinson* extended beyond status crimes to involuntary acts, including drunken behavior by an alcoholic. To so hold might have been scientifically unsound or unwise, and it might not have been the most persuasive interpretation of *Robinson*, but given *Robinson* it could hardly have been described as a blatantly lawless decision. It would have been the sort of expansive but plausible interpretation of a precedent that courts have been handing down for centuries.

A decision in Powell's favor would also have been consistent with some of the neolegalistic criteria fashioned by jurisprudents to identify fields in which the Supreme Court's activism is legitimate. Criminal law is an area in which the courts have traditionally played a major role, and properly so because of their expertise and the tendency of popular majorities to be insensitive to the need for fairness toward criminals. Criminal defendants can be thought of as the functional equivalent of racial and religious minorities. In displacing a state court's rules of criminal responsibility, the Supreme Court is not overriding democracy but merely correcting other judges.

Although not violative of the rule of law, a broad reading of *Robinson* would have vastly expanded the Court's role, for it would have made a potential constitutional case out of every issue of free will—for example, defenses based on drunkenness and insanity. Legalistic arguments for judicial restraint do not adequately describe the implications of this sort of decision. On one side of the scale are the virtues, real or imagined, of uniformity and rationality. On the other side is the impact not only on the Court's caseload but on the values of FEDERALISM: freedom, diversity, and relatively widespread citizen participation in government. Federalism's values are embedded in our constitutional order, but in a case like *Powell* they are not "the law" in the usual sense of an authoritative rule of decision on whose binding force well-trained lawyers would agree; they are, rather, the political virtues without which constitutional jurisprudence becomes sophistry.

DAVID P. BRYDEN
(1992)

Bibliography
BRYDEN, DAVID P. 1986 Politics, the Constitution, and the New Formalism. *Constitutional Commentary* 3:415–437.
HARLAN, JOHN M. 1964 The Bill of Rights and the Constitution. *American Bar Association Journal* 50:918.
NAGEL, ROBERT F. 1989 *Constitutional Cultures: The Mentality and Consequences of Judicial Review.* Berkeley: University of California Press.

THAYER, JAMES BRADLEY 1893 The Origin and Scope of the American Doctrine of Constitutional Law. *Harvard Law Review* 7:129–156.

JUDICIAL STRATEGY

That judges shape much public policy is a fact of political life. The significant questions are how, how often, how effectively, and how wisely they influence policy. Each of these inquiries poses normative as well as empirical problems. Here we shall be concerned only with legitimate strategies that a Justice of the United States Supreme Court can employ to maximize his or her influence. We shall focus mainly on marshalling the Court.

A Justice, like any strategist, must coordinate limited resources to achieve goals. He or she must make choices—about goals and priorities among goals and also about means to achieve those goals. Intelligent choices among means depend in part on accurate assessments of the resources the Justice controls and of the limitations that others may impose on use of those resources.

The Justices can order litigants, including government officials, to act or not act in specified ways. Less tangibly, judges also have the prestige of their office, supported by a general cultural ethos of respect for the RULE OF LAW. In particular, a Justice has a powerful weapon, an opinion—a document that will be widely distributed by the Government Printing Office and several private firms. That opinion will justify—well or poorly—a particular decision and, explicitly or implicitly, the public policy it supports.

A Justice's power is limited by the nature of judicial institutions. Judges lack self-starters. Someone has to bring a case to them. Furthermore, while they can hold acts of other public officials constitutional or unconstitutional and so allow or forbid particular policies, it is much more difficult for judges to compel government to act. The Supreme Court can rule that blacks are entitled to vote, but it cannot force Congress to pass a CIVIL RIGHTS law to make that right effective. Moreover, the Court can hear only a limited number of cases. It depends on thousands of state and federal judges to carry out its jurisprudence. And no Justice plays an *official* role in selecting, retaining, or promoting judges.

Second, a Supreme Court Justice needs the agreement of at least four colleagues. And each Justice can write a separate opinion, dissenting or concurring, in any case.

Third, and more broadly, the Court is dependent on Congress and the President for appropriations and enforcement of decisions. Each of these branches has other important checks: The House can impeach and the Senate can then remove a Justice. Congress can increase the size of the Court, remove at least part of its APPELLATE JURIS-DICTION, propose constitutional amendments to erase the effects of decisions or strike at judicial power itself, and use its access to mass media to challenge the Court's prestige. The President can even more effectively attack the Court's prestige, and he can persuade Congress to use any of its weapons against the Justices. He can also choose new judges who, he hopes, will change the course of CONSTITUTIONAL INTERPRETATION.

Fourth, state officials can influence public opinion to pressure Congress and the President. State officers can also drag their heels in carrying out judicial decisions and select judges who are hostile to the Court's jurisprudence.

Fifth, leaders of interest groups can pressure elected officials at all levels of government. And when judicial decisions threaten or support their values, these people seldom hesitate to apply whatever political leverage is in their self-interest.

Commentators—journalists and social scientists as well as law professors—constitute a sixth check. If judges make law, EDWARD S. CORWIN said, so do commentators. Justices who want their jurisprudence to endure must look not only to immediate reactions but also to the future. What commentators write may influence later generations of voters, lawyers, and public officials.

A Justice confronts these limitations simultaneously, and each of these groups will include a range of opinion. Any ruling will elate some and infuriate others, and the political power of various factions is likely to vary widely. In short, problems of synchronizing activities are always present and are typically complex.

The first audience a Justice must convince is composed of other Justices. The most obvious way of having one's views accepted by one's colleagues is to have colleagues who agree with one's views. Thus ability to influence the recruiting process is a difficult but fruitful means of maximizing influence. (See APPOINTMENT OF SUPREME COURT JUSTICES.) Justices who cannot choose their colleagues must consider how to persuade them.

Although treating others with courtesy may never change a vote or modify an opinion, it does make it more likely that others will listen. When others listen, intellectual capacity becomes critical. The Justice who knows "the law," speaks succinctly, writes clearly, and analyzes wisely gains distinct advantages.

Practical experience can be a valuable adjunct. Logic is concerned with relations among propositions, not with their desirability or social utility. According to WILLIAM O. DOUGLAS, several Justices were converted to Chief Justice EARL WARREN's position in BROWN V. BOARD OF EDUCATION (1954) because of his vast political experience. Strength of character is also crucial. Although neither learned nor gifted as a writer, Warren led the Court and the country through a constitutional revolution. It was his "passion for justice," his massive integrity, Douglas also recalled, that made Warren such a forceful leader. "Is it right?" was his typical question, not "Do earlier decisions allow it?"

In another sense, intellect alone is unlikely to suffice. Justices are all apt to be intelligent, strong-willed people with divergent views about earlier rulings as well as public policy. They are also apt to differ about the Court's proper roles in the political system—in sum, about fundamentals of jurisprudence. At that level of dispute, it is improbable that one Justice, no matter how astute and eloquent, will convert another.

Facing disagreements that cannot be intellectually reconciled, a Justice may opt for several courses. Basically, he can negotiate with his colleagues or go it alone. Most often, it will be prudent to negotiate. Like policymaking, negotiation, even bargaining, is a fact of judicial life. Writing the opinion of the Court requires "an orchestral, not a solo performance." All Justices can utilize their votes and freedom to write separate opinions. The value of each depends upon the circumstances. If the Court divides 4–4, the ninth Justice, in effect, decides the case. On the other hand, when the Court votes 8–0, the ninth Justice's ability to negotiate will depend almost totally on his capacity to write a separate opinion that, the others fear, would undermine their position.

To be effective, negotiations must be restrained and sensitive. Justices are likely to sit together for many years. Driving a hard bargain today may damage future relations. The mores of the Court forbid trading of votes. The Justices take their oaths of office seriously; and, while reality pushes them toward accommodation, they are not hagglers in a market, peddling their views.

The most common channels of negotiating are circulation of draft opinions, comments on those drafts, and private conversations. A Justice can nudge others, especially the judge assigned the task of producing the OPINION OF THE COURT, by suggesting additions, deletions, and rephrasings. In turn, to retain a majority, the opinion writer must be willing to accede to many suggestions, even painful ones, as he tries to persuade the Court to accept the core of his reasoning. OLIVER WENDELL HOLMES once complained that "the boys generally cut one of the genitals" out of his drafts, and he made no claim to have restored their manhood.

Drafts and discussions of opinions can and do change votes, even outcomes. Sometimes those changes are not in the intended direction. After reading FELIX FRANK-FURTER's dissent in BAKER V. CARR (1961), TOM C. CLARK, changed his vote, remarking that if those were the reasons for dissenting he would join the majority.

Although the art of negotiation is essential, a Justice should not wish to appear so malleable as to encourage efforts to dilute his jurisprudence. He would much prefer a reputation of being reasonable but tough-minded. He thus might sometimes find it wise to stand alone rather than even attempt compromise. It is usually prudent for a Justice, when with the majority, to inject as many of his views as possible into the Court's opinion, and when with the minority to squeeze as many hostile ideas as possible out of the Court's opinion. There are, however, times when both conscience and prudence counsel standing alone, appealing to officials in other governmental processes or to future judges to vindicate his jurisprudence.

Although Justices have very limited authority to make the other branches of government act, they are not powerless. Judges can often find more in a statute than legislators believe they put there. OBITER DICTA in an opinion can also prod other officials to follow the "proper" path. The Court might even pursue a dangerous course that might push a reluctant President to carry out its decisions lest he seem either indifferent to the rule of law or unprotective of federal power against state challenges.

Lobbying with either branch is also possible. Indeed, judicial lobbying has a venerable history running back to JOHN JAY. Advice delivered through third parties may have been even more common. Over time, however, expectations of judicial conduct have risen so that even a hint of such activity triggers an outcry. Thus a judge must heavily discount the benefits of direct or indirect contacts by the probability of their being discovered.

The most obvious weapon that a Justice has against unwelcome political action is the ability to persuade his colleagues to declare that action unconstitutional or, if it comes in the shape of a federal statute or EXECUTIVE ORDER, to disarm it by interpretation. These are the Court's ultimate weapons, and their overuse or use at the wrong time might provoke massive retaliation.

A Justice must therefore consider more indirect means. Delay is the tactic that procedural rules most readily permit. The Justices can deny a WRIT OF CERTIORARI, dismiss an REMAND, the case for clarification, order reargument, or use a dozen other tactics to delay deciding volatile disputes until the political climate changes.

Under other circumstances, it might be more prudent for a Justice to move the Court step by step. Gradual erosion of old rules and accretion of new ones may win more adherents than sudden statements of novel DOCTRINES. The Court's treatment of segregation provides an excellent illustration. If MISSOURI EX REL. GAINES V. CANADA (1938) had struck down SEPARATE BUT EQUAL, the Court could never have made the decision stick. Indeed, years later, when it excommunicated Jim Crow, enforcement created a generation of litigation that still continues.

Strategy is concerned with efficient utilization of scarce resources to achieve important objectives. Its domain is that of patience and prudence, not of wisdom in choosing among goals nor of courage in fighting for the right. The messages that a study of judicial strategy yields are: A web of checks restrains a judge's power; and If he or she wishes to maximize his or her ability to do good, a judge must learn to cope with those restrictions, to work within and around them, and to conserve available resources for the times when he or she must, as a matter of conscience, directly challenge what he or she sees as a threat to the basic values of constitutional democracy.

WALTER F. MURPHY
(1986)

Bibliography

BICKEL, ALEXANDER M. 1957 *The Unpublished Opinions of Mr. Justice Brandeis.* Cambridge, Mass.: Harvard University Press.
——— 1961 The Passive Virtues. *Harvard Law Review* 75: 40–79.
DOUGLAS, WILLIAM O. 1980 *The Court Years, 1939–1975.* New York: Random House.
KLUGER, RICHARD 1976 *Simple Justice.* New York: Knopf.
MURPHY, BRUCE 1982 *The Brandeis/Frankfurter Connection.* New York: Oxford University Press.
MURPHY, WALTER F. 1964 *Elements of Judicial Strategy.* Chicago: University of Chicago Press.
O'BRIEN, DAVID M. 1986 *Storm Center: The Supreme Court in American Politics.* New York: Norton.

JUDICIAL SUPREMACY

Stripped of the partisan rhetoric that usually surrounds important decisions of the Supreme Court, debate about judicial supremacy raises a fundamental question: Who is the final, authoritative interpreter of the Constitution? The response of judicial supremacy is that courts perform that function and other officials are bound not only to respect judges' decisions in particular cases but also, in formulating future public policy, to follow the general principles judges have laid down.

JUDICIAL REVIEW does not necessarily entail or logically imply judicial supremacy. One can, as THOMAS JEFFERSON did, concede the legitimacy of courts' refusing on constitutional grounds to enforce statutes and EXECUTIVE ORDERS and still deny either that officials of a coordinate branch must obey a decision or follow its rationale in the future. This view, called "departmentalism," sees the three branches of the national government as equal in CONSTITUTIONAL INTERPRETATION. Each department has authority to interpret the Constitution for itself, but its interpretations do not bind the other two.

There are other possible answers to the basic question: Congress, the President, the states, or the people. A claim for the states presupposes the Constitution to be a compact among sovereign entities who reserved to themselves authority to construe their obligations. Such was Jefferson's assertion in the KENTUCKY RESOLUTIONS (1798), and it echoed down decades of dreary debates on NULLIFICATION and SECESSION. The CIVIL WAR settled the matter, though some southern states briefly tried to resurrect nullification to oppose BROWN V. BOARD OF EDUCATION (1954).

A claim for the President as the ultimate, authoritative interpreter smacks too much of royalty for the idea to have been seriously maintained. On the other hand, Presidents have frequently and effectively defended their independent authority to interpret the Constitution for the executive department.

A case for the people as the final, authoritative interpreter permeates the debate. American government rests on popular consent. The people can elect officials to amend the Constitution or create a new constitution and so shape basic political arrangements as well as concrete public policies. Jefferson advocated constitutional conventions as a means of popular judging between conflicting departmental interpretations.

Although even JAMES MADISON rejected Jefferson's solution, indirect appeals to the people as the ultimate interpreters are reflected in claims to the supremacy of a popularly elected legislature. On the other hand, in THE FEDERALIST #78, ALEXANDER HAMILTON, rested his argument for judicial review on the authority of the people who have declared their will in the Constitution. Judicial review, he argued, does not imply that judges are superior to legislators but that "the power of the people is superior to both."

Although JOHN MARSHALL partially incorporated this line of reasoning in MARBURY V. MADISON (1803), neither he nor Hamilton ever explicitly asserted that the Supreme Court's interpretation of the Constitution was binding on other branches of the federal government. One might, however, infer that conclusion from Marshall's opinions in *Marbury* and in *McCulloch v. Maryland* (1819), where he expressly claimed supremacy as far as state governments were concerned.

We know little of the Framers' attitudes toward judicial supremacy. In *The Federalist* #51, Madison took a clear departmentalist stand, as he did in the First Congress. In 1788 Madison wrote a friend that the new Constitution made no provision for settling differences among departments' interpretations: "[A]nd as ye Courts are generally the last in making the decision, it results to them by refusing or not refusing to execute a law, to stamp it with its final character. This makes the Judiciary Dept paramount in fact to the Legislature, which was never intended and can never be proper."

In the Senate in 1802, however, GOUVERNEUR MORRIS argued that the judges derived their power to decide on

most civil suits brought by the United States and over the then negligible federal criminal caseload. Notably, the act did not give the federal trial courts jurisdiction over cases "arising under" federal law, leaving these to be adjudicated in the state courts.

The appellate structure of the new court system was rudimentary. Federal criminal cases were left without direct review (and remained so for a century). The circuit courts were given a limited APPELLATE JURISDICTION over the district courts, and the Supreme Court was authorized to review civil cases decided by the circuit courts involving more than $2,000.

Finally, in its famous section 25, the act—consistent with the Framers' intention to assure the supremacy of federal law—gave the Supreme Court power to review final state court judgments rejecting claims of right or immunity under federal law. (State court judgments upholding claims of right under federal law were not made reviewable until 1914.) Supreme Court review of state judgments involving questions of federal law has been a feature of our judicial FEDERALISM ever since 1789, and has served as a profoundly significant instrument for consolidating and protecting national power.

The institutional structure created by the first Judiciary Act proved to be remarkably stable; major structural change did not come until 1891. The Supreme Court has had a continuous existence since 1789, with changes only in the number of Justices. So also have the district courts (though their number has of course undergone major change). Even the circuit courts—architecturally the weakest feature of the system—survived for more than a century.

As to the jurisdiction of the federal courts, changes were incremental in the pre-CIVIL WAR period, with the state courts acting as the primary enforcers of the still rudimentary corpus of national law. But the Civil War brought a sea change: Congress was no longer prepared to depend on the state judiciaries to enforce rights guaranteed by the new FOURTEENTH AMENDMENT and by the Reconstruction legislation. By the HABEAS CORPUS ACT of 1867 and the various CIVIL RIGHTS ACTS, Congress extended the lower federal courts' jurisdiction to include claims against state officials for invasion of federal constitutional and statutory rights. These extensions were in turn overtaken by the JUDICIARY ACT OF 1875, giving the federal courts a general jurisdiction to adjudicate civil cases arising under federal law, subject only to a minimum amount-in-controversy. These expansions, supplemented by subsequent numerous specific extensions of federal trial jurisdiction over various sorts of actions involving national law, signaled the transformation of the federal courts from narrow forums designed to resolve maritime and certain interstate disputes into catholic tribunals playing a principal role in enforcing the growing body of national rights, privileges, and immunities.

The growth of the federal judicial business in the post-Civil War era placed an ever-growing pressure on the federal judicial system. The Supreme Court was especially burdened by the duties of circuit riding and by an increasing caseload. By 1890 the Court had a backload of 1800 cases; in the same year, 54,194 cases were pending in the lower federal courts. Congress responded to the crisis in the CIRCUIT COURTS OF APPEALS ACT (Evarts Act) of 1891, which fixed the outline of the contemporary federal judicial system. The act established a system of intermediate appellate courts called Circuit Courts of Appeals (not to be confused with the old circuit courts, which were finally abolished in 1911), one for each of (the then) nine circuits and staffed with its own judges. Although a narrow category of district court decisions continued (and continue) to be reviewed directly by the Supreme Court, the Evarts Act created the standard modern practice: appeals went normally from the district courts to the new courts of appeals; the judgments of the latter were in turn reviewable by the Supreme Court.

The second major and seminal innovation of the Evarts Act related to appellate review in the Supreme Court: the act introduced the principle of review at the Court's own discretion (by writ of CERTIORARI) of judgments in the lower courts. This principle was in turn greatly expanded in the so-called Judges' Bill of 1925, which sharply reduced the availability of Supreme Court review as of right of decisions of state and federal courts and substituted for it discretionary review on certiorari—the method of review that, to this day, dominates the Court's docket.

Changes in the structure of the federal judicial system have been few and minor since 1925, although both the statutory jurisdiction and the business of the courts have undergone major transformations. In essence the system remains a three-tier system, with the district courts serving as the trial courts, the courts of appeals as the appellate tribunals of first instance, and the Supreme Court as the court of final review (having also the power to review state court decisions involving issues of federal law). The picture is completed by the existence of special federal tribunals empowered to decide particular categories of cases, and by numerous federal administrative tribunals; the decisions of all of these are typically subject to review in the regular federal courts.

The most important component of the contemporary statutory jurisdiction of the UNITED STATES DISTRICT COURTS encompasses diversity cases involving more than $10,000, criminal prosecutions and civil actions brought by the United States, a large range of actions against the United States and its agencies and officials, federal HABEAS CORPUS, and—most significant—all civil cases in which a plaintiff sues on a claim arising under the Constitution and laws of the United States. The latter, all-encompassing rubric includes not only cases brought pursuant to the hundreds of federal statutes specifying a right to sue but also the numerous cases where that right is a judge-created ("implied") right to enforce a federal statutory or—(of profound significance)—constitutional provision not itself explicitly containing a right of action. In addition, the statutes allow certain diversity and federal question cases brought in the state courts to be removed for trial to a federal district court. Finally, the district courts exercise a significant jurisdiction to review the work of many federal administrative agencies and to review and supervise the work of the system of bankruptcy courts. The jurisdiction of the district courts is occasionally specified as exclusive of the state courts (for example, admiralty, COPYRIGHT, and PATENT); most of their civil jurisdiction is, however, concurrent with that of the state courts.

The country is, in the mid-1980s, divided into ninety-seven districts (including the DISTRICT OF COLUMBIA and PUERTO RICO). Each state has at least one district; districts have never encompassed more than one state. The district courts are staffed by 576 active district judges—almost three times the 1950 figure (182 new district judgeships were created between 1978 and 1984 alone). The growth in number of judges has, nevertheless, failed to keep pace with the explosive increase in the caseload that has occurred since the 1960s. In 1940 about 70,000 criminal and civil (nonbankruptcy) cases were filed in the federal courts; in 1960, about 80,000; by 1980, the figure was almost 200,000, and in 1984 it exceeded 275,000. (The compound annual rate of increase in the federal district court case load was under one percent between 1934 and 1960; it has been five percent since 1960.) The increase is due primarily and naturally to the vast growth in the total corpus of federal (constitutional, statutory, common, and administrative) law applied in turn to a growing country with an expansive and mobile economy. It has also been fed, however, in the past twenty-five years by congressional and court-initiated changes in substantive and remedial rules that have made the federal courts into powerful litigation-attracting engines for the creation and expansion of rights and the redistribution of entitlements and powers in our society. Thus open-ended constitutional and statutory formulas have been used to fuel aggressive judicial review of the validity of federal and state legislative and administrative action and to create an expansive system of remedies against federal and state government (including affirmative claims on the resources of these governments). JUSTICIABILITY requirements (such as STANDING) that previously narrowed the scope of jurisdiction over public law actions have been significantly eroded. And federal court litigation has become increasingly attractive to plaintiffs

as a result of provisions for attorneys' fees, the elimination (or inflation-caused erosion) of amount-in-controversy requirements, and the increasing use of CLASS ACTIONS.

These developments are reflected in the changing content of the federal district courts' workload. There were 6,000 suits against the United States in 1960, and almost 30,000 in 1983. There were only 300 CIVIL RIGHTS cases in 1960, almost 20,000 in 1983; 2,100 prisoner postconviction cases in 1960, more than 30,000 in 1983; 500 social security law cases in 1960, more than 20,000 in 1983. In general, about thirty-five to forty percent of the mid-1980s district court civil caseload involve the United States or its officials as a plaintiff or defendant; sixty to sixty-five percent of the civil caseload is "private" (including, however, litigation against state and local governments and officials). Diversity cases have contributed about twenty percent of the caseload since the 1970s. The number of criminal prosecutions has, historically, fluctuated widely in response to special federal programs (peaking during PROHIBITION); since the mid-1970s the criminal caseload has been quite stable and in the mid-1980s contributed about fifteen to twenty percent of the total.

In response to the explosive caseload Congress has acted to allow the district courts to rely substantially on the work of so-called federal magistrates—officials appointed by district judges with wide powers (subject to review by the district judge) to issue warrants, conduct preliminary hearings, try minor criminal offenses, supervise civil discovery, rule on preliminary motions and prisoner petitions, and (with the consent of the parties) even to hear and enter judgment generally in civil cases. The conferring of additional powers on magistrates has evoked controversy as well as some (so far unsuccessful) constitutional attacks.

The UNITED STATES COURTS OF APPEALS (as they are now called) have jurisdiction to review all final (and some interlocutory) decisions of the district courts. Pursuant to special statutory provisions they also review some cases coming directly from federal administrative agencies (this being an especially significant component of the business of the Court of Appeals for the District of Columbia Circuit). About fifteen percent of their cases are criminal cases, and another fifteen percent are federal and state prisoner postconviction and civil rights cases; only fourteen percent of their docket consists of diversity cases.

The caseload of the courts of appeals has increased dramatically in the last twenty-five years and is, in the mid-1980s, commonly described as constituting a crisis. In the forty years before 1960 that caseload hovered between 1,500 and the peak of 3,700 reached in 1960. In 1970 the figure was almost 11,500, and in 1980 it was over 21,000. From 1980 to 1983 the caseload jumped again to 29,580. From 1960 to 1983 there was an increase of almost 800 percent in the number of appeals from the district courts; the compound annual rate of increase for all cases from 1960 to 1983 was 9.4 percent (compared to 0.5 percent in the preceding twenty-five years).

To manage this workload there exist (in the mid-1980s) twelve courts of appeals assigned to geographical circuits (eleven in the states and one for the District of Columbia) and an additional one (described below) for certain special categories of subject matter. The number of judges in each circuit ranges from six (First) to twenty-eight (Ninth). There are 156 authorized circuit judgeships; in 1960 there were sixty-eight (and as recently as 1978 only ninety-seven). Cases are typically heard by panels of three judges; a few cases of special importance are in turn reheard by the court sitting EN BANC. The increase in number of judges has by no means kept pace with the expansion of the caseload since 1960. As a result, there have been substantial changes in the procedures of these courts: opportunities for oral argument (and even for briefing) have been sharply curtailed and an increasing proportion of cases is disposed of summarily, without opinion. Central staff attorneys (as well as a growing army of conventional law clerks) assist the judges.

From the beginning of our national history Congress has perceived a need to create special tribunals for the adjudication of cases falling outside the traditional areas of federal court jurisdiction. Military tribunals have, from the outset, administered a special body of law through special procedures. The administration of justice in the TERRITORIES in transition toward statehood was perceived as requiring special temporary federal tribunals that would become state courts upon statehood; the District of Columbia and the territories and dependencies of the United States also require a full panoply of special federal courts to administer local law. Beginning in 1855, with the establishment of a rudimentary Court of Claims, Congress has created a series of special tribunals to adjudicate money claims against the United States. And, particularly with the advent in this century of the modern administrative state, Congress has created numerous administrative agencies and tribunals whose business includes adjudication.

Unlike the ordinary federal courts, the institutional hallmark of most of these tribunals has been specialization. Further, the transitory nature of some of these tribunals, the perceived need to allow some of them to function inexpensively with expeditious or informal procedures, and (in the case of the administrative agencies) the equally strongly perceived need to endow them with a range of policymaking functions in addition to adjudicative functions, has typically led Congress to create them not as tribunals constituted under Article III (with lifetime judges performing an exclusively judicial function) but as special LEGISLATIVE COURTS or administrative tribunals.

Their judges typically serve temporary terms and are removable for misfeasance without IMPEACHMENT. The constitutional authority for such tribunals has been much discussed and litigated; Congress's authority to constitute them has virtually always been upheld.

The most important specialized tribunals in the current federal judicial system are: the local courts of the District of Columbia, Puerto Rico, and the territories and dependencies; the system of military courts; the system of bankruptcy courts; the TAX COURT and the CLAIMS COURT, adjudicating certain tax refund claims and certain damage actions against the federal government; the Court of International Trade, adjudicating certain customs disputes; and a large and variegated array of administrative tribunals and agencies. The work of all of these tribunals is typically subject to review, through various forms of proceedings, in the regular federal courts.

In addition, in 1982 Congress created a thirteenth court of appeals, the UNITED STATES COURT OF APPEALS FOR THE FEDERAL CIRCUIT. This is a regular Article III court, whose jurisdiction is not territorial but is defined in terms of subject matter, including appeals from the Claims Court and the Court of International Trade and many patent and trademark cases.

Continuously since 1789 the Supreme Court has been the single institution with nationwide authority to supervise the inferior federal courts and to give voice to a uniform national law. The Court's size has varied from five to ten Justices; since 1869 it has consisted of a Chief Justice and eight associate Justices. The Supreme Court acts *en banc*, not in panels, though individual Justices have the conventional authority to issue stays and take emergency action. The Court acts by majority, but in this century the practice has been to grant a certiorari petition (setting the case for plenary review) if four Justices are in favor.

The caseload explosion in the lower federal courts has imposed major burdens on the Court. The Court disposed of over 4,000 cases in its 1983 term (compared to about 3,300 in 1970, 1,900 in 1960, and 1,200 in 1950). The task is possible because only a small number of cases (usually about 150) are decided on the merits by full opinion after plenary briefing and oral argument. Another 100 to 150 cases are decided on the merits by MEMORANDUM ORDER. The remaining dispositions consist of summary denials of petitions for certiorari (or other writs); there were almost 3,900 of these in 1983–1984. In 1960 there were just under 2,000 new cases docketed in the Court; in 1970, about 3,400; in 1983, about 4,200. The increase in cases docketed means more and more resources devoted to "screening" cases for decision and less to the hearing and disposition of cases on the merits. Thus the time devoted to oral argument has shrunk steadily in this century and now almost never exceeds one hour per case. The length of briefs is limited; and an ever-growing battery of law CLERKS assists in legal research and in the drafting of opinions.

The content of the Court's work reflects the scope and content of the national law. In the 1983 term the Court's decisions by full opinion included three cases within the original jurisdiction; ninety-six civil cases coming from the lower federal courts (of which forty-six involved the federal government, twenty-eight involved state and local governments, and twenty-two were private cases); sixteen federal habeas corpus cases; and thirty-two cases from the state courts (eighteen civil and fourteen criminal). Diversity cases are rarely reviewed. The Court is, increasingly, a constitutional court; about half of its cases tend to involve a constitutional question as the (or a) principal issue. The United States (as party or AMICUS CURIAE) participates in over half of the cases that the Court decides on the merits.

Although the federal judicial system has grown substantially in its 200 years, the federal courts continue to constitute only a small—though disproportionately powerful—component of the American judicial system. (Fewer than three percent of the country's judges are federal Article III judges; the biggest states have judicial systems larger than the federal system.)

The relations between state and federal courts are multifarious and exceedingly complex. Except where Congress has specified that federal court jurisdiction is exclusive, state courts of general jurisdiction exercise a normal competence to adjudicate cases involving issues of federal law (particularly in that many such issues arise by way of defense in civil and criminal cases arising under state law). Their decisions of these cases are subject to Supreme Court review, usually on certiorari; but that Court's jurisdiction in such a case is limited to the federal question in the case and may not be exercised at all if the judgment rests on a valid and dispositive state-law ground. State court judgments on issues of federal law (unless reversed by the Supreme Court) have normal RES JUDICATA effect.

The federal district courts, in turn, adjudicate many questions of state law, not only in diversity cases but also in cases arising under federal law where state law governs one or more issues. No provision for review by the state courts of the correctness of federal court decisions on issues of state law has ever existed; but in a narrow class of cases federal courts will abstain from exercising an otherwise proper federal jurisdiction in order to allow a state law issue to be determined in the state courts. (See ABSTENTION DOCTRINE.) Under the decision in ERIE RAILROAD v. TOMPKINS (1938), on issues of state law (including issues of state common law) state court precedents are accepted as authoritative by the federal courts.

Special problems are presented by the politically sensitive role of the federal courts in controlling the legality of the actions of state and local governments and their officials. Although the ELEVENTH AMENDMENT bars the federal courts from asserting jurisdiction over actions against a state as such, a wide range of remedies against state and local governments and their officials exist in the federal courts. Federal courts routinely review the constitutional validity of state criminal convictions through the writ of habeas corpus. Since the adoption of the Civil Rights Act of 1871, they have exercised jurisdiction to grant INJUNCTIONS and DAMAGES against state and local officials (and, more recently, against local governmental entities as such) for conduct under color of state law—including conduct by officials asserting official power even where the conduct is prohibited by state law—that infringes on the ever-growing corpus of federal constitutional and statutory rules governing STATE ACTION. Federal courts may enjoin state officials from enforcing unconstitutional state statutes and administrative schemes; moreover, the courts' injunctive remedial powers are frequently exercised to assume broad managerial supervision over state agencies and bureaucracies (for example, schools, mental hospitals, prisons). And the ever-burgeoning array of federal conditions and restrictions that accompany federal economic and social programs available to the states are, as a matter of routine, enforceable in the federal courts.

The political sensitivities aroused by the federal courts' jurisdiction to control the validity of state and local government action has led to some statutory and judge-made restrictions on the exercise of this jurisdiction. For over half a century federal court actions to enjoin the enforcement of state statutes on constitutional grounds had to be litigated before THREE-JUDGE COURTS and were subject to direct review by APPEAL to the Supreme Court. (The institution of the three-judge district court was virtually abolished in 1976.) During the NEW DEAL, statutory restrictions were placed on the jurisdiction of the federal courts to interfere with state tax statutes and public utility rate orders. Statutory and judge-made rules restrict the power of the federal courts to enjoin or interfere with pending state court proceedings; and state prisoners who fail to exhaust state court remedies or fail to comply with state procedural rules do not have access to federal habeas corpus.

The federal judicial system appears to operate on one-hundred-year cycles. The structure created in 1789 became increasingly unwieldy after the Civil War and was—after some twenty years of pressure for reform—finally transformed by the Evarts Act of 1891. That act created a stable system which has, in turn, come under increasing pressure from the caseload explosion that began in the 1960s. Relief could come in the form of diminutions in the district courts' original jurisdiction (such as a long-discussed abolition of or reduction in the diversity jurisdiction); but the need for architectural revision has also become increasingly clear in the 1970s and 1980s.

Structural problems center on the appellate tiers. Further substantial increases in the number of circuit judges is an uncertain remedy. Some circuits are already unwieldy and are finding it increasingly difficult to maintain stability and uniformity in the intracircuit law. Increasing the number of circuits would increase intercircuit instability and disuniformity and place further pressure on the finite appellate capacity of our "one Supreme Court"—the latter constituting the obvious structural bottleneck in the system.

More generally, a judicial system administering an enormous and dynamic corpus of national law and adjudicating a rising caseload (approaching 300,000 cases a year) cannot operate forever on an appellate capacity that is limited to some 150–200 judicial opinions with nationwide authority. There is rising concern, too, about the quality of federal justice as the growing caseload leads to an increasing bureaucratization of the federal judicial process, with the judges reduced to an oversight capacity in managing a growing array of magistrates, central staff, and law clerks.

Since the 1970s, two methods of increasing the system's capacity to provide authoritative and uniform judicial pronouncements on issues of national law have been discussed. One consists of greater subject-matter specialization at the appellate level, with special courts of appeals having nationwide authority to deal with specified subjects of federal litigation (for instance, tax cases, administrative appeals); such courts would remove pressure from the regional courts of appeals and the Supreme Court. The alternative (or additional) possibility is to create an additional appellate "tier": a national court of appeals with power to render decisions of nationwide authority, receiving its business by assignment from the Supreme Court or by transfer from the regional courts of appeals. In addition, if the number of certiorari petitions continues to mount, the Supreme Court will eventually have to make some adjustments in its screening procedures (perhaps dealing with these petitions in panels).

Behind these structural problems lie more fundamental questions about the enormous power that the federal courts have come to exercise over the political, economic, and social policies of the nation. Throughout our history intense controversy has surrounded the question whether (and to what extent) a small corps of appointed life-tenured officials should exercise wide-ranging powers to supervise and invalidate the actions of the political branches of federal, state, and local governments. From time to time these debates have threatened to affect the independence of the federal judicial system. Thus, in the 1930s, facing wholesale invalidations of the New Deal program by a "conservative" Supreme Court, President FRANKLIN D. ROOSEVELT proposed to "pack" the Court with additional judges; his plan was widely perceived to be contrary to the spirit of the Constitution and was defeated in Congress. (Shortly thereafter a Court with a new membership and a new judicial philosophy in effect accomplished Roosevelt's purposes.)

In the second half of the twentieth century retaliatory proposals have mostly consisted of attempts to strip a "liberal" Supreme Court of appellate jurisdiction in certain categories of constitutional litigation (for example, REAPPORTIONMENT or abortion), leaving the state courts to be the final arbiters of federal law in these areas. Intense controversy surrounds the question whether Congress has constitutional power to divest the Supreme Court of appellate jurisdiction over specific categories of constitutional litigation. (The one explicit Supreme Court pronouncement on the question, the celebrated EX PARTE MCCARDLE [1869], in sweeping language upheld this power pursuant to the explicit provision of Article III providing that the Court's appellate jurisdiction is subject to "such Exceptions" and "such Regulations" as "the Congress shall make.") Even if Congress has jurisdiction-stripping power, however, its exercise—much like the exercise of the power to "pack" the Court—would be widely perceived as anticonstitutional in spirit. In fact, no such legislation has come near to achieving acceptance, attesting to the vast reservoir of ideological and political strength that the ideal of an independent federal judiciary continues to possess.

The more important and authentic debate that continues to rage as the federal court system enters its third century relates to the proper role of an independent federal judiciary in a nation that is democratic but also committed to the ideal of fidelity to law. The federal courts have come to exercise a power over the political, economic, and social life of this nation that no other independent judicial system in the history of mankind has possessed. Whether that power is wholly benign—or whether it should and can be reduced—is one of the great questions to which the twenty-first century will have to attend.

PAUL M. BATOR
(1986)

Bibliography

AMERICAN LAW INSTITUTE   1969   Study of the Division of Jurisdiction Between State and Federal Courts. Washington D.C.: American Law Institute.

BATOR, PAUL M. et al.   1973   *The Federal Courts and the Federal*

System, 2nd ed., with 1981 Supplement. Mineola, N.Y.: Foundation Press.

CARRINGTON, PAUL D.; MEADOR, DANIEL J.; and ROSENBERG, MAURICE 1976 *Justice on Appeal*. St. Paul, Minn.: West Publishing Co.

DIRECTOR OF THE ADMINISTRATIVE OFFICE OF THE UNITED STATES COURTS [annually] *Annual Reports*. Washington, D.C.: United States Government Printing Office.

FRANKFURTER, FELIX and LANDIS, JAMES M. 1928 *The Business of the Supreme Court: A Study in the Federal Judicial System*. New York: Macmillan.

FRIENDLY, HENRY J. 1973 *Federal Jurisdiction: A General View*. New York: Columbia University Press.

POSNER, RICHARD A. 1985 *The Federal Courts: Crisis and Reform*. Cambridge, Mass.: Harvard University Press.

WRIGHT, CHARLES ALAN 1983 *The Law of Federal Courts*. St. Paul, Minn.: West Publishing Co.

JUDICIARY ACT OF 1789
1 Stat. 73 (1789)

Article III of the Constitution constitutes an authorizing charter for a system of national courts to exercise the JUDICIAL POWER OF THE UNITED STATES, but is not self-executing, needing legislation to bring it to life. Accordingly, the First Congress, in its twentieth enactment, turned to the creation of a JUDICIAL SYSTEM for the new nation. Its work—the First Judiciary Act, approved September 24, 1789—has ever since been celebrated as "a great law." The statute, obeying a constitutional command, constituted a SUPREME COURT. It created the office of Attorney General of the United States. It devised a judicial organization that was destined to survive for a century. And, by providing for Supreme Court review of state court judgments involving issues of federal law, it created a profoundly significant instrument for consolidating and protecting national power.

But it is the decision of the First Congress to take up the constitutional option to establish a system of federal courts "inferior" to the Supreme Court that has been characterized as the act's "transcendent achievement." The Constitution does not require the creation of inferior courts. Nevertheless, the decision to do so came swiftly, actuated by the unanimously shared view that an effective maritime commerce—trading lifeblood for the thirteen states—needed a dependable nationwide body of maritime law, and by a consensus that the most reliable method to assure its development would be to entrust it to a distinctive body of national courts. (Far more controversy surrounded the view, also finding expression in the act, that national courts were needed to assure out-of-state litigants protection against parochial prejudices.)

The act thus created a system of federal courts of original (trial) jurisdiction, establishing a tradition that has survived without interruption to this day. On the other hand, the act gave these courts the authority to adjudicate only a small fraction of the CASES AND CONTROVERSIES encompassed by the federal judicial power, attesting to the clear contemporaneous understanding of the Constitution that it is for Congress to determine which, if any, of the cases, within the federal judicial power should be adjudicated in the first instance in a federal tribunal.

The first section of the act provided for a Supreme Court, consisting of a Chief Justice and five associates. Below this, the act created a curious bifurcated system. The country was divided into districts generally coterminous with state boundaries (Massachusetts and Virginia each had two districts), each with a district court manned by a district judge. In addition, the act divided the country into three circuits, in each of which another trial court, called a CIRCUIT COURT—manned not by its own judges but by two Supreme Court Justices and a district judge—was to sit twice a year in each district within the circuit. These circuit courts, in addition, received a limited APPELLATE JURISDICTION to review district court decisions. The system of circuit courts set up in 1789, with its requirement that Supreme Court Justices sit on circuit as trial judges, persisted for more than a century; it proved to be the weakest architectural feature of the first Judiciary Act.

The act exploited only a fraction of the constitutional potential for original federal court jurisdiction. Significantly, the constitutional grant of federal judicial power over cases arising under the Constitution and laws of the United States (FEDERAL QUESTION JURISDICTION) was largely unused and remained so until 1875. (A notable exception was section 14, the All Writs Act, which, among other matters, authorized Supreme Court Justices and district judges to "grant writs of HABEAS CORPUS" to inquire into the legality of federal detentions.) The act made important use, however, of the power to locate litigation affecting out-of-staters in the new national courts. Thus, the circuit courts were given CONCURRENT JURISDICTION with the state courts over civil cases involving more than $500 "between a citizen of the State where the suit is brought, and a citizen of another State," as well as over civil cases involving more than $500 in which an ALIEN was a party.

The most important grant of jurisdiction to the new district courts gave them "exclusive original cognizance of all civil causes of ADMIRALTY AND MARITIME JURISDICTION," subject to a savings clause preserving COMMON LAW remedies.

The litigation interests of the national government were given narrow recognition in the First Judiciary Act. The circuit courts were given power to adjudicate civil cases involving more than $500 in which the United States were "plaintiffs or petitioners" (suits against the United

States were not contemplated); the district courts had power to adjudicate suits at common law involving $100 brought by the United States. The act gave the district courts exclusive original cognizance over certain seizures, penalties, and forfeitures. And, finally, Congress provided for the then tiny criminal business of the national government by giving the circuit courts "exclusive cognizance of all crimes and offenses cognizable under the authority of the United States," subject to a concurrent jurisdiction in the district courts to try certain minor criminal offenses.

The circuit courts were given the authority to review final decisions of the district courts in civil and admiralty cases involving more than $50 or $300, respectively. In addition, the first Judiciary Act originated the device, in continuous use ever since, of providing for pretrial removal of certain cases from state to federal court (for example, removal in civil cases to a circuit court by alien defendants and by out-of-staters sued in the plaintiff's home-state court).

The framers of the first Judiciary Act, notwithstanding the later established DOCTRINE that the ORIGINAL JURISDICTION of the Supreme Court does not depend on legislative grant, specified in section 13 what this original jurisdiction was to be; the listing nearly (but not completely) exhausted the constitutional grant, encompassing controversies between states, between a state and a citizen of another state, and suits involving foreign diplomats. Setting another lasting precedent, the act designated only a portion of the original jurisdiction of the Supreme Court as exclusive jurisdiction. In his opinion for the Court in MARBURY V. MADISON (1803), Chief Justice JOHN MARSHALL read section B to give the Supreme Court original jurisdiction over certain cases that Article III had not expressly placed within the Court's original jurisdiction. Accordingly, the Court held this narrow provision of the 1789 act unconstitutional.

Not all lower federal court decisions were made reviewable. For instance, no provision at all was made for review of federal criminal cases (which remained, in the large, unreviewable for a century). The act authorized the Supreme Court to review final judgments in civil cases decided by the circuit courts if the matter in dispute exceeded $2,000.

In its celebrated section 25, Congress asserted the constitutional authority—sustained in MARTIN V. HUNTER'S LESSEE (1816) and COHENS V. VIRGINIA (1821)—to give the Supreme Court authority to review certain final judgments or decisions in the "highest" state court in which a decision "could be had" (language that survives to this day). Significantly, this authority did not encompass all cases involving issues of federal law: review was limited to cases where a state court had *rejected* a claim of right or immunity under federal law. (This limitation eventually proved to create an unacceptable institutional gap and was eliminated by the Judiciary Act of 1914.) A seminal feature of section 25 was its specification that Supreme Court review is limited to the question of federal law in the case.

The first Judiciary Act originated a fundamental structural feature of our legal topography in its section 34, called the Rules of Decision Act, providing (in language that still survives) that, except where federal law otherwise requires, the laws of the several states shall be regarded as "rules of decision" in trials at common law in the federal courts "in cases where they apply." Interpretations of this delphic provision—including the reversal from SWIFT V. TYSON (1842) to ERIE RAILROAD V. TOMPKINS (1938)—have had a significant impact on our judicial FEDERALISM. In addition, the act contained elaborate boilerplate with respect to many matters no longer of current interest, (for example, the exact days for court sessions, quorums, clerks, forms of oaths, bail).

The first Judiciary Act, passed by a Congress many of whose members had participated in the framing of the Constitution, has had a lasting effect, not only on the shape of the federal judicial system but on our thought about the constitutional and structural premises on which that system is based. Created by great statesmen, it set on foot an enterprise that 200 years later still bears its imprint.

PAUL M. BATOR
(1986)

Bibliography

FRANKFURTER, FELIX and LANDIS, JAMES M.   1928   *The Business of the Supreme Court: A Study of the Federal Judicial System.* New York: Macmillan.

GOEBEL, JULIUS   1971   *History of the Supreme Court of the United States: Antecedents and Beginnings to 1801.* Pages 457–508. New York: Macmillan.

WARREN, CHARLES   1923   New Light on the History of the Federal Judiciary Act of 1789. *Harvard Law Review* 37:49–132.

JUDICIARY ACT OF 1801
2 Stat. 89 (1801)

This maligned congressional enactment was the final achievement of the Federalists and one of their most constructive, but the Federalists so enmeshed it in partisanship that the first important action of THOMAS JEFFERSON's administration was the repeal of the act. It created resident circuit judgeships and enormously expanded federal JURISDICTION. The JUDICIARY ACT OF 1789 had created circuit courts consisting of district court judges and Supreme Court Justices. From the outset the Justices complained about the arduous duty of riding circuit and the necessity of deciding in their appellate capacity the same cases they had decided on circuit. Congress had done nothing to separate the Justices from the circuit courts, despite presidential recommendations. The Republican victories in 1800 spurred judicial reform that was "worth an election to the [Federalist] party," said a Federalist leader. A lameduck Congress belatedly passed a much needed bill that created six circuit courts staffed by sixteen circuit judges. More important, the bill extended the JURISDICTION OF THE FEDERAL COURTS to include virtually the entire JUDICIAL POWER of the United States authorized by Article III, including a general grant of FEDERAL QUESTION JURISDICTION—something which Congress did not grant again until 1875. But the bill also reduced the size of the Supreme Court to five when the next vacancy occurred, to prevent Jefferson from making an appointment. Also, President JOHN ADAMS at the last hour appointed sixteen Federalists to the new circuit judgeships. Enraged Republicans determined to pass the JUDICIARY ACTS OF 1802.

LEONARD W. LEVY
(1986)

Bibliography
TURNER, KATHRYN   1965   Federalist Policy and the Judiciary Act of 1801. *William and Mary Quarterly* 22:3–32.

JUDICIARY ACT OF 1837

See: Circuit Courts

JUDICIARY ACT OF 1869

See: Circuit Courts

JUDICIARY ACT OF 1875
18 Stat. 470 (1875)

For three-quarters of a century after the abortive JUDICIARY ACT OF 1801, federal courts lacked any general FEDERAL QUESTION JURISDICTION, that is, JURISDICTION over cases arising under federal law. The 1875 act, adopted on the same day as the CIVIL RIGHTS ACT OF 1875, was one of Congress's last pieces of nationalizing legislation during the era of RECONSTRUCTION; its primary purpose was to provide a federal judicial forum for the assertion of newly created federal rights. Using the language of Article III of the Constitution, Congress gave the CIRCUIT COURTS jurisdiction over cases "arising under the Constitution or laws of the United States" or under national treaties, provided that the matter in dispute exceeded $500. The act also

authorized the REMOVAL OF CASES from state to federal courts by either plaintiffs or defendants, when those cases could have been brought originally in the federal courts.

In part, the 1875 Judiciary Act's sponsors justified this widening of federal jurisdiction as a response to a commerce that had become national in scope. In particular, they sought to relieve railroads from the need to contend with unfriendly state courts in cases involving foreclosure, receivership, taxation, and even injuries to person and property—an objective which Populists came to criticize. In the *Pacific Railroad Removal Cases* (1885) the Supreme Court read the new jurisdictional grant so expansively that in 1887 Congress increased the jurisdictional amount, eliminated removal by plaintiffs, and insulated from APPEAL federal court orders remanding removed cases to the state courts.

The chief long-term significance of the 1875 act was its establishment of a generalized federal question jurisdiction—the jurisdiction that is seen today as the federal courts' indispensable function. In FELIX FRANKFURTER's words, in 1875 the lower federal courts "ceased to be restricted tribunals of fair dealing between citizens of different states and became the primary and powerful reliances for vindicating every right given by the Constitution, the laws, and treaties of the United States."

KENNETH L. KARST
(1986)

Bibliography
CHADBOURN, JAMES H. and LEVIN, LEO   1942   Original Jurisdiction of Federal Questions. *University of Pennsylvania Law Review* 90:639–674.
FRANKFURTER, FELIX and LANDIS, JAMES M.   1928   *The Business of the Supreme Court.* Pages 64–69. New York: Macmillan.

JUDICIARY ACT OF 1891

See: Circuit Courts of Appeals Act

JUDICIARY ACT OF 1911

See: Judicial Code

JUDICIARY ACT OF 1925
43 Stat. 936 (1925)

The Supreme Court's desire to reduce the burden of postwar litigation reaching its docket, combined with Chief Justice WILLIAM HOWARD TAFT's aggressive program of reform, resulted in the Judiciary Act of 1925. As litigation increased, efforts to expand the Court's discretionary control over its JURISDICTION—begun in the CIRCUIT COURTS OF APPEALS ACT of 1891—gained favor. Taft took the administrative functions of the Chief Justiceship seriously and sponsored a three-man committee of justices charged with formulating a detailed plan to regulate the Court's workload. The eventual proposal, framed mainly by Justice WILLIS VAN DEVANTER, entailed what Professor FELIX FRANKFURTER would later describe as a "drastic transfer of existing Supreme Court business to the circuit courts of appeal." This draft bill was submitted to Congress in 1922. The patchwork appearance of existing national legislation regulating the federal judiciary had prompted confusion and delay, and Taft, testifying in favor of the bill, applauded its "revision and restatement—a bringing together in a harmonious whole" of the earlier "wilderness of statutes." After three years of inaction, Congress finally passed the "Judges' Bill" in early 1925.

The new act reorganized the Court's APPELLATE JURISDICTION, allowing it to center its energies on constitutionally or nationally significant issues. Henceforth, cases would reach the Court from three avenues. Some district court decisions would go directly to the Supreme Court, but most would be shunted to the circuit courts of appeals. Among those exceptional cases that could be directly appealed because of their national importance were those arising under INTERSTATE COMMERCE or antitrust statutes, suits to enjoin enforcement of either ICC orders or state laws, and appeals by the federal government in criminal cases. Review of circuit courts of appeals' decisions was made largely discretionary; unless the Court chose to examine such a case by means of a WRIT OF CERTIORARI, most circuit decisions would be final. This provision thus superseded some of the reforms enacted in the 1891 legislation. Only two kinds of cases might be appealed directly from state courts: where a state law had been sustained against federal constitutional attack or where the state court had voided a federal law or treaty. Although the act left some problems unsolved, it successfully abated the flood of cases inundating the Court.

DAVID GORDON
(1986)

Bibliography

FRANKFURTER, FELIX and LANDIS, JAMES M. 1927 *The Business of the Supreme Court.* New York: Macmillan.

JUDICIARY ACTS OF 1802
2 Stat. 132, 2 Stat. 156 (1802)

Gloating Federalists declared that the JUDICIARY ACT OF 1801 was as valuable for their party as an election victory. The appointment of only Federalists to the new circuit judgeships, the attempt by a new circuit court to get a

Jeffersonian editor indicted for SEDITIOUS LIBEL, and the issuance in 1801 of the show cause order in MARBURY V. MADISON (1803) convinced President THOMAS JEFFERSON's administration that the Federalists meant to continue party warfare against them from the bench. Republicans also opposed the expanded JURISDICTION OF THE FEDERAL COURTS; they wanted litigants to remain primarily dependent on state courts and the United States as dependent as possible on the states for the execution of its laws. The upshot was the repeal of even the constructive reforms of 1801.

Federalists in Congress argued that repeal would subvert the independence of the judiciary and was unconstitutional because the circuit judges had tenure during good behavior. The Republicans answered that the Constitution empowered Congress to establish and therefore to abolish inferior federal courts. The debate on the repealer triggered a prolonged congressional discussion on national JUDICIAL REVIEW. Federalists supported the power of the Supreme Court to hold acts of Congress unconstitutional, while Republicans assaulted judicial review as an undemocratic judicial usurpation, a violation of SEPARATION OF POWERS, and a subversion of LIMITED GOVERNMENT. The only proper check on the popularity elected and politically responsible branches of the national government, Republicans argued, was the outcome of elections. Chief Justice JOHN MARSHALL's opinion in *Marbury* was the Federalist reply from the bench.

Apprehensive about the possibility that the Supreme Court might declare the repealer unconstitutional, Congress passed another judiciary act which abolished the August term of the Court. By fixing one term a year, to be held in February, Congress managed to postpone the next meeting of the Court for fourteen months, allowing a cooling-off period, during which time the Justices could resume their circuit duties. They did, and in STUART V. LAIRD (1803) they sustained the power of Congress to assign them to circuit work. The Judiciary Act of 1802 also increased the number of circuits from three to six. Until the Reconstruction period, the federal judicial system remained basically unchanged after 1802.

LEONARD W. LEVY
(1986)

Bibliography

ELLIS, RICHARD E. 1971 *The Jeffersonian Crisis: Courts and Politics in the Young Republic.* Pages 4–60. New York: Oxford University Press.

JUDICIARY REFORM ACT
50 Stat. 751 (1937)

This act, a remnant of President FRANKLIN D. ROOSEVELT's court-packing proposal, provided that "whenever the constitutionality of any Act of Congress affecting the public interest is drawn in question in any court of the United States . . . the court shall permit the United States to intervene and become a party." The act further provided for direct APPEAL to the Supreme Court when a lower court held a congressional act unconstitutional in a case to which the United States or a federal officer was a party. Moreover, such appeals were to be expedited on the Court's calendar.

The act also forbade the issuance by any district court of an INJUNCTION suspending enforcement of an act of Congress upon constitutional grounds, unless approved by a specifically convened THREE-JUDGE COURT. (A single judge might grant temporary injunctive relief to prevent "irreparable loss" to a petitioner.) The three-judge court's grant or denial of an injunction was directly appealable to the Supreme Court. The remainder of the act amended the JUDICIAL CODE to provide a replacement when a district court judge was unable to perform his work. The constitutionality of the act was never challenged; although the three-judge court requirement was largely repealed in 1976, other sections are still good law.

DAVID GORDON
(1986)

JULIAN, GEORGE
(1817–1899)

An Indiana abolitionist, lawyer, and congressman (1849–1851; 1861–1871), George Washington Julian was an early advocate of emancipation under the government's WAR POWERS. In 1862 he guided the HOMESTEAD ACT through Congress. Julian advocated confiscation of rebel lands and black suffrage. In 1867 he was a member of the committee of seven which drew up ARTICLES OF IMPEACHMENT against President ANDREW JOHNSON. In 1868 he introduced a constitutional amendment that would have granted women's suffrage. After 1871 Julian became a liberal Republican and then a radical Democrat. He published much, including his political memoirs (1884) and a biography of his father-in-law, Congressman Joshua R. Giddings (1892).

PAUL FINKELMAN
(1986)

Bibliography

JULIAN, GEORGE W. 1884 Political Reflections, 1840–1872. Chicago: Jansen, McClurg & Co.

JULLIARD v. GREENMAN

See: Legal Tender Cases

JUREK v. TEXAS

See: Capital Punishment Cases of 1976

JURISDICTION

Jurisdiction is a magical and protean term. In American law it refers to the power of legislatures, the competence of courts to deal with certain types of cases, the allocation of cases between state and federal courts, the power of both state and federal courts over defendants who have only peripheral attachments to the locale of the court, and the territory in which a unit of government exercises its power. Not surprisingly the word shifts its meanings as it moves among these quite different tasks.

The term's confusing spread of meanings has its roots in the English medieval experience. What modern observers would think of as political power accompanied the grant of property; the landlord was lord of more than land; he exercised powers of justice over the people who tilled that soil. Yet that jurisdiction also had limits: above it stood the powers of the monarch, who at least in theory had the power and responsibility to see that the lords rendered justice. Thus the word emerged from the Middle Ages carrying several meanings: the power to make law, the power to adjudicate cases, and, loosely, the territory within which that power was exercised.

We use all three senses today. We speak, for example, of legislative jurisdiction, meaning legislative power, generally allocated by state and federal constitutions. Thus the earliest opinion of the Supreme Court applying the limits of SUBSTANTIVE DUE PROCESS to state economic regulation, in Allegeyer v. Louisiana (1897), said that the state had exceeded its territorial jurisdiction. Territorial considerations aside, any decision holding a law unconstitutional can be described as a holding that the legislative body has transgressed the limits of its jurisdiction—its lawful authority. The courts have employed this rhetoric especially in defining a state's jurisdiction to tax.

We use the extended, territorial sense of the term when we write of a fugitive's having fled a jurisdiction, or when lawyers ask about which jurisdiction's law applies. Article IV, section 3, of the Constitution uses the term in this sense when it prohibits creation of a new state within the jurisdiction of an existing state without the latter's consent.

The most distinctively legal, though not exclusively constitutional, sense of the term refers to the authority of a court to decide a matter or to issue an order—its subject matter jurisdiction. Some state courts are courts of so-called general jurisdiction, competent to decide all cases within the ordinary bounds of the law. Other state courts are courts of limited jurisdiction, empowered only to decide specified types of cases or to grant only specified forms of relief. A municipal court, for example, may have jurisdiction to award damages only up to a limited dollar amount and may have no jurisdiction at all to grant an INJUNCTION.

In constitutional law jurisdiction has two special meanings, both involving civil cases. One flows from the limitation of the subject matter jurisdiction of the federal constitutional courts in Article III of the Constitution; the other grows from the due process clauses of the Fifth and FOURTEENTH AMENDMENTS.

Fundamental to the constitutional scheme is the proposition that each branch of the federal government must share powers and observe limits not only in regard to the other two branches of government but also in regard to the states. Article III and many statutes thus limit the subject matter jurisdiction of the federal courts to certain types of cases; that article, for example, ordinarily would prohibit a federal court from deciding a case between two citizens of the same state in which no question of federal or maritime law was involved. Because the limitations of Article III describe a fundamental division of authority between state and federal governments, the federal courts have been scrupulous, some would say zealous, not to overstep those subject matter boundaries. Thus even though no party to a lawsuit evinces the least concern about it, a federal court has an independent duty to investigate the basis for its subject matter jurisdiction and to dismiss the suit if jurisdiction is lacking. Such dismissals, like the jurisdictional rules that require them, protect the interests of the state court systems, to which the litigation must go if the federal courts cannot hear it.

The Constitution also limits the powers of the federal government and the states over individual citizens. State courts, for example, must observe a limitation that flows from the Fourteenth Amendment's due process clause. Since *Pennoyer v. Neff* (1878) the Supreme Court has insisted that, regardless of the kind of case involved, the defendant have some connection with the state in which the suit occurs. Over the past century the Court has remolded the basis and expanded the range of personal jurisdiction—changes that, some have suggested, have come in response to an increasingly mobile population and an economy increasingly national in scope. The Court has sometimes based the requirement of personal jurisdiction on the state's lack of power over persons not within its borders—thus harking back to the territorial sense of the term; more recently it has tended to speak less of territorial power and more of unfair inconvenience to a defendant forced to litigate in a distant forum. Whether it has grounded the requirements in FEDERALISM or in fairness to the defendant, however, the Court has insisted that such connections exist in order for a judgment of a court to be entitled to FULL FAITH AND CREDIT.

Whether similar constitutional restrictions on personal jurisdiction apply to federal courts is a more obscure matter. Because the federal government is sovereign throughout the United States, notions of geographical territoriality play no role, and only the inconvenience to the defendant would be at issue in such a case. In a number of instances involving the national economy, such as federal securities law cases, Congress has provided for nationwide personal jurisdiction in the federal courts, and such grants of power have been upheld, presumably because any harm to the defendant is outweighed by the need for a nationally available system of courts supervising the national economy. The outer limits of congressional power have not been tested, for in most cases either venue statutes (controlling the districts in which civil suits may be brought) or the FEDERAL RULES OF CIVIL PROCEDURE limit federal courts to essentially the same reach of personal jurisdiction that a state court would have.

Unlike subject matter jurisdiction, personal jurisdiction can be waived by those entitled to its protection: the Supreme Court has repeatedly held that either by prior agreement or by the simple failure to raise the issue at an early stage of litigation defendants may lose their opportunity to challenge the court's power to decide the case. COLLATERAL ATTACK on a judgment on the ground that the court lacked personal jurisdiction is available only to a defendant who did not appear in the original suit.

Article III's limits on the subject matter jurisdiction of federal courts allocate cases as between state and federal courts; the due process limitations in personal jurisdiction allocate cases between a court, either state or federal, in a particular place and courts in other places more convenient to the defendant. Though both doctrines in their more technical aspects are quintessential lawyer's law, their roots lie in the Constitution's allocations of governmental power and in a tradition of individualism. The same origins underlie the idea of jurisdiction as the limitations on the power of various branches of government. Ultimately all the uses of "jurisdiction" derive from the medieval Western tradition that distinguished between power and justice, making the ability to dispense the latter a function of allocations of the former.

STEPHEN C. YEAZELL
(1986)

Bibliography

BATOR, PAUL M. et al. 1973 *Hart and Wechsler's The Federal Courts and the Federal System.* Mineoloa, N.Y.: Foundation Press.

HAZARD, GEOFFREY C. 1965 A General Theory of State-Court Jurisdiction. *Supreme Court Review* 1965:241–289.

MECHREN, ARTHUR T. VON, and TRAUTMAN, DONALD 1966 Jurisdiction to Adjudicate: A Suggested Analysis. *Harvard Law Review* 79:1121–1179.

JURISDICTION, FEDERAL

As ALEXANDER HAMILTON stressed in THE FEDERALIST #78, the power and obligation of federal judges to measure the conduct of public officials and bodies against the precepts of the Constitution mean that federal courts must sometimes act to thwart these officials and bodies. On occasion this is, at least in some quarters, a very unpopular enterprise. From time to time, Congress has entertained the possibility of responding to controversial decisions by the Supreme Court or the lower federal courts by strategically removing the JURISDICTION of part or all of the federal judiciary over the controverted matters.

Proposals of this sort raise the important and sensitive question of whether the lower federal courts and, possibly, even the Supreme Court, ultimately act at the sufferance of Congress or whether the Constitution secures the existence of an independent federal judicial voice. Article III of the Constitution, which provides for the establishment of the federal judiciary, invites rather than stills speculation on this fundamental question of institutional structure. The first sentence of Article III provides: "The judicial power of the United States, shall be vested in one supreme Court, and in such inferior Courts as the Congress may from time to time ordain and establish." Following this is the provision without which Hamilton felt the Constitution would have been "inexcusably defective": "The Judges, both of the supreme and inferior Courts, shall hold their Offices during GOOD BEHAVIOR, and shall, at stated Times, receive for their Services a Compensation, which shall not be diminished during their Continuance in Office."

Section 2 of Article III begins with a menu of matters over which the judicial power "shall extend." Nine categories are delineated. The first three are styled as classes of "cases," the most important being cases "arising under this Constitution, the Laws of the United States, and treaties." The remaining six are styled as classes o "controversies," the most prominent being controversies "between Citizens of different States." Section 2 then specifies two narrow classes of cases over which the Supreme Court has ORIGINAL JURISDICTION and concludes with the following stipulation: "In all the other Cases before mentioned, the supreme Court shall have APPELLATE JURISDICTION, both as to Law and Fact, with such Exceptions, and under such Regulations as the Congress shall make."

Remarkably, there is no well-settled understanding of the scope of Congress's authority under these provisions to restrict federal jurisdiction. Cooler and more responsible heads have usually prevailed in Congress when "court-stripping" proposals have been floated, and the Supreme Court has been carefully diplomatic in sounding deference to Congress when it can afford to do so; as a result, there is little authority on the question. Most of the Court's pertinent statements have been by way of broad OBITER DICTUM and have been Janus-faced. Broad statements welcoming Congress's plenary license to sculpt federal jurisdiction have been balanced by the Court's insistence that the very fabric of national union depends on the existence of final federal judicial authority over legal affairs.

The two most prominent cases in this area both grew out of the CIVIL WAR. In EX PARTE MCCARDLE (1869) the Court faced jurisdiction-limiting legislation plainly intended to protect Reconstruction LEGISLATION from constitutional invalidation. Although the legislation gestured at pushing the Court aside, it only touched one statutory basis of the Court's appellate jurisdiction, leaving—as the Court itself pointedly observed—another statutory route to the same end. With an angry and somewhat dangerous Congress in the wings and with little at stake for the moment, the Court gave broad deference to Congress's power to reduce its appellate jurisdiction. Three years later, in an attempt to prevent the presidential pardon of supporters of the Confederacy from entitling them to compensation for property lost during the hostilities, Congress denied the federal courts jurisdiction over property claims that depended on presidential pardon. In *United States v. Klein* (1872) the Court promptly struck down this law as a means to the unconstitutional end of interfering with the President's authority to grant pardons and as an unconstitutional attempt to dictate how federal courts otherwise seized with jurisdiction should decide cases. Most commentators are skeptical about the applicability of either the generous tone of *McCardle* or the special circumstances of *Klein* to modern court-stripping issues.

A few propositions are reasonably clear. In one sense, the lower federal courts do indeed exist at the sufferance of Congress. Although there is some scholarly dissent, most commentators agree that Congress was not obliged to create the lower federal courts at all and could disband them today. Most also agree that when Congress does establish lower courts it need not give them all or any particular part of the jurisdiction enumerated in Article III. Events at the CONSTITUTIONAL CONVENTION OF 1787 support the conclusion that the Framers intended to resolve their sharp division over what form, if any, the lower federal judiciary should assume by leaving the matter for congressional resolution, and the first sentence of Article III plainly executes this compromise. Although it is logically possible to hold that Congress must give all of the federal judicial power to any lower federal court it creates, such an inflexible view seems arbitrary and at odds with the idea of remanding the shape of the lower federal courts to the judgment of Congress in the first place. Congress has never given all of Article III jurisdiction to the lower federal courts, and the Supreme Court, from *Sheldon v. Sill* (1850) forward, has firmly assumed that Congress can order à la carte from the Article III menu.

Sheldon v. Sill can be read to say that Congress can choose any package of lower-court jurisdiction it likes, as long as the bounds of Article III jurisdiction are not exceeded. But this is surely not the case. Were Congress to parse access to civil plaintiffs on the ground of their religion or political affiliation, for example, the FIRST AMENDMENT would surely be violated. A diversity case with no pertinent wrinkles, *Sheldon* reliably stands only as a negation of the binary view of congressional authority over the lower federal courts.

With respect to the Supreme Court, once it is observed that the first sentence of Article III clearly contemplates the existence of a Supreme Court with some modicum of jurisdiction, the textual focus shifts to the last sentence of Article III: "In all the other Cases before mentioned, the supreme Court shall have appellate Jurisdiction, both as to Law and Fact, with such Exceptions, and under such Regulations as the Congress shall make." Most commentators agree that Congress's authority under this provision includes the power to remove some Article III CASES or CONTROVERSIES from the appellate jurisdiction of the Supreme Court. Congress has always kept some classes of cases from the Supreme Court, and the Court consistently has endorsed this reading of the exceptions language. Substantial housekeeping concerns support this institutional consensus. Some Article III matters have seemed unnecessary or even inappropriate candidates for the Court's appellate jurisdiction, such as controversies between citizens of different states that have been fully adjudicated in the courts of one of the states.

But beyond the propositions that the Supreme Court must have some jurisdiction and that Congress can take some cases out of the Court's appellate jurisdiction, little is clear, and much remains open to scholarly reflection. The orthodox view among legal scholars has been very generous to Congress. As long as Congress leaves the jurisdiction of state courts intact, avoids patent constitutional problems such as selecting plaintiffs on the basis of their religious beliefs, and avoids untoward interference with the federal courts that do have jurisdiction, the orthodox view licenses Congress to tailor federal jurisdiction, including that of the Supreme Court, as it pleases. On this view, for example, Congress could respond to decisions by the Supreme Court that extended the protections of the First Amendment to the burning of the American flag by depriving the entire federal judiciary of jurisdiction over FLAG DESECRATION cases. Most, if not all, of the scholars who hold this view—their ranks have included Paul Bator, Charles Black, Gerald Gunther, Michael Perry, and Herbert Wechsler—would deplore such an event, and they would urge Congress not to trifle with the federal judiciary in this fashion. But the orthodox view rests on the unshakable conviction that the first section of Article III gives Congress unlimited plenary authority over the Supreme Court. For some, this reading of the Constitution has been a cause for regret; but others have seen an important institutional virtue in the federal judiciary's vulnerability to such treatment. Charles Black and Michael Perry, for example, have urged that Congress's power to silence the federal, when not exercised, supports the claim that Congress has acquiesced in the general run of the courts' decisions and, hence, lends democratic legitimacy to these nonmajoritarion tribunals.

A revisionist strand of Article III scholarship has developed, arguing for substantial constitutional restraints on Congress's power to shape federal jurisdiction. The claims for such restraints group around two propositions: first, that the Constitution secures a core function for the federal judiciary against congressional interference; and second, that Congress cannot act to reduce federal jurisdiction selectively out of manifest hostility to federal judicial doctrine.

Henry Hart, in a famous written dialogue on Congress's jurisdiction-limiting authority, first argued that there was an essential role of the Supreme Court that Congress could not constitutionally impair. Leonard Ratner has given more concrete content and support to what is called the "essential functions" thesis, arguing that the demands of supremacy and uniformity require that the Supreme Court be available to review all matters of federal legal substance. Although lacking in explicit textual support in its Hart-Ratner form, the essential-functions thesis can draw support from the commitment of the Constitutional Convention and its product, the Constitution, to subordinate the states to federal authority and to do so through the federal judicial process. In some of its variations, the thesis can also draw support from congressional precedent: in the course of two centuries of meandering Supreme Court appellate jurisdiction, the Court has always been permitted jurisdiction to review unrequited claims of constitutional right against state and local conduct.

A structurally distinct form of the essential-functions thesis has also emerged, attached not to the Supreme Court alone but to the Article III federal judiciary as a whole. The claim is that there are certain matters for which *some* Article III court must be provided. Only in default of Congress's having provided a lower federal court with jurisdiction over these matters does the Constitution require that the Supreme Court be available to them. Although given modern voice in the past decade, this appears to have been Alexander Hamilton's view, as reflected in *The Federalist* #82, and is familially related to Justice JOSEPH STORY's views in MARTIN V. HUNTER'S LESSEE (1816). The scholars who have been attracted to this version of the essential-functions thesis have regarded it as better supported by legally relevant materials. This author, in the first modern statement of this form of the essential-functions thesis, has argued that Article III's textually explicit commitment to an independent judiciary can be honored only if politically sensitive cases—those involving claims of constitutional right being the strongest possible candidates—are assured review in an Article III forum. Robert Clinton has argued from a close analysis of events at the Constitutional Convention that the Framers intended to oblige Congress to distribute all Article III jurisdiction among the federal courts and used the "exceptions and regulations" language only to permit Congress to distribute Article III matters among Article III courts. Akhil Amar, observing, in effect, that every instance of the word "cases" in Article III is modified by a preceding "all," has argued that the first three items on the Article III menu—those styled as categories of "cases"—are textually required to be assigned to some Article III court.

The alternative revisionist claim, that Congress cannot act to reduce federal jurisdiction selectively out of manifest hostility to federal judicial doctrine, has been advanced on a number of connected grounds. Laurence Tribe has borrowed equal-protection analysis from the HUNTER V. ERICKSON (1969) tradition to argue that it is unconstitutional for Congress to burden the exercise of particular constitutional rights by depriving those who claim such rights the benefits of a federal forum. John Hart Ely has argued that the motive of Congress in such cases—hostility to federal judicial doctrine—is impermissible and can serve to invalidate selective removals of jurisdiction. This author has argued that some selective deprivations of jurisdiction carry the appearance of congressional hostility to controversial constitutional claims, invite the disregard of those claims, and are for that reason unconstitutional.

Although the best possible protection against untoward congressional manipulation of federal jurisdiction is the sound judgment of Congress, there is a growing, but still much disputed, view among academic commentators that the Constitution protects against a lapse of congressional responsibility here as elsewhere.

LAWRENCE G. SAGER
(1992)

Bibliography

AMAR, AKHIL 1985 A Neo-Federalist View of Article III: Separating the Two Tiers of Federal Jurisdiction. *Boston University Law Review* 65:205–272.

BATOR, PAUL M. 1982 Congressional Power over the Jurisdiction of Federal Courts. *Villanova Law Review* 27:1030–1041.

CLINTON, ROBERT L. 1984 A Mandatory View of Federal Court Jurisdiction: A Guided Quest for the Original Understanding. *University of Pennsylvania Law Review* 132:741–866.

EISENBERG, THEODORE 1974 Congressional Authority to Restrict Lower Federal Court Jurisdiction. *Yale Law Journal* 83:498–533.

GUNTHER, GERALD 1984 Congressional Power to Curtail Federal Court Jurisdiction: An Opinionated Guide to the Ongoing Debate. *Stanford Law Review* 36:895–922.

HART, HENRY M., JR. 1953 The Power of Congress to Limit the Jurisdiction of Federal Courts: An Exercise in Dialectic. *Harvard Law Review* 66:1362–1402.

REDISH, MARTIN H. and WOODS, CURTIS E. 1975 Congressional Power to Control the Jurisdiction of Lower Federal Courts: A Critical Review and a New Synthesis. *University of Pennsylvania Law Review* 124:45–109.

SAGER, LAWRENCE GENE 1981 Foreword: Constitutional Limitations on Congress' Authority to Regulate the Jurisdiction of the Federal Courts. *Harvard Law Review* 16:129–156.

TRIBE, LAURENCE H. 1981 Jurisdictional Gerrymandering: Zoning Disfavored Rights Out of the Federal Courts. *Harvard Civil Rights-Civil Liberties Law Review* 16:129–156.

WECHSLER, HERBERT 1965 The Courts and the Constitution. *Columbia Law Review* 65:1001–1014.

JURISDICTION, FEDERAL
(Update)

In the 1990s, there have been two notable statutes, and one bill not yet enacted, regulating the jurisdiction of the federal courts to accomplish particular policy goals.

The ANTITERRORISM AND EFFECTIVE DEATH PENALTY ACT OF 1996 cuts back federal HABEAS CORPUS for state prisoners and limits JUDICIAL REVIEW in deportation proceedings against ALIENS. In habeas cases, the act limits the APPELLATE JURISDICTION of the Supreme Court. A prisoner whose first habeas petition has been denied may file a second petition only if authorized to do so by the court of appeals, and a denial of authorization may not be appealed to the Supreme Court. In *Felker v. Turpin* (1996), the Supreme Court upheld the constitutionality of this provision, finding that the act had not entirely eliminated review because the prisoner still had a right to file an original habeas petition in the Supreme Court. This construction of the act allowed the Supreme Court to avoid the constitutional question that would have been presented if Supreme Court review had been entirely foreclosed. In deportation

that a society of this sort would be deeply unjust—they still might resist a constitutional right to sexual independence on grounds of procedural fairness. They might say that democracy is the only acceptable form of government, and that it is undemocratic to use a constitution to prevent the majority from having the law it thinks best, even when the majority is profoundly wrong. This last claim—that individual constitutional rights are undemocratic—is one of the two most widely discussed issues of foundational constitutional jurisprudence in America and will be discussed further.

The second, interpretive part of constitutional jurisprudence considers issues closer to those of traditional jurisprudence and also closer to constitutional legal practice. It asks not what constitution would be ideal but what constitution we actually have, both in general and in detail. The central question of interpretive jurisprudence is a methodological one. It is only indirectly concerned with the right answer to the substantive questions the Supreme Court must eventually decide, like the question as to how far the Constitution as it stands, properly interpreted, now grants individuals constitutional rights to free speech, abortion, or economic protection. Interpretive jurisprudence is concerned, rather, with the strategies of investigation and argument that should be used to answer these questions.

The clauses of the Constitution that grant individual rights are drafted in very abstract language. The FOURTEENTH AMENDMENT, for example, says that no state may deny DUE PROCESS OF LAW or EQUAL PROTECTION OF THE LAW. How should lawyers and judges decide whether the legal effect of that language is to create a constitutional right for blacks to attend integrated rather than segregated schools, for whites to resist AFFIRMATIVE ACTION, or for a woman to have an abortion when she and her doctor believe it necessary or desirable? One answer, which is particularly popular among conservative politicians, insists that CONSTITUTIONAL INTERPRETATION can only be a matter of discovering and respecting the wishes of those who made the Constitution, who are often called, compendiously, the "Framers." Did the framers of the Fourteenth Amendment intend blacks (or whites or women) to have such a constitutional right? If so, then the correct interpretation of the amendment's legal force includes that right; but if not, then it does not.

The question as to whether this ORIGINAL INTENT method of constitutional interpretation is appropriate is the second of the two most debated issues of constitutional jurisprudence and will be further discussed. Two other answers to the methological question as to how the abstract language of the Constitution should be interpreted each have support among constitutional lawyers and teachers. "Passivism" holds that when the language of the Constitution is abstract or its legal effect is for another reason unclear or debatable, then it should be interpreted to interfere least with the power of state or national legislators or other political officials to do what they think best for the community. Passivism presupposes the foundational thesis that individual constitutional rights are in principle antidemocratic. It therefore acts to shrink the scope of such rights whenever possible.

The method of "integrity" presupposes a very different interpretive attitude: the Constitution is not just a set of discrete political decisions allocating power in different ways but a system of principle. It therefore insists that each of the abstract clauses and provisions should be interpreted and applied in a way that makes it coherent in principle with accepted interpretations of other parts of the Constitution and with principles of political morality that provide the best available foundational justification for the constitutional structure as a whole.

This brief and schematic discussion illustrates the inevitable interconnections between foundational and interpretive issues. Although the original-understanding method denies that foundational morality should figure prominently in constitutional interpretation, it cannot be applied without relying on controversial foundational positions, as will be discussed. The passivist method presupposes a contoversial foundational position about the conflict between CONSTITUTIONALISM and democracy, and the method of integrity insists that foundational morality must play an overt, although limited, role in detailed constitutional interpretation.

The Constitution contains both structural and disabling provisions. The structural provisions describe the various branches of the national government, provide methods for electing or selecting their members, and define the powers of these institutions and officials vis-à-vis the institutions and officials of the various states. These structural provisions constitute the American form of democracy; they create government by the people. In contrast, the disabling provisions of the BILL OF RIGHTS and the Civil War amendments, like the FIRST AMENDMENT and the due process clause and the equal protection clause, set limits to the overall authority of elected officials. Many lawyers and politicans believe these provisions impede government by the people and are undemocratic for that reason.

Some who take this view regard this friction as a cardinal defect of our constitutional system. They argue that the antidemocratic provisions should be narrowly interpreted to give individuals as few trumps over majority decision as possible. Other lawyers who agree that the disabling provisions are antidemocratic do not agree this is a cause for regret; they believe that a limited democracy is superior to a pure one simply because the former respects individual rights. Is the assumption both these views share—that the Constitution impedes as well as creates democracy—correct? This depends on what we take democracy to be.

Democracy is collective government by the people. But which sense of collective is meant? There are two kinds of collective actions—statistical and communal—and our conception of democracy will turn on which kind we take democratic government to require. Collective action is statistical when what the group does is only a matter of some function—rough or specific—of what the individual members of the group do on their own, that is, with no sense of doing something as a group. In contrast, collective action is communal, when it cannot be reduced to some statistical function of individual action because it is collective in the deeper sense that requires individuals to assume the existence of the group as a separate entity or phenomenon. An orchestra can play a symphony, although a single musician cannot. This is a case of communal rather than statistical action because it is essential to an orchestral performance, not just that a specified function of musicians each plays some appropriate score, but that the musicians play *as* an orchestra, each intending to make a contribution to the performance of the group and not just as isolated individual recitations.

On the statistical understanding, democracy is government according to the wishes of a majority or at least a plurality of the eligible voters. Under communal understanding, democracy is government by distinct entity— the people as such—rather than any set of individuals one by one. These two conceptions of democracy take different views of the distinction previously drawn between the structural and disabling provisions of the Constitution. By the statistical reading, structural provisions are mainly limited to those that are procedurally structural—those that define how members of Congress are elected, what proportion of them it takes to enact legislation, and so forth. By the communal conception, the structural provisions include not only those that are procedurally structural in these ways but also provisions needed to create a genuine political community that can be understood to be acting as a collective unit of political responsibility. A genuine community is one in which government is not only of and for the majority, but of and for all the people, and a genuine community will therefore need to insure not only that each citizen have an opportunity to participate in political decisions through a vote, but that each decision allows each citizen equal concern and respect.

Several of the apparently disabling constitutional provisions can be understood as necessary to guarantee equal respect and concern and, therefore, to be functionally structural rather than disabling of democracy understood by the communal conception. The First Amendment guarantee of free speech, for example, might be thought nec-essary not only to full and equal participation, but to equal respect as well, and the equal protection clause can be interpreted as requiring equality of concern for all citizens in the deliberations that produce political decisions. Thus, the foundational question of constitutional jurisprudence—whether and how far the Constitution is undemocratic—is actually a deep question that draws on the most fundamental parts of moral and POLITICAL PHILOSOPHY.

But how should lawyers and judges decide whether some state or statute violates the requirement that states follow "due" process, deny no one the "equal" protection of the laws, or avoid punishments that are cruel and unusual? The original-understanding thesis insists that abstract constitutional provisions should be interpreted to have only the force that the Framers intended or expected them to have. Although this thesis has generally been rejected in Supreme Court practice, lawyers and politicians have offered various arguments in its support. Some say, for example, that because the Framers were the people whose decision made the Constitution our FUNDAMENTAL LAW, their convictions about its correct application should be respected.

We must recognize three points about this kind of argument, however. First, any such argument for the original-understanding thesis necessarily draws on normative assumptions about the proper allocation of authority in a democracy among remote constitutional architects, contemporary legislators, and past and contemporary judges. Second, these normative assumptions cannot be justified, without the most blatant and absurd circularity, by appealing to the intentions, wishes, or decisions of the people whose authority they propose to describe. It would absurd to argue that judges should respect the expectations of the Framers because the Framers expected that they would or believed or decided that they should.

The third point is particularly important: Such arguments, even if supported by independent normative assumptions, are radically incomplete if they purport to establish only the general proposition that lawyers and judges should respect the Framers' wishes or intentions. In most pertinent cases, the question at issue is not whether judges should respect the convictions of the Framers but which of their convictions judges should respect, and how. Suppose the following historical information is discovered: All the framers of the equal-protection clause believed, as a matter of political conviction, that people should all be equal in the eye of the law and the state. They were convinced that certain forms of official RACIAL DISCRIMINATION against blacks were morally wrong for that reason, and they adopted the amendment mainly to prevent states from discrimination against blacks in those ways. They agreed, for example, that it would be morally wrong for a state to create certain special remedies for breach of contract and make these remedies available to white plaintiffs, but not black ones. The framers assumed that the clause they were adopting would prohibit that form of discrimination.

They also shared certain opnions about which forms of official discrimination were not wrong and would not be prohibited by the clause. They shared the views, for example, that racial SEGREGATION of public schools did not violate the clause. (Many of them, in fact, voted to segregate schools.) None of them even considered the possibility that state institutions would one day adopt affirmative-action RACIAL QUOTAS designed to repair the damages of past segregation; therefore, none of them had any opinion about whether such quotas would violate the clause. Some of them thought that laws that discriminate in favor of men treat women unjustly. Most framers of the equal protection clause did not outlaw the gender-based distinctions then common. Most of them thought that homosexual acts were grossly immoral and would have been mystified by the suggestion that laws prohibiting such acts constituted an unjustified form of discrimination.

Many contemporary lawyers and judges think that some or all these concrete convictions are inconsistent with the framers' more abstract intention to establish a society of equal citizenship. Almost everyone now agrees, for example, that racially segregated schools are inconsistent with this ideal. Many people think that affirmative action is inconsistent with the ideal as well, and many people, although not necessarily the same people, think that laws that subordinate women or homosexuals violate the ideal. If a contemporary judge believes that the framers' concrete convictions were inconsistent with their abstract ones on one or more of these matters because the framers of the clause did not reach the correct conclusions about the moral consequences of their own principles, then that judge has a choice to make. It is unhelpful to tell him or her to follow the framers' intentions. The judge needs to know which intentions—at how general a level of abstraction—he or she should follow and why.

In other words, a judge can compose sharply different versions of the original understanding of the equal protection clause, each of which has support in the collection of framers' convictions and expectations. The judge might adopt a reductive version that emphasizes the framers' concrete opinions and hold that the clause condemns only the cases of discrimination that the framers of the clause collectively expected it to condemn. So understood, the clause forbids discrimination against blacks in legal remedy for breach of contract, but it does not forbid racially segregated schools, affirmative-action quotas that disadvantage whites, or discrimination against women or homosexuals. Or, the judge might adopt an abstract version of the original understanding that emphasizes the framers' general conviction to provide equal citizenship, properly understood, for all Americans. Under this version, if we assume that equality is in fact denied by school segregation, quota systems, or laws that subordinate people on the basis of gender or sexual orientation, the clause condemns these discriminations, despite what the framers themselves thought or would have approved.

The important choice judges and other interpreters of the Constitution must make, therefore, is not between the original understanding and some other method of interpretation but between reductive and abstract versions of the original understanding. Many proponents of the original-understanding method have not made this choice coherently; they believe the equal protection clause outlaws racial segregation and affirmative action quotas, but does not outlaw laws discriminating against women or homosexuals, for example. Lawyers and judges must not only choose between the reductive and abstract versions coherently but also on principle, that is, with adequate support in foundational jurisprudence. The passivist interpretive method, which supports the choice of reductive understanding of the framers' intention, is based on the statistical conception of democracy and, accordingly, fails if this conception is rejected. The method of integrity, which presupposes an abstract understanding, is based on a communal conception in which individual rights are not subversive, but constitutive of genuine democracy. Even at the practical level of adjudication, constitutional law is deeply embedded in political philosophy.

RONALD DWORKIN
(1992)

Bibliography

DWORKIN, RONALD 1985 *A Matter of Principle.* Cambridge, Mass.: Harvard University Press.
——— 1986 *Law's Empire.* Cambridge, Mass.: Belknap Press of Harvard University Press.
PERRY, MICHAEL J. 1988 *Morality, Politics, and Law.* New York: Oxford University Press.

JURORS AND THE FREEDOM OF SPEECH

See: Witnesses, Jurors, and the Freedom of Speech

JURY

See: Blue Ribbon Jury; Grand Jury; Petit Jury; Trial by Jury

JURY CHALLENGES

See: Peremptory Challenges

JURY DISCRIMINATION

Jury discrimination was first recognized as a constitutional problem shortly after the CIVIL WAR, when certain southern and border states excluded blacks from jury service. The Supreme Court had little difficulty in holding such blatant RACIAL DISCRIMINATION invalid as a denial of the EQUAL PROTECTION OF THE LAWS guaranteed by the recently adopted FOURTEENTH AMENDMENT. But, beyond such obvious improprieties, what should the principle of nondiscrimination forbid? Some kinds of "discrimination" in the selection of the jury are not bad but good: for example, those incompetent to serve ought to be excused from service, whether their incompetence arises from mental or physical defect, from demonstrably bad character, or from bias. No one has seriously argued that American jury service ought to be determined wholly by lot, as it was among the citizens of Athens. In addition, it has been the uniform policy of American jurisdictions to excuse from service some who are competent, but whose service would work a hardship on them or others: doctors, ministers, and parents who care for small children have been exempted from service on such grounds.

The history of the constitutional law regulating jury composition has been a story of expanding and compulsory democratization. In our early national history property and voting qualifications were common, and women were systematically excluded or exempted from jury service. At COMMON LAW, indeed, special juries were sometimes employed: a jury of merchants to decide certain kinds of mercantile questions, for example, or in the trial of an ALIEN, a jury half of which spoke his language. Even in the early and middle decades of this century, the Supreme Court upheld against constitutional attack a BLUE RIBBON JURY system, by which jurors were selected supposedly for intelligence and character in a way that resulted in the vast overrepresentation of professional and business classes, in *Fay v. New York* (1947); a highly discretionary and easily abused "key man" system for selecting potential jurors by consultation with community leaders, in SWAIN V. ALABAMA (1965); and the voluntary exemption of women from jury service, in *Hoyt v. Florida* (1961). At present, however, a federal statute requires that the federal jury be drawn from a pool that represents a "fair cross section of the community," and a similar constitutional standard has been imposed by the Supreme Court on the states as well, in TAYLOR V. LOUISIANA (1975).

There are normally three stages in the selection of an American jury at which improper discrimination may occur: the establishment of the master list of all persons eligible for jury service within the JURISDICTION of a particular court (this is called the jury roll); the selection of the panel of potential jurors (called the venire) who will be asked to appear at the courthouse; and the selection from that panel of those who will actually serve on a jury in a particular case or set of cases. The question of discrimination can arise in both civil and criminal cases, but the courts have paid far more attention to the criminal jury. Two distinct provisions of the Constitution of the United States bear upon jury selection: the equal protection clause of the Fourteenth Amendment and the SIXTH AMENDMENT.

In STRAUDER V. WEST VIRGINIA (1879) and NEAL V. DELAWARE (1880) the Court held that the equal protection clause forbade a state to try a black defendant by a jury from which members of his race had been affirmatively excluded, either by statute or by administrative practice. A federal statute passed shortly after the Civil War made such discrimination a crime.

In *Hernandez v. Texas* (1954), dealing with the exclusion of Mexican Americans, the Supreme Court extended the *Strauder* ruling to other ethnic groups. On the other hand, the Court has repeatedly said that the Constitution does not entitle a defendant to a jury that consists in whole or in part of members of his race, or of any other particular composition. The idea of the jury affirmed in these cases is not that it is a microcosm of society at large, but that it is an institution of justice for which participants may properly be required to be qualified. The equal protection clause does not guarantee a particular mix but protects only against improper exclusions.

What exclusions, beyond racial ones, are improper? In *Hernandez* the Court said that where any group in a community is systematically discriminated against it will need the protection of the Constitution, and added: "Whether such a group exists within a community is a question of fact. When the existence of a distinct class is demonstrated, and it is further shown that the laws, as written or as applied, single out that class for different treatment not based upon some reasonable classification, the guarantees of the Constitution have been violated." But what is a reasonable classification? This question is complicated by the fact that the law has traditionally imposed qualifications for jury service which may, or may not, have differential impact on racial or other protected groups. The Court has accordingly upheld, against equal protection attack, qualifications for jury service that are extremely vague and easily susceptible to abuse—"generally reputed to be honest and intelligent . . . esteemed in the community for their integrity, good character, and good judgment." The burden is on the defendant to show that such qualifications have in fact been abused. Generally speaking, racially disproportionate impact alone is not enough to invalidate a classification under the equal protection clause: actual intent to discriminate must be proved, by direct or circumstantial evidence, as the Court held in WASHINGTON V. DAVIS (1976). But in jury discrimination, proof of a substantial disproportionality in racial (or sexual) balance between the jury pool and the community at large constitutes a prima facie case of intentional discrimination which the government must rebut. (The Sixth Amendment is more protective than the equal protection clause, in those cases to which it applies, for it has no intent requirement, and the Court held in *Duren v. Missouri* (1979) that it not only prohibits discrimination but affirmatively requires that the pool from which the jury is drawn contain a "fair cross section" of the relevant community.)

Who may object to an improper exclusion? In *Peters v. Kiff* (1972), the Supreme Court held that any defendant is entitled to object to improper exclusions from the panel from which his jury is selected, whether or not he is a member of the excluded race. In addition, the Court held in *Carter v. Jury Commission of Greene County* (1976) that members of the excluded race who wish to serve on juries are entitled to bring independent proceedings to attack their exclusion, for they are deprived of equal protection with respect to an important right of CITIZENSHIP.

A separate source of constitutional restrictions on jury discrimination is the Sixth Amendment's guarantee of an "impartial jury" in criminal cases. DUNCAN V. LOUISIANA (1968) held that this provision, which originally applied only to the federal government, was "incorporated" within the Fourteenth Amendment's due process clause, and thus was applicable to the states as well. (See INCORPORATION DOCTRINE.) In *Taylor v. Louisiana* the Court held that the concept of the jury as a "fair cross section of the community" was at the core of the Sixth Amendment and thus applicable to the states. Thus exclusions will be tested not merely under the equal protection clause, which focuses on improper exclusions, but by the affirmative "cross section" principle. The latter principle conceives of the jury not as a group of citizens who are qualified for a task and chosen in a manner free from INVIDIOUS DISCRIMINATION, but as a body fairly chosen from a group that represents the community of which it is a part.

But what does "fairly chosen" mean? The federal statute requires that the jury roll reflect a fair cross section of the community, and that the venire be drawn at random from the roll; this scheme meets any standard of fairness. The courts might impose similar standards on the states. But there remains the crucial stage at which the particular jury panel is selected from the venire, and none of the rulings cited above speak to this matter. This selection is made just before trial in a process in which lawyers and the judge cooperate. Certain jurors are excused "for cause," that is, because there are good reasons why they should not sit in the particular case: admitted bias, acquaintance with one of the parties, and so on. In addition, the parties are allowed a limited number of discretionary, or "peremptory," challenges to other potential jurors. What happens if the prosecution should exercise its peremptory challenges to keep blacks or women off the jury? If that can be done with impunity, the insistence upon fairness at the other stages of jury selection becomes an empty ritual; but how can a discriminatory exercise of peremptory challenges be established? To require the prosecutor to accept any juror of a particular race or class would be unfair to the state, and upset the balance of the selection process. The Supreme Court held in *Swain v. Alabama* that the use of peremptory challenges against potential minority jurors is not always unconstitutional, but that systematic racial discrimination is impermissible under the equal protection clause. In *Batson v. Kentucky* (1986) the Court partially overruled *Swain*, holding that a prosecutor cannot constitutionally use peremptory challenges to exclude potential jurors solely on account of their race. If the circumstances raise an inference of such a use of peremptory challenges, the burden shifts to the state to provide "a neutral explanation" for the exclusions.

The effect of the antidiscrimination holdings has also been undercut by the Supreme Court's decision in APODACA V. OREGON (1972) that the states are not required to insist upon unanimous verdicts. (See JURY UNANIMITY.) Even if some members of a discriminated-against class make it to the jury, *Apodaca* means that their views can be disregarded by the majority. On the other hand, the proposition that jurors of the defendant's race or sex will be especially likely to vote for him is an assumption more easily made than proved, and arguably demeaning both to the jurors and to the class to which they belong. And even minority jurors who are outvoted will have a chance to have their views considered. The true basis of the fair cross-section requirement is assurance of the kind of diversity of view and experience that will most advance the kind of collective decision making that, as Harry Kalven and Hans Zeisel show, represents the jury at its best.

As for the distinct institution known as the GRAND JURY, which sits before trial to decide whether the evidence of a particular defendant's guilt is sufficient to justify his INDICTMENT, racial discrimination in its selection is also a violation of the equal protection clause. The indicted individual is entitled to the dismissal of his indictment, as the Court held in *Carter v. Texas* (1900), even though in some sense the defect may be thought to be cured by a properly composed trial jury. The Court has not applied the affirmative "fair cross section" requirements to the state grand jury, nor indeed, as the Court held in HURTADO

v. CALIFORNIA (1884), are the states required to employ the institution of the grand jury at all. Discrimination in the selection of state grand juries remains regulated by the equal protection clause, which forbids only intentional discrimination. The federal statute does apply the "fair cross section" requirement to federal grand juries as well as trial juries.

The continued existence of both the grand jury and the trial jury appears to rest on two assumptions. First, judicial decisions, especially in criminal cases, are assumed to be more just when they are not left to professionals but are also influenced by the views of ordinary people. Second, jury service—again, especially in the criminal process—is seen as popular participation in government. Our constitutional protections against discriminatory selection of jurors are aimed at promoting the ends of justice and the ideal of citizenship.

JAMES BOYD WHITE
(1986)

Bibliography

JUDICIAL CONFERENCE OF THE UNITED STATES 1961 The Jury System in the Federal Courts. *Federal Rules Decisions* 26: 411–504.

KALVEN, HARRY and ZEISEL, HANS 1966 *The American Jury.* Boston: Little, Brown.

LARUE, L. H. 1976 A Jury of One's Peers. *Washington & Lee Law Review* 33:841–876.

JURY DISCRIMINATION
(Update)

The problem of improper discrimination in the jury selection process was considered repeatedly by the Supreme Court throughout the 1990s. Since its decision in BATSON V. KENTUCKY (1986) involving race-based jury selection in criminal cases, the Court has decided a dozen or so cases involving claims that impermissible selection criteria have been used to constitute GRAND JURIES and, more commonly, PETIT JURIES. Most of the cases have focused on the PEREMPTORY CHALLENGE device, and the way in which it may be used by lawyers to remove members of disfavored groups from serving on petit juries. Certainly, most observers would agree that trail courts often find it difficult, if not impossible, to police lawyers' use of peremptories to ensure that an impermissible criterion such as race is not motivating challenges. For this reason, many have argued that the peremptory challenge device itself— which has historical but not constitutional foundation— should be abandoned as a prophylactic matter, to make good *Batson's* promise of racial equality in criminal jury decision-making. This prophylactic argument seems even more

forceful now that the Court, in *J. E. B. v. Alabama* (1994), has extended the reasoning of *Batson* to invalidate gender-based peremptories as well. As the Court is faced with challenges to more and more arguably impermissible criteria in the selection and constitution of juries, such as age, class, and SEXUAL ORIENTATION, the Court may have an increasingly harder time reconciling the peremptory challenge device with the inclusionary impulse that has characterized most of the Court's jurisprudence in the last half-century concerning access to political participation. The more the Court thinks and writes about JURY SERVICE AS A POLITICAL RIGHT, the more the Court will be constrained to hold various selection criteria to be impermissible, and the more vulnerable the practice of peremptories will become.

Two underdiscussed aspects of the modern jury exclusion cases are their STATE ACTION and STANDING analyses. As to state action, in *Batson* the race-based peremptories were exercised by a state prosecutor, so that government action was apparent. But what about peremptories exercised by private criminal defense counsel, or by plaintiffs' counsel and defense counsel in civil cases? The Court has found state action in all these circumstances, emphasizing that the trial judge—undoubtedly a state actor—is the person who formally implements the peremptory challenge, regardless of the private character of the lawyer who may initiate it. Perhaps more crucial is a recognition that picking jurors, like picking voters, is quintessentially a public function, so that the state cannot avoid constitutional constraints by delegating the selection process to private lawyers.

As to standing, the Court has held that litigants, regardless of their race, have third-party standing to assert the rights of excluded black would-be jurors. Behind these standing holdings is the idea that courts cannot presume that black jurors would be sympathetic to the interests of black litigants alone. On the one hand, this notion is in perfect keeping with the Court's emerging colorblind constitutional vision most forcefully articulated in the racial restricting cases such as SHAW V. RENO (1993) AND ITS PROGENY. In these cases, the Court has explicitly stated that government may not constitutionally presume that persons of one race will, because of their race, have any distinct viewpoint and exercise voting and other political power to support particular persons or political causes. On the other hand, a number of earlier lines of Court authority had suggested that racial minorities could be assumed to hold distinct political points of view, at least in the main. These earlier cases involved topics such as minority vote dilution, restructuring of political decision-making processes, and exclusion of women and blacks from juries. The modern Court's insistence that government not think nor act based on assumptions about racial minority group political attitudes is also in tension with the history of the FIFTEENTH AMENDMENT itself. The drafters and ratifiers of the Fifteenth Amendment assumed, expected, and indeed counted on the idea that, when it comes to political activity, voters, because of their race, would—to use the Court's words in *Shaw*—"think alike, share the same political interests, and prefer the same candidates at the polls." Whether the insistence of the REHNQUIST COURT on colorblindness is justifiable or not, the Court certainly has not adequately explained how its modern reasoning fits in with this constitutional tradition and history. When this tradition is taken into account, arguments could be made that not each and every instance of governmental RACE-CONSCIOUSNESS in the political-rights realm is equally constitutionally problematic.

VIKRAM D. AMAR
(2000)

(SEE ALSO: *Hunter v. Erickson; Voting Rights.*)

Bibliography

ABRAMSON, JEFFREY   1994   *We the Jury: The Jury System and the Ideal of Democracy.* New York: Basic Books.
AMAR, VIKRAM DAVID   1995   Jury Service as Political Participation Akin to Voting. *Cornell Law Review* 80:203–259.

JURY NULLIFICATION

Jury nullification occurs when the prosecutor convinces a jury beyond a REASONABLE DOUBT that the defendant committed the crime charged, but the jury nevertheless decides to acquit. Also called an "acquittal against the evidence," nullification represents a conclusion by the jurors that the literal application of the penal law would be inappropriate on the facts presented, and they thus effectively "nullify" the criminal law by refusing to convict.

There are many reasons a jury might nullify, but cases where the power is exercised generally fall into one of two groups. The first is when the jury decides that the law itself is unfair or unpopular, regardless of what the defendant has done. Juries have acquitted against the evidence when defendants were charged with minor vice crimes like gambling, liquor law violations, or other offenses that are sufficiently common or underenforced that a conviction of one offender seems unfair. Crimes that carry an especially harsh sentence are also candidates for nullification. The Supreme Court has recognized, for example, that when crimes carried a mandatory death penalty, some juries preferred to acquit a factually guilty defendant rather than impose CAPITAL PUNISHMENT. More recent examples include a refusal to convict a defendant accused of simple possession of drugs, where the prescribed punishment is severe and mandatory.

The second, and more common, group of cases is when the law itself is uncontroversial, but there is something about the defendant that makes an acquittal seem appropriately merciful. Cases where the defendant's motives seemed good, or where the defendant has already suffered great harm can result in nullification—a mercy killing, or a parent's negligent killing of his or her own child, for example. Other instances include cases in which the police officers or prosecutors seem to be overreaching in trying to convict a particular defendant, or in which the victim brought much of the harm on himself, as when an unarmed thief is shot by the defendant while fleeing the scene of a crime. In each of these cases, the jury is using its power to acquit to make a statement about the prosecutor's judgment in bringing this defendant to trial.

Jury nullification has a long but murky history. The practice has its roots in English COMMON LAW, where the rule gradually emerged that juries had a power to acquit that was beyond the judge's power to overrule. One English case often identified with the nullification power is the 1670 trial of WILLIAM PENN and William Mead, who were charged with disturbing the peace and unlawful assembly for holding a public meeting in defiance of the Anglican Church. Although the evidence of guilt was clear, the jury refused to convict. When the jurors refused the court's request to reconsider, the judge fined and jailed them for CONTEMPT. The foreman of the jury, named Bushell, filed a HABEAS CORPUS petition, and the court eventually ordered that the jurors be released. Although BUSHELL'S CASE (1670) is sometimes erroneously said to have approved the right to acquit against the evidence—the English court never made such a determination—it did help establish the important principle that jurors cannot be coerced into reaching a particular verdict.

The jury's power to nullify found a welcome home in the American colonies, where the power was sometimes used as a form of political protest. The best known colonial example was ZENGER'S CASE, in which the jury acquitted John Peter Zenger, accused of SEDITIOUS LIBEL for publishing articles critical of the Royal Governor. His acquittal in the face of strong evidence of guilt helped solidify the view that juries generally, and the power to nullify in particular, were a critical protection against government tyranny.

Despite its deep historical roots, there is little evidence that the jury's power to nullify was critical to those who drafted or ratified the Constitution and the BILL OF RIGHTS. Perhaps this is because the power was assumed to exist—jurors were frequently instructed by the trial judge that they had the duty to "find the law" as well as the facts, an instruction that allowed juries to decide whether the criminal law should be applied to the case before them. But as judges became better trained and as the criminal law became more complex, courts increasingly came to instruct juries on the precise law that they were obligated to apply to the facts before them.

As the relationship between judges and juries changed, so did the nature of the nullification debate. There was never any doubt that juries had the raw power to acquit against the evidence, and so the controversial question became whether juries must be told of the power. When the Supreme Court finally addressed the issue in *Sparf & Hansen v. United States* (1895), it implicitly rejected the idea that the constitutional right to a TRIAL BY JURY included the right to a jury instructed that it might acquit against the evidence. Although the Court's opinion did not use the phrase "jury nullification," it left little doubt that the ability to nullify was merely a power incident to the jury system, not a right that could be enforced by a defendant.

Sparf & Hansen resolved the issue, at least in the federal courts. Although the question of instructing the jury was revived during the mid-twentieth century, often in criminal cases filed against those involved in political protests over CIVIL RIGHTS and the VIETNAM WAR, federal courts again rejected the view of nullification proponents. State courts are in accord: although a few state constitutions still provide that juries have the power to find the law, it does not appear that any state routinely permits argument to the jury on the nullification power.

Still, jury nullification continues to occur, although it is hard to say how often. There are enough examples of it in high-profile cases to create the impression that juries frequently acquit against the evidence, and in some jurisdictions for some crimes (usually nonviolent ones) there is evidence to support this view. Most observers believe, however, that juries in general rarely exercise the power, and when they do, they limit its use to cases that are close on the evidence. As a leading jury study put it, "the jury does not often consciously and explicitly yield to sentiment in the teeth of the law. Rather it yields to sentiment in the apparent process of resolving doubts as to the evidence."

Nevertheless, the mere possibility that a jury might nullify has a significant impact on the criminal law. One example is the legal system's tolerance of inconsistent verdicts. Sometimes two defendants are tried together, and the evidence against them is identical, yet the jury convicts one and acquits the other. Logic suggests that if the jury had a reasonable doubt against one defendant, it must have had a reasonable doubt about the other. In federal courts, however, the conviction may stand despite the inconsistency; the Supreme Court has said that because the jury might have decided to nullify when it acquitted the second defendant, the first defendant's conviction will not be disturbed if there was enough evidence to sustain that conviction. This inconsistency will be tolerated even if there is no evidence that the jury intended to nullify with respect to the defendant it set free.

A second example of the influence of jury nullification is the legal system's distrust of the "special" verdict—a verdict that requires the jury to answer specific questions that explain its decision. Although there are many reasons why special verdicts are disfavored, one reason is that forcing a jury to be too specific in its decision might interfere with its power to nullify. As one court put it, in *United States v. Desmond* (1982), "Underlying this aversion [to special verdicts] is the feeling that denial of a general verdict might deprive the defendant of the right to a jury's finding based more on external circumstances than the strict letter of the law."

The exercise of jury nullification evokes strong reactions, both for and against. Advocates of nullification argue that without this power, the jury would not be able to fulfill its role as the conscience of the community, dispensing individual justice in appropriate cases. Proponents note that laws prohibiting drug use, for example, may be fair in almost every case, but the legislature may not have anticipated the exceptional one, such as the use of marijuana for medical purposes. If the prosecutor decides to charge a patient with a crime for using marijuana, the jury is free to step in and prevent an injustice from occurring. If such nullifications are repeated, juries can also perform an important function by signaling the legislature that certain laws should be reassessed because they are no longer in line with community values.

Some proponents have argued that juries should take an even more aggressive role in monitoring and shaping the laws. Advocacy groups lobby for "fully informed jury" laws, under which jurors would be told by the judges that they are the ultimate decisionmakers in all criminal cases about both the law and the facts. Some scholars have echoed similar themes, arguing that jury nullification should be encouraged both in and outside the courtroom to help bring about desired social change.

There are also those who criticize the exercise of jury nullification. They note, for example, that when a jury nullifies, it often does so on the basis of incomplete, even misleading information. Jurors who believe that a young defendant should not have his future ruined by one drunk driving conviction, for example, would surely want to know before nullifying that the defendant had been in trouble with the law before; yet, that evidence often will not be admissible at trial. Because the jury has the power, but not a right, to acquit against the evidence, relevant information that the jury would like to hear on this issue will never be presented.

One remedy for the problem of imperfect information would be to change current practice and allow lawyers to argue to the jury for nullification. Critics object to such a candid course of action, however, arguing that if juries were told of the power to nullify, they would nullify much more often, thereby undermining the RULE OF LAW. Critical federal judges have agreed that explicit allowance of nullification would give "every individual the option of disregarding with impunity any law which by his personal standard was judged morally untenable."

A related concern of critics is that although the power to nullify can be used for wise and merciful ends, it can also reflect a jury's improper motives. When juries refused to convict white defendants who had violated the civil rights of minority citizens trying to register to vote, this was an exercise in jury nullification. Likewise when defendants in sexual assault cases are treated leniently because the victim was allegedly "asking for it," jurors may well be expressing the sentiments of the community, but most would not defend these actions as just or merciful.

Finally, those who oppose instructing the jury on the power to nullify note that many controversial political questions are played out in the courtroom, and that the resolution of those issues should not be left to randomly selected juries. Questions about ABORTION are raised in cases where defendants are charged with trespassing at family planning clinics, just as questions about the legitimacy of GUN CONTROL may be raised in a case charging illegal possession of assault rifles by hunters. Critics contend that social issues like these should be resolved in the legislature, and that once they are, a proper respect for the rule of law means that juries should be required to apply the law as written.

The strength of the jury's power to nullify is also its weakness. Juries have the discretion to acquit any defendant for any reason, a power that can be used for both proper and improper purposes. Jurors are quite properly charged with making an important, perhaps life-and-death, decision about whether a defendant is guilty of the crime charged. Whether the jury should be more specifically charged with their power to consider larger issues that go beyond the law and the facts presented—a procedure that is today rejected by almost all courts—is at the heart of the jury nullification debate.

ANDREW D. LEIPOLD
(2000)

Bibliography

ABRAMSON, JEFFREY 1994 *We the Jury*. New York: Basic Books.
KALVEN, HARRY, JR. and ZEISEL, HANS 1966 *The American Jury*. Boston, Mass.: Little, Brown.
KING, NANCY 1998 Silencing Nullification Advocacy Inside the Jury Room and Outside the Courtroom. *University of Chicago Law Review* 65:433–500.
LEIPOLD, ANDREW 1996 Rethinking Jury Nullification. *Virginia Law Review* 82:253–324.
WEINSTEIN, JACK B. 1993 Considering Jury "Nullification": When May and Should a Jury Reject the Law to do Justice? *American Criminal Law Review* 30:239–254.

JURY SERVICE AS A POLITICAL RIGHT

In his article in this encyclopedia on JURY DISCRIMINATION, James Boyd White identified a, if not the, central question as being "[w]hat exclusions, beyond racial ones, are improper?" The dozen or so cases the Supreme Court decided during the 1990s have served to heighten the need for a CONSTITUTIONAL THEORY to identify the groups whose exclusion from or underrepresentation on juries ought to be troubling. In the 1970s the Court invoked the Sixth Amendment, which guarantees to criminal defendants the right to a TRIAL BY JURY. This amendment, however, offers an explanation that is incomplete in at least two respects. First, few would doubt that jury discrimination raises constitutional problems outside the criminal setting. Second, and more basic, the Sixth Amendment tells us only about some circumstances in which a jury must be provided, not about how juries must be constituted. That is, there is nothing in the text or history of the Sixth Amendment that tells when exclusion of certain groups or individuals renders a body less than a "jury."

An approach that would focus on the DUE PROCESS OF LAW rights of litigants to a fairly selected jury would also be plagued with problems. If a jury that, because of intentional official action is all white, was held to deprive a black litigant of her due process rights, then why shouldn't the same be said for a jury that turns out to be all white not because of official design but rather because of random chance? Moreover, a due process approach that stressed the possibility that jurors of different races will treat litigants differently would not provide a basis for attacking exclusion of black jurors when the litigants are white. This due process approach can create unfortunate dilemmas when black jurors are excluded in a case where the defendant is white but the victim is black.

For these reasons, the Court in recent jury exclusion cases beginning with BATSON V. KENTUCKY (1986) and continuing with cases such as *Powers v. Ohio* (1991), *Edmonson v. Leesville Concrete Co.* (1991), and *J. E. B. v. Alabama* (1994) has focused less on the rights of the litigants, and more on the rights of excluded jurors—in particular, their rights to EQUAL PROTECTION OF THE LAWS under the FOURTEENTH AMENDMENT. The newfound focus on the rights of the would-be jurors is welcome, but the equal protection analysis employed by the Court thus far is at best incomplete and at worst incorrect. Traditional equal protection analysis may be too narrow; the use of wealth and age criteria ordinarily does not trigger any heightened scrutiny under equal protection, and yet the use of these criteria to exclude jurors ought to be troubling. Indeed, the Court has already (and quite properly) suggested that wealth ought play no part in jury selection, *Thiel v. Southern Pacific Co.* (1946).

More generally, a problem with the traditional equal protection approach is that the equal protection clause—like everything else in the Fourteenth Amendment—was originally intended to be limited to what nineteenth-century lawyers called "CIVIL RIGHTS" such as PROPERTY RIGHTS, FREEDOM OF CONTRACT, and inheritance rights. Political rights, which included voting and jury service, were excluded from the coverage of the Fourteenth Amendment and were addressed more specifically in the VOTING RIGHTS amendments, beginning with the FIFTEENTH AMENDMENT and running through the TWENTY-SIXTH AMENDMENT. And the groups protected by these voting amendments are not necessarily the same as those protected under a traditional equal protection approach.

The modern Court is beginning to understand the close linkage between jury service and other political rights, such as office holding and especially voting. In both *Powers* and *Edmonson*, Justice ANTHONY M. KENNEDY writing for the Court likened jury service to voting, both to support its finding of STATE ACTION, and to draw strength from PRECEDENT removing race from voter selection. This "juror as voter" theme in Kennedy's writings has surface plausibility. After all, jurors vote to decide winners and losers in cases. Thus, the plain meaning of various constitutional provisions concerning the "right to vote" might be interpreted literally to apply to jurors. Beyond this plain meaning, jury service eligibility historically has been limited as a general matter to those who are registered voters.

The connection, however, runs deeper still. The link between jury service and other rights of political participation such as voting is an important part of our overall constitutional structure, spanning three centuries and eight amendments: the Fifth Amendment, Sixth Amendment, SEVENTH AMENDMENT, Fourteenth, Fifteenth, NINETEENTH AMENDMENT, TWENTY-FOURTH AMENDMENT, and the Twenty-Sixth. The voting–jury service linkage was recognized by the Framers, who saw juries as a lower branch of the judicial department, just as the House was the lower branch of the legislature. Indeed, THOMAS JEFFERSON thought that as between electing legislators and doing direct law administration through juries, the people's voice in the latter was more important than in the former in order to preserve liberty and democracy. This connection noted at the founding between voting and jury service was recognized by the Framers and ratifiers of the RECON-STRUCTION amendments—who used the phrase "right to vote" in the Fifteenth Amendment as a shorthand for political participation more generally, including serving on juries—and by the authors of twentieth-century amendments patterned after the Fifteenth.

Thus, when deciding which criteria cannot be used to select jurors, we should self-consciously ask ourselves whether the criteria under consideration would be permissible as a basis for excluding voters. Given the modern Court's characterization of voting as a FUNDAMENTAL RIGHT whose burdening usually triggers STRICT SCRUTINY, many grounds for excluding jurors are constitutionally dubious. Indeed, the fact that we would never think of permitting peremptory challenges to voters should cause us to consider whether peremptories in juries are consistent with our modern commitment to inclusion and REPRESENTATION in political participation. Some believe that the Court's characterization of voting as a fundamental right under the Fourteenth Amendment itself raises problems. This position has some support in ORIGINAL INTENT; as suggested above, political rights were excluded from the scope of the Fourteenth Amendment. At the very least, however, the criteria the Constitution prohibits as bases for selecting votes are impermissible bases for selecting jurors as well. These include race (Fifteenth Amendment); sex (Nineteenth Amendment); class, at least in federal forums (Twenty-Fourth Amendment); and age (Twenty-Sixth Amendment).

VIKRAM D. AMAR
(2000)

(SEE ALSO: *Procedural Due Process of Law, Criminal.*)

Bibliography

AMAR, AKHIL REED   1995   Reinventing Juries: Ten Suggested Reforms. *UC Davis Law Review* 28:1169–1194.

AMAR, VIKRAM DAVID   1995   Jury Service as Political Participation Akin to Voting. *Cornell Law Review* 80: 203–259.

JURY SIZE

Traditionally, in the United States, a criminal trial jury—the PETIT JURY—has been composed of twelve persons. Early Supreme Court opinions assumed that in federal criminal cases juries of that size were required by the Constitution. In PATTON V. UNITED STATES (1930) the Court ruled that during the course of a federal trial a criminal defendant could, with the consent of the prosecutor and judge, waive the participation of one or two jurors and agree to have the verdict rendered by less than twelve.

In DUNCAN V. LOUISIANA (1968) the Supreme Court held that under the FOURTEENTH AMENDMENT a person accused of a serious crime in a state court is guaranteed the right to TRIAL BY JURY according to the same standards applied under the Sixth Amendment in the federal courts. Later, in BALDWIN V. NEW YORK (1970), the Court held that a serious, nonpetty crime for purposes of the jury trial guarantee is one where imprisonment for more than six months is authorized. In the wake of *Duncan*, the Court in WILLIAMS V. FLORIDA (1970) decided that trial of a serious crime by a jury of six persons did not violate the constitutional right to trial by jury. Eight years later, the Court in BALLEW V. GEORGIA (1978) ruled that six was the constitutional minimum—that a jury of five persons did not meet the constitutional standard. In *Colgrove v. Battin* (1973) the Court had also ruled that a six-person jury in a civil case in the federal courts did not violate the SEVENTH AMENDMENT right to jury trial.

In early England, the number of jurors on a petit jury came to be firmly fixed at twelve some time in the fourteenth century. The reasons for choosing the number twelve for the jury at common law are shrouded in obscurity; the same number was also in wide use in other countries of Europe from early times. Some writers ascribe this number to mystical and religious considerations, for example, the twelve tribes and the twelve apostles. At the time of the adoption of the Constitution and the BILL OF RIGHTS, the idea of the twelve-person jury was entrenched in the English COMMON LAW system and practice of the colonial society.

In *Williams*, the Court rejected the idea that the history of the drafting of the Sixth Amendment jury trial provision enshrined the twelve-person jury in the Constitution. Instead, the Court adopted a functional approach, relating jury size to the purposes of jury trial. The goals of the jury system were seen as interposing the common-sense judgment of laypersons, permitting community participation in the decision-making process, and making the group large enough to promote group deliberation and obtain a fair cross-section of the community. With respect to these various goals, the court majority found "little reason to think" that there is a significant difference between six and twelve, citing in support "the few experiments" and asserting that neither currently available evidence nor theory suggested contrary conclusions.

The interval between *Williams* and *Ballew* saw the publication of a significant body of SOCIAL SCIENCE RESEARCH examining the effects of changes in jury size. In *Ballew*, although the Court was unanimous on the jury size issue, only two Justices relied on these social science studies in concluding that five-person juries did not adequately fulfill the functions of jury trial outlined in *Williams*. Three Justices had "reservations as to the wisdom—as well as the necessity—of . . . heavy reliance on numerology derived from statistical studies." The same three Justices

suggested that the Constitution does not require every feature of the jury to be the same in both federal and state courts, implying that a different, presumably higher, minimum size standard might be applied in the federal courts.

The studies done since *Williams*, through experiment, use of statistical analysis, and theorizing, have inquired whether the size of the jury affects: the likelihood of representation on a jury of ethnic and racial minorities and minority viewpoints that might influence results or the incidence of hung juries; the propensity of juries to reach compromise verdicts; the consistency of verdicts; the likelihood that verdicts reflect community sentiment; and the overall quality of group decision making. A few researchers have also studied the cost savings that might be achieved by reductions in jury size.

In the main, the social scientists have criticized the Court's conclusion in *Williams*, and have argued that decreasing jury size has undesirable effects. Some of these studies have been subjected to methodological criticism, such as the objections to their reliance on small group research. Definitive research on the subject remains to be done. On the issue of the jury's representative character, however, social science has already contributed fairly definitive conclusions. Although it is not possible for a single jury to be representative of the community, six-person juries are less likely than twelve-person juries to contain individuals from minority groups or those who have minority viewpoints. Richard Lempert has suggested that "there may be a positive value in minimizing the number of situations in which minority group members are judged by groups lacking minority representation. . . ."

In other constitutional contexts, judges often rely on intuition and common sense to reach judgments on functional issues, or they take into account constitutional values that transcend a functional approach. The jury size issue, however, involves specific numbers, and intuition and other constitutional values do not provide an adequate basis for drawing the required fine distinctions. One who is not persuaded by the social science studies is therefore relegated to the type of statement made by Justice Powell in *Ballew*, defending the line between five and six: "[A] line has to be drawn somewhere." Under such an approach, the constitutional line could as easily have been drawn between twelve and eleven, and with more historical justification.

Because of the Court's reluctance to overrule recent precedents and because of uncertainty whether social science research can ever demonstrate a sufficient basis for drawing a different line, it seems probable that, for a long time to come, six will remain the constitutional minimum for a criminal jury in the state courts under the Fourteenth Amendment. (Whether the Court will some day adopt Justice Powell's view and apply a different minimum size standard for juries in federal criminal trials is problematic.) Perhaps in some future century when legal historians try to deduce the reasons for choosing six as the constitutionally significant number, they, like their predecessors, may speculate about the possible mystical value of the number. In the end, they are likely to conclude that its origins, like those of the number twelve, are shrouded in obscurity.

NORMAN ABRAMS
(1986)

Bibliography

LEMPERT, RICHARD 1975 Uncovering "Nondiscernible Differences: Empirical Research and the Jury Size Cases. *Michigan Law Review* 73:644–708.

JURY TRIAL

See: Trial by Jury

JURY UNANIMITY

The requirement that a jury in a criminal case reach a unanimous decision became generally established in England during the fourteenth century—about the same time that juries came to be composed of twelve persons. Unanimity began to be generally required for jury verdicts in the American colonies in the eighteenth century. The unanimity requirement as commonly applied means that all the members of the jury must agree upon the verdict—whether for conviction or acquittal. If any of the jurors fail to agree, the jury is "hung"—that is, unable to reach a verdict. Under well-established DOCTRINE, after a hung jury the defendant may be retried.

In a series of cases dating back to the end of the nineteenth century, the Supreme Court has assumed that under the Sixth Amendment the verdict of a criminal jury in the federal courts must be unanimous. This assumption has not been tested, however, for there is no provision for less than unanimous criminal verdicts in the federal courts. The decision in DUNCAN V. LOUISIANA (1968) opened the way for the Court to consider the constitutionality of efforts made by many states to change elements in the COMMON LAW jury system. *Duncan* ruled that the FOURTEENTH AMENDMENT protected the right to TRIAL BY JURY in state courts according to the same standards applied under the Sixth Amendment.

To understand the Court's subsequent decisions regarding jury unanimity, it is necessary also to consider its related decisions on JURY SIZE. The Court in WILLIAMS V. FLORIDA (1970) upheld the use of six-person juries for serious criminal cases. The question whether state criminal juries must reach unanimous verdicts was presented for the first time in 1972 in two companion cases, APODACA V. OREGON and JOHNSON V. LOUISIANA. In *Apodaca*, the constitutionality of 10–2 verdicts was sustained under the Sixth and Fourteenth Amendments. In *Johnson*, 9–3 verdicts were upheld under the Fourteenth Amendment alone. In *Apodaca*, a state case, five Justices (one concurring Justice and four dissenters) also expressed the view that the Sixth Amendment required unanimity in federal criminal trials.

In BALLEW V. GEORGIA (1978) the Court rendered its second size-of-jury decision, holding five-person juries to be unconstitutional. Thus, by the time the Court considered the issue in BURCH V. LOUISIANA (1979), it had upheld six-person juries, sustained the constitutionality of 10–2 and 9–3 majority verdicts, and held five-person juries to be unconstitutional. In *Burch*, the Court held that conviction by a 5–1 vote of a six-person jury violated the constitutional right to trial by jury.

The Court has not in modern times decided whether the SEVENTH AMENDMENT requires unanimity in federal civil trials. It can be argued that it so held in two early cases, *American Publishing Company v. Fisher* (1897) and *Springville v. Thomas* (1897), but the Court's nonunanimous verdict decisions in state criminal cases and its decision in *Colgrove v. Battin* (1973) that six-person juries are constitutional in federal civil trials, arguably have undermined those early decisions.

In addressing the unanimity issue in *Apodaca* and *Johnson*, the Court relied heavily on the analysis used in the first size-of-jury case, *Williams v. Florida*, and applied the same functional approach relating the size of the jury to the purposes of a jury trial. From a functional perspective, the unanimity issue has much in common with but is not identical to the jury size question. For example, both involve concerns that juries represent a cross-section of the community and that minority viewpoints be represented. In connection with jury size, the concern is that if the jury is too small, it will not reflect minority views. Where unanimity is departed from, the concern is that minority viewpoints represented on the jury will simply be disregarded and outvoted. A majority of the Court in *Apodaca* rejected this latter claim on the grounds that there was no reason to believe that majority jurors will fail to weigh the evidence and consider rational arguments offered by the minority. The dissenters argued that jury reliability was diminished in a nonunanimous system because there is less pressure to debate and deliberate. Professor Hans Zeisel has made a similar point: "[T]he abandonment of the unanimity rule is but another way of reducing the size of the jury. But it is reduction with a vengeance, for a majority verdict requirement is far more effective in nullifying the potency of minority viewpoints than is the outright reduction of a jury to a size equivalent to the majority that is allowed to agree on a verdict. Minority viewpoints fare better on a jury of ten that must be unanimous than on a jury of twelve where ten members must agree on a verdict" (1971, p. 722).

The less than unanimous verdict also poses a question not raised in the jury size cases. A majority of the Court in *Johnson* held that nonunanimous verdicts are not inconsistent with proof beyond a REASONABLE DOUBT and therefore do not violate DUE PROCESS. The fact that some members of the jury are not convinced of guilt does not itself establish reasonable doubt, a concept that apparently applies only to the standard of proof that each individual juror subjectively must apply, not a concept applicable to the jury as a group.

Are criminal defendants as well protected from conviction under a nonunanimous verdict system as under a unanimity requirement? The majority in *Apodaca* and *Johnson* conceded that juries would be hung somewhat less frequently under a nonunanimous system but also relied on SOCIAL SCIENCE RESEARCH for the proposition that "the probability that an acquittal minority will hang the jury is about as great as that a guilty minority will hang it." Data in the same study, however, persuaded some of the dissenters that the prosecution would gain "a substantially more favorable conviction ratio" under a nonunanimous system.

By the time *Burch* was decided in 1979, the Court, following the pattern suggested in the 1978 jury size case of *Ballew*, appears to have abandoned any attempt to rely on social science to support its conclusions regarding required jury attributes. In holding 5–1 verdicts unconstitutional, the Court concluded that "having already departed from the strict historical requirements of jury trial, it is inevitable that lines must be drawn somewhere" and relied upon "much the same reasons that led [us] in *Ballew* to decide that use of a five-member jury threatened the fairness of the proceeding. . . ."

The constitutionality of other numerical combinations—for example, 8–4 or 7–5 verdicts or the various possible majorities on juries of seven to eleven members—remains in doubt. In *Burch*, the Court expressly reserved opinion on the constitutionality of nonunanimous verdicts by juries of more than six. Only Justice HARRY A. BLACKMUN, concurring in *Apodaca*, commented that a 7–5 verdict standard would afford him "great difficulty."

The Court's decisions in the nonunanimous verdict cases have been designed to leave room for the states to experiment with different majority verdict systems. But the uncertainty produced by these decisions may discourage experimentation. If the states do introduce additional variations, the notions that "lines must be drawn somewhere" and that at some point "the fairness of the proceeding" is threatened hardly provide an adequate basis for selecting among the numerous lines that may be presented. If the Court is unwilling to rely upon social science research to back up its functional approach, it may find itself without a calculus for resolving constitutional issues in which specific numbers count.

NORMAN ABRAMS
(1986)

Bibliography

ZEISEL, HANS   1971   And Then There Were None: The Diminution of the Federal Jury. *University of Chicago Law Review* 38:710–724.

JURY UNANIMITY
(Update)

The issue of jury unanimity is tied to, among other things, JURY SIZE. The Supreme Court has allowed states to deviate from the historical norm of twelve-person juries, and has upheld criminal convictions by juries composed of as few as six persons. In criminal cases, where juries were intended to protect defendants against oppression and governmental overreaching, allowing a jury composed of less than twelve persons to convict by less than unanimous agreement may present a dangerous slippery slope. But there may be stopping points along this slope. Unlike the number six, majority rule and SUPERMAJORITY RULE have unique and stable mathematical properties. Surely, everyone would agree that there is a difference between majority and minority rules, and no one would permit conviction of a defendant by less than a majority. Majority and supermajority rules also govern political institutions other than juries, such as legislatures and appellate judicial panels, to which juries were analogized by the Framers. If jury service is similar in essence to voting and other forms of majoritarian political participation, then the historical tradition of unanimity may not be sacrosanct. Moreover, unanimity traditions at the time of the framing of the Constitution were easier to justify given the homogeneity of jurors at that time. It bears recalling that initially only white men could serve as jurors. As juries have become more racially and sexually diverse, a rule that gives each individual an absolute veto seems less necessary, and perhaps unwise. The challenge for those who advocate a departure from unanimity, of course, is to find a way to ensure that majorities on juries listen to and in good faith consider the views of minorities whose votes can be overridden. Minority vetoes may be problematic; however, minority voices need to be heard.

VIKRAM D. AMAR
(2000)

JUS DARE

(Latin: "To give the law.") This is the traditional function of the legislature in a constitutional government with SEPARATION OF POWERS and is contrasted with JUS DICERE, the function of courts. A court may be said to have invaded the realm of *jus dare* when it engages in JUDICIAL POLICYMAKING.

DENNIS J. MAHONEY
(1986)

JUS DICERE

(Latin: "To say [what] the law [is].") This is the traditional function of courts, and it is usually understood as a limitation upon their power (*jus dicere, et non jus dare*). "It is emphatically the province of the judicial department to say what the law is"—Chief Justice JOHN MARSHALL in MARBURY V. MADISON (1803).

DENNIS J. MAHONEY
(1986)

JUST COMPENSATION

The just compensation clause of the Fifth Amendment demands that a private PROPERTY owner be made whole financially when property is taken by the federal government for PUBLIC USE. The same requirement is made applicable to the states by the DUE PROCESS clause of the FOURTEENTH AMENDMENT. The requisite compensation is the monetary equivalent of the property taken, putting the owner in as good a position pecuniarily as before the taking, as the Supreme Court held in *Monongahela Navigation Co. v. United States* (1893). Compensation for losses peculiar to the owner, such as loss of investment or business profits, litigation expenses, and relocation costs, is not constitutionally required, but often is made payable by statute.

In recognition of the somewhat elusive nature of the "monetary equivalent" standard, a variety of working rules have been developed to aid the courts. The most important of these rules is the concept of fair market value. Under this concept, the owner is entitled to receive, as just compensation, the price for the property interest taken that would be agreed upon, as of the time of the taking, by a willing and informed seller and a willing and informed buyer, considering the highest and best use for which the property was available and suitable.

The market value test, however, is not an inflexible one, and other methods of estimating value have been held appropriate when reference to actual market data is im-

possible because there is no actual market for the property, or when the market value test would result in manifest injustice by diverging to an impermissible degree from the full indemnity principle of the Fifth Amendment.

If the property taken is only a part of a single parcel, just compensation includes payment to the owner for any diminution in value of the remainder resulting from the planned use of the part taken, but the value of benefits to the remainder may be offset against the value of the "take." These results, which ordinarily can be measured by the difference in value of the property before and after the taking, can theoretically, although seldom in fact, result in a zero award. Many states, deeming it unfair to deduct enhancements to the remainder, reject the "before and after" test and award the full value of the part taken plus any net consequential damages realized by the remainder after offsetting any special benefits thereto. That either approach is constitutionally permissible was affirmed in *Bauman v. Ross* (1897).

ARVO VAN ALSTYNE
(1986)

Bibliography
ORGEL, LESTER   1953   *Valuation under the Law of Eminent Domain*, Vol. 1. Charlottesville, Va.: Michie Co.

JUSTICE DEPARTMENT

See: Attorney General and Department of Justice

JUSTICIABILITY

Federal judges do not establish legal norms at will or on demand, but only when deciding cases that are justiciable, that is, appropriate for federal court decision. What makes a case justiciable is thus itself an important threshold question, because it determines whether a federal court will exercise its power to formulate and apply substantive law, rather than leaving the issues in the case to be resolved by political or other means. Hence, when the Supreme Court fashions the criteria of justiciability for itself and the lower federal courts, it effectively defines the nature and scope of the JUDICIAL POWER of the United States—the power to make decisions in accordance with law.

Most justiciability issues arise when litigants who are primarily motivated to vindicate public rights seek to contest the validity of government behavior, especially on constitutional grounds. Such public interest suits are usually designed not so much to redress traditional personal grievances as to vindicate fundamental principles. Commonly the plaintiffs seek DECLARATORY JUDGMENTS or INJUNCTIONS to prevent government officials from carrying on objectionable practices that affect a wide segment of the population. These actions often test and illustrate the degree to which federal judges, particularly Supreme Court Justices, view their power of constitutional oversight as warranted only by the necessity to resolve traditional legal disputes or, instead, by a broader judicial mission to ensure government observance of the Constitution.

In demarcating the federal judicial function, the law of justiciability comprises a complex of subtle doctrines, including MOOTNESS, ADVISORY OPINIONS, and POLITICAL QUESTIONS, among others. The Supreme Court has derived that law from two sources: Article III, which limits federal judicial power to the decision of CASES AND CONTROVERSIES, and nonconstitutional "prudential" rules of the Court's own creation. Both Article III and the rules of prudence incorporate notions of the attributes or qualities of litigation that make the legal issues presented appropriate for judicial determination. The difference between the two is that if Congress wants to have the federal courts entertain public actions, it may override the Court's prudential barriers, but not the constitutional limits of "case" and "controversy."

Three primary, and often mutually reinforcing, conceptions of appropriateness shape the many manifestations of justiciability. One concerns judicial capability. It centers on making federal court adjudication competent, informed, necessary, and efficacious. In this conception, a judicial decision is proper only when adversely affected parties litigate live issues of current personal consequence in a lawsuit whose format assures adversary argument and judicial capacity to devise meaningful remedies. The second conception of appropriateness concerns fairness. It promotes judicial solicitude for parties and interests not represented in the lawsuit, whose rights might be compromised unfairly by a substantive decision rendered without their participation. The third conception concerns the proper institutional and political role in our democracy of the appointed, electorally unaccountable federal judiciary. It cautions federal courts to be sure of the need for imposing restraints, especially constitutional restraints, on other, particularly more representative, government officials.

Whether the policies underlying justiciability doctrine are (or should be) applied in a principled, consistent fashion, depending on the form and characteristics of litigation alone, as the Supreme Court professes, or whether the Court does (or should) manipulate them for pragmatic reasons, is a subject of major controversy among the Court's commentators. Inevitably, the Court has discretion

to adjust the degree to which these imprecise and flexible policies must be satisfied in particular cases, given individual variations in the configuration of lawsuits and the inherently relative nature of judgments about judicial capability, litigant need, and the propriety of JUDICIAL ACTIVISM AND RESTRAINT. Assessments of the information and circumstances needed for intelligent, effective adjudication will vary with the levels of generality at which issues are posed and with judicial willingness to act under conditions of uncertainty. Appraisals frequently diverge concerning hardship to, and representation of, present and absent parties who will be affected by rendering or withholding decision. Perhaps most dramatically, Justices differ in their evaluations of the relative importance of judicial control of government behavior and the freedom of politically accountable officials to formulate policy without judicial interference.

In view of the latitude and variation in the Court's self-conscious definition of federal judicial power, it is not surprising that justiciability is a sophisticated, controversial, and difficult field, or that many decisions provoke the skepticism that justiciability DOCTRINE has been manipulated to avoid decision of some issues and advance the decision of others. The Court certainly considers (and is willing to articulate) the degree of concrete focus and clarity with which issues are presented, and how pressing is the need for judicial protection of the litigants. The Court may also consider (but almost certainly will not articulate) a number of the following factors: how substantial, difficult, and controversial the issues are; whether a decision would likely legitimate government action or hold it unconstitutional; how important the Court believes the principle it would announce is and whether the principle could be expected to command public and government acceptance; the possibility of nonjudicial resolution; whether a decision would contribute to or cut off public debate; the expected general public reaction to a decision; the Justices' own constitutional priorities; and a host of other practical considerations that may implicate the Court's capacity to establish and enforce important constitutional principles.

Such judgments appear to have influenced a number of notable justiciability rulings in diverse ways. For example, in *Poe v. Ullman* (1961) the Court held a declaratory judgment challenge to Connecticut's contraception ban nonjusticiable because the statute was not being enforced, but later held the ban unconstitutional in the context of a criminal prosecution. By contrast, in a declaratory judgment challenge to an unenforced prohibition on teaching evolution, the Court, in EPPERSON V. ARKANSAS (1968), held the case justiciable and the prohibition unconstitutional without awaiting a prosecution. Similarly, the Court twice dismissed a seemingly justiciable appeal challenging Virginia's ban on MISCEGENATION, as applied to an annulment proceeding, within a few years of declaring public school segregation unconstitutional in 1954, but in 1967, following the CIVIL RIGHTS advances of the early 1960s, held the law unconstitutional on appeal of a criminal conviction. Moreover, although the Court has deferred decision in some cases where it ultimately held state statutes unconstitutional, it also occasionally appears to have lowered justiciability barriers and rushed to uphold the constitutionality of important federal legislation (the Tennessee Valley Authority and nuclear liability limitation statutes) or to invalidate it when Congress wanted constitutional assistance with ongoing legislative reform (the FEDERAL ELECTION CAMPAIGN ACT.)

Perhaps the Court is inclined to insist on a greater showing of justiciability where it expects to hold governmental action unconstitutional than where it expects to uphold the action, in part because of a substantive presumption of the constitutionality of government conduct. Yet any generalization about the relations between justiciability and the Court's substantive views is hazardous, given the many factors and subtle judgments that may be weighed in any given case. What seems certain is that decisions on questions of justiciability will always be influenced by visions of the judicial role and will be difficult to comprehend without understanding those visions.

JOHNATHON D. VARAT
(1986)

Bibliography

BICKEL, ALEXANDER M. 1962 *The Least Dangerous Branch: The Supreme Court at the Bar of Politics.* Chap. 4. Indianapolis: Bobbs-Merrill.

GUNTHER, GERALD 1964 The Subtle Vices of the "Passive Virtues": A Comment on Principle and Expediency in Judicial Review. *Columbia Law Review* 64:1–25.

VARAT, JOHNATHON D. 1980 Variable Justiciability and the *Duke Power* Case. *Texas Law Review* 58:273–327.

WRIGHT, CHARLES A.; MILLER, ARTHUR R.; and COOPER, EDWARD H. 1984 *Federal Practice and Procedure.* Vol. 13:278–293. St. Paul, Minn.: West Publishing Co.

JUVENILE CURFEW LAWS

Curfew laws generally run counter to American constitutional principles of freedom and liberty. Consequently, the state's power to restrict the movements of its citizenry has been limited to times of civil unrest, crisis, or emergency and is justified by legitimate governmental concerns for the health, safety, and welfare of the community. Juvenile curfew laws, however, differ: usually there is no emergency; only a discrete segment of the population is affected; and the curfew may remain in effect for years.

Public concern about juvenile delinquency and victimization has renewed support for curfew ordinances and has encouraged government officials, primarily at the local level, to enact curfews for youths.

Although curfew laws aimed at youths have proliferated, only a few juvenile curfew ordinances have been challenged in the courts. The Supreme Court has never ruled on the constitutionality of any juvenile curfew ordinance, but some state courts and a few lower federal courts have considered the issue. Most of these challenges are based on alleged violations of the FIRST AMENDMENT rights of children and their parents to FREEDOM OF ASSOCIATION, movement, and expression; the FOURTEENTH AMENDMENT rights of children to EQUAL PROTECTION OF THE LAWS, SUBSTANTIVE DUE PROCESS, and PROCEDURAL DUE PROCESS; and the Fourteenth Amendment rights of parents to parental autonomy and familial privacy. Unfortunately, the opinions do not clearly define the parameters of state authority to enact curfew ordinances, in part because the laws themselves vary significantly from jurisdiction to jurisdiction, thus making it difficult to draw comparisons across cases.

Curfew opponents have had mixed success when challenging curfew ordinances on constitutional grounds. Most courts reject the equal protection claim that the state cannot treat minors differently because of their age or because a FUNDAMENTAL RIGHT is infringed; but even when a fundamental right is affected, some courts have upheld such regulations on the ground that the state has compelling interests in the protection of children and the reduction of juvenile crime. Of course, if no fundamental right is implicated then a substantive due process claim also will fail; some courts thus have rejected such a challenge on the ground that the curfew ordinance does not violate a fundamental right. If a fundamental right has been implicated, some courts have found the state's interest sufficiently compelling to warrant the intrusion while others have found the curfew unconstitutional. Similarly, First Amendment claims that the ordinances infringe on expressive or associative rights have been rejected because of the state's greater authority to regulate minors or the importance of the governmental interest, while others have been upheld.

Fourteenth Amendment challenges to curfew ordinances, however, have been upheld on the grounds that the laws are too vague and fail to apprise children and their parents of the prohibited conduct. VAGUENESS challenges also have been sustained when the ordinances delegate too much legislative authority or discretion to those charged with enforcement of the laws. The Fourteenth Amendment claims of parents that juvenile curfew ordinances invade familial privacy and infringe on parental autonomy also have had some limited success, although the courts appear willing to permit some degree of governmental intrusion. The boundaries of state and parental power, however, remain uncertain as do the nature and extent of children's constitutional rights.

KATHERINE HUNT FEDERLE
(2000)

Bibliography

FEDERLE, KATHERINE H. 1995 Children, Curfews, and the Constitution. *Washington University Law Quarterly* 73:1315–1368.

JORDAN, MICHAEL 1993 From the Constitutionality of Juvenile Curfew Ordinances to a Children's Agenda for the 1990's: Is It Really A Simple Matter of Supporting Family Values and Recognizing Fundamental Rights? *St. Thomas Law Review* 5:389–431.

VEILLEUX, DANNY R. 1993 Annotation: Validity, Construction, and Effect of Juvenile Curfew Regulations. *American Law Reports*, 4th ed. 83:1056–1123.

JUVENILE PROCEEDINGS

In a juvenile proceeding, a state court is asked to decide whether and how to intervene in the life of a child who may need supervision or protection. These proceedings often take place in a juvenile or family court and usually have two distinct phases: a "jurisdictional" stage, at which the judge must decide whether there are grounds for intervention; and a "dispositional" phase, in which the judge decides how to intervene. Juvenile court statutes typically provide for JURISDICTION in three types of cases: the delinquency case, where a young person is found to have violated a criminal law; the case where the child's conduct is not criminal, but the child is found to be beyond parental control, or in need of supervision because of improper or protocriminal conduct, such as truancy, or running away; and the dependency case, where by reason of parental neglect or abuse the child is in need of protection. Once jurisdiction is established, the court typically has broad discretionary authority in the "dispositional phase" of juvenile proceedings to intervene into the child's life through supervision, or out-of-home placement in foster care or a residential institution.

At COMMON LAW, there were neither special courts nor separate proceedings for minors accused of violating the law. "Infancy" provided a defense, somewhat akin to insanity, in a case where because of immaturity a child lacked the capacity to form the requisite criminal intent. Presumptions made it impossible to find the requisite intent in children under seven, and difficult to find it in those between seven and fourteen. Youths over fourteen were presumed capable. Except for this possible defense, a child could be arrested, indicted, tried, and convicted just like an adult. Minors were regularly charged with crimes, tried like adults, and jailed and imprisoned with adult offenders.

In the nineteenth century, reformers began questioning the appropriateness of treating youthful and adult offenders alike. A revolution began in 1899, when Illinois established the first juvenile court. Hailed as a more humane and effective way of helping children in trouble get back on the track to good citizenship, the Illinois court became a model; by 1925 nearly every state had adopted LEGISLATION providing for some sort of juvenile proceedings. For these new juvenile proceedings, the implicit model of authority was not the traditional criminal trial with adversarial procedures but the family itself, with the state as *parens patriae*.

The philosophy of the early juvenile court emphasized four tenets. The first was rehabilitation, rather than deterrence or punishment. The state's goal was to save the wayward child through appropriate treatment. The second was individualization: justice for children was to be personalized. The court's primary goal was to determine whether a child needed help, and then to prescribe on an individualized basis the appropriate treatment. The third was separation: children were to be kept away from adult criminals who might physically brutalize minors or teach them criminal habits. Finally, juvenile procedure emphasized procedural informality. Although the adversarial determination of facts might be appropriate for a criminal trial where the purpose was punishment, legalistic formalities were thought to be counterproductive in a juvenile proceeding where the purpose was rehabilitation.

Before 1967, because of the philosophy of the juvenile court and its traditions of procedural informality, juvenile proceedings typically offered none of the safeguards afforded adults in criminal trials. Juvenile court practices were virtually unaffected by the recent decisions of the Supreme Court interpreting DUE PROCESS to impose increasingly high procedural standards imposed on state criminal proceedings. Except in a few states, a young person accused of delinquency would not be assigned counsel, had no broad RIGHT AGAINST SELF-INCRIMINATION, was judged by a preponderance of the evidence standard (not proof beyond a REASONABLE DOUBT), had no right to TRIAL BY JURY, and often faced HEARSAY evidence.

The Supreme Court had hinted that due process might demand more. *Haley v. Ohio* (1948) held that a confession given by a fifteen-year-old boy and used in a criminal trial was involuntary. Justice WILLIAM O. DOUGLAS wrote that "[n]either man nor child can be allowed to stand condemned by methods that flout constitutional requirements of due process of law." More pointed doubts about the procedural informality of juvenile proceedings were expressed in *Kent v. United States* (1966). The Court's holding could be read narrowly: the District of Columbia must use fair procedures to transfer minors from juvenile to adult courts. But in Justice ABE FORTAS's opinion the landmark ruling that was to come the next year was foreshadowed in two respects: first, in the suggestion that the *parens patriae* doctrine of the juvenile court is not "an invitation to procedural arbitrariness"; and second, in the expression of the fear that notwithstanding the paternalistic philosophy of juvenile proceedings, the child may in fact receive "the worst of both worlds: that he gets neither the protections accorded to adults, nor the solicitous care and regenerative treatment postulated for children."

The constitutional watershed came in IN RE GAULT (1967), which held that due process required the states to apply various procedural safeguards to the guilt (or jurisdictional) phase of delinquency proceedings. The Court found that fifteen-year-old Gerald Gault, who had been committed for up to six years at an Arizona Industrial School for making an obscene telephone call, had been deprived of his constitutional rights to adequate written NOTICE of the charges, notice of his RIGHT TO COUNSEL, including assigned counsel, and of his right to confront and cross-examine witnesses; and advice of his privilege against self-incrimination. In a broad opinion rejecting the claim that *parens patriae* and the rehabilitative ideal justified procedural informality, Fortas declared that "unbridled discretion, however benevolently motivated, is frequently a poor substitute for principle and procedure." Although the holdings of *Gault* were expressly limited to the guilt phase of delinquency proceedings, *Gault* broadly declared a principle that children have constitutional rights of their own: "Whatever may be their precise impact, neither the FOURTEENTH AMENDMENT nor the BILL OF RIGHTS is for adults alone."

During the years following *Gault*, the Supreme Court decided several cases that expanded the constitutional rights of children in delinquency proceedings. IN RE WINSHIP (1970) held that the "beyond a reasonable doubt" standard of proof was constitutionally mandated in the adjudicatory stage of delinquency proceedings. *Breed v. Jones* (1975) held that the protections of the DOUBLE JEOPARDY clause were applicable to minors. The juvenile in *Breed* had been put in jeopardy by the original adjudicatory hearing where jurisdiction was established, and the Court found that the juvenile's subsequent criminal trial for the same offense constituted double jeopardy. But in *Swisher v. Brady* (1978) the Court held that the double jeopardy clause did not prohibit Maryland officials from taking exceptions to a SPECIAL MASTER's nondelinquency findings.

Despite the decisions in *Gault*, *Breed*, and *Winship*, the Court's decision in MCKEIVER V. PENNSYLVANIA (1971) reflects the Court's continued commitment to a separate system of justice for children and adults. In *McKeiver* the Court held that jury trials are not constitutionally required in delinquency proceedings. The Court reasoned that because a jury is not "a necessary component of accurate factfinding," denying a juvenile a jury trial would not violate the FUNDAMENTAL FAIRNESS component of the due process clause. In addition, the Court pointed out that "the jury trial, if required as a matter of constitutional precept, will remake the juvenile proceeding into a fully adversary process and will put an effective end to what has been the idealistic prospect of an intimate, informal protective proceeding."

Since *Gault*, juvenile proceedings involving noncriminal misbehavior, or juveniles thought to be beyond parental control, have been questioned on both procedural and substantive grounds. What does *Gault* imply about appropriate procedural safeguards? To what extent may a state restrain the liberty of a minor on the basis of acts that if committed by adults would not be criminal? The Supreme Court has not yet ruled on the due process requirements applicable to these proceedings, and most states do not provide the procedural safeguards now applicable in delinquency proceedings. In addition to voicing procedural concerns, critics have also criticized as vague and overly broad the language defining these "status offenses": running away from home, sexual promiscuity, truancy, and the like. With few exceptions, however, appellate courts have upheld the constitutional validity of these statutes against such attacks. The Supreme Court, which has written no opinion dealing with such proceedings, has sent mixed signals in summary opinions.

Today every state has juvenile proceedings that allow a court, typically a juvenile or family court, to assume jurisdiction over a neglected or abused child and remove the child from the parents' care. Although not protected by explicit language in the Constitution, the interest of parents in their children's upbringing plainly carries great constitutional weight. Beginning with MEYER V. NEBRASKA (1923), the Supreme Court has recognized the constitutional right of parents to direct the rearing of their children. The parents' claim to authority, however, is not absolute. Since the early nineteenth century, the *parens patriae* power has been held sufficient to empower courts of equity to remove a child requiring protection from parental custody and to appoint a suitable person as guardian.

Statutes authorizing state intervention have been criticized on substantive and procedural grounds. Vague substantive standards of abuse and neglect often leave judges to base their determinations on their own subjective values. As the Supreme Court noted in *Santosky v. Kramer* (1982), the Court has not precisely determined what forms of parental conduct justify state intrusion.

The Court has, however, decided several cases with respect to the procedural requirements where parental rights are terminated on grounds of abuse or neglect. In *Stanley v. Illinois* (1972) the Court relied on the doctrine of IRREBUTTABLE PRESUMPTIONS to hold that it is a denial of DUE PROCESS for unwed fathers to be disqualified from custody of their children without individualized hearings on their fitness. In *Santosky* the Court decided that the "fair preponderance of the evidence" standard, applied in New York parental rights termination proceedings, violated due process: "Before a State may sever completely and irrevocably the rights of parents in their natural child, due process requires that the State support its allegations by at least clear and convincing evidence." In LASSITER V. DEPARTMENT OF SOCIAL SERVICES (1981), however, the Court held that due process does not require assignment of counsel in every case involving the termination of parental rights. Although most jurisdictions do provide counsel for parents in such cases, few provide separate counsel for the children.

Gault has forced revolutionary changes in delinquency proceedings, but the requirements imposed in other sorts of juvenile proceedings have been modest. In the twenty years since that landmark, Supreme Court decisions have extended to young people accused of crime those procedural safeguards essential to an accurate determination of their guilt. To that extent, the Constitution no longer permits the procedural informality that characterized juvenile proceedings for over half a century. *Gault* and its progeny have substantially narrowed but not obliterated the differences between the adult criminal justice process and the juvenile justice process for delinquents. *McKeiver* underlines the conclusion that the Constitution does not require identical procedures for delinquents and adults. The Court has never held that equal protection requires the legal system to treat all those accused of crime the same, whether adults or minors.

Outside the guilt phase of delinquency proceedings, the Court has shown substantial caution, notwithstanding the potentially expansive announcement in *Gault* that children have rights, and that juvenile proceedings will be judged by their performance, not their promise. A number of factors probably underlie this caution. For one thing, the protective and rehabilitative aspirations of the juvenile court have never been rejected by the Court. As *McKeiver*

suggests, the traditions of the juvenile court and the values of informality, flexibility, and protection still may carry some weight in constitutional adjudication. More fundamentally, decisions affecting children are special in two important respects that must affect constitutional analysis. First, defining constitutional rights in juvenile proceedings implicates defining parental rights, particularly in cases involving noncriminal misbehavior where the state may be reinforcing parental prerogatives, and in abuse and neglect proceedings, where the state directly challenges parental adequacy. Second, by reason of immaturity, young people may be more susceptible to coercion, and less able to make informed and responsible decisions. Whether considering the VOLUNTARINESS of a confession, the "knowing" WAIVER OF CONSTITUTIONAL RIGHTS, or the need for supervision and control, it would be foolish for the courts to conclude that age is irrelevant.

ROBERT H. MNOOKIN
(1986)

(SEE ALSO: *Children's Rights; Schall v. Martin.*)

Bibliography

FLICKER, BARBARA   1982   *Standards for Juvenile Justice: A Summary and Analysis.* Juvenile Justice Standards Project. Cambridge, Mass.: Ballinger Publications.

FOX, SANFORD J.   1970   Juvenile Justice Reform: An Historical Perspective. *Stanford Law Review* 22:1187–1239.

MACK, JULIAN W.   1925   The Chancery Procedure in the Juvenile Court. Pages 310–319 in Jane Addams, ed., *The Child, the Clinic, and the Court.* New York: New Republic, Inc., and the Wieboldt Foundation.

PLATT, ANTHONY M.   1977   *The Child Savers: The Invention of Delinquency.* Chicago: University of Chicago Press.

PRESIDENT'S COMMISSION ON LAW ENFORCEMENT AND ADMINISTRATION OF JUSTICE   1967   *Task Force Report: Juvenile Delinquency and Youth Crime.* Washington, D.C.: Government Printing Office.

STAPLETON, W. VAUGHAN and TEITELBAUM, LEE E.   1972   *In Defense of Youth: A Study of the Role of Counsel in American Juvenile Courts.* New York: Russell Sage Foundation.

J. W. HAMPTON, JR. & CO. v. UNITED STATES

See: *Hampton & Co. v. United States*